The New
Healthcare
Market

The New Healthcare Market

A Guide to PPOs for Purchasers, Payors and Providers

Edited by
Peter Boland

DOW JONES-IRWIN
Homewood, Illinois 60430

ISBN 0-87094-534-3

Library of Congress Catalog Card No. 84–71429

Printed in the United States of America

2 3 4 5 6 7 8 9 0 K 2 1 0 9 8 7 6

□ To Ann

FOREWORD

Writing a foreword to this book puts me in the position of someone trying to define "preferred provider organization." It is difficult to capture richness and diversity. Just as PPOs themselves take many forms, the chapters that make up this book approach their subject from many angles. This diversity—within preferred provider organizations themselves and within this book—is both inevitable and desirable.

In the case of PPOs, diversity is inevitable because the idea behind these organizations is really quite simple. Consumers get more health care for their money when they go to more efficient doctors and hospitals; by limiting consumer choice, we can contain health care costs. That's it. All of the fancy definitions are irrelevant.

At the same time, flexibility and diversity are desirable. One of the greatest assets of PPOs right now is the fact that they are unencumbered by elaborate legislative definitions, such as those that briefly slowed HMO development in the 1970s. Lack of regulatory restraint makes PPOs the simplest form of entry vehicle into the world of price-competitive medical care. But they are not *the* business of price-competitive medical care. Rather, they are a convenient starting point for developing a whole array of high-quality, cost-effective medical care products.

Developing an amalgam of price-competitive health plans is perhaps the key to survival for the medical care firm of the future. Multiple payment schemes are already becoming the norm. Soon there will be no such thing as a pure prepaid group practice or a pure fee-for-service group practice. Rather, health care organizations will accommodate a range of financial options. Individual organizations will embrace fee-for-service reimbursement, preferred provider arrangements, and every permutation between these two extremes. My feeling is that this movement toward diversity is the only way to simultaneously stimulate competition in terms of price, quality, and access.

What makes the PPO extraordinarily important right now is that it fits so well into the transformation already underway in the health industry. The PPO is not monolithic but protean. It is inherently flexible and varied. Because of these characteristics, it is perhaps the most appropriate or the easiest way for organizations to enter an evolving health system.

I commend *The New Healthcare Market* for capturing so effectively both the essence and the salience of the PPO. Peter Boland and an outstanding group of health care leaders provide a range of perspectives and conclusions that is diverse as the organizations they examine. The result is a rich and rare publication—one that honors inconsistency as well as consensus.

Paul M. Ellwood, Jr., M.D.
InterStudy

PREFACE

The health care industry is undergoing a fundamental change in philosophy, structure, and direction. The impact of these changes is unclear, and the roles of the major participants remain undefined. As a result, there is widespread uncertainty and confusion among health care providers, insurers, and purchasers.

This book attempts to identify the nature of the changes taking place and to provide a framework for assessing the impact of this restructuring on the health care market. What is at stake is control over health care resources. Who decides the amount of resources used? Where services are provided? How they are consumed? What trade-offs are made? How accountability is determined?

What is evident in the health care industry is that increasing competition among providers is creating innovative approaches to meet the business needs of purchasers for more affordable health care. This competitive environment is producing a variety of new contracting agreements between purchasers and providers for medical care services that are price-competitive. These transactions are referred to as *preferred* provider arrangements because purchasers negotiate selective contracts with more efficient and therefore preferred providers.

The most popular phrase for these new arrangements is preferred provider organizations or PPOs. They are a generic type of administrative structure to accomplish service agreements between providers and purchasers. Preferred provider contracting is a *process* for negotiating specific medical services between health care buyers and sellers at agreed-on prices.

Preferred provider arrangements such as PPOs lack a common definition because they vary according to the objectives of the participants and the characteristics of the local marketplace. However, the contributing authors in this book offer dozens of definitions, descriptions, and explanations of preferred provider arrangements and organizations. Each one is valid and reflects the unique perspective of the author.

The economic and social dynamics shaping the new marketplace represent contrasting and often conflicting viewpoints. An underlying rationale of this book is that major participants in the health care field must understand each other's point of view to successfully define their respective roles and achieve their business objectives. This book contains the perspectives of 107 distinguished experts—corporate benefits managers, physicians, insurance executives, attorneys, hospital administrators, health data specialists, economists, health care researchers, labor union representatives, health plan sponsors, and management consultants. Their practical experience and breadth of knowledge offer health care participants a wealth of pragmatic advice about how to take advantage of the changing health care market—its pitfalls as well as its opportunities.

Peter Boland, Ph.D.

LIST OF CONTRIBUTORS

Gary D. Aden, Senior Vice President, Pennsylvania Hospital

Leslie M. Alexandre, Cost Containment Specialist, U.S. Corporate Health Management

Michael F. Anthony, Partner, McDermott, Will & Emery

Joyce L. Batchelor, Programmer/Analyst, The Commons Management Group

Dennis F. Beatrice, Associate Director, Health Policy Center, Florence Heller Graduate School, Brandeis University

Judith D. Bentkover, Research Fellow, Kennedy School of Government, Harvard School of Public Health, Harvard University

Thomas C. Billet, Consultant, Johnson & Higgins

Peter Boland, President, Boland Healthcare Consultants

Edward M. Bosanac, President, E. Michael Associates

Robert C. Bradbury, Director, Master of Health Administration Program, Graduate School of Management, Clark University

Alan C. Brewster, Medical Director, Saint Vincent Hospital, Inc.

Robert L. Broaddus, President, California Preferred Professionals, Inc.

Robert P. Brook, Vice President, Employee Benefit Plans, Inc.

Gary Brukardt, Senior Vice President, VHA Health Ventures

Robert A. Chernow, President, Corporate Health Strategies, Inc.

Jon B. Christianson, Associate Professor, Department of Management and Policy, Department of Economics, College of Business and Public Administration, University of Arizona

Robert W. Coburn, President, The Commons Management Group

Gerald W. Connor, Wood, Lucksinger & Epstein

Bertram M. Cooper, Partner, O'Melveny & Myers

David DeCerbo, Partner, Hayt, Hayt & Landau

Paul R. DeMuro, Attorney, Carpenter, Higgins & Simonds

Bryan E. Dowd, Assistant Professor, Center for Health Services Research, University of Minnesota

Carol B. Emmott, Executive Director, California Association of Public Hospitals

Douglas L. Elden, Douglas L. Elden & Associates

Alain C. Enthoven, Marriner S. Eccles Professor of Public and Private Management, Graduate School of Business, Stanford University

Roger Feldman, Associate Professor, Center for Health Services Research, University of Minnesota

Jonathan E. Fielding, Professor, Schools of Public Health and Medicine, UCLA and President, U.S. Corporate Health Management

Max Fine, President, Max Fine Associates

Frederick S. Fink, Vice President, Booz, Allen and Hamilton

Robert D. Finney, Manager, Healthcare Cost Containment, Hewlett-Packard Company

Raymond R. Flachbart, Vice President, InterQual, Inc.

Donald C. Flagg, Vice President, Human Resources, Corporate Relations, The Stouffer Corporation

Jennifer B. Flink, Hewitt Associates

Gerald L. Glandon, Assistant Professor, Department of Health Systems Management, Rush University

Peter N. Grant, Weissburg and Aronson, Inc., San Francisco

Frank J. Greaney, Vice President, Cost Containment, American General Group Insurance Company

Janett C. Greenberg, Vice President, Group Life and Health Cost Containment, Massachusetts Mutual Life Insurance Co.

Stephen A. Gregg, President, Family Health Plan, Inc.

Charles H. Harrison, Partner, Arthur Andersen & Co.

Randi L. Harry, Principal, Arthur Young & Company

Mark A. Hartman, Associate, Hayt, Hayt & Landau

Richard A. Hinden, Douglas L. Elden & Associates

William H. Hranchak, Manager, Arthur Andersen & Co.

Karen Ignagni, Assistant Director, Department of Occupational Safety, Health and Social Security, AFL-CIO

Donald A. Jackson, Kimble, MacMichael, Jackson & Upton

W. Mark Jasper, President, Benefit Panel Services

Alan Jeffery, Vice President, Manager, Employee Benefits, Security Pacific Bank

Lucy Johns, Independent Consultant, Health Care Planning and Policy

Robert T. Jones, Vice President, Corporate Development, National Medical Management, National Medical Enterprise, Inc.

Leonard Kalm, Director of Special Programs, AmeriCare Health Corporation

Linda L. Kloss, Senior Vice President, InterQual, Inc.

Michael Koetting, Abt Associates, Inc.

Robin Kornfeld, Consultant, Laventhol & Horwath

Michael E. Kove, President, Health Ventures

John E. Kralewski, Professor and Director, Center for Health Services Research, University of Minnesota

Bettina Kurowski, Associate Professor of Health Administration, University of Colorado at Denver

Linda L. Lanam, Executive Director, Private Market Programs, Blue Cross and Blue Shield Association

Susan Leal, William M. Mercer-Meidinger, Incorporated

Arthur N. Lerner, Assistant Director for Health Care, Bureau of Competition, Federal Trade Commission

Philip M. Levine, Contract Manager, Saint Francis Memorial Hospital

Walter McClure, President, Center for Policy Studies

Angelo M. Masciantonio, Director of Cost Containment, Advanced System Applications

Richard A. Maturi, Director, Preferred Provider Product Development, Blue Cross and Blue Shield Association

Stanley Mendenhall, Commission on Professional and Hospital Activities (CPHA)

Arnold Milstein, Director, National Medical Audit, Inc.

David M. Narrow, Attorney, Bureau of Competition, Federal Trade Commission

Jonathan P. Neipris, Deputy Insurance Commissioner for Policyholder Services and Enforcement, Commonwealth of Pennsylvania

Hallie Katz Normington, Project Consultant, VHA Health Ventures

Marvis Oehm, Executive Director, Area XXIV, PSRO, Inc.; Director, District V, California Medical Review

Nellie O'Gara, President, First Health Associates, Inc.

Adele Palmer, Economist, Rand Corporation

Charles L. Parcell, Senior Vice President, Marketing Group, Blue Shield of California

Thomas A. Pedreira, Kimble, MacMichael, Jackson & Upton

Roy F. Perkins, Scripps Clinic and Senior Consultant, Booz, Allen and Hamilton, Inc.

William T. Phillips, Phillips & Associates, Inc.

Theodore M. Raichel, Executive Director, Product Management and Research, Blue Cross and Blue Shield Association

Charles P. Reilly, Executive Vice President, American Medical International

Sheila Riley, Corporate Law Department, State Farm Mutual Automobile Insurance Company

Brenda P. Roberts, Executive Director, Cooperative Health Corporation, Presbyterian Hospital

Robert D. Roberts, Partner, Arthur Young & Company

Fred Rothenberg, Fred Rothenberg and Associates

Mary T. Rushka, Administrator, Worksite Health Promotion Program, Mattel Corporation

Christopher W. Savage, Associate, O'Melveny & Myers

Kathryn A. Schroer, A. S. Hansen, Inc.

Elliot A. Segal, Principal and Manager of Health Programs, William M. Mercer-Meidinger, Incorporated

Janet Shapiro, Research Associate, Center for Health Services Research, University of Minnesota

Roberta J. Shapiro, Executive Director, Choice Health Care Plan

Patricia R. Sher, Vice President, Cost Containment, Gulf Group Services Corporation

Douglas E. Smith, Director of Project Management, Corporate Health Strategies, Inc.

John L. Smith, Scripps Clinic and Senior Consultant, Booz, Allen and Hamilton, Inc.

Sandra W. Smith, President, Health Plan of America

Dennis W. Strum, Vice President Planning and Development, Lutheran Hospital Society of Southern California

James D. Suver, Professor of Accounting and Health Administration, University of Colorado at Denver

Samuel J. Tibbitts, President, Lutheran Hospital Society of Southern California

Gordon R. Trapnell, President, Actuarial Research Corporation

Robert N. Trombly, President and CEO, Mutual Health Services Company

Larry J. Tucker, Hewitt Associates

Ann Venable, Senior Health Care Staff, Arthur D. Little, Inc.

Robert E. Ward, Kimble, MacMichael, Jackson & Upton

Richard C. Warmer, Partner, O'Melveny & Myers

Terry Warren, Director of Marketing, PriMed

William A. Weinberg, Department of Hospital Finance, American Hospital Association

Charles D. Weller, Jones, Day, Reavis & Pogue

Richard E. Wesslund, Director of Financial Planning/Revenue Diversification, Mission Services Corporation

Walter Wieners, Account Representative, Health Systems International

Esther Wu, Senior Employee Benefits Representative, McDonnell Douglas Corporation

Edward Zalta, Chairman, California Preferred Professionals, Inc.

CONTENTS

PART 1

DYNAMICS OF MARKET COMPETITION

1. The Changing Environment for Healthcare Services
2. Economics of Marketplace Competition
3. Impact of New Trends
4. Regulatory Responses to Competition

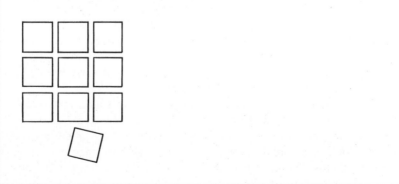

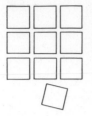
THE ROLE OF PREFERRED PROVIDER CONTRACTING IN THE HEALTHCARE MARKET

Peter Boland, Ph.D.

President
Boland Healthcare Consultants
Berkeley, CA

Steeply rising health care costs are the driving force behind the development of alternative delivery systems and the proliferation of new preferred provider arrangements on the market. Health care purchasers[1] are searching for ways to stretch available health care dollars without cutting back on medical services. Health care providers[2] are being forced to compete on the basis of price because fewer health care dollars are now available for each provider, in part because of a surplus of physicians and hospital beds in most urban areas.

Preferred provider contracting is changing the traditional relationship between purchasers and providers of medical services. Large purchasers are beginning to intervene in the market and negotiate contracts with providers, or through intermediaries such as insurance carriers and third-party claims administrators, for medical care at "preferred" or reduced rates. Health insurance carriers are also being forced to define a new role for themselves and carve out a niche in this process; otherwise, purchasers and providers could bypass them altogether and deal directly with each other.

This article addresses the role of preferred provider contracting in the current health care market and speculates about how this process may change as local market conditions mature in the next few years. The first part discusses the importance of preferred provider organizations (PPOs) within the context of how providers and purchasers approach health care delivery and how their roles are changing. The second section describes the range of incentives for purchasers, insurers, and providers to negotiate medical services agreements. The third section analyzes the changing dynamics of the marketplace in relation to the predominant features of preferred provider arrangements. A typology of characteristics is then proposed for the current generation of preferred provider arrangements and the generations to follow.

IMPORTANCE OF PPOs

The most important effect of preferred provider contracting is likely to be educational in the short run and economic in the long run. While individual preferred provider products may generate increased market share for providers and reduce health care spending for purchasers during the rest of the 1980s, the way health care services are bought and sold is being fundamentally altered by the selective contracting mechanism. The process of negotiating for medical services will accelerate the restructuring of the health care industry because of what purchasers and providers learn about each other. Two major consequences are that:

— Purchasers will gain a better understanding about influencing the dynamics of the delivery system, about the practice of medicine, and about the inherent problems of providing medical care.
— Providers will learn more about the advantages of a working partnership between hospitals and physicians and will become more aware of purchaser needs and constraints.

Employers and other purchasing organizations are coming to view health care as a commodity like other goods and services on the market. As such, purchasers are beginning to ask standard business questions about a product that has rarely been analyzed or negotiated by commercial purchasers before. For hospitals and physicians, this process will increase their perception of abuses in the delivery system as they become more aware of cost issues and incentives for unnecessary medical expenses within the system. It will also increase provider appreciation of commercial business priorities like predictability of costs, performance specifications, and product accountability.

Providers will likewise gain more of an appreciation for the corporate culture that purchasers represent in bargaining for reduced health care costs. So long as providers remained sellers in a seller's market, they did not have to understand the constraints and needs of their customers. Now that market conditions have changed and the roles are reversing, health care providers are being forced to devise strategies and products that respond to, and in some cases anticipate, purchaser interests and priorities. Providers who work closely with purchasers in designing a preferred provider arrangement are far more likely to be successful in marketing that product than if they develop it primarily to reflect and protect their own interests. In each case, providers and purchasers are learning more about each other's viewpoints, financial objectives, and business requirements.

Employers and purchaser organizations are learning more about how the health care system functions and about the economics of hospital administration and reimbursement incentives. The process of negotiating, implementing, and monitoring health service agreements will largely demystify health care management and hospital finance for purchasers. This experience will prepare them to approach buying health care services in much the same way as other goods and services involved in business transactions.

Greater knowledge about how the health care system operates will also increase purchasers' appreciation for the technical constraints and the complexity involved with improving the efficiency and effectiveness of medical care. Purchasers cannot assume that using standard business principles will quickly transform the health care system into a more rational and humane arrangement of medical services. Its economic incentives, which are largely the result of historical reimbursement patterns, reward inefficiency and penalize efficiency. The diversity of delivery systems resist rapid across-the-board application of many effective management techniques. At this stage, business pricing techniques and purchasing procedures are still relatively foreign to hospital managers, physicians, and other allied health practitioners.

One of the effects of preferred provider contracting is linking efficiency and productivity to financial reward. Theoretically, efficient providers are rewarded with service agreements that channel patients to them while inefficient providers are left with decreasing market share and must compete with others in the same situation for remaining sources of revenue. However, when purchasers cannot readily identify efficient providers, the providers with the most effective marketing capability will likely increase their share of the market.

This economic reality is forcing hospitals to develop management systems to calculate the real cost of individual services just as businesses determine the cost of products as a basis for marketing and sales activities. Relatively few hospitals have management information systems sophisticated enough to calculate and assign overhead operating costs to individual services that are provided to patients. This is a far more complex and expensive task for hospitals to accomplish than is the case in most other production-oriented businesses. Hospital information systems have to track numerous events that often occur simultaneously. Different types of medical personnel provide a wide range of services to patients with varying degrees of illness in many treatment settings. Accounting for all of these interactions requires advanced information systems.

INCENTIVES FOR PARTICIPATION

Negotiating health contracts gives purchasers an opportunity to stabilize costs and develop greater predictability for overall health care expenses and offers financial incentives to consumers to select more cost-effective medical care providers. Numerous hospitals and physicians support negotiated provider arrangements as a means of improving their position in the market and remaining competitive in the future. Preferred provider plans include a multiplicity of organizational and financial arrangements that offer more flexibility and control over health care resources. Both purchasers and providers of medical care can benefit as a result of this new negotiating environment. Whichever party has better data and more sophisticated negotiators is likely to benefit the most from the arrangement. There are numerous reasons why preferred provider arrangements are attractive options in the current health care market. Some of the reasons why purchasers (employers, enrollees), third-party payors (insurance carriers, Blue Cross-Blue Shield), and providers (physicians, hospitals) participate in this particular type of health delivery system can be outlined below:

PURCHASER INCENTIVES
Employers

— Achieve cost savings by obtaining competitive or reduced prices and decreased utilization.
— Improve predictability of health plan costs by fixed-term prices with performance specifications for cost control.
— Improve purchasing power by contracting with cost-effective providers for particular health services.
— Reduce impact of cost shifting on private health plan premiums.
— Maintain existing provider contracts while negotiating new approaches to health care delivery and payment.

Preferred provider organizations enable employers to offer an alternative health plan option (to traditional high-cost plans) that can financially compete with HMOs. Employers can influence employee choice of lower cost health care coverage through financial incentives and can exert more direct control over provider practices and services than through other alternative delivery systems such as HMOs. Businesses can promote cost-effective medical practice patterns and lower cost treatment options in a service area by means of PPOs. Employers can also maintain flexibility in benefits mix design and maintain control over the amount of employee premium sharing and copayment through preferred provider arrangements.

Enrollees

— Reduce financial risk and out-of-pocket expenses due to lower premium cost or percent of contribution.
— Freedom to choose providers within the plan.
— Retain traditional doctor-patient relationship.
— Improved quality of care by receiving services from providers whose treatment and referral practices are closely monitored.

Enrollees often have a broader choice of health plan options and services in a PPO as an inducement for participation. Likewise, employees and their dependents may realize increased access for health care through an organized network of providers near both residence and work site.

THIRD-PARTY PAYOR INCENTIVES
Insurers

— Retain current accounts by satisfying customer demand for more cost-effective health care coverage and better information.
— Opportunity to increase market share in health care finance sector and compete with Blue Cross-Blue Shield, HMOs, and self-insureds.
— Reduce rate of increase in premiums and health care expenditures.
— Develop a comprehensive information base to evaluate resources and to compete with health data companies.
— Improve benefit package by broadening traditional product line emphasis on catastrophic coverage to include comprehensive medical coverage.

Insurance carriers and third-party administrators will expand their service capacity by integrating established billing and claims payment operations with new financial and utilization review functions called for by PPOs. As a result of these activities, they will gain increased familiarity with the technical operations of provider medical systems and the health care industry.

PROVIDER INCENTIVES
Physicians

— Increase or at least maintain a volume of patients and a referral network.

— Retain independence of fee-for-service practice.

— Improve cash flow and level of profit through quicker claims payment.

By participating in preferred provider arrangements, physicians will become better prepared for future reimbursement schemes requiring greater financial risk and performance monitoring. In general, the quality of the care they provide will improve by compliance with performance protocols and closer peer review called for in preferred provider arrangements. Physicians will also be rewarded for cost-effective practice patterns through financial incentives and profit-sharing formulas.

Hospitals

— Enhance financial position by improving cash flow through prompt payment agreements, increasing patient revenues, and decreasing bad debts and disallowances.

— Increase market share by obtaining exclusive contracts to provide hospital services in a larger geographical area than would normally be served.

— Increase profits if unit costs are held below the negotiated price of services and generate additional revenue if the volume of services increases per patient (i.e., intensity of services).

— Attract a higher proportion of low medical risk individuals and families, which would result in higher profitability.

— Promote corporate diversification into alternative delivery systems and product specialization that are competitive on the basis of price.

Preferred provider arrangements will encourage hospitals to become more competitive by implementing internal cost-saving features and increasing operating efficiencies. These activities require cooperative agreements between hospital and medical staff, and the process of reaching these agreements will result in stronger hospital-physician relationships. Selective contracting agreements, with built-in performance standards and utilization control requirements, also better prepare hospitals for future payment mechanisms based on sophisticated health data systems and reimbursement methodologies.

DEFINING CHARACTERISTICS

The long-term success of preferred provider arrangements depends on the major participants—providers, insurers, and purchasers—reaching an accommodation on how to share the risks and rewards of affordable health care services. Preferred provider arrangements reflect the diverse goals and objectives of providers and purchasers in each contracting arrangement. While most preferred provider arrangements share a number of defining principles, the mix of characteristics that define them vary according to key elements, 15 of which include:

— Sponsorship.
— Risk sharing.
— Payment method.
— Financial incentives and disincentives.
— Utilization review components.
— Utilization review organization.
— Quality assurance program.
— Provider network.
— Provider membership criteria.
— Choice of providers.
— Benefits coverage.
— Service area.
— Organizational structure.
— Administrative services.
— Information management.

The way in which these elements are organized and implemented determines the success of a preferred provider arrangement in a particular area.

How a product is developed will depend on the sponsor's philosophy, business objectives, level of sophistication, and interpretation of local market conditions. These factors will likewise be influenced as more information becomes available on what makes a preferred provider arrangement successful and how to structure each element most effectively. Some of the 15 elements will be emphasized more than others, depending on which "generation" of PPO model the product corresponds to. While there are no definitive management prescriptions on what makes a successful preferred provider arrangement, their long-term viability will most likely depend on two overriding factors:

— Maintaining or improving the provider's market position.
— Responding to the needs of health care purchasers in the local marketplace with a competitive product.

The circumstances for each market will differ according to the extent of competition among health care providers and the level of awareness among purchasers about how to buy medical services. Market conditions are likely to be dominated by provider preferences as long as competition among and between physicians and hospitals remains low. As competition increases—due to the surplus of physicians, an excess of hospital beds, a decreasing pool of available patients, or a shrinkage of reimbursement dollars—market forces of supply and demand begin to balance one another so that more of an equilibrium is reached between provider and purchaser needs. As purchasers become more knowledgeable about how the health care market functions, they can influence the price of services and how they are delivered by negotiating selective agreements with providers for medical care. When purchasers gain the analytical tools to bargain with providers from a position of relative parity, then purchaser preferences begin to supersede the needs of providers in a competitive health care environment.

The types of PPO models currently on the market are largely "provider driven" and reflect the objectives of a provider-dominated market that is experiencing the initial pressure of competition within the health care industry. In this model, physicians and hospitals respond first to their perception of provider market forces (e.g., excess hospital beds, surplus physicians) and secondarily to their sense of purchaser concerns such as overall costs. The current generation of PPOs are designed to increase market share (i.e., fill more beds, capture more patients) in exchange for discounting usual fees and rates by a large percentage.

The next generation of PPOs are emerging in some parts of the country and reflect a deepening awareness on the part of providers that purchaser concerns about quality, access, and cost of medical care need to be addressed in a more sophisticated manner. Purchasers are pressing for more accountability in three areas:

1. Costs:
   Total health plan costs.
   Predictability of costs and the rate of increase.
   Per capita costs.
   Internal cost management programs offered by providers.
   Shared financial risk.
2. Data:
   Comparative reports generated on a regular basis.
   Case mix adjusted data.
   Provider profiles and trend data.
   Utilization data by enrollee and service.
3. Access:
   Preventive as well as curative services.
   Administration of benefits for multisite employees.

While these purchaser priorities are being addressed in contract negotiations, quality of care is only recently becoming a serious bargaining issue. There are two reasons for this. Providers do not generally agree on what constitutes quality medicine, nor do they have the means of measuring it at the present time. Purchasers are unfamiliar with the technical and professional issues concerning quality of care and leave that to the province of practitioners.

Future generations of PPOs are at the conceptual stage at the present time but are apt to reflect three general trends that are emerging in the marketplace:

1. Increased emphasis on business management principles by both for-profit corporations and nonprofit organizations as a result of an industry-wide shakeout precipitated by tighter controls on reimbursement.
2. Increased awareness and willingness of purchasers to channel their health care resources to meet corporate objectives of cost control.
3. Increasing acceptance of and growing enrollment in closed provider networks such as HMOs by purchasers (because of lower costs) and providers (because of reduced market share).

EMERGING TRENDS

Fifteen key characteristics (e.g., sponsorship, risk sharing, payment method) are used to define and distinguish different generations of preferred provider arrangements in this section. A typology of "current," "next," and "future" generations is presented as a vehicle for discussing how key characteristics differ according to local market conditions. The influence of local market conditions on these arrangements can be characterized as provider driven, purchaser driven, or in a state of relative equilibrium.

In theory, the evolutionary cycle of these three models (current, next, and future generations) corresponds to the early 1980s, mid-1980s, and late 1980s, respectively, with development phases of two to five years for each model. The future generations category is likely to include a number of development cycles and subsequent models over a multiyear period. In practice, however, regional markets develop at different times and mature at varying rates. At the present time, some regions are experiencing a transition from current generation to next generation models, while other areas have yet to develop any preferred provider arrangements. A typology of such models is shown below in Exhibit 1.

Some of the key characteristics that hypothetically describe current generation models may not appear at all in health services markets that initiate next generation models as a first step. This "jump" in the evolutionary cycle generally occurs when local market influences such as intense provider competition and aggressive business coalition activities create pressure to develop a preferred provider arrangement that is more purchaser driven than provider driven.

EXHIBIT 1
Evolving Models of Preferred Provider Arrangements

	Typology of Different Models		
	Current Generation	*Next Generation*	*Future Generations*
Market influence	Provider driven	Provider/purchaser equilibrium	Purchaser driven
Corresponding date	Early 1980s	Mid-1980s	Late 1980s
Development cycle	2–5 years	2–5 years	2–5 years each

In this discussion, each of the three models is described in relation to 15 key characteristics and is summarized below in Exhibit 2. While the discussion of current and next generation preferred provider arrangements is empirical, the comments presented on future generations are highly speculative.

CURRENT GENERATION

The current generation of preferred provider arrangements is largely sponsored by hospitals and physicians attempting to protect market share in the face of increasing competition from other providers in their communities. Since most plans are provider driven and defensive in nature, they generally do not include risk sharing for providers. The selling point to purchasers is reduced charges, often as much as twenty percent or more off billed hospital charges or "usual, customary and reasonable" physician fees. In order to effectively channel employees into the lower cost health plans, employers frequently reduce the amount of deductible and copayment attached to preferred provider care.

Patient use of services is generally monitored by participating hospitals (i.e., delegated review) according to their own standards for such utilization management techniques as preadmission review and hospital claims review following discharges. Quality assurance measures are not usually distinguished from utilization review procedures.

The focus of preferred provider arrangements is to bring together a threshold number of primary care physicians, specialty resources, and acute care hospitals to offer a comprehensive package of services to employers in a particular area. In most cases, physicians can join these plans as a way to market themselves without having to alter their practice patterns and with little modification in their fee schedules. Hospitals are selected according to range of services, location, number and type of physicians with admitting privileges, charge structures, and price competitiveness.

EXHIBIT 2
Selected Characteristics of Preferred Provider Arrangements

	Current Generation	Next Generation	Future Generations
Sponsorship	Hospital and physician based	Multihospital network Health and hospital service plans Insurance carriers Third-party administrators	Insurance carrier and provider joint venture PPO network
Risk sharing (physician)	None	Minimal risk pools (e.g., 5%)	Productivity incentives Cost-effectiveness standards
Payment method: Physician	Discount from UCR	Discount based on relative value scale conversion	Flat fee for specific procedures Full fee for cost-effective practice patterns
Hospital	Discount from billed charges Negotiated per diem	Multiple per diem Case mix based on DRGs	Capitation
Financial incentives and disincentives (enrollee)	Decreased deductibles and copayment	Lower premiums Decreased copayment for cost-containing procedures	Increased copayment and deductibles for non-PPO services
Utilization review components	Hospital claims review	Preadmission review Physician and hospital profiling	Ambulatory and ancillary services review
Utilization review organization	Delegated hospital review	Predetermined review policies Dual review	Nondelegated review Penalty provisions
Quality assurance	Standard utilization review	Diagnosis and procedure-specific screening criteria DRG validation	Medical appropriateness evaluation Case mix management and intensity of service criteria
Provider network	Primary care resources and referrals	Alternative treatment resources	Exclusive enrollee channeling

EXHIBIT 2 *(concluded)*

	Current Generation	*Next Generation*	*Future Generations*
Provider membership criteria:			
Physician	Staff of participating hospital	Premembership screening criteria	Practice pattern standards adjusted for case mix and profitability performance
Hospital	Range of services Charge profiles	Cost and utilization profiles adjusted for case mix	Efficiency and appropriateness performance factors
Choice of providers	Flexible enrollment	Flexible enrollment	Designated enrollment
Benefits coverage	Acute care and specialty services	Outpatient services in alternative settings	Ambulatory and alternative health care services Health promotion and illness prevention services
Service area	Local	Regional and state-wide	Multistate and national
Organizational structure	Subsidiary or multiple product line of sponsor	Independent product line	Network of participating PPOs Vertically integrated systems of care
Administrative services	Internal operations with limited utilization review	Confined to internal operations	Preadmission review and quality assurance Health insurance coverage
Information management:			
Purchaser reports	Undifferentiated summary statistics	Utilization and cost experience of enrollees per service Physician and hospital profiles	Cost management performance results Cost and utilization experience compared for PPO and non-PPO enrollees
Provider reports	Inpatient statistics based on UHDDS	Physician and hospital profiles adjusted for case mix and financial performance	Inpatient data linked to ambulatory data for planning and budgeting models Physician and hospital financial data

Unlike health maintenance organizations, one of the most attractive features of the plan for enrollees is the freedom to select providers. Enrollees can also elect at any time to be treated by nondesignated providers for an additional copayment or fee. A full range of acute care and specialty services is generally available to participating enrollees in a local area.

Many early preferred provider arrangements have been sponsored by a parent organization as a supplement to their normal line of business, e.g., acute care services for hospitals, major medical insurance for carriers. Purchasers usually receive very limited information about the actual level of savings for two reasons. First, diagnosis and procedure data were generally not collected and analyzed for purchasers. Second, most preferred provider information systems are not able to compare plan utilization and costs for subscribers using PPOs exclusively, employees combining PPO and non-PPO care, and enrollees participating exclusively in traditional coverage plans. Provider information systems are primarily based on the Uniform Hospital Discharge Data Set (UHDDS) and additional summary billing data.

NEXT GENERATION

The next generation of preferred provider arrangements is being introduced in some metropolitan areas at the present time by a broad spectrum of sponsors that include Blue Cross and Blue Shield plans in most states, for-profit hospital management companies, multihospital networks, insurance carriers, third-party claims administrators, independent management and investor organizations, and purchasers themselves. The effects of provider competition have influenced some physician-affiliated PPOs to begin assuming a minimal amount of financial risk as a way to achieve greater provider compliance with utilization control targets and as a marketing tool to purchasers. Payment to physicians continues to be predominately based on a percentage discount from UCR and relative value scale conversion factors. Hospital reimbursement is shifting away from straight discount agreements to per diem, multiple per diem, and case mix payment schedules.

Incentives for channeling enrollees to preferred providers will likely be reinforced by lower copayment levels for a range of procedures that have proven to be cost effective. These include preadmission testing, second surgical opinion, ambulatory surgery, home health care, and outpatient treatment for drug, alcohol, and psychiatric care.

Utilization review and volume control functions will play a larger role in this generation of preferred provider arrangements because comprehensive data systems are being introduced in the market that can develop extensive profiles on physician practice patterns and hospital use of resources. Delegated hospital review will be supplemented and, to some extent, replaced by outside third-party review organizations—independent from the hospital—that will take more responsibility for specific monitoring functions such as preadmission review and retrospective bill review. Combined third-party and hospital review (i.e., shared review) is becoming more frequent because sole reliance on delegated review systems have generally been less successful than shared review and independent review agencies in two key areas: (1) reducing unnecessary utilization and intensity of services and (2) persuading potential purchasers that preferred provider arrangements can reduce per capita costs because of tough review mechanisms.

Physician and hospital profiles may become the basis of quality assurance and may be used to define practice standards in relation to specific medical diagnoses and procedures. An increasing emphasis will be placed on validating diagnosis related group (DRG) information, since it will be the basis for many management protocols and reimbursement systems.

The increased emphasis on cost effectiveness and quality assurance is resulting in the application of premembership screening criteria for provider participation in many preferred health plans. In most earlier plans, physicians could join largely at their own discretion. Preferred health plan sponsors elected to admit physicians without a strict screening process in order to lessen organized resistance to the new type of delivery system and to limit potential legal exposure. This approach assumed that physicians whose practice patterns conflicted with the objectives of the plan could be educated and disciplined to adopt more cost-effective treatment behavior "after the fact." This approach is difficult to implement and, with the availability of more sophisticated profiling tools, is beginning to give way to defined standards of physician practice patterns.

The intent of clearly defined performance norms is to discourage nonconforming physicians from seeking membership in the first place so that overutilization and inappropriate care can be avoided. Hospital profiling is likewise becoming more sophisticated and in many cases will be able to compare facilities in terms of performance characteristics adjusted by the common denominator of diagnosis related groups (DRGs).

The provider base in many emerging preferred provider arrangements is expanding to accommodate more traditional care providers (in alternative treatment settings) and allied health professionals such as dentists, pharmacists, psychologists, chiropractors, and podiatrists in response to market pressure for cost management and greater choice of therapeutic regimens. Prepackaged benefits coverage is also integrating a wide spectrum of cost-effective services outside the hospital such as ambulatory surgical centers, birthing centers, skilled nursing facilities, home health agencies, and hospice care.

In response to employer demand for multisite employee coverage, preferred provider arrangements are beginning to expand into regional organizations and network on a statewide basis. Preferred provider arrangements are increasingly being marketed as separate product lines whose images are distinctly different from traditional health care delivery systems and indemnity insurance health plans. Because of the increasing demand for management-oriented information systems, PPOs are developing flexible reporting formats for employers that detail the cost and utilization experience of individual enrollee groups.

FUTURE GENERATIONS

The growing participation of insurance carriers in the field will bring greater institutional stability and uniformity to multistate and national preferred provider arrangements. Carriers are apt to enter into joint venture relationships with local and regional providers in an effort to market complementary resources. Many preferred provider arrangements will become multistate and national operations sponsored by networks of PPOs to compete with Blue Cross and Blue Shield. These new models will represent vertically integrated systems of health care that provide multiple levels and types of care in one organization.

Future generations of preferred provider arrangements will be strongly influenced by the capacity of information systems to link quality assurance and utilization statistics with cost-management mechanisms and by the trend toward capitation reimbursement. Physicians will assume greater financial risk in these models and may be evaluated according to predetermined cost-effectiveness standards. Financial reward will probably be related to their level of productivity and clinical efficiency. Physician reimbursement will move toward flat fees for specific procedures and, in many cases, capitation. However, with the advent of sophisticated data systems to monitor physician behavior, full fees may be paid to doctors who have been identified as the most cost-effective practitioners in their communities.

Hospitals will be paid according to a continuum of reimbursement methods—percentage discount from billed charges, per diem rates, per case arrangements—that place the hospital at greater financial risk. Most hospitals will likely be paid according to DRGs or other product-specific schedules (adjusted for case mix) and capitation. The latter will gain influence as information systems develop into sophisticated planning and budgeting tools.

The network of providers may be restricted to practitioners in each area with records of cost-effective treatment patterns. Providers could be selected on the basis of how closely their style of medical practice corresponds with the plan's performance standards (adjusted for case mix), which would be clearly defined as part of premembership screening criteria. Hospitals could be judged primarily on efficiency and appropriateness of care factors.

In return, patient channeling may approach the restrictive level of exclusive provider organizations (EPOs). Copayments and deductibles for non-PPO services could be raised as a disincentive to go outside the network. The strategy might be to approach the level of disincentives used by HMOs to retain enrollee participation within the system. Enrollee incentives may be boosted by gradually lowering total premium costs so that preferred provider health coverage will be significantly less than traditional health plans. Coverage will be expanded to include disease prevention services and health promotion programs, which are relatively low cost options and attractive marketing features to enrollees.

In order to effectively channel enrollees to the most cost-effective providers in an area, choice of providers will be more controlled than in past models of PPOs. Flexible enrollment plans, which employees favored because of minimal paperwork requirements, may give way to designated enrollment plans or exclusive provider organizations. The shift could be spurred by employer demand for reliable information on whether the preferred provider option did in fact save money or at least dampened the rate of increase in company health care costs. To best determine whether a net savings occurs, a defined group of enrollees should be tracked, compared with a control group, and evaluated over time. This cannot be done when subscribers switch back and forth between PPO and non-PPO sponsored health plans without the use of sophisticated data tracking systems.

In future generations of PPOs, utilization review will extend to hospital ancillary services and ambulatory settings such as physician offices. As a condition of participation in preferred plans, providers may be required to agree to financial penalty provisions as a disciplinary device for not conforming with established performance protocols. Physicians will probably be obligated to furnish valid and timely medical practice data as a condition of membership. The predominant form of hospital review will likely be nondelegated. Quality assurance standards will be able to evaluate the appropriateness and necessity of specific medical care regimens. Individual episodes of care will be judged according to case mix management and intensity of service criteria for quality assurance purposes.

In order to remain financially viable, PPOs will need to develop considerable expertise in measuring quality of care and conducting prior authorization reviews. They will be able to sell these and other claims processing services as a vendor to other providers and purchasers of care. Some PPOs may assume substantial financial risk by offering health insurance coverage to defined groups of purchasers as part of a broad diversification approach.

At this stage, purchasers will be able to evaluate the PPO's capability compared with other health care options. Routine cost and utilization reports will be generated for clients to describe the results of specific cost-management programs. Hospital information systems will be linked with ambulatory statistics so that a comprehensive utilization and financial database can be used for planning and budgeting activities. This will enable PPOs to assume greater risk and to allocate resources more efficiently and with greater predictability.

CONCLUSION

The dominant trends that support the creation of PPOs—rising health care costs, increased provider competition, government price regulation, physician surplus, and excess hospital capacity—will continue to shape the market for the foreseeable future. These trends point to increasing proliferation of alternative delivery systems and price-sensitive health care arrangements. Hospitals and physician group practices that develop the management tools to function as preferred providers and alternative health care delivery systems will be better prepared to respond to new opportunities in the health care industry.

As a process for developing concepts and arrangements that reflect changing market conditions, preferred provider contracting is a bridge between the traditional practice of medicine and an evolving health care system that remains undefined and in flux. PPOs may prove to be transitional vehicles for moving traditional medical care into a new generation of better managed health care systems.

NOTES

1. Purchasers include employers, employee organizations, third-party payors (such as insurers and government), health and welfare trust funds, and labor unions.

2. Providers include physicians; hospitals and other medical facilities; and allied health professionals such as dentists, pharmacists, psychologists, chiropractors, and podiatrists.

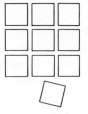

The Changing Environment for Healthcare Services

PREFERRED PROVIDER ARRANGEMENTS: MARKET AND DELIVERY SYSTEM PERSPECTIVES*

Richard A. Maturi

Director, Preferred Provider Product Development
Blue Cross and Blue Shield Association
Chicago, IL

Theodore M. Raichel

Executive Director, Product Management and Research
Blue Cross and Blue Shield Association
Chicago, IL

During the past two years, health care providers, group health benefit plan managers, insurers, entrepreneurs, and health care policymakers have shared a growing interest in preferred provider arrangements. Most of what has been written about preferred provider arrangements has focused on (1) their potential as provider marketing vehicles or (2) the organization of providers associated with preferred provider arrangements as new types of competitive "alternative delivery systems."

---

*The views expressed in this article are those of the authors and do not necessarily represent the views of individual Blue Cross and Blue Shield Plans.

The primary focus of this article is on preferred provider arrangements as an emerging type of health care benefit program. The article begins with a discussion of the provider marketing principles and health benefit plan cost control principles that are driving the development of preferred provider arrangements.

The article then proposes and discusses a definition of preferred provider arrangements. The definition is intended to accommodate wide variation in the design of preferred provider arrangements. At the same time it includes the basic characteristics that distinguish them from other established health care benefit options, such as traditional indemnity and service benefit programs and HMOs.

Building from this definition is a discussion of the types of products that a variety of vendors are developing to service a health benefit plan's preferred provider arrangement. The discussion provides a framework for sorting out the diverse products and vendors that are being labelled preferred provider organizations (PPOs).

In addition to presenting a market-oriented framework for preferred provider arrangements, this article also considers the effects of these arrangements on the health care delivery system. This includes a discussion of the factors that may determine whether preferred provider arrangements will become accepted and prevalent, as well as a discussion of how preferred provider arrangements could affect the organization and effectiveness of the health care delivery system.

UNDERLYING PRINCIPLES

It is useful to view preferred provider arrangements most fundamentally as vehicles for underlying provider and health benefit plan strategies. There are several strategic principles that appear to be operating in preferred provider arrangements. These can be grouped as provider marketing principles and health benefit plan cost control principles.

Provider marketing principles include

1. A provider can compete for patients on the basis of price (or, more generally, "cost effectiveness") by achieving special status in a health care benefit program.
2. A closer linkage to health care financing services can make the provider a stronger competitor in the future.

Health benefit plan cost control principles include

1. The health benefit plan can increase its control of benefit cost by channeling subscribers or beneficiaries to more cost-effective providers for service.
2. The health benefit plan can share with the individual subscriber the responsibility for selective purchasing of health care services.

3. The group purchaser[1] can negotiate more effective cost-containment provisions with providers if the benefit program gives competitive advantages to providers that agree to such contracts.

The following is a discussion of these principles:

PROVIDER MARKETING PRINCIPLES

The provider marketing principles underlying preferred provider arrangements are based on competition for patients on the basis of price (or, more generally, cost effectiveness). Provider competition is not new, but its nature is changing. The growing priority that public and private health benefit plans place on cost is shifting the emphasis of provider competition from prestige, service capacity, amenities, and medical staff makeup towards price. In addition, the growing excess capacity of traditional providers—reflected in average hospital occupancy rates of 60 percent in some areas and rising physician/population ratios—is making many providers more anxious to compete. Finally, the flow of revenue from health care benefit programs has become less secure, as coverage has been reduced in some private benefit programs, payment has been constrained by government payors, and—most recently—unemployment has risen dramatically in many provider service areas. As a result, there is a growing need not just to compete for patients, but to compete for patients for whom adequate payment is assured.

However, the way consumers purchase health care services is different from the ways consumers purchase most other goods and services. Health care service charge structures are complex and most consumers have limited ability to discern which providers make more efficient patient care management decisions. Thus, the ability of most health care consumers as purchasers is questionable. Further, when people incur serious illness requiring expensive and complex health care services, they will—within their economic means—place priority on receiving the best possible care, not the most efficiently delivered care. Society has responded to this priority by making available relatively comprehensive private and public health care coverage programs that remove the financial barriers to high quality health care. The limited ability of consumers to "shop" for health care services on the basis of price, and the diminished need to do so because of comprehensive health care coverage, dampens the ability of providers to directly market to patients on the basis of price.

An underlying principle of preferred provider arrangements is that by competing for special position in a benefit program, a provider can compete for patients on the basis of price. The precedent for this type of price competition has been well established with HMOs, where the benefit program covers services only when received from or ordered by the HMO providers. In areas where HMO market penetration has grown to over 20 percent, such as Minneapolis/St. Paul and California, fee-for-service providers have learned the power of benefit-program–based price competition. Hospitals have become increasingly dependent on HMOs for patient referrals, and fee-for-service physicians have lost patients and income.

There is an additional marketing principle underlying the involvement of some providers with preferred provider arrangements: a closer linkage to health care financing services can make the provider a stronger competitor in the future. Again, the precedent was set with HMOs. Some providers may extend this strategy by acquiring or joint venturing with insurance companies to offer other types of nontraditional health care financing arrangements, such as preferred provider arrangements.

HEALTH BENEFIT PLAN COST-CONTROL PRINCIPLES

There are several cost-control principles associated with preferred provider arrangements. First, the health benefit plan can increase its control of benefit cost by channeling subscribers or beneficiaries to more cost-effective providers for service. HMOs are the ultimate channeling vehicle, because coverage is provided only for services received from or ordered by HMO providers. However, offering an HMO only creates channeling for those individual members of a group who choose to enroll in the HMO. In most groups, HMO enrollment has been constrained due to the limited number of providers participating in many HMOs and the absence of coverage for services received from non-HMO providers. Thus the major proportion of members in groups where HMOs are available as an option are still concentrated in the traditional benefit program, where there usually is no channeling. A benefit program that is less restrictive regarding choice of provider but still has channeling incentives for members might be offered as either (1) the only benefit program, thus affecting all the group members, or (2) an individual option that enrolls members of the group who would not enroll in the HMO.

Second, the health benefit plan can share responsibility with the individual subscriber for selective purchasing of health care services. The health plan is unable to make the decision of where an individual member should receive care at the time of service. Individual members generally do not have the information or expertise to make prudent purchasing decisions on their own. However, if the health benefit plan takes responsibility for prospectively identifying "preferred" providers, the individual member can be given financial responsibility (as reflected in different coverage levels) for following this guidance. This approach to making the member a more selective consumer of health care services may be viewed by some group health benefit plans and members as preferable to the financial incentives resulting from across-the-board reductions in benefits.

Third, group purchasers can negotiate more cost-containing contracts with providers if the benefit program gives competitive advantages to providers that agree to such contracts. A purchaser can give incentives to providers that are cost effective, innovative, or competitive for patients to agree to cost-containment provisions, by giving such providers special status in a health care benefit program. By securing the agreement of preferred providers to price controls and participation in innovative pricing methods, utilization-control programs, and/or risk-sharing arrangements, purchasers can control total benefit cost, even if they are not confident of their ability to a priori identify "cost-effective" providers.

A BASIC DEFINITION

There is significant variation in the definitions of preferred provider arrangements. To some extent, this may be because early definitions have usually been either empirical descriptions of the characteristics of observed PPOs or statements of the authors' opinion on the characteristics that a PPO should have. As a result, some definitions are too constraining.

In addition, the definition is affected by the perspective of the definer. If the author of a definition is interested in alternative delivery systems or in health care provider marketing strategies (the perspectives most common in the literature), then the definition will focus on organizational relationships among providers and the new roles that providers can assume. From the perspective of a Blue Cross and Blue Shield Plan or of a commercial insurance carrier, the definition is more likely to focus on the design of a health care benefit contract and the associated methods for designating preferred providers. An employer or union trust fund's definition is also likely to focus on the benefit program features of the arrangement.

A basic definition of preferred provider arrangements should be broad enough to accommodate the possibilities for different designs. In addition, the basic definition should focus on the group health benefit plan's concerns. Regardless of the organizer of the arrangement, there are effectively no preferred providers until a health benefit plan decides there are preferred providers. Thus, the following basic definition is proposed:

> *Preferred Provider Arrangement:* A health care benefit program arrangement designed to control benefit costs by giving members incentives to use health care providers designated as preferred, but that also provides substantial coverage for services from other health care providers.

This basic definition implicitly includes four defining characteristics that, in combination, distinguish preferred provider arrangements from other health care financing arrangements. These are discussed in detail in the following paragraphs.

TWO TYPES OF PROVIDER DESIGNATION

First, there are (at least) two types of designations for providers in the benefit program: preferred provider designation and nonpreferred provider designation. In every preferred provider arrangement we are aware of, there is a contractual relationship between the purchaser and the preferred providers.

There may or may not be contracts with nonpreferred providers. In many cases, there is no contract with nonpreferred providers, and the benefit program merely reimburses subscribers (at some level) for covered services they receive from nonpreferred providers. Blue Cross and Blue Shield Plan preferred provider arrangements usually do involve contractual relationships with some or all nonpreferred providers. In these cases, the Plans either developed a separate contract with preferred providers or a "preferred provider addendum" to a basic provider contract.

PROVIDER SELECTION

Second, there is a process for designating or selecting preferred providers. In some cases, the group purchaser may simply respond to the approaches of one or more providers marketing themselves as preferred and may not make any active procurement effort.

In other cases, the group purchaser will actively select preferred providers from among all available providers, using a formal selective contracting process. Three methods of active selective contracting are commonly considered:

1. All providers are offered a contract that includes price and, generally, utilization-control provisions. The providers then "self-select" by accepting or rejecting the contract. In some cases, the price is determined by a uniform percent reduction from each provider's current charges, without consideration of variations in provider prices. However, the more sophisticated preferred provider arrangements use some combination of offering a flat price schedule for all providers (e.g., physician fee schedule or hospital DRG prices), provider-specific price offers up to a ceiling price for any provider (e.g., UCR payment or hospital-specific per-diem levels up to a maximum per diem), and/or controls on future price increases.

2. All providers are given an opportunity to submit competitive proposals, and the purchaser selects the best proposals. This method appears to be most applicable for selecting institutional providers. The criteria for competitive selection have included relative unit price bids, financial stability, service mix, geographic location, and evidence of past cost-conscious behavior.

3. Only certain providers are offered, or invited to submit, proposals for preferred contracts. The objective of this method is to select the already cost-effective providers. Unfortunately, this method will be limited until techniques are developed to evaluate historical cost effectiveness in a comprehensive way that accounts for price, patient care practices, and patient characteristics.

FINANCIAL INCENTIVES FOR MEMBERS

The third defining characteristic of a preferred provider arrangement is that members are given financial incentives to use the preferred providers. Two general types of financial incentives are commonly used. In some preferred provider arrangements both are used:

1. The first type of financial incentive is decreased cost sharing for services obtained from preferred providers. This most often is reduced (or waived) coinsurance but may also be reduced (or waived) deductibles.

2. The second type of incentive is a guarantee that the member will not be billed by the preferred provider for charges in excess of benefit program payment levels. In this case, the health benefit plan will limit the unit payment for services received from any provider and may limit the unit payment for services received from nonpreferred providers to a level below the contractual levels paid to preferred providers. The preferred providers agree to accept the contractual price as payment in full. In general, the nonpreferred providers have not agreed to such a limitation on balance billing.

SUBSTANTIAL COVERAGE AT ALL PROVIDERS

The fourth and final defining characteristic of preferred provider arrangements is that subscribers have substantial coverage for services received from other providers. There is no set definition of "substantial" in this regard. The health benefit plan market—or different market segments—will likely set effective standards for substantial coverage.

This characteristic of preferred provider arrangements distinguishes them from HMO benefit programs and so-called exclusive provider organizations where there is no coverage for nonemergency services received from nondesignated providers.

There is potential for wide variation among preferred provider arrangements that have the four characteristics presented above. Some variations have already been noted. These should be interpreted only as examples of how current preferred provider arrangements manifest the four defining characteristics.

Preferred provider arrangements can vary in the same ways that any other type of benefit program varies. These include, for example, the general scope and level of benefits, the extent of coverage for cost-containing services such as ambulatory surgery and home health care, and selective use of cost sharing to stimulate subscriber utilization of lower cost alternatives to inpatient care. In addition, there are possibilities for variation regarding provider selection, benefit incentives, and cost-control methods, which are emphasized in preferred provider arrangements.

The key variables regarding provider selection are the methods for selection, as discussed above, and the proportion of area providers that are preferred. Provider selection methods will vary in response to legal considerations, the sophistication and judgment of the purchaser, and the characteristics of local providers (e.g., number, types of overutilization, variations in price, and discernable patient care practice patterns).

The proportion of area providers that are designated as preferred will also vary widely. The extremes have already been reached in this regard. In some cases, a single provider in a community has been designated as preferred by a group purchaser. At the other extreme, in Blue Cross and Blue Shield of Minnesota's AWARE program, twenty of twenty-seven hospitals in Minneapolis-St. Paul agreed to preferred contracts in 1983, and all hospitals agreed to preferred contracts in 1984.

Preferred provider benefit programs may vary in several ways (in addition to normal benefit program variations). The first is the scope of services for which there are preferred provider incentives. Most preferred provider arrangements have included such incentives for hospital inpatient services and medical services. However, some preferred provider arrangements have extended (or limited) the scope of services affected by incentives to dental services, prescription drugs, mental health, clinical laboratory services, or podiatry.

A second way the benefit program can vary is in the types of incentives for members to use preferred providers. As noted before, the two common types of incentives are reduced cost sharing and balance billing protection. However, other types of incentives are being explored, such as cash rebates and expanded scope of benefits at preferred providers.

A third way the benefit program can vary is in the level of incentives. In some cases the level of incentive will be very explicit, for example the difference between no coinsurance and 20 percent coinsurance. In other cases the level will be less explicit. For example, the effective level of a balance billing incentive will depend on the difference between benefit payment limits for nonpreferred providers and each nonpreferred provider's unit charge level. The member may not know the amount of the additional out-of-pocket expense for using a nonpreferred provider until after the services are delivered.

A fourth way the benefit program can vary is in the conditions for receiving incentives. For example, most preferred provider arrangements currently award the financial incentive to the member if he uses any preferred provider. It is also possible to have each member designate a single preferred provider as a patient care manager and only award the incentive when services are delivered or ordered by the member's designated provider.

Currently, the major cost-control methods used with preferred provider arrangements are pricing methods and utilization controls. Different types of price controls can be used. These include percentage reductions from normal charges, provider-specific price limits, limits on the unit price for any provider in a geographic area or service category, and controls on the rate of price increases from year to year. Price units will vary from negotiated fee-for-service charges to intensity-adjusted per-case price schedules. Capitation payment and other population-based, risk-sharing arrangements, such as incentive pools for physicians, are being explored.

Utilization control methods may include a variety of preadmission, admission, concurrent, and retrospective review programs; provider profile programs; and associated utilization-management incentives and penalties.

It should be noted that these types of cost-control methods are designed to control the price and utilization practices of preferred providers. Most of these methods are derived from experience with contractual relationships between purchasers and providers in traditional benefit programs. However, there may be significant advances in the future in the development of cost control programs that help the provider to be more cost effective. One area of particular interest is restructuring the hospital medical staff relationship to foster more cost-effective delivery of the health care services they jointly produce. Another approach of interest is to have a designated preferred provider for each member that is responsible for "managing" all of that member's care. This approach may allow member-specific responsibility and incentives for providers.

Finally, it bears repeating that preferred provider arrangements are evolutionary. Trying to define them according to the specific characteristics that are evident (or make theoretical sense) today will add to confusion as "PPO-like" arrangements that meet the fundamentals but not the specifics of restrictive definitions continue to emerge. It is likely that additional variations will emerge that have not been discussed above. However, any arrangement that does not meet the four basic defining characteristics discussed above is fundamentally different—probably a traditional indemnity or service benefit program, an HMO, or a so-called EPO—and not a version of the basic preferred provider arrangement.

PREFERRED PROVIDER PRODUCTS AND VENDORS

An employer or union trust fund can in principle develop, fund, and administer a preferred provider arrangement without outside assistance. However, it is more likely that it will purchase all or some of the services required for a preferred provider benefit program from an outside vendor. In this case there is a tangible product being sold to the health benefit plan by the vendor.

A comprehensive preferred provider product is a benefit program fully supported by traditional administrative services (e.g., claims processing, data reporting), preferred provider selection, management of provider cost-control services, and financial arrangements for the benefit program. In essence, this product is a variation of the health care benefit programs traditionally purchased by most groups. Such comprehensive preferred provider products are being developed by Blue Cross and Blue Shield Plans, as well as by some commercial carriers, HMOs, and hospital chains.

However, in the past decade, the traditional health care benefit product has been unbundled into component services. For example, some groups self-fund their benefit programs and perform some administration themselves, while contracting with a vendor (e.g., a third-party administrator) for certain services such as claims processing.

Similarly, the preferred provider product is being unbundled into component services such as provider selection and contract negotiation, utilization control, and claims processing, as the following examples illustrate.

— The Prudent Buyer Plan is a comprehensive preferred provider product offered by Blue Cross of California. The product includes all services necessary for a preferred provider arrangement, including provider selection and contracting, payment and claims processing, cost control program administration, benefit packaging, and underwriting.

— Med-Network is a product offered by AdMar, a third-party administrator. With Med-Network, AdMar offers a developed provider network (provider selection and contract negotiation), utilization-review services, and claims processing services.

— Mountain Medical Affiliates is a hospital-sponsored PPO that offers affiliated hospitals and medical staff as preferred providers (provider selection), offers a contract to the purchaser (provider contracting), and conducts a utilization control program (cost-containment program administration).

— Insurance Dentists of America (IDOA) is organizing a national pool of dentists that it is marketing to commercial insurers offering dental coverage. IDOA is contracting with the dentists (provider selection) and has contracted with several major commercial insurers. The commercial insurers will individually make fee schedule offers to the pool of dentists. IDOA will also provide utilization data management services to participating insurers (cost-containment program management).

— Humana's Group Health Division is offering health benefit products regulated as HMOs. In some cases these are offered as preferred provider arrangements. The preferred provider products are comprehensive, with Humana Care Plus assuming the underwriting function and contracting with a commercial carrier for claims processing services.

These examples are not presented as comprehensive descriptions of the products but to illustrate that different vendors are offering different sets of component services.

The concepts of preferred provider products and of their unbundling are helpful in understanding the activity of PPOs. The term *PPO* is generally not used to refer to the preferred provider arrangement as defined above. Instead it usually refers to (1) the product being offered to a group health benefit plan (e.g., the Prudent Buyer Plan, Med-Network), (2) the vendor offering the product (e.g., Insurance Dentists of America, Mountain Medical Affiliates), (3) the group of providers that are designated as preferred by either a group health benefit plan or a vendor's product, or (4) one of the providers designated as preferred.

The tremendous diversity among preferred provider products and vendors can be viewed as an extension of the general trend of unbundling health benefit products into underwriting, claims processing, and benefit design services. The addition of provider selection and benefit incentives makes preferred provider arrangements more complex than traditional benefit programs and adds additional possibilities for unbundling the product. Thus, in comparing preferred provider products (or PPOs) it is useful to consider both the characteristics of the resulting preferred provider arrangements and the mix of component services included in the product.

The unbundling of the traditional health insurance product was accompanied by the emergence of new types of vendors—third-party administrators (TPAs)—that could offer component services without taking on the underwriting and other functions of insurers, HMOs, and Blue Cross and Blue Shield Plans. Similarly, the unbundling of the preferred provider product is being accompanied by the emergence of a variety of new vendors, in particular, entrepreneurial brokers that assemble preferred provider panels. It is also being accompanied by the diversification of established organizations, such as TPAs and hospital chains, into offering component services for a preferred provider arrangement.

The unbundling of preferred provider products has a variety of implications for health benefit plan managers, vendors, providers, and regulators. Health benefit plan managers will have a wide and perhaps confusing array of options regarding (1) the mix of services they purchase from a vendor and (2) whether they purchase different component services from different vendors. In addition, whether and how responsibilities are divided and coordinated between the health benefit plan and one or more vendors may have implications for the effectiveness of the preferred provider arrangement in terms of benefit cost control and service to members.

Vendors that are not capable of offering a comprehensive product will have to choose among merging, joint venturing, acquiring, or cooperating with other component service vendors. They will also have to assess which mix of services are attractive to which market segments.

Interested providers will have to decide whether to directly offer component services or participate in a preferred provider product organized by someone else. In principle, providers could pursue multiple avenues—offering themselves directly to group health benefit plans as preferred providers and participating in several preferred provider panels organized by different vendors. However, over time, such providers may find that they are competing with themselves, and some may reposition themselves to be more aligned with, or to exclusively participate in, a single product.

The unbundling of preferred provider products also presents special concerns for regulators. Some of the components of a preferred provider arrangement are already regulated in all (insurance) or some (provider rate setting) states. Other components are so new (provider selection), that there is little experience to draw from in judging the need for regulation. It will be important for regulators to sort out the component services and vendors into a manageable framework. If attempts are made to regulate PPOs as a uniform type of organization or product rather than as a collection of distinct functions, there will be risks that vendors will end-run regulation by adjusting the mix of services in their product or be constrained from offering their product because it does not fit an enabling definition.

EFFECTIVENESS ISSUES

The success of preferred provider arrangements will depend on their ability to meet the needs of health benefit plans in three performance areas: (1) benefit cost containment, (2) member access to and choice among preferred providers, and (3) stability.

BENEFIT COST CONTAINMENT

The ideal preferred provider arrangement may be a perfect symbiosis of the objectives of providers and health benefit plan managers. If it is possible to identify providers whose current practice patterns make them substantially more cost effective than the norm and to channel members to use these providers, then the cost-effective preferred providers will achieve marketing and financial objectives with little change in behavior. Likewise, the health benefit plan will achieve cost-control objectives and be better able to maintain more comprehensive coverage for its members.

In practice, neither provider selection nor patient channeling is likely to work so effectively. Developers of preferred provider arrangements do not have at their disposal tested methods for identifying the most cost-effective providers. In many cases, the 'preferred' providers are those that are affiliated with an organizing entity (e.g., a hospital chain), or those that offer or are willing to accept price controls and to participate in utilization-control programs. In addition, the ability to channel patients via benefit incentives is unclear. It is not known to what extent people will respond to these incentives.

The differences between the ideal scenario and current real world limitations can be expected to bring out some underlying inconsistencies between the motivations of providers and health benefit plans. The major motivation for providers to participate in preferred provider arrangements is to secure an adequate patient load that generates adequate net revenue. The health benefit plan is motivated by an interest in controlling the total flow of dollars to providers.

As a result of these different motivations, another form of competition could emerge—the competition between providers trying to maximize revenue while retaining preferred status and group purchasers trying to control provider prices and utilization patterns. In the short-run, the performance of preferred provider arrangements in controlling cost may depend on the outcome of this competition and thus will depend on the quality of the vendor's management of cost-control methods. In the early stages of the evolution of preferred provider arrangements, benefit program design, price controls, payment program administration, and utilization-control programs will be the driving forces for benefit cost control.

In the long term, the keys to cost-containment performance may be the purchaser's ability to identify cost-effective providers and the joint development of programs to facilitate their improved cost effectiveness. Identifying cost-effective providers will be at best an extremely complex task. It is well recognized that relative unit price is an inadequate measure, since low-unit prices can be offset by patient care management practices that cause excessive utilization.

Comparisons of some utilization indices are possible, but in most cases it will be extremely difficult to compare population-based indices such as admissions per thousand. In the traditional (i.e., non-HMO) delivery system, there is usually no population that can be exclusively associated with a given provider. Thus, it is extremely difficult to determine which providers are likely to make referral and hospitalization decisions that result in increased per-capita costs.

Finally, provider price and utilization performance is affected by the socioeconomic characteristics of the population the provider serves. For example, where housing conditions are poor, it may be inadvisable to discharge patients as early as would be possible where better home care can be expected.

These technical difficulties do not mean that purchasers or vendors of preferred provider products will be unable to evaluate cost effectiveness, but that the ability to do so will evolve over time. The approach of some preferred provider arrangements is to not exclude providers up front based on cost-effectiveness measures, but to be prepared to terminate contracts with preferred providers in the future based on poor performance. Given the state of the art of evaluating cost effectiveness, this may be an appropriate middle ground.

Where preferred provider arrangements create mutual benefit for group health benefit plans and providers, they may stimulate the development of more substantive programs to facilitate provider cost effectiveness. Vendors of preferred provider products could develop new information systems that help providers improve productivity, management consultant services for providers, and educational programs on effective patient-management techniques. The precedent for these types of activities is well established in the historic relationship between Blue Cross and Blue Shield Plans and their participating providers. As part of their contractual relationships with providers, many Plans fund or directly participate in experimental provider cost-containment programs; provide management information or consulting services; or sponsor cost-containment education programs for providers. Provider trade associations and multi-institutional organizations have also offered education and technical assistance programs to help member providers improve their efficiency. However, the symbiotic importance of cost-effective delivery of care to the objectives of group health benefit plans, vendors of preferred provider products, and preferred providers could support substantially enhanced development of cooperative cost-containment programs.

CHOICE AMONG PREFERRED PROVIDERS

The preferred provider arrangements and products under development vary in terms of the proportion of available providers that are preferred and the specialty service capacity of the preferred provider panels. From the health benefit plan's perspective, the preferred provider panel should be of adequate size and specialty mix to give members an adequate choice of quality providers to meet their health care needs. Otherwise, members will have no option but to go to nonpreferred providers for service.

In many cases, the PPOs approaching purchasers represent a small group of affiliated providers. In such cases, the purchaser may be able to contract with several PPOs to achieve an adequate set of preferred providers for its members.

However, if an insufficient proportion of local providers are participating in PPOs, the group purchaser may be unable to secure enough preferred providers through contracts with PPOs. Even if a large number of providers are participating in local PPOs, contracting with multiple

PPOs will require the purchaser to negotiate and administer a variety of different PPO contracts, and there still may be geographic and specialty gaps in the service capacity of the total group of preferred providers the purchaser can assemble.

An alternative is for the group purchaser to develop a single panel of preferred providers for an entire community, by selectively contracting among the total population of individual providers. The types of vendors most likely to do so include Blue Cross and Blue Shield Plans, commercial carriers, and entrepreneurial "brokers."

There are no empirical guidelines on what proportion of area providers should be included in a preferred provider panel. The initial trend in PPO development was toward panels with a very small proportion of area providers—but this was more likely driven by the desires of the organizing providers to gain a relatively exclusive competitive advantage than by an assessment of the needs of health benefit plans. While it can be argued that the preferred provider panel should be a small elite group of the most cost effective, the importance of adequate choice, geographic access, and specialty capacity should not be underestimated.

STABILITY

The third performance factor that will affect the success of preferred provider arrangements is stability, both of the preferred provider panels and of the vendors of preferred provider products. Regardless of how successful a preferred provider arrangement is in containing benefit costs, it may not be acceptable over the long run if too many members have to change providers too often because the 'preferred' providers keep changing.

Also of concern is the stability of the vendors of preferred provider products. A shakedown in the vendor market has already begun, with many vendors unable to get their products off the drawing board. It is likely that there will be further shakedowns with vendors withdrawing from the market, as the HMO market has experienced.

IMPLICATIONS FOR HEALTHCARE FINANCING AND DELIVERY

Preferred provider arrangements could foster changes in the roles of health care delivery and financing organizations, affect the competitive positions of these organizations, and have both positive and negative effects on access to affordable quality health care.

Employers, union trust funds, Blue Cross and Blue Shield Plans, and commercial carriers may become more active and selective purchasers of health care services for their members. While elements of selective purchasing are evident in the practices of some of these participants today (most notably, Blue Cross and Blue Shield Plans), their role as buying agent for members could more fully evolve.

Providers will gain a better understanding of the relationship between their role in health care delivery and the health care financing system. Some may become more active participants in the development of health care coverage programs, as an extension of their marketing efforts.

Preferred provider arrangements could substantially affect who are the winners and losers in health care delivery and financing competition. If preferred provider arrangements gain substantial enrollment, and benefit incentives channel patients to preferred providers, the survival of some providers may depend on whether they are in a preferred provider panel and in which one(s) they participate.

It is also possible that preferred provider arrangements could affect the competitive positions of Blue Cross and Blue Shield Plans, commercial insurers, and third-party administrators, while creating substantial new competition in the health care financing market. Blue Cross and Blue Shield Plans may extend their current competitive strength of effective contractual relationships with providers. Commercial carriers and third-party administrators could begin to establish this competitive strength, through a benefit program arrangement that may not require contracts with a major proportion of providers.

Competition among established and new health care financing organizations could subdivide the group benefit plan market into different segments desiring different characteristics in a preferred provider arrangement and seeking different mixes of services from vendors. To the extent there is a substantial market for preferred provider arrangements, it may be easier to secure a small market share than to maintain a large market share with a single product.

Any prediction as to who the competitive winners and losers will be is premature. However, it is possible to speculate that vendors who are experienced in all aspects of a preferred provider arrangement, are well organized, and are able to offer a variety of health care benefit arrangement options (in addition to preferred provider arrangements) to meet the needs of different market segments will be more likely to succeed.

The implications discussed above focus on the roles and competitive prospects of the organizations participating in health care delivery and financing—group health benefit plans, vendors of products to health benefit plans, and providers. Preferred provider arrangements could also have major implications for the social policy objective of maintaining and improving population access to high quality health care.

Preferred provider arrangements could contribute to more affordable health care in several ways. First, if preferred provider arrangements can help contain benefit costs, they may allow health benefit plans to maintain more comprehensive coverage, with access to the fee-for-service delivery system. Enrolled members will have maintained financial access to health care services, and the flow of needed resources to the health care delivery system will be more assured.

Second, preferred provider arrangements may promote greater provider cost effectiveness. They may give providers more powerful, competition-oriented incentives for the efficient delivery of health care services. The cost control programs developed by vendors and providers can help providers become better patient care managers. New innovations in financing and delivery may develop in an environment where experimentation can be more readily conducted with a limited set of providers. These cost-containment effects need not be limited to members enrolled in preferred provider arrangements, but can spill over to all patients served by the preferred providers.

Third, ideally, financial resources will be directed to the more efficient providers. Less efficient providers will become less viable financially. The reduction of excess provider capacity, and the development of new capacity such as ambulatory care and long-term care facilities, will hopefully be biased towards retention and expansion of the more cost-effective, well-managed providers.

The growth of preferred provider arrangements could also present serious social policy dangers. These dangers are inherent in any movement towards price and premium competition. They are not so much the result of preferred provider arrangements as they are byproducts of strategies to control health care costs via competition.

First, preferred provider arrangements can be inadvertantly or purposely designed to penalize the less healthy members of enrolled groups. For example, the group health benefit plan's cost may be shifted to less healthy members in the form of higher out of pocket expense if the set of preferred providers does not include adequate capacity to treat high-cost illness and coverage for services received from nonpreferred providers is reduced from current levels.

If a preferred provider arrangement with such inadequate design is offered as an option for individual selection by members of a group, it might attract the healthier members. The resulting concentration of the less healthy members in the other benefit programs would drive up their premiums and possibly drive up the less healthy members' contribution to premiums.

A second concern is that the growing stress on provider price competition could detract from the quality of care. This could result if providers respond to cost reduction incentives by providing too little care. In addition, providers may choose not to invest in health care delivery capacity that is needed in the community but that does not enhance their price competitiveness. It might be argued that if there is a need for such capacity, there will be demand and thus—in the long run—competitive advantage for some provider to develop the capacity. However, the lack of access on the way to a long-run, theoretical equilibrium may be an unacceptable price to pay for market efficiency.

A related concern is possible adverse impacts on providers that provide community services—such as medical education or high levels of charity care—that potentially make them poor price competitors. Such institutions might face choices such as being unable to join a preferred provider panel, having to deeply discount their charges in order to join one, or having to reduce their community service role.

Another danger is that provider price competition in general, and in particular as stimulated by preferred provider arrangements, will engender predatory pricing by institutional providers that have the resources to subsidize deeply discounted prices. For example, some hospitals could offer prices below their unit resource costs and finance the discount from reserves, in order to compete in the short-term for preferred status. A more efficient provider without discount subsidy resources could suffer a loss of patients when faced with competition from such a provider.

Finally, as noted earlier in this article, some vendors of preferred provider products are very new. Indeed, the health care benefit market may soon be flooded with new entrants. Some vendors could encounter the financial and managerial difficulties possible with any new business venture. This is a risk that must be accepted if health care cost solutions are to be sought through competition and innovation. But there should also be concern that distressed vendors could provide poor service to health benefit plans or providers or could collapse altogether, leaving a health benefit plan in disarray.

CONCLUSION

Most fundamentally, preferred provider arrangements are vehicles for achieving provider marketing strategies and health benefit plan cost-control strategies. These strategies are being put into action through the development of health care benefit program arrangements that are designed to control benefit costs by giving members incentives to use health care providers designated as preferred but that also provide substantial coverage for services from other health care providers. While several basic characteristics distinguish preferred provider arrangements from other established types of health care benefit programs, there is room for wide variation in terms of provider selection, benefit program design, and cost-control methods.

Preferred provider products are combinations of services offered to support a group health benefit plan's preferred provider arrangement. Just as the traditional health insurance product has been unbundled into component services, the comprehensive preferred provider product is being unbundled into component services.

The wide variety of activities and organizations referred to as PPOs, and the associated disagreement and confusion regarding what a PPO is, can be explained by:

— The variation possible in the specific characteristics of different preferred provider arrangements.
— The different mixes of services that can be included in a preferred provider product.
— The variety of established and new organizations acting as vendors of preferred provider products.
— The fact that the term PPO is alternatively used to refer to the preferred provider arrangement, the associated products, their vendors, and providers participating as preferred.

It remains to be seen whether preferred provider arrangements will play a significant role in health care financing. To achieve such a role, these arrangements will have to meet the needs of group health benefit plans for cost containment, member access to an adequate choice of preferred providers, and stability.

As they evolve, preferred provider arrangements could stimulate significant changes in health care delivery and financing. Health care purchasers and providers could take on new roles, and there may be major competitive winners and losers among health care providers and health care coverage vendors.

Of more fundamental concern is how these arrangements will improve or detract from population access to high quality health care services. Competitive forces alone will not be sufficient to ensure that the potential benefits of preferred provider arrangements are realized while their possible dangers are avoided. It will be necessary for local community leaders to influence the vendors and purchasers of preferred provider products to be accountable to the needs of the communities in which they operate. Thus the key to ensuring that preferred provider arrangements contribute to affordable, quality health care will be to achieve a balance between competitive forces and community accountable leadership.

NOTES

1. We will use the term "group purchaser" to refer to an organization responsible for negotiating and administering contracts with providers for the provision of health care services to members of a group health benefit program.

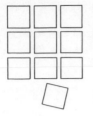

The Changing Environment for Healthcare Services

REDEFINING PREFERRED PROVIDER CONTRACTING MODELS

Peter N. Grant, J.D.
Weissburg and Aronson, Inc.
San Francisco, CA

The purpose of this essay is to provide a definitional context for discussing California preferred provider contracting activities, to describe current contracting models, and to discuss the future relationship between fee for service preferred provider arrangements and the growing number of capitated, closed panel plans in California.

Since the beginning of 1984, hospital selective contracting activities have been on the increase in California. Hospitals in certain urban areas gained limited experience through contracting with individual practice associations (IPAs) and group model health maintenance organizations (HMOs) during the 1970s. However, it was only in the fall of 1982 and spring of 1983, after the passage of AB 799, that Medi-Cal established the precedent for a statewide selective contracting effort with hospitals.

Following in the footsteps of the Medi-Cal program and based on the authority of AB 3480, Blue Cross commenced contractual negotiations to create a network of providers for its Prudent Buyer Plan preferred provider program in March of 1983. In the context of contemporary selective contracting, the Prudent Buyer Plan did for physician contracting what the Medi-Cal program did for hospital contracting: transformed it from abstraction to reality. Of course, Blue Shield had pioneered large scale physician contracting almost 40 years earlier. These successive contracting waves by the major public and private purchasers of health care services in the State were accompanied by major publicity efforts and have received significant media coverage on both a statewide and national basis.

Following the lead of Medi-Cal and Blue Cross, in 1984 a broad variety of entities have moved into the alternative delivery system marketplace. These plans involve provider discounts, increased utilization review (including preadmission certification, admission review, and concurrent review), and financial incentives for beneficiaries to seek care from contracting providers.

In early 1985 various private sector and governmental initiatives appear to be precursors of even more fundamental changes in California's health care marketplace. The federal regulations which authorize the Medicare program to contract on a capitated basis with federally qualified HMOs and state licensed competitive medical plans (CMPs) went into effect on February 1, 1985. On February 10, 1985, California's Medi-Cal Expanded Choice waiver request was granted by the Health Care Financing Administration (HCFA). Pursuant to this program it is anticipated that up to 25 percent of the Medi-Cal population will be enrolled in capitated systems.

The institution of these new governmental programs in conjunction with the growth in private sector HMO enrollment has resulted in an expansion of the service areas and marketing efforts of existing plans and in a growth in the number of plans seeking state licensure and federal qualification. In many cases providers either individually or in joint venture are integrating forward to create new licensed plans. These developments have also brought about basic changes in the relationships between the plans and contracting providers. While the physician component of the plan's provider network, either IPAs or integrated groups, have generally been capitated for professional services, hospitals have traditionally been compensated on the basis of discounted customary charges or per diem rates. However, with amazing rapidity California hospitals are now accepting capitated payment for the provision of all inpatient services.

A DEFINITIONAL FRAMEWORK

CURRENT VIEW

The selective contracting activities described above have generally been discussed under the broad and ill-defined aegis of preferred provider organizations (PPOs). The health care industry has tended to divide the various PPO arrangements into three types: payor-based PPOs, intermediary or entrepreneur-based PPOs, and provider-based PPOs. However, such a definitional framework is no longer reflective of the dynamic health care marketplace, and its continued use has actually made it more difficult to discuss the evolution of California's alternative delivery systems. Indeed, discussions of marketplace development often seem to bog down because of a lack of shared terminology.

BASIS FOR A NEW APPROACH

Articulating a definitional framework for the purpose of discussing preferred provider contracting in California has been made all the more challenging by the changes in the health care and health insurance industries over the past several years. In the early 1980s the health care marketplace has become increasingly complex. The categories of health care providers have expanded greatly with the advent of new delivery modes, such as freestanding "urgi-," "emergi-" and "surgi-centers," and the expanding role of allied health professionals. Correspondingly, in the health insurance industry there has been an unbundling of services such as data analysis, claims administration, and billing.

Certain generalities can be cited as a basis for categorizing contracting activity in California. The individual consumer in the health care marketplace purchases one product, health care coverage, which consists of two fundamentally distinguishable major functions. The first and most obvious function is *the direct provision of health care services* by health care providers, including physicians, other health care professionals, acute care hospitals and alternative delivery modes such as freestanding urgent care and surgical centers. The second necessary function is *the underwriting of health care benefits,* which involves the acceptance of the economic risk of the cost of health care for others in return for a predetermined payment. Underwriting is generally associated with the creation of the benefit package, actuarial expertise, and the marketing of the total plan package to groups or individual consumers. Other related functions include claims processing and billing, which are often performed either by the underwriting entity or by independent third-party administrators, and utilization review services, which are becoming increasingly important as a cost-containment strategy.

The underwriting function has been performed traditionally by carriers that include indemnity insurers or service plans such as Blue Cross and, more recently, health maintenance organiztions. These underwriting entities accept economic risk by contracting for predetermined rates with individuals or groups to cover the costs of health care services and are subject to numerous governmental regulations, including significant financial reserve requirements. More recently, however, business and labor has tended to self-insure for health benefits with reinsurance used in some cases to limit overall risk.

ALTERNATIVE FRAMEWORK

Based upon this understanding of the marketplace, preferred provider activities can be divided into the following categories: purchaser-based preferred provider arrangements, preferred provider plans, and provider networks. These three categories are not mutually exclusive in that provider networks contract with both purchaser-based preferred provider arrangements and preferred provider plans to serve as a provider panel. This framework is only partially reflective of the variety of preferred provider contracting arrangements in California. It is anticipated that further definitional efforts will be made as the marketplace evolves.

Purchaser-Based Preferred Provider Arrangements

A purchaser-based preferred provider arrangement is instituted by a self-insured entity, such as a self-insured employer or union trust, which contracts either directly with individual providers of care or with a preexisting provider network to render health care services to members of the self-insured group. Examples of self-insured entities contracting with providers for the provision of health care include two California companies: Hewlett-Packard in Santa Clara and Cubic in San Diego.

Such purchaser-based preferred provider arrangements enjoy a great deal of creative flexibility because state insurance regulatory schemes are preempted by the Employee Retirement Income Security Act of 1974 (ERISA).

Preferred Provider Plans

A preferred provider plan is generally formed by a carrier that sells the service of underwriting health care benefits for others. Health benefit underwriters are licensed by the state and include indemnity insurers, nonprofit hospital service plans such as Blue Cross, and state licensed health plans such as Blue Shield. These carriers of health benefits may either create their own provider panels by directly contracting with hospitals and physicians or by entering into contracts with a preexisting provider network. As noted below, Blue Cross and Blue Shield have chosen to form their own unique system of providers in California while certain indemnity insurers have contracted with preexisting provider networks. Another model of preferred provider plan entails a joint venture between the carrier and providers. In several states, including Oregon and New Mexico, Blue Cross is entering into such joint ventures with providers. After the preferred provider plan that consists of both the underwriting and health care provider components is created, the plan is marketed to nonself-insuring groups or individuals.

As well, it is possible for an insurer to offer its provider component to a self-insured employer on an administrative services only (ASO) basis, thereby essentially abandoning its underwriting function.

Provider Networks

A provider network is a group of health care providers that have been organized to offer a system of care to the consumer. Provider networks do not underwrite health benefits. Provider networks can be formed by providers, independent entrepreneurs, insurance brokers, or third-party administrators. Most provider networks in California include both hospitals and physicians. However, separate hospital and physician networks do exist, and specialty networks have been formed by dentists, pharmacists, and psychologists. The goal of a provider network is to offer a group of institutional and noninstitutional providers that provide high quality care, are efficient and cost effective, include the full range of needed services, and are geographically accessible. Provider networks formed by providers often involve the creation of a new corporation that markets the network either directly to self-insuring purchasers or to carriers to serve as the provider component of a preferred provider plan.

The relationship of preferred provider plans to provider networks is ambiguous. Provider networks are created in part to contract with a carrier to serve as the provider component of a plan to be marketed to non-self-insuring groups. Such a relationship is often described as the underwriting of a provider network. Alternatively, a provider network may enter into a joint venture with a carrier in order to offer a preferred provider benefit package in the marketplace. However, provider networks concurrently seek to approach purchasers, both employers and unions, directly to offer the services of the provider network in the hope that the entity would desire to self-insure. In this latter situation the carrier would be precluded from offering underwriting services to the self-insured entity.

In organizing their preferred provider plans, certain California carriers, such as Blue Cross and Blue Shield, have chosen to create their own provider panel through direct contact rather than to contract with preexisting provider networks. The reasons for this decision appear to vary. The carriers that have contracted with providers directly have generally been large enough to absorb the cost of such a selective contracting effort. As noted above, there seems to be some fear that contracting with provider networks will legitimize them in the eyes of employers and unions and potentially spread the trend toward self-insuring. Some carriers wish to base the selection of participating providers on the basis of their own data. Finally, there is some concern that provider-controlled provider networks will tend to be less cost efficient because of economic self-interest.

Other carriers have chosen to contract with existing provider networks. The creation of a network of providers and, in particular, the physician component of such a network, can be both costly and time consuming. Existing provider networks can offer a cost-effective method of obtaining provider participation in the plan. Further, many provider networks exhibit a certain flexibility in contracting with carriers or purchasers that allows for consideration of a purchaser's unique needs. For example, provider networks will often alter the network of contracts pursuant to negotiations with purchasers. Networks also often offer a convenient utilization-review program.

The constraints of the antitrust laws are also of key concern to provider networks. Provider-controlled networks, in contracting with both carriers and self-insured purchasers, are confronted with significant antitrust inhibitions. After the decision in *Arizona* v. *Maricopa County Medical Society* 457 U.S. 332 (1982), it is uncertain whether a provider-controlled network would be able to sufficiently integrate its activities so that it can act as a single economic unit in the marketplace unless it is willing to take on at least some level of economic risk. Accordingly, provider-controlled networks must take care that their activities do not fall afoul of the antitrust prohibitions against price-setting and concerted refusals to deal with purchasers.

Provider networks are now confronted with several major strategic issues. Increasingly, provider networks may find it appropriate to joint venture with carriers to offer preferred provider plan options. Further, provider networks must deterine whether it would be advantageous to either acquire or apply to become a health benefits underwriter, such as an insurance company, nonprofit hospital service plan, or State licensed HMO. Whether or not California environment will nurture the creation of numerous new provider-controlled alternative delivery systems, the progeny of Blue Cross and Blue Shield, is a most intriguing and important question.

CURRENT MARKETPLACE ACTIVITY

The following is a partial listing of PPOs that are currently being implemented in California and a brief commentary regarding the unique approaches being utilized in creating the system.

PURCHASER-BASED PREFERRED PROVIDER ARRANGEMENTS

Hewlett-Packard

Hewlett-Packard Company (HP), a Santa Clara self-insured employer that employs 16,000 in Santa Clara County, has chosen to create a preferred provider arrangement for the benefit of its employees by contracting directly with providers. They have contracted with El Camino Hospital and the El Camino Preferred Physicians Medical Group, a group of physicians on the medical staff of El Camino Hospital.

Other Arrangements

A variety of public and private entities including self-insured employers and union trust funds are in the process of establishing smaller, local preferred provider arrangements. Examples of such direct contracting include the activities of public entities, such as the City and County of San Francisco and several local school and fire districts; employers, such as Cubic of San Diego; and unions, such as the Retail Clerks, Carpenters, and Butchers Unions.

PREFERRED PROVIDER PLANS

Blue Cross Prudent Buyer Plan

In March of 1983, Blue Cross began contracting with California hospitals and physicians to create the provider panel for its preferred provider plan, the Prudent Buyer Plan. Currently Blue Cross has Prudent Buyer Plan contracts with 197 hospitals and approximately 15,500 physicians. Initially Blue Cross only offered the Prudent Buyer Plan to groups of 25 or more. However, in order to increase enrollment, many Blue Cross individual freedom of choice plan members were converted to the Prudent Buyer Plan in October of 1984. Approximately 500,000 of the total Blue Cross enrollment of 5 million are currently Prudent Buyer Plan members.

Blue Shield Preferred Plan

Blue Shield began limited hospital contracting to create a preferred provider panel in April of 1983. Blue Shield's physician membership of 37,500 comprises the preferred physicians. Currently, Blue Shield has contracts with 184 hospitals. Under the hospital contract, rate discounts are made available to all Blue Shield subscribers, not only Preferred Plan members. Approximately 100,000 of the total Blue Shield enrollment of 1,300,000 are Preferred Plan members.

PruNET

This preferred provider arrangement is being created by Prudential Life Insurance Company. It is the PPO sister to Prudential's HMO product, PruCARE. As one of the major health insurers in the state, PruNET is viewed as an important competitor in the alternative delivery system marketplace.

PruNET is actually a hybrid of a preferred provider plan and an insurer-based provider network. It contracts directly with providers to provide health care services for enrollees who have purchased coverage from Prudential. As well, the PruNET network will be available to self-insured groups with Prudential marketing claims administration services in conjunction with the provider network.

PruNET is currently contracting with hospitals on the basis of multiple per-diem rates and with physicians on the basis of a 15 percent discount off of the physicians' usual fee or 15 percent off of the usual and prevailing fee for the service area, whichever is less.

PruNET established a PPO program in Santa Barbara effective October 1, 1983 and has recently completed its provider directory for the Santa Clara/Santa Cruz area. PruNET's East Bay provider network is almost complete, and PruNET is preparing to commence provider contracting activities in San Francisco and Los Angeles.

Aetna CHOICE

The Aetna Life Insurance Company is another major underwriter of health care benefits in Northern California. Aetna has chosen to implement its experimental CHOICE program in three locations nationwide: Santa Clara, California; Washington, D.C.; and Evanston, Illinois.

The CHOICE program constitutes a unique reversal of the Safeco primary care case management alternative delivery system model. Subscribers are allowed freedom of choice to select primary care physicians but must receive all specialty care and hospital-based services only from designated providers.

CHOICE has executed risk-sharing contracts for specialty services with the Palo Alto Clinic and San Jose Clinic. It has entered into contracts with Stanford University Hospital, San Jose Health Center, and El Camino Hospital for inpatient services. CHOICE has obtained a Knox-Keene license for its operations in California.

Other Plans

Other preferred provider plan arrangements include those established by Transamerica Occidental (Transamericare), Fireman's Fund (Health Plus), Pacific Mutual, Metropolitan Life, and New York Life. Like Prudential, several of these carriers are developing hybrids of preferred provider plans and provider networks. Several state licensed plans are in the process of spinning off PPO products. These reportedly include Bay Pacific and Health Plan of America.

PROVIDER NETWORKS

Preferred Health Network (PHN) and SELECT Health

These two hospital/physician joint venture provider networks offer comprehensive provider networks either individually or in combination.

Northern California Health Care Cooperative, Inc., doing business as SELECT Health, is a multi-hospital–based Preferred Provider Organization that is comprised of well-respected hospitals and associated physicians in Northern California.

SELECT Health is organized as a California Cooperative Corporation, with the seven hospitals acting as equal members of the Corporation. The hospitals and the associated physician groups are represented on the Board of Directors. Business and community representatives will also serve on the Board.

Each of the hospitals and individual physicians associated with the hospital is available to enter into agreements with employers, health and welfare trust funds, and insurance companies for negotiated, predetermined rates for services. The SELECT Health providers are committed to participating in a strict utilization-review program to be monitored by the SELECT Health staff and a utilization-review committee.

SELECT Health providers are geographically accessible to residents throughout Northern California. Another four to six hospitals and associated physician groups are expected to join the network shortly. SELECT Health is actively marketing the services of its member providers.

Preferred Health Network (PHN) is a California corporation that is owned, governed, and operated by equal participation of member hospitals and physicians. There are no outside investors or outside stockholders. Members of the medical staff associated with each member hospital are organized into a legal entity referred to as a professional practice group (PPG). A representative of each hospital and each PPG has a seat on the Board of Directors. Hospitals, PPGs, and physicians in PPGs each sign a participation agreement that incorporates standard terms and conditions. The standard terms and conditions describe how payors, hospitals, PPGs and physicians relate to each other, including an integrated utilization-review system. Contracts are negotiated between payors and member providers utilizing the super messenger concept. The 18 network hospitals were selected based on their strong reputations and low operating costs. Network physicians, numbering more than 2,000, were selected for their dedication to quality health care as well as their prudent use of health care services. Geographically, the PHN hospitals and related PPGs are uniformly distributed across both Los Angeles and Orange Counties.

The PPO Alliance

Three hospital-based PPO organizations—UnitedHEALTH (sponsored by Adventist Health System-West), CarePLUS (sponsored by Health West), and Universal Health Network (sponsored by the Lutheran Hospital Corporation)—have joint-ventured a new, for-profit market entity called PPO Alliance that is headquartered in Cypress, California. PPO Alliance builds on the increasing growth of all three member organizations and will add more hospitals and physicians and close gaps in geographic access to services. The number of contracting hospitals are expected to increase from the current 55 to approximately 90. The number of contracting physicians is expected to grow from 700 to approximately 1,500. PPO Alliance now has 57,000 subscribers from among several employer groups, union trusts, and insurance carriers. By joint-venturing under a common marketing entity that also draws on allied consulting and UR services, PPO Alliance could become a prominent force in the state's marketplace. While the present pattern of payment for participating hospitals follows contract per-diem arrangements, PPO Alliance plans a test of DRGs.

National Medical Enterprises Healthpace

National Medical Enterprises (NME), the Los Angeles based investor-owned hospital holding company, and Carroon & Black, the New York based insurance services company, are preparing to market health benefits to employers in California by mid-1984 and nationwide by late 1984. Carroon & Black will provide marketing, claims processing, and actuarial services. The provider network will consist of NME hospitals, where available, and nonaffiliated hospitals in areas with no NME facility.

Foundations for Medical Care, PPO, Inc.

Many of the local Foundations for Medical Care in California are in the process of establishing local provider networks. Existing physician members of the Foundations are serving as the physician component of the networks while the Foundations are contracting with hospitals on the basis of multiple per-diem rates. The First Far West Insurance Company underwrites the Foundation network in certain parts of the state. Recently, the First Far West/Foundation PPO received contracts with the influential California Public Employees Retirement System (PERS) in three large counties of the state.

Other Networks

Other provider-based networks include Preferred Providers of America (PPA) (a joint venture of the state's multispecialty clinics) and California Preferred Professionals (CPPI) (a physician-controlled physician network). Specialty provider networks, such as dental, podiatrist, psychologist, and pharmacy PPOs, are also being created.

CAPITATION AND THE FUTURE OF PREFERRED PROVIDER CONTRACTING

Many observers of the health care marketplace have argued that the development of discounted, fee for service preferred provider arrangements should be seen as an interim step in the development of a system of fully capitated, competing plans. From this perspective, the recent expansion in private sector enrollment in capitated plans and the implementation of new governmental programs which would allow Medicare and Medi-Cal beneficiaries to enroll in such plans is cited as a natural step in the evolution.

Others concede that enrollment in closed panel, capitated plans will inevitably increase. However, it is argued that this trend will serve to increase the importance of preferred provider arrangements. Underlying this view is the concept of adverse selection. As adverse risks are more and more concentrated in the PPO modified freedom of choice plans, it becomes even more essential for health care purchasers to channel these adverse risks to efficient providers who have agreed to rate discounts and are subject to strict utilization review.

Whether or not the latter view of the competitive market prevails and continues to include full freedom of choice options, either version contemplates at least a temporary coexistence of PPO and HMO options. This situation raises a particularly difficult and sensitive issue regarding the appropriate manner in which physicians should be organized for alternative delivery system contracting. While the physician components of California preferred provider arrangements generally consist of large, nonintegrated, multispeciality professional corporations or unincorporated associations, most capitated plan physician components are made up of smaller partially integrated IPAs or fully integrated primary care or multispeciality groups. The solution to the issue of the most effective and politically palatable form of physician organization and interaction is perhaps the next challenge for California providers in this era of competition.

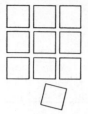 **Economics of Marketplace Competition**

COMPETITION STRATEGY, MARKET MODELS, AND PREFERRED PROVIDER PLANS

Walter McClure, Ph.D.

President
Center for Policy Studies
Minneapolis, MN

☐ A new approach to assuring adequate medical care and coverage at acceptable cost is being implemented in various forms around the country. This approach has come to be known as the *competition strategy* because it emphasizes increased use of competitive market principles rather than sole reliance on strong and direct economic regulation and control of providers by government. This chapter will describe and discuss some of the strengths and weaknesses of this new approach in relation to different market models including preferred provider plans.

The competition strategy is a comprehensive approach to medical care policy that should be understood as a means to an end, not an end in itself. The underlying principle is to give medical consumers the means and incentives to choose efficient health care providers over inefficient ones.

In the last 20 years, the United States has made substantial progress in extending adequate medical care and financial protection to most of its population through a combination of private and public insurance. However, the adoption of increasingly universal and comprehensive health insurance has been accompanied by a persistent and excessive rise in medical expenditures that has proven difficult to control. The problem is to control these expenditures without sacrifice to adequate medical care and insurance protection.

There are legitimate reasons causing medical expenditures to rise: the aging of the population, new medical technology, and the increased cost of resources in general. But the principal reason for the excessive rise in medical expenditures is the increasing overelaboration of medical practice style far beyond the point of diminishing marginal returns to health improvement (i.e., the point at which the health benefit resulting from additional medical care becomes less than the cost of the additional care). A shift to more conservative and efficient practice styles would bring the annual rate of increase in medical expenditures down without sacrificing the quality and availability of medical care.

OVERLY ELABORATE MEDICAL CARE

In the hands of competent providers, conservative as well as elaborate practice styles appear capable of equally good patient results and represent high quality. For example, the Mayo Clinic practices a conservative style requiring 30 percent less hospitalization than the national average for comparable patients (800 versus 1,200 hospital days per 1,000 population, respectively), whereas the city of Boston, equally noted for medical excellence, practices an elaborate style with higher hospital use rates than the national average.

These differences in style can be conceptually represented by Exhibit 1.

EXHIBIT 1
Community Health Status versus Utilization and Expenditure Rates (services and expenditures per capita)

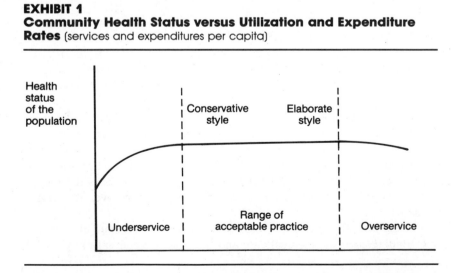

For any given population, the diagram suggests that below the most conservative utilization rates, services are inadequate and health status falls. Above the most elaborate rates, patients are subjected to excessive risk and health status again falls. In between is the range of acceptable practice, and it is quite broad; given competent providers, health status appears to be equally good all across this range.

While both elaborate and conservative medical practice styles appear to get equally good results and are clinically acceptable, they are not equally financially acceptable. The most elaborate styles cost almost twice as much per capita as the most conservative styles. For example, the more conservative styles require about 1.3 to 1.5 physicians and 600 to 800 hospital days per 1,000 population; whereas the national average, which tends toward the elaborate style, is about 1.9 physicians and 1,200 hospital days per 1,000 population.[1] Thus, if the United States were to shift to the more conservative practice styles, it might save up to 20 percent or more on national medical expenditures.

It should be emphasized that a shift to conservative style does not represent denial or rationing of services. For example, the Mayo Clinic, a conservative provider, can hardly be accused of denying services; it simply does all that medical care can do with fewer services per patient than more elaborate providers. Also, conservative style should not be equated to "low technology," nor elaborate style to "high technology." Every sophisticated medical technology known is available at Mayo Clinic. Rather, it appears that conservative providers deploy both low and high technology conservatively, and elaborate providers deploy both low and high technology aggressively. From the standpoint of accepted clinical practice, both styles appear equally good.

The style of medical practice can be endlessly elaborated to absorb every dollar that society is willing to spend. Thus, a kind of medical Parkinson's Law operates: style of practice rises to absorb the dollars available. Such medical care is not bad, it is simply cost ineffective. More health and well-being would result if the money were spent on other priorities such as adequate nutrition, improved lifestyles, safer workplaces, and decreased toxins in the environment.

MARKET FAILURE

The medical care system has been thrown into serious market failure by present health insurance. The present elaboration of medical practice style stems from an underlying cause—the perverse incentives created by present health insurance.

These perverse incentives act on both patients and providers. Consider the patient. Under present comprehensive health insurance, the patient pays little or nothing for most services, and so is indifferent to their cost. Thus, consumers have little incentive to use medical care prudently or to seek out conservative, efficient providers. In fact, because the insurance pays, they do not even have the means to identify conservative providers. Medical consumers do not necessarily demand elaborate services, they only want relief from illness. But if costly elaborate services are offered, the patient has little reason to refuse them.

Consider the provider. Present health insurance pays for services; the more services provided and the more complex those services, the more it pays. Thus, elaborate providers are rewarded, the more elaborate they are. Conversely, conservative providers lose revenue, the more conservative and efficient they are.

Presumably a conservative provider rendering fewer services per patient could make up revenues by caring for more patients. But because present insurance makes patients indifferent to the cost, conservative providers gain no new patients by their more economical style. Quite the contrary, a patient indifferent to cost is likely to be impressed by elaborate services even when they add little or nothing to their health outcome. Thus under present insurance, the elaborate provider is more likely to gain patients than the conservative provider.

Given two equally acceptable styles of practice, one well paid the other poorly paid, providers will certainly choose the better paid one. Indeed, in many areas insurance is now supporting so many physicians and hospitals that they must practice the elaborate style to stay in business. With fewer patients for each provider, the providers must provide more services to each patient to keep up revenues. A conservative provider would simply go broke.

The problem is not bad patients or bad providers, it is a badly designed insurance system. As long as the insurance system rewards elaborate providers and punishes conservative providers, no policy to encourage more conservative practice is likely to succeed.

Present health insurance removes the price mechanism from consumer choice and provider competition, and thereby eliminates all considerations of cost from consumers and providers. In effect, present health insurance hands consumers and providers a blank check to do whatever they wish. A spare-no-expense mentality develops, and providers compete solely on nonprice factors. Since present health insurance rewards elaborate practice styles, this provider competition tends to focus on increasing elaboration of practice style. Thus under the present market failure, provider competition is, in fact, cost generating rather than cost saving with little additional benefit to health status.

MARKET REMEDIES

There are basically only two fundamental remedies for market failure:

— *Market reform:* This strategy would restructure the medical care and health insurance systems sufficiently to establish the struc-

tural conditions of a sound market. This must be done in ways that respect equity so that low-income persons are assured of adequate medical care and insurance.
— *Government regulation and control:* This strategy would impose direct economic regulations or controls on providers to keep expenditures under control while not altering the present incentives on consumers.

Usually the first type of economic regulation imposed is to place limits on physician fees and hospital charges, i.e., to limit service prices. Almost universally, this type of regulation alone has been found inadequate; indeed, it tends to aggravate the rise in expenditures because it aggravates elaboration of practice style.

To see this, observe that it is average expenditure per capita, not service prices, that reflects the true burden of expenditures. Average expenditure per capita is made up of three factors: (1) service price, (2) services per capita, and (3) complexity of service mix. Or, expressed in a different way:

$$\text{Expenditure per capita} = \text{Service price} \times \text{Services per capita} \times \text{Complexity of service mix.}$$

Simply limiting the service price (e.g., physician fee and hospital per diem) does not limit expenditures because providers will maintain their revenues by increasing the quantity and complexity of services offered each patient. In other words, providers will beat a fee schedule by elaborating style. Thus expenditures per capita will rise, despite service price controls, with no commensurate improvement in health status.

The best index of conservative practice is high-quality medical care at low-expenditures per capita. Conversely, the index of elaborate practice is high-quality medical care at high expenditures per capita.[2] If regulation could identify conservative providers, it would do better to reward these conservative providers with a higher fee because they keep the quantity and complexity of services so much lower than elaborate providers. But even were this done, the problem remains that there is no incentive directing the patient to the conservative providers in preference to the elaborate providers. Indeed, government usually finds itself alone trying to resist style and expenditure increases while under attack from both providers and consumers.

To solve this problem, the government control strategy always moves toward more complete government control. Eventually it must place a budgetary ceiling on total expenditures per capita and then institute controls, not only on service prices but on the quantity and complexity of services.[3] Attempts to directly control the quantity and complexity of services (e.g., through "utilization review") have not worked well. Since providers themselves disagree on whether conservative or elaborate style is more appropriate, it has been impossible for bureaucrats to enforce more conservative practice.

As an alternative, the market reform strategy can achieve the advantages of the government control strategy without its disadvantages. Market reform, or the term *competition strategy,* does not refer to just any kind of competition. As shown above, provider competition under market failure is cost generating rather than cost saving. Rather, it refers to competition that occurs in a market that meets all the structural conditions required for a sound market.

Also, the competition strategy does not refer to some doctrinaire, laissez-faire ideology. In a market as charged with the public well-being as medical care, there must be proper oversight and safeguards. Physician licensure, hospital safety codes, quality, and peer review safeguards, as well as antitrust regulation, must be maintained. Further, the market must be designed to assure equity: there must be adequate subsidies, via one mechanism or another, to assure that low-income persons have equitable purchasing power for medical care and health insurance in the new reformed market.

In sum, the essence of the competition strategy is to give consumers the means to identify more efficient and more conservative providers and fair incentives to choose them in preference to more elaborate providers. In turn, this will compel more costly and elaborate providers to compete for patients by adopting more conservative and efficient practice styles or else lose their patients to providers that do.

SOUND MARKETS

The problem can be usefully restated in the language of economics. The perverse incentives described above do not arise in sound markets. In sound markets, consumers are rewarded for seeking out efficient producers because they get better value for money. Thus, inefficient or poor quality producers lose customers to efficient, good quality producers, creating powerful incentives for producers to compete on efficiency, quality, and responsiveness to consumers.

The competition strategy attempts to overcome perverse incentives in the current market by creating the conditions for a sound market. The strategy consists of two parts: First, it must spell out a model for the future medical care and insurance system that meets the structural requirements of a sound market. Second, it must spell out a practical implementation strategy to gradually move the present system from its current form to the new future model.

A sound market must satisfy at least the following structural conditions:

— A sufficient number of competing producers.

— A fair price mechanism felt by consumers and producers.
— Free entry and exit from the market for producers.
— No collusion or cartel behavior by producers.
— Adequate consumer information about alternative producers.

Any proposed market model must be examined against each of these conditions. The better it approximates them, the more likely it will perform well. The less it approximates them, the more poorly it will perform.

If one or more of these structural requirements is seriously violated, the market is said to be in failure, which produces perverse incentives leading to wasteful, unresponsive, poorly distributed goods and services. The present system performs poorly exactly because it so seriously violates a majority of the required conditions for a sound market.

There are at least four different market models that appear to satisfy these conditions: (1) major risk insurance, (2) competing health care plans, (3) preferred provider plans, and (4) a combined market model. They differ mainly in the price mechanism used. Each has distinct strengths and weaknesses and will be discussed in turn with special emphasis on preferred provider plans.

MAJOR RISK INSURANCE MODEL

This model uses service prices as the price mechanism for provider competition. Since present comprehensive insurance masks service prices from consumers, this model replaces comprehensive insurance with "major risk insurance."[4] Under major risk insurance, the insurance pays for medical services only if and when family medical bills exceed, say, 10 percent of household income. Until this threshold is exceeded, consumers must pay medical bills out of their own pocket.

This model radically alters the incentives on consumers and providers while still assuring excellent financial protection. No consumer will have to pay more than 10 percent of household income; this is probably too high for low-income persons, so the threshold could be reduced to 5 percent of income for the near poor and to 0 percent (total coverage) for the most poor. On the other hand, most families will be paying most of their medical bills out of pocket. They, therefore, have strong incentive to use medical care more prudently (empirical evidence supports this), and to seek out providers who charge reasonable service prices, and who treat conservatively (empirical evidence is not yet available).[5] This empirical evidence also suggests that consumers will not deny themselves necessary medical care as long as their share of the cost is not excessive relative to their ability to pay.[6] Although consumers lack the expertise to make perfect choices among providers every time, the theory is that enough consumers will make appropriate choices enough of the time to alter provider practice style over time. Elaborate providers will gradually lose patients to more conservative providers unless and until they change to more conservative styles themselves.

There are many other forms of major risk insurance besides that above. For example, a different major risk insurance plan might require consumers to pay 50 percent of the first $3,000 of medical expenses incurred in any year; the insurance would pay the other half and pay for all medical expenses exceeding $3,000. Thus, the consumer would never pay more than $1,500, but would be highly conscious of the cost and quantity of services received. (Both the 50 percent coinsurance rate and the maximum of $1,500 would be substantially lowered or subsidized for low-income consumers.) The technical term for any requirement that consumers pay part of their medical expense under an insurance plan is *cost sharing,* and includes such devices as deductibles, coinsurance, and copayment. Any plan that covers most medical services with little or no cost sharing is called *comprehensive.* The point of major risk insurance is to introduce substantial cost sharing as an incentive for the consumer to use medical care wisely and seek out conservative providers, but to limit the maximum cost share so that consumers are always assured of adequate financial protection.

An advantage of this model is that only the insurance system must be changed, and then efficiency and conservative practice style gradually result without direct policy intervention in medical care organization and practice itself. There are several disadvantages. First, providers may elaborate their practice style in treating "catastrophic episodes" whose cost exceeds the maximum cost share. In such cases, some regulation may be needed. Second, this model puts a greater, but not undue burden (consumer expense never exceeds the maximum cost share), on the sick than on the well; depending on societal values, this may be deemed appropriate or not. Third, the consumer is asked to shop for services when a family member is ill. Even though most medical services are elective, it is difficult for consumers to become informed buyers of individual services because services are so complex and serious illness occurs so rarely to an individual family.

However, the greatest difficulty is political. It is very hard to get consumers to accept major risk insurance after they have had comprehensive insurance. One remedy to overcome consumer resistance might be to introduce modest cost sharing initially, and gradually increase it in subsequent years. A second remedy might be to offer consumers a choice between a comprehensive plan and a major risk plan and give consumers choosing the major risk plan a cash rebate equal to the difference in the cost of the two plans; this has other problems, however. (See discusiosn of Combined Market Model below.) It is not certain that consumers will accept either approach. If only a few consumers accept major risk insurance, or if they purchase private insurance to supplement it, then the incentives on providers to change style are too weak,[7] and the model fails.

COMPETING HEALTH CARE PLAN MODEL

This model uses premiums as the price mechanism for provider competition.[8] If consumers demand comprehensive insurance, then the major risk model is untenable, and service prices cannot be used as a price mechanism for provider competition. Under comprehensive insurance, the only price mechanism available for provider competition is the premium itself. To create provider price competition over premiums, the key is to divide providers into competing groupings, called *health care plans.* The health care plan not only provides the insurance, it provides all the medical care. (Actually, the plan may refer certain specialized services to nonplan providers, but will pay for these services only when approved by a plan provider. Emergency services away from the plan are also paid by the plan.) The consumer is annually offered a multiple choice of health care plans as well as a conventional plan. Employees, employee organizations, or the government pay a fixed capitation toward the plan chosen by the consumer. (This combination of multiple choice of plans and fixed capitation is called *fair multiple choice.*) If the consumer is willing to enroll in a health care plan with conservative efficient providers, then this plan can offer more comprehensive benefits; however, consumers must agree that services of nonplan providers are not covered unless approved by a plan provider. On the other hand, if consumers enroll in a health care plan with elaborate providers, or in an insurance plan that covers any provider no matter how conservative or elaborate, they get less comprehensive benefits or must pay any additional premium out of their own pocket.

As one practical example illustrating fair multiple choice, the Polaroid Corporation in Boston offers its employees a choice of several different plans. One is a conventional comprehensive insurance plan with a premium of $53 per month per employee. (All premium data here refer to 1980–81 plan offerings.) The others are all health care plans, each with its own set of providers. The exact benefits vary among the health care plans, but all of them have more comprehensive benefits than the insurance plan. The least expensive health care plan charges a premium of $41 a month, the most expensive plan charges $52 a month, the others are in between. The Polaroid Corporation contributes a capitation of $41 a month to any plan chosen by an employee; the employee pays the balance. For example, if the conventional insurance plan is chosen, Polaroid would pay $41 and the employee would pay the balance of $12; if the employee, instead, chose the least expensive health care plan, Polaroid would pay $41 and the employee would pay nothing. Each year the company gives its employees a booklet that describes and compares the benefits and premiums of each of the plans offered; this allows employees to make an informed choice. Each year they may choose to remain in their present plan or switch to a different plan.

In this model, financial protection and equity are again excellent, since all plans are comprehensive (some more so than others), and the government can subsidize the capitation for low-income persons at any desired level of equity. And again, the incentives on consumers and providers are radically changed. The consumer has the means to identify conservative providers by comparing the benefits and premiums of their plans with other plans. Consumers have the incentive to choose them because they offer more benefits and lower premiums. Of course if the plan sponsors have a questionable reputation (poor quality or unresponsive, uncaring service), consumers will avoid their plan no matter what its benefits or premiums. Thus, unless they improve their performance, elaborate or unattractive providers will lose consumers to plans with conservative and attractive providers.

Note that in this model, price competition occurs not between individual providers, as in the major risk model above, but rather between groupings of providers. The providers in each health care plan compete as a group against providers in other health care plans. Conventional providers (i.e., providers not in any health care plan) also compete as a group against the health care plans; there is no price competition between individual conventional providers in this model because they are covered through conventional insurance plans, which, as mentioned earlier, eliminate the price mechanism. (By price competition, it is understood that providers compete on nonprice factors—competent, responsive, compassionate service—as well as on premiums or service prices.)

Great diversity among health care plans is possible in this model. Some plans, called "hospital-based, prepaid, group practice plans," tightly organize the whole spectrum of care within the plan, including multispecialty clinics with both primary physicians and specialists, and a hospital. Other plans, called "individual practice plans," would be less tightly organized; plan physicians would practice solo in their individual offices, and specialty and hospital services would be purchased by the plan (at no charge to the consumer) from appropriate nonplan specialists and hospitals, who would compete (in the secondary market) for plan business. Between these two extremes, many other kinds of plan organization are possible.[9] The plans could thus organize themselves and pay plan providers in any way they deemed most attractive in the market. The common requirement on all health care plans, however, is that they provide or arrange all insured medical services for enrollees on a prepaid basis, and that no plan have a provider monopoly in its area.

The advantage of this model is that all consumers can have comprehensive benefits. Further, plan competition should encourage more integrated systems of medical care, which should improve quality and continuity. Also, consumers can make more informed choices. They do not have to shop for individual services, as in the previous model, but rather they shop for a comprehensive plan, and they choose it when they are well, not when they are sick.

This plan model also poses several disadvantages. First, policy must stimulate providers to develop health care plans, a difficult but not impossible task. Health care plans are now being organized in most larger cities with the support of employers and government. Second, policy must encourage employers and public insurance programs to offer fair multiple choice. This is just beginning. Unless most consumers have a fair multiple choice, there is little incentive for conventional providers to compete with the health care plan providers; rather they will make up any loss of patients to the health care plans by elaborating their services to consumers who have no choice of plans. (There is good empirical evidence that under fair multiple choice, nonmonopolistic health care plans shift to more conservative, efficient practice.[10] However, because fair multiple choice is not yet widespread, empirical evidence is not yet available on whether health care plans induce conventional providers to practice more conservatively. However, it is known that a good health care plan frequently induces conventional providers to start their own plans, a promising sign.)

Third, health care plans may try to enroll only healthier consumers so as to keep their costs below their premium. This problem, called *risk selection,* can be handled in two ways. The capitation can be adjusted for the health status of the consumer, higher for sicker consumers and lower for healthy consumers, so that sick consumers are just as attractive to the plans as healthy consumers; the technical methods for this adjustment are still crude, however. Also, administrative rules can prohibit risk selection by plans; however, there are subtle ways for plans to engage in risk selection that make enforcement difficult, such as using marketing schemes designed to select favorable risks or imposing cost-sharing requirements at the time of plan renewal (to encourage sicker enrollees to move back to comprehensive insurance plans). In practice, it seems likely that the combination of adjusted capitation rates and administrative rules will be sufficient to minimize risk selection, but the question is still open.

PREFERRED PROVIDER INSURANCE MODEL

This model combines elements of the two previous models in a unique way.[11] A preferred provider insurance plan is somewhat like a combination between a health care plan and a major risk plan. In a major risk plan, the consumer may go to any provider but must pay a share of the cost. In a health care plan, the consumer may go to a plan provider and the plan pays all the cost, but if the consumer goes to any other provider without a referral from the plan provider, the consumer must pay all the cost. In a preferred provider plan, consumers may go to any provider, but if they go to certain "preferred" providers identified by the plan as conservative and efficient, the plan pays all or most of the cost, whereas if they go to any other providers they must pay substantial coinsurance, say 20 to 30 percent, for their services.[12]

In this model it is the plan sponsor who identifies the conservative providers to the consumer as preferred and provides the incentive of full coverage (little or no cost sharing) to use them in preference to elaborate providers, for whom consumers must pay a cost share. (The plan could be sponsored by a set of providers, an insurer, or an employer.) In this model, the real price competition occurs in negotiations in the secondary market between the plan sponsor and the providers. Providers compete to convince the preferred provider insurance plan that their average expenditures per capita are lower than other providers so as to win preferred status. Price competition on service prices in the primary market between consumer and provider occurs only after this negotiation, and involves only the nonpreferred providers.

This model has several advantages. The only policy intervention is in the insurance system; no direct intervention in medical care organization and practice is needed. It does not require fair multiple choice arrangements, at least in principle. Coverage is comprehensive if preferred providers are used, and yet consumers are not penalized so severely for going outside the preferred providers as they would be in a health care plan.

A substantial advantage of both the preferred provider and competing health care plan models is that they offer opportunities to move away from strictly fee-for-service reimbursement. A plan sponsor can use modified fee-for-service and other provider payment methods that exert direct economic incentives on providers for efficient conservative practice. While some direct incentives on providers are possible under conventional or major risk insurance, the possibilities are usually greater in plans with a small number of providers.

Finally, a particular advantage of preferred provider plans over competing health care plans (HMOs) is that they are easier to initiate and dismantle. In the simplest arrangement, a plan sponsor, such as an employer, simply identifies a set of providers whose efficiency (both in terms of unit cost and practice style) it has some confidence in, and gives them preferred status in an existing insurance plan. It pays them on a fee-for-service basis or perhaps according to some other negotiated method of payment. If the preferred providers prove unsatisfactory, the plan sponsor simply removes their preferred status. Patients may continue to use these providers as before but now pay coinsurance as with any other nonpreferred provider. In contrast, if an HMO is dropped from a multiple choice arrangement, enrollees cannot usually continue with their HMO providers, and consumer relations problems may arise.

The preferred provider insurance model also has very practical difficulties. First, preferred provider plans are illegal for insurers in many states but usually not for self-funded employers. Insurers are forbidden in these states to treat or pay one provider differently than another, even if certain providers are more efficient than others. The remedy is for employers, unions, insurers, and other potential plan sponsors to push for enabling legislation, as has been successfully accomplished in California, Minnesota, and a growing number of other states.

Second, it is technically difficult to identify conservative efficient providers when the population served by the providers is not enrolled with them exclusively (i.e., expenditures per capita cannot be explicitly calculated for preferred providers, unlike a health care plan). It is fairly easy to identify providers whose fees and charges are reasonable (i.e., unit-cost efficient) simply by comparing fees and charges for the same services across several providers. The real difficulty is to identify providers who are also conservative in their use and intensity of service mix (i.e., practice-style efficient). Unlike health care plan providers, there is no defined service population for preferred providers, so utilization rates usually cannot be constructed let alone compared across providers. For example, if a preferred surgeon performs 25 operations, it is possible to determine roughly whether the average cost per patient is reasonable by comparing fees and hospital charges for similar operations, but it is impossible to tell how many of these operations the surgeon could have avoided with more conservative treatment unless much more patient information is available.

Because of the difficulty of identifying conservative providers, some employers have moved to "discount provider plans." These are plans that simply give preferred status to any provider who agrees to a negotiated discount on fees and charges. Discount provider plans encourage providers to elaborate their practice style, and are, therefore, unlikely to be effective. Providers can usually beat a discounted charge system by increasing the number and intensity of services they provide to patients. For the reasons given earlier, utilization review apparently offers only a partial corrective to elaborated practice style. Hence, discount plans tend to punish conservative providers and reward elaborate providers—exactly the opposite of how proper incentives should work. Employers and other plan sponsors would be better off to limit plans to conservative providers and pay them reasonable but attractive fees as a reward for remaining conservative.

A third problem is that providers strongly resist any attempt by plan sponsors to treat one limited set of providers differently than another, even if this differential treatment is economically fair. This appears to be the reason that preferred provider plans have been historically the last and least common plan to appear (cost-shared plans and health care plans developed much earlier). Finally, there is a real threat to freedom of entry for competing providers. Unless there is fair multiple choice, a group of conservative providers cannot identify and offer themselves directly to consumers on a full-coverage basis; they must get approved by the insurance plan first. This makes such a plan vulnerable to cartel behavior. Consumers may also object to plan sponsors deciding which providers will be given preferred status.

These problems have potentially serious implications. Instead of choosing conservative providers (who are difficult to identify) as preferred, plan sponsors tend to choose any provider who will sign a fee schedule. As noted earlier, fee schedules reward elaborate practice. Next, providers place pressure on the insurer (threaten to refuse service to insured consumers) to sign up the great majority of providers as preferred. Public insurance programs are particularly vulnerable to such pressure. If all or most providers have preferred status, the whole mechanism of choice and competition is vitiated. Finally, the insurer and the preferred providers may develop a marriage of mutual convenience, and act as a cartel to exclude troublesome competitive providers. However, the model appears technically sound and attractive, and economic conditions are ripe for its development. As long as there are several competing preferred provider plans and the preferred provider plans are offered under fair multiple choice with other plans, freedom of entry is reasonably assured.

COMBINED MARKET MODEL

It may be more realistic and practical to have a flexible way to combine any or all of these models to fit given situations or areas. One combined model with this flexibility has the following structure:

— *A diversity of competing plans* in each area, which, in addition to one or more conventional insurance plans, must include health care plans, preferred provider plans, major risk plans, and/or any other plans which give consumers the means to identify conservative providers and fair incentives to choose them in preference to elaborate providers.

— *Fair multiple choice* must be available to the great majority of consumers in each area.

This model operates just like the competing health care plan model as far as fair multiple choice is concerned. But the plans offered need not be just health care plans, they could also include cost-shared plans and preferred provider plans, as well as a conventional comprehensive insurance plan.

There are several advantages to this model. First, it is flexible. If, for example, one employer did not want a major risk plan, there would be no need to include it; an employer could still encourage provider competition by offering health care plans or preferred provider plans. If an employer were located in an area with no health care plans, cost-shared plans and preferred provider plans could be used. Thus, each employer or public program could tailor the mix of plans it offered to its own needs and desires. If new kinds of competitive plans are innovated, they can be easily added to the choices. Second, fair multiple choice permits the employer or public program to place a budgetary ceiling on its medical expenditures. It changes medical care expenditures from fixed benefits and open-ended dollars to fixed dollars and open-ended benefits. In the present insurance system, benefits are specified and then the employer, employee organization, or government must pay whatever open-ended expenditure the medical care system charges it. In contrast, under fair multiple choice each employer or government program specifies the capitation it will pay, and the competing plans must then offer the best benefits they can for this amount. The consumer is free to choose among the plans to obtain the benfits and providers he desires. Third, the market can be appropriately supervised by the employer or public program. If an employer believes that a plan is actuarially worthless, or has poor quality providers, or is engaged in risk selection, the employer can refuse to offer that plan to employees. The employer can require all plans to include whatever standard minimum benefits the employer wants for its employees, and it can exclude any plans that charge an excessive premium. (Some employers may wish to prohibit plans from charging more than the employer capitation rate; in this case, plans compete for these employees solely on benefits.)

A problem occurs when major risk plans are put in competition with comprehensive plans. There is some likelihood that healthier consumers will join the major risk plans while sicker consumers will join the comprehensive plans. This will drive up the costs of the comprehensive plans. Depending on societal values, this may or may not be considered inequitable. If it is considered equitable that the sick pay somewhat more than the healthy, then there is no problem. If it is considered inequitable, there are several remedies. First, the capitation paid by the employer or government can be adjusted for the health status of the consumer. Second, the amount of cost sharing permitted can be reduced by the employer; if the differences in benefits among the plans are not too great, the problem is minimized. Third, major risk plans can be eliminated from the choice.

A typical way for employers to implement this model is as follows. Suppose the employer has been offering a simple comprehensive insurance plan whose premium has been increasing 15 percent per year. The employer specifies that it will pay only a 12 percent increase, which then becomes its capitation. The employer then requires that the insurance plan introduce modest cost sharing to reduce its premium to equal this capitation. (Alternatively, the employer can require the insurance plan to collect the balance of the premium from the employees.) Simultaneously, the employer offers this same capitation to any health care plans or preferred provider plans that can provide benefits equal or greater than its insurance plan. This helps minimize employee resistance to the introduction of modest cost sharing in their insurance plan. Thereafter, the employer increases the company's capitation at a controllable rate, say 10 percent per year, and plans must offer the best benefits they can for this amount. (An alternative mode of implementation is for the employer to convert the original insurance plan into a preferred provider plan, set the capitation at the cost of this plan, and then offer a fair multiple choice of other plans.)

Note in this model, as in the competing health care plan model, that until most consumers have fair multiple choice, the pressure on conventional providers to compete on service prices and premiums is rather weak. Thus, if only one employer implements fair multiple choice, little change in provider behavior can be expected. If all employers and public programs in an area adopt fair multiple choice, then the entire market environment for providers is altered, and they must compete by shifting to more conservative and efficient practice.

EXPECTED PERFORMANCE

The above models show that the competition strategy is not one strategy but a flexible combination of several strategies, all with the same essential intent: to give consumers the means to identify more conservative and efficient providers, and to offer fair incentives under sound market conditions for consumers to choose between them and more elaborate and costly providers. These market models could restrain health care expenditures because of the strong market incentives for providers to shift to more conservative and efficient practice. Moreover, sound markets are usually more effective in reducing costly and excessive provider capacity (conservative style requires fewer providers) than are government controls, which are subject to political pressure from providers. Finally, there is less danger of underspending and undercapitalization in a sound market than in a government-controlled system.

Quality of medical care in a sound market is likely to be at least equal or superior to that in a government-controlled system. Some critics argue that health care plans may underserve their patients in order to keep their costs below their premiums and earn greater profits; however, both theory and experience suggest that such plans will fail not long after they start.[13] Research suggests that the quality of care in mature health care plans is at least equal, if not superior, to that of conventional providers generally.[14] Nevertheless, government licensure and periodic inspection of all providers, whether conventional or in health care plans, seems highly desirable to assure that every provider meets minimum standards of quality. Provider responsiveness to consumer needs and desires is likely to be greater in a competitive market than in a government-controlled system; the unresponsive and uncaring provider will lose patients to more responsive and compassionate providers, and the pluralism of a market is more likely to satisfy the diversity of consumer tastes than the uniformity characteristic of government-controlled systems. This pluralism and flexibility of markets also tends to make them much more innovative than government-controlled systems, which tend to be more rigid. Thus, the advantages of markets tend to increase with time.

The threat of increasing government regulation and control may be the best way to motivate providers, insurers, and employers to implement various models of the competition strategy.

NOTES

1. Walter McClure, *Reducing Excess Hospital Capacity* (Springfield, VA: National Technical Information Service, Report No. HRP–0015199, October 1976), chapter 1.

2. It is useful to distinguish two types of efficiency: "microefficiency" is the cost of each unit of service; "macroefficiency" is the average expenditure per capita necessary to produce a given level of health status in a population. A medical care system could have high microefficiency by producing each service efficiently and yet still have low macroefficiency by utilizing more numerous and complex services than conservative practice would suggest. The focus of policy should be on macroefficiency rather than just microefficiency.

3. Walter McClure, *Comprehensive Market and Regulatory Strategies for Medical Care* (Springfield, VA: National Technical Information Service, Report No. HRP–0902178, February 1979), chapter 5.

4. This model was developed independently by Martin Feldstein, "A New Approach to National Health Insurance," *Public Interest* 23 (Spring 1971), p. 93, and by M. Pauly, *National Health Insurance: An Analysis* (Washington, DC: American Enterprise Institute, 1971).

5. Joseph Newhouse, et al., "Some Interim Results from a Controlled Trial of Cost-Sharing in Health Insurance," *New England Journal of Medicine* 305, no. 25 (December 17, 1981), pp. 1501–7.

6. Robert Brook, et al., "Does Free Care Improve Adults' Health?", *New England Journal of Medicine* 309, no. 23 (December 8, 1983), pp. 1426–34.

7. Charles Link, et al., "Cost-Sharing, Supplementary Insurance, and Health Services Utilization," *Health Care Financing Review* Fall 1980, pp. 25–31.

8. This model was first suggested by K. White, "Primary Medical Care for Families," *New England Journal of Medicine* 277 (October 19, 1967), pp. 847–852, and developed more fully by Paul Ellwood, "The Health Maintenance Strategy," *Medical Care* 1 (May 1971), pp. 291–98. See also Clark Havighurst, "HMOs and the Market for Health Services," *Law and Contemporary Problems* 35 (Fall 1970), pp. 716–95; Scott Fleming, *Structured Competition* (Washington, DC: United States Department of Health, Education and Welfare, 1972, unpublished); Walter McClure, "Three Memoranda on National Health Insurance," (Minneapolis: InterStudy, 1974, unpublished); and Alain Enthoven, "Consumer Choice Health Plan," *New England Journal of Medicine* (March 23, 1978), pp. 650–8.

9. Walter McClure, "Broadening the Definition of a Competitive Health System," *Journal of Health Politics, Policy and Law* 3 (Fall 1978), pp. 303–27; Paul Ellwood, and Walter McClure, "Health Delivery Reform" (Minneapolis: InterStudy, 1976, unpublished).

10. Harold Luft, *HMOs: Dimensions of Performance* (New York: Wiley-Interscience, 1981), chapter 14; Walter McClure, *Comprehensive Market and Regulatory Strategies for Medical Care,* chapter 4, section A2.

11. This model has no definite author. Contributions were made by Joseph New-house, "How Shall We Pay for Hospital Care," *Public Interest* 23 (Spring 1971), pp. 78–92; Clark Havighurst, "Controlling Health Care Costs," *Journal of Health Politics, Policy and Law* 1 (Winter 1977), pp. 471–98; Robert Sigmond (1977 personal communication); and Walter McClure, *Comprehensive Market and Regulatory Strategies for Medical Care,* chapter 4, section A3.

12. A preferred provider plan is defined by some to mean or include a closed panel insurance plan paying panel providers on a fee-for-service basis (usually discounted or modified in some way), with no coverage for nonpanel provider services. Such a closed-panel insurance plan is not a preferred provider plan, it is an alliance, a form of health care plan. It becomes a preferred provider plan only if enrollees can receive at least partial coverage when they use nonpanel providers. Any health care plan can become a preferred provider plan if it adds this feature of partial coverage for services not rendered or ap-proved by plan providers.

13. Jon Christianson, and Walter McClure, "Incentives for Quality in a Restructured Medical Care System," *Policy Studies Journal* 9 (Special Issue 1980), pp. 271–78.

14. Frances Cunningham, and John Williamson, "How Does the Quality of Care in HMOs Compare," *Group Health Journal,* Winter 1980, pp. 4–13.

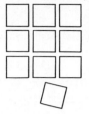

Economics of Marketplace Competition

ECONOMICS OF PPO PARTICIPATION

Adele Palmer, Ph.D.

Economist
Rand Corporation
Santa Monica, CA

To succeed, a PPO needs four kinds of participants: one or more hospitals, some physicians, a number of insurance beneficiaries, and one or more payors. The PPO cannot begin operations unless it has participants in each category—and it cannot maintain operations without continuing participation in each category. Hence, an examination of the motives for PPO participation can reveal a great deal about the causes of PPO success or failure.

Anticipated economic gains are among the most common motives for PPO participation. Providers typically hope to maintain or improve *revenue-generating* utilization. Beneficiaries are attracted by access to care at reduced cost—whether through increased scope of insurance coverage, lower copayment requirements, or lower insurance premiums. And payors aim for lower reimbursement payments per insured beneficiary. Health care markets are not extraordinary in this respect: Buyers want to pay less, while sellers want to earn more.

To earn these benefits, PPO participants are expected to make concessions. For example, providers often offer discounts and special utilization control (UC) programs, the payor's insurance plan may provide first-dollar coverage, and beneficiaries can obtain that coverage only by selecting PPO panel providers.[1] Like potential gains, such concessions have economic consequences.

The economic forces that shape participants' gains and concessions are examined in this chapter. It views PPO prospects and pitfalls from the perspective of each type of PPO participant. The findings suggest at least partial answers to these questions:

— What determines the size of the concessions each party is willing to make? Which hospitals, physicians, payors, and beneficiaries are likely to make the largest concessions? Which have the strongest bargaining positions?

— Which PPO design features help most in reducing health care costs and insurance premiums? Which are likely to attract the most enrollment?

— How can a potential participant evaluate the concessions being offered by others? For example, is the hospital's discount rate offer a good indicator of savings to the payor?

— Does society gain from development of a successful PPO? What does the answer to this question mean for PPO participants and nonparticipants?

Throughout the discussion, two concepts will prove to be essential: rechanneling and demand effects. PPOs invariably include some provision to induce patients to select panel providers—to rechannel patients from one set of providers to another. However, a PPO often enrolls a number of beneficiaries who are not rechanneled—who were already using panel providers and would continue to do so even without the PPO. An evaluation of the PPO's economic situation requires a careful distinction between enrollment and rechanneling.

As explained below, the incentives that are designed to generate rechanneling will also affect demand for health care by all enrollees. Effects on the amount of care sought by beneficiaries can play a larger role than rechanneling in determining PPO economic outcomes. This chapter will show how and why demand as well as rechanneling effects are critical to PPO success or failure.

HOSPITAL PARTICIPATION

The most popular description of the hospital's participation motive is *to maintain (or improve) its patient base.* For some hospitals, this means attracting a larger fraction of the local community's insured beneficiaries; for others, it means expanding the effective catchment area. In either case, the aim is to serve patients who might otherwise be treated elsewhere.

An ultimate goal is to maintain or increase revenue-generating utilization of the hospital's services. However, the hospital must also recognize the payor's goal of reducing reimbursements per insured beneficiary. Accordingly, the PPO premise is that the hospital's aggregate utilization can rise without hurting the payor if the utilization is spread over a larger number of beneficiaries. Thus, the hospital's ultimate gain is to be derived from serving rechanneled patients.

It is very difficult for a hospital to induce rechanneling directly. As a rule, privately insured patients pay very little of their hospital charges, so discounts or other charge-related concessions would have limited direct effect on the patient's choice of provider. (Patients often choose their physicians without knowing which hospital the physician uses.) Improved amenities or increased scope of services might be attractive to patients or their admitting physicians, but the added costs would have to be recovered somehow, and both public and private payors have begun resisting cost increases. An alternative is for the hospital to obtain cooperation from a payor who will offer incentives that will rechannel beneficiaries to the hospital.

In exchange, the hospital offers some set of concessions. A frequent one is a discount on the hospital's typical charges; another is a utilization-control program, which might include preadmission screening and length of stay review. A less common offer is a fixed per-diem rate. In any of these cases, the concessions apply to any and all PPO beneficiaries, but not to the hospital's other patients. In this way, the hospital assures that a payor can reap gains only by participating in the PPO program.

HOSPITAL'S DECISION PROCESS

Rationally, the hospital should only participate in the PPO if it expects to do better with PPO participation than without it. The proper comparison is *not* between future years (with the PPO) and recent years (without it), but between the two alternative *expectations* for future years. If the hospital is considering the PPO option because of changing market conditions, both expectations may be quite uncertain. Nonetheless, some assessment of the difference between the two (uncertain) prospects is a critical element of the decision process.

Ideally, the first step is to project future utilization and net revenues in the absence of PPO participation. (It may be necessary to suppose that some other local hospital(s) will join a PPO, but that consideration is reserved for later in this chapter.) The projection must assume some schedule of costs and charges per patient and some rate at which the local community will generate inpatient utilization.

Among the community's insured beneficiaries is a group of particular interest—the group insured through the payor(s) who would participate in the PPO. Unless the hospital's typical charges or its treatment patterns for other patients would change under the PPO, utilization by those other patients should be unaffected and can therefore be ignored in making the

PPO participation decision. Thus, the principal objective in step one is to project what utilization by the potential PPO group might be if the hospital does *not* join the PPO.

The second step is to project the PPO's potential rechanneling effect for the beneficiaries who could participate. Some of those beneficiaries might be expected to use the hospital even in the PPO's absence. It is usually safe to assume that such beneficiaries will also use the hospital if they join the PPO plan and that they will select the PPO plan if it is offered. If so, those beneficiaries will be covered by the discounts, the utilization control program, and any other concessions the hospital provides. Though these beneficiaries would show up in a count of PPO patients, they are *not* rechanneled patients. All true concessions made to these beneficiaries will represent a net loss to the hospital.

Net gains are nonetheless possible if the PPO generates enough rechanneling. To illustrate, suppose the hospital offers a discount (but no special utilization controls); if the average net revenue for a non-PPO patient would be $1,000, then the PPO net revenue might be, say, $700. To keep this illustration simple, suppose that PPO participation would have no effect on the number of admissions per 1,000 beneficiaries, but only on their channeling among hospitals. The following cases indicate how the hospital's total net revenue would be affected if only 10 percent of the PPO patients are actually rechanneled:

	Net Revenue	
	Without PPO	With PPO
Number of beneficiaries admitted to the hospital	1,000	1,000
900 not rechanneled	$900,000	$630,000
100 rechanneled	—	70,000
Total net revenue	$900,000	$700,000

In this hypothetical situation, the extra net revenue from rechanneled patients is not enough compensation for the loss from concessions to unrechanneled patients. Here, even though the hospital would earn net revenue from PPO patients who would not otherwise be admitted, joining the PPO would not be economically rewarding—not, at least, with such a high discount.

However, the hospital might consider offering a smaller discount. A simple trial-and-error exercise (as well as more sophisticated mathematical analysis) shows that the hospital would benefit if its net revenue per PPO patient rose above $900. At exactly $900 the hospital breaks even;

any discount that yields a higher net revenue per patient would make it economically beneficial to join the PPO.

Alternatively, the hospital might consider offering special utilization-control provisions for PPO patients. For example, there might be special procedures designed to discourage some admissions (e.g., in cases where minor surgery or diagnostic testing can be performed on an outpatient basis). In terms of net revenue, the effect can be very similar to that of the discounting alternative: net revenue per unrechanneled beneficiary falls because such beneficiaries generate a smaller number of inpatient days than they would without the PPO; this must be offset by admissions of rechanneled patients.

At least in principle, a UC program can be designed to have the same effect on hospital net revenue as any alternative discounting offer. A discount that reduces net revenue by 10 percent is, from the hospital's net revenue perspective, equivalent to a UC program that reduces the admission rate by 10 percent—provided the UC program has no negative effect on the number of participating (rechanneled and unrechanneled) beneficiaries. (If there is an effect on beneficiary participation, the UC program would have to be tailored accordingly, but can still render the desired net revenue outcome.) Similarly, a UC program can reach the same revenue target by reducing average lengths of stays so that net revenue per stay declines 10 percent.

There are important practical differences between UC programs and discounts. The UC program must solve different administrative problems and typically requires more cooperation and participation by physicians and other health care practitioners. With a UC program, revenue "tailoring" is perhaps more difficult to achieve, since the professionals who implement the program will undoubtedly be concerned with matters of patient welfare and proper modes of care that can conflict with net revenue goals. These issues are critical to a hospital considering whether to offer discounts or UC programs, or some combination of the two, and the issues are not purely economic. Nonetheless, having determined which UC options are feasible, the hospital can (and surely should) evaluate the net revenue effects and compare them with discounting alternatives.

In making the evaluation, notice that a discount and a UC program that have the same effect on *net* revenue have quite different effects on *total* revenue. When a UC program reduces admissions by 10 percent, it reduces *both* net and total revenue by 10 percent; the hospital incurs no costs for admissions that do not occur, and receives no reimbursement for them. In contrast, a discount that reduces net revenue by 10 percent reduces total revenue by much less than ten percent; the hospital would be reimbursed for 100 percent of the treatment costs, as well as 90 percent of its normal net revenue.

Thus, a hospital should *not* be indifferent between a 10 percent reduction in total charges and a 10 percent reduction in admissions. If D is the percentage reduction in charges, which is commonly labeled the PPO discount rate, then the corresponding percentage reduction (P) in net revenue is given by:

$$P = D/(NY/Y)$$

where NY and Y are net and total revenue, respectively. The hospital achieves the same net revenue target from a given percentage admissions reduction or from an equivalent value for P—not D. Offered a choice between a 10 percent reduction in admissions and a 10 percent PPO discount rate, the hospital would earn a higher net revenue by selecting the utilization control option.

The hospital may also evaluate a *combined* offer of a discount and a special UC program. The rechanneling rate still establishes the extent to which the hospital would be willing to make concessions for PPO membership, but the concessions can consist of a package that includes some discounting and some controls on admissions, lengths of stay, or other aspects of utilization.

Though the joint effect is easy to calculate, there is a small trick to the calculation. The objective is to meet some target for the percentage of net revenue *retained*. Setting P equal to 10 percent, for example, allows the hospital to retain 90 percent of net revenue per admitted patient. If that same target is to be met using a discount in combination with a percentage utilization reduction, U, then the requirement is:

$$(1 - P)(1 - U) = 90.$$

For example, this 90 percent net revenue target can be met by lowering P to 5 percent and setting U equal to 5.3 percent. Other combinations of P and U can also meet the same target.

The target percentage would change under different assumptions about the amounts of channeling, rechanneling, and typical net revenues per case, but this would not alter the fact that various combinations of discounts and UC features can yield the same combined net revenue effect.

Yet another type of hospital concession is the fixed per-diem charge. It combines discount and UC features by establishing a flat daily rate (usually within a broad service category) which may be less than the hospital's usual average daily charge, while holding the charges constant regardless of the patient's actual utilization during each day of care. In this way, the hospital can internalize the savings from its own success in controlling utilization, though the hospital also absorbs some risk that utilization controls will not prove sufficient to justify the reduction in charges. The financial implications of per-diem rates are also somewhat easier to monitor; data on lengths of stay and admissions rates tell much of the story. Yet, despite these special features of the per-diem pricing approach, the analysis of the rechanneling effect and its importance to the hospital's economic gains are essentially like those of other types of concession packages.

Examining the PPO's economic prospects from a particular hospital's perspective reveals some explanations for the crucial role of *negotiations* in a PPO's formation and renewal. While the hospital may have to make some concessions in order to participate in the PPO, there will often be a range of concession levels that would be considered satisfactory if not ideal. (For example, in the hypothetical case considered above, the hospital would gain as long as the discount is between zero and $100 per admission.) Moreover, a given overall concession level is consistent with a variety of concession "packages" (e.g., combinations of UC and discount offers). In negotiations, the hospital can adjust its concession package in response to the concerns of other potential participants, while aiming for the highest possible net gain consistent with achieving membership in the PPO.

There is also a lesson in all this for payors: A hospital can offer payors larger savings if the hospital's concession package relies more heavily on UC than on discounts. For the payor, a 5 percent saving on reimbursements per admission has the same financial effect as a 5 percent reduction in admissions. Nevertheless, in PPO negotiations, some payors focus all their attention on setting the discount rate. This may reflect their scepticism about the hospital's ability to enforce UC standards or about the hospital's sincerity in offering them (especially given the hospital's expressed desire to provide more services). However legitimate the scepticism might be, the fact remains that the highest discount rate a hospital can afford to offer will always be less than the highest UC rate it can afford. By insisting on a high discount rate, a payor forsakes an opportunity for even greater reimbursement savings through utilization controls.

MAKING CONCESSIONS WHEN INFORMATION IS LIMITED

As a rule, PPOs are formed under conditions of limited information. In particular, a hospital may find it difficult to identify the current channeling pattern for an insured group, and may consider rechanneling to be very unpredictable.

Given uncertainty about the potential amount of rechanneling, the hospital might resort to a simple rule of thumb that dictates that the discount rate should not exceed net revenue per case as a percent of total charges; for example, if net revenues are 12 percent of charges currently, then the PPO can yield positive net revenues per case as long as the discount rate is less than 12 percent. This strategy for setting the discount may seem appealing because it assures that every PPO patient will generate positive net revenue.

However, a hospital that pursues this strategy can do itself a great disservice. Suppose, for example, that the hospital, after noting that its net revenue rate is 12 percent, decides to offer a 5 percent discount. This apparently conservative offer actually presumes the PPO will increase the insured group's use of the hospital by more than 71 percent! If that target is not met, PPO membership with a 5 percent discount is ill-advised for the hospital.

The problem with the rule of thumb, and a preferable decision-making approach, can be found by reference to the formula:[2]

$$D* = (NY/Y) \times R,$$

where $D*$ is the break-even discount rate (in percent), NY is net revenue, Y is total revenue, and R is the number of *additional* inpatient cases as a percent of the total number of PPO cases. Thus, if NY/Y is .12 (the net revenue percentage is 12 percent) and D is 5 (the offered discount rate is 5 percent), the value of R needed just for the hospital to break even is 42 (i.e., 42 percent of all PPO admissions would not occur without the PPO). Measured as a percent of admissions that would occur without the PPO, the increase in admissions is $R/(100 - R)$, so an R value of 42 means a 71 percent increase in the insured group's inpatient cases.

Even if the hospital cannot predict R very well, the discounting formula should help hospital administrators judge how much rechanneling is needed to warrant a given discount rate (or to warrant a given concession package of discounts and utilization controls). Even without detailed data and analysis, an experienced administrator should be able to assess whether the requisite value of R is a reasonable or farfetched possibility.

RECHANNELING VERSUS DEMAND EFFECTS

So far, it has been assumed that the principal way for the hospital to improve overall utilization is to "capture" patients who would otherwise use alternative providers. This attitude is certainly in keeping with the hospital's message to the payor, namely, that there is a way for the hospital to gain without increasing the payor's reimbursement expenses. However, the incentives offered to beneficiaries to induce rechanneling will generally affect the amount of utilization they demand, and the result can be important to payor and hospital satisfaction with the PPO.

Compared to a more standard insurance plan (e.g., one with open choice of provider, a deductible, and perhaps 25 percent coinsurance), a PPO plan commonly offers reduced copayments for services from panel providers. Over the last few years, an increasing body of evidence shows that copayments have marked effects on utilization per beneficiary. For example, interim results from the Rand Health Insurance Study[3] show that compared to a plan with zero copayments, a 25 percent coinsurance plan reduces total health care expenditures by 20 percent; in particular, the reduced expenditures reflect a 20 percent reduction in hospital admissions. In short, a PPO that offers a reduced copayment as the rechanneling incentive should expect increased hospital admissions even if there is no rechanneling.

This good news for the hospital should pose no special problem in its concession-making evaluation. Instead of interpreting R in the discount formula as just the percentage increase in the number of beneficiaries using the hospital, R should include an expected increase in the number of admissions per beneficiary.

On the other hand, this is not such good news for the payor. Consequently, the payor might resist using reduced copayments as the rechanneling incentive or insist on other PPO provisions, such as externally monitored admissions controls.

Reducing copayments is not the only available mechanism for rechanneling. Later in this chapter, the distinction between a "reward" structure based on reduced copayments and a "penalty" structure based on *increased* copayments will be considered. Then it will become even clearer that demand effects deserve special consideration by both payors and providers when negotiating a PPO's rechanneling incentives.

COST-SHIFTING OPTION

This discussion has assumed that the hospital will not change its non-PPO charges just because it joins a PPO. If that assumption is wrong, the concessions evaluation should be altered. Specifically, if non-PPO charges can be raised, the hospital can compensate itself for any PPO-related concessions, even if rechanneling and demand effects are minimal.

To shift costs, a hospital must have patients whose non-PPO payor will accept and reimburse higher charges. Many private payors have done so for many years. On the other hand, one of the reasons for so much hospital and payor interest in PPOs and other "alternative delivery systems" is that payors are no longer so accomodating. Some payors may suspect that they can get large concessions through a PPO because the hospital will merely shift the costs elsewhere. But the hospital must consider whether other payors will sit back idly while their average reimbursements rise when the hospital has joined a PPO.

There are two important questions a hospital should answer before attempting to recover PPO-related concessions through cost shifting:

a. If non-PPO payors will reimburse higher charges, what prevents obtaining those higher reimbursements regardless of whether the PPO forms?

b. What would higher non-PPO charges do to the existing trend away from payor acceptance of hospital charges?

A hospital administrator may judge that higher charges are not possible for a variety of reasons; in most cases, those same reasons would prevent PPO-related cost shifting. Exceptions may occur, but then the hospital must evaluate how long those higher reimbursements will be accommodated by payors.

PHYSICIAN PARTICIPATION

For some physicians, the motive for PPO participation is very similar to the hospital's motive. Through rechanneling, the PPO may improve or help maintain the physician's practice. It is often suggested that younger physicians who are still developing their practices would find the PPO option especially attractive. In addition, more experienced physicians may view the PPO as desirable if they are losing patients to a new HMO, to local population decline, or to other physicians arriving in the community. In all of these situations, rechanneling of insured patients to panel physicians promises them higher incomes.

For physicians attracted by the rechanneling prospect, the issues involved in making concessions might appear like those facing the hospital. However, major differences can result from the slightly different forms of the concessions physicians typically consider.

Although the most frequently encountered physician concession is sometimes described as a fee "discount," fixed percentage discounts from the physician's private fees are relatively rare. Instead, the most common financial concession entails agreement to a fixed fee schedule. Where the fee schedule is uniform for all panel physicians (or for panel members within various specialty categories), the true amount of any discount will vary among physicians depending on how their own customary fees compare with the scheduled ones. Frequently, the fee schedule is established by reference to usual fees in the local community, using perhaps the 70th or 80th percentile as the schedule norm. Accordingly, 70 or 80 percent of the community's physicians could (in principle) accept the schedule without any actual reduction in their fees.

As a rule, physicians do not offer to implement special ambulatory UC programs. A few PPOs have tried to implement gatekeeping arrangements, particularly for specialist referrals, but some organizers of new PPOs (e.g., Universal Health Network) have foresworn gatekeeping on the grounds that previous attempts have proven difficult and costly; patients have bypassed the system by making their own appointments, and specialists legitimately have argued that such gatekeeping contradicts the purpose for joining the PPO panel. In general, therefore, PPO utilization controls typically apply only to inpatient care, and the physician's nondiscount concessions usually entail just compliance (and perhaps assistance) with the hospital's UC program.

Whereas a hospital clearly loses revenue by preventing admissions, limiting lengths of stay, or controlling ancillaries, it is less clear that these actions have much effect on physician incomes. To some extent, less inpatient care may be replaced with greater ambulatory care, particularly through increased numbers of preadmission and postdischarge office visits. The substitution of ambulatory for inpatient care can genuinely reduce overall reimbursements because the expense for a single inpatient day will pay for multiple ambulatory visits. Nevertheless, the result can also be greater physician revenue per case.

But even if the fee schedule and/or UC program reduces physician revenue from a given episode of care, very little rechanneling may be necessary to compensate the physician. The reason: Low PPO copayments tend to increase the amount of care demanded by a given beneficiary. In short, the unrechanneled beneficiaries may increase their utilization enough to compensate the physician even if few patients are rechanneled by the PPO.

It may seem curious to infer that physicians' concessions are modest when actual observation suggests that physicians are often difficult to recruit for a PPO panel. One explanation may be physicians' concern with financial risk; some early PPOs failed because the third-party administrators that sponsored them went bankrupt, leaving many physicians (and hospitals) with substantial unpaid bills. Many PPOs now insist on having only reputable payors and include a provision for direct reimbursement by the payor so that physicians receive rapid payment in full.

Even the inducements of more patient visits and simplified billing will have little to offer physicians whose practices are full and lucrative. In fact, some evidence suggests that physicians actually reduce their practices once their incomes pass some target level. For such physicians, participation in the PPO must be motivated by other factors.

Some physicians are undoubtedly motivated by personal (or perhaps financial) interest in a hospital that is seeking a larger patient base. To some extent, a hospital may have to rely on this type of motivation, both to recruit a sufficiently large physician panel and to obtain a commitment to the PPO's success.

In practice, it is difficult for hospital or PPO administrators to control utilization and costs of care without physician cooperation. A utilization control program can prevent abuse, but attempts to change generally accepted practice patterns will have little success without medical staff support. And, as will be seen below, a hospital that does not control its costs stands to suffer from the competitive pressures that promote development of PPOs and other alternative care systems.

Moreover, physicians who do not have to make real concessions to participate in a PPO may find it attractive to participate in many competing PPOs. (This phenomenon appears especially prevalent in the well-publicized Denver area PPOs.) Consequently, many more PPOs can form in a community than would be feasible if each had to recruit a separate physician panel, and none of the individual PPOs can hope to garner as much rechanneling as otherwise. Avoiding this outcome also requires a degree of personal commitment to a hospital on the part of panel physicians.

As a PPO attempts to expand its physician panel, it will generally find that selectivity in physician recruitment and informal standards for cost-effective practice patterns are both weakened. Such growth may be at the expense of physician commitment that would assist the PPO's survival.

Consider the reasonable proposition that there is some distribution of cost effectiveness among physicians. Some may be especially conscious of costs, or may prefer to avoid extensive treatment unless a health condition is quite serious, or may simply be so experienced with some conditions that their approach to diagnosis and treatment has become streamlined. Other physicians, in contrast, may be unfamiliar with costs or extremely adverse to any chance of misdiagnosis or incomplete treatment. The majority of physicians presumably fall between these two extremes.

To the extent that a PPO can be selective in recruiting, it can hope to empanel mostly cost-effective physicians. If the PPO aims to empanel only, say, 10 percent of the community's physicians, then the panel might be composed of the community's least costly 10 percent—rendering an advantage in the effort to control costs. However, if the PPO expands membership to 20, 30, or 40 percent, even the most careful recruitment strategy cannot avoid the fact that the additional physicians will be drawn from an increasingly costly portion of the physician distribution. Where recruitment is designed to attract the community's most cost-effective physicians, average cost effectiveness will tend to decline as the panel encompasses a larger fraction of the local community's physicians.[4]

BENEFICIARY PARTICIPATION

In considering the economic "gains" to a PPO's participating beneficiaries, it is important to note that the introduction of a PPO plan can occur against a backdrop of reduced health insurance coverage or benefits. As in the case of provider participation decisions, the proper comparison is between alternative *futures* with and without the PPO. A new PPO plan may be less generous than last year's insurance but better than the current alternative. It is the latter comparison that determines whether there is a gain to beneficiary participation in the PPO.

There remains a sense in which history can affect beneficiary participation decisions: The beneficiary may have a previously established relationship with a provider, and may not be indifferent about whether a PPO plan requires or permits a change in that relationship. If a previous insurance plan provided the same coverage for any choice of physician, the beneficiary may find that the PPO changes the out-of-pocket costs associated with retaining the familiar provider. On the other hand, if the previous plan covered care only from selected providers, the beneficiary may find that the PPO makes a wider provider choice possible.

To account for the effect of history, the following discussion considers two different situations. In one, the previous insurance plan provided the same coverage for any choice of provider—a traditional fee-for-service/cost-reimbursement plan. In the other, the previous insurance plan was an exclusive, closed-panel HMO, like Kaiser.

In each case, the discussion will proceed initially as though individual insurance subscribers can choose between PPO enrollment and an alternative plan similar to the preexisting one (though perhaps with revised premium schedules, copayments, or scope of benefits). For the most part, the same factors are relevant even when the PPO plan will replace the preexisting one as the only insurance option available to the beneficiary group. After those basic factors have been examined, the discussion will turn to the special issues raised when the PPO plan is introduced as a single replacement option.

PPO VERSUS TRADITIONAL INSURANCE

From a beneficiary's perspective, the salient differences between a PPO plan and a traditional insurance alternative are likely to be financial in nature. Because PPO panel providers are usually drawn from physicians and hospitals that also provide health care under traditional insurance plans, the choice between a PPO plan and a traditional plan does not inherently require a change in the set of providers from which a beneficiary can obtain care. Some beneficiaries will find that they can retain their familiar providers while taking advantage of any PPO-related financial benefits. And even if a beneficiary's familiar provider is not on the PPO panel, PPO enrollment would not preclude the use of that provider if and when the beneficiary is willing to pay the additional cost.

The PPO plan might have special utilization controls that would not apply under traditional insurance, and these might exert some influence over beneficiary preferences for the PPO plan compared to traditional insurance. There is some debate over whether, on the one hand, beneficiaries believe that UC programs protect them from unnecessary or incompetent care or, on the other hand, beneficiaries view the programs as undesirable interference in the doctor-patient relationship. It is also unclear whether a patient, upon seeking care in a particular instance, would be aware that a UC program has had any effect on the patient's treatment. What is clear is that a patient who is willing to pay to circumvent a PPO's UC program can do so by turning to a nonpanel provider. Thus, preferences for or against UC programs also translate into willingness to accept the special financial characteristics of the PPO.

A PPO plan has three design features that combine to determine whether a beneficiary will experience a financial benefit from PPO enrollment:

— the channeling incentive (i.e., the differential in patient-paid expenses between panel and nonpanel providers);
— the reward or penalty structure relative to traditional insurance; and
— the premium relative to traditional insurance.

The way these features are combined has important effects on size and characteristics of PPO enrollment, but that will be easier to appreciate after each feature has been examined individually.

The Channeling Incentive

A basic design feature of any PPO plan is its channeling incentive. Typically, the deductible and/or coinsurance rate differs depending on whether a PPO enrollee uses a panel or nonpanel provider. A few systems, often called *Exclusive Provider Organizations* or EPOs, deny coverage if the beneficiary uses a nonpanel provider. Yet another design provides a differential scope of benefits depending on choice of provider. Still, in all these cases, there is some direct financial incentive for enrollees to choose panel providers.

The size of the channeling incentive can be an important PPO design decision. Enrollees whose familiar providers are not on the panel will weigh the incentives against the need to seek out a different provider, perhaps travel farther or wait longer to obtain care, or otherwise sacrifice some preference for a nonpanel provider. Other things equal, a larger channeling incentive will induce more of these enrollees to change providers and thus will cause more rechanneling within any given group of enrollees.

But the channeling incentive, in itself, is *not* the critical factor in determining PPO enrollment. That depends especially on insurance premiums and the reward or penalty structure relative to the traditional insurance alternative.

The Reward or Penalty Structure

A PPO plan can be designed to reward the use of panel providers or to penalize the use of nonpanel providers. For example, if the traditional plan imposes a 25 percent coinsurance rate, a reward-structure PPO would set the same coinsurance for nonpanel usage but a lower rate when the panel is used. In contrast, a penalty-structure PPO would set the rate for panel usage at 25 percent but *raise* the rate for nonpanel usage.

Unless the premium for the PPO is higher than for traditional insurance, a reward structure should attract high enrollment. Beneficiaries whose familiar providers are on the panel will find the PPO reduces their out-of-pocket costs without any change in their provider choices; virtually all such beneficiaries may enroll in the plan, though they will not be rechanneled.

In addition, the reward-structure plan may attract many beneficiaries whose familiar providers are not on the panel. They face no financial disadvantage even from retaining their favorite providers, and the PPO will reward a change if that is desired in the future. Having enrolled, some of these beneficiaries will choose to be rechanneled, and more of them will do so the larger is the reward. Thus, a reward-structure PPO is likely to experience high enrollment, with a degree of rechanneling that depends on (a) the number of potential rechannelees in the group and (b) the size of the rechanneling incentive.

In contrast, a penalty structure will attract little or no enrollment at all unless there is a difference in premiums between the PPO plan and traditional insurance. Otherwise, beneficiaries who already use panel providers have no incentive to join the PPO (because their premium and coinsurance remain the same and the PPO closes off the option of using any provider at that same coinsurance rate). And beneficiaries who use nonpanel providers are necessarily better off with the traditional plan's coinsurance rate. To attract enrollees, a penalty structure plan should offer a premium lower than for the traditional insurance alternative.

The PPO Premium

Though there is little (if any) evidence on how people select insurance plans, many economists believe that the selection may be *biased.* That is, people who differ in the extent to which they expect or want to consume health care services will systematically differ in their selection among plans that offer different combinations of premiums and copayment provisions.[5]

Suppose individuals can choose between two traditional plans: a high-premium/low copayment plan and a low-premium/high copayment plan. A subscriber who rarely uses health care services might find the latter more attractive; it provides insurance against the unexpected occurrence of illness, but it costs the beneficiary little so long as utilization is low. On the other hand, a subscriber who frequently visits the doctor is more likely to accept a higher premium, judging that it will be offset by the copayment savings as the beneficiary goes about consuming health care services. In extreme cases, the differences between the two health plans may be so great that all subscribers will choose one or the other, but when the subscribers split between the two plans, it is likely that the split will not be random. The high premium/low copayment plan will tend to attract high-utilization subscribers, while the low premium/high copayment plan will tend to attract low-utilization subscribers.

A reward-structure plan is, by definition, a plan that offers lower copayments (for use of panel providers) than the traditional alternative. If its premium is higher than for the traditional plan, only some enrollees may enroll. In that case, the plan will not only encourage increased demand (since enrollees face a lower copayment than before) but may also attract enrollees whose utilization is higher than average at any copayment rate. This may be good news for the PPO providers, but it will be a revolting development for the PPO plan's payor.

In contrast, a penalty-structure plan can be combined with a reduced premium. (Few if any subscribers would enroll otherwise, as noted above.) In this case, the PPO plan will tend to attract low-utilizing patients. The low-premium, penalty structure plan will not generate the demand effect and will yield a selection bias that favors *low* PPO utilization. Providers will not be too pleased with this result since it means that more rechanneling must be achieved in order to gain from PPO participation, but this design will help the plan save money for payors.

There is a lesson in all this for payors considering PPO participation. Given uncertainty about the PPO's ability to control costs, some payors have taken the position that the PPO should match their traditional plan's premium until PPO experience provides a basis for revision. With the premium held constant, however, a penalty-structure plan would not attract beneficiary enrollment—so the payor offers a reward structure. The result is likely to be increased utilization per subscriber (from both the demand effect and a selection bias). In short, the strategy of maintaining premiums may prove to be self-defeating for payors.

For subscribers, the reward structure with a matched premium may look desirable at first, but may fail to yield a long-run benefit. Premiums for health insurance necessarily reflect the levels of reimbursement payments per subscriber. If those payments turn out to be higher for the PPO plan than for an alternative, then PPO premiums will rise. A reward-structure plan can save money over the longer run only if the panel providers can face both selection bias and a demand effect without generating higher expenses for the payor. (More about this below.) Alternatively, a penalty-structure plan with reduced premiums will not pose such a challenge and may thus, over the long haul, prove more durable and rewarding for all concerned.

PPO VERSUS HMO INSURANCE

A closed-panel HMO consists of providers different from those available on the PPO panel or, for that matter, as nonpanel providers under the PPO plan; a beneficiary who leaves the HMO to join a PPO is automatically rechanneled. In the beneficiary's choice between a PPO and an HMO, a central issue is preferences for choice of provider.

HMOs generally have very low copayments. A reward-structure

PPO may offer similarly low copayments (for use of panel providers), but a penalty-structure PPO would have higher copayments than the HMO.

HMOs also generally have relatively low premiums. The reason seems to be effective rationing of utilization. (Recent results from the Rand Health Insurance study, for example, indicate that an HMO offers about the same ambulatory care per subscriber as fee-for-service providers, but much less hospitalization; effective gatekeeping is a likely explanation.) While HMOs have low copayments that tend to encourage increased demand, the combination of limited provider choice and gatekeeping are able to control costs enough to keep premiums low.

If a penalty PPO's copayments are enough higher, the PPO may come close to matching the HMO's low premium. The penalty plan substitutes a financial disincentive for gatekeeping as the means for controlling demand, and also makes the payor responsible for paying a smaller fraction of fees and charges. By limiting the payor's expenses, the penalty plan helps limit premiums. If the PPO and HMO premiums are similar enough, the beneficiary's choice is between a low-copay, limited choice plan (the HMO) and a higher copay, more open choice plan (the penalty PPO).

A reward-structure PPO, though offering similar copayments, will probably have to charge a higher premium than the HMO. Without a truly closed panel—and without high copayments—the reward-structure plan is ill-equipped to match an HMO in controlling utilization. The reward plan's premium will probably have to be higher to pay for its higher costs. Still, beneficiaries will enroll in the PPO if they are willing to absorb the added cost in exchange for wider provider choice and less gatekeeping.

In principle, a PPO could prosper in competition with an HMO—provided the PPO is not expected to be less costly. Not all beneficiaries are happy in HMOs, and there seems little reason to deny them an alternative they are willing to pay for. The potential pitfall here is that the payor and the beneficiaries may initially underestimate the PPO's costs (and that providers will overestimate their ability to control utilization), in which case the PPO's survival will be threatened by its failure to meet inappropriate expectations.

PPO PLAN AS THE ONLY OPTION

Essentially the same factors are involved in a beneficiary group's acceptance of a PPO plan when only one insurance option will be made available. If most beneficiaries in a group would choose the PPO option when given a choice, there will be high acceptance of the PPO as the only option. If few beneficiaries would freely choose the PPO, acceptance of that as the only option will be poor.

Acceptance will be lowest when the preexisting insurance was a traditional plan and the PPO maintains that same premium under a penalty-structure design. Many beneficiaries (especially those whose familiar providers are not on the PPO panel) will correctly conclude that their benefits have been cut in the transition from the traditional to the PPO plan. What they may not recognize is that premiums or copayments might have risen if the old plan had been continued. The employer/payor has an important educative duty to perform in these circumstances.

However, it is worth noting that the transition to a PPO plan almost necessarily affects beneficiaries differentially. Even if the traditional plan became more expensive, some beneficiaries might have chosen to pay the higher cost to keep it. Such beneficiaries fail to benefit from the PPO plan. Other beneficiaries, those who would freely choose the PPO, are better off.

PAYOR PARTICIPATION

The term *payor* can apply to an insurance company or a self-insured employer—an entity that writes the checks to pay providers for covered services. In this chapter, the term can also apply to an employer or other party who pays insurance premiums. Since premiums reflect the cost of reimbursement payments to providers, those who pay the premiums have at least as much interest in controlling health care costs as those who write the payment checks.

Subscriber groups differ in their objectives; some demand more coverage for child health services, for example, while others require ample coverage for occupational illness. Accordingly, payors may differ in their evaluations of a particular PPO provider panel, and a panel with, say, a strong occupational health program may find it especially easy to attract a payor for whom occupational health is a major concern.

Beyond that, however, the payor cares whether the PPO can offer a given capability at low cost per subscriber. Lower costs permit the payor to cut (or prevent growth in) premiums or to expand coverage; an insurance company may then find itself better able to compete for subscribers, while a self-insured employer may find that reduced costs for fringe benefits make the company more profitable or able to offer a compensation package that helps attract desired employees. The following discussion of the payor's perspective emphasizes evaluation of the cost-reduction potential of PPO participation.

Traditionally, payors have not extensively analyzed differences among providers in their ability to offer low-cost health care. Instead, the payor would observe reimbursement expenses for a subscriber group (or for all those within a community or region) and set commensurate premiums. But as health care costs have risen, payors have faced the challenge of identifying causes and seeking remedies. Differences in the costliness of various providers is one aspect of the problem that has received increasing attention.

Because of differences in case mix, quality of care, and other factors, comparing the costs of alternative providers is extremely difficult. Ideally, the payor would like to be able to say which providers would provide quality care for a particular subscriber group at least cost. In practice, payors cannot make this judgment with certainty.

Judging the cost-reduction potential of a PPO plan is even more difficult. Evaluating the costliness of prospective panel members is only one aspect of the problem. In addition, the payor must judge how changes in premiums and copayment terms will influence beneficiary behavior (enrollment and demand for services); how discounts and changes in copayment terms will affect payments for services; and how UC programs will affect utilization of services per subscriber. Placing dollar values on all these effects would be a heroic task, involving more than a little speculation about important unknowns.

Nonetheless, much can be learned by considering how such an analysis would proceed if accurate values could be placed on the component effects. The following discussion begins by describing how reimbursement expenses are affected by different PPO design characteristics. Then the discussion turns to the issue of setting premiums under a PPO plan.

Like other potential PPO participants, the payor should evaluate a PPO relative to the alternative *future* without one. However, many payors—insurance companies, business coalitions, and some large employers—also have the option of selecting providers to form a PPO panel. That topic is also considered below.

EVALUATING EFFECTS ON REIMBURSEMENT EXPENSE

The payor can reasonably presume that reimbursement expense for beneficiaries who do not enroll in the PPO will not be affected by it (though the payor should be alert for any evidence of PPO cost shifting). Thus, the evaluation procedure focuses on those subscribers who do enroll.

For purposes of this simplified illustration, suppose that potential enrollees currently use two local hospitals, A and B, and suppose that hospital A would be on the PPO panel. Each potential enrollee belongs to one of three categories, labeled and defined as follows:

— Type A: Enrollees who would use hospital A regardless of whether the PPO forms.
— Type B: Enrollees who would use hospital B regardless of whether the PPO forms.
— Type C: Enrollees who would use hospital B in the PPO's absence, but would be rechanneled to hospital A under the PPO plan.

Reimbursement expenses per subscriber will be affected differently for each of these categories. The overall effect on reimbursement expenses depends on the number of enrollees in each group and whether the plan has a reward or penalty structure.

Reward-Structure Effects

Suppose that, in the absence of the PPO, average charges per subscriber at hospitals A and B are $A and $B, respectively, and the payor would reimburse the same fraction of the charges, c, in either case. With a reward-structure PPO, however, the payor would continue to pay fraction c only for Type B enrollees (who continue to use hospital B). For Type A and Type C enrollees, the payor would pay a higher fraction, $c*$, of hospital A's PPO charges. Since beneficiaries who use hospital A would pay a smaller fraction of the bill under the PPO, their utilization would rise by some proportion, d (which would include effects of selection bias as well as the demand effect). Finally, hospital A's PPO concessions reduce expense per beneficiary by some fraction, h. For each type of beneficiary, then, the effect on reimbursement expense per enrollee would be approximated by the following simplified formulas:

$$\text{Type A change} = \$A(1 - h)(c*)(1 + d) - \$Ac,$$

$$\text{Type B change} = \$Bc - \$Bc = 0, \text{ and}$$

$$\text{Type C change} = \$A(1 - h)(c*)(1 + d) - \$Bc$$

For Type B subscribers, the reward-structure plan causes no change in reimbursement expense. For Type A, a change is likely, but whether it is an increase or decrease depends on whether the hospital's concessions are sufficient to offset the demand and change-in-copayment effects. A change is also likely for Type C subscribers, but for them the effect depends critically on whether hospital A is intrinsically less costly than hospital B.

Consider the following numerical example: Suppose the PPO plan reduces the beneficiary's copayment rate from 25 percent ($c = .75$) to zero when panel providers are used ($c* = 1.00$); hospital A's concessions reduce its charges per Type A or Type C subscriber by 25 percent ($h = .25$); and the demand effect associated with the copayment reduction is 20 percent ($d = .20$). Under these conditions, expense per Type A subscriber would *rise* by .15$A, Type B expense would remain unchanged, and the change in Type C expense would be .9$A − .75$B. For the subscriber group as a whole, the effect on average reimbursement expense also depends on how many of the subscribers are of each type. For example, if 80 percent of the subscribers are Type A, and the remainder split evenly between Types B and C, the change in average expense per subscriber would be:

$$.8(.15)\$A + .1(0) + .1(.9\$A - .75\$B) = .21\$A - .075\$B$$

Accordingly, average expense per subscriber would be unchanged by the PPO if $A is about 35 percent of $B; if hospitals A and B were equally costly in the PPO's absence, however, the PPO would *raise* average expense per subscriber by about 30 percent.

The basic formulas suggest some useful generalizations about reward-structure PPOs:

— Type A expense will rise unless hospital concessions fully offset both the change in the payor's share of the reimbursement burden and the demand (and/or selection) effect.
— Type B expense is unchanged.
— Type C expense falls if panel providers are intrinsically less costly than nonpanel providers.
— If panel providers are intrinsically less costly, a reward-structure plan can reduce average expense if rechanneling is substantial.

Penalty-Structure Effects

The reimbursement effect formulas for a penalty structure plan are:

$$\text{Type A change} = \$A(1 - h')c - \$Ac,$$

$$\text{Type B change} = \$B(1 - d')(c') - \$Bc,$$

$$\text{Type C change} = \$A(1 - h')c - \$Bc.$$

Since the penalty-structure plan does not change beneficiaries' copayment rates for hospital A, there is neither a demand effect nor an increase in the payor's share of expenses for Type A or Type C subscribers.[6] However, Type B subscribers experience an increase in their copayment rate (which reduces the payor's share from c to c', and this should cause the subscribers to *reduce* their utilization by some fraction (d'). Finally, hospital A offers some concessions, indicated by $(1 - h')$.

A penalty-structure plan surely reduces reimbursement expense per Type A and Type B subscriber. For Type A, the reduction is due to hospital concessions; for Type B, the reduction results from the payor's reduced share of the bill as well as the reduction in beneficiary demand that causes.

However, a penalty-structure plan does *not* guarantee a reduction in the overall expense for the subscriber group as a whole. If hospital A is intrinsically more costly than hospital B, there could be an increase in Type C expense, and if rechanneling is substantial enough (i.e., if the number of Type C enrollees is large enough relative to the numbers of Type A and Type B subscribers), the penalty structure could result in increased average expense for the subscriber group as a whole.

Suppose, though, that it has already been determined that hospital A (and not B) will be on the PPO panel if it forms. The formulas for the reward- and penalty-structure designs seem to suggest that the penalty structure would offer the best chance for reducing average expense per subscriber. Should the payor insist on a penalty structure as a condition for PPO participation?

The short answer: not necessarily. As a rule, the penalty plan would have to offer a lower premium than the reward plan in order to attract beneficiaries (either individually or as a group). Therefore, what the payor should do is estimate what the differences in insurance premiums would have to be and how that compares with expected differences in the expense effects of alternative PPO design options. And in doing so, the payor must consider how providers and beneficiaries will respond to different insurance premiums.

SETTING PPO PREMIUMS

As was noted in the discussion of beneficiary participation, a penalty-structure plan would gain little (if any) enrollment unless its premium is lower than for a traditional (or reward-structure) plan. The question the payor must answer is whether the reduction in the premium necessary to induce enrollment will be permissible given the expense reduction that can be achieved.

There is no simple, assured answer to this question. What can be said is that the payor's chances of successfully walking the tightrope between reduced premiums and reduced expense improves markedly if panel providers are intrinsically less costly than their nonpanel competitors.

The premium reductions necessary to induce penalty plan enrollment surely differ for the three types of subscribers. Type A subscribers should accept a fairly small premium reduction since they retain their familiar provider and copayment rates. Type C subscribers might require more reduction in the premium since they must change providers to retain their familiar copayment rate. And Type B subscribers will not freely enroll unless the premium reduction compensates them for the increase in their copayment rates.

Unfortunately, the payor must offer the same premium to all enrollees. After all, there is no way for the payor to know in advance which enrollees would be of which types.

If the premium reduction is large enough to attract Type B enrollees, it will be larger than necessary to attract Type A enrollees. It is possible (perhaps even likely) that a premium reduction large enough to attract Type B enrollees is greater than the average reimbursement savings over all the subscribers who would enroll at the new premium. The payor should not count too heavily on Type B enrollment, since it may cost a good deal more than it is worth.

Type A enrollment may be easy to achieve but make little contribution to reimbursement savings. Under a penalty plan, the savings for Type A enrollees come from provider concessions, but providers have no good reason to offer concessions unless the PPO rechannels patients. That requires Type C enrollment. If the premium reduction is not large enough to attract Type C enrollment, the penalty structure offers minimal (if any) reimbursement savings.

So, in the end, a central issue is whether Type C enrollees will generate enough reimbursement savings to warrant the premium reductions necessary to enroll them. One thing is clear: The answer is far more likely to be *yes* if the PPO rechannels these patients from more costly providers to less costly ones.

Penalty-structure plans appear to be gaining in popularity, especially for insurer-sponsored plans marketed to employer-supported subscriber groups. As evidence has mounted that utilization can be controlled through increased coinsurance, both insurers and employers have turned to coinsurance benefit changes as a way of stemming the increase in insurance premiums. Beneficiaries, on the other hand, resist such benefit cuts. A penalty-structure PPO offers a compromise solution: a technique for raising coinsurance for beneficiaries willing to pay while holding the line for others.

Many of these penalty-structure plans are of too recent vintage to have proved that the premium savings they promise are consistent with the reimbursement expense savings they generate. Furthermore, while many of these plans have negotiated for provider concessions, there is little evidence to date on whether the plans generate the degree of rechanneling panel providers anticipate.

If, as many people believe, the time is ripe to convince beneficiaries that they gain in the long run from contributing to health care cost control, then penalty-structure PPOs are a design well suited to the times. For a given set of panel providers, a penalty-structure plan may have lower reimbursement expenses than a reward-structure plan; so it should have lower premiums as well. In this sense, a penalty structure is the superior offering to subscribers who want to use more of their incomes for purposes other than health care.

However, a reward-structure design cannot be ruled out as a viable option where subscribers want low coinsurance but are willing to use a community's least costly providers if that will help keep premiums down. HMOs have attracted this type of subscriber for many years. A reward-structure PPO offers a similar option with perhaps somewhat higher premiums and a less restricted choice of providers. At least in principle, a reward-structure plan can be less costly than traditional insurance, provided the PPO is careful in its selection of panel providers.

PAYOR'S OPTION TO SELECT THE PANEL

Recently, insurance companies and business coalitions have been taking the initiative in sponsoring PPOs. Among other things, PPO sponsorship entails the right and responsibility to select panel providers. At some stage in the process, the sponsors often solicit discounts or other concessions from providers interested in joining the PPO panel. In effect, the sponsors encourage providers to compete for the privilege of PPO participation.

By soliciting competitive offers, the payor is attempting to exercise some leverage on provider concessions. Suppose, for example, that most of the payor's subscriber group already uses hospital A. They can offer hospital A very few "new" patients. But by pointing out that hospital B is a candidate for a panel slot, the payor implicitly threatens to rechannel many of hospital A's current patients to hospital B. Since hospital A is comparing two alternative *futures* (with and without PPO participation), the rechanneling rate under consideration can be quite high. Consequently, hospital A will consider making a much larger concession than it would if there were no competitors for the PPO panel position.

Though the payor that establishes this kind of competition reaps a stronger bargaining position, there are some potential pitfalls. In particular, if the payor chooses the panel provider(s) solely on the basis of the discount rate offer, the payor may unintentionally empanel some of the community's most costly providers.

The discount rate offered by a hospital is not a good indicator of the cost savings it will generate. A hospital may offer a high rate because it expects a lot of PPO rechanneling, or because its net revenue is a large fraction of its total revenue, or both. Neither of these factors is clearly associated with efficiency. In particular, a hospital may have a high net revenue rate simply because it has a lot of excess capacity (a lot of underused facilities and equipment) and it recovers the investment in the excess capacity by charging its patients high prices. Such a hospital may offer a high PPO discount rate, but still charge the PPO more than its competitors would.

FORMING A SUCCESSFUL PPO

In recent years, a large number of preferred provider organizations have formed throughout the United States. A few are in operation; many more hope to begin operations in the near future. Some are strictly local in scope while others aim to spread throughout a state, a region, or even the whole nation. Some are sponsored by insurers, others by employers, and others by their provider members. Some offer special programs, while others rely primarily on discounts. Much experimentation is underway, and it is too early to assess how successful the concept is likely to be in practice or which of the many PPO forms is best suited to particular circumstances.

This chapter has analyzed, and to some extent speculated about, the economic forces that can reinforce or impede a PPO's formation and survival. The chapter reaches no general conclusion about which PPO design is best, nor even that any single design is likely to be best in all situations. Instead, the chapter has suggested some perspectives and insights about some of the central issues in PPO survival.

A central argument in this chapter is that a PPO stands the greatest chance of meeting all its participants' expectations if it channels patients to the community's most efficient providers. Rechanneling is key to providers' satisfaction with the program, and to their willingness to make concessions. Rechanneling can help payors reduce their expenses and thus offer lower premiums to beneficiaries or their employers. But rechanneling can raise reimbursement expenses, and hence insurance premiums, if panel providers are more costly than their competitors.

Large PPOs will not necessarily be more successful. If the PPO attempts to attract the most cost-effective providers in a community, growth of the panel may imply that additional members are increasingly costly ones. In terms of earning provider concessions, the overall number of subscribers in the group is less important than the amount of rechanneling that might be generated. This depends primarily on the size of the rechanneling incentive the payor offers.

If two (or more) providers are competing for PPO membership, each should evaluate the rechanneling effect by considering what its patient load would be if the other provider(s) gained membership. A provider may currently serve most subscribers in a group, but (if the rechanneling incentive is large enough) might lose many of them if a different provider is admitted to the PPO panel.

Utilization controls can be an important contributor to PPO cost control. Given any net revenue target, the utilization-control rate a hospital can offer is larger than the discount rate it can offer. Thus, holding the hospital's financial benefit constant, the payor should achieve greater reimbursement savings with the utilization-control option.

Many payors are skeptical of providers' abilities (and perhaps willingness) to control utilization. In some cases, the skepticism may be warranted. However, the payor might do better to establish some monitoring capability (and perhaps negotiate for some rebate from providers if utilization-control targets are not met) than to rely entirely on discounts.

Penalty-structure PPOs offer an especially promising technique for reducing health care expenditures, but largely because such PPOs raise copayments for at least some beneficiaries. There is no guarantee that a penalty plan will save money, and even if it does, beneficiaries may ultimately determine that the premium savings they earn do not compensate them for the higher out-of-pocket expenses they incur. At the same time, reward plans still offer some opportunity for savings, and may be the preferred alternative for some beneficiary groups.

Historically, there have been very limited incentives for beneficiaries or providers to emphasize cost effectiveness as a criterion for evaluating health care delivery. During the 1970s, costs rose dramatically as medicare, medicaid, and rising incomes spurred demand for health care. To economists, the effect was hardly surprising; increased demand combined with poor mechanisms for cost-based competition was a recipe for inflation.

Today, a wide variety of new programs—including alternative delivery systems such as PPOs—are introducing mechanisms to promote cost-based competition. To the extent that a market's suppliers succeed by using their resources efficiently to produce the products consumers desire most, society as a whole benefits by making the fullest use of all the resources at its disposal. This chapter has argued that a PPO that empanels a community's most efficient providers stands the best chance of meeting all its participants' objectives. Such PPOs contribute to a larger movement in the direction of more efficient health care markets.

To say that society as a whole gains is not to say, however, that every individual in society gains. Providers that do not manage their resources wisely, or that must repay large debts, or that otherwise suffer some disadvantage in cost competition will lose. Some providers, to become competitive, may have to sacrifice long-standing commitments to providing charity care or educational programs. Participants in poorly designed PPOs will suffer disappointment, as will participants in other new programs that prove ill suited to the needs of their communities. Cost competition and the process of learning how to participate in it will change health care delivery. Not everyone will be happy with the changes.

The health care industry is in a state of flux, and there are no guaranteed outcomes. The best anyone can do is be alert to new options, evaluate them carefully, and make a well-reasoned judgment.

NOTES

1. For a general description of various PPO models, see Joan B. Trauner, "Preferred Provider Organizations: The California Experiment," Institute for Health Policy Studies, UCSF (August 1983).

2. To use the formula, NY should be defined as the difference between Y and variable costs plus any increment in annualized fixed costs (e.g., additional equipment) incurred as part of PPO implementation. The formula is a good approximation if variable costs per case are fairly constant over the caseload range under consideration and if the insured group's casemix is unchanged; otherwise, the formula should be modified.

3. An excellent survey of evidence on cost-sharing effects is in Charles E. Phelps, "Health Care Costs: The Consequences of Increased Cost Sharing," The Rand Corp., R-2970-RC (November 1982).

4. Of course, this argument does not apply to PPO expansion from one local community to another. In each new community, the PPO can again begin to recruit from among the most cost-effective local physicians.

5. For some groups, premiums are paid by an employer or other party. When alternative plans are offered in this circumstance, it is commonplace for one of the plans (sometimes called a Basic Plan) to be fully paid and for subscribers to be assessed for the premium increment associated with any more costly alternative. Thus, a penalty-structure PPO plan can offer a reduced premium by making it the Basic Plan and requiring subscribers to pay some of the premium for the traditional alternative.

6. This statement, and the formulas it describes, are slightly simplified. Even when the coinsurance rate is constant, the amount a beneficiary must pay for care changes whenever the total charge changes. Because a discount changes the charges, it changes what beneficiaries must pay, and this can affect their demand for care. The simplified formula ignores this effect on demand since it is likely to be very small in magnitude.

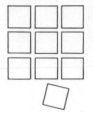

Economics of Marketplace Competition

AN ECONOMIC ANALYSIS OF THE "PREFERRED PROVIDER ORGANIZATION" CONCEPT*

Alain C. Enthoven, Ph.D.

Marriner S. Eccles Professor of
  Public and Private Management
Graduate School of Business
Stanford University
Stanford, CA

☐ Preferred provider organizations or PPOs are the latest hot product of the health care financing industry. Employers who have experienced very large increases in the costs of their employee health benefits are searching for ways to get those costs under control without appearing to roll back covered benefits. Many are looking hard at the PPO idea.

What is a PPO? It is not an organization; it is a kind of contract between providers of and payors for health care services. The key idea is *selective* contracting in advance for the services of health care providers, an idea the medical profession had, until recently, successfully resisted

---
*The author acknowledges with gratitude valuable criticisms and suggestions on a draft from John M. Harris, Jr., Harold Luft, Roger Noll, Richmond Prescott, and Boyd Thompson.

since the beginnings of health insurance. Beyond that, the concept becomes elusive. There are infinite possible financial arrangements among providers, patients, and payors. Between conceptual opposites such as "free choice of provider" and "closed-panel plans" lies a continuum of intermediate possibilities. So there is bound to be some arbitrariness in drawing lines. It would not be useful to define the concept to include any use of selective provider contracting. To define the PPO so broadly that it includes traditional Blue Cross or Blue Shield would be to render the definition meaningless or to say that it is not anything new. The definition we need describes something that is new.

WHAT A PPO IS

The buyer side of the PPO contract consists of employers and labor-management trust funds. These agencies may deal directly with providers or deal indirectly through claims administrators or financial intermediaries. Researchers at InterStudy, a leading health policy research institute, have defined the PPO as made up of the following components:

1. A provider panel.
2. A negotiated fee schedule, frequently considered a discount.
3. Utilization or claims review and some form of control mechanism.
4. No "lock in" of consumers.
5. Administrative and marketing arms.[1]

The provider panel consists of a limited number of physicians and hospitals presumably selected for their cost effectiveness. The focus may be hospitals and their medical staffs or medical groups or members of a medical society. The negotiated fees are accepted as payment in full by contracting providers. Utilization controls may consist of such devices as prior authorization for nonemergency hospital admissions, concurrent review of inpatients with discharge planning, utilization review with disallowance of payment to providers for unnecessary services, and/or the use of a primary care physician as "gatekeeper." Consumers are offered additional benefits for using the panel providers. Waiver of coinsurance payments is a frequent example. Or patients may have to pay additional coinsurance if they go outside the panel. A lock in refers to the patient's agreement, usually for a year at a time, that the only services covered by insurance will be those received from panel providers. This is typical of Health Maintenance Organizations. The absence of a lock in means that insurance does pay substantial, if reduced, benefits to patients using non-panel providers.

PPOs are being sponsored by physicians' organizations, hospitals, traditional insurers, employers, foundations for medical care, and claims administrators.

WHAT A PPO IS NOT

On the other hand, a PPO is not:

1. A traditional indemnity or service benefit insurance.
2. A health maintenance organization.
3. A provider risk-sharing arrangement.
4. A financial intermediary.
5. A cohesive provider organization.

Traditional indemnity insurance pays fixed sums to indemnify patients for amounts they are charged for specific services. This is usually backed up by insurance that pays 80 percent of the patient's remaining covered expenses. Patients have complete free choice of provider, as far as the insurance plan is concerned and all providers are treated equally. There is no contract between the insurer and the provider. Thus, the provider can charge whatever the patient will agree to in the knowledge that the insured patient has little knowledge, incentive, or power to bargain effectively. By contrast, in the PPO, insurance covers the services of contracting providers preferentially, and prices are negotiated in advance by a cost-conscious buyer with the power to bargain effectively.

The service benefit insurance plans, Blue Cross and Blue Shield, traditionally have contracts with participating providers who agree to accept the contractual fee-for-service payments as payment in full. But these plans usually involve no significant provider selection—any licensed provider can participate. For example, the overwhelming majority of fee-for-service doctors in each state participate in Blue Shield. There is no serious bargaining over fees, and there are no serious attempts to control use of services. Because a licensed physician who wants to accept the Blue Shield contract may do so, Blue Shield gives the physician no incentive to be a low bidder. By contrast, the PPO attempts to negotiate reduced fees in a competitive environment. It offers providers increased volume in exchange for reduced fees.

The health maintenance organization or HMO pays its provider organizations on the basis of periodic per capita amounts set in advance, not directly linked to fees or charges for services rendered. The HMO limits coverage to the services of participating providers. The member agrees for a year at a time to receive all covered services from participating providers. By contrast, PPO enrollees can receive some, if less favorable, insurance coverage for the services of nonparticipating providers. The HMO member who goes outside for services must pay for them himself, while the traditionally insured can go to any provider and expect his insurance to pay equally. The PPO is somewhere in between, with something that might be called *a soft lock in*. PPO coverage can get to look a lot like an HMO or an EPO (exclusive provider organization) if coverage of the services of nonparticipating providers is poor enough.

In principle, the PPO concept does not include "at risk" physician contracts. Unlike the HMO, in which the physicians' organization receives a per capita payment, set in advance, independent of the number of services actually used, PPO physicians do not suffer financially if use of services increases, and they are not directly rewarded for reducing the use of services or for treating patients in less costly ways. (If all physicians in a particular PPO do treat their patients in less costly ways, the PPO's premium can be reduced and the PPO can attract more patients. To the individual physician, this is a very indirect reward.) PPO contracts may include risk sharing on the part of hospitals in the form of contracts specifying all-inclusive fixed payments per day or per case. And, as will be suggested later, the PPO concept could be adapted to include incentive payments to providers for controlling per capita costs.

A PPO is not a financial intermediary. It does not collect premiums or pay bills. The actual payments to PPO providers are made through whatever financing vehicle the employer wishes to use, such as traditional insurance or a self-funded plan.

And finally, while an effective PPO will include a utilization review system, the PPO is usually not a cohesive provider organization with a unified management structure able to allocate resources and control quality and cost. A PPO is not like prepaid group practices (PGPs) that have these attributes.

WHY PPOs NOW? WHAT IS GOOD ABOUT THEM?

The PPO idea contains several important advances over traditional insurance. First, it is an attempt to select cost-effective providers and to reward insured patients, who otherwise would not be cost conscious, for selecting them for care. The PPO uses coinsurance, which is an incentive for patients to be cost conscious at the time of medical need. But in the hands of a PPO, this tool can have an important advantage over the flat coinsurance rate typical of traditional insurance. A flat 20-percent coinsurance rate applicable to all providers may reduce use of services, but it can do little to direct patients to economical providers. The PPO can use coinsurance to direct patients to cost-effective providers. It is almost impossible for the ordinary patient to assess the economic efficiency of a provider, especially where complex costly care is involved. An aggregate buyer, with a broader data base and specialized expertise is more likely to be able to identify efficient providers in advance. In turn, this informed cost consciousness on the demand side may allow providers to compete on the basis of overall economy.

Second, the PPO includes contracting in advance for prices by someone who has the bargaining power, the knowledge and time to shop, and an incentive to make economical arrangements. Organized medicine has resisted this in the past. Physicians have not wanted external third parties to get involved in the transaction between doctor and patient.

Contracting for prices in advance gives the PPO an opportunity to inform the patient about the likely out-of-pocket costs of use of the services of PPO providers. In the absence of such a contract, the insurer is reduced to telling the patient something like "we pay 80 percent of UCR (usual, customary, and reasonable)," which tells the patient very little about what he or she is likely to have to pay. Thus the PPO can give the patient a much clearer economic signal, to which he or she is more likely to be able to respond.

Third, the PPO has the potential to include some quality control, for example, by directing patients *away from* physicians who provide poor quality care and *to* experienced physicians for complex procedures. As employers limit or influence choice of provider, they will be held responsible by the employees for the quality of care and service that is provided. To gain employee acceptance of the concept of limited choice, employers will need to make credible efforts to assure quality. In any case, quality of care is in the employer's interest. It will be reflected in less sick leave and disability.

The PPO allows *the physician* to continue in his or her existing fee-for-service practice setting, yet to compete on economic terms with other physicians and with HMOs. It is not surprising that nearly half the PPOs are in California; nearly half the HMO members are also in California. (The enactment in 1982 of a clear legal mandate in AB 3480 has also been an important contributor to this development.) The PPO does not require the physician to enter a risk-bearing contract. And PPOs do offer prompt payment.

The PPO appears to offer *the employer* a way of quickly getting a grip on the health care costs of those employees who choose to remain with fee-for-service physicians while continuing to offer comprehensive coverage, at least to those who choose preferred providers. Most employees are not members of HMOs, and it will take many years before most will be. Moreover, the PPO does not have to disturb existing financial arrangements. The financial vice president who last year proudly told the board of directors that she would save money by switching from an insurance policy to self-funding can contract with a PPO without going back to tell the directors that she was wrong. And the PPO format does not restrict the employer's freedom to design the benefit coverage or to negotiate it with employees. In contrast, the Federal HMO Act requires HMOs to offer quite comprehensive benefits.

The PPO offers *the employee* a reward for going to economical providers, yet it does not require a *hard lock in*. This may be quite attractive for a family in which some members are happy to use preferred providers while others want the freedom to continue to use other doctors.

Related to this idea are two claims made for PPOs that are exaggerated and misleading. The first claim is that in the PPO the patient does not have to change providers and the doctors do not have to change practice style. This is the same illusion on which many unsuccessful individual practice associations were built in the 1970s. If nobody changes behavior, the PPO concept is worthless. For the PPO to be effective, patients using costly providers must switch to economical ones and/or costly providers must change practice styles and participate in reorganization of the delivery system to make it more efficient.

The second claim is that unlike HMOs, employees do not have to enroll in the PPO: the employer can simply contract with the preferred providers and offer them on a preferential basis to employees in the context of the existing insurance plan that covers all the employees. If the employer wants to know that the preferred providers are actually saving him money, not merely offering lower prices and "making it up on volume," then he needs a population denominator.[2] The dollars and hospital use rates he cares about are per capita. Moreover, as will be suggested later, it will be in the interest of employers to include incentives in PPO contracts for providers to control per capita costs. For this to be possible, there must be a defined population to serve as a denominator. The pure PPO model does not include an election and a lock in, hence it does not generate a natural population denominator. Who would be called the patients of the preferred providers for purposes of evaluation? Patients who went to them exclusively? Partly? And what about patients who went to no doctor at all that year? To define a satisfactory population denominator, there has to be some equivalent to enrollment and a lock in. Moreover, employers seeking to control costs are likely to be reluctant to "give away" better benefits to those using preferred providers without "taking away" benefits from those who use nonpreferred providers. A natural way to do this is to offer a PPO plan with a balance of give away and take away as an alternative to the existing insurance plan.

Why are PPOs happening now, especially in California? PPOs existed many years ago. In the states of Washington and Oregon, for example, they were called "hospital associations" or "contract medicine" because these lay-controlled organizations contracted with closed panels of physicians. These organizations negotiated uniform prices with physicians, and they actively reviewed medical care for necessity and appropriateness. Organized medicine systematically destroyed them.[3] The American Medical Association described their practices as unethical. The medical societies created physician-controlled insurance plans and then boycotted non-physician-controlled plans. Physicians cooperating with contract medicine were threatened with censure and expulsion from medical societies, which could lead to loss of referrals and hospital staff privileges.

In these and other states, concerted political action by organized medicine was also a key factor. For example, prior to 1982 and the enactment of AB 3480, the Insurance Code in California prohibited insurance companies from offering PPOs: "Nothing in this section shall be construed to authorize an insurer . . . in any manner to direct, participate in or control the selection of the hospital or physician and surgeon from whom the insured secures services."[4]

In recent years, the ability of organized medicine to control the financing of medical care has been breaking down. Systematic enforcement of antitrust law, culminating in the 1982 Supreme Court decision in the case of *Arizona* v. *Maricopa County Medical Society,* has been a major factor. On the West Coast, Prepaid Group Practice, led by Kaiser-Permanente, overcame the resistance of organized medicine, due in substantial part to the support of organized labor and public sector employers. Prepaid group practice has become an established part of "mainstream" medicine, at least on the West Coast, and in Minnesota, and is rapidly becoming so in Illinois, Massachusetts, and Michigan. This has helped to legitimize the idea of "limited provider" health care plans and the economic competition of alternative delivery systems. An increasing supply of doctors and the proliferation of subspecialties have weakened the ability of organized medicine to control physician behavior.

In 1981, the Congress changed the Medicaid law to allow States to engage in selective contracting for providers to serve Medicaid beneficiaries.[5] In 1982, Congress put firm comprehensive limits on the growth in the cost per hospital case that Medicare would pay for.[6] And the California state legislature enacted selective provider contracting for Medi-Cal, the state's Medicaid program.[7] Employers, labor, and insurance companies feared that if they did not do something to prevent it, providers would seek to make up their revenue losses resulting from Medicare and Medicaid controls by shifting costs to insured private patients. So they campaigned successfully for AB 3480, which added the provision "that an insurer may negotiate and enter into contracts for alternative rates of payment with institutional providers (and after July 1, 1983, professional providers) and offer the benefit of such alternative rates to insured customers who select such providers."

ECONOMIC ANALYSIS OF THE PPO CONCEPT

While the PPO idea embodies some significant advances over traditional insurance, some cautions about their real effectiveness are in order. The successful PPO must identify, select, and contract with economical providers and induce patients to go to them for care. As they attempt to do this, they will meet the cohesive social fabric of the provider communities and find that these steps are easier said than done. Substantial problems will emerge.

IDENTIFYING ECONOMICAL HOSPITALS

Identifying economical hospitals is relatively easy. An interested purchaser can submit typical orders for typical diagnoses (length of stay, procedures and tests ordered, etc.) and ask what the bill would be. From this, a purchaser can estimate what its cost would be to hospitalize patients in each hospital.

Some PPOs use all-inclusive cost per day as the measure of hospital cost. This is a poor measure because it does not allow for the severity or complexity of the cases being treated; it is likely to favor hospitals with long stays because the first days that include active treatment are more costly than later days that are usually more convalescence; and it confounds the prices charged by the hospital with the practice patterns of the physicians. Cost per case based on diagnosis related groups (DRGs) would be a better measure, because it attempts to control for severity of case mix. However, it too confounds hospital prices and physician practice patterns.

SELECTING ECONOMICAL HOSPITALS

Selecting economical hospitals, to the exclusion of others, is somewhat more complex. Special provisions may need to be made for tertiary care and other specialized services not offered at participating low-cost hospitals.

Sick people go to doctors, not to hospitals. Doctors order tests, hospitalize patients, and recommend and perform procedures. That argues for selecting economical doctors rather than hospitals. Hospital care is the joint product of doctors and hospitals. And doctors have staff relationships to particular hospitals. At least the selections of hospitals and doctors must recognize the relationships between the two. It would not do an employer much good to offer a particular hospital as a preferred provider if few of his employees' doctors practiced there.

CONTRACTING WITH HOSPITALS

Some PPOs, such as the Blue Cross of California Prudent Buyer Plan, contract on the basis of a negotiated all-inclusive price per day. Any mode of contracting has its problems, including this one. Cost per day rewards hospitals for admissions of easy cases, some of which might be unnecessary, and it rewards longer stays. Contracts based on cost per day and cost per case—the two leading candidates—share the important deficiency that they do not reward hospitals for the single most important source of economy in health care, that is, reduced hospital use. Prepaid group practices typically hospitalize their patients some 25 to 45 percent less often than do their fee-for-service counterparts.[8]

These modes of contracting can be contrasted with the way in which Kaiser Foundation Health Plan and Hospitals are paid, which is primarily per capita payment set in advance. In some cases, the physicians in the Permanente medical groups share in the net incomes of the hospitals. Under this type of contract, reduced hospital use is to the benefit of hospitals. And physicians are rewarded for their efforts to hold down hospital costs.

Contracts based simply on prices per item of service, per day or per stay are poor proxies for what the purchasers care most about—total cost per capita. A better contract, from the employer's point of view, would include incentives for physicians and hospitals to reduce hospital admissions. This should be possible in a modified PPO format without introducing explicit risk sharing. (See below.)

IDENTIFYING ECONOMICAL DOCTORS

Identifying economical doctors is not easy to do. Just looking at fees is not nearly enough. The key issues are in the timeliness and accuracy of diagnosis, in the proficiency with which procedures are performed, and in decisions concerning use of costly resources such as hospitals. To identify economical doctors, one needs a data base with total costs of treatment by provider and by type of case, something that is far beyond the capabilities of most insurers and employers. The apparently high-cost doctor might actually be an economical doctor with an excellent reputation to whom the difficult cases are referred. Or he or she might be a marginally competent occasional surgeon with a high rate of complications. To tell these two apart, one needs either reliable judgment by an experienced knowledgeable doctor or a reliable index of the severity of illness. Development of the latter is still in the research stage. The former lacks objective verifiability.

SELECTING ECONOMICAL DOCTORS

Actually selecting economical doctors, to the exclusion of others, will also prove to have its difficulties. For example, hospital-focused PPOs hope to identify economical doctors through the staffs of participating hospitals. But a hospital is likely to have a hard time excluding those of its physicians who are high utilizers of services, those who admit the most patients and order the most tests. After all, these doctors are now the hospital's best customers. PPOs are likely to be under a lot of pressure to take a whole hospital medical staff, the costly along with the economical. How serious a problem this will be depends on the strength of the hospital's utilization-control system and the willingness of the medical staff to support it. In the 1970s, many individual practice associations found it politically impossible to exclude physicians. Insurer-sponsored PPOs may be able to exercise greater selectivity. Employers would do well to take a careful look at these aspects of a proposed PPO arrangement.

Physicians are linked to each other by patterns of professional ties, such as hospital medical staff relationships, and by patterns of referrals. They refer patients to doctors in other specialties for various reasons, some good and some not so good. The list includes confidence and respect for professional competence, ease of communication, confidence that the patient will be returned to the referring doctor, reciprocity for other referrals, and social ties. Many physicians will be reluctant to change referral and collaborative relationships merely because some patients are in a PPO that does not include some of their colleagues. Patients, in turn, may become dissatisfied if the specialists to whom they are referred are not preferred providers. And if the pattern of referrals outside the PPO persists, the economic effectiveness of the PPO will be attenuated.

Finally, the PPO remains basically a fee-for-service concept, likely to pay doctors more for doing more costly procedures. There is likely to be "coding creep," that is, classifying patient visits into more complex and better paid categories, and "diagnosis creep," that is, classifying patients into more remunerative diagnoses. The PPO might negotiate fees for routine visits and for complex procedures, but driving a hard bargain on prices will not do much good if the physician can make up his or her loss by increasing the volume of complex procedures. So the employer or other cost-conscious payor needs some kind of defined population to serve as a denominator, and an ability to track costs, hospital days, and procedures per person per year.

All this is not to argue that PPOs will not work at all. But it is to say that there will be more and less effective PPOs. Effective implementation of the PPO idea is likely to prove to be a lot more complex than might initially appear to an inexperienced observer. And the achievement of significant savings is far from guaranteed.

MEASURING THE PPO AGAINST THE PGP STANDARD

While some individual practice associations compete effectively with them, the evidence supports the view that prepaid group practices (PGPs) are the most cost-effective system of health care in actual operation today. Among the leading examples are Kaiser-Permanente, Group Health Cooperative of Puget Sound, and Harvard Community Health Plan. In a review of a large body of comparison studies, Harold Luft found that the total cost of health care, premium and out-of-pocket, for members of PGPs was 10 to 40 percent lower than the cost for similar people under fee-for-service and traditional insurance.[9] So a useful perspective may be gained by examining the ways in which PGPs achieve their economies and whether PPOs are likely to be able to duplicate their performance.

APPROPRIATE INCENTIVES FOR PHYSICIANS

The fee-for-service system, as it actually operates in the United States, pays physicians a greater net income per unit of time for hospital care than for office care and for complex procedures than for history taking and advice, as well as more for doing more generally, whether or not more is necessary or beneficial to the patient.[10] By contrast, in cost-effective PGPs such as the above-mentioned examples, as well as in the Mayo Clinic, an efficient multispecialty group practice, the physicians are salaried, and their incomes are independent of decisions with respect to one mode of care versus another. Indeed, the PGP model may include disincentives to hospitalize. Planned workload may be based on scheduled office visits, with hospital visits done "on the physician's own time."

Salaries may not be the optimal incentive to reward extra effort to give good service. Some efficient organizations such as St. Louis Park Medical Center in the Minneapolis area, pay physicians what might be called "attenuated fee-for-service" in which adjustments are made that take the edge off the cost-increasing incentives, but in which greater productivity is still rewarded.

A PPO could, in part, correct the cost-increasing incentives with a fee schedule that pays the same net income per unit of time for history taking and advice and for procedures. Mark Blumberg has recommended this as a reform of the fee-for-service system in general.[11] Employers ought to insist on it. But it will take time for PPOs to figure out how to do this. At best, the PPO format does not reward physicians for refraining from giving unnecessary or ineffective care.

Generally speaking, PGPs employ physicians full time, so their careers are bound up with the success of the organization. One can therefore expect the needs of the PGP to have a large impact on their practice styles. By contrast, fee-for-service solo practitioners are able and likely to join several PPOs as well as participating in Blue Shield and one or more individual practice associations. As a consequence, their interest in any one PPO will be diluted, and the impact of the PPO's incentive and utilization-control scheme on their practice style will be attenuated. It is less likely that they will work hard to make a particular PPO a success. This is a problem that has limited the effectiveness of many individual practice association HMOs.

MULTISPECIALTY GROUP PRACTICE

PGPs are generally multispecialty group practices (MSGP). Studies show that MSGP is frequently much more economical in hospital use than is solo practice, even in the absence of the incentives of per capita payment.[12] One reason is that multispecialty groups do not add a doctor until the ones they already have are busy. Solo practitioners in "over-doctored" areas can be quite underutilized and under economic pressure to find new ways to make themselves useful, including recommending procedures that yield no benefit to the patient. MSGP also provides systematic professional checks and balances. Before the surgeon operates, it is likely that the primary care physician must be persuaded that the operation will benefit the patient. Complex cases are likely to be the subject of multispecialty consultations, which are more easily and naturally arranged in the MSGP setting. This is likely to enhance the quality of care. Finally, there are no economic disincentives to making appropriate specialty referrals. The primary care physician need not fear losing the patient and associated income if he or she refers to a partner specialist.

While the PPO format can embrace both MSGPs and solo practice, many PPOs are targeted to the solo practitioner through hospital staffs. The more effective ones are likely to be those based on a cohesive organization of physicians.

MATCH RESOURCES USED TO THE NEEDS OF THE POPULATION SERVED

Victor Fuchs found that, other things equal, 10 percent more surgeons per capita are associated with 3 percent more surgery. Thus, more surgeons are likely to mean more surgery and less proficient surgeons.[13]

Most of the United States is oversupplied with hospital beds: 4.4 beds per 1,000 population, much more than what the leading PGPs would need to take care of the same population. At best this entails excess overhead costs. And hospitals in overbedded areas have weakened incentives to organize effective utilization controls.

An important source of economy for the PGP is in matching carefully the numbers of physicians in the various specialties and the numbers of facilities to the needs of the population served. Then each specialist can be kept busy seeing patients with the problems he or she was trained to treat and can make a good living at a low cost per case. And excess overhead costs are avoided.

In theory, a sophisticated PPO could attempt to tap the same source of economy by trading greater patient volume for reduced price and by adding participating providers only when existing providers are busy. Most solo practitioners will regard any PPO as only one of several or many sources of payment, and they will be reluctant to reveal their total patient workload, a key indicator of bargaining position, to a PPO. With all the other considerations they must balance in provider selection, it seems doubtful that a PPO would be able to achieve this kind of fine tuning.

APPROPRIATE REGIONAL CONCENTRATION OF SPECIALIZED SERVICES

In complex surgery, experienced providers achieve better results at a lower cost.[14] Large PGPs organize services to concentrate costly specialized services at regional centers to achieve economies of scale and experience. Small PGPs buy such services from high volume regional centers. PPOs ought to be able to do the same thing, that is, contract with high volume regional centers for open-heart surgery, elective neurosurgery, and other costly specialized services. Employers checking out the effectiveness of a proposed PPO should look for this.

ORGANIZE CARE IN LESS COSTLY SETTINGS

PGPs save money by organizing care in settings that are less costly than the acute care hospital: outpatient surgery in day surgery centers and home nursing care. Under the per capita prepayment mode of finance, the hospital is rewarded with more net income, not punished by loss of revenue for organizing these modes of care, and the payment system provides a ready source of finance. The development of these economical modes of care has been retarded by the irrational incentives of traditional insurance that pays providers more for using more costly modes of care. The "pure PPO model" does not reward hospitals for helping to keep patients out of hospital. Picture a curve relating the resources spent on a treatment to the health benefit produced (Exhibit 1). Usually, as more

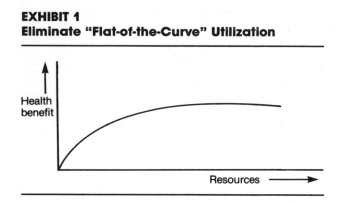

EXHIBIT 1
Eliminate "Flat-of-the-Curve" Utilization

Health benefit

Resources ⟶

resources are spent the curve flattens out. After a point, little or no additional health benefit is produced. Excess medical care may even be harmful to the patient's health. Think of longer versus shorter hospital stays, more versus less frequent tests, or a procedure performed on more and more people with fewer and fewer clear indications for it.

There is a great deal of "flat-of-the-curve" care in the United States today. PGPs do less of it than their fee-for-service solo practice counterparts. PGP physicians include avoidance of overtreatment in the professional norms of their groups. PPOs try to restrain the urge to overtreat by utilization controls and by use of primary care physicians as gatekeepers. But utilization controls are negative restraints, more costly, and less effective than training and motivating the doctor to do the right thing in the first place. And the primary care physician as gatekeeper concept has not proven to be effective.[15]

Basically, the problem is that unlike PGPs, PPOs do not organize the delivery system for effectiveness and efficiency. They merely attempt to shop for economical providers in the context of a fundamentally inefficient system. In the long run, it seems unlikely that PPOs will be nearly as efficient as PGPs, unless they evolve into PGPs, for example by hospitals and their medical staffs contracting to provide care on a per capita prepayment basis. Indeed, the most promising aspect of the PPO idea may be that it may be a transitional step to PGP.

RECOMMENDATIONS TO EMPLOYERS CONSIDERING PPO CONTRACTS

First, employers should pay a great deal of attention to the quality of care and service. A prompt accurate diagnosis and the appropriate procedure done right the first time are likely to do a lot more for the economy of care and the return of the employee to a productive status than any price discounts. Moreover, employees are likely more willingly to accept limitations on their choice of provider if they know the employer is genuinely concerned with quality of care. Thus, it makes sense to inquire carefully into the quality assurance systems in operation in the PPO that proposes to serve your employees.

Second, most employers will not like managing medical care in detail and are not likely to be very good at it. Most of the cost of medical care is in costly treatments for sick people.[16] Arguments with doctors about the necessity of tests and procedures in individual cases are not likely to be arguments most employers can win. The expertise is all on their side. Employers will not be able to save much money merely by curbing obvious abusive overutilization.

Rather than buying medical care by the piece and attempting to judge the necessity of each piece, it makes more sense to buy care in the form of a prospective price for a comprehensive package. For example, an all-inclusive price per day is better than paying discounted hospital charges. An all-inclusive price per case is better than price per day. And per capita prepayment is better still. Such arrangements give providers greater freedom to allocate resources to achieve the best overall results. The process of care is less distorted by the payment arrangement. Contracts based on fixed prices for more global units are easier to administer.

Third, if you are developing a PPO contract, try to phase in provider accountability for total per capita costs.

Per capita costs are the product of prices and quantities of services. There are wide variations in the per capita consumption of many medical services associated with no apparent difference in medical need or health produced.[17] Thus, attention to the volume and appropriateness of services is at least as important as attention to price. Mere "discount medicine"—descriptive of many PPOs—is not likely to be a good deal in the long run.

Some providers may offer discounts in order to be included in a company plan as preferred providers without an annual election by employees to join the PPO plan. One trouble with that arrangement is that the employer will not be able to know whether the preferred providers are really saving money. It is better to offer the PPO plan as alternative choice, require an annual election, and include reduced benefits for seeing non-panel providers as well as increased benefits for seeing panel providers. This will give the company a defined population that will help it to evaluate overall cost effectiveness. Also, it may allow employers to offset some "give away" with some "take away."

Next, work with local hospitals and physicians to set up a payment formula that includes incentives to reduce hospital days and dollars per capita. For example, set up a target for reduction in hospital days per capita and offer to split the savings if the target is exceeded. Hospitals can do many things to help keep people out of hospital: good utilization control seriously implemented; good management to perform tests and return results quickly so that patient stays will not be prolonged by waits for tests; discharge planning; and arranging less costly alternatives such as home nursing care, transfer to a nursing home, and an outpatient surgery center. But one cannot expect hospital managers to put their hearts into these cost-reducing innovations if it means destroying their business.

Fourth, try to make your payment system rational. As Blumberg and others have observed, fees for complex procedures are set early in their life cycles, when costs are high and the expertise to do them is concentrated in a few hands.[18] As these procedures become widespread, economies of scale and experience bring down their costs. But, in the health care economy dominated by traditional insurance, no competitive economic force brings down the fees. As a result, the net income per unit of physician time is much higher for procedures than for taking histories, thinking, and giving advice. This creates powerful incentives to do procedures, even when less aggressive treatment would be as good or better for the patient. Similarly, as Blumberg has shown, the traditional fee-for-service system has paid more net income per unit of time for care in the hospital than for care in the office. An effective purchaser should therefore be concerned about relative prices as well as absolute price levels. It is in the purchaser's interest to negotiate prices that equalize the net income per unit of physician time for procedures, history taking, and giving advice and for hospital and office care. For example, a purchaser should be careful to see that the physician does not earn more for the same procedure if done in hospital than if done in an outpatient surgical center.

CONCLUSION

The PPO idea has important positive elements that make it timely in today's increasingly competitive environment. But it is not a panacea. PPO contracts will be more or less effective, depending on how they are designed and implemented. In the most effective PPOs, the provider side will evolve into cohesive organizations capable of managing the quality and total per capita cost of care.

NOTES

1. Linda Ellwein and David Gregg, M.D., *An Introduction to Preferred Provider Organizations (PPOs),* (Excelsior MN: InterStudy, April 1982).

2. Because of the possibility of risk selection, the problem of evaluation can be quite complex. PPOs might show lower per capita costs merely because they have selected healthier patients. Thus, employers need to compare the per capita costs on an age-, sex- and other health-risk-adjusted basis, and they need to look at total costs for their employee group and somehow compare them with what they otherwise would have been in the absence of the PPO.

3. Lawrence G. Goldberg and Warren Greenberg, "The Emergence of Physician-Sponsored Health Insurance: A Historical Perspective," in *Competition in the Health Care Sector, Past, Present, and Future,* ed. Warren Greenberg (Germantown, MD: Aspen Systems Corp., 1978).

4. Insurance Code of the State of California, Section 10133.

5. The Omnibus Budget Reconciliation Act (OBRA) of 1981.

6. The Tax Equity and Fiscal Responsibility Act (TEFRA) of 1982.

7. Assembly Bill 799, California 1982.

8. Harold S. Luft, "How Do Health Maintenance Organizations Achieve Their 'Savings'?" *New England Journal of Medicine* 298, no. 24 (June 15, 1978), pp. 1336–43.

9. Luft, ibid.

10. Mark S. Blumberg, "Rational Provider Prices: Provider Price Changes for Improved Health Care Use," in *Health Handbook,* ed. George K. Chacko, (Amsterdam: North Holland Publishing Co., 1979).

11. Blumberg, ibid.

12. Fred T. Nobrega, M.D., Iqbal Krishan, M.D., Robert K. Smoldt, MBA, Charles S. Davis, MS, Julie A. Abbott, M.D., Eda G. Mohler, RRA, Walter McClure, Ph.D., "Hospital Use in a Fee-for-Service System," *Journal of the American Medical Association* 247 (February 12, 1982), 806–10. Anne A. Scitovsky and Nelda McCall, "Use of Hospital Services Under Two Prepaid Plans," *Medical Care* 18, no. 1 (January 1980), pp. 30–43.

13. Victor R. Fuchs, "The Supply of Surgeons and the Demand for Operations," *Journal of Human Resources* 13 (Supplement, 1978), pp. 35–36.

14. Harold S. Luft, John P. Bunker, and Alain C. Enthoven, "Should Operations be Regionalized? The Empirical Relation between Surgical Volume and Mortality," *New England Journal of Medicine* 301, no. 25 (December 20, 1979), pp. 1364–69. Steven A. Finkler, "Cost Effectiveness of Regionalization: The Heart Surgery Example," *Inquiry* 16, no. 3 (Fall 1979), pp. 264–70. Ann Barry Flood, W. Richard Scott, and Wayne Ewy, "Does Practice Make Perfect? Examining the Relation between Volume and Outcomes in Acute Care Hospitals," *Medical Care* (in press).

15. Steven H. Moore, Diane P. Martin, and William C. Richardson, "Does the Primary-Care Gatekeeper Control the Costs of Health Care? Lessons from the SAFECO Experience," *The New England Journal of Medicine* 309, no. 22 (December 1, 1983) pp. 1400–4.

16. Christopher J. Zook and Francis D. Moore, "High-Cost Users of Medical Care," *The New England Journal of Medicine,* 302 (1980), pp. 996–1002. Steven A. Schroeder, Jonathan A. Showstack, MPH, and Judy Schwartz, "Frequency and Clinical Description of High-Cost Patients in 17 Acute-Care Hospitals," *The New England Journal of Medicine,* 300 (1979), pp. 1306–9.

17. Alan M. Gittelsohn and John E. Wennberg, "On the Incidence of Tonsillectomy and Other Common Surgical Procedures," in *Costs, Risks and Benefits of Surgery,* ed. John P. Bunker, Benjamin A. Barnes and Frederick Mosteller, (New York, 1977) pp. 91–106. Also Paul M. Gertman, "Surgery in an Era of Constrained Resources," in *Surgical Clinics of North America,* 62, no. 4, ed. Ira M. Rutkow, M.D. (Philadelphia: W. B. Saunders Company, August 1982), pp. 781–791.

18. Blumberg, "Rational Provider Prices: Provider Price Changes for Improved Health Care Use." Benson B. Roe, "The UCR Boondoggle: A Death Knell for Private Practice?", *The New England Journal of Medicine,* 305 (July 2, 1981), pp. 41–45.

THE IMPACT OF CURRENT TRENDS ON FUTURE PATTERNS OF MEDICAL PRACTICE

Roy F. Perkins, M.D.

John L. Smith, M.D.

Both with
Scripps Clinic
La Jolla, CA
and
Senior Consultants
Booz, Allen and Hamilton, Inc.
San Francisco, CA

☐ No one can claim omniscience in forecasting the medical service delivery system of the future. Indeed, there is always uncertainty in prognostication, whether it relates to health care or the world of international politics. The imprint of changes in national political leadership, financial crises, and public pressures can abruptly alter otherwise orderly patterns of transitional change.

Nonetheless, the study of evolutionary trends usually permits a reasonably definitive presumption of forthcoming change, and in the case of medical service organization and function, it is anticipated that modifications in the next decade will be more profound than in the previous 50 years.

Changing organizational and reimbursement mechanisms for medical services have evolved gradually, but at an accelerated pace in recent years, driven largely by inexorably rising health care costs. Prospects for their continuing growth and development will depend upon the influence of more comprehensive medical trends, encompassing demographic, clinical, technologic, and fiscal factors. In aggregate these indicate that:

1. Demand for health care services will continue to increase but at a slower pace than in past years.
2. Scientific and technologic advance will provide improved methods of disease detection and treatment.
3. There will be increased emphasis upon preventive medicine.
4. Competition in the medical marketplace will be a growing and prevalent phenomenon.
5. Hospitals will have to develop new strategies to maintain financial and programmatic strengths.
6. Health care costs will continue to rise, provoking increased public sector and corporate consumer resistance.
7. Physicians organized into larger collective units will be able to fare more successfully in a competitive environment.
8. Alternate delivery system growth will be abetted by:
   a. Availability of physicians willing to work under different organizational and fiscal conditions to achieve financial security and successful practice growth.
   b. Organized consumer support, seeking high quality care at reasonable cost.
9. Organizational arrangements among health care providers and medical service delivery systems will continue to be modified and refined.

The rationale for these conclusions is borne out by more critical assessment of individual future trends.

A NUMBER OF FACTORS WILL CONTRIBUTE TO GROWTH IN VOLUME OF MEDICAL SERVICES

1. There will be further population growth, though at a slower pace than in the past three decades and at a disparate rate in different sections of the country.
   a. As noted in Exhibit 1, growth rate reached a peak of greater than 1.75 percent annually in 1960, then fell steadily to a low point in the latter 1970s. Despite a temporary annual incre-

EXHIBIT 1
U.S. Population Growth Rate, 1950–2000

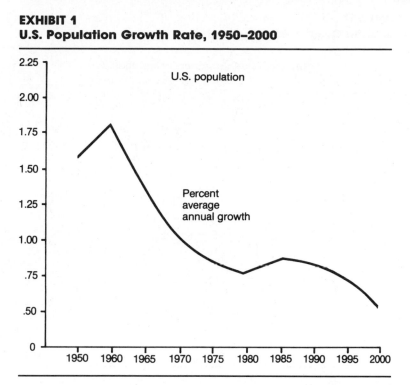

SOURCE: Booz, Allen and Hamilton Inc.

ment in the first half of this decade, there will be a projected annual decrease in growth rate, remaining as less than 1 percent annually, until the end of the century.

b. Exhibit 2 depicts the rate of population growth in different sectors of the nation, noting that increase will be greatest in the western, southwestern, and southeastern states, slowest in the midwestern and northeastern regions. Assuming that the geographic distribution of physicians remains the same in the future, there will be more competition for market share of patients in the slower growing areas of the country.

2. The proportion of senior citizens will increase, and these members will require more medical services, as well as more complex, time consuming, and costly care.

a. The percentage of population in the 65 and older age group will increase from 11.2 percent to 17 percent by the 21st century, as noted in Exhibit 3.

b. The elderly population has a significantly higher hospital use

EXHIBIT 2
Population Growth Rate by Region

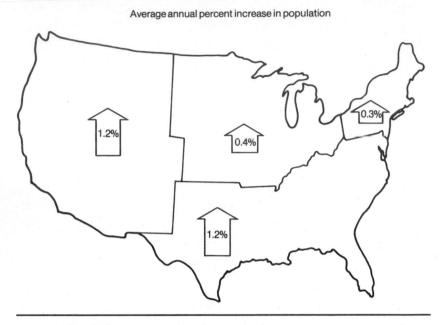

Average annual percent increase in population

SOURCE: Booz, Allen and Hamilton Inc.

rate and accounts for more outpatient visits to physicians than
other age groups.

3. Growth in the supply of physicians will result in greater service
volume, providing greater access to medical service and generating its own demand for follow-up and continuing care.

4. Public education encourages patients to seek early assessment of
symptoms and enhances awareness of the need for timely intervention in the management of disease.

5. Growth of scientific knowledge will enable larger segments of the
population to obtain health care benefits not currently available.

6. As an offsetting factor, physicians might limit service demand as
they are financially at risk as part of prepayment plan organizations.

THERE WILL BE MORE SOPHISTICATED METHODOLOGIES FOR DISEASE DETECTION, MANAGEMENT, AND PREVENTION

1. Rapid technologic development will continue in several areas,
including:

EXHIBIT 3

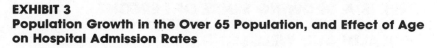

Population Growth in the Over 65 Population, and Effect of Age on Hospital Admission Rates

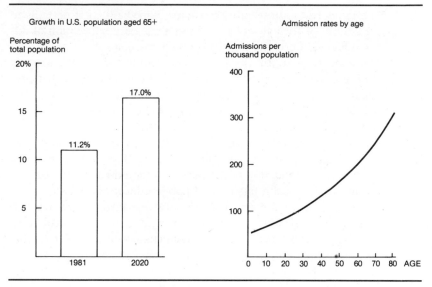

Growth in U.S. population aged 65+

Admission rates by age

Percentage of total population

Admissions per thousand population

SOURCE: Booz, Allen and Hamilton, Inc.

    a. Nonclinical systems—computerized medical records and management of patient flow such as admissions and appointment scheduling.

    b. Preventive technologies, as exemplified by DNA research, gene replacement, synthetic vaccines.

    c. Diagnostic technologies—miniaturization, computerized medical history analysis, real-time monitoring, computerized imaging, digital subtraction radiography, nuclear magnetic resonance.

    d. Therapeutic technologies—improved radiation therapy, microsurgery, artificial organs, transplantation, dissolution of stones through extracorporeal shock waves.

  2. Pharmaceutical advance and new research techniques will provide improved methods of disease control.

    a. New drugs and treatment protocols will be particularly effective in cardiac disease, hypertension, cancer therapy, hematologic disorders, and diabetes.

    b. Trace proteins (interferon, antihemophilic globulins, clotting factors) may prove to be of value in a variety of currently untreatable diseases.

    c. Monoclonal antibodies (specialized immune mechanism reactors) will become a major weapon in disease detection and management.

THERE IS A GROWING SENSE OF PERSONAL RESPONSIBILITY FOR THE MAINTENANCE OF HEALTH AND WELL-BEING

1. Public interest in preventive medicine, especially as it pertains to the control of lifestyle-related illness through modification of adverse habit patterns, is a growing phenomenon.
2. The concept of wellness is attracting strong interest and support from the corporate sector, based upon the presumption that prevention of illness will not only reduce health expenditures, but will increase employee productivity through reduced absenteeism and disability, as well as improved morale.
3. Program efforts apply most particularly to the containment of cardiovascular disease and are directed toward screening and risk identification, reduction of disease likelihood through elimination of unfavorable health habits, and public education.
4. Corrective factors are centered around stress management through behavior modification techniques, weight control, cessation of smoking and substance abuse, and maintenance of a regular aerobic exercise routine to promote cardiovascular stimulation.
5. Physician skepticism remains in some quarters about the virtues or potential promise of preventive medicine efforts. They claim that such programs contain more advocacy than reality, and suffer from overpromotion in the face of underachievement.
6. Of the public and intermediary funds expended for medical services, only a fraction has been dedicated to the support of health promotion.
7. Despite the fact that it will take additional decades to determine the cost effectiveness of prevention programs and their influence on morbidity and mortality, the short-term impact of health promotion efforts has been favorable, motivating patients to take responsibility for their future health destinies and to maintain sound living habits. It has also enabled them to acquire relaxational techniques, improve muscle tone, and increase cardiovascular tolerance.

THERE WILL BE A PHYSICIAN SURPLUS IN THE COMING DECADE, LEADING TO INCREASING COMPETITION IN THE MEDICAL MARKETPLACE

1. From 1970 to 1980, the physician growth rate was 3 times that of the general population, with a 70 percent increase in output of medical graduates, and a 24 percent increment in the nation's population during the same period.
   a. At present one third of all actively practicing physicians have graduated from medical school since 1970.

EXHIBIT 4
Projected Growth in Physician Supply

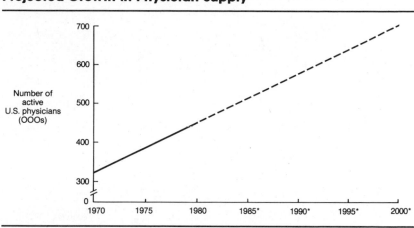

*Projected by BAH.
SOURCES: Projections of Supply of Manpower in Selected Health Occupations: 1950–1990;
U.S. DHHS.

  b. As noted in Exhibit 4, the number of practicing physicians in
    1990 will be double the number in 1970.
2. Apart from the large annual output from U.S. medical schools,
  there has been a substantial immigration of foreign medical graduates to this country, many of whom have remained here to enter
  active practice. Only very recently has there been a tightening of
  immigration policy, but on a continuing basis, 20 percent of
  newly licensed physicians in the United States annually have been
  foreign medical graduates.
3. While the growth in physician supply affects all specialties, internal medicine, radiology, and pediatrics are experiencing the
  greatest increases, as illustrated in Exhibit 5.
4. At present, there is no relationship between estimated physician
  and specialty requirements for the future and the number of training programs and output of new specialists at U.S. institutions.
5. Growth in physician supply has seemingly outpaced demand and
  is projected to do so increasingly in the future, resulting in loss of
  market share by individual practitioners. These trends are depicted in Exhibits 6, 7, 8, and 9.
  a. Weekly patient visits per physician decreased 15 percent from
    1970 to 1980, with 10 percent decline in hospital admissions
    by each physician, reduction in surgical procedures per sur-
    geon, and loss of real net income during the same period.
  b. Downward income pressure has been accentuated by ever in-

EXHIBIT 5
Growth in Physician Supply by Selected Specialties

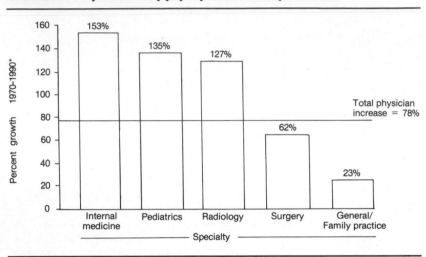

*Projected.
SOURCE: Physician Characteristics and Distribution in the U.S., 1981, AMA; Summary Report of the Graduate Medical Education National Advisory Committee, 1980, USDHHS.

EXHIBIT 6
Patient Visits per Physician, 1970–1990 (physician supply outpaced patient visit demand resulting in a 15 percent decline in patient visits per physician from 1970 to 1980)

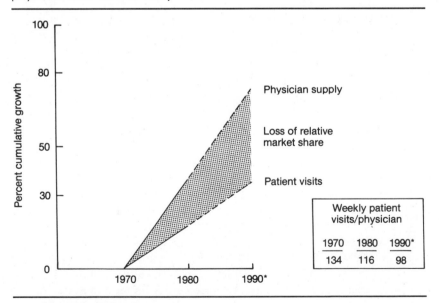

Weekly patient visits/physician		
1970	1980	1990*
134	116	98

*Projected by BAH.
SOURCES: Profiles of Medical Practice, AMA; DHHS.

EXHIBIT 7
Hospital Admissions per Physician, 1970-1990

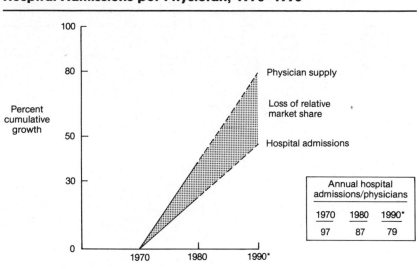

*Projected by BAH.
SOURCES: Hospital statistics, 1981, 1971, AHA; DHHS.

EXHIBIT 8
Surgical Procedures per Surgeon, 1975-1990

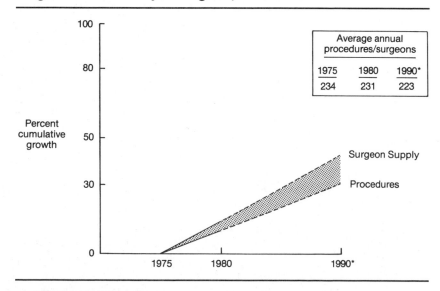

*Projected by BAH.
SOURCES: Hospital statistics, 1981, 1976, AHA; DHHS.

EXHIBIT 9
Effect of Increased Physician Supply and Decreased Market Share on Professional Net Income

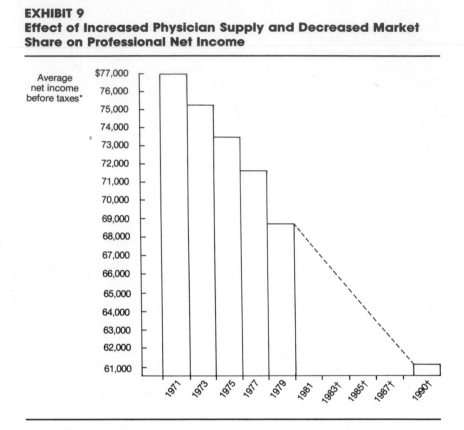

Average net income before taxes*

*Constant 1979 dollars.
†Projected by BAH.
SOURCES: Periodic Survey of Physicians, 1970–1980, AMA; U.S. DHHS.

creasing expense of medical practice, as depicted in Exhibit 10.
c. These trends are projected to continue into 1990.

COMPETITIVE, REGULATORY, AND FISCAL PRESSURES WILL AFFECT THE VIABILITY OF SOME HOSPITALS, ALTER PHYSICIAN-HOSPITAL RELATIONS, AND REQUIRE CHANGE IN MANAGEMENT PERSPECTIVES

1. There will be increased competition among community institutions, even as inpatient utilization decreases, and there is a shift to ambulatory care.
2. Regulatory and reimbursement constraints will erode the capital base of institutions, making it increasingly difficult to acquire fiscal resources for the support of highly specialized programs and

EXHIBIT 10
Effect of Increased Professional Overhead Expense on Physician Net Income (1970–1990)

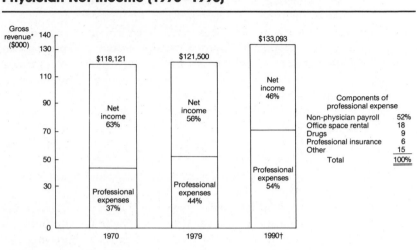

*Constant 1979 dollars.
†Projected by BAH.
SOURCES: Medical Economics Continuing Survey, 1980; Profiles of Medical Practice, 1971, 1980, AMA.

services, advanced technology, and facility modernization or renovation.

   a. Community hospitals will be unable to maintain their role of being "all things to all people" and will have to more carefully select and refine their product line.

   b. The inability of hospitals to maintain financial integrity from inpatient revenues alone will result in strategic decisions to diversify their service portfolios, including ambulatory care.

3. Institutional entry into new health care markets will make it necessary for hospitals and medical staffs to redefine their relationships and explore means of more mutually productive and rewarding endeavors.

4. Hospital management perspective will have to focus increasingly upon sound operational, fiscal, and programmatic policies.

ORGANIZATIONAL AND DELIVERY PATTERNS OF HEALTH CARE SERVICES WILL CONTINUE TO UNDERGO EVOLUTIONARY CHANGE

1. Aggressive health care providers will establish decentralized resource networks to capture new markets and offer more ready accessibility and availability of services.

    a. The public has increasingly come to expect availability of all the services they require, including health care, at their doorstep, preferring to minimize significant travel or inconvenience in securing these amenities.

    b. Hospitals, physician offices, and clinics experiencing erosion of patient support because of location in older, central urban neighborhoods of population decline are seeking to regain or expand their service volume by establishing satellite facilities in more peripheral, rapid growth suburban areas.

    c. The most successful satellite programs are those that are well organized, offer unique services not otherwise available in the community, or are part of an integrated system of comprehensive patient care.

2. There will be a continuing shift from inpatient to ambulatory care.

    a. Younger populations, lower birth rates, high costs, and alternatives to inpatient care have resulted in reduced admission rates and declining length of stay in hospitals; this, together with surplus supply, has resulted in lower occupancy levels and greater unused occupancy.

    b. With fiscal pressures imposed by DRGs and other cost-containment programs, alternatives to inpatient care will become an increasingly desirable objective.

3. Group practice has displayed rapid and continuing growth.

    a. As depicted in Exhibit 11, medical groups currently comprise almost 40 percent of the actively practicing physician population, nearly quadruple the proportion in 1965.

    b. Larger business units offer scale advantages and market leverage for physicians, with lower practice expenses due to shared cost of staff wages, medical and office equipment, and office rent.

    c. Larger groups offer market leverage for physicians by giving patients greater accessibility to care through multiple practice locations, more convenience in hours of operation, and a broader range of professional and ancillary services. They also attract patient support by greater community visibility and exposure and by advertising.

    d. Increase in revenue per physician can result from greater sophistication of services that are available to patients and larger patient volume (Exhibit 12).

4. Physicians are affiliating with marketing organizations for access to patients.

    a. Health maintenance organizations and preferred provider organizations are marketing mechanisms for hospitals and physicians. HMOs and PPOs contract with employers for low-cost, comprehensive health care services. Through these contracts,

EXHIBIT 11
Growth in Percentage of Physicians in Group Practice

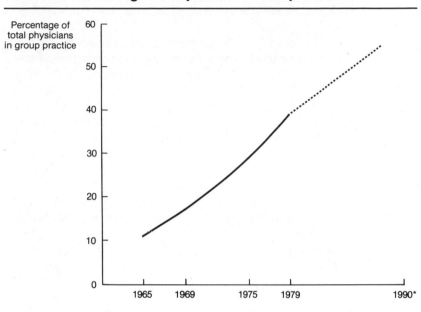

*Projected.
SOURCES: Medical Economics Continuing Survey, 1966; Profiles of Medical Practice, 1970, 1976, 1980, AMA.

EXHIBIT 12
Potential for Increased Physician Revenue in Large Groups

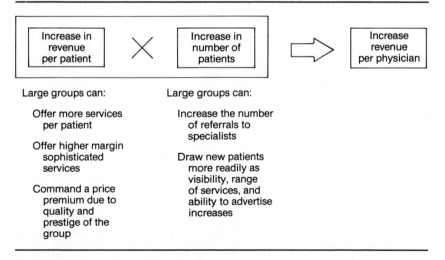

Large groups can:

  Offer more services
    per patient

  Offer higher margin
    sophisticated
    services

  Command a price
    premium due to
    quality and
    prestige of the
    group

Large groups can:

  Increase the number
    of referrals to
    specialists

  Draw new patients
    more readily as
    visibility, range
    of services, and
    ability to advertise
    increases

SOURCE: Booz, Allen and Hamilton Inc.

affiliating hospitals and physicians are assured access to an attractive patient base.

    b. HMO and PPO development is initiated by health care providers or purchasers.

5. Recent and rapid growth in HMOs is expected to continue, spurred by government and industry interest in controlling costs.

    a. Despite the fact that prepayment care dates back to the 1930s, growth in enrollment was slow during the next 40 years, with a membership of only 3 million members by 1970.

    b. During the next decade, the annual compounded growth rate was 11.9 percent with 10.3 million enrollees in 1981.

    c. Further rapid growth is projected at a 9 percent compounded annual rate, with an anticipated population of more than 22 million members by 1990.

    d. Prepaid plans have found appeal among members of the health insurance industry and include numerous Blue Cross/Blue Shield plans, INA, CNA, Prudential, Connecticut General, and Traveler's insurance companies.

6. Capital venture investors are entering the health care industry in service activities with large market potential and high growth rates.

    a. As noted in Exhibit 13, these include commercial laboratories, ambulatory surgery centers, urgent care centers, home health services, and specialized imaging or therapy resources.

EXHIBIT 13
Price/Service Oriented Competitors in the Health Care Market

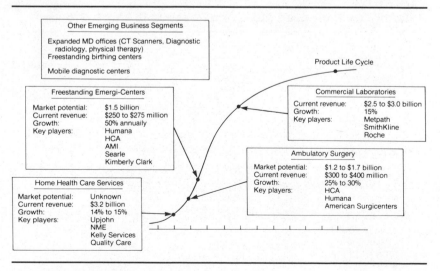

SOURCE: Booz, Allen and Hamilton Inc.

    b. Ample capital is available for the entrepreneurial support, development, and growth of these enterprises.

7. As patient care becomes more complex, time consuming, and comprehensive, delivery of services will become more of a collaborative effort, with a team of multidisciplinary providers and physicians, as well as allied health professionals.

    a. Adaptational problems will become evident among components of the multidisciplinary team, centered around recognition, control, and rewards.

    b. Some allied health professionals will strive to achieve autonomy through licensure and award of privileges in directing patient care.

RISING HEALTH CARE COSTS IS THE PARAMOUNT ISSUE OF THE TIMES AND WILL BE THE DRIVING FORCE IN AFFECTING FUTURE TRENDS

1. The public sector, which accounts for 40 percent of total health care expenditures in the nation through its federal programs, has applied fiscal constraints through changing reimbursement mechanisms in what has been a largely unsuccessful effort to contain costs. Organized medicine has been effective in consolidating the opposition of its members to increased governmental efforts to alter existing service or reimbursement patterns, claiming that there is too much preoccupation with cost and too little concern about quality.

2. The entrance of the corporate consumer into the cost-containment picture represents a new collective and powerful entity among the purchasers of health care. Through its organized coalitions, industry is expected to leverage its buying power to gain greater control of its health care costs.

    a. It will seek to purchase comprehensive systems of care at a defined price. Solo practitioners and isolated specialists will be unable to participate as providers in these systems unless they become part of a larger organizational unit that is able to provide a total package of service benefits.

    b. The trend toward self-insurance is expected to continue, providing incentives to reduce utilization and costs.

    c. HMO development will be supported, fueled by industry interest in reducing costs.

    d. Preferred provider organizations will grow as hospitals and physicians seek to maintain market share, providing industry with direct access to lower charges and utilization review.

3. As summarized in Exhibit 14, dollar concerns will trigger differ-

EXHIBIT 14
Pressures Produced by Rising Health Care Costs

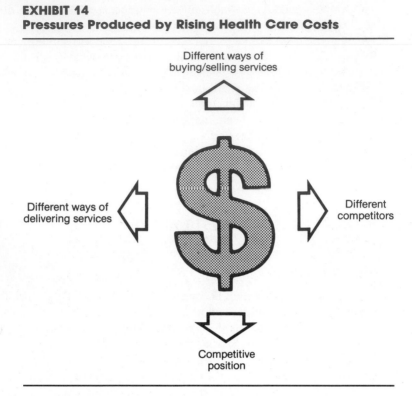

SOURCE: Booz, Allen and Hamilton Inc.

ent ways of buying, selling, and delivering services and will un-veil new competitors who seek an advantageous position in the market.

What do all of these trend factors portend for the predominantly fee-for-service delivery system?

As the output of graduates from U.S. institutions continues at a brisk pace, augmented by a consistent influx of trainees from foreign medical schools, it will become increasingly difficult for those newly entering clinical practice to attract the patient volume requisite to professional gratification and financial success, especially those starting in solo practice. A greater proportion of physicians, especially those in medical and surgical subspecialties, will settle in nonmetropolitan areas where there is an underrepresentation or unavailability of such expertise.

Physicians joining existing partnerships and single or multispecialty groups will usually enter clinical settings where a flow of patients and income return are assured. Increasingly, physicians are purchasing the practices of those who are retiring or have withdrawn from practice. In some instances, hospitals are purchasing the practices of their non-hospital-based retiring physicians, upon whom they have depended for referrals, and are making them available to new practitioners under favorable financial terms to assure continuing patient and medical staff succession support. Family practitioners will be able to move successfully into some areas where primary physicians are underrepresented.

There will be left a repository of new practitioners unwilling or unable to make the investment to enter solo practice and unlikely to attract a stable patient base over the short term (one to three years). These will be attracted to larger organizational units in alternate delivery systems (HMOs or PPOs) where there is an adequate patient base, regular hours, assured income, and a variety of additional financial and professional benefits.

Under a fee-for-service (FFS) system, there is no cost control in either the fee or the frequency of service—FFS (total cost) = fee $\times$ frequency. This model has resulted in a dramatic increase of health care costs, although some of the constituent elements responsible for the increment are beyond physician control, including scientific and technologic advance, the application of more intensive, complex, and time consuming care to patient management, the team delivery of services, and the greater overhead expense of maintaining a professional practice. On the other hand, some facets of total cost are more directly influenced by physicians, including encouragement of more frequent utilization of services, the tendency to raise fees without increasing productivity in order to assure income return, and the growing trend toward a pricing system based upon unbundling of services (billing for each unit of a total service or procedure, so that the aggregate cost is greater than that previously charged for the service as a whole).

Deepening concern about rising health care costs and its effect in stimulating alternatives to traditional fee-for-service reimbursement have extended into the ranks of organized medicine, prompting the California Medical Association and the American Medical Association to call for a voluntary one-year freeze on physician fees during 1984.

The perceived need to control or reduce fees and discourage frequency of services has encouraged the growth and development of prepaid care. In an HMO, the formula: cost = fee $\times$ frequency becomes less meaningful because cost is fixed and predictable, and the fee and frequency of service are not relevant, being largely the responsibility of the provider. The need to exercise control places the physician at risk. Access to utilization of subspecialty services can be controlled through the gatekeeper function of the primary care physician. Additionally, with copayment, a surcharge can be placed on the patient to further limit utilization.

Newer reimbursement systems, apart from HMOs, have been variably identified by terms such as contract medicine, discount medicine, or preferred provider organizations (PPOs). In the formula: PPO (cost) =

fee × frequency, it is anticipated that cost will be most favorably affected by a negotiated discount fee, but this will also have to be coupled with assurance of appropriate utilization (to curb excess frequency). It will be incumbent upon PPOs to exercise timely and adequate utilization review if they are to remain viable and competitive with HMOs, and some PPO providers are planning to offer service on a traditional fee basis, relying upon strong appropriateness and utilization-review surveillance measures to contain costs.

Conceptually, the PPO model is preferable to an HMO for most practicing physicians, involving less disruption of the current medical delivery system. For the most part, the physician, physician referral patterns, and the hospital delivery system remain the same as in a fee-for-service setting. The physician and hospital are not at risk, and there is no gatekeeper containment of patient self-referral to specialists. The comparative features of an HMO and PPO system are summarized in Exhibit 15.

EXHIBIT 15
Comparison of HMO and PPO Features

Characteristics	HMO	PPO
Capitation and guarantee for providers	Yes	No
Shared risk for hospital and ambulatory care	Yes	No
Accepted fee schedule with volume discount	No	Yes
Need for gatekeeper concept	Yes	No
Full coverage required or preferred	Yes	Yes
Easy access to specialties	No	Yes
Danger of adverse selection in small number of enrollees	Yes	No
Need for quality assurance	Yes	Yes
Need for utilization review	Yes	Yes
Overall risk to physician group	Yes	No
Overall risk to hospital	Yes	No
Contract required	Yes	Yes
Need for marketing to employers	Yes	Yes
Attractive to large employers	Yes	Yes/No
Guaranteed budget cost to employers	Yes	No
Need for extensive data processing	Yes	Yes

PPOs are developing under a variety of sponsors, including marketing and physician organizations, hospitals, large multispecialty groups, university medical centers, and networks of single and multispecialty providers. No single model has emerged as the most desirable one, but clinicians would prefer the organization that is under physician control and governance. The larger and more widely dispersed PPOs offer greater choice of physicians and more widespread geographic access to services but will be the ones most difficult to monitor and the ones in which cost-containment efforts will be the most challenging. The well-organized, tightly knit, and unified groups will be able to exercise more optimal quality assurance and utilization-review procedures and offer the most attractive marketability.

At this stage, PPOs are an unknown entity to mass purchasers of health services, and their ability to contain costs and fall within budgeted limits for health care expenditures is less certain than for HMOs. It is too early to predict whether they will become the reimbursement mechanism of the future, but much will depend upon the performance of the pioneer organizations that become operational.

Earlier in the chapter, it was noted that most community hospitals would be unable to remain viable if they relied solely on inpatient services and revenues and that they will have to develop more diversified programs and services, including ambulatory care, if they are to survive. This will place them in a potentially adversarial position with their medical staffs, since physicians will regard ambulatory care activity as an incursion into their own practice domain.

It was also pointed out that solo practitioners or small physician groups will not be able to gain access to large patient populations covered by corporate purchasers of health care unless they become part of larger organizational units. This would be possible if hospital medical staff physicians became part of a larger collective service entity.

Notwithstanding their apprehension over changing institutional roles, physicians will have to sustain and fortify their hospitals of choice upon whom they depend for highly sophisticated and inpatient services and upon whom they will have to rely increasingly for resource support as market competition stiffens. At the same time, hospitals will have to depend more crucially upon their medical staffs for sustained program and service support and implementation of their strategic plans for the future.

Indeed, this must be a new era and a period of new opportunity for hospital and medical staff interaction and interdependence, based upon mutual gain for each constituency. Hospitals and professional staffs that aggressively nurture this concept will fare more successfully, while those that adopt an attitude of mutual confrontation will be drawn more deeply into a morass of inaction, and will fall by the wayside.

It is suggested that medical staffs corporately organize, accepting physician members who voluntarily wish to participate in new programmatic opportunities. As indicated in Exhibit 16, this will permit board representatives from the hospital and professional corporation to function as the governance body of a joint venture health services corporation. The service corporation would be empowered to formulate plans for specific jointly sponsored programs and services and would develop contracts to assure physician providers for these services, whether they relate to HMOs, PPOs, or more conventional medical service plans. It

EXHIBIT 16
Organizational Model for Individual Practitioner Participation in Alternate Delivery Systems

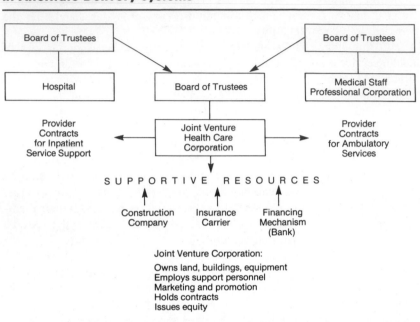

Joint Venture Corporation:

Owns land, buildings, equipment
Employs support personnel
Marketing and promotion
Holds contracts
Issues equity

might own land, buildings, and equipment, employ support personnel, engage in marketing and promotion, hold contracts, and provide tax shelter advantages for physician members.

At a time when medical service expenditures are being constrained, innovative and imaginative organizational relationships among entities of the health delivery system will have to be encouraged and actively pursued in order to assure care of optimal quality and to preserve incentives for those who provide that level of care.

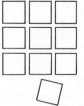 **Impact of New Trends**

ROLE OF PHYSICIANS AND HOSPITALS IN SELECTIVE CONTRACTING

Gary Brukardt
Senior Vice President
VHA Health Ventures
Irving, TX

Hallie Katz Normington
Project Consultant
VHA Health Ventures
Irving, TX

☐ As the hospital utilization rate declines and dollars shift from the acute care setting to ambulatory care settings, hospitals will need to develop a broad spectrum of health care delivery systems and position themselves to compete effectively in the competitive health care marketplace of the 1980s. During the 1980s, hospitals and physicians could be each other's major competitors along with those who manage the payment system. In order to be successful, each party will need to recognize the managerial and financial resources and capabilities of each other and pursue jointly the opportunities that are presented by the competitive marketplace.

The shift from hospital to alternative delivery systems has resulted in the proliferation of a large variety of ambulatory care programs that include home health care, home intravenous therapy, urgent care centers, imaging centers, and birthing centers. The development of these programs and the associated introduction and development of other nonacute care products such as hospice, geriatric, and day care has significantly impacted the hospital environment. It has forced hospitals to seek new strategies and lines of business. Given these delivery system developments and the major changes in the hospital payment mechanisms, it is essential that hospitals position themselves to respond to these changes. Hospital management and boards must develop alternative revenue sources that will offset their losses in the acute care setting. The individual hospital will be confronted by a variety of challenges while attempting to develop alternate products and services. These challenges will come from other hospitals, physician-sponsored systems, and purchaser-sponsored systems.

While developing alternative nonacute care programs, the not-for-profit hospital will have to be especially sensitive to limitations placed on their access to capital. As utilization rates continue to decline nationally, DRGs take effect, and all-payor prospective payment plans are implemented, the hospital's ability to generate profit margins will be significantly reduced. As profit margins decrease, the nonprofit hospitals will find it increasingly difficult to receive favorable bond ratings and obtain debt financing. Further, as a result of decreasing admissions, hospitals will find it increasingly difficult to demonstrate consistent profits from operations. Thus, investors will be hesitant to purchase bonds from these institutions. These reductions in capital availability will limit the ability of individual hospitals to capitalize on opportunities to develop alternate delivery systems and thus maintain pace in an environment of rapid technological and social change. Reimbursement changes will also reduce the ability of investor-owned systems to generate pretax profits and raise equity capital.

Further, investors and newly organized health care management firms will find it increasingly difficult to enter the acute care market. However, reduced acute care market activity could result in a tremendous availability of capital for the development of alternative delivery systems.

In order to minimize the deterioration of profits and enhance their access to competitively priced capital, hospital providers will need to demonstrate the following: (1) the ability to retain or increase their total market share, (2) the ability to influence consumer access to the system, (3) their involvement in the governance and ownership of alternate delivery systems, (4) the development of joint venture activities with physicians who have significant influence over consumer utilization of health care resources.

The PPO addresses many of the issues outlined above. As an organizational and functional joint venture, it enables both the physician and hospital to jointly manage health care resources and patient access to the system. The PPO, through its ability to control access, guarantees providers a source of patients and offers the provider an opportunity to furnish a full continuum of care to the marketplace. Further, the PPO offers stability, because once consumers select a health care option, they generally remain loyal to this option and resist further change.

PPOs also provide hospitals the opportunity to change payor mix and payment sources. If hospitals are to survive under the new reimbursement systems, they will need to reduce the percentage of patients who are financed through government entitlement programs. The financial viability of these institutions will be dependent upon their ability to attract new private pay patients and increase their marginal profits. In addition to changing patient mix, PPOs offer hospitals the opportunity to develop new pricing strategies.

The development of PPOs has forced hospitals to identify the true cost of their services and develop a competitive, cost-based pricing structure. Hospitals will need to determine, through detailed cost analyses, where to set the marginal and incremental prices of their products. Because of the need to develop competitive delivery systems like PPOs, hospitals need to price their products and services at different levels. Pricing levels may be developed based upon a variety of pricing schemes:

— Price concessions based on volume utilization by selective purchasers.
— Caps on rate increases for predetermined and negotiated time periods.
— Pricing mechanisms directly related to the CPI.
— Per-diem payments.
— Guaranteed rates for a specific contract period.
— Incentive savings programs.

IMPACT ON HOSPITALS

Ultimately, the financial impact of a PPO on a hospital is determined by how the PPO affects hospital admissions and profitability. In general, the PPO financial impact should be projected at a variety of patient penetration levels. One method for hospitals to market their PPO product successfully, and gain market share quickly, is to become a model employer and enroll their employees in their own PPO.

In the 1980s, the health care industry will become increasingly technical. Hospitals, particularly acute care facilities, will become increasingly expensive to operate and an increasing number of programs will be developed on an outpatient basis. In the years ahead, it is conceivable that hospitals will experience a total restructuring. The new configuration will most likely exhibit a product orientation. Rather than being responsible for areas of care, management will be responsible for the pricing, packaging, and management of products throughout the hospital. As a result, nonprofitable products may be discontinued. The hospital will be highly sophisticated and technical. In many instances, the hospital will be significantly sized down. Hospitals, along with physicians, will have to identify the market demand for services and develop products that can effectively and efficiently respond to these demands. These changes will create a plethora of social, ethical, and moral conflicts.

MARKET FACTORS SUPPORTING DEVELOPMENT OF ALTERNATIVE DELIVERY SYSTEMS

In this decade, the health care business will be market driven. Price competition and price sensitivity will be key issues confronting those who purchase and deliver health care. The ability to price, package, and distribute the health care product will be essential for market success. Under the old cost reimbursement system, providers of health care simply added up costs, decided what the profit margin would be, and set rates. Under the new payor-regulated environment, health care providers must become price sensitive.

In addition to increased competition and price regulation, several other market characteristics also support the development of alternative delivery systems. These characteristics include a more mobile population, a physician surplus, and excess capacity in the hospital sector.

As a result of population shifts in major metropolitan areas, frequent relocation, and an increased number of women in the workforce, middle-class suburban Americans no longer identify with the individual family physician. In general, individuals are primarily concerned with the price and convenience of medical care. As a result, the health care market has begun to emphasize "episodic care" and has responded to the market demand for price and convenience through the development of urgent care centers. Urgent care centers, open nights and weekend hours, are a response to the needs of the family where both husband and wife work. Because of the proliferation and success of urgent care centers, the successful PPO of the future must provide a vertically integrated network of services.

The health care industry is faced with an increasing surplus of physicians, and the basic characteristics of this group is changing. The increase in the number of female physicians who may seek two careers, and total number of physicians, has resulted in an increase in the number of physicians who desire salaried positions with regular hours. This physician demand for an eight-hour work day enhances the ability of alternative delivery systems to attract physicians and supports the proliferation of freestanding ambulatory care centers and alternative delivery systems that can offer physicians regular hours. The ability of the closed panel HMO, or group practice model, to attract a number of highly motivated and qualified physicians is one result of this increased physician availability. The recruitment of quality staff has enabled the HMO product to become increasingly competitive. Again, the goal of these HMOs is to significantly reduce hospital utilization. A closed panel or group practice model HMO can quickly impact fee for service solo practitioners and hospitals. Frequently, these HMOs offer comprehensive facilities, including hospitals.

An increasing number of Medicare and Medicaid recipients are being provided the option to purchase contract services on a capitated basis. The competition among HMOs, PPOs, and other selective contracting arrangements for their patronage will intensify. If providers desire to maintain these population sectors as users of their facilities, they will need to develop competitive alternative delivery systems. To survive, PPOs will need to successfully approach this segment.

FACTORS FOR PPO SUCCESS

Recent market research that analyzed the effectiveness of PPO marketing indicates that buyers are interested in the price of services, service accessibility, provider quality, effective quality assurance/utilization review, and the availability of utilization and cost information.

If PPOs are to be successful in capturing market share, the PPOs must sell purchasers on price rather than cost. Historically, hospitals have priced their services on the basis of cost-based formulas that were encouraged by regulatory agencies. This pricing approach resulted in the development of pricing structures that had little in common with the costs of services. Price is critical to the success of a PPO.

The successful PPO must predetermine physician and hospital price before entering the marketplace within applicable anti-trust laws. In addition to developing a competitive pricing strategy, PPOs must be sensitive to purchaser concerns regarding price shifting. It is exceedingly important that the PPO be responsive to price competition, price sensitivity, and the payor regulated environment. These issues must be addressed in the hospital's pricing strategy and negotiated physician fee schedules.

The provider-sponsored PPO is uniquely positioned to be responsive to market pressures. The provider-sponsored PPO may offer one of the last opportunities for physicians and hospitals to manage the health care system and be competitive.

Provider ingredients for a successful PPO require that the hospital and/or physician are organized, provide good access and a wide range of services, and are price competitive in the marketplace. It is essential that the PPO provide an adequate mix of physicians by specialty and location. The successful PPO will emphasize the development of a strong base of primary care physicians. The benefit designs that are offered to the community must meet the needs of group purchasers, union contracts, and

Medicare and Medicaid recipients. If the PPO is to be successful, it is essential that benefit packages that encourage PPO utilization through a series of economic incentives be developed. Secondly, this benefit design must contain cost-sharing features that discourage patient overutilization. This is a delicate but essential ingredient. Provider-sponsored PPOs will need to be sensitive to buyer, third-party administrator (TPA), insurance company, broker, and consumer needs. Plan design is a fundamental element.

The organizational structures should encourage physician representation, hospital representation, and payee representation at the governance level. As a result of the development of strong business coalitions, many PPOs have had substantial payor input into the development and design of the product. This inclusion of payors in the governance of PPOs has often been unsettling to the providers. However, the tripartite involvement of physicians, hospital representatives, and payors is essential to the development of quality and acceptable product. In operational PPOs, this involvement has proven to provide an excellent balance between hospitals and physicians. Responsible representatives can prove to enhance product marketability and provide excellent director skills.

It is essential that hospitals conduct a comprehensive financial analysis before developing a PPO. Financial feasibility should be measured in terms of both the direct rate of return and the indirect rate of return. In the simplest sense, the financial feasibility of a PPO depends upon the physician financial contributions, the hospital contribution, and a monthly maintenance fee that is charged to the users of the plan. Before entering into a PPO arrangement, providers need to determine the financial impact. Physicians need to assess whether the PPO will have a positive impact on patient volume and income. Is the PPO a source of additional revenue or replacement income in a declining market? Will the PPO generate sufficient income to offset potential revenues from a predetermined fee schedule? In short, for the cost of enrollment, will the physician realize short-term and long-term gains?

The hospital will need to conduct a similar assessment. Given the plethora of options in the market, will the return on dollars be adequate to justify expense or should another option be explored? Hospitals are quick to accept quick fixes to complex management issues. Hospitals must weigh heavily the cost of the opportunity that they will lose by choosing not to accept a PPO or other selective contracting vehicle.

The financial integrity of the PPO as an organization is essential to financial viability. Can the PPO generate sufficient user fees to operate and maintain viability? Should the PPO seek a joint venture relationship with an established third party intermediary? Is the PPO properly capitalized to be competitively positioned? What is its financial role vis-à-vis other payor-sponsored PPOs (BC/BS, commercial carriers, etc.)?

However, if PPOs are to survive and maintain their own financial viability and integrity, they may choose to sell claims processing services, market preadmission certification, and quality assurance programs. However, it is important to recognize that these selective contracting vehicles may choose to simply remain providers. The function of providing administrative services may be restricted to a contracting agreement with a TPA. When PPOs choose not to enter this highly competitive market, they have greater flexibility in accessing a wide variety of markets because they are not competitors.

Providers do not usually have the expertise to enter the TPA market. It is a highly competitive market and offers only marginal returns. The ability to provide excellent claims processing capability, good output reports, and systems support are essential elements to success in this product line. Once providers enter this product line, they risk alienation from other administrators and diminish their distinct role as providers.

Market research conducted by VHA Health Ventures and others has indicated that network development is a key element in PPO success. The network enables the PPO to provide a differentiated product and offer a wide range of services in multiple locations. This is appealing to the purchaser, as it reduces their need to select one provider and offers the individual consumer access to a wide range of providers.

In addition, the formation of provider networks, which include a range of hospitals (primary, secondary, and tertiary care facilities), enables the PPO to aggressively price their products and offer multitiered pricing. The development of a network system provides the PPO with increased access to the financial and human resources that are necessary to support product development activities. Regional and national linkages will become an increasingly important strategy for PPO success.

Although PPOs were organized initially to address the needs of group purchasers of health care through fully insured indemnity plans, partially insured multiple employer trusts, or self-funded trusts, Medicare and Medicaid group purchasers are becoming an increasingly important market sector. Since Medicaid and Medicare account for a high percentage of total health care dollar expenditures and hospital revenues, PPOs must become active in these markets and address the special needs of these populations. It will be important to develop a PPO within a vertically integrated system that is responsive to the potential implementation of a government-voucher payment system.

For example, Mountain Medical Affiliates, Inc., and Presbyterian/ St. Luke's in Denver was one of the first PPOs to apply for a Medicare demonstration waiver from the Health Care Financing Administration (HCFA). This program has resulted in the development of a joint venture product between a commercial insurance carrier, a physician's organization, and three hospitals.

JOINT VENTURE CRITERIA

Although doctors and hospitals share the dual objectives of retaining current market share and capturing additional market share in a declining and stagnated market environment, it is probably more important to develop a system to retain existing market share. In fact, if current market trends continue, it will be necessary to review the financial feasibility of a PPO in terms of an "opportunity lost" formula. Such a formula would enable a hospital to determine, given declining lengths of stay and admission rates, the negative differential that might result if a hospital does not develop a PPO.

Since the health care market will become segmented into three distinct areas (HMOs, PPOs, and the traditional purchaser system), physicians and hospitals will need to be competitive in all three markets. As the market becomes increasingly segmented, hospitals may diversify into third party claims administration. Ultimately, hospitals may develop national business strategies that include the formation of risk-taking insurance companies. In such an environment, the health care providers might function as intermediaries. In the areas of function, governance, and ownership, PPOs will need to be flexible and respond rapidly to changes in market conditions. In addition, the joint venture PPO corporation will need to have flexibility to extend its provider lines beyond PPOs.

As increasing numbers of hospitals spin off for-profit corporations, there will be an increasing number of hospitals that joint venture PPOs and other ambulatory care systems with their medical staffs. Joint ventures will enable hospitals and physicians to work together in the development of products that attempt to meet the common goals and objectives of both parties. This process is generally alien to physicians who have, traditionally, prided themselves on their individuality and the solo practice of medicine. It is equally foreign to hospitals, which have historically managed physicians on a fragmented basis.

Several other factors support the development of hospital/physician joint ventures. In order to remain financially viable, hospitals require the capital resources of physicians. At the same time, in order to provide their patients a continuum of care, physicians need the resources of the hospital. If doctors and hospitals are going to survive the competitive market of the 1980s, it is essential that they develop joint ventures. The PPO represents an excellent and safe first step in that direction. However, both hospitals and physicians must recognize that they may not possess, internally, the resources that are necessary to manage these systems effectively. They must be willing to hire the expertise necessary to develop and implement a successful new product. If they are not willing to commit substantial resources, they should not try to develop alternative delivery systems.

CONCLUSION

The PPO itself should not be looked upon as a panacea to resolving the complex issues that face the health care industry. As business coalitions and government continue to pressure the health care industry to contain costs, hospitals and doctors must actively and innovatively respond to marketplace demands. Traditional providers of care must recognize that the new alternative health care delivery mechanisms were developed by entrepreneural physicians and managers who recognized that product response to marketplace demand was an exceedingly important ingredient in the 1980s.

This recognition of the need to respond to consumer demands represents a dramatic change in health care delivery. Historically, the health care market has only responded to provider pressures, and it has generally ignored the purchaser and consumer of care. Suddenly, consumers and other purchasers are requiring providers to be sensitive to their changing needs. Hospitals and doctors must be responsive to consumer needs and provide services that offer competitive prices, convenience, and quality. PPOs offer traditional providers of health care the opportunity to meet these needs without sacrificing the ideal of a self-managed system that strives to maintain quality care and patient/physician relationship.

Impact of New Trends

PPOs: Issues for Hospitals

Kathryn A. Schroer
Consultant
A. S. Hansen, Inc.
Deerfield, IL

William A. Weinberg
American Hospital Association
Chicago, IL

Hospitals in today's health care environment are facing changes and uncertainty that affect all aspects of their ability to function as a primary provider of health care services. A cutback in governmental payment, new market forces, and a surplus of physicians and hospital beds are forcing hospitals to reevaluate their business and creatively develop and work with new health care delivery and financing systems. One such system, the preferred provider organization (PPO), is being tried by many.

As PPOs multiply, many important managerial, financial, and legal issues arise for hospitals. Hospitals' ability to address these issues depends in part on management sophistication and linkages with other institutions. Of major importance is the hospital administration's understanding of the financial impact PPO involvement could have on the institution. Originally designed to manage the financial risk for providers, PPOs now are gradually placing more and more risk on hospitals and physicians. The PPOs, like other alternative delivery systems, emphasize decreased length of stay and providing care in ambulatory or less intensive settings, and these may have a long-term effect on hospitals' occupancy rate. For example, inpatient days per thousand decreased from an estimated rate of 750 in fee-for-service arrangements to 400 in health maintenance organizations (HMOs) over the last year. As usage of HMO and PPO health benefits increase, this could have a major impact on hospitals. Therefore, an understanding of financial impacts and a close evaluation of the hospital's mission as a provider of care are important to the hospital's success in a PPO setting.

This chapter will provide a perspective that emphasizes hospital issues in PPO development, contracting, and sponsorship. It will specifically highlight financial and utilization issues. PPO payment mechanisms will be addressed at length.[1]

The first section will look at study results from research conducted by the American Hospital Association (AHA) in 1982, 1983, and 1984. Analysis will emphasize growth trends in PPOs, sponsoring changes, and trends in PPO structuring as identified by the research. The second and third sections will review managerial, organizational, and financial issues, and hospital participation and nonparticipation in PPOs. The discussion will highlight both hospital-sponsored and non–hospital-sponsored PPOs, with particular emphasis on financial implications for the hospital.

AHA STUDY HIGHLIGHTS

In September 1982 the AHA facilitated a survey of all community hospitals within the United States to ascertain the level of interest or participation in preferred provider organizations. Results showed that 84 hospitals in 22 states were participating in operating PPOs, and over 700 hospitals were interested in PPO development.[2] Hospitals sponsoring or participating in these PPOs generally had between 50 and 300 beds. This was also the range in size of hospitals indicating interest in PPOs. Survey results indicated that the majority of these hospitals were located in metropolitan areas and most were not-for-profit hospitals. These hospitals were facing market impacts such as overbedded service areas, increases in alternative delivery systems such as surgicenters, emergency centers, HMOs, and others, and a tightening of health benefit dollars by employers. Upon further investigation of the 84 participating hospitals, the AHA identified 35 operational PPOs. An in-depth study of those PPOs revealed that:[3]

> The composite model PPO responding to the survey was developed through hospital sponsorship and legally organized as a corporation. It is controlled in a joint venture between hospital(s) and physicians. It has a formal governing board made up of a more or less equal number of physician and nonphysician members. Utilization review, generally performed through hospital/physician committee is in place. The PPO provides inpatient hospital, ambulatory and physician services as well as several other types of programs and/

or services. It markets to a variety of purchasers ranging from its own hospital employee group to major employers, union trusts and insurance groups.[4]

Although 75 percent indicated that utilization review and quality assurance systems were operational, few had actually developed definite review criteria separate from what had previously been implemented in participating hospitals. Most PPOs had been operating with a minimal number of buyer contracts. Further, the PPO with greatest reported claims ($5 million in 1982) offered a hospital discount of only 4 to 7 percent, and a physician discount of 20 percent.

The American Hospital Association recently completed an updated survey of hospital participation in PPOs. Preliminary results identified 115 operating PPOs (operational defined as marketing a fully developed product). Although these PPOs are in varying stages of development, each have provider panels in place and a functioning administrative staff. These PPOs are located in 26 states with the greatest number in California (44 PPOs). Unlike the previously mentioned survey (July 1983), many responding hospitals indicated participation in two or more PPOs. Also, the emergence of the Blue Cross and Blue Shield PPO plans has dramatically penetrated markets in California, Missouri, Ohio, and Virginia. Blue Cross and Blue Shield PPOs are also developing in Florida, Minnesota, Michigan, Maryland, Massachusetts, and Georgia. The survey indicated that sponsorship of PPOs by insurance carriers, third-party administrators, and employers is growing. Based on their sponsorship, PPOs were identified as follows: 22 were hospital-sponsored, 30 physician, 19 hospital/physician joint venture, 9 Blue Cross or Blue Shield plans, 5 insurance, 5 multihospital systems, 6 third-party administrator, 5 HMO/IPA, 7 entrepreneur, 4 employer/union, and 3 by combinations of the above. PPOs continue to develop most rapidly in highly populated urban areas, although interest in PPO development in smaller and rural community hospitals continues. These small hospitals view the PPO as one tool for slowing the loss of patients to neighboring communities.

TRENDS

Trends in PPO development seem to be leading to the following:

— Greater growth in non–provider-based PPOs.
— Growth of PPO networks.
— Change in payment schedules to place more financial risk on providers and to emphasize utilization review mechanisms.

Growth of Non–provider-sponsored PPOs

Although PPO sponsorship by hospitals and physicians is still growing rapidly and continues to represent the major sponsoring mechanism, a surge of development by insurance carriers, third-party administrators and other entrepreneurial groups is evident. Blue Cross and Blue Shield plans across the country are rapidly implementing plans involving physician and hospital contracting. Buyers are increasingly encouraging development of non–provider-based PPOs, which they view as possibly more responsible in terms of containing health care cost.

PPO Networks

Networks of existing PPOs are developing nationwide. These networks differ from PPO plans developed uniformly (a "cookie cutter" approach) across the United States. They are composed of previously existing PPOs, developed independently to meet specific market demands. They are loosely structured as consortia, associations, or alliances. Some national corporations are requesting a PPO network to meet the demands of health benefits at all the company's locations.

Payment Schedule Changes

A shift in payment method is occurring away from the earlier system of discounts on charges for hospital and doctor fees, toward per diems, and DRG payment mechanisms for hospitals and negotiated fee schedules and relative value systems for physician payment. These systems increase financial risk for providers and are more attractive to buyers of health care. Further, utilization management, central to these newer payment systems, has become a key ingredient in PPO marketing strategies.

ISSUES FOR HOSPITAL-SPONSORED PPOs

A hospital's decision to sponsor a preferred provider organization, to contract with a PPO, or *not* to become involved incorporates a number of key considerations.

The following issues will be discussed in terms of hospital-sponsored PPOs:

- Market considerations.
- Medical staff relations.
- Staffing.
- Hospital governing board concerns.
- Information systems.
- Legal implications.
- PPO board structure.
- Long-term planning.
- Utilization-control mechanisms.
- Financial considerations.
- Hospital payment mechanisms.

MARKET CONSIDERATIONS

The first exploratory step in PPO development must include an analysis of the hospitals' competitive market through comprehensive market research. A hospital could suffer a significant financial loss by neglecting this first step. Marketing is an area of expertise that is sometimes unfamiliar to hospital executives, although marketing activity is dramatically increasing in hospitals across the country. The hospital developing a PPO must thoroughly understand *all* competitive organizations and factors that may be indicators of their PPO's potential market success. HMOs, PPOs, and other alternative delivery systems must be scrutinized for level of penetration in the marketplace. Detailed market research should further identify buyers' interest levels, trends in employee health benefits, and future economic and demographic impacts within the marketplace. When information is available, private payors' use of the hospital during the last several years should be analyzed, and the percentage of patient days represented by each potential buyer should be scrutinized. This type of market research and analysis is imperative in developing an appropriate marketing strategy and plan for the PPO. Hospitals should recognize the importance of adequate staffing and financial commitment for this initial process. Market analysis must be thoroughly completed identifying a go/no-go point at which investment in development will be further analyzed.

When this phase is completed, the hospital should develop a PPO product that is attractive to the buyer. A lack of flexibility in the arrangement, a noncommital utilization control mechanism, or a poorly organized and designed product will make sales difficult. Hospital sponsored PPOs should work to avoid the perception that theirs is a "fox-in-the-hen house" or "quick-fix" approach. Hospital-sponsored PPOs should also be able to prove the physicians' commitment to strong utilization control and cost containment.

In summary, the hospital sponsoring a PPO must know its market, develop a thorough market strategy, and develop a product (PPO) that is most acceptable to the hospital, the physicians, and importantly, the buyers.

MEDICAL STAFF/PHYSICIAN RELATIONS

Before any major PPO development begins, a hospital must look to its medical staff. When a PPO is sponsored by the hospital itself, the medical staff's cooperation and receptivity is of great importance. The PPO should strive to develop a structure that is satisfying to its entire medical staff and, specifically, to the physicians that would be most beneficial to the PPO provider panel. An uncooperative physicians group has the potential power to undermine a PPO before it is operational. This may be done by refusal to adhere to a fee schedule, refusal to develop appropriate UR mechanisms, or refusal to accept other terms offered by the PPO. The hospital should evaluate its medical staff in terms of:

— Practice patterns: a review of general practice patterns, including use of ancillaries.
— Involvement in other alternative delivery systems (which may encourage or preclude participation): a physician involved in an HMO or IPA will be accustomed to the type of UR used in a PPO. However, if the physician has an exclusive contract with other organizations, participation in the PPO would be precluded.
— Loss of market share (potential future loss): a physician with a "healthy" practice is less interested in PPO participation.
— Incentives to best motivate physicians to participate and practice cost effective medicine: what financial incentives are appropriate (bonus, shareholder status, other).
— Average age: a younger medical staff may be more receptive to the PPO concept and to changes in their medical practice.

The physician panel should be involved to a degree in the development of the fee schedule and in determining what, if any, other incentives would be necessary. Physicians should play a key role in developing the PPO's utilization-control system as well as in the selection of their peers for the panel. The hospital-sponsored PPO must also be sensitive to the impact the PPO may have on members of the medical staff *not* participating. The hospital must avoid alienating non-PPO physicians or allowing a negative political situation to arise among physicians on staff. Overall, clear communications, collaboration, and an understanding of the issues impacting physicians can foster a strong working relationship between the hospital sponsor and its partner, the medical staff.

STAFFING

Administrative expertise is another managerial consideration for hospitals sponsoring PPOs. An assessment of needed talent should be undertaken by the hospital. Staff skilled in the following are essential:

— Administration of alternative delivery systems.
— Contract negotiation.
— Sales.
— Marketing.
— Information system development or evaluation.
— Health benefits design.
— Physician relations.
— Utilization control.
— Finance.

Many of these staff may already be working within the hospital's administration. But some new talent will be required.

HOSPITAL BOARD RECEPTIVITY

Whether the hospital governing board is receptive to the PPO concept is also key to developing the organization. As with the medical staff, and with other hospital ventures, the board has the power to make or break a PPO. If several board members are from corporations or large employers and are familiar with health benefits trends and market pressures, the board members may be supportive of the PPO concept and may potentially be a good marketing tool. Many hospital boards will need to be educated concerning alternative delivery systems. Some concerns that may be raised by the board include:

— Untested form of organized health care delivery. Little information on PPO financial performance is currently available. The board will question the PPO's effect on the hospital's overall financial stability. A forecast of potential gains and losses should be presented to the board. As it becomes available, other PPOs' experiences should be related to the board.
— Loss of control over the PPO. If the PPO has its own governing structure, the hospital board may feel a loss of power while financially backing the organization. Emphasizing the importance of the PPO as a separate organization is important.
— Concern for malpractice liabilities and insurance regulations that directly affect the hospital. A clear explanation of all legal impacts that might affect the hospital should be provided to board members.
— Hospital mission to serve its community. The board may question the appropriateness of PPO involvement in light of consistency with its overall mission. This question should be addressed early in the development of the PPO.

To summarize, the hospital board should be thoroughly educated on the issues implicit in PPO development, and clear communications between the staff who are developing and implementing the PPO and the governing board are essential.

INFORMATION SYSTEM CAPABILITIES

The need for sophisticated data and information systems is key to a PPO's success. The ability to generate utilization reports and to handle claims at one level or another will be demanded by the buyer. Further capacity to relate specific services and physicians to the hospital and the PPO financial status and to incorporate cost information into case mix information systems will be needed. A management information system with this capacity is expensive and many hospitals may not have the capability in-house to provide this function. The need to cautiously evaluate the hospitals' available system, other systems for purchase, or potential contracting for these services is important. Hospitals need to develop a credible data system that will meet their own needs as well as the needs of buyers. Generation of physician profiles, cost data, ancillary usage reports and more will help dispel the buyers' fox-in-the-hen house perceptions. Some systems, developed to address DRG case mix, may be transferable to PPO users and should be considered for this purpose.

LEGAL IMPLICATIONS

Legal issues are of great importance in developing or contracting with a PPO. Legal counsel should analyze state insurance laws and HMO laws and regulations as well as federal antitrust laws. Provider-based PPOs must be developed with care to avoid price-fixing or other allegations. Further, tax laws should be considered in designing the PPO. A hospital's own legal counsel may or may not be adequate in structuring the PPO.

THE PPO GOVERNING BOARD

While there are many legal models for structuring a provider-based PPO, structuring of the PPO governing board is often not carefully considered. Choosing the appropriate members and distributing power adequately within the PPO board is crucial. The majority of existing PPOs have relatively small boards with a large number of physicians participating. This serves as both an incentive for physician performance and as a method for closely involving physicians in credentialling of the panel and developing or approving the utilization-control process. The board should be structured in terms of:

— Appropriate size: a small board facilitates quicker action/reaction.
— Composition: the number of physicians, hospital representatives, buyer representatives, and others that best reflect the controlling parties in the PPO (i.e., physician sponsors).
— Responsibilities: clear definition of the powers of the board should be outlined when the board is developed. The extent of the board's responsibility for approving the provider panel, for expansion of services, or for terminating the PPO activities should be determined during the initial phase of development.

LONG-TERM PLANNING AND GOALS

A hospital's involvement in alternative delivery systems should be viewed in terms of its long-term goals. PPOs foster the use of nonacute care settings and strive to decrease length of stay.

This is in contrast to hospitals' traditional emphasis on inpatient acute care. Hospitals must define their business and their goals in terms of what impact this may have on their current operations. They must evaluate whether a PPO fits into long-term planning and goal setting for the institution, as well as whether it is in accord with the basic mission of the institution.

UTILIZATION-CONTROL MECHANISMS

Utilization may be controlled in a variety of ways in both provider-based and non–provider-based PPOs. Its structure is often dependent on the payment mechanism utilized. Utilization review may be structured as follows:

1. Performed internally by each hospital participating in the provider panel (no central UR function within the PPO).
2. Performed by the PPO.
3. Contract for utilization-review services performed by outside organization.

In any of these arrangements, the hospital as PPO sponsor may be exposed to a certain degree of malpractice liability and should be adequately insured. Utilization review performed by individual hospitals within the PPO (standing hospital committee) will be the least marketable option while exposing the PPO to the least malpractice liability. Buyers may not view this as a meaningful approach to changing or monitoring medical practice. Outside utilization-control programs, performed by the PPO or contracted for will prove most acceptable to buyers but may place greater malpractice liability on the PPO. Utilization control elements commonly implemented by PPOs include preadmission certification, concurrent review, second surgical opinion, discharge planning, and others frequently used in HMOs.

Any of the three systems mentioned above should be designed to effectively control the use of health care services. It should generate data for managerial use and for patient and physician profiles, and it should be flexible enough to meet demands of purchasers. The system should have the capacity to carefully track and channel patients as they progress through the health care system. As mentioned previously, the physician panel should be partners in developing and monitoring the system.

FINANCIAL CONSIDERATIONS

Before devising a PPO payment system and moving ahead with PPO development, hospitals must carefully analyze their costs, a difficult process for many institutions. Developing a financial plan for the PPO can be riddled with uncertainties. Often marketing costs alone can escalate well beyond estimated implementation budgets. Implementation costs for hospital-based PPOs have averaged $250,000 to $500,000 depending on the size of the provider panel, the region of the country, and variables such as extent of marketing efforts required. Developing a pricing schedule the hospital can live with is not a simple matter; simply discounting on "gut feeling" can be costly. A clear understanding of the PPO's effect on the hospital's fixed and variable costs, as well as analysis of all marketable payment options should be adhered to when determining the cost effectiveness of the initial investment and the feasibility of payment systems.

HOSPITAL PAYMENT MECHANISMS

There are a variety of different payment methodologies that a hospital may select when developing a PPO arrangement. In this section the strengths and weaknesses of a number of alternative systems are reviewed. Emphasis is sometimes placed on things to watch out for, not to discourage hospitals from taking the initiative in developing PPOs or contracting with them but rather to insure that costly mistakes are not made. Given the appropriate set of variables, a payment system that serves the hospital's interests and is acceptable to the payor is possible.

Discounting

One option is to discount charges across the board. This is based on the theory that the losses incurred from the reduced charges will be offset by volume increases as payors offer financial incentives for subscribers to use preferred providers. In determining an appropriate discount, the hospital must examine a number of issues. The hospital must recognize that a discount will be offered to a payor for *all* the payor's cases. Some of those cases will be new cases where the consumer selects the preferred hospital as a result of the financial incentives built into the benefit package. At the same time some of the patients the hospital receives would have selected the hospital even if there had been no PPO arrangement and no financial incentives. These patients would have generated revenue at a nondiscounted rate in the absence of a PPO arrangement. Under the PPO arrangement they are discounted in the same manner as additional "PPO generated cases." The hospital must recognize that revenue will be lost when cases it would have received under any circumstances are discounted. The next variable to consider is the marginal cost of new cases. Marginal costs are the additional costs incurred as a result of additional cases and is lower than average cost because many cost components are fixed. For example, part of the average cost per case for a hospital is the director of nursing's salary. If the PPO adds a hundred cases, it does not result in another director of nursing being hired or even in a salary increase in most cases. While the director's salary is part of the *average* cost, it is *not* part of the *marginal cost*. This article does not attempt to provide a formula for determining marginal cost as there is no simplistic solution; nonetheless, a carefully derived estimate of marginal costs is essential.

Thus far in the analysis, the hospital has reduced revenue and increased costs as a result of the PPO discount. Balancing off the additional costs and lost revenue is the revenue to be received from additional PPO-generated cases. The hospital must estimate the revenue that the additional cases will generate. A simple procedure for doing so is to assume that additional cases will by and large be similar to the cases the hospital is already receiving from the payor. The average revenue for cases already being received is known and can be multiplied by the anticipated number of additional cases to determine additional PPO-generated revenue. The final step is to estimate what the additional volume will be. This is essential not only in determining additional revenue but also marginal cost. If the anticipated volume increase does not occur, a hospital can easily find itself in the red.

Nonetheless, estimating additional volume may be difficult. PPOs usually do not restrict subscribers to preferred providers but only provide financial incentives to utilize preferred providers. In selecting a provider, consumers will consider many variables in addition to price, making it difficult to estimate volume increases. The hospital can structure its contract so as not to put itself at risk for volume increases or lack thereof. This can be achieved by arriving at a discount based on an assumed volume, and then incorporating into the contract the provision that the discount is contingent upon the agreed upon volume of patients and/or services being attained. The level of discount can be tied to the volume increase actually received, in a balloon-type arrangement, offering an increasing discount when greater volume is achieved. The specific mechanics of a guaranteed discount system vary. It is in a hospital's interest to determine a discount based on an assumed volume and then provide that discount if and only if the volume is actually realized. Even though the volume guarantee request is based on sound business considerations, payors may nonetheless not always agree to it. And if the payor refuses to provide the guarantee? The hospital has to determine whether the required volume level will be reached even though there are no written guarantees. To estimate whether it will be realized the hospital must examine all variables that will determine what the actual increase will be including but not limited to:

— The financial incentives being given to subscribers to choose the preferred hospital: are they sufficient?
— Do the subscribers live within a reasonable distance from the hospital. People do not drive 60 miles to save $100 (20 minutes rule of thumb).
— Are the physicians currently treating the patients on the hospital's

staff? People tend not to change their physicians. Do they understand their choices?
— Are subscribers aware of the PPO alternative? How much education and marketing is being performed?

The hospital must examine these and other variables in order to determine if the necessary volume will be reached.

In summary, if the payor agrees to a volume guarantee, then the hospital is not at risk for shortfalls in expected volume increase and need only determine the discount given the guaranteed volume. If there is no volume guarantee, then not only must the hospital determine the discount, it must also be confident that the volume, while not guaranteed, will be reached, and that confidence should be based on a comprehensive study. What if the study shows the volume will not be reached?

Again the hospital has options to consider, including the following:

— Discontinue PPO development.
— Set a new discount based on a realistic volume increase figure.
— Have the payor increase financial incentives for the subscriber to insure a volume increase.

Emphasis is often placed on the discount aspect of PPOs. Payors nonetheless realize that total costs are a function of unit costs and the number of units consumed. With a discount the hospital has addressed unit cost, but the number of units consumed is addressed by incorporation of utilization review (UR) into the contract. UR further complicates the hospital's analysis. The UR program will probably review admissions and length of stay and may review ancillary utilization as well, since total charges (i.e., the payor's total costs) are related to each of these.

Utilization review will not only impact additional admissions that the PPO contract may generate, it will also impact the average revenue received from PPO cases already using the institution, by reducing lengths of stay and ancillary utilization (if reviewed). Some cases may even be lost altogether due to preadmission review. These revenue losses must be factored in when evaluating how much of a discount to offer and what type of volume guarantee to require.

In summary, then, the hospital must consider the following in arriving at a discount rate:

— What will the volume increase be?
— Is the volume increase guaranteed?
— What will the revenue loss be from discounting cases the hospital would have received even without a PPO arrangement?
— What is the marginal cost of the additional PPO generated cases?
— What effect will utilization review have on the revenue of PPO-generated cases and cases the hospital would have received in any case?

Low-Cost Provider

An alternative lower risk approach is to provide no discount. A low-cost hospital can negotiate this if its charges are already below its competition. From the payor's perspective, total payments will be less if subscribers utilize the low-cost hospital. The payor may still seek a discount so as to increase potential savings further. Employers are also likely to request utilization review just as they do in a discount charge system.

Per Diem

The payor community appears to be moving away from the charge discount approach. One alternative is a prospectively negotiated per diem, where the hospital receives a fixed payment per patient day to cover all costs. In establishing a proper per-diem rate, the hospital must take into account a number of cost and volume factors. The per diem will probably be, at least in part, based on a historical per diem discounted by some percentage rolled forward by an inflation factor. For example, a hospital determines that total costs last year for Smith Insurance subscribers was $1 million. The total number of days these patients were in the hospital was 10,000. One million dollars divided by 10,000 days equals a $100 per diem. Assume a prorated inflation rate of 10 percent and the per diem is $110. In return for volume increases, the hospital discounts the $110 per diem.

A volume estimate is again essential to the analysis for the same reasons outlined for the charge/discount system, and a volume guarantee is appropriate. In the per-diem system, volume is measured in terms of patient days since each patient day generates a fixed revenue amount. Still paralleling the charge/discount system discussion, the analysis must take into account the impact of UR. The per-diem arrangement breaks the unit of service/revenue relationship for *ancillary* services. In other words, ancillary utilization is *not* related to the amount the payor will pay for the services rendered: The payor pays the *same* amount regardless of the ancillaries used. Therefore the payor is not at risk for overutilization of ancillary services and need not require ancillary review. In terms of admissions and days, the payor will probably still seek UR to reduce its risk exposure for those variables that are still related to payor costs. Since the per-diem payment system is based on patient days, the hospital must give careful consideration to the effect UR will have. Each day that UR eliminates from a patient stay results in a fixed revenue reduction equal to the per-diem rate. There will be a cost reduction that will partially offset the revenue loss. Many of the costs associated with the lost days are fixed and will just be reallocated to the remaining days, thus raising the actual per diem. Furthermore, while the revenue received for any given day is equal to the per diem, the per diem is only an *average*. All days may generate the same revenue, but every hospital day does not cost the same amount. The last days in a patient's stay tend to be the least costly and also tend to be the days most likely eliminated by a UR program. In short, the revenue lost from these days may be far more than the cost reductions that result from their elimination. The hospital must give careful consideration to this in setting a per-diem rate.

A weakness of the per-diem system is that it does not adjust for changes in case mix. As already stated, per diem generates the same revenue for each day regardless of actual costs incurred, which vary from day to day and case by case. Should the types of cases being treated move towards a mix of more costly cases, the hospital could suffer a loss; where the shift is towards less costly cases the hospital may gain. If, on the other hand, the hospital's case mix remains the same over time despite the addition of new cases resulting from PPO usage, the per-diem system can function quite adequately. The potential problem of a significantly shifting case mix will vary from hospital to hospital, and from payor to payor, depending on how the characteristics of potential new patients compare to the hospital's current case mix and the number of cases involved. Each hospital must examine the potential for changes in case mix over time.

A variation on flat per-diem contracting is a multiple per-diem arrangement based on service. For example, different per diems can be set for medical, surgical, and obstetrical cases. Surgical cases may be subdivided into such things as orthopedic, neurologic, etc. In a hospital-sponsored PPO, the hospital is free to establish whatever payment "hybrid" it desires and attempt to sell that proposal to the payor. Furthermore, the two systems already mentioned, discounts and per diems, can be utilized together. A hospital may be quite comfortable agreeing to a per diem for some services and not others. Open heart surgery cases might be paid on a discount system or not included in the PPO arrangement at all. The PPO arrangement is a negotiated agreement between two parties, each with its own set of needs, and the payment methodology should be tailored specifically to the needs of the parties involved.

In summary, in developing a per-diem rate the hospital has to consider

— Expected volume increase.
— Revenue lost as a result of the discount for cases it would have received under any circumstances.
— Reduced revenue resulting from utilization review of cases the hospital would have received under any circumstance.
— Marginal cost of additional cases resulting from PPO contract.
— Stability of case mix.
— Volume guarantee if any.
— Revenue generated by additional cases.

Per-Case System

A per-case system is one that includes the diagnosis-related group (DRG), as well as an average payment per case unadjusted for case mix.

An advantage the DRG system has over the per diem is the addition of an automatic adjustment for changes in case mix. Furthermore, economic incentives in a PPO-DRG system will be consistent with those in the Medicare DRG system. This may be helpful for hospitals under the Medicare prospective pricing system. Many hospitals will have established complex data systems for Medicare prospective pricing and these systems can be utilized under a PPO-DRG system at minimal additional cost. These hospitals also have internal management systems that can be utilized under the PPO arrangement contract. Adopting a PPO-DRG system of course does not mean adopting Medicare prices or even the Medicare methodology for arriving at DRG prices.

Utilization review under a DRG-based system will be similar to that for a per-diem system. Admissions are still related to total payor costs— so preadmission review is a likely requirement from the payor standpoint. The payor in a DRG system is not at risk for length of stay (LOS) variations, so concurrent review for LOS is less likely unless there is a provision in the contract for additional payment when LOS exceeds certain points. In that case, review will probably be limited to the additional days.

While the DRG approach has many advantages, the hospital is "at risk" for variations in the severity of illness within each DRG. A severity adjustment would subdivide a DRG into different classes based on the patient's degree of illness. The rate of payment could then be based on both the DRG and severity of illness for the case. This area is receiving considerable attention, in part because of Medicare's interest in possibly using a severity of illness adjustment with the DRG classifications. As alternative severity indexes are developed and evaluated, hospitals will be able to employ them in their PPO payment arrangements.

It should be emphasized that DRGs are not the only case mix measure that can be employed in a payment scheme; there are others that may be used. A disadvantage of utilizing another system is that it may create unnecessary confusion within a hospital that is on Medicare DRGs. Another disadvantage is that the data system developed for the DRG may not be entirely transferable to another case mix system, resulting in increased data management expenses.

The biggest hurdle to overcome in a DRG system is determining the payment rates. If the hospital historically has a small number of cases in a given DRG, then the costs for those cases may not be a statistically accurate estimate of the actual average cost for treating that DRG. A hospital may prefer to establish DRG rates only for those categories with a sufficient number of cases on which to base rates, and where the cost variation is likely to be limited. Once again it should be emphasized that the hospital can be creative in using DRG payments where appropriate and using another methodology for other cases.

Capitation

The final payment option to consider is a capitation approach. Capitation is used by HMOs in which payment covers hospital and physician services. But, a hospital could utilize a capitation approach for its services only. In a capitated arrangement, the hospital would provide all the agreed-upon services in return for a prospectively set amount for a given individual. Patients would be encouraged to utilize the preferred hospital by paying lower deductibles and/or coinsurance, just as they are in any PPO arrangement. For the hospital, a major shortcoming to this program is that the capitated hospital will have to reimburse other institutions for care provided to capitated patients. The risk can be minimized by restricting patients to preferred institutions (EPO approach) or by making the financial penalties incurred in using a nonpreferred provider high enough to effectively preclude use of nonpreferred providers. An additional problem with capitation is the need for a large enough population to set capitated rates.

Outpatient Services

The payment discussion thus far has been restricted to inpatient services only. The PPO contract can be further complicated by adding provisions for outpatient services as well.

Payors are interested in outpatient services because they are usually less costly than inpatient. In negotiating a contract, payors may push for substituting outpatient for inpatient services enforced through the UR process. Hospitals must be very careful in negotiating for outpatient services. If the average inpatient cost is compared to the average outpatient cost, outpatient may be far less. The hospital can then negotiate outpatient rates that are lower than inpatient but still generate a higher revenue margin nonetheless. This makes outpatient services an attractive alternative to both the hospital *and* payor. A note of caution: As inpatient utilization is shifted over to outpatient, much of the inpatient costs will remain and be re-allocated to the remaining inpatients, thus raising inpatient costs. This problem can be addressed if the inpatient volume lost to outpatient can be made up. The essential point is that when outpatient services substitute for inpatient, much of the inpatient costs remain and must be addressed in the PPO cost analysis.

In summary, a few basic principles will apply to all payment alternatives:

— Payment arrangements must meet the needs of the hospital.
— Payment arrangements must be acceptable to the payor.
— The hospital need not lock itself into any single payment methodology but should be creative and flexible. It may develop a hybrid that incorporates different types of payment into the agreement.

— Hospitals should recognize that they control certain variables while they have no control or limited control over others, general inflation and volume. Hospitals should minimize their risk exposure for costs they cannot control.

— Developing a PPO should not be done in a vacuum. Consideration must be given to the PPO pricing system's effect on *other* payors who might end up paying higher rates based on average, rather than marginal costs. Essentially, they may be covering the fixed costs and subsidizing PPO patients. If this occurs, such payors may demand the same payment rates or seek legislated cost-control measures. In developing PPOs, hospitals must recognize that when negotiating with a customer other customers will be watching carefully.

ISSUES FOR HOSPITAL CONTRACTING—NONSPONSORSHIP

Insurance carriers, third-party administrators, employers, and physicians are sponsoring PPOs. Along with many of the issues discussed under hospital sponsorship of PPOs, there are a number of things to be evaluated by the hospital when considering a contractual relationship with a PPO. A hospital contracting with one or more PPOs sponsored by the above organizations or by other hospitals should consider the reputation and financial viability of the sponsor. The reputation of participating hospitals should also be assessed in terms of its impact on the first hospital's own position in the marketplace. Financial statements of the sponsor should be reviewed when possible, and detailed contract negotiations are required.

Careful consideration should be given to a contract that demands exclusive contracting with that PPO alone. Further, if the PPO is requiring a financial investment by the hospital, the hospital should carefully analyze what services will be provided by the PPO in return for funding, and whether it will be a worthwhile investment. As in the hospital-sponsored PPO, market analysis should be provided to contracting hospitals to assist in determining market share represented by the PPO. Also, the medical staff and the governing board should be well informed and thoroughly in agreement before contracting begins. Utilization-control mechanisms should be analyzed in terms of their impact on hospital inpatient usage, medical staff receptivity, and adherence to the hospital's basic mission.

SELECTION MECHANISMS AND ALTERNATIVE PAYMENT SYSTEMS IN PPO CONTRACTING

For a hospital contracting with a PPO, payment issues, like other managerial issues, are similar to those in hospital-sponsored PPOs. The contracting arrangement may not provide the hospital with as much flexibility in structuring contracts. Payors may offer terms on a "take it or leave it" basis, although hospitals always have the option of nonparticipation.

Methodologies used in selecting preferred hospitals in a non–hospital-sponsored PPO generally fall into two general categories: "unlimited participation" and "limited participation." The mechanics and impact of each of these alternatives are briefly discussed below.

Unlimited Participation

The unlimited participation approach offers a standard contract or a hospital specific contract to any hospital that wishes to participate and may use any payment unit (e.g., DRG, discount, per diem). Any hospital willing to accept the contract's term is free to participate as a preferred hospital. The advantage of this approach is that the hospital knows what is being offered and can determine whether the contract is in its own best financial interest. In an unlimited participation system a scenario can easily develop whereby all hospitals in an area elect to accept the contract and all hospitals are preferred. In this situation, no hospital will receive a volume increase to offset reduced revenue since subscribers will have no financial incentive to select one facility over another. On the other hand, electing not to participate may lead to a volume reduction, as patients go to other preferred facilities. Should a volume reduction occur, the hospital would receive less revenue and might not be able to offset the loss with cost reductions because of a high proportion of fixed costs.

If most of the costs are fixed, the hospital may find that not contracting reduces revenue more than costs. In that case, it may be wise to accept the contract since additional costs resulting from the PPO payments are minimal and any revenue, no matter how small, will help offset the fixed costs even without a volume increase.

Limited Participation/Competitive Bid

Another selection methodology is limited participation/competitive bid. Hospitals are asked to submit bids, and preferred hospitals are selected based on criteria that usually include quality, location of hospital, and current subscriber utilization of the hospital. Competitive bidding presents the hospital with considerable uncertainty. What is certain is that some hospitals will *not* be selected and a hospital that wants to be selected must come in with a low enough bid. The facility does not want to bid any lower than is necessary to be selected. Bids are often awarded for a year, allowing hospitals not selected in a given year to be selected in subsequent years. However, any payor using this approach will probably also want some stability from year to year in terms of which hospitals are preferred. This may tend to lock some hospitals in and others out on a long-term basis.

Under the competitive bid approach, the hospital is more certain of a volume increase than under the unlimited participation approach because not all hospitals will be selected. Some hospitals will be selected and subscribers given incentives to use *only* those facilities. Nonetheless, it is still in the hospital's interest to have a volume guarantee built in if possible. This may be impossible in a payor-sponsored program because the payor will issue a request for bids with no volume adjustments, leaving hospitals little choice.

Limited Participation/Payor Pre-selection

The third selection mechanism is for the sponsor to make the selection of a limited number of hospitals based on historical information and approach those facilities. Hospitals have no option to bid against each other in this arrangement. The specific manner of selecting facilities can vary from sponsor to sponsor.

Alternative Payment Options

Flexibility is the essential difference in terms of payment between the hospital- and non–hospital-sponsored PPO. In a hospital-sponsored PPO, the payment arrangement can be tailored to the individual payor/hospital relationship. For the hospital arrangement, standardized contracts are very likely because they are less costly.

In determining what discount is acceptable when deciding to accept a contract or in determining what discount to incorporate into a bid the analysis is consistent with what the hospital must do when sponsoring the PPO. This also applies to a per-diem, DRG, and capitation arrangement.

In summary, many of the issues relevant to hospital-sponsored PPOs must be considered in hospital contracting with outside PPOs. The key is to closely analyze payment options, market analysis, and legal issues before signing a contract.

CONCLUSION

PPOs as a form of selective contracting are indicative of the vast changes occurring in hospitals' environments. The impact on hospitals is and will continue to be great. As hospitals move into PPO arrangements, it is important to remember these basic points:

1. Be innovative. Whether designing a self-sponsored organization or contracting with another, hospitals should create a situation that will best fit the hospital's and the buyer's needs. Management should be creative in structuring and contracting.

2. Consider the options. When analyzing the feasibility of developing or contracting with a PPO, it is important to examine other types of organizations that might better serve the hospital. Perhaps an HMO,

EPO, or other arrangement would be most appropriate. Also, perhaps a decision not to enter an arrangement would be advantageous.

3. Examine the financial investment and long-term consequences of PPO involvement. Is it worth a $500,000 initial investment? What will be the long-term effect on the hospital's bottom line? What are the best options?

4. Consider the moral obligation or mission of the hospital. How will the concept of selecting out a certain group of consumers mesh with a hospital's mission to provide care to all? Would filling beds with PPO patients necessitate turning away other patients and thus conflict with the hospital's obligations?

5. Look at the effect on other payors. Will PPO involvement have negative or positive connotations for other payors? Will they demand the same payment schedule? Will they fear cost shifting? Can the hospital prove cost shifting will not occur?

The PPO movement is continuing, providing many options for hospitals. Success has yet to be fully evaluated from the hospital's, physician's, or buyer's perspective, but it seems a viable option. PPOs are currently relatively unregulated, with few constraints placed by state governments. Hospitals that adequately address issues raised in this chapter and become involved with PPOs have the opportunity to become a major force in the health care marketplace. Furthermore, these hospitals have opportunities for retention or expansion of market share that might otherwise be controlled through regulation.

NOTES

1. The chapter does not convey official policy of the American Hospital Association.

2. John Hatfield, and Joseph Kubal, "Preferred Provider Organizations," *Urban Health* January 1983.

3. Study completed July 1983.

4. K. Schroer, and E. Taylor, "A survey of preferred provider organizations," *Hospitals.* 58, no. 6 (March 16, 1984), pp. 85-6, 88.

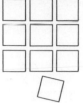

Impact of New Trends

COPING WITH COMPETITION

William T. Phillips, M.B.A.

Phillips & Associates, Inc.
Bethesda, MD

☐ The status quo for hospitals has been visably shaken by three recent competitive developments. They are excess capacity, employer utilization and cost review, and limitation of employer-provided health benefits.

Excess capacity refers to the number of generally unfilled hospital beds and/or a disproportionate ratio of physicians to population in a community. Both of these surpluses resulted from federal funds being used to expand hospitals and subsidize medical education. The funds were provided to alleviate or avert shortages of institutions and health care professionals, as predicted by several blue ribbon study groups.

The second factor in promoting competition is employer utilization and cost review. Although business has traditionally used the management techniques of quality control and accountability, it is a fairly new concept in health care. Employers are now using several methods for this purpose, including asking for more understandable reports from their insurance companies, contracting with professional standards review organizations (now called peer review organizations or PROs) to monitor and evaluate health care provided to employees, and hiring specialized firms to provide analytical tools and reports to document their health care spending. This enables them to make specific and comprehensive changes in their health care plans. For example, an employer may change a benefit within an existing health insurance plan or contract with a group of providers who have been identified as being cost-effective (the basis for PPO development). Utilization and cost review techniques used by employers are a direct result of the tremendous increases in the cost of health care in the past decade.

A third reason for the new competition is the limitation of employer-provided health benefits. These limitations have been occurring voluntarily through the rise of flexible benefit plans whereby employees may elect to reduce health care coverage in exchange for other types of benefits (the so-called cafeteria plans). Proposed changes in the IRS code could also limit future health benefits. For example, the Reagan Administration has advocated a limit on tax-free contributions by employers toward employee health insurance in order to raise revenue and instill greater cost consciousness.

SOURCES OF COMPETITION

New organizations are rapidly being formed to "capture" patients and place them in an alternative delivery system designed to have a favorable impact on the cost and use of health services. Two of the more common new arrangements are the health maintenance organization (HMO) and the preferred provider organization (PPO).

An HMO is a complete health care organization that combines the delivery and the financing of comprehensive health care services.

A PPO, on the other hand, is a health care delivery system comprised of hospitals and physicians who contract on an established fee-for-service basis and provide comprehensive medical services to subscribers.

Both HMOs and PPOs developed because of the continuing pressures of government and industry to contain the rate of increase in health care costs in recent years. Enrollment in each of these plans has reached substantial proportions in areas like Minneapolis/St. Paul and California. Other, more conservative areas, have multiple PPOs as well such as Tulsa, Oklahoma, and Birmingham, Alabama.

A third source of competition for hospitals, further segmenting the health care market, is free-standing emergency centers. These walk-in, fee-for-service centers are usually conveniently located in communities and provide physicians' services and ancillary services (such as X-rays and laboratory tests). The growth of these centers may have a negative impact on the number of emergency room visits, and therefore, on the total number of hospital admissions.

GROWTH OF COMPETITION

The introduction of HMOs or PPOs in an area also introduces substantial competition to a hospital. The growth of these organizations has the potential to restrict traditional sources of patients or divert patients from a hospital.

Hospitals are frequently unprepared for the rapid growth rate experienced by an HMO or multiple HMOs in some locations, due partly to historical perceptions. In the first two years of Kaiser's presence in Washington, D.C., their plan grew from 60,000 to almost 125,000 members. Of the approximately 175 qualified HMOs in 1982, over 10 percent experienced annual enrollment growth in excess of 10,000 members. In New Jersey, enrollment among the 11 HMOs grew from 164,805 members as of June, 1982 to 189,615 enrollees one year later, or an annual growth rate of 15 percent.

These new competitors in effect capture the hospital's patients by offering their services at a competitive price. The HMO member is essentially removed from the fee-for-service practice or captured by the HMO, usually for one year. Thus, HMO growth damages the hospital by substantially lowering its use. The damage indicator to hospitals may be difficult to perceive. To illustrate, assume HMO growth has started in a community, and the HMO has 15,000 members. The community has an under-65 hospital utilization rate of 875 days per 1,000 population. The HMO has a hospital utilization rate of 350 days per 1,000 members. The HMO has reduced the number of hospital days by 7,875 (15,000 members × (875 − 350)/1,000). If a 300-bed hospital does *not* have a contract with the HMO, patients that may have been previously admitted to this hospital may now be captured by the HMO and channeled to another hospital with whom the HMO has a contract.

Conversely, if the hospital has a contract with the HMO, it actually would gain about 5,250 patient days, most of which would be new patients (15,000 × 350/1,000).

While some continue to debate whether HMOs will be around, others are recognizing that a larger number of HMOs are now for profit and that they are viable. With a relatively modest growth rate of only 50 percent and 33 percent respectively for the next two years, HMO enrollment would grow to 22,500 and 30,000 members.

Assuming that the hospital utilization rates will remain about the same, then total hospital utilization will decline by almost 16,000 patient days. For the hospital without an HMO contract, patient days will decrease. For the two hospitals with an HMO contract, patient days will increase 6,125 for each of the hospitals (see Exhibit 1).

The damage indicators for a PPO are similar, particularly if the hospital (and its physicians) are *not* preferred providers. A community with a limited number of HMOs may offer more potential for a PPO, since PPOs are easier to form, are less costly, and develop more quickly.

Consider the following: two hospitals and an insurance company each develop PPOs in the same community, which greatly magnifies the

EXHIBIT 1
Loss of Patient Days

HMO membership × (Average hospital utilization rate − HMO hospital utilization rate)

$$30,000 \times \left(\frac{875 - 350}{1,000}\right)$$

	Lost Patient Days	Gained Patient Days	Net Change
Hospital A (No contract)	5,250	—	(5,250)
Hospital B (HMO contract)	5,250	6,125	875
Hospital C (HMO contract)	5,250	6,125	875
	15,750	12,250	

capturing effect. If each hospital-sponsored PPO achieves a participation level of 10,000 patients in two years, and the insurance company PPO achieves a participation level of 15,000 patients, the total number of people in alternative delivery systems (HMO or PPO) has increased from a modest 15,000 to 65,000 in just three years (see Exhibit 2).

EXHIBIT 2
Total Year-End Enrollment

	Year 1	Year 2	Year 3
HMO			
1	15,000	22,500	30,000
PPO 1	—	5,000	10,000
PPO 2	—	5,000	10,000
PPO 3	—	7,500	15,000
	15,000	40,000	65,000

Assume further that the PPOs collectively lower the hospital utilization rate from 875 days per 1,000 to 750 hospital days per 1,000 participants. The total reduction in hospital days for the community may be determined by adding the number of hospital days reduced by the PPO (4,375), yielding a total of 20,125 less hospital days in two years (see Exhibit 3).

For the two hospitals sponsoring PPOs, the number of hospital days generated by the PPO may be as many as 7,500 (750 days per 1,000

EXHIBIT 3
Total Loss of Hospital Days
(Year 3 enrollment)

HMO		
1	15,750	
PPO 1	1,250	
PPO 2	1,250	4,375
PPO 3	1,875	
	20,125	

population × 10,000 participants) if all PPO admissions are to the sponsoring hospital.

If there are five hospitals in the community with basically the same services, the hospital that does not contract with either the HMO or a PPO will have a decline in patient days of 4,025, as shown in Exhibit 4.

EXHIBIT 4
Net Gain (Loss) of Patient Days

	Patient Days Lost (HMO)	Patient Days Lost (PPO)	Patient Days Gain (HMO)	Patient Days Gain (PPO)	Net
Hospital A	3,150	875	—	—	(4,025)
Hospital B	3,150	875	6,125	5,625	7,725
Hospital C	3,150	875	6,125	5,625	7,725
Hospital D	3,150	875	—	7,500	3,475
Hospital E	3,150	875	—	7,500	3,475
	(15,750)	(4,375)	12,250	26,250	18,375

COMPETITIVE OPTIONS

Hospitals have tried to retain their autonomy by opening satellite clinics and other outpatient facilities to assure a steady flow of referrals in direct competition with private physicians and group practices. As such, it may not represent a politically viable solution.

One option is for hospitals to expand their lines of business and diversify into other health care businesses, as many voluntary hospitals are doing. Chief executive officers (CEOs) see diversification as a way to generate new revenues and raise additional capital for renovation and expansion. Often they are reorganizing their corporate structures at the same time. In one model, the hospital becomes the parent organization for a variety of subsidiaries. In another, it establishes a parent holding company, which owns the hospital as well as other subsidiaries.

Earlier, consideration of a PPO or HMO by a hospital was rare. Now, with declining patient days and PPO/HMO growth, diversification into HMO or PPO ownership and development is growing. Accomplished through subsidiaries or joint ventures, the hospital continues operating as in the past, but these new companies can pursue new nontraditional ventures and use the profits as it chooses.

CONCLUSIONS

The growth and development of alternative delivery systems represents a tremendous challenge and significant opportunities for hospitals and health care providers. As private sponsorship of HMOs and PPOs continue, hospitals and physicians must recognize that the new organizations will capture their patients and inflict damage on the traditional source of patients.

This will require a nontraditional competitive response, if the hospital and physician are to retain their present market share of patients. Direct sponsorship of a preferred provider organization by a hospital, a coalition of hospitals, or multihospital system is now emerging. Similarly, group practices and other physician groups are now sponsoring PPOs. Both have recognized the need for an effective response to competition. The PPO is one excellent strategic response. In tough times, new strategies are required for a hospital or physician.

PREFERRED PROVIDER ORGANIZATIONS: AN INVESTOR-OWNED PERSPECTIVE

Charles P. Reilly
Executive Vice President
American Medical International
Beverly Hills, CA

☐ Of the many measures proposed to control rising health care costs, the preferred provider organization (PPO) is perhaps the least controversial. The PPO seems to offer something for everyone. For health care purchasers, it provides a means of negotiating lower rates. For health care providers, it offers a potential way to increase their market share. And for consumers, it offers savings by lowering or eliminating copayments and deductibles if they are treated by a preferred provider, while still allowing them the option of choosing a physician or health facility outside the preferred network.

While PPOs come in so many different forms as to defy a tidy definition, at the heart of every PPO is an elemental concept—the interaction of supply and demand. PPOs offer advantageous fees to purchasers in exchange for improving their market share. Simply put, the PPO is a mechanism for discounting the unit price for health services in exchange for greater volume.

CHANGING MARKETPLACE

Although discounting products and services to garner a greater market share is a common practice in most industries, it is a relatively new one to health care. In recent years, however, health care costs have risen to the level where they are meeting resistance from major purchasers.

For example, American business has experienced a 250 percent increase in expenditures for employee health benefits in the last decade. In 1983, Atlantic Richfield Co. spent more than $100 million on health insurance. Ford Motor Co.'s health bill exceeded $743 million—up $33 million from the year before—and General Motors Corp. paid out a staggering $2.2 billion in medical benefits.

In all, business spent more than $77 billion on health insurance in 1983, more than $100 billion if related administrative costs are factored in. Faced with these formidable and ever increasing costs, American business is taking a more active role in negotiating their employee health benefits. Employers are looking to alternative forms of insurance, plans that encourage cost sharing, second surgical opinions, preadmissions testing, and payment procedures that are not biased in favor of more costly treatment.

This new determination to contain costs comes at a time when changing utilization patterns have also resulted in unprecedented competition among providers. There is no longer a shortage of hospital beds in this country, nor is there a shortage of physicians. Hospitals, physicians, and other health care facilities find themselves competing for patients at a time when the purchasers of health care, namely government and business, possess a firm resolve to lower cost. In such a competitive and cost-conscious market the PPO concept has arisen.

Although the efficacy of PPOs in reducing health care costs is as yet undetermined, the PPO does attempt to rectify some of the inefficiencies of our third-party payment system. Historically, physicians have prescribed treatment for which neither they nor their patients were paying. It has been a system that has provided little incentive for cost efficiency. The consumer was not compelled to consider cost when choosing a physician, the physician had no incentive to shop prices at competing hospitals, and the hospital did not have the authority to question the cost of the physician's prescribed course of treatment.

The third-party payment system has also helped to mask the true cost of health care by dispersing rising costs over such a broad spectrum of the economy that no particular constituency became alarmed enough to demand reform. Business and industry, for example, passed on the cost of higher health insurance premiums to the public in the form of higher prices for goods and services. The government offset higher medicare costs through higher social security taxes. And the health care consumer, who was usually well insured by either government or industry, suffered under the dangerous illusion that health care was a lot cheaper than it really is. The third-party payment system helped create a climate in which cost efficiency was more the exception than the rule.

What the PPO attempts to do is bring the buyer and seller of health services closer together—to allow the traditional market forces of supply and demand to interact. It tries to match up what the purchasers of health care want (lower costs) with what the providers of health care services want (more market share). The theory is simple, though the development of a successful PPO is obviously a complex process in which the various needs of all the parties involved (physicians, hospitals, employer, employees, and insurance companies) must be met.

THE PPO AND THE INVESTOR-OWNED HOSPITAL INDUSTRY

The investor-owned hospital industry is playing an increasingly vital role in the delivery of health care. The industry has grown dramatically in recent years—up 40 percent since 1977—and now accounts for about one in five community-based, nongovernment facilities.

Although the investor-owned industry still accounts for a limited share of the total U.S. health care delivery system, it has been an active force in the marketplace. The larger investor-owned companies all have aggressive acquisitions and marketing programs. And like all successful businesses, they are continually looking for new ways to make their products and services more attractive to consumers.

The leading investor-owned companies have been broadening their mix of products and services for a number of years. Industry giants such as AMI, HCA, Humana, and NME have, to varying degrees, invested in outpatient surgical centers, urgent care centers, clinics for the treatment of alcoholism and drug abuse, home health care services, diagnostic imaging laboratories, psychiatric hospitals, and nursing homes. There is a clear trend toward the development of regional health care networks that will offer consumers a complete menu of health care services. In a competitive marketplace, expanding the range of services and facilities is a way to generate more patient referrals by covering more points of entry into the health care system. Obviously, such integrated networks provide a ready framework for marketing PPOs, HMOs, or other insurance products.

Because investor-owned companies are competing in the same health care market as nonprofit facilities are, their approach to developing provider-based PPOs is much the same. Most investor-owned companies view the PPO as a viable and potentially profitable marketing tool.

One of the advantages of the PPO is that it can be tailored to meet the needs of specific markets. Some provider-initiated PPOs include a limited menu of health services, such as hospital care only. Others include a comprehensive provider network of physicians, hospitals, diagnostic laboratories, pharmacies, and outpatient surgical centers. PPOs can be targeted at either large or small groups. Some PPOs are marketed directly to self-insured employers, while others are part of a standard insurance product.

Although PPOs defy a tidy definition, they do share certain family resemblances. Most PPOs, whether initiated by a nonprofit or a for-profit provider, include most of the following characteristics (features peculiar to the investor-owned industry are given special mention).

1. Negotiated Fees. At the heart of every PPO is an attempt to negotiate lower fees in exchange for a predictable and potentially greater market share. In addition to simply lowering current rates, some PPOs include a formula that is agreeable to the purchasers for future price changes. Employers, for example, are apt to be more concerned about lowering the cost of their employee health benefits over the long haul than about simply securing a short-term gain. PPOs can be developed to provide a guaranteed cap on employer costs over a specific time period.

2. Prompt Payment. In exchange for lower fees, some PPOs stipulate prompter payment to improve the provider's cash flow.

3. Provider Network. The product of the PPO is its network of providers. A provider network can be composed of physicians, hospitals, or a comprehensive network of health care facilities. In general, the broader the scope of services offered by a PPO, the more attractive it will be to the purchaser. A self-insured employer, for example, would find it far simpler to contract with 1 provider than with 20. In areas where a leading investor-owned company already has a network of hospitals and alternative facilities in place, it might have the edge. We seem to be moving toward an era of "brand name" medicine, where purchasers might be more inclined to contract with a known entity, such as AMI or HCA, rather than with an ad hoc affiliation of providers.

PPOs developed by investor-owned hospital companies have been of all types. Some offer only preferred hospital rates; others include a wide variety or services. Because large, investor-owned companies may operate a number of different hospitals and alternative centers in a given market, they can use their own facilities as the core of a comprehensive provider network, contracting with physicians and other providers as required.

Naturally, if an investor-owned company is to develop a provider network beyond the scope of its own facilities, the cooperation of physicians is essential. Physicians must agree to charge lower fees in the hopes of boosting their patient loads. With the ratio of physicians to population continuing to rise, more and more physicians are apt to find such an arrangement attractive.

To help recruit physicians, investor-owned companies are offering a number of support services. AMI, for example, offers management and marketing advice to help its physicians run their practices more efficiently and boost their patient loads.

4. Quality. The sine qua non of any health care transaction is quality. The American people traditionally place the highest value on human life, and demand the best in health care for themselves and their families. It is difficult to conceive of American consumers accepting any health care service that they consider to be less than the best medical science has to offer. Moreover, no responsible physician, hospital, or other provider would lower the standard of care as a means for lowering fees. Quality is the most essential element in health care and can not be compromised in the interests of competition.

5. Accessibility. Accessibility is another dimension of quality. Providers obviously must be located in reasonably convenient locations. The PPO should also include provisions to address other patient concerns, such as minimized waiting time. These concerns, from the investor-owned perspective, are simply good business. Many employers, for example, have strong union or other employee groups which have a voice in the selection or change of health benefits. If a PPO does not address the concerns of its potential membership, it is unlikely to be a viable product in the marketplace.

One of the great strengths of the investor-owned industry is the recognition that patients are *customers*—and ensuring customer satisfaction is an integral part of any successful business. AMI, for example, has ongoing market research programs designed to monitor the attitudes of patients, physicians, and other key audiences toward its facilities and services. Investor-owned companies often have more aggressive marketing strategies designed to determine what consumers want and to adapt their health care services to meet those needs.

6. Utilization Review. Utilization review (UR) is accepted by both business and health care providers as an effective tool for cost control. UR ensures that care is given in an appropriate but cost-effective manner. Though systems vary widely, they may include provisions for preadmission certification, continued stay review, second surgical opinions, and ancillary services review. Surgical reviews in a PPO that includes outpatient surgical centers can offer significant savings by routing surgical procedures—when appropriate—to outpatient facilities.

An effective UR program is essential to the success of any PPO. A provider-based PPO can not expect to lower fees solely on the prospect of increasing volume. Provisions must be made to continually refine the system and monitor it for cost efficiency. A comprehensive UR program also ensures that providers do not increase the number of services merely to offset lower fees.

Investor-owned companies are also using UR as an effective tool for recruitment. UR can identify physicians with a track record of cost-effective utilization of hospital and alternative services. Many PPOs also include provisions for dropping physicians or other providers from the network if their style of practice suggests a consistent disregard for cost-efficient treatment.

7. Choice. Patient participation in a PPO is never mandatory—although a related concept, the exclusive provider organization (EPO), is also being tried in some areas. In the typical PPO, the patient still receives partial coverage, usually 80 percent, for treatment from physicians and facilities outside the preferred network. Though one of the selling points of PPOs is freedom of choice, they nevertheless create a financial incentive to use the preferred provider. In addition, the PPO tends to make the patient a more cost-conscious and responsible consumer of health care services—something that the traditional third-party payment system did not encourage.

8. Flexibility. PPOs are designed to meet the needs of a specific market place and specific health care purchasers. For example, a PPO can be tailored to meet the specific needs of an employer in terms of deductibles, copayments, and so forth. This flexibility in design also allows the provider to construct a plan with sufficient patient incentives to ensure the desired increase in patients.

THE FUTURE OF PPOs IN FOR-PROFIT HEALTH CARE

The large investor-owned health care companies are, in general, well positioned to develop effective PPOs. First, as was mentioned earlier, many of the industry giants, such as AMI, HCA, and Humana, already have in place a nationwide network of hospital and outpatient services. These facilities are linked to centralized systems of management review and cost control and can serve to anchor a provider network organized to meet the needs of the multilocationed employer or insurer.

Though investor-owned companies may have to contract with physicians or other providers outside their network to develop a PPO in a given market, they have an umbrella organization in place that is potentially attractive to the employer or insurer who would otherwise have to deal with multiple provider groups.

The investor-owned health care companies are perhaps better positioned to develop provider-based PPOs than nonprofit facilities are for the following reasons.

INTERNAL MANAGEMENT CAPABILITIES

Management systems, such as financial reporting, cost accounting, clinical, and patient data, are expensive both to develop and run. Despite the operating savings these systems might ultimately generate, many smaller, nonprofit providers cannot afford to develop them.

Where small providers do implement such systems, they may have to sell excess capacity to other providers to justify the investment and to absorb operating overhead. Such sales programs require additional personnel and generate costs of their own. The small provider that chooses to buy excess capacity may generate some savings for itself, but will bear the hidden costs of having to use a system designed to meet the specific needs of an institution or management other than its own.

The large, investor-owned systems, however, have had the capital to develop sophisticated management systems, to acquire the equipment and personnel required to run them, and to justify the ongoing operating costs. Since the facilities of investor-owned companies are already part of an integrated system with a single operating philosophy, use of the system does not demand that facilities accommodate the needs of an outside vendor.

The industry giants thus have the potential, through their financial data processing systems, to price potential business on factual data, knowing (1) what it costs to treat their present base of business, and (2) how that cost can be decreased incrementally as volume of new business increases accordingly.

Since investor-owned systems own most if not all of their facilities, this centralized management capability allows them to price effectively and to respond to contract market bids quickly.

CAPITAL STRENGTH

Developing and marketing a PPO or related product involves many of the financial risks of starting a new business. The capital strength of large, investor-owned systems allows them to assume these risks and to absorb short-term losses in exchange for potential long-term gains. Undercapitalized nonprofit institutions may lack the financial resources to assume an aggressive, risk-taking stance in the marketplace.

The capital strength of the investor-owned giants also gives them other options in developing PPOs. In addition to marketing a PPO to employers through an insurance intermediary, or directly to self-insured employers, large investor-owned companies can choose to underwrite their own insurance plans. They can, in effect, buy or establish their own insurance companies for the purpose of marketing a health benefits package directly to business and industry.

The current industry trend toward the development of regional health care networks with a broad range of services is a strategy designed to facilitate a wide variety of options for selective contracting—PPOs, HMOs, and other insurance products.

PRODUCT DEVELOPMENT AND MARKETING

The entrepreneurial spirit that founded the investor-owned health care industry is well suited to today's highly competitive health care market. The large investor-owned companies already have in place the core strategic planning, market research, and marketing staff to develop effective PPOs and related products for given markets.

Though the same capabilities often exist in nonprofit health care systems, many smaller nonprofit institutions have lagged behind in the development of an effective marketing effort. Many of these smaller providers simply lack the personnel and capital to undertake sophisticated market research, product development, and promotion.

PPOs being developed by smaller nonprofit providers are often defensive—offering discounts in order to retain their current business, but lacking long-term potential to increase the provider's market share. Some investor-owned giants, however, have aggressive long-range marketing plans that include underwriting insurance risks, guaranteeing a cap on employee health costs, and offering a combined product line of PPOs, HMOs, and other health care plans.

Although the PPO is too recent a phenomenon to predict what ultimate form the concept may take, investor-owned companies are actively exploring its potential to improve their market share. The PPO is obviously just one of many possible provider responses to an increasingly competitive and market-driven health care environment.

The investor-owned health care companies, for the most part, see the PPO as a *transitional* strategy in the evolution of more comprehensive health care products. The capital resources of the larger investor-owned companies, combined with their internal management capabilities and their penchant for aggressive marketing and promotion, are apt to give them the edge over many nonprofit facilities in the development of both PPOs and the still evolving health care products of the future.

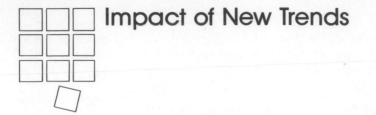 Impact of New Trends

PUBLIC HOSPITALS IN A COMPETITIVE ENVIRONMENT: CAN THE SAFETY NET SURVIVE?

Carol B. Emmott, Ph.D.
Executive Director
California Association of Public Hospitals
San Mateo, CA

Through a wide variety of governance structures and subsidy practices, public hospitals across the country serve as an institutional "safety net" in meeting health needs that are inadequately addressed in the private sector. Widely varying regulatory practices, eligibility patterns, and reimbursement mechanisms in both publicly and privately sponsored payment systems have resulted in a patchwork medical "system." With no centralized planning or uniform coverage, eligibility, or payment principles, a large proportion of the population and a costly range of services fall through the cracks of the "mainstream" system.

The nation's public hospitals were created and have been maintained to meet these complex needs. Through this complementary mission, these facilities care for patients routinely excluded from the private sector and often provide services that have been determined to be economically unattractive to private providers.

Nationally, public hospitals provide 23 percent of medicaid supported indigent care and up to 43 percent of bad debt and charity care. California has the most extensive of the states' public hospital systems, constituting 11.9 percent of the State's available bed complement. Recently published statistics[1] provide detailed insights into the unique patient and service mix of California's county hospitals, a pattern that is probably illustrative of public health care systems throughout the country. For example, with only 11.9 percent of the state's available beds providing 12.7 percent of all hospital services, California's public hospitals

— Provide 70.5 percent of all psychiatric emergency services, 59.2 percent of all hospital clinic services, 32.3 percent of all burn care, 24.7 percent of all rehabilitation care, and 19.9 percent of all coronary intensive care services.

— Prior to recent eligibility cutbacks, provided 27.7 percent of all Medi-Cal hospital services, 39.0 percent of all hospital services to costly medically indigent adults (MIAs), and 42.4 percent of all hospital services to costly medically needy users.

— Experienced a 45 percent annual increase in their uncompensated care burden as a result of recent Medi-Cal eligibility cutbacks.

— Provide a broad range of public health, mental health, and substance abuse programs, as well as linguistically accessible services to the State's monolingual and immigrant populations.

— Have little opportunity to cost shift, as the role of private insurance in their revenue base is only 37 percent of that of their private sector counterparts.

— Have deteriorating physical plants that are 67 percent older than private facilities and capital investment rates of less than one quarter of private hospitals, despite increased service demand and the spectre of competition for their sponsored patients.

Even before the recent wave of major reforms in health care organization and payment practices at both national and state levels, public hospitals often faced overwhelming odds in maintaining their uneconomical service and patient mix. In fact, closures of public hospitals throughout the country have become routine. For example before 1965, 49 of California's 58 counties operated 65 county hospitals. By 1982 that number had dwindled to only 31 general acute hospitals in 24 counties. At best, these closures have required local government to purchase more expensive private care or have imposed burgeoning charity care demands on private providers. At worst, public hospital closures have left many indigents without reasonable access to necessary care. Almost all of the many changes in reimbursement practices in all public and private payment systems hold the possibility of increasing the fiscal pressures on these "safety net" institutions. Unless corrective action is undertaken, the increasing gap between demands and resources could well result in further closures—with now predictable effects on patients, private providers, and/or local governments.

Despite the lack of coherent organization and planning, the American health care system is in fact a system in the technical meaning of the word. Change or reform in one sector produces significant spill-over effects on related parts. Whether viewed as mirror images or hand-in-glove relationships, public and private systems of care are intimately linked. For example, constraints on reimbursement in medicaid programs over the last few years have resulted in reduction in private participation and increased medicaid usage of public facilities. Currently, institution of prospective payment in medicare has created the incentive to identify "unprofitable" patients. Software vendors are actively marketing systems to identify these patients and assist hospitals in tailoring their case mix or "product line" to contribute to a healthy "bottom line." Public hospitals will be the most likely recipient of patients referred or transferred from private facilities. Many California county facilities report increases in their medicare caseload subsequent to the phased implementation of the prospective payment system that began in October of 1983.

COMPETITION AND PUBLIC PROVIDERS AND PATIENTS

Private insurance only constitutes 14 percent of the revenue base of California's public hospitals, compared to 38 percent in private institutions. In contrast, 73 percent of their revenues are attributable to Medi-Cal (California's medicaid program) and subsidy programs for unsponsored indigents. As a result of this unique financing structure, California's public hospital administrators concentrated on Medi-Cal hospital contracting and the transfer of the medically indigent adults (MIAs) during debate on the reforms enacted by the California Legislature in 1982.

Relatively little attention was paid to the significant 1982 reforms in private insurance practices imposed by AB 3480. This legislation, like similar reforms in other states, permits insurers and employers to play a more active role in cost containment through direct purchase of care. As the dust settles and the potential impacts of these multifaceted reforms are being better assessed, it is becoming clear that too little attention was paid to possible impacts of introducing "competition" into private payment systems.

The interdependence of public and private systems of care can be expected to produce significant shifts in patient demands. Unlike shifts of Medi-Cal and medicare patients, however, the shifts anticipated as a result of private sector competition and PPO contracting will impose increased demands for totally uncompensated care on public facilities.

This conclusion derives from two assumptions:

— The importance of price discounts in meeting the cost-containment objectives of PPO developers.
— The poorly understood but effective historical partnership between public and private providers in meeting the needs of unsponsored patients.

Debate has raged for years as to whether competition or regulation is the best approach to health cost containment. California stands in the forefront of adherents to the competition approach. As a result of overly generous retrospective reimbursement, the health care system has developed inefficient wasteful practices that may, in theory, be improved as a result of "competitive" pressure or the need to provide services with less resources. The efforts of PPOs to stimulate greater health care efficiency should be universally applauded and will, no doubt, improve the cost consciousness of providers without necessarily compromising quality of care.

While the cost-containment approaches of developing PPOs are difficult to assess definitively at this time, academic and other observers of this quiet revolution confirm public hospital administrators' worst fears.[2] It appears clear that during the initial development phase, PPOs are relying primarily on price discounting for their cost savings, rather than developing sophisticated utilization-control mechanisms. Providing price discounts to private payors as well as to Medi-Cal will create an incentive to reduce unit costs and improve efficiency. Improvements of this sort will be slow in coming, however, and cannot be assumed to cover the level of price discounts requested by PPO negotiators. As a consequence, the most readily available method of adapting to reductions in private reimbursement levels will be decreases in the level of bad debt and charity care carried by private providers.

This anticipated phenomenon will produce a "reverse cost shift" whereby private sector economies will be effected at the expense of public providers to whom unsponsored and inadequately covered individuals will be referred or transferred. One might argue that one of the major explicit objectives of competitive strategies has been reduction in the "cost shift" through which private providers have compensated for contractual, bad debt, and charity losses by raising charges to private payors. It can also be argued that the role of California's county hospitals is to meet the needs of unsponsored patients. Both are true.

Nevertheless, policymakers failed to understand the scope and size of this imperfect but effective means of spreading the costs of indigent care or the impact of cost-shift reduction on public providers. In addition, policymakers have thus far failed to take account of the more subtle secondary ways that private sector savings will be achieved at the expense of public providers.

PRIMARY IMPACTS

Indigent care is subsidized in California, as in most states, through a combination of direct subsidies to public providers by means of state and local tax revenues and through provider assumption of a bad debt and charity care burden. Because of the latitude providers have had in escalating charges to charge-paying insurers, uncompensated costs have been "cross-subsidized" by private payors.

This indirect approach to indigent care finance has little to commend it conceptually or in terms of its impact on escalating costs of private care. Its only defense is that it *worked*—worked in successfully spreading indigent costs and worked by keeping a substantial proportion of these costs off the tax rolls.

Consider these facts: In 1980-1981, 31 California public hospitals shouldered 7 to 10 times the burden of bad debt and charity care costs as compared to segments of the private hospital community. ($115 per patient day in public hospitals, compared to $11 to $16 per patient day in private hospitals.)[3] This trend was dramatically exacerbated in 1983 with repeal of Medi-Cal eligibility for the Medically Indigent Adults, raising public hospitals' share of uncompensated costs from an estimated 35 percent to 45 percent of the state's total burden.[4] Despite the concentration of 45 percent of uncompensated costs in only 5 percent of the state's hospitals, private facilities still recorded an estimated $456.3 million in uncompensated costs in 1983, up an estimated $38.1 million or 9.1 percent from 1982. Despite this increased burden, private hospitals recorded increases in profits of 7 to 40 percent in this year following the Medi-Cal reforms as a result of their continued ability to increase charges to private payors.

It is not difficult to deduce the likely behavior of private facilities as they begin to feel the financial pinch from negotiating price discounts with private payors. In fact, California Hospital Association's 1983 survey data have documented the beginning of the shift. A 32 percent increase in uncompensated care in the first six months of 1983, shifted in the third quarter to only 19 percent over 1982 levels.[5] While fiscal pressures will no doubt encourage some actual decreases in the costs of care, PPO reliance on sizeable price discounts will force private providers to intensify their financial screening practices. Those that fail their "wallet biopsies," owing to lack of insurance or inadequate insurance, will be referred or transferred to public facilities where available.

The private sector can be expected to continue some level of care to unsponsored patients, due to remaining Hill-Burton free care obligations, hospital trustee commitments, and the requirement under California law that hospitals operating emergency rooms serve emergency patients without regard to their ability to pay. Nevertheless, the volume of uncompensated care provided by private facilities is large enough that a shift of any magnitude will place unmanageable demands on public facilities. To understand the potential scope of the problem, complete elimination of the private sector cost shift through a transfer of all private hospital uncompensated care costs to public facilities would increase the county facilities' burden 123 percent. This data, it should be noted, does not incorporate any physician costs.

With augmented indigent care support, California's public hospitals can assume some of this burden previously borne by private hospitals. However, there are limits on the state's understanding of the potential reverse cost-shift phenomenon and on the current political commitment to needs of the poor. In addition, transfer of the MIAs has utilized a good portion of the slack capacity of county hospitals, bringing occupancy levels now up to 80 percent. Therefore, both operating support and capacity limits will make any wholesale shift of the private sector's indigent care burden most difficult.

Far more subtle than the general incentive to reduce the indigent care cross-subsidization are incentives within the PPO movement to reduce cross-subsidization for other noneconomic patients. Those charged with purchase of health care for younger, healthier employees whose health costs are predictable are clearly seeking to "segment" their populations and remove them from risk-pooling arrangements. Current insurance practices require that these employers contribute to the costs of care for older, more costly, less predictable groups of employees.

Through the rapid proliferation of plans, employers now have broad choices. Not only can they self-insure and develop their own contracting process if their size warrants it, but they can choose from a vast array of plans tailored to their exact needs. Through this process, the imperfect but effective system for distributing the costs of high-risk groups over a broader population will be lost. As a consequence, older employee groups and those with special health risks will find limited access to PPOs. These groups, along with small employee groups whose health cost experience is less predictable, will face rapid escalation in already unacceptably high rates from indemnity carriers. Some will be able to pay. Many will purchase inadequate coverage that will provide only limited access to private providers. Others will simply be forced out of the private insurance market and will rely on public facilities whose "open door" philosophies dictate that medical needs transcend ability-to-pay considerations. For the elderly, who have previously purchased "medicare wrap around coverage," rapid escalation in insurance costs can be expected to swell the numbers of those who become dually qualified for medicare and Medi-Cal, thereby increasing both State and federal health costs.

SECONDARY IMPACTS

A review of some of the more technical cost-containment devices under consideration by developing PPOs suggests additional "reverse cost-shift" mechanisms that will increase the burden on public safety net systems.

Developing PPOs appear to be considering modest to rather extreme benefit limits. Limits on dental and psychiatric care are widespread among existing plans. Such limits can be expected to expand significantly as PPO plan developers seek to limit their liability for some of the more costly types of services. Should such practices be permitted, otherwise covered individuals will become "therapeutic orphans" when they encounter certain costly health needs. Public facilities are particularly vulnerable to these pressures because they tend to concentrate their service mix in exactly those high-cost areas, such as rehabilitative care, which may well be excluded from benefit packages.

Another major device in reducing premium costs appears to be significant increases in copays and deductibles. Experience has shown that young and healthy populations are most inclined to take their chances with potentially high out-of-pocket costs. While this pattern may appear to be a relatively good risk for such populations, younger employees can require very costly services but are rarely in a financial position to assume heavy out-of-pocket costs. Such individuals will be viewed as bad financial risks by private facilities. As a result, a portion of this population can be expected to turn to public facilities for partially subsidized care.

A final, still more subtle, proposed PPO practice that may shift an increasing burden onto public facilities is limits on the accessibility of care. Some plans are considering access barriers, such as only 9 A.M. to 5 P.M. coverage for nonemergent care. Others may misgauge the numbers of providers required and impose delays on accessing needed care. Both intended and unintended barriers to care can be expected to result in some spill-over to public systems, particularly their busy emergency departments.

All or some of these cost-cutting devices may be adopted in the name of PPO premium reductions. Certainly, the public has demanded more affordable health coverage. However, the smorgasbord of widely varying plans that will soon confront the consumer will require complex risk/benefit calculations. Some would argue for the individual's right to opt for inadequate, inexpensive coverage. Few, however, are prepared to acknowledge that the consumer's choice between high premiums, good coverage, and low out-of-pocket costs versus low premiums, poor coverage, and high out-of-pocket costs will often be poorly informed. Furthermore, part of the costs of bad decisions will be borne neither by enrollees or their PPOs but by public providers and/or public payment systems. Through these subtle mechanisms, premium savings will often result in increased demands on the public hospital system and eventual public subsidy of private payment systems.

IMPACT OF CONTRACTING AND PAYMENT POLICIES

Although public hospitals are only 37 percent as reliant on the contribution of private insurance to their revenue base as their private sector counterparts, their tenuous financial base requires that they be concerned about reductions in these revenues. PPO development can impose two distinct threats to this portion of the public hospital revenue base: failure of PPOs to directly contract with them and PPO policies regarding out-of-plan emergency and tertiary care.

Public hospitals view the competition arena across a distinctly uneven playing field. In California, Proposition 13 has precluded use of general obligation bonds to meet the widening gap between capitalization in public and private facilities. In addition, the reliance of public hospitals on state and county annual appropriations for now almost one half of their revenues has prevented most of them from utilizing revenue bonds in meeting their capital needs. As a result, these facilities are 67 percent older than private hospitals and fall 62 percent to 83 percent below private facilities on various measures of capital investment rates. Aging capital plants contribute to the remaining stigma attached to these "indigent care" facilities. Despite the efforts of some public facilities whose private insurance base constitutes 20 percent of revenues and whose capital plants approach the amenities available in the private sector, PPO entrepreneurs have displayed little interest in directly contracting with the facilities on whom they depend for many of their cost-cutting measures. In addition, PPO developers have failed to develop tertiary care contracts with public hospitals, even in the specialty care areas (such as burn and rehabilitation care) where public facilities play a predominate role.

The second means by which public facilities will be directly disadvantaged by PPO policies is through policies established regarding reimbursement for out-of-plan care. Public facilities typically serve as the major trauma providers in their communities. While private hospitals only admit 28 percent of their patients through their emergency rooms, public facilities admit 58 percent through their emergency rooms. As a result, a good proportion of their private patient caseload enters as a result of trauma or other emergency care needs.

If PPOs are permitted to impose excessively rigid definitions of covered "emergency" services or to pay for care at rates substantially below costs, public facilities could be dealt yet another "competitive" blow. The California HMO industry has already attempted to limit their payments for out-of-plan emergency care to Medi-Cal contract rates. Yet public hospitals' total costs for emergency room admissions exceed average inpatient costs by 35 percent. PPOs should be required to compensate fairly for legitimate emergency care needs of their enrollees.

CONCLUSION

Through their short-sighted pursuit of cost savings, private purchasers of health care, competition advocates, policy makers, and PPO developers have paid little attention to the destructive impacts of their actions on the fragile indigent care system. PPOs could well provide the final blow that would make the public hospital system financially unviable by

— Reducing the level of uncompensated care delivered by private providers.

— Pricing affordable, adequate health insurance out of the reach of older, sicker, or less predictable populations.

— Imposing limits on coverage or access to necessary services to enrollees.

— Failing to contract directly with high quality public providers.

— Undercompensating emergency care providers for services to their enrollees.

More importantly, the vulnerable populations that depend on public providers for service could be set adrift in a competitive private market place where private providers must focus almost exclusively on the "bottom line." Private providers can hardly be expected to reverse the pattern of reducing their uncompensated costs and significantly expand their indigent care commitment in response to public hospital closures or cutbacks.

As noted above, complete elimination of the indigent care cost shift and transfer of almost a half billion dollars worth of uncompensated hospital care to public facilities overstates the problem but does give a sense of its scope. Similarly, it is useful to consider that 1980-1981 data show that closure of all public facilities and distribution of their bad debt and charity care costs to private facilities would increase the per patient day uncompensated care burden on these facilities from 176 percent to 211 percent in various sectors of the private hospital community.[6] In view of a 56 percent increase in uncompensated care costs in public facilities since that time and the declining utilization in private hospitals, these figures grossly understate the impact of public hospital closures.

Regardless of the need to provide affordable health care options to private purchasers and a political climate that is ill-disposed to concern itself with the poor and needy, simple pragmatism requires that this potential problem be addressed. What is at stake is far more than public hospitals themselves. What is at stake is the quality of this country's social contract with the sick and poor.

Congress is highly unlikely to extend medicaid to all the unsponsored poor. As a result, the "safety net" must be preserved to ensure access to life-preserving services to indigents who fall through the schism that separates private and public payment systems. Operating and capital support for public facilities must be augmented to meet the growing needs of those excluded from the mainstream competitive system. Adequate funding of the resulting two-tiered system may well be sufficient. However, policymakers must also be ready to complement this approach with a means of enabling some private providers to continue a contribution to meeting indigent needs that exceed the physical resources of public facilities. In addition, methods must be identified to address indigent care needs in areas that lack safety net providers. In California, the medically indigent adult transfer, through which counties have served as both direct providers of care and also as brokers of privately purchased care, may provide a useful model.

The debate must begin, before a further diminution in the ranks of public facilities occurs. Without this invaluable resource, competition will not succeed and will have to be replaced by an approach that distributes and pays for indigent care costs in the context of a regulated cost-containment system.

NOTES

1. *Health Care in the 80's—Can the Safety Net Survive?*, White Paper of the California Association of Public Hospitals, March 1984.

2. Joan B. Trauner, "Preferred Provider Organizations: The California Experiment," *Monograph Series,* Institute for Health Policy Studies, University of California, San Francisco, August 1983.

3. California Association of Public Hospitals analysis of California Health Facility Commission data. Charge data was adjusted to "costs" by a ratio of operating expense to charges.

4. California Association of Public Hospitals analysis of 1983 Third Quarter Year-to-Date data regarding "revenue reductions," using an estimate for the fourth quarter and 1981–82 ratios for the proportion that bad debt and charity care represent of total revenue deductions.

5. "MIAs Reappear in County Hospitals," *CHA Insight,* March 1984.

6. California Association of Public Hospitals analysis of California Health Facility Commission data. Charge data was adjusted to "costs" by a ratio of operating expense to charges.

Impact of New Trends

FROM INDEMNITY INSURANCE TO HEALTHCARE DELIVERY *

Sheila Riley, J.D.

Corporate Law Department
State Farm Mutual Automobile Insurance Company
Bloomington, IL

Why should employers and health care providers care whether insurance companies create and operate PPOs? The answer to this question lies in avoiding problems that are created when employers group together to form a PPO or when health care providers group together for the same purpose.

Preferred provider organizations, like health maintenance organizations, are arrangements to provide medical care. They are by their nature regional and local. Thus, except for the largest employers who are also centralized in their employees' location, employers must group together to form a PPO. It is that collective action that creates problems that a single company, such as an insurance company, does not have.

The first and most immediate problem is that in grouping together, they may take themselves out of ERISA's[1] protections from state regula-

*The views expressed in this chapter are those of the author and do not necessarily represent the views of State Farm Insurance Companies. I wish to express my appreciation to Elizabeth Grantham for her assistance and research.

tion. An employer may "self-insure," assuming risks that would otherwise be the business of insurance, only if the employer meets the definitions of an ERISA trust. Otherwise, if a group of employers are assuming risk that is normally within the definition of the business of insurance, they are subject to state insurance regulatory laws. They must comply with the solvency laws relating to insurance companies, and if they are not to qualify as a multiple employer trust pursuant to ERISA, then they must qualify under the insurance code to continue to do business. The state insurance commissioners have announced their intention to enforce these requirements, and a 1982 amendment to ERISA has made it procedurally easier for them to do so.

The second risk is that when employers (or health care providers) group together to purchase health care services, it raises antitrust issues that are unresolved. It is not an area in which an attorney specializing in antitrust can give an opinion that if the employer group (or health care provider group) creates and operates their PPO within a certain framework, they will be relatively safe from antitrust litigation. All they can say is that there are substantial unresolved risks at this time. Such groups are subject to the risk of a full-blown trial.

There are two reasons that make the threat of antitrust litigation particularly onerous. The first is that such litigation which is not dismissed by summary judgment, is vastly more expensive than virtually any other type of litigation. The importance of this point is that the great majority of antitrust litigation expenses are incurred in preparation for and during the conduct of a trial on the facts. Summary judgment would decide the case on the legal issues, prior to preparation for trial on the facts. The second reason is probably the lesser risk. In the event the defendants lose, they must pay plaintiff three times plaintiff's damages plus attorney's fees.

A third risk to an employer group PPO is that one or more employers may drop out of a PPO to pursue another health care delivery system or because of bankruptcy or other causes. This leaves employers still in the PPO with unfunded liabilities for medical care.

HEALTH CARE FINANCING OPPORTUNITIES

There are compelling reasons why some insurance companies are increasingly interested in organizing and operating PPOs. PPOs give them an opportunity to increase their market share in the health care financing market. A number of large group health insurers have long been losing market share to the Blue Cross and Blue Shield organizations, HMOs, and to self-insured status. The PPO form and operation gives them a real opportunity to compete with the former advantages of all three; advantages that have resulted in a decreasing market share for insurance companies to date.

PPOs CAN AVOID DISADVANTAGES OF HMOs

The aspects that potential subscribers to group and staff HMOs do not like include the following: they usually cannot choose their own doctor; they often do not have a doctor they can call their family physician but instead may see a different one each time they visit the HMO; and they are locked into the HMO for a year unless they want to pay for their own medical expenses in full. If they are dissatisfied with the quality of care, or if the HMO doctor will not prescribe more radical care when the patient thinks it is warranted, they have only two alternatives: they can pay the full amount for their medical care, or they can appeal to the HMO management to overrule the decision of the treating physician.

The PPO offers an approach to these situations that is more accommodating to the patients' interests.

There are two aspects of group and staff HMOs which are particularly onerous to potential physician members: the degree of management control which HMOs retain over physicians' total income, and management interference with the doctor-patient relationship. They are paid on a capitation basis rather than on a fee-for-service basis. A PPO, on the other hand, controls only that part of the physicians' income that comes from the PPO arrangement, and it is usually a fee-for-service arrangement. It also allows competition among physicians for patient care at the time care is sought. This results from the "dual options" the patient has of obtaining treatment from a participating physician or going to a non-participating physician and paying a larger part, but not half, of the medical expense.

PPOs CAN ADOPT COMPETITIVE STRENGTHS OF HMOs

The competitive strength of HMOs that PPOs can adopt, without adopting the other aspects of HMOs, is strict utilization review. HMOs' hospitalization rate is approximately 420 hospital days per 1,000 enrollees. Health insurance hospitalization rates are usually much higher. The Rand study indicates that is not primarily due to the type of enrollees attracted to HMOs as has been theorized in the past to explain the difference in the hospitalization rates. At least a major part of the low HMO hospitalization rate is due to utilization review (UR). The primary UR tools are preadmission screening, concurrent review of hospital length of stay, and developing a physician and hospital admissions profile for each particpating physician and hospital. PPOs can adopt those strengths to their competitive advantage.

PPOs CAN ADOPT WELL-ESTABLISHED COMPETITIVE STRENGTHS OF BLUE CROSS AND BLUE SHIELD ORGANIZATIONS

One competitive strength that Blue Cross and Blue Shield organizations have long had over insurance companies is that they actually negotiate with physicians and hospital administrators about prices and services. There is nothing new about negotiating with doctors and hospitals. Since their inception during the 1930s, Blue Cross and Blue Shield have operated by doing just that. They were in the beginning a PPO and may be looked to as a model of what may be expected from a provider-based PPO. They should demonstrate clearly to insurance companies searching for methods to improve their group health care financing experience, that health care providers are willing to negotiate rates and terms of payment. Nationally, the Blue Cross and Blue Shield organizations enjoy an average of over 10 percent lower rates charged by hospitals than insurance companies do.

WHY HAVEN'T MORE INSURANCE COMPANIES FORMED PPOs?

For the reasons stated above, hundreds of insurance companies might be expected to be developing at least one PPO on an experimental basis, instead of the few companies who actually are doing so. What, then, is different about these few companies?

PRACTICAL FACTORS

PPOs are local or regional. In the beginning the predecessors to Blue Cross were operated through a single hospital. Each PPO will by the nature of the market serve only patients within the geographic area of concentration of the physicians, allied health practitioners, and hospitals who contract with it. People generally go to the hospital nearest to them or not many miles farther.

Hospitals are a good model to look at. They do not usually attract an entire city (unless they have some exclusive service). Each hospital only attracts a few neighborhoods. Health care outside of specialists is a very local market. It is not immediately compatible with a centralized, national operation. Insurance companies, and health insurance companies more than other lines, are centralized operations, and national or multi-state.

PPOs are viewed as experimental by insurance companies. They represent a fundamental change in business philosophy—from indemnity for expenses to direct involvement in health care. In the years since 1938 when the first Blue Cross prototype was formed in Texas, not one insurance company has created a similar organization. HMOs began operating first in Seattle in the mid-1920s and in California in 1929. And yet it was not until 1966 that the first insurance company formed an HMO. Several others followed, but only a few national insurance companies have had long-term ownership of HMOs. They are Prudential, CIGNA, CNA, Nationwide, John Hancock, and Wausau. Most of these companies all sponsor at least one PPO. A few companies have for some time offered HMO coverage to employer groups through unaffiliated HMOs. They are Gulf Life of Florida, Metropolitan Life, Northwestern National Life, and Travelers. One company whose insurance program included a plan resembling a PPO in four cities (Safeco) has discontinued that plan.

PPOs lend themselves only to large group cases. On a small group or individual basis, the PPO cannot quickly represent a large enough market in a local area to efficiently operate a UR program. This was one of the major factors that led to Safeco's withdrawal from its PPO plan. The PPO relies upon the health care provider's attention to its UR procedures. The health care provider must have a volume of PPO patients to do that. The PPO must represent a significant number of local patients to negotiate a separate contract with a hospital.

Catastrophic versus comprehensive coverage. For those insurers who have not owned or marketed an HMO or a PPO, one difference is that they may have had a product line that was more oriented to catastrophic coverage with deductibles and copayments. By increasing the deductibles and copayments, by involving the patients in payment for a portion of their own health care and limiting the maximum amount of catastrophic coverage, they did not in the last 10 years suffer the degree of loss that the other carriers did. They never adopted the philosophy of providing comprehensive health care. Rather, their business philosophy stemmed from the fact that insurance is spreading of a risk. If an expense is a certainty, or a near certainty, there is no risk involved. That people will obtain ordinary health care is a near certainty.

To make such a basic change from hands-off indemnity to entering separate contracts with the health care providers would require a driving force—more a smashing force. It is a fundamental change in business requiring development of a new philosophy and a new set of skilled employees to deal with health care providers and procedures.

Indemnity system failed for some. Most of the companies referred to above got into direct involvement in providing health care in large part because they were losing market share and their health insurance line was awash in a sea of red ink. The indemnity system had failed for those companies. They were forced to look beyond the indemnity hands-off approach or consider discontinuing their health insurance line. For one company, Prudential, market conditions were so unfavorable that they did in fact discontinue their individual health insurance line. They sold no new individual business for a year while they redesigned their product.

Prudential's experience, and their product before and after a one year hiatus, reflect the changes in the health care financing market over the last ten years. It is in a transition from a cost-plus system to a budget-based system. They began imposing a system of utilization review. No longer was the choice of care completely in the control of the patient and the health care provider.

PUBLIC RESPONSE TO PAYMENT SYSTEMS

People consider elective health care less necessary if they pay all or a significant portion of the costs. This factor is the heart of the policy issues faced by insurance carriers. It is a very serious matter to contemplate directly involving a nonmedical operation, as insurance companies are, in the choice of health care, and necessarily in the choice of care in particular cases, on a case-by-case basis. That is what UR requires and what the choice of providers for PPOs requires.

Examples. The development in three benefit areas exemplifies the difficulty: podiatry, mental health treatment, and alcoholism treatment.

In podiatry, the Auto Workers' Union have for a number of years had a provision in their contracts for podiatry coverage. All auto workers and their families are covered. In Detroit people are five times as likely to have a particular foot operation as in the rest of the country.

In mental health care, federal workers have for many years enjoyed much broader mental health benefits than other industries. All federal workers and their families are covered. Washington D.C. supports three times as many psychiatrists and psychologists as other cities in the country.

In alcoholism treatment, in those states that did not have mandatory insurance coverage for alcoholism treatment centers and then enacted such legislation, numerous alcoholism treatment centers sprang up. Previously it was considered economically infeasible to build in those locations. The usual length of stay in alcoholism treatment centers is closely related to the minimum required insurance coverage for length of stay in that state, even though that minimum coverage varies from state to state. Once a law is on the books concerning minimum coverage, the utilization expands to that minimum coverage level.

In matter of need and payment, people who may, however desperately, need elective medical care, will usually not seek out that care if they have no insurance to pay for it. If their health insurance pays up to 80 percent of the expenses, most of them will elect to have the care. If it is fully covered by insurance, almost all of them will have the care. For those who have the care, their pain will usually be reduced. Their lives will usually be at least somewhat enhanced.

The choice of providers in a PPO and the UR to which they agree, offer third-party payors an opportunity to obtain some control over the degree of utilization of covered medical services. At the same time the dual option offers the patients an opportunity to make their own policy decision. In a traditional health care financing system, they will not usually pay all or even half the bill for care. However, they will regularly pay 20 percent up to a maximum of a few hundred dollars. Side by side with the comprehensive health care insurance system is the deductible and coinsurance system. Patients pay the first $100 or so in full, and then they pay 20 percent up to some limit, usually not more than $1,000 out-of-pocket. Their employer uses the deductibles and coinsurance to keep the premium down and as a form of UR. Millions of people accept that system as adequate.

If an employer substitutes PPO coverage at 90 to 100 percent for care by a medical provider who agrees to UR and perhaps a discounted fee and offers the incentive proved over many years of small deductibles and 20 percent copayment for going outside the PPO, the patients will continue to refrain from seeking more care in the outside health care market because of those incentives. They will also accept the incentives as providing adequate coverage, as they now accept deductibles and co-payments. That is also not experimental. The market has proved it. It needs to be pointed out.

Elective versus nonelective care. The incentives of small deductibles and 20 percent copayment work as a form of UR in cases of "elective" surgery and treatment. "Elective treatment" is not a well-defined medical term. The PPO offers a self-correcting method to distinguish the elective from the nonelective cases. If the preferred provider does not offer necessary care, the patient who suffers more than they are willing to bear will go outside and pay the difference in price. That is why the public policy issues are very different for exclusive provider organizations (EPOs). With an EPO there is no competition at the time treatment is sought. There are EPOs in the health care market now called HMOs. They are regulated rather carefully. They should be, because the patients do not have a real choice concerning elective treatment. If they elect to get treatment outside the HMO, they pay the full fee.

Instinctively, many people who are asked whether or not they would accept an HMO instead of their current insurance answer no. The individual relationship and trust in the doctor may be part of it. An important part of that relationship is that if they suffer more than they are willing to bear, that doctor will not usually deny more radical, more expensive treatment. If the doctor does deny more radical treatment, the patient will seek another doctor without having to confront the first doctor on the issue of necessity. An HMO doctor can deny more radical treatment, and the patient is left with no alternative but to pay in full for the more expensive treatment or to confront the doctor on the issue of necessity. It would be the same in an EPO, or in a PPO that required patients to pay half of their medical expenses for services from health care providers outside the approved list.

If EPOs are allowed and not regulated, abuses will follow because the patient has no choice.

PPO incentives should be at 20 percent. To summarize, *necessary* and *elective* health care are terms of art and not fact. The public response to a payment system that requires the patient to pay most or all of the costs for elective health care is often destructive to patients' health. The health care financing market has established 20 percent as a widely acceptable level of copayment that does not discourage seeking necessary health care. Therefore, PPOs should set their differential at 20 percent for an incentive to the patient to get their health care within the PPO. There should be a real choice.

LEGAL IMPEDIMENTS TO CONTRACTS WITH INSURERS

Many legal issues are raised as impediments to PPO contracts with insurers. As a whole, most of the legal problems are ones that can be avoided by good planning at the negotiation stage especially, and careful drafting of the agreements. The questions involve issues of taxation, antitrust activity by purchasers, free choice of provider statutes, allied health care provider statutes, and whether the PPOs should be regulated.

TAXATION

Is contracting with medical providers the business of insurance? The U.S. Supreme Court has said it is not.[2] Is the income "premium" income that is subject to state premium taxes? On one hand, Blue Cross and Blue Shield operations have always claimed it is not a premium. The states regulate Blue Cross and Blue Shield under separate authority and tax them differently. On the other hand, the definition of insurance in codes is broad. The fact that a patient who seeks care outside the PPO is partly indemnified raises premium tax issues. Companies would like to avoid premium taxes (which are levied on gross income, like sales tax) and have their income taxed as ordinary income.

ANTITRUST ISSUES AGAINST PAYORS (INSURANCE COMPANIES)

One insurance company working alone does not usually have a large enough market share to operate a PPO. In any one state, usually fewer than 10 insurance companies have 1 percent or more of the health insurance market. All other sales organizations are geared to handle less than 1 person in 100. That is not enough concentration of subscribers for a PPO. The PPO market must be concentrated in a local area. So smaller companies can enter the PPO market only by banding together to do so. This raises antitrust questions.

They can form a joint venture if they meet the test of joint ventures for antitrust exemption. If they do that, they lose some or all of their individual control over the PPO. However, the cure for this problem should not be any blanket antitrust exemption for a group negotiating rates with health care providers. To do that would enable such a group to enter into conspiracies with impugnity to restrain other such groups in their negotiations.

FREE CHOICE OF PROVIDER STATUTES

Many states have statutes providing that no policy or subscriber contract may require that the service be rendered by a particular hospital or person. These statutes are obstacles to EPOs (exclusive provider organizations) that do not qualify as an HMO. But they are not an impediment to PPOs. PPO contracts provide an alternative to the preferred provider and do not require the service be rendered by the members of the PPO.

Several states have statutes relating to Medical or Hospital Service Corporations (Blue Cross and Blue Shield) that require payment for services by physicians or hospitals outside the area in which the corporation does business but that would not be a serious limitation. Most services are provided locally, and a very small portion of the payments would be affected by these laws.

Depending on the interpretation, one common statute could be an impediment to formation of a PPO. Typical language reads as follows: "The patient shall have a free choice of any provider of health care..." If this statutory language means there can be no incentives to choose among participating health care practitioners, then it is an impediment. States that have similar statutes are Idaho, Missouri, and Montana (as to commercial insurance policies) and Maine, New Hampshire, and Nevada (as to hospital or medical service corporations).[3] Several other states have miscellaneous statutes that may be interpreted as legal impediments to PPOs by commercial insurers or Blue Cross and Blue Shield Organizations. Those states having statutes affecting commercial insurance policies are Illinois, North Carolina, Rhode Island, South Dakota, and Utah.[4] Those states having statutes affecting hospital or medical service corporations are Georgia, Illinois, Ohio, South Dakota, and Texas.[5]

ALLIED HEALTH CARE PRACTITIONERS

The PPO form offers an opportunity to obtain utilization review of allied health care practitioners. Rather than a legal obstacle for PPOs, this may prove to be one of the most important benefits from participation in a PPO. These statutes only require paying specified allied practitioners (e.g. chiropractors, podiatrists, psychologists, counselors, nurse practitioners) on the same basis as physicians. The basis of payment for physicians in a PPO is a contract including utilization review. For allied practitioners who want to contract in order to obtain referrals, the key will be utilization review.

For example, if utilization among doctors for a particular DRG (Diagnosis Related Group) is a weekly office visit during the acute phase plus medication, and monthly visits thereafter, then a similar general rule should be applied to other health care providers. Standards for utilization should be developed that apply to allied practitioners.

Attempting to eliminate allied health care practitioners raises serious antitrust boycott questions, especially if the practitioners are licensed by the state to provide health care. The UR portion of the PPO contract, on the other hand, can be drafted to comply with antitrust laws and gain the benefit of utilization review.

PPO MODEL LAW DRAFTING GROUP

The NAIC/NAHMORS[6] joint task force and its advisory committee studied the question of state regulation of PPOs. After months of study and discussion, it was decided that this is an experimental business form. It should be allowed to develop and not be frozen into a single form. Before a state can regulate an entity, it must define it. That very definition often interferes with further development of the business entity. HMO laws are examples of this.

No instances of specific PPO abuses that require additional regulations were discovered by the task force. During discussions, many attempts were made to anticipate problems that have not yet arisen and to draft laws on regulations for those anticipated areas. It was pointed out that state health care regulators have authority to regulate quality of care issues, as they do with physicians and allied health care practitioners, and Departments of Insurance have authority to regulate solvency and risk assumption issues. Thus, the PPO business form can be left to develop within existing legal parameters. The legislation required will be to remove impediments in those states where they exist.

The joint task force will be an information source on proposed and enacted laws on PPOs, both in the states and in Congress. But it will not at this time prepare any model law to regulate PPOs.

CONCLUSION

About 10 percent of PPOs are being formed by insurers and a like amount by Blue Cross and Blue Shield organizations. Whether the incentives for insurance companies to create and operate PPOs are sufficient to motivate members of the group health insurance industry to become directly involved in health care delivery, can only be appreciated over time. PPOs offer insurers a vehicle to adopt the competitive strengths of business entities that have for years taken a progressively greater share of the health care financing market. The potential is now there to increase the group health insurance company share of that market. Many of these changes can also be adopted within the traditional insurance system, on a more conservative scale. Most supposed legal impediments are really straw issues. Good planning and contract drafting can avoid them. However, a change in philosophy of business will be required by each insurance company entering the PPO market. That change will be from insurance indemnity plans to direct involvement in health care delivery which is both the highest quality and budget-based.

NOTES

1. Employees Retirement Income Security Act, 29 USC 1001 et seq.

2. *Group Life & Health Insur. Co.* v. *Royal Drug. Co.* (1979) 99 S. Ct. 1067, 440 U.S. 205, 59 L Ed 2d 261, *rehearing denied* 99 S. Ct. 2017, 441 U.S. 917, 60 L Ed. 2d 389; *Arizona* v. *Maricopa County Medical Society* (1982) 1025 S. Ct. 2466, 457 U.S. 332, 73 L Ed. 2d 48.

3. Idaho §41-2103(8); Maine 24 §2303(1); Missouri §375.936(11)(b); Montana §33-22-111(1); Nevada §695B.180(10); New Hampshire §420-A:16.

4. Illinois 73 §982b; North Carolina §58-260; Rhode Island §27-18-25; South Dakota §58-17-54; Utah §31-20-3.

5. Georgia §56-1708; Illinois 32 §555; Ohio §1739.06; South Dakota §§58-39-9 and §58-40-10; Texas Art. 20.12.

6. National Association of Insurance Commissioners and National Association of HMO Regulators.

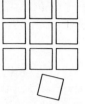 Impact of New Trends

CAN WORKERS AFFORD PPOS?

Karen Ignagni
Assistant Director
AFL–CIO
Washington, D.C.

☐ The popularity of PPOs is a manifestation of a new willingness on the part of payors and providers of health care to attempt to bring about through private action what Congress has failed to enact—a comprehensive program to reduce the rate of growth in private and public expenditures for health services. Whether PPOs can play a significant role in reducing health care inflation across the board or merely provide short-term discounts to certain groups is a crucial issue for legislators, employers, and workers to address. However, experience with other alternative delivery systems suggests ways to maximize the cost-cutting potential of PPOs. To understand how organized labor views preferred provider arrangements, it is necessary to place PPOs in their historical and political contexts.

In 1965, Congress enacted medicare and medicaid legislation. Shortly thereafter, organized labor began to work for the passage of a comprehensive national health care program to make affordable quality health care available for all Americans. This program would have established a prospective budgeting system for hospitals and doctors and improved access to care for those without insurance protection or with inadequate coverage. Had this program been enacted, private as well as public expenditures for

195

health care services would be lower than they are today, and 40 million Americans would not be without insurance protection.

In 1970 very few members of Congress, with the exception of Senator Edward Kennedy and his co-sponsors of the Health Security Bill, were interested in supporting national health care legislation. Federal outlays for all health care programs were $18 billion, compared to approximately $100 billion last year. Private health insurance premiums were going up approximately 5 percent per year, as compared with increases today as high as 40 percent. As inflation in the general economy worsened, health care costs began doubling every five years and consuming a greater and greater share of the country's gross national product (GNP).

The recession of the mid-1970s eroded the purchasing power of workers' wages and made it difficult to maintain health care coverage. During that time organized labor continued to work for a national health care program as well as other legislative efforts to improve the health care delivery system and reduce the cost of care. The AFL–CIO worked for the enactment of legislation that provided loans and grants for the development of health maintenance organizations (HMOs) as an alternative to the fee-for-service medical system. Its affiliated unions and state and local bodies organized community HMOs at the local level. Unions were directly involved in starting group model HMOs in Providence, Rhode Island; New Haven, Connecticut; Cleveland, Ohio; and Detroit, Michigan.

The AFL–CIO also supported the Carter Administration's cost-containment program, which would have done away with the so-called "cost-plus" system of reimbursing hospitals by putting a cap on the annual rate of increase in hospital costs. This legislation was defeated by a strong coalition of legislators who were persuaded that a voluntary effort could contain the growth in hospital costs without resorting to federal legislation. Between 1976, when the Carter legislation was first proposed, and 1978, hospital inflation declined slightly and then resumed its rapid growth once the threat of legislation subsided.

About the time when Congress was debating whether to regulate the hospital industry, health care economists began to discuss a free-market or "procompetitive" alternative for controlling costs. Advocates of this approach believe that if consumers became more economically sensitive to the price of health insurance, they would become more conscious of cost when utilizing services. Pro-competition theory implies that consumers are largely responsible for the current crisis in health care costs even though physicians and other providers function as purchasing agents for patients.

Since the defeat of the Carter cost-containment program, Congress has been debating the issue of competition versus regulation. Two years ago Congress took action toward controlling health care inflation by requiring that hospitals participating in medicare be paid on a prospective basis. Although organized labor has long advocated a prospective reimbursement system, the AFL–CIO believes it must apply to private as well as to public payors of care, and to physicians as well as to hospitals. If only medicare is reducing its payment to hospitals, facilities will have a strong incentive to turn away beneficiaries, shift costs onto employers, employees, and state and local governments and penalize inner-city and public hospitals, which treat a disproportionate number of elderly and poor patients. The DRG program, which was designed by the Reagan Administration to achieve short-term savings in federal programs, may only exacerbate the "cost-crunch" experienced by the private sector because of the strong financial incentive it creates for hospitals to compensate for reductions in reimbursement under public programs by charging private payors more.

Ironically, despite the Reagan Administration's opposition to a systemwide cost-containment program, passage of such legislation could bring down the rate of increase in the overall health care spending and mean significant savings for public as well as private programs. For example, cost estimates for the Medicare Solvency and Health Care Financing Reform Act of 1984, introduced by Senator Edward Kennedy and Congressman Richard Gephardt, indicate that if this legislation were enacted in 1985, by 1989 the federal deficit could be reduced by $30 billion and private expenditures could be reduced by $74.2 billion

Until such legislation is enacted, health care costs will continue to rise and fewer and fewer people will be adequately protected against the high cost of getting sick. Last year national health care spending reached almost 11 percent of our gross national product and amounted to $355 billion. If current trends continue, it is estimated that by 1990 the national tab for health care will be a whopping $756 billion and amount to 12 percent of our GNP. Per capita expenditures will reach approximately $3,000, almost double current levels (see Exhibit 1).

Because of Congress' unwillingness to pass comprehensive cost-containment legislation, state and local governments and employers and employees have developed unique responses to this problem. Eleven states have now established their own cost-containment programs that limit the rate of growth in annual hospital revenues. According to the National Conference of State Legislators, more than 300 pieces of health care cost-containment legislation were introduced last year. Business and management have also begun to develop strategies to fight health care inflation. They have established programs to monitor unnecessary utilization by providers, encourage preventive care, create financial incentives for certain surgical procedures to be done on an outpatient basis, require mandatory second surgical opinions, and promote HMO involvement.

PPOs represent a private sector response to the problem of rising health care costs, which combines features of the regulatory and competi-

EXHIBIT 1
National Health Expenditures

Year	Total Expenditures (billions)	Per Capita	Percent of GNP
1950	$ 12.7	$ 82	4.4
1960	26.9	146	5.3
1970	74.7	358	7.5
1975	132.7	604	8.6
1980	249.0	1,075	9.5
1982	322.0	1,365	10.5
1985 (a)*	456.4	1,882	10.8
1990 (a)*	755.6	2,982	12.0

*(a) estimates.
SOURCE: Health Care Financing Administration, Department of Health and Human Services, 1983.

tive approaches to health care cost containment. Generally when people refer to PPOs they mean a hospital or group of hospitals and/or physicians that contracts on a fee-for-service basis with employers, insurance carriers or third-party administrators to provide health care services to subscribers. In exchange for a stable patient base, less paperwork, and rapid claims payment, hospitals and physicians agree to provide care to subscribers at discounted prices that are negotiated in advance.

Employees in groups that join PPOs will pay less out-of-pocket costs for health care services, in exchange for giving up the freedom to choose their provider and agreeing to use designated hospitals or participating physicians.

The notion that smart shopping on the part of consumers can significantly reduce health care inflation will lead many to conclude that workers should take advantage of PPO discounts, and anyone wishing to go outside the list of participating providers for treatment deserves to pay more. The prospect of little, if any, deductibles and/or coinsurance could provide a strong financial incentive for workers to choose to participate in a PPO.

Unfortunately, choosing a provider is much more difficult than simply comparing prices. Consumers must consider quality and accessibility as well as cost. Organized labor is concerned that employers who have experienced health insurance premium increases of 20 to 30 percent every year for quite some time will choose from competing PPOs solely on the basis of price, giving little consideration to other factors. This could be a catch-22 for workers who might become dissatisfied with quality of care offered by the PPO. They would have no option but to pay more for services. Difficulties could also arise in connection with employees who live in areas that are inaccessible to participating providers. They too would have no option but to seek care from nonparticipating practitioners and pay more for services. Although PPOs may save employers money, they may also contain exclusions and limit actions that reduce health care coverage for workers.

Another problem associated with PPOs is the question of what happens to small employer groups that, because of their size, have no clout with which to bargain with hospitals and doctors for reduced rates. Anecdotal evidence indicates that the sole PPO option open to these employers will be exclusive contracting arrangements whereby the plan enrolls members on an all or nothing basis and requires employees who seek the services of providers not participating in the plan to pay for all of their own health care costs.

PPOs offer volume discounts to employer groups. Such discounts may do little to reduce the nation's total health care bill. For years the Blue Cross Association was able to take advantage of its substantial market share within communities by offering premium discounts to subscribers. There is no evidence that these discounts held down overall health care costs. In fact, private health insurance companies have continually made the argument that their clients paid higher premiums as a result of Blue Cross arrangements with hospitals. Similarly, although preferred provider organizations may produce short-term savings for subscribers, they may result in higher costs for nonmembers. As more large groups join PPOs, there will be a growing gap between what they are charged and total health care costs. Small groups and those which, for whatever reasons, are unable to join PPOs will pay more in addition to carrying an unfair share of the burden of uncompensated care.

PPOs may only exacerbate some of the largest problems confronting the health delivery system. Giving the competitive edge in the health care market to large and healthy groups could result in a great deal of adverse selection and pressure on doctors and hospitals to recoup lost revenue by shifting costs onto other payors or to minimize bad debts by refusing to serve jobless workers, the poor, and others without health insurance protection.

The AFL–CIO believes that no real health care reform is possible without moving away from the cost plus reimbursement system for hospitals and the fee-for-service system for physicians. That is why organized labor has been instrumental in the formation of group practice HMOs and has strongly encouraged its members to join these plans. Given a choice between a viable group practice HMO and a preferred provider organization, labor clearly favors HMOs and will continue to urge its members to join them.

Union members who join HMOs can be sure that the care they will receive is adequate. HMOs must meet standards established by the federal government to be qualified to offer health care services in their communities. Physicians in group practice HMOs agree to provide health care services to subscribers on a capitated basis. Unlike the fee-for-service system, they do not have a financial incentive to hospitalize patients unnecessarily or to perform unnecessary tests and procedures.

Not all employees can or wish to join HMOs. And some unions, as an alternative to the current system, have formed contracted relationships with preferrred provider organizations. Small unions that lack the economic clout to negotiate discounts with providers are exploring the possibilities of joining together and forming a master trust to negotiate with providers.

The AFL–CIO has developed a list of minimum standards that it believes PPOs should meet before being licensed to do business. Until fairly recently, commercial carriers in most states were not permitted to provide or arrange for the direct provision of health care services. As a result, state departments of insurance never had a need to audit quality of care or monitor access to and availability of services. Insurance commissioners traditionally confine their review of health care plans to the design of the contracts and the financial statement of the carrier. Since preferred provider organizations are more than third-party intermediaries and are actually brokering the care patients receive, the functions of state insurance departments should likewise be broadened to adequately monitor these new entities in at least six ways:

1. PPOs should be required to disclose information concerning out-of-pocket costs associated with certain standard medical services to enable consumers to weigh cost savings associated with PPOs against the advantages, in their own minds, of maintaining a relationship with a nonparticipating physician.
2. PPOs should be required to disclose to all subscribers and potential subscribers any limitations on services or services excluded under the plan to enable beneficiaries to know before signing up what will and will not be covered.
3. PPOs should be required to have established procedures for providers or subscribers to file grievances. This will assure that consumer and provider complaints can be dealt with promptly and that services might be improved.
4. PPOs should be required to establish procedures for admitting emergency patients to nonaffiliated hospitals or for consultation with and transfer to nonparticipating physicians. Otherwise, patients in life-threatening situations could find themselves without protection.
5. PPOs should be required to monitor utilization of affiliated providers and hold patients harmless.
6. PPOs should be required to meet minimum solvency requirements in the interest of protecting patients and asssuring continuity of care.

Because of the projected future growth in PPOs, it would be impractical for the federal government to monitor compliance. All of these requirements could be readily monitored by state insurance commissioners who are now involved in licensing carriers and approving rate increases. When practicable, insurance commissioners should set standards for PPOs that are consistant from state to state to assure that the public health is adequately protected.

Even the most efficient PPOs will not reduce total health care costs. Organized labor has a three-pronged strategy to deal with the problem of rising health care costs: support comprehensive across-the-board federal cost-containment legislation that would establish broad guidelines for states to use in developing and implementing their own programs; work with payors and providers on the local level to develop joint programs that reduce the cost of care and improve access to services; and strongly resist health care takeaways at the collective bargaining table by putting forth alternatives, which may include PPOs, to reduce health care costs without requiring workers to pay more out of pocket for health care services.

A number of employers have attempted to cut back employees' health care benefits under the guise of improving competition in the health industry and reducing cost. An increasing number of companies offer employees cash rebates if they select a low-option health insurance plan with high deductibles and coinsurance rates. Other companies set aside a certain amount of money for health insurance benefits for their employees and allow workers to receive cash refunds for unused benefits at the end of the year. These plans reward people for underutilizing or avoiding health care services so that employers will realize short-term reductions in health insurance premiums. The result is that workers are encouraged to go without appropriate treatment, which leads to higher health care costs in the long run when the untreated illness becomes more serious and requires more expensive levels of treatment.

PPOs are far better alternatives to the arbitrary cutbacks that some employers have imposed on their workers' health care plans. However, it may be too high a price for society to pay for PPOs if they control the rate of increase in health care costs for their subscribers at the expense of small groups of employees, the economically disadvantaged, or those with chronic conditions.

On the other hand, in states that have already implemented some type of reimbursement controls, PPOs may have a major role to play in offering employer groups real savings by monitoring utilization and controlling the fees of participating providers. PPOs are not likely to be as cost effective as group practice HMOs but they do provide another alternative to the present, inefficient delivery system.

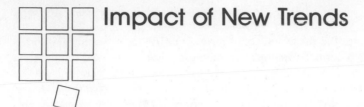

BARGAINING FOR HEALTH BENEFITS: UNIONS AND EMPLOYERS CAN CUT COSTS

Max Fine

President
Max Fine Associates
Washington, D.C.

In early 1984, 80 of the top decision makers on employee health benefits in the state of Maryland gathered together and agreed it was time to stop being casual about medical costs. The 80 represented the largest corporations and the largest unions in the state. Just a few weeks before, the management and union cochairs of the meeting—from which physicians and other providers were barred—had been shouting at each other across a picket line set up when the company planned cuts in health care benefits and the union struck.

All 80 participants agreed to strike out at doctors and hospitals instead of each other. They will jointly direct their members and employees to preferred providers and "patronize only those hospitals and doctors providing quality care at a reasonable cost. . . ."

At about the time of the strike in Baltimore, several unions in the New York metropolitan area dropped their Blue Cross insurance and made arrangements to obtain hospitalization benefits for their members directly from hospitals.

"We can do it better on our own," said a negotiator for the unions, representing factory workers and longshoremen. The decision followed Blue Cross's demand for a 30 percent rate increase.

Even in a city of seven million people, with high hospital occupancy rates, the 30,000 union members involved were able to make arrangements for discounts with three hospitals easily accessible to most members. They figure they will save the 30 percent.

In California, during that period of trade union awakening to a long-developing health care cost crisis, state and regional affiliates of two of the nation's largest unions were calling special meetings to deal with the problem. The meetings of the Western Conference of Teamsters and of the California Branch of the United Food and Commercial Workers, as well as the activities in Baltimore and New York, were prompted by changes in collective bargaining agreements or by management finally becoming sensitive to the burden of health benefits as a rapidly growing business expense. The contract changes require union members to pay increased health benefit costs out of their own pockets. Other unions face similar dismal prospects.

The cost problem seemingly sneaked up on corporate America while the top brass were not looking. Only four years ago, a survey by a social scientist from MIT found a general indifference among chief executive officers of Fortune 500 companies to the mounting costs of health care and health benefits programs. One CEO commented, "If I paid much attention to that, I wouldn't be CEO very long." Meanwhile, the undetected medical cost problem worsened so rapidly that in 1984, more money was spent by corporations for health insurance than was paid to all U.S. stockholders in dividends—an estimated $77 billion.

Corporations and unions are now in hot water, like Henry's frog. (The frog was kept in a tank of water as the temperature was increased a few degrees each day. The unwitting frog was eventually boiled to death without knowing it; he would have jumped from the tank if the temperature had been turned up rapidly.)

Lee A. Iacocca, chairman of the Chrysler Corporation, a company hard hit by auto workers' growing medical bills, said that if the nation's system of health care is not revamped, "You'll see a lot of broke companies."

GENESIS OF THE PROBLEM

How did the unions, corporations, and other major purchasers of health benefits get in this mess?

It all began in 1944, when President Franklin D. Roosevelt prodded the National War Labor Board, which had frozen wages and salaries, to

permit unions to negotiate for employer contributions to employee benefit plans. Shortly after VJ Day, federal courts ruled that the "fringe benefits" such as group insurance and pensions were conditions affecting employment and, therefore, subject to collective bargaining under the National Labor Relations Act. These decisions spurred the growth of fringe
benefits and were the real genesis of private health insurance. At the start
of World War II, there were fewer than 13 million Americans with any
form of hospital insurance; by 1950, there were 76 million. Over the next
one-third century, only the *costs* of health insurance plans increased
faster than the *numbers* of those covered. The number of Americans with
coverage nearly tripled to 200 million, while the premiums skyrocketed
from $2 billion in 1950 to $77 billion in 1980. But the unions cared little
about the cost so long as they could negotiate more and more benefits,
with increasing employer assumption of the premiums. And the employers, even penny-pinching industrialists, strangely enough said, "No
problem." It took decades and expenditures of tens of billions of dollars
before that nonchalant attitude changed. Not until Blue Cross replaced
U.S. Steel as its major supplier did General Motors begin to take the
medical cost problem seriously. (In 1983, health care costs at General
Motors amounted to at least $480 for every vehicle produced in the
United States. At Chrysler, the health insurance tab added $600 to the
price of every car.)

Bombarded with statistics telling them that health costs were consuming over 10 percent of the gross national product, the major purchasers of group health benefits, like Pogo, finally met the enemy in themselves. They had hammered out agreements that provided excellent insurance for hospitals and surgeons at costs arbitrarily established by the
latter. In a perverse redistribution of funds made available through collectively bargained agreements, they had overprovided sickness coverage
and underprovided for preventive medicine, early diagnosis of disease,
and health maintenance. They had produced a lopsided health care delivery system that was costing the pace-setting companies and unions,
and all others following the pace, far more than they needed to be spending. And they had directed the delivery system away from the reforms
that could reduce rates and costs of sickness.

When you borrow from Peter to pay Paul, Paul does not complain.
There were no outcries from Blue Cross and the hospitals and surgeons
whose costs and fees, even in days of general adversity, were paid fully
by the plans. Hospital bed occupancy actually rose by 9 percent in Michigan during the most recent economic recession, with the hospitals and
surgeons welcoming well-insured, laid-off auto workers. The negotiators
had provided well for sickness benefits for the laid-off workers who in
the past might have been treated free of charge through public programs.
But now they represented an increased supply of full-paying patients, and
the costs were additive.

SOLUTION TO THE PROBLEM

How will the unions and corporations solve the cost problem?

It will not be by holding their present arrangements as sacrosanct and cast in stone. The plans were not divinely inspired. They were jerry-built. They started with hospital benefits, then add-ons such as surgical benefits, major medical, drug plans, dental plans, vision benefits, hearing aids, and whatever could be purchased by the leftovers in the overall economic settlement between the union and the management.

And the white collar workers and nonunion employers followed the pattern.

Most of corporate America is not ready, yet, to take strikes over its desire to reform health benefits. Union leaders who have made concessions on wages, vacations, and other items, insist they will make no concessions on health insurance benefits. MOB—maintenance of benefits—is the demand of their members. The corporations and the unions in Baltimore established a "first" in active cooperation to solve the problem. They stopped shouting at each other, and each side agreed to work with the other. After all, they had proved over many years that negotiating and hard bargaining with each other only increased the costs they paid to others. It was time to negotiate with those receiving the hard-earned health care dollars.

Is it not amazing that it took labor and management so long to recognize their own self-interest?

Other labor officials are still mad at corporate leaders for not supporting labor's efforts to enact national health insurance in the 1970s. Other corporate leaders are still reluctant to accept labor as a negotiating partner rather than an adversary.

But many local unions and many companies have been hurt by health care costs. Some are escaping from the 40-year-long rut of more benefits at higher costs, and others will follow.

Several large unions and the AFL–CIO itself have long supported the concept and development of HMOs. But only about 10 percent of UAW members belong to HMOs even though the union has been their strongest booster for decades. The AFL–CIO Executive Council also supports other alternative delivery systems, presumably including IPAs and PPOs. The latter have features that may attract many members who have shunned HMOs. If the unions actively begin to "buy smart" by negotiating with sponsors of these various systems, they can control health benefit costs, and far more of their members will accept membership in health care plans. By providing incentives for employees to join PPOs and other forms of quality-assured delivery systems, the corporations and unions can rapidly control their costs. In fact, the competing plans offer the most practical solution to the cost escalation problem.

By late 1984 the UAW had negotiated the PPO alternative for their members at General Motors and the Ford Motor Company. At the same time, other large unions were preparing similar demands in major industries and the public employment sector.

COMPETITION VERSUS REGULATION

When Senator Edward M. Kennedy, backed by organized labor, campaigned to enact national health insurance, his plan was strongly opposed by the American Medical Association as too radical. Three years after Kennedy abandoned his fight, sweeping changes began taking place in health care financing. Physicians in some areas were competing fiercely to attract patients. Others started worrying about empty waiting rooms and prepared to offer fee discounts and incentives to fill them. Hospitals all over the country were positioning themselves for possible price wars.

In Arizona, four industrial giants led an unsuccessful drive supported by 1,300 other companies to regulate hospitals. In South Florida, employers pinpointed 17 "cost-effective" hospitals and began channeling patients to them. Insurance companies, Blue Cross and Blue Shield plans, and independent groups were challenging charges as never before, sponsoring HMOs, developing utilization review and control software, and forming PPOs.

Measured against the procompetitive tumult and its prognosis for cost containment, the old Kennedy plan looked tame indeed. Along with the procompetitive Congressman Richard A. Gephardt, Kennedy introduced new legislation with both regulatory and competitive features. Union leadership quickly endorsed the bill and vowed to press for its enactment in 1985.

However, the unions must recognize that much of what needs to be done to hold down health plan costs will not have anything to do with regulations or government. Government cannot require people to take care of themselves and cannot force unions and management to work together and "buy smart."

The unions that cannot wait years for legislation to solve their health plan cost problem should look for the answers by turning to what they do best—bargaining.

In bargaining for high-quality health care at lower costs, the conditions are quite different than union-management negotiations. Few of the traditional consultants that labor unions or companies have employed to select the best insurance plan or to redesign the benefit structure have experience in negotiating with providers. Some do not know the difference between an ophthalmologist and an optometrist. But in weighing the overtures and merits of competing PPOs or other plans, there are specific features to consider. The following set of guidelines are proposed to assist unions and/or union/management teams in negotiating improved health care coverage with the providers and in avoiding lures and traps.

TEN THINGS TO KNOW IN CHOOSING A NEW HEALTH PLAN

1. Beware of doctors bearing discounts. Some plans rely strictly on physicians who agree to discount their fees for a designated list of services. Doctors' fees take only about 20 cents of the medical dollar. But doctors' orders determine hospital, lab, X-ray, prescription drug, and other costs that consume 70 percent of all health care expenses. The best qualified and most experienced doctors may not join a plan that simply cuts fees. These are the same doctors that you want in your plan. They provide the best care and they can do the most to reduce overall costs. Selecting a plan because of physician fee cuts is like treating symptoms but ignoring the disease.

2. Make sure the doctors have agreed to be guided by strong utilization-review procedures, e.g., doctors who reduce their fee but order more services than patients need can run up charges faster than a computer. You are interested in the total costs. The best way to reduce total costs is to get the physician to control them. The plan selected should have strong incentives for the member physician to cut costs through utilization-review procedures and provisions to drop those who abuse the system.

3. Require the insurance company or plan administrator to make arrangements with hospitals to reduce unnecessary hospital admissions and lengths of stay. This means that the insurance plan should not pay hospital charges for procedures that can safely be done in the doctor's office. (But these procedures should be covered and paid for outside the hospital.) It means that the hospital should be required to accept utilization review aimed at (*a*) eliminating unnecessary admissions, (*b*) improving medical review of patients to assure that they are kept in the hospital only as long as they need to be there, and (*c*) comparing the hospital's record to other hospitals.

4. Check the relationship between the hospital and the doctors. The doctors must be able to admit their patients to the hospitals that have agreed to decent rates and to high standards of utilization review. A hospital can recover any discount it offers by keeping patients an extra day, thereby running up plan costs. Doctors working with unions and employers are in the best position to reduce costs.

5. If necessary, redesign the health insurance benefits program to eliminate any incentives for overhospitalization or for overordering of procedures by physicians. It may pay to make compensating changes in the benefits, for example, by including some cost sharing on hospital stays but encouraging preventive care and outpatient visits. Data from some plans that have done this, such as Plantronics, Inc., American Family Corporation, and General Telephone, indicate redesign of the benefit provisions can be a tranquilizer for cost inflation.

6. Easy access to medical care is essential, so it is important to select a plan with doctors whose offices are easily accessible to members and their families. A full range of primary and specialty care must be available from fully qualified physicians participating in the plan. The number of doctors should be adequate to assure a minimal waiting time for appointments.

7. The plan should require all participating physicians to submit to audits, review of medical services rendered, second opinions, and similar measures shown to be cost effective and quality enhancing.

8. Having to change doctors can be a tough pill to swallow, so insistence upon nonexclusivity in the Plan is important. That is, qualified physicians already serving the members should have an opportunity to become participating members in the Plan.

9. Be sure the Plan has established methods to control high-charging physicians. The sky is no longer the limit, and fees paid to the Plan's participating doctors should be reimbursed at reasonable amounts. Also, once the Plan has been selected, members should be encouraged to discuss fees frankly with their individual doctors.

10. True control over medical costs will require more than tightening up on expenditures for sickness and injury. Structure your health benefits to include programs that promote good health and help members to avoid chronic ailments that reduce the active lifetimes for working people.

The advent of a competitive environment in health care—with PPOs and alternative delivery systems vying for customers—opens new opportunities for wise purchasers. If employers and labor unions adapt these simple guidelines to the unique situations that are found in every medical care community and begin bargaining together for the health care they provide for their employees and members, they can effectively control inflation of those costly health benefits without impairing the quality of the vital services people need.

Regulatory Responses to Competition

EMERGING INDIRECT ROLE IN HEALTH FINANCING REGULATION

Michael Koetting, Ph.D. *

Abt Associates, Inc.
Cambridge, MA

◻ Most discussion of the role of state government in health care cost containment has centered around direct state intervention: Should or should not states undertake rate review? One of the unfortunate consequences of this debate has been a lack of attention to the *indirect* role of state government. The indirect role of state government in health care cost containment has to do with the functions influencing the health care environment, particularly the impact on markets and market-oriented approaches. "Market-oriented approaches" refer to health organization and financing structures that create market incentives for controlling costs. Generally these consist of PPOs, HMOs, and a whole spectrum of hybrid alternative health plans (AHPs).

These alternatives are appearing, in one degree or another, in virtually all states. The pressure for cost containment is enormous and ap-

---

*My thanks to Terry Stoica of the Illinois Governor's Office (and formerly the Illinois Department of Insurance) for her many valuable comments on an earlier version of this paper. An intellectual debt is also owed to Joan B. Trauner whose monograph of PPOs in California confirmed many of my earlier speculations and provided numerous specifics from California.

parently growing. In some cases, this pressure will create state rate regulation mechanisms, but it will everywhere create further experimentation with market-oriented approaches. Even in states with some form of rate review, businesses and other payors will use market-oriented approaches to supplement whatever results are obtained by rate regulation.

Consequently, states will be forced to embrace some indirect role in health care cost containment. Their only choices will be to choose a more or less activist role in encouraging market-oriented approaches or to be more or less assertive in shaping responses from the market. It will be impossible for states to avoid some role in dealing with market-oriented approaches to health care.

This article will offer a preliminary assessment of the state role in the indirect regulation of health care costs. Three levels of involvement are identified: Market Activist—steps states can take to actively encourage market approaches; Consumer Protection—steps necessary for basic protection; and Long-Range Planning and Protection—steps to monitor and cope with broader range policy issues.

MARKET ACTIVIST RESPONSE: ENCOURAGING THE MARKET

There are steps that can be taken at the state level that would facilitate the growth of market-oriented approaches to cost containment. The steps outlined below are low-cost initiatives that have minimal direct impact on the health care industry but contribute to an environment where market pressures for lower-cost health care can develop. There is little to lose from experimenting with such pressures, particularly when combined with appropriate safeguards.

REMOVE LEGAL OBSTACLES

The most important thing for a state to do is make sure its laws allow for direct contracting between insurance companies and providers. In most states the legal situation is sufficiently ambiguous that it has retarded development of PPOs. Merely clarifying the legal status of contracting may have salutory effects.

In California, for instance, there was substantial hesitation on the part of the insurance industry to enter into contracts with providers because of uncertainties in the insurance code prior to 1982. Although the California Department of Insurance was in fact approving group plans with such contractual arrangements, many insurance companies felt these plans were vulnerable to litigation. California AB 3480, passed in June of 1982, explicitly spelled out the ability of insurance companies to enter into PPOs. The results were an immediate rush to create PPOs, which is apparently transforming health care financing in California.

Changes on such a scale cannot automatically be expected elsewhere. California is unique: the large HMO penetration, a general acceptance of the proprietary role in health care, the excess of hospital beds and doctors, and the absence of direct controls on health care costs made it ripe for such a dramatic change. The fact that this change was accompanied by the introduction of contracting for medicaid hospital care (medicaid PPOs, in essence) magnified the impact of AB 3480.

The change or clarification of the legal status of contracting will not always be easy. Some degree of opposition from the organized medical community is likely. Medical societies have been bitterly opposed to such changes and can be expected to oppose even clarification of laws on contracting. The response of hospital associations and other providers is harder to predict. It will depend in part on the overall regulatory environment of the state. For instance, hospitals may be quite willing to accept such a concept if the alternative is perceived to be an all payor rate regulatory system.

Providers may use the discussion of contracting as an opportunity to pass laws effectively prohibiting contracting. This can be done in the guise of permitting contracting, then so overloading the bill with protections and safeguards that the net effect is to restrict flexibility in financing and insurance regulations. In 1983, discussion of dental contracting in the Texas legislature led to the passage of a law that the Health Insurance Association of America generally considers anticompetitive.

COORDINATION WITH RATE SETTING

While this is not a universal problem, rate regulation merits at least some mention. Ten states have mandatory rate-review systems for private payors and several more are seriously considering them. These states are Connecticut, Maine, Maryland, Massachusetts, New Jersey, New York, Rhode Island, Washington, West Virginia, and Wisconsin. Eight other states are expected to consider proposals to establish such systems in the 1984 legislative session.[1]

Rate regulation systems are not inherently inimicable to market-based approaches. Market-oriented approaches (particularly HMOs, but also utilization reviews and various benefit redesigns related to PPOs) can have a very powerful effect on utilization, which supplements the focus on unit costs in rate review systems.

Unfortunately, ideological debates over the desirability of rate setting have treated market approaches as alternatives rather than as complements. As a result, rate regulation programs have not been as sensitive to the problems of meshing these two strategies as might be desired.

Examples of the kind of problems encountered are:

— Payment on a uniform DRG basis weakens the incentive of non-hospital-based AHPs to monitor hospitalized patients (since the

hospital, not the AHP, will benefit from the reduction in length of stay, ancillaries, and so forth).
— Regulation of charges may make it difficult or impossible for AHPs to negotiate for discounts in their dealings with hospitals.

The latter is the more general problem and is beginning to receive wide recognition. For instance, the language in the Social Security Amendments of March 1983, which makes it possible for individual state rate regulatory systems to receive waivers from Federal cost limitations, requires that such systems allow for direct HMO and AHP negotiation with hospitals. However, the degree of allowance that the state can make will depend to some degree on how much it wants to actively foster market-oriented approaches to health cost containment.

The specific solutions to this problem depend to a great extent on the technical aspects of the rate-review system. The problem of coordination can generally be resolved by allowing discounts based on demonstrated reductions in hospital per unit charges to the contracting party without shifting these charges to other payors. An alternative is to allow hospitals that have a certain share of their revenues under contractual agreements to opt out of the regulatory system.

DEVELOPMENT OF A STATE DATA BASE

In the short run, a sophisticated data base is desirable but not necessary for the development of PPOs. Analysis of current claims information allows the prospective purchaser of provider services to know its own client base. Moreover, the solicittion of bids minimizes the need for independent comparative data because it is possible to compare bids with each other.

But over a longer time frame, more sophisticated data will be necessary to account for variations in case mix. For instance, is one hospital per diem more or less than another's when case mix is taken into account? Likewise, third-party payors will want to know how programs they have initiated compare to other alternatives. A data base is also necessary to understand and monitor the directions of government programs by private payors. A survey of 167 business coalitions concerned with health care costs found that the greatest single need identified by these coalitions was the need for improved data bases.[2]

Comparative data bases do not have to be developed by the state; private consortia or groups of insurance companies can undertake their development. However, it may be more appropriate for the state to undertake the effort to develop accessible health cost data.

First, there is the question of efficiency. Because of its ability to mandate participation, the state can create an all-inclusive data base with much less effort than any other group. In fact, it is unlikely that any other group could get an all-inclusive data base since their resources would be limited to what they had at hand (their own claims data) or what they could persuade hospitals to provide. Voluntary efforts, such as the Illinois Cooperative Health Data System, have not been generally successful because key actors always have incentives (cost, proprietary information, etc.) for withholding cooperation. The limitations of voluntary data collections have led coalitions in Arizona and Iowa and elsewhere to push for state data collection efforts.

Another important argument for a central data base is that it simplifies the data provisions for hospitals: If the vast bulk of information need be provided only once to a central agency, which then bears the responsibility for making this data available to users, the burden on hospitals to provide data to potential contractors will be lessened. Administering, and bidding on, multiple contracts will be a growing problem for hospitals as the number of PPO agreements grows. Steps such as centralizing data submissions will minimize the problem.

A third reason for developing a state data base is that the availability of such information may serve as a catalyst to purchasers to consider PPOs and other AHPs. The availability of data that clearly documents differences and similarities in hospital costs graphically demonstrates the potentials for alternative financing arrangements. The ready availability of comparative data also will be perceived as an asset for contracting activities and makes contracting that much easier. It is an indirect state intervention that will encourage market contributions.

A final reason the state should be involved in developing a data base is to guarantee access to comparative data for small insurers, individual employers, and other groups that might otherwise get locked out of the PPO market. These groups do not have a large enough market share on their own to develop effective information bases and would be forced to throw in their lot with larger groups. While this has some favorable aspects, it might well inhibit the formation of new, small initiatives that could be an important ingredient of a new health care market.[3] A market-activist approach would encourage the development of a maximum number of different possibilities.

The notion of state data bases has gained increasing acceptability. Within the last year, Iowa created a health data commission and clearing-house, and Arizona enacted a system to collect hospital prices by DRG. Maine, at the same time it created an all-payor, rate-regulation system, gave that commission the power to collect billing data and combine it with discharge data. The ability to combine these two elements is the key to making a data base useful.

Rate-regulation states, in general, have good state data bases. One of the more interesting is the Maryland Information Center, a self-supporting legal entity separate from the Maryland Health Services Cost Review Commission, but affiliated with the Baltimore PSRO. The Information

Center accesses data from the Health Services Cost Review Commission (including patient level charges and abstracts) and a variety of other local and national data sources. Users can purchase reports from a catalogue or have special reports tailored to their specification.

The California Health Facilities Commission, which has been in existence for several years, exists solely to collect such data. The Commission's mandate was extended in 1982, as part of the bill specifically allowing PPOs, to collect billing information that combines discharge abstracts with other cost data. Data collected and published by the California Health Facilities Commission has been used extensively by state and some private agencies involved in writing PPO agreements.

CONSUMER PROTECTION: A MINIMALIST RESPONSE

The fundamental notion behind market-oriented approaches to health cost containment is to increase consumer incentives to choose health care coverage that moderates the rate of cost growth. The cutting edge of this strategy, however, is to put the consumer at increasing risks for routine care—or to pay more to minimize routine risks. Additional protections are therefore necessary to make sure that the consumer knows the risk and is protected from risks beyond certain limits. The consumer may not be able to know how much he or she will be sick in the coming year, so there will be some gamble involved. But the consumer should have the right to know that whatever risk he or she takes, there are no hidden loopholes in the coverage and the coverage will be of an acceptable quality level.

On the other hand, excessive zeal in the area of consumer protection can unnecessarily delay all market reforms. A reasonable argument can be made that some of the requirements of the Federal HMO Act, for instance, have been a major brake on the development of HMOs. And health care provider organizations may make "consumer protection" a strategy to stymie competitive reforms by loading on "protections" to the point that proposed changes would sink of their own weight. This has long been a strategy of medical societies, and, as mentioned earlier, dentists in Texas have apparently taken the same tack.

Thus, it is necessary to strike a reasonable balance between the need to allow new initiatives such as PPOs to develop without being prematurely stifled and the need to offer some basic protections to consumers that are commensurate with the increased risk they are bearing.

REGULATING ADVERTISING CLAIMS

State agencies that regulate insurance programs have been monitoring advertising claims for years, but there are a number of aspects of market-oriented approaches that might make the job more difficult.

One factor is the large growth in employers offering multiple plans. In some companies the range of plans from which employees must choose can be overwhelming. With more people making more choices, there is greater risk because people will differ in the amount of understanding they bring to the issue or the amount of time they can devote to it.

Second, the growth in numbers of plans reflects a growth in the type of plans. For several years alternatives to conventional insurance were limited to HMOs and those in only certain portions of the country. That is changing. The last few years have seen such a proliferation of combinations and permutations of types that even a typology of offerings becomes difficult. Both statutes and regulations tend to lag behind the development of alternative types of health care plans.

The situation of multiple employer trusts (METs) is an obvious case. These sprang into existence following the passage of the federal Employee Retirement Income Security Act (ERISA) in 1975. METs initially claimed exemption from various state regulations under the terms of ERISA. However, federal regulation proved vastly insufficient. While METs fell through the regulatory crack, some plans were marketed at actuarially unsound rates, charged exorbitant commissions, and skimmed off funds for personal use. A number of these plans went out of business leaving millions of dollars in unpaid medical bills.

As other types are developed, state insurance departments will have to continually survey their statutes and regulations to make sure that they have sufficient statutory authority to regulate emerging entities for at least the basic protections that are offered to consumers of more conventional insurance coverage.

Another factor that makes this task all the more difficult is the increase in the number of plan features that might impinge on the consumer share of costs. PPOs, for instance, negotiate contracts with "preferred" providers that allow for the payment of lower rates for medical treatment than would be the case without such contracts. Some of these savings are passed on to the consumer in the form of lower premiums. But typically the insurer protects itself by limiting payments to nonparticipating providers to a level not more (or even less) than that given to participating providers. The consumer who used the nonparticipating provider then bears the payment responsibility for any difference in treatment cost. This feature is not significantly different from current co-pay features as long as there are sufficient providers within the PPO network. *Sufficient* in this context refers to geography, availability, and type of specialists. If specialists are not available, the consumer might end up with greater out-of-pocket expenses than originally envisioned.

These kinds of features place considerably greater demand on the insurance regulator than a simple indemnity policy that offers to pay wherever the subscriber seeks treatment. Now the insurance regulator must also develop criteria for monitoring the claims of PPO networks with regard to the sufficiency of participating providers.

INFORMATION FOR INFORMED CHOICE

The adequacy of information is a problem for the employer choosing a policy for its employees and for the employee who must choose among policies. Both can be protected by requiring that certain information be included in marketing materials. For example, sufficient information on actual service coverage should be required. It is not only necessary to make sure that claims about access are accurate; it may also be necessary to regulate what information about access is reported and in what format.

While this may seem elementary to some, this level of protection should not be taken for granted. Few, if any states currently have statutes that give the insurance regulator sufficient latitude to set out a format for describing the actual degree of access that a PPO will offer.

Another area of concern is the area of co-payments and deductibles. Marketing material should be required to clearly describe the magnitude and structure of the co-payments and deductibles. While this is covered under most existing insurance regulations and statutes, it is unlikely that there are requirements to spell out the full implications of these co-pays. This will become a more important issue as more complicated co-payment arrangements come into use.

Consider a group insurance plan currently being offered by one California insurer. The policy pays 80 percent of the provider charge for participating physicians, but only 75 percent of the fee schedule for nonparticipating physicians. However, the contract with the PPO stipulates that the charges of participating physicians will be 17 percent less than the fee schedule. Thus, the consumer pays only 16.6 percent (i.e., 83 percent $\times$ 20 percent = 16.6 percent) of the fee schedule amount of participating physicians but 25 percent of the fee schedule amount for nonparticipating physicians. the out of pocket difference to the consumer is greater than the 5 percent, which would be suggested by a superficial reading of the difference between in and out of plan usage. Moreover, there is no guarantee that the nonparticipating physician will limit his or her billing to the fee schedule, which could make the difference even greater.

This is not a simple concept and the PPO marketing material may have reason to minimize the difference in order to stress the plan's apparent flexibility. Insuring that marketing materials contain clear examples illustrating the implications of various plan copay features may require increased sophistication from insurance regulators.

Information on sufficiency of coverage and co-pay arrangements can be addressed by requiring some historical information on out of pocket expense by subscribers. This could take the form of information on average out of plan expenditures within given geographical areas or by developing some average out of pocket expenditure limits which, when exceeded, would require a specific mention in the marketing material.

The underlying rationale for these regulatory concerns stems from the fact that emerging forms of health insurance increase risks for consumers. As a consequence, consumers will need additional information to make adequate assessment of those risks. Relying on traditional forms of regulation will not be sufficient.

CHANGES IN THE INCENTIVE STRUCTURE

Regulating quality will be the most important—but most difficult—assignment for states if market-oriented approaches are to succeed over time. This is because as cost containment becomes a major issue, the entire incentive structure of the health care industry is revised.

In a fee for service system, the provider has absolutely no incentive to underprovide services and has incentives to overprovide. This offers enormous protection to the consumer of medical care who can be confident that every possible treatment will be tried. But in a more cost-conscious atmosphere, the incentives will definitely switch. The provider will have strong incentives for underprovision of services.

For instance, one comparison of a prepaid practice showed that for certain relatively common surgical procedures the prepaid practice had lower rates of surgery "than would be expected under well-established, explicit criteria."[4] The general issue is clearly a serious one. The incentives have been changed. One cannot help but wonder how "pulling-the-plug" arguments will be different when the provider is at risk for each additional day of care.

These issues are not limited to prepaid health plans. An essential element of the market-oriented strategy is that all providers eventually face the same set of incentives—because they are all competing with each other. Thus, PPOs that are competing with each other and with HMOs will have the same basic incentives to reduce admissions, length of stay, ancillary use, and surgical procedures. (These incentives may not be as strong during the initial stages of PPO contracting, which will focus primarily on price; but it is clear that in the long run, PPOs must control utilization as well if they are to compete with HMOs.)

The same change in incentives will impact other alternative financing arrangements. Recently, for instance, Humana announced its plans to offer its own health insurance related to its hospitals.[5] It is not clear whether this plan will legally be classified as an indemnity plan or a service contract. (It would probably be an indemnity plan if it were structured so that the policy provided some coverage for providers other than Humana hospitals.) But, however it is legally classified, the incentives to Humana will be very similar to those of traditional HMOs: The fewer in-hospital services, the greater profit. It is doubtful there is a single state with an insurance code that anticipates such a blend of insurer and provider and the resulting change in incentive structure with regard to the provision of care.

IMPLICATIONS OF NEW INCENTIVES FOR QUALITY REGULATION

Some people, particularly members of the provider communities, will attempt to base arguments against market-oriented approaches on this change in incentive structure. While their concerns are real, their argument should not prevail. Quantity does not necessarily equal quality. Society can no longer afford a style of medicine which guards against adverse outcomes by providing incentives for the overprovision of care. It is necessary to develop a consistent set of incentives for controlling costs—throughout the entire health care system. Half-way changes that result in a checkerboard of uneven incentives will not accomplish the change.

Nevertheless, it must be understood that this is a major rules change. Mechanisms of social regulation must adjust to these new rules. It would be irresponsible to advocate these changes, as necessary as they are, without considering the implications of the changes and the need for corresponding checks and balances.

At the other extreme from those who would overregulate are market advocates who suggest that market forces are completely self-regulating i.e., that quality will be maintained by fear of loss of enrollment or by disenrollment in plans that do not adequately meet member needs. Again, there is some truth in the contention, but it must be approached very skeptically. Disenrollment is after the fact, and allowing people to experience poor quality of care is not an appropriate social policy. Choosing health care coverage is not like choosing a restaurant or an automobile where consumers get immediate feedback. A consumer can purchase health care coverage for years without actually using it to any great extent. If quality judgments are left to the consumer, it may be too late by the time the consumer has data to judge, if indeed the consumer ever has the ability to judge quality.

Malpractice is another type of safeguard. But that too is after the fact. Moreover, many of the existing problems in medicine are partially caused by the system's approach to malpractice and the resulting "defensive medicine." It is to be sincerely hoped that changes can be made in the determination of malpractice that make that system less of a factor in shaping medical practice. Reliance on malpractice as a quality regulatory device is a step in the wrong direction. It would make much more sense to fashion quality control mechanisms that reduce the need for malpractice. In fact, if this is not done, malpractice problems may be the undoing of market-oriented approaches.

Yet, however strong the necessity for improved quality regulation, there is a very strong practical argument for moving slowly in this area: There is no consensus on what should be done. Standards of appropriate medical care have not been defined in such a way that they lend themselves to useful regulatory intervention. Quality regulation, therefore, must proceed on two fronts. It must take immediate steps to provide minimal guarantees, and it must undertake steps to develop standards of medical care that lend themselves to the task at hand.

MINIMAL QUALITY CONTROLS

As a first step, state regulators must take steps to insure that their statutory basis and regulatory structure reflect the possible impact of the new incentives and structures. It must be understood, for instance, that the divisions between indemnity and service contracts are considerably blurred. PPOs, depending on their actual structure, may be more like HMOs than not. PPOs are explicitly designed to exert extreme pressures on subscribers to use participating members. For instance, the Prudent Buyer Plan of California Blue Cross will reimburse nonparticipating hospitals only at a flat per-diem rate that is well below charges from most hospitals, particularly for expensive procedures. Thus, subscribers to this plan are going to be under considerable economic pressure to receive care at participating sites.

This suggests that quality control mechanisms in the state regulatory structure should be similar to those for HMOs. But it is unlikely any state statutes reflect this. Not even California statute recognizes this, and California is probably the state that is most advanced in both PPOs and in the protection of consumers under HMOs.

The most important specific quality control mechanisms at this time are insurance of adequate grievance procedures and adequate internal quality reviews. States can accomplish this by extending their HMO regulations to other forms of organizing and financing that implicitly or explicitly lock consumers into certain providers. It may also be necessary to require procedures by which providers can appeal the decisions of a plan's utilization-review program. It is bad for both the consumer and the practitioner to leave the practitioner with no recourse when he or she believes the utilization-review process is in error on a particular patient. This not only has implications for quality of care, but also for malpractice coverage. Failure to allow an adequate appeal process could result in increased malpractice costs. (This is an area where regulations for PPOs may have to be more explicit than HMO regulations because of the differences in legal structures: closed panel HMOs actually employ the physicians while PPOs do not. Consequently, differences of opinion with a utilization-review process could result in real economic transfers among entities in a PPO structure. That is, physicians could in fact be penalized for their decisions in a much more direct fashion than under an HMO.)

As pressure for cost control grows, it may be necessary to extend requirements for these safeguards to almost all providers. Under a truly competitive system, all providers will be under pressure to reduce utilization to the lowest possible level.

BROADER QUALITY ISSUES

Beyond specific steps, state regulators must broaden their notion of what quality regulation involves to reflect the change in incentive structure that is fundamental to the entire shift in the market. There must be more concern with quality as an outcome rather than solely as a matter of the inputs into the process.

Some progress has been made in this area with regard to HMOs, but the progress is uneven, and states differ substantially. In some states, there appears to be a greater concern for the outcome of the medical care, and review includes more inspection of medical records and utilization-review minutes than used to be the case. But it is not clear how much of this is actually being done and how the results are being interpreted by regulators. In other states, HMO regulation still focuses almost entirely on financial issues. To the extent quality is an issue, emphasis tends to be on the condition of the physical plant and on the existence of agreements with specialists.

HMO regulation still suffers from unclear direction, and in most states, responsibility is fragmented across state departments (usually Insurance and Public Health) with neither department understanding how the two interests are joined. Moreover, the amount of funding devoted to HMO regulation is often a problem. HMO regulators frequently lament that they do not have sufficient resources to adequately address the issue of health care outcomes. Yet medical outcomes are an area where consumers have little ability to judge.

An outcome-based view of quality of care is also important for developing the information that people need to make informed choices. There is currently no efficient way of conveying information about quality of care to consumers. Most of the mechanisms proposed by consumer advocates (such as opening state files for consumer inspection or consideration of complaints and malpractice claims) are too cumbersome to solve the problem. Only the largest and most sophisticated purchasers (e.g., large corporations or professional brokers) can meaningfully use such information because of difficulty in access and interpretation. And even then the information is often too anecdotal to be of much systematic use. Some more direct measures are needed.

Unfortunately, such direct measures do not yet exist. States, therefore, should think seriously about what type of regulations will be needed in the future and, particularly, about what kind of quality information will be required for monitoring purposes.

The first step will be to realize that quality consists more of *patterns* of care than isolated incidents since individual factors contribute so heavily to single incidents. With the universal development of discharge data bases, it is feasible to consider computer searches of discharge abstracts for certain conditions or patterns that would suggest quality problems.

The current problem is that there are few clear notions of what patterns to seek.

One approach that has been tried is to identify a number of diagnosis categories that are "care sensitive." That is, expert medical opinion is used to identify a limited number of diagnoses, the outcome of which are believed to actually depend on the care received. Outcome is measured in terms of readmission and mortality rates.[6] Other process and outcome variables could be used (such as complications or recovery rates). These measures could be taken across different health plans to determine if there were significant variations in the outcome patterns from one plan to the next.[7]

Similarly, standards currently exist on the expected number of ruptured appendices per appendectomy; or on the expected number of birth complications for a population of a given composition. Comparisons of actual outcomes by health plan to these standards might be either useful summary information or used to trigger more intensive investigation.

The point is not that these are the best or even appropriate measures in themselves. The point is that this kind of regulation is not being done—for the most part is not even being thought about—by the people who are regulating health plans. Under the market-oriented health system that is emerging, this kind of regulation will be a necessity. And it will take a great deal of time and effort to develop and implement.

LONG RANGE ISSUES: MONITORING, PLANNING, AND PROTECTING

The need for government planning is not lessened because of the introduction of significant market forces into health care; indeed, the need may be greater than ever.

Three general functions must be met:

— State government must have some systematic mechanism for monitoring the "big picture" of health care within a state.
— It must have some capability of identifying problems before they become intractable.
— It should be able to propose alternatives and solutions that can be undertaken to address these problems.

Developing mechanisms that can carry out these functions will be difficult. Experience with Certificate of Need has shown that certain kinds of direct "planning" intervention are often ineffective or even counterproductive. Other health planning functions of state government have often drifted off into political irrelevancy by churning out thick documents oblivious to the immediate needs of providers, purchasers, or political actors.

In order to be effective, state health planning agencies must avoid both of these pitfalls. They will need to create products that are designed to either develop a consensus for political action or that make a compelling case for individual actors to pursue certain courses of action. In either case, the key will be to focus planning more clearly on specific problem areas rather than to indulge in general theory and data gathering which has no constituency.

Focused collection of data and development of quality standards, discussed earlier, are prime examples of constructive planning that can be integrated with market approaches. However the planning function goes beyond these and must consider certain broader issues that will greatly color the introduction of market mechanisms into health. These issues include providing for uncompensated care, encouraging regionalization of services, supporting medical education, and solving malpractice problems.

UNCOMPENSATED CARE

Providing care for the uninsured has always been a problem, but indications are that this will become an even bigger issue. Government payors are ratcheting down their reimbursements. As a result, hospitals and other providers will have declining revenues from paying customers. In addition to cutting rates, government retrenchment often includes restricting the number of people who will be covered or instituting co-payment for people who may have difficulty paying. This increases uncompensated care.

As market mechanisms take continued hold, private payors will use contracting to obtain discounts against hospital and practitioner changes. But the current charge levels are what defray uncompensated care and contractual allowances. Those hospitals with larger uncompensated care or contractual allowances will be at a relative disadvantage since their prices to paying customers must include a larger mark-up over costs to cover these. Thus, hospitals with large charity loads and large government utilization (particularly medicaid) will have to cut their costs more than their counterparts to offset the added mark-up. This can become self-defeating if the reduced costs result in a lower level of amenities, making the hospital less attractive to private payors.

This general problem is compounded by the fact that uncompensated care is not evenly spread. Lack of insurance coverage is worse in certain areas, and those are typically areas with the greatest concentration of medicaid recipients. If the uncompensated care problem is allowed to run to its logical conclusions, hospitals will separate into "charity" hospitals (primarily government hospitals with large medicaid and uninsured populations) and private pay hospitals that can afford to compete for PPO contracts.

Geographical concentration of uninsureds is only one dimension of the problem. Another is stratification by health status. As competition for lower-cost health insurance increases, insurers, prepaid or otherwise, will be concerned about minimizing risks. This results in the familiar problem of adverse selection, which seriously feeds on itself. The more a particular form of coverage attracts sicker people, the higher the premium becomes, which in turn creates incentives for the less sick to look elsewhere.

There will be no easy solutions. It is not even clear what part of state governments should take the lead—insurance regulators, public health departments, or welfare agencies.

One possible solution is regionalization of uncompensated care coverage as has been done in conjunction with rate-review programs in New York and New Jersey. Or states may have to increase the amount of effort (and funding) devoted to creating high-risk pools, as has been done in Minnesota, Connecticut, and other states. Or perhaps the answer will be to allow Blue Cross or other insurance companies to develop patterns of internal subsidies. Massachusetts Blue Cross has funded, as part of its master contract with hospitals, a feasibility study for a line of low-income insurance possibly based on a case management approach. This insurance would be funded by subscriber contributions, uniform hospital discounts, and a Blue Cross subsidy.

As market mechanisms come to play a greater role in determining the price of health care, greater attention must be given to defraying some of its hidden costs.

REGIONALIZATION OF SERVICES

In order to develop long-run efficiencies, there will have to be some reorganization of the practice of medicine. The desire for immediate savings through market-oriented approaches, however, might push that reorganization in undesirable or suboptimal directions.

For instance, most PPOs are being negotiated on a per-diem basis, perhaps with some allowance for different kinds of per diems (e.g., open heart surgery). Rough allowances are made for case mix differences by trying to contract with hospitals of varying intensity so that even complex cases can be handled by participating hospitals. This, however, places two constraints on the cost savings. First, the inclusion of more complex hospitals, with higher costs, necessitates inclusion of more lower-cost hospitals to avoid increasing net costs; otherwise people currently receiving care at less complex hospitals would be pushed into more complex hospitals, usually at higher costs. The necessity of including relatively large numbers of hospitals reduces contracting leverage. Second, the general approach foregoes any attempt to match services with type of hospital. Thus, the problem of seeking relatively routine care at tertiary institutions will be continued.

Neither of these would be insurmountable problems except for the dynamics of price competition that are gradually emerging. Some PPO (or other AHP) will eventually try to gain a market advantage by either reducing the proportion of tertiary hospitals with which it contracts or by channeling subscribers into hospitals in a more "efficient" manner. HMOs are in practice accomplishing the latter. In either case, the effect is to reduce the number of nontertiary cases in tertiary hospitals, which will further drive up unit costs in tertiary hospitals and could touch off a vicious cycle.

It is not yet apparent how serious a problem this may become, but the possibility is real enough. The need for the state to monitor this process is yet another reason for the development of a state data base. Moreover, to the extent that a data base can be used by insurers to develop more sophisticated contracting terms (DRGs, for instance), there will be incentives for a more logical sorting of the provision of service than simply putting a financial squeeze on the more complex institutions.

Or, perhaps such a data base will facilitate an orientation away from contracts with individual providers toward contracts with a network of providers who then have the incentive to improve the match between the patients' needs and the appropriate institution.

In any event, it is necessary to systematically monitor the health of tertiary centers which, although they look least vulnerable now, may turn out to be most vulnerable in future market situations.

MEDICAL EDUCATION

Medical education has long been recognized as a problem area for market approaches. Generally, the answer has been to postulate the necessity for some direct funding of medical education and then act as if the problem has gone away. The problem may not go away. Perhaps the problem should go to the national government, because the implications for health manpower are truly nationwide. Some states export a large number of doctors, while others import a large number of doctors.

However, states may be the appropriate laboratory to deal with the issue before it is tackled by the federal government. More creative health care initiatives have come from the state level than the federal level.

Two important steps would be for states to develop budgeting techniques that allowed them to measure the full costs of their state medical schools and then to fund those directly. To the extent that these costs are currently being underwritten by the federal government through a portion of the patient reimbursement from medicare and the match on medicaid, it is unlikely any state will take on this problem without substantial help from the federal government. Perhaps a waiver could be worked out so that funds that otherwise would be applied to those purposes through medicare and medicaid, could be given directly to the state for medical education, thereby allowing the state the latitude to develop ways of supporting education other than through patient charges.

Without some new payment structures, medical education will eventually be severely squeezed by market pressures similar to those on tertiary care centers. For a while such pressure is in fact tolerable since the current system is producing unnecessary physician surplus. A longer-run goal is to avoid allowing the pendulum to swing too far in the other direction.

MALPRACTICE INSURANCE

The present standards for determining malpractice and malpractice settlements have contributed to the overutilization of medical services by encouraging defensive medicine. In some respect, this provides a useful check on tendencies to reduce utilization past the point of safety. But in the long term, the health care community would be better served with a general restructuring of the approach to malpractice.

One important aspect of such a restructuring will be the development of a more realistic method for assessing liability than the current system. One interesting aspect of that problem is the link between quality regulation and malpractice. More explicitly defined quality standards might provide better standards for assessing malpractice than the current implicit rule of whether the practitioner tried every conceivable test and procedure. The existence of a coherent utilization-review network, with appropriate appeals processes, might also make it easier to establish new standards for the determination of malpractice.

If better defined quality standards and tighter utilization review procedures by providers can be accomplished, this might also help the problem of malpractice insurance by making it more difficult for consistent offenders to go undetected. While it is doubtful that individual problem practitioners are the main cause of higher malpractice premiums, curtailing the practices of these providers would have some beneficial effect.

CONCLUSION

An increase in the number of market-oriented approaches to health care cost containment is a desirable, and probably inevitable, development in health finance during the coming years. This change will cause a number of problems, in general because any social change is traumatic, but also specifically because the nature of market solutions is to dramatically alter the relative risks to the provider and, ultimately, to the consumer.

Under the system of health financing as it existed just a few years ago, providers had little incentive to do anything other than provide more services, and consumers had little incentive other than to accept them. Society is in transition to a different health care system. It will be a less expensive system, but a system with greater risks.

The existence of possible problems does not imply that states should oppose these changes. Nor should states create numerous regulations to protect against every foreseeable problem. But states, and other levels of government, must approach the emerging health marketplace with their eyes open to the possible problems.

Even with a sense of restraint as to when intervention is necessary, some steps will be necessary to protect consumers during this time of transition. These will include the extension of basic notions of consumer protection into new areas and new problems. Thoughtful monitoring of potential problem areas is also needed so that developing problems are addressed before they reach the crisis stage. Further, there are steps that states can take if it wishes to actively encourage the evolution of positive market forces.

NOTES

1. "States Are Moving to Control Costs for Health Care," *New York Times* (February 27, 1984).

2. Dunlop Group of Six/American Hospital Association, *National Data Base on Health Care Coalitions* (Chicago, Illinois: American Hospital Association, 1983), p. 3.

3. A number of "information broker" cottage industries have sprung up in California interpreting and analyzing California Health Facilities Commission information both for payors and for hospitals. These small firms are often more creative sources of ideas than the larger insurance companies and employers that are the only type of agencies who would be able to build data bases in the absence of a state clearinghouse.

4. William Richardson, et al., "Comparisons of Prepaid Health Care Plans in a Competitive Market: The Seattle Prepaid Health Care Project," in *National Center for Health Services Research* (USDHHS, DHEW Publication No. (PHS) 80–3199, August, 1980), p. 28.

5. *Blue Sheet* 27, No. 6 (February 8, 1984), p. 13. At least two other payor proprietary hospital chains are considering such arrangements.

6. Gary Gaumer and Jerry Cromwell, "Impacts of Prospective Reimbursement Programs on Patient Care in Hospitals," Abt Associates; Monograph prepared under contract HCFA 500–78–0036; January, 1983.

7. In undertaking across-plan comparisons, it is of course necessary to standardize for factors that would lead to systematic differences in outcome, such as differences in age, sex, or racial composition. The research done by Abt Associates addresses this issue by considering patterns for specific age-sex categories within each of the care sensitive diagnoses.

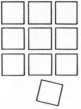

Regulatory Responses to Competition

THE HYBRIDS—
A REGULATOR'S DILEMMA

Linda L. Lanam, J.D.
Executive Director
Private Market Programs
Blue Cross and Blue Shield Association
Washington, DC

Jonathan P. Neipris
Deputy Insurance Commissioner
 for Policyholder Services and Enforcement
Commonwealth of Pennsylvania
Harrisburg, PA

☐ The most frequently cited key to health care cost containment in the 1980s is increased competition in the marketplace.[1] One part of the overall effort necessary to achieve this goal is the development of alternative health care delivery and financing systems at the state and local levels. Preferred provider organizations (PPOs) are among the newest and the simplest of these systems. However, PPOs present a particular dilemma for regulators.

The dilemma begins with the initial determination of what a PPO is. The basic component of a PPO is an agreement with a defined set of health care providers whereby the providers will render some or all of their usual range of services for a predetermined price or for a discount off their usual and customary charges. The economic savings are intended to accrue to both payor (usually an employer) and patient from use of the contracting providers in preference to others. Of course, there must be some incentive established to encourage the exercise of this preference. That usually involves making the contracted-for fee serve as payment in full for the preferred providers while applying a deductible to the payment of the charges of those providers outside the PPO arrangement. An additional characteristic of PPOs may well be the one on which long-term success depends—effective utilization review.[2]

While the PPO concept has come to mean discounted fee for service, there is reason to believe that effective utilization review will also have an effect on the units of service to be charged for as well as on the cost to be charged per unit. Even with no charge discount, agreement to reduce the number of units of service through utilization controls can yield significant savings. Second surgical opinions, preadmission certification, and concurrent utilization review are fast becoming part of the traditional health insurance plans in an attempt to reduce use of expensive procedures. It would hardly be considered efficient for the PPO to pay for unnecessary services, regardless of the discount provided. It is important to note that the existence of utilization controls has yet to be used as a basis for classifying an entity for regulatory purposes. Insurance laws generally do not speak to the issue of administrative control over services to be purchased by insurance consumers.

The regulator must then look at the whole operation of a PPO. PPOs are often characterized as something between an insurance company and a health maintenance organization (HMO), designed to deal with the delivery and financing of health care services. The fact that such arrangements are "neither fish nor fowl," and therefore essentially unregulated, raises a variety of conflicting issues that must be dealt with as PPOs develop. For example, efforts to provide comprehensive consumer protection against possible abuses could serve to seriously limit the potential of PPOs and result in enactment of unnecessarily elaborate legislative and regulatory definitions and constraints. At the same time, however, if PPOs concentrate primarily on providing more cost-effective medical care, with the emphasis on cost, there could be an impact on the quality of care delivered.

Looked at from a state insurance regulator's point of view, PPOs are a new entry in the list of "hybrids," i.e., mechanisms for delivery or financing of health care that exhibit characteristics of existing regulated entities such as insurance companies and health maintenance organizations (HMOs) but are unregulated. One of the first hybrids, and still the most prevalent, was the multiple employer trust (MET), in which a group of small employers banded together to provide employee benefits for the total group at a more economical price than that available to individual employers. Initially the "economical price" was lower insurance premiums. Eventually these groups sought to limit up-front costs further by creating a group version of self-insurance. They provided the equivalent of a standard commercial insurance policy of the fee-for-service type with claims payments made from a pool of funds contributed by members of the group. During the 1970s a number of these trusts went bankrupt. They were run by third-party administrators (TPAs) who were not licensed as insurance agents, brokers, or insurance companies but who were employed to administer the claims process. Insurance departments were faced with risk-bearing entities that were not insurance companies, run by unlicensed entrepreneurs operating within their states; since, under the provisions of ERISA (Employees Retirement Income Security Act of 1974),[3] METs were considered to be exempt from state insurance regulation, there was little state insurance commissioners could do to protect the public.

In an effort to deal with the gap between the federal regulatory scheme contemplated by ERISA with its narrow focus on fiduciary and disclosure requirements and the broader concerns of the states, California developed and enacted a "jurisdiction to determine jurisdiction" act.

> This bill creates a presumption that any entity providing certain health care benefits in California is presumed to be under [the insurance department's] jurisdiction unless it can prove to the contrary.[4]

The California act has been accepted as a model and subsequently enacted in several other states. In addition, the National Association of Insurance Commissioners (NAIC) actively supported an amendment to ERISA that was passed by Congress in 1982 and that specifically allows states to regulate reserves and employee contributions and to apply existing enforcement procedures to these group self-insurance arrangements.

As a result of this first confrontation with new efforts to reduce the cost of employee benefits, insurance commissioners are relatively skeptical about further unregulated developments in the health care benefits area, particularly those that are concerned primarily with price competition. In an effort to determine how to approach this hybrid called a PPO, state regulators must examine the arrangements from an understanding of existing regulatory frameworks such as insurance codes, HMO laws, and ERISA, their interrelationships, and overlapping jurisdictions, and the deficiencies in the current regulatory environment.

Insurance is regulated by the states as a business "affected with the public interest"[5] and is exempt from federal regulation under the specific provisions of the 1952 McCarren-Ferguson Act,[6] which declared state regulation to be in the public interest. The underlying responsibilities of insurance regulation are to assure fair competition, monitor the solvency of insurance companies, help to make adequate insurance coverage more widely available, and to make certain that the insuring public is treated equitably.

Solvency is of primary importance to effective regulation, because insurance, unlike other products, is a promise to be collected on at some future time.

> Insurers promise to pay if and when the event insured against occurs, but payments from buyers are required in advance...If an insurer becomes insolvent and is unable to honor its promises, its customers lose not only the purchase price but also resources relied upon to meet...claims, provide income during periods of disability, pay medical expenses or care for surviving dependents.[7]

In the early 1900s, the abuses resulting from uncontrolled competition showed that a freely competitive system could not assure either the continuing solvency of insurers or the equitable treatment of consumers. Today the insurance codes of the various states contain provisions requiring that specific amounts of capital and surplus be maintained in order to do business, that annual financial reports be made by the company, and that the Insurance Commissioner regularly examine the financial condition of companies. The amount of capital and surplus varies with the lines of insurance business for which a company is licensed. In Pennsylvania, for example, the requirements range from $150,000 required of a casualty insurance company writing health and accident coverages to $1,650,000 for a life insurance company writing all types of life and health insurance. Annual statements report on income and expenditures and reinsurance transactions and include comprehensive information on investments. They allow regulators to track the development of companies and, since the reports are on forms that are standard in all the states, to exchange information with other insurance departments. State insurance department financial examiners perform regular on-site reviews of the financial condition of companies domiciled in the state. This occurs usually every three or four years, more often for new companies or those showing large underwriting losses or evidence of significant underreserving, i.e., failure to set aside adequate funds to cover expected claims.

Financial considerations can be crucial when dealing with group health benefits where the potential liability could be substantial. When an employer contracts with an insurance company to provide these benefits, there is the above-mentioned set of statutory requirements to be met, which are intended to minimize the risk of insolvency. Insurance companies can still go bankrupt, but policyholder protection remains a primary aim of the regulator.

Every state insurance code contains standard provisions defining "unfair insurance practices" and prescribing enforcement actions to be instituted by the regulator. These laws prohibit such things as misleading advertising, premium rebates or other inducements to purchase insurance, excessive delays in adjusting and paying claims, and unfair discrimination in rating or selling insurance. They provide for specific civil penalties, including stiff fines, and also allow for potential license revocation. Of course, they also include administrative hearing provisions to limit potential abuse of authority by the regulatory agency.

Unfair insurance practices acts (UIPA) were originally enacted in accordance with the provisions of the McCarren-Ferguson Act

> by defining or providing for the determination of all such practices in this State which constitute unfair methods of competition or unfair or deceptive acts or practices and by prohibiting the trade practices so defined or determined.

As the heart of the consumer protection aspect of the traditional state regulation of insurance, all insurance companies, Blue Cross and Blue Shield plans, and, in states such as Pennsylvania, HMOs are subject to the UIPA.

When an employer or union wants to "self-insure" (financing certain employee benefits through its own resources) workers compensation or health care, the transaction moves outside the scope of standard insurance regulation. This option has historically been available only to extremely large organizations, because the number of employees must be sufficient to allow for accurate prediction of the frequency of loss. However, under the provisions of ERISA relating to employee welfare benefit plans, self-insurance programs became a possibility for groups of small employers. Multiple employer trusts (METs) were a result of such small employers seeking to self-insure. These trusts have none of the safeguards inherent in either an insured plan or one based on the employer-employee relationship, and the bankruptcies of several large trusts have led employers to look for other options to limit the cost of employee benefits. This is one of the reasons for the attractiveness of PPOs in the employer community.

The similarities between PPOs and insurance companies arise from the type of benefits that are arranged for (typically those included in a group health insurance policy) and the financing method used (discounted fee-for-service arrangements are used by Blue Cross and Blue Shield plans in the various states). But what is it that would make a PPO an insurance company? If the simplest definition of an insurance company is a company that issues or arranges for insurance contracts, then the regulatory focus must be primarily on the nature of the contract. The essential component of an insurance contract is risk—where one party agrees to assume the risk of the other for a fee, or a group may agree to share its risks and apportion the cost among the members of the group. When an insurance regulator looks at a PPO, the first question relates to whether or not there is risk. If the answer is affirmative, then concern shifts to the entity taking the risk.

In the standard description of a PPO contract between an employer and a group of providers, there are risks. The employers assume the risk that their annual payments will not be less than without this arrangement. The providers assume the risk that increased patient flow will not materialize or will not be sufficient to offset the loss of income from the agreed-upon discount. However, under this scenario, the risks involved are self-insured and therefore outside the scope of standard insurance regulation. When groups of employers or groups of providers seek to share or apportion their risks in some way, it begins to look more like the generally accepted description of an insurance transaction, particularly if a third-party is responsible for the arrangement.

Health maintenance organizations (HMOs) are the other relative of this hybrid. HMOs are regulated at both the state and federal levels. The federal HMO act was passed in 1973 after three years of discussion and analysis and has subsequently been amended to reflect continuing development in the field. In addition, a majority of states have enacted their own HMO laws and the National Association of Insurance Commissioners (NAIC) has developed a model HMO act, which contains the following description of "the nature of an HMO."

> A health maintenance organization may be described as an organization which brings together a comprehensive range of medical services in a single organization to assure a patient of convenient access of health care services. It furnishes needed services for a prepaid fixed fee paid by or on behalf of the enrollees. An HMO can be organized, operated, and financed in a variety of ways. For example, an HMO may be organized by physicians, hospitals, community groups, labor unions, government units, insurance companies, etc. Generally speaking, an HMO delivery system is predicated on three principles. (1) It is an organized system for the delivery of health care which brings together health care providers. (2) Such an arrangement makes available basic health care which the enrolled group might reasonably require, including emphasis on the prevention of illness or disability. (3) The payments will be made on a prepayment basis, whether by the individual enrollees, medicare, medicaid, or through employer-employee arrangements.[8]

Of these three principles, only capitation is generally not a part of existing preferred provider arrangements. When PPOs utilize the "closed-panel" approach, they exhibit great similarity to an HMO. However, capitation payment has historically been the crux of the HMO concept and to date PPOs have utilized the discounted fee-for-service method of payment.

Does another of a PPO's main attributes, use of a financial incentive to encourage obtaining service from a contracting provider, give rise to any regulatory jurisdiction? HMOs have the strongest type of incentive built into their program since they will not pay for care provided other than by a contracting provider. This extreme incentive is inherent in the operations of HMOs and has traditionally been offset by "quality of care" regulation. This regulatory scheme commonly involves assurance of an adequate supply of competent providers with a grievance procedure for the relief of consumer complaints regarding care. This jurisdictional line may be crossed by an exclusive provider organization (EPO), which would limit consumer choice of providers who could be reimbursed. This jurisdictional regulatory boundary appears to be theoretical at the present time since there are no state laws creating a quality of care regulatory scheme based solely on the limitation on provider reimbursement.

The question will get more difficult to answer in situations where the reimbursement to noncontracting providers is less than fully equivalent to that available to contracting providers. The less the reimbursement to the noncontracting provider, the greater the disincentive to go outside the PPO network. Logically, the creation of a disincentive significant enough to, in effect, serve as a bar to using noncontracting providers could trigger quality of care concerns similar to those applied to HMOs. Paying only 80 percent of the bill of a nonparticipating provider is a generally acceptable standard, but what if only 50 percent were paid? Again, there is no existing statute that makes distinctions in regulatory status based on this criterion. Insurance departments routinely approve policy forms and would be loathe to authorize a policy that granted such limited benefits as to be illusory or grossly unfair. The regulatory protection would seem to exist in such situations, in the assurance that something of value was being purchased.

Regardless of the desires of state regulators to protect the public, whether by seeking to apply existing laws or by creating new ones, it is important to note that "employee welfare benefit plans," as defined in ERISA are exempt from state laws. As such, the limits of state insurance regulation may apply only with regard to the issue of solvency. Such arguments will likely be raised. The intent of the statutory preemption of state insurance regulation for such things as PPOs remains to be determined.

To date, legislative and regulatory activity dealing with PPOs has tried to help providers and purchasers engage in selective contracting. State "antidiscrimination" and "freedom of choice" laws have been perceived to limit such contractual arrangements. Many states are moving to clarify the situation. In addition, federal legislation has been introduced to achieve this end and encourage the development of PPOs in all states. But the questions of whether regulation is or will become necessary and, if so, who should regulate remain open.

One strength of PPOs lies in their adaptability to the specific needs of a particular employer or geographic locality. While this attribute is well suited to a developing marketplace, it is the one that would probably be most limited by regulation.

Regulation seeks uniformity in order to eliminate identifiable abuses. The majority of regulators want to encourage the marketplace to develop on its own at the present time, rather than trying to second-guess it by applying controls in advance. However, there is no guarantee that this attitude will continue to hold sway.

NOTES

1. Alain Enthoven, "The Need for Fundamental Reform through Economic Competition and Rational Economic Incentives," *Issues in Health Care* II, No. 1 (1981).

2. "Utilization Review for the PPO," *Hospital Forum,* (Nov./Dec. 1982).

3. Pub. L. No. 93–406, 88 Stat. 829 [codified at 29 U.S.C.A. Sections 1001–1381 (1975)].

4. Testimony by Frank L. Damon, Chief Deputy Insurance Commissioner, State of California, before the House Labor Management Relations Committee, March 5, 1982.

5. *German Alliance Insurance Company* v. *Lewis,* 233 U.S. 380 (1914).

6. Pub. L. No. 79–15, 59 Stat. 33–34 [codified at 15 U.S.C.A. Sections 10011 (1946)].

7. Mehr and Cammack, *Principles of Insurance,* 6th ed. (Homewood, Ill.: Richard D. Irwin, 1976).

8. Model Health Maintenance Organization Act, *NAIC Proceedings–1982* I, p. 503, available through National Association of Insurance Commissioners (NAIC), 1125 Grand Avenue, Kansas City, Missouri 64106.

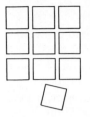

Regulatory Responses to Competition

STATE APPROACHES TO REGULATION OF PPOS

David DeCerbo
Partner
Hayt, Hayt & Landau
Great Neck, NY

Mark A. Hartman
Associate
Hayt, Hayt & Landau
Great Neck, NY

This chapter explores the statutory and regulatory responses to PPOs in four states: California, Florida, New York, and Ohio. California and Florida are two of six states that have so far enacted explicit pro-PPO statutes. (The other states are Minnesota, Virginia, Wisconsin, and Indiana.) By contrast, no legislation specifically intended to address the issue of PPOs currently exists in either New York or Ohio. However, the development of PPOs in those two states will be affected, to some extent, by other factors such as the particular hospital rate-setting methodology currently in use in New York and recent actions by the state's attorney general in Ohio.

Although recent activity in most states has generally been conducive to the establishment and development of PPOs, it must be remembered that the overall regulatory climate in which this activity is taking place is one that has generally been favorable to the concept of deregulation of the health care industry and to the injection of competition into the health care market. Thus PPOs have appeared at the same time that the federal government has changed medicare reimbursement for inpatient hospital care from a cost-based to a diagnosis related group (DRG) methodology, and many states are considering relaxing their certificate of need (CON) laws. It may not be coincidental that the only state discussed in this chapter that appears to be placing obstacles in the path of PPO development (New York) is currently exempt from medicare's DRG reimbursement and is contemplating expanding its CON requirements. It remains to be seen how well PPOs will fare in the future if the deregulation ultimately is not successful and the pendulum of government policy swings away from the increased competition and back towards greater governmental controls.

CALIFORNIA

The current statutory and regulatory ciimate in California actively promotes and encourages the development and operation of PPOs. Although PPOs were never explicitly illegal in California, their development was stymied because of concerns relating to the financial support and viability of noninsurer-based PPOs and because of regulatory and legal constraints that affected insurer-based PPOs. Until relatively recently, the California Insurance Code prohibited insurers from discriminating "between insureds of the same class in any manner whatsoever." In addition, California law also provided that insurers could not in any manner direct, participate in, or control the selection of the hospital or physician from whom the insured received services. In its classic form, a PPO would probably run afoul of both types of provisions. Effective January 1, 1983, however, these limitations, and others restricting the development of PPOs, were eliminated. New legislation authorized insurance companies to negotiate alternative rates of payment with selected health care providers and to sell insurance policies that either require the insured to use preferred providers or that contain financial incentives to encourage the insured to use those preferred providers.

The California legislature enacted this pro-PPO legislation as an adjunct to other legislation that sought to reduce California's Medi-Cal (medicaid) costs. California opted for increased competition in its Medi-Cal program by allowing hospitals to contract with the State for Medi-Cal patients. This reform raised the fear on the part of California insurers that hospitals would attempt to shift costs from the Medi-Cal program to private insurers, a problem that the insurance industry has been aware of for a number of years. This concern prompted the California legislature to permit insurance carriers and employers also to negotiate alternative rates of payment with health care providers. Such negotiated rate structures are the essence of PPOs.

The pro-PPO legislation is contained in Assembly Bill 3480. The key provisions of this bill relating to PPOs amend various portions of California's Insurance Code. Assembly Bill 3480 extensively amends Section 10133 of the Insurance Code and carves out certain exceptions to the general rule prohibiting an insurer from furnishing medical services or in any manner directing, participating in, or controlling the selection of the hospitals or physicians from whom an insured obtains services. Specifically, portions of Section 10133 of the Insurance Code have been amended to permit

> an insurer [to] negotiate and enter into contracts for alternative rates of payment with institutional providers, and offer the benefit of such alternative rates to insureds who select such providers. Alternatively, insurers may, by agreement with group policy holders, limit payments under a policy to services secured by insureds from institutional providers, and after July 1, 1983, from professional providers, charging alternative rates pursuant to contract with such insurer.
>
> When alternate rates of payments to providers are applicable to contracts with group policy holders, such contracts shall include programs for the continuous review of the quality of care, performance of medical personnel, utilization of services and facilities and costs, by professionally recognized unrelated third parties utilizing in the case of professional providers similarly licensed providers for each medical or dental service covered under the plan, and utilizing in the case of institutional providers appropriate professional providers.

These amendments to the Insurance Code permit insurers to negotiate and enter into contracts for alternative rates of payment with both institutional and professional (i.e. physician) providers. Furthermore, these amendments promote not only PPOs but also contemplate the development of exclusive provider organizations (EPOs), by which the insured's choice of a provider can be completely limited to a set of preferred providers. The EPO concept appears to be an extension of the PPO model by which the financial incentives to use a preferred provider have been replaced by permitting the insured no choice at all.

Other amendments to the Insurance Code pertain directly to the issue of EPOs. Section 10133.5 of the Insurance Code requires the commissioner of insurance to promulgate regulations and guidelines applicable to EPOs. According to the statute, these regulations are to ensure:

1. Adequate number and locations of institutional facilities, professional providers, and consultants in relation to the size and location of the insured group and that the services offered are available at reasonable times.
2. Adequate number of professional providers, and licensed classifications of providers, in relation to the projected demands for services covered under the group policy plan.

3. The policy or contract is not inconsistent with standards of good health care.

4. All contracts including those with providers, and other persons furnishing services, or facilities shall be fair and reasonable.

Regulations pursuant to Section 10133.5 were put into effect by the insurance commissioner on February 23, 1984. The regulations are contained in Title 10, California Administrative Code, Chapter 5, Subchapter 2, Article 6.

Section 2240 of the Regulations sets forth definitions.

Exclusive provider is defined as:

> an institution or a health care professional which renders exclusive provider services to covered persons under a group contract pursuant to a contract with the insurer to provide such services at alternative rates.

Exclusive provider services is defined as:

> health care services which are covered under a group contract only when rendered by an exclusive provider within the service area.

Section 2240.1 of the regulations provides that insurers shall ensure that (1) exclusive providers are duly licensed and of sufficient number to provide the services projected; (2) that all decisions pertaining to health care services to be rendered be based upon medical need; (3) that facilities used by exclusive providers for basic health care services be located within reasonable proximity to the work places or principal residences of the primary covered persons and are reasonably accessible to public transportation and the physically handicapped; (4) that basic health care services excluding emergency care are available at least 40 hours each week except for weeks including holidays and that such services be available until at least 10 P.M. at least one day each week or at least 4 hours each Saturday, except for Saturdays falling on holidays; (5) that emergency health care services be available and accessible within the service area at all times; (6) that the ratios of covered persons to health care professional staff members and administrative and other support staff of institutional exclusive providers are such that services will be accessible to covered persons without delays detrimental to their health; (7) that health care professionals that may legally render the services covered as exclusive providers are accessible to covered persons through staffing, contracting, or referral; (8) and that exclusive provider services be rendered pursuant to written procedures that include a documented system for monitoring and evaluating accessibility of care.

Section 2240.1 also prescribes certain requirements with respect to physician's services that constitute exclusive provider services. This section requires that insurers shall ensure that: "there is the equivalent of at least one full-time physician to each 1,200 covered persons and at least the equivalent of one full-time primary care physician for each 2,000 covered persons." Section 2240.1(b) requires that "medically required specialists who are certified or eligible for certification by the appropriate specialty board are accessible to covered persons through staffing, contracting or referral." Section 2240.1(c) provides that the commissioner shall consider to the extent deemed necessary, the practices of comparable health care service plans licensed under California's Knox-Keene Health Care Service Plan Act. Knox-Keene applies to prepaid health plans and provides for extensive regulation and licensure of those plans by the commissioner of corporations.

Assembly Bill 3480 also amended section 10401 of the Insurance Code. That section had previously provided that "any incorporated insurer admitted for disability insurance and any agent of such insurer, that makes or permits any discrimination between insurers of the same class in any manner whatsoever with relation to such insurers, is guilty of a misdemeanor." This section was amended to provide that, in addition to the above quoted language, "the payment to insureds by any insurers of alternative rates of payments negotiated and contracted for with institutional providers shall not constitute a violation of this section." Consequently, insurers are now free to negotiate contracts for alternative rates without being concerned that similarly situated insureds are being discriminated against.

Based upon this legislative activity, it appears that California is actively promoting and encouraging development of PPOs and EPOs with respect to both institutional and professional providers of health care. What appears to have begun as a legislative initiative to reduce the cost of the state's medicaid expenditures, has expanded to become an attempt to open other segments of the health care market to competitive pressure. The effectiveness of such a plan among institutional providers may be attributed in part to relatively low hospital utilization. An excess of underutilized hospital beds has undoubtedly made hospital providers more willing to negotiate with PPOs and EPOs in an attempt to preserve and expand their market share. These same forces are also at work with respect to Medi-Cal reimbursement. The surplus of hospital beds throughout the state may enable the marketplace to reduce the price of hospitalization by making contracting with selected groups attractive to those hospitals with low occupancy.

The recently adopted statutes and regulations provide the necessary legal support for the development of alternative payment rates. These provisions create the necessary exceptions to otherwise applicable requirements that a patient be able to choose a hospital or physician freely; that an insurer not direct, participate in, or control the selection of the hospital or physician from whom the insured obtains services; and that insurers not differentiate between insureds in the same class with respect to negotiated rates.

However, several concerns remain to be addressed in the future. There is some concern tht PPOs will be considered prepaid health plans and therefore subject to Knox-Keene. Application for a license is contingent upon the submission of contracts with providers and subscribers and a demonstration that the plan is financially responsible. With respect to financial matters, the commissioner is mandated to consider "the financial soundness of the plan's arrangements for health care services and a schedule of rates and charges adopted by the plan."

Although PPOs do not fit into the traditional health care service plan format, the commissioner of corporations has continued to scrutinize PPOs and recently issued two options (OP 4664H and OP 4730H) on the subject. These opinions concluded that under the set of facts presented, particular PPOs were not subject to Knox-Keene. There are, however, reasons to suspect that other PPOs will not be able to escape the commissioner's jurisdiction. The commissioner of corporations concluded that the particular PPOs in question were not subject to Knox-Keene primarily because of the fact that the payors contracted directly with providers. However, it is still open to question whether the commissioner will assert jurisdiction over those PPOs that function in a different fashion. The potential applicability of Knox-Keene is of concern to providers because the risk of the insurer's insolvency could be shifted from the insured to the provider. In addition, the application of Knox-Keene to PPOs may have the effect of placing a regulatory overlay on some PPOs, which may retard their development.

In conclusion, California has provided ample latitude within which PPOs may operate. With the exception of EPOs, which are carefully regulated, there does not seem to be any attempt to implement all-encompassing PPO regulations. However, the existing Knox-Keene regulatory framework, if applied to PPOs, will undoubtedly cause some reduction in the rapid growth of PPOs in California.

FLORIDA

Effective October 1, 1983, several amendments to Florida's Insurance Code became law that facilitated the establishment of PPOs in that state. This legislation (contained in Senate Bill No. 28–B) generally allows insurers or groups of insurers providing health insurance to contract with licensed health care providers for alternative rates of payment, permits insurers to limit payments made on behalf of insureds to the preferred payor rate, and provides that such insurance agreements do not constitute a deceptive or unfair trade practice.

Senate Bill 28–B contains a detailed legislative rationale for approving alternative rate contracts in the health care industry. In enacting this bill the legislature specifically referred to the fact that health care spending increased in 1982 almost three times as much as did the Consumer Price Index. According to the Florida legislature, expenditures for hospital care in 1982 increased 19.4 percent, which was considered especially burdensome upon older residents of Florida who, according to the legislature, account for 50 percent of all hospital inpatient days.

In the Preamble to Senate Bill 28–B, three related objectives are referred to. The Florida legislature appears to have endorsed the view that price competition is needed in the health care marketplace in order to reduce costs. This can be done in general by reducing legal barriers to price competition and specifically by permitting third-party payors to negotiate directly with providers to determine rates of payment.

In order to accomplish this goal, Senate Bill 28–B employed an approach similar to that used in California. Section 626.9541 of the Florida code currently enumerates various unfair methods of competition and unfair or deceptive acts or practices applicable to insurers. Senate Bill 28–B added a broad exception to the examples of unfair or deceptive practices:

> (25) ALTERNATIVE RATES OF PAYMENT—Nothing in this Section shall be construed to prohibit an insurer or insurers from negotiating or entering into contracts with licensed health care providers for alternative rates of payment, or from limiting payments under a policy pursuant to agreement with insureds, as long as the insurer offers the benefit of such alternative rates to insureds who select designated providers.

This language specifically carves out an exception to Section 626.9541 (7)(b) of the code. That section provides that intentionally permitting unfair discrimination between actuarially similar individuals for the same premium, policy fees, rates charged, or benefits payable is considered an unfair or deceptive act or practice. The exception to this provision and the broad language contained in the new subsection permit the negotiation of an agreement for alternative rates between insurers and health care providers. However, it would appear necessary that the insurer offer the benefits of such alternative rates to insureds who select designated providers. Insurers who do not "offer the benefit" of the alternative rates to insureds are not protected by the exception.

In general, the Florida legislation is less extensive than that adopted in California. This may be partly because Florida has not considered the possibility of an exclusive provider organization as has California. Consequently, the Florida legislation encourages the development of PPOs by removing some legal barriers to their existence and does not attempt to respond to the unique types of issues raised by EPOs. Although Florida's PPO legislation does not appear to regulate PPO activity directly, it remains to be seen (as was the case in California) whether PPOs will nevertheless fall under regulatory supervision. For the present, PPOs should be able to avoid such regulatory supervision.

NEW YORK

In contrast to the legislative activity encouraging PPO development in both California and Florida, the legislature of the State of New York has not yet enacted specific PPO legislation. However, regulatory action recently taken by the New York State Department of Health has made it arguably illegal for any organization, including PPOs, to negotiate reduced rates of payment with hospitals. The lack of legislation directly relating to PPOs means that any PPO seeking to do business in New York risks regulatory involvement with several different state agencies, depending on the particular form the PPO takes. If a PPO bears the financial risk of its subscribers, or the PPO furnishes medical and/or health or hospital services to its subscribers, it may fall under the jurisdiction of the Superintendent of Insurance. In addition, a PPO may be subject to regulation under New York's Public Health Law (as health maintenance organization) if it offers a comprehensive health service plan to an enrolled population for a basic advance or periodic charge.

In addition to the lack of specific PPO legislation, the ability of PPOs to negotiate discounted special payment rates with hospitals appears to have been severely curtailed as a consequence of New York's hospital reimbursement methodology contained in Section 2807–a of the Public Health Law and the implementing regulations in Part 86 of Title 10 of New York Codes, Rules, and Regulations. New York is currently one of the four "waiver" states (Massachusetts, New Jersey, and Maryland are the others) that have been granted an exemption by the federal government from participating in the medicare prospective payment system (PPS)—the reimbursement system for medicare beneficiaries based on diagnosis related groups. Under New York's Prospective Hospital Reimbursement Methodology or NYPHRM, the State has adopted a revenue cap model for hospital inpatient reimbursement, under which the operating revenue of every hospital is limited to an amount calculated by the Department of Health as the amount necessary for that hospital to operate efficiently. More important, according to the Department of Health, hospitals are required to charge all third-party payors "full charges" and are not permitted to allow any payor to pay a discounted rate. The only non-charge-paying payors are medicare, medicaid, Blue Cross, and more recently, health maintenance organizations. A hospital's average charges, in turn, may not exceed a prescribed differential of the Blue Cross per-diem reimbursement rate. According to the Department of Health, the only exception would be for those groups that had agreements in effect prior to May 1, 1982. Those agreements could continue in effect.

Hospitals are therefore prohibited by regulation from agreeing to accept less than full charges from any payor, even though some hospitals may be willing to grant price concessions in return for other benefits (such as increased utilization or cash flow). In addition, NYPHRM essentially guarantees that Blue Cross will be given a competitive rate advantage over other third-party payors (other than health maintenance organizations, which are to reimburse hospitals at the Blue Cross rate).

In late 1983, these provisions were challenged in federal court by plaintiffs seeking to enjoin those portions of NYPHRM which made it illegal for hospitals to negotiate discount rates with certain third-party payors. This lawsuit, entitled *Rebaldo* v. *Cuomo and Axelrod,*[1] was brought by a self-insured employee welfare fund governed by the Employee Retirement Income Security Act of 1974 (ERISA).[2] The welfare fund raised a number of issues, some of constitutional dimension, relating to the arbitrariness of a statutory scheme that protected Blue Cross's competitive position and that would have the effect of forcing the Fund to relinquish its self-insured status in New York and purchase Blue Cross coverage in order to obtain satisfactory coverage for its members. The welfare fund argued that purchasing Blue Cross coverage would lead to the perverse result of the welfare fund paying more for health care coverage while hospitals would be receiving less in reimbursement. The State respondents (Blue Cross attempted unsuccessfully to intervene in the litigation but was instead permitted to participate as an *amicus*) argued that the challenged portions of NYPHRM constituted insurance regulations and stressed the state's primary role in that area. Without addressing the plaintiff's other allegations, the district court held that Public Health Law Section 2807–a.6(b) is preempted by ERISA insofar as it relates to ERISA funds and enjoined enforcement against all such funds. The Court rejected the State's argument that the ERISA savings clause, which exempts from preemption "any law of any State which regulates insurance," was applicable to NYPHRM.

Relying on *Group Life & Health Insurance Co.*[3] (which construed the phrase "business of insurance"), the court reasoned that by negotiating with third parties for the delivery of health care services at a discount, the welfare fund was not engaged in the "business of insurance." The district court, therefore, narrowly construed the specific exceptions to ERISA's general preemption rule. Accordingly, Section 2807–a.6(b) was not saved from preemption under ERISA's savings clause.

Furthermore, the court did not find, as was contended by *amicus* (Blue Cross), that the provisions of NYPHRM were converted into federal law by the medicare waiver granted to New York State by the federal government. The court, accordingly, held that Section 2807–a.6(b) was not saved from preemption under Section 514(d) of ERISA which states:

> Nothing in this subchapter shall be construed to alter, amend, modify, invalidate, impair or supersede any law of the United States or any rule or regulation issued under any such law.

The state appealed the lower court decision in *Rebaldo* to the United States Court of Appeals for the Second Circuit. On appeal, the Hospital Association of New York State submitted an amicas brief on the state's behalf. The sole issue on appeal was whether Congress, in enacting

ERISA, had intended to preclude the subsequent adoption of a medicare reimbursement "demonstration project" to the extent that the demonstration projected affected hospital rates charged to self-insured employee benefit plans. Reversing the District Court, the Second Circuit held that NYPHRM was not preempted by ERISA and ruled that the preemption provision was intended to prevent state interference with federal control of ERISA plans but did not exclude such plans from regulation of any purely local transaction. The Court found that the containment of hospital costs was a proper exercise of a state's police powers, writing as follows:

> The purchase of hospital service is like the purchase of public utility service, or of any other service or commodity whose price is controlled by the State. Insofar as the regulation of hospital rates affects a plan's cost of doing business, it also may be analogized to State labor laws that govern working conditions and labor costs, to rent control laws that determine what employee benefit plans pay or receive for rental property, and even to such minor costs as the Thruway, bridge and tunnel tolls that are charged to plans' officers or employees. In short, if ERISA is held to invalidate every State action that may increase the cost of operating employee benefit plans, those plans will be permitted a charmed existence that never was contemplated by Congress. Where, as here, a State statute of general application does not affect the structure, the administration, or the type of benefits provided by an ERISA plan, the mere fact that the statute has some economic impact on the plan does not require that the statute be invalidated.

Although the Second Circuit vacated the District Court judgment, the matter was remanded for further proceedings consistent with the opinion.

Although there is no specific PPO legislation in New York, the legislature and the Department of Health have thus far indicated through its statewide hospital rate-setting methodology that it opposes discounts for nongovernmental payors other than Blue Cross and health maintenance organizations. More fundamentally, the New York regulatory climate currently favors a public utility model for health care regulation and cost containment, rather than the competitive model which is in favor in California and Florida. In order to control costs, the Health Department has acted to reduce health care expenditures by direct control over reimbursement rates. In exchange, the hospital industry appears to have achieved a certain amount of rate stability and protection from price competition.

Four additional observations are appropriate:

1. New York is currently exempt from DRG reimbursement. DRG reimbursement, unlike cost-based reimbursement which continues to be used in New York, places substantial pressure on hospitals to consider health care as a product (actually 467 different products). DRG reimbursement then puts pressure on hospitals to determine which of those products it can produce in a cost-effective fashion.

2. New York hospitals are generally operated by not-for-profit corporations.
3. Under New York's Public Health Law, publicly traded corporations are prohibited from directly operating hospitals.
4. Hospital utilization in New York is generally quite high. In fact there is a long-running dispute between the Health Department and the Hospital Industry as to whether there is a surplus of acute care beds in New York State in general and New York City in particular.

This combination of factors may contribute to a regulatory climate that is generally not conducive to PPOs and the free market environment in which they seem to thrive. It remains to be seen whether changes in the regulatory structure, notably in the area of utilization review, and competition for certificate of need approval in the future will alter this assessment.

OHIO

As is the case in New York, there is no legislation directly pertaining to PPOs in Ohio. The development of PPOs in Ohio, however, has been fostered by two recent events. In September 1983, a consent decree was entered into by the parties to an antitrust action brought by the attorney general of the state against the Greater Cleveland Hospital Association. This consent decree has the effect of allowing individual hospitals in the greater Cleveland area to negotiate with third-party payors for reductions from a hospital's charge schedule. The second development, probably less significant, was an opinion issued by the antitrust section of the Ohio attorney general's office to the Department of Insurance relating the legality of PPOs under federal antitrust laws.

The opinion of the Ohio attorney general, issued on November 17, 1983, generally discussed the legality of PPOs under the Sherman Act,[4] and included an analysis of whether participating providers engage in illegal price fixing and concerted refusals to deal (i.e., group boycotts). The opinion concluded that PPOs would generally be viewed as lawful.

The opinion carefully distinguished between "naked" price-fixing agreements that are invalid per se and those agreements in which the restraint on prices is secondary to a valid business purpose and are consequently to be reviewed under the Rule of Reason standard of antitrust liability. Under the Rule of Reason, courts are to examine and balance the procompetitive effects of a practice against its anticompetitive effects, scrutinize the degree of market power possessed by the participants, and determine whether there are less restrictive alternatives to achieve the same legitimate business goals. The attorney general concluded that price agreements by PPOs should be assessed under the Rule of Reason. The likelihood of finding unlawful price fixing will depend upon the organizational form of the PPO and its share of the applicable market.

In the opinion of the Ohio attorney general, nonprovider-controlled PPOs (i.e., carrier-based PPOs; employer or union fund PPOs) and third-party, administrator-based PPOs, which negotiate payment rates with physicians or hospitals on an individual basis, can minimize price-fixing concerns. However, where the providers act to set reimbursement rates collectively, illegal price fixing is more likely. Collective rate setting by providers is not a prerequisite for the establishment or successful operation of PPOs.

According to the attorney general, provider-controlled PPOs are able to avoid per se liability for price-fixing because their agreements are secondary to the creation of the PPO entity. As opposed to the maximum fee agreements held per se unlawful by the United States Supreme Court in *Arizona* v. *Maricopa County Medical Society,*[5] the Ohio attorney general views the rate-setting activity of provider-based PPOs as more than naked price fixing: "Physicians or hospitals who combine to form a PPO do much more than fix prices, they pool their capital and undertake the risks associated with the establishment of a new method of marketing their services. The integration of marketing, claims administration, billing and other functions warrants the conclusion that the resultant price restraint is ancillary in nature."

While traditional insurers usually provide reimbursement at the same level regardless of the particular provider, PPOs provide their subscribers with an economic incentive to seek health care from member providers. Because of utilization review and other quality-control mechanisms frequently employed by the PPO, providers have an incentive to render efficient, high-quality, patient care services. The Ohio attorney general warns, however, that where nearly all of the community's providers are members of a PPO, the procompetitive benefits may tend to be outweighed by the anticompetitive effects of such a monopoly. Under the attorney general's analysis, a 15 percent to 20 percent share of a community's market by a PPO would not raise these monopoly issues.

A similar approach is taken in analyzing PPO liability under an illegal boycott theory. Again the attorney general concludes that a Rule of Reason analysis is appropriate inasmuch as the exclusion of some physician or hospital competitors is merely an incidental consequence of the formation of the PPO. Absent undue market power, provider- and nonprovider-based PPOs may contract with the providers of its choice without engaging in an illegal boycott. The purpose of the PPO is not to exclude competitive providers but rather to create new markets for the preferred providers. "Excluded providers remain free to pursue other available business opportunities, such as competing for the business of subscribers of traditional insurers, or by affiliating with other health plans."

To the extent that potential antitrust liability in the form of illegal price fixing or claims of a boycott create uncertainty to PPO organizers, the opinion of the Ohio attorney general provides some limited degree of comfort. Perhaps of greater interest to PPOs is the terms of a settlement of an antitrust case brought by the attorney general against the Greater Cleveland Hospital Association.

In July, 1980, the State of Ohio brought a lawsuit against the Greater Cleveland Hospital Association (GCHA) alleging violations of federal and state antitrust laws with respect to third-party reimbursement by insurance carriers. GCHA's conduct, which allegedly violated state and federal antitrust provisions, had the effect of virtually eliminating competition from the hospital insurance industry. Apparently GCHA had developed an insurance plan in which its members, approximately 90 percent of the hospitals in the greater Cleveland area, could participate. At the same time, it was alleged that GCHA had attempted to prevent individual hospitals from negotiating alternative plans with third-party payors, notably commercial insurance carriers.

The State further alleged that GCHA and its members created Blue Cross of Northeast Ohio to administer its joint insurance plan and that GCHA acted to negotiate collectively to set inpatient charges at its member hospitals at levels in excess of the rates charged to Blue Cross. Other health insurance plans were therefore unable to compete effectively. After three years, the suit was settled with the signing of a consent decree in which GCHA admitted no wrongdoing but agreed to a permanent injunction being entered against it that enjoined a number of activities.[6]

As part of the consent decree, GCHA was permanently enjoined from entering into any agreement that prevents, restricts, hinders, or discourages any hospital from organizing, operating, or contracting with insurance prepayment plans. GCHA was also restrained from carrying on activity that has the purpose and effect of restraining competition among hospitals in the marketing of hospital services to prepayment plans.

Additionally, GCHA was prohibited from interfering with any attempts by individual hospitals to negotiate a special payment rate for hospital services, to require that GCHA or Blue Cross approve any such agreement, or to allow GCHA to negotiate hospital reimbursement rates for hospitals that control greater than 10 percent of the market in any standard metropolitan statistical area (SMSA). In addition, the consent decree attempts to sever the special relationship between GCHA and Blue Cross by restricting their ability to attend meetings together.

In summary, while Ohio does not have legislation encouraging the development of PPOs, preferred plan arrangements should be encouraged by the recent actions of the attorney general. Although the attorney general's opinion is certainly not binding upon private litigants or the United States government, it does provide some encouragement to PPOs. Although there are no assurances that individual hospitals will want to negotiate with PPOs, the GCHA case provides some encouragement that the attorney general in Ohio is taking an aggressive posture with respect to artificial barriers being set up to impede the negotiation process.

CONCLUSION

At the present time, PPOs appear to be popular and generally are being encouraged. Much of this success can be attributed to the fact that PPOs appear to be responsive to current policy considerations such as cost containment and deregulation of health care services and insurance. Both California and Florida are attempting to reduce health care costs to consumers and third-party payors by reducing entry barriers for third-party payors and thus increase competition for the health care dollar. At the same time these states are permitting new third-party payors to negotiate directly with health care providers for rates of payment. PPOs also offer consumers readily apparent financial incentives to choose "preferred providers." "Deregulation" is another important policy consideration that is currently popular. The development of PPOs can be viewed as an important step in the potential deregulation of two previously highly regulated industries—insurance and health care. Thus the pro-PPO actions taken in California and Ohio and to a lesser degree in Florida constitute primarily insurance deregulation. The effect of this deregulation on the hospital industry is less clear and does not appear to have been directly addressed by the legislatures in California and Florida. In New York, the PPO issue has been viewed from the perspective of the health care provider. Consequently a policy decision has been made to protect the hospital industry from negotiated rates other than those set by the State Department of Health. It remains to be seen how health care providers will fare with PPOs and whether the increased competition they portend will be beneficial to the overall health care delivery system.

NOTES

1. No. 83-8707 (S.D.N.Y., March 1984).
2. 29 U.S.C. Section 1001 *et seq.*
3. A/K/A/ *Blue Shield of Texas* v. *Royal Drug Co.*, 440 U.S. 205 (1979).
4. 15 U.S.C. Section 1.
5. 102 S. Ct. 2466 (1982).

6. *State of Ohio, ex rel. Celebrezze* v. *Greater Cleveland Hospital Association*, Trade Cases (CCH) par. 65,685 (N.D. Ohio, September 21, 1983).

PART 2

PREFERRED PROVIDER ARRANGEMENTS

1. Marketplace Fundamentals
2. Purchaser Objectives and Priorities

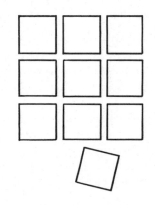

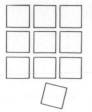
EVALUATION CRITERIA FOR ASSESSING NEGOTIATED PROVIDER AGREEMENTS: A GUIDE FOR HEALTHCARE PURCHASERS

Peter Boland, PhD

President
Boland Healthcare Consultants
Berkeley, CA

The starting point for assessing preferred provider arrangements should be to approach buying health care services or insurance coverage as a commodity like other goods and services. It is a standard purchasing decision that should be scrutinized at least as closely as other products with comparable costs.

In assessing different preferred provider arrangements, purchasers should ask questions such as the following: Is it a creditable and reliable product? How will it save money? Why is it a better managed health care system? Does it include the necessary cost-control functions and quality-assurance features to produce cost-effective health care services? If it provides services more efficiently, the results should be evident in the premium or in the anticipated cost to self-insured groups.

A difficult task facing purchasers is to identify and assess important issues about preferred provider arrangements. This article addresses many of the major issues and the nature of preferred provider contracting. It includes an executive summary of key negotiating issues, which is followed by a 10-point evaluation framework covering the following topics:

1. Cost Management Incentives.
2. Organizational Issues.
3. Payment Mechanism.
4. Utilization Management and Quality Assurance.
5. Geographic Coverage and Access.
6. Scope of Services.
7. Legal Considerations.
8. Financial Issues.
9. Performance Monitoring.
10. Consumer Satisfaction.

These topics can be used as a guide for making the decision to contract for health care services through a preferred provider arrangement.

PREFERRED PROVIDER CONTRACTING

The market for health care services has become increasingly competitive. This is due to a variety of reasons. First, there is an oversupply of physicians and hospitals in most metropolitan areas. Second, the growth of health maintenance organizations is an increasing economic threat to traditional medicine. Third, legal prohibitions on selective contracting have been removed in many states. Fourth, business, organized labor, and government are using their buying power to gain greater control over health care costs.

Preferred provider organizations capitalize on the current oversupply of doctors and hospitals. In theory, they encourage competition among providers—on the basis of price, quality and access—to render services to designated patients. In turn, patients are channeled to efficient providers who may be willing to accept competitive prices, have another party review services they provide, and meet other contracting requirements. If the system works accordingly, noncontracting providers may find a dwindling pool of available patients.

Preferred provider arrangements are a product of this new competitive contracting environment among providers as well as a contributing factor in making the market itself more competitive. These arrangements have become known as preferred provider organizations (PPOs) even though there is not always an organization as such. They often entail *selective* arrangements between different contracting parties for health care services rather than a particular organization like an HMO, which provides medical care. Preferred provider contracting is a process for negotiating specific medical services between health care purchasers and providers at agreed-upon prices. A preferred provider organization is a generic type of administrative structure designed to accomplish such service agreements. It will vary according to the objectives of the participants and the characteristics of the local marketplace.

The basic concept of PPOs is that consumers get better value for their health care dollar if they utilize more efficient (i.e., the ability to achieve the desired result at a minimum of cost) doctors and hospitals. This could include the following: (1) obtaining enriched benefits coverage or more appropriate services than before at comparable or less cost, (2) getting the same amount of care as before at less cost, or (3) receiving less services at lower cost from providers who are more cost effective than previous hospitals, physicians, and other health professionals.

The purpose of selective contracting is to slow the rate of cost escalation. It addresses some of the fundamental issues by changing purchaser,[1] patient, and provider[2] incentives. The traditional incentives rewarded inefficiency. Preferred provider arrangements offer purchasers a potentially cost-effective mechanism for buying health care services. By influencing consumers to choose more efficient physicians and hospitals, purchasers stretch their health care dollars. This is an attractive employer option as an alternative to reducing employee benefits. Employers would rather shift to more efficient providers than reduce benefits and risk employee dissatisfaction.

Selective contracting makes both purchasers *and* providers more sensitive to the price of health care services. While preferred provider arrangements have the potential to save the purchaser money, the amount of money saved is due to a number of factors, such as (1) the level of reimbursement negotiated, (2) the types of preferred arrangements available in the service area, (3) demographic and utilization characteristics of the employees, (4) geographic concentration of employees (and their dependents) at job sites or residential areas, and (5) the degree to which financial incentives are developed to influence beneficiary choice.

The underlying premises of each major participant about preferred provider contracting should be clarified at the beginning of the negotiation process because they bear directly on the expectations of each party and how the program is evaluated. Providers are interested in whether the arrangement is viewed as long term and whether the purchaser is willing to include the right mix of incentives and disincentives to attract adequate enrollment in the preferred plan. Purchasers are concerned about three basic issues. First, whether provider motivation is reflected in plan design as a defensive posture to maintain market share or as aggressive positioning to take advantage of a new market opportunity. Second, whether provider business objectives support effective utilization-management controls and a willingness to share financial risks and rewards with purchasers. Third, whether providers are flexible enough to develop service agreements with purchasers that respond to particular needs and constraints.

As with other standard purchasing functions, employers and employee organizations should negotiate preferred provider agreements in relation to their own business objectives for health services or insurance coverage. In formulating these objectives, purchasers can use their own internal resources to develop protocols for evaluating different preferred provider arrangements on the market. Businesses can draw on the recommendations of corporate functions such as materials and logistics, purchasing, finance, legal, medical director, and benefits compensation. In-house staff can then be supplemented by outside resources skilled in hospital pricing, provider reimbursement, utilization management, and contract negotiation.

The following executive summary presents an overview of key *purchaser* issues to address in negotiating preferred provider agreements.

EXECUTIVE SUMMARY

Cost Management Incentives. The employee *benefits structure* should be designed to incorporate an appropriate mix of financial incentives and disincentives that discourages both unnecessary utilization and underutilization of services. The level of *financial risk* borne by providers is an indication of their willingness to accept accountability. Information should be provided on physician cost performance, utilization patterns, and financial incentives. Using *treatment alternatives* to hospital care can result in cost reduction and more appropriate medical care. These include outpatient surgery clinics, surgi-centers, preadmission diagnostic tests, birthing centers, hospice care for the terminally ill, and home care or extended care for rehabilitation.

Organization. The organizational structure of a preferred provider arrangement should encourage representation of providers and purchasers at the governance level to ensure accountability. Purchasers should be cautious in contracting with an organization that is not *fully operational* at the time agreements to provide services are negotiated.

Preferred provider arrangements can be sponsored by providers, health insurers, entrepreneurs and purchasers. There are pros and cons for each type of arrangement. *Hospital based* PPOs usually rely on internal utilization review programs and have difficulty screening out physicians who do not practice cost-effective medicine but already have admitting privileges at the hospital. *Physician based* PPOs tend to focus on ambulatory care to the exclusion of hospital care. *Jointly sponsored* arrangements require cooperation and commitment among physicians and hospitals on common management policies.

Health insurer sponsored PPOs provide stability and a large client base that offers potential leverage in the market. Insurance carriers have generally been slow to implement effective cost containment techniques for reducing health care premiums. *Entrepreneur based* PPOs are free to contract with any provider but often lack the technical resources to identify the most efficient physicians and providers in a community.

Purchaser initiated PPOs can develop contracts that fit the specific needs of employers and employee organizations rather than those of providers. A serious drawback is purchaser unfamiliarity with the technical aspects of medical care, insurance, and health information systems.

Membership Selection Standards. Provider selection standards should be based on hospitals and physicians that have demonstrated cost-effective medical care before participating in the PPO.

Utilization Review. Internal cost control functions are necessary to change traditional provider practice patterns. *Utilization control* procedures should monitor physician behavior for inappropriate and unnecessary services. Utilization management activities performed by an independent review organization or in conjunction with the hospital are generally more effective than sole reliance on internal hospital review ("the fox guarding the hen house"). Hospital monitoring programs include the following types of reviews: preadmission, concurrent, retrospective, ancillary services, physician services, and outpatient. Utilization review and quality assurance procedures should include disciplinary sanctions and financial penalties to encourage physician compliance.

Payment Method. The single best indicator of a PPO's capacity to monitor costs and utilization of services is the payment method. The most prevalent reimbursement schemes are based on per diem rates, negotiated discounts from billed charges, price based on diagnosis related groups (DRGs), and capitation. Information on hospital per diems are available to form a negotiating base for providers. Without a strict utilization review mechanism, this method can act as an incentive to keep patients in the hospital longer than medically necessary.

Negotiated discounts are problematical because they can both reduce the basic hospital rate per day and encourage the frequency of treatments and number of procedures ordered for a patient. Negotiated provider agreements will not succeed on discounts alone because it is not the percentage of discounts that determines the amount of savings. Discounts without proper utilization controls are illusory. Utilization control results in greater savings than discounts because it reduces the frequency of unnecessary services and the amount of resources used in providing those services.

Per case reimbursement schemes such as *per discharge* and *diagnosis related groups* (DRGs) discourage unnecessary length of stay and intensity of services by tying a fixed amount of reimbursement to different types of care or illness categories regardless of how much it costs to treat a particular case. There is a tendency to diagnose certain illnesses according to the most lucrative reimbursement categories ("DRG creep") in order to maximize the revenue per patient.

Capitation reimbursement based on a predetermined rate for each covered employee is difficult to administer for current PPOs with flexible enrollment policies. Providers could be paid for enrollees who may never be treated as patients due to "freedom of choice" provisions.

Access and Services. A network of primary care and specialty physicians is necessary to ensure choice of providers and convenient access to preferred providers in the service area. Participating hospitals should provide a full range of acute care services.

Performance Monitoring. The provider-purchaser agreement should establish the content, format, and frequency for standardized reports. Data gathering and statistical analysis should be targeted to user needs and priorities concerning utilization, costs, and program operations in order to be a useful management tool. Penalty provisions should be built into the contract specifications to assure full compliance on reporting requirements.

EVALUATION FRAMEWORK

COST MANAGEMENT INCENTIVES

The incentives in the traditional fee-for-service payment system have rewarded health care providers for providing more services, performing more tests, and often generating a more intense level of care than necessary. This incentive system has given rise to numerous alternative health care delivery systems and case management systems that place the provider at financial risk for services provided. PPOs will be effective in reducing costs to the extent that they incorporate two types of financial inducements: (*a*) incentives and disincentives for doctors and hospitals to be efficient and compete for patients, and (*b*) incentives and disincentives for employees to appropriately use the most cost-effective providers of service.

It is necessary to review cost control functions available in a preferred provider arrangement in order to judge whether price reductions will be offset by potential increases in both inpatient and outpatient utilization. Without adequate internal cost-control functions, providers will be unlikely to change their method of practicing medicine because traditional payment mechanisms have rewarded a liberal use of tests, procedures, and hospital stays. The following features should be considered by employers and employee organizations in evaluating the impact of cost-management incentives associated with different preferred provider arrangements:

— Utilization control.
— Risk sharing.
— Uninflated rates.
— Treatment alternatives.
— Health promotion and illness prevention.
— Administrative controls.
— Benefits redesign.

Utilization Control

Patient misuse of the health care system occurs most often through lack of basic awareness and skills in dealing with common problems (e.g., the fever of a common cold) and understanding how the health care is organized (e.g., inappropriate use of the emergency room as the point of entry for routine medical care). Utilization management activities can be performed in one of three ways: internally delegated to the hospital, contracted to an external review organization independent from the hospital, or shared hospital and third-party review.

Delegated review can be a serious disadvantage if existing hospital review programs are inadequate or if participating hospitals have different review criteria that would compromise comparison among facilities. Nondelegated review is costly but overcomes the problem of comparability among hospitals. It can be hampered if different enrollee groups are too small to generate an adequate database of cases for performance evaluation. There is an additional cost for utilization review functions that can be paid for directly by consumers on a case-by-case basis, indirectly by consumers through administrative fees passed on by the PPO, directly by the PPO out of revenues, or directly by the insurance company, which would be uncommon.

Most provider sponsored PPOs claim to have a high quality internal provider monitoring program. However, independent hospital review by third-party review organizations or combined third-party and hospital review (e.g., nondelegated preadmission authorization and retrospective bill review coupled with delegated concurrent review) are generally more successful than sole reliance on internal hospital review to reduce unnecessary utilization and intensity of services. Effective provider monitoring procedures should be an integral part of the PPO for two reasons: inappropriate and unnecessary services are sometimes provided by doctors and hospitals, and consumers find it almost impossible to make judgments about the appropriateness of medical care after such care has been initiated.

Effective prior authorization programs result in more appropriate use of hospital services and protect patients from unnecessary risk. Patient screening programs like preadmission review/certification for hospital confinements are only as effective as the screening criteria used and the competence of the reviewers. PPOs should provide clear and comprehensive information on such programs to the employer and employee organizations. Employees should be educated about the purpose, structure, function, and financial implications of the preadmission system. Complicated or delayed patient preadmission screening systems or second opinion programs may result in a lack of appropriate care and high dissatisfaction among both providers and enrollees. Overly complicated systems may also result in lack of use by patients and providers. For example, preadmission review systems based on lists of specific medical procedures may not be understood by enrollees who are not used to medical terminology. The proliferation of different preadmission lists by different groups increases confusion among providers. A preadmission program applied to all elective admissions may be easier to explain to employees and may help assure more consistent use of a program.

One effective control in preventing unnecessary surgery has been the successful implementation of programs that require a second opinion by another independent physician before surgery is performed. Many successful programs permit the enrollee to inform the physician recommending surgery that the enrollee's plan requires a second opinion. This permits the patient to seek the opinion without alienating the recommending physician. The second opinion should be sought from a physician who has no professional or social association with the first. The enrollee then makes the final decision about whether to undergo surgery unless a prior authorization program is also in place. In that event, both programs should be coordinated so conflicting decisions are not made that confuse the employee and the provider. This can be accomplished by including questions about the second opinion on a preadmission request form or by instructing enrollees to provide a report of the second opinion to the hospital.

A range of utilization review procedures are available to providers for controlling unnecessary and inappropriate utilization. The most common procedures are listed below in Exhibit 1.

The way in which preferred provider arrangements collect and analyze data and conduct utilization review programs will reflect how serious they are about cost-effective treatment. Predetermined utilization-control policies and advance provider endorsement of penalty provisions may be necessary to encourage compliance with established performance protocols. Fee schedules that are diagnosis and procedure specific enable plan sponsors to link efficiency and productivity to financial reward. Despite the added paper work, physicians should be required to furnish a specified minimum record documenting office services so the plan can link together inpatient and outpatient data.

EXHIBIT 1
Utilization Review Procedures

Prior authorization:
  Preadmission review
  Second opinion for surgery and invasive procedures

Concurrent review:
  Admission certification
  Continued stay review
  Discharge planning

Retrospective review:
  Medical claims review
  Hospital claims
  Ancillary services and procedures review
  Claims pricing and auditing

Data analysis:
  Physician profiling and trend analysis
  Hospital profiling and trend analysis
  Service profiling and trend analysis

Risk Sharing

Financial incentives for providers are intended to influence physician practice patterns. Without a sufficient financial incentive (i.e., reward or penalty), providers are not likely to change traditional practice styles. Since PPO payment is usually on a negotiated fee-for-service basis, risk is normally borne by the insurance carrier or the self-insured employer or purchaser group. However, risk can be assumed or shared at any level, as shown below in Exhibit 2, as long as it is legal in the state where the

EXHIBIT 2
Typical Preferred Provider Organization Structure

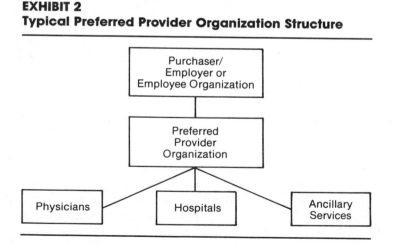

PPO is offered. The level of shared risk is an indication of provider willingness to accept accountability for the performance of the organization.

A common mechanism used in independent practice associations to increase individual physician risk is to withhold a percentage from their fee-for-service claims payment, which is placed in a risk or retention pool. A retention pool can likewise be created to reward cost-effective physicians in PPOs. Under this arrangement, an agreed-upon amount is taken out of provider payments and set aside (e.g., 10 percent). Funds are later distributed based on how well providers meet individual performance goals or if the overall objectives of the PPO are reached.

Financial incentives for physicians to develop cost-effective medical practices may range from continued participation in the PPO to direct "bonuses" for cost-effective care. Some purchasers, however, do not support the bonus concept on the grounds that providers should not be rewarded extra for doing what is expected in the first place. PPOs should provide information on physician cost performance, utilization patterns, and financial incentives to the buyers of care.

Uninflated Rates

Negotiated payment methods (e.g., reduced hospital charges) should be linked to an uninflated price index like the Consumer Price Index. From a purchaser's standpoint, this is preferable to inflated standards based primarily on medical price indices. Likewise, hospital charges should reflect a relatively constant cost profile over a multiyear period to guard against artificially raising charges prior to negotiating discounts. Basing hospital discounts on current charges rather than on costs will automatically be starting at an inflated level. Little money will be saved if a PPO has contracted with the most expensive hospitals at a 20 percent discount, and employees move from less expensive hospitals to more expensive hospitals that have been discounted. However, by identifying more efficient, less expensive hospitals to begin with, discounting could be deemphasized in favor of fixed payment methods like per diems or diagnosis related groups.

Using the "usual, customary, and reasonable" (UCR) schedule as the basis for negotiating price reductions may in some cases (and for some services) be starting from an inflated rate, particularly if there is an oversupply of physician specialties in the community. It would be advantageous for PPO price negotiators to have information on the range of costs for any given service in a community and be prepared to actively bargain for reductions below the UCR schedule.

Treatment Alternatives

Using the most appropriate level of care for a patient's medical condition is an important part of cost-effective treatment. More and more services can be safely performed outside the hospital at greatly reduced cost without inconveniencing the patient or jeopardizing quality of care. These services include outpatient surgery clinics, licensed surgi-centers, and conducting preadmission diagnostic laboratory tests and X rays. Offering families the option of birthing centers, hospice care for the terminally ill, and home care or extended care for rehabilitation when these programs are available in the community is important to appropriateness of care issues. Care provided in settings other than the hospital is often more effective and comfortable as well as less expensive.

It is also necessary to monitor the use of alternative health care services and the utilization patterns of alternative health care providers. A form of case management is required to assure cost-effective treatment, since some hospitals, for example, charge as much for outpatient surgery as for inpatient surgery. Using treatment alternatives to hospital care could result in cost reduction in several areas, including the setting where the service is provided, the personnel used, and in some cases, the style of practice. PPOs should collect and make available the data necessary to evaluate the appropriateness and use of treatment alternatives.

Health Promotion and Illness Prevention

Health education and health promotion programs can selectively reduce costs and have been integrated into a number of corporate and public employee plans. Such programs can be included in the benefit structure of the PPO and should concentrate on employee needs. These would include stress management, smoking cessation, alcohol and substance abuse, weight control and nutrition, physical fitness, management of chronic illnesses such as hypertension and diabetes, and consumer education on how to use health care services effectively.

The economic return-on-investment in most health promotion programs is long range. However, the effect of many illness prevention services on health care costs and health status is much more immediate. Illness prevention services are attractive low-cost options for consumers. Preventive services include prenatal visits, well-baby care, immunizations, self-help medical care, and screening programs for hypertension, diabetes, and glaucoma.

Administrative Controls

Preferred plan arrangements should incorporate provisions to administer coordination of benefits (COB) and to make medical payments to injured employees whose injuries are the fault of a third party. These measures are evolving to account for various cost containment programs. However, PPO administrators need to define their approach carefully and ensure proper execution of procedures to generate savings. The National Association of Insurance Commissioners' model for COB and subrogation do not apply very well to these measures for PPOs because they involve negotiated rates rather than regular rates (i.e., billed charges).

Benefits Redesign

The difference in out-of-pocket costs between using a preferred provider rather than a nonpreferred provider should be significant for enrollees but not so precipitous as to "lock" them into using only contracting providers. A "lock in" provision contradicts the freedom of choice concept, which from many employees' perspective is one of the current attractions of a PPO over an HMO.

Increasing employee contributions (i.e., cost sharing) in order to lower utilization of health care services is a source of controversy between employer and employee organizations and is of prime concern at the bargaining table. The purpose of cost sharing by employees can be to reduce unnecessary utilization as well as to shift health plan costs from the employer to the employee. If the incentive to not utilize is "too low" then unnecessary utilization will likely occur. Conversely, if the disincentive is "too high" then plan costs may rise substantially over time since underutilization can result in more serious illness. In a PPO, these incentives and disincentives can be balanced through an appropriate design of copayments and deductibles and selected expansion of low-cost benefits. This will protect the actual value of the health plan benefits from being eroded by unnecessary utilization, which needlessly wastes resources and results in higher costs.

Clear communication and employee education on how to use health plan services most effectively is essential for the success of the program. Employees should be advised that to obtain the most benefit from a health plan they should check to see if their physician or clinic would be covered at the maximum rate. Statements like "free choice of physician" should be qualified. The success of the program also depends on purchasers notifying the utilization-review organization that a particular patient is with a PPO. One way of achieving this is to provide incentives for enrollees to tell providers they are in a preferred provider arrangement.

Where hospital utilization and cost data are available for prior periods, employers and employee organizations should assess which hospitals and physicians are most frequently used by employees under existing health plans. This information can serve two purposes. First, if particular facilities are heavily used by a group, the volume could provide some negotiating leverage, especially for self-insured groups. Second, if facilities in a proposed PPO network are infrequently used, the success of getting large numbers of employees to exchange physicians and hospitals is doubtful in the short run and may result in dissatisfaction with the program in the long run.

The extent to which employee education is needed will depend on the past use of health services and the shift in behavior expected under a new health plan arrangement. Employees generally select health coverage when they are well and the selection may be heavily influenced by price, especially if payroll deductions are made for dependent coverage. However, when employees become ill, they are likely to rely on an existing physician, clinic, or hospital relationship for services.

ORGANIZATIONAL ISSUES

The organizational characteristics of a PPO are important to examine. They indicate a great deal about why the PPO was formed, who controls it, and the scope and quality of health care services it offers. Three of the most important organizational issues are the structure of the plan in relation to limiting corporate liability, sponsorship of the PPO, and the operational status of the plan.

Structure

The PPO can be organized as a nonprofit corporation, i.e., a nonprofit health plan, a product line of a nonprofit corporation, a hospital service sponsored plan; or as a separate profit line of a corporation, i.e., an entrepreneur/investor sponsored plan, an insurance carrier indemnity option.

Sponsorship

There are pros and cons for each type of preferred provider arrangement. The advisability of one versus another depends on the particular needs of the purchaser. The most common forms of preferred provider arrangements are those organized or initiated by providers, insurers, purchasers, and entrepreneurs. Different sponsors for each of these four types of PPOs are listed below.

Provider Based PPOs. Sponsors include:

— Hospital.
— Multihospital network.
— Hospital based independent practice association (IPA).
— Hospital-physician joint venture.
— Health maintenance organization (HMO).
— Independent practice association network.
— Foundation for medical care or clinic network.
— Physician network.
— Allied health professionals.

Provider based PPOs generally offer physicians and hospitals larger roles in shaping the operating policies of the organization, which creates strong incentives to make it work. However, a consensus style of management in such PPOs may compromise the flexibility of the organization.

Hospital sponsored systems usually rely on internal utilization review programs rather than combined third-party and hospital review or contracting with independent review organizations outside the hospital. This may be a serious disadvantage that could lead to unnecessary utilization. Hospital based PPOs also tend to have problems with screening out physicians who do not practice cost-effective medicine but who already have admitting privileges at the hospital. Hospitals rely on physicians for admissions and are reluctant to restrict PPO membership to any staff physicians and risk alienating them, especially when the initial volume of PPO patients is expected to be a relatively small part of the hospital's business. A hospital based PPO can be perceived by employers as "the fox guarding the hen house." On the other hand, PPOs organized by physicians tend to concentrate on ambulatory care to the exclusion of hospital care, where the majority of health care costs occur. Treating patients on an ambulatory basis who might otherwise be treated as inpatients could lead to substantial savings.

A joint venture sponsored by physicians and hospitals tends to overcome some of the disadvantages of PPOs separately sponsored by physicians and hospitals. The biggest advantage of jointly sponsored arrangements is the commitment of both parties to clearly defined management goals and policies. Stability becomes the issue in such ventures. A further drawback of most joint ventures is that relatively little input is sought from purchasers in designing the PPO.

Insurer Based PPOs. Sponsors include:

— Health/hospital service plans (Blue Cross and Blue Shield).[3]
— Commercial insurance carriers.

PPOs sponsored by health insurers offer a track record of experience in underwriting, risk assumption, and claims administration, which are important features in operating a successful alternative delivery system. Insurance carriers also represent a large client base, which offers potential market leverage in negotiating favorable service agreements with providers.

To date, insurance companies have generally been slow to implement effective cost containment techniques for reducing health care premiums. While a number of the largest carriers operate successful health maintenance organizations, most carriers have been reluctant to encourage the growth of alternative delivery systems so far. However, sponsorship of a PPO by an insurance company indicates an increased interest in stemming costs and in developing a competitive product line for health care purchasers.

Entrepreneur Based PPOs. Sponsors include:

— Third-party administrator.
— Insurance broker.
— Investor/independent management company.

Entrepreneur-based PPOs are usually initiated by independent third-party claims administrators of group health care benefit plans. Since they do not usually have an allegiance to a particular group of providers, in theory they are free to contract with the most efficient physicians and hospitals available in a community. On the other hand, some entrepreneur-sponsored plans do not have the technical resources or the management commitment to identify and sign up the most efficient providers in an area. Many providers are discouraged from working with them because of their independence and for-profit orientation to medical care. Entrepreneurial plans can be structured as independent organizations where ownership and sponsorship are separate and operate at an "arms length" from each other or they can be owned and sponsored by the same investors or shareholders.

Purchaser Initiated PPOs. Sponsors include:

— Employer (self-insured).
— Business coalition/trade association.
— Health and welfare trust fund.
— Labor organization.

Purchaser-initiated health plans offer the advantage of developing contracts that fit the specific needs of the employees and employee organizations rather than those of the providers. The biggest drawback to this approach is the purchaser's unfamiliarity with technical aspects of the medical system and insurance industry and the lack of sophisticated health care information on which to make decisions.

Operational Status

A great deal of uncertainty and confusion has developed about purchasing a new product like a PPO. Employers and employee organizations can gain a great deal of familiarity about a new PPO by evaluating its operational status. The first step is to identify whether the plan is "preoperational" or "operational." Preoperational means the PPO is not actually providing services but is still in its formative stage, which normally begins with an initial feasibility phase, then proceeds to a planning phase, and culminates with a development phase before becoming operational. During each of these preoperational phases the PPO could be actively marketing its services in anticipation of beginning operations on an expected date. Purchasers should be very cautious in contracting with an organization that is not operational at the time agreements to provide services are negotiated. They still may not be fully operational when the contract period is set to begin. Potential purchaser groups should find out what date the organization became operational and whether it has had prior experience in alternative delivery systems or in the health care field. However, an advantage to contracting with a new organization is to come in on the ground floor and receive additional concessions in terms of extra services or lower rates.

It is likewise important to evaluate how many major service agreements have been negotiated with the PPO by both purchasers and participating providers. This will indicate the level of operational readiness, whether the plan is likely to provide the range of services it proposes, and the size of the client base supporting the new operation. In order to gauge provider participation, it is necessary to identify the number of letters of interest, contracts pending and signed, physicians by specialty and board certification, dentists, allied health providers, hospitals by type, foundations for medical care, clinics, laboratories, and pharmacies. In order to assess purchaser participation, it is necessary to ascertain how many employers, employee organizations, insurance carriers, third-party administrators, and health and welfare trust funds have already subscribed to the PPO (e.g., as evidenced by contracts or memoranda of understanding) or are in the process of subscribing (e.g., via letters of intent).

PAYMENT MECHANISM

The actual details of a PPO's *overall* design and operational capability are the best indicator of its cost effectiveness. However, since a comprehensive review is not usually possible, the second best indicator is the payment mechanism used by the PPO. How participating hospitals and physicians are paid is a critical issue to address because it is the best indicator of provider motivation and of the PPO's capacity to effectively monitor costs and utilization of services. Cost-conscious physicians and hospitals are more likely than inefficient providers to assume financial risk for patient care. Inefficient providers generally do not realize how their practice patterns compare with more cost-conscious providers or what they can do to become more cost-effective practitioners.

There is a general hierarchy of payment mechanisms based on the capacity of a health care organization to provide cost-effective medicine. It is directly related to the degree of provider risk and the extent of utilization review. The most prevalent payment schemes for hospital and physician services are summarized below.

Hospitals

Price per patient day or per diem. This is a payment method that can be based on (*a*) an all-inclusive single rate that reflects an estimated mix of cases and average per diem rates or (*b*) multiple per diem rates reflecting different bed classifications or types of services provided.

An overriding practical advantage of this payment method is that per diem price histories are readily available to form a negotiating base.

Price per patient day does not account for the severity or complexity of the case being treated except as measured by length of stay. It favors hospitals with long stays because the first days of care, which involve more costly treatment procedures, are masked behind the "average cost," which includes the less costly convalescent days toward the end of the hospitalization period. This payment mechanism also blurs the distinction between the prices charged by the hospital and the practice patterns of the physicians, which makes it difficult to evaluate the efficiency of the hospital itself. The more separate per diem rates that are negotiated can create less financial protection for purchasers because multitiered per diems represent more of an incentive for hospitals to provide care at the highest cost or most intense level of service. They are also far more difficult to administer than single per diem rates.

Without a strict utilization review mechanism, price based on a per diem rate serves as a reward to keep patients in the hospital longer than medically necessary and acts as an incentive to admit easy cases that cost less than the average to treat. Some of those cases can be more appropriately treated outside the hospital in a less expensive setting. Contracts should require this.

Negotiated discount from established hospital charges. This can be (a) across the board or based on (b) multiple per diem rates by hospital services (e.g., routine medical/surgical, obstetrical, pediatric, and intensive care).

Negotiated discounts from established charges (not costs) has a dampening effect on the basic hospital rate per day but it does not decrease the length of hospital stay or the amount of medical services provided. Medical bills are based on the daily room-and-board charge as well as the length of stay and the number of additional procedures performed like lab tests, X rays, and other ancillary services. By discounting the average rate, this payment mechanism can become an incentive to increase the frequency of treatments and the number of procedures that are ordered for a patient.

Discounting implies arbitrary across-the-board reductions regardless of the efficiency or inefficiency of particular services. Since price discounting can mask the real problem of inefficient and inappropriate medical care, it does not reward cost-effective providers. Taken alone, negotiated discounts have more of a tendency to shift costs around than to change physician practice patterns or stimulate hospital efficiency.

Discounts are problematic because purchasers do not generally know what the discount really means, what it is based on, whether it will be a one-time only occurrence, how it compares with other cost reduction mechanisms, and if it merely means shifting costs to other payors. It has little value as a quick fix because an objective of selective contracting is to reduce not only overall costs, but per capita costs and unit costs as well.

Any discount arrangement should be taken from a predetermined set base (e.g., schedule of charges) and linked to an uninflated price index (e.g., Consumer Price Index). Controls are needed to prevent price discounts from being eroded by inappropriate use of resources such as an increase in units or frequency of services. Discounts without proper utilization controls are illusory. Limitations on future price increases are also needed to reduce unit costs.

Negotiated provider agreements will not succeed on discounts alone because it is not the percentage of discounts that determines the amount of savings. PPOs must have the capability of managing physicians and hospital resources to generate purchaser savings. Since providers have the capacity to increase revenues in response to limiting fees (e.g., billing for individual services, changing the mix of services, prescribing additional services), it is necessary to closely monitor utilization of resources. It is better to contract with hospitals and physicians that offer both efficiency and cost savings rather than providers that only offer an attractive price discount. A volume discount, however, is favorable for employers when they are unable to channel employees to preferred providers through benefits design changes.

Price per case based on a prospectively determined rate. This is determined according to (*a*) per discharge or (*b*) diagnostic related groups (DRGs).

Per case arrangements offer the advantage of discouraging unnecessary length of stay and intensity of services. Per-discharge reimbursement sets one flat fee for hospital stays or can be adjusted for broad categories of care (e.g., maternity, cardiac, orthopedic). It puts the hospital "at risk" for variations in the severity of illness (and cost) within each specified category. Per discharge payment provides employers with more information about the type and frequency of illnesses than per diem data but far less than DRG systems.

DRGs depend on the reliability of the data regarding the final diagnosis and the patient condition. This is a major shortcoming of DRG reimbursement because of frequent recording errors of medical records systems. There is also a tendency to diagnose certain illnesses according to the most lucrative reimbursement categories (known as "diagnosis coding creep" or "DRG creep") in order to maximize the revenue per patient. Many cases are excluded from this system altogether because of inherent limitations in the classification scheme. DRGs require far more sophisticated claims payment systems than other reimbursement methods. When hospital pricing is based on DRGs, a severity adjustment factor should be included in order to offset the incentive to not treat sicker patients, which would lose revenue for hospitals.

Capitation based on a predetermined rate for each covered beneficiary regardless of plan utilization or treatment costs. This is a payment method that offers employees and employee organizations a contract based on total costs per employee, which is the single most important variable to most purchasers. Since it puts the organization "at risk" for providing all negotiated services at a set price, capitation rates favor reduced hospital use and efficient treatment at each level of health care provision. However, this type of reimbursement mechanism would be very difficult for PPOs to administer with flexible enrollment policies. Providers would be paid for enrollees who may never be treated as patients due to freedom of choice. The PPO would need nearly 100 percent penetration of the particular employee group and would function more like an exclusive provider organization (EPO).

Physicians

A negotiated discount from the established physician fee schedule (which may include a regional adjustment factor) or *from "usual, customary and reasonable" (UCR) fees.* The rationale for reimbursement methods that applies to hospitals also applies to physicians.

Capitation based on a predetermined rate for each covered beneficiary regardless of plan utilization or treatment costs. Payment based on per capita reimbursement encourages cost-conscious physician practice patterns by placing the provider "at risk" for health care.

PPOs are also reimbursed for general operating costs and administrative services that range from basic overhead functions to conducting utilization review. It should be clarified what these services include, what they cost, and how they are paid. Three common ways to pay for these functions are:

— Purchasers pay a percentage of premium or claims, a monthly member fee, or a one-time, set-up fee based on the services provided and the size of the group.
— Physicians pay a monthly fee.
— Hospitals pay a monthly fee.

UTILIZATION MANAGEMENT AND QUALITY ASSURANCE

The purpose of utilization-review programs is to evaluate the appropriateness of care by monitoring the behavior of health care providers. Unnecessary and inappropriate utilization of health care services can not only be costly but also detrimental to a patient's health status. Purchasing organizations should begin the process of evaluating quality of care by asking the PPO what internal measures it uses to assess quality. Three approaches can be used to address the extent to which the PPO monitors quality of care: (1) patient outcome, (2) process measures, and (3) analytical reports. Patient outcome occurs after the service has been provided and is helpful in evaluating long-term effects of providing care in particular settings or short-term evaluation of specified procedures.

Process measures are used to indirectly suggest quality of care. They relate primarily to the structure of the system and selected characteristics of the provider. If enough process measures are incorporated in the health care plan, there will be a greater likelihood that a higher quality of care will be provided than if the process factors are not present. Some specific process measures are shown in Exhibit 3.

EXHIBIT 3
Quality of Care Process Measures

Primary care physician-to-patient ratio.
Turnover rate of physicians.
Availability of specialty care in the plan and contractual agreements for a full range of outside specialists.
Percentage of service involving outside specialty referrals.
Method of controlling access to specialists.
Internal utilization-review mechanism, particularly prior authorization and concurrent review.
Utilization review contract with an independent review organization or shared review arrangements.
Independent second surgical opinion.
Continuing education program for medical staff professionals.
Selection standards for hospitals and physicians.

Membership Selection Standards

Provider selection should ideally be based on hospitals and physicians that have demonstrated cost-effective medical care before participating in the PPO. One of the advantages of purchasers creating a preferred provider panel themselves is to make sure that inefficient and ineffective providers are screened out. It is much more difficult to change the behavior of inefficient physicians once they are in a PPO than it is to screen them out through appropriate selection criteria. Hospitals that are selected should have a performance record that can be audited. It is important to know the average charges for services provided based on actual charges rather than publicly cited charges.

Membership selection standards for hospitals can range from virtually none at all (except for price agreements) to comprehensive selection criteria that would include many of the features in Exhibit 4. Subjective selection standards can also be used in evaluating medical facilities. These could include the reputation of the hospital in the community and the number of physicians with admitting privileges who are interested in participating in selective contracting and alternative health care delivery

EXHIBIT 4
Hospital Membership Selection Standards

State license.
Professional liability insurance.
Accreditation by the Joint Commission on Accreditation of Hospitals (JCAH).
Financial liability (i.e., specific financial parameters).
Historical cost and utilization performance as measured by local or state data.
Full range of acute care services.
Specific specialty services (e.g., secondary and tertiary care).
Number of board-certified physicians by specialty.
Geographic accessibility to clients.
Cost competitive status (e.g., operational indices like utilization review, acceptance of
    risk).

systems. The opinion of local or state health planning agencies and business coalitions could also be considered.

Physicians who are cost-conscious practitioners tend to hold down
costs by appropriate use of technology, limited use of additional physician consultations, and increased use of less costly treatment alternatives.
Possible membership selection standards are included in Exhibit 5. Pur-

EXHIBIT 5
Physician Membership Selection Standards

State license.
Professional liability insurance.
Malpractice suits awarded or pending.
Review of pending or past accusations by any local or state medical quality assurance
    agency.
Practice pattern profile of Professional Review Organization (PRO).
Office located in service area.
Hospital privileges at participating hospitals.
Specialty board certification and board eligibility.
Participation in a group medical practice.
Involvement in utilization review controls or risk-sharing activities.
Involvement in alternative delivery systems.

chasers may also want to consider the physicians' reputation and longev-
ity in the community to be served as well as their history in providing
service to low-income and elderly patients.

Agreements to accept utilization restrictions such as preadmission review and certification are less effective than excluding high-cost providers to begin with. The inclusion of high utilizers in the provider panel
undermines the potential savings of negotiated price discounts. The ob-

jective of reducing the growth of medical costs without jeopardizing reasonable access for consumers can be achieved by contracting with cost-effective providers.

Analytical reports are based on the acquisition of patient encounter data from claims submitted for payment or from data collected specifically for the purpose of assessing the quality of care. In analytical systems, performance criteria are established for different symptoms, diagnoses, procedures, and services. Encounter data between the patient and the provider is reported and evaluated against the criteria, and when unusual patterns of care are detected a more comprehensive system of inquiry is initiated. Profiles of both provider and individual patient behavior can be developed through such analytical systems. Over and under-utilization, as well as patterns of inappropriate medical treatment can be detected.

Utilization Review

The key to the success of an effective quality assurance program is the extent to which the buyer has access to and utilizes a valid and comprehensive management information system *and* is prepared to make provider contract decisions based on the information. The effectiveness of the utilization control techniques will depend on the management support provided to monitor activities. Strict utilization management is a prerequisite for successful business operations. Control over the use of resources, especially hospital services, is essential because utilization is a more significant cost factor than charges or price of services. An important objective of the review process is to assess whether the admission is clinically justified (i.e., medically necessary) and if treatment is cost effective. A key to reducing unnecessary costs is an effective and efficient utilization review and control mechanism. Utilization control results in greater savings than discounts because it reduces the frequency of unnecessary services and the amount of resources used in providing those services.

Hospitals are the focus of most utilization review activities because hospital services are more costly than any other aspect of health care. PPO purchasers also want high-quality ambulatory services, which can be aided by ambulatory care case management. Any health care cost-containment strategy must include comprehensive utilization review to provide some assurance of appropriate health care and to reduce costs.

Hospital review programs are a cost-containment measure designed to control the patient's utilization of hospital facilities and services. Their primary objectives are to (1) reduce the number of inappropriate inpatient hospital admissions, (2) reduce the length of stay for inpatient services, (3) monitor ancillary services, and (4) direct the use of outpatient facilities when medically feasible. Review programs can also offer additional cost reductions through evaluation and control of ancillary services and physician services attendant to hospital stays. These programs can decrease claim processing costs and expedite payment because the review also acts as a preaudit procedure for claims.

Hospital reviews can be conducted prior to, during, or after the hospitalization and are performed by either physicians or nurse coordinators who work with physician consultants. The major components of a hospital review program include:

Preadmission review. The attending physician must request and receive prior approval for all elective hospitalizations or request authorization at least 24 hours before hospitalization. When request is made, the review team will either authorize the admission and assign the number of approved days for stay or deny medical authorization and recommend a second opinion or outpatient services. This evaluation prevents unnecessary cost incurrence, retroactive denial of claims, and possible patient liability for payment. Preadmission certification and prior authorization programs work together to redirect admissions and selected procedures. Preadmission certification can substantially reduce the number of inappropriate hospital admissions by channeling unnecessary admissions to more appropriate (and less costly) settings like ambulatory surgery centers and skilled nursing facilities. Prior authorization can also be applied to all specialty referrals.

Concurrent review. While the patient is hospitalized, nurses or medical records technicians under the supervision of doctors periodically evaluate the hospital records to ensure than the appropriate level of medical services are being provided (e.g., intensive care room versus semiprivate room). They also determine the appropriate date of discharge and, during this review, the preauthorized length of stay may be either shortened or lengthened depending on the patient's medical condition. Like preadmission review, concurrent review can substantially reduce the number of days of hospitalization and attendant costs by moving patients into less acute (and less expensive) levels of care such as a skilled nursing facility, home health care, or ambulatory care. Emergency care is also reviewed within 24 hours after admission to the hospital.

Retrospective review. Unlike preadmission and concurrent review, retrospective review takes place after the patient has been discharged. This review typically examines the appropriateness of admission, diagnosis, length of stay, and procedures performed. Billed charges can be compared with the medical record of services provided and with coverage provisions. Findings of inappropriate use or charges can result in denial of claims and loss of hospital revenue. Since retrospective review can require after-the-fact adjustments in provider payments, PPO contracts should clearly indicate the procedures and sanctions associated with this review.

Ancillary services review. This quality control review can occur before, during, or after concurrent review and evaluates the appropriateness of the hospital services that the patient receives such as laboratory tests, X rays, and physical therapy.

Physician services review. During concurrent review, the team can also evaluate the appropriateness and medical necessity for the services that the attending physician provides to the patient during the hospital stay.

Outpatient review. Statistical profiles of outpatient treatment patterns can be used to assess overutilization of office visits, X rays, laboratory, diagnostic, and other ancillary services.

Specific procedures and services can automatically trigger utilization review services. A list of these services should be identified. The mechanism for administering the review can be in person, often with the medical director of the plan; by telephone; or by mail. The status of the review program should also be ascertained as to whether it is advisory, binding, or phased-in over a designated time period. The PPO should also have a management plan for ensuring that the impact of its utilization control and referral procedures does not adversely affect continuity of care.

It is important to clarify the role and responsibility of the physician directing the utilization review process and to understand the incentives within the plan that will influence physician practice patterns. Physician compliance with utilization review and quality assurance procedures should be stated in the contract agreement and should include disciplinary sanctions and financial penalties. It is difficult to enforce provider compliance effectively without explicit protocols.

GEOGRAPHIC COVERAGE AND ACCESS

A network of primary care and specialty medical care physicians is necessary to ensure choice of providers and convenient access to participating providers in the service area. Geographic availability of PPO services is determined by the number and location of medical resources in the service area. It can be measured in terms of patient travel time and the distance from the patient's residence to the medical facility. To assess geographic coverage, providers should be listed according to their location (i.e., address, city, county). Those data can then be compared to the distribution of the employee population on a map showing the location of physicians' offices, laboratories, pharmacies, hospitals and all other services available to plan members in the area.

Patient convenience is the principle factor in evaluating access to care. It includes factors such as those shown in Exhibit 6. The PPO must also make sure that emergency care is provided for throughout the designated service area.

EXHIBIT 6
Patient Convenience Factors

Hours and days of the week routine care is available.
Arrangements for 24-hour access to primary care providers.
Procedures for emergency care in and out of service area.
Average waiting time at each facility.
Clearly defined and easily understood point of entry into the system.
Average waiting time to obtain an appointment for primary care, each major specialty
    area, routine physical examinations, and nonemergency conditions.
Average length of time it takes to get a referral appointment within and between each
    facility.
Efficient screening procedures to channel member inquiries and patient appointments.
Availability of translators and multilingual staff.
Availability of staff to write instructions and prescriptions in the primary languages of
    plan members.
Average length of time from member enrollment until an identification card is issued.
Provision of temporary identification cards.
Parking at the facility and if there is a charge.
Availability of public transportation to the facilities.
Availability of after-hours telephone consultation.

SCOPE OF SERVICES

A comprehensive PPO should include a full range of acute care hospital
services and physician specialty areas (see Exhibit 7). PPOs can contract
with high volume regional medical centers for specialized high-cost procedures like open heart surgery and elective neurosurgery.

EXHIBIT 7
Acute Care Hospital Services

The following basic acute care services should be provided by hospitals:
Ambulance service arrangements
Anesthesia
Clinical laboratory
Dietetic
Emergency medical care
Intensive care
Intermediate care
Medical
Nuclear medicine
Nursing
Occupational therapy
Pharmaceutical
Radiological
Rehabilitation center
Respiratory care
Social service
Speech pathology and audiology
Surgical

Some PPOs emphasize the concept of patients utilizing the primary care physician to manage the overall care of the client. If this "gate-keeper" appraoch is emphasized, a core group of primary care physicians should be available (see Exhibit 8). All physicians should be identified as to whether they are certified or eligible to be certified by a specialty board.

EXHIBIT 8
Primary Care and Specialty Physicians

Primary care physicians that should be available include:
  Family practice
  General practice
  Internal medicine
  Obstetrics and gynecology
  Pediatrics

Other physician specialists that should be accessible include:
  Allergy
  Anesthesiology
  Cardiology
  Dermatology
  Endocrinology
  Gastroenterology
  General surgery
  Neurology
  Ophthalmology
  Orthopoedic medicine
  Otolaryngology
  Pulmonary medicine
  Psychiatry
  Urology

In addition, the PPO could offer a wide range of supplemental health care services that stress nonhospital treatment, lifestyle behavior programs, alternative health care regimens, allied health care services, illness prevention care, and health education programs (see Exhibit 9). As a means of clarifying the scope of benefits covered, the PPO should furnish a written description of the following: all services to be provided, conditions on eligibility to receive services, procedures to follow to obtain covered services, circumstances under which benefits may be denied, and a full explanation of the claim and denial review procedures.

LEGAL CONSIDERATIONS

Significant legal issues can be raised about the structure and operation of PPOs even though they are currently operating in a relatively unregulated market. The PPO should provide to health care purchasers all legal docu-

EXHIBIT 9
Supplemental Health Care Services

The following health care programs and services could be offered:
  Alcohol treatment
  Chiropractic
  Consumer education
  Convalescent and extended care
  Corrective appliances
  Dental
  Drug dependency
  Eye glasses/hearing aids
  Health education
  Health promotion
  Home health
  Hospice care
  Mental health
  Nutrition
  Podiatry
  Prenatal
  Reproductive health care
  Smoking cessation
  Voluntary sterilization
  Weight management
  Well-baby care

ments including articles of incorporation and provider contracts. The most important and potentially litigious areas relate to antitrust considerations, organizational structure, contractual obligations, malpractice liability, utilization review, and quality assurance procedures. Each of these topics is briefly summarized below.

Antitrust. A PPO cannot engage in unreasonable restraint of trade through agreements among competing providers to affect prices, to divide service or geographic markets, or refuse to deal with other providers.

Organization. To minimize potential antitrust issues, a PPO should be structured so that no single group of providers will control price negotiations with payors or decide which groups of providers will be eligible for patient referrals. Agreements with payors should be accepted by participating providers on an individual basis. This procedure is cumbersome and one of the biggest impediments to selective contracting for physicians.

Operation. The rights and responsibilities of providers and purchasers should be clearly stated in the terms of the PPO contract.

It is very important to understand fully the extent to which the PPO has disclosed any limitations, exceptions, or exclusion of plan coverage. There should be "hold harmless" provisions in the contract that protect subscribers, employers, and employee organizations from overcharges by providers and from claim denials when procedures are found to be medically unnecessary. Hold harmless provisions are usually between providers and payors. In many instances these provisions are being eliminated from contracts or being worded to indicate a bilateral condition. Many malpractice insurance carriers will no longer accept unilateral hold harmless provisions.

Some of the most important contract considerations involve the following issues: claims payment responsibilities, utilization review and control plans, scope of services, patient termination rights, provider obligations to accept patients, controls on referrals, and providers' rights to pursue collections. Participation agreements should clearly state policies for dispute resolution, grievance procedure, and arbitration guidelines.

Liability. Professional liability is viewed as a major reason why some providers have been reluctant to become involved in PPOs. Many providers are concerned about potential malpractice exposure and are "waiting for a court case to test it." Since hospitals participating in a preferred provider arrangement can be viewed potentially as agents of the PPO, hospitals ad PPOs should each establish physician selection standards and performance criteria to evaluate the competency of participating providers. Hospitals will want to structure a PPO relationship in such a way that avoids being viewed as their agent.

Utilization Review. The utilization control and quality assurance procedures of a PPO should be coordinated to avoid erroneously withholding covered medical benefits, inappropriate denial of authorization for further treatment, or improper breaches in continuity of care. The PPO participating agreement should clearly state what type of utilization and quality assurance reviews will be performed, what the review standards are based on, what the procedures are for carrying out the different types of review, and how utilization review is paid for.

FINANCIAL ISSUES

The financial solvency of *current* PPOs is not a critical evaluation issue because most do not involve sufficient financial risk. As the market matures in the coming years, however, PPOs will probably assume far greater risk. Financial solvency will then become an important issue. At that juncture, the most important questions to ask will concern provisions for insolvency, how the operating budget was developed, and long-range financial plans.

The PPO's approach to the risk of insolvency should allow for three things:

— Continuation of benefits for the duration of the contract period.
— Continuation of benefits for enrollees who are confined in an inpatient facility on the date of insolvency until their discharge.
— Payments to unaffiliated providers for services rendered to enrollees. Plan members should be "held harmless" for any outstanding medical claims in the event of insolvency.

Prospective purchasers should also ascertain what level of reserves, if any, is available as a margin against unanticipated claims expense. This applies especially to Exclusive Provider Organizations and PPOs that function as an insurer.

The budget and financial plans of the PPO should be available to the purchaser and be based on a number of interrelated factors that should be clearly understood by potential purchaser organizations before negotiating a service agreement. The main features of a comprehensive PPO should include:

Enrollment projections and the assumptions used to make the projections. Accurate enrollment projections are critical to planning and maintaining an adequate cash-flow sytem to support health plan operations.

The underlying assumptions for projecting enrollment are based on estimates of how well the health plan will fit the employee benefit design objectives of potential purchasers, whether the scope of services and the location of health care providers adequately meet the needs of potential subscribers, and whether the financial incentives in the plan are sufficient to overcome the existing pattern of relationships between employees and their physicians.

Expected break-even point (where profit and loss are equal) and the assumptions behind the projection. The PPO should explain how operating deficits will be covered until the break-even point is reached.

This indicates the level of indebtedness, the degree of capitalization, and how much revenue the PPO needs to become self-sustaining.

Cost and utilization assumptions for each category of health services used to establish rates. Utilization assumptions indicate a great deal about how well plan sponsors understand the interplay of demographic characteristics, physician practice patterns, financial incentives and disincentives, and cost management techniques. The greater the degree of provider risk (e.g., reimbursement based on diagnosis related groups of illnesses or capitation) involved in the plan, the more accurate these assumptions must be in order for the plan to be actuarially sound.

Current and projected rate structure (cost) for each health service.

The rate structure is the most important "bottom line" financial issue for potential purchasers to consider. It represents how effectively and how efficiently the health plan can deliver health care services. In order to understand how the overall rate structure was determined, potential purchasers should examine the different rates developed for each medical service.

Policy for coordination of benefits (COB), subrogation, and worker's compensation. Unless specific guidelines are developed to handle these policies, the health plan could incur far higher costs than need be, since recoveries are readily available in these areas.

Outstanding loans and loan commitments and projected repayment schedules. Details about loan obligations may indicate how well plan sponsors were able to arrange for favorable terms and rates. The terms and schedule for repaying the loan will bear directly on the price charged for health plan services.

Financial and contractual arrangements with medical professionals, hospitals, and other providers of health care services. Any contingent compensation such as incentive or profit-sharing arrangements with medical providers should be described.

From a purchaser's standpoint, financial incentives and profit-sharing agreements for physicians can be favorable or unfavorable. If incentives are tied to rigorous provider performance standards, then profit sharing can have a positive effect on the quality and quantity of health services provided. On the other hand, if financial inducements are inappropriately structured, then patient care could suffer. Profit-sharing programs should be accompanied by strong quality assurance measures to support high-quality care.

Questions about the financial stability of preferred provider arrangements apply to agreements negotiated directly with providers as well as those with insurance carriers and intermediaries. The financial and operational history of each of the participating corporate entities involved in the plan is particularly important to take into consideration. If it is a joint venture between physicians and hospitals, the extent to which each has a financial stake in the venture is relevant.

Additional criteria for evaluating financial soundness are based on whether the PPO follows acceptable accounting, budgeting, and record-keeping practices. It should provide financial reports including operating statements, capital requirements, and a statement about indebtedness. A complete financial statement should be requested that includes the following: balance sheets, statements of income and expense, statements of changes in financial position, capital expenditures, and descriptive material to analyze the flow of all funds. The PPO's most recent financial statements should have been audited by an independent certified public accountant.

PERFORMANCE MONITORING

One of the most important aspects of a preferred provider arrangement is the accumulation of accurate data for assessing the success of the product. Monitoring provider performance is a complex task that is central to achieving adequate cost control and quality of care. Without a focused monitoring system, purchasers must rely on provider assurances about fulfilling contract requirements and practicing cost-effective medicine.

With a sophisticated reporting format, purchasers can continuously review the success of the preferred provider arrangement. It should be flexible enough to accommodate changes in coinsurance and deductible policies, shifts in utilization behavior and intensity of services, and modifications in the benefits coverage and payment methods.

What employers need most of all is accurate and timely data. However, provider-purchaser contracts often overlook specific reporting requirements. The contract negotiation process should clarify two factors: (*a*) to what extent purchasers understand their data needs and (*b*) to what extent the provider has the operational capacity to furnish such information. The resulting service agreement should establish the content and format for standardized reports, arrangements for ad hoc or custom-tailored reports, and the frequency of these statements. Penalty provisions should be built into the contract specifications to assure full compliance on reporting requirements. In the case of individual and small group subscribers, these reports should be provided at least on a limited basis.

One of the objectives of data activities should be to make the purchase of health care services analogous to other business purchasing decisions. Purchasers can negotiate with providers from a position of relative parity when they have access to necessary data on utilization, quality, costs, and price.

Purchasers will need comparative reports that indicate preferred health plan savings over traditional insurance options in order to justify the administrative resources required to rechannel employees to preferred providers. Employers will be interested in multiyear trend data and comparisons between specific types of employee groups (i.e., by job classification and demographic characteristics) in relation to potential savings. The information system should be based on management criteria that measures provider performance and productivity on a full range of medical activities. Consumers are more apt to receive cost-effective medical care from providers whose performance is monitored by a comprehensive data system that is used to discipline inefficient practitioners.

It is important that the information system be oriented toward new trends in data gathering and analysis such as DRGs and provider profiling. This capacity will enable purchasers to take advantage of medicare's reporting requirements and prospective reimbursement system based on DRGs in negotiating with providers in the future. DRG-specific analysis will enable purchasers to evaluate hospitals from a comparative database so that similar services can be assessed. Employers will be able to develop profiles of their employee's utilization experience with specific physicians and compare that with other providers who treat similar enrollee groups.

The purpose of providing summary and detailed information about PPO utilization is to enable employers and employee organizations to understand where medical dollars are going. Information about PPO use can be compared with the utilization profiles of national, state, and local population groups and can be compared internally with various groups within the membership to identify unusual trends and inappropriate utilization patterns.

An organization purchasing comprehensive PPO services will want to know per capita costs as well as the overall health plan costs. Per capita costs are important because they are an indication of how well the PPO is monitoring appropriate utilization, intensity of services (i.e., amount of medical resources per patient), and referral patterns.

At a minimum, the reports should generate statistical averages based on aggregate claims data by major lines of coverage (e.g., hospital room and board, surgery, outpatient services), by major diagnostic category, by provider, by employee and dependent, and by age and sex of claimant. Reports that include more detailed information categories would enable purchasers to gain a better understanding of what specific utilization patterns were responsible for the leading categories of health plan costs. This would allow them to design an intervention strategy that focuses on specific cost-containment activities in plan design, utilization review and control, and treatment alternatives to inpatient hospitalization and patient-initiated overutilization.

Detailed information should be furnished on utilization statistics, cost data, and cost-saving features (see Exhibit 10). The latter should inform employers and payors about the effectiveness of each cost control function, e.g., expected savings from nonconfirmed surgery (second surgical opinions), days saved (retrospective review), procedures and days shifted (preadmission review). Data gathering and statistical analysis should be targeted to user needs and priorities concerning utilization, costs, and program operations in order to be a useful management tool.

CONSUMER SATISFACTION

Consumer satisfaction is the real "bottom line" for preferred provider arrangements. The most important index of client satisfaction is whether

EXHIBIT 10
Utilization Statistics and Cost Data

The following data sets represent a comprehensive range of data elements for three categories of information: utilization statistics, cost data, and cost-saving features.

1. Utilization statistics:
   Hospital days per 1,000 enrollees
   Admissions per 1,000 enrollees
   Surgeries per 1,000 enrollees
   Most prevalent inpatient procedures
   Total number of days per admission
   Readmission rate per 1,000 enrollees
   Average length of stay by age, sex, relationship to member, and diagnostic category (i.e., case mix adjusted, if possible)
   Distribution of hospital days by patient characteristics
   Number of paid hospital days
   Frequency of claims by diagnostic category including the percentage of total claims and the average length of stay
   Frequency of number of paid days by diagnostic category, including the percentage of total claims and the average length of stay
   Outpatient visits per 1,000 enrollees
   Frequency and type of outpatient services and visits
   Ratio of inpatient to outpatient procedures
   Average number of family members
   Average number of physician visits per family per year
   Ratio of females to males per case mix

2. Cost data:
   Total reimbursement paid and the average reimbursement paid per hospital day
   Total number of visits and amounts of reimbursement for age groups by type of service and relationship to employee
   Number of claims
   Total paid claims, reimbursement and cost per employee and plan enrollees
   Comparison of normal charges and negotiated rates for each provider, major provider services, and paid claims
   Profile of charges that were billed, covered, and paid per admission, per day, and per service
   Charges paid for most frequent conditions and procedures
   Ancillary charge data by diagnosis for each hospital
   Profile of individual physicians and hospitals on costs; length of stay; number of admissions, visits, and procedures
   Profile of employee group and individual enrollees on physician visits, costs by medical specialty, and number of services per procedure
   Profile of nonpreferred plan use including provider, procedures and services, costs, and identification of consumer

3. Cost saving features:
   Coordination of benefits (COB) recoveries
   Third-party recoveries
   Weekend hospitalizations and short-stay elective admissions
   Ambulatory surgery
   Pre- and post-operative lengths of stay
   Second surgical opinions
   Preadmission testing
   Preadmission review
   Concurrent review
   Retrospective review

enrollees elect to maintain their coverage with the PPO health plan. In the case of exclusive provider organizations (EPOs), disenrollment data should be evaluated and should account for "voluntary disenrollment," which includes people who are moving out of the service area, as well as the primary reasons for regular disenrollment. The waiting time for disenrollment should also be indicated.

The PPO should provide a written description of the procedure for handling member suggestions, complaints, and grievances. It should indicate how and where a member initiates a complaint, whether there is a designated patient advocate or ombudsperson in the system, and the rights and responsibilities of members and management at each step of the process.

CONCLUSION

Preferred provider organizations are a vehicle for developing price competition in the health care industry. As such, they may be a means of transition to more sophisticated reimbursement mechanisms for health care services (e.g., diagnostic related groups and capitation) that will be heavily influenced in the future by employers and employee organizations. PPOs may also act as a midwife as employee benefits structures move from traditional insurance coverage, which insulated beneficiaries from the cost of medical care, toward more tightly managed health care systems. These new systems of care are likely to emphasize cost sharing between employees and employers and risk sharing between purchasers and providers.

Preferred provider arrangements alter the way purchasers do business with health care providers. They are an open agenda for purchasers and providers to develop bilateral service agreements. Preferred provider contracting matches up what health care purchasers want (high quality at lower costs) with what providers of care need (maintaining market share). In theory, it is a mechanism for buying, selling, and delivering health care services more efficiently. Many providers are flexible enough to offer a range of services to suit the needs of individual groups as long as purchasers are willing to pay for them. This is particularly true for medium to large employers and employee organizations.

With the advent of preferred provider arrangements, employers and employee organizations can improve bottom-line performance by selectively buying health care services and insurance coverage at more competitive prices. Negotiating health care agreements with physicians and hospitals gives purchasers an opportunity to stabilize costs, develop greater predictability for overall medical care expenses, and stretch their health care dollars without reducing employee benefits. Purchasers should carefully evaluate the pros and cons of different preferred provider arrangements in terms of their own priorities and business objectives.

NOTES

1. Purchasers include employers, employee organizations, third-party payors such as insurers and governments, and health and welfare trust funds.

2. Providers include physicians; hospitals and other medical facilities; allied health professionals such as dentists, pharmacists, psychologists, chiropractors and podiatrists; and vendors of alternative health care services.

3. Blue Cross and Blue Shield are technically classified as nonprofit hospital service plans and licensed health plans respectively rather than as health insurance carriers. While they are combined organizations in most states, Blue Cross and Blue Shield operate as separate businesses in states such as California.

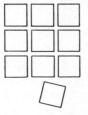

Marketplace Fundamentals

ACTUARIAL PROBLEMS IN PPOS

Gordon R. Trapnell, F.S.A.

President
Actuarial Research Corporation
Annandale, VA

☐ To some it is a surprise that there are actuarial concerns in developing or contracting with PPOs. PPOs are viewed primarily as delivery systems and not as insuring mechanisms. In this view, a PPO either provides the services more efficiently or it does not, and the effects should be evident in the resulting premium rate. Hence at least prima facie, PPOs should not have the same rating problems as HMOs and other prepaid plans.

But verifying the presence of savings and determining who will benefit from them turn out to require complex actuarial analysis. The first actuarial problem is to determine whether there are in fact real, significant savings. For example, PPOs are usually offered as an alternative to an existing plan, usually with some significant cost advantage to those using the preferred providers. If the PPO is to avoid *increasing* an employer's cost, the savings from reduced payments for those using preferred providers must at least offset the reduced cost sharing or other inducements given to enrollees to use the preferred providers. It may be a crucial actuarial calculation to determine whether the savings will pay for these promises.

Much more complex actuarial problems also arise. The most difficult to handle, and most dangerous to the payor, are the effects of biased selection. This refers to a patient's nonrandom choice of plan or provider that reflects their perceptions of their need for care as well as economic factors. Not only may selection undermine an employer's projected savings but it could also make the plan cost more than it would have without the PPO. Selection may also produce substantial losses for participating hospitals or sponsoring insurers.

EVALUATION OF THE POTENTIAL FOR SAVINGS

The lure of savings, or of at least a slower growth rate of expenditures, is the main attraction of PPOs for employers and other purchasers. In fact, the potential savings must be substantial for an employer to be willing to impose any real restraints on the free choice of providers by employees. Until recently, employers have been extremely reluctant to reduce or restrict their employee benefit programs. The potential for misunderstandings and ill will has been regarded as too high a price to pay for the relatively modest savings to be obtained. These considerations have been particularly inhibiting in unionized industries or where the formation of unions has been feared, since most unions have adamantly opposed any restrictions on freedom of choice. Although in the current business climate the inhibitions have begun to be overwhelmed by the employers' need to control the cost of their health insurance programs, the prospects for success in controlling outlays must be quite tangible to induce employers to tangle with such nettlesome issues.

As frequently noted, there is a great diversity of features in PPOs. From an actuarial perspective these can be arranged in a hierarchy that reflects their potential for cost containment.

— Simplified billing and prompt payment.
— Provider discounts and agreement to accept payment as full compensation.
— Competitive advantages for preferred providers ranging up to exclusive contracts (EPOs) in return for higher patient volume.
— Requirement for prior selection among options, including a PPO with reduced cost sharing and/or reduced employee contribution.
— "Lock-in" to preferred providers in the PPO option.
— Agreements for precertification of admissions and to abide by the results of utilization review.
— Formal gatekeepers, i.e., a single physician must approve all nonemergency care for any patient.
— Acceptance of risk sharing by providers.

In addition, the interactions among features of a specific plan, the emphasis provided by sponsors, and the full context of circumstances may transform their importance. For example, agreements to accept reduced fees create strong incentives for physicians to make up the lost revenue by increasing utilization. Physicians have the capacity to increase revenues in response to fee controls by prescribing additional services, altering the mixture of services, or changing how services are billed. An administrative framework that can address this tendency may be necessary to prevent the disappearance of potential savings from fee discounts.

When PPOs are included in employer benefit plans, employees are usually offered the choice of using preferred or other providers. An advantage, usually lower cost sharing (i.e., deductibles, coinsurance, copayments), is given to those using the preferred providers. This may be accomplished by offering lower cost sharing relative to the existing plan (a "carrot" approach) or by substantially increasing the cost sharing for those using the nonpreferred providers (a "stick" approach). A more forceful variation is to require employees to elect in advance (via open enrollment) to use only preferred providers, in return for a reduced employee premium contribution. Offering only preferred providers (an exclusive provider organization or EPO) is a far stronger approach.

Agreements to accept precertification and utilization restrictions tend to be less effective than excluding high-utilization or high-cost providers to begin with. Risk pools and capitation payments may cross the line into prepaid arrangements, but a continuum of possible arrangements exists, and determining what is a PPO and what is an IPA may be a matter of taste.

IMPACT OF SPONSOR'S OBJECTIVES

The specific features to be included in a particular PPO reflect both the perceived effectiveness of the measures and the strategic objectives of the organizers or sponsors. These frequently reflect objectives other than obtaining a lower cost of care for employer purchasers. Some typical sponsor objectives are illustrated in the following examples.

— Blue Cross plans to seek a substantially larger discount from a majority of the hospitals in their service area.
— Provider organizations, especially hospitals and large group practices or clinics, seeking to retain patients under competitive conditions.
— Established commercial insurers to seek to maintain market share by reducing the cost of their product compared to competition and thus retain enrollees in competition with HMOs in open enrollments.
— Hungry entrepreneurs who seek an opportunity to seize a significant share of the market, including insurance companies that do not presently have a substantial market share, hospital chains, physicians, nonmedical entrepreneurs, and organizations with re-

view experience (e.g., IPAs and utilization review organizations such as PSROs).

These perspectives may lead to different approaches and features being emphasized. For example, Blue Cross plans typically emphasize the price they pay for hospital care. Preferred providers are those willing to meet their price (and perhaps shift the rest of the real cost to other payors). Nonpreferred providers are those that are not willing to cut their charges to the offered level. Most hospitals are willing to comply, at least as long as PPO patients are a relatively small part of the overall market. Although any restriction on revenues puts obvious pressure on hospitals to control costs, this approach represents more of an application of market power to the detriment of their competitors and the hospitals than a cost control technique. An additional feature may be explicit agreements to accept utilization controls. Although it remains to be seen how much emphasis these controls will receive or how different they will prove in practice from similar measures already implemented, a framework exists in which coersion can be applied, reinforced by the threat of dropping a hospital from the PPO. As competition among insurers tightens, the motivation to implement these measures will increase.

To assess the financial impact of a PPO, it is necesary to go beyond the form of the organization to the substance of the procedures followed and the effectiveness of execution. Having a preadmission certification program, for example, does not necessarily guarantee any change in the admission rate. Unfortunately, since most PPOs are new, there is no data from which to measure their performance. Further, measurement under the best of circumstances would be difficult.

Judgments concerning the probable effectiveness of utilization management, the selection of providers, and other organizational features of PPOs bring the actuary to the limits of professional expertise. In addition, estimates may be needed for planning purposes before the details of design and implementation are known.[1] Frequently, however, estimates must be made in order to project the appropriate premium rates or level of self-funded benefits that require allowances for the effects of such features. The best that can be accomplished in these circumstances is to project a range of costs depending on the effectiveness of implementation. But this is not always satisfactory. The natural tendency of many managements is to assume an optimistic stance concerning the effectiveness of their own actions. This may in turn lead to the incorporation of undesirable features in a plan. Projected savings from reduced utilization, for example, may be used to reduce employee contributions or to increase provider payments.

These are situations that each actuary will have to solve using the best professional judgment in the circumstances. A few observations may be useful. One is to be sure to identify the losers. At least in the short run the reduction in costs through PPOs is basically a zero sum proposition, in that the savings must be obtained at the expense of some affected party. For there to be savings, some sums that would have been paid will not be paid, and it is prudent to identify the party that will forego such payments. One may place greater faith in estimates where the loser has been identified and is acting accordingly, than in situations where all affected are participants to the transactions and are sanguine concerning its impact on them.

Another observation is that the strategic objectives of the organizers or sponsors may have a profound impact on the effectiveness of any of the features incorporated in a PPO. Further, the real objectives may be only peripherally concerned with generating savings for the employers or governments that ultimately pay the cost. For example, many PPOs are sponsored by providers concerned chiefly with preserving their present revenues. Employers should approach such fox-guarded hen house varieties of PPO with care.

CASH FLOW AND THE NEED FOR INCURRED ANALYSIS

Some PPOs promise to improve providers' cash flow through more prompt payment of bills, accomplished by quick processing and direct payment to providers. An additional benefit of direct payment may be to reduce provider bad debts. This is especially true if the level of payment has been fixed in advance (e.g., through a negotiated fee schedule), so that the provider knows the correct copayment to collect from each patient at the time of service.

These characteristics of PPOs may improve the cash flow of providers and reduce the paperwork burden of patients and hence may be advantageous to all parties. But in the short run, employers introducing a PPO are likely to have to increase their outlays for health benefits, since they may still be paying off old claims while paying the new ones. The increased cash outlays in the first year may not only eat up the savings that were projected for the first year, but even increase the employer's outlays over what they would have been. (By the second year, of course, the impact of the discount would be felt.) The prevalence of self-insurance arrangements among the larger employers could make it difficult to adopt a PPO that promised prompt payments or reduced paper work. This could restrict the marketability of such PPOs.

Valid comparisons of costs of a PPO and the existing plan can only be made on an incurred basis, attributing all outlays to the time at which services are performed rather than when they are paid. In addition, delays in payment affect their value, through the time value of money. This is properly reflected by discounting payments between the time of service and the time of payment.

DISCOUNTS AND PITFALLS IN THE DESIGN OF REIMBURSEMENT

A frequent feature found in PPO arrangements is negotiated fee schedules or discounts from usual charges. For discounts to benefit plan members, the discounts must be combined with a provider agreement not to charge the patient for any excess over any applicable copayments.

Although discounts may appear to present the surest source of savings, there are many threats to their realization. The most important of these are increased utilization, changes in the mix of services provided toward more expensive services, an increase in charge rates reflecting reduced utilization, a pattern of selection of providers that undermines the savings, and technical problems in the design of the savings formulas themselves.

The threat of offsetting increased utilization is well known and has been extensively commented upon. Even reduced utilization may fail to generate corresponding savings if overall utilization of an institution is reduced in proportion. This can be most easily seen if a PPO purchases the entire services of a nonprofit hospital. In the long run there is an additional problem for discounts obtained from nonprofit institutions. As more patients become covered by discount arrangements, there are fewer patients paying full charges to make up the lost revenue, and the amount of feasible discount decreases.

The problems of the selection of providers chiefly concern the possibility of promising savings that will not materialize. An obvious example is for those providers that already charge less than the fee schedule to agree systematically to be preferred and for those that charge more to refuse, and not for patients to actually change providers. Under these conditions there would never be any savings regardless of where the fee schedule was set. Similarly, a very deep discount from one hospital may leave the payment above the full charges of another. Although this is an obvious pitfall, examples can be found in which providers were preferred on the basis of the size of the discount rather than the resulting level of payment for services.

Subtle technical complications may also arise in the design of discounts and fee schedules. One class of problems concerns a shift of reimbursement basis between how the insurer normally paid claims and how claims are paid through the PPO. For example, if inpatient hospital claims have been paid on the basis of hospital charges, and the PPO negotiates an average per diem or average payment per admission, then the potential exists to pay more rather than less for inpatient hospital services.

This effect can be seen even with only one hospital involved. Suppose the charges of a hospital average $450 per patient day for privately financed patients, and the hospital agrees to a per diem rate of $400. This may represent a saving for all insured groups, but there may be some employment groups that have average charges per diem of less than $400. Such groups may have a lower than average need of the most expensive hospital services or have a much longer average length of stay, which spreads the expensive services over more days. On the other hand, there will be groups with a much larger savings than indicated by the discount. This latter effect can cause major problems for the hospital, since it is likely that groups joining such a PPO would systematically be those that benefited from the change in reimbursement basis.

With more than one hospital the same problem may occur but is more difficult to detect. In addition, further problems may be introduced if the PPO offers a set price across the board for all takers (e.g., a specific dollar amount per diem, per admission, or per DRG admission). In this case the average rate paid may be well below the average charges for all hospitals but above that paid in specific hospitals. If patients from a particular group are concentrated in such hospitals (with average charges to the group below the negotiated rate), payments for the group will rise in the PPO.

Similar problems can arise if the PPO negotiates a rate per admission and enrolls from groups that presently pay on the basis of charges. In this situation, it is wise to obtain detailed tabulations of the claim experience of the group to determine how the group is likely to fare in the PPO.

In the examples discussed above, where payment would have otherwise been made on the basis of charges (or a percentage of charges), negotiating a discount in terms of charge rates would assure an even distribution of savings, at least as long as the pattern of utilization remained unchanged. Another alternative would be to use a more precise reimbursement system. For example, a schedule of reimbusement amounts based on diagnostic related groupings (DRGs) may reduce significantly the differences attributable to the change in reimbursement basis.

The same type of problems can occur if an insurer normally pays hospitals on a per-diem rate. Here the shift would be to a discounted charge or a per admission basis. For example, one Blue Cross plan decided to pay hospitals on a per admission basis to improve hospital incentives to control costs and negotiated a fixed fee per admission with a number of hospitals in a metropolitan area. In offering this PPO to specific employment groups, however, the insurer had to check which hospitals were actually used by the patients of each group. Although in general the payment levels were below the cost of hospital services in the area, the possibility existed that the agreed payment in the PPO might be higher than the average charges per admission in the hospitals previously used by a particular employment group.

The general principle running through all these examples is that it is not necessarily the discount that determines the savings. Savings can only be determined by comparing the amounts that will be paid under a PPO arrangement with what would have been paid in the absence of that arrangement for the patients in a specific employment group. These calculations must be determined on a group-by-group basis.

Further, problems are considerably more complicated if enrollees can choose whether to use the PPO or not. If an entire group is being converted to a PPO, a few summary claim statistics from a prior year will provide adequate assurance that the reimbursement shift will not undermine savings for that group. Analysis of the potential for reimbursment shifts caused by employer choices, however, requires utilization data for individual providers (especially the hospitals). Further, it may be necessary to model the choices of employees to obtain an estimate of the impact of the shift. The choices to be modeled may be either the initial enrollment or changes of providers during the year.

A final consideration is that over the long run, if PPOs become widespread, many institutional providers will not be able to maintain the level of discounts obtainable now. For those providers who can only offer discounts by cost shifting, there will be an insuffcient base of patients to whom the discounts can be passed on. In the long run, unless true efficiencies are introduced, hospitals agreeing to substantial discounts are likely to be forced to discontinue them.

Once a network of providers is established, however, it may be difficult to change. Large groups of patients cannot be shifted arbitrarily from one hospital to another without disrupting the network of physicians and institutions and hence affecting the quality of care. Since the stability of the preferred provider set is important for the quality of care and the credibility of the organization, PPOs that concentrate on lower long-term costs will wind up in the best competitive situation.

In response to these factors, some employers have ignored discounts from hospitals altogether and concentrated on the cost structure and efficiency of operation of the institutions. In the long run these will be more important to the cost of care than the level of current discounted prices that can be negotiated. Thus it may be wise to contract initially with institutions that have lower cost and practice medicine efficiently rather than those that can only provide a competitive rate with a substantial discount.

UTILIZATION CONTROLS

It is well known that achieving savings through fee negotiations with preferred providers depends on avoiding offsetting utilization increases. Such increases may appear because a different mix of services is charged or a different definition of services (e.g., charging separately for injections) is used, rather than an increase in days of care, admissions, or visits. The capacity of providers to increase apparent utilization has been demonstrated with respect to attempts to control fees or charges through regulation (e.g., the 1972–74 price controls). Further, as competition increases and providers become willing to accept discounts or lower fees without gaining an increased volume of patients (which must happen if the overall cost of care is to be lower), the incentive to raise revenues becomes very strong.

One of the most effective opportunities that PPOs present to control health care costs is the introduction of effective utilization controls, backed by the capacity to exclude providers that do not cooperate fully. Measures such as preadmission certification, concurrent admission review (usually by a nurse coordinator), and professional review of cases exceeding specified norms have been demonstrated to reduce inpatient hospital utilization by 15 percent to 25 percent in most areas of the country. To be effective, the reviews must be backed by the capacity and the will not to renew contracts with providers that consistently fail to meet the established norms. Provider agreements to accept the reviews and to forego compensation for unapproved stays are also effective.

Gatekeepers are also an effective utilization control technique. A gatekeeper is a primary care physician (usually chosen in advance by the patient) who must give prior authorization for any nonemergency specialist or hospital services before the plan will pay for them. Like most other utilization control techniques, however, the impact depends on the style of medical practice of the specific gatekeepers, their financial interest in the plan, and the management support provided. Normally, gatekeepers are given a direct financial incentive to control utilization, such as risk pools or capitation payments.

Other models have proved to be effective. One employer has achieved a major reduction in claim payments by using independent walk-in clinics as gatekeepers. The physicians operating the clinics tended not to have established networks of referral physicians and had a financial incentive not to refer patients beyond the clinic for fear of losing the patients to established physicians. In other situations, gatekeepers may have no impact whatsoever. This may be a problem especially where the gatekeepers are the staff of the hospital establishing the PPO; there are no real incentives on either side to reduce utilization other than to preserve the PPO. Whether or not the hospital will reduce utilization at the expense of itself and its staff for the long-run welfare of both is a question that can only be answered in practice. Further, the process of implementation may be halting and sporadic. The history of many IPAs shows that the measures necessary to control utilization were only taken when financial insolvency was an immediate threat. Others have failed to take the required steps even then and failed.

One very interesting development from an actuarial perspective is the development of PPOs by IPAs and peer review organizations that see an opportunity to expand operations by applying lessons learned in their review operations to select the most efficient providers and cut utilization. An experience base of several years in attempting to police utilization in an IPA permits these organizations to determine inefficient providers far more effectively. Further, although new techniques are being developed to analyze utilization data and determine efficient utilization and providers, the current practice is more an art than a science and experience is critical.

PROVIDER SELECTION CRITERIA

The original idea behind the PPO was to limit participation to efficient providers, defined as those with low costs or who make efficient use of services. The main appeal of the PPO, compared with certain other organizational forms that provide incentives for efficient care (i.e., prepaid group practice plans), however, is a wide selection of providers, especially at the personal physician level, without forcing employees to choose among a restricted set of physicians or to accept the physician assigned by a group. These conflicting objectives can be reconciled through the precise selection of providers and the policing of renewal provider contracts. There is evidence that very substantial savings can be obtained through eliminating only a minority of physicians and hospitals. The expertise to accomplish these objectives can be found in the IPA/peer review organization field. It exists as a result of the need of these programs to police utilization as a prerequisite of staying in business.

The usual tool of analysis is the provider profile, standardized for case mix, and other factors. The most important elements would appear not to be the format or the analytic techniques (although these have advanced rapidly), but the judgment of the individuals involved in gathering, interpreting, and applying the data. The conventional wisdom among these experts is that data have been most helpful both in convincing HMO managements to act and in getting provider boards to accept conclusions.

Progress has also been made in the capacity to process and standardize claims data to determine efficient providers.[2] How effective these will be, however, in the selection of providers for a PPO remains to be seen. At present, the most effective aproach would appear to be to make use of the expertise available from both practitioners and claim data base analysts and to design contracts in such a manner that renewal is optional to the PPO. Specific provider profiles would appear to be a necessity.

BIASED SELECTION BY ENROLLEES

Biased selection is the tendency for individuals to make decisions to join a plan or use providers in ways that distribute the cost of a program among plans or among providers in a nonrandom fashion. Biased "selection in health insurance is the phenomenon of persons who are relatively low users of service choosing those plans with less extensive benefits."[3]

An important application of biased selection for PPO's is the behavior of individual patients when faced with a choice among insurance plans that involves a trade-off between cost sharing and restrictions on choices of physicians. Experience suggests that patients with existing conditions tend to be less likely to change providers when an economic incentive is provided to change (e.g., a reduction in cost sharing).[4]

A similar type of choice occurs in competition between IPA-type HMOs and reimbursement plans, and the evidence shows that those enrolling in the HMOs tend to have lower costs than those that do not. (These results appear, however, to have been highly specific to the particular circumstances of the competing plans so that it is very difficult to generalize.) Two general principles can be hypothesized. First, selection is very sensitive to the relationship between the employee contribution rate for the HMO and the regular plan. If the HMO contribution rate is higher, the HMOs tend to get larger families (but not necessarily ones with high health care costs). If the HMO premium rate is lower (and the employee gets the benefit), the HMO will pick up a number of single employees with relatively low health care costs. Second, the impact of selection is roughly proportional to the degree of restrictions on access to providers. Hence, a much greater impact would be expected in the case of closed panel plans than in the case with IPAs that include most physicians in a community.

These behavioral tendencies have several important implications for calculating actuarial rates for PPOs. First, if employees must select the PPO at the beginning of a year, those with relationships with nonpreferred providers would be less likely to join, especially if they are currently under treatment for an existing condition. In contrast, those not under current treatment and those without a serious condition are likely to feel freer to join the PPO. Thus, those joining the PPO would be expected to have lower average claims than those remaining in the reimbursement plan. Second, in many plans the inducement to join the PPO is a significantly lower employee premium rate, but if the difference in premium rates for joining the PPO was calculated on the average experience of all employees, the employees joining the PPO are likely to be overcompensated for doing so. This is because the average saving for the particular employees joining the PPO are likely to be lower than for all employees.

Similar selection problems can occur if the choice of providers is made at the time of service, with lower copayments for those using the preferred providers. For example, a uniform fee schedule may be substantially below the average level that would have been paid for all plan members but still above what would have been paid for those using the preferred providers. This is likely to occur, since the terms of the transaction are more favorable for the employees and physicians where full payment is applicable. In some cases, employers offering a PPO on a service by service basis are counting on incentives to obtain significant shifts to preferred providers. Such shifts are in fact necessary if the plan is to have an impact other than as a way of rewarding some employees for using certain providers or a penalty for not using them.

In these cases there are three important questions to answer. First, are the financial incentives to change adequate to influence a significant number of employees? Second, how will the relative health needs of those shifting providers compare to that of the entire group? Finally, how do the amounts that will be paid for the shifters to the new providers compare with those that would have been paid to the old? For these reasons it is prudent to determine which providers were used in a base period and to make explicit assumptions concerning employee behavior to model the impact of provider selection. No set formulas can be offered concerning the analysis required. Experience does suggest, however, that patients with existing conditions tend to be less likely to change providers when an economic incentive is provided to change (e.g., a reduction in cost sharing). As more PPO experience is gained in similar situations, more data will be available concerning the potential impact of these types of problems.

The most severe selection problems occur when the PPO is funded independently of the reimbursement plan (i.e., offered by an organization that is financially independent of the regular insurer), and the relative experience is reflected in the premium rates charged. Thus if PPOs are permitted to compete in open enrollments for members of an employment group and charge a "community rate" (or other rate that does not reflect the experience of the specific employees enrolled from that group), the employer could pay more for the employees joining the PPO than they would have cost under the reimbursement plan.[5] In these situations, the selection battle will determine the viability of both options. The loser is likely to go by the wayside, regardless of efficiency.

CONCLUSION

A final caution is that the field is still so new that it is not always possible to pin down what a PPO will actually do. Many of these organizations are in the formation stage, and there may be large discrepancies between the original plans and the actual implementation. In addition, there is very little operating experience and consequently it is not possible to project with confidence the effects of the various features. Finally, any particular situation is likely to have enough unique features that it will be prudent to exercise actuarial judgment based on a careful study of all relevant factors.

NOTES

1. An actuary should specify all features in detail that are assumed in the estimates and restrict the applicability of the estimates accordingly. It is not always possible to do this. The actuary may find himself effectively accountable for estimates in an absolute sense despite the violation of numerous conditions noted in his footnotes.

2. The work of the Health Data Institute and others in developing computer programs to analyze claim data are discussed elsewhere.

3. U.S. Congress, "Tax Subsidies for Medical Care: Current Policies and Possible Alternatives," Congressional Budget Office, 1980, p.19. For an analysis of selection see James R. Price and James W. Mays, "Biased Selection in the Federal Employees Health Benefits Program," *Inquiry,* forthcoming.

4. See for example, Paul Eggers, "Risk Differentials between Medicare Beneficiaries Enrolled and Not Enrolled in an HMO," *Health Care Financing Review* 1, no. 3 (Winter 1980).

5. This frequently occurs in the dual choice options presently given HMOs.

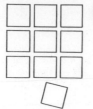

Marketplace Fundamentals

UTILIZATION REVIEW METHODS AND INCENTIVES

Marvis Oehm

Executive Director, Area XXIV, PSRO, Inc.
Director, District V, California Medical Review
Los Angeles, CA

Utilization review (UR) is a generic term currently applied to various means of monitoring the use or controlling the "abuse" of inpatient hospital services paid by third-party insurance plans. UR has existed nationally since the inception of the medicare program.

Utilization review is generally viewed as a "cost-containment mechanism." However, it is difficult to separate cost containment from quality of care. Hospitals are high-risk, high-cost treatment settings. Persons admitted to hospitals unnecessarily always run the risk of acquiring hospital-based infections or experiencing side effects from medicines or surgical or diagnostic procedures. Further, unnecessary surgeries have their own potential problems. For example, if a person is admitted for an unnecessary cataract extraction and has not had an adequate physical examination prior to this elective surgery, death is a possible (not probable) outcome.

In a practical sense appropriate utilization and quality of care are analogous. However, the overriding concern for most hospitals and most payors is economic. Hospitals want to maximize their revenues while payors want to reduce their costs. Thus, there is an immediate conflict. Good UR can mediate this conflict.

BACKGROUND

Both the medicare and medicaid programs have required hospitals to monitor utilization of hospital services paid for by public funds. To participate in these programs, hospitals formed Utilization Review Committees to review cases and assure that public funds are spent only for medically necessary services.

In several parts of the country, local groups of physicians organized medical care foundations that had a peer-review component in the private sector. It was largely on these foundation programs that later national legislation mandating peer review was based.

Under this national legislation, UR was applied primarily to patients whose care was paid for through a Federal or State (medicare or medicaid) program. The Joint Commission on Accreditation of Hospitals (JCAH) standards recommended UR be applied to a sample of private pay patients.

The major impetus behind current UR programs came with the 1972 Amendments to the Social Security Act (PL 92–603) and the implementation of the Professional Standards Review Program (PSRO). The PSRO Program represented a national effort to curb escalations in the costs of the medicare and medicaid programs. Until that time, utilization review activities had been token in nature and ineffective in curbing unnecessary use of institutional care and services. UR was further characterized as more form than substance.[1]

PSROs were intended to be local physician membership corporations. Within local areas, the physician community was to develop and implement consistent areawide review programs. PSROs were to develop and apply objective norms, standards, and criteria for monitoring the use of hospital services. Through application of these objective measures, PSROs were to determine the medical necessity, appropriateness, and quality of services provided to patients whose care was publicly funded. Payment was then to be made only on the basis of decisions by the PSRO.

The original peer review legislation was based on models of voluntary and community review efforts of some local medical societies and foundations for medical care as well as federally funded Experimental Medical Care Review Organizations (EMCRO). In many areas, these precursor organizations applied for and received federal funding as PSROs.

PSRO review, in many areas, applied only to medicare patients because of lack of adequate funding and changes in legislation that made medicaid review optional.

Preferred provider organizations, regardless of structure or membership, all depend on reducing or maintaining the lowest possible use of inpatient hospital services.

All PPOs have some form of UR built into the system because its long-term financial stability will, in part, depend on the effectiveness of the UR program.

REVIEW METHODS AND PROVIDER BEHAVIOR

UR PROCESSES AND GOALS

All forms of UR are intended to assure that

1. Services are *medically* necessary—specifically, is the patient's medical condition or problem such that he or she needs the services provided or proposed to be provided?
2. Services are *appropriate*—specifically, is the patient's medical condition such that the services he or she requires can only be delivered in the hospital and cannot be delivered in an outpatient setting (e.g., clinic or doctor's office), skilled nursing facility, or home?

Some UR programs, generally those developed by physician-based groups, will also address whether the services meet professionally recognized standards of health care. This review deals with such issues as the timeliness and quality of services provided. For example, if an outmoded or potentially harmful treatment is provided, this type of review can result in an immediate contact between a physician representing the review organization and the patient's physician. Other review programs may not offer this service. However, various private review services and insurance carriers have either borrowed PSRO criteria or have established medical policy committees, comprised of physicians, to address these quality issues.

UR is most frequently based on written information provided by the patient's physician and documented in the hospital medical record or reported on the hospital bill. This information may often be supplemented by telephone discussions with the attending physician or surgeon. Each UR method is designed to accomplish a specific purpose or prevent a certain behavior. The PPO payment structure and the local health care market environment should determine which methods are emphasized. The following are the major review activities being performed across the country:

— Preadmission Review/Certification.
— Concurrent Review.
— Admission Review.
— Continued Stay Review.
— Discharge Planning.

— Retrospective Review.
— Ancillary Services Review.
— Data Collection/Analysis.
— Second Opinion Programs.

Preadmission Review or Certification and Prior Authorization

Regardless of label, this review is intended to discourage or prevent unnecessary admissions to hospitals. If the reason for admission is an elective surgery, this type of review can also identify and discourage potentially unnecessary surgeries.

This review requires the physician and patient to provide basic diagnostic and/or planned procedural information to a review organization *before* the patient goes to a hospital or receives a service. The information can be provided by telephone or on a written form. If the information is incomplete, the attending physician is often contacted by telephone. This type of review is normally applied to elective admissions. An elective admission is normally defined as a planned treatment that can be delayed for an indefinite period without risk of permanent disability. Such procedures might include vasectomies, cataract extractions and implants, and certain hernia repairs.

Some preadmission review programs may include a telephone authorization for "urgent" admissions. There is no common definition of urgent admissions, and in retrospect, some are elective and some are true emergencies. Emergency admissions are not subject to this type of review because, by definition, treatment in these cases must be provided immediately or there is a risk of permanent disability or death. When a patient is admitted for a significantly debilitating symptom (such as an immediate onset of pain from a kidney stone), this is normally an urgent admission and is not subject to preadmission review. If, on the other hand, the patient has a history of several weeks or months of low-back pain, this would normally be subject to preadmission review. This would include a case of back pain intractable to outpatient management.

In evaluating the potential savings of a preadmission review program, the cost of substitute services should be considered. Most preadmission review programs will result in more services being provided in an outpatient clinic or doctor's office and less services performed in the hospital. But, the services in most cases will still be rendered.

Preadmission review can also educate the patient and physician community on services that are covered on an outpatient basis. Despite changes in health benefit plans over the years, misconceptions about the extent of outpatient coverage still persist. Some private insurance plans are structuring benefits to provide for a lower hospital benefit (e.g., 50 percent instead of 80 percent or 80 percent instead of 100 percent) if preadmission review is not obtained. This has the advantage of involving the insured in making decisions about the types of services used. It has the disadvantage of requiring substantial employee educational activities.

Concurrent In-Hospital Review

This includes admission review (admission certification) and continued stay review (length of stay review) and was, under PSRO, the most widespread type of review. This review is begun immediately (usually within one working day) after a patient is admitted to the hospital. At admission review, the patient's record is assessed to determine whether the admission is medically necessary and appropriate (as defined above for preadmission review). If admission is medically necessary and appropriate, a follow-up review date is set and the continued stay review process begins. During continued stay review, the patient's continued hospitalization is assessed for medical necessity and appropriateness.

Concurrent review is primarily oriented toward reducing the number of days a patient stays in the hospital. Further, with a large enough patient base, over a period of time, concurrent review, by the so-called sentinel effect, may reduce any unnecessary admissions. This type of review does not normally involve the patient or insured unless a question about medical necessity arises. Concurrent review (CR), was a mandated activity under the PSRO program and all PSROs developed sophisticated CR programs. Thus, where PSROs exist, this is often the easiest review to implement in some parts of the United States. It is also the most labor-intensive part of any UR program.

Example of Admission Review. John Smith had a fainting episode on Sunday. He was taken to the hospital Emergency Room by his wife on Sunday afternoon. At the hospital, he was admitted for evaluation.

On Monday, the medical record is screened. The doctor plans to perform a diagnostic workup with several different studies. Mr. Smith is reported as feeling fine, is receiving no medications, and is walking in the hallway. The studies planned normally do not require the acute hospital, so the case is referred to a peer-review physician who contacts Mr. Smith's physician. Any of the following situations may occur:

1. Mr. Smith's physician may decide to discharge him and to do other studies on an outpatient basis.
2. Mr. Smith's physician may agree that hospitalization is not medically indicated, but for convenience to the patient's family, the studies would be performed in the hospital. In this situation, what happens depends on who is the reviewing organization and how benefits are structured.
3. Mr. Smith's physician may report that laboratory and clinical data, not yet in the record, indicate a serious neurological prob-

lem and thus the record will be regularly reviewed until further stay is not medically needed.

Example of Continued Stay Review. Mrs. Jones was admitted to the hospital for acute appendicitis. Her Tuesday admission was appropriate; her surgery early Wednesday morning was timely and appropriate. On Friday morning, she is walking and eating and is receiving no significant pain medication, but there are no plans for discharge on Friday or Saturday. The case is referred to a review organization physician who may discuss the case with Mrs. Jones' physician with the following possible results:

1. Mrs. Jones' physician reports he is going out of town for the weekend and has not written the order for discharge.
2. Approval of continued stay if Mrs. Jones requires additional services that can be provided only in the hospital.

Notices of Review Decisions. In many concurrent programs, the review organization provides a written notice if services are not medically necessary or appropriate. This is usually a letter to the patient or insured, the hospital, and the attending physician. It documents the review organization's decision and gives any appeal procedures to contest the recommendation.

Discharge Planning

Discharge planning is often a part of a concurrent review program and involves Social Service personnel in hospitals. Effective discharge planning can reduce the number of days in a hospital by identifying and arranging for alternate services to be provided at home or in a skilled nursing facility. This would include such activities as arranging for temporary homemaker, meal services, or visiting nurse assistance. This part of a review program can be effective if the health benefits provide coverage for such posthospital alternate services.

Retrospective Review

Retrospective review has traditionally been performed by many insurance companies and has consisted of bill review and coverage review for medical necessity and coordination of benefits. This type of review is performed after a patient has received all services and has been discharged from a hospital. Review may include an assessment of the medical record but most often consists of a review of the hospital bill and a summary of the hospitalization. One major problem with retrospective review is that the patient and provider may not know until several months after the fact that services will not be covered. Further, since all the services have already been rendered and the costs already incurred, they must be written off as uncollectible costs or bad debts by the provider if the patient cannot pay. This increases the overall costs of care because uncollectible costs and bad debts contribute to raises in hospital rates.

Ancillary Services Review

Ancillary review is similar to retrospective review, as it generally occurs after a patient has been discharged from a hospital. Ancillary services are defined as those hospital services for which separate charges are made. Such services appear on a hospital bill as separate line items. The term includes both those services that a hospital itself provides and those which it provides via a contract with an outside agency or individual. Common ancillary services include

- Laboratory studies—blood tests, urine tests.
- Respiratory therapy—oxygen, Intermittent Positive Pressure Breathing (IPPB).
- Physical therapy.
- Operating room.
- X-ray studies.
- Special care units—intensive care, coronary care.
- Personal comfort items—admission packs (toothbrushes, cups, washbasins, etc.).

Ancillary review consists of two parts:

1. A comparison of items ordered by a physician; items performed, as evidenced by appropriate reports in the medical record; and items billed. Ideally, these three items should match, and this review is always retrospective.
2. An assessment of the medical necessity of particular ancillary services.

Ancillary review will identify double-billing errors and overcharges.

Ancillary review is labor intensive and expensive because the hospital itemized bill is compared, line by line, with the physician orders and laboratory, X ray, and operative reports in the medical record. On a 15-day hospital stay, the bill may be 10 to 15 pages, and the record 100 pages. Each item on the bill is located in the record in two places—the physician order for the item and the report that it was done or provided. This should only be considered on a general basis where problems are known or suspected to exist. Where a local review organization has done ancillary review, it may offer a source for identifying problems. Sample bill review may reveal frequent double billings for such items as surgery or routine billings of a specific set of tests regardless of the patient's problem.

Some companies are offering employees rebates or reduced deductibles if the employee identifies and reports errors on his or her bill. Hospitals are required to give the patient an itemized bill. These bills often list the services provided on each day, starting with the room charge. Major errors, such as billing for the room twice on one day, billing for the surgery twice, or billing for intensive care when the patient did not get intensive care, can be identified by a person without medical training. Since these are frequent, high-cost errors, an employee can easily identify and report them. Such employee programs won't identify nonmedically necessary services, but they can effectively identify major billing errors.

Second Opinion Programs

Second opinion programs have not traditionally been included in the usual UR mechanisms. They are included here because these programs are gaining in popularity as a means to deter unnecessary surgery. These programs are aimed at reducing unnecessary elective surgeries because, by definition, only an elective surgery can be delayed without risk of permanent disability or death. A second opinion program requires that, for specified elective procedures (e.g., hernia repairs, cataract extractions), the patient be examined by a second physician. This is different from traditional UR, which depends on the documentation provided by the patient's attending physician.

The American College of Surgeons recommends the second opinion be provided by a qualified specialist in the appropriate field of surgery. This means if a cataract extraction is recommended, the patient would see another ophthalmologist, or if a coronary bypass were recommended, the patient would see another cardiologist or cardiovascular surgeon.

Normally, the physician giving the second opinion will have agreed not to perform the proposed procedure. The second opinion physician is to be independent of the first physician and would not have any personal or professional relationship with the original physician. Second opinion programs are often targeted on specific high-cost, frequently performed or frequently questioned procedures such as cataract extractions, coronary bypass surgery, hysterectomies, or laminectomies.

Second opinions have always been a standard part of accepted medical practice, and such programs can be voluntary or mandatory. In a voluntary program, the second opinion is encouraged but benefits are not reduced for failure to obtain a second opinion. In a mandatory program, benefits are reduced if surgery is performed without a second opinion. In most programs, full benefits are paid if the insured complies with the process and benefits are not modified based on the second opinion recommendation.

Since some surgeries are very costly (e.g., coronary bypass), deferring only one such surgery can result in a $20,000 savings. However, in estimating potential savings, the cost of the second opinion and frequently a second set of tests should be considered.

Data and Information Systems

Most review organizations offer computerized data collection and reporting to support the review services. The data elements collected routinely vary, and the more detail collected (e.g., ancillary service data detail on charges), the more expensive the system. Most review organizations collect a basic set of data called the Uniform Hospital Discharge Data Set (UHDDS). This contains basic information on the patient (age, sex, zip code, identifying information on the insurance plan); the principal diagnosis (defined as that reason, established after study, to be responsible for the hospital admission); up to four additional diagnoses; and up to five procedures performed. Other information often includes where the patient was discharged to (e.g., home, extended care), dates of procedures performed, number of reviews, and information on which physicians provided the care.

Much of this same information is contained on claim forms submitted by hospitals to the insurance companies. The extent of data available on a group's past utilization will depend on how much detail from claims has been entered in the computer. The extent to which the data are comparable to national data, such as medicare, depends on the coding systems used to input data. The current medicare data system using diagnosis related groups (DRGs), is based on the *International Classification of Diseases*—Ninth Edition—*Clinical Modification* (ICD–9–CM). A variety of other coding systems are in use and these are summarized in the chart below. However, it is only where diagnoses and procedures are coded in ICD–9–CM, that DRGs can be calculated for comparison with medicare DRG pricing.

To be able to compare utilization across plans or with federal or state programs, a consistent coding scheme is desirable (see Exhibit 1).

EXHIBIT 1
Major Coding Schemes

ICD9-CM	Codes for diagnoses and procedures. Basis for the medicare payment system by DRGs. Mandated by the Federal government for use on Uniform Hospital Billing forms (UB 82).
ICDA-8	Prior edition of ICD-9-CM. Less specific than ICD-9-CM; contained fewer procedures.
HICDA-2	A clinical modification with more specificity than ICDA-8. Replaced by ICD-9-CM.
DSM I, II, III	Coding for psychiatric hospitals. In medicare, replaced by ICD9-CM.
CPT	Current Procedural Terminology—largely used for physician services billing and is the basis of such fee guidelines as the California Relative Value Studies (RVS).

Regardless of the coding system used or data element collected, a comprehensive data reporting capability will be necessary to, at a minimum:

— Evaluate the effects of the review program over time.
— Compare utilization in different groups that may have different benefit structures.
— Identify which services and which hospitals are used most frequently.
— Identify differences in costs of similar services at different hospitals.

IMPLEMENTING A REVIEW PROGRAM

All the review functions discussed above can be performed independently by individual hospitals (called delegated review) or by an outside, third-party review organization (called nondelegated review).

Hospital based UR (delegated review) is carried out by internal hospital medical staff committees operating under a variety of different plans and procedures. Nonphysician staff who support the activities of the hospital UR committees are employees of the hospital. They may be organized in a variety of ways with some review personnel reporting to hospital administration, others to nursing staff, and others to medical records or medical staff. In third-party UR (nondelegated review), the personnel, physicians, and nonphysicians, are employed by the review organization rather than the hospital. Some third-party review organizations pay hospitals to carry out concurrent review in a delegated mode.

.Regardless of which structure (delegated or nondelegated) is used for implementing review, the basic medical record/information screening process is carried out by trained nonphysician personnel. These personnel are most often registered nurses but also include licensed vocational nurses, medical records personnel, registered record administrators or accredited records technicians, or social service personnel such as social workers and discharge planners.

When the nonphysician reviewer (usually called a review coordinator) cannot find sufficient information in a medical record to approve a case, the review coordinator will normally refer the case to a physician advisor or reviewer (called a PA). Depending on the requirements of the specific review program, the PA may or may not contact the attending physician to discuss the case. In most programs, however, only a physician may recommend that services are not "medically necessary and appropriate." Often this decision is transmitted in the form of a letter to the patient (called a noncertification or denial letter). In almost all private review programs, final benefit, payment, and coverage decisions rest with the insurer or employer, and medical necessity decisions are advisory.

Delegated Review

In delegated review, each hospital employs, trains, and pays the nonphysician screening personnel. These staff may have a variety of responsibilities such as infection control, medical records supervision, and/or medical staff support. The review function, therefore, may be only one of a variety of responsibilities. In these cases, review, especially for an outside group, may assume a low priority as internal demands on a day-to-day basis take precedence. Hospitals are businesses and they must make money. To the extent review conflicts with internal operating objectives, review personnel will respond to internal rather than external goals.

Review staff may report to administration, nursing, medical records, or medical staff with corresponding incentives and priorities. In delegated review, the physician review responsibilities often rest with the hospital medical staff's utilization-review committee. In some hospitals, these committees change annually, while in others, there may be one or more permanent physician advisors who are paid by the hospital for review work. Continuity of physician involvement in the review process is important because it takes time for a physician reviewer to become well grounded in principles of medical necessity and appropriateness. For example, for most new PAs, family or physician convenience is readily accepted as justification for hospitalization.

Currently, most hospital medical staff by-laws and procedures provide for review of specific cases on a request basis, and at least theoretically, any patient or insurance company should be able to request a hospital review of a particular case at no charge. For purposes of JCAH accreditation, all currently accredited hospitals do maintain some form of UR program.

Some third-party review organizations are building on the delegated hospital review systems by offering the preadmission and retrospective review program components while paying the hospital $20 to 30 per case to perform the concurrent review portion of the program.

Nondelegated Review

In nondelegated review, the nonphysician and physician personnel are employed, trained, and paid by an organization outside an individual hospital. This may be a peer review organization (PSRO/PRO), medical care foundation, insurance carrier, or other private review corporation. Some review organizations offer combinations of delegation and nondelegation or may only perform specific activities such as preadmission review.

Most PPOs will offer some variation on the foregoing UR themes as part of the PPO package. Evaluating the package will be more or less difficult, depending on the past information available for hospital use for a particular group.

PROVIDER INCENTIVES AND UTILIZATION REVIEW

Good UR can be delegated or nondelegated depending on the local market environment, because the market environment will influence hospital and physician incentives. For example, in areas with excess bed capacity, hospitals may encourage physicians to admit more patients to keep beds full. Hospitals in areas with shortages of beds are more likely to encourage physicians to discharge patients sooner.

Exhibit 2 shows some general market characteristics and possible corresponding overutilization incentives on the part of providers and consumers of services.

EXHIBIT 2
Provider Incentives for Overutilization

Market Characteristic	Potential Utilization Incentive
1. Overbedding or excess hospital capacity. This occurs when many hospitals in a geographic area routinely fill less than 75 percent of their beds. Some metropolitan areas have hospital occupancy rates of less than 50 percent with some hospitals at less than 30 percent.	1. To increase admissions or lengths of stay in order to fill excess capacity and maximize revenue.
2. Number of physicians and surgeons. Because physicians admit patients to hospitals, the number of physicians in an area will largely determine utilization rates in general and surgical rates in particular.	2. Increased numbers of admissions, increased numbers of specific surgical procedures.
3. Competition for physicians. Hospitals, especially in an overbedded area, compete with each other to attract physicians to the medical staffs who will admit patients. Some hospitals may purchase the latest in diagnostic equipment; others may reduce barriers by facilitating the credentialing process or encouraging maximum use of hospital services.	3. Increased use of sophisticated diagnostic tools (e.g., CT scans); increased admissions for diagnostic evaluations, and more services per day per patient.
4. Lack of alternative types of services such as home health, ambulatory care, or extended care beds in an area.	4. Longer stays in the hospital or admission to the hospital when ambulatory diagnostic services are not available.

5. Method of payment:
  a. Cost reimbursement: This method was used by the medicare program until the 1982 Tax Equity and Fiscal Responsibility Act. Most comprehensive
	5. Method of payment:
	  a. The more services provided, the more revenues generated.

EXHIBIT 2 *(concluded)*

Market Characteristic	Potential Utilization Incentive
5. a. *(continued)* or major medical insurance plans pay on the basis of claims submitted by hospitals. Under this type of system, the per-diem room, board, and routine nursing service costs were paid, plus the costs of ancillary services.	
b. Per-diem, all-inclusive reimbursement. Under this system, a per-diem rate that includes all ancillary services is negotiated with individual hospitals. This method is being used by many PPOs, which often offer a higher benefit, if a patient uses a participating provider.	b. Provide fewer ancillary services per patient day; longer length of stay to cover costs of ancillary services provided early in the stay; refusal of services to potentially high care/high cost patients.
c. Per-case (per discharge) reimbursement. This is the basis of the Medicare Prospective Payment System (PPS) based on diagnostic related groups (DRGs). In Kansas, Blue Cross/Blue Shield moved to payment based on DRGs. This method of payment formed the basis for New Jersey's all party payor system. Although there may be various exceptions (as in very long lengths of stay where extra payment is made), the intent in a DRG system is to pay a single amount (determined in advance) for the entire set of services associated with particular groups of medical problems.	c. Reduced length of stay; reduced use of ancillary services; increased number of admissions and re-admissions; premature discharges.
d. Capitation: This method forms the basis of the Kaiser system and most HMO programs. In this method, a monthly fee is paid, which covers all services.	d. Reduced admissions; reduced length of stay; reduced use of ancillary services; premature discharges.
6. Benefit structures that focus on in-hospital coverage with low deductibles and copayments or no deductible and copayments are usually associated with higher hospital use than those that cover a broader range of outpatient or extended care services.	

EXHIBIT 3
Utilization Review Activities

Problem	UR Activity
Unnecessary admissions/Unnecessary surgeries	Preadmission review and second opinion programs for selected procedures.
Too many days in the hospital.	Admission and continued stay review (concurrent review).
Overuse of ancillary services.	Retrospective ancillary/bill review.
Premature discharges and re-admissions.	Admission and continued stay review (concurrent review).
Lack of alternative services and/or lack of coverage for alternative services.	Admission/continued stay review and data collection.

Each of the general provider incentives noted above can be mediated by an effective UR program. The review activity and expected results are shown in Exhibit 3.

EVALUATING A REVIEW PROGRAM

Since there are various organizational models for performing UR and since any local market environment will influence the effectiveness of any UR program, there is no single set of variables by which all UR programs can be evaluated. The most detailed statistical evaluations have been performed by the Federal government on the PSRO review system. However, many questions about the effectiveness of particular review models have been left unanswered due to the uneven implementation of the program, changing federal regulations, reductions in funding, and the lack of measurable evaluation criteria.

However, even where statistical study data are not available, there are some generic considerations that can be used to decide if a UR program has the potential to modify or control utilization. First, if a program is to modify physician behavior, it must be active. There must be some interaction between the reviewers and those whose cases are reviewed. The interaction serves two functions (especially if the interaction is among physicians): first, education of the attending physician as to appropriate levels of care or service and, second, potential reduction of length of stay or avoidance of admission in the particular case.

For example, in a 1981 problem-oriented study of elective cataract extractions in medicare patients, one physician was identified as having an overall length of stay of 4 days for all his cataract patients, regardless of medical condition. A peer-review discussion occurred. This attending physician was the only ophthalmologist on the staff of this delegated hospital and indicated this was his routine pattern of practice. Following the peer discussion, his length of stay was reduced to two days which, at the time, was the community standard of practice. In the absence of the peer-review discussion, this change probably would not have occurred. Currently, this surgery is an outpatient procedure.

An effective program should be based on communitywide, regional, or national professional standards. As indicated by the above example, hospital-based physicians and staff may not be aware of changes or advances in treatment or practice patterns.

PROFESSIONAL CREDIBILITY AND OBJECTIVITY

For example, in an areawide assessment of physical therapy services in all Central Los Angeles hospitals, significant overutilization was identified in one delegated hospital. The utilization level was so high that the review agent implemented 100 percent nondelegated review of this service and referred all cases to an outside registered physical therapist. The 100 percent review continued for three months and was based on standards developed by the Southern California Physical Therapy Association with the following dramatic reduction in units of service per patient per day, from 2.51 to 1.53. This reduction was statistically significant at the 95 percent level of confidence. The total number of procedures was reduced from 80.8 per day to 24.3 procedures per day. Average per-diem physical therapy charges were reduced from $11.08 to $6.35, resulting in an annual savings of approximately $200,000.00.

In the absence of professionally developed norms supported by peer reviewers, this dramatic a change in behavior could not have been achieved. Because the review criteria used had been developed with input from a regional professional body and because the RPT reviewer was a peer of those whose cases were being reviewed, all interactions were on a professional peer level. Where those being reviewed question the validity of criteria used, the professional competence of the reviewers, or the lack of objectivity of the process, resistance is often encountered. This takes the form of appealing every decision, refusal to cooperate with the review process or, in an extreme case, lawsuits against the review agent and payor. In this case, the results of review were accepted by the hospital and department, and behavior was changed to a professionally acceptable level.

The process for developing community-based or regional review criteria requires extensive peer involvement in and support of a local review organization. The professional credibility and objectivity of a review organization maximizes the potential educational effects of review because changes in practice patterns and treatment modalities are exchanged between hospitals and physicians during review interactions. Where professional credibility is lacking, review is seen as a negative process that places the interests of the payor over those of the patient.

The program should have stability of personnel or structure and community support over time. This is important because it facilitates provider acceptance and response to review interventions on a day-to-day basis.

Thus, there are three basic generic considerations that are indicative of an effective UR program—activity level, use of professional norms and criteria supported by peer reviewers, and program stability and community support over time.

The activity level of a UR program can be measured in three ways. At least one of these measures should be available, regardless of the organization of the UR program, i.e., delegated, nondelegated, PSRO/ PRO, or other review system:

1. Number of cases identified by a review coordinator and given to a physician for peer review as a proportion of cases reviewed during a specific time period. At least a year is desirable. These are known as referrals. In some programs and in some delegated hospitals, no notification letters are used, therefore, there may be no noncertifications or advisory letters. Where notification letters are not used, it is important to determine on how many of the cases referred, was the attending physician actually contacted (sometimes by the nonphysician reviewer); by the reviewing physician, resulting in discharge.

2. Where notification letters are used, the actual number of denials (or noncerts), as a proportion of cases reviewed (denial rate), is a useful measure of review activity. Again, at least a year is desirable.

3. Actual reductions in utilization for any groups under review. This can include reductions in length of stay or admission rates. This could be in the form of pre- and postreview implementation experience or in the form of reductions in specific problem areas over the review period.

In the absence of documented utilization changes, often the higher the referral and denial rates, the more potentially effective the UR program. Referral and denial rates may decrease over time as employees, hospitals and physicians are educated about coverage requirements. Further, there is some evidence for delayed effects of a review program. A study of the first two years of the application of the Certified Hospital Admission Program (CHAP) by the Medical Care Foundation of Sacramento to medicare patients, showed a decrease in length of stay in the first year and a decrease in admission rates in the second year. The program consisted of a preadmission review of all elective admissions and concurrent review of all admissions.

Where review has been performed for a number of years, recent referral and denial data may be as low as 0 to 1 percent of cases reviewed, indicating that a maintenance level of utilizations has been achieved. In this situation, historical data of the type described in item 3 should be available.

PEER INVOLVEMENT AND USE OF PROFESSIONALLY DEVELOPED CRITERIA

The level of peer involvement in the direct review process can likewise be measured by items 1 and 2 above. Inquiries about the sources and uses of review criteria should include a group or organization developing the basic review criteria used. These criteria sets in wide use across the country are listed below.

— American Medical Association—model diagnosis and procedure-specific screening criteria.
— SI/IS (Severity of Illness/Intensity of Service) criteria developed by InterQual.
— ISD Criteria (Severity of Illness/Intensity of Service and Discharge Screens)—an expansion of the SI/IS criteria.

In addition to using one or more of these criteria sets, local review organizations may have developed local modifications or special criteria for problems unique to that area. Other criteria sets such as the Appropriateness Evaluation Protocol (AEP) or Systemetrics criteria may also be in use in some areas.

For consistency of the review program, a recognized criteria set should be in use. This reduces the possibility of different reviewers making different screening decisions on the basis of similar information.

Most PSROs adopted local versions of these criteria sets because of the extensive clinical input into their development and the ease of use by trained personnel. Both the clinical input and literature search activity for in-depth criteria development are expensive and time consuming and most organizations could not support this level of effort.

In addition, a method and structure for updating or expanding criteria are necessary because of changes in medical technology and practice patterns. Ideally, those whose practice or whose treatment patterns are to be judged should have some involvement in the criteria development process. For example, the procedure of a carpal tunnel release currently appears on ambulatory surgery lists for numerous organizations, including the federal government. In some areas, the procedure is still routinely done in a 2-day hospital stay. Based on the criteria, the cases are referred by review coordinators but are approved by physician advisors who simply disagree with the criteria set because they or their national society had no input in developing the criteria. It is possible to simply deny payment, but to achieve a change in behavior, the practicing physicians should be involved, even if only in a review, and comment made.

A recent example of updated, new, or expanded criteria should be requested.

AVAILABILITY OF PEER REVIEWERS TO REVIEW STAFF

The number and location of peer reviewers available to the review coordinator is a measure of the activity level of the review process. Where the review coordinator has no regularly scheduled access to a physician advisor, peer intervention is minimized because the review coordinator may be reluctant to refer cases. Peer reviewers should be directly available to review coordinators every working day, either by telephone or at a specific location. Where access is restricted or physicians are not easily reached by telephone, the number of referrals is reduced and peer opportunities for interaction are reduced.

The availability and location of peer reviewers can be assessed by asking whether the review coordinator can contact a peer reviewer directly on any working day either in person or by telephone.

The number of peer reviewers is important because it reflects the overall level of physician resources available for the review process. The review organization should have sufficient physician resources to provide specialty review in any areas covered by the organization.

In some delegated hospitals, members of the medical staff rotate through the UR committee, so training or orientation of the peer reviewers is important to assure consistency of the review process over time. In other hospitals, a single physician may be paid by the hospital to perform all the reviews.

Review organizations may have different physicians in different specialties performing peer review activities on a consulting basis, while other review organizations may use one or two salaried physicians to perform the review.

Between the extreme of rotating all medical staff members (whether they want to do review or not) through a UR Committee and the extreme of having one paid physician reviewer, most PSROs and private for-profit review organizations are using practicing physicians on a consulting basis. These organizations have some training or orientation for new physician reviewers and an evaluation of the quality of the review. This latter evaluation normally depends on how clearly the reviewer is able to record his or her reasons for either approving or denying medical necessity in cases reviewed. These reasons should be understandable to the nonphysician reviewers and should be consistent with acute care criteria.

Any review organization should be able to provide copies of physician reviews (without names or other identifying information) as evidence of peer involvement in the review process.

Where a single physician performs all the review, there are potential problems with specialty coverage and appeals.

DELEGATED AND NONDELEGATED REVIEW

There are advantages and disadvantages to both delegated and nondelegated review systems. In its initial implementation of review for the Medicare Prospective Payment System (PPS), the federal government is requiring that review functions related to DRG payment be nondelegated. The stated reason for non-delegation is " . . . it has been determined that a provider cannot conduct review effectively or efficiently because of the extreme conflict between review responsibilities and financial incentives." Under the Medicare Prospective Payment System, if an admission is denied, the entire DRG payment is denied. The hospital, in order to maximize revenues, may increase admissions by reducing any barriers to admissions such as preadmission or admission review. Thus, under prospective payment, the review goal (to reduce or maintain admission rates) is in conflict with the hospital financial goal (to maximize revenues).

In a per-diem reimbursement system where the hospital is paid per day, the review goal to reduce length of stay may be in conflict with the hospital financial goal of maximizing revenues.

In an environment of low hospital occupancy and excess beds the economic incentive is to fill beds and may be in direct conflict with the internal review program of a delegated hospital. Such conflicts can cause the hospital to lose medical staff members who may go to hospitals with less strict review systems. An active nondelegated system can have a similar result where there are less active nondelegated review systems operating in close geographic proximity.

A nondelegated system over a large enough geographical area can minimize this problem because the hospital and physician community would be aware that everyone was subject to the same rules. This objective application of a reasonably uniform review process facilitates community acceptance and may significantly reduce resistance to the review process. Where, because of different systems (delegated or not) in one hospital, a practice or service is approved and in another the same practice or service is denied, provider resistance to any review is strong. An active nondelegated system over a wide geographic area has the potential for educating physicians to appropriate use of inpatient hospital services and changes in treatment patterns. In a delegated system, reviewers may only be aware of their *own* patterns and may not have a comparative basis of experience.

Delegated concurrent review coupled with a nondelegated preadmission and retrospective bill review, is a common combination of services offered by many review organizations. In this situation, the frequency and type of monitoring of the delegated review and findings should be assessed. Weekend admissions are often classified by the patient and physician as emergency admissions. These will often be subject to preadmission review, but would be subject to concurrent review as would all other emergency admissions. To be certain the emergency admissions are reviewed appropriately and are not a means of bypassing preadmission requirements, some monitoring of delegated review is needed.

This can be part of a review organization contract or could be done by an insurance company or employer directly.

The monitoring is normally in the form of sampling of individual review decisions. Where problems are identified, there should be some mechanism, such as withdrawing delegation, for modifying the review to resolve the problems. Delegated review may sometimes be used to obtain provider cooperation as part of the PPO contracting process. A review program may be a major or very minor part of a PPO package, depending on the particular structure, benefit package, payment methods, and any built-in financial incentives for appropriate utilization.

When review is a part of a PPO package, even the most effective system may not, by itself, reduce total costs. This is because review can only affect utilization in an advisory capacity and does not generally involve decisions about charges.

Fee review and use of uniform fee schedules coupled with medical necessity decisions could involve the review organization in antitrust problems.[2] Many review organizations thus make advisory medical necessity decisions and final payment decisions rest with the carrier or employer.

REVIEW AND COST SAVINGS

Where charges are not controlled as in many charge or cost-reimbursement systems such as most standard insurance plans, reductions in utilization may result in higher charges and no net savings might be realized from a review program. Review may result in more dollars spent for outpatient, home, day treatment, or extended care facilities. An effective review program should be able to differentiate between services that are not necessary *at all* and those that are necessary but can be delivered in a less expensive setting. Therefore, reductions in payments for inpatient services may be offset, at least in part, by increases in payments for outpatient services.

Since charges generally increase at a slower rate than changes in utilization, over the short run (one to three years), a review program can show some dramatic net savings. This is because at the time hospital use drops, the cost of the substitute services is generally lower at that same time. According to the *Utilization Review Letter,* Blue Cross hospital use in Iowa dropped from 878 days per thousand subscribers to 738 days per thousand in 1983.[3] The reported $24 million reduction in rates is attributed to the Iowa Foundation For Medical Care's utilization review for

Blue Cross. The report also noted gradual hospital price increases as utilization decreased. Prices tend to increase because hospitals' fixed costs are spread over fewer patient days. As patients may be forced to pick up a higher deductible, higher co-payments, or the whole bill where review or plan rules for second opinions or preadmission review are not followed, the patient may not be able to pay. Increases in bad debts will be translated into overall price increases.

Working with two PSROs, the Iowa Foundation for Medical Care and the Mid-State Foundation for Medical Care in Western Illinois, Deere and Company estimated savings in 1982 of $11 for each review dollar spent. In Western Illinois, since 1977, days per 1,000 insured dropped by 29 percent and admissions by 19 percent. In Iowa, days per thousand declined by 33 percent and admissions by 30 percent.[4]

DATA ANALYSIS AND LONG-RUN BENEFITS OF REVIEW

Where detailed data on utilization patterns are not readily available, data collected as a product of the review program can be a valuable tool to assess benefit packages. Where claims detail is available, review data can provide a comparative basis for evaluating changes in utilization resulting from a review program. The larger the group, the faster a data base is accumulated and the sooner evaluation and future planning can occur.

With one to two years of review and data collection, which includes specific diagnoses for a large group, procedures or DRGs that were frequently questioned or denied can be identified. Analysis of overall use can indicate the need for a targeted second opinion program, the need for modification of benefit and coverage structures, and the lack of specific types of services available in some areas.

For example, if tonsillectomy and adenoidectomy or laminectomies are frequently performed procedures within a group, these would be areas for a targeted mandatory second opinion program. Second opinions have always been a standard medical practice, and employees can be encouraged to obtain such opinions if they are covered under the benefit structure. Where employees have a family physician (internist, general, or family practitioner), this physician often refers to a surgeon and is often consulted again by the patient prior to elective surgeries. The family physician is often the source of second opinion referrals.

An evaluation of services most frequently questioned can reveal two potential types of problems. First, despite changes in benefit packages over the years, some patients and physicians still believe that some services are covered only in the hospital setting. If a benefit package does cover outpatient or extended care services, then the problem is one of employee education. For example, a new employee may already have a relationship with a primary care physician. The employee selects a PPO option and receives the literature without any verbal orientation or explanation of the benefit. When the employee becomes ill, he goes to his regular physician who admits this 29 year-old man to a hospital for a cystoscopy. He is hospitalized one day and discharged. However, few if any benefits will be paid in this case because all the PPO option requirements were violated. Neither the physician nor the hospital used were PPO contract providers. The particular plan required preadmission review and preadmission approval for use of a nonparticipating provider, neither of which was sought according to the brochure instructions. The cystoscopy is listed as a procedure normally done on an outpatient basis and only covered in the hospital where the patient's overall medical condition is such that the procedure cannot safely be performed outside the hospital. In this case, admission was not medically necessary, because the patient was in good health except for the specific urinary problem.

Where problems like this arise and there are denials of hospital use, the employer must reevaluate how employees are oriented to use the benefits. Mailing or distributing literature may not be sufficient. These types of denials and lack of understanding of program benefits can result in angry employees (who must pay the bills) and angry physicians and hospitals who will not be paid, but who must try to collect from the employee. In this situation, the employee would likely be turned over to a collection agency, and, if the money was not recovered, the provider would write it off as a bad debt. The larger these bad debts and uncollectible costs, the greater the pressure to increase prices to cover them.

This same situation could indicate the need for modifying benefits. For example, if cystoscopies, vasectomies, and excisions of skin lesions are frequently performed unnecessarily in the hospital, an analysis of the benefit package may reveal insufficient coverage for outpatient services. Some insurance plans still provide *NO* outpatient benefits, but 80 to 100 percent for services provided in hospitals. Further, the reimbursement may be lower for the same procedure outside the hospital, or it may not be covered at all. Another type of situation may occur where day treatment or other outpatient follow-up is not a benefit for certain special programs such as alcohol rehabilitation. Coverage may, in fact, reinforce the problems they are supposed to solve. For example, coverage of multiple hospitalizations for alcohol rehab can result in frequent readmissions for "drying out." In cases where some portion of patients leave against medical advice after a detoxification period, it may be necessary to consider limiting inpatient coverage to some maximum number of hospitalizations while expanding outpatient and day treatment coverage.

In some areas, alternative services may not exist or may be insufficient in either number of facilities or quality of services. Some areas are short of skilled nursing facility beds. In other areas, there are limited outpatient surgical facilities and few home health services. As the needs are identified in the private sector, community efforts to fill resource gaps can be initiated. Joint efforts based on this type of data between the business and medical communities, may have significant results in improving both the quality and continuity of health care services in local communities.

CHANGES IN MEDICARE REIMBURSEMENT AND IMPLICATIONS FOR OVERALL COSTS

As the medicare program implements reimbursement based on diagnosis-related groups (DRGs), hospitals may, over the short run, begin shifting more costs to the private sector. Since medicare rates are public, private sector groups who have access to their own utilization data based on diagnosis related groups can compare how much they are paying by DRG with how much medicare is paying by DRG. Generally, medicare patients stay longer in hospitals and often have multiple medical problems requiring more resources than other patients. This type of analysis can help identify the level of cost shifting. If a group wishes to consider payment based on DRGs, then another review function should be added. In a DRG payment scheme, the in-hospital review and certification could be expanded to include a process called DRG validation. In this process, the diagnoses, procedures, and other information on which the DRG is calculated are verified. Since DRG payment is made per case, regardless of length of stay within certain thresholds, the importance of regular continued stay review is diminished, and a DRG validation review at the time of discharge can be substituted.

There is concern in the physician and hospital community that new payment systems may stifle medical practice. Specifically, physicians are concerned that services that are not profitable will be eliminated with resulting compromises in the quality of care. There is also the possibility that payment system changes will force a greater scrutiny of the actual improvements to care created by new technologies. Is the $735 lens for an implant after cataract surgery really that much better than the $320 lens? Would spending more time with the patient and performing a detailed physical examination result in the need for fewer laboratory tests? Do technological advances result in such an increased diagnostic capability that other technologies can be discarded?

As more services are provided in ambulatory care centers, extended care facilities, or free-standing surgicenters, the focus of review will shift to these services. Some companies are emphasizing "wellness" programs including exercise, smoking, and dietary programs. The trends toward both out of hospital services and preventive care should, over the long run, help contain health care costs.

Despite the increasing sophistication of medical review technologies, the provision of health services and utilization review programs are among the most personal of services. On any individual case in the review process, the needs of the patient and the goal of cost containment must be balanced.

NOTES

1. Senate Finance Committee Report 92-1230 in *Legislative History of Professional Standards Review Organization; Provisions of the Social Security Act Amendments,* U.S. Department of Health, Education, and Welfare, Health Care Financing Administration, Health Standards and Quality Bureau (September 1972), p. 2.

2. Douglas A. Hastings, Becker Borsody Epstein, P. C. Green, "Legal Issues Raised by Private Review Activities of Medical Peer Review Organizations," *Journal of Health, Politics, Policy and Law* 8, no. 2 (Summer 1983), pp. 308–309.

3. *Medical Utilization Review,* McGraw-Hill, Inc., 12, no. 4 (February 15, 1984).

4. Regis D. Rulifson, "Deere and Company Battle Costs through Peer Review," *The Internist* 25, no. 1 (January 1984), p. 21.

BIBLIOGRAPHY

American College of Surgeons ACS, *Socio-Economic Factbook for Surgery,* 1983–1984.

Health Systems Plan for Los Angeles County, 1982, Compendium, Los Angeles Health Planning and Development Agency, May 1982.

Paul D. Sanazaro, M.D., Ed., *Private Initiative in PSRO, Final Report,* Published for the W. K. Kellogg Foundation by the Health Administration Press, Ann Arbor, Michigan, 1978.

"An Evaluation of a Medicare Concurrent Utilization Review Project. The Sacramento Certified Hospital Admission Program," *Health Insurance Statistics,* Dept. of Health Education and Welfare, Social Security Administration, Office of Program Policy and Planning, Office of Research and Statistics. HI-80 March 17, 1978.

Nancy E. Adler, Ph.D. and Arnold Milstein, M.D., MPH; "Evaluating the Impact of Physician Peer Review: Factors Associated with Successful PSROs," *American Journal of Public Health* 73, no. 10 (October 1983).

Robert V. Patteson, Ph.D., and Hallie M. Katz, MBA, MSPH, "Investor-Owned and Not-for-Profit Hospitals—A Comparison Based on California Data," *New England Journal of Medicine* 399 (August 1983), pp. 347–353.

Report to Congress Required by the Tax Equity and Fiscal Responsibility Act of 1982, December 1982.

PSRO Transmittal 107, Health Standards and Quality Bureau, Health Care Financing Administration, March 1984.

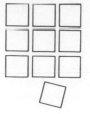

Marketplace Fundamentals

OPPORTUNITIES TO CONTROL UTILIZATION THROUGH PREFERRED PROVIDER ARRANGEMENTS

Arnold Milstein, M.D., M.P.H.
Director
National Medical Audit, Inc.
San Francisco, CA

☐ Preferred provider arrangements offer substantial opportunities to curb medically unnecessary health service utilization. This chapter will lay out these opportunities for large employers and other purchasers such as employer coalitions, trusts, or carriers that are able to (1) redesign benefits to create a preferred provider option within an employer medical plan and (2) actively shape or shop for characteristics of a preferred provider utilization control system. For small employers or other purchasers not meeting these two criteria, this discussion may be of use in evaluating the adequacy of efforts made by a PPO to control service utilization.

UTILIZATION CONTROL TARGET

What is an appropriate target for utilization control efforts in a PPO setting? Though this may vary among PPO purchasers, a common objective is to reduce hospital utilization levels within the PPO's fee-for-service provider system to the level achieved by group practice HMOs. Expressed in days of hospital care per 1,000 health plan enrollees, this objective translates into a 30–40 percent reduction in the rate of hospital utilization.[1]

Any other health care service may also be a target for utilization control efforts under a preferred provider arrangement. Examples include hospital ancillary services; physician services in hospital, home, or office settings; home health services, outpatient lab, pharmacy, and imaging services; nursing home care; and ambulance services.

Objectives may range from reducing current utilization levels (as was the case for hospital bed utilization discussed above) to simply maintaining favorable preexisting levels. When PPO unit prices are substantially below market rates, maintaining preexisting utilization levels may be as important an objective as using preferred provider arrangements to reduce utilization levels. This is because available research suggests (1) that physicians respond to lower unit prices by increasing the frequency and length of office visits, as well as the amount of ancillary services they order;[2] and (2) that hospitals respond to price controls by increasing utilization levels.[3]

GENERIC IMPLEMENTATION VEHICLES

While determinants of, and interventions against, unnecessary utilization are numerous, preferred provider arrangements lend themselves to the use of three basic vehicles to control utilization. These are:

- a. utilization review,
- b. provider agreements, and
- c. benefit design.

UTILIZATION REVIEW

Utilization review (UR) is the evaluation of proposed or prior care to determine if care is or was medically necessary. UR may also include an assessment of whether or not the quality of care was adequate. Quality of care is not only an important purchaser concern in its own right, but since poor quality has been shown to increase utilization,[4] review directed at quality is likely to curb avoidable utilization. UR can be used to control preferred provider service utilization in a number of ways: premembership screening, individual claim reimbursement, and monitoring preferred provider practice patterns.

Premembership Screening

One method of using UR to control utilization is via analysis of physician or hospital utilization practices prior to granting preferred provider status. This can be accomplished via review of a random sample of medical records from all providers being considered for PPO membership. Or, if reliable utilization statistics are available, review can be focused on providers whose multicase utilization practices exceed normative data for length of hospitalization, ancillary service use, referrals for specialty consultation, and other parameters of efficiency. Unfortunately, reliable utilization statistics, controlled for case mix, are sometimes not available for hospitals and almost never available for individual physicians.

Premembership screening via UR is seldom employed by PPO sponsors because of their worry that not enough physicians will join if forced to submit to a UR "audit" prior to membership. A second impediment is its expense, especially for new, minimally capitalized PPOs. A third reason why results of UR are not used as a criterion for membership is the belief that provider utilization practices are highly changeable, and that PPOs, which reward conservative utilization practices, can transform providers who previously were extravagant utilizers. Alternatively stated, "bad" candidates for preferred provider status cannot be reliably identified by examining their utilization practices prior to PPO membership. This hypothesis remains untested.

As a result of these perceived barriers, premembership screening via UR is seldom used. However, it should be noted that PPO sponsors who are able to use UR in this manner may be able to operate more economically than others since they will (1) face a reduced need for and cost of ongoing UR, (2) not have to incur unnecessary utilization in the process of learning which of their provider members overutilize services, and (3) not have to incur the administrative and legal expenses associated with taking away previously granted membership status.

Individual Claim Reimbursement

A second use of UR in the preferred provider setting is to affect individual claim reimbursement. This may be accomplished via *prevention* of unnecessary services before or during service delivery (e.g., preadmission or concurrent hospital utilization review) or it may be accomplished via *nonreimbursement* for previously provided services that UR determined to be medically unnecessary (i.e., retrospective review). Successful implementation of either approach requires supportive clauses in preferred provider agreements and/or the employer's medical plan. These will be discussed in later sections of this article.

Monitoring Provider Practice Patterns

A third use of UR in the preferred provider setting is to monitor provider performance over multiple cases. This may be preferable to the prior two uses of UR in locations where a PPO sponsor faces substantial provider resistance to preferred provider arrangements, and multiple instances of overutilization are the only politically feasible basis for expulsion or other forms of provider penalty.

Under such circumstances, the organizer would establish (1) rate-based UR performance thresholds (e.g., a maximum tolerable percent of ordered or provided services that UR determined to be unnecessary) and (2) a system of penalties to be imposed if a provider exceeded these thresholds. Penalties might include nonreimbursement, in whole or in part, for future unnecessary services that are ordered or provided or expulsion from PPO membership if unacceptable performance is repeated.

Special Considerations

There arc multiple other dimensions of UR pertinent to its use in the preferred provider setting.[5] However, four deserve special consideration.

The first is *the relationship between UR and claims data*. UR and claims data each represent an independent method for identifying inefficient providers. The critical differences between them are that (1) UR yields much more conclusive evidence regarding lack of medical necessity, and (2) claims data analysis is much less expensive. There are vocal proponents of each as an exclusive method of identifying overutilizing providers. However, in the absence of evaluations of their comparative efficiency, it is probably sensible to use both and gradually rely more heavily on claims data, if, over the long run, it provides sufficiently reliable and sensitive "footprints" of overutilization identified via UR.

The second is the *scope of UR*. The principal considerations in deciding which services should be subjected to UR are the cost of comprehensive UR and the sorry state of primary care physician office records from which UR judgments regarding office visits must be drawn. One sensible approach is (*a*) to subject relatively expensive services (e.g., hospital care, substantial physician outpatient procedures, long-term allergy/dermatology/psychiatric care services) to 100 percent utilization review, (*b*) to specify minimum PPO medical record documentation requirements for services provided in physician offices, and (*c*) to subject all other services to utilization review via samples rather than 100 percent of claims. Samples may be random, random subject to the requirement that a minimum sample of claims from each provider be reviewed, or guided by aberrant patterns gleaned from claims screens or aggregate claims data.

A third consideration is *governance of the UR system*. The central issue here is whether or not UR staff governed by the PPO's sponsor or providers can be trusted to ignore potentially conflicting loyalties to peers or the PPO itself and judge cases strictly on clinical merit.

While evidence from comparable settings, such as PSRO review, would seem to favor maximum independence of UR system governance, the issue has not been conclusively resolved. Often PPO sponsors face overwhelming political barriers to using fully independent UR systems, even though their intuition tells them that independent review looks "cleaner." Use of third-party UR audit, discussed in the following paragraph, is a means of resolving this dilemma. By giving PPO sponsors a neutral measure of UR system efficacy, it allows assessment of whether or not insisting on an independently governed UR system is worth associated political risks.

A final consideration is *UR system performance*. UR systems can vary dramatically in their ability to correctly identify unnecessary services (see Exhibit 1). However, since UR is a complex and medically technical service, an employer or PPO sponsor is usually unable to judge UR system performance. Claims data performance measures, such as PPO hospital utilization levels relative to other fee-for-service providers, are sometimes used. However, these measures may be confounded by extraneous variables such as adverse selection. One solution is to subject UR systems to independent audit before and/or after use. This could be arranged by a preferred provider organization as a means of establishing its credibility to employers, or it could be arranged by an employer prior to deciding to offer a PPO to its employees. Exhibit 1 summarizes the results of such an audit performed for a regional cost-containment coalition prior to PPO implementation. The audit permitted selection of the most effective of three UR systems under consideration.

EXHIBIT 1 *
Percent of Estimated Total Unnecessary Hospital Days in Audit Sample Correctly Identified by Three UR Vendors

UR Vendor A	68 percent
UR Vendor B	43 percent
UR Vendor C	34 percent

*Provided by National Medical Audit, Inc., San Francisco. 1984 Benefits Manager's Audit Series. (Vendor and client identity confidential.)

PROVIDER AGREEMENTS

Agreements with preferred providers offer five mechanisms to control utilization: reimbursement basis, cooperation with UR system requirements, predetermined utilization control policies, advance provider endorsement of penalty provisions, and development of alternative services.

Basis of Provider Reimbursement

Agreements with preferred providers represent an opportunity to create powerful provider incentives for appropriate utilization by modifying the basis for reimbursement. A simple example of this, used by the California Medicaid Program in its preferred provider contracts with hospitals, was to peg reimbursement to all-inclusive, per-diem prices. This created pressure on contracting hospitals to curb unnecessary utilization of ancillary services, since their provision would incur expense without associated incremental revenue.

The general principal underlying the use of reimbursement to control utilization is that of shifting the risk of overutilization to the provider in order to let provider self-interest drive utilization control. The generic means to this end is to lump reimbursement for services currently paid on an individual unit price basis into more inclusive prices. The maximum extension of this approach is represented by HMOs, which are paid a single price per enrollee for all services and are thereby highly motivated to control utilization. Multiple reimbursement bases, incorporating various degrees of inclusive prices and provider risk, are possible within preferred provider agreements. Exhibit 2 summarizes some of these possibilities.

EXHIBIT 2

Scope of Single Unit Price	Example of Purchaser	Entity Receiving Payment
Total hospital charges and physician's fees for selected inpatient surgeries	Fortune 500 electronics firm	Attending surgeon
Per-diem room and board, and ancillary charges for all hospitalizations	California medicaid agency	Hospital
Per admission hospital room and board, and ancillary charges within specified diagnostic groups	Medicare Prospective Payment System	Hospital

Pros and Cons of Reimbursement-Based Strategies. The principal advantages of using provider reimbursement strategies rather than UR to control utilization are three. First, relying on provider incentives may prevent (rather than permit but not pay for) unnecessary services and their attendant iatrogenic threats to patient health and safety. Second, it substantially reduces the need for and expense of UR (see below). Third, it shifts responsibility for curbing utilization from the employer (or their agent, the UR system) to the provider. This shift may reduce the employer's vulnerability to lawsuits based on an overly stringent UR system that may be alleged by a plaintiff's attorney to be the employer's agent.

Two disadvantages are associated with using reimbursement to control utilization. The first is that newly created incentives for efficiency can generate pressures for cutting corners, poor quality, underutilization, and compensatory overutilization in categories of services not subject to reimbursement incentives. An example of the latter phenomenon would be increased unnecessary admissions by physicians seeking to protect hospital revenues under a reimbursement system based on a predetermined all-inclusive price per admission.[6] These inadvertently created perverse provider incentives increase dependence on residual UR activities (e.g., those directed at quality of care or necessity of hospital admission). If these residual UR functions are less effectively implemented than the UR functions replaced by reimbursement incentives, unnecessary service utilization could be accentuated rather than reduced.

A second disadvantage of a reimbursement based utilization control strategy is that its successful implementation relies on the availability of claims data that is accurate and sufficiently detailed to account for differences in case mix. Without such data, it is difficult to judge whether a particular provider reimbursement rate reflects efficient utilization practices rather than variations in case mix or limitations of the data from which the rate was derived. Many employers do not have such data and those that do may have it for hospitals, but not physicians.

Recommended Strategy. The best mix of UR and reimbursement-based utilization control methods will vary with the particular circumstances faced by a PPO sponsor. However, the following general decision-making factors should be considered: Reimbursement based incentives are generally preferable because they cost less and prevent iatrogenic illness. However, they should only be used to the extent a PPO purchaser and/or sponsor has (a) a reliable claims data base and (b) UR systems with a strong track record in the identification and control of underutilization and problems in quality of care.

Cooperation with UR System Requirements

Many UR systems are substantially impaired by irregularity in provider cooperation with procedures that are necessary for UR systems to function effectively. Required provider activities include: (1) full, timely, and legible documentation (in medical records and/or treatment authorization requests) of clinical investigations, interventions, diagnoses, and treatment plans; (2) making such records and requests easily available to UR staff in a timely manner at a reasonable charge, if any; (3) responding promptly and constructively to telephone inquiries from UR staff; (4) adhering to predetermined avenues for appealing UR decisions; (5) adhering to UR decisions unless they endanger patient health and safety; (6) refraining from encouraging patient lawsuits over UR decisions with which the provider disagrees; and (7) timely collection and provision of patient encounter data required by the PPO to monitor utilization via its automated data system.

Obligating preferred providers to these required procedures via provider agreements will enhance review system effectiveness and provide a more defensible legal basis for expelling noncooperating providers.

Cooperation with Predetermined Utilization Policies

Locking preferred providers into predetermined utilization policies via the provider agreement itself represents a highly cost effective means of controlling utilization. Such an arrangement eliminates the need for, and cost of, UR. However, the applicability of this approach is limited to clinical circumstances in which (*a*) prevailing clinical wisdom justifies less extravagant utilization practices than commonly prevail; and (*b*) variation among patients is low enough that general treatment policies will be valid.

Examples of such policies are (1) lists of surgeries to be done on an outpatient or same-day admit basis; (2) predetermined lengths of stay for uncomplicated maternity cases; (3) prohibition of elective medical admissions on Fridays and Saturdays; (4) prohibition of automatic repeat inpatient ancillary service orders beyond three days; and (5) limiting the types of surgeries for which assistant surgeons and/or assistant anesthesiologists can be billed.

Because the applicability of this utilization-control technique is limited, it is inadequate as a sole method of controlling utilization.

Advance Provider Endorsement of Utilization Related Penalties

Preferred provider agreements can also serve the cause of utilization control by prospectively establishing a provider's written concurrence with penalties used to enforce compliance with UR system requirements and decisions. This is likely to reduce the frequency of provider complaints and lawsuits based on allegations of unfair review processes and penalties, since these were part of the explicit conditions of membership to which the provider had previously agreed. Stemming and winning lawsuits by providers supports the credibility and courage of UR staff. Credibility and courage, in turn, enhance UR staff performance in their sometimes adversarial interactions with providers.[7]

Development of Alternative Services

A final means by which preferred provider agreements can enhance utilization control is by serving as a vehicle for the creation of services that substitute for more expensive existing services. Examples of such services in preferred hospital agreements might include (*a*) opening an outpatient alcohol detoxification and rehabilitation service to substitute for an inpatient service, (*b*) opening an urgicenter to substitute for emergency room services, and (*c*) opening an off site half-way house to substitute for inpatient psychiatric services.

Physician agreements could include provisions requiring use of these new services, unless use of the more expensive preexisting service was certified as necessary for a particular patient by the PPO's UR system.

BENEFIT DESIGN

Benefit design lends itself to a variety of methods to control utilization within preferred provider arrangements. Some methods may be viewed as intrinsic to the concept of preferred provider contracts. An example of this would be lowering of enrollee copayment in order to encourage the use of preferred providers which, in turn, are presumed to practice more efficiently or be subject to more effective utilization controls.

Other methods are not specific to preferred provider arrangements. Rather, they are opportunistic in the sense that creating a preferred provider option within a medical plan is used as an opportunity to incorporate effective utilization control methods that may be viewed as too administratively burdensome to employees or otherwise controversial to incorporate in an employer's regular indemnity plan. An example of the latter is preadmission review of hospital admissions. The following uses of benefit design to control utilization in a PPO setting encompasses both intrinsic and opportunistic uses of preferred provider agreements.

Four Uses of Benefit Design to Control Utilization

Benefit design may be used to (1) encourage the use of preferred providers instead of other providers, (2) encourage the use of lower levels of care within a preferred provider network, (3) discourage frivolous enrollee use of preferred providers, and (4) enhance physician cooperation with UR systems. Examples of these are summarized in Exhibit 3.

EXHIBIT 3

Utilization Objective	Example	Enabling Benefit Design Feature
Encourage use of preferred providers instead of other providers	All health services	Reduce copay or deductible for PPO service use; and/or Increase copay or deductible for use of nonpreferred providers; and/or Share savings associated with PPOs with employees exclusively using PPO services.
Encourage use of lower levels of care within the preferred provider network	Outpatient surgery Same day surgery admits	Further reduce copay or deductible for adhering to a list of surgeries recommended for delivery on an outpatient or same day admit basis.
	Outpatient alcohol detoxification	Add new benefit of alcohol counselor home visit.
Discourage frivolous use of preferred providers	All health services	Retain sufficient copay or deductible to prevent enrollee perception of "free" service. Hold enrollees financially responsible (in whole or in part) for entering or remaining in hospital after being notified of UR denial.

EXHIBIT 3 *(concluded)*

Utilization Objective	Example	Enabling Benefit Design Feature
Enhance MD cooperation with UR systems	All health services	Penalize employees by raising copay or deductible if attending MD refuses to comply with UR requirements such as obtaining preadmission review of elective hospital admissions.

CONCLUSION

There are three general paths to utilization control in the context of preferred provider arrangements: utilization review systems, preferred provider contracts, and benefit design. Each path has, in turn, a variety of implementation options with associated advantages and disadvantages. The combination of options best suited to a particular preferred provider purchaser or sponsor depend on a variety of factors. Among the most important are provider negotiating strength, efficacy of available UR systems, and the availability of accurate historical and ongoing comprehensive claims data systems.

The task of selection and implementation of utilization control methods for a preferred provider organization is complex and demanding. Faulty execution risks unnecessary services and, in its extreme form, complete reversal of the value of provider unit price concessions. Accordingly, utilization control, including surveillance of quality of care, may well evolve as the single most important determinant of PPO survival in the increasingly competitive American health care market.

NOTES

1. H. S. Luft, "Assessing the Evidence on HMO Performance," *Milbank Memorial Fund Quarterly/Health and Society* 58 (1980), pp. 501–536. W. G. Manning, "A Controlled Trial of the Effect of a Prepaid Group Practice on Use of Services," *New England Journal of Medicine* 310, no. 23 (1984), pp. 1505–1510.

2. T. Rice, "The Impact of Changing Medicare Reimbursement Rates on Physician Induced Demand," *Medical Care* 21 (1983), pp. 803–815.

3. "Rate Setting May Increase Length of Hospital Stay," *Washington Health Costs Newsletter,* (January 1983), p. 7.

4. K. Steel, P. Gertman, C. Crescenzi, and J. Anderson, "Iatrogenic Illness on a General Medical Service at a University Hospital." *New England Journal of Medicine* 304 (1981), pp. 638–642.

5. A. Milstein and J. Bush, *An Employer's Guide to Utilization Review,* California Chamber of Commerce, 1984. A. Milstein and J. Trauner, *An Employer's Guide to Preferred Provider Organizations.* California Chamber of Commerce, 1984.

6. J. E. Wennberg, "Will Payment Based on DRGs Control Hospital Costs?" *New England Journal of Medicine* 311, no. 5 (1984), pp. 295–300.

7. N. Adler and A. Milstein, "Evaluating the Impact of Physician Peer Review: Factors Associated with Successful PSROs," *American Journal of Public Health* 73 (1983), pp. 1182–1185.

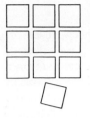

Marketplace Fundamentals

DATA AND DATA-RELATED ACTIVITIES

Robert W. Coburn, M.B.A.
President
The Commons Management Group
Columbia, MD

Joyce L. Batchelor, M.C.R.P.
Programmer/Analyst
The Commons Management Group
Columbia, MD

☐ The emphasis on PPO formation and more formal efforts to control health care costs focus attention on the significant problems associated with beginning, operating, managing, and monitoring PPO operations.

Providers entering into a preferred provider arrangement must understand their costs, the financial impact any discounts will have on income, and any increase in volume required to offset the decrease in prices. Purchasers must know their historical utilization and cost experience, which providers are currently being used by their employees, and what type of health care services they have historically purchased, in order to determine accurately whether the discounts offered in the PPO contract have the potential to decrease (or minimize the increase in) expenditures. Without these data, both purchasers and providers enter into potentially ineffectual arrangements that may neither help purchasers contain costs nor help providers stabilize their market share or their income.

Data analysis is important at the outset when the services to be offered are determined, providers to participate in the PPO are selected, and the prices or rates for services are determined. It is important on a continuing basis when the success of the PPO in controlling both levels of cost and levels of utilization must be monitored. Other factors that should also be monitored on an on-going basis include profiles of individual providers and individual services, changes in the quality of care delivered, and changes in access to appropriate health care services by beneficiaries of the PPO's programs.

From the PPO perspective, the objective of data activities will be to make the provision and the purchase of health care services analogous to other business purchasing decisions. Such other decisions usually involve precise understanding of the commodity or service being purchased, the amount being purchased, the price the commodity or service will cost, the specific vendor from whom it will be obtained, and comparable terms available from other vendors.

Traditionally, health care purchases made under a corporate benefit plan, for example, have been handled in a vastly different manner than nonhealth care purchases: the health care service may not be well defined even during the time it is being delivered, the quantity to be delivered is determined virtually solely by the vendor, the price is also determined by the vendor, and the vendor in each instance may be selected by each individual covered under the plan.

Despite the importance of the data, however, data collection and analysis will be problematic in most PPO environments, whether due to political concerns, financial concerns, access to data, or a variety of other problems. Successful implementation and operation of the PPO will require that these problems be overcome, that baseline data be obtained, and that a successful management reporting system be installed.

The remainder of this chapter will focus on specific aspects of data activities and on the manner in which some of these problems have been addressed in the past. The chapter discusses data requirements, sources of data, data collection, processing and analysis, special issues related to data quality and data management, and cost aspects of data projects.

DATA REQUIREMENTS

While the potential applications of data are numerous, the specific requirements will be a function of the applications in each instance. If utilization patterns are to be studied, then data are required about the specific types of services delivered, the providers by whom the services were delivered, and the average frequency or duration of the services delivered by each provider. If cost patterns are to be analyzed, data are required about the specific services delivered, the providers by whom the services were delivered, the average cost and range of costs for each service provided, and the components of cost that comprise the total amount charged.

The minimum data requirements suggested might be summarized as including the Uniform Hospital Discharge Data Set (UHDDS) adopted by the U.S. National Committee on Vital and Health Statistics as a suggested minimum set of data to be collected for each patient discharged from an acute-care hospital, the corresponding type of utilization data for ambulatory patients, and at least summary billing data, aggregated at the departmental or procedure level.

The UHDDS contains primarily sociodemographic and patient identification information and consists of:

— Patient identification (name or number).
— Date of birth.
— Sex.
— Social characteristics (e.g., race, marital status).
— Residence information (e.g., zip code).
— Hospital identification.
— Physician identification.
— Source of referral.
— Admission date.
— Discharge date.
— Date of principal surgical procedure.
— Service to which the patient was admitted.
— Diagnoses treated and procedures performed.
— Patient disposition (or discharge status).
— Payment source.
— Total charges.

The analagous data set for ambulatory care excludes admission and discharge data but includes most of the other data. Such measures of service as DRGs or relative value units (relative measures used to quantify professional services) are later assigned to each type of data.

The "total charges" data element suggested above is not sufficient from a financial perspective, and inpatient financial data retained should include, at a minimum, charges summarized within major routine service and ancillary service categories, as follows:

— Room and board (preferably broken into semiprivate, private, and special care unit accommodations).
— Laboratory (pathology).
— X ray (radiology).
— Drugs (pharmacy).
— Operating room.
— Supplies.
— Other charges.

Finally, it is extremely important that these data be *saved* over time. In numerous instances it will be found that the provider has actually reported some or all of these data (most of the data elements suggested above are now considered "standard" data elements for reporting and payment purposes by most providers and payors), but that the payor has actually processed and adjudicated the claim without saving the data, at least in any automated mode. This is due to both the volume of data processed and the cost of saving the data. Many providers will also discover that the data have not been saved internally.

The importance of *baseline data* also cannot be overemphasized. It is all too possible to undertake a cost-containment effort because overall cost increases have become unmanageable, proceed through the first year of the program, and then be completely unable to determine whether the cost-containment effort has had any positive impact at all. Since the overall cost of health care services can be influenced by a myriad of factors, it is possible that the cost of services purchased declined by a significant amount, but that the cost-containment program was a total failure. The ability to measure the results of specific program activities against a quantifiable baseline is requisite.

DATA SOURCES

In many PPOs, especially those started by organizations that do not generate or routinely handle health care data, availability of and access to data will be a significant problem. Since many PPOs are still in the development phase, this section will focus especially on background and start-up types of analyses. For most PPOs, three of the main sources of data will be:

— Government agencies.
— Hospitals' records.
— Bills or claims forms.

The following sections discuss briefly each data source, the type of data available, and problems associated with accessing the data.

GOVERNMENT AGENCIES

Both state and federal government agencies collect aggregate statistics on health care. Most states require hospitals to submit long range plans that provide aggregate statistics on the number of beds, physicians, patients and patient days, average length of stay, and types of services provided (i.e., OB/GYN, pediatrics, etc.). In addition, states and local agencies collect sociodemographic data, usually by county, which are useful in market analyses. These data, however, are almost always aggregated and do not provide detailed analyses of services offered or rendered.

The most useful government data are often those that can be used as standards for comparison. With the new prospective payment reimbursement system, the federal government has calculated average prices and average lengths of stay for medicare patients within each of 467 diagnosis related groups (DRGs). Several states have also followed suit and have made this information available not only for medicare patients but for all patients (New Jersey and Maryland are two examples). These data can be compared to a purchaser's inpatient experience and can be used in establishing standards on which to base subsequent cost/benefit analyses.

Data *generated* by the government (generally aggregate statistics at the regional or national level) are usually available to the public; some data *collected* by the government are also available. However, except for DRG-specific data, such aggregate data are not extremely useful in determining the viability of a PPO arrangement for either the individual company or the provider. Instead, individual patient data are required, which can be aggregated to form hospital, physician, and company profiles of services provided and received. These detailed data can be obtained from the other two sources, hospitals and bills or claims forms.

HOSPITALS

For every patient discharged from most hospitals, an information sheet, called a discharge abstract, is prepared. The discharge abstract contains the UHDDS elements for that patient and that episode of care. From this information, length of stay and preoperative length of stay utilization statistics can be calculated. There is no uniform instrument analogous to the abstract for ambulatory patients, and all of the required data must be collected on—and saved from—the provider's bill or on separate summary forms prepared by the provider.

Patient-specific data are confidential. However, several states now require hospitals to submit patient level information to a central clearinghouse. Frequently, the clearinghouse removes patient-identification information, and then makes these data available to the general public upon request. Detailed data on hospital costs and charges however, are generally not available routinely to the public (if they exist at all), and these may have to be recreated or estimated using data from other sources.

BILLS OR CLAIMS FORMS

For employers who wish to enter into a PPO agreement, historical insurance claim forms often provide the only realistically accessible patient level data for analysis. Although there are numerous inpatient hospital claims forms and ambulatory billing forms, most now contain much of the UHDDS and more significantly, a detailed breakdown of charges by ancillary and routine services. In the past, most businesses have received very aggregate data from their insurer or claims administrator, including such data as number of hospital days, number of claims, and cost per claim. Now, by collecting historical claims data, a company can determine the types of health services purchased by its employees, which hospitals and physicians its employees patronize for medical care, and how much is being spent for each type of service among the different providers.

Use of historical claims data for analysis remains limited for several reasons. Ironically, most hospitals do not save claims data for more than three to six months, so information necessary to establish historical trends is often unavailable, even within the hospital. Insurers or administrators may have saved hard copy claims data (e.g., actual claims forms), but often have not saved the required data in automated files.

When data have been saved, the quality of the diagnostic and procedural data has been uniformly poor, although this has changed significantly since the inception of the Medicare Prospective Payment System. Finally, and probably most important, no uniform hospital billing form has existed in most states. Instead, it was possible for every payor in every state to require a different claims form, which makes collection and analysis of these data both time consuming and expensive. However, this is changing. National implementation of a standard claim form (Uniform Bill 1982 Version, or UB82) to be used for all patients and by all payors begins January 1, 1986, and earlier in many states. Following implementation, all claims, including inpatient hospital care, will be filed on the UB82. The UB82 will enable businesses to collect and analyze claims data more easily, provided that insurance companies and third-party administrators begin to save the data.

Despite the problems identified, unfortunately, claims data for inpatient care are still far easier to access than data for ambulatory care. Ambulatory claims frequently involve:

— Bills only from the provider group, so that development of profiles on individual practitioners is impossible.
— Bills for ambulatory care coded similarly to inpatient care, so that the setting is not easily determined.
— Billing cycles that differ significantly from inpatient facilities, and multiple bills for different services, so that linking all bills for one episode is extremely difficult.
— Bundling services into one aggregate piece, so that fees for specific services cannot readily be determined.
— Information designed specifically to maximize the amount payable under the insurance plan, regardless of the actual conditions that may have been present.
— The same problems with inaccurate, incomplete, or inconsistent data found with other claims data.

Developers of the PPO must recognize all of these problems; it must be realized also, however, that physicians still order and deliver most medical services, and practice profiles on individual practitioners are the single most critical element in the selection and monitoring of members of the preferred provider panel.

DATA COLLECTION AND PROCESSING

Once the available source(s) of data are identified and the commitment made to analyzing data for the PPO venture, the processes of data collection, editing, processing, and analysis commence. The amount of time and expense involved in this phase of PPO development depends on the quality and availability of the data and on the results desired from the analyses. Regardless of the source, however, all data must be edited for quality to ensure reliable analyses.

It is almost always preferable to obtain data in an automated medium; this reduces the time, cost, and processing required for data entry. If data collection efforts begin with hard copy forms (i.e., insurance claims forms or hospital discharge abstracts) a great deal of initial effort must be expended to prepare the forms for key entry and eventual data processing. The DRG case mix grouping system requires that diagnoses and procedures be coded in ICD–9–CM (*International Classification of Diseases,* 9th Revision, Clinical Modification, which is the most widely used diagnosis and procedure coding taxonomy). If the data do not contain ICD–9–CM codes, medical records professionals must be hired to translate the English descriptions to the numeric codes necessary for computer analysis. In addition, claims data should be examined by clerical personnel for completeness and accuracy. Once this is accomplished, the data must be transferred into machine-readable format so computer editing and analysis can be performed.

Some data, especially ambulatory data, may be coded in CPT–4 (*Current Procedural Terminology,* 4th Revision) or other coding taxonomies. While these systems are useful for describing services for purposes of analysis, they are less than optimal for management use. There does not appear to be a case mix grouping approach analagous to DRGs for such systems, and no satisfactory crosswalk between CPT–4 and ICD–9–CM has been developed.

The next step is to edit the data. Although often not discussed as widely as the analysis phase, the editing process is critical to achieving reliable results from the data analysis. It is extremely important to create as clean a database as possible for analysis. Much of the editing to be performed consists of common sense checks on the accuracy and validity of the data. For example, edits should check to see if the admission date reported falls before the discharge date, whether the admission and discharge dates fall within the specified time period of study, if fields for age, sex, and discharge status contain valid and consistent values, and whether the sum of the ancillary and routine charges equals the total charges listed.

The edit process should be used to establish flags on the record indicating which edit or edits the record failed. At this point, error records can be investigated further to ascertain whether any of the errors may be corrected. Edits must also be classified as either fatal or nonfatal. Fatal errors are those errors that, if not removed from the data, would bias the results. Nonfatal errors must be flagged; records containing fatal errors must be purged from the database or at least placed in a suspense file until the errors have been corrected.

Finally, during the editing process, the data should be checked for duplicate records. If each patient record contains a unique identification number, checking for duplicates is fairly easy. The use of check digits enhances the accuracy of such identification numbers. If no unique identification exists, it is possible to search for duplicates using variables such as admission, discharge and birth dates, sex, and principal diagnosis. Any duplicates discovered should be removed from the database in order that subsequent findings not be overstated.

Following editing, it is usually necessary to group the data into some case mix groupings to enable further analysis. The most widely used grouping method is diagnosis related groups (DRGs), the system currently in use by the government for reimbursement under medicare. A patient is assigned into one of 467 DRGs based on the diagnoses, procedures, age, sex, and discharge status data from the record. The 467 DRGs represent clinically meaningful categories of patients with similar hospital resource consumption (or cost).

DATA ANALYSIS

Once the data are edited and grouped, the monumental (and tremendously important) task of data analysis is the next step. Whether the PPO is initiated by a hospital, employer, or other entity, the data analysis phase is the most critical aspect of making informed, reasonable business judgments. Establishing a PPO and contracting out health services is a business decision and should be based on a thorough understanding of the costs, benefits, and risks involved.

PROVIDER-BASED PPOs

For hospitals and other providers considering a PPO arrangement, the questions should focus on internal assessment and should address, at a minimum:

— The most frequent services provided.
— The most profitable services provided.

— The highest quality services provided.
— Those services that must be maintained for community service or public image purposes.
— The geographic market area served, and census data related to the growth of that area.
— The mix of patients treated most frequently, sorted by age, sex, types of illness, and payor source.
— Trends in admissions, length of stay, and ambulatory care over time.
— Utilization profiles on physicians and other providers to be associated with the preferred provider panel.
— Financial (performance) profiles on physicians and other providers to be associated with the preferred provider panel.

Nonhospital organizations starting a PPO will note that many of the same questions and issues also apply to their situations; the obvious complexity, of course, is access to these kinds of data.

By analyzing such sources as abstract and claims data, many of these issues can be examined. The DRG case mix system provides the means to group patients into categories with similar hospital resource consumption patterns. The provider can then perform financial and utilization analyses to determine which patients, illnesses, and physicians provide the optimal experience.

Where a particular DRG is more expensive to treat than anticipated, further analysis by physician or ancillary service should be conducted. For example, if Hospital A determined that charges for patients with coronary artery (heart) disease appeared exceptionally high, further analysis by physician might reveal one cardiologist who habitually keeps patients in the hospital three days longer than his or her colleagues, or another who routinely uses vastly more ancillary services than the norm. Understanding the costs of providing its health care "products" is requisite for making sound pricing, marketing, and management decisions within the terms of a PPO contract, and in deciding which providers are to be invited to join the provider panel.

In summary, detailed analysis of its wealth of internal data should be a major component of any provider's preparation for PPO activities. The hospital, especially, has ready access to vastly more data than any other party who will enter a PPO relationship, and it is a grave error not to take full advantage of this data analysis opportunity.

NONPROVIDER BASED PPOs

Business entities, payors, and other organizations that cannot access such detailed data must focus analyses on both internal experience and the external health care system in their area. Internally, businesses should determine the types of health care services their employees are purchasing, the total costs, and the cost per service paid to each hospital and physician providing care to its employees. Attention should also be directed to the number of inpatient admissions, the average length of stay per hospital visit, and whether utilization of hospital services is increasing or decreasing among its employees. Trends in each of these factors over time should be examined. Where no other data are available, claims data must be used as the data source.

In addition, however, business must come to understand fully the existing health care system, its reimbursement methodologies, and its terminologies. Further, since it is buying services rather than selling, business must be able to compare services rendered by different providers with respect to price and utilization statistics. Specifically, business purchasers of health care services should be able to answer questions such as the following:

— Do cost differentials exist among providers for the same health service?
— Do lengths of stay differ among providers for the same diagnoses?
— What percentage of a hospital's admissions does the company account for?
— Which providers should be included in the PPO?
— How can practice patterns be monitored to ensure appropriate and quality care?

The answers to these questions will enable business entities to become more informed and knowledgeable purchasers of health care services. The information contained in hospital billing forms is, in most instances, sufficient to answer these questions.

PRACTICE PROFILES

For purposes of illustrating the types of analyses that can be performed, assume Company A, the major employer in the area, has collected its inpatient hospital claims for the past two years in an attempt to determine if a PPO arrangement with area providers will be beneficial. The data have been edited and each record assigned a DRG. The first step in the analyses is to determine, in the aggregate, the company's utilization and cost experience.

By simple counting and averaging, Company A can determine where its employees sought health care, the total charges paid to each hospital, and, on the average, how long patients stayed and how much each episode cost the company. With multiple years of data, the percentage change in admissions and total dollars expended can also be calculated. The data can be displayed in Exhibits 1 and 2 as follows:

From these exhibits, Company A discovers that the majority of its employees use Hospitals 1 and 2; that $3,185,919 was spent on health care in 1984 (representing a 46 percent increase in total dollars spent

EXHIBIT 1

		1983		
Hospital	Number of Admissions	Total Charges	Average LOS	Average Charge
Hospital 1	727	$ 998,898	5.1	$1,374
Hospital 2	521	654,897	5.0	1,257
Hospital 3	279	527,310	6.0	1,890
	1,527	$2,181,105	5.2	$1,428

EXHIBIT 2

		1984				
Hospital	Number of Admissions	Total Charges	Average LOS	Average Charge	Percent Change Admissions	Percent Change Average Charge
Hospital 1	979	$1,557,589	5.1	$1,591	+35%	+16%
Hospital 2	616	1,058,904	5.9	1,719	+18%	+37%
Hospital 3	242	569,426	6.3	2,353	−13%	+25%
	1,837	$3,185,919	5.5	$1,734	+20%	+21%

over 1983), and that total hospital admissions rose 20 percent in one year. It also points out that Hospital 3 is a higher cost, longer length of stay (LOS) hospital compared to Hospitals 1 and 2, in the aggregate. The experience at Hospital 3 should be examined closely to determine whether it treats a more complex mix of patients or whether it is simply more expensive for all types of cases.

This type of analysis provides a general description of Company A's health care experiences for 1983 and 1984. To examine the services consumed and the costs of these services in detail, analysis by DRG is required. Typically, the top 10 volume DRGs (including such things as normal deliveries, medical back problems, stomach and intestinal diseases, and gynecological procedures) for a company represent 25 percent or more of its admissions, which provides a good starting place for DRG specific analyses. The average charge, average length of stay, average preoperative length of stay (where appropriate), average per diem, and number of admissions should be calculated by DRG within each hospital to produce a comparison data base. From these data, prices (reflected as average charges per case) and lengths of stay can be compared across hospitals for similar services. A simple table similar to that below can be developed for any number of DRGs (see Exhibit 3).

EXHIBIT 3

| | 1984 | | | | | |
| | Hospital 1 | | Hospital 2 | | Hospital 3 | |
DRG	Average LOS	Average Charge	Average LOS	Average Charge	Average LOS	Average Charge
373 Normal delivery	3.1	$1,135	2.3	$1,279	3.2	$1,351
243 Back disorders	8.6	2,795	4.0	1,954	6.8	4,114
355 Hysterectomy	6.3	2,793	8.2	5,956	9.0	8,362

Company A is paying approximately the same amount for normal deliveries among the hospitals. However, charges for back disorders range from $1,954–4,114 and for hysterectomies from $2,793–8,362. This represents a significant difference in prices for the same type of service.

In addition to cost and utilization analyses by DRG, physician profiles should be prepared detailing the average charge, average length of stay, and the percent of total charges that ancillary charges represent for each DRG. In this manner, high or low cost physician profiles can be identified. A word of caution; however, if the majority of hospital billing forms are not complete with physician identifiers or are not accurate in identifying attending physicians, gross misrepresentations of individual physician practice patterns will almost certainly occur.

Finally, utilization analyses may also be conducted from this database. For example, certain procedures are now commonly performed on an outpatient basis. Utilizing these data, Company A could determine whether any of these procedures were being performed frequently on an inpatient basis. A few examples of such procedures would include tooth extractions, routine D & Cs, arthroscopies, and vasectomies.

Another statistic often used to measure the appropriateness of care is the preoperative length of stay (the number of days a person is in the hospital before surgery is performed). Ideally, this number should be as close to one day as possible. Any hospital with a significantly longer average preoperative length of stay should be examined closely since these days involve significant cost for services that could often be delivered prior to admission.

The above analysis offers a business purchaser a wealth of knowledge on which to base PPO decisions. Businesses can establish profiles on their own health care experiences and on the providers from which they purchase care. This is only the beginning, however, for a variety of factors will influence the selection of providers for a PPO. For example, even though a hospital may offer a lower per-diem cost per case, if its length of stay is much higher than other hospitals, the "savings" may only be imaginary, as Exhibit 4 illustrates:

EXHIBIT 4

DRG X	Per Diem	Average LOS	Charge/ Case
Hospital 4	$322	6.8	$2,190
Hospital 5	379	5.1	1,932

Knowledge of the relative charges and utilization of hospital services by provider presents an informed basis on which to negotiate PPO discounts: If Hospital 4 offered Company A a 10 percent discount on each patient's bill for DRG X and Hospital 5 offered no discount at all, it is readily apparent that Hospital 5 still represents the optimal purchase decision for this particular type of care, despite its higher per-diem rate, as long as quality factors or other mitigating circumstances are not at issue.

DATA QUALITY

Initial access to the data does not solve all of the problems. The quality of decisions made can be no better than the quality of the data on which they are based. The importance of editing the data was stressed above, and even this step will not solve all of the problems. There are several difficulties that will be present; foremost among these are:

— Timeliness of the data.
— Completeness of the source data.
— Accuracy of the source data.
— Consistency of data among multiple sources.
— Availablility of adequate detail in the data.

Many providers do not bill for services rendered for 3 to 4 weeks, or longer, after services are delivered. If claims data are to be used as the data source, access to the data cannot begin until the claim has been generated. If it must also be adjudicated before the data are accessed, the delay is even greater. Providers have rarely been required to submit complete data. Unless this is made a condition of PPO participation and of program payment, data that are not readily available will continue to be underreported.

Another aspect of completeness is linkage of hospital and physician claims data for inpatient episodes. Until such claims are linked, it is virtually impossible to accord the physician financial responsibility for his or her actions, and the hospital will continue to bear all of the brunt for inappropriate patterns of care.

Of all the data reported, the least accurate and complete have usually been diagnostic and procedural data, since these were considered only incidental to the payment process. These data are the basis for analysis of the services purchased and should be considered mandatory data elements. Finally, where similar data are obtained from different sources, the problems of different formats and data elements must be resolved, as must the problem of different definitions for the same data elements.

In summary, the focus must be on defining a minumum data set and on improving the quality of those data on a continuing basis. Virtually the only way to develop accurate provider profiles and valid pricing structures is through patient-specific data, to continue to demand more complete and accurate data, and to tie both reimbursement and continued participation in the PPO to such reporting.

DATA-RELATED ACTIVITIES

As in any business entity, there are numerous management and operational activities that must be supported by the data generated. Some of the most important of these include selecting participating providers, pricing services, and monitoring and managing all aspects of PPO operations.

In basic economic terms, the total cost of operations (measured as cost by the payor or revenue by the provider) will be a function of both price and volume. Review of price and volume information implies the availability of practice profiles by disease or procedure, and by provider. Ideally, practice profiles are developed in advance and are used to select the initial members of the provider panel. Subsequent additions to or changes in the provider panel will be based on similar profiles. At a minimum, these profiles must reflect patterns of both utilization and cost. Future profiles should be expected to include a quantifiable means of examining quality of care.

The financial profiles will also serve as a key source of data for establishing prices. Significantly, the prices established must benefit both the provider and the purchaser of services. This is the essence of a solid business relationship, and it is clearly less than optimal for one party to be so disadvantaged that it cannnot continue the arrangement past the first year. Prices for services will obviously be related to direct and indirect costs, along with some amount of surplus. Where possible, the analyses should also identify fixed and variable costs, so that marginal costs and revenues can be identified. Finally, price data should be compared to data from state sources, fee schedules, or directly from other providers, to ensure that the price schedule established is both reasonable and competitive.

Finally, monitoring and management includes regular, thorough review of all aspects of operations—and especially those related to provider performance and price schedules. It is recommended that strict performance standards be established in advance and adhered to carefully. For example, it might be specified that physicians whose performance was above the 90th percentile of all physicians with the PPO on both utilization and charges for any three quarters during the year would be subject to dismissal from the preferred provider panel. Similar monitoring should address other aspects of utilization, as well as quality. Practice patterns and trends should also be evaluated.

COSTS OF DATA-RELATED PROJECTS

Data collection and processing can be expensive activities, and the cost of a data effort should be considered carefully before such a project is started. The cost can vary widely depending on the scope of the activity and the amount of data to be involved. It should be noted, however, that significant economies of scale can be achieved in those portions of the process that are automated. It should also be noted that, taken in the proper perspective, the cost will appear quite reasonable: if a data project or data system leads to the identification of problems that subsequently result in only a 5 percent reduction in overall cost or utilization (a rather conservative estimate, in most instances), then a data effort that costs only 1 to 2 percent of total annual health care expenditures becomes an excellent investment.

As described in the sections above, the major activities associated with a data project are usually initial data collection, data entry, editing and processing, and analysis. Obviously, cost will be a function of both volume and price, but such factors as data sources, data format, and the familiarity of the responsible individuals with health care data will also be key variables.

The elements of cost likely to be involved in such a project or ongoing system will include some or all of the following components:

- Obtaining (access to) the data.
- Clerical preparation of the data.
- Professional medical records input.
- Data entry.
- Editing and processing.
- Reporting.
- Data analysis.

The initial requirement is to obtain the source data, usually some form of utilization and cost data, and possibly planning data, about the environment and the population to be enrolled. Providers are almost always the optimal source for utilization and cost data, since they have the complete source data. Depending on the environment in which the PPO is to be started, however, providers may or may not be willing to provide source data for the effort. If data from providers are unavailable, claims data are usually the next best alternative.

The optimum situation is for the desired data to be available in some machine-readable mode, in a specified format. Cost elements in this situation will involve primarily the cost of conversion of the data to a host computer and a specified format. If only hard copy data are available, copies of each source document must be obtained and processed. In such situations, cost estimates should include time for personnel to assign a unique identifier to each document, to count and batch the documents carefully, and to ensure that all documents are legible for key entry purposes.

If specific identification of the medical services delivered is not present in some coded form, additional effort will be required by medical records coding professionals to convert the information provided by the provider into codes for computer processing. This is an especially important step and must be done both thoroughly and accurately. The codes assigned to the diagnosis and procedure information are often the only data that provide insight into the actual services provided and billed, and these will be the basis for the profiles developed on each provider. Determination of accurate codes will frequently be complicated by the lack of adequate information provided on the provider's bill, and it is very important to ensure that the information available is coded as completely and accurately as possible.

The next significant cost elements will be editing and processing the data. If previously prepared programs are not readily available for this function, the least expensive means of starting this process is through prepared computer packages or database management systems. Familiarity and experience with health care data processing becomes especially important at this point.

Following editing, it will be necessary to group the data into some diagnostic or case mix groupings to enable further analysis. For hospital claims, the most commonly known and used grouping method is DRGs. The DRG "Grouper" software uses the specific diagnoses and procedures reported for each inpatient episode and assigns patients into one of 467 discrete categories for analysis (and frequently for payment purposes). The Grouper software can be obtained for a large IBM mainframe computer for a very nominal price, but the size, complexity, and medical intricacies of the Grouper indicate that it may be both less expensive and more efficient to obtain this service from an organization that already uses the software on a regular basis.

To repeat, if prepared computer programs are not readily available, a database package is extremely helpful at this point. The key requirement is the ability to sort and subsort within a variety of variables. For example, it is extremely desirable to be able to examine length of stay and average charges per case within DRG. Additionally, it is useful to have this capability by individual company, preferably showing experience at each individual hospital. It is also helpful to examine such data by individual hospital, preferably showing the aggregate experience for each company.

Similar data are also necessary with respect to other providers, such as physicians. In this instance, the data will resemble a "usual and customary" profile, which reveals the physician's most frequent or customary charge for a given procedure or type of visit. Such information also enables comparison of each physician to similar profiles developed for the community as a whole and for other individual practitioners in the same medical specialty.

CONCLUSION

From any perspective, the importance of information on which to base management decisions cannot be overstated. The cost of health care services now requires that purchase decisions be made more carefully than ever before. The complexity of the problem mandates extensive analyses before decisions are actually reached. The confidential and proprietary nature of the data and the lack of uniformity in collecting and processing these data have created extensive problems for initial analyses, but these problems do not necessarily defy solution, and can usually be overcome. As in other aspects of business, the party that controls the data is likely to control the direction of the PPO. Experience, perseverance, adequate resources, and the availability of the appropriate technical skills will usually be the key components in achieving such control.

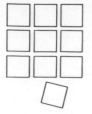

Marketplace Fundamentals

DATA AND NEW FORMS OF ALTERNATIVE DELIVERY SYSTEMS

Elliot A. Segal

Principal and Manager of Health Programs
William M. Mercer-Meidinger, Incorporated
Washington, DC

The past decade in this country has witnessed a steady increase in the development of alternative delivery systems. These systems are alternatives to the traditional fee-for-service and cost-plus practice of medicine. These alternatives began about a half century ago, with the first variety being the closed panel prepaid group practices. It is noteworthy, as large corporations now begin to embrace this concept, that the dominant and most important group practice arrangement was originally developed by Kaiser Industries. This was in response to a need in the late 1920s to make health care available for employees who were involved in construction projects on the West Coast.

The term for alternative group practices, health maintenance organizations or HMOs, has been of recent vintage, coming into prominence in the past 10 to 12 years. This term generally describes an entity that provides specific health services to its members for a prepaid fixed payment. A monthly payment insures some portion of the cost of health services that a subscriber may incur during a period of time.

350

There are basically two broad HMO models: the prepaid group practice model and the individual practice association (IPA) or medical care foundation model. In both models, the HMO receives periodic payments of fixed amounts in return for the services it provides to members.

HMOs, in concept, allow for an opportunity to provide cost controls or cost-management incentives. The providers of services are at risk for the total care package and, therefore, are not reimbursed for each of the services they provide. This is an alteration from the usual economic incentives in medical care. HMOs tend to collect more relevant utilization data, particularly of hospitalizations; and often for marketing purposes, they have provided information on days of hospital care for every 1,000 plan members, a statistic just beginning to be acquired by insurance companies.

EMERGENCE OF PPOs

The past two years have seen the emergence of a new form of an organized health care structure, the so-called preferred provider organization (PPO). Although new in nomenclature, the PPO can be thought of as a hybrid of existing alternative delivery systems most resembling the independent practice association form of a health maintenance organization (HMO), but with an attempt by the providers not to assume any risk. PPOs generally appear to be entities that will offer discounts (usually off total charges), provide utilization review, and maintain fee for service, while they seek increased market share in return.

There are certain data items that should be considered by purchasers in evaluating their participation in PPOs. For example, when a PPO offers a 10 percent discount, does this necessarily mean that the end result is advantageous to an employer. The answer depends upon the base used for calculating the discount. If a hospital raises its charges by 15 percent and then offers a 10 percent discount, it would be foolhardy for a purchaser to accept such an arrangement. But an employer must have the appropriate data beforehand in order to know this is happening.

A hospital may be able to camouflage such a situation by keeping its room and board charges relatively fixed and seek other ways to boost the charges. Examples of such arrangements will be spelled out later.

For a company, the data needs to evaluate a PPO are obvious. A corporation should be able to standardize the health care it pays for in a system of quantifiable measures. The new emerging diagnosis related groups (DRG) technology provides such opportunities.

FORCES LEADING TO PPOs

In order to place the data needs and the resultant opportunities that preferred provider organizations (PPOs) offer to purchasers of care in perspective, it might be helpful to attempt to isolate the forces that have brought about this movement. From a national policy perspective, the federal government has been struggling with the creation of a national financing system for health care for almost 50 years. Such a system was first considered for inclusion within the Social Security program enacted during the Roosevelt era. The Murray-Wagner-Dingell proposals of the mid- to late 1940s were the first major attempts at a comprehensive total health program for the total population. These proposals did not result in enacted legislation. The late 1950s saw the enactment of legislation designed essentially to provide financial assistance to people considered indigent.

This legislation was a prelude to the major legislation passed in 1965 that created the medicare and medicaid programs, Titles XVIII and XIX of the Social Security Act. The medicare program was created as an entitlement program to cover individuals 65 years or older. This is handled federally through the creation of two trust funds, one for hospitalizations and a supplementary medical trust with voluntary payments by recipients. The medicaid program was structured to cover indigent individuals with the funding to be supplied by a matching federal-state formula. States were given substantial latitude in determining the levels of eligibility inclusion. The policies set by these statutes in effect created the national health insurance policies for the country. Limiting federal financial participation to the indigent and the elderly left individuals not in these categories to the private market place. Insurance coverage for the bulk of this middle class working population has increased dramatically over the past thirty years and has been made available by Blue Cross/Blue Shield service type plans and private insurer indemnity plans. During this same period, the McCarran-Ferguson Act assigned the regulation and administration of these plans to the authority of state insurance commissioners.

Over the past two decades the nation's health outlays have increased substantially, both publicly and privately. Private outlays have become more and more the purview of employers who have taken on the responsibility for the financing of care for their employees. Much of this growth has been as a consequence of union bargaining for benefits.

The result is that employers now pay for a substantial portion of health care and are recently becoming aware that they should seek to become prudent buyers of services. Probably the major public policy struggle in the health arena in recent years has been over the extent of health insurance coverage provided and who should be included. Since enactment of medicare and medicaid in the mid-1960s, there have been other legislative proposals for more comprehensive coverage that have not become law.

Simultaneously, there have also been significant public debate and continuing efforts to control cost, stimulate competition, or impose regulatory actions on the health care system. The Regional Medical Program and the Comprehensive Health Planning Programs, the Health Manpower and Nursing legislation were all legislative attempts of the 1960s to increase resources, create more planning efficiencies, and potentially stimulate competition.

The early 1970s saw the enactment of regulatory legislation that included the establishment of Professional Standard Review Organizations to monitor care, Certificate of Need to hold down new construction, and Medicare Section 223 to limit price increases for medicare payments.

Section 223 was a part of the medicare amendments of 1972 and set up a reimbursement situation that has had large scale implications for cost management. Essentially, Section 223, covering hospital payments, set reimbursement limits for room and board charges but not for ancillary charges. This split set off an artificial balkanization of separate a la carte-like charges for items such as x-rays, drugs, and lab tests. Hospitals, always anxious to maximize income, isolated out these ancillary services and raised these prices much more rapidly than room and board costs. Government and private data tracking programs were able to measure internal dramatic hospital cost shifts.

Room and board charges have declined from the predominant cost of a hospitalization to a distinct minority in less than 10 years. These room and board charges were likely to be over 80 percent of the hospital bill and now could be as low as 30 percent.

Throughout this cornucopia of federal health legislation, few changes were imposed on the structure or methods of payment. Hospitals would continue to charge on a cost plus per-day stay basis. Physicians would generaliy charge on a fee-for-service basis. The one set of legislative changes that stimulated alterations in reimbursement, was the establishment of health maintenance organizations. Federal legislation (P.L. 93-222) enacted in 1974 established standards for federal designation of HMOs and the basis for obtaining grants and loans. This act provided a thrust toward alternative deliveries and a prepayment environment.

Partially as an alternative to HMOs, PPOs have now emerged as provider entities that contract with insurers, employers, and other third-party payors. They claim to offer subscribers a dual choice. This choice suggests that plan members can choose the preferred provider, or they may also use nonpreferred providers at an additional financial cost.

Many PPOs have been disappointed at the slow pace with which they have been embraced by employers. On the other hand, PPOs have not yet demonstrated that their "product" is well defined, that their price is competitively superior, that their organizational structure is compatible with employer plans, or that their utilization and quality provisions are acceptable. Employers are asking for, but are not receiving, data to answer such questions.

For PPOs to be successful in marketing to sophisticated employers, they will have to provide information on utilization and price. PPOs will have to accumulate and demonstrate, with case-mix profiling, that they can save employers money.

NEW PAYMENT AND DATA MANAGEMENT SYSTEMS

PPOs are becoming another alternative available to purchasers. Beginning this decade, three major purchasers of health care have begun to seek more cost-effective alternatives to their previous methods. First, the federal government, on behalf of medicare recipients, has established a prospective payment system based upon casemix, diagnosis related groups (DRGs). Medicare will also allow HMOs and qualifying PPOs to sign up medicare recipients on an at-risk basis. Under this approach, a provider will get a fixed annual payment per person compared to per case payments under DRGs.

Second, medicaid programs have made changes that have varied widely by state. Some states have curtailed services while others have specifically circumvented the recipients freedom of choice, thereby stimulating the rise of preferred providers. In a state such as New Jersey, medicaid cases also are paid on a diagnosis related group basis.

Thirdly, private employers have moved to expand alternative delivery and financing systems that have included HMOs and evolving PPOs. Much of the movement toward alternatives has been as a result of escalating costs and a search for more cost effectiveness. This search has led, particularly among employers, to a desire to incorporate appropriate management principles in their health care expenditures. This movement has led to corporations demanding better statistics and data accounting from their carriers and third-party administrations (TPAs), in order to make more informed choices and decisions about their plans.

As corporations search for ways to curb skyrocketing health costs, they wish to curtail open-ended uncontrolled expenditures. They want to monitor the care in order to become (along with their employees) more prudent purchasers. Most companies have recently come to believe that HMOs are a legitimate (and likely cost-effective) alternative to their own plan. Suddenly, the PPO movement has added a new dimension to the scene. Will these organizations be a positive or negative force? In order to answer the question rationally, some important data must be acquired and evaluated.

One of the more useful ways to accumulate such data for monitoring hospital use is via the diagnosis related group technology. DRGs have now emerged as a patient classification system that can serve several functions. They can be helpful in utilization review, hospital budgeting, cost control, prospective reimbursement, and regional planning. Medicare has recently adopted DRGs as the basis of a prospective reimbursement program. Blue Cross plans in Kansas and Oklahoma have followed suit. For purposes of PPO evaluation, price and utilization review information is essential.

This paper will describe the use of DRGs for data reporting and management and the resultant opportunities for price negotiations with providers. Knowing what DRGs are and what they can do makes this evident.

DRGs are really a classification system of hospital patients. They are grouped into 23 major diagnostic categories (MDCs), which are essentially grouped by medical clusters of speciality such as circulatory problems, musculoskeletal problems, and ear, nose, and throat cases. They are based upon the premise that these medical products are essentially similar amd require the same bundle of resources.

Using this classification system, a corporation is able to set up a data management information system. Such a system can pinpoint by medical and surgical specialty where costs are occurring. The location including the hospital and the physicians can also be identified.

Once such an information profile is gathered for a company, it can then be compared with matched national and regional standards that can identify overutilization and above-normal charges. Such a systematic approach allows for an evaluation of whether to enter into agreements with PPOs.

If a PPO is composed of hospitals that are standard or better than standard for utilization and are reasonable from a cost standpoint, they become prime candidates to be sought out for negotiated agreements.

Under the new medicare reimbursement system, hospitals will be seeking new ways to become efficient in order to maximize reimbursements. Those that are efficient will "earn a profit" under the medicare approach. It is a natural extension that if efficiencies can be developed to enhance a hospital under medicare, those same efficiencies could be extended to enhance marketplace standing with private payors.

OPPORTUNITIES FOR CORPORATIONS

An important question is how an enlightened employer and an efficient hospital can work together. An employer armed with regional price information by hospitals for the same DRGs can go to the efficient providers and work out negotiated provider agreements (NPAs). Such arrangements can mean substantial savings opportunities for purchasers and increased market share for participating hospitals, while simultaneously fostering potential difficulties for hospitals unaware, unwilling, or unable to participate in such arrangements.

At this point in time, it appears that some PPOs are composed of efficient hospitals, some are composed of inefficient hospitals, and some have a mixture. This is also true of physicians.

A company that takes the initiative to set up a data management program will be able to evaluate and determine the variations. Having such information will allow a company to initiate provider agreements rather than wait to be approached.

An employer, armed with its utilization information, can decide to pick and choose from among PPO members. For example, a PPO might include several hospitals. Among this group might be some of the most expensive hospitals in the area and some of the most economical. A prudent purchaser would seek NPAs with the latter institutions and avoid relationships with the former. A data wise employer would also seek to avoid an affiliation agreement with the PPO if such an alliance required participation of all institutions.

A DRG-based or case-mix cost management system provides several advantages for employers seeking to work with PPOs and can also be helpful to corporate group insurance plans in other ways. In dealing with PPOs, strong data accumulation can be useful in three aspects of an affiliation program. These include: discount agreements, utilization review, and revised reimbursements.

DISCOUNT AGREEMENTS

PPOs offering discounts to employers generally provide these lowered charges as a reduction below charges. These charges are usually established as a fixed-price per diem plus ancillaries. Because the basis of charges is the per diem rate, length of stay by a payor becomes essential. For example, if Hospital A has a base per diem of $350 compared to Hospital B at $300, that does not mean Hospital B is more cost effective. (See Exhibit 1.) If B normally has four-day stays for normal deliveries

EXHIBIT 1

	Per Diem Rate	Length of Stay (days)	Charge
Hospital A	$350	3	$1,050
Hospital B	300	4	1,200

while A has three-day stays, the base hospital difference favors A at $1,050 vs. B at $1,200. Hence, the issue of utilization review (which will be discussed below) is an important factor.

In addition, the discount percentage offered may not be as important as the base upon which discounts are offered. For example, if both Hospitals A and B had similar lengths of stay for deliveries (e.g., three days) and Hospital A offered a 10 percent discount while Hospital B offered 5 percent, B would be most cost effective with the final charge of $810

EXHIBIT 2

	Price per Day	Stay in Days	Charge	Dis-count	Minus Discount	Final Charge
Hospital A	$350	3	$1,050	10%	$105	$945
Hospital B	300	3	900	5%	90	810

compared to $945 (see Exhibit 2), even though A provides a "bigger discount."

Utilization review also has serious implications for a company. Having a lower length of stay for a hospital bout can often have geater savings impact. For example, if the average length of stay for Hospital A can be reduced for normal deliveries from three days to two days, the savings are much more extensive than a discount. (See Exhibit 3.)

EXHIBIT 3

	Day Rate	LOS	Charge	Dis-count	Final Charge
Hospital A (discount)	$350	3	$1,050	10%	$945
Hospital A (no discount)	350	2	700	0%	700

Further, if a proportion of maternity cases could be done out of hospital (e.g., via use of a birthing center) even the nondiscounted $700 could be reduced significantly.

UTILIZATION REVIEW

Alternative delivery systems, such as HMOs generally have established programs of utilization review. Since HMOs suffer the risk when costs exceed projections, they have strong incentives to keep utilization down. In fact, most closed panel HMOs have utilization rates per 1,000 plan members of about 500 or less hospital days compared to indemnity plans, which usually exceed 700 hospital days per 1,000 plan members.

In contrast, PPOs, especially the noncarrier variety, do not necessarily take on a cost risk. Many of the existing PPOs are hospital based and indeed may have been established to seek to replenish dwindling hospital occupancy rates. Most of these hospital-inspired PPOs will, of course, profess to have appropriate utilization review or peer review programs that they will self-administer.

Historically, the federal medicare program in 1972 created Professional Standard Review Organizations (PSROs) to police hospital admissions because self-administered peer review was considered to be a failure. With lower hospital occupancy rates in 1983, what evidence can hospitals set forth to demonstrate they can self-administer utilization review. A forward thinking corporation should, as part of an NPA, jointly establish standards and build in a surveillance, monitoring, and reporting system. Profiling past utilization data will pinpoint the areas of concentration.

CASE MIX REIMBURSEMENT

Medicare began reimbursing hospitals by DRGs on October 1, 1983. This provides hospitals with a chance to "make a profit" when the DRG amount exceeds the actual cost incurred, and "lose money" when the cost exceeds the reimbursement amount.

A corporation can seek to become a prudent purchaser by attempting to establish a similar program. Of course, an individual company, unlike medicare, need not deal with all providers. Indeed, states such as California and Virginia have recently enacted statutes that encourage companies to carefully select only certain providers.

When a purchaser undertakes a program with a fixed price per DRG, it mitigates the need for a detailed concurrent UR program. In this type of a program, the hospital accepts the risk for overly long stays. On the other hand, preadmission reviews become essential. Because a fixed price will be paid for a specific DRG, such as a hernia, a hospital could benefit from short stay "easy" hernia cases. These, of course, are the cases that may also be handled on an outpatient basis. Hence, it behooves a company to establish a review program to ascertain the necessity of such an admission.

A strong data program can also measure excessive health problem areas. For example, a company can expect a certain number of cases of illnesses based upon population and other demographics. When this rate is exceeded, problems and questionable areas can be identified. A strong data profile allows tracking on an on-going basis.

A company that gathers this price information by DRGs can also negotiate fixed-price DRG payments. Because hospital charges vary significantly, often as much as two or three fold in similar geographic areas, such negotiations can mean extensive savings. Currently, there are no constraints to negotiating different agreements with different providers. A negotiating package for an NPA might include fast-pay discounts, volume discounts, utilization-review standards and their administration, fixed-price agreements by case mix, and risk-sharing reimbursement using a system such as DRGs.

In order to be a knowledgeable negotiator and prudent purchaser of care, a strong data acquisition and profiling system is essential.

CONCLUSION

Corporations, because of a variety of forces over the past several decades, have undertaken a broader level of responsibility for the payment of their employees and dependents. As health costs have escalated, companies have begun to use alternative delivery and financing systems in order to introduce incentives and cost efficiencies. These alternative arrangements have included HMOs and IPAs.

Recently, providers have evolved a new model known as a preferred provider organization (PPO), which they hope will satisfy purchasers demands for cost-effective care while maintaining features of the traditional fee-for-service arrangement.

Purchasers who have, or are developing, a strong data analysis and management information system can be in a position to take advantage of this PPO movement. Enlightened purchasers can seek out efficient PPOs and negotiate provider agreements with these groups. A data utilization profiling system appears to be a necessary step for employers who wish to establish such arrangements.

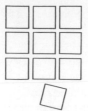

Marketplace Fundamentals

Data Issues in the Selection of Preferred Providers

Robert A. Chernow, Ph.D.
President
Corporate Health Strategies, Inc.
New Haven, CT

Douglas E. Smith, Ph.D.
Director
Corporate Health Strategies, Inc.
New Haven, CT

By definition, the concept of a "preferred provider" in the medical industry embodies the notion of "preference" or selection. Largely for economic reasons (perceived lower cost), incentives are provided by an employer (such as a corporation) to encourage their employees to use a specific group of providers (doctors and/or hospitals) in an area. In addition, certain safeguards are usually built in (such as utilization review) to ensure that the *total* dollars charged by these preferred providers remain below those of other providers in the area.

A major issue, therefore, becomes the *selection* of preferred providers. What is needed is a measure of performance (i.e., a performance index). Since preferred providers are generally considered the most cost effective in a community, charges are probably the best measure of performance. Using this measure, a good performance index might be defined as the following:

$$\text{Performance index} = \frac{\text{Total excess or unnecessary charges}}{\text{Total expected charges}}$$

Since excess charges can be thought of as the difference between actual charges and expected charges, the key is defining the expected charges, or those charges that can be attributed solely to volume and the types of patients being treated and not to poor performance. Given this measure, the lower the value of the performance index (PI) the better is the performance of the hospital (or doctor).

First, what contributes to poor hospital performance must be considered. Insight can be gained from past experience. Employers, for example, may contract inappropriately with a group of providers that initially appears cost effective but in fact are not. Consider the case of an employer who contracted with a hospital whose average charge per admission was the lowest in the community. Upon further investigation, it was uncovered that this institution was treating a much less complex (and hence, a much less expensive) mix of patients. More difficult to detect, however, was the situation in which the employer considered the different types of patients being treated but failed to consider that a number of admissions were not medically necessary. The result was that the employer's total costs were far greater than they needed to be. Even after implementing a preadmission certification program (and substantially decreasing the number of inappropriate admissions), this hospital turned out not to be a good choice as a preferred provider. By eliminating the medically unnecessary admissions, particularly the least expensive patients, the average charge per admission for the hospital increased. In fact, the average charge per admission increased to the point where it exceeded the norm for the community, even after the different types of patients being treated were considered. In such situations, utilization safeguards are only partially successful at best.

While the necessary data items were available in both instances to make a correct decision, they simply were not organized and interpreted in the proper manner. In the selection of preferred provider hospitals (or doctors), a method is needed that "double adjusts" for the factors contributing to poor performance as illustrated by the above examples. That is, the method must consider at a minimum both of these performance factors: (1) the cost *efficiency* of hospitals, taking into account the different types of patients these hospitals treat (i.e., case mix) and (2) the *clinical appropriateness* of the admissions (i.e., their medical necessity).

The purpose of this article is to discuss these key performance factors, their measurement, and how they should be used *together* in the selection of preferred provider hospitals. (The method can also be used to identify physicians, but this discussion will be restricted to hospitals to illustrate the concepts.) The method also provides insight into areas where further intervention and monitoring is warranted for the preferred provider (e.g., the use of ancillary services). To facilitate the discussion, the authors have used data from an actual corporation (call it Corporation XYZ) to illustrate some of the data issues involved in the selection process.[1] While these factors are not the only ones to be considered, they do provide information essential in making informed judgments. In the final analysis, however, a variety of factors (political, geographic, quality related, scope of services offered, and economic) will determine which providers will be preferred.

HOSPITAL PERFORMANCE FACTORS

To reiterate, at least two factors should be examined in evaluating hospital performance:

1. *Efficiency,* or whether patients are treated cost effectively, once admitted.
2. *Appropriateness,* or whether admissions to a hospital are medically justified in the first place.

Most employers will want to restrict their consideration of preferred providers to hospitals in the area that are already treating a relatvely large number of the employer's patients. Thus, volume of admissions is a convenient way of identifying a subset of hospitals in the area that warrant further in-depth study with respect to overall performance.

VOLUME

It is not unusual that in any given geographic area, a relatively small number of hospitals treat a disproportionate number of a corporation's employees and their dependents. Thus, for Corporation XYZ, a company with about 5,000 employees located in a medium-sized community (150,000 to 200,000 population), four hospitals, or about 10 percent of all hospitals in the area during 1983 accounted for 72 percent of Corporation XYZ's admissions and 63 percent of Corporation XYZ's room and board and ancillary service (lab, X-ray, drug) charges.

These four high-volume hospitals appear to be prime candidates for closer scrutiny because of the concentration of Corporation XYZ's patients in each one. In addition, high volume (1) indicates acceptance of the hospital as a provider of care by employees (or their doctors, at least) and (2) places the employer, because of the dollars involved, in a better position to negotiate favorable arrangements with the hospital.

After having limited the hospitals for in-depth study to the high-volume institutions, attention can now be turned to the key performance factors, efficiency and appropriateness. Both factors are amenable to measurement assuming the technology employed is sensitive enough to identify individual patient and provider differences.

EFFICIENCY

To analyze efficiency, the four high-volume hospitals treating Corporation XYZ employees and dependents were compared one to another (in terms of their charges) after having taken into account the unique types of patients (cases) each hospital treated. Thus, if some hospitals treated more difficult patients (i.e., more expensive) than others, this was taken into account and adjusted for when determining the expected charges. This type of adjustment is called case-mix adjustment, and it relies on the accurate definition and measurement of the various types of patients each hospital treats. While there are numerous ways to categorize patients,[2] the patient classification scheme used by Corporation XYZ was based on diagnosis related groups, or DRGs. Originally developed at Yale University in the 1970s, DRGs consider a variety of factors known to affect the amount of hospital services (resources) used by patients during their stay. Some of the major factors considered are the patient's principal diagnosis, age, whether or not a procedure was performed in the operating room, and the type of procedure performed. Thus, two patients admitted to a hospital may have had the same admitting diagnosis, but consumed very different services (resources) because of a difference in age or whether surgery was performed.

One advantage of DRGs is that they collapse thousands of different medical diagnosis and procedure codes into a few hundred distinct groups. This facilitates an analysis as the number of patient groups become more manageable and the sample size of each group increases. The various codes that are combined into each DRG are medically related and statistically similar in terms of their use of hospital resources. This means that the patient groups created based on the DRG technology are well defined; therefore, the same type of patients comprise each patient group. Thus, for Corporation XYZ, it was possible to compare one hospital's actual charge experience with expected charges (i.e., the charges of all other hospitals in the database) based on the types of patients (DRGs) that hospital treated. The expected charge in Exhibit 1 below, therefore, represents a total charge figure (room and board and ancillary services only) that has been case-mix adjusted.

This analysis, which adjusted for differences in case mix, reveals that for Corporation XYZ, Hospital H performed best (when considering efficiency alone) of the four high-volume hospitals. Averaging across all diseases and disorders, its patients were treated for 7.8 percent less (or $57,928 less) than expected compared to the other high-volume hospitals treating the same types of patients. On the other hand, Hospitals A and F

EXHIBIT 1
Corporation XYZ
Hospital Performance
Case-Mix Adjusted

		Total Charges			
Hospital	Admis-sions	Actual	Expected	Excess Charges	Performance Index
A	558	$1,322,294	$1,167,074	+$155,220	+13.3
F	51	165,888	141,906	+ 23,982	+16.9
E	650	1,156,350	1,098,223	+ 58,127	+ 5.3
H	172	688,200	746,128	(− 57,928)	(− 7.8)

both performed poorly (again, considering efficiency alone) compared to the other two high-volume hospitals. Patients admitted to these two institutions cost Corporation XYZ 13.3 percent and 16.9 percent, respectively, more than expected (again, after adjusting for the unique types of patients treated at these institutions).

In many instances, however, certain admissions to a hospital are not appropriate because the admission was not medically justified (i.e., the patient could have been safely treated as an outpatient). Since these inappropriate admissions could have biased the results of the previous analysis, it is necessary to adjust for these inappropriate admissions.

APPROPRIATENESS

To examine the impact of inappropriate admissions on hospital efficiency, criteria and computer programs (based on physician judgment) were developed to select those admissions that were considered "most questionable admissions" (MQAs). These MQAs largely consisted of short-stay nonsurgical admissions whose lengths of stay varied by disease category (but were most frequently one day or less), and surgical admissions that usually can be safely performed on an outpatient basis. Exhibit 2 illustrates the results of this analysis for Corporation XYZ. Exhibit 3 shows the distribution of the MQAs among the four high-volume hospitals treating Corporation XYZ's employees and dependents.

Exhibit 3 shows great disparity in the percent of questionable admissions among the four high-volume hospitals. In Hospital A, approximately one out of every five admissions (21.0 percent) could be deemed questionable. This compares with Hospital F and Hospital H where the number of questionable admissions is closer to one in three. Conversely, Hospital E had only 14 questionable admissions, or only 2.1 percent of its admissions were considered questionable.

EXHIBIT 2
Corporation XYZ
Most Questionable Admissions

Diagnostic Category	MQAs	Percent of Total
Nervous system:	9	4.35
Nonsurgical cases	(9)	
Ear, nose and throat:	36	17.39
Nonsurgical cases	(15)	
Tonsillectomy, age 0–17	(10)	
Rhinoplasty	(4)	
Sinus and mastoid procedures	(7)	
Respiratory system:	10	4.83
Nonsurgical cases	(7)	
Laryngoscopy	(3)	
Circulatory system:	4	1.93
Nonsurgical cases	(4)	
Digestive system:	30	14.49
Nonsurgical cases	(26)	
Hernia procedures, age 0–17	(2)	
Proctosigmoidoscopy	(2)	
Musculoskeletal system:	8	3.86
Nonsurgical cases	(3)	
Soft tissue procedures	(2)	
Arthroscopy	(3)	
Skin, subcutaneous tissue and breast:	11	5.31
Nonsurgical cases	(6)	
Plastic procedures	(3)	
Skin grafts	(2)	
Kidney and urinary tract:	16	7.73
Nonsurgical cases	(16)	
Female reproductive system:	32	15.46
Nonsurgical cases	(7)	
D&C, conization and radio-implant	(16)	
Tubal interruption for nonmalignancy	(3)	
Laparoscopy and endoscopy	(6)	
Neoplasms:	13	6.28
Malignant, nonsurgical cases	(10)	
Benign, nonsurgical cases	(3)	
Other cases (in diagnostic categories with fewer than 10 MQAs)	38	18.35
Total	207	100.00

EXHIBIT 3
Corporation XYZ
Most Questionable Admissions by Hospital

		Admissions	
Hospital	Number	Most Questionable	Percent Questionable
A	558	117	21.0
F	51	15	29.4
E	650	14	2.1
H	172	61	35.5
Total	1,431	207	14.5

SELECTION OF PREFERRED PROVIDERS

The next challenge was to determine the effect on hospital efficiency of removing the MQAs. In this way, Corporation XYZ could identify the best hospital candidates for a preferred provider arrangement. To accomplish this, a new *performance index* had to be developed for each high-volume hospital. As in the previous analysis, the performance index was calculated by dividing total excess or unnecessary charges by total expected hospital charges. However, for the new index, cost efficiency was determined after having removed MQAs from each hospital's case mix. Thus, the expected charges on Exhibit 4 reflect

1. What would have been anticipated had each hospital admitted Corporation XYZ "patients" only when it was appropriate (i.e., medically justified).
2. What charges would have been anticipated for *appropriate* admissions had each hospital treated these patients according to the norm for the area after having adjusted for case mix.

EXHIBIT 4
Corporation XYZ
Hospital Performance
Adjusted for Most Questionable Admissions and Case Mix

Hospital	Admissions	Actual	Expected	Excess Charges	Performance Index
A	558	$1,322,294	$1,141,622	+180,672	+15.8
F	51	165,888	114,651	+ 51,237	+44.7
E	650	1,156,350	1,076,569	+ 79,781	+ 7.4
H	172	688,200	636,079	+ 52,121	+ 8.2

The removal of MQAs effectively modified each hospital's mix of patients (i.e., case mix) and therefore its efficiency level. It is conceivable that one or more of Corporation XYZ's high-volume hospitals went from being efficient to inefficient once MQAs were removed. This is because the efficient treatment of a large number of MQAs can mask the inefficient treatment of patients that are admitted appropriately to the hospital. (The reverse, of course, is also possible.) Therefore, the difference between the actual and the expected total charges shown in Exhibit 4 is a measure of each hospital's total excess or unnecessary charges after having adjusted for MQAs and case mix. The table clearly reveals that Hospital E now becomes the leading candidate for a preferred provider type arrangement. The table also strongly suggests that Hospital H may not be a suitable preferred provider candidate after adjusting for MQAs because its performance worsened. Further, the performance of Hospital F has considerably worsened; in fact, its performance index increased from 16.9 (unadjusted for MQAs, see Exhibit 1) to 44.7 (after having adjusted for MQAs, see Exhibit 4).

Despite the fact that Hospital E appears initially to be an excellent preferred provider candidate among the four high-volume hospitals, it is still having an adverse impact on Corporation XYZ's costs. In fact, as shown in Exhibit 4, this hospital accounted for $79,781 in excess charges despite the fact that overall it performed the "best" of the high-volume hospitals. (In our experience, preference is a relative thing; while one hospital may be performing in a clearly superior fashion compared to others, it does not mean its performance is ideal with no room for improvement.) Thus, Hospital E treated so many of Corporation XYZ's patients (650) that even marginally poor performance was translated into high excess charges.

CONTRIBUTION OF PERFORMANCE FACTORS TO EXCESS CHARGES

Since Hospital E appears initially to be the best candidate for a preferred provider type of arrangement, Corporation XYZ targeted this institution for a more in-depth analysis. In this way, Corporation XYZ hoped to assist Hospital E to further improve its performance. (Both parties had something to gain at this point by working together closely.) The analysis that follows illustrates the type of insight that can be gleaned by focusing on the factors contributing to Hospital E's excess charges.

$1,076,569 or 93.1 percent of Hospital E's total charges of $1,156,350 was attributable to volume (the 650 admissions). Therefore, the remaining $79,781, or 6.9 percent, represent the total excess charges for this hospital. The table below (Exhibit 5) indicates the relative contribution of inefficient operation and MQAs to these excess charges.

EXHIBIT 5
Contribution of Performance Factors to Excess Charges
Hospital E
Case-Mix Adjusted
Adjusted for MQAs

Total Excess Charges	*Amount Attributed to:*	
	MQAs	*Inefficiency*
$79,781	$80,002	−$221

The results of this analysis are clear: 100 percent of the excess charges were due to MQAs, or inappropriate admissions. Further, by removing the MQAs and, therefore, altering Hospital E's case mix, it became a more efficient institution. Had Hospital E admitted patients only when medically justified, the analysis reveals that it would have treated these patients approximately equal to the norm for the region.

However, the efficiency factor is simply an average of several other factors, which also are subject to analysis. (Further analysis is only worth undertaking at this point because Corporation XYZ—through greater insight—could achieve additional savings.) Hospital E may be keeping Corporation XYZ patients longer than expected (ALOS factor), or it may be charging Corporation XYZ more than expected for its room and board (R+B factor) and/or ancillary services (ancillary factor) compared to other hospitals treating the same type of patients (case mix). After adjusting for the types of patients treated in this hospital, it was possible to analyze the contribution of these factors to Hospital E's efficiency.

The contribution to total excess charges (−$221) due to efficiency shown in the previous table is not distributed uniformly among the three efficiency factors (i.e., ALOS, R+B charges, and ancillary services charges) that contribute to the difference. For Corporation XYZ, the difference is primarily due to much greater than expected charges for ancillary services (see Exhibit 6).

In the future, it would be worthwhile to analyze the contribution of each of the various ancillary services for Corporation XYZ to total ancillary charges (e.g., operating room, lab, X ray, drugs).

From the analysis, it appears that initially Hospital E is not only the best *candidate* for a preferred provider type of arrangement, but also is a good candidate for direct medical intervention (i.e., initiatives aimed at altering existing modes of practice) for several clearly documented reasons:

1. It is admitting a large number of Corporation XYZ's patients (650).

EXHIBIT 6
Corporation XYZ
Contribution of Efficiency Factors
Hospital E
Adjusted for Case Mix and MQAs

Efficiency Factor	Difference from Expected
ALOS	−$ 5,242
R+B charges	− 6,411
Ancillary charges	11,432
Total	−$ 221

2. It is having a large impact on Corporation XYZ's costs ($79,781).
3. This adverse impact is due to admissions that are highly questionable, that is, medically unjustified (2.1 percent).
4. Ancillary service charges are much greater than expected given the unique types of patients being treated ($11,432).

Finally, it is interesting to note that Corporation XYZ did negotiate a "preferred" contract with Hospital E, and thus far (nine months), the arrangement has worked well for both parties. In addition, Hospital E has established preadmission and ancillary service review procedures for Corporation XYZ patients. Moreover, Corporation XYZ, through its database, continually monitors Hospital E's performance and provides feedback to the hospital on a periodic basis.

A final word of caution: the method described in this article for identifying "preferred providers" should only be used as a general guide. The method is restricted to the consideration of cost efficiency and the appropriateness or medical necessity of admissions. Other factors such as geographic accessibility, scope of services provided, and quality of care are also important. (All these factors were considered by Corporation XYZ before finally selecting Hospital E.) Nevertheless, the method does provide initially a convenient way of combining a considerable amount of hospital utilization and cost data into a relatively simple format for evaluating hospital performance overall. This method can be a valuable starting point in the selection of "preferred providers" and has led to successful arrangements in a number of different medical communities.

NOTES

1. Unless some basic data items are available in an area, either from hospitals or from insurance companies, a detailed analysis cannot be performed. These basic elements include medical diagnostic and procedural information, age and sex of the patient, hospital

charges, and provider identification. In addition, the size of the employee base must also be considered. A minimum of 1000 employees in nonmetropolitan and smaller cities (100,000 population or less) is desirable; many more employees are required in large cities, but this depends on the size of the city and the number of providers in the area.

2. R. B. Fetter, Y. Shin, J. L. Freeman, R. F. Averill, and J. D. Thompson, "Case Mix Definition by Diagnosis-Related Groups," *Medical Care,* 18, no. 2, Supplement, (February 1980), pp. 1–53.

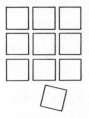

Purchaser Objectives and Priorities

TODAY'S MEDICINE BUYER: A CHANGE FROM THE LAST TO KNOW AND THE FIRST TO PAY

Robert D. Finney, Ph.D.*

Manager, Health Care Cost Containment
Hewlett-Packard Company
Palo Alto, CA

☐ In business transactions, businesses define their interests and actively seek their accomplishment. Each party to a transaction wants and pursues value in balancing quality and economy. An exception to this principle has been in payment for health care. In the health care field, providers (physicians, hospitals, and others) have dictated needs and prices, insurers have passed them along after making their own profits, companies have paid, and consumers have demanded both more and better services from all parties. The word "business" in the medical context has been decried. Good medicine and economical business practices have been portrayed as opposites. To practice good medicine has been to ignore economy and unconditionally to praise "quality."

*I want to acknowledge the contributions that my wife, Jackie, made to this paper.

Rationally, however, cost and quality are two sides of the same coin. Cost management is not antithetical to quality. Superior management will both improve quality and effect a reduction in high cost trends, as in every business.

Wise buyers and wise medical practitioners understand both the business and professional sides of medicine and agree that skyrocketing health care costs are unacceptable, although for different reasons. These buyers and providers of health care know that the treasuries funding health are being depleted and that actions to control this situation are unpleasant to most parties. Everyone, however, knows that the results of these actions can benefit those who effectively respond to the problems.

One thing is certain, the days of business being a "payor" are over. Business is today becoming a "buyer" of health services. Payors pay. Buyers shop and seek value.

BUSINESS-SPONSORED PPOs— A RECOMMENDATION FOR BETTER DECISION MAKING

A PPO sponsored by business is one mechanism to challenge long-standing power relationships, system resource allocations, and cultural expectations. It is capable of reversing 30-plus years of unquestioned giving, of putting providers of health care at risk, and through competition, of creating an environment that will produce deserved winners and losers in addition to more knowledgeable consumers. Thus, a PPO is one remedy for the acknowledged failure of the medical marketplace.

During the spring of 1984, a PPO began functioning in Santa Clara County, commonly referred to as "Silicon Valley." This alternative delivery system was developed because of the needs of the Hewlett-Packard Company and its employees and through the mutual efforts of the Company, its third-party administrator, one hospital, and one physicians' group comprised of about 300 multispeciality members.

Sponsorship here refers to a joint venture in which the buyer participates actively with providers from feasibility planning into operational and through evaluation stages to meet its own unique needs. The focus is on hospitals and broad-based physician groups being major provider parties, although the model does not exclude other providers of health care. The reasons for excluding a broker or "middleman" between the company and the providers are to have more control over the program and more incentives to allocate among the sponsors.

Each party to the negotiations retains its autonomy and independence in determining what it will contribute and on what basis. Thus, while the process is collaborative, it is also on an arms length basis. In this process, the buyer disclaims any liability for the practice of medicine.

Sponsorship may be undertaken by one company only or through a business coalition. Variations on sponsorship exist in San Diego, Cleveland, and southern Florida. For the buyer considering sponsorship of a PPO, an initial requirement is to include problem solvers and to exclude problem makers from the negotiations. This approach tends to convert troublemakers into troubleshooters.

This article is not a case study. Rather, it proposes conceptual and practical issues that a buyer, who wishes to optimize the rewards that such a system of care could generate, may find relevant. What is presented is not an end product but rather a beginning. Experience has demonstrated that it is not unusual to consume hundreds of hours and involve many talents between the time of developing a valid concept and agreeing to finely tuned contracts. The reader should note that concepts that are reiterated throughout this paper are addressed in different contexts to illustrate their interrelationship and linkage in the PPO.

DRAWBACKS TO SPONSORSHIP

Sponsorship does not progress along a predictable critical path. It is not orderly. It requires diplomacy, patience, determination, and the dedication of resources. While the program hopefully is "simple" in design and operation, the development process to form the program is complex. A simple process produced by simple participants will likely result in simple, but costly failure. However, "practice makes perfect," and the buyer will become conversant with the issues that will lead to greater mastery over health policy, delivery, and financing problems.

DEFINITION OF THE BUSINESS-SPONSORED PPO

Writings about PPOs have increased geometrically over the past three years. One of the first and most widely quoted came from InterStudy in 1981. Currently, there exist numerous survey articles designed to educate constituencies, stacks of legal documents prepared to protect clients, some "how to" approaches, position papers, and other sundry expositions with a wide swing between pro and con positions. Major business periodicals contain articles on PPOs. PPO conferences are in fashion. Again, the proof is in the results produced, that is, in making concepts operational.

In California, the location of the largest operational PPO, the state medicaid (Medi-Cal) program, there exists no statutory definition. However, the state's actions are a de facto definition. Recognition should be given to the government's leadership, at the federal (medicare) and state levels. Both are acting to control health costs, although the thrust of some of government's actions is repugnant to many in the provider community as its past virtually unlimited, unchallenged authority and freedom to operate is curtailed. This is one area that business is learning from government. So often, the opposite is true. Providers are learning that the PPO methods are more benign, though not less results oriented, than regulatory government control.

Unlike HMOs, the PPO has eluded legal definition. This is not bad in that it provides latitude for creative thinking and different approaches to the central PPO theme, i.e., contracting for health services.

Instead of reiterating the common features of PPOs that are found pro forma in the literature, below are summarized ideas that can help formulate operational programs.

— A PPO should be an alternative delivery system, not "discount medicine" as some detractors insist that it is.

— A PPO is a method to promote competition in the health care marketplace. This marketplace defies the economist's definition of "market." It tests the extent to which the "market" can regulate price and product. It is a "free market" approach as compared to regulatory approach, with all the flexibility and risk that this approach implies.

— A PPO is a set of quid pro quos that together create a strong set of incentives and responsibilities for all parties.

— A PPO is an opportunity for proactive players to manage change in health care. It is a specific market strategy that providers of care can use to adapt to revolutionary change in their field.

— A PPO is a hybrid between traditional fee-for-service and HMOs.

— A PPO is a method of restructuring risks and rewards in a system that has traditionally provided high financial and status rewards to providers of care.

— A PPO is a method of avoiding costly hospital admissions, a principle on which HMOs are based. It is a method of attempting to avoid the most expensive care while also providing appropriate and quality services.

— A PPO is an initiative that will have to survive on a long-term basis to qualify as part of the solution to health costs. Otherwise, PPOs will be catalysts to produce other approaches. The benefits of a catalyst to produce desired change cannot be denied and are valuable in themselves.

With these thoughts in mind, on what basis would a buyer be willing to become a participant, a sponsor of a joint venture?

PREREQUISITES TO BUSINESS SPONSORSHIP

Evaluation of the prospects for PPO success is the first step. Prerequisite conditions are the focus of this evaluation. The following conditions are prerequisites to business sponsorship, though not an exhaustive listing.

MANAGEMENT SUPPORT

This ingredient is the basis for getting anything accomplished. Without this commitment, look elsewhere than the PPO for solutions to rising health care costs. Remember that management controls resources, and a PPO requires a portion of those resources in order to achieve savings over and above the resources it requires to function in itself.

FAVORABLE ENVIRONMENT

The environment should contain many of the following elements:

1. *A health delivery system with multiple providers having broad geographic coverage.* Employees should have as many choices as feasible, as their personal perceptions of convenience and quality will affect their willingness to participate in a PPO.

2. *Leadership and business acumen in the provider community.* Health care providers are experiencing a permanent upheaval from their past ways of operating, because they have failed to recognize and/or have ignored important considerations. They must be in the vocal vanguard, actively expressing their knowledge and support for efficiently delivered health care.

3. *Low hospital occupany rates.* When hospital occupancy rates are low, the hospital is deprived of revenue it needs to operate and, ultimately, to survive. Raising prices to compensate for low volume is a practice now challenged by buyers. This situation creates hospital administrators hungry for more volume, i.e., increased revenue.

4. *Reduced inpatient utilization.* The medical literature has shown that a substantial amount of medical care can be provided just as effectively and much more efficiently on an outpatient basis. Buyers must insist upon and reward efficiency in the use of such appropriate types of facilities and treatment modalities.

5. *High variation in hospital and physician charges.* Such variation gives the buyer the opportunity to select providers of care that deliver identical quality services at better prices. In health care, the buyer must realize that a direct correlation between high price and high quality is nonexistent. In fact, in too many cases, the opposite is true, which is a well-known fact in the medical world.

6. *High physician to population ratio.* "Surplus" physicians create a buyer's market. As stated in the section about low hospital occupancy rates, a high ratio of physicians to population, given present and future treatment modalities, cost-effective technologic innovation, and buyer cost consciousness, tends to deprive physicians of revenue. Harsh economic reality will facilitate the physician's desire to accommodate his/her customers.

7. *A concentrated employee work force experienced with alternative delivery systems.* A concentration of employees coupled with their collective experience with alternative delivery systems (e.g., health maintenance organizations) facilitates "buying power" and the demand for innovative, cost-efficient alternative delivery systems as long as quality care is achieved. For purposes of this article, the term "employee" refers to both employees and their dependents. Knowledgeable employees are flexible in accepting nontraditional approaches to health care as long as the incentives in each approach are fully explained and are attractive.

8. *Buyers mobilized for action provide an ideal climate for exploring PPO feasibility.* To maintain value, companies have identified and controlled cost centers. Health care benefits are a significant cost center for business. When examined, this cost center should be targeted for better management. PPOs are one manifestation of businesses' initiative to control costs.

QUALIFIED PROVIDERS

The buyer is seeking cost-effective providers who deliver a comprehensive range of quality services. In the absence of information a buyer may have to evaluate providers. Opting for a "request for proposal" (RFP) approach has the advantage of systematically asking area providers (hospitals and associated physician groups) to respond to buyer information needs based on a standard set of criteria. This approach attempts to minimize subjectivity while affording the buyer a valid, reliable evaluation tool to determine the benefits of contracting with specific parties.

DATA/DATA SYSTEMS

Historically, data have been the "missing link" in the process, and no one cared. Purchasers, insurers, providers, and consumers, year in and year out, made decisions on "gut feeling" that eventually contributed to creating a cost problem that threatens the financial viability of some businesses and the well-being of their employees. Economists state that the Medicare Trust Fund is currently going bankrupt and is headed for a several hundred billion dollar deficit during the 1990s.

The buyer should require that his sponsorship of a PPO be both information (factually) and data (analytically) driven. Information and data are essential to establish management confidence in and support of the PPO, in addition to expanding initial management confidence, support, and interest in generating further innovation in health care cost management.

Health information sources include claims data, state data collected on all hospitals, data from hospitals themselves, data from Health Systems Agencies (HSA), data from Professional Review Organizations (PRO) for medicare beneficiaries, and private review organizations that a purchaser may be using. In the future, different PPOs may share data bases in order to provide greater precision and overall analysis that can work to the PPO improvement of each data contributor.

These data make possible analyses of intra-regional hospital performance, comparisons of physicians' performance by groups in and out of a PPO, the linking of physician and hospital charges to obtain complete case costs and other pertinent studies.

The "trust me" approach espoused by providers in the past is incompatible with business PPO sponsorship. Businesses will require facts in addition to well-documented assurances.

CLAIMS ADMINISTRATION

The claims administrator is a key participant. With the modified indemnity benefit provisions of the PPO, the administrator must be able to manage the new program. Ideally, the role will go beyond this to being a partnership, although business must remain the "buyer" in this area also. A good administrator can be a source of creative thinking as well as a party with whom to work through problematic issues. The administrator also stands to learn from the experience and thus adds to his own capabilities and market share. Claims administrators stand to gain financially, as they are used to help manage PPO claims and other possible activities such as aspects of utilization review.

PROJECT MANAGEMENT

Taking an objective from intent to operation requires project management capabilities. The buyer must assess the abilities of each participant to carry out its purpose in the project. Further, the personalities must form a productive working relationship. All participants in the process have their own goals and expectations from the PPO. Since they must function cooperatively for the PPO to succeed, the project must satisfy their individual motives and interests, in addition to achieving the objectives of the PPO.

Assuming a buyer's prerequisites are met, reasons for businesses to undertake sponsorship must be assessed.

BUYER RATIONALE FOR PPO SPONSORSHIP

For many years, accountability for unacceptably high health care costs was attempted through "finger pointing" by payors, insurers, physicians, hospitals, government, teaching institutions, and consumers. This has changed considerably with more appreciation by all that each party has played a part in creating the cost problem. This enlightened understanding is leading to a revised view of what the advantages of PPO sponsorship can be to the buyer. Cooperation and accommodation are preferable to conflict in problem resolution. It is vital to remember that business disclaims any intent to practice medicine and, therefore, cannot function independently of providers in managing costs.

BETTER MANAGED HEALTH SYSTEM

The sponsor wants to assure the well-being of employees and needs the means to do so. To do this, an "informative rich" system is required where the data are analyzed to ask and answer questions, make suggestions, gain insight, and be a catalyst in system evolution. Provisions can be built in, such as cost caps, to predict future costs. The buyer can play a central role in the design of the utilization management, usually referred to as utilization review. Control of referrals can be accomplished. Many of the proven cost-control mechanisms that characterize HMOs can be used, outpatient surgery being one. These are only examples.

One of the criticisms of PPOs is that they are unregulated. In a buyer-sponsored PPO, the buyer can be demanding regarding the standards of performance and safeguards. Government regulations are often spawned from free market abuse. Regulations, however, are less vital to the extent the system can and will police itself.

SHORT-TERM AND LONG-TERM SAVINGS

The use of discounts, as well as the use of cost-effective providers will yield immediate short-term savings. Long-term savings will result from superior management and continued innovation to maintain cost effectiveness. Discounts are not the answer, although they are a prominent part of the current PPO thinking.

To seek or not to seek discounts has both business and policy implications. Arguments against discounts include the potential cost shifting to other buyers/payors, their "one time only" effect, and not knowing what the discount really means. Arguments for discounts include the fact that they are one way of decreasing charges to the buyer and that using the clout of a buyer to get better prices is a common business practice.

KNOWLEDGE OF SYSTEM OPERATIONS

Buyer knowledge is power. One way to obtain knowledge is for the PPO sponsor to seek involvement in the information production process. Engagement in system development and operation strips away much of the mystique that characterizes the health care system. This knowledge about the PPO can be used for many purposes including employee education, benefits redesign, and program evaluation. It also increases the intangible factor of buyer confidence when interacting with providers. A provider that excludes a buyer from first-hand knowledge of its operations may have something to hide and should either be avoided or be required to provide buyer information requirements that can be verified.

EMPLOYEE RELATIONS

The PPO is an attractive health care option. It can provide convenience, as well as financial and programmatic incentives. Freedom of choice exists, accessibility to a broad range of providers is preserved, and the employee is protected from financial risk. The program must serve the needs of the consumer, or the PPO will fail.

RISK MANAGEMENT

A PPO is a microcosm of the larger health care system. Today's buyers are considering many options to manage costs. The PPO provides the opportunity to introduce change on a limited basis and thus contain possible adverse effects. From this vantage point, the PPO becomes a laboratory in which the buyer can test cost management approaches with minimized risk. Further, the buyer can view the program itself as an experiment and therefore not be committed to it over a long period if it does not produce expected results. However, the buyer should plan to make a long-term commitment to the PPO due to such factors as stability, cost, morale, and community relations.

If the prerequisite elements are met and the projected benefits meet the buyer's objectives, both a structure and process for the PPO must be devised. While conceptual design may be viewed as academic, flawed conceptual design has been identified as a major factor leading to unsatisfactory results in any undertaking. Without proper attention to structure and process, the "flexibility" advantage to the PPO could readily be its downfall, because it lacks necessary management direction and control.

WHAT THE BUYER SHOULD EXPECT

Two dimensions of design are to identify (1) critical result areas or objectives and (2) the methods to achieve them. Four examples of objectives and means to reach them are discussed below.

REDUCE HEALTHCARE UNIT PRICES

The "quick fix" is the discount, and more PPOs are seeking them than not. The meaning of discounts must be scrutinized. One provider offered a six percent discount with a promise of more depending on volume of patients delivered. Upon further questioning, the administrator conceded that his prices had been increasing at 25 percent per year for several years. The six percent was negligible in the context of this economic circumstance.

Policy and business sense will dictate whether to seek discounts. For example, some major businesses in Arizona have chosen a regulatory route to cost management, one reason being their concern about how discounts could shift costs to others. A buyer could, from a business perspective, seek discounts selectively. For example, if data analysis demonstrated that one hospital stood apart from a group of peers having significantly lower prices while maintaining the same high quality, the buyer might accept those prices (e.g., per diems), recognizing that he is hopefully buying superior management reflected in the lower prices. To the extent that program incentives bring more employees to that hospital, and away from higher cost hospitals, the buyer will realize a savings.

If the buyer found another hospital that appeared to be a quality prospect, but prices were unacceptably high, a discount, in the form of reduced prices, could be considered.

Other approaches to reduce unit prices would be to negotiate limitations on future price increases (caps) and insist on cost-effective delivery approaches such as ambulatory surgery, the use of generic drugs, and the elimination of the emergency room as a general purpose clinic.

From the physician side, a negotiated fee schedule is a common approach to manage price. The method of calculating fees and the reasonableness of those fees relate to significant cost centers that must be controlled as part of the PPO system. Probably the most important aspect of reducing unit prices from the physician side is for physicians to recognize and practice the art and science of total case management, not medicine, at any cost. That is, the physician must note the cost of every element in a case and control it wherever possible.

ELIMINATE UNNECESSARY UTILIZATION OF HEALTHCARE SERVICES

There are wide variations nationally in costly inpatient utilization for the same diagnosis and treatment. Hospital-based care, being the most expensive, is the prime target for cost management especially given the fact that frequently the same quality health care can be provided outside the inpatient setting. A major tool to manage hospital costs is utilization review (UR). Utilization review has been defined as a process whereby the medical necessity and quality of services are evaluated for the purpose of ensuring medical necessity, appropriate level of care, and professionally recognized standards for quality of care. Based on selected Hewlett-Packard data comparisons, where UR was present in HMOs used by the company and not present under the standard indemnity plan, over a 25 percent difference existed in length of patient stay in the same hospital.

Although the data were not adjusted for case mix, the implication is clear. Utilization review should be negotiated before any PPO arrangement is implemented.

To illustrate the importance of selecting UR organizations, a consultant, whose expertise is UR, was recently retained by a large private buyer to evaluate the actual review decisions made by six well-established, large-volume UR contractors. Four of the six review companies served clients nationwide and two served clients in specific geographical regions.

The consultant used a method in which the review contractor's justifications for approving hospital admissions for payment were evaluated by an independent physician reviewer. The independent reviewer assessed whether or not the reasons which the UR contractor cited for approving the patient admission fully documented the need for hospitalization. In the case of the strongest contractor, 80 percent of the UR contractor's reasons for approving hospital admissions were judged fully adequate. In the case of the weakest performing UR contractor only five percent of the reasons were judged fully adequate.

These findings dramatically show that the uncritical buyer of utilization-review services risks purchasing utilization review in name only. Not only does this represent a loss of opportunity to gain the quality and cost benefits of UR, the buyer may also pay more for the review itself than is yielded in utilization savings. Buyers should get references from UR contractors and evaluate them carefully.

Other methods of controlling unnecessary utilization include choosing cost-conscious physicians for participation in the PPO and providing financial incentives to physicians for doing a superior job of being efficient. Patients can also be rewarded for efficiency and should be educated to demand quality, economical care as part of their treatment process.

IMPROVE THE QUALITY OF CARE

Assuring quality of care is a significant element of cost management. Quality of care will be fostered by selecting quality hospitals and physicians. Utilization review should positively affect quality. Experts have determined the difficulty of measuring quality. Nonetheless, there are quantitative as well as qualitative criteria correlated to quality. Indicators include outcomes of cases treated, status of referrals, change in services, medical staff demographics such as education and age, infection rates, mortality rates, age of medical equipment, diagnostic errors, malpractice suits, and down time of medical devices.

Providers can assess quality and explain its meaning to each other, and they can explain this concept in nonprofessional language to buyers, patients, and the general public. This explanation is an aspect of successful consumer marketing of the PPO.

Another dimension of quality is the "quality of caring." This is an intangible element that is nonetheless real. It refers to a humanistic approach to deliver care that addresses a patient's mental distress including uncertainties associated with a strange environment, and replaces them with positive values such as confidence and a sense of well-being. Quality of caring overcomes an otherwise mechanistic, "high-tech" environment that may put more emphasis on efficient processing of the patient than on a balance between efficiency and a protective, attentive, conscientious, and humane approach. Buyers should require this and eliminate providers from the PPO who take an "assembly line" approach to their patients.

REWARD EMPLOYEES WHO USE THE PPO

Waiving health plan coinsurance and deductibles is common. The buyer wants to create a benefits package of incentives to motivate employees to use the PPO. One suggestion is to reduce out of pocket expenses, but not to eliminate them. Even programs that provide special features to patients should not be "free," because this reinforces the insulation from actual costs that insurance has perpetuated for years. Employees must be educated that health care is not free, even if they do not pay a cent out of pocket. A decreased overall benefits package, layoffs, and actual loss of jobs may be negative by-products of uncontrolled health care expense.

Other incentives can include reduced paperwork for the patient by insisting that providers complete claims forms. Acceptance of payment "assignment" on the part of providers is essential. This means that, except for any cost-sharing requirements, the patient will not be billed for anything over and above PPO reimbursement arrangements. Program features such as health promotion should be sought by the buyer to broaden the spectrum of incentives, thus increasing the appeal of the PPO to as many employees as possible. This strategy also increases consumer points of entry into the PPO, because the health promotion component can be used to educate employees to become better shoppers.

The objective is to reach employees' motivational threshold to use the PPO while maintaining a conservatism in the benefit structure. It is easier to increase incentives than to reduce or eliminate them, once in place.

These four objectives and the means discussed to achieve them can be viewed as a system of incentives and responsibilities, for all parties to the PPO (the quid pro quos referenced earlier).

A GRAPHIC DISPLAY OF PPO EXPECTATIONS

The distribution of incentives and responsibilities among program participants is depicted in Exhibit 1. It identifies five major participants and

EXHIBIT 1

Sample Program Elements	Buyer	Employee	Physician	Hospital	TPA
System "friendliness" (user ease)	R	I	R	R	R
Marketing	R/I	NA	R/I	R/I	NA
Reimbursement schedule	I	NA	R	NA	R
Utilization control	I	NA	R	R	R
Quality	I	I	R	R	R
Lower out of pocket cost	R	I	NA	NA	NA
Lower cost hospital	I	I	R	R	NA
Cost-effective services	I	I	R	R	NA
Low unit price	I	I	R	R	NA
One year contract	I	I	R	R	NA
Fee for service	R	NA	I	NA	NA
Minimum financial risk	I	I	I	I	NA
Increased volume	R	NA	I	I	NA
Product line diversification	NA	NA	I	I	NA
M.D. financial incentives	R	NA	I	NA	NA

NOTE: "I" stands for Incentive, "R" for Responsibility, and "NA" for Not Applicable.

indicates how they relate to program elements. Participants may vary. For example, if a buyer is self-administered for claims, the third-party administrator (TPA) or insurance company may be excluded.

This exhibit shows motives and actions to which all parties to the PPO must commit. Incentives and responsibilities hold parties accountable and can be modified in any renegotiation process. The PPO appeals to both direct and subtle motivations of all parties. As in any business transaction, it is each participant's estimate of the value that the program has personally for him/her that will be the deciding factor concerning any voluntary participation.

OTHER CONSIDERATIONS TO PPO SUCCESS

RISK ASSESSMENT

This factor must be analyzed over and above the prerequisite elements for business sponsorship discussed earlier. Questions of risk are more far ranging and include legal concerns such as antitrust, potential adverse publicity from a program that does not succeed, and other considerations that can be grouped under a category of factors leading to unsatisfactory results. Risk assessment applies to all participants. In the case of providers, the down side represents economic security, and they have every right to expect that potential risk is commensurate with potential reward. An example of a question a buyer should ask is what the relationship of risks to benefits is between directly participating in a business-sponsored PPO versus offering one through a third party such as an insurance company or provider.

REFERRAL CONTROL

Many HMOs and some PPOs use a primary care physician as a "gatekeeper." The purpose is first to treat the patient at the lowest cost-effective appropriate level of care and then, if necessary, refer the patient to a specialist. However it is approached, control over referrals inside and outside the PPO is necessary if the program is to succeed financially. Providers should understand the terms of referral and be held accountable for unnecessary costs generated by their referrals. The buyer should require a report from the physician group detailing information about referrals. This would include referrals both inside and outside the PPO.

EVALUATION

The PPO, as described here, is a substantial undertaking that is evolutionary. To encourage timely, productive change, evaluation must be ongoing. Buyers' integral position in the negotiations makes them more sensitive to the PPO's functioning. They should require reports on regular and periodic bases to maintain a current knowledge base and, thus, a strong bargaining position. This situation presents one strong argument favoring a buyer's sponsorship versus adopting an "off-the-shelf" PPO developed entirely by others. Employee satisfaction surveys also are an invaluable information source. As a generalization, evaluation should focus on PPO structure, process, and outcomes. If all responsibilities and incentives are valid and have been fulfilled, it is likely that the PPO will be successful.

Evaluation will be more difficult for a PPO as distinguished from an EPO, Exclusive Provider Organization. In the case of the PPO, the program operates as an option out of the buyer's indemnity plan, thus offering the plan participant the freedom of choice to use either a PPO provider or not. The EPO is a "defined plan" that the participant formally joins like an HMO, thus "locking in" the user. Because membership is exclusive in an EPO, it makes evaluation easier, because the total number of medical "transactions" of each member is recorded. Tracking employees who move in and out of the PPO option makes evaluation a significantly greater research challenge.

PPO VERSUS EPO

To reiterate, the EPO, through enrollment, "locks in" employees, because they must use it exclusively once they enroll. With "lock in" comes control. Clearly, providers want as much control as possible in these uncertain times. However, the EPO removes from the employee the unique market option of broader choice that exists with the PPO. If the buyer already offers an EPO option(s), including HMOs, the inherent diversity of choice of offering a PPO is attractive in a marketplace that has, as tradition, defied consumer choices.

Nonetheless, various rationales are given to support the EPO, including the evaluation argument. However, the buyer can create the lock-in effect and still use the PPO approach, first, through the choice of hospitals and, second, through incentives and penalties to employees. The loyalty of many patients can be gained and changed through benefit plan changes that alter incentives.

PROVIDERS AT RISK

Programs that place providers at an agreed upon risk will be the most successful from the buyer's perspective. Aside from any PPO considerations, research has suggested that moderate risk takers tend to be the highest achievers. Buyers should insist on a moderate degree of risk on the part of PPO providers, because risk motivates them to assume greater responsibility for the overall management of the care they deliver. Prospective reimbursement, caps on future prices, and financial incentives and disincentives tied to performance should be attempted. Structuring reasonable and timely risk into the PPO is one of the major challenges for the buyer. Further, providers should be cognizant that buyers and many consumers have almost always been at financial risk for health care charges.

ACCESSIBILITY

A buyer needs to provide the program to employees who work and reside in geographic specific locations to assure convenience. One option may mean a network of providers to achieve this easy accessibility. Another option may also involve other buyers linked in a network to use collective "clout" purchasing with providers to meet company and employee needs. The use of coalitions or other groups of buyers, such as trade groups, to insure acceptable employee access to care has been used. This approach still leaves any individual buyer the option to participate or not, but at the same time achieves a superior position for any buyer in negotiating with providers.

COST SHIFTING

This issue is important, because the PPO goal is cost management, not cost shifting. Nonetheless, PPOs have cost-shifting implications. It is even possible that a buyer using an EPO could have costs from those providers shifted back onto its own indemnity plan. Two protections against cost shifting are (1) to use a hospital that offers the same economies to all buyers and (2) to gather buyers, particularly smaller ones, under the protection of an organization that will represent their interests when contracting, while not violating antitrust considerations.

Medicare's prospective diagnostic-related group-based reimbursement system (DRG) is putting pressure on hospitals to cost shift to the private sector. Thus, private buyers have an additional powerful party forcing their costs up, because government has mandated cost control and competition with its volume purchasing clout.

CONTRACT REQUIREMENTS

It is preferable that the buyer's legal counsel draft contracts in conjunction with the administrative program development staff. The concentrated attention and thought of this process produces a high order of discipline that is a basic ingredient needed to frame a contract that balances the buyer's objectives with those of the provider. The contract(s) should address administrative elements as well as legal provisions. Contracts with physicians and hospitals may include provisions addressing the following areas: definitions, specifics of the offer, scope of covered services, obligation by the buyer to promote the program, reimbursement schedule payment, most favored customer adjustment, claims administration, utilization review, referral, medical records, nonexclusive relationship, eligibility, termination, liability and insurance, general provisions (e.g., assignment, modification, notices), admission practices, obligations of providers, inpatient-outpatient ambulatory surgical center and emergency reimbursement, special programs (e.g., health promotion), generic drugs, open staff, participant eligibility, and contract confidentiality.

One further issue is whether the buyer should play any management role in the PPO. The buyer, in this PPO definition, does not deliver medical services. Nonetheless, by virtue of the joint venture, role in marketing, administration of employee claims, data collection, and evaluation, there is a management role in the program for the buyer that is distinct from the practice of medicine and hospital administration. There must be communication among the parties that can occur without disturbing the integrity of the relationships. Buyers manage other business contracts, and there are good reasons why buyers would want to perform certain management functions as an ongoing part of the PPO program for which they pay.

RELATION TO BENEFITS PACKAGE

A PPO offering would be one part of a buyer's health package offered to its employees. The buyer could provide HMOs of different types in addition to an indemnity plan. Since a buyer's goal is to have employees seek the most cost-effective quality care, a consideration must be how PPO incentives would cause employees to choose one system over another and what the cost implications would be. This question should be considered in the evaluation of the PPO.

PAYMENT MECHANISMS

The way providers are paid will have effects on other parts of the system. The buyer should consider all apparent alternatives and also evaluate new ones.

One PPO reimbursement option that will probably make broader appearance in the future is the lump sum payment that covers all costs (physician, hospital, and others) attributed to patient treatment. This approach is particularly adapted to surgical procedures. This financial structuring provides strong incentives to the physician to practice case management from both health quality and cost perspectives, as he or she is placed at risk. If managing physicians do not hold total costs under a negotiated level, they lose part of what would otherwise be paid to them to other health care providers instead. Positive financial incentives should also be provided if total costs for the care are below the negotiated level. That is, the managing physician could use the opportunity to make a "profit."

Another payment mechanism is diagnostic related groups (DRGs) mentioned earlier. DRGs represent a sophisticated technique for hospital pricing which is available to the buyer. DRG-based payments for physician reimbursement are being considered in the medicare system. Although there are detractors of the DRG system, the advantages may outweigh the disadvantages. DRGs are one analytical tool the buyer should consider when determining payment proposals.

MARKETING

A marketing plan is a "must" component of the program. The buyer has a lead role in motivating employees to use the PPO, but physicians and hospitals can help and indeed profit by assuming part of the responsibility. Physicians, for example, can make brochures available in their offices, and nurses or other staff can take time to reinforce the program with patients. Marketing can also occur as part of the health promotion. Creation of volume will largely depend on a good program that is aggressively marketed to potential consumers. As a sign of both good faith and intent to market the program, the buyer should consider including this as part of the contract.

SPONSOR COMMUNICATION

This PPO approach is impossible to develop without productive communications and good working relationships among the participants. Both formal and informal communication must continue once the program is operational. At a minimum, once a month sessions should be required initially, perhaps quarterly thereafter, and ad hoc as necessary. This process also provides direct feedback required for evaluation and corrective action.

CONSULTANTS

Ironically, health cost management is a growth industry. This is true nowhere more than with consultants, including lawyers. A consultant can be helpful in the conceptualization of the PPO, serving as a sounding board, and providing advice in specialty areas such as utilization review.

However, one of the goals of the buyer who sponsors a PPO is to gain more mastery over health care costs. The buyer wants to become an equal with providers, recognizing the unique roles of each party. Therefore, the buyer wants consultants that are both teachers and technicians. In the case of PPOs, many consultants will not have the ability to serve the buyer with required professional expertise. It should be kept in mind that the consultants are learning themselves, as PPOs are a new concept, especially in the context of the buyer-sponsored approach. Buyers must constantly assure themselves that they are receiving the services for which they pay.

In sum, while consultants can be a valuable resource, the admonition *caveat emptor* should be closely regarded for the buyer's protection.

FROM THEORY TO PRACTICE

Insurers, hospitals, physicians, clinics, brokers, buyers, and others are sponsoring PPOs. Programs are significantly different in design, sophistication, acceptance, depth of resources, etc. For a buyer to sponsor a PPO, to offer a PPO developed by others, or not to offer a PPO are management decisions. Regardless, the buyer should not feel pushed to join the PPO movement. Rhetoric and "hype" must never substitute for substance and results, or the buyer and employees will be harmed.

Change is a constant in the health care system. It is also a hallmark of good business practice that constantly seeks to improve services to customers. Employees, in this case, should be regarded and treated as customers to satisfy through the PPO program.

PPOs purport to make the business sponsor among the first to know why and what he is buying. The success of PPOs is not the major issue. A substantial improvement in the economics of health care decision-making is. The point is that, if PPOs are unsuccessful, buyers can go on to other methods to manage health care costs. If successful, the buyer has incrementally added one more solution to unnecessary and unacceptably high health benefit costs, while assuring that the company's employees and their dependents receive nothing less than quality health care.

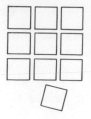

Purchaser Objectives and Priorities

HEALTHCARE BUYERS' APPROACH TO SELECTIVE CONTRACTING

Fred Rothenberg

Fred Rothenberg and Associates, Inc.
Woodland Hills, CA

☐ The PPO offers the purchaser of health care the opportunity to effectively address many of today's cost-containment issues. Just as important, it gives the seller of those services a chance to design an effective product that allows the capture of a larger share of the health care market. The degree to which the product succeeds in accomplishing these complementary goals depends on the purchaser's clear understanding of its needs and the success of the seller in meeting those needs.

It is the purpose of this article to identify the critical issues in PPO design and provide various alternative ways of addressing them.

The PPO can be

— Designed by the consumer of health care, usually one or more large employers who wish to develop a more cost-effective provider delivery system for their employees.
— Designed by an insurer or third-party administrator (TPA) who wants to develop a new product line to protect or capture additional market share.
— Designed by a group of providers, usually hospitals and physi-

cians, who want to jointly market their services directly to employers, insurers, and TPAs.

Each of these groups goes about its job in a different way. This article examines PPO design from the purchaser or ultimate payor's point of view, thus adhering to one of the cardinal rules of marketing. That rule is "always remember who the buyers are and design the product to suit their needs."

Therefore, this article will

1. Define a PPO: that definition contains essential points that differentiate a PPO from other health care delivery systems. Failure to adequately address each of these points will lessen the PPO's chances for success.
2. Examine the payor's objectives: there are eight categories of product requirements that every payor should be concerned about. Payor understanding of those product requirements, and the ways in which they can be satisfied, will lead to achieving its cost-containment objectives.

DEFINITION OF A PPO

Webster has not yet chosen to define the PPO. Perhaps he is waiting to see if it lasts. Nevertheless, a PPO can be described as:

> An organization of fee-for-service providers who have a contractual arrangement to provide health care services at a discount to a defined pool of patients who have free choice of provider but have an economic incentive to utilize PPO member providers.

There are several essential elements in that definition. Each element must be properly addressed.

Organization of providers. The delivery system can be either formed by providers, organized by a third party such as an insurance company, or developed by a self-insured employer. There are contractual and operational links between the providers and the organizing entity.

Fee for service. The provider's income is based on the units of service provided. The price of each unit of service is generally determined through negotiations between the provider and the payor. Unit prices may differ for the various purchasers of the PPO services.

Contracts. The development and negotiation of written agreements, specifying the terms of the relationships between the parties, consume much time and expense. Contracts can exist between:

— The PPO organizing entity and each of its providers.

— The PPO and the payor.
— The payor and each provider.

The contracts will normally contain provisions dealing with:

— The range of services to be provided.
— Compensation arrangements and prices.
— Utilization review procedures.
— Inspection of records.
— Insurance and general liability issues.
— Dispute resolution processes.
— Referrals to non-PPO providers.
— Termination, contract renewal, and price renegotiations.

Discount.   Not many buyers will be satisfied that the providers' normal price structures, regardless of how low they may be, are sufficient to guarantee a savings. Each hospital within the PPO may negotiate a different price for the same service. Discounts among the PPO hospitals in the same network will vary depending on their relative customary price structures and the negotiating skills of the parties. A payor will find it nearly impossible, however, to negotiate different prices with each of several hundred physicians in a PPO. Physicians in a given geographic area, therefore, normally receive the same price for the same service.

Defined pool of patients.   This defined pool consists of the subscribers, employees, or insureds who have enrolled in a special benefit program that directs them to the PPO providers. Examples of such distinctive programs are marketed by Blue Cross of California (Prudent Buyer), Blue Shield of California (Preferred Program), and Blue Cross of Virginia (Key Care).

Free choice.   In contrast to the health maintenance organization (HMO), PPO patients may use the services of any provider within the PPO network and receive full benefits. The patient may also use the services of a non-PPO provider; however, a significant additional payment by the patient will normally be required.

Economic incentive.   While the patient can use the services of non-PPO providers, it will be costly to do so. Increased deductibles and coinsurance are the usual penalities. The payor must agree to and the provider should insist on, a well designed set of penalties or financial incentives to keep the patient in the PPO network. These are the providers' "quid pro quo" for discounting and other contract concessions.

All the elements in the PPO definition must be carefully considered in the design phase. They are all interrelated and therefore should be continually reviewed as the PPO is being constructed. Various options are available to the designer. As with any other product, careful design will help avoid major alterations after the product is introduced.

PAYOR OBJECTIVES

Upon entering the PPO marketplace, there are eight major elements that a buyer must consider, set objectives for, and make decisions about. A summary of these eight are as follows:

Financial

— Required savings.
— Components of product cost.
— Hospital and physician rate structure.
— Cost of administration.

Provider Network

— Types of providers.
— Number of providers.

Benefit Programs

— Scope of benefits.
— Financial incentives.

Utilization Review

— Potential savings.
— Administration.
— Risks.

Operating Systems

— Modifications to existing systems.
— Implementation.

Marketing

— Clear product definition.
— Understanding the contracting process.
— Enrollment potential.

Program Evaluation

— Reporting systems.
— Monitoring provider performance.

Custom Design versus Established PPO

— Payor considerations.
— Overcoming payor concerns.

A more detailed examination of each of these areas occurs in the following paragraphs.

FINANCIAL OBJECTIVES

Required Savings

In order to market the PPO product, it must be priced lower than the purchaser's current fee-for-service benefit program. This cost savings is the purchaser's reward for dealing with a delivery system that has fewer providers and therefore less choice than in its present benefit program.

The cost savings must be large enough to compensate the ultimate payor, the employer, for the effort of moving employees from their present program to the more restrictive preferred product. The employer may encounter difficulty in making such a move, since employees will view the program as a reduction in their current benefit levels.

Generally, at least a 10 percent savings must be achievable. If it is not achievable, the changes required in moving to the new program will be viewed as not being worth the effort. There is nothing terribly scientific in identifying 10 percent as an appropriate differential. It is, however, a level commonly mentioned when pricing objectives are discussed. It, therefore, may have become a standard simply because enough people have talked about it.

The required savings may even be set at higher levels. This can occur when the employer, in order to convince the employee of the benefits of the PPO, decides to share the savings with the employees who join the PPO product. This sharing of savings can take the form of

— Reduction of current copayments and deductibles.
— Decreased employee payroll contributions.
— Increased or new benefits.

The employer must be certain that PPO savings are at least equal to the cost of any combination of the above three alternatives. To do otherwise would place the employer in the position of paying more for the PPO product than for the employer's standard fee-for-service program.

Insurers with several health product lines, including fee-for-service and HMO programs, may choose to subsidize one product line with the savings from another. For example, in order to maintain or improve the insurer's market position in the standard fee-for-service program, savings from the PPO product may be used to artificially reduce premium levels on the underwritten standard product. The reverse is also a possibility.

All of these considerations have an impact on the savings objective, and that objective will therefore vary by geographic area, competitive market conditions, and individual employer circumstances.

Components of Product Cost

Several components make up the total cost of the PPO product. These components must be identified by the payor and a target cost established for each. The aggregate of those individual components should then produce the total desired savings (e.g. 10 percent) relative to the payor's current benefit program.

These cost components are

— Hospital unit prices: These are the contracted rates of payment for hospital care. These can be either a (or several) price per day, price per case, or discount from billed charges.

— Physician unit prices: These are the contracted payment rates for physician services. They are the stipulated fees for specific services.

— Inpatient service volume: This is the payor's expectation concerning any change in historical hospital service volume due to utilization review programs, provider selection, or provider financial incentives.

— Outpatient service volume: This is the payor's expectation concerning the volume of outpatient services. Change in historical patterns can result because of reduced hospital lengths of stay or the substitution of outpatient care for what historically may have been a hospital admission.

— Emergency care in non-PPO hospitals: The patient's financial penalty for the use of a non-PPO hospital is normally waived if the admission is the result of an emergency. The cost of such care will usually be paid for at the non-PPO hospital's customary billed charges. Such charges will, on average, be higher than the contracted rates in PPO hospitals. The extent of emergency care in non-PPO hospitals will depend on the number of PPO hospitals and their geographic placement. This cost component is also directly related to the scope of service in the network. For example, the absence of cardiovascular surgery or neonatal intensive care in the PPO would cause the payor to pay billed charges for such services.

— Price "creep": Payors may be concerned about some providers attempting to offset price discounts through performing and billing for more complex services than were actually required. Examples could include physicians who inappropriately bill for complex procedure codes. Hospitals paid on a diagnosis-related group (DRG) payment system may inappropriately move patients into a more costly diagnostic category.

— Program administration: The payor will have both a significant developmental investment as well as relatively higher ongoing costs of administering the PPO program. These costs include the design, negotiation, and contracting with providers as well as alterations to existing payment systems. Relatively higher operational costs result from utilization review activities, maintenance and renewal of the contracting provider network, and an improved reporting system to monitor program results and provider performance.

All of these cost components should be examined in the aggregate to determine the potential level of PPO product price savings relative to current benefit programs. One example of such an aggregation is contained in Exhibit 1.

EXHIBIT 1
PPO Cost Components

	Component	Percent of Total Product Cost (a)	Percent Savings (added cost) Relative to Present Benefit Program	Percent Savings
A	Hospital unit price	55	18	9.90
B	Physician unit price	35	5	1.75
C	Inpatient service volume	55	10	5.50
D	Outpatient service volume	35	(4)	(1.40)
E	Emergency care	55	(3)	(1.65)
F	Price creep	90 (b)	(1)	(.90)
G	Program administration	10	(30)	(3.00)
			Net Savings	10.20%

(a) The example presumes:

55%	hospital care
35%	physician care
10%	administration
100%	Total

(b)

Hospital care	55%
Physician care	35%
	90%

Any number of component cost aggregations are possible. Each depends on the payor's present benefit program, the prices currently paid to providers, the potential for reduced utilization, and the number of providers who want to participate in the payor's program.

Hospital and Physician Rate Structure
The payor has four basic objectives in selecting the method of provider payment. They are

— Provide more financial certainty for the payor by fixing the payments at stipulated dollar amounts.

— Shift the risk of case mix variations to the provider by limiting the number of rates in the payment structure.
— Control the ability of the provider to manipulate the system in order to compensate for discounts.
— Minimize the number of operational changes to the payor's existing payment system by structuring the system as closely as possible to the payor's existing system.

The payor approaches these objectives armed with several alternatives. In the area of hospital payments, those alternatives include percentage discounts from the provider's normal charge structure, all-inclusive per-diem systems, and per-case payment systems.

Discounts from billed charges can provide a degree of savings for the payor. It may, however, not satisfy the objectives related to shifting the risk of case mix variation, additional financial certainty, or minimizing the provider's ability to manipulate the system.

Per-diem systems usually include daily room costs and ancillaries. These systems range from a single all-inclusive per diem regardless of diagnosis or level of service to multiple per diems that are dependent on case type or location of patient in the hospital. Separate per diems may be negotiated for cardiovascular surgery, neonatal intensive care, other intensive care, maternity, psychiatry, substance abuse, general medicine, and general surgery. The greater the number of per diems in the rate structure the less financial certainty for the payor. The trade-off for minimizing the number of per diems may be higher overall prices due to adverse case mix protection sought by the provider. Provider manipulation of the system may also occur through inappropriately extending the patient's length of stay. Effective utilization-control systems can help to minimize this concern.

Per-case payment structures as extensive as the 470 medicare diagnostic rates may do a good job of matching payment rates with the level of required service. The ability of the provider to manipulate per-case payment systems through "creative diagnostic coding" is an issue that is, however, of concern to some payors. The term "DRG Creep" has been coined to describe the movement of a case from one DRG to another in an effort to obtain a higher payment. That same case, prior to a DRG payment system, may have been classified in a less costly grouping. The level of financial certainty for the payor may, therefore, be lower than that provided by the per-diem system.

It is important that the payor have historical hospital payment data. That data should be in the form of the preferred method of payment to PPO hospitals. If the payor does not have per-case data that is segregated by diagnosis, entertaining such a system for the PPO is probably unwise. The DRG system also usually requires extensive modifications to the payor's existing payment system.

EXHIBIT 2
Alternative Hospital Payment Structures: Level of Attainment of Payor Objectives

	Financial Certainty	Shift Risk to Provider	Free from Manipulation	Minimize System Changes	Availability of Historical Data
Billed charges	Low	Low	Medium	High	High
Per diems	High	High	Medium	Medium	Medium
Per case	Medium	Medium	Medium	Low	Low

A chart summary of the attributes of each of the alternatives is contained in Exhibit 2.

The per-diem approach, based on Exhibit 2, would appear to offer the payor a system that most nearly attains its overall objectives. It is, however, one which places the provider under the most uncomfortable of circumstances. The ability of a per-diem system to survive long term, while at the same time maintaining the required discount levels, is therefore questionable. That question will be answered primarily by the degree to which the payor's population consistently uses the average service levels contemplated by the per-diem rate structure. Major variations in service levels from year to year will cause the provider either to seek a payment system that is more sensitive to case mix variations or to significantly increase prices.

Fewer options are available when addressing the issue of the physicians' payment structure. The payor has probably previously paid for physician services under either a usual, customary, and reasonable system (UCR) or an indemnity system with maximum stipulated benefit levels. In nearly all cases, except for those Blue Shield plans that may already have contracts with physicians, the patient has been responsible for that portion of the physician's billing in excess of the payor's UCR or stipulated indemnity. The PPO payor wants to negotiate a payment arrangement with the physician that stipulates the specific payment amount for each service and relieve the patient of any payment other than the usual copayments or deductibles.

The payor will require far more physicians than hospitals in the PPO network. Blue Cross of California has, for example, more than one hundred and fifty participating hospitals and nearly eleven thousand participating physicians in their PPO. It is possible to individually negotiate varying prices with a limited number of hospitals but almost impossible to individually negotiate prices with large numbers of physicians.

A UCR system is an option for the PPO; however, it does not provide the payor with the level of financial certainty that a stipulated fee system does. In contrast to the small number of per diems used in the hospital setting, the physician fee system normally assigns individual fees to every possible physician service. These individual services may number in the thousands, with each represented by an assigned service code.

The payor can either assign a price to each procedure or, as is more customary, use one of several relative value systems (RVS). Examples of such systems include the California Relative Value Studies and the Mountain Medical Relative Value System developed in Colorado. Under the RVS, the payor needs only to establish "conversion factors" or a price per relative value unit for each major category of physician services. Those major categories are generally five in number: medicine, surgery, radiology, anesthesiology, pathology.

The conversion factors are multiplied by the number of relative value units for each procedure to establish the fee for each procedure. An example of this process is contained in Exhibit 3.

EXHIBIT 3
Use of Relative Value Systems to Establish Fees for Physician Services (California Relative Value Studies—1974)

Code	Service Type	Relative Value Units	Conversion Factor for Major Category	Fee
90000	Brief evaluation, new patient	5.9	$ 6.50	$ 38.35
44900	Appendectomy	5.8	150.00	870.00
44900–30	Anesthesia during appendectomy, 2 hours	9.0	35.00	315.00
72010	X ray of spine	27.0	12.00	324.00
86068	Blood, crossmatch	40.0	1.50	60.00

In establishing stipulated fees or conversion factors, the payor must normally set them at a level that will not cause a higher payment in the aggregate than what would have occurred under the payor's present system. The fees must be set so that they are reflective only of the payor's expenditures. They should not include any patient payments that were in excess of the payor's UCR or indemnity allowances. The PPO physician fees are an average of the payor's historical physician payments trended, as appropriate, for inflation. Exhibit 4 demonstrates this process.

Exhibit 4 shows that the average payment level is $37 even though the UCR limit is $40. If the payor establishes $37 as the PPO fee for that procedure, the payor's total payments will not exceed what would have been paid under the existing system. It should also be noted that three of the five physicians in the example will view the proposed fee as being too low while two of the five will be satisfied with it. The degree to which

EXHIBIT 4
Establishing a PPO Physician Fee Schedule
Procedure #90000 (brief evaluation, new patient)

	Billing No.	Historical Billed Charge	Maximum Historical UCR Level	Payor Payment
	1	$ 50	$ 40	$ 40
	2	45	40	40
	3	40	40	40
	4	35	40	35
	5	30	40	30
Totals	5	$200	$200	$185
Average		$ 40	$ 40	$ 37

the payor's prior payment system matched physician billed charges and the willingness of the payor to forego any savings attributable to PPO physician unit prices will, in large measure, determine the number of physicians who are willing to join the PPO program.

As was previously noted, fee negotiations with individual physicians usually is not a practical alternative. Much care needs to be exercised, therefore, in setting these fees so as to obtain good physician response to the payor's contracting overtures. The success of the PPO program is, to a major degree, contingent on the number, range of specialties, and quality of the contracting physicians. Extraordinary attempts to save money by severely restricting physician fees is somewhat shortsighted. The physicians can engage in "RVS creep" much like the hospitals can engage in "DRG creep." Additionally, the physician's active involvement in hospital utilization control is more important than the relatively small savings available from physician price discounts.

Cost of Administration

The cost of developing and operating a PPO program is higher than for a standard fee-for-service benefit program. Development costs include

— Product design and planning.
— Development of provider contracts.
— Development of utilization-review program.
— Establishment of provider network.
— Employee benefit description and certificates.
— Revision of existing claims payment systems.
— Design of reports that monitor the program after implementation.

The expertise needed to complete the development may be higher than that customarily employed by the payor in employee benefit activities. While the development time schedule is to some degree a function of the number of people on the development team, the process will normally require at least a six-month period. Much of the time will be devoted to program design (and redesign), as well as the provider contracting process.

Following the development stage, the payor will continue to experience higher PPO operating costs than in the previous benefit program. These additional costs will result from

— Utilization-review activities.
— Provider contract renegotiation.
— Monitoring the provider network.

The utilization review component alone may increase the cost of program administration by fifteen percent or more. It is hoped that this additional cost will be more than offset by reductions in service utilization.

Payors are generally disproportionately concerned about increases in the cost of administering benefit programs. Perhaps it is easier for the payor to distinguish and quantify changes in the cost of administration than it is to determine the real reasons for changes in benefit costs. As a result, they pay close attention to the differences in administration charges among competing insurers and TPAs. One way of minimizing the administration charges for the PPO product is for the insurer or TPA to recover these charges by sharing in the program benefit cost savings achieved by the insured group.

PROVIDER NETWORK

Types of Providers

The payor's emphasis is on the reduction of inpatient services and costs. However, its sophistication in creating a network is highest in dealing with hospitals and physicians. They have moved slowly in contracting with home health agencies, skilled nursing facilities, and outpatient surgical centers. This is perhaps attributable to the relatively low level of such benefits provided for in the payor's current benefit programs. These other agencies offer real alternatives to acute hospital care and, therefore, can be expected to become part of the payor's long-term provider network design.

In addition to including these alternative providers, the payor is likely to begin experimenting with financial incentives that promote the use of these providers. Such an incentive system was developed by the Community Care Network of San Diego. That PPO designed acute hospital admission and length of stay targets for network primary care physicians. Savings attributable to decreased hospital utilization are to be shared among the participating physicians.

The inclusion of alternative providers in the PPO and the development of incentive systems will tend to reduce the quantity of service required of the acute hospital. It will also tend to make the level of care provided to PPO inpatients more intensive due to a greater proportion of PPO enrollees receiving service on an outpatient basis or being discharged earlier from the hospital. Unit costs per patient day for hospital care are therefore likely to increase for the PPO patient population while the total cost of PPO care declines.

PPOs will begin to include such medical specialties as psychologists, physical therapists, chiropractors, and podiatrists. The enrollee's current benefit program normally includes such services. Since contract physicians have agreed not to bill the PPO patient for charges in excess of the contract rates, the patient is likely to avoid any provider, such as a psychologist, without a PPO contract. Discriminatory practices may then be leveled at the payor by the psychologist.

Number of Providers

There is a conflict between having the largest number of providers in the PPO so as to offer the prospective enrollees the widest choice and limiting the number of providers to offer hospitals and doctors a relative degree of exclusivity in return for discounted prices. Some payors appear to understand the provider's need for exclusivity and have designed their programs accordingly. Awareness by the potential contracting provider of the payor's desire to establish exclusivity will also result in more favorable pricing proposals.

Payors that have adequate payment data bases can review them to identify which providers currently serve the bulk of their enrollees. The payor can then set out to contract with those providers. Normally, large, full-service hospitals have served the bulk of the payor's patients. These hospitals also tend to have the highest average charges and costs.

When PPO networks for payors were first developed, the assumption was that it would be difficult, if not impossible, to design a hospital network that included large, full-scope, tertiary care providers while at the same time achieving the required cost savings. That was not the case. The payor can build a provider network that consists of attractive providers at a level of savings commensurate with its needs.

It is somewhat more difficult to limit the number of participating PPO physicians. Generally, the PPO will accept as many physicians as are willing to participate. In its initial stages, the PPO may not be attractive to a majority of eligible physicians. Many physicians may avoid the PPO due to fixed, and generally reduced, payment levels as well as stringent utilization-review requirements. Any who wish to join are usually welcomed.

A limitation on participation in the PPO can be accomplished by requiring PPO physicians to be on the staff of the PPO hospitals. The payor is wise to make this a condition of physician participation. Linkage between hospital and physician is required with regard to the utilization-review process. The participating physician also must be able to admit patients to the participating hospital. The payor should therefore either design the PPO or examine existing PPOs with this linkage in mind.

As the PPO matures, further restrictions on physician membership may evolve. An examination of individual practice patterns may become a determining factor for both the physician's initial entry as well as continued PPO participation.

BENEFIT PROGRAMS

Scope of Benefits

The payor, such as a large employer group, will probably want to keep its present scope of benefits relatively intact even if moving to a PPO program. Improvement in benefit levels may be desirable, however, in order to offset the employees' perception of limited choice of provider in the PPO. The employee is likely to associate that limited choice with a reduction in benefit levels.

Large employers have generally tailored their benefit programs to suit their individual circumstances. The likelihood of major alterations to those programs in order to join a PPO is somewhat remote. The third-party payor is therefore confronted with the need to continue to administer any number of benefit programs for its clients, even in the PPO model. Nevertheless, the third-party payor hopes to be able to move much of its enrolled population into a few standard benefit programs from a myriad of present benefit options. This reduction in the number of existing benefit programs reduces the third-party payor's current cost of benefit administration and generates another element of indirect savings for the PPO product.

The payor may decide to alter its benefit program to discourage the use of inpatient hospital services. Alterations can include an increase in the number of covered home health visits or a waiver of the patient's coinsurance when surgery is performed on an outpatient basis.

Another element of savings for the payor can occur depending on the way in which copayments are structured. If the payor wants to pass some of the discount obtained from the providers over to the patient, the copayment percentage is applied to the per diem, per case, or fees negotiated with the provider. If the payor is greedy, however, the copayments are calculated on the higher billed charges and the enrollee bears a greater share of the total claim cost. This latter approach will also tend to produce higher bad debts for the provider than the former approach. However, it can result in additional savings for the payor, depending on the level of discount negotiated with the providers. An example of this can be seen in Exhibit 5.

EXHIBIT 5
Impact of Copayments on Share of Total Claim Cost

	Copayment Based on:	
	Billed Charges	*Negotiated Rate*
Billed charges	$2,000	$2,000
Negotiated rate	1,700	1,700
Patient liability at 20 percent	400	340
Payor payment	$1,300	$1,360

Exhibit 5 indicates that calculating the copayment on billed charges produces a $60 savings for the payor. This is about a four percent savings when compared to the $1,360 the payor would have disbursed if the co-payment had been calculated on the negotiated rate.

PPO negotiated hospital rates are theoretically an average of the hospitals' anticipated per-diem or per-case costs. Some hospital billings during the contract period are therefore likely to reflect lower total billed charges than the negotiated rates. It may be difficult to explain to the patient why the copayment, if based on the negotiated rate, is more than it would have been if based on the billed charges. Payors therefore may wish to consider basing the copayment on the lesser of the charge or negotiated rate. This approach will cost the payor. It does, however, always share the PPO savings with the patient and encourages use of the network.

Financial Incentives

Of concern to both the payor and the participating provider is the structure of the financial incentives. These incentives are in place to encourage the patient to use the PPO provider to the exclusion of the non-PPO provider. This is one of the most important elements in assuring the viability of the PPO system. These incentives normally take the form of additional copayments and deductibles when the enrollee uses non-PPO providers. Without properly designed incentives to keep the enrollee from using providers outside the system, the following is a likely scenario:

1. Patients will continue to use their present non-PPO provider.
2. PPO providers will not increase their volume.
3. Discounts and provider interest will erode.
4. The payor will not reduce present benefit costs.
5. The PPO program will be abandoned.

Careful structuring of these incentives is important. They must be

effective enough to keep the patient in the PPO network yet not so onerous as to make the availability of services outside the PPO illusionary.
Too tight an incentive system may even subject the PPO to a different set
of laws and regulations. The State of California has relatively few rules
relating to PPOs. It does, however, have some very specific requirements
for an exclusive provider organization (EPO). The difference between a
PPO and an EPO is that in the EPO benefits are payable only when a
network provider is used. Onerous PPO financial incentives could be
viewed as converting the PPO to an EPO.

Some financial incentive structures are better than others. For example, the use of an annual deductible of $500 whenever non-PPO physi-
cians are used may be more effective than 20 percent copay. Twenty percent copay when applied to a $50 office visit produces only a $10 disincentive. On the other hand, the $500 deductible forces the patient to pay
for the entire $50 office visit. A $750 per admission hospital deductible
may also be more effective in keeping the enrollee in the PPO system.
An incentive system that uses a limited indemnity per diem by geographic area may be understandable to the payor. It may, however, be
unintelligible to the enrollee who has no idea of what total hospital daily
costs are in a non-PPO hospital. The patient does, however, understand a
$750 deductible.

Exhibit 6 is a list of various incentive alternatives to keep the patient
in the PPO system. Some may be more effective than others. The important considerations are:

— Is the incentive understood by the patient?
— Will it keep the patient in the system while providing a degree of
freedom to use services outside the system?
— Does the incentive produce no greater payment for the payor than
had the patient used the PPO network?

EXHIBIT 6
Additional Cost to Patients Using Non-PPO Providers

Alternative	Hospital	Physician	Comments
Additional copayment applied to billed charges, e.g., 25 percent	X	X	Can result in payor payment in excess of PPO rates
Stipulated per diem	X		Questionable understanding by patient
Payor pays a percentage of PPO fee structure (e.g., 75 percent)		X	
Deductible per admission	X		
Payor does not accept assignment	X	X	

Payor and provider interests are both served by effective incentives. The short-term success of the PPO and its long-term viability are dependent on those incentives.

UTILIZATION REVIEW

Potential Savings

While a payor does not need a PPO to improve the quality of its utilization-review program, the two typically go together. The PPO contract between the payor and the provider can serve as a vehicle that binds the provider to the use of the utilization-review system. Failure to follow the rules of that system can free the payor from any payment obligation to that provider.

The principal cost savings to occur in the PPO product may result from the utilization-review component. Claims have been made that the mere sentinel effect of having this feature can result in as much as a 15 percent reduction in inpatient utilization. Given the current disparity in the use of inpatient care between fee-for-service and HMO programs, there obviously can be some reduction in fee-for-service usage.

Administration

The HMO relies on the physician to be self-motivated in controlling the quantity of inpatient care, since the physician normally shares in the savings generated by such control. The payor-organized PPO, on the other hand, relies on external controls. These may include preadmission certification, concurrent review, and retrospective review. All are intended to limit the patient's access to the hospital. These external controls may be administered either directly by the payor, by a third party under contract to the payor, or by the PPO providers themselves.

Generally, providers will react negatively to externally imposed controls. They will view those controls as an imposition on the way they practice medicine. They will also feel that the system is likely to be administered by persons who do not have a clear understanding of the care required by their patient. Care should therefore be exercised by the payor in designing such a system and establishing its credibility in the eyes of participating providers. A system acceptable to providers will have the following characteristics:

— Provider involvement in the program design.
— Clear rules and procedures.
— Physician reviewers representing the major medical specialties.
— Prompt and consistent responses to provider requests.
— Appropriate reconsideration process.
— Joint payor and provider review of overall results.

Risks

The payor will, in the beginning, be somewhat reluctant to override the recommendations of the patient's physician due to medical malpractice issues and possible exposure to lawsuits. But limited success in reducing utilization will strengthen the payor's resolve.

Utilization review has some offsetting costs and risks for the payor. These include

— The expense of administering the program whether through employed personnel or contracts with third-party reviewers. Such third-party costs are typically stated either as a cost per admission (e.g., $25) or a fee per enrollee per month (e.g., 75 cents).

— Malpractice insurance premiums, legal defense costs, and court-awarded damages. Payors, in addition to determining the appropriateness of the admission and length of stay, also put themselves in the position of directing enrollees to the specific providers in the PPO network. As a result, the payor may find itself drawn into a liability case caused by the provider's medical negligence.

— Outpatient care substituted for inpatient services. The extent of this additional cost will depend on the effectiveness of the utilization-review program.

Despite these additional costs, the perception is that the controls are required. Payors feel they can save money through reduced utilization. They also believe these controls are needed in order to prevent price discounts from being eroded through an inappropriate increase in units of service.

OPERATING SYSTEMS

Modifications to Existing Systems

A major payor concern involves the required changes to the way claims are paid to PPO providers and the new reports that are needed to monitor program performance. Frequently, a payor who believes there is much to gain by contracting with a PPO will rush into that activity without first analyzing its available systems capability and the time required for changes to those systems.

Some of the issues that must be addressed are

1. Can hospital providers be paid on a per-diem or per-case basis? The payor's present system has probably been designed to pay billed charges. System modifications will include the need to maintain several per diems or case rates for each provider. In addition, a history of the periodic changes to those rates and their effective dates is needed in order to match payment rates with dates of service.

2. Can the system pay physicians using a relative value system? The payor will need to maintain a table of relative value units for several thousand different procedures against which appropriate conversion factors can be applied. The conversion factors may be different by geographic area. The effective dates of fee revisions must also be maintained.

3. How will non-PPO provider claims be identified and paid? Identifiers will be necessary in the provider database. The system must be capable of determining that the claim is from a non-PPO provider. It must also calculate the level of payment due to a non-PPO provider. In some instances, such a non-PPO claim will be for emergency care. Since financial penalties are customarily waived in emergencies, the system must be capable of differentiating between emergency and nonemergency situations.

4. Can the system calculate copayments on the basis of negotiated rates? The payor's system has probably been designed to calculate copayments on the basis of billed charges. Further modification may be needed if deductibles are waived when outpatient surgery is performed.

5. How will preadmission and length-of-stay approvals be transmitted to providers, recorded, and linked to the claim when it arrives? Timely responses to providers are essential. The system must be able to match the claim with the approval in order to avoid delays in provider payments.

6. What are the required changes to the employee's explanation of benefits and the provider's remittance advice? Care must be exercised in reflecting the employee's proper copayment amount. Financial penalties for the use of non-PPO providers must be accurately stated. The provider must be able to clearly see that the correct negotiated rates were used in payment of the claim.

7. What new data elements must be captured in order to process claims and produce reports? Some payors may not currently capture patient days or the detail charges from the hospital claim form. Both elements will be needed: the days in order to pay claims and the charges in order to monitor possible underutilization. The physician's zip code or other location identifier may now be required in order to pay the proper geographic negotiated rate.

Implementation

These issues are of concern both to the self-insured payor and to the insurer or TPA. The employer who wants to move rapidly to a PPO product may find that its claims administrator is not yet willing or ready to make the required developmental effort. That effort involves significant cost, and the administrator may not believe that it is recoverable due to the product's uncertain future.

The payor's claims and systems personnel may already believe they are overburdened. Assigning a major effort to them, such as one based on PPO concepts, is likely to meet with a certain level of resistance from internal operating personnel. It is best to begin that developmental effort as soon as the PPO program design has been established. Waiting for the PPO contracts to be signed by the providers will delay program implementation for some months while the system is being modified to reflect those terms. Significant benefit cost savings are likely to be lost due to the delay.

The payor's interests can be best served by involving operating personnel from the beginning of the PPO design. Modifications to the product design necessitated by system limitations are most easily accomplished early on. Those limitations are usually best described by the payor's claims and systems personnel.

MARKETING

Clear Product Definition

The PPO program product line will not sell itself for two reasons:

— There are many potential purchasers who do not understand it.
— There are purchasers who understand it but think that other buyers should be given a chance to work the problems out of the system.

Some PPOs have been organized in a defensive posture, that is, in an attempt to protect market share rather than to take advantage of a market opportunity. Physicians, for example, have to some degree been driven into the system out of the fear of loss of patients. This defensive approach generally produces an ill-defined PPO with little sense of the marketing efforts that are to be employed.

An effective marketing effort should involve an assessment of the competition, establishment of realistic enrollment objectives, effective training and incentive systems for marketing people, and clear concise promotional material for potential buyers. The PPO should put itself in the payor's position and ask itself, "What does the payor want to know?" Some of those questions include:

— Who is in charge of and accountable for the PPO delivery system?
— Which hospitals are included in the PPO and what are their service capabilities?
— Where are the physicians located and what are their medical specialties?
— Are there other types of providers in the PPO?
— What is the utilization review system, and how does it work?
— What are the various alternative payment methods that the PPO can accommodate?

— What other buyers are currently enrolled in the PPO?
— How are providers added to, monitored, and eliminated from the PPO?
— Does the PPO have a standard price structure? If not, how are prices negotiated?
— What are the terms of the contract between the PPO and the providers, the PPO and the payor, or the payor and the provider?
— What kinds of regular reports are provided to the payor?

The more clearly these questions are addressed in the initial contact with a prospective payor, the easier it will be to complete the contracting relationship.

Understanding the Contracting Process

In addressing the above questions, there is the issue of the contracting process between the payor and the PPO providers. Provider-based PPOs generally require individual contracts between each provider and the payor. In addition there usually is a contract between the PPO entity and the payor. Therefore, completion of the contracting process may not be easy. It can involve a negotiation of price and other terms with each hospital as well as a payor price offer and provider acceptance process with each PPO physician. Much of this has been caused by the need to comply with antitrust requirements.

The possible approaches to the contracting process are numerous, and many have been designed with the provider in mind instead of the payor. The average payor is somewhat leery of the PPO to begin with. The payor also has little knowledge of or is bewildered by the various PPO contracting process alternatives. It is in the provider-based PPO's interest, therefore, to clearly define the process in its promotional material and assist the payor through it.

The PPO that can quote prices and require only a single contract between the PPO and the payor has an advantage in the marketplace. The closer the PPO can get to this approach the greater its chances of success.

Enrollment Potential

PPOs should not be wild-eyed about potential enrollment. Realistic objectives need to be set. Employer groups and their brokers move slowly when major changes to employee benefit programs are required. While some PPOs may talk in terms of first year PPO enrollment equivalent to 20 percent or more of their present fee for service business, that is probably more for the providers' benefit than theirs. These kinds of glowing projections are often used to convince the prospective PPO provider of the need to join the PPO and grant significant discounts. Projections of significant enrollment in HMO programs occurred when HMOs were first conceived. Those projections have not yet been met, although significant added enrollment has occurred in recent years. PPO enrollment will probably follow a similar course.

How rapidly the payor or its enrollees will move from its present benefit program to the PPO depends on several things. These include

1. The degree to which the payor wants to subsidize its present benefit program with savings from the PPO product or vice versa: Some insurers may wish to protect or improve their standard underwritten fee for service market share by subsidizing it with PPO savings. This may be somewhat short-sighted; especially if other insurers have taken an opposite point of view. The potential for long-term product price effectiveness is in the PPO.

2. The financial incentive system for use of PPO providers: Without such a system, there is no PPO. A careful balance needs to be achieved that allows the perception that movement outside the system is possible yet keeps the great bulk of patients in the system. Other incentives include the degree to which the employer is willing to share PPO savings with the employee through reduced copayments, deductibles, and employee payroll contributions.

3. The inclusion of other benefits in the PPO product relative to the current benefit program: Examples include well-baby care, innoculations, and improved skilled nursing and home health benefits.

4. Whether both the PPO product and the standard benefit program will be permitted to exist side by side as a dual option for the payor's enrollees or employees: Obviously, if the PPO program is the only one offered to the employees, all will enroll in it. A self-insured employer may simply maintain its present benefit program and waive or reduce deductibles and coinsurance when PPO providers are used. Insurers are generally concerned about offering a dual option of PPO and standard fee-for-service because of the risk of adverse selection. Those employees who are less likely to need health care services will choose the PPO option, leaving a generally sicker population in the standard program. As the cost of the standard program increases due to excessive benefit use, more employees will leave it and costs will again escalate. Insurers have found that they are unable to continue to charge enough to cover these costs. Underwriting losses result. Nevertheless, the desire to introduce the PPO program to employees as painlessly as possible will probably lead the insurer to offer a dual option.

There are certainly other factors that will determine the success of the PPO. The most important ones are the savings generated by it and the enrollees' perception of the quality of service received.

PROGRAM EVALUATION

The payor's data needs and reports in the PPO product are more significant than under a standard fee for service program.

The program, and the individual providers in it, must be regularly evaluated after implementation to be certain it

— Is saving the payor money. The PPO system has been sold on the basis that it is less expensive than the payor's current program. Comparative reports will be required that demonstrate this.

— Is providing reasonable satisfaction to its enrollees or employees in terms of their perception of the quality and accessability of their care. Limited choice of provider requires more attention to this factor than in the past.

— Does not contain problem providers who may do harm to the network. Since the PPO network is small, relative to the total number of available providers in the community, a single hospital or physician group can have major impact on the overall performance of the PPO product.

Many of the reports are appropriate for a standard benefit program as well as the PPO product. Some payors, including insurers and third-party administrators, have been slow to develop reports that monitor and help evaluate their benefit programs. The PPO that develops a total information system for its clients will have an additional advantage over its competitors. Some suggestions for such reports are contained in Exhibit 7.

Employers want this data in simple-to-understand formats to determine

— Where their money is going.
— How the PPO costs compare with their prior benefit program.
— When changes are needed to the PPO delivery system or the benefit program.

The reporting system should include trend data, comparisons to non-PPO product lines and providers, and a comparison of the specific employer group to the total product line.

While the data development costs may be substantial, the credibility of the PPO can be enhanced by the willingness to provide such reports. Without such data as a standard feature, the PPO runs the risk of each participating payor developing its own reports. That individual development could produce both inaccurate and misleading conclusions.

CUSTOM DESIGN VERSUS ESTABLISHED PPO

Payor Considerations

A major decision for a payor is whether to develop a provider network by designing a program and directly contracting with individual providers or

EXHIBIT 7
PPO Information System Possible Reports

Type of Report	*Purpose*
Admissions, length of stay, hospital costs, and number of cases per diagnosis category both in total and per enrollee	To review trends relative to prior experience and a non-PPO based program
Physician visits, costs by specialty, and number of services per procedure both in total and per enrollee	To review trends relative to prior experience and a non-PPO benefit program
Cost, length of stay, and number of admissions/visits/procedure type by individual physician or hospital	To examine trends, relative volume of activity among providers, possible abuses of billing procedures, practice patterns
Use of non-PPO providers, including identification of patient, provider procedure, and costs	To examine the degree of use and purpose of the services as well as to compare the net cost of such services to PPO rates
Comparison of billed charges and negotiated payments for each PPO provider	To compare the negotiated fee schedule to billed charges
Results of preadmission certification and concurrent review	To evaluate the impact of and savings attributable to the utilization-review program including approvals relative to denials, second opinion results, and appeals
Enrollee surveys and examination of medical records	To evaluate enrollee satisfaction with the PPO system
Claims cycle times	To examine the length of time required to receive and process claims
Ancillary charge data by diagnosis by hospital	To review for possible over- and under-utilization

whether to deal through an established provider-based, or third-party payor–designed PPO. This decision process involves the following issues:

1. The size of the payor: Generally, the smaller the payor the more difficult it will be to establish a unique provider network. The dispersion of the payor's enrollees or employees throughout a large geographic area would offer a relatively small number of patients to each provider. Generation of significant interest among the providers is, therefore, difficult at best. If the payor is an employer with 500 or more employees, most of whom live within a few miles of each other, contracting with a limited number of providers should be explored.

2. The cost and effort required under the alternative approaches:

The payor that designs and implements its own PPO program may end up with one better suited to its needs than if it were to join an existing PPO. On the other hand, more time is required with the custom design approach. This time is devoted to design, contract development, and contacting and negotiating with large numbers of unaffiliated providers.

Expertise that is not presently on the payor's staff will be required in the formation of its own unique PPO network. Such expertise will include legal assistance in contract development, persons who are aware of the varying characteristics, costs, and services available from the provider population and who are able to speak the provider's language during a sometimes lengthy process of contract negotiations.

Further costs will be incurred in the development of utilization-review programs, claims system modifications and program reporting. These services may already be available from an existing PPO. Maintenance of the provider network through annual renegotiations with each provider is another costly activity.

The following items should be evaluated in deciding whether to custom design a PPO or enroll in an existing one.

1. The time required to take advantage of PPO savings. Usually, less time is required to join one or more exisiting PPOs than to form a unique one. Even though the established PPO may not offer everything the payor seeks, adjustments can be made over time to make the PPO more reflective of the payor's needs.

2. The level of investment in the payor's current benefit program. Many large employers maintain their own benefit analysts and claims processing personnel. These payors are not likely to immediately dismantle that organization and delegate the functions to an outside PPO. They are more likely to attempt to form a PPO or find one that can interface with their existing structure.

3. The risk of loss of an entire PPO network. The payor, in moving to the PPO product, begins to direct many of its employees or enrollees away from their present providers to a new set of providers. This redirection and establishment of new provider relationships is not something that can or should be done frequently. Contracting with an established PPO, as opposed to one of the payor's own design, can result in higher exposure to potential major changes in the provider delivery system. If, in subsequent years, the payor is unable to renegotiate prices and other terms with the established PPO, the entire provider network can be lost. It may, therefore, be more comforting for the payor to think in terms of the loss of a single provider from the payor's custom-designed PPO than to risk the loss of the entire delivery system.

4. Control of the provider network. The provider-based PPO has the additional problem of image. Providers are not entirely trusted by payors due to prior real or imagined abuses. These payor concerns may be highest with regard to potential utilization abuses to offset PPO price discounts. Unfortunately, the banding together of providers into the PPO network can tend to magnify this problem for the payors. The payor wants to feel in control of the network rather than to feel controlled by it.

5. Stability of the established PPO. Some established PPOs, and perhaps most significantly those that are provider-based, have the appearance of a certain looseness or disorganization about them. The need in most instances for the payor to deal with each physician or hospital in the contracting relationship seems to belie the notion that the established PPO is really an organized system with common goals and objectives. Further, the lack of promotional materials, the changing size and nature of the delivery system as it either expands or contracts, and the sometime absence of a single point of accountability adds to the PPO's problem. Perhaps these issues are merely signs of a maturing organization. The payor, however, cannot afford to risk this apparent instability in addition to the other issues involved in movement to the PPO program.

Exhibit 8 summarizes the above issues and the degree to which the employer-designed, insurer/third party administrator, and provider-based PPOs address the purchaser's concerns.

EXHIBIT 8
PPO Sponsorship in Relation to Payor Objectives

Payor Objective	Degree of Satisfaction		
	Employer Sponsored	Insurer or Third-Party Administrator Sponsored	Provider Sponsored
Appropriate for large or geographically concentrated employer	High	Medium	Medium
Minimal development cost	Low	High	Medium
Minimal development time	Low	High	Medium
Ability to maintain current method of benefit administration	High	Low	Medium
Protection against risk of loss of entire provider network	High	Medium	Low
Payor control of delivery system	High	Low	Low
Stability of network	High	Medium	Low

Overcoming Payor Concerns

The provider-based PPO would appear to have a number of issues that preclude it from being the PPO of choice. It can, however, minimize those problems and enhance its position in the marketplace by effectively addressing the following points:

1. Facilitate the payor contracting effort through a single contract rather than multiple contracts. The current legal concerns over price-setting and antitrust issues must be overcome before this can become a reality. In the interim, a clearly defined contracting process, assisted by the PPO organizers, can help the payor through this activity.

2. Design a provider selection and monitoring process that clearly addresses quality and utilization issues. The payor should be able to determine that the PPO has established criteria that measure provider performance, reports that reflect provider activities against those criteria, educational programs that assist the provider in improving performance, and disciplinary measures that provide for the elimination of problem providers.

3. Be flexible in dealing with the payor's utilization-review requirements. The PPO should have its own well-designed utilization-review program. It should also be willing to accommodate and assist those payors who have developed their own. Feelings of "them versus us" can hopefully be sublimated.

4. Minimize the degree to which initial discounts can erode over time. Unless significant volume increases occur, a hospital that has discounted its price significantly below its average cost will have difficulty maintaining that discount. PPOs that contain institutional providers whose costs compare favorably with other providers in the community will best be able to maintain good PPO price structures and network stability.

5. Be able to cope with the payor's desired method of payment. The PPO providers should be willing to consider various payment methods including per diems, per case, and RVS approaches. The PPO may even have developed a claims processing capability that the payor may wish to use.

6. Contain enough committed professional providers of all specialties. The PPO should not be dependent on several physicians without whom serious harm can come to the delivery system. The network should be capable of functioning even though there are dropouts.

Provider-based PPOs are possibly the most numerous form of PPO. Undoubtedly there will be some that can effectively address the above issues and successfully capture a share of the market. It would be fortunate if all three types of PPOs were to get a chance to demonstrate their wares in order to ultimately develop the best product.

FUTURE FOR PPOs

In order for PPOs to occupy a significant place in the health care system certain problems need to be recognized and addressed. The following four issues are most important to the long-term viability of PPOs:

1. Wariness of the payor. The PPO can address this issue by designing a program that meets the purchaser's needs, satisfies the enrollees' service requirements, and produces the expected savings. Initial success will increase enrollment.

2. Inability to cope with administrative changes. The payor has to resolve that one and be willing to make the required investment in operating system changes. The PPO can help by being flexible and not insisting on just one way of doing business.

3. Willingness to alter benefit programs. Payors want the savings that come with discounts. They may, however, be reluctant to make appropriate benefit changes, such as financial incentives for the use of PPO providers, in order to maximize savings. The PPO can encourage incentive development by the way their services are priced or by making such incentives a contracting requirement.

4. Ignorance of how to seek out PPOs and other marketing short comings. General payor awareness, especially of provider-based PPOs, is slim. Perhaps this is attributable to their early stage of development. The PPO can improve upon this situation by simply developing, adopting, or buying the necessary expertise and tools. The contracting process between the payor and the providers is also unclear and therefore a deterrent in developing a buyer-seller relationship. Clarifying the process and providing a single contracting point will help.

If the above issues can be effectively addressed, the future of PPOs may look something like this:

1. PPO failures will occur. Presently, many providers are members of several PPOs. Each PPO is different in design and many may not be adequately addressing the kinds of issues described in this article. Many PPOs will fail due to these design issues. Providers will also become more selective by casting their lot with the most viable organization.

2. Government regulation of PPOs will increase. Regulation is likely to occur as some PPOs fail or do not provide adequate service levels to enrollees. Providers who have rendered services to payors who then fail to pay their bills may also be in the forefront of such regulation.

3. PPOs will be another part of the health care system. The PPO will probably grow at about the same rate as the HMO has.

CONCLUSION

Some observers feel that the PPO is merely fee-for-service medicine's last gasp. The combination of physicians and hospitals forming delivery networks and the development of incentive systems or utilization controls to contain service volume may just be someone's clever way of moving all of us further into the HMO model.

Nevertheless the PPO, even if it is just a transitional phenomenon, offers both payors and providers an opportunity to address some of today's health care cost-containment issues. Understanding the PPO design issues explored in this article will assist in taking full advantage of that opportunity.

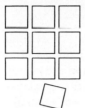

Purchaser Objectives and Priorities

MEDICAL PROGRAM DESIGN AND FUNDING

Thomas C. Billet, M.B.A.
Consultant
Johnson & Higgins
New York, NY

☐ The importance of employee benefits as a part of the total compensation package is dramatically illustrated in the growth of benefit costs as compared to that of wages and salaries. From 1969 to 1980, wages and salaries in the United States increased 123 percent. During the same period, benefit costs increased 197 percent. Rising costs in existing benefit programs, new benefit programs such as dental and long-term disability insurance, and increases in the employer-paid portion of Social Security are partly responsible for these increases. However, the most significant factor has been the rise in the cost of medical benefits: 265 percent in the same period.

This trend has fueled the development of alternative delivery systems aimed at slowing the rate of cost escalation. As a new delivery system, PPOs are changing the way health care is delivered to employee groups by instituting direct contractual arrangements between and among employers, health care providers, and insurance carriers. This new mode of contracting for health services has important implications for employee benefit plans. New ideas in the areas of medical program design and funding are needed for employers to effectively use PPOs as a cost-containment vehicle. This article explores some alternatives to conventional insurance arrangements.

The first part deals with plan design considerations and offers some alternative plan designs that would be appropriate for integrating a PPO option. The second part explores the possibility of including a PPO option within a flexible benefit program. The last part assesses the relative advantages and disadvantages of self-insurance as an alternative funding mechanism when implementing a PPO option.

Each of these design and funding arrangements is analyzed in the context of their implications for employer interactions with preferred provider organizations.

PLAN DESIGN CONSIDERATIONS

As health care costs continue to escalate, more employers are focusing their attention on benefit plan design and cost-containment measures. This section is based on an example of an employer integrating a PPO option into its regular medical benefit plan. For discussion purposes the PPO is assumed to be a network of hospital providers, although the same logic would apply if the PPO consisted of only one hospital provider. An evaluation of employer medical plan design considerations is made, with recommendations provided to facilitate the implementation of a PPO option.

As purchasers of health care services, employers find themselves with a unique opportunity to dramatically effect positive changes in their benefit plan designs and utilization patterns through the use of a PPO. Not only can costs be maintained or reduced through innovative plan design but also revenues can be increased by the redirection of benefit dollars throughout the PPO network.

There are a number of key issues that focus on the design of the medical program. The program should

— Increase employees' utilization of *network* medical resources as much as possible.
— Limit the escalation of future costs.
— Provide employees with catastrophic medical protection.
— Increase employee awareness of medical costs.

To address these objectives, it is necessary to incorporate two concepts into the medical program: (1) Build in incentives to control utilization and (2) Build in disincentives for utilization outside the PPO network.

While there is not one specific design that will answer all needs or meet all objectives, a typical medical program (Plan I) can be compared to two alternatives (Plans II and III) that will contain costs (see Exhibit 1). The design of each plan is coupled with a disincentive strategy outlining reimbursement for services performed outside the PPO network.

EXHIBIT 1

Medical Benefits	Plan Design I*		Plan Design II*		Plan Design III*	
	Within PPO Network	Outside PPO Network	Within PPO Network	Outside PPO Network	Within PPO Network	Outside PPO Network
I. Hospital Benefits						
Daily room and board and miscellaneous charges (average semiprivate charge limit)	100%	70%	90%	70%	Paid under major medical	Paid under major medical
Physician visits (in-hospital)	100%	100%	100%	100%	Paid under major medical	Paid under major medical
Maximum length of confinement	Unlimited	365 days	Unlimited	365 days	Unlimited	365 days
Deductible per confinement	None	None	$100	$250	N/A	N/A
Exceptions†						
Mental/nervous	Maximum 30 days in a 12 month period	Maximum 30 days in a 12 month period	Maximum 30 days in a 12 month period	Maximum 30 days in a 12 month period	Maximum 30 days in a 12 month period	Maximum 30 days in a 12 month period
Drug/alcohol	Maximum 28 days, 33 days detoxification	Maximum 28 days, 33 days detoxification	Maximum 28 days, 33 days detoxification	Maximum 28 days, 33 days detoxification	Maximum 28 days, 33 days detoxification	Maximum 28 days, 33 days detoxification
Lifetime maximum confinements	2 confinement periods	2 confinement periods	2 confinement periods	2 confinement periods	2 confinement periods	2 confinement periods
Lifetime maximum benefits—drug/alcohol/mental/nervous disorders	$25,000	$25,000	$25,000	$25,000	$25,000	$25,000

*Benefits listed are limited to (UCR) usual, customary and reasonable.

†Reimbursement for these services will be reduced under the Outside Network plan once contracts are reached with providers of these services.

EXHIBIT 1 *(continued)*

Medical Benefits	Plan Design I*		Plan Design II*		Plan Design III*	
	Within PPO Network	*Outside PPO Network*	*Within PPO Network*	*Outside PPO Network*	*Within PPO Network*	*Outside PPO Network*
II. Emergency room						
Sickness (sudden and serious) and accidental injury	100%	100%	100%	100%	100%	100%
Sickness	75%	50%	75%	50%	75%	50%
Deductible	None	None	$50 per occurrence	$50 per occurrence	None	None
III. Diagnostic X ray and Lab	100%	100% with $100 calendar maximum (remainder paid under major medical)	100%	100% with $100 calendar maximum (remainder paid under major medical)	Paid under major medical	Paid under major medical
IV. Physician Office Visits	Paid under major medical	Paid under major medical	Paid under major medical	Paid under major medical	Paid under major medical	Paid under major medical
V. Surgery						
Surgical services	100%	100%	100%	100%	100%	100%
Voluntary second opinion	100%	100%	100%	100%	100%	100%
Surgeries requiring second opinion						
Opinion required/obtained	N/A	N/A	100%	100%	N/A	N/A

	Col 1	Col 2	Col 3	Col 4	Col 5	Col 6
Opinion required/not obtained	N/A	N/A	75%	75%	N/A	N/A
Voluntary ambulatory procedures	100%	100%	100%	100%	100%	100%
Mandatory ambulatory procedures						
Inpatient with plan approval	N/A	N/A	100%	100%	N/A	N/A
Inpatient without plan approval	N/A	N/A	75%	75%	N/A	N/A
VI. Skilled Nursing Facility† (Average semiprivate charge limit)	100%	100%	100%	100%	Paid under major medical	Paid under major medical
Maximum length of confinement	120 days	120 days	60 days	60 days	120 days	120 days
VII. Home Health Care†	N/A	N/A	100%	100%	N/A	N/A
Maximum visits	N/A	N/A	100 visits per 12 month period	100 visits per 12 month period	N/A	N/A
VIII. Hospice Care†	N/A	N/A	100%	100%	N/A	N/A
IX. Utilization Review Preadmission certification (nonemergency)	Required	Required	Required	Required	Required	Required
Concurrent monitoring	Required as can be obtained	Required	Required as can be obtained	Required	Required	Required as can be obtained

*Benefits listed are limited to (UCR) usual, customary and reasonable.

†Reimbursement for these services will be reduced under the Outside Network plan once contracts are reached with providers of these services.

EXHIBIT 1 (concluded)

Medical Benefits	Plan Design I*		Plan Design II*		Plan Design III*	
	Within PPO Network	Outside PPO Network	Within PPO Network	Outside PPO Network	Within PPO Network	Outside PPO Network
X. Major Medical Expense						
Lifetime maximum	$500,000	$500,000	$500,000	$500,000	$500,000	$500,000
Calendar year deductible						
Individual	$100	$250	$100	$250	$250	$1,000
Family limit	$300	$750	$300	$750	None	None
Coinsurance	80%	70%	80%	70%	80%	70%
Outpatient mental/ nervous	50%	50%	50%	50%	50%	50%
Calendar year maximum	$1,000	$1,000	$1,000	$1,000	$1,000	$1,000
Stop-Loss						
Individual	None	None	$1,000	None	$1,000	None
Family	None	None	$3,000	None	$3,000	None

*Benefits listed are limited to (UCR) usual, customary and reasonable.
†Reimbursement for these services will be reduced under the Outside Network plan once contracts are reached with providers of these services.

PLAN I

Plan I uses a typical medical program to define the benefit payable within the PPO network. Hospital reimbursement to any non-network facility is limited to 70 percent of charges. All physician and major medical benefits are reimbursed at the same level whether services are rendered within the PPO network or outside of it.

In summary, Plan I affords the easiest transition into the PPO network structure. The "inside" benefits are structured to remain consistent with an existing employer-sponsored medical program. This could serve to reassure employees of the maintenance of current benefit levels and high quality of care.

PLAN II

Plan II uses the same general design as Plan I, while adding more cost-effective alternatives. Specifically, Plan II incorporates the following cost-containment measures within and outside the PPO network:

1. Hospital admission deductibles: $100 within and $250 outside.
2. Hospital coinsurance: 90/10 within and 70/30 outside.
3. Mandatory second surgical opinion program for specific procedures, with reduced benefits payable for noncompliance.
4. Mandatory ambulatory surgery program for specific procedures, with reduced benefits for noncompliance.
5. Emergency room deductibles and increased employee coinsurance for non–life-threatening illnesses.
6. Hospice/home health care reimbursement at 100 percent of UCR.
7. The introduction of out-of-pocket employee limitations for all medical services.

The above measures would serve to minimize hospital utilization by creating economic incentives for the patient to be treated at the most appropriate level of medical care.

Plan II enables the employer to implement a cost-containment program within the current structure of benefits. This plan would promote a high level of cost awareness among employees in helping them to become better health care consumers.

PLAN III

Plan III introduces employee cost sharing for all health care services.

Plan III is a simplified benefit program that implements strict utilization controls in the form of high deductibles and coinsurance. This plan would serve well in an environment where an employer would provide financial incentives to encourage participation.

There are several advantages to Plans I, II and III that apply to all PPO network participants. First, each plan design is constructed to encourage the highest possible utilization of PPO network facilities by employees. Second, Plans II and III permit the introduction of structuring mechanisms designed to shift utilization to the most appropriate PPO network facility. Finally, because each plan design has built-in disincentives for utilization outside the PPO network, the general level of employee cost awareness will be raised whether the employer chooses to adopt Plan I, Plan II, or Plan III. In addition, as a result of varying the medical benefits payable according to the use of the PPO or non-PPO plan, the employer can achieve effective cost containment.

However, there are other alternatives for promoting use of the PPO without varying payment levels. One viable option is to include the PPO within the context of a flexible benefit program.

EMPLOYEE FLEXIBLE BENEFIT PROGRAMS

RESTORING COST CONTROL

Many employers are seeking to respond to ever rising medical benefit costs by offering preferred provider organizations as part of their medical plan. By including a PPO option within a flexible benefit program, an employer can both increase general employee cost awareness and encourage participation in the PPO.

With a flexible benefit program, the employer can redefine the company's financial commitment to the benefit program. Rather than providing certain distinct benefits, the costs of which may be difficult to control, the employer commits to an overall level of expenditure.

While cost containment may be the major goal of a flexible program, there are other advantages that can be equally important. These include

— Increasing the perceived value of benefits to employees.
— Providing more satisfaction per benefit dollar.
— Providing employees with a more personalized benefit package by responding to demographic changes in the workforce.

A flexible program can both slow escalating benefit costs and make what is spent more effective in the eyes of the employees.

STRUCTURING A FLEXIBLE PROGRAM

Under a flexible program, employees are given a package of benefits with basic and optional items. Basics may include a core plan of medical, life, and disability insurance, as well as vacation and retirement benefits. Optional items could include dependent medical care, dental insurance, additional life and disability insurance, and some form of profit sharing or savings plan.

Above the basic plan, the employer decides what is to be spent and then allocates "credits" to employees on the basis of salary, seniority, merit, or some other combination of predetermined variables. The employees use these credits to "buy" the options available within the flexible program. As a result, costs are fixed rather than being dependent on the funds needed to support distinct benefit programs.

A flexible benefit program would easily permit the introduction of a PPO option. The employer could simply make the PPO the core medical plan, and then offer the regular medical plan as an option. Employees wishing to use the regular plan would then "buy" that option with their flexible credits. Aggregate benefit costs would be controlled, since employee use of flexible credits on one or more chosen options would preclude their use on other options.

By placing the PPO within the framework of a flexible program, the employer can maintain the benefits payable in the PPO and non-PPO options at a consistent level. The non-PPO (or regular) medical option would simply cost more to the employee. As a result, both employee cost awareness and participation in the PPO would be promoted.

The only "disadvantage" in this method is that the employee would have to elect one or the other medical plan at the beginning of the year and then participate in it for the full benefit plan year. Thus, employees would not be able to choose the PPO or non-PPO plan at the point of each medical episode. However, this can be an advantage to the employer since, at the end of the year, management would have separate PPO and non-PPO experience profiles for cost and evaluation analysis purposes.

FLEXIBILITY AND COST CONTAINMENT

The method described above permits flexibility within well defined financial limits. No employee will be seriously damaged economically regardless of which medical or other benefit option he or she chooses. The employee has a margin of flexibility, while the employer can achieve cost containment.

A flexible benefit program can be an effective vehicle for implementing a PPO medical option. Moreover, while costs have steadily risen in standard benefit programs, the flexible approach enables the employer to control costs while simultaneously providing employees with a more personalized benefit package.

THE SELF-INSURANCE OPTION

The preceding two sections have focused on PPO integration within the context of benefit plan design. However, plan funding can be a consideration as important as plan design. Placing a PPO medical option within the framework of a properly funded benefit plan should rank high on an employer's list of priorities.

Self-insurance as an alternative to conventional fully insured medical program funding is becoming increasingly common. Self-insurance offers the advantages of improved cash flow, increased flexibility in program design, and the possibility of obtaining better management information reporting systems. These considerations may ease the integration of a PPO option into the regular medical program.

FINANCIAL CONSIDERATIONS

An employer's decision to self-insure its medical program should be made independently of the decision's potential impact on the development of a PPO option, because the financial implications of self-insurance are significant. Self-insurance involves more risk than does a fully insured arrangement. All claim payments and any financial risk of loss under the program are the liability of the employer, though this may be tempered by the purchase of stop-loss insurance that would take over when paid claims reach a certain percentage (e.g., 125 percent) of expected claims. The normally cited advantages and disadvantages of self-insurance are:

Advantages

— The employer should realize improved cash flow through the use of money normally held by the insurance company for reserves and margins.
— The employer may have no state premium tax liability.
— The employer or a third-party administrator (TPA) may be able to administer the plan for less money than is presently being paid to the insurance company for administrative expenses.

Disadvantages

— The employer assumes the full risk of adverse claims fluctuations and full claim liability (unless there is a stop-loss provision).
— The employer may have difficulty in budgeting for monthly claim payments because the flow of claims made can vary over time.
— The employer loses the "insurance" element of its employee medical program.

Once the decision to self-insure is made (again, based solely on its financial implications) the employer may then consider its relevance to the integration of a PPO option into the medical program. Here, the employer must assess both the demographic concentration of its employees and the size and distribution of dollars paid to providers.

Although self-insurance is available to smaller employers (e.g., fewer than 1,000 covered lives), the decision to integrate a negotiated PPO option into a self-funded medical program will be affected by several important variables. Specifically, the employer should have a large concentration of employees in an area where the hospital providers are limited in size and distribution. It would make little sense for an employer acting independently in an area with several large hospitals, and whose employees and their physicians are widely distributed, to integrate a PPO option into its medical plan. The employer's bargaining power in obtaining discounts and improved services from providers would be constrained because the financial power of its employees' medical dollars would be geographically diluted. Further, should one or a few hospital providers be selected for contracting it may be inconvenient and undesirable for many employees to sever relationships with other area hospitals. Consequently, based on both employee levels and distribution, as well as provider size and distribution, the point of self-insurance at which PPO integration makes sense could be substantially higher than 1,000 employees.

FLEXIBILITY IN PROGRAM DESIGN

In a fully insured arrangement, an employer may be somewhat limited in structuring its medical program design. Most states require that benefits, rates, and financial mechanisms of insurance be approved by the State Department of Insurance. By self-insuring its medical program, an employer can avoid most of these regulations and design contractual arrangements that it deems most appropriate.

Further, smaller employers are sometimes limited in structuring their programs by the business practices of major insurance carriers. Depending on the size of the employer, many carriers may only offer a standard medical insurance product that might not meet the needs of an individual employer. By self-insuring, the employer has the opportunity to design its program to its own specifications. Thus, the levels of cost sharing, the coverage of particular services and other factors can be determined by the individual employer.

MANAGEMENT INFORMATION SYSTEMS

Without complete and accurate data reported on a timely basis, it is impossible for an employer to manage its medical program and to make adjustments based on utilization. A sophisticated program of administration will provide detailed information for effective decisions in the areas of cost containment, employee and provider involvement, data base management, and credible cost and utilization projections.

Although many major insurance carriers have fairly sophisticated management information reporting systems, their flexibility in designing custom reports for individual employers may be limited by the employer's size. Smaller employers in particular may have some difficulty in getting reports designed to their own specifications. However, a self-insured employer may contract with a carrier on an ASO (administrative services only) basis or elect to hire a TPA to process claims. Consequently, self-insurance allows for a greater measure of flexibility in shopping around for the best administrative agreement.

The administrative services package should be evaluated on the basis of cost and the ability to deliver a quality data management reporting system. This latter consideration is of particular importance to an employer with a PPO option in its medical program. The employer must have a sophisticated reporting system in order to effectively track and compare utilization and cost patterns between the PPO and non-PPO medical options.

To achieve these goals, an efficient administrator must meet certain requirements. The administrator (be it insurance carrier or TPA) should have the ability to

- Efficiently administer claim payments.
- Provide sophisticated, detailed claim data quickly and efficiently.
- Generate a sophisticated bank of reports including, but not limited to
  - Claims by I.C.D.A.-9s (illness by coding).
  - Claims by diagnosis related groups (DRG).
  - Claims by provider, employee, and dependents.
  - Claims paid within the PPO by procedure and amount.
  - Claims paid outside the PPO by procedure and amount.
- Respond to the needs and objectives of the employer, i.e., be flexible.

Based on the considerations listed above, the employer must evaluate its objectives to determine which vendor can deliver the services best suited to meeting those objectives.

CONCLUSION

The rapid and continuing development of PPOs indicates that, in one form or another, direct contracting in health care will be here for some time to come. Therefore, employers should take action to assure that the process works effectively to control costs.

This action may take the form of multiple medical program options, flexible medical benefit programs, and self-insurance of the medical program, as discussed in this article. Whether it is these or other techniques that are used, employers should be prepared to mold preferred provider arrangements to meet their needs. An action-oriented cost-containment strategy aimed at designing effective preferred provider arrangements offers employers an excellent opportunity to control spiraling health benefits costs.

Purchaser Objectives and Priorities

Promoting Health Through Preferred Arrangements

Jonathan E. Fielding, M.D., M.B.A.

Professor, Schools of Public Health and Medicine,
*   UCLA*
President, U.S. Corporate Health Management
Santa Monica, CA

Leslie M. Alexandre, M.S.P.H.

Cost Containment Specialist,
U.S. Corporate Health Management
Santa Monica, CA

Mary T. Rushka, M.P.H.

Administrator, Worksite Health Promotion Program
Mattel Corporation
Hawthorne, CA

During the past 40 years, employers have been forced to accept greater responsibility for the health of their employees, retirees, and dependents. The employer's role is no longer limited to that of the unquestioning payor of health insurance premiums, worksite injury claims, and disability compensation. Numerous government regulations regarding worksite safety and occupational health have created a fertile ground for the adoption of employee health screening activities and safety and health

431

education programs. Concurrently, union demands and employers' efforts to attract employees have encouraged expansion and diversification of health benefits packages.

Interest in disease prevention and health promotion programs has also emerged from employer concern with health insurance costs that have grown at a faster rate than any other cost of doing business. Much of this increase is due to medical care inflation, which has frequently run more than 150 percent of the consumer price index.[1] The escalating cost of providing health insurance, coupled with the desire to maintain a healthy workforce, has encouraged many employers to pursue organized efforts aimed at keeping employees well.

A strong rationale for employer investment in disease prevention is that many of the principal causes of death and disability can be prevented, or at least forestalled. Cardiovascular disease, cancer, cerebrovascular disease, accidents, and cirrhosis of the liver together account for at least 75 percent of all deaths in the United States.[2] Many of these deaths occur during employees' most productive years and could be averted or postponed by adoption of healthier lifestyles.

Employers interested in reducing the incidence and severity of these debilitating conditions in their workforce usually begin by assessing individual risk for a variety of health problems and then offering health promotion programs to reduce these risks. Health promotion program activities include smoking cessation, hypertension screening and follow-up, nutrition/weight control, exercise/fitness, drug and alcohol abuse control, stress management, accident prevention, and general health education.

Common sense suggests that use of proven preventive approaches can yield greater rewards (both in health status and dollars) than attempting to cure preventable medical problems once their manifestations become apparent. In the long run, employers investing in health promotion programs believe they will see a return on their investment in terms of improved health and lower health benefit costs. In the short run, these employers often benefit from reduced absenteeism, improved morale, and higher productivity.

Another driving force behind the increase in employer-sponsored health promotion/disease prevention activities is consumer demand. The proliferation of research touting the benefits of disease prevention, along with heightened public interest in health, has resulted in a plethora of health information in popular magazines, on television and radio news programs, and in employer and union newsletters. Since most adults devote at least half of their waking hours five days a week to their job, it is not surprising that many employees are anxious to work in an environment that enhances health and supports good personal health habits. Employees are also increasingly requesting medical coverage for preventive services such as well-baby care, immunizations, and periodic examinations that include mammography and Pap smears.[3]

In industries where competition for technically skilled employees is keen, sponsoring health promotion activities can provide a competitive edge over other companies in terms of recruitment and retention. Evidence of this is seen in California's "Silicon Valley," where some on-site company fitness centers have replaced the employee cafeteria as the gathering place of young, energetic workers. For these "high tech" employers, the health and fitness program is part of the benefits package and marketed prominently by company recruiters.

PROVIDERS AND DISEASE PREVENTION

Over the past decade, there has been a slow but steady increase in the availability of preventive services from the medical community. Three major forces that have moved physicians and other health care providers in the direction of prevention are (1) a growing emphasis on comprehensive primary care services in the delivery of health care, (2) rapidly expanding competition among health care providers, and (3) greater availability of third-party reimbursement for nontraditional types of care.

GROWING EMPHASIS ON PRIMARY CARE

For decades the trend in both medical education and post medical school training was toward greater and greater levels of specialization. The position of the primary care physician in the health care delivery system was notably subordinated to that of the specialist. Now, the major payors for health care services are looking to make primary care physicians the gatekeepers to the rest of the health care system.

High-quality medical care is marked by coordination and continuity of services. Primary care physicians are the logical candidates to assume responsibility for this type of care, since they generally have the patient's complete medical history and are trained to handle a much broader array of somatic and nonsomatic problems than most specialists. Primary care physicians can refer their patients to specialists when necessary and be responsible for following up the results of the referral. The gatekeeper approach assigns responsibility for monitoring a patient's use of specialty services to a single primary care physician. This promotes cost effectiveness by minimizing duplication of services and unnecessary use of more intense levels of care.

Good primary care goes far beyond the provision of routine clinical services. The primary care physician must be an educator, counselor, motivator of behavior change, and reinforcer of positive changes in health habits. Preventive services, including the identification of high-risk individuals, early detection of disease, health education, and health maintenance, fall naturally within the domain of the primary care physician. An increasing supply of primary care physicians, particularly family practitioners trained and interested in preventive services, portends a greater availability of preventive health services in the community.

PROVIDER COMPETITION

Based on projections by the Graduate Medical Education National Advisory Committee (GMENAC), by 1990 the United States will have nearly 70,000 more physicians than necessary, and more than 145,000 extra physicians by the year 2000.[4] Physicians throughout metropolitan and suburban communities are already feeling the impact of considerable direct competition brought about by the physician surplus.

Physicians are competing for patients not only with other physicians but also with a growing array of nonphysician practitioners. Allied health practitioners have become a more viable option for many insurees as a result of greater availability of third-party reimbursement for these lower cost substitutes for physician services. A national survey of more than 600 major employers found that about 90 percent provide coverage for chiropractors and psychologists, 80 percent for podiatrists, 40 percent for medical and psychiatric social workers, and between one fourth and one third cover certified acupuncturists, certified nurse midwives, and Christian Science practitioners.[5]

One visible offshoot of these trends is that many physicians are striving to differentiate their services from those of their competitors. Preventive services, frequently overlooked in the practice of medicine, are gaining in popularity with both purchasers and consumers of health care services. These services offer physicians a positive way to attract and retain new patients.

Hospitals, particularly those with lower occupancy rates, are also facing intense competitive pressures. Hospital inpatient utilization is dropping without a commensurate decline in hospital capacity. New ambulatory care services, including freestanding surgicenters and emergicenters, are directly competing with hospitals for patients. Health maintenance organizations and selective provider contracting programs are channeling large groups of patients into some hospitals, increasing the number of empty beds in others.

In an attempt to improve their competitive posture, many hospitals are vertically integrating their acute care services with other levels of care.[6] The goal of vertical integration is to provide a set of services that will direct patients from one level of care to another according to their health care needs. For example, a patient coming to a hospital's outpatient clinic for a periodic assessment that reveals a malignant breast lump is likely to have surgical follow-up at that hospital.

One way that a number of hospitals have expanded their scope of services has been to develop and/or market wellness programs that include such activities as a health risk appraisal, work-related screenings, occupational health services, smoking cessation and other behaviorally-oriented classes, and blood pressure screening and follow-up. Hospital-sponsored wellness activities are typically used to improve visibility in the community, promote a positive image, and, most importantly, attract patients to the hospital for the use of inpatient services.

ALTERNATIVE CARE COVERAGE

The most common cost-control activity undertaken by employers in the first half of the 1980s is the redesign of their medical benefit plans to create consumer incentives for more appropriate use of the health care system. One of the most positive outcomes of this activity is the addition of coverage for a broad array of alternative providers, services, and settings for care. Examples include home health care, hospice, birthing centers, extended care, and non-hospital alcohol rehabilitation. There has been a significant shift from excluding coverage for many of the newer, less costly health care alternatives to providing at least limited and sometimes full coverage for these options.[7] Cost control is the major reason for the shift, with employers attempting to direct employees and their families toward the lowest cost source of care that will produce good health outcomes.

A number of employers have begun to cover preventive services in their medical benefits plans. For example, in 1983 Bank of America added coverage under its fee-for-service indemnity plan for childhood immunizations up to age 12 and for Pap smears.[8] A national survey of employer health care cost-containment activities found that 13 percent of respondents provided coverage for screening services (early detection or multiphasic), 13.3 percent for well-baby care, 17.3 percent for childhood immunizations, and 40 percent for Pap smears.[9] Some of the reasons why employers add preventive services to health benefits packages include: (1) a belief that covering preventive services will provide a substantial return on investment in the long run, (2) a desire to bring the benefit plan in line with the employer's overall emphasis on health improvement, and (3) the perception of preventive services as a positive low cost tradeoff for other benefit plan changes that are expected to be met with disfavor by employees.

OPPORTUNITIES FOR PREVENTION

Private health insurance coverage for preventive services has generally been unavailable for fully insured plans. Commercial carriers have traditionally expected the patient to pay for non-illness-related routine care and Blue Cross/Blue Shield coverage for prevention has usually been limited to hospital-based inpatient health education.

Many employers are moving to self-insure their medical benefits and can therefore exercise greater discretion as to what services are covered.

However, many of the self-insured employers are reluctant to provide coverage for additional services in the face of escalating health insurance costs. Preventive services are often viewed as an add-on rather than an integral component of the medical plan. Even when there is interest in covering preventive services of proven effectiveness, there may be lack of consensus regarding which services meet this criterion.

Increasingly, employers are turning to preferred provider arrangements when faced with mounting pressure to offer a rich employee benefits smorgasbord without incurring avoidable health benefit cost increases. Preferred provider arrangements offer employers an opportunity to add health insurance coverage for preventive services. Within a preferred arrangement employees can be encouraged, through economic incentives and education, to obtain routine preventive care at appropriate intervals. Contracting directly with preferred providers for preventive services allows employers to establish guidelines for proper utilization and to monitor provider behavior.

From a marketing perspective, preventive services can provide a positive incentive for employees to utilize selected providers. Based on the experience of health maintenance organizations, offering comprehensive preventive services is a very attractive feature. Coverage for preventive services holds special appeal for younger employees and their families who are often oriented toward prevention.

Providing coverage for preventive services is also desirable for any employer trying to create a "corporate norm" of good health. Encouragement of good health practices, including the appropriate use of preventive services, is being integrated into the corporate culture of many U.S. companies, often following the example of a committed CEO or other senior ranking employee.[10] Increasingly, employers are establishing smoking (or NO smoking) policies and publicizing the undesirability of this habit.[11] More visible testimony to the creation of good health norms in American business are the par courses, employee health information resource centers, and "relaxation rooms" at a growing number of worksites. Sponsorship of a preferred arrangement that incorporates preventive services is a natural complement to these actions.

Some preferred arrangements, particularly those with hospitals, may even involve the preferred provider bringing health risk screening and follow-up educational programs on-site. This service may be especially valued by smaller employers without the internal resources to develop and staff an employee health promotion program.

SELECTED EXPERIENCES

Incorporating preventive services into preferred arrangements has not been accorded high priority by most participants (employers, providers, insurers) in these arrangements. For example, employers contemplating preferred arrangements are frequently too busy sorting out the confusing array of providers and plans to consider the advantages of such a marriage. There are, however, representatives from each of the relevant parties who have followed their inclination that preventive services are a natural component of a preferred arrangement and have established pioneering efforts in this direction. A few of these efforts are described here.

Employer Example

One employer that has placed a high priority on the inclusion of preventive health services in negotiating preferred arrangements with providers is Cleveland-based Ameritrust Company, National Association. In June 1983, Ameritrust began offering its 3,300 covered employees several new options for medical coverage. In addition to their traditional basic medical-supplemental major medical plan, employees could select among an 80 percent comprehensive plan, three HMOs, and two PPOs. The PPOs offered, Ohio Health Choice Plan and Emerald Health Network, are similar in design, each involving a group of hospitals that have joined together with virtually all of their admitting physicians to form a network of preferred providers.

Ameritrust made it a point to incorporate coverage for preventive services into their agreements with both PPOs, motivated by a belief in the cost effectiveness of health promotion and disease prevention and a desire to make the preferred provider options at least as attractive as the HMOs. Preventive services covered are similar to those provided by the HMOs and include well-baby care, periodic examinations, childhood and adult immunizations, and eye refractions. The content of periodic examinations is left to the discretion of the providing physician, but the services included are expected to be appropriate to the age and sex of the patient. The Ohio Choice Health Plan also provides patients with a computerized health risk appraisal, which is administered at their health center. Preventive services under both arrangements can be received either from a primary care physician or a specialist, can be used as frequently as desired, and, like all other services covered under the preferred plans, do not require coinsurance.

Although information on insurees' use of these preferred arrangements is not yet available, the company believes that the inclusion of preventive services, particularly well-child care, was an important reason for many employees selecting the preferred plans. This belief is supported by the fact that enrollment in the PPOs (approximately 20 percent of the covered employees) is comprised of a larger percentage of families than enrollment in the Blue Cross plans, which do not cover preventive services.[12]

Insurer Example

Through its CHOICE plan, Aetna Life and Casualty has been one of the strongest promoters of the gatekeeper approach to preferred provider arrangements. The CHOICE plan is structured to encourage consumers to be efficient users of the health care system.[13] To belong to CHOICE, each enrollee must designate a personal physician through whom all non-emergency care will be initiated. Any licensed physician is acceptable for this role, primary care or otherwise. If specialty services are required by the patient, he or she must be referred to physicians and surgeons with whom Aetna has contracted. Any nonemergency surgery that is necessary must be performed in a recognized referral hospital.

By eliminating the financial barriers to primary care, which is broadly defined to include virtually all nonemergency, nonspecialty services, Aetna's plan provides consumers with greater access to preventive health care services. The CHOICE plan eliminates deductibles and covers 100 percent of the cost of primary care up to the maximum expenditure specified by the employer, which is generally in the range of $200 to $400 per insuree. If the maximum is reached, a 20 percent coinsurance is attached to additional primary care services up to a maximum family out-of-pocket expenditure of $500. All inpatient and specialty services are fully reimbursed by the plan.

Provider Example

El Camino Hospital in Mountain View, California has created a preferred provider arrangement that reflects its belief that innovative employers want not only a comprehensive, well-run health promotion program but also access to a medical care delivery system that has a proven track record of quality and efficiency. Three hundred of the 380 staff physicians have formed the El Camino Preferred Physicians Medical Group, Inc. (PPMG) and have contracted with the single largest employer in the area, Hewlett-Packard Company.

Membership in the PPMG plan is open to all Hewlett-Packard employees and family members enrolled in the company's self-funded health plan (a total of 38,000 covered lives). Financial and promotional attractions for the group's services include a reduction in copayments and deductibles for primary and specialty care plus the opportunity to participate in El Camino Hospital's *Lifecheck* health promotion program. *Lifecheck* is a health risk screening and health promotion program that can be offered either at the worksite or at the hospital's facilities to groups of employees and their family members.

Lifecheck generally consists of the following five health education workshops:

1. *Orientation:* This is a general education session during which the concept of health risk factors and their relationship to disease and disabil-

ity are discussed. After the session, participants may choose to make an appointment for a health risk screening.

2. *Screening:* The lifestyle screening program is designed to motivate employees to take positive action toward improving their health habits. Participants receive a personal computerized health risk evaluation after completing a lifestyle questionnaire and having key physical parameters (e.g., blood pressure, height, weight) measured.

3. *Interpretation of Results:* At this meeting, a computerized interpretation of each participant's health risk appraisal is returned to him or her with an explanation of the meaning of the scores. Participants also complete a health plan that includes a commitment to take action to reduce ameliorable health risks.

4. *Review of Risk Factors:* This session centers primarily on discussion of the major "risk reduction" areas of stress management, hypertension control, nutrition/weight management, exercise, and smoking cessation.

5. *"Dollars and Sense":* The final session teaches participants how to be wise health care consumers. Topics include choosing a physician, assertiveness in the patient-physician encounter, prudent use of the health plan, and an introduction to the El Camino PPMG.

The novelty of El Camino's model program has engendered considerable interest from other local employers who await employer/employee/provider reaction as they develop their own preferred arrangements.[14]

CRITICAL EMPLOYER QUESTIONS

When using a preferred arrangement as a vehicle for making preventive services available to their insurees, employers should be careful to structure the details of the arrangement in the way that will best meet both their health and health care cost objectives. Important questions employers should consider in negotiating for preventive services as part of a preferred arrangement will be discussed in the following sections.

WHAT ARE THE GOALS OF INCLUDING PREVENTIVE SERVICES IN THE CONTRACT?

Employers may incorporate preventive services into their preferred arrangements in order to: (1) make the preferred option more attractive relative to other plan choices, (2) offer employees a positive new benefit, (3) reduce health care costs, (4) ensure competitiveness of the company benefit package with other employers, and/or (5) supplement services provided in the company's health promotion program.

If the primary goal is selection of the preferred arrangement by a larger number of employees, the employer will need to decide what degree of coverage for preventive services is necessary to entice its workers to select that option. In one case it may be a sufficient incentive to include reimbursement for two or three preventive services that have either frequently been requested for coverage by employees or that an employee survey reveals to be most desired. Where the insuree population is comprised of many young families, for example, the availability of coverage for well-baby care and childhood immunizations may attract many employees to the preferred arrangement. In a different case, where the alternative plan options already contain coverage for at least some preventive services, it may be necessary to offer insurees a much broader package of preventive services under the preferred arrangement and eliminate any cost sharing requirements for their use.

When employers have a strong interest in pursuing the long-range health and cost benefits of disease prevention among their insured population, their primary goal will be to increase the use of preventive services among their insurees. Employers can best meet this goal by incorporating a well-defined, comprehensive set of preventive services into the preferred arrangement, working with the providers to ensure that these are delivered in the most effective manner and eliminating any financial barriers to their use.

WHAT PREVENTIVE SERVICES WILL BE OFFERED TO INSUREES, IN WHAT SETTINGS, AND WHAT RESTRICTIONS, IF ANY, WILL BE PLACED ON THEIR USE?

Prenatal care (including amniocentesis and genetic counseling), well-baby care, childhood and adult immunizations, periodic examinations that include screening for early detection of health problems, and patient education and counseling about health habits and risk factors for disease all constitute disease prevention services. Which combination of these services is most appropriately provided through a preferred arrangement depends both on the nature of the preferred arrangement and the employer's current prevention activities.

Some preventive services, such as prenatal and well-child care, are personal health care services that are generally provided in a physician's office or clinic by trained medical practitioners. Many preventive services, however, can be effectively provided in a group setting by nonphysician health professionals. Behaviorally oriented lifestyle change activities and counseling about proper nutrition and stress reduction are good examples of these types of services. Preferred hospitals and some preferred physician groups may be willing to offer these activities at the employer's site, which encourages greater employee participation. In addition, preferred providers gain from a positive introduction to employees prior to any occasion when they or their families might require the use of their medical services.

Settling on a package of preventive services for which provider reimbursement will be available is generally less difficult than establishing a set of reasonable guidelines to govern the provision and use of these services. Guidelines are particularly important when periodic examinations are one of the covered services. Sometimes physicians, as well as their patients, are not familiar with the recommended content and frequency of these health assessments. As a result, some physicians have a tendency to include procedures for which there is no medical justification, such as chest X rays as a screen for lung cancer in the "well" (i.e., asymptomatic, nonoccupationally exposed) population, or broad blood chemistry panels. Inappropriate screening can lead to unnecessary patient discomfort and added benefit plan expense due to insurees undergoing extensive diagnostic work-ups to rule out possible disease after a false-positive screening test result.

There are a number of resources available to assist employers in defining the content and frequency of periodic exams.[15] One aid to employers is a set of criteria that can be applied to diseases and conditions under consideration for inclusion in a periodic exam. Screening for a disease or condition is appropriate if it meets all of the following criteria:

— It is an important cause of illness, disability, or death.
— It has an asymptomatic or minimally symptomatic period during which detection and treatment can substantially reduce illness and/or death.
— Treatment in the asymptomatic state yields a better outcome than treatment begun after symptoms appear.
— Patients are willing to comply with treatment.
— The natural history of the disease is sufficiently well known, risks resulting from screening are low enough (medically and psychologically), and treatments are sufficiently effective in reducing illness, disability, and/or death to conclude that screening-initiated diagnosis can lead to a net benefit in the target population.
— The screening tests used are acceptable, accurate (i.e. acceptable number of false-positives and false-negatives), available at reasonable cost, and relatively easy to administer.

Over the past decade several prominent groups of scientists and physicians have applied these and other similar criteria to available screening approaches to develop a set of recommended procedures for inclusion in a periodic exam, usually for each age and sex-specific group at suggested frequencies. Among these groups are the Institute of Medicine Ad Hoc Advisory Group on Preventive Services for the Well Population, the Canadian Task Force on the Periodic Health Examination, the American Cancer Society, and, most recently, the INSURE Project, sponsored by the commercial insurance industry and the Robert Wood Johnson and MacArthur Foundations.[16-19]

The Lifecycle Preventive Health Services (LPHS) Guidelines developed by the INSURE Project are based on a complete review and modification of all of the earlier sets of recommendations. These guidelines are particularly applicable to employers, since the purpose of the INSURE Project is to determine the feasibility and impact of providing reimbursement for a defined set of preventive services as a health insurance benefit.[20] The LPHS Guidelines for young and middle-aged adults are displayed in Exhibit 1.

HOW CAN THE PREVENTIVE SERVICES COMPONENT OF A PREFERRED ARRANGEMENT BEST BE MONITORED AND EVALUATED?

If the purpose of incorporating coverage for preventive services is primarily to encourage employees to utilize preferred providers, an employer may be content with merely tracking insuree use of different providers. Utilization of preferred providers should be easy to measure, but without knowing what it would have been in the absence of coverage for preventive services, it is not possible to attribute use of a preferred provider directly to their inclusion. A random sample survey of the workforce can be useful for determining why employees selected particular providers and for ascertaining insurees' level of satisfaction with plan features and services. By including the proper questions, such a survey can also reveal the general extent to which preventive services are being used, and the likelihood of increasing selection of the preferred option(s) by including coverage for additional preventive services.

Some employers who incorporate coverage for preventive services in their preferred arrangements will want to know the degree to which these services are being used over time and the approximate cost to the plan. Most claims payment systems, however, do not encourage or require accurate description or coding of many preventive services by a physician. Because insurance coverage has traditionally been unavailable for disease prevention, physicians seeking third-party reimbursement for preventive services have learned to indicate specific medical diagnoses for which services are reimbursable instead of preventive care, which is generally not paid for under most benefits plans.

Even if physicians are willing to fill out the claim form accurately, most standard claims forms are not designed to accommodate coverage for preventive services. For example, in many instances it is impossible to distinguish services that were provided preventively from those that were follow-up to a suspected disease or condition.

Employers who are genuinely concerned with monitoring the use of preventive services under the benefits plan will probably need to work with their carrier and/or claims administrator, and preferably some phy-

EXHIBIT 1. Summary Table of LPHS Guidelines

	Young and Middle Adults (18–59 Years)	*18–24 Years*	*25–30 Years*	*40–59 Years*
	One LPHS exam *every 5 years* plus interim exams every 2–3 years beginning at age 40.	Health problems: 1) Deaths and disability from motor vehicle accidents. 2) Transition from adolescence to adulthood. 3) Development of unhealthy lifestyle.	Health problems: 1) Deaths and disability from motor vehicle accidents. 2) Development of unhealthy lifestyle.	Health problems: 1) Control of cardiovascular risk factors. 2) Deaths and disability from cancer of lung, colon/rectum, and breast. 3) Health hazards associated with alcohol consumption.
	Minimum preventive services as listed below plus history, physical exam and lab work as indicated	Every 5 years	Every 5 years	Every 5 years Every 2–3 years as indicated

INTERVAL & RISKS — HISTORY

	18–24 Years	25–30 Years	40–59 Years
1) Blood pressure	✔	✔	✔
2) Cigarette smoking	✔	✔	✔
3) Alcohol & drug use	✔	✔	✔
4) Diet	✔	✔	✔
5) Exercise	✔	✔	✔
6) Auto & seat belt use	✔	✔	✔
7) Family planning	✔	✔	✔
8) Accident prevention	✔	✔	✔
9) Breast and skin self exam	✔	✔	✔
10) Oral hygiene	✔	✔	✔

PHYSICAL — EXAM

	18–24 Years	25–30 Years	40–59 Years
1) Height	✔	✔	✔
2) Weight	✔	✔	Every 2–3 years
3) Blood pressure	✔	✔	Every 2–3 years
4) Rectal exam			Every 2–3 years
5) Hearing screening			Every 2–3 years
6) Breast exam	✔	✔	Every 2–3 years and annually 50+

LAB PROCEDURES & IMMUNIZATIONS

	18–24 Years	25–30 Years	40–59 Years
1) Serum cholesterol		Males once	Females once
2) TBC skin test	High risk, once		
3) Stool occult blood			Annually
4) Blood glucose			✔
5) Pap smear	Every 3 years after 2 neg.	Every 3 years after 2 neg.	Every 3 years after 2 neg.
6) Mammography			Annually after 50 yrs.
7) Tetanus	Every 10 years	Every 10 years	Every 10 years
8) Polio	High risk		
9) Rubella	Unimm/nonpreg. fem.		
10) Pneumococcal vaccine	High risk	High risk	High risk

PATIENT EDUCATION

	18–24 Years	25–30 Years	40–59 Years
1) Cigarette smoking	✔	✔	✔
2) Diet cholesterol	✔	✔	✔
3) Weight control	✔	✔	✔
4) Salt intake	✔	✔	✔
5) Alcohol & drug use	✔	✔	✔
6) Exercise	✔	✔	✔
7) Family planning	✔	✔	✔
8) Accident prevention	✔	✔	✔
9) Breast and skin self exam	✔	✔	✔
10) Oral hygiene and dental referral	✔	✔	✔

sicians, to modify existing claims forms. Employers will also need to educate both employees and physicians about how to use the form. In a preferred arrangement the opportunity for this type of provider education is greater than in a traditional plan, since the employer is dealing with an identifiable group of physicians that are interested in maintaining a contractual relationship with the employer, the employer's insurer, or its medical claims administrator.

There are several utilization and cost variables that employers should review when assessing the impact of adding coverage for preventive services. For each specific service covered, variables periodically reported to the employer by its carrier or administrator should include: (1) total number of visits, (2) number of visits per 1,000 insurees, (3) total number of services, (4) number of services per 1,000 insurees, (5) number of unique claimants, (6) total dollars paid, and (7) average dollars paid per service.[21] Although this is frequently difficult to accomplish, it is particularly useful to display these variables by age/sex distributions of the insuree population to determine which types of insurees have the highest utilization rates for different preventive services.

In the long run, most employers will want to know if offering preventive services leads to better health outcomes in those employees who use the services properly. The strength of such an evaluation will be enhanced by knowing whether employees who selected a plan covering preventive services differed notably from those who did not select such a plan with respect to age, sex, prior use of the health care system, and other factors that might suggest that employees who select a plan that covers prevention are more (or less) healthy initially.

Assessment of the long-term health impacts of preventive services requires a two-part analysis. First, the extent to which preventive services were actually used by insurees must be established. Only if it can be determined that preventive services were in fact used by insurees is it appropriate to examine the potential effects of their usage on disease rates or on the cost and utilization of health care services.

One obvious measure to include in such an evaluation is the frequency and benefit plan costs of various diseases and conditions for which preventive services were available. For example, a preventive services package typically includes screening procedures for several cancers. Variables that might be compared over time include: (1) age-adjusted rates of overt cancers for which early screening was covered, (2) age-adjusted per capita dollars paid for these conditions, (3) age-adjusted per capita hospital-related dollars paid for these conditions, (4) frequencies and lengths of short and long-term disabilities arising from these cancers, and (5) per capita absenteeism.

However, when conducting this type of evaluation, there are significant methodological problems for employers to overcome in order to reach valid conclusions. If at some point the employer decides to cover preventive services for all employees, a different evaluation scheme will have to be used that relies on an external population for purposes of comparison.

Even greater methodological difficulties arise when employers attempt to compute the dollar savings of offering preventive services. It would be desirable to compute the ratio of costs to benefits, where benefits would include reductions in expenditures for health insurance, worker's compensation, disability, turnover, and absenteeism. However, definitive conclusions require large comparable populations, high utilization of preventive services benefits, and many years of comparison.

Benefits of improved health from early identification of preventable problems can be estimated from other studies, such as those cited by the American Cancer Society in developing its guidelines for cancer screening.[22] In addition, some behavioral changes, such as smoking cessation, can be reasonably expected to reduce the toll and known costs of excess morbidity and mortality associated with specific health risks.[23]

CONCLUSION

In these days of fiscal retrenchment in health benefits, preferred provider arrangements that include preventive services represent a positive option for both employers and employees. Preferred arrangements allow employers to offer the services of a selected group of practitioners who have indicated a greater than average interest in the provision of high quality preventive care. In addition, preferred arrangements may permit employers to more readily monitor the use of preventive services over time by tracking simple cost and utilization variables.

Employees, often inundated by news of their plans' latest cost-containment feature, will be pleasantly surprised to find preferred arrangements that include preventive services among their benefits options.

NOTES

1. J. E. Fielding, *Corporate Health Management* (Palo Alto, CA: Addison-Wesley, 1984).

2. U.S. Department of Health, Education and Welfare. Public Health Service. *Healthy People: The Surgeon General's Report on Health Promotion and Disease Prevention.* DHEW (PHS) Publication No. 79–55071. Washington, D.C.: U.S.G.P.O.

3. D. N. Logson, M. A. Rosen, and M. M. Demak, "The INSURE Project on Lifecycle Preventive Health Services: Cost Containment Issues," *Inquiry* 20, no. 2 (1983), pp. 121–126.

4. U.S. Department of Health and Human Services. Public Health Service. *Summary Report of the Graduate Medical Education National Advisory Committee* September 30, 1980. Vol. 1. Washington, D.C.: U.S.G.P.O.

5. Health Research Institute, *Health Care Cost Containment Third Biennial Survey Participant Report* (Walnut Creek, CA, Winter 1983), p. 16.

6. J. Goldsmith, *Can Hospitals Survive?* (Homewood, IL: Dow Jones-Irwin, 1981).

7. Health Research Institute, *Health Care Cost Containment.*

8. Personal communication, Bank of America, April 1984.

9. Health Research Institute, *Health Care Cost Containment,* p. 17.

10. R. M. Cunningham, Jr., *Wellness at Work: A Report on Health and Fitness Programs for Business and Industry* (Chicago, IL.: Inquiry Books, 1982), p. 56.

11. Personal communication, California Council on Smoking and Health, January 1984.

12. Personal communication with Emily Kane, Health Care Benefits Administrator, Ameritrust Company, National Association, March 1984.

13. Personal communication with Dr. John Harper, CHOICE Medical Director, Aetna Life and Casualty, March 1984.

14. Personal communications with Jim Norris, Associate Chief Executive Officer, El Camino Hospital, Mountain View, CA, and Dale Turner, Director of Lifecheck Program for El Camino Hospital, March 1984.

15. J. E. Fielding and L. M. Alexandre, "Assessing Health: What Can Employers Do?" *Business and Health* 1, no. 4 (March 1984), pp. 5–12.

16. J. E. Fielding, "Preventive Services for the Well Population," in *Healthy People: The Surgeon General's Report on Health Promotion and Disease Prevention, Background Papers.* U.S. Department of Health, Education and Welfare. Public Health Service. DHEW (PHS) Pub. No. 79–55071A, 1979, pp. 277–304. Washington, D.C.: U.S.G.P.O.

17. Canadian Task Force on the Periodic Health Examination. *Periodic Health Examination: Report of a Task Force to the Conference of Deputy Ministers of Health.* Canadian Government Publishing Centre, 1980.

18. American Cancer Society, *The Health-Related Checkup,* 1980.

19. D. N. Logsdon et al., *The Lifecycle Preventive Health Services Physicians Manual* (INSURE Project: New York, NY, 1982).

20. Ibid.

21. Where it is not possible to determine or estimate the total number of covered lives under the plan, the number of covered employees can be used to calculate this rate. However, if the composition of insurees in the plan changes notably from year to year comparisons of this rate over time become less reliable.

22. American Cancer Society, *The Health-Related Checkup.*

23. J. E. Fielding, "Effectiveness of Employee Health Improvement Programs," *Journal of Occupational Medicine* 24, no. 11 (November 1982), pp. 907–916.

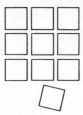

Purchaser Objectives and Priorities

EMPLOYER APPROACHES TO INITIATING A PPO

Jennifer B. Flink
Hewitt Associates
Lincolnshire, IL

Larry J. Tucker
Hewitt Associates
Newport Beach, CA

Preferred provider organizations began in a provider-based atmosphere. As the health care environment became more competitive, hospitals and physicians pursued PPO arrangements as a way to compete more effectively in the marketplace. Considering that employers who sponsor health care plans also pay the majority of the costs, employers were natural targets for their marketing efforts.

Today, the majority of operational PPOs are provider sponsored. Most employers do not have the immediate resources to sponsor or control a PPO. However, employer involvement in initiating a PPO can influence the effectiveness of the arrangement. While not all PPOs are managing health care costs effectively, early experience indicates that PPOs can work if organized and managed properly.

Not surprisingly, the primary objective of employer-initiated PPOs is to manage health care costs. PPOs may improve provider efficiencies through the setting of competitive prices and lessening the intensity of services used by patients. By establishing cost controls and monitoring treatment methods, PPOs have the potential to minimize the cost-shifting impact that has come as a result of medicare cuts and the new medicare reimbursement system.

The more employers learn about the potential of PPOs, the more information they will need to organize this alternative form of health care delivery. For that reason, information in this chapter is written specifically to guide the employer in considering all the alternatives for developing a PPO—from initially asking whether a PPO is feasible to working with others to establish one. If an employer finds that existing PPOs are not available or do not meet the organization's expectations, then the employer may decide to initiate a PPO through one of the following approaches:

— Establish a PPO as a single employer.
— Work with a local coalition or other employers on an individual basis.
— Work with claims administrators.
— Work with providers.

The first section will focus on these approaches and consider the employer's ability to undertake any one of them.

APPROACHES TO EMPLOYER-INITIATED PPOs

A decision tree can be used to identify the approaches an employer may take (see Exhibit 1) to initiate a PPO. First, some initial consideration needs to be given to whether a PPO is a feasible alternative at all.

The key issue is whether the health care environment is competitive. Most industries and professions benefit from at least a modest amount of competition; the health care industry is no different. As more hospitals and physicians feel the effects of competition, the health care system should become more efficient. Communities with low hospital occupancy rates and excess physicians are highly competitive. If little or no competition is present in a given geographic area, it may be difficult to create the necessary incentives to form a workable PPO.

On the other hand, in some communities without sufficient competition an employer's historical relationship may be strong enough to encourage providers into a PPO.

Assuming the community *is* an appropriate environment for a PPO, the second branch of the decision tree (Exhibit 1, B) can be addressed: an evaluation of existing PPOs. This is a critical step in the overall decision-making process.

SELF-INITIATING A PPO

There are three major considerations of an employer initiating its own PPO.

EXHIBIT 1

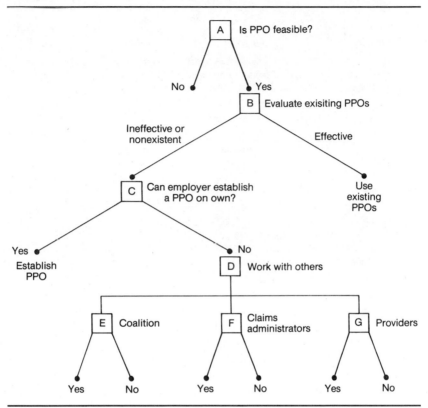

- Employer must have strong market power in the community.
- Health care environment must be right to support a PPO.
- Financial commitment must be there.

STRONG MARKET POWER

Market power is the most important element to consider when establishing a PPO. Whether a company has the market power to start a PPO on its own will be determined largely by such tangible factors as the size of the organization in relation to the size of the community (see Exhibit 2). On one level, the ideal situation involves a large company located in a medium-sized community. There are numerous medium-sized communities where a large company employs a substantial portion of the population. This arrangement would more naturally lend itself to establishing a PPO.

Although the relationship between the size of the employer and the community is a key to market power, other less tangible factors are also

EXHIBIT 2

Size of Community	Size of Employer		
	Large	Medium	Small
Large (many hospitals, many doctors)	Work with others; may work alone if densely populated in one area.	Work with others.	Work with others.
Medium (few hospitals, many doctors)	Develop PPO on own or with others. Evaluate market power.	Join with others.	Join with others.
Small (one hospital, few doctors)	Limited possibilities.	Limited possibilities.	Limited possibilities.

important. In general, the employer should be perceived as a "dominant force" in the community. While the size of the employee workforce and the economic impact the group can have is part of what determines that dominance, there are other elements, such as the employer's leadership participation in the community. That participation can be through grant contributions to cultural affairs, athletic events, health care research, or other philanthropic activities; development arrangements to set up community programs such as a health fair; or contributions of time and expertise through education.

Has the employer been part of community problem solving or problem creating? In most communities, the same organizations' names surface again and again. The employer will consider whether any past events have created tension between the employer and the community. What historical role, if any, has the employer played in the health care delivery system? And, the employer will consider whether it is perceived as knowledgeable in the area of health care and preferred provider organizations. Raising these questions will identify whether the company is perceived as a threat or an ally. This is also dependent on the size of the community.

ANALYZING HEALTHCARE ENVIRONMENT

If an employer is in a good position to initiate a PPO based on market power, the next step is to analyze the health care environment. If there are already active PPOs, the employer will assess the competition and evaluate the wisdom in establishing an additional PPO. Finding out whether providers will contract with multiple PPOs will be critical in staffing the organization.

Part of that assessment also will include understanding the medical community's attitude toward PPOs. Some physicians feel threatened by PPOs because they are seen as a departure from the traditional mode of an office-based, private practitioner relating to the individual patient. In other cases, there is a concern among physicians that quality of health care might suffer because the new environment places limitations on costs and lacks the continuity of patient care. However, since the health care market is now more competitive in many parts of the country, physicians are turning to PPOs as potential career alternatives. For that reason, employers will find more physicians willing to contract with a PPO.

FINANCIAL COMMITMENT

After assessing competition and community attitudes, the employer will analyze the financial risks involved. Initiating a PPO, independent from other groups, requires a significant financial commitment. Coordinating the information needed, making the analyses, and organizing utilization-review procedures—while at the same time soliciting providers—can be costly and time consuming. In addition, the employer will incur costs related to developing contracts, reviewing all the legal implications, employee communication, and plan documents. This initial expense of planning and research can be very costly. Although an employer can reduce this cost by eliminating data analysis and other aspects of PPO coordination, skimping on start-up costs will have an adverse impact on the long-term effectiveness of the PPO.

FORMING A PPO WITH OTHERS

If an organization does not meet the criteria for initiating a PPO alone or would prefer to share the responsibility, then the employer can look to others. There are three possibilities: employer coalitions, claims administrators, or providers.

COALITION-INITIATED PPO

One way to share the start-up costs and responsibilities of a PPO is to participate in a local health care coalition. More than 200 coalitions have been organized nationwide by employers who recognize a need to work together in addressing the rising costs of medical care.

Some coalitions ask hospitals and physicians to join the organization to assure a provider perspective; most are restricted to employers. And, although coalitions' objectives vary, their most common goal is to find creative ways to combine patient volume with health care dollars to control costs and, at the same time, keep health care quality high.

If an active community coalition exists, the first steps toward establishing a PPO may have already been identified, such as:

— Cost control measures have been discussed and evaluated.
— Community resources have been identified.
— Employers that represent substantial patient volumes have been recognized and included in the coalition.

Beyond these issues, the employers must confirm their commitment to the success of a coalition-initiated PPO. To do so, first, they must be prepared to offer and even to promote the PPO to their employees. Second, they must be willing to commit the time and money required. In order to finance the study, the coalition might seek other employers looking for future savings in their employee medical plans.

Like an employer-initiated PPO, the coalition is faced with demands for time and money. A major advantage to a coalition-initiated PPO is the ability of each employer to share the responsibilities of time and money.

HEALTHCARE CLAIMS ADMINISTRATORS

Another alternative is for an employer to approach an insurance carrier, third-party administrator, or foundation for medical care (FMC) to become involved in the PPO development process. Certainly, the larger administrators can lend some advantages to the process since they

— Can increase an employer's market power by selling the PPO to the administrator's other clients.
— Have in-house expertise, such as medical consultants, to assist in planning and possibly implementing a PPO.
— Have in-house counsel to review state laws and develop the PPO contract.
— Have access to data that can be used to identify efficient providers.
— Have utilization-review programs (in some cases).

Already, a number of insurance carriers and third-party administrators are developing PPOs in certain geographic areas as pilot studies. However, others have to be sold on the concept. Many TPAs and carriers do not have the budgets or staffing to develop a PPO product, and large national carriers do not always recognize the needs and opportunities in particular geographic areas. Employers, then, must approach administrators with the PPO concept and initiate their involvement.

Claims administrators may profit from some education by interested employers and, as a result, recognize that a PPO product can be an excellent marketing tool. During this period when health care cost management is a high priority to employees, a PPO product may be attractive to them.

Some administrators are currently marketing their PPO contracts as separate products from claims processing services. Although many claims administrators prefer to sell these services jointly, they recognize the competitive importance and financial gain in marketing their PPO contracts as a stand-alone product. Also, it enables administrators to

— Attract large patient volumes among potential clients.
— Introduce other products and services to this potential client group.

Foundations for Medical Care are another type of claims administrator that may be approached to initiate a PPO. Prior to the establishment of the Medicare System, Foundations for Medical Care or FMCs were developed as peer-review mechanisms. Today, these physician-organized foundations sell services to employers that include the following:

— Claims processing.
— Reduced physician fees.
— Utilization-review systems.

Like other claims administrators, FMCs often recognize the advantage of having a comprehensive PPO included in its product package. Those employers who currently use a local foundation to administer claims may have taken a major step toward the development of a PPO.

If an employer is satisfied that the FMC provides responsive service, accurate processing, effective cost controls, and proper management reporting, the FMC might be convinced to take the additional step of introducing hospitals into their programs. For example, in California, each FMC has developed its own PPO, which is part of a statewide PPO system linking 24 foundations through an umbrella organization. Hospitals are also to be included in these arrangements.

One disadvantage to using a claims administrator is that additional fees may be required in development, implementation, and/or administration of the project. These fees might be collected as an hourly fee, a per-employee charge, an offset to some of the savings, or an added expense in the administrator's standard charges. The value of the claims administrator's expertise and increased market power must be balanced with the costs when deciding on a suitable approach.

Another issue to consider when using a claims administrator is that the employer has limited control over the cost management mechanisms. This might be a disadvantage to the employer if the claims administrator lacks the necessary sophistication to effectively manage the PPO. Employers might consider the administrator's capabilities and how to be more involved in controlling the PPO.

PROVIDERS

Another approach to initiating a PPO involves working directly with health care providers. Employers may approach efficient hospitals to work together to form a PPO, since the employer could benefit from access to the hospital's medical staff, the use of internal utilization review, and established administrative procedures.

In approaching specific providers, the employer needs to establish criteria for measuring efficiency. Some employers have data available comparing hospitals' and physicians' patterns of medical practice. This information is beneficial in the selection process. Other considerations include the internal method for utilization review. Does the hospital have a strict or lenient internal review process? Is the hospital sophisticated in terms of productivity measures and administrative controls? An extensive process needs to be established for identifying efficient providers.

Employers who intend to work directly with providers in developing PPOs need to keep in mind that sensitive issues abound, and a number of pertinent questions must be asked:

— Will the local medical society accept reduced fees and/or the proposed utilization-review process?
— Does the community have a larger or smaller ratio of physicians to population than other areas?
— Are hospital occupancy rates high or low?
— Will the quality of medical care be compromised with the introduction of a PPO?
— Who are the local hospital board members and how might this approach affect them?
— Will other employers in the area consider the PPO a move to shift costs to them?

The employer needs to understand that the PPO arrangement touches on numerous sensitive issues such as physician incomes, hospital revenue, and quality of care. To establish a successful PPO, these issues need to be researched, solutions developed, and the results tactfully presented.

ADDITIONAL EMPLOYER ISSUES

Since the objective in initiating a PPO is to provide quality health care within manageable costs, the employer needs to evaluate the cost savings implications. The financial impact of the following three areas should be considered in the initiation phase:

— Financial incentive to influence employee behavior.
— Impact a PPO will have on employee attitudes.
— Communication program necessary to introduce the PPO.

Each of these areas will influence the effectiveness of a PPO within an organization in terms of cost and savings, as well as employee relations.

FINANCIAL INCENTIVE

To encourage employees to use the preferred providers, a financial incentive in the plan is necessary. Employers offering a PPO usually reimburse at a higher percentage for PPO use and pay a lower percentage for non-PPO use. The plan might be designed in the following way:

	Deductible	Coinsurance	Stop Loss
Preferred providers	$ 50	95 percent	$500 out-of-pocket
Other providers	$200	75 percent	$3,000 out-of-pocket

Under this arrangement, there is a strong incentive for using preferred providers. However, many employers offering PPOs waive the cost sharing portion altogether for PPO use. These health care plans are organized so that an employee using a preferred provider does not pay a deductible and often does not pay any portion of the bill.

An arrangement that eliminates employee cost sharing is overlooking the need for employees to be active participants in the financial aspect of health care. The Rand Corporation concluded in their extensive study on cost sharing that employee decisions are influenced when they pay part of the bill.[1] Utilization decreased by almost 20 percent when employees paid 25 percent of the bill with a $1,000 limit on out-of-pocket costs. That study also found cost sharing does not affect the health status of those employees involved in cost sharing with the exception of myopia and hypertension. Therefore, in creating an incentive for preferred providers, cost sharing is needed for both PPO and non-PPO use as a method of making employees more responsible for their health care decisions.

EMPLOYEE ATTITUDES

It is easy to identify the way a financial incentive *should* be designed. However, the incentive will be dependent upon the present plan design. Employee attitudes toward the current plan and their reaction to potential changes are important factors in introducing an effective preferred provider arrangement.

Generally, health care plans can be categorized into two groups: first-dollar coverage and comprehensive coverage. Under first-dollar coverage, most hospital services are covered at 100 percent, with no front-end deductible. Introducing a PPO option will require reduced coverage for non-PPO use (see Exhibit 3). Although the preferred provider portion is 100 percent reimbursed with no cost sharing, employees may

EXHIBIT 3

	Present Plan	*PPO*
First-dollar coverage	No deductible/100 percent of hospital services plus major medical with $50 deductible/80 percent coverage of nonhospital services	No deductible/100 percent of PPO services $250 deductible/70 percent of non-PPO services
Comprehensive	$100 deductible/80 percent coverage of all medical costs	$50 deductible/90 percent of PPO services $250 deductible/65 percent of non-PPO services

still view the change as a "take away" of benefits due to decreased coverage for providers not included in the PPO.

Companies using a comprehensive approach, however, are in an excellent position to include cost sharing in the PPO alternative. The plan already shares the costs with employees, and the incentive may be perceived as a "give back." So the PPO reimbursement level can be higher than the original plan, with lower reimbursements for non-PPO use as shown in Exhibit 3.

An increasing number of employers are implementing employee choice into their medical plans. Multiple medical plan options usually include a comprehensive plan design with various choices of deductible and, in some cases, a first-dollar coverage alternative. When such a choice-making system is combined with a PPO, employee reactions to adding higher coverage for the PPO will be positive because the PPO coinsurance level is usually higher than the original plan. The difficulty is in communicating both the choice and the PPO concept. One Midwest employer found a solution in the following design:

	Deductible	*Coinsurance*	*PPO/Coinsurance*
Plan A	$100	80 percent	90 percent
Plan B	$300	80 percent	95 percent
Plan C	$500	80 percent	90 percent

This employer varied the plans by the deductible and added an incentive for Plan B by raising the PPO/coinsurance level to 95 percent. This arrangement, along with an extensive communication program, worked very well in this particular setting.

Beyond considering the present plan design and how employees might perceive any changes, an employer has other issues to consider. Employee demographics, in particular, may influence PPO participation and employee perceptions. Experience with HMOs in the Twin Cities area, where health care cost management is at the forefront, is a good example. Some employers in the area have experienced adverse selection of HMOs, where younger, healthier employees select the HMO. Often, those employees have not yet developed relationships in the medical community. An employer with a younger population might experience higher PPO use for the same reasons as HMO experience has shown. Evaluation of age status may aid in determining how effective a financial incentive might be.

A company with a large percentage of employees with working spouses may experience no significant change in employee behavior from the PPO due to dual coverage. Example: One employee is reimbursed 75 percent of her medical bills because she did not use the PPO. However, her husband's company plan will coordinate their benefits and pay the remaining 25 percent. Under this situation, the purpose is defeated and employee attitudes and behavior will remain essentially unaffected.

COMMUNICATION EFFORT

Because the PPO concept is new to employees, it is not easily understood. Clear communication is essential to effective implementation and positive employee attitudes. Thorough programs generally take a three-phase approach:

— Assessing employee attitudes and reactions.
— Introducing and implementing changes.
— Ongoing or "maintenance" communication.

Assessing employee attitudes can help to identify employees' level of understanding of the existing health care problem. It can also pretest employee reactions to various approaches. Many employers use techniques to "listen" to employees, to assess their reactions to proposed changes, to get an indication of employees' preferences among various alternatives, or to obtain additional employee ideas. This sort of input can affect employee involvement in the PPO significantly. When the final plan design has been determined, a program to communicate the PPO and the new plan will be developed. The methods of communication vary by employer. However, programs are likely to utilize different media. Some employers implement their program using a self-activated sound-slide presentation supported by posters and group discussions. Others have introduced changes primarily through employee meetings featuring a knowledgeable presentor with a few key visual aids. The approach taken depends upon the corporate culture of the individual employer and the characteristics and interest of the employee audience.

Communication does not stop when the PPO has been implemented. Many employees will continue to learn about the new plan and the PPO concept after it begins. Communicating PPO cost savings, reminding employees of the preferred providers, and informing employees of other cost-management efforts the company is taking will help reinforce the logic of using the preferred provider organization.

CONCLUSION

With the advent of cost shifting from medicare and continuing escalation of health care costs, it is up to the employer to take the initiative in considering PPOs as one potential solution to the health care problem.

Employers can no longer afford to wait for others to develop PPO models. For those employers unable to make such a move alone, they can influence other interested groups to collaborate. The alternative is all too clear. Without some form of effective cost controls, employers will continue to pay the rising medical bills for its employees, in addition to supporting providers' losses from increased medicare regulations.

NOTES

1. Robert H. Brook, M.D., Sc.D. et al. "Does Free Care Improve Adults' Health?" *New England Journal of Medicine* 309, no. 6 (December 8, 1983).

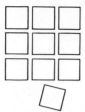

Purchaser Objectives and Priorities

PAYOR'S PERSPECTIVE ON REIMBURSEMENT METHODS UNDER A PREFERRED PROVIDER ARRANGEMENT

Susan Leal, J.D.
William M. Mercer-Meidinger, Inc.
San Francisco, CA

The preferred provider concept is a relatively new addition to the health care delivery system, yet one that is gaining increased popularity. Preferred provider organizations are being established by insurance carriers, third-party administrators, and progressive employers who view preferred provider arrangements as a serious means of reducing health care costs.

As a cost-containment measure, under such arrangements, an employer will negotiate with a group of select hospitals and/or physicians for reduced rates. In some cases, the employer may not want to negotiate directly with providers but instead purchase the services of a PPO (established by an insurance carrier, third-party administrator, or group of providers) that has negotiated with providers on behalf of the employer.

In either case, the payor must be aware of the various methods of reimbursement. A variety of ways to establish reimbursement under these arrangements have been developed as a means of achieving reduced or discounted rates, such as reimbursements based on per diem, volume discounts. However, the payor should realize that what appears to be a reduced or discount rate may not necessarily be the case. The payor should understand the advantages and disadvantages of these methods as well as the precautions that can be taken.

This chapter focuses on reimbursement methods that are already in place in a preferred provider arrangement and those currently in the process of negotiation. Because hospital costs often comprise the largest portion of an employer's health care cost, emphasis will be on methods of reimbursing hospitals.

Before reviewing the various methods of reimbursement, it is important to list the major prerequisites for negotiating a reimbursement method for reduced rates.

For example, it is required (and will be assumed in this chapter) that the payor will have gathered detailed hospital utilization data before entering into negotiations with providers. Detailed hospital utilization data will give the payor extensive information, as follows:

1. The data will indicate the volume of business the payor reimburses at each hospital. The volume of business should be arrayed by patient days, number of admissions, and dollars reimbursed.

2. The data will show the payor its case mix at each hospital utilized. Specifically, this means that the data will show the types and number of cases (e.g., appendectomy, tonsillectomy) performed at each hospital. One of the reliable systems now available for displaying case mix is the diagnostic-related group (DRG) system that breaks hospital treatment into 467 distinct case types. For example, DRG #373 is vaginal delivery without complications, and DRG #374 is vaginal delivery with complications. This case-mix data should also link physicians and charges to each case.

3. The data will also indicate those hospitals that, when matched with regional and national norms, are above or below the standards in terms of length of stay and number of admissions. It will also indicate whether the hospital charges per case are above or below the regional and national norms.

Another important prerequisite is that utilization review play an important role in all methods of reimbursement. For the purposes of this chapter utilization review is defined as a process whereby the medical necessity and quality of health care services are evaluated for the purpose of ensuring:

1. That health care services are provided only when medically necessary.

2. That the services are delivered at the appropriate level of care.
3. That they meet professionally recognized standards for quality of care.

METHODS OF REIMBURSING A HOSPITAL

There are a variety of methods for reimbursing under a preferred provider arrangement involving discounts from billed charges. These include first dollar discount, volume discount, and fee schedules.

FIRST-DOLLAR DISCOUNT FROM HOSPITAL CHARGES

For every dollar spent (hospital charges billed), there is a discount of x percent. While the advantages of this straightforward method seem clear, it has a number of pitfalls that must be overcome.

First, the payor must look at its hospital utilization data and compare the costs of competing hospitals. If, for example, the costs of the prospective preferred hospital are higher than its competing hospitals (for comparable services), the percentage of discount should compensate for this difference. For example, if the target hospital's charges per case (e.g., delivery, appendectomy) are an estimated 5 percent over its competing hospital's charges, then the discount should be set at 15 percent of billed charges to receive an uninflated 10 percent discount from billed charges.

As a second precaution, the discount should be taken from a pre-established, set base. An example of such a base would be a discount from a hospital's "schedule of charges" already in place prior to the discount arrangement (pre-established base). Schedule of charges means a hospital's charges related to daily room and board, daily service charges, radiology, laboratory, and all other ancillary charges. The payor-hospital agreement should contain a definition of schedule of charges and should provide that the schedule of charges be available to the payor upon request. Further, this schedule of charges should also remain in effect for a time certain, e.g., 12 months (set base).

Protections against a future rate increase that will offset any prior discount arrangements should also be taken. This can be accomplished by providing in the payor-provider agreement that an increase in the schedule of charges be linked to increases in the Consumer Price Index (CPI). Specifically, the payor should link increases to the CPI based on *all goods and services* rather than to a specific medical CPI which reflects the fast-rising inflation connected with medical costs. Agreeing to link rate increases to a medical industry CPI would eliminate any incentives for the hospital to be cost effective.

Finally, this method of reimbursement should be coupled with a provision in the agreement that the hospital be subjected to strict utilization controls. Discounted rates can appear to achieve savings, but savings are only achieved when the services are provided efficiently. For example, a discount from hospital charges will be worthless if it is offset by an increased utilization of services. In addition, a discount rate at an inappropriate level of service (a more intense level of service than is necessary) is an illusory saving.

VOLUME DISCOUNT

Under this arrangement, the hospital will give a discount only after the payor has directed a certain volume of business to it (volume can be measured by patient days, number of admissions, or dollars billed). A volume discount may be determined in the following manner:

All billed charges that exceed $500,000 in a 12-month period will be discounted by 15 percent. This would mean if the billed charges for the 12-month period were $700,000 there would be a discount or rebate to the payor of $30,000 ($200,000 × .15) for the hospital charges.

The advantages of this type of arrangement over the first-dollar discount are that they will easily be accepted by hospitals. The hospital will not have to provide any discount unless a certain volume of business is provided. This type of arrangement may be appropriate when an employer cannot provide a financial incentive (normally involves changes in the health plan design) to direct its employees to the preferred provider.

The same cautions apply as in the first-dollar discount. In addition, care should be taken in setting the discount trigger or volume minimum. In the earlier example, a $500,000 volume had to be reached before the discount went into effect. This trigger may be set too high if the payor did only $300,000 of business in the previous year and can only direct enough employees to the preferred hospital to increase the volume by another $100,000. The payor can avoid this problem, however, if it has gathered detailed hospital utilization data that will indicate the amount of money paid at each hospital utilized by its employees. With this utilization data, the payor can make a fairly reasonable estimate of how much business may be directed to the preferred hospital from the nonpreferred hospitals.

FEE SCHEDULES

Other methods of reimbursement can best be termed "fee schedule arrangements." In these types of arrangements, the hospital is paid a set amount for each unit. The most common units are per diem or per case, explained as follows:

Per Diem

In the per-diem arrangement, the hospital is reimbursed a set amount for each day of inpatient care provided.

This type of arrangement has the potential of placing some risk on the hospital to provide care in an efficient manner. Specifically, the hospital has to cover all its costs within the set daily rate. The hospital should therefore be concerned about ancillary charges (e.g., laboratory tests) and treatment at a more intense level than is medically necessary (e.g., use of intensive care bed instead of a regular acute bed).

On the other hand, the hospital can offset risk that may exist through negotiation of a per-diem arrangement that is much higher than its current per-diem charges. For example, the current reimbursement from the employer may develop an average per diem of $600. To avoid any possible risk, the hospital may negotiate a $750 per-diem rate. At the higher per diem, the hospital will not be under pressure to bring about efficiencies in its operation. By referring to hospital utilization data that includes charge information, the payor can determine whether the per diem being negotiated is above the hospital's current average per-diem rate.

The payor must also take precautions against being unduly influenced by a low per diem, if the low per diem is being offered by a hospital that does not have the capacity or capability to provide complex medical services. Specifically, a hospital offering a low per diem, but with limited capability or capacity for handling relatively complicated cases may, in effect, be more expensive than the hospital with a higher per diem and a capability to handle more complex cases.

Increased admissions or extended length of stay can also offset the potential savings and in some cases result in a higher reimbursement level. Therefore, the per-diem arrangement must work in tandem with strict utilization review, which should include both preadmission review to avoid unnecessary admissions and concurrent review to prevent continued hospital stay that is not medically necessary.

Multitiered per Diem

Many hospitals will want to cover the risk of being inundated by cases requiring complex, expensive services (i.e., burn unit, neonatal ICU, cardiovascular surgery). Therefore, it is quite likely that a hospital will not agree to a flat per-diem rate (unless the rate is set very high). Rather, the hospital will negotiate a multitiered per diem. The following is an example of such an arrangement:

Medical/Surgical	$ 600 per diem
ICU	$1,200 per diem
Obstetrics	$ 750 per diem

However, the disadvantage of such an arrangement is that there is less incentive on the hospital to provide care at the least intensive level of service. What, for example, is the incentive for a hospital being reimbursed at $1,200 per diem for ICU to encourage movement to a medical/surgical bed where the per diem is $600?

Case-Mix Reimbursement

A third type of fee schedule arrangement is referred to as case-mix reimbursement. Would a prudent purchaser pay for an automobile through an arrangement to reimburse the auto manufacturer for each day it took to manufacture the car; or, would the prudent purchaser agree in advance to a set price for the automobile? There are obvious reasons for agreeing to a set price for a product: the manufacturer has definite incentives to make the product in an efficient and timely manner. The same holds true in purchasing hospital products.

As indicated in the automobile scenario, there are advantages in setting a price per product, but this method of reimbursement can have its pitfalls.

The first hurdle that the payor will encounter is defining and pricing the hospital product. The payor can establish the price per product, if it has hospital utilization data broken into DRGs linked to hospital charges.

Because this reimburses a set amount for each hospital product, the main pitfall to avoid is allowing unnecessary hospital admissions—especially admission of cases that are more appropriate in an outpatient setting. Therefore, DRG based reimbursement should be combined with strong preadmission review.

Finally, while the DRG method places some incentive on the hospital to be efficient (if the DRG price is set at a reasonable level and utilization is controlled) it does not place any incentive on the physician. It is important to remember that the physician orders the procedures and discharges the patient. With this in mind it is important to consider still other reimbursement methods that combine hospital and physician reimbursement.

PHYSICIAN REIMBURSEMENT

There are primarily two types of physician reimbursement. One method is to target reimbursement to a percent of usual and customary fees. The main advantage of this arrangement is that it appears to be one of the most straightforward ways of achieving a discount. Yet, there are a number of disadvantages.

"Usual and customary" may be difficult to define. Usual and customary for one physician may be cut-rate for another. The payor must take adequate steps to insure that high-priced physicians in the community do not skew the usual and customary fees.

This method also encourages physicians to increase their fees so that the level of "usual and customary" will continue to inflate and thus give these physicians a higher level of fees.

Another method is the establishment of a fee schedule for specific medical and surgical procedures. This method is easier to establish and the savings are simpler to quantify than the discount from usual and customary fees. It places limited risk on the physician because the physician has to perform a specific procedure for a set price. But, this risk can be offset if there is increased utilization.

COMBINED REIMBURSEMENT

Reimbursement methods are also being considered to combine physician and hospital reimbursement. An example of a combined reimbursement would be as follows:

The employer will pay $1,000 for a normal delivery without complication (DRG #373). The $1,000 would be allocated between the physician and the hospital. This reimbursement method gives both the physician and the hospital an incentive to provide care in an efficient manner.

The payor should also consider combining some DRGs to bring about greater incentive for efficient delivery of care. For example, the employer may offer to pay the physician and hospital $1,200 for all deliveries combining vaginal deliveries (DRG #371) and Cesarean deliveries (DRG #371). This combination would be an incentive to avoid the more expensive Cesarean deliveries.

CONCLUSION

Based on the previous discussion, the payor (employer) may conclude that the DRG-based reimbursement and the combined physician-hospital reimbursement methods have the greatest potential for reducing costs because these methods place a risk on the provider and therefore provide an incentive for cost effectiveness. In general, all the methods outlined in this chapter have a potential for reducing costs. The effectiveness of any method used will depend on how well the payor uses certain tools (hospital utilization data and utilization review) to avoid the pitfalls associated with each method.

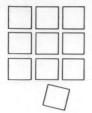

Purchaser Objectives and Priorities

EMPLOYER DEMAND FOR PREFERRED PROVIDER ORGANIZATIONS[1]

Roger Feldman, Ph.D.
Associate Professor

John E. Kralewski, Ph.D.
Professor and Director

Bryan E. Dowd, Ph.D.
Assistant Professor

Janet Shapiro
Research Associate

All of Center for Health Services Research
University of Minnesota
Minneapolis, MN

☐ The goal of PPOs is to identify efficient health care providers and to form them into a health care delivery system. Widespread interest in PPOs stems from the belief that they can contain health care costs while offering consumers a choice of physicians and hospitals. To date, however, there is little information available about the potential demand by employers to offer PPOs as a health plan option to their employees. This article presents information gathered on employers' demand for PPOs by a survey of employers in Minneapolis. Twenty-seven employers were surveyed prior to the offering of PPOs. Information was obtained about employer attitudes toward PPOs and their willingness to offer this new form of health care delivery system. The same firms were resurveyed one year later to determine how many employers had offered a PPO and why the decision to offer or not to offer a PPO had been made.

Most of the surveyed firms are self-insured and offer a choice of health care plans, including HMOs. As knowledgeable buyers of health insurance, many firms wished to be involved in setting PPO policy, conducting utilization review, and designating preferred providers. The firms' primary interest was in premium savings promised by PPOs, but they insisted that quality of care and convenient access to providers be maintained. The firms were hesitant to offer a PPO as an additional health plan. They were skeptical of claims by HMOs regarding reduced utilization and were aware of the administrative costs of offering a new health plan.

After one year, only one firm had offered a PPO, and four firms were planning to offer a PPO during the next 12 months. Lack of data to show cost savings over other plans, concern over lack of administrative and management experience, and limited selection of providers were shared concerns of the firms that were not interested in offering a PPO.

During 1983 several groups initiated efforts to develop PPOs in the Minneapolis/St. Paul metropolitan area. The purpose of this study was to gather market information from employers that would be helpful in determining the potential acceptance of and demand for a PPO plan and the desired design for such a plan.

INITIAL SURVEY

Data were collected through structured interviews using two survey instruments. One questionnaire was designed to gather information from the chief executive officer (CEO), and a more detailed questionnaire pertaining to the firm's health care benefits was designed for the benefits or personnel officer. This latter questionnaire requested information regarding health plans offered, number of employees enrolled in each plan, the firm's cost per plan for individuals and their dependents, and the employee share of monthly premiums for individuals and their dependents.

The survey questionnaires were designed to assess:

1. Employer attitudes toward health care and health care costs.
   Importance of health care costs compared to other costs of doing business.
   Satisfaction with present health insurance plans being offered.
   The employers' perceived need for an alternative health care delivery system to contain costs.

2. Employer strategies regarding health insurance.

   What types of health insurance plans are being offered in each firm, number of employees in each plan, and the costs of the plans to the firm.

   What is being done within the firm to contain health care costs.

   The use of incentives to influence employee choice of health insurance plans.

3. Employer perspectives regarding PPOs.

   The desired components of a PPO plan.

   Who should own a PPO and the activities in which the firm would wish to be involved.

   The firm's interest in risk sharing and willingness to contribute to capitalization of a PPO.

   Acceptable limits on choice of physicians and hospitals.

   Desired incentives to encourage employees to join a PPO.

   Desired employee cost sharing arrangements.

SURVEYED FIRMS

Twenty-seven firms were surveyed in January and February of 1983. Of these firms, 60 percent had operations outside of the state. Three firms were in their respective Fortune 50 categories, and five companies interviewed were in the Fortune 500 for industrial firms. The survey, therefore, represents the opinions of large national corporations that will eventually impact employee health benefits around the country.

The firms ranged in size from 250 to 17,000 employees. Five firms had under 1,000 employees, and two firms had over 10,000 employees, but the majority were in the 1,200 to 8,500 range. Seventeen of the 27 firms interviewed had some union members, but only 31.8 percent of their employees belonged to unions. The firms interviewed employed over 100,000 persons locally, approximately 25 percent of the Minneapolis metropolitan work force.

In order to obtain a broad corporate perspective, the CEO or someone at the vice president level in the firm was interviewed in addition to the benefits officer. In many instances, an interview was obtained with the CEO. When this was not possible, the interview was most frequently conducted with a senior vice president of human resources or personnel.

HEALTH INSURANCE ENVIRONMENT

Of the firms in the sample, 88 percent were found to be self-insured. This largely reflects national trends among large employers as reported by several recent studies.[2] The plans are administered by a number of insurance companies including Blue Cross and Blue Shield and commercial carriers. Movement from one plan administrator to another appears to be rather common. Two reasons mentioned for changing administrators and claim payors were the firm's inability to get adequate claims data and a sense of inefficiency in administrative services. All but four of the surveyed firms make equal, level dollar contributions to their employees' insurance premiums regardless of the cost of the chosen plan. In these four firms there was a desire to move to level dollar contributions but, to date, strong unions in those firms had made it impossible. Over half the employees in each of these firms were union members. However, the percent of unionized employees in a firm does not appear to be related to the cost of health insurance, the amount of premium the employee pays out of pocket, or the number of plans offered by the firm.

All but one of the surveyed firms offer more than one health care plan, and 92 percent of those with multiple plans offer a health maintenance organization (HMO) as one of the alternatives. The mean number of plans offered by the companies was six and ranged from one to nine. Among those offering more than one plan the percent of enrollees in the self-insured plan ranged from 15 to 90 percent with a mean of 54.7 percent (Exhibit 1). Twelve of the firms had more than half of their employ-

EXHIBIT 1
Range and Mean Number of Employees in Health Insurance Plans ($N = 25$)

Indemnity			IPA			HMO		
Min	Max	Mean	Min	Max	Mean	Min	Max	Mean
15%	90%	54.7%	0	48%	12.9%	4%	62%	32.4%

ees in the company's own plan. Among the firms offering HMOs the percent of enrollees ranged from 4 to 62 percent with a mean of 32.4 percent. Only five of the firms had more than half of their employees in HMOs. Among the 11 firms offering independent practice associations (IPAs) the percent of enrollees ranged from 0 percent to 48 percent with a mean of 12.9 percent. A few firms had dropped or were considering dropping their IPAs due to their high costs. However, employee benefits officers stressed the difficulty in dropping plans once they have been offered to employees. While these IPA and HMO enrollment rates generally reflect the penetration of those plans in the community, it is important to note that in this study most of this enrollment resulted from the patterns in two large firms, both of which encouraged HMO development in the past.

Exhibits 2 and 3 show ranges and means of total plan cost by type of plan. The means for single coverage premiums are relatively similar for indemnity, IPA, and HMO plans. HMO premiums are lowest at $51.27

EXHIBIT 2
Range and Mean of Single Coverage Premiums ($/month) .

	Minimum	Maximum	Mean
Indemnity (N^* = 19)	9.88	87.66	52.34
IPA (N = 11)	54.55	85.24	60.84
HMO (N = 19)	47.45	57.61	51.27

*N refers to the number of firms. When a firm offered more than one indemnity plan option they were averaged together and are counted as one plan.

EXHIBIT 3
Range and Mean of Family Plan Premiums ($/month)

	Minimum	Maximum	Mean
Indemnity (N = 20)	33.40	197.90	144.39
IPA (N = 11)	156.67	192.15	173.91
HMO (N = 20)	132.50	163.86	150.35

per month, on average, and exhibit a smaller range (less difference between low and high values) than indemnity plan premiums. This probably results from the greater variance in coverage in indemnity policies and the HMOs' practice of community rating. Among family plan premiums, the cost of the indemnity plan is lowest, on average, followed by HMOs. The range of indemnity premiums is quite large, from $33.40 to $197.90 per month, again reflecting variance in coverage in these plans. IPA premiums are $24 higher than HMO and $30 higher than indemnity premiums, on average.

Due to the HMOs' policy of community rather than experience rating, it is not possible to compare HMO premiums to the quantity of services delivered by HMOs. Community rating may be a profit-maximizing strategy for HMOs for that reason.[3] Thus, while the maximum HMO premium in these firms was less than the maximum indemnity plan for similar coverage, employers remain skeptical over the actual savings.

Employees pay very little of the single coverage premium, on average. Exhibits 4 and 5 show that employee contributions range from an average of $2.14 per month for single coverage indemnity plans to $8.12 for IPAs. The employee's contribution to family plan coverage is higher, however, ranging from $16.32 per month for indemnity plans to $37.15 for IPAs, on average.

EXHIBIT 4
Range and Mean of Employee Contribution to Individual Plan ($/month)

Indemnity			IPA			HMO		
Min	Max	Mean	Min	Max	Mean	Min	Max	Mean
0	10.00	2.14	0	30.04	8.12	0	22.14	5.70
	N = 19			N = 10			N = 19	

EXHIBIT 5
Range and Mean of Employee Contribution to Family Plan Premium ($/month)

Indemnity			IPA			HMO		
Min	Max	Mean	Min	Max	Mean	Min	Max	Mean
0	54.03	16.32	0	99.14	37.15	0	67.30	26.33
	N = 17			N = 11			N = 18	

These results are consistent with earlier findings regarding employers' methods of contributing to health plan premiums. In large Twin Cities firms, full payment of the single coverage premium by the employer is common, while full payment of the family plan premium is rare.[4] Generally, the formula for employer contributions consists of an equal, level dollar contribution to all family plans (sometimes set at the lowest cost plan's premium) or a level percent contribution. Thus, one would expect the higher cost IPA plans to be associated with higher employee out-of-pocket costs.

FINDINGS OF INITIAL SURVEY

Contrary to previous studies,[5] the firms in this sample view the cost of health insurance as a serious problem. Forty-four of 53 respondents rated the problem as "important," and the remaining 9 rated cost "somewhat important." None of the respondents rated the problem as "not very important" or "unimportant," the two categories of least concern. On an item-by-item comparison, health care costs were rated as a greater problem for the firm than life or dental insurance, worker's compensation, social security, pension plan, sick pay and holidays, wages and other production costs, interest expenses, and federal, state, and local taxes. Wages and other production costs were the only expenses that closely approached health care costs in terms of importance. The firms' concerns about health care costs are two-fold: the rate of increase in costs (rather than the level of costs) and the firms' lack of control over health insurance costs.

Ninety percent of the respondents said their firms were taking steps to reduce the cost of health insurance. The most frequently cited step was increasing employee cost sharing at the point of purchase through changes in deductibles and copayment rates. Other strategies include encouraging ambulatory surgery and second opinions, discouraging weekend admissions for elective surgery, and participating in business coalitions and utilization-review programs. While health promotion has received a great deal of national attention as a cost-containment measure, few of these companies were pursuing that strategy in any substantive manner. However, the companies sponsoring health promotion programs were developing very innovative approaches and were attempting to market their program to other firms.

Generally, firms were satisfied with the quality of care delivered by their health insurance plan. Sixteen percent reported dissatisfaction with their HMO plans, however. The primary reasons for dissatisfaction were lack of availability of claims data, a perceived inadequate use of referrals outside the HMO, and concern over actual cost savings.

Following these introductory questions, the general PPO concept was described to the respondent and a series of questions was asked to determine under what circumstances the respondent would be willing to offer and support a PPO. The survey asked which characteristics of PPOs were most important to firms and which were least important. Firms were also asked who should own the PPO and to what extent firms should be involved in the PPO's activities. In effect, the firms were encouraged to design a PPO of their own liking. Finally, firms were asked what incentives they would be willing to offer employees to encourage enrollment in a PPO.

The first set of questions identified the characteristics of PPOs firms would consider most important. The findings are presented in Exhibit 6. For each characteristic, an average score was computed using the following weights: very important = 4, important = 3, not very important = 2, unimportant = 1. Quality of care delivered by preferred providers received the highest score, followed closely by premium savings over other insurance plans and inclusion of both hospitals and physicians among the preferred providers. A good geographic distribution of preferred providers and inclusion of a full range of services, including access to tertiary care, also received high scores. Not surprisingly these findings indicate that firms would like PPOs to have all the features of their present insurance plans but at lower prices. A PPO may be able to accomplish that goal if the correct providers are identified, but even within a well-designed PPO, there will be tradeoffs among the premium cost, the coverage and the amenities the plan can offer. Thus it is important to know the firms' intensity of preferences for each of the plan characteristics in Exhibit 6.

EXHIBIT 6
Importance of PPO Characteristics to Firms

	Average Rating (1–4, where 4 represents "very important")		Number of Times Cited as the Most Important Characteristic				Number of Times Cited as the Least Important Characteristic			
			CEO		CEO & Benefits Officer		CEO		CEO & Benefits Officer	
	CEO	CEO & Benefits Officer	Number (total N = 28)	Per-cent	Number (total N = 52)	Per-cent	Number (total N = 28)	Per-cent	Number (total N = 52)	Per-cent
	(N = 28)	(N = 52)								
1. The premium savings of the PPO relative to other insurance plans in your firm.	3.86	3.85	17	61	30	58	1	4	1	2
2. Open enrollment period more than once a year.	1.61	1.62	0	0	0	0	13	46	29	56
3. Coverage of preventive care such as comprehensive physical exams and well-baby care.	2.89	3.00	1	4	1	2	1	4	1	2
4. Coverage of mental health services (beyond state-mandated minimums).	2.89	2.92	0	0	0	0	0	0	3	6
5. Coverage of chemical dependency programs (beyond state-mandated minimums).	3.25	3.15	0	0	0	0	0	0	0	0

EXHIBIT 6 (concluded)

	Average Rating (1–4, where 4 represents "very important")		Number of Times Cited as the Most Important Characteristic				Number of Times Cited as the Least Important Characteristic			
	CEO	CEO & Benefits Officer	CEO		CEO & Benefits Officer		CEO		CEO & Benefits Officer	
	(N = 28)	(N = 52)	Number (total N = 28)	Per-cent	Number (total N = 52)	Per-cent	Number (total N = 28)	Per-cent	Number (total N = 52)	Per-cent
6. Good geographic distribution of preferred providers.	3.75	3.75	1	4	3	6	0	0	1	2
7. Inclusion of both hospitals and physicians in PPO.	3.89	3.85	0	0	0	0	1	4	1	2
8. Inclusion of specific hospitals or physician groups as preferred providers.	2.25	2.33	1	4	2	4	2	7	3	6
9. Periodic review of utilization of services by preferred providers.	3.11	3.39	0	0	1	2	1	4	1	2
10. The quality of care delivered by preferred providers.	3.89	3.85	5	.18	11	21	1	4	1	2
11. Offer a full range of services including access to tertiary care.	3.79	3.67	0	0	0	0	0	0	0	0

To assess the intensity aspect, firms were asked which of the characteristics were most important and which were least important. Premium savings was most frequently cited as "most important," followed by quality of care and a good geographic distribution of preferred providers. Frequent open enrollment periods was by far the least important characteristic.

When firms were asked the number of hospitals that should be designated preferred providers, the number chosen most often was "2–5." The categories "1" and "6–10" received less support. Firms feel that a low number of preferred providers sacrifices enrollee convenience in travel time and provides too restricted a choice, while a larger number may result in inadequate premium savings. Only 20 percent of the CEOs who wanted "2–5" or "6–10" hospitals in the PPO plan would be willing to reduce the number of hospitals to obtain an additional 10 percent premium savings. However, 42 percent of the benefits officers would accept such a reduction.

The situation was somewhat different for physician groups. The number of firms indicating "support" increased as the number of physician groups increased. Both CEOs and benefits officers appear to be reluctant to reduce the number of PPO physicians to a single group even if the reduction results in additional premium savings. While they recognize the savings that potentially can be achieved by limiting choice of physicians to one group, they are concerned over access to services and lack of proper referrals. Employers remain reluctant to curtail benefits or access to services as a means of controlling health care costs.

Next, firms were asked who should own the PPO (Exhibit 7). Third-party payors, physicians, and hospitals were the favored alternatives. Firms are not particularly interested in owning the PPO themselves, and they are largely opposed to union ownership.

Although firms generally do not wish to become involved in ownership, they would like to be involved in several activities associated with

EXHIBIT 7
Favored Groups for PPO Ownership ("Yes" answers)

	CEOs		CEOs and Benefits Officers	
Group	Number (Total N = 26)	Percent	Number (Total N = 53)	Percent
Your firm	4	14	10	19
Employees enrolled in the plan	5	18	7	13
Union(s)	0	0	0	0
Third-party insurer	18	64	30	57
Physicians	14	50	31	58
Hospitals	16	57	34	64
Other	6	21	11	21

EXHIBIT 8
Desired Involvement by Firms in PPO Activities ("Yes" answers)

Activity	CEOs		CEOs and Benefits Officers	
	Number (Total N = 28)	Percent	Number (Total N = 53)	Percent
Policymaking	12	43	24	45
Hiring the PPO's administrator	3	11	4	8
Rate setting	10	36	24	45
Plan administration	8	29	12	23
Utilization review	9	32	22	42
Designating preferred providers	9	32	17	32
Establishing reimbursement schedules for providers	6	21	12	23
Risk sharing	15	54	25	47
None	6	21	8	15
Other	5	18	7	13

the PPO (Exhibit 8). Many firms felt they should be involved in setting PPO policy, conducting utilization review, and designating preferred providers. In most cases, they prefer to carry out these tasks through an industry advisory process. Over 50 percent of the firms indicated that they would be willing to enter into some type of risk sharing agreement with a PPO if a simple procedure could be developed.

Finally, firms were asked what type of cost sharing (or disincentive) arrangement they would support for PPO enrollees who used out of plan providers and what type of incentives they would support to encourage employees to join the PPO. As shown in Exhibit 9, there is considerable support for rather stringent disincentives for out-of-plan use of providers. The $200 deductible and 20 percent coinsurance approach was supported by 41 percent of the firms, and 63 percent indicated support for a plan where the employee would pay all of the charges in excess of the PPO fee schedule. As previously noted, most of these firms are moving toward higher deductibles and coinsurance in their self-insured indemnity plans, and most view PPO out-of-plan cost sharing as an extension of that trend. Some, in fact, noted that they would support a PPO that had some deductibles and coinsurance for use of services within the plan.

These findings are reinforced by the findings of a survey of Twin Cities firms conducted in 1981, which found the average deductible for single coverage enrollees to be $87.40 and $226.70 for family plan enrollees.[6] However, the coinsurance rate (portion paid by the enrollee) for

EXHIBIT 9
Corporate Support for Employee Incentives
(those indicating support)

	CEOs		CEOs and Benefits Officers	
	Number (Total N = 27)	Per-cent	Number (Total N = 43)	Per-cent
Employee Cost-Sharing Arrangements				
$50 deductible per family and a 5% coinsurance rate	4	15	5	12
$100 deductible per family and a 10% coinsurance rate	8	30	11	26
$200 deductible per family and a 20% coinsurance rate	11	41	21	49
The employee pays charges in excess of the PPO fee schedule	17	63	28	65
Employee Incentives to Encourage PPO Enrollment	(Total N = 22)		(Total N = 43)	
Cash bonus	0	0	1	2
In-kind benefits such as vacation time	3	14	5	12
A share of the difference between PPO and fee-for-service premiums	15	68	28	65
A share of the difference between PPO premiums and actual expenditures if a surplus exists	4	18	14	33
No incentive	7	32	13	30

Importance of incentives (1–4, where 4 represents very important):

	CEOs (N = 26)	CEOs and Benefits Officers (N = 47)
Average Rating	3.00	3.13

inpatient hospital services was only 6 percent on average, and 18 percent for major medical coverage.

Exhibit 9 also shows the firms' support for various incentives to encourage enrollment in the PPO. The most striking finding is that firms are unwilling to pay bonuses to employees who enroll in the PPO. However, most of the firms are willing to share savings with their employees if any savings are realized. Most firms indicated that the PPO should have lower deductibles and coinsurance than their self-insured plan as an employee incentive to join and use the PPO. Firms do believe that incentives are important, although CEOs rate them somewhat less important than benefits officers, in general.

INTERPRETATION OF INITIAL SURVEY RESULTS

Several streams of events are taking place in the employer sector that will have a direct impact on the health care delivery system. First, every firm interviewed noted that health care costs, or more precisely, the costs associated with their health insurance plans, are a major problem area and they have all targeted those areas for cost control programs. Second, as a result of the above, virtually all of the firms are changing their health insurance plans to include higher deductibles and coinsurance.

Most of those interviewed believe that increased deductibles and coinsurance will create price sensitivity among their employees and will thus cause them to "shop" for the lowest cost provider. Less talked about is the fact that these changes lower the cost of the health insurance plan to the employer by transferring some of the costs to the employee. Clearly, the current economic conditions, the weakened position of unions, and high unemployment rates create a favorable climate for these changes. The deductible and coinsurance portions of health insurance plans offered by firms in this study will, therefore, likely increase rather dramatically during the next 12 to 18 months. Deductibles may reach $500 per family in plans with the coinsurance rate increasing to 15 to 20 percent.

Although firms appear willing to support high levels of employee cost sharing, they are concerned that dramatic increases in coinsurance and deductibles may damage labor-management relations. In addition, most of those interviewed believe that major savings can be achieved without reducing the services covered or the choice of providers. They view the PPO concept as a means of maintaining current coverage of health care costs for employees choosing a preferred provider while increasing the cost sharing for employees who wish to use other sources of care. The firms are, therefore, restructuring their self-insured plans, mainly by increasing deductibles and coinsurance while seeking arrangements with PPOs that will provide the same services but will forego collecting at least a portion of the coinsurance and deductible payment. In many ways, the PPO concept is providing a safety valve that allows the firms to accomplish the restructuring of their self-insured plan while maintaining good employee relationships. Employees will have the option to pay the deductibles and coinsurance costs associated with the self-insured plan and be able to use any provider, or they can use the preferred providers and pay no or fewer out-of-pocket costs.

Both benefits officers and CEOs believe that this will be a powerful cost-containment strategy and that it will create price sensitivity among employees, stimulate price competition among providers, and shift services to cost-effective physicians and hospitals.

A second and less pronounced strategy being pursued by these firms is a systematic review of utilization to determine problem areas. The majority of firms interviewed are self-insured, and, consequently, they have direct access to a great deal of utilization data from their indemnity plans.

The benefits officers are extremely knowledgeable and are continually looking for ways to alter their plans so that services will be provided at a lower unit cost. They are greatly concerned over the fact that they cannot get utilization data from the HMOs and therefore cannot determine the true costs of those programs. While most of the firms offer HMOs, they are skeptical about the alleged savings, and some believe that HMOs are in fact increasing the cost of their company's overall health insurance. There will be increased pressure on the HMOs to provide company-specific utilization data in the future, and this will carry over to any other health care plan offered by these firms.

Health care costs, of course, include both unit costs and the number of units of services (i.e., physician visits or hospital days) used by the providers. Employers believe that price competition created by offering a PPO option will lower unit costs. Moreover, the employers plan to control the number of units of services used by providers through an ongoing utilization-review program. Some plan to conduct this review in-house, while others are considering contracts with Professional Review Organizations (PRO) programs or private firms to conduct the review. In either case, utilization of health services will be monitored, and high-cost providers can be removed from the preferred provider program.

RECENT PPO DEVELOPMENT IN MINNEAPOLIS

During the twelve months following the initial survey, five PPOs have organized or are in the process of organizing in the Twin Cities. The two plans presently being marketed are both sponsored by hospitals. One of these plans is sponsored by seven hospitals with leadership emanating from a local nonprofit hospital system. The plan is offered as a dual choice to employees, either as a new plan or as an option under the company's existing indemnity plans. Participating hospitals guarantee a per-diem charge of 10 percent less than their usual charge. Enrollees who use the PPO hospitals will receive more generous benefits, in the form of lower coinsurance rates, than enrollees who use nonpreferred hospitals. This plan is presently being offered to employees of the participating hospitals, and it is being marketed to other employers.

Another PPO is sponsored by a large metropolitan hospital with affiliations with two other local hospitals: a children's hospital and an outlying metropolitan hospital. This plan is being marketed to local employers. One corporation from our study is offering this PPO to all its indemnity plan members.

Two hospitals, one from Minneapolis and one from St. Paul are organizing a third PPO that is not yet being marketed to employers.

The two remaining PPOs are physician-sponsored. One is built around 250 primary care doctors plus medical specialists, the other is organized by 14 specialty groups. Neither has reached the stage where it can be marketed to employers.

FOLLOW-UP SURVEY

The rapid development of PPOs in Minneapolis has given the surveyed firms an opportunity to translate their attitudes toward PPOs into actual demand to offer a PPO to their employees. To measure the extent of demand to offer a PPO, a second survey was conducted during February 1984. The corporate benefit officers of the 27 firms were contacted by telephone to find out what actions had been taken during the year regarding PPOs. Only one firm was unavailable for discussion, and in four companies the interviewer spoke with either a new benefits officer or was referred to someone else with more direct knowledge of PPOs.

At the time of the follow-up telephone survey, one firm was offering a PPO, and five more firms were very close to offering a PPO. All of these firms had rated the cost of health insurance as "an important problem" in the initial survey, yet none of them viewed health insurance costs as an overriding concern compared to other costs of doing business.

The company presently offering a PPO already had a very active health promotion program, and top management was very interested in the entire health issue. That company is offering the PPO as an option within its fee-for-service insurance plan. Enrollees in that plan are automatically eligible for PPO benefits if they use one of the three participating hospitals, otherwise they may continue to use their existing provider without paying penalty deductibles or coinsurance rates. Thus, the plan resembles a hospital discount to the employer rather than a PPO that would feature financial incentives for consumers to use preferred hospitals. The only consumer incentive for participation in the PPO is freedom from paperwork compared to the previous fee-for-service plan. The company estimates that about 30 to 35 percent of the eligible employees are using the preferred hospitals, and some are switching back from HMOs to the fee-for-service plan.

The benefit structure in this PPO remained the same as in the indemnity plan. High-technology procedures are included, there is prescription drug coverage at no additional charge, and psychologists are included if they are on the participating hospitals' staffs. The firm has no management role and is not risk sharing with the PPO.

At the time of the initial survey only one corporation was planning to offer a PPO within the year. One year later this corporation has not yet offered one but is planning to offer one or two in 1985. The firm has found that the most important obstacle to offering a PPO has been that the provider organizations have not had an actual plan to present. The providers are knowledgeable about providing services but are not familiar with developing the insurance benefits side of health. Therefore, the employer has found it necessary to educate the providers during the negotiation period. The PPO(s) will be offered as a modification within the existing fee-for-service plan. The final decisions on the physician and hospital component are yet to be made, but there was some skepticism expressed over hospital-based PPOs. Payment will be a negotiated fee-for-service arrangement with some kind of risk sharing. There will be no organizational involvement with the PPO. It has not been decided whether to pay 100 percent for use of PPO providers (compared with 80/20 for non-PPO providers) or to have some kind of coinsurance and deductible for PPO providers.

Another firm will be offering a PPO as a new plan within the year. Seven hospitals and their medical staffs are involved as the preferred providers, and outside physicians will be chosen by a board of peers looking for a conservative practice style. Payment is being negotiated and will not go above present levels. There will be no firm involvement in the organizational structure, nor will there be risk sharing. Benefits will be the same as with the existing plan. For those who go outside the plan there will be 30 percent coinsurance, compared to 15 percent within the plan. Financial incentives for members are still being discussed.

Two other firms felt that in the next 12 months they would be offering a PPO, but they had not yet decided on which PPO to offer. One firm did not yet have any details. The other company planned to offer the PPO as an option under the existing indemnity plan. The company does not intend to risk share and is considering contracting for utilization review. Benefits covered are to be the same as the standard indemnity package. As yet the company has not decided to offer employees any incentive to join the PPO. That PPOs have no track record is considered to be the most important obstacle to offering a PPO.

The remaining 21 firms stated complete lack of interest in offering a PPO, but when probed, all but nine showed some interest in watching the development of PPOs. Of the nine, two stated that corporate decisions were made elsewhere in the country. The remaining 12 firms had a variety of reasons for holding back on offering a PPO. Lack of data to show a cost savings over other plans, concern over lack of administrative and management experience, and limited selection of providers were shared considerations. These organizations looked at PPOs in relation to HMOs and expressed concern that there could be adverse selection from the HMOs.

In addition, 2 firms of the 12, when looking back on their HMO experience, were not convinced there had been a cost savings. They felt it was necessary to have more information before becoming involved in another health plan concept. One firm stated that there seemed to be little difference between HMOs and PPOs. One organization had actually sought out the available PPOs, but the PPOs were not willing to assume the firm's actuarial risk.

INTERPRETATION OF FOLLOW-UP SURVEY

Although there was considerable interest expressed by employers in the PPO concept during the initial survey, only one firm resurveyed in the study had introduced a PPO. Four more firms were close to introducing a PPO one year after the original survey. Several common features may be noted among the PPO designs chosen by these firms. In three of four cases where information was available, the PPO will be offered as an option or modification within the firm's existing indemnity plan. This choice reflects the firms' desire to avoid the administrative costs of offering a new health plan.

All of the PPO arrangements involve the same benefit coverage as existing indemnity plans. Firms are aware of the cost of adding new benefits and want to avoid these costs when they offer a PPO.

Despite the firms' stated wish to be involved in PPO activities such as setting PPO policy, designating preferred providers, and conducting utilization review, little evidence was found for such involvement among these firms. The firms' management role in the PPOs was limited, and there was no evidence for any form of risk sharing with the PPOs. Such lack of organizational involvement may reflect, in part, a failure by the PPOs to make knowledgeable proposals to the firms. PPOs might be well-advised to hire individuals who know about the insurance business if they hope to find suitable "partners" among large business firms.

CONCLUSION

Twin Cities firms are concerned about the costs of their health insurance plans and are searching for ways to control these costs. The PPO concept is attractive, because it allows firms to introduce cost sharing into their indemnity plans while maintaining access, choice, and coverage at present levels. One firm has offered a PPO, and four are close to offering PPOs. The initial evidence suggests that PPOs will be offered as an option within the firms' indemnity plans; however, there is a good deal of diversity in the PPO organizational form. Lack of sophistication in plan development on the part of the available PPOs has hindered their adoption at this time.

NOTES

1. We gratefully acknowledge funding provided for this study by the following hospitals: Abbott-Northwestern Hospital, Health Central Systems, Methodist Hospital, Metropolitan Medical Center, North Memorial Medical Center, and St. Francis Regional Medical Center. Portions of this article appeared previously in *Hospital and Health Services Administration*.

2. Health Insurance Association of America, *Source Book of Health Insurance Data 1982–1983* (Washington, DC: Health Insurance Association of America); National Loss Control Service Corporation. *Trends of Self-Insurance in the 80's* (Long Grove, IL: National Loss Control Service Corporation, 1980).

3. Roger Feldman and Bryan Dowd, "Simulation of a Health Insurance Market with Adverse Selection," *Operations Research* 30, no. 6 (November-December 1982), pp. 1027–1041.

4. Roger Feldman and Bryan Dowd. "Executive Summary of the 1982 Business and Health Survey," unpublished report by University of Minnesota Center for Health Services Research and the Minnesota Coalition on Health Care Costs, February 1983.

5. Harvey M. Sapolsky, Drew Altman, Richard Greene, and Judith D. Moore, "Corporate Attitudes Toward Health Care Costs," *Milbank Memorial Fund Quarterly/ Health and Society* 59, no. 4 (Fall 1981), pp. 561–585; Jacqueline Wallen and Sherman R. Williams, "Employer-Based Health Insurance," *Journal of Health Politics, Policy and Law* 7, no. 2 (Summer 1982), pp. 366–379.

6. Gail Jensen, Roger Feldman, and Bryan Dowd, "Corporate Benefit Policies and Health Insurance Costs," *Journal of Health Economics,* forthcoming 1985.

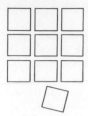

Purchaser Objectives and Priorities

PPO Attributes: What Benefit Managers Look For[1]

Raymond R. Flachbart, M.A., M.B.A.
Vice President, InterQual, Inc.
Chicago, IL

Robin Kornfeld, M.S.
Consultant, Laventhol & Horwath
San Francisco, CA

Gerald L. Glandon, Ph.D.
Assistant Professor
Department of Health Systems Management
Rush University
Chicago, IL

Roberta J. Shapiro, M.B.A., M.P.H.
Executive Director, Choice Health Care Plan
Des Plaines, IL

☐ Preferred provider organizations (PPOs) are a recent response to changing forces in the health care market. As such they are not well known by potential purchasers and consumers, i.e., employers and employees. Consequently, for PPOs to be successful, they must market effectively to both of these groups as well as to others that influence the group benefits market.

484

An effective marketing program is predicated on a number of factors, one of which is market research.[2] "The marketing research system consists of the systematic design, collection, analysis, and reporting of data and findings relevant to a specific marketing situation or problem facing an organization."[3] Many PPOs have been formed without conducting systematic market research. As such, their relative success or failure cannot be understood unless the market's response to various PPO alternatives is systematically associated with specific PPO design features.

To date, most employers have only been approached through attitudinal questionnaires by organizations attempting to study PPO design. This technique has done little to assess the trade-offs that occur as part of the decision-making process. Although mailed questionnaires retrieve factual information such as the comprehensiveness of health benefits being offered, the general satisfaction with group health benefits options, and potential interest in PPOs, these questionnaires are not designed to estimate the relative importance of the individual components of the PPO package.

In order to address this situation, market research was conducted to evaluate the choice behavior of health benefit managers in the selection of a preferred provider alternative. The study discussed in this article used a quantitative marketing technique to evaluate benefit managers' preferences concerning the product design of PPOs. Before discussing this study, the results of three other studies involving purchasers' PPO preferences are discussed.

In a study conducted in Minnesota, researchers attempted to assess basic attitudes toward health insurance costs, as well as to find out how employers in the Twin Cities would react to various PPO characteristics.[4] The data collection tool, a nine-page questionnaire, was mailed to each firm's health benefits manager and chief executive officer (CEO). The study showed that there was not a statistically significant difference in the responses of the benefit managers and the CEO. The major finding was that quality of care and expenditure savings were the two characteristics deemed "most preferred" by respondents when evaluating attributes of a PPO package. However, the researchers noted that what really needs to be measured is "the firm's intensity of preferences for each of the plan's characteristics."[4]

A survey was conducted of 135 firms in the Milwaukee area ranging in size from 200 to over 10,000 employees.[5] When asked which of a list of seven features were among the most important for a PPO, the three highest-ranked features and the number of responses for each were as follows (respondents were allowed to indicate more than one feature as important):

— Quality of providers.   93
— Accessibility/availability to larger number of employees.   82
— Low relative cost.   62

In another study, interviews were conducted with 28 firms in the Indianapolis area ranging in size from 170 to 30,000 employees.[6] The interviews were conducted to ascertain each firm's views on a proposed PPO under development by a large area hospital and its medical staff. The concern most frequently cited by the employers interviewed was that there would be a decline in the quality of care that the PPO provided. The distance between employee residences and the PPO hospital was the second most commonly cited concern.

These three studies indicate that quality, accessibility, and cost are important attributes to PPO purchasers. The surveys required respondents to indicate whether any single attribute was deemed "most preferred" or "least preferred" but did not require the respondents to indicate their preferences for various groups of attributes combined to form alternative PPO plans. While these studies fulfilled their objectives, they raise additional questions. How important is a change in one or more attributes to the marketability of the overall PPO plan? Can improvements in two attributes offset a decline in a third attribute? Attempting to answer these questions requires assessing the trade-offs inherent in the benefit manager's decision-making process. An assessment of this process, using conjoint analysis as a marketing research tool, is discussed below.

GENERAL DESCRIPTION OF CONJOINT ANALYSIS

For many years, marketing researchers have been using a technique called conjoint analysis to analyze the potential acceptance of multiattribute products in the marketplace.[7] While commercial use of this analysis as a marketing tool for determining the demand for new multiattribute products is widespread, application in the health care field is limited.[8] The advantage of conjoint analysis is that it quantifies preference data and provides a way to accurately predict the aggregate behavior of people through a model based on individual responses. The methodology is based on an approach in which respondents rate a set of "total product descriptions" rather than reacting to separate product attributes as in the aforementioned studies. Thus, the rating process on the product descriptions is designed to force the respondent to make trade-offs among the individual components of each product description.[7] In this context, conjoint analysis simulates the decision-making process.

Additionally, conjoint analysis can provide information about the relative value to each respondent of the individual attributes. Therefore, conjoint analysis provides information that is useful in modifying current products or services and in designing new ones for select buying publics. Its advantage in relation to PPO market research is that it can determine the preferences of the purchaser market in terms of a number of PPO attributes simultaneously, as well as calculate the importance of individual attributes in relation to each other.

METHODOLOGY

The various tasks and processes involved in the study methodology are outlined in Exhibit 1. The first step was to identify those attributes or characteristics of PPOs that were considered important by health care purchasers. Next, profiles or descriptions of alternative health plans were developed as composites of these important attributes. Each health benefit manager was then asked to rank these alternative health plans in terms of those "most likely" to those "least likely" to be offered by their firm. These rankings were then analyzed using conjoint analysis. The various steps in the study are discussed in greater detail in the next four sections.

EXHIBIT 1
Tasks and Processes Involved in Conjoint Measurement[9]

Step	Task	Process*
1	Identify important attributes of PPOs	Literature review and focus group interviews
2	Develop varying profiles of PPO health plans	Use orthogonal array to select a subset of all possible combinations of attribute levels
3	Obtain respondents' rating of various PPO profiles and attributes	Questionnaire sent to employee health benefit managers
4	Develop utility scales for the levels of each attribute and derive relative importance weights for each attribute	Conjoint measurement analysis
5	Compare utility functions among sample segments	Segmentation

*These processes are described in the accompanying text.

IDENTIFICATION OF ATTRIBUTES

The first task was to identify salient characteristics of PPOs. Typically the conjoint measurement approach defines each attribute in terms of a certain number of discrete levels. The following criteria were considered in generating the attributes and their levels:[9]

1. The attributes should be able to be implemented, that is, attributes should represent tangible benefits or factors that could occur as a consequence of offering a PPO.
2. The attributes and their levels should be important to both health care providers and purchasers.

EXHIBIT 2
Selected Attributes and Levels

Attribute	Level Number	Level Description
Perceived level of provider care		"Designated providers" who are perceived by the community to provide:
	1	Above average
	2	Average
	3	Below average patient care.
Annual cost savings		A reduction on your annual cost of providing health benefits per employee of:
	1	1 to 8 percent
	2	9 to 16 percent
	3	17 to 24 percent
Utilization review program	1	Comprehensive Review Program (includes preadmission certification, second surgical opinions, concurrent inpatient review).
	2	Retrospective Review (medical/claims data reviewed periodically to identify designated providers who are too inefficient or costly).
Designated providers	1	Only hospitals as designated providers.
	2	Both physicians and hospitals as designated providers.
Geographic distribution of designated providers		Designated providers are located:
	1	Within 10 minutes of at least 50 percent of the employees' place of residence
	2	Within 20 minutes of at least 50 percent of the employees' place of residence
	3	Within 30 minutes of at least 50 percent of the employees' place of residence

3. The levels of any particular attribute should vary substantially from each other and yet taken as a whole represent a meaningful and realistic range.

The actual process of selecting the attributes and their levels consisted of a literature review and a focus group interview with a pre-test sample of health benefit managers. The focus group interview was used to reduce the initial preliminary list of ten attributes drawn from the literature review to a final list of five attributes. The resulting five attributes and their corresponding levels are summarized in Exhibit 2.

DEVELOPMENT OF PROFILES

The second major step in the study required the development of descriptions of alternative health plans. These were developed by selecting a subset of all possible combinations of attribute levels. A special type of design called an orthogonal array was used to reduce the 108 potential combinations of the five attributes and their levels to 16 combinations. Simply stated, the design used reduces "the number of combinations to a manageable size while at the same time maintaining orthogonality"[10] (complete independence). This type of design "assumes away most (sometimes all) interaction effects."[10] An example of a typical profile used in the questionnaire is presented in Exhibit 3.

EXHIBIT 3
Typical Health Plan Profile

IF OFFERED, THIS ALTERNATIVE HEALTH PLAN WOULD INCLUDE:

Characteristics:
- "Designated providers" who are perceived by the community to provide ABOVE AVERAGE patient care.
- A 1–8 percent reduction on your annual cost of providing health benefits per employee.
- RETROSPECTIVE REVIEW (medical/claims data reviewed periodically to identify designated providers who are too inefficient or costly).
- Only HOSPITALS as designated providers.
- Designated providers are located WITHIN 10 MINUTES OF at least 50 percent of the employees' place of residence.

PLAN RATING SCORE: _____
(0–100)
0 = LEAST LIKELY to offer
100 = MOST LIKELY to offer

DATA COLLECTION

The data for this study were obtained through a mailed questionnaire sent to 365 health benefit managers in the Chicago metropolitan area, representing manufacturing, financial, and service firms. The first part of the questionnaire was used to obtain statistical information regarding the firm's size, type of industry, health benefits coverage, and cost-containment activities.

In the second part of the questionnaire, respondents were asked to assess the likelihood of their organization offering the 16 proposed alternative health benefit plans, which were comprised of varying levels of the five attributes. The ratings were obtained in a two-step process. The benefits managers were provided with directions that instructed them to first sort the plans into two groups: those "most likely" to be offered and those "least likely" to be offered. The second step required the benefit manager to rate each of the plans in the two groups. This technique for obtaining preference ratings is a commonly used technique in studies using conjoint analysis.[7,9]

DATA ANALYSIS

The data were analyzed by the conjoint analysis procedure. Conjoint analysis measures the effects of two or more independent variables (the attribute levels) on the rating of the dependent variable (the likelihood of a PPO profile being chosen). This analysis requires ranked data on a respondent's overall judgment of a set of alternative packages. Analysis of this ranked data determines the importance of the individual characteristics that comprise the total package. In addition, the "part-worth" utility of each level of each attribute is generated. These part-worth utility measurements allow one to identify the most preferred bundle of attributes. The computation of an attribute's preference measurement is arrived at by various computer programs.

RESULTS

Of the 365 health benefit managers who received the survey questionnaire, 110 questionnaires were properly returned, representing a 30 percent response rate.

DESCRIPTION OF SAMPLE

The 110 firms responding to the questionnaire had the following characteristics:

— Of the 110 respondents, 54 percent were manufacturing firms, 10 percent financial service institutions, 18 percent distribution facilities, and the remaining 18 percent consisted of other types of firms.

— Approximately 66 percent of the respondents employ less than 250 employees, while the remaining 34 percent employ 250 or more employees within the Chicago metropolitan area.

— The principal health benefits funding mechanism was a fully-insured plan for 50 percent of the firms, self-funded plan for 36 percent, and a minimum premium or other plan for the remaining 14 percent.

— Approximately half the firms had recently increased the deductibles and/or copayments associated with their health benefits plan.

— Forty percent of the firms offered at least one HMO or IPA plan, and for those firms that did, an average of 13 percent of the employees were enrolled in these plans.

CONJOINT ANALYSIS RESULTS

The graphs in Exhibit 4 display the preference measurement results of the conjoint analysis model used in this study. The graphs reflect an aggre-

EXHIBIT 4
Average Attribute Utility Scales*

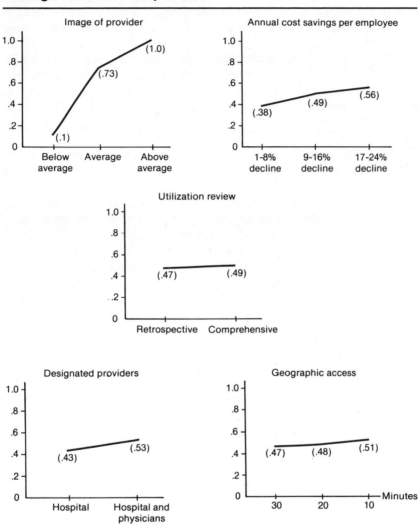

*Measurements represent utility values as the average of all respondents; 1.0 represents the greatest possible value for any attribute level, and 0.1 represents the least possible value.

gate of all respondents' preferences for the attribute levels used to define PPO plans. In each graph, the horizontal axis represents the varying levels of each attribute, and the vertical axis represents the respondents' part-worth utility as calculated by the computer algorithim.

Part-worth utility and utility scales are scores that represent the "value" of each attribute level to the respondent(s). "These utilities provide unbiased information about the relative importance of the various attributes, the value of various levels of each of the attributes and an estimate of the trade-offs respondents make when they evaluate several attributes together." [11]

The numbers along the vertical axis in Exhibit 4 are rescaled part-worth utility measurements, with 1.0 representing the highest score possible (i.e., the most preferred level of any attribute). As an example, the utility scale for below average provider image is 0.1, or the least possible score, while the utility scale for an average provider image is 0.73, which is fairly high.

The slopes of the graph measure the degree of importance to the respondents of a change in a level of an attribute. The steeper the slope between any two attribute levels, the greater the value respondents placed on a change in that level. For example, a change from an above average to average provider image was not as important to respondents as a change from an average provider to below average provider image.

The averages of utility estimates for each level of the five attributes were internally consistent. That is, as the level of an attribute changed, the utility measure for that level also changed in the anticipated direction. For example, as cost savings became greater, the associated part-worth utility became greater. This internal consistency and compatibility is a measure of the study's validity.

From these utility measures, minimum and maximum values as well as relative importance measurements were derived for the five attributes. These values are provided in Exhibit 5. The minimum and maximum values displayed for each attribute represent the average utility for the least preferred level of that attribute and the average utility for the most preferred level, respectively. The relative importance measurement of an attribute is that attribute's range (maximum value less minimum value) divided by the sum of ranges for all attributes. As such, the relative importance value measures not only the importance of the distribution of

EXHIBIT 5
Conjoint Values of the Attributes

	Minimum Value	Maximum Value	Range	Relative Importance
Image of provider	4.88	13.46	8.57	56.1%
Cost savings	7.21	9.70	2.49	15.5
Utilization review	7.87	9.18	1.31	8.4
Designated providers	7.66	9.39	1.73	11.0
Geographic access	7.85	9.28	1.43	9.0
Total			15.53	100.0%

NOTE: Due to rounding, items may not add up to total.

part-worth utility measures for any given attribute, but also an attribute's importance in relation to the other attributes.

The results of this study reveal that the image of the provider was overwhelmingly viewed as the most important attribute to respondents in their selection of alternative PPO plans. A distant second to the image of the provider was potential cost savings to the firm.

In trying to define image of the provider from the viewpoint of those who completed the survey, it is important to review the description of this attribute as seen by the respondents. As provided in Exhibit 6, the attribute is described as: providers who are perceived by the community to provide above average, average, or below average patient care. In trying to interpret the meaning of this to respondents, one can speculate that the word "perceived" raised connotations of "image" while the level of "patient care" implied a quality issue. For purposes of identification, the term image of provider will be used for this attribute; however, it should be kept in mind that this is merely a proxy for the actual description noted above.

EXHIBIT 6
Relative Importance of Attributes by Type of Industry

Attributes	Manufacturing	Financial Service	Distribution	Other
Image of provider	53.1%	59.7%	52.9%	60.1%
Cost savings	17.9	10.5	12.9	13.9
Utilization review	8.1	10.2	10.0	6.6
Designated providers	11.2	9.1	10.7	11.8
Geographic access	9.7	10.5	7.5	7.7
Total	100.0%	100.0%	100.0%	100.0%

NOTE: Due to rounding, items may not add up to total.

The results generated for type of industry, provided in Exhibit 6, reveal that while cost savings are viewed as the second most important attribute by all types of industries, manufacturing firms would place a slightly greater emphasis on potential cost savings than would the other types of firms.

Results based on financial expenditure for health benefit coverage, provided in Exhibit 7, depict an inverse relationship between the amount of money spent on health benefits and the relative importance of potential cost savings. This result contradicts the expectation that the greater the amount spent on health care coverage, the greater the sensitivity towards cost savings.

Part of the reason for this inverse relationship may be explained by the results concerning the image of the provider. Those firms with

EXHIBIT 7
Relative Importance of Attributes by Health Benefit Expenditures per Employee

Attribute	Number of Dollars Spent per Employee	
	$1–$1,999	Greater Than $2,000
Image of provider	55.6%	59.3%
Cost savings	15.8	13.6
Utilization review	8.9	8.3
Designated providers	11.2	10.0
Geographic access	8.4	8.7
Total	100.0%	100.0%

NOTE: Due to rounding, items may not add up to total.

greater than $2,000 expenditure per employee placed more importance on the image of the provider than those with less than $2,000 per employee. One interpretation is that these firms do not mind paying more for health care coverage, as long as they believe they are being treated by higher quality providers.

Finally, an analysis based on principal funding mechanism revealed the greatest change in the degree of importance for each of the attributes, as shown in Exhibit 8. Firms that utilize a minimum-premium plan seem most interested in the image of the provider, but least concerned with geographic access of these providers. On the other hand, in comparison to all other population segments, those utilizing a funding mechanism other than the fully insured by a third party, minimum premium, or self-funded plan expressed the lowest degree of importance for the image of the provider and the highest degree of relative importance for cost savings. However, the number of respondents for the "other" category was extremely small, and therefore these results may change with a larger sample size.

EXHIBIT 8
Relative Importance of Attributes by Funding Mechanism

Attributes	Fully-Insured	Minimum Premium	Self-Funded	Other
Image of provider	54.6%	59.3%	57.6%	48.2%
Cost savings	14.6	18.4	15.8	21.4
Utilization review	8.4	7.7	8.7	8.1
Designated providers	11.4	8.5	11.4	8.8
Geographic access	11.0	6.1	6.5	13.5
Total	100.0%	100.0%	100.0%	100.0%

NOTE: Due to rounding, items may not add up to total.

DISCUSSION

The results of this study are useful in designing a PPO product that will maximize the product's marketability to employers, while minimizing its marketing costs. A scenario involving a provider-sponsored PPO will be discussed in order to illustrate how the study's results can be interpreted. If a provider has a below average image, it may decide to offer increased PPO cost savings in order to compete with a PPO that has a provider with an average image. The study's results suggest that the below average image cannot be offset by increases in cost savings, geographic accessibility, or other attribute improvements. This is shown in Exhibit 9 using the utility scales provided in Exhibit 4.

EXHIBIT 9
An Example of PPO Design Using the Study's Results

Competing PPO		PPO Being Designed	
Average image	.73	Below average image	.10
1–8 percent cost savings	.38	17–24 percent cost savings	.56
Retrospective utilization review	.47	Comprehensive utilization review	.49
Hospital provider only	.43	Hospital and physician providers	.53
30 minutes geographic access	.47	10 minutes geographic access	.51
Total utility	2.48		2.19

Therefore, in designing a PPO with a below average provider in terms of image, it would be more advantageous to spend an equivalent level of resources on improving the provider's image than on improving any of the other PPO attributes included in this study. This assumes that the target employer groups of the PPO would have similar characteristics to those firms included in this study. In determining whether to make "product design" changes, the relative costs of such changes must be weighed against the marginal impact in the product's marketability and, in turn, on the amount of projected net income.

Likewise, if a PPO sponsored by a hospital with an average or above average image was seeking other hospital partners with which to network, the results suggest that it should not choose any partners with a below average image. This is true even if the inclusion of a provider with a below average image would reduce the PPO's costs and increase its accessibility (within the ranges measured in this study).

The above scenario is true only to the extent of the study's limitations. These limitations include: a small number of firms (110), parochial (Chicago area), and mainly one type of industry (manufacturing). Another study using conjoint analysis was completed by benefit managers in the St. Louis area.[12] This study used three attributes, quality, cost savings, and accessibility. As with the study involving the Chicago managers, the findings of the St. Louis study indicated that the quality of the providers was more important than the other two attributes combined. However, a more important limitation of these studies may exist with the methodology's implicit assumption that the benefit managers' answers to this survey replicate the decisions they would make for their firm. This limitation is discussed in light of the study's results below.

As noted previously, the potential cost savings provided by the plan ranked a distant second in importance to the image of the provider. This was surprising given the literature on PPOs, the study's focus group interview, and the descriptive results obtained by the data in the first half of the questionnaire. These data indicated that the majority of firms responding to the survey had instituted a wide variety of cost-containment programs in an attempt to reduce their health care expenditures.

Two possible reasons for the low rating of cost savings are suggested. First, respondents may have felt.that the study's levels of cost savings were not realistic. If so, they may have placed lesser significance on the presence of this attribute, thus lowering its relative importance. However, evidence to suggest that these cost saving levels were believed to be realistic is found in the attribute's part-worth utility measurements. These measurements increase as the level of cost savings increase. This pattern of utility measurements would not have been as likely to result if respondents' had viewed the cost savings patterns as unrealistic.

A second possible explanation noted earlier is that benefit managers may respond in one fashion to a survey and in another fashion when presenting recommendations to their superiors. It may be easier to voice a concern for quality and image in a survey as opposed to making a selection of plans based on a firm's limited resources. In the latter case, cost may be more important.

Another finding somewhat inconsistent with the literature on PPOs is the low relative importance placed on utilization review by the respondents. One potential explanation, supported by the comments from the focus group interview, is that benefit managers do not understand these programs and their potential impact on quality and cost savings. Another possible explanation is that because utilization review is not an end unto itself, but a means to achieving more efficient resource utilization and, as a result, cost savings, some benefits managers may have "chosen" plans offering high cost savings in the study and felt they did not need to also differentiate between utilization-review methods.

However, as mentioned previously, conjoint analysis minimizes if not eliminates the interaction effects among variables. This fact would tend to support the first explanation given, that of benefits managers not understanding these programs and their purposes. It is also important to note that while the results suggest that utilization review may not be perceived to be important to marketing a PPO, this does not mean that utilization review is not important to achieving other goals of the PPO, including cost savings and quality assurance.

CONCLUSION

Conjoint analysis was utilized in this study to measure the preferences of health care purchasers towards various attributes comprising alternative PPO plans. The study reveals that of the five attributes used to describe alternative plans, image of the provider was the most important in terms of affecting the likelihood that health benefits managers would offer a particular plan. The data show that of the 13 attribute levels tested, respondents placed the greatest importance on a provider perceived by the community as having an "above average" image and felt most negatively about a provider perceived by the community as having a "below average" image. The findings indicate that in no instance could any other combination of the study's attribute levels overcome a below average image for the PPO's designated providers.

Despite the study's limitations, the high importance placed on image of the provider, which was more important than the other four attributes combined, cannot be overlooked. This fact suggests that even in an era of increased cost-containment activities, purchasers are still concerned about provider image and are willing to trade-off other attributes to use high-image providers.

NOTES

1. The study discussed in this article represents the work of Ms. Robin Kornfeld as required for successful completion of her Master's degree from The Department of Health Systems Management, Rush University, Chicago, Illinois.

2. Philip Kotler, *Marketing for Nonprofit Organizations,* 2d ed. (Englewood Cliffs, N.J.: Prentice-Hall, Inc., 1982), Chapter 6.

3. Ibid., p. 167.

4. Bryan Dowd, Roger Feldman, John E. Kralewski, and Janet Shapiro, "Corporate Perspective on the Preferred Provider Concept," Center for Health Services Research, University of Minnesota, March 1983.

5. Conducted by William M. Mercer—Meidinger, Inc., 1983.

6. Conducted by William M. Mercer—Meidinger, Inc., 1984.

7. Paul E. Green and V. Srinivasan, "Conjoint Analysis in Consumer Research: Issues and Outlooks, *Journal of Consumer Research* 5 (September 1978), pp. 101–123.

8. Paul E. Green, "On the Design of Choice Experiments Involving Multifactor Alternatives," *Journal of Consumer Research* 1 (1974), pp. 61–68.

9. Naresh K. Malhortra and Arun K. Jain, "A Conjoint Analysis Approach to Health Care Marketing and Planning," *Journal of Health Care Marketing* 2, no. 2 (Spring 1982), pp. 35–44.

10. Paul E. Green, "Conjoint Analysis in Consumer Research," p. 110.

11. Yoran Wind and Lawrence K. Spitz, "Analytical Approach to Marketing Decisions in Health Care Organizations," *Operations Research* 24, no. 5 (September–October 1976), pp. 973–990.

12. This study was conducted by InterQual, Inc. for the Regional Health Network, Inc., a provider-initiated PPO.

PART 3

DESIGN AND DEVELOPMENT OF PREFERRED PROVIDER ARRANGEMENTS

1. Planning and
   Design Features
2. Management Functions
3. Contracting Requirements
4. Legal Issues

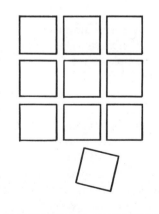

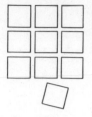

Planning and Design Features

MYTHS AND MISCONCEPTIONS ABOUT PREFERRED PROVIDER ARRANGEMENTS

Peter Boland, Ph.D.
President
Boland Healthcare Consultants
Berkeley, CA

☐ Preferred provider arrangements have to accommodate divergent interests and goals in order to succeed and remain competitive. Investors and shareholders of private for-profit PPOs, for example, have far different expectations than sponsors of employer-initiated preferred provider arrangements. The points of view each participant brings to the contracting process have an impact on shaping the nature of the arrangement and on the subsequent transaction of providing and consuming medical services. Major participants have different ideological and professional assumptions about the nature of preferred provider contracting and about their involvement. For example: How much financial risk should providers assume? How strong of an economic incentive should be built into the benefits package to encourage enrollees to use preferred providers? What kind of management reports should be generated on a routine basis for purchasers?

A number of assumptions about the nature of PPOs have been made by providers and purchasers that have not been borne out by the experience of preferred provider arrangements to date or by other alternative delivery systems such as health maintenance organizations. These misconceptions are important to identify because the design of many current preferred provider arrangements is based on the "conventional wisdom" of these assumptions. By recognizing common misconceptions that are inherent in many design features, providers and purchasers are more apt to reach accord on how to structure a preferred provider arrangement to meet the needs of each party.

Twelve common misconceptions about preferred provider arrangements are discussed below and address the following issues:

— Definition.
— Price.
— Membership criteria.
— Fee-for-service medicine.
— Medical staff relationships.
— Risk sharing.
— Discount agreements.
— Marketing.
— Enrollment.
— "Win win" scenario.
— Hospitals as preferred providers.
— PPOs as fad.

MYTHS AND MISCONCEPTIONS

THE LACK OF A COMMON DEFINITION IS AN OBSTACLE TO DEVELOPING AND MARKETING PPOs

There are numerous conceptions of PPOs that reflect different points of view, types of sponsorship, organizational arrangements, and benefit structures. While there are common principles guiding the development of a broad range of preferred provider arrangements, there is no single definition for two reasons. First, local market conditions largely determine the nature and predominant characteristics of the product. Second, preferred provider contracting is a *process* for negotiating specific medical services between health care buyers and sellers at agreed-upon prices. A PPO is a generic type of administrative structure designed to accomplish such service agreements. It will necessarily vary according to the objectives of the participants and the dynamics of the local marketplace.

The lack of a common definition, however, does make it more difficult to readily understand what a PPO is and what it is not, since they vary according to local market conditions. It also makes it harder to assess different PPOs according to a uniform set of performance standards or to evaluate different components of preferred provider arrangements.

Unlike HMOs, PPOs have thus far escaped rigid regulatory definitions and compliance requirements. The lack of regulatory definition enables providers and purchasers to negotiate more flexible service agreements and contract conditions than is possible within a strict HMO structure.

One of the strengths of PPOs is their flexibility to respond to new consumer needs and changing market opportunities. The diversity of preferred provider arrangements that results from this process offers purchasers a wider choice of services, prices, and provider arrangements than ever before. The lack of a common definition supports the range of contracting opportunities available to purchasers and providers for negotiating medical service agreements.

PRICE IS BY FAR THE MOST IMPORTANT MARKETING FEATURE

The uncontrolled cost of health care has forced purchasers to reexamine their role in buying medical care and to require accountability from medical suppliers similar to that expected from vendors of other business services. Benefit managers are under pressure to reduce the rate of increase in health care costs without jeopardizing employee relations. What they are looking for is an acceptable level of access to high-quality services at more affordable rates. They are particularly sensitive to accusations of cutting costs at the expense of quality and would generally maintain quality despite the cost if there was a choice. In the past, exorbitant benefit costs could more easily be passed on and absorbed than the even higher costs of employee dissatisfaction and anger. The latter situation can lead to lower productivity and morale, increased absenteeism and medical claim expenses, and labor union discord.

Human resource managers are as concerned about the predictability of health care costs as they are about the actual level of costs. Both create havoc for senior management responsible for planning and budgeting activities.

The decision of whether to enter into a preferred provider arrangement goes beyond the issue of price and includes factors such as predictability of costs, access, quality of care, and internal operating costs. In selling a preferred provider arrangement to employers, the most important purchaser concern may not be cost alone but "image," which is a subjective assessment of consumer satisfaction factors such as product quality, convenience, reliability, prestige, *and* cost.

HIGH-COST PROVIDERS WILL CHANGE THEIR PRACTICE PATTERNS WITH THE RIGHT INCENTIVES IN A PPO

Many PPOs take the position that membership criteria should be broad enough to enable most physicians to qualify in a locale. This approach may prove to be financial suicide. It suggests that physicians should be given an opportunity to meet PPO performance standards once they are participating members rather than establishing performance standards as a criterion for membership. This misconception is based in part on the assumption that practice pattern data to assess physician behavior are available and accessible, which is not the case in most preferred provider arrangements. The latter approach would screen out or discourage inefficient practitioners from seeking membership.

A hospital sponsored PPO may not want to risk alienating part of the medical staff identified as high-cost providers, since only a small percentage of the hospital's revenue would be generated by PPO volume during the first few years of operation. The hospital may choose to let an internal utilization management committee or the Board of Directors battle out the policy issue over a period of years based on whatever data are available to them.

PPOs that encourage most physicians to apply up front do so for a number of strategic reasons. These include (1) minimizing legal challenges from rejected applicants, (2) undercutting medical association opposition, (3) ensuring a broad physician network as soon as possible, (4) generating operating capital from membership fees, and (5) believing the myth that inefficient physicians can be readily identified and motivated to become more efficient practitioners. This policy decision generally rests on two assumptions. First, physicians with unnecessarily high-cost practice styles can be educated or disciplined to modify their behavior. Second, the organization lacks reliable information to judge whether a physician practices cost-effective medicine.

Very few physicians are eager to modify their practice patterns except for compelling reasons. These patterns are usually ingrained and reinforced by patient gratitude and financial reward. Physicians are unlikely to change their professional behavior, especially if there is little financial threat or risk involved. The current generation of PPOs generally shield participating physicians from financial risk. Even preferred provider arrangements that withhold a portion of physician payment (e.g. 5 percent) as an incentive for meeting performance objectives are not going to influence high-cost providers who can readily make up that loss in other ways.

A preferred provider sponsor that does not have an information system or access to data on physician profiles is at a serious disadvantage. If a sponsor does not place a high priority on this level of information and analysis, it probably will not take utilization management seriously enough to run a cost-effective operation. Utilization review and control mechanisms need to be fully capitalized and integrated with other automated management functions in order for the PPO to succeed in the long run.

It is far more effective to establish appropriate performance standards as a prerequisite for membership. By setting a tone early on that the organization is committed to providing high-quality efficient medical care, the PPO will be able to attract better physicians and market a more competitive product. Some preferred provider arrangements have been able to achieve this by having a core group of physicians choose who they want on their PPO panel as cost-efficient providers. This prevents unnecessary medical costs due to inefficient practice patterns and avoids disruptive and demoralizing disciplinary procedures required to weed out overutilizers.

PPOs PRESERVE TRADITIONAL FEE-FOR-SERVICE MEDICINE

Fee-for-service reimbursement is one of the most important features of preferred provider arrangements to physicians. Preferred provider arrangements also introduce a new level of performance monitoring and peer review that requires substantial changes in traditional practice styles of participating physicians.

In order to remain financially successful, utilization review standards will become increasingly strict and sophisticated in order to generate adequate cost savings to satisfy the cost saving needs of local purchasers. As providers develop new strategies for competing more effectively in the future, they will become increasingly price sensitive as a result of marketplace demand. Preferred provider contracting offers physicians the familiarity of fee-for-service reimbursement, but it generally imposes new cost containment mechanisms and quality assurance protocols. It is a bridge from the traditional style of medicine typified by fee-for-service practice to a new era of alternative delivery systems marked by risk sharing and performance-based reimbursement.

At the present time PPOs offer physicians and hospitals an opportunity to experiment with price-competitive medical care with relatively little financial risk for physicians and little or (at most) moderate financial risk for hospitals. In the future, preferred provider organizations are likely to involve greater risk sharing based on capitated reimbursement and hybrid capitation models or "product-based" payment methods (e.g., DRG-based reimbursement).

Current preferred provider arrangements on the market serve as an introduction to a new era of price-competitive medical care. In the long run, they may serve as a major catalyst for changing fee-for-service medicine.

PPOs CREATE AN ADVERSARIAL RELATIONSHIP BETWEEN MEDICAL STAFF AND HOSPITAL

The process of developing a PPO brings hospitals and physicians together for a common purpose—to compete effectively in a changing marketplace that they have less control over than in the past. Hospitals depend on practitioners for admissions, referrals, and case management expertise, while physicians need hospitals to provide high-technology resources, continuity of care, a continuum of services for their patients, and a place to practice. Regardless of whether a PPO is provider based (physician, hospital) or payor initiated (employer, health and welfare trust fund, insurance company), physicians and hospitals must cooperate with each other in order to survive.

The adversarial environment that surrounds PPOs is a result of health care competition among similar types of providers in an area, e.g., hospital A versus hospital B, obstetricians versus other obstetricians. Since physicians admit patients to competing hospitals, there is a need for hospitals to establish loyalty between medical staff and their institution in order to develop a successful PPO. Conflict can arise over specific policies such as fee schedules and utilization review within a particular preferred provider arrangement like a PPO. When this occurs it is often the result of physicians (medical staff) not being adequately consulted, involved, and advised by the PPO sponsor. Even a hospital sponsored PPO can be interpreted as an economic threat to physicians if they are not given an adequate opportunity to participate in its development and share in its success.

The biggest source of potential conflict, however, is due to a lack of understanding about current trends in the marketplace that are restructuring the practice of medicine. Both physicians and hospitals are being forced to adapt to stricter reimbursement regulations, a shrinking patient base, alternative health care delivery systems, and more demanding medical consumers and purchasers. Each of these trends can be perceived as an economic threat as well as the strategies devised to cope with them. On the other hand, the same dynamics that are creating competition can also be interpreted as new business opportunities to create health care products that better respond to consumer needs.

Preferred provider contracting represents a unique situation in which physicians and hospitals can work together for common objectives. Joint venture opportunities for contracting provide a vehicle and a rationale for hospitals and medical staffs to benefit from new cooperative relationships.

PPOs PROTECT PROVIDERS FROM FINANCIAL RISK

There is little incentive to meet performance goals such as cost efficiency when neither the PPO nor the individual practitioner is at risk. Without a sufficient financial incentive (i.e., reward or penalty), providers are not likely to change traditional practice styles. Many current preferred provider arrangements have been designed by hospitals and physicians to protect and advance their financial interests in the face of increasing competition. Until recently, there was little pressure for providers to place themselves at risk for the performance of their organization since the market did not demand it.

PPOs are generally seen by providers as a marketing tool to increase market share rather than as a vehicle to reduce consumer health care costs. With that as their objective, there is no immediate reason for providers to place themselves at risk for an untested product in a volatile market. The main provider rationale for joining a PPO is to lessen risk by defending against future competition. Physicians affiliate with PPOs to protect their sources of revenue, retain their patient base, and maintain their chosen style of medical practice. Nonetheless, PPOs will not be able to financially survive without producing significant cost savings for employers to justify the administrative expense and effort of channeling employees to preferred providers.

In order to reduce health care costs, strict utilization review policies will be applied to physicians. These review mechanisms can be most effective when enforced through penalty provisions (e.g., denial of payment, expulsion from panel). Without penalty sanctions for noncompliance, there is far less incentive to adopt cost-efficient medical practice patterns. Preferred provider models in the future will include greater risk sharing because it rewards efficiency and effectiveness, which are the basis of competitive health care.

The other trend that could propel providers to accept increased risk is that purchasers may eventually require it as a prerequisite of good faith bargaining. However, financial accountability (as opposed to clinical accountability) and shared risk are not usual provider objectives. If providers will not accept some financial responsibility for their performance, purchasers are likely to remain skeptical about their motives.

Many purchasers are interested in developing more of an "arm's length" partnership approach to health care delivery with providers. This approach includes the mutual objective of distributing risk and rewards equitably through negotiation. The concept of risk *sharing* between providers and purchasers will attract wide purchaser support because it signals accountability for the financial burden of health care.

DISCOUNT AGREEMENTS REDUCE HEALTH CARE COSTS

Discount agreements can apply to a variety of physician and hospital payment schedules and each may appear to save purchasers as much as 15 to 20 percent off billed charges. Discount agreements in and of themselves however only apply to the projected price of specific services for a particular time. They do not necessarily reflect the actual cost of the service, the difference between what was charged and the amount actually collected, how it was priced the past few years, or whether different components that used to be included in those services will instead be priced separately. Without additional information, purchasers will have a difficult task trying to determine what effect the discount could have on both per capita costs and overall costs.

Lower prices do not mean that lower costs will necessarily result. Cost savings depend on many factors in addition to the price of individual services. The frequency with which services are provided as well as the complexity or intensity of the services ordered are as important as individual prices. Likewise, the scope of services covered greatly affects health care costs for consumers. Purchasers also need to determine how the price of specific services compares with that of other providers in the area.

Since utilization review monitors what care is given and how it is provided, review mechanisms are more important than price discounts in achieving cost savings. So too are physician and hospital selection standards for participating in PPOs. It is far more cost effective to screen out inefficient providers than to give a discount on their services that, to begin with, may not have been appropriate.

Because cost is based both on the price of services *and* the volume of services provided (i.e., cost = price × volume), price alone will not guarantee an actual reduction in either overall costs or per capita costs. In fact, a price discount given by a high-cost inefficient provider may be less advantageous to purchasers than the normal charges of an efficient provider. However, a competitive price discount offered by cost-effective physicians and hospitals does represent true cost savings.

Discount medicine implies "cheap" medical care to some consumers. In such situations, benefits managers would not sell a preferred provider option to employees who consider it cheap medicine. Price discounts become less attractive as purchasers learn more about how anticipated savings can be diluted or eaten up by offsetting provider actions. At that point, the importance of price discounts should be reexamined in relation to the impact of other techniques for reducing health care costs.

MARKETING IS THE KEY TO A SUCCESSFUL PPO

A primary reason for PPO failures is an overemphasis on marketing strategy prior to resolving questions about conceptual design, product pricing, and support system development. While the importance of marketing should not be underestimated, it cannot make up for a flawed product that does not meet the needs of potential purchasers in a particular locale.

Inadequate product design often results from not resolving internal policy issues during preoperational planning. Issues such as how to structure risk and reward sharing, the extent and nature of utilization review, and membership criteria for physicians each influences the design of the product and the effectiveness of the delivery system. These kinds of policy issues and design features will determine how well the product responds to local market conditions.

One of the most frequent mistakes being made by preferred provider sponsors is prematurely rushing PPOs into the marketplace without adequate development time and consultation with key payor organizations in affected local areas. Providers cannot assume that their product will be well received solely on its own merits, particularly if the program is perceived as provider oriented. PPO sponsors will benefit from involving potential purchasers in the design stage and should follow through with extensive educational activities informing subscribers about the benefits of preferred provider arrangements in order to win their support and secure their participation.

Each of these actions is an integral part of successful marketing. It is an ongoing activity of preferred provider contracting, which includes extensive market research and product design in addition to direct sales activities. In the long run, the success of marketing a preferred provider arrangement rests on the strength and characteristics of the product, not vice versa.

FLEXIBLE ENROLLMENT IS A FUNDAMENTAL DESIGN PRINCIPLE OF PPOs

The ability of subscribers to choose a preferred provider or a non-PPO physician at the onset of illness is widely considered one of the most important selling points of preferred provider arrangements. It offers more flexibility and wider discretion than health maintenance organizations or exclusive provider organizations. This feature has been well received by employee benefits administrators because it is perceived as expanding employee choice rather than restricting benefit options.

The shortcoming of this approach to enrollment is that purchasers will not be able to tell whether preferred providers are in fact saving money on a per capita basis, which is the most important standard for comparison. There is no effective means of evaluating the performance of different providers treating undifferentiated groups of patients at different time periods. It is essential to determine per capita costs rather than overall costs because the latter masks increased volume of services (i.e., frequency or intensity). For this to be calculated, there must be a defined population to serve as a denominator. For example:

$$\text{Per capita savings} = \frac{\text{Treatment costs}}{\substack{\text{Number of PPO} \\ \text{enrollees } not \\ \text{using preferred} \\ \text{providers}}} - \frac{\text{Treatment costs}}{\substack{\text{Number of PPO} \\ \text{enrollees using} \\ \text{preferred} \\ \text{providers}}}$$

Since current PPO models do not require a designated enrollment or a "lock in," which is necessary to define a population denominator, it will be difficult to accurately judge whether preferred providers are saving purchasers' money or merely offering lower prices and recouping the loss on volume.

In the future, purchasers may be more likely to require designated enrollment for a one-year period in order to assess the extent of cost savings through preferred provider contracting. This will require using sophisticated administrative systems that can track costs and cost savings.

EVERYBODY WINS IN PREFERRED PROVIDER CONTRACTING

The restructuring taking place in the health care industry will inevitably produce winners and losers. As a reflection of this process, preferred provider contracting will likewise generate gains and losses for providers as well as purchasers.

The revenue base supporting the health care industry is shrinking and shifting to alternative delivery systems. One of the purposes of preferred provider contracting is to reduce purchaser costs by developing a more cost-effective mix of services than traditional inpatient acute care. Selective contracting for such services means showing preference to cost-effective providers, or "bargain basement" bidders, while withholding business (and revenue) from others. This means that many preferred providers will gain a better market position over their competitors who are not selected. Hospitals that will most likely be hit the hardest by selective contracting are facilities with the following features: high cost, low utilization, small percentage of private patients, and major referral center activities.

As a result of being selected a preferred provider, hospitals may realize a lower profit margin for each PPO case in relation to non-PPO patient admissions. This could reduce net revenue in the short run and would create additional pressure for hospitals to make up the decreased revenue and improve their competitive financial position in two ways: (1) by charging more for regular patients, and (2) by shifting some high cost/low reimbursement cases to public hospitals (i.e., state, county, municipal). The cost shifting to public hospitals will further strain their capacity to remain in operation without substantial government subsidy. Other hospitals that serve poor populations at medicaid prices will be further squeezed by competition, particularly if their clientele does not pay charges that include some margin for making up losses. Many hospitals with a high percentage of medicaid patients often run in the red but cannot afford to operate at a deficit over an extended period of time.

Groups of high risk/low reimbursement medical care consumers may be adversely affected by selective contracting because staff physicians at preferred provider hospitals will feel additional pressure to redirect unprofitable cases to other facilities. Because of their adverse medical conditions, these consumers will not be covered by private insurance programs that participate in preferred provider arrangements.

On the purchaser side, smaller employers that do not have enough leverage to bargain with providers for preferred rates may be damaged by exclusion and by having to pay potentially higher health insurance premiums or provider charges to make up for the price reductions granted to larger purchasers who negotiated preferred provider agreements. In the future, insurance carriers and Blue Cross and Blue Shield will likely offer smaller employers discounted premiums for PPO coverage.

HOSPITALS NEED TO BE PREFERRED PROVIDERS TO REMAIN COMPETITIVE IN METROPOLITAN AREAS

Preferred provider organizations are not panaceas for struggling hospitals. While selective contracting arrangements offer attractive marketing advantages for some medical centers, they also involve potential risk in two key areas—financial impact and medical staff relations.

Whether a hospital decides to become a preferred provider or whether a chosen PPO is the right type of preferred provider arrangement, the decision should be based on an assessment of the strengths and weaknesses of various competitive strategies. Each strategy has inherent risks and opportunities. The particular strategy that is adopted will depend on the hospital's role and competitive position in the community and the capacity of the institution's leadership for directing its internal and external resources to new product development.

Every hospital does not have the necessary resources to be a successful preferred provider. One of the minimum prerequisites is a thorough understanding of the hospital's cost structure on a service by service basis. This should be supported by a cost accounting system and an information system capable of modeling the impact of different utilization, staffing, and pricing assumptions on the financial operations of the hospital.

Hospitals that enter into preferred provider contracts without a sophisticated analytical base for making that agreement run the risk of financial loss. Facilities could find themselves worse off due to adverse patient mix, unrealized patient volume, and bad debt left behind by failing PPOs.

If preferred provider contracting is adopted as a one-shot strategy to increase market position, it is less likely to be successful than if it is part of a broader strategy of corporate diversification. The latter strategy could include a range of alternative delivery systems—including PPOs—aimed at creating a vertically integrated structure of client services. Within this framework, it makes more sense to evaluate the pros and cons of PPO involvement as a strategic option for remaining price competitive. If current market trends of declining lengths of stay and admission rates continue, it will be more realistic for hospitals to view selective contracting as a means of retaining existing market share rather than capturing additional market share in the future.

PPOs ARE A PASSING FAD

Preferred provider arrangements are an outgrowth of specific market conditions—surplus hospital beds, oversupply of physicians, tightened reimbursement standards, and spiralling health care costs—which created a more competitive environment for medical services. Although these market forces are restructuring the health care industry, the shakeout period will take a number of years and will generate numerous alternatives for providing competitive health care services.

Preferred provider organizations are the most widely recognized model of preferred provider arrangements that are being developed to compete on the basis of price, quality, and access. Since PPOs are still developing as an organizational model, it remains to be seen whether both the provider objective of increased market share and the purchaser objective of reduced health costs can be achieved. In order to meet provider and purchaser objectives, both increased market share and reduced health costs will have to be achieved simultaneously. A variety of organizational models with diverse characteristics and different economic incentives will test whether increased volume, decreased costs, and fee-for-service payment are compatible in a competitive medical environment.

The particular organizational design of different PPO models is likely to change during the next few years in response to local conditions and opportunities. Just as the health care industry is in a state of transition, so too are the current models of PPOs. They are responding to the changing dynamics in the market and will be evolving with it.

CONCLUSION

During the negotiation process it is useful for major participants to question and carefully consider the basic assumptions of preferred provider arrangements and to thoroughly understand what they are getting into. This is critical to the success of the organization and to the satisfaction of the consumers. Different viewpoints and values need to be clarified before and during the negotiation process in order for purchasers and providers to develop a mutual level of understanding and trust. Unless divergent values and assumptions are made explicit and resolved through negotiation, they will resurface during the course of the contracting period as unmet expectations, dissatisfaction, and disagreement about program operations.

The process of negotiating preferred provider agreements is new to both purchasers and providers. It will necessarily be marked by a high degree of initial confusion and uncertainty as each party tries to define their respective roles and responsibilities. By clarifying each other's assumptions and objectives, purchasers and providers will be able to identify areas of common interest, which is the starting point for developing cost-effective preferred provider arrangements.

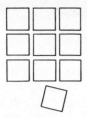

Planning and Design Features

PPO DECISION MAKING: BUSINESS PLANNING PRINCIPLES APPLY*

Michael E. Kove, M.P.H.
President
Health Ventures
San Rafael, CA

Nellie O'Gara, M.P.H.
President
First Health Associates, Inc.
Chicago, IL

☐ An article recently appeared in *Business Week* about "the upheaval in health care" that has caused the health care provider community to respond by "putting on a business suit." The current crisis in health care is forcing health care providers to think and act more like businesses and corporate entities by borrowing successful management and planning

---

*The strategic planning/strategy management techniques used in this chapter were developed by the staff of Arthur D. Little, Inc. The techniques were adapted for health care provider use by the company's heath care consulting staff in Cambridge, Massachusetts and San Francisco, California, where Mr. Kove directed the Western Region Health Care Consulting Practice. Much of the material in this chapter was adapted from a seminar presented by the Arthur D. Little, Inc. staff, in Houston, Texas in 1983.

techniques from industry. Along with this "suit," health care providers are adapting and implementing business planning and management methodologies as they move toward "corporate" organization, consider diversification, and manage their organizations in a more complex and competitive environment.

The purpose of this chapter is to explore the process of strategic planning/strategy management adapted to the health care provider and see how it applies to the decision-making process for PPOs. Within this context each of the five elements of the strategic planning/strategy management process will be discussed. These include the following:

— Strategic business unit definition.
— Industry/Market maturity.
— Classification of competitive position.
— Strategy selection.
— Risk analysis.

First, however, it would be useful to provide a brief perspective behind the development of strategic planning/strategy management within the business community and to look at some of the same patterns and trends that have occurred within the health care industry.

PERSPECTIVE

The use of business planning and management techniques is not surprising, considering the fact that the health industry as a whole has a history of adapting and utilizing business and industrial technologies. For example, basic ultrasound and x-ray technologies were developed and used elsewhere before their diagnostic and treatment capabilities in health care were recognized.

Parallels also exist in the phases of business development, including planning and management techniques, and those events that have shaped the provision of health care services. Both the business world and health care providers have been dramatically influenced by the tremendous social, technical, economic, and political changes that have transformed the United States (and the rest of the world) in the third quarter of this century.

For business and industry the 1950s were marked by an emphasis on increased production and new plant capacity in response to the pent-up consumer demands of the postwar era. This was a period of corporate decentralization and the development of professional management. Management by objectives became popular, practical computer development was just beginning, and real management information systems were still unknown. Business planning involved revising one year's production goals to the next year's sales objectives.

When consumer demand had been satisfied, the emphasis switched to marketing and creating new demand for more products. The latter part of the 1960s saw corporations creating profit centers controlled by budgetary processes and organizational hierarchies. Planning utilized formulas and budgets, while advances in computer technology permitted standardization.

As the 1960s drew to a close, the profit center approach was beginning to be replaced by an overall approach to product development, markets, and competition. This market-oriented view became increasingly popular during the late 1970s as corporate business activity moved from multiple to fewer units. It was also an era during which a corporation's businesses were found to be significantly different from one another in characteristics, revolving around industry maturity and competitive position. These differences suggested that generic strategies could be applied to resource allocation and product/market development. Managing a diversified business had become the corporate challenge, and contemporary strategic planning/strategy management was used to meet that challenge.

Similarly, as the health care provider industry underwent change during the 1960s and 1970s, planning concepts and management techniques within this industry also evolved.

The general economic expansion of the postwar decades brought with it a dramatic growth in American medicine. By the end of the 1950s national health expenditures represented more than 7 percent of the gross national product, the health care workforce more than tripled, and medical care became one of the largest industries in the nation. Medical research and technology were the focus of postwar health policies, while the Hill-Burton Act of 1946 caused hospital planning of the 1950s to focus on the design, development, and construction of physical facilities.

With the enactment of medicare and medicaid legislation in the mid-1960s, the need to consider consumer demands and regulatory controls came to the fore. Management and planning techniques were designed to satisfy medical staff, accrediting bodies, unions, and third-party payors. Planning was short term and focused on operating budgets as the need for greater fiscal management increased.

Health care planning in the 1970s was dictated by the requirements of the National Health Planning and Resources Development Act of 1974. During this time, Health Systems Agencies replaced Comprehensive Health Planning Agencies, and institutional long-range planning became the focal point of planning endeavors. These activities included a definition of mission, development of programmatic and departmental objectives, and resource allocation decisions—in response to regulation and demonstrated community need.

The 1980s will be characterized by a competitive awareness among health care providers. Both businesses and health care providers have become increasingly concerned with maintaining competitive positions as advancements are made in transportation, in computer and communication systems, and in service delivery technologies. Growing pressure is being brought to bear on health care providers by the intense interest of business and government in controlling medical costs.

The provision of health care is a business—a big business. External factors must be recognized and monitored, and alternative strategies must be developed to cope with rapid change. Because of these conditions, it will be important to plan and manage strategically. These two activities are embodied in what is called strategic management systems.

There are two reasons why both strategic planning and strategic management are appropriate for health care providers. First, there are issues such as increasing competition; limited resources; changing regulations and reimbursement patterns; demographic, social, and cultural shifts; new technology; and health personnel trends. These require an increased ability to plan for and manage change.

Second, health care providers are being pressured to adopt business-like, efficient management techniques because of physician surpluses and DRG reimbursement systems. These influencing factors are also transforming the institutional structure of medical care itself into a management-oriented corporate model. This can be seen in the rise of HMOs and PPOs, in the development of multihospital systems, in the emergence of diversified health care companies, and in the growth and proliferation of profit-making firms in medical services.

PPO DEVELOPMENT

Preferred provider organizations have evolved in response to increasing health care competition, based on the following factors:

— Declining and unfavorable revenue mix.
— Oversupply of hospital beds and declining demand for use.
— Increasing supply of physicians.
— Radical changes in financial incentives tied to treating medicare patients.
— Growing buyer concern with increasing and unmanaged health care costs.
— Increasing consumer cost sharing and the resulting "shopping" for facilities and physicians.

These variables require that health care providers, especially hospitals, consider new competitive strategies. Determining the appropriate strategy can be a time-consuming task, and if not done properly, may result in an outcome that is little better than guesswork. Much of the provider rush into the PPO marketplace is a reaction to increased competition rather than the result of a well-thought-out strategy.

The application of business planning techniques, particularly strategic planning and strategy management, can lead to successful PPO planning and implementation. The utilization of a structured (but not binding) planning process can do much to eliminate many errors and misjudgments and ensure that development resources are well spent.

Like their business counterparts, health care providers are significantly different from one another in terms of characteristics such as industry/market maturity, competitive position, and market potential. It is important to accurately define and understand these differences because they will dictate the selection of a generic strategy.

While health care providers must pay attention to national trends, it is also important to recognize regional and local trends in planning PPOs. At this point in time, all available information concerning PPO development and operations must be viewed against the backdrop of the local environment.

Like hospitals, the operating environment of PPOs is more condition driven than ambition driven. This means that the purchasers and payors of health care services are playing more active roles in determining how health care services will be provided and in determining the cost/charge structures for the services. These external factors are the "conditions," and they appear to outweigh the "ambitions" of the providers. The term *condition driven* can be further explained in relation to attributes that a health care provider acquires over time. These, in turn, define strategic condition and influence options.

STRATEGIC BUSINESS UNITS

The concept of the strategic business unit (SBU) is used by many corporations in their strategic planning and strategy management endeavors. This concept is used to identify business areas with different markets and to allow for more focused definitions of the line of business of an organization.

An SBU is defined as an area of operation with an external market for services for which it is possible to determine objectives and execute strategies independent of other areas of operation.

The process of defining SBUs is not an exact science, and its application (as part of strategic planning and strategy management) is relatively new to health care providers, although pharmaceutical companies and medical supply firms have used the concept for years. In viewing hospitals from a business perspective, business units can be defined in relation to the way a hospital is functionally organized, managed, and budgeted. There are also examples of hospital strategic planning where the major clinical services were determined to be SBUs. Nonhospital providers and/or brokers of care, such as HMOs, free-standing PPOs, third-party administrators, and third-party payors, would also have to adapt the basic industry approach to their own unique circumstances.

Since determining SBUs in health provider organizations has had limited application to date, some generic guidelines can be useful for initially determining SBUs within health provider organizations. These include:

— Charges.
— Patients.
— Competitors.
— Quality.
— Substitutability.
— Termination.

While the above list may be clearly understood by some, the term *substitutability* should be explained further. The term raises the question of whether a particular unit can be substituted for the one being considered an SBU. For example, a nursing home is not a substitute for an acute care facility. Another example is seen in the comparison of cardiac and pediatric services. Because these services have different patients, have separate charge structures, and cannot substitute for one another, then they indeed might be viewed as separate business units. Most health care provider organizations contain one or more SBUs.

SBUs might include the major clinical services of a hospital or (in the case of a diversified health care provider organization) acute services, long-term care services, and auxiliary enterprises. PPOs, HMOs, and even home health services might qualify as SBUs or together they could be grouped under the heading "alternative delivery systems." The answer depends as much on meeting the generic criteria previously stated as on the definition of the particular entity. Some might argue that a PPO is a business unit, while others consider it just a marketing device.

Once SBUs are defined, the concepts of maturity and competitive position can be applied individually.

INDUSTRY/MARKET MATURITY

One key component of strategic condition is maturity. Maturity is a concept that enhances the understanding of an industry or market in a systematic fashion and then guides the strategy selection and management processes. This concept suggests that an industry or market will look different at different points in time and that there are specific characteristics closely related to time or evolution (maturity).

Industry/market maturity can be broken into four generic stages: emerging, growing, maturing, and declining (Exhibit 1).

An industry or market's life span is defined by the dynamics affecting volume rather than time. Volume accelerates, peaks, and begins to decline. There are no good or bad points on the curve. What is critical, however, is that the behavior and strategies chosen be both appropriate and consistent with the stage of maturity.

Eight descriptors are useful in determining maturity. They are:

EXHIBIT 1
Maturity Stages

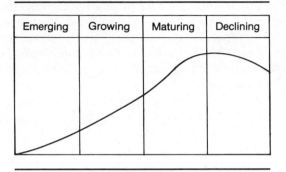

Emerging	Growing	Maturing	Declining

— Growth rate.
— Growth potential.
— Products/Services.
— Number of competitors.
— Market share stability.
— Referral patterns.
— Ease of entry.
— Technology.

An example of these descriptors can be seen in the the coal mining industry, which can then be compared to the hospital marketplace. With the increased availability and relatively inexpensive cost of both oil and natural gas, the need for coal diminished and industry volume declined. There was little or no growth potential, since supply exceeded demand. The product line shrank and was tailored to major customer needs. The number of competitors declined, which led to small regional providers. Market share became concentrated, customers and suppliers became tied to each other, and there was little incentive for new companies to enter the field. Technology changed very little. However, the oil crisis in the mid-1970s changed the picture somewhat, and the coal industry moved from a declining position back toward a mature or growth stage.

For hospitals, whose major product is inpatient care, a similar situation is developing. Volume, as measured by patient days or discharges is declining. The supply of hospital beds exceeds the current demand for them, and new hospital development has slowed dramatically. In most areas, market share is stable and each year sees the total number of hospitals decrease. Existing market share stability is therefore based on physician and patient loyalty. Technological advances have fostered increases in the utilization of outpatient services. Thus, inpatient care can be viewed in the mature/aging stage.

Since hospitals face increasing competition for both inpatients and outpatients, PPOs are seen as one way of increasing patient volumes. This is particularly important for inpatient services, where significant investments in resources exist. Although much has been written about the "graying" of the population and the positive effect this may have on the use of inpatient services, this effect must be considered in light of both technological changes and political pressures to lower health care cost by reducing in-hospital stays.

While the concept of industry/market maturity is straightforward, it requires a level of understanding and acceptance that is relatively new to health care planning and management. Demand forecasts must accurately reflect trends impacting the industry. Although much attention is focused on the financial aspects of PPOs, and even DRGs, more must be understood about utilization dynamics, because this addresses issues of growth rate and potential.

The business community in general has always conducted market and product research. Historically, the providers of health care have created the demand for their services, while the purchasers of those services had little or no say as to how the services would be provided and at what cost. This has now changed, and health care providers must carefully understand what the users and payors of health services want and expect. These needs and expectations will help determine industry potential—a potential that can be viewed by providers as market potential.

Few organizations have taken the time to study PPOs in terms of the eight industry/market maturity descriptors previously listed. Considering the concept of maturity will provide structure and substance to the PPO decision-making process.

Since we have seen market share stabilize in many areas, it remains to be seen if the PPO concept will change referral pattern strength and loyalty. This is especially important, because there appear to be no barriers to entry and few distinguishing characteristics from PPO to PPO.

PPO development is in the emerging phase. The real issue is how long it will take before the activity matures. There is evidence to suggest that the maturing process will occur quickly for the following reasons:

— Growth rate for inpatient services has already slowed.
— Market saturation will be reached sooner rather than later because of the number of entrants into the marketplace.
— Most if not all PPOs offer similar incentives for utilization.
— The number of competitors will stabilize or decline slightly.
— Market share will stabilize as major providers become entrenched.
— Buying patterns will be established bringing with them customer loyalty and increasing price sensitivity.
— The market will become difficult to enter because competitors have solidified their positions and growth is slowing.

In summary, the concept of maturity provides a framework for understanding the environment that impacts the health care delivery system—a system that includes PPOs. Maturity positions are neither good nor bad but are useful in defining strategic thrust and strategy selection, which are covered later in this chapter. In attempting to determine maturity, the stage of maturity for a particular strategic business unit may be different in a local market than that found in a national market. A good example of this phenomenon is open-heart surgery, which is on the decline nationally, as nonsurgical techniques become the procedure of choice. This has caused open-heart surgery to be mature in medically sophisticated urban centers, while it is still enjoying reasonable growth in other locales.

COMPETITIVE POSITION

While the concept of industry/market maturity helps determine the range of strategies available, competitive position can be an even more powerful tool for understanding a condition-driven environment. There are four steps that comprise the competitive position analysis. These steps are:

— Define the competition.
— Describe the competition.
— Determine the bases of competition.
— Assess competitive position.

Defining the competition is not as simple as it sounds. Often a hospital will consider all other hospitals in a given area as competitors. This is usually not the case. The number of real competitors can be narrowed by analysis factors such as market share, geographic distribution, and service/product mix. Defining the competition is critical, since few hospitals can compete effectively with 8 or 10 other facilities in a given area. This particular point is interesting because of a "lemming-like" rush to form PPOs within the hospital sector.

Unlike general businesses, health care providers seldom take the time to clearly identify and dissect their rivals in the marketplace. The historical reason for this behavior is lack of perceived need. Times have changed, however, and the results of such a dissection process are often surprising and usually increase understanding. For example, a competitor may not have the ability to move quickly into new markets and take advantage of emerging opportunities. This may be due to internal political (medical staff-administration disagreement) or financial (poor cash flow and lack of borrowing power) reasons. It is also interesting to consider that an objective assessment could lead an organization to discover other competitive handicaps. These could also limit opportunities, especially those that require the concurrance of the medical staff and/or financial resources.

As competition increases, so does the need to understand competitors. This can be best accomplished by "profiling" rivals based on such factors as ownership, growth rate, service mix, market share, degree of integration, management, geographic coverage, utilization review, cost effectiveness, and medical staff.

A competitive analysis can be undertaken on a number of levels— product/service, business unit, and corporate. The desired outcome is a thorough and complete analysis consistent with the complexity of the competitive environment.

In determining the bases of competition, it is essential to identify criteria upon which competition actually takes place. Although each market situation has unique characteristics, generic bases of competition do exist, and these can be used in the PPO arena. These include the following:

— Facilities.
— Resources.
— Medical staff.
— Support services.
— Management systems.
— Price.
— Location.

Within these competitive factors it is possible to consider such PPO-related issues as geographic coverage, service mix, medical staff support, pricing strategy, utilization review, and timing of entry. What is also important is that the above elements influence not only physicians but also more and more consumers, employers, and insurers in the market for health services. While not all of the factors have equal importance, all can have an effect on referral patterns and, hence, utilization. This is especially true of employer, consumer, and insurer choice of provider. An objective assessment of competitive position increases the likelihood that the strategic planning and management processes reflect the reality of the sponsor's position in the marketplace.

Once the competition has been defined and described and the bases for it determined, it is time to assess competitive position.

Competitive position can be described in six ways:

— Dominant.
— Strong.
— Favorable.
— Tenable.
— Weak.
— Nonviable.

Each of the competitive positions differ in the degree to which a participant can perform, control, and act in the marketplace. A dominant competitor controls the behavior of other competitors while also having the widest choice of strategic options. A favorable competitor has particular strengths that are exploitable in particular strategies and has an average opportunity to improve position. Weak competitors are plagued by unsatisfactory performance and have limited opportunities for improvement, and their position cannot be tolerated in the long-run.

Examples of the above are IBM, which is the dominant competitor in the computer industry; ABC-NBC-CBS, which are all favorable in television broadcasting; and A&P, which is weak in retail grocery.

In a condition-driven environment, it is important that the assessment of competitive position be objective and realistic. The issue is not so much what position is but rather what is done based on that position.

At this point, it is important to link the concepts of competitive position and industry/market maturity. This linkage will permit the determination of strategic condition, which guides the strategy selection process.

In relating strategic condition to PPO development, it is obvious that two organizations with different positions on the matrix (as in Exhibit 2)

EXHIBIT 2

Strategic condition

	Emerging	Growing	Maturing	Declining
Dominant				
Strong				
Favorable				
Tenable				
Weak				
Nonviable				

will behave differently in the marketplace. While organization A has the financial resources and skills to negotiate meaningful discounts, organization B may be struggling financially as a result of poor financial skills and cash position. Organization A may also have a good working relationship with its medical staff, including a history of successful joint ventures, while the opposite is true for organization B.

Behavior should and does differ among organizations, and these differences should reflect both market conditions and organizational strengths and limitations in response to those conditions. Likewise, different strategies may be necessary in order to improve, maintain, or gain position.

In summary, the concepts of strategic business units, maturity, and competitive position allow a business to define those areas of its operation for which there are separate markets, to identify and understand seemingly diverse trends, to anticipate and prepare for change, and to assess its position in the marketplace. These elements allow a business to systematically analyze the differing external and internal factors it must consider in the determination of strategic condition. It is equally important for those planning a PPO to go through the same type of analytical process.

STRATEGY SELECTION

There are two key elements in strategy selection. They are:

— Identifying the strategic objective.
— Selecting and defining the strategy or strategies.

These two elements are the link between the analysis of strategic condition and the successful implementation of a strategy in the marketplace.

A strategy is defined as a coherent set of actions aimed at gaining a sustainable advantage over the competition, improving position vis-à-vis customers (patients, physicians, insurers), and allocating resources.

Selecting a strategic objective is based upon strategic condition, as defined previously, and upon an organization's goals, culture, and resource availability. Here again, strategy is more condition driven than ambition driven. Since goals, culture, and resources are specific to individual situations, this section concentrates on the role of strategic condition in strategy selection.

As stated earlier, a dominant competitor in a growing industry can behave differently than a weak competitor in a maturing industry. In fact, depending on where a business is on the matrix, its strategic options vary.

EXHIBIT 3

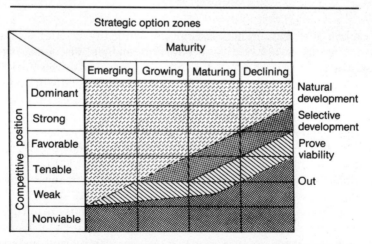

Exhibit 3 illustrates the four zones of strategic options, which include:

— Natural development.
— Selective development.
— Prove viability.
— "Out."

A business that is in the "natural development" zone has the greatest strategic freedom. Some typical objectives in this zone include:

— *Start-up:* The introduction of a new program, service, or product with a clear, significant technical breakthrough.
— *Grow with Industry:* Limit efforts to those necessary to maintain market share and to ensure that relative competitive position remains stable.

Within the "selective development" zone, options are more limited and include the following objectives:

— *Focus/Develop Niche:* Select a particular segment of the market more narrow in scope than competing programs. For health care providers, subspecialty programs often reflect a niche in the market that can be protected.
— *Differentiate:* Achieve the highest degree of service difference in market with acceptable costs. Alternative birthing centers in hospitals are examples of differentiation, as are urgency care clinics within an emergency room facility.

A business entity in the "prove viability" zone needs to do just that. The options are to:

— *Hang in:* Prolong the existence of a business unit in anticipation of some favorable changes in the environment. For example, the small rural hospital that maintains empty medical/surgical beds in the hope that the "swing bed" concept would be embraced by third-party reimbursers.
— *Retrench:* Cut back investment in the business unit to reduce the level of risk and exposure to losses and to free up capital.

Finally, a business entity in the "out" zone has little choice but to withdraw, that is, to remove the business unit from competition in the marketplace.

Once strategic objectives have been determined, the next task is to select and define the strategies necessary to support them. The following categories provide a framework for this strategy selection:

— *Market Strategies:* Given a particular objective, appropriate marketing activities are chosen. These might include hiring a marketing director and meeting with large employers.

— *Product Line:* Should the existing product line be expanded or contracted, or are there ways to add value to existing services to bolster the strategic objective? For those who do not view a PPO as a separate strategic business unit, the PPO could be viewed as a product and the decision to develop one should support the business's objectives. (Some view a PPO as a marketing strategy in and of itself.)

— *Technology:* How is the service provided? Are there new/emerging systems of delivery that require investment by the business unit under consideration?

— *Operations:* Can the organization function more efficiently? This particular strategy is important since most PPO schemes involve some sort of discount arrangement and increased efficiency is one way to make up for lost revenue.

— *Retrenchment:* Are there areas within a business unit where resources can be freed to support the strategic objective? This becomes an important issue for an organization with limited resources that desires to get into the PPO marketplace but lacks some of the necessary financial resources to do so.

— *Financial:* What are the implications for pricing, investment, and profitability? Since PPOs involve some type of discount arrangement, strategic considerations in this area are of utmost importance.

Strategy selection, therefore, details the steps to be taken to achieve the strategic objective(s). While the above should be considered by organizations considering PPOs, the strategies likewise apply to the viability and success of functioning PPOs.

Once strategic objectives and the strategies to support them have been chosen, the next step is to assess the risks associated with executing a given strategy. Each strategy should be assessed to determine the probability of successful implementation in the marketplace.

RISK ANALYSIS

The level of risk associated with any given strategy can be considered low, medium, or high, and there are several risk factors to evaluate. This is illustrated in Exhibit 4.

The characteristics of an industry itself may affect the risks associated with executing some or all strategies. The level of risk may be different for two business units because of uncertainties associated with each. For example, tertiary care programs are more risky than are prevention programs because of the investment required in technology.

When considering maturity, executing strategies in maturing and aging industries/markets is less risky than doing so in emerging ones. This

EXHIBIT 4

Risk analysis

Factor	High	Medium	Low
Industry			
Maturity			
Competitive position			
Strategy			
Assumptions			
Past performance			
Future performance			
Overall rating			

is because mature industries/markets are more stable and more predictable than less developed ones.

The stronger the competitive position, the lower the risk involved in carrying out strategies because of the business's ability to withstand and influence external forces.

Some strategies are inherently riskier than others. Market and product line strategies generally involve more risk than operations strategies because they deal with factors beyond the control of the institution (e.g., physician preference, consumer demands, and competitors' responses).

Furthermore, optimistic assumptions about market growth, industry condition, or the state of the economy tend to increase risk. The greater the positive change that is assumed from current conditions, the greater the risk.

Past performance also needs to be considered. If previous efforts have led to growth and profitability and have been successful in marketing and operations, then there is every reason to assume that this performance record will continue and therefore contribute to lower risk.

Finally, the higher the expectation, the greater the risk that the expectation will not be met. Thus an assessment of risk is an extremely important part of the overall strategic planning/strategy management process.

All elements of the strategy selection process (strategic objective, strategy selection, risk analysis) are necessary to determine a coherent and rational direction. A key consideration of selected strategies is that they be "do-able." A strategy cannot be conceived without consideration as to implementation and impact.

Strategic condition is the cornerstone of strategy selection. Every strategy selected must "fit" within the business objectives, culture, and available resources, unless a conscientious effort is made to alter one of the elements to create a new fit. While there are natural areas of strategy selection, they must be used as guidelines to incorporate the realities of the business's situation.

As health care providers come under increasing external pressures, risk assessment becomes even more important.

CONCLUSION

Strategic planning/strategy management is an adaptable business tool that has relevance for health care providers. It can be a very powerful tool in the decision-making process surrounding PPOs. It is also useful in evaluating and considering such concepts as corporate reorganization and diversification. Its use can help eliminate the continuation of reactive and potentially unguided responses to an environment that is becoming increasingly complex and threatening.

PPOs present but one option in the struggle to maintain or increase market share or to just remain competitive. Although it would be wrong to conclude that all health care providers or payors are ready to jump on the PPO bandwagon, the intense activity in this arena suggests that many organizations are indeed jumping on.

While there are no substitutes for sound judgment, the decision-making process outlined in this chapter is designed to force a logical thought process and to present an analytical approach to support "gut" reactions.

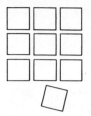

Planning and Design Features

ORGANIZING AND DEVELOPING A PPO

Raymond R. Flachbart, M.A., M.B.A.
Vice President
InterQual, Inc.
Chicago, IL

☐ The purpose of this article is to describe a generic approach to the development of PPOs. The first part of the article describes PPOs and the incentives for developing them. It also attempts to create a common base of terminology and perspective. The remainder of the article addresses the PPO development process. The following basic and often-asked questions will be addressed:

— What distinguishes a PPO from other forms of health care delivery?
— What are the various incentives for employers, consumers, physicians, and hospitals to be involved in a PPO?
— Is it necessary for a PPO to offer price discounts?
— What are the advantages and disadvantages of various PPO organizational structures?
— How can hospitals and/or physicians go about the process of starting and developing a PPO?
— Are PPOs just a fad that will fade in a couple of years?

GENERAL DESCRIPTION

There are many significant changes occurring in the way health care is being managed and delivered today. These changes are being driven by a number of factors, including reimbursement limits imposed by third-party payors, increased market competition among providers, and the belief of business leaders and consumers that the cost of health care is increasing annually at an unacceptably high rate. One example of a reaction to this high cost perception is the formation of business coalitions that are seeking ways to control and reduce health care costs.

These changes in the competitive environment have created and fostered the development of PPOs as well as other alternative forms of health care delivery. Because the structure and form of PPOs are still evolving and because of the absence of federal legislation regulating PPOs, no commonly accepted definition of PPOs is available. In its basic conceptual form a PPO is an intermediary organization that offers cost savings to health care purchasers if their constituents use select (preferred) providers to receive their care. Common characteristics and definitions germane to PPOs are listed below. Most PPOs usually involve:

1. A group of preferred providers, usually including at least hospital(s) and physicians.
2. Contractual relationships between providers and purchasers. Purchasers can be employers (private and public), welfare (union) trust funds, or multiple employer trusts.
3. The providers' promise of cost savings to the purchaser. This can be accomplished through a variety of means including:
   a. Discounts on hospital and/or physician prices.
   b. Prospectively negotiated prices for physician procedures and for hospital services, either on a per diem or a per DRG basis.
   c. Utilization controls that attempt to increase the efficiency of health care resource allocation. When appropriate, these controls attempt to reduce the following factors for patients using the preferred providers:
      (1) Rate of hospital admissions.
      (2) Length of hospital stay.
      (3) The use of inpatient and outpatient ancillary services.
      (4) The rate of specialty referrals.
      These reductions result in fewer charges to the purchaser, thereby reducing the purchaser's total costs if all other factors remain equal.
   d. Quality improvement measures that are an attempt to increase the effectiveness of health care services, thereby avoiding the use of additional health care resources so often necessary with ineffective care.

    e. Some combination of price discounts, prospectively negotiated charges, utilization controls, and quality improvement measures.

4. Incentives provided to encourage patients to use the preferred providers. These incentives are usually in the form of reduced out-of-pocket expenses (lower deductibles and/or copayments) for the patient.

5. Freedom of patients to choose between preferred and nonpreferred providers each time they require health care services. If patients use a nonpreferred provider their out-of-pocket expenses will be greater than if they use a preferred provider.

6. Retention of the fee-for-service structure for physician reimbursement.

A PPO can be viewed as a hybrid of the traditional fee-for-service insurance plan and a Health Maintenance Organization (HMO). The PPO offers some benefits of the HMO, such as cost savings to employers and employees and financial incentives to patients to use the panel of providers. It retains some of the more attractive benefits of fee-for-service insurance:

— Patients retain freedom of choice to receive services through a preferred provider, or other provider of their choice, without losing coverage.

— A wider range of physician or hospital services and locations are usually present on PPO panels than on some HMO panels.

INCENTIVES TO PARTICIPATE

A list of potential incentives for purchasers, consumers, physicians, and hospitals is provided in Exhibit 1. The incentives for each group are discussed separately below.

EXHIBIT 1
Incentives to Participate in a PPO

Purchaser	*Providers*	*Consumers*
Financial savings	Maintain or increase market share	Lower out-of-pocket expenses
Ability to offer benefits to their constituents: Lower out-of-pocket expenses Increased benefits High-quality providers More attractive to some than HMOs	Retain fee-for-service structure	Retains freedom of choice
	Rapid claims payment (in some cases)	Enriched benefits package (in some cases)
	Mechanism to develop foundation for other cooperative ventures among providers	High quality of care

PURCHASER INCENTIVES

The major incentives for purchasers to involve themselves with a PPO are the promise of financial savings and the ability to offer their employees additional benefits. These benefits include lower out-of-pocket expenses and a health benefits plan that may be more attractive to a greater number of employees than an HMO.

As previously noted, there are various methods by which providers attempt to accrue these cost savings; two common methods for PPOs are price discounts and utilization controls. Price discounts can take various forms as well. For instance, providers can offer discounts on room rates, per-diem rates, ancillary charges, per-case charges, or charges per Diagnostic Related Group (DRG). Many employers view discounts on room or per-diem rates with suspicion because providers can make up the difference by charging more for other items or by increasing the length of inpatient stay or intensity of services.

To some employers discounts also have other negative aspects, including the connotations of "cheap health care" (and therefore poor quality) or prices that have been artificially inflated before applying the discount.

Many employers realize that externally imposed utilization controls can yield greater savings than price discounts. Utilization controls attempt to reduce the number of episodes of care and the amount of resources used in these episodes of care. Successful utilization controls typically include prior authorization and concurrent review of hospital services and adjudication conducted prior to claims payment of ambulatory care services.

The difference between the cost saving methods of price discounts and utilization controls can best be illustrated by the equation that determines a purchasers' health care costs:

$$\text{Price per unit}(A) \times \text{Number of units}(B) + \text{Profit to carrier} = \text{Cost to purchaser,}$$

where B is defined as each episode of health care, such as a hospital stay, an ancillary test, or a physician's visit.

Price discounts or prospectively negotiated charges can reduce the price per unit (A) while utilization controls reduce the number of units (B). A PPO that emphasizes utilization and quality measures as well as negotiates prospective prices for its services is offering purchasers:

— well-monitored, high-quality providers and
— financial savings through limits on prices and the utilization of fewer units.

PROVIDER INCENTIVES

The most important incentive for hospitals and physicians to participate in a PPO is to retain or increase market share and patient volume. This potential exists because the PPO's incentive system of lower out-of-pocket expenses encourages patients to use the preferred providers. In an environment free of alternative delivery system (ADS) competition, a PPO can be an offensive strategy to gain market share from competitors. In an environment in which ADSs are highly competitive, a PPO may be necessary just to protect a provider against its current users' switching to a competitor to enjoy the incentives of its ADS. This is a major reason why PPOs have flourished in metropolitan areas where there is an over-supply of hospital beds and physicians and where consumer awareness is high. As one PPO develops in response to decreases in patient volumes, others follow in order to prevent loss of market share.

Another incentive for physicians to participate in a PPO is that the PPO retains fee-for-service reimbursement. This is different from most HMOs, which reimburse physicians on a capitation basis. Additionally, a PPO sometimes guarantees rapid claims payment, which improves cash flow.

To be successful, a provider-sponsored PPO requires that hospitals and physicians work together cooperatively. A potential advantage of a PPO is that it lays the foundation for a hospital and its medical staff to work together on other cooperative ventures. Regardless of the future of PPOs, hospitals and physicians that can jointly work to control the expenditure of health care dollars will be in a stronger position to negotiate successfully with an increasingly more sophisticated and selective purchaser market.

CONSUMER INCENTIVES

The major incentive for consumers to use a preferred provider is that with most PPOs a consumer's out-of-pocket expenses (deductibles and/or co-payments) will be reduced or eliminated when using one of the preferred providers. Since a PPO is merely an option within a traditional indemnity insurance plan, consumers do not have to give up their freedom to decide which provider to use for each episode of care. This differs from an HMO, in which a consumer must enroll in advance and then stay with that option for a specified period of time, usually one year. The consumer may also enjoy other benefits with a PPO including an enriched benefit package and access to well-monitored, high-quality providers.

ORGANIZATIONAL STRUCTURES

PPOs have adopted many organizational forms, the determination of which is influenced by factors which include:

— The type of sponsoring agency.
— The sponsoring agency's willingness to accept financial risk.
— The size of the sponsoring agency's market share.
— Local political conditions.

Although most entities that sponsor PPOs also retain control of the PPO, this in not always the case. This section will discuss PPOs as controlled by purchasers, providers, and distribution channels, such as insurance carriers.

PURCHASER-CONTROLLED PPOs

Some self-funded employers have long offered dual choice programs using price discounts with selected providers. The advantage of a purchaser's controlling a PPO is that the purchaser can review its own claims experience to identify the most cost-effective providers in its area and in turn offer incentives to its employees to use these providers. Depending on the cost effectiveness of certain providers, a purchaser may be able to offer these incentives to the employees without bargaining for additional concessions from providers, and still save money.

PROVIDER-CONTROLLED PPOs

Provider-controlled PPOs can be formed by:

— A hospital or group of hospitals.
— A group of physicians.
— An HMO.
— A group of hospitals and physicians jointly.

The physician/hospital joint venture model has long-term advantages not present to the same degree in the other provider-controlled models. Together hospitals and physicians control the majority of health care expenditures. By creating a PPO in which hospitals and physicians share jointly in the decision making and operating costs, both groups will be more committed to the success of that PPO than one in which they have no voice or financial stake. Regardless of the organizational structure, the provider-controlled PPO:

— should be able to negotiate with purchasers for both hospital and physician services.
— must have both hospitals and physicians committed to the PPO's goals and policies, especially utilization control.

PPOs CONTROLLED BY DISTRIBUTION CHANNELS

Insurance companies, third-party administrators, and insurance brokers can assemble provider panels, contract with them, and encourage and endorse their use. Some carriers are contracting with only hospitals, others with both hospital(s) and physicians.

PPOs formed by insurance carriers can have significant impact in the marketplace due to existing relationships with major purchasers as well as their position with other market segments. For instance carriers can approach segments of the market, such as associations and smaller industrial or manufacturing firms and underwrite them, thereby reducing the risk exposure of insuring individual firms for PPO options.

DEVELOPING A PROVIDER-CONTROLLED PPO

This section discusses the development process of provider-controlled PPOs and is based upon the development of PPOs in 12 metropolitan areas ranging in size from 150,000 to 7 million people.[1]

Some firms involved in helping develop PPOs suggest that providers should conduct PPO feasibility studies to determine whether a market exists for a PPO in their area. However, in most major metropolitan areas, PPOs already exist and many more are forming. The problem is that many of the PPOs that have been formed do not have contracts with purchasers, either because the PPO has not been formed properly or because it has not been marketed properly. The question for providers in most metropolitan areas is not whether to participate in a PPO, but how to develop a PPO in such a fashion that it is marketable and has competitive advantages over other alternative delivery systems that are or will be present in their area. In order to develop a marketable PPO with competitive advantages, several recommendations should be followed. Namely, the PPO should:

— Include a network of high-quality hospitals and physicians that provide geographic accessibility to employees and their families.
— Rely on stringent quality and utilization measures and prospectively negotiated charges to create cost savings for purchasers as opposed to large price discounts.
— Develop and implement a marketing plan that promotes and sells the PPO to employers and employees as well as to insurance carriers and HMOs.

This section of the article addresses networking and marketing issues as well as the PPO's overall development process.

OVERALL DEVELOPMENT PROCESS

The PPO is a new business venture; as with most entrepreneurial efforts it requires a good deal of sweat equity. That is, the success of the endeavor will be enhanced if volunteer labor (at least initially) is provided by those parties who have the knowledge, influence, and contacts to make a provider-controlled PPO viable. These people include key physicians, senior hospital management, and influential Board members. Therefore, in order to guide the development process, a steering or coordinating committee should be formed of interested physicians and hospital administrators. Steering committees vary in size, but usually range from 8 to 16 members.

The steering committee has several responsibilities. First, with the help of legal counsel it should evaluate and select the organizational structure of the PPO. Second, it should review the recommendations of the subcommittees that it establishes and choose a course of action. Although the appropriate functional areas for subcommittees investigation vary by provider and local area, four common functional areas include: physician issues; networking; marketing; and quality and utilization management. As with the steering committee, each subcommittee should include both physician and hospital representatives. Alternatively, some steering committees will directly deal with the issues related to these areas without establishing subcommittees.

A third responsibility of the steering committee is the development of appropriate guidelines for the PPO staff to use in negotiating hospital prices and physician fees with purchasers. Existing hospital prices should be analyzed, and if several hospitals are participating in the PPO, a single charge, by service or by DRG should be used in negotiations. Sales experience indicates that a hospital charge per DRG is attractive to purchasers because it reflects some degree of risk-sharing by the provider.

In terms of physician pricing, the use of a Relative Value Scale (RVS) has gained acceptance in many metropolitan areas. The RVS assigns weights to physician procedures which are multiplied by a single price to determine the payment of each procedure. The single price is negotiated between a purchaser and the PPO. Starting with the current charges of physicians in a PPO, InterQual has modified existing nationally recognized RVSs for local conditions and determined negotiable prices that would meet the dual goal of being acceptable to the majority of the PPOs' physicians while also ensuring cost savings to the purchaser.

The physician subcommittee is responsible for determining PPO membership criteria for physicians and for making decisions related to the establishment of a physician's association. Since the PPO is designed to save money for purchasers, only efficient and effective practitioners can further the PPO's goals. However, not many providers have objective data by which to bar nonefficient practitioners without incurring a risk of being sued. Therefore, many physician associations (PAs) that have formed to link with hospitals for operating a PPO initially accepted all physicians who are on the staff of the hospital(s) of the PPO. Some PAs limit membership to just certain classes of staff membership. Some PAs, though, are developing standards and criteria by which to evaluate practitioners when they reapply for PA membership after one year.

Additionally many PAs have included provisions in the shareholders agreement that states that each physician will abide by the utilization measures of the PPO and that they will pay an initial membership fee ranging from $300 to $1,000. These two measures, especially utilization mechanisms, will help serve to limit the number of physicians joining the PA to those who believe in the provision of efficient and effective health care services.

NETWORKING ISSUES

Networking is the term used to describe the strategy by which the institution that is acting as the organizer or sponsor of a PPO establishes linkages with other providers. Networking, or establishing some form of organizational or service relationship with other institutions, can enhance an institution's market attractiveness. Market research and experience has shown that potential purchasers of the PPO evaluate the plan relative to three important attributes:

— quality
— cost
— accessibility

To ensure a PPO's market attractiveness, it is useful for the institution sponsoring the plan to evaluate itself in relation to these three attributes during the developmental phase. An institution must look very closely and objectively at itself, especially in terms of its strengths and weaknesses relative to developing a marketable plan. Next, an institution sponsoring a PPO should also evaluate potential networking partners, i.e., those providers who enhance and/or complement the lead institution's strengths and improve the plan's overall market position. The specific steps in evaluating an institution's networking position follow:

1. Identify specific evaluation criteria that reflect the key attributes of quality, cost, and accessibility.
2. Evaluate the sponsoring institution relative to these criteria. Try to identify specific areas that the institution lacks; such areas represent gaps that may be filled through networking.
3. Based on the number and types of gaps identified for the institution, determine whether a marketable PPO can be sponsored without networking partners. If it can, then proceed accordingly. If, in the likely event that it cannot, the following two steps should be completed as well.
4. Identify potential institutional networking candidates.
5. Evaluate these networking candidates relative to the same set of criteria as above in terms of the ability of each candidate to help the sponsoring institution fill the gaps identified earlier.

In order to complete the identification of networking candidates, the networking subcommittee should develop a list of hospitals that are not its major competitors. The hospitals listed should be evaluated according to

EXHIBIT 2
Criteria to Be Used in Evaluating Networking Candidates

Evaluation Criteria	Criterion Questions for Networking Candidates
Dispersion gaps	Does networking with this candidate enhance the accessibility of the PPO relative to the dispersion of target employees and their families?
Program and service gaps	Does networking with this candidate add highly utilized programs and services that are not available through the sponsoring hospitals?
Image	Does networking with this particular candidate provide the PPO with a positive public image?
Cost	Is there data available to determine the cost effectiveness of the networking candidate? If so, would networking with the candidate help the PPO provide cost effective care?
Affinity	Is there a natural affinity between the candidate and the sponsoring hospital? (To the extent that an affinity exists between institutions, establishing networking arrangements between these institutions is facilitated.)
Industry contacts	Does networking with this candidate provide increased access to purchasers for marketing the PPO plan?

the criteria chosen under step 1 above. One possible list of criteria and the criterion questions that should be evaluated is provided in Exhibit 2.

Once networking candidates are chosen, a strategy for inviting them to participate in the PPO must be developed. This strategy will largely depend on local conditions and the actors involved. Whatever the approach used, the sponsoring hospital should include a discussion of its own strengths as well as those of the PPO that it is developing, also being sure to emphasize the potential benefits of the PPO to the networking candidate.

MARKETING THE PPO

The marketing subcommittee has three major tasks to oversee and coordinate:

— Developing a marketing approach that is based upon marketing research, emphasizes promotion and direct sales, and includes professionally developed collateral, such as brochures, video-tapes, and slide presentations.
— Identifying a list of priority prospects (potential purchasers).
— Deciding upon who will market the PPO to prospective purchasers.

Each of these areas is discussed below.

Developing a Marketing Approach

Theoretically, a PPO entity is no different than any other vendor seeking a customer or client base. The successful marketing campaign must first begin with product identification to:

— Clarify the provider's role and enhance its image.
— Demonstrate the providers' concern for efficient and effective health care.
— Delineate the mechanisms and protocols for assuring appropriate monitoring of utilization, quality, and cost, which employers prefer.
— Emphasize the patient's freedom to choose providers for which they have a preference.

Through effective market research, different customer and consumer categories can be identified and segmented appropriately for market potential. Simply stated, the function of researching the PPO marketplace is to assure that the voice of the customers (employers and employees) will be properly factored into the PPO's marketing campaign. This is a process which successful HMOs have employed.

Identifying Priority Prospects

As mentioned previously, the provider-controlled PPO has multiple marketing targets: self-funded and minimum premium firms (both private and public), welfare (union) trust funds, multiple employer trusts, insurance carriers, and in some cases HMOs. Many insurance carriers have or are forming their own PPOs, and usually they want to select the providers and product features of their PPO. However, a PPO comprised of well-organized, cost effective providers can save an insurance company time and money. This is accomplished through the carrier's contracting with these providers for the PPO services it plans to market. Therefore insurance carriers represent an important distribution channel for provider-controlled PPOs, especially as a method to gain access to small and medium size firms.

Other important markets for the PPO are self-funded and minimum premium firms. These firms usually employ at least 30 percent of all workers in most metropolitan areas, and over 40 percent in those markets with a preponderance of large firms. In some large metropolitan areas, these firms number over 1,000. Identifying which firms are most interested in negotiating with PPOs without having to make a large number of sales calls is one goal of the PPO marketing process.

This process of identifying interested firms starts with procuring or developing a universal list of employers in the geographic area of the PPO and, through the steps listed in Exhibit 3, reducing the list to those firms most likely to be interested in offering the PPO to its employees.[2] This is accomplished through the elimination of firms of certain sizes and

EXHIBIT 3
Identifying Priority Prospects

I.   Develop a list of firms whose employees frequently use the hospital.

II. Order from vendor a universal list of firms meeting size range criteria.

III. Review universal list and select categories according to size and Standard Industrial Codes.

IV. Order revised list by:
 A. Line of business.
 B. Size.
 C. Service area zip code sequence.
 D. Executive contacts.

V.   Initiate market surveying process to firms remaining on list.

VI. Analyze survey results according to:
 A. Organizational characteristics.
 B. Benefit scope.
 C. Union contract expiration (if any).
 D. Financial incentives.
 E. Decision-making process.

VII. Combine contact list (from item I above) with employer firms assessed as "marketable" (by survey process), to develop list of priority prospects targeted for immediate solicitation.

---

industrial codes. For example, self-funded firms usually employ more than 300 people. Firms with fewer than approximately 300 employees should be eliminated from this list. Once the list of firms is reduced, market surveys are sent to gather information on these firms and to judge which firms may be interested in the PPO.

Those firms that are deemed to be priority prospects through this process are viable candidates for direct sales calls by the PPO. Other firms are best approached through distribution channels such as insurance companies, third-party administrators and/or benefit brokers. The distribution channels that are most prevalent in a local area can also be identified through the surveying process discusssed above and in Exhibit 3.

Marketing Staff

Like all new products, for a PPO to be successful, it must be marketed properly. As demonstrated by HMOs, sophistication of the marketing staff can greatly affect the viability of the organization.

Some provider-controlled PPOs have relied on hospital marketing personnel to initially market the PPO. However, using marketing and sales personnel who have worked for or sold health benefits to purchasers is considered important to the PPO's success. PPO sales personnel also need to be knowledgeable of hospital issues, especially those related to quality and costs. Consideration should also be given to the use of a PPO negotiating team comprised of marketing, operations, and financial personnel. Whatever the background of those who will market the PPO, they should be trained in negotiation and sales techniques and should become familiar with the purchasers' mentality and concerns, as well as providers' issues.

CONCLUSION

The PPO development process is time-consuming and at times arduous. Being a new venture, the PPO requires expertise not always available among providers.

While it can be accomplished in a shorter time period, most PPOs take six to twelve months to develop. The start up costs of provider-controlled PPOs currently in operation have ranged from $50,000 to $200,000. Those PPOs at the high end of this range have involved multiple hospital and physician groups. Other factors that affect development costs include the amount of donated time made available to the PPO by physicians and administrators, the degree of consultant use, and the thoroughness of the development process undertaken.

In order to develop a PPO, a series of committees of physicians and administrators should be formed to investigate various functional areas that are important to the PPO. Most PPOs require more than one institutional partner to meet the concerns of the purchaser market. A systematic evaluation process of potential candidates that employs criteria based upon the purchasers' concerns increases the likelihood of choosing the most suitable partners.

Funds will be saved in marketing the PPO if a systematic approach is followed in deciding on priority prospects. This process should use data concerning the employer market, mail surveys, and personal interviews to decide on priority prospects for sales calls. This profiling process should be undertaken simultaneously to the PPO development process, so that contracts can be negotiated as soon as possible after the PPO is formed.

Successful PPOs have provided financial savings for purchasers, market share for providers, and reduced health care expenditures without a lock-in provision for patients. Regardless of the life span of the "PPO movement," hospitals and physicians that can link together in provider networks and successfully decide upon product, pricing, and marketing strategies will be in a more viable position than those that do not. Additionally, providers who successfully negotiate with purchasers will have developed contacts and experience that will become increasingly important as the purchaser market becomes more sophisticated. Expertise in both areas—networking and negotiations with purchasers—can be achieved through the development of a PPO. This expertise will be valuable to providers attempting to survive in the shrinking health care market.

The PPO may also be described as a "managed health care plan," the emphasis of which is stringent utilization management and quality improvement measures. This managed arrangement could also facilitate offering health services on a capitated basis as a competitive medical plan (CMP) or an HMO that could qualify to serve private pay and medicare patients. The development of a PPO becomes a means by which to achieve a variety of ends, including cooperative ventures, credibility with purchasers, and a means to protect a provider's commercial insurance and medicare market share.

NOTES

1. This material is based upon InterQual's role as a consultant to hospital and physician groups in 12 metropolitan areas, in the areas of organizational and networking development, hospital and physician pricing, marketing plan development, sales calls, utilization management, information systems analysis, and recruiting and training of PPO staffs.

2. To facilitate an appropriate market analysis profile, statistical information should be secured from a viable source having:

— A current and comprehensive computerized data base, from which to assemble statistical reports to identify the types of employers that meet the PPO's marketing criteria.
— A number of optional reports by which to identify
   The market universe, that is, the number of all businesses in the PPO service area.
   How the market is dispersed geographically.
   Which (if any) business classifications are predominant in the marketplace.
   The size of the establishments in those markets.

InterQual researched data sources and has identified the following two:

— Dun's Marketing Services, a division of Dun and Bradstreet. Dun's has the capacity to report on business and industry throughout the United States.
— Harris Publishing Company. Harris limits reference directories to industrial and manufacturing firms in the following states: Ohio, Michigan, Illinois, Indiana, and Pennsylvania.

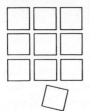

Planning and Design Features

PRODUCT DESIGN AND PROVIDER INVOLVEMENT IN SELECTIVE CONTRACTING

Robert P. Brook
Vice President
Employee Benefit Plans, Inc.
Walnut Creek, CA

Michael F. Anthony, J.D.
Partner
McDermott, Will & Emery
Chicago, IL

☐ Can you imagine starting a business without a marketing or financial plan? Would you sign a contract with a supplier and not know what the deliverables were? Would you create an organization with unfamiliar partners? Maybe so—probably not. Yet many hospitals and physicians are responding to the opportunity or threat of selective contracting in exactly this fashion.

Why? Perhaps the phenomenon, in part, is attributable to a less than complete understanding concerning the business of developing, implementing, and managing a complex health care financing and delivery system. Also, competition, which is being championed as the means to a more efficient, less expensive health care delivery system begs the question, do health care providers know how to compete? Can the health care system deal with winners and losers in an industry that has historically been characterized by plenty for all? One thing is for sure: in selective contracting and the transitional period the industry is facing, there is far more at stake than merely "rearranging the deck chairs on the Titanic."

The focus of the following discussion will address the business considerations of sponsoring or participating in an organization to pursue selective contracting. Emphasis will be placed upon product design, provider involvement in organizational selection, and potential pitfalls for a hospital, network of hospitals, and physicians in considering selective contracting opportunities.

SELECTIVE CONTRACTING

The concept of selective contracting includes an organized form of health care financing and delivery capable of accepting patients and the responsibility for serving them on a negotiated rate basis. The various parties involved promise to provide quality medical services to patients at reduced overall costs. Unlike a health maintenance organization (HMO), the selective contracting process does not guarantee the provision of health care services. Rather, it merely arranges for access to a "preferred" panel of providers. Currently, the most popular design to achieve these results is the preferred provider organization (PPO).

In many respects, PPOs are the "little brother" of the increasingly successful HMO. Presumably, PPOs appeal to a broader segment of providers who find the concept more palatable than HMOs, namely the retention of fee-for-service medicine. PPOs were initially touted as a relatively simple "solution" or "option." In short, a contract between a purchaser and a supplier on a preferred basis. This is not an uncommon venture in business. However, in the health care market this is no simple task, indeed.

The experience of providers in developing PPOs has revealed several interesting trends. The natural emphasis thus far for providers in developing PPOs has been the medical service component. That is, a contractual network of hospitals and physicians, a utilization management system, and some form of governance and management. No small effort to be sure. Nonetheless, it is only one component of a PPO, albeit an important one.

The important point to introduce is that the working definition of a PPO should include more than just the provider component. A PPO should be considered a health plan that is composed of distinct integrated elements: selected group of providers, marketing and management systems, medical care management structure, comprehensive service benefit design, and supportive administrative and insurance services. All elements must be in place before a PPO can begin to achieve desired results. So far providers have been more successful in organizing the medical service component than marketing it to purchasers and patients. There are several reasons for this.

The best explanation is the lack of definition given to product design and to a reasonable sales approach. Product design encompasses all of the components and interrelationships necessary to make a PPO work. It also involves the ability to differentiate a product from those of competitors with reasonable assurances about desired results. In designing a PPO product common pitfalls providers are encountering include lack of clear business concept, administratively infeasible organizational design, lack of a reasonable market plan, lack of control over critical functions, and undercapitalization. As a result, there tends to be an obvious level of frustration on behalf of the sponsors.

It is no small venture for a hospital and its medical staff to participate in or become involved in sponsoring a PPO. Among other things it requires a well thought out strategy that recognizes the nature of hospital/medical staff relations, the needs of the marketplace, and the absolute requirement for understanding the management resources and support systems required to operate a PPO. Also it is crucial to understand the key role insurance companies and benefit consultants play in the decision to purchase and the mechanics of administering and financing health care.

To better grasp the requirements of organizing a PPO effort, two major aspects should be focused on: PPO product design and provider involvement in selecting an organizational model.

DESIGNING A PPO PRODUCT

It is important to understand that somewhere in the PPO purchase decision someone is selling a health benefit plan that will serve to complement an employer's existing coverage. As such it will compete directly with standard medical plans offered by commercial insurance carriers, Blue Cross and Blue Shield Associations, and HMOs. As a result, the provider-sponsored PPO must define its product within competitive parameters and keep the purchaser's needs in mind.

The first step in product definition includes a preliminary determination of the market and provider feasibility of establishing a PPO. This strategic assessment process is essentially a period of fact finding and interpretation. There are three major areas for consideration.

PURCHASER BEHAVIOR

It is important to recognize who are the market leaders and innovators and what trends are occurring. An assessment must be conducted on the behavior of the various purchasing and market segments. Most purchasers can be classified into two purchasing segments: premium and direct purchasers of health care services. Premium purchasers deal directly through insurance organizations and are basically a fixed-cost purchaser for a defined period of time. Direct purchasers are self-funded or self-insured organizations, and basically pay medical service claims directly to providers. Their arrangements with insurers or third-party administrators are secondary in nature—purchasing administrative support services and insurance policies to minimize financial risk exposure. Each segment has a significantly different impact on the approach for a PPO in accessing patient markets.

PROVIDER ATTITUDES

The major question is what competitive threats are providers experiencing and what are they willing to do about it. Important areas to assess include the provider's willingness to (*a*) comply with strong utilization controls, (*b*) discount fees and/or accept alternative payment arrangements, including the assumption of risk, (*c*) come together to form an organization, and (*d*) provide capital for development and operations. Furthermore, an understanding of how real the competition is perceived to be and what types of providers are feeling the pinch is required. In most instances educational efforts will be required to facilitate fact finding and decision making in assessing provider attitudes.

INSURANCE ORGANIZATION BEHAVIOR

A sense must be reached on which insurers, if any, are in a position to "shake up" the market by selectively contracting and redirecting patient flow. If an insurance organization is pursuing alternative delivery system development and participation is an objective, it is paramount to understand its requirements for participation prior to designing a product.

It is likewise important to understand who else in the market is attempting to shake things up. For example, business coalitions have become increasingly vocal about health care costs. Certain coalitions have even gone so far as to facilitate or sponsor the development of PPO arrangements. Other important players who may be active in a given market include benefit consultants, third-party administrators, and unions. In most instances the health care purchasing equation includes some combination of the above and insurance companies. Relationships between purchasers (employers) and intermediary organizations (insurance companies, third-party administrators) have been solidified over time and by political ties. It is not a simple proposition to displace or significantly modify existing relationships. Current arrangements of the purchaser must be considered in evaluating the demand for and approach to marketing a PPO.

Once intelligence has been gathered in these three areas, a preliminary determination on feasibility can be made. At this point a go/no go decision can be made. Also, the ingredients for the conceptual design of the initial product and approach to pursuing development have been collected. The conceptual design should address the following:

— Provider configuration
— Health care delivery system
— Organizational design
— Marketing strategy
— Financing sources
— Legal issues

Assuming a promising finding and a decision to move forward, the next level of PPO product design must answer several questions. What functions is the PPO to perform? What functions will be under contract? What is the best organizational design to achieve desired results? In addressing these questions it is useful to consider Exhibit 1, PPO Building Blocks. The PPO building blocks are classified into four levels. A systematic analysis at each level will yield a definition on the functions the provider-sponsored PPO is to perform, and therefore, its business purpose. It will also be a useful tool for gaining a better understanding of all the systems and services required for a complete PPO product.

EXHIBIT 1
PPO Building Blocks

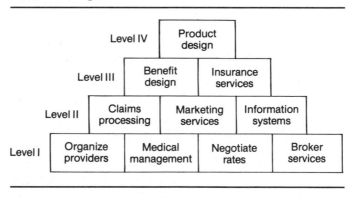

Level I functions are those most commonly performed by the providers sponsoring a PPO. In essence these functions are what is being sold by the sponsoring providers. Level II functions are typically purchased or arranged for through contract management. Level III functions are performed by existing relationships of the purchaser. The PPO must work with them, displace them, or add to them. Level IV is the finished product design, which accounts for all the other functions and the appropriate organizational arrangements to complete the system. Exhibit 2, PPO Product Design Matrix, presents further definition on each Level's functions, who typically is responsible for performing it, and potential opportunities and pitfalls in each area.

EXHIBIT 2
PPO Product Design Matrix

	Provider PPO Functions	*Contract Management*	*Opportunities and Pitfalls*
Organize providers	Major function of provider PPO that includes education, selecting appropriate provider configuration, utilization management system, and contract negotiation.	Not a common approach for provider PPO. However, may use consultants to assist in development. Inherent distrust of insurance organization's motives.	There is potentially economic worth in creating an organization of providers. Pitfalls include inexperience and inability to work together toward common purpose.
Medical care management	Major function of provider PPO either in terms of the design of utilization controls, operating and policing the system or both. Usually involves stringent peer review and sanctions.	May use outside organization to assist in implementation or operations (e.g., PSRO). May delegate to participating hospitals and/or physician groups.	May have opportunity to sell utilization controls to purchaser. Internally run program should have greater commitment and enforcement. Suspicion by purchasers about providers policing themselves.
Negotiate rates	Depending on legal considerations PPO either sets rates or accepts a purchaser's offer. PPO may determine level of discount and payment terms.	May accept rates tendered by purchaser or insurance organization.	Far greater flexibility if PPO negotiates, however, raises antitrust concerns. PPO may lose control over key area and be frustrated in its inability to negotiate rates.
Broker services	Major function of provider organization is to broker access to a preferred panel of physicians and hospitals at negotiated rates and utilization management controls.	Insurance organization may serve as brokering agent on behalf of the PPO. This may also include benefit consultants and TPAs.	Depending on the approach to the marketplace, competitive situation, and growth expectations, the PPO may provide a valuable service to providers.

EXHIBIT 2 *(continued)*

	Provider PPO Functions	*Contract Management*	*Opportunities and Pitfalls*
Claims processing	Provider PPO may be involved in claims adjudication. Costly to develop systems for start-up.	Major function of administrative agent(s) of PPO. PPO either ties in to existing arrangements or has exclusive arrangement with its own administrative agent.	Difficulty lies in PPO obtaining and coordinating information needed to manage from the claims form under contract management approach.
Marketing services	Provider PPO usually has limited marketing staff. A Marketing Director conducts direct sales to accounts and relies on contract management sources for account servicing and access to market.	Provider PPO usually augments its marketing through relationships with insurance companies to access the market quicker.	Control over types of accounts and marketing services gives PPO greater flexibility and identity. PPO loses control and it is difficult to hold insurers accountable when under contract with insurance organization. However, PPO gains quicker access to the market.
Information systems	Expensive start-up cost. PPO may develop information requirements and specifications.	Major function of contract management. Modifications to existing systems required.	Many software programs under development. State-of-the-art not available to manage total PPO needs.
Insurance services	Not an area of involvement.	Purchaser establishes arrangements independent of relationship with PPO.	All major groups purchase a range of insurance services. PPO with established insurer relationship may have a more complete product.

EXHIBIT 2 *(concluded)*

	Provider PPO Functions	*Contract Management*	*Opportunities and Pitfalls*
Benefit design	May determine benefit package features, e.g., copayments and deductibles. Assist purchaser in this area.	Major function of contract management. Insurance companies and benefit consultants have expertise in this area.	To complete the PPO equation purchasers must be willing to modify benefits to include incentives and disincentives. Usually a slow process, particularly if benefits are negotiated.

BUSINESS PLAN

After careful consideration is given to each level, a more detailed business plan should be developed. The business plan will serve three primary purposes. First, the process of gathering information and decision making serves the purpose of education and consensus building. This will be valuable in establishing provider commitment and creating realistic expectations. In the case of a network of sponsors it may also weed out the less than serious participants up front. Second, it will serve as a means to prioritize development tasks, define the various functions and responsibilities of all parties, and forecast expected results. Finally, the business plan is essential to implementation activities and provides the master plan for bringing all the necessary components together in a logical, planned fashion.

The business plan should not be considered merely an academic process. Rather, it should be developed in conjunction with planning and implementation activities and be a driving force in decision making. In the development of the business plan the following are the principal components:

MARKET PLAN

The key ingredients of the PPO market plan include: market strategy, product positioning and differentiation, enrollment plan, and promotion and sales plan. The first major consideration is determining the strategy for how the PPO will access patient populations. In large part, this should have been determined in the initial market research. It involves two basic choices. Access can be accomplished through an intermediary organization, like an insurance organization or third-party administrator,

EXHIBIT 3
PPO Market Access

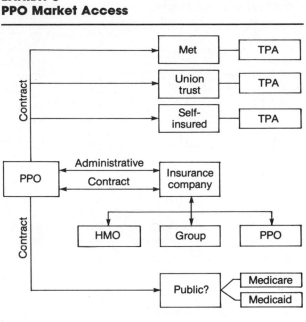

or through direct contracting with the purchaser. Exhibit 3, PPO Market Access, displays the various market segments for a PPO. Each segment will have different requirements which must be fully understood.

It is also important to determine how the PPO will position itself against its competitors and how it plans to differentiate its services. Most developing PPOs answer this in terms of quality of care and cost effectiveness. The former is elusive and the latter has no proven results. These two factors alone are not enough. Exhibit 4, Product Design Positioning, displays three primary product design features. An illustrative example is provided to work through the product positioning issue. It is important to recognize that the positioning of the product is applicable to both the purchaser (employer) and the patient (employee).

Once the approach to market access and product positioning has been determined, an enrollment plan, including member (user) projections, is required. Enrollment projections should include a time-phased plan for offering the PPO to accounts. Projecting enrollment, or the level of PPO patient volume, is essential to resource planning and financial projections. Projections will also serve as a measure of operational performance for the PPO.

Little attention by providers has been directed to the fact that the PPO plan will require significant selling and education to its users at the

EXHIBIT 4
Product Design Positioning

	PPO Product Design		
Competitor	*Price*	*Access*	*Covered Services*
Blue Cross			
Employer	15% Less	Equal	Better
Employee	Less	Equal	Better
Commercial Insurer			
Employer	20% Less	Less	Better
Employee	Less	Less	Better
HMO			
Employer	Equal	Better	Less
Employee	Equal	Better	Less
Other PPO			
Employer	Less	Equal	Better
Employee	Equal	Equal	Better

workplace. The PPO has the potential for misunderstanding by the user on how to use it to obtain maximum benefits. A sales plan that includes educational and promotional activities should be developed. Even if the PPO has determined that it will not perform these types of activities, it must be aware of how they are to be done. There is enough evidence from the HMO industry to create suspicion of contract management for marketing services, and a PPO would be wise to be cautious in this area.

FINANCIAL PLAN

The PPO financial planning process should include six major components: (1) financial objectives, (2) development budget, (3) payment arrangements, (4) forecasted operating expenses and revenue sources, (5) approach to financial incentive programs, if any, and (6) pro forma financial projections. There should also be a plan for capitalizing PPO development and initial operating losses. Essentially two major outputs from the financial plan occur: the determination of financial feasibility and identification of sources of funds.

The provider-sponsored PPO is in a peculiar situation in the financial planning process. Hospital managers will recognize the need to set prices competitively; however, when the time comes to accept payment arrangements on behalf of their respective institutions, another role surfaces. The corollary role is that of negotiating the best deal for their organization. To haggle over initial hospital prices and physician conversion factors can be time-consuming, unhealthy organizational behavior. The potential for this to occur is compounded in a network model with varying cost structures of different sponsors. It is more important to agree upon the payment methodology and positioning of charges in the marketplace as the first step. Physician involvement in setting the payment methodology may lessen the ensuing political turmoil that typically arises. Likewise, the sponsoring hospitals must make their position known early on, especially the acceptability of discounting and/or alternative payment arrangements from billed charges. Initial financial exposure for the sponsoring hospital will be minimal in most cases, because start-up PPO patient growth will most likely be slow and represent a small portion of total hospital business. Therefore, the PPO may provide an excellent vehicle for experimenting with alternative payment arrangements.

ADMINISTRATIVE ARRANGEMENTS

Careful consideration must be given to how the PPO expects to arrange for administrative services for each group account. The PPO either complements an existing arrangement or develops an exclusive arrangement with an organization that performs administrative services, or it may become a component of an insurance company PPO that will perform all administrative services. Combinations of these options are possible as well. The major administrative functions include claims processing, maintenance of eligibility files, management information systems, and account servicing.

Two caveats are worth mentioning. First, the total administrative expense for PPO operations must be competitive. Based on current market experience a 7 to 12 percent range is a reasonable expense to the purchaser. Remember, PPO administrative requirements are greater than a straight administrative services only (ASO) arrangement for a self-funded account. The PPO's expense will probably be more in line with that of an HMO. Finally, under multiple administrative arrangements, the task of information collection and coordination becomes increasingly difficult. PPOs require sophisticated, timely management information on utilization and financial performance. Absent this information, management and control of PPO operations will be seriously impaired.

HEALTH CARE DELIVERY SYSTEM

The nature of the PPO health care delivery system must be established. There are two basic considerations: (1) the design of the provider or network configuration and (2) the medical care management system to be incorporated.

Considering which hospitals are to be in the PPO network requires an understanding of each one's cost structure and comparative patterns of admissions and length of stay. For example, if a hospital charges high costs and/or has high lengths of stay, the question becomes one of how much of a discount and how much decrease in length of stay are required? For the hospital, the consideration is how much of an increase in volume is expected to offset discounting and decreased length of stay.

For physicians, the nature of the relationship between primary and specialty care will require definition. Will the PPO be an open system allowing patients to select providers at will? Or will it require a primary care gatekeeper approach for the authorization of specialty care and inpatient services? This question must be answered in the context of political feasibility and the number and types of physicians the PPO will require to assemble a competitive network.

Development of a centralized, enforceable medical care management system is crucial to PPO success. A scheme must be developed for reducing hospital utilization and to assure that utilization of physician office services is conducted at an appropriate level. The medical care management system will require four interrelated major components: utilization control systems, quality assurance programs, clinical management information systems, and an administrative body composed of PPO providers (e.g., medical care management committee). The business plan must address the types of utilization controls to be used, who is to perform the control functions, what incentives and sanctions will be employed, and what information is needed to monitor and enforce desired outcomes.

Design considerations will have an impact on whether providers, particularly physicians, will cooperate with and participate in the PPO. The design of the health care delivery system must be carried out with a constant emphasis on the economic feasibility of participating providers, as well as the political and technical feasibility of assembling the network.

CORPORATE ORGANIZATION

The selection of the appropriate corporate structure will take into consideration all of the steps discussed up to this point. Typically, most PPOs begin the development process with a preference for one particular corporate design. It may be a mistake to finalize the corporate structure at the onset, however. This is due to the changing nature of the PPO product design throughout the development phase. The selection of a particular organizational model will have ramifications concerning the flexibility of business purpose, the relationship between hospitals and physicians, and legal feasibility.

The business plan should detail the legal design of the corporate organization, organizational relationships, management structure, and the responsibilities and functions of each component.

IMPLEMENTATION PLAN

The final approval of the business plan by the PPO directors in a sense will be perfunctory. In most cases, commitment to move forward and ante up will have already been made in dealing with the major decisions points in the business planning process. However, the fact is that the development of a PPO health plan is a complex, multifaceted, management-intensive business. Chances are that all systems cannot be completed for initial operations. Competitive needs may dictate entering the market with a less than complete product. This does not obviate the need for developing and fine tuning management systems, practices, and processes. A time-phased implementation plan identifying the minimum requirements to begin operations and longer-term enhancements will be very useful.

The business planning process for PPOs must by necessity be dynamic. This is largely due to the situation of bringing together substantial numbers of participants with diverse interests and varying experiences in working together. This can create the situation of a difficult time in reaching consensus and making enforceable decisions. The business planning process should help to minimize tensions and provide much needed direction.

PROVIDER INVOLVEMENT

PPOs have developed with a myriad of sponsorship combinations. For example, third-party administrators, insurance companies, employer coalitions, self-funded employers, union trust funds, hospitals, physician groups, and entrepreneurs have become interested in controlling the organizational unit that coordinates contractual arrangements between providers and purchasers of medical, hospital, and other health care services. Regardless of sponsorship, health care providers by necessity play a key role in the PPO, because a full complement of hospital and medical services must be offered.

Individual physicians and hospitals would appear to have significant leverage in negotiating the agreements for the provision of services through a PPO. After all, the market assessment is likely to indicate that purchasers must make health care services available to a group of subscribers or employees who seek medical care within a dispersed geographic market. Purchasers understand that subscribers and employees want convenient access to a full range of health professionals and facilities. This would seem to favor a PPO product including several hospitals and physicians. This would further imply that individual hospitals and physicians should be able to be selective about PPO involvement. However, purchasers are often willing to offer economic incentives for employees and subscribers to utilize the services of less convenient facilities and health care professionals who are proven, cost-efficient providers. Therefore, some providers will be excluded from the selective contracting process and individual hospitals and physicians may not be in the best position to go it alone in direct negotiations with PPOs and other purchasers. The remainder of this section will focus on some of the options available to hospitals and physicians in developing an organizational model and increasing their negotiating leverage and direct involvement in the selective contracting process.

Physicians' interest in PPOs and selective contracting tends to be more fragmented than hospitals. To overcome the potential of divergence of objectives with hospitals and other physicians in the selective contracting process, medical staff members may elect to form a negotiating unit to represent their collective interests. This unit could take the form of an independent practice association (IPA), which is a corporation organized for specific selective contracting purposes. Other alternatives include physician committees, fully integrated group practices, or partnership arrangements. Oftentimes hospitals will seek to avoid pressuring physicians into these kinds of arrangements as they tend to become a unifying element in medical staff negotiations with hospitals on matters other than selective contracting. Nonetheless, hospitals recognize that dealing with individual physicians rather than an organization representing the interests of the physicians is burdensome and tends to inhibit the development of economic incentives that create a successful selective contracting product.

Cooperative hospital/physician approaches to the selective contracting process appear to offer perhaps the greatest promise in assuring that providers will assume a productive role in molding PPOs and the selective contracting process. The cooperative approach may involve the formation of a provider-sponsored PPO or merely a provider unit to work through other PPOs. Following are four key advantages of the cooperative hospital/physician approach:

1. *Negotiating Leverage.* Hospitals and physicians are in a position to provide a product that includes a full range of services, including medical and hospital services, ancillary and support services, and outreach programs. What would otherwise be a series of individual contractual negotiations by purchasers with providers is simplified in a cooperative approach to one negotiation between purchaser or PPO and a business unit representing the collective interests of participating providers.

2. *Risk Sharing and Incentives.* A properly structured cooperative hospital/physician approach recognizes that both physicians and hospitals must share risks in order to share attendant rewards. The cooperative approach facilitates the development of incentive structures such as mechanisms that ensure that physicians and hospitals mutually benefit.

3. *Equity Participation.* When all providers have capital at risk in a cooperative approach, an economic dimension is added to what would otherwise be a relationship of convenience between a hospital and its medical staff members. Return on investment becomes a concept that melds the interest of all participants in the provider component of the PPO.

4. *Coordinated, Controlled Delivery System.* It is often heard that the key element necessary to ensure the long-term viability of PPOs is a strong medical care management system. By tying risk sharing, incentives, and equity participation to medical care management decisions, cooperative hospital/physician arrangements can be tailored to provide assurances to employers that utilization will be held in check without sacrificing the quality of care provided. The economic stake of the providers serves as the incentive to accomplish the cost-containment objectives of the cooperative hospital/physician approach.

Many models are available for the development of the cooperative hospital/physician approach. To some extent, a new partnership between the hospital and its medical staff must be forged in developing models that will become or contribute to successful PPOs. In exploring the various models, hospitals and physicians must seek to develop a systematic evaluation technique that sorts through the many elements that affect achievement of providers' collective objectives.

EVALUATING HOSPITAL/PHYSICIAN COOPERATIVE MODELS

It is important that the participation of physicians be clearly defined before analyzing available hospital/physician cooperative models. Once physicians' roles are defined, models can begin to take on meaningful shape. What better way to evaluate such models than the application of the mnemonic "DOCS!," which represents a four-step analysis addressing organizational and operational issues affecting the cooperative approach. The DOCS! analysis can be summarized as follows:

1. **D**octors Role.
    a. In relation to hospitals and other providers.
    b. In the decision-making process.
    c. In contribution of risk capital.
    d. In negotiations and system design.
    e. In selection of other providers.
2. **O**rganizational Structure of the Administrative and Marketing Services.
    a. The "PPO" or brokering organization.
    b. Provider unit.

3. Contracts to be negotiated.
   a. Clinical.
   b. Administrative.
4. Systems to Support Contracts.
   a. Utilization management.
   b. Quality assurance.
   c. Management information.
   d. Claims processing.

To illustrate the utility of this four step analysis, DOCS! will be applied to four cooperative hospital/physician models. Two of these models involve an individual hospital and selected medical staff members, and two involve several hospitals and selected members of their corresponding medical staffs.

Individual Hospital-Controlled PPO

Exhibit 5 depicts an individual hospital-sponsored PPO designed to generate active participation by involving members of the hospital's medical staff while the hospital remains in control of the business decisions and selective contracting process. The DOCS! analysis would be applied to this exhibit as follows:

Doctors. Because the hospital wishes to control the PPO, physicians are afforded nonmajority representation on the PPO's Board of Directors, with such representation assured in the contractual arrangements

EXHIBIT 5
Individual Hospital Controlled PPO

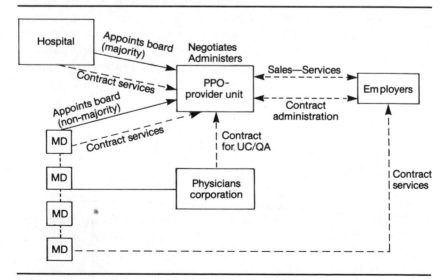

between the PPO and the individual physicians. The physicians are not asked to put capital at risk as a tradeoff for playing a lesser role in the business decisions made by the PPO. Physicians have organized their interests in a physician corporation to sell services to the PPO, but the physician corporation does not represent the collective interests of the physicians in negotiations with the PPO on contractual arrangements for the provision of professional services. Because this PPO is not designed to provide equal input by the physicians in the decision-making process, the hospital selects the members of its medical staff who will participate in the PPO. The hospital must carefully select participants to avoid alienating members of its medical staff while focusing on the necessity for including only cost-efficient providers.

Organization. The hospital seeks to control the PPO and thus serves as the sole shareholder of a for-profit corporation, which the PPO is in this model. In the alternative, the PPO could be set up as a not-for-profit corporation with the hospital serving as sole or controlling member. Because physicians have only a minority interest on the Board of Directors, they are not asked to put capital at risk. Thus the hospital, through the purchase of stock and/or loans to the PPO, provides necessary working capital for the organization. As the PPO develops contractual arrangements with purchasers, further revenues will be generated by charging purchasers on a percentage of revenue, per claims, or per enrollee basis for administrative services provided. Because the hospital controls the Board of Directors, it also is in a position to mandate negotiating postures, selection of purchasers with whom the PPO will deal, and selection of the physician panel.

Contracts. The PPO in this exhibit enters into contractual arrangements with the hospital and the physicians whereby each agrees to provide a defined package of clinical services and to abide by certain rules and regulations established by the Board of Directors of the PPO. The PPO then uses these provider contracts as the basis for negotiations with various purchasers of hospital and medical services. Because only one hospital is involved in this structure, the hospital can agree with the PPO on price terms, and the PPO can act as the hospital's agent in negotiating such terms with purchasers. Because several competing physicians are likely to enter into contracts with the PPO, combined with the fact that physicians do have some representation on the PPO Board of Directors, a careful evaluation of antitrust issues should be completed before the PPO binds individual physicians to price terms. It may be necessary for the physicians to directly negotiate with purchasers on price terms to avoid an allegation that competing physicians have collaborated to establish prices for the provision of services to purchasers. An argument could be made that the PPO is not a collaboration of competing physicians to set prices if it is not controlled by physicians and price schedules are agreed upon in direct negotiations by the PPO with each individual physician who wishes to enter into a contract with the PPO. If this argument were to hold true, the PPO then would be in a position to negotiate directly with purchasers on all terms (including price terms) on behalf of the physicians as well as the hospital. Extreme care must be taken to ensure that the contractual scheme developed is properly cloaked to avoid, to the extent possible, any potential antitrust violation.

Systems. The PPO is likely to enter into arrangements with the hospital to provide certain administrative services such as data and claims processing, and will contract with the physicians' corporation for the provision of medical care management services. Often, contracts with physicians to provide medical care management services include incentive mechanisms for the physicians to effectively reduce utilization of both hospital and medical services. For example, in Exhibit 5, the physicians' corporation may participate in a percentage of savings attributable to a strong utilization review program.

The PPO may wish to enter into arrangements with third-party administrators for the provision of claims processing and other administrative services. The need for such arrangements will depend in large part upon the market identified by the PPO and in-house capabilities to provide necessary administrative services.

Multihospital-Sponsored PPO Marketing Organization

Exhibit 6 illustrates a collaborative mechanism to market the services of four individual hospital-sponsored PPOs as shown in Exhibit 5. Following is the DOCS! analysis of Exhibit 6.

Doctors. Each hospital participating in this exhibit develops a PPO similar to Exhibit 5. Each individual hospital in Exhibit 6 is restructured and, through a subsidiary corporation, develops a PPO that is controlled through stock ownership or membership by the hospital subsidiary. The PPO enters into contractual arrangements with individual physicians that define the representation (if any) of the physicians on the PPO board. Also, a medical advisory committee of participating physicians is formed to provide input to the PPO on issues affecting professional medical services. Physicians are not asked to put capital at risk and, in this case, have not formed a separate physicians' corporation to provide medical care management services.

Organization. In addition to the PPO, a new corporation is formed as a joint venture by all hospitals wishing to collaborate on a marketing effort. As shown in Exhibit 6, each of four individual hospital-sponsored PPOs participate in the formation of a PPO marketing corporation. The corporation is organized as a for-profit entity with one fourth of the stock owned by each of the participating hospitals or a subsidiary. The Board of

EXHIBIT 6
Sample Organizational Structure: Multihospital Sponsored PPO

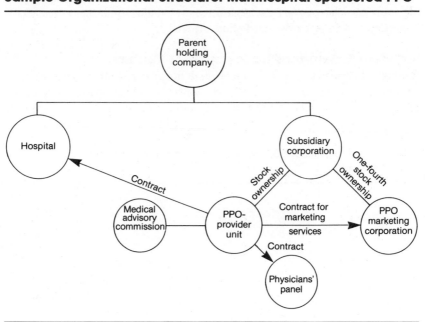

Directors of the PPO marketing corporation includes equal representation of these four hospitals, and any profits derived from its activities will be equally distributed to the participating hospitals.

Contracts. Each hospital-sponsored PPO enters into the appropriate contractual arrangements with its hospital and affiliated physicians. The PPO marketing corporation then enters into separate contractual arrangements with each PPO whereby the PPO marketing corporation agrees to market the services of the individual hospital-sponsored PPOs on the terms and conditions dictated by the PPOs. The PPO marketing corporation is in a position to then negotiate with purchasers of service to provide a full range of hospital and medical services covering a broad geographic area. Because the individual hospital-sponsored PPO mandates the terms and conditions of participation and the contractual arrangement with the PPO marketing corporation, significant autonomy is retained by each individual hospital-sponsored PPO. Many would argue that consistency is needed for a successful marketing effort by the PPO marketing corporation; however, programs organized much like Exhibit 6 have been successfully implemented in the market.

Systems. The PPO marketing corporation does not set policy for the individual hospital-sponsored PPOs. Thus, different pricing schemes, utilization management, quality assurance, claims processing, and management information systems may be developed by each of the participating individual hospital PPOs. Again, many would argue that consistency is needed for an effective marketing effort.

Individual Hospital/Physician Joint Venture

Exhibit 7 represents an equal individual hospital/physician joint venture organized to serve as a PPO and also as the organization responsible for entering into contracts with IPA-HMOs. Following is the DOCS! analysis:

EXHIBIT 7
Individual Hospital PPO/IPA: Equal Hospital/Physician Joint Venture

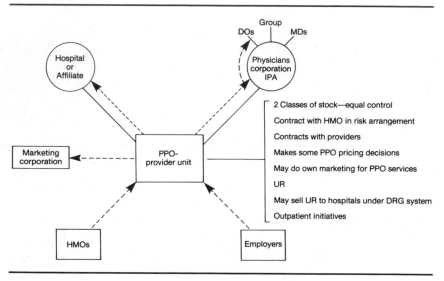

Doctors. In Exhibit 7, physicians are more directly involved in developing an organization that specifically represents their interests in the selective contracting process. Moreover, physicians work closely with the hospital in developing a joint venture organization that represents the interests of both the hospital and the physicians. Participating physicians initially form a physicians corporation, which can be for-profit or not-for-profit. The Board of Directors is elected by all physicians participating as either shareholders or members. Through this physicians corporation, participating physicians have equal input on all decisions made by the joint venture PPO; put equal capital at risk in the PPO venture; have equal say in the selection of the physician panel; and have equal input on systems design.

Organization. The PPO is set up as a for-profit corporation with two classes of stock, one designated for the hospital or an affiliate and another for the physicians corporation. By defining voting rights of the shareholders for each class of stock, the joint venture provides equal input by both classes of shareholders on all decisions made in the selective contracting process. The physicians corporation and hospital put at risk an equal amount of capital; profits developed in the PPO are distributed to the physicians corporation and hospital on an equal basis; and a two thirds majority is required for any resolution adopted by the directors of the corporation, thus ensuring input by at least some representatives of each shareholder on all decisions made by the joint venture PPO.

Contracts. The physicians corporation and hospital enter into contractual arrangements with the PPO whereby all terms of participation are agreed to, including price terms. It is important again to analyze carefully all antitrust issues before designing a mechanism for establishing pricing decisions. Because Exhibit 7 is a true joint venture between a hospital and its medical staff with sharing of risks and rewards, additional insulation may be available in dealing with potential antitrust issues, especially in the price setting area. Many organizations have included community representation on the joint venture Board of Directors in order to further insulate the joint venture PPO from antitrust violations. The theory is that since the organization is not controlled by either the hospital or participating physicians, it can make some decisions on pricing issues. Once the PPO has contracted with physicians and the hospital, it is then in a position to negotiate with purchasers, including, as shown in Exhibit 7, health maintenance organizations.

Systems. The hospital is in a position to provide on a contractual basis various administrative services such as management, marketing, and claims processing. The physicians corporation is postured to enter into a contractual arrangement for the provision of medical care management services such as utilization management and quality assurance.

Hospital/Physician Joint Venture PPO Network

The concept developed in Exhibit 7 oftentimes must be extended to include several hospitals and their corresponding medical staffs. Exhibit 8 depicts a PPO network arrangement whereby three hospitals and physicians from their respective medical staffs enter into a joint venture arrangement to provide hospital and medical services with easy access in a broad geographic area. Following is the DOCS! analysis of Exhibit 8.

Doctors. Interested physicians on the medical staffs of each of the three hospitals form an IPA to represent physicians' interests. Each IPA then controls the selection of participating physicians and monitors the

EXHIBIT 8
**Provider-Sponsored PPO Network: Equal Hospital/Physician
Joint Venture**

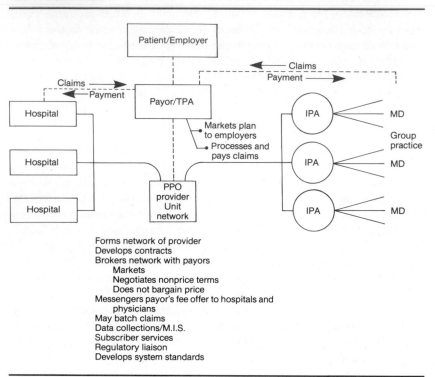

Forms network of provider
Develops contracts
Brokers network with payors
    Markets
    Negotiates nonprice terms
    Does not bargain price
Messengers payor's fee offer to hospitals and
    physicians
May batch claims
Data collections/M.I.S.
Subscriber services
Regulatory liaison
Develops system standards

activities of the physician panel. The three IPAs serve as equal share-holders in the PPO network with the three hospitals, thus ensuring equal control of all activities of the PPO network through equal Board representation. Through its participating physicians, the IPA also provides medical care management services through the PPO network.

Organization. The PPO network is a for-profit corporation with stock held equally by each individual hospital and its corresponding medical staff IPA. The IPAs and the hospitals each elect an equal number of representatives on the board of directors of the PPO network. They also share equally in capitalization of the PPO network.

Contracts. Because the IPA of each hospital will include several competitors, many attorneys would be hesitant to provide an unqualified antitrust opinion if the PPO network agrees to price schedules with the individual hospitals and their corresponding IPAs. Therefore in Exhibit 8, the PPO network agrees with the IPAs and the hospitals on all non-price terms and initiates negotiations with purchasers based on these contractual arrangements. Individual physicians and hospitals negotiate with the purchasers directly on price terms, with the PPO network serving as a messenger of offers and counteroffers emanating from both the purchasers and individual providers. If the PPO network does establish price schedules with significant risk sharing and incentive structures, the PPO network may also be able to negotiate price terms on behalf of all participating providers.

Systems. The PPO network purchases utilization management and quality assurance services from the respective IPAs. Thus, each hospital's IPA is in a position to tailor its medical care management programs to the hospital's environment while maintaining consistent standards throughout the system. The PPO network enters into contractual arrangements with the hospitals to provide certain data collection and management information services as well as other administrative support systems.

The network PPO may also enter into a contractual arrangement with a third-party administrator to assist in the marketing of the hospital and medical service plans to employers and other purchasers and also to assist in the processing and payment of claims.

Because several providers are involved in the PPO network, the scope of services negotiated through the PPO network may mandate developing in-house capabilities in the PPO network corporation, including the coordinating of regulatory liaison, monitoring of system standards, defining of subscriber services, completing claims batching, and coordinating of marketing services.

These four exhibits have been designed to illustrate the many permutations available in implementing a cooperative hospital/physician entry in the PPO selective contracting market. By applying the DOCS! analysis, a common thread can be tied through alternative available structures. Each hospital and its medical staff must work closely in identifying objectives and melding them to the extent possible in a model that will facilitate achievement of those objectives.

MAKING IT WORK

The business planning and provider involvement processes as described should afford the PPO a well-organized, carefully planned product and increase the likelihood of success. Successful selective contracting relies on a system of interlocking incentives for employers, employees, physicians, and hospitals. The PPO organizers must be able to affect each of these areas. This will require the proper application of economic incentives and sanctions to affect changes in treatment patterns, service efficiencies, and patient expectations that have been developed and embedded through decades of experience.

Perhaps the best way to answer the question of how to make it work is to look at the experience of HMOs. The following lessons would be sound advice for PPO health plans to adhere to:

— Understanding the market and designing a competitive product are essential ingredients to enrollment growth and fiscal viability.
— The transition from a developing organization to a fully operational entity requires sophisticated management systems and practices.
— Control over the consumption of health care resources, especially hospital services, is essential.
— A merging of shared economic rewards and risks between physicians and hospitals, to effectuate cost-effective behavior, is essential.

In addition to these HMO lessons, experience of early providers in sponsoring or becoming a component of a PPO has added the following desired characteristics: (1) cooperative arrangement between hospitals and physicians, (2) coordination of economic incentives, (3) a target group of willing purchasers, (4) prevention of further HMOs, and (5) the flexibility to adapt to whatever competitive opportunity becomes available.

Trying to identify successful factors in making the "first generation" PPO work is speculative at this point in time. The entire field is evolving so rapidly that it may never be possible to isolate "success" factors of the early PPOs. Those that succeed may have to be flexible enough to evolve into second generation PPOs. Essentially, this means a maturing of the selective contracting concept into that of a *PPO health plan*. Those PPO health plans that are successful will be so because they are right for their marketplace, contain costs and control utilization, and practice sound business principles without sacrificing quality.

CONCLUSION

PPOs are a relatively new approach to competition for health care providers that is restructuring the nature of the financing and delivery of health care services. The magnitude of provider activity in developing PPOs suggests unparalleled enthusiasm for this competitive model versus others introduced to date. The new competitiveness calls for different economic incentives, greater financial risk on behalf of providers, and changed relationships among hospitals, physicians, patients, insurers, and purchasers.

PPOs as currently conceived are an unproven business opportunity. The concept does represent a transitional way for providers to deal with the totality of changes occurring in the industry. Those providers who recognize the opportunity and adequately address the issues will survive and perhaps prosper. Some will be successful, others will not. Regardless of whether or not PPOs become an important method of cost containment, the changed relationships between hospitals and physicians are likely to persist.

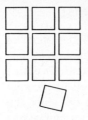

Planning and Design Features

FINANCIAL MANAGEMENT TECHNIQUES

James D. Suver, D.B.A., C.M.A.

Professor of Accounting and Health Administration
University of Colorado at Denver
Denver, CO

Bettina Kurowski, D.P.A.

Associate Professor of Health Administration
University of Colorado at Denver
Denver, CO

One of the key factors that appeals to all parties considering a PPO is the opportunity to minimize or control the financial impact of providing quality health care. These benefits are not automatic, however, and all participants must be aware of and practice sound financial management. The purpose of this chapter is to define the role of financial management and to illustrate some of the techniques that can be used to help in the process.

ROLE OF FINANCIAL MANAGEMENT

Financial managers in preferred provider organizations must take an active role in ensuring that the costs and benefits of alternative health care delivery systems are fully understood. The organization contracting with the PPO promises (or implies a promise) that a defined group of subscribers will be encouraged to use the services of the PPO instead of other providers. The PPO needs to be assured that the volume discounts granted to the purchaser of the services will result in an increased volume of services in order to maintain or increase the existing levels of income. This requires that the amount of the discount and the price on which the discount is based be negotiated so as to attract purchaser organizations while minimizing the risk to the provider.

The establishment of a proper fee schedule requires that the provider have adequate cost information on which to base the price of the services and the discounts to be offered. Many provider organizations do not have this type of cost information. Associated with the determination of a full cost per service is the understanding of the cost allocation process in the PPO. Improper use of the allocation process can lead to unrealistic prices being established by the PPO. For example, if the volume of services provided to the subscribers does not represent new services or subscribers, then the provider is not better off with the contractual arrangement than before. This scenario could occur if the majority of the demand in the area is already covered by discounted fees, which would result in very little opportunity to increase volume for any one provider. Only deeper discounts would attract subscribers in the short run, which would quickly be matched by other providers. The net result would be diminished revenues for all and a weakened financial condition in the long run. Financial managers must be extremely cautious of this type of behavior.

Not all the financial benefits of a PPO accrue from the increased volume of subscribers. It is possible to negotiate prompt payment of claims, which can reduce working capital requirements and provide financial incentives. This benefit will only be received if the billing system of the provider is designed to provide more rapid claims information to the purchaser. Unfortunately, provider billing systems are notably deficient in this respect.

Another attractive financial benefit of a contractual arrangement is the minimizing of bad debts associated with the self-pay status of many subscribers who are not members of a formalized plan. Other factors to be considered include the ability to manage the inflow of cash in such a manner as to maximize investment income.

Another potential cash outflow could be created if the contracting organization requires additional utilization controls to ensure that the volume of services provided by the PPO are medically necessary and reflect quality medical care standards. All of these factors can require additional outflows of cash that should be added to the cost of the contractual arrangement.

The financial management process in a PPO must continually be monitored to ensure that the most effective information is being provided for management decision making.

FINANCIAL MANAGEMENT TECHNIQUES

Financial managers have available several techniques to help in the financial management process. Cost/volume/profit models, cash flow analysis, and contribution margin concepts offer considerable potential to improve management decision making. The effective use of these techniques requires a basic understanding of cost behavior. For example, cost behavior can be segregated into two major categories depending upon the objective for which the cost information is being used.

COST DEFINITIONS

Cost information, which is primarily used to establish prices and determine income levels, is usually segregated into fixed and variable components. Cost information that is needed for responsibility and control purposes can be divided into direct and indirect components. These two categories are not mutually exclusive because direct and indirect costs can also be used in the pricing decision. More of this dual use of information will be explained in greater detail later.

Other cost definitions include the distinction between total costs and per-unit costs. Total costs are vital in the pricing decision and contract negotiation. Per-unit costs are the costs most usually quoted. Both of these key concepts are vital components of the relationships among cost, volume, and profit that are discussed next.

COST/VOLUME/PROFIT MODELS

One of the key aspects of the PPO concept is the potential for increased volume due to the contractual relationships between the major participants. The development of a cost/volume/profit model requires the separation of costs into fixed and variable components. Fixed costs are defined as those costs that do not vary with changes in volume, within a prescribed range of volumes. A graphic portrayal of total fixed costs is illustrated in Exhibit 1.

Exhibit 2 illustrates this concept within a specific range, $0-X_1$. Total variable costs are defined within the context of a cost/volume/profit model as linear in nature within the relevant range of volumes being considered. This variable cost behavior is protrayed in Exhibit 3.

The slope of the curve

$$\frac{(TVC_3 - TVC_2)}{V_3 - V_2} \quad \text{or} \quad \frac{(15 - 10)}{3 - 2} = 5$$

is defined by the variable cost factor, and the constraint of linearity means that within the volume covered by the graph in Exhibit 3, each additional unit adds an equal amount to the total variable cost curve.

EXHIBIT 1
Total Fixed Cost Behavior

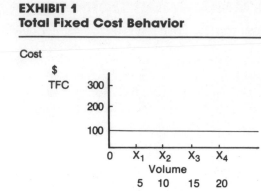

(Relevent ranges are O-X_1, X_1-X_2, X_2-X_3, etc.)

EXHIBIT 2
Total Fixed Costs within a Specified Range

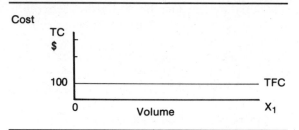

EXHIBIT 3
Total Variable Costs

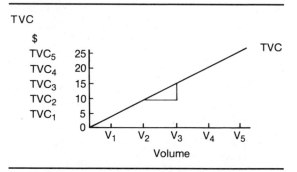

This equal amount concept is equivalent to the development of a per-unit cost curve where the TVC/volume is equal to the per-unit variable cost. This concept is illustrated in Exhibit 4.

The per-unit fixed cost curve is developed in a similar manner with TFC/volume equal to per-unit fixed costs. This is graphically illustrated in Exhibit 5.

The impact of cost behavior on full costs and per-unit costs leads to an interesting definitional conflict. For example, the basic definition that fixed costs do not vary with volume changes and that total variable costs increase with volume pertains only to total fixed and total variable costs. As illustrated in Exhibits 4 and 5, fixed costs do vary with volume changes and variable costs do not vary with volume changes as per-unit costs are calculated. The PPO that bases its discount prices on full costs

EXHIBIT 4
Per-Unit Variable Cost Curve

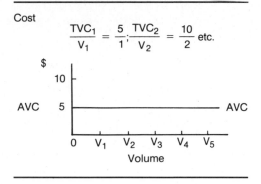

$$\frac{TVC_1}{V_1} = \frac{5}{1}; \frac{TVC_2}{V_2} = \frac{10}{2} \text{ etc.}$$

EXHIBIT 5
Per-Unit Fixed Cost Curve

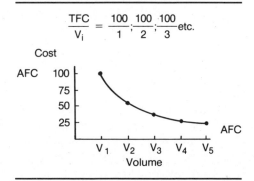

$$\frac{TFC}{V_i} = \frac{100}{1}; \frac{100}{2}; \frac{100}{3} \text{ etc.}$$

must be fully aware of the importance of the volume estimate in determining prices if all costs are to be recovered.

Based on the preceding discussion of volume-related cost definitions, it is possible to make use of the cost/volume/profit model. Basically, a cost/volume/profit model can be expressed in the following manner:

$$\text{Total revenue (TR)} = \text{Total costs (TC)} + \text{Profit (I)}$$
$$\text{or}$$
$$TR = TC + I$$

Total revenue can be further expressed as the price of services (P) times the quantity of services sold (Q) or

$$TR = (P) \times (Q)$$

Total costs can be further defined as total fixed costs (TFC) plus total variable costs (TVC)

$$TC = TFC + TVC$$

Total variable costs can also be defined as the variable cost per unit (VCU) times the number of units (Q)

$$TVC = (VCU)*(Q)$$

Combining the expanded definitions into the basic model results in the following equation.

$$(P)(Q) = TFC + (VCU)(Q) + I$$

From the model, various "what if" analyses can be accomplished to test the impact of proposed contractual arrangements on profit.

CONTRIBUTION MARGIN ANALYSIS

The development of cost/volume/profit models also facilitates the development of a contribution margin approach to decision making. The contribution margin can be defined as the amount remaining to cover fixed costs and profits after the out-of-pocket or incremental costs have been covered. The contribution margin for a service procedure per patient day can be determined by taking the price for the activity (P) minus the variable costs (VCU) for delivering the service (P − VCU = Contribution margin). This type of information is useful in short-run decisions where excess capacity is available and the pricing of services at less than full cost will not have an impact on services currently provided at full cost. This type of analysis is also referred to as marginal cost pricing, incremental cost analysis, or the "out-of-pocket" concept.

The use of the contribution margin approach is illustrated below.

Sample Problem

Given:

Total cost per DRG 103	$ 2,500
Fixed component per DRG	2,000
Total fixed costs	2,000,000
Variable component	500
Desired profit 10 percent of TC	250 per DRG
Estimated volume of services	1,000 DRGs
Determine required price	?

Computations:

$$(P)(Q) = TFC + (VCU)(Q) + I$$
$$(P)(1,000) = 2,000,000 + (500)(1,000) + 250(1,000)$$
$$(1,000)P = 2,000,000 + 500,000 + 250,000$$
$$P = 2,750,000/1,000$$
$$P = \$2,750$$

What-If Analysis:

Q. What would the price be if the volume of services were increased to 1,500 due to PPO contractual arrangements?

Computations:

$$1,500P = 2,000,000 + 500(1,500) + 250,000$$
$$1,500P = 2,000,000 + 750,000 + 250,000$$
$$P = 3,000,000/1,500$$
$$P = \$2,000$$

$$\text{Discount} = \frac{750}{2,750} = 27\%$$

Thus the impact of increases in volume on the required price can be determined using the What if capability of cost/volume/profit models.

What-If Analysis:

Q. What increase in volume must be obtained to offer a 20 percent discount on charges? Basic data remains the same except for the following.

Standard price	$2,950
Price after discount (1–20 percent)	.80
Discount price	$2,200

Computations: Solve for quantity required

$$\$2,200Q = 2,000,000 + 500Q + 250,000$$
$$(2,200 - 500)Q = \$2,250,000$$
$$1,700Q = 2,250,000$$
$$Q = 1,323.53 \text{ or } 1,324$$

$$\text{Percent increase in volume} = \frac{1,324}{1,000} = 32\%$$

Thus, a 20 percent discount granted to a purchaser of services must lead to an increase in volume of 32 percent in order to meet financial requirements.

$$PDRG102 = \$2,200$$
$$TFC = \$2,000,000$$
$$VCU = \$500$$
$$\text{Desired profit} = \$250,000$$

Q: Determine break-even quantity.

$$PDRG102 - VCU = \text{Contribution margin}$$
$$\$2,200 - 500 = \$1,700$$

From a contribution margin approach, the break-even can be expressed as:

$$\frac{TFC}{CM} = Q_{BE}$$

or

$$\frac{2,000,000}{1,700} = 1,176.47 \text{ or } 1,177 \text{ units}$$

If a profit margin is desired, the equation becomes:

$$\frac{TFC + Profit}{CM}$$

or

$$\frac{2,000,000 + 250,000}{1,700} = 1,323.53$$

This answer is the same as determined by the CVP model used in *what if* analysis above. The contribution margin approach represents a "short-cut" to the normal cost/volume/profit model.

DIRECT VERSUS INDIRECT COSTS

Another useful dichotomy is the separation of costs into direct and indirect categories. For some decisions on whether to offer or discontinue a service, only direct costs are relevant to the decision. For example, direct costs would be the only costs that would be changed by a decision of this type.

Direct and indirect costs are also useful in assigning responsibility for control purposes. For example, all costs that can be traced to a specific product, service, procedure, function, or activity fall into the category of direct costs. Direct costs of a laboratory procedure would be lab supplies, materials, technical personnel, and specific equipment required for the procedure. Indirect costs would be supervision, floor space, office supplies, and housekeeping. Direct costs can be either fixed or variable. The key distinction is that they are directly traced to an activity. Indirect costs are all other necessary costs of the organization, and since they are not traced directly to the activity, they must be allocated. Allocation always involves a certain degree of subjectivity, therefore costs should be made direct whenever possible to maximize their "control" potential. Since direct costs can be traced specifically to some activity or function, individuals can be held responsible for their control, while indirect costs are much more difficult to monitor. Indirect costs can also be fixed or variable in nature and present a challenge to the individual manager for control purposes.

DIRECT COST CONTRIBUTION MARGIN

It is possible to determine a direct cost contribution margin similar to the contribution margin approach explained above. This technique is particularly useful when fixed and variable cost information is not available. Although it presents some difficulty in arriving at per-unit cost, it is useful when analyzing total costs. For example, given an organization with the following characteristics:

Total patient revenue	$3,000,000
Total direct costs	1,000,000
Total indirect costs	2,500,000

A direct cost contribution margin could be constructed in the following manner:

Total revenue	$3,000,000
Total direct costs	1,000,000
Direct cost contribution margin	2,000,000
Indirect costs	2,500,000
Income (loss)	$ (500,000)

The decision to continue the service, at least in the short run, should be based on the positive contribution margin, not on the "negative bottom line." The organization would be $2,000,000 worse off if the service was discontinued. This approach also focuses on the incremental cost concept, since decisions should be based on the impact on the organizations' covering of all costs and not just the accounting bottom line.

OPPORTUNITY COSTS

One category of cost that is important to the decision-making process is the concept of opportunity costs. These costs represent the benefits that are given up by making one decision over another. For example, offering a discount to increase demand for one service must be considered in the light of what is given up when using the resources in another area.

Opportunity costs are generally not part of the accounting system and will not show up on the financial statement. However, they are a real cost and must be included in the evaluation of the cost/benefit of the decision. Resources that do not have alternative uses do not have opportunity costs.

CASH FLOW ANALYSIS

As discussed earlier, one of the negotiated areas in a PPO contractual arrangement is the timing of payment for services rendered. This quicker payment of billings results in reduction of working capital needs, since a lower balance of accounts receivables can be maintained. For example, cash received 30 days earlier under the PPO agreement has an increased out value that can be computed in the following manner:

Amount of PPO billings	$1,000,000
Length of time saved	30 days
Opportunity cost for funds	12 percent

Interest saved/earned by not having $1,000,000 in receivables:

Monthly	1% × 1,000,000 = $ 10,000
Annual	12% × 1,000,000 = $120,000

DISCOUNT VERSUS FIXED-FEE PRICING MODELS

One of the major issues confronting many purchasers and providers of services under PPO contractual arrangements is the choice between offering a discount or negotiating a fixed price per unit of service. There are several factors that need to be considered in utilizing the discount approach. For example, determining the size of the discount to be offered is a major issue. From a marketing perspective, the discount should be large enough to make it attractive to the purchaser but not so high as to jeopardize meeting the total financial requirements of the provider. Typically, discounts range from 3 to 30 percent. The cost/volume/profit model can also be useful in this decision. For example, given the following choice between a discount and expected increases in volume, which system should the provider choose?

	Discount	Expected Increase in Volume
Option 1	5 percent	20 percent
Option 2	10 percent	30 percent

This decision can be addressed by computing the contribution margin of each option. Given a price of $2,500 per service, a variable cost of $500, and an existing volume of 1,000 services, the financial aspects of the decision could be calculated as shown.

$$\text{SP} \quad - \text{VCU} = \quad \text{CM} \qquad\qquad\qquad \text{TCM}$$

$$2,500(.95) - 500 = \underline{1,875} \times 1.2(1,000) = \$2,250,000$$

$$2,500(.90) - 500 = \underline{1,750} \times 1.3(1,000) = \$2,275,000$$

The 10 percent/30 percent option increase in volume represents a $25,000 financial advantage over the 5 percent/20 percent option. Clearly, the volume estimate plays an important part of the decision process but is also subject to the most uncertainty.

Another approach to analyzing the problem is the determination of the volume necessary to make the decision-maker indifferent to either discount. This could be determined in the following manner.

$$.95(2,500 - 500)(1,200) = .90(2,500 - 500)Q$$
$$2,250,000 = 1,750 \; Q$$
$$Q = 1,285.71$$

Therefore, if the increase in discount to 10 percent resulted in an increase in volume of greater than 7 percent, the decision-maker would be better off offering the higher discount.

The fixed fee approach depends on having reasonable estimates of the fixed and variable components and the total volume to be anticipated for the negotiating year. For example, assume the following cost data:

$$\text{Variable cost} = \$500$$
$$\text{Fixed cost} = \$2,000,000$$
$$\text{Other financial requirements} = \$250,000$$
$$\text{Volume} = 1,000$$

At what fixed price should the services be offered?

$$\frac{\text{Total financial requirement}}{\text{at a volume of 1,000}} = 2,000,000 + 500(1,000) + 250,000$$

$$\text{Per unit price} = \frac{2,750,000}{1,000}$$

$$\text{Price} = \$2,750$$

If 1,000 procedures can be performed, then the provider will meet their total financial requirements. Since the 1,000 estimate plays a key role in the computation of the price, what should the penalty be if the volume estimate is not made or what should the incentive be to exceed the volume estimate?

The financial aspects of this question can be determined by separating the total financial requirements into fixed and variable components on a per-unit basis. This can be accomplished in the following manner:

$$VCU = \quad \$500 \; \text{(given)}$$
$$FCU = \frac{2,000,000 + 250,000}{1,000} \quad \text{or} \quad \underline{\$2,250}$$

If the purchaser only requests 900 days of service, what would the financial impact be? If only 900 days of service are furnished, the variable costs for the remaining 100 units will not be incurred. However, since the fixed cost portion would not be reduced by the decrease in volume, a shortage of $100 \times \$2,250$ or $\$225,000$ would result and a penalty equal to the change in days times the fixed cost per unit should be established.

In the event that the purchaser demands more than the 1,000 days specified in the contract, the incentive could be determined by multiplying the days in excess of 1,000 by the variable cost factor. Subtracting this amount from the agreed-upon price would equal the amount of the incentive. For example, if 1,100 patient days were demanded, this would result in an increased cost to the provider of $100 \times \$500$ or $\$50,000$. If the purchaser paid $\$50,000$ to the provider, then their financial position would be the same as if 1,000 days were delivered. The incentive clause to the purchaser could be the difference between the $\$2,750$ and $\$500$ prices, or $\$2,250$, which represents the fixed components of the price.

Although the fixed price has intuitive appeal in the sense of fairness and equity, it probably requires better accounting information and greater trust than is currently available from purchasers and providers. It should be cautioned that the discount method does not have to result in any savings to the purchaser. Providers must meet their total financial requirements, and any time the discount is expressed as a percentage of price, it becomes possible to give significant discounts on an increased price base, which lets the provider obtain the desired margin regardless of the volume impact and leaves the purchaser paying the same total amount.

Illustrated Example

A local hospital decided to offer the following contract to a local industry:

ST. JOSEPH COUNTY HOSPITAL, INC.
Analysis of Hospital Inpatient Charges for
Industry and Patient
January 1, 1984

Assuming:

The hospital grants a 5 percent discount from the total charges and this is applied before deductible and coinsurance. The industry has a $200.00 deductible contract with its employees.

The industry has a 20 percent coinsurance that applies after the deductible. St. Joseph County Hospital is named the Preferred Provider and the employee will only have to pay $100.00 deductible if this hospital is used. The length of the stay is 5 days.

The following analysis was completed to determine the impact on the purchaser and the subscriber.

	St. Joseph County Hospital		Other Hospital per Diems	
Average per diem charge	$ 225	$ 275	$ 300	$ 325
Total charges (5 days)	$1,125	$1,375	$1,500	$1,625
Less:				
5% discount	56	—	—	—
Net charges	$1,069	$1,375	$1,500	$1,625
Deductible by patient	100	200	200	200
Amount to apply coinsurance	$ 969	$1,175	$1,300	$1,425
Coinsurance at 20%	194	235	260	285
Amount industry to pay	$ 775	$ 940	$1,040	$1,140
Summary:				
Patient pay	$ 294	$ 435	$ 460	$ 485
Industry pay	775	940	1,040	1,140
Discount	56	—	—	—
Total charges	$1,125	$1,375	$1,500	$1,625
Percent difference in per diem	—	22%	33%	44%
Percent difference in patient pay	—	48%	56%	65%
Percent difference in industry pay	—	21%	34%	47%

Advantages accrue to both parties as the exhibit indicates. However, what is the impact on the hospital of accepting the reduced price? The amount of the discount ($56) per patient stay must be recovered through increased volume if the contract is not to hurt the financial condition of the provider.

This increase in required volume could be determined from the contribution margin approach discussed earlier. For the purpose of this analysis, assume the variable costs represent 10 percent of the total revenue or $112.50. The contribution margin for each stay of five days would be:

$$\$1,125 - \$112.50 = \$1,012.50$$

In other words, attracting one more patient would result in an increased contribution of $1,012.50. Thus, the hospital would be better off financially if only one additional patient is attracted by the offer.

Since the hospital was already the low-cost institution in the area, it was possible to offer a low discount to the industry that was appealing to them in terms of financial incentives. The subscriber also benefited through the lower deductible and reduced cost of the coinsurance.

CONCLUSION

There are financial benefits to be derived from PPOs, but they will not be realized without sound financial analysis and management on the part of all participants in the arrangement. Financial management techniques offer the decision-makers some insights into the dollar impact of alternative proposals and the opportunity to evaluate them under varying scenarios of volume and price. The use of these techniques will also highlight the more sensitive financial aspects of the decision and where more information is needed. This basic understanding should help the decision-makers decide when to seek additional financial expertise and guidance.

REFERENCES

Richard A. Blacker and Robert W. Lundy, Jr., "Preferred Provider Organizations: The Latest Response to Healthcare Competition—An Overview," *Healthcare Financial Management,* July 1983, pp. 14–16, 18.

Richard A. Blacker and Angela A. Mickelson, "Practical Considerations: Negotiating Contracts with PPO's," *Healthcare Financial Management,* September 1983, pp. 48–51.

Jeffrey G. Craft, "Preferred Provider Organizations: Addressing the Legal Issues," *Healthcare Financial Management,* August 1983, pp. 10–12, 14, 16.

M. Orry Jacobs, "Competition and Regulation: Do They Make a Difference in Hospital Reimbursement?" *Health Care Management Review,* Summer 1983, pp. 53–56.

Fred Rothenberg, "PPO's: Critical Elements in Their Design," *Healthcare Financial Management,* October 1983, pp. 32–34, 40, 42.

John P. Schmitt, Ph.D., "Preferred Provider Organizations: A Fiscal Perspective," *Healthcare Financial Management,* November 1983, pp. 58–64.

Planning and Design Features

MODELING A FINANCIAL APPROACH TO PPO DECISIONS

Randi L. Harry

Principal
Arthur Young & Company
San Francisco, CA

Robert D. Roberts

Partner
Arthur Young & Company
San Francisco, CA

☐ The decision of whether or not to participate in a PPO is complicated and fraught with potential conflict between a hospital and its medical staff. The purely economic aspects of the decision-making process can best be approached by financial modeling. In the following account of a hospital with a choice of accepting a PPO or facing serious economic setbacks, the financial variables and projections are presented from different points of view and with different solutions.

Consider this scenario: Four employers in a small community, representing a substantial portion of the population, band together to form a PPO for their employees. Their representative approaches all three hospitals in the area—St. Anywhere Memorial Hospital, Community Hospital, and University Hospital—for bids on the PPO contract.

How are hospitals and physicians to approach the process of deciding whether or not to pursue a PPO? The financial issues are varied and complex, but the reality of the situation is that hospitals simply cannot offer incremental costs to every PPO, HMO, EPO, medicare, and medicaid organization that comes to their door. The first and most basic question that must be addressed is whether the PPO needs the hospital and its physicians more than they need the PPO. The solution, which is determined through a process of selective negotiation, will entail hard answers to questions like: What must the hospital give up? What will it get in return? What is the break-even point? Highly developed negotiating tactics are crucially important, as well as an understanding of health care economics and the relevant cost behaviors.

As illustrated in the following scenario of St. Anywhere Hospital, sometimes the answers will not be definite. Although St. Anywhere clearly needs the PPO, not all of the physicians on the hospital's staff will gain from accepting the PPO's conditions. In a case like this, long-term interests may have to be balanced against short-term gains or losses. While physicians might gain by rejecting a PPO, with its discounted fee schedule and relative loss of autonomy, over the long term their financial survival will depend on cooperation with the hospital. Hospitals and their medical staffs are increasingly at financial odds as their incomes are being eroded. But, financial and professional survival for everyone involved depends on cooperation between the hospital and its medical staff.

Another crucial issue to consider is the relative advantages and disadvantages of committing to volume discounts in order to have a PPO arrangement. Can the institution handle the increase (if any) in volume? Is the medical staff willing to participate at the discounted fee schedule? Will the relationship between volume and discounted fees bring in enough revenue to justify having the PPO?

The financial advantages to a hospital of having a PPO include an increase in revenues and patient occupancy from PPO subscribers, as well as possibly attracting new physicians and patients.

The financial disadvantages to a hospital of having a PPO can include a loss of revenue if the patient volume is not sufficient. Having a PPO does not guarantee a hospital a basic minimum of income or occupancy. And if the occupancy of the hospital is too high, will patients who pay the full rate be forced to seek care at other hospitals? Furthermore, the hospital/medical staff relationship might be upset by the new incentives and procedures.

Approaching these questions involves keeping the issues firmly in mind while negotiating for the best balance. In the St. Anywhere example, problems of a contemporary hospital looking at the PPO issue are presented from different points of view: an overall look at the hospital's financial history, position in the community, and competitive stance with regard to other hospitals in the area; a consideration of the advantages and disadvantages of accepting the terms of a PPO from the points of view of various doctors and administrators; determining the hospital's negotiating position (e.g., full services, costs, accessibility, medical staff acceptance, whether it needs the PPO more than the PPO needs it); and selecting the best hospital to fulfill the needs and requirements of the subscriber from the point of view of the negotiator for the health plan. These examples provide one methodology a hospital might use in approaching this problem. The first step is to appoint a PPO task force to design and implement an administrative action plan and a financial action plan.

ADMINISTRATIVE ACTION PLAN

— Analyze the hospital's strategic position, i.e., how much does it need a PPO? What are its present financial strengths and weaknesses? Will it gain additional patients or lose the capacity to service more? What is the broad financial picture for the hospital if it bypasses PPO consideration at this time? Will there be a second opportunity?

— Determine the hospital's competitive position with regard to other hospitals and medical providers in the area.

— Delegate negotiating authority to a selected portion of the administrative staff and clarify the chain of command for this action.

— Consider the legal implications of signing a PPO contract, i.e., antitrust problems such as price-fixing and restraint of trade, securities, insurance, and other regulatory implications.

— Work with the medical staff to examine the mutual benefits that will accrue from contracting with a PPO. In addition to accepting a discounted fee schedule, there may be issues of utilization controls, prior authorization, and curtailment or strict limitation of privileges. Another consideration to bring to their attention, if the hospital is not successful in obtaining the PPO contract, is that there will be less money available in the budget for equipment, staffing, and special programs.

— Define the service package: service mix, potential stop-losses, auxiliary networking, limitations on patient type, etc. Some of this information might come from the PPO itself in statements of its needs, requirements, and utilization history. Also analyze the service mix and financial history of the PPO subscribers currently being served.

— Consider what alternatives are available if the hospital does not join this PPO, for example, other PPOs or HMOs, or starting its own.

FINANCIAL ACTION PLAN

After the administrative action plan is well underway, the PPO task force can consider a financial action plan in the following three parts. First, define the project. The steps involved in this process include analyzing the hospital's strategic position, estimating the negotiations timetable, formulating alternatives to be evaluated, determining the degree of precision required, identifying all available data, defining additional data requirements, and assigning data collection tasks.

Second, collect the financial data. With regard to competition: consider the service area, competing institutions, respective market share, expected contracts, and specialized services. With regard to services: consider admissions, rate of change in admissions, average length of stay, intensity, financial class utilization by patient type, standard treatment protocol, charge per unit of service, and specialized service types. With regard to costs: consider fixed costs, semi-variable costs, variable costs per unit, and fixed and variable inflation rates. With regard to reimbursement: consider medicare adjustments and reclassifications, full cost allocation (stepdown), payor utilization, and reimbursement type (per diem, discount, cost plus).

Third, analyze the data. The steps involved in this process include finalizing the alternatives to be evaluated, evaluating the alternatives, performing sensitivity analyses, and developing a negotiating strategy. Data analysis contains so many variables, it is almost impossible to process all the alternatives manually. At this point in the process it is very helpful to have a microcomputer to do the job of forecasting and creating scenarios. For the St. Anywhere example, a microcomputer model (CASE-PLAN) developed by Arthur Young was used to analyze the data and project the variables into meaningful concepts.

The key to the analysis is to evaluate "what if" questions: What if the hospital does not get the contract? What if the hospital contracts at $400 per day and volume remains constant or decreases? What if the hospital contracts at $4,000 per discharge and the mix of patients or acuity changes? What will be the financial result of subcontracting certain services? What if the PPO contract is limited only to specialized services? What if Blue Cross or Aetna wants to negotiate the same or more favorable terms?

No matter what a hospital's costs are, if they are out of line with the marketplace, the hospital will probably not be able to negotiate a higher charge. If a hospital's costs are significantly higher than the competition, for whatever reason (e.g., higher capital costs, higher staffing, inefficiencies), it will be difficult to pass these costs on. However, patients are often willing to absorb higher charges if a hospital's quality and scope of services, reputation, and accessibility are first rate. On the other hand, a hospital should not limit its charges to merely covering costs.

Consideration of these factors in finer detail can be accomplished by a best-case, worst-case, and most-likely-case approach. For example, hospitals and physicians need to know what it will cost to treat a PPO patient: fixed costs, variable costs, and semivariable costs. Although few costs are 100 percent completely fixed or variable, most of them can be so classified within a reasonable range. An example of fixed costs might be nonmedical supplies and equipment rentals and clerical support salaries. Variable costs fluctuate in response to volume, for example, laboratory tests, emergency room visits, and intensive care patient days.

The following are questions to ask in projecting a worst-case, best-case, and most-likely-case scenario:

— How many patient days will be lost or gained and how much revenue do they amount to?
— How much will costs be affected with a loss in patients and with a gain? This requires an understanding of the hospital's fixed, variable and semi-variable costs.
— What is the difference between the lost or gained revenue and the reduced or increased operating cost?
— Are there any other patient days that will be lost or gained along with the PPO contract? (How will the physicians respond to the PPO?)
— What is the difference between the hospital's standard rate and the negotiated PPO rate with regard to patients who currently pay full rate and will become PPO subscribers?

The above questions are asked and the answers are quantified in the St. Anywhere scenario.

SCENARIO: MEDICAL STAFF/ HOSPITAL RELATIONSHIPS

St. Anywhere Memorial Hospital is a 250-bed, general acute-care hospital in Anywhere, Colorado. Anywhere is a small suburban community approximately 40 miles from the business center of Anyopolis. The Hospital serves the population of Anywhere, adjoining communities to the north and northwest, and portions of adjoining towns to the east and south. The Hospital service area spans about 200 square miles.

St. Anywhere Memorial Hospital was chartered as a not-for-profit charitable corporation in 1921. The Hospital's mission is to provide quality health care to serve the physical, emotional, and spiritual needs of the community regardless of the ability of individual patients to pay for services. The Hospital began operations in a small wooden frame structure about three miles from its present location. That structure was extensively remodeled in 1958, and a new structure to replace that facility was constructed on the present site in 1975.

The construction of the replacement facility was financed largely through intermediate and long-term borrowing. The Hospital borrowed $15 million in 1975. Bonds and notes now mature twice each year through 1990. Current maturities include $300,000 each in April and October. Total debt service for this year is $1,670,000.

From 1970 to 1980, Anywhere's population increased by 50 percent and the State Department of Human Resources forecasts continued growth through 1990. Beginning in 1980, with the closure of an oil and gas field near town, the economic climate of the community began to decline. Unemployment climbed to 15 percent and some long-term residents were forced to leave the community. Still others were unable to find work and became eligible for Medicaid benefits when their unemployment benefits were exhausted.

The economic downturn led to a small but steady decline in St. Anywhere's occupancy, which was shared with the other hospitals in the community. Occupancy had been running at over 80 percent, but declined last year to about 75 percent. In addition, the number of patients covered by private insurance decreased, with a shift of some of the patients to self-pay and medicaid coverage.

The medical staff has not organized into an Individual Practice Association (IPA) or other organization designed to contract with an insurance company. The staff has a strong loyalty to the Hospital, but they have resisted any attempts to form large groups for purposes of contracting with insurance companies.

St. Anywhere shares its service area with two other hospitals. The first is University Hospital. This is a larger hospital, with 350 beds. This hospital provides *all* services. Its occupancy has historically run at about 65 percent. Its rates have historically been higher than St. Anywhere's by 10 to 15 percent, and its costs are also about 10 to 15 percent higher. Its medical staff is largely organized around an IPA, which was formed for the purpose of setting rates for its faculty members and billing for their fees.

The other hospital is Community Hospital. It has about 150 beds and provides all services except OB, burn, pediatrics, neonatal, and cardiovascular surgery. It is located in suburbia. Its medicaid population has historically been very low and its private patient population has been very high. It is presently operating at about 85 percent of capacity. Its charges have run about 10 percent lower than St. Anywhere's and its costs, similarly, about 10 percent lower. Community Hospital has announced that it plans to apply for a Certificate of Need (CON) to request a significant bed expansion. If it is able to obtain a preferred contract, its bid for a CON would be significantly enhanced. This CON bid is viewed by St. Anywhere's administrative and medical staff as highly threatening to their hospital's future.

The entire state has been affected by high inflation and unemployment, resulting in additional state expenditures for welfare benefits and decreased revenues. In an attempt to balance a large state deficit, a new program of stringent limitations on medicaid per-diem reimbursement was recently announced. The medicaid ceilings limit each hospital's reimbursable inpatient costs to annual increases of 5 percent for last year and 3 percent for next year, and cut outpatient reimbursement by 10 percent. These limitations reduced St. Anywhere's profit from a budget of approximately $522,000 last year to a loss of $277,000.

Hospital administration prepared a budget for this year to generate a bottom line of $827,000 (an excess of revenues over expenses of $770,000 is necessary just to cover the excess of debt service over building depreciation).

Four of the major employers in St. Anywhere's service area have joined into an employer's coalition, Affordable Health Care (AHC), with the objective of reducing the amounts they spend for health care benefits. They plan to begin a self-insurance program and have approached the Hospital with a proposal to begin negotiating to provide exclusive services to their employees. They have also approached the other two hospitals in the service area. Patients covered by these employers' plans represent approximately 14 percent of St. Anywhere's admissions, and historically these patients have made the difference between a slight net profit at the end of the year and a significant loss.

AHC has asked St. Anywhere to develop a proposal defining the inpatient per-diem rate and outpatient percentage discount it would be willing to offer in return for an exclusive contract. AHC is willing to consider contracts for all of the services the hospital has to offer or only certain specialized services. However, its strong preference is to contract with the hospital for all of its services.

AHC has also announced that it has developed a fee schedule, which it expects at least a majority of the physicians on the staff of the contract hospital to accept.

Community Hospital's medical staff does not have an organized IPA or PPO. Approximately 11 percent of its patients are represented by AHC.

The University Hospital IPA has announced that it can deliver all of its physicians, which comprise about 85 percent of the total medical staff, to AHC at the proposed physician's compensation rates. AHC has traditionally amounted to about 5 percent of its patients. Many AHC patients have not enjoyed the impersonal character of this teaching hospital.

St. Anywhere's administrators estimate that the contract would approximately double the volume of patients from these employers. They also estimate that a discount of at least 35 percent will be necessary to win the contract.

St. Anywhere's controller provides the following information about the range of all-inclusive per diems the hospital can logically submit:

— Medicare hospital costs are $520 per day.
— If a bid based upon current hospital charges to AHC were submitted, it would be $680 per day.
— Reducing this by 35 percent would result in a bid of $442 per day for inpatient services.
— Assuming the volume doubled after the contract was awarded, the hospital could come out about even with current profit margins if the bid was discounted to $576 per day with an additional 15 percent discount on outpatient services.
— The hospital could bid as low as $489 per day with a 15 percent discount on outpatient services and still essentially break even, again assuming the AHC patient load would double.

Administration believes that granting a 35 percent hospital discount ($442/day inpatient, 65 percent of charges outpatient) and accepting the proposed physician fee schedule is not feasible. If such a rate were negotiated, a two-percent across-the-board cut in all expenses, including physician fees, would be required to maintain solvency and meet debt service.

As an alternative, administration has proposed that the hospital and the medical staff form a Medical Staff/Hospital network (MeSH)[1] in order to offer potential buyers an integrated package of services and utilization controls. If such a network could be formed, administration estimates that a contract with AHC could be signed for an overall 20–25 percent discount.

Attached are four sets of reports:

— The original budget.
— An analysis of the impact of losing all of AHC's patients.
— An analysis of the impact of doubling AHC's volume at an inpatient per diem of $442 and a 35 percent outpatient discount.
— An analysis of the proposed MeSH network with a hospital per diem of $545 and a 20 percent discount on outpatient *and* physician fees.

All reports, in order to maintain comparability with the MeSH network results, include physician revenues and costs. (Note: Totals on some reports may not agree due to rounding.)

The following individuals will negotiate a contract between St. Anywhere and Affordable Health Care:

— Dr. Slide, hospital-based pathologist.
— Dr. Atam, hospital-based radiologist.
— Dr. Morphia, hospital-based anesthesiologist.
— Dr. Triage, emergency room physician.
— Dr. Swab, surgeon.
— Dr. Noah, family practitioner.

ST. ANYWHERE MEMORIAL: ORIGINAL BUDGET
Case Plan
Arthur Young
Patient Type Analysis
7/84–6/85

	Units of Service		Gross Revenue	Deduct from Rev	Net Revenue	Variable Costs	Contrib. Margin	Fixed Costs	Net Profit
	Admissions	Days							
Inpatient types:									
Medicine	3,074	18,444	14,218	1,748	12,470	4,814	7,657	5,284	2,373
Surgery	3,172	20,616	19,624	4,901	14,723	6,065	8,658	7,306	1,352
Intensive care	573	5,444	4,742	1,479	3,263	1,826	1,436	1,557	−121
Obstetrics	1,532	4,597	6,090	1,956	4,135	1,999	2,135	2,138	−2
Open-heart surgery	467	4,158	5,844	2,857	2,988	2,022	965	1,933	−968
Pediatrics	535	1,374	1,185	210	975	442	533	680	−147
Nursery	1,627	4,882	1,122	−667	1,789	553	1,236	441	795
AHC surgery	595	4,057	4,035	0	4,035	1,284	2,751	1,465	1,285
AHC primary care	690	3,897	3,014	0	3,014	1,045	1,969	1,183	786
AHC ob/gyn	274	821	1,088	0	1,088	357	731	382	349
Total inpatient	12,539	68,290	60,962	12,483	48,479	20,408	28,071	22,369	5,702
	Visits								
Outpatient types:									
Urgent care center	0	n/a	0	0	0	0	0	0	0
Outpatient clinic	10,429	n/a	1,469	−3	1,473	566	907	1,551	−644
Emergency	19,384	n/a	2,814	350	2,464	1,069	1,395	1,192	203
Physician offices	28,144	n/a	1,087	226	861	271	589	215	374
AHC physician visits	7,209	n/a	278	0	278	70	209	55	154
Total outpatient	65,165	n/a	5,649	573	5,076	1,976	3,100	3,013	87
Total hospital and physicians	12,539	68,290	66,611	13,056	53,555	22,384	31,171	25,383	5,788
Total hospital									827
Total physicians									4,961

ST. ANYWHERE MEMORIAL: ORIGINAL BUDGET
Case Plan
Arthur Young
Patient Type Analysis–Per Unit of Service
7/84–6/85

Patient Type	Per Admission						Per Patient Day			
	Admissions	Net Rev.	Var Cost	Tot Cost	Net Prof	Patient Days	Net Rev.	Var Cost	Tot Cost	Net Prof
Inpatient:										
Medicine	3,074	4,057	1,566	3,285	772	18,444	676	261	547	129
Surgery	3,172	4,642	1,912	4,216	426	20,616	714	294	649	66
Intensive care	573	5,694	3,187	5,905	−211	5,444	599	336	622	−22
Obstetrics	1,532	2,698	1,305	2,700	−1	4,597	899	435	900	0
Open-heart surgery	467	6,395	4,329	8,466	−2,071	4,158	719	486	951	−233
Pediatrics	535	1,824	827	2,099	−274	1,374	710	322	817	−107
Nursery	1,627	1,099	340	611	488	4,882	366	113	204	163
AHC surgery	595	6,782	2,158	4,622	2,160	4,057	994	316	678	317
AHC primary care	690	4,369	1,515	3,230	1,139	3,897	773	268	572	202
AHC ob/gyn	274	3,975	1,305	2,700	1,275	821	1,325	435	900	425
Total inpatient	12,539					68,290				
	Visits									
Outpatient:										
Urgent care center	0	0	0	0	0	—	—	—	—	—
Outpatient clinic	10,429	141	54	203	−62	—	—	—	—	—
Emergency	19,384	127	55	117	10	—	—	—	—	—
Physician offices	28,144	31	10	17	13	—	—	—	—	—
AHC physician visits	7,209	39	10	17	21	—	—	—	—	—
Total outpatient	65,165									

ST. ANYWHERE MEMORIAL: NO AHC PATIENTS

Case Plan
Arthur Young
Patient Type Analysis
7/84–6/85

	Units of Service		Gross Revenue	Deduct from Rev	Net Revenue	Variable Costs	Contrib. Margin	Fixed Costs	Net Profit
	Admis- sions	Days							
Inpatient types:									
Medicine	3,074	18,444	14,218	1,748	12,470	4,817	7,654	5,944	1,710
Surgery	3,172	20,616	19,624	4,901	14,723	6,071	8,653	8,222	431
Intensive care	573	5,444	4,742	1,479	3,263	1,825	1,438	1,761	−324
Obstetrics	1,532	4,597	6,090	1,956	4,135	2,003	2,132	2,503	−372
Open-heart surgery	467	4,158	5,844	2,857	2,988	2,021	967	2,180	−1,213
Pediatrics	535	1,374	1,185	210	975	448	528	840	−313
Nursery	1,385	4,155	955	−668	1,623	472	1,151	385	766
AHC surgery	0	0	0	0	0	0	0	0	0
AHC primary care	0	0	0	0	0	0	0	0	0
AHC ob/gyn	0	0	0	0	0	0	0	0	0
Total inpatient	10,738	58,788	52,659	12,482	40,177	17,655	22,522	21,835	686
	Visits								
Outpatient types:									
Urgent care center	0	n/a	0	0	0	0	0	0	0
Outpatient clinic	9,282	n/a	1,308	−23	1,331	500	830	1,477	−647
Emergency	17,640	n/a	2,561	321	2,240	969	1,271	1,214	57
Physician offices	28,144	n/a	1,087	215	873	271	601	271	330
AHC physician visits	0	n/a	0	0	0	0	0	0	0
Total outpatient	55,065	n/a	4,956	513	4,443	1,741	2,702	2,962	−260
Total hospital and physicians	10,738	58,788	57,615	12,995	44,620	19,396	25,224	24,797	427
Total hospital									−2,942
Total physicians									3,368

ST. ANYWHERE MEMORIAL: NO AHC PATIENTS
Case Plan
Arthur Young
Patient Type Analysis–Per Unit of Service
7/84–6/85

Patient Type	Per Admission					Patient Days	Per Patient Day			
	Admissions	Net Rev.	Var Cost	Tot Cost	Net Prof		Net Rev.	Var Cost	Tot Cost	Net Prof
Inpatient:										
Medicine	3,074	4,057	1,567	3,500	556	18,444	676	261	583	93
Surgery	3,172	4,642	1,914	4,506	136	20,616	714	294	693	21
Intensive care	573	5,694	3,185	6,259	-565	5,444	599	335	659	-59
Obstetrics	1,532	2,698	1,307	2,941	-243	4,597	899	436	980	-81
Open-heart surgery	467	6,395	4,325	8,991	-2,596	4,158	719	486	1,010	-292
Pediatrics	535	1,824	838	2,409	-585	1,374	710	326	937	-227
Nursery	1,385	1,172	341	619	553	4,155	391	114	206	184
AHC surgery	0	0	0	0	0	0	0	0	0	0
AHC primary care	0	0	0	0	0	0	0	0	0	0
AHC ob/gyn	0	0	0	0	0	0	0	0	0	0
Total inpatient	10,738					58,788				
Visits										
Outpatient:										
Urgent care center	0	0	0	0	0	—	—	—	—	—
Outpatient clinic	9,282	143	54	213	-70	—	—	—	—	—
Emergency	17,640	127	55	124	3	—	—	—	—	—
Physician offices	28,144	31	10	19	12	—	—	—	—	—
AHC physician visits	0	0	0	0	0	—	—	—	—	—
Total outpatient	55,065					—				—

ST. ANYWHERE MEMORIAL: AHC DISCOUNT
Case Plan
Arthur Young
Patient Type Analysis
7/84–6/85

	Units of Service		Gross Revenue	Deduct from Rev	Net Revenue	Variable Costs	Contrib. Margin	Fixed Costs	Net Profit
	Admis- sions	Days							
Inpatient types:									
Medicine	3,074	18,444	14,218	1,748	12,470	4,812	7,659	4,870	2,789
Surgery	3,172	20,616	19,624	4,901	14,723	6,045	8,678	6,808	1,870
Intensive care	573	5,444	4,742	1,479	3,263	1,833	1,430	1,479	−50
Obstetrics	1,532	4,597	6,090	1,956	4,135	1,992	2,143	1,964	178
Open-heart surgery	467	4,158	5,844	2,857	2,988	2,023	964	1,836	−871
Pediatrics	535	1,374	1,185	210	975	437	538	582	−44
Nursery	1,873	5,620	1,292	−1,163	2,455	635	1,820	503	1,317
AHC surgery	1,186	8,090	8,045	2,909	5,136	2,555	2,581	2,733	−152
AHC primary care	1,380	7,795	6,028	1,384	4,644	2,088	2,556	2,160	396
AHC ob/gyn	548	1,643	2,176	543	1,633	712	921	702	219
Total inpatient	14,340	77,780	69,245	16,823	52,422	23,132	29,290	23,638	5,652
	Visits								
Outpatient types:									
Urgent care center	13,622	n/a	2,012	312	1,699	644	1,056	1,201	−145
Outpatient clinic	0	n/a	0	0	0	0	0	0	0
Emergency	15,847	n/a	2,300	369	1,932	904	1,028	1,081	−54
Physician offices	28,144	n/a	1,087	234	853	271	582	179	403
AHC physician visits	14,418	n/a	557	0	557	139	418	92	326
Total outpatient	72,031	n/a	5,956	915	5,041	1,958	3,083	2,553	530
Total hospital and physicians	14,340	77,780	75,201	17,738	57,463	25,090	32,373	26,191	6,182
Total hospital									−355
Total physicians									6,537

ST. ANYWHERE MEMORIAL: AHC DISCOUNT
Case Plan
Arthur Young
Patient Type Analysis–Per Unit of Service
7/84–6/85

Patient Type	Admissions	Per Admission				Patient Days	Per Patient Day			
		Net Rev.	Var Cost	Tot Cost	Net Prof		Net Rev.	Var Cost	Tot Cost	Net Prof
Inpatient:										
Medicine	3,074	4,057	1,565	3,150	907	18,444	676	261	525	151
Surgery	3,172	4,642	1,906	4,052	590	20,616	714	293	623	91
Intensive care	573	5,694	3,199	5,781	−87	5,444	599	337	609	−9
Obstetrics	1,532	2,698	1,300	2,582	116	4,597	899	433	861	39
Open-heart surgery	467	6,395	4,331	8,260	−1,865	4,158	719	487	928	−210
Pediatrics	535	1,824	818	1,907	−83	1,374	710	318	742	−32
Nursery	1,873	1,311	339	608	703	5,620	437	113	203	234
AHC surgery	1,186	4,331	2,154	4,457	−126	8,090	635	316	654	−19
AHC primary care	1,380	3,365	1,513	3,079	286	7,795	596	268	545	51
AHC ob/gyn	548	2,980	1,300	2,582	398	1,643	994	433	861	133
Total inpatient	14,340					77,780				
Visits										
Outpatient:										
Urgent care center	13,622	125	47	135	−11	—	—	—	—	—
Outpatient clinic	0	0	0	0	0	—	—	—	—	—
Emergency	15,847	122	57	125	−3	—	—	—	—	—
Physician offices	28,144	30	10	16	14	—	—	—	—	—
AHC physician visits	14,418	39	10	16	23	—	—	—	—	—
Total outpatient	72,031									

ST. ANYWHERE MEMORIAL: MESH NETWORK

Case Plan
Arthur Young
Patient Type Analysis
7/84–6/85

	Units of Service		Gross Revenue	Deduct from Rev	Net Revenue	Variable Costs	Contrib. Margin	Fixed Costs	Net Profit
	Admissions	Days							
Inpatient types:									
Medicine	3,074	18,444	14,218	1,748	12,470	4,812	7,659	4,870	2,789
Surgery	3,172	20,616	19,624	4,901	14,723	6,045	8,678	6,808	1,870
Intensive care	573	5,444	4,742	1,479	3,263	1,833	1,430	1,479	−50
Obstetrics	1,532	4,597	6,090	1,956	4,135	1,992	2,143	1,964	178
Open-heart surgery	467	4,158	5,844	2,857	2,988	2,023	964	1,836	−871
Pediatrics	535	1,374	1,185	210	975	437	538	582	−44
Nursery	1,873	5,620	1,292	−1,356	2,647	635	2,012	503	1,509
AHC surgery	1,186	8,090	8,045	2,390	5,655	2,555	3,100	2,733	367
AHC primary care	1,380	7,795	6,028	579	5,449	2,088	3,361	2,160	1,201
AHC ob/gyn	548	1,643	2,176	1,028	1,148	712	436	702	−266
Total inpatient	14,340	77,780	69,245	15,792	53,453	23,132	30,320	23,638	6,682
	Visits								
Outpatient types:									
Urgent care center	13,622	n/a	2,012	254	1,758	644	1,114	1,201	−87
Outpatient clinic	0	n/a	0	0	0	0	0	0	0
Emergency	15,847	n/a	2,300	312	1,988	904	1,084	1,081	3
Physician offices	28,144	n/a	1,087	234	853	271	582	179	403
AHC physician visits	14,418	n/a	557	111	446	139	306	92	215
Total outpatient	72,031	n/a	5,956	911	5,045	1,958	3,087	2,553	534
Total hospital and physicians	14,340	77,780	75,201	16,703	58,498	25,090	33,407	26,191	7,216
Total hospital									1,750
Total physicians									5,466

ST. ANYWHERE MEMORIAL: MESH NETWORK
Case Plan
Arthur Young
Patient Type Analysis–Per Unit of Service
7/84–6/85

Patient Type	Admissions	Per Admission				Patient Days	Per Patient Day			
		Net Rev.	Var Cost	Tot Cost	Net Prof		Net Rev.	Var Cost	Tot Cost	Net Prof
Inpatient:										
Medicine	3,074	4,057	1,565	3,150	907	18,444	676	261	525	151
Surgery	3,172	4,642	1,906	4,052	590	20,616	714	293	623	91
Intensive care	573	5,694	3,199	5,781	-87	5,444	599	337	609	-9
Obstetrics	1,532	2,698	1,300	2,582	116	4,597	899	433	861	39
Open-heart surgery	467	6,395	4,331	8,260	-1,865	4,158	719	487	928	-210
Pediatrics	535	1,824	818	1,907	-83	1,374	710	318	742	-32
Nursery	1,873	1,413	339	608	805	5,620	471	113	203	268
AHC surgery	1,186	4,767	2,154	4,457	310	8,090	699	316	654	45
AHC primary care	1,380	3,949	1,513	3,079	870	7,795	699	268	545	154
AHC ob/gyn	548	2,097	1,300	2,582	-485	1,643	699	433	861	-162
Total inpatient	14,340					77,780				
	Visits									
Outpatient:										
Urgent care center	13,622	129	47	135	-6	—	—	—	—	—
Outpatient clinic	0	0	0	0	0	—	—	—	—	—
Emergency	15,847	125	57	125	0	—	—	—	—	—
Physician offices	28,144	30	10	16	14	—	—	—	—	—
AHC physician visits	14,418	31	10	16	15	—	—	—	—	—
Total outpatient	72,031									

ST. ANYWHERE MEMORIAL: MESH NETWORK
Case Plan
Arthur Young
Financial Class Analysis
7/84–6/85

	Units of Service		Gross Revenue	Deduct from Rev	Net Revenue	Variable Costs	Contrib. Margin	Fixed Costs	Net Profit
	Admissions	Days							
Inpatient types:									
Blue Cross	1,646	8,927	7,935	0	7,935	2,648	5,287	2,701	2,586
Medicare	3,396	22,635	20,722	7,186	13,536	6,855	6,682	6,994	-313
Medicaid	3,161	14,590	12,919	5,099	7,820	4,382	3,438	4,407	-969
Self-pay	916	4,573	3,957	198	3,759	1,340	2,419	1,353	1,066
Aetna	279	1,360	1,254	0	1,254	422	831	433	398
Other commercial insurers	1,336	6,698	5,872	0	5,872	1,966	3,906	2,023	1,883
Affordable health care	3,602	18,994	16,586	3,309	13,277	5,520	7,757	5,726	2,030
Total inpatient	14,337	77,778	69,245	15,792	53,453	23,132	30,320	23,638	6,682
	Visits								
Outpatient type:									
Blue Cross	6,836	n/a	639	0	639	218	420	285	135
Medicare	14,593	n/a	1,286	0	1,286	429	858	569	288
Medicaid	15,193	n/a	1,361	565	796	457	339	604	-265
Self-pay	9,507	n/a	802	80	722	262	460	352	108
Aetna	1,367	n/a	128	0	128	44	84	57	27
Other commercial insurers	4,854	n/a	413	0	413	136	278	182	96
Affordable health care	19,679	n/a	1,327	265	1,062	413	649	503	145
Total outpatient	72,030	n/a	5,956	911	5,045	1,958	3,087	2,553	534
Total hospital			75,201	16,703	58,498	25,090	33,407	26,191	7,216

ST. ANYWHERE MEMORIAL: MESH NETWORK
Case Plan
Arthur Young
Department Profitability
7/84–6/85

Cost Center	Unit Serv. Name	Unit of Service	Gross Revenue	Deduct from Revenue	Net Revenue	Direct Costs	Direct Profit	Allocated Costs	Net Profit	Total Cost per Unit
Routine:										
Med/surg		53,578	20,151	4,186	15,966	7,995	7,970	7,587	383	291
ICU		6,422	4,561	1,359	3,202	2,324	878	966	−88	512
Obstetrics		6,239	2,347	847	1,500	1,262	237	657	−420	308
CCU		3,565	2,508	790	1,718	1,312	406	646	−241	549
Pediatrics		2,357	717	114	603	584	19	450	−431	439
Nursery		5,620	950	−997	1,948	616	1,332	278	1,054	159
Total routine:		77,780	31,235	6,299	24,936	14,093	10,842	10,585	258	
Ancillary:										
Dr. Morphia	procedures	7,642	172	51	121	23	98	0	98	3
Anesthesiologists	procedures	929	24	7	17	7	10	0	10	8
Dr. Swab	admissions	343	398	106	293	156	137	0	137	453
Surgeons	admissions	4,701	6,079	1,746	4,333	2,412	1,921	0	1,921	513
Dr. Noah	admissions	310	180	24	156	81	75	0	75	261
Primary care MDs	admissions	5,032	4,456	597	3,859	2,014	1,845	0	1,845	400

Dr. Natale	admissions	437	619	223	395	257	138	0	138	589
Obstetricians	admissions	1,643	2,803	1,012	1,791	1,166	625	0	625	710
Surgery and recovery	procedures	7,618	5,448	1,540	3,908	2,501	1,407	1,147	260	479
Anesthesia	procedures	8,489	1,027	306	721	358	362	344	18	83
Labor and delivery	births	1,872	1,140	411	728	826	−97	325	−422	615
Radiology-diagnostic	films	77,771	4,207	944	3,264	1,460	1,804	919	885	31
Radiation therapy	treatments	9,981	263	34	229	236	−7	182	−189	42
Laboratory	cap units	4,016,323	5,101	918	4,183	2,153	2,030	1,345	686	1
EKG	procedures	12,165	658	172	486	374	111	149	−38	43
EEG	procedures	622	93	18	75	59	16	55	−39	183
Physical therapy	treatments	32,505	702	139	563	244	319	423	−105	21
Drugs sold	cost reqns	734,926	3,039	755	2,283	0	2,283	1,426	857	2
Medical supplies	cost reqns	391,442	1,290	180	1,110	0	1,110	1,209	−99	3
Inhalation therapy	pt days	72,160	1,679	391	1,288	831	457	317	141	16
Blood bank	units	6,459	612	176	435	460	−24	134	−159	92
Total ancillary		39,989	30,238	15,619	14,619	6,644	9,751	7,975		
Outpatient:										
Urgent care center		13,622	967	122	845	422	423	501	−78	68
Outpatient clinic		0	0	0	0	0	0	0	0	0
Emergency room		15,847	1,366	185	1,180	732	449	674	−225	89
Physician offices		42,561	1,644	346	1,299	681	617	0	617	16
Total outpatient		72,031	3,977	653	3,324	1,835	1,489	1,175	314	173
Total hospital and physicians		75,201	16,703	58,498	31,547		26,951	19,735		7,216

— Dr. Natale, obstetrician/gynecologist.
— Mr. Caesar, president of the board, St. Anywhere.
— Ms. Facilitator, administrator, St. Anywhere.
— Mr. Arbit, negotiator, Affordable Health Care.

The problem in all of its facets, with all optional solutions, is presented from each of their individual points of view.

HOSPITAL-BASED PATHOLOGIST

Dr. Slide is one of the hospital's two pathologists. His gross professional compensation is budgeted at $137,000 for the fiscal year and is included in the operating expenses of the laboratory. His contract calls for professional compensation of $0.077 per College of American Pathologists workload measurement unit (CAP unit). The hospital combined bills for lab services and retains 5 percent of compensation as a billing fee and to cover bad debts and medicaid contractual allowances. Dr. Slide supervises the operations of the laboratory, performs quality control functions, and consults on individual patient test results. He spends 10 percent of his time on activities that qualify under medicare as direct patient care. Under the current contract, Dr. Slide's net fees for the year would be $130,107. With the new Medicare Prospective Payment System, the hospital would have to pay this amount from its predetermined rate rather than billing Medicare (as was done in the past). In addition, the medicaid limitations have increased non-medicare contractual allowances in the laboratory, and the hospital has informed Dr. Slide of the need to renegotiate his contract. With this new proposal from AHC, the hospital will need to achieve further reductions in compensation in order to survive. Dr. Slide estimates he could negotiate a contract with the hospital that would result in the following levels of compensation, depending on the outcome of the AHC negotiations:

	No AHC	AHC Discount
Gross compensation	$118,517	$154,628
Less contractuals	(22,824)	(33,830)
Less billing fee at 2%	(2,370)	(3,093)
Net compensation	$ 93,322	$117,706

He does not have staff privileges at Community or University Hospital, both of which currently have sufficient pathologists on their staffs.

Under the MeSH network proposed by administration, Dr. Slide's compensation would be as follows:

Gross compensation	$154,628
Less contractuals	(27,828)
Less billing fee at 2%	(3,093)
Net compensation	$123,708

HOSPITAL-BASED RADIOLOGIST

Dr. Atam is one of the hospital's three radiologists. His professional compensation is budgeted at $146,000 for the fiscal year, and this is included in the operating expenses of the Radiology-Diagnostic Department. His current contract provides for compensation of $6.05 per film, less a billing fee and bad debts of $7\frac{1}{2}$ percent. Dr. Atam has some limited administrative and supervisory duties, but about 80 percent of his time is spent reading films (which qualifies as direct patient care for Medicare). Under the current contract, his net compensation for the year would amount to $135,297. Under Medicare Prospective Payment, he could bill Medicare directly for patient care activities, but his administrative compensation would have to be paid by the hospital out of its predetermined rate. Medicaid contractual allowances for radiology have increased and the hospital has notified Dr. Atam that his contract needs to be renegotiated. AHC's proposal will require additional decreases in compensation if the hospital is to remain in operation. He believes the hospital would sign a new contract, depending on the AHC contract, as follows:

	No AHC	AHC Discount
Gross compensation	$128,496	$156,838
Less contractuals	(28,853)	(40,375)
Less billing fee at 2%	(2,570)	(3,137)
Net compensation	$ 97,073	$113,327

Dr. Atam does not have staff privileges at Community or University, and neither of those hospitals are recruiting for radiologists. However, he believes that if one of the other hospitals gets the AHC contract, it might well need another radiologist to handle the increased volume.

The effect on Dr. Atam's compensation of the MeSH network proposal by administration would be:

Gross compensation	$156,838
Less contractuals	(35,193)
Less billing fee at 2%	(3,137)
Net compensation	$118,509

HOSPITAL-BASED ANESTHESIOLOGIST

Dr. Morphia is St. Anywhere's anesthesiologist. She supervises a staff of 10 nurse-anesthetists and handles particularly difficult cases herself. With this number of nurse-anesthetists, she generally supervises six or seven concurrent procedures. Her contract with the hospital is not exclusive, and some of the surgeons prefer to bring in their own anesthesiologists. About 10 percent of the hospital's surgeries are done by others. The hospital bills for her services (including supervision) on the basis of a fee schedule that averages $17.50 per case. The hospital charges her a 10 percent billing and bad debt fee. She expects that her gross billings for the fiscal year will amount to $152,000 (this is not included in St. Anywhere's financial statements). Before the Tax Equity and Fiscal Responsibility Act (TEFRA), Dr. Morphia's fees were reimbursed on a reasonable charge basis. Under the new regulations, the hospital will be required to treat all of her time as nonpatient care because of the number of concurrent cases she supervises. She would be entitled to net fees of $136,800 under the current contract, and the hospital would not be allowed to bill Medicare for any of these services. Anesthesia medicaid contractual allowances have also increased. A contract needs to be negotiated so that Dr. Morphia can receive compensation from the hospital, since she can no longer bill Medicare directly. Dr. Morphia is not currently a member of the staff at Community or University Hospital, both of which use outside anesthesiologists. She believes she would have no problem getting staff privileges at either hospital. If she were to do so, however, she would need to open her own office and assume her own billing costs. She believes she would net approximately 65 percent of gross fees after the costs of billing and maintaining an office.

She expects the hospital would agree to contracts, depending on how AHC is resolved, as follows:

	No AHC	AHC Discount
Gross compensation	$131,000	$172,000
Less contractuals	(38,000)	(57,000)
Less billing fee at 2%	(2,620)	(3,440)
Net compensation	$ 90,380	$111,560

She does not believe she would be able to maintain her patient base initially, and would expect her volume in the first year to average the level originally projected even with some additional AHC patients. So she is faced with the choice of remaining at St. Anywhere and losing 13 percent of her patients for a net compensation of $90,380, or moving to another hospital to maintain her patient volume and reduce her net fees to 65 percent ($85,150).

The effect on Dr. Morphia's compensation of Administration's proposed MeSH network would be:

Gross compensation	$172,000
Less contractuals	(51,000)
Less billing fee at 2%	(3,440)
Net compensation	$117,560

Her compensation is included in the MeSH Network reports as net profit of $98,000 plus direct costs (insurance, pension, etc.) of $23,000, less the billing fee.

EMERGENCY ROOM PHYSICIAN

Dr. Triage is one of St. Anywhere's three emergency room physicians. Her contract with the hospital provides for guaranteed minimum compensation of $8,500 per month. The hospital bills for her services on a fee schedule that averages $16.38 per visit and also charges her a 7½ percent billing and bad debt fee. This will result in net fees for the year of $97,899. Her compensation is included in St. Anywhere's financial statements as an emergency room operating expense. Dr. Triage and the hospital have agreed that her administrative time is minimal, so all of her time is treated as direct patient care for Medicare. St. Anywhere is considering establishing a free-standing urgent care center to see patients both on an appointment and a walk-in basis. Administration estimates this would allow them to close the hospital-based clinic and would reduce current ER volume by about 25 percent. Dr. Triage is considering the possibility of transferring to such an urgent care center. She would supervise a staff of another physician (currently assigned to the clinic) as well as several residents and would receive an administrative salary of $12,000 in addition to professional fees. Administration estimates this plan would not be feasible without the additional AHC volume.

If the hospital does not get the AHC contract, her fees would not exceed the guaranteed minimum, and the intermediary would be required to test the reasonableness of the minimum. If the intermediary imposed the TEFRA Reasonable Compensation Equivalent (RCE), her compensation might be reduced still further. In any case, her compensation will be reduced to $87,210, as follows:

Gross compensation	$102,000
Less contractuals	(12,750)
Less billing fee at 2%	(2,040)
Net compensation	$ 87,210

If the hospital negotiates a 35 percent discount with AHC, her compensation would increase to $101,926:

Gross compensation	$123,564
Less contractuals	(19,167)
Less billing fee at 2%	(2,471)
Net compensation	$101,926

Both of the other hospitals in town use a closed-panel ER group to staff their emergency rooms. This group has a waiting list of applicants from other cities to fill any vacancies in Anywhere.

If the urgent care center were opened and a 35 percent discount was negotiated, Dr. Triage would receive compensation of $113,926 ($12,000 plus 6,811 visits at $16.38 for gross fees of $123,564 less billing fees of $2,471 and contractuals of $19,167).

The effect on Dr. Triage's compensation if the urgent care center were opened and the MeSH network were implemented would be:

Gross compensation	$123,564
Less contractuals	(15,589)
Less billing fee at 2%	(2,471)
Net compensation	$105,504

SURGEON

Dr. Swab is one of the more active surgeons on the staff at St. Anywhere, averaging about 300 admissions a year. He does not regularly admit patients to University or Community Hospital, although he is on the medical staff at all three hospitals in town. He is a member of a large, multi-specialty medical group that handles all billing and administrative functions for his practice. He has a well-established practice and expects his gross fees for this year to be approximately $347,000.

Dr. Swab's group, the Somewhere Medical Clinic, has been discussing the possibility of approaching some of the town's larger employers and offering to take over responsibility for monitoring and authorizing all care provided to their beneficiaries. Under such an arrangement, Somewhere would control the flow of patients from the employer(s), and no services (including hospital services) would be paid for unless they had been authorized by one of Somewhere's physicians. AHC has not contacted Somewhere to ask for a proposal of any kind.

Most of Somewhere's physicians are members of the medical staff of all three of Anywhere's hospitals. Many divide their practices among two of the hospitals because of differences in equipment and facilities.

Dr. Swab also chairs the Quality Assurance Committee of St. Anywhere's medical staff, and he believes strongly in the necessity for physician involvement in quality assurance and utilization review. He says, "Anyone who believes that a layman can judge whether a physician is practicing good medicine is a dangerous fool." Despite this role, his patients typically have longer hospital stays and higher bills than the average for St. Anywhere's medical staff.

The MeSH network proposed by St. Anywhere's administration would result in net compensation to Dr. Swab of $137,000. This is less than he had originally expected this year ($190,850) because of his higher length of stay and charges. It is also less than he would net if St. Anywhere did not get the contract ($162,250), again because of higher length of stay and charges. It is not as much as he would net if St. Anywhere took a 35 percent discount and he continued to be reimbursed on a fee for service basis ($218,900), but administration has indicated that it just cannot afford that kind of discount and will *have* to take a chance at losing the contract by offering a smaller discount, if the MeSH proposal is not accepted.

FAMILY PRACTITIONER

Dr. Noah is a family practitioner who was born and raised in Anywhere. After several years' absence for college, medical school, and completion of his residency, he returned to Anywhere five years ago to establish his practice. Despite his home-town roots, he has had some initial difficulty in attracting patients. One problem, in particular, relates to patients he referred to some of the specialists in town. Many of these specialists practice in large, multidisciplinary groups, which usually include internists and sometimes family practitioners. Many of the patients he referred found it more convenient to select a new primary care physician from among the group so that all their records would be in one place and because coordination between the group primary physician and the specialists seemed to be smoother.

Dr. Noah's goal is to make a comfortable living, but he has said repeatedly that he will not sacrifice his close relationship with his patients in order to increase his own income. He expects to make about $156,000 in gross fees this year, for a net income of $74,880, and will admit about 270 patients to St. Anywhere. He does not practice or belong to the staff at University or Community. About 15 percent of his patients work for the AHC employers. If St. Anywhere does not get the contract and these patients are required to go to another physician, Dr. Noah's net compensation will be reduced to a little less than $64,000. With the economy down and many families postponing elective care, he does not believe he would be able to attract sufficient new patients to replace the AHC patients he would lose. Besides, many of those patients have been with him for a number of years and he feels very strongly that they should not be forced to choose another doctor.

The MeSH network proposed by St. Anywhere's administration would result in net compensation to Dr. Noah of $75,000. This is about what he had originally expected this year ($74,880). It is more than he would net if St. Anywhere did not get the contract ($63,840), since the loss of his AHC patients would cost more than the discount. It is not as much as he would net if St. Anywhere took a 35 percent discount and he continued to be reimbursed on a fee for service basis ($86,400), but administration has indicated that it just cannot afford that kind of discount and will *have* to take a chance at losing the contract by offering a smaller discount, if the MeSH proposal is not accepted.

OBSTETRICIAN/GYNECOLOGIST

Dr. Natale is one of the obstetricians in Anywhere. She practices as part of a small group (four physicians) and admits virtually all of her patients to St. Anywhere because of its convenient location, its alternative birth center, and the warm friendly attitude of the nursing staff. She also has staff privileges at University and Community, but since Community does not have an OB service it is inconvenient for her to admit gynecology patients there. A number of her patients have complained of the cold, impersonal atmosphere at University, so she generally admits only high-risk mothers there (because of the neonatal nursery).

Dr. Natale has an active practice and expects to admit 379 patients to St. Anywhere this year. In fact, she is so busy now that she could not handle any additional patients if they were offered to her. She expects to gross about $537,000 next year and net $279,240.

The MeSH network proposed by St. Anywhere's administration would result in net compensation to her of $279,159. This is not reflected in the MeSH Network financial reports, because the MeSH members have agreed to allocate a higher per diem payment (reflecting short length of stay) to obstetrics patients. This allocation will eliminate any AHC contractuals on Dr. Natale's patients. This is a little more than she had originally expected for this year ($279,240) because she cannot take on any of the additional patients. It is more than she would net if St. Anywhere did not get the contract ($237,120), since she expects to lose a few patients to other obstetricians. It is the same as she would net if St. Anywhere took a 35 percent discount and she continued to be reimbursed on a fee-for-service basis ($279,159), but administration has indicated that it just cannot afford that kind of discount and will *have* to take a chance at losing the contract by offering a smaller discount if the MeSH proposal is not accepted. Dr. Natale would be almost as well off if St. Anywhere did not get the contract, since she would make almost the same amount of money and would see fewer patients.

PHYSICIAN COMPENSATION SUMMARY

St. Anywhere Memorial Hospital

	Original Budget	No AHC Patients	35 Percent AHC Discount	MeSH
Dr. Slide	$130,107	$ 93,322	$117,706	$123,708
Dr. Atam	135,297	97,073	113,327	118,509
Dr. Morphia	136,800	85,150*	111,560	117,560
Dr. Triage	97,899	87,210	113,926†	105,504†
Dr. Swab	190,850	162,250	218,900	137,000
Dr. Noah	74,880	63,840	86,400	75,000
Dr. Natale	279,240	237,120	279,159	279,159

*Assumes Dr. Morphia opens a nonhospital-based private practice.
†With urgent care center.

PRESIDENT OF THE BOARD

Mr. Caesar is an attorney who is president of the board of St. Anywhere Memorial Hospital. He has been a member of the board for 15 years and is strongly committed to the long-range success of the hospital. He has worked very hard to maintain St. Anywhere as a financially viable institution, while still carrying out its mission, by major fund-raising efforts and good management.

As chair of the long-range planning committee, three years ago he spearheaded a drive to develop the tools and capability for strategic and financial planning. The reports being presented to the board and others for evaluating the current situation are the product of his support for effective planning tools, and he is glad to see that his efforts have finally paid off.

Mr. Caesar has somewhat mixed emotions about the proposal made by AHC. Although it appears to place St. Anywhere in an untenable position, he can sympathize with the employers' plight. His own health insurance, carried through the state bar association, was subject to a 32 percent increase in premiums last year.

Mr. Caesar is interested in administration's proposal for a Medical Staff/Hospital network (MeSH), but he has some concerns about the idea. For one thing, although he does not specialize in antitrust matters, he believes this kind of arrangement might expose the hospital to an antitrust action by one of the other hospitals in town if St. Anywhere is successful in getting the AHC contract.

Another concern relates to the ability of the members of the medical staff to work together. In his years on the board, he has seldom seen more than two or three members of the medical staff agree with one another for very long on *any* subject, except perhaps the way they feel about malpractice attorneys.

Particularly since the proposal, in effect, asks the private practice physicians to accept a discount that will increase the compensation of their hospital-based colleagues, Mr. Caesar believes there may be little support for the idea among the physicians.

ADMINISTRATOR

Ms. Facilitator is administrator of St. Anywhere. She has been at the hospital for four years and has developed a good relationship with the board and the medical staff. The hospital is well respected in the community and is financially sound.

The series of changes in health care reimbursement that have taken place in the last few months is staggering. Ms. Facilitator has attended a number of meetings and seminars to keep abreast of the changes and assess their impact on St. Anywhere. It was at one of these seminars that she was first introduced to the concept of a Medical Staff/Hospital network, organized to offer potential buyers an integrated package of services and utilization controls.

The current proposal from AHC puts St. Anywhere in a difficult position. Management has already implemented a number of cost-saving measures, and there is not much "fat" in the budget. Nonetheless, costs at St. Anywhere run 10 percent to 15 percent higher than at Community Hospital.

The primary reason for St. Anywhere's higher costs lies in utilization. The hospital's length of stay has remained higher than at either Community or University Hospital. Ms. Facilitator suspects that the longer length of stay is accompanied by overutilization of ancillary services, but she has been unable to collect data to confirm her suspicions.

She recognizes the difficulties in getting St. Anywhere's traditional, conservative medical staff to accept the idea of such a network, but she believes that the AHC proposal and the projections of its impact on the hospital may be enough to at least generate serious consideration of the idea.

The real justification for creating a MeSH organization, in her opinion, is to establish a vehicle for effective control of utilization in a fixed-price or flat-fee environment. Attempts by administration to impose such controls are bound to fail because of the medical judgment required to evaluate the appropriateness of practice patterns. Ms. Facilitator sees the MeSH as an opportunity to develop physician awareness and acceptance of the critical need for monitoring and control of utilization.

AFFORDABLE HEALTH CARE

Mr. Arbit is the negotiator for Affordable Health Care. The four employers have compiled the following data on their health care benefit payments for the last year:

	Inpatient	*Outpatient*	*Total*
Payments to hospitals			
St. Anywhere	$ 6,165,000	$415,000	$ 6,580,000
University	3,284,000	221,000	3,505,000
Community	3,408,000	228,000	3,636,000
Total hospitals	$12,857,000	$864,000	13,721,000
Payments to physicians			
Family practice			1,781,000
Obstetricians			1,397,000
Surgeons and specialists			1,862,000
Total physicians			5,040,000
Total			$18,761,000

The goal of each of the AHC employers is to achieve a 20 percent reduction in total health care expenses. They believe it will be impossible to secure significant savings on physician fees because of the difficulties in contracting with large numbers of physicians. So, to meet their objectives, they will need to achieve approximately a 30 percent discount from the hospital selected to serve all of the AHC-covered employees.

There are three hospitals in Mr. Arbit's negotiating area, and all three are interested in bidding for his contract. Historically, AHC has paid charges for its patients and thus its continued business is considered to be very valuable by all three hospitals. AHC has in fact made the difference between a profit and loss picture at at least two of the hospitals, St. Anywhere and University Hospital. Mr. Arbit knows the following about all three hospitals:

1. St. Anywhere is a suburban hospital with a good quality medical staff. There have historically been problems with length of stay as its physicians have resisted efforts by the local Peer Review Organization (PRO) to control utilization. Nevertheless, its length of stay is within a normal range, although it is higher than at either of the other two hospitals.

2. St. Anywhere offers the complete range of services except for burns and neonatal. If Mr. Arbit contracts with St. Anywhere as AHC's primary hospital, he would have to contract with University Hospital for at least those services that St. Anywhere does not provide. The same is true if he contracts with Community Hospital as it does not provide obstetric, burn, pediatric, or neonatal care, or cardiovascular surgery. St. Anywhere operates at about 75 percent of capacity and has 250 licensed beds.

3. University Hospital has 350 licensed beds and has operated at about 65 percent capacity. AHC's patients amount to only about 5 percent of its volume, as they historically have not liked University Hospital's impersonal setting. Nevertheless, the quality of care by its teaching staff is excellent. This teaching staff is organized into an IPA-type organization that has announced that it will accept AHC's proposed physician fee schedule. By contracting with University Hospital, Mr. Arbit could completely fill the capacity needs for AHC's patients. However, University Hospital's costs have traditionally run quite high, about 10 to 15 percent higher than at either Community or St. Anywhere.

4. Mr. Arbit has announced that he wishes the hospitals to submit all-inclusive per-diem bids for hospital services. University Hospital has submitted a hospital bid of $598 per day. According to his data, this appears to be approximately equal to University Hospital's medicare costs at a per-diem rate.

5. Community Hospital has 150 licensed beds. It is a highly desirable hospital, since it is located in the suburban area in which many of AHC's patients reside. However, it has been running near maximum capacity, around 85 percent, and additional patients would impose severe strains. The hospital has applied for a CON for bed expansion; however, at the earliest this would permit additional beds about twelve months in the future. Community's medical staff is not organized, but responses from a majority of them indicate an interest in accepting AHC's proposed physician fee schedule. Its all-inclusive per-diem bid for the contract is $499, a price that is about 25 percent below its charge levels.

CONCLUSION

The foregoing case study and accompanying tables and charts indicate the complexity of the problem without providing a clear-cut solution for St. Anywhere's administrators and physicians. It seems that there is little financial advantage to refusing the PPO, given the population, unemployment, and economic factors of the community. On the other hand, it is not certain that the PPO will provide an acceptable level of net revenue.

The purchaser, AHC, probably would prefer to sign a contract with St. Anywhere rather than Community or University Hospital, but to what degree? Is it worth another $25 a day to their clients? Is it worth another $100 a day? Perhaps Mr. Arbit, AHC's negotiator, will opt to sign two contracts; one with Community and one with University. This would result in full coverage for the PPO subscriber, and therefore AHC does not need St. Anywhere. The other possibility is that Mr. Arbit could opt to award the PPO contract to St. Anywhere, and contract with University Hospital for only those special services St. Anywhere cannot provide.

If St. Anywhere does not get this contract, it will lose all 1,500 PPO patients that it presently serves. This would be a loss of $8.4 million in revenues. Also, physicians who practice at St. Anywhere are going to have to make some decisions of their own, depending on how many of their PPO patients will move to Community or University Hospital. Physicians can elect to simply lose their market share, although if that amounts to as much as 25 percent of their patients, it will affect their practices considerably. Doctors can elect to practice at both hospitals, with 25 percent of their patients subscribers to the PPO at one hospital and 75 percent private admissions to the other hospital. This requires making rounds at two hospitals and it creates new problems of paperwork and administration. Or physicians could elect to move to the PPO hospital and keep 100 percent of their patients.

Other factors besides provider finances have to be considered in a plan as far-reaching in its consequences as a PPO will be for this hospital and its service area. But it is clear from the scenario that the hospital must consider the financial impact before submitting a bid, or it will be courting financial disaster.

The financial advantages to a hospital in pursuit of a PPO contract will be decided by how effective it is in the negotiating process. MeSH provides another avenue St. Anywhere and its physicians can actively pursue in seeking a satisfactory solution to the problem. The discount can make all the difference. The figures can give an indication of the high and low limits the hospital should consider, and indeed, they should be a primary consideration.

If St. Anywhere loses the AHC contract, it will potentially lose more patients. If its physicians move to another hospital, they may move their practices with them. Since most physicians do not want to practice at two hospitals, the hospital that has the contract is the hospital that will be most attractive to the physicians.

PPOs also have major impacts on the general operations and financial viability of participants. Evaluating and developing PPOs requires the systematic application of expertise in strategic planning, operations management, finance, marketing, and law. Successful PPOs must be effectively planned, developed, and implemented.

There is potential for tremendous conflict about PPOs between hospitals and physicians, and it seems clear that they are going to have to learn to resolve it together. In purely short-term considerations, it might seem that there are more advantages for physicians to be independent, but over the long-term their financial survival as well as the hospital's is going to depend on everyone working together. While the particulars of MeSH may not be the best possible answer for everyone in this scenario, cooperation is going to be absolutely crucial in reaching a solution that everyone can live with.

NOTES

1. MeSH is a model for a joint venture arrangement between a hospital and its medical staff designed by Paul M. Ellwood, M.D., and InterStudy, Excelsior, Minnesota.

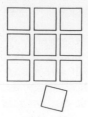

Planning and Design Features

FACTORS AFFECTING DRG PROFITABILITY

Stanley Mendenhall

*Commission on Professional and Hospital Activities
(CPHA)
Ann Arbor, MI*

In negotiating a preferred provider contract, the need for reliable and comprehensive information for determining payment schedules is critical. Many preferred provider organizations are considering following medicare's lead by basing hospital payment on 468 mutually exclusive case types known as diagnosis related groups (DRGs).

Medicare's DRG-based prospective payment system is an attempt by the federal government to deal with rising health care costs by providing greater incentives for efficient hospital management. Under the prospective payment system mandated in the Tax Equity and Fiscal Responsibility Act of 1982 (TEFRA), payment is no longer based on what a patient costs the hospital, but instead is based on the "products" the hospital produces.

Products provided by the hospital have been defined as 468 DRGs classified in 23 major diagnostic categories. Assignment to a particular DRG is based on principal and secondary diagnoses (including comorbidities and complications), principal and secondary surgical procedures, age, and discharge disposition. (A comorbidity is a patient's condition in addition to the basic cause for hospitalization at the time of admission. A complication is an additional condition that develops during the patient's stay at the hospital.)

In some cases, only one diagnosis factor is necessary to make the assignment; a bloody nose assigns a patient to DRG 66 (Epistaxis). However, other DRGs may contain a wide variety of diagnoses and/or surgical procedures. For example, DRG 229 (Hand Operation, except for Ganglion) has 1,574 diagnoses and 100 surgical procedures that can result in its assignment. Other DRGs are assigned based on secondary procedures and other factors; a coronary bypass performed as the principal surgical procedure is DRG 107; if a catheter is inserted as a secondary procedure, it's DRG 106. A victim of acute myocardial infarction is assigned to DRG 122 if the patient leaves the hospital alive, but DRG 121 if the patient expires.

In order to calculate hospital reimbursement for each DRG, a blend of a hospital-specific rate and a regional rate is multiplied by the Health Care Financing Authority (HCFA) weight for the DRG. For example, the weight of DRG 39 (Lens Operation) is 0.5010; this multiplied by a blended rate of $3,000 yields a reimbursement for the DRG of $1,503. If the hospital spends less than $1,503 to treat the patient, it retains the profit; if it spends more, the hospital remains at risk for the difference.

Over the long-term, medicare envisions phasing out of the "blended rates" so that hospitals from Maine to California will receive the same payment for any DRG.

Some advantages of using DRGs to negotiate a preferred provider contract are:

— DRGs provide a comprehensive rating structure for all inpatient services.
— Thorough testing went into setting up the grouping system.
— A large part of the hospital community understands DRGs and has taken steps to manage its institutions based on DRGs.

Disadvantages are that the system is relatively new and requires further refinement, and DRG payments are for inpatient services only. In addition, study is needed on questions of potential weaknesses or possibilities for abuse. These include:

— *Gaming:* Is there temptation to "play games" with diagnoses and procedure assignment to maximize reimbursement?
— *Physician Practice:* Do the DRGs, in fact, provide incentives to practice medicine more efficiently?
— *Patient Condition:* Do DRGs adequately account for patients who are more severely ill?
— *Weights:* Was the use of billing data to develop the DRG weights appropriate, given their known deficiencies and possible inaccuracies in the new context?

The last issue was addressed in research conducted by the Commission on Professional and Hospital Activities (CPHA) early in 1983, after the initial introduction of DRGs. CPHA investigated the differences in DRG reimbursement based on medicare billing data as compared to reimbursement based on the use of a hospital's medical record data. CPHA found that 80 percent of the hospitals would have higher reimbursement from medical record data as opposed to the billing data submitted to HCFA in 1980 and 1981.

The accuracy of medical record data versus billing data has been fairly well established. Medical record data have historically contained more complete information on secondary diagnoses and operative procedures, since the main users of the data were the clinicians of a hospital. There were never strong incentives for billing departments to have as accurate data as medical records since the physicians seldom, if ever, saw the bills. The important fact is that Medicare set the DRG payment rates from the billing data in its base. The resulting issue of concern becomes whether the known deficiencies of Medicare's database have created artificial "winners" and "losers" among the DRGs.

Further CPHA studies indicated potential weaknesses in the DRGs themselves. That is, there appear to be some deterrents to practicing medicine more efficiently.

The research focused on variations in profitability. "True" profitability is typically defined as the difference between medicare reimbursement and the hospital's cost of covered services; in this study, the profitability was estimated by examining the differences between hospital charges and medicare reimbursement. This is more accurately described as contractual allowance or discount. The assumption here is that the larger the contractual allowance, the less profitable the case; the smaller the contractual allowances, the more profitable the case. The most profitable cases will have negative contractual allowances; that is, medicare reimbursement *exceeds* hospital charges.

The research used over 350 hospitals' data from October 1983 through June 1984. Over 580,000 medicare cases are represented in this study. Three types of problems were encountered, and specific DRGs were identified as more or less profitable for the nine hospitals studied. These three problems are

1. Comorbidity adjustments.
2. "Garbage can DRGs."
3. DRGs that pay more for doing less.

COMORBIDITY ADJUSTMENTS

The first category in which profitability was affected was the complex case, one involving comorbidities or complications. In 208 DRGs (104 pairs) the presence or absence of comorbidities or complications determines DRG assignment. There are 2,800 diagnoses that are considered comorbid or complicated.

For example, DRG 84 is a noncomorbid DRG with a principal diagnosis of open fracture of three ribs and approximate reimbursement of $2,321. DRG 83, an open fracture of three ribs with a fracture of the sternum, is comorbid and carries a reimbursement of $2,943.

One major problem in the treatment of comorbidities and complications was that no adjustment was made for the impact of multiple comorbidities and complications. Thus, a patient who has kidney failure, a postoperative infection, and diabetes (all as secondary diagnoses) is classified as no different than a patient who simply has a secondary diagnosis of diabetes.

Increased reimbursement would be expected for comorbidities and complications, but as Exhibit 1 indicates, the extra reimbursement allowed ranges widely, from an increase of over $1,200 to actually less reimbursement in three pairs of DRGs when comorbidities or complications are present. The overall average reimbursement for a comorbidity is about $362 per case. This raises significant questions as to whether this is adequate, especially in the case of multiple comorbidities.

EXHIBIT 1
Differences in Reimbursement for Comorbid versus Noncomorbid DRGs

Reimbursement Differences between Comorbid/Noncomorbid DRG Pairs	Number of DRG Pairs	Percent of Cases in CPHA Sample
$ 1,200+	4	1.1
1,000–1,199	9	8.7
800– 999	4	2.2
600– 799	9	3.2
400– 599	18	12.4
200– 399	34	45.2
0– 199	23	24.9
(0) (199)	3	2.2
	104	99.9%

Total Cases = 8,976

When looking at the overall profitability of comorbid DRGs, 2 comorbid/complicated DRGs were more profitable than their noncomorbid/complicated counterparts, but in 102 DRGs the reverse was true. (See Exhibit 2.)

Outliers are the cases that are extremely expensive to hospitals, either because they are long-term (day outliers) or highly resource intensive for a shorter term (cost outliers). Exhibit 2 also shows that comorbid/complicated DRGs produce more cases in both categories. The conclusion is that complicated/comorbid DRGs are less profitable, have more outliers, and are greater business risks for the institution providing care.

EXHIBIT 2
Comparison of Profitability of Comorbid/Complicated versus Noncomorbid DRG Pairs

	Number of Cases	Number of DRGs	Number of DRGs Where Profitability Was Greater	Percent Day Outliers	Percent Cost Outliers
Comorbid/ complicated DRGs	239,836	104	2	2.9%	1.7%
Noncomorbid/ complicated DRGs	40,477	104	102	0.9%	0.3%
	280,313	208			
Total cases in sample	583,908				

"GARBAGE CAN" DRGs

In creating the DRGs, medicare had a problem. From over 12,000 diagnoses and 3,000 procedures, they had to come up with a manageable number of categories. Some of the resulting DRGs are precise in terms of which diagnoses and procedures are assigned to them. These are typically conditions that carry a relatively high volume of cases, or those describing very specific situations, e.g., DRG 66, cited earlier, in which a bloody nose is the only condition that would warrant that assignment.

The "leftovers" are assigned to what can be called "garbage can" DRGs. These DRGs contain descriptions that include such terms as *other* (54) DRGs, *except for* (48 DRGs), *major* (22 DRGs), *minor operations* (5 DRGs), and *miscellaneous*. DRGs lumping these low-frequency cases tend to be far less homogeneous. For example, DRG 46 (Other Eye Disorders) contains 844 diagnoses.

The profitability problem with these garbage cans is that they allocate the same reimbursement for conditions that may be associated with wide ranges of costs. For example, DRG 12 (Degenerative Nervous System Disorders) contains Alzheimer's disease, hemiplegia, Parkinson's disease, as well as Kuru which is caused by cannibalism among the natives of New Guinea. Each of these diagnoses would have widely different diagnosis and treatment paths, and thus a hospital treating a disproportionate number of hemiplegias would definitely consume more resources than those treating a less severely ill patient.

An associated difficulty arises when a hospital administrator tries to evaluate staff performance in these DRGs. For example, in the profit margins of physicians who treated DRG 12 in Exhibit 3, note that physician 142 made $2,210 a case, and physician 206 lost an average of $5,288 a case. One might conclude that doctor 206 provides less efficient

EXHIBIT 3
DRG Profitability by Physician

DRG 12: Nervous System Degenerative DX
  Expected LOS 9.4   Trimpoint 29   Medicare Price $3,462
  HCFA Weight 1.1136

					Profitability Analysis		
Phys	Cases	ALOS	Var Exp LOS	Total Reimb Case	Avg Cost/ Case	Est Margin Case	Total Income (Loss)
014	2	40.5	31.1	8,409	14,636	6,137−	12,275−
026	1	25.0	15.6	3,884	8,151	4,267−	4,267−
037	1	2.0	7.4−	3,884	515	3,369	3,369
126	3	10.7	1.3	3,884	2,505	1,379−	4,140
142	3	6.3	3.1−	3,884	1,674	2,210	6,633
206	55	27.0	17.6	5,448	10,736	5,288−	290,878−
224	11	15.9	6.5	4,456	6,779	2,323−	25,548−
310	46	27.4	18.0	5,713	11,073	5,360	246,574−
312	2	9.0	0.4−	3,884	2,199	1,685	3,371

care to patients, when in fact the doctor is treating the more severely ill patients, which included hemiplegias in this case.

DRGs THAT PAY MORE FOR LESS

The third anomaly is the DRG that pays more money for a less complicated hospitalization. Each DRG weight reflects statistical averages of how physicians treated medicare patients in 1981 and how sick their patients were. The CPHA research indicated that these data do not necessarily result in rates that provide incentives to practice medicine more efficiently.

This situation carries ethical implications if a sophisticated but unscrupulous physician learns to use DRGs to work to the institution's advantage. For example, DRG 197 is Cholecystectomy (gallbladder removal), which carries an approximate reimbursement of $4,460. To be assigned to this DRG, a patient must have a principal diagnosis of cholelithiasis (gallstones), pancreatitis, hepatitis, or another hepatobiliary condition. The patient must also have a surgical procedure of cholecystectomy (gallbladder removal). During a cholecystectomy, it is common to do a type of X-ray called a cholangiogram to see if there are gallstones in the common bile duct that connects the gallbladder to the duodenum.

DRG 200 is called Hepatobiliary Diagnostic Operations, Not for Cancer. The diagnoses that assign a patient into this DRG are basically the same as to 197; the procedures that would assign a patient to this DRG are gastroscopy, liver biopsy, pancreas biopsy, laparotomy, and intraoperative cholangiogram—all relatively simple diagnostic procedures; the reimbursement is $7,745. Thus, if the doctor had a patient who would *normally* receive *both* a cholecystectomy as well as a diagnostic intraoperative cholangiogram, the hospital would make an extra $3,285 if the cholangiogram was performed but the gallbladder was left in, since the patient would be assigned to DRG 200 instead of DRG 197.

Another surprising case is one in which *not* doing a simple procedure that seems called for results in greater profitability. DRG 411 is "History of Cancer, *No* Endoscopy" with reimbursement of $2,166; DRG 412 is History of Cancer, *with* Endoscopy, and pays $1,020. Endoscopy is an inexpensive, noninvasive procedure that provides valuable information about current status of the patient, but the hospital would lose $1,146 by performing it for a patient admitted with history of cancer.

Finally, there are three pairs of DRGs shown below in which a comorbidity actually results in a lower level of reimbursement. A comorbidity would normally be expected to consume more resources and therefore the reimbursement would be greater; however as can be seen in Exhibit 4, up to $158 per case can be lost for a complicated/comorbid case.

EXHIBIT 4
Three DRGs Where Comorbidities Are Reimbursed
Less than Noncomorbid DRGs

	HCFA Weight	Appropriate Reimbursement
168 Mouth OP w/cc (comorbidity/complications)	.8631	$2,589
169 Mouth OP w/o cc	.8992	2,698
Difference		(109)
403 Lymphoma, Leukemia w/cc	1.1715	$3,515
404 Lymphoma, Leukemia w/o cc	1.1787	3,536
Difference		(21)
452 Complications of Treatment w/cc	.8492	$2,548
453 Complications of Treatment w/o cc	.9020	2,706
Difference		(158)

HOW DID IT HAPPEN?

The immediate questions here are how were these rates developed and how will these "incentives" affect the practice of medicine.

In order to understand where the rates came from, the quality of the data used to set the rates must be reviewed. Much of the 1980 and 1981 billing data submitted to medicare by fiscal intermediaries did not contain complete diagnostic information; much of it did not have the discipline in coding normally associated with medical record professionals.

HCFAs response is that the rates and the DRG methodology itself will be under review over the next couple of years and refinements will take place. In the meantime, however, there may be certain classes or types of DRGs that are more consistently profitable than others. CPHA research with hospital Profit and Loss Statements by DRG are summarized in Exhibits 5 and 6.

From the list of the most profitable DRGs, it is interesting that three out of the top four DRGs are for cardiac procedures. The most profitable DRG is DRG 108—Other Cardiac Operation except Coronary Bypass

EXHIBIT 5
Ten Most Profitable DRGs

			Cases	HCFA Weight*
108	SUR	Other Cardiac Operation, Pump	1,039	4.3756
431	MED	Childhood Mental Diagnoses	39	2.2519
125	MED	Other Circulatory Diagnoses, Catheter	4,595	1.6455
124	MED	Major Circulatory Diagnoses, Catheter, except AMI	2,575	2.2200
171	SUR	Other Gastrointestinal Operation	73	2.3976
155	SUR	Upper GI Op A −	549	2.3336
86	MED	Pleural Effusion PA −	38	1.1217
407	SUR	Myeloproliferative Diagnoses, Major OR Operation −	139	2.1366
347	MED	Cancer, Male, PA −	133	0.8304
349	MED	BPH, PA −	205	0.6998

*Weights in Federal Register, September 1, 1983, for DRG reimbursement.

EXHIBIT 6
Ten Least Profitable DRGs

			Cases	HCFA Weight*
302	SUR	Kidney Transplant	172	4.2279
104	SUR	Cardiac Valve OP, Pump, Catheter	426	6.8527
457	MED	Burns, Extensive	13	6.8631
109	SUR	Other Cardiac Operation, No Pump	271	3.6963
4	SUR	Spinal Operation	222	2.2452
105	SUR	Cardiac Valve OP, Pump	450	5.2308
106	SUR	Coronary Bypass, Catheter	2,027	5.2624
2	SUR	Craniotomy, Trauma, AG	290	3.2829
456	MED	Burn, Transfer to Other Hospital	15	2.0902
191	SUR	Major Pancreas, Hepatobiliary Shunt Operation	276	4.1791

*Weights in Federal Register, September 1, 1983, for DRG reimbursement.

with pump. This DRG includes the surgical procedures for PCTA, percutaneous transluminal angioplasty. The procedure involves the insertion of a balloon-like instrument into a vein or artery; when the instrument is inflated, it removes obstruction. This relatively simple procedure has been grouped into the same DRG as correction of congenital heart defects with open heart surgery. The former procedure, through new technology, has made this particular DRG very lucrative from the hospitals' point of view since it is much simpler than open heart surgery.

What is significant is that, when the DRG rates were developed in 1980 and 1981, this procedure was extremely rare. CPHA statistics show that this procedure was performed 2,000 times in the United States during 1980 and 1981, 15,000 times in 1982, and 32,000 times in 1983. Thus, the data that medicare used to set the DRG rates with in 1980 and 1981 showed relatively few incidences of PCTA, which would tend to inflate the rates.

The same generalization would apply to cardiac catheterization, which again has become more widespread in the last several years.

PROFITABILITY FACTORS

There are many factors that could impact the profitability of a hospital operating under a DRG-based payment system. These include physician practice, patient condition, and the inability of hospitals to identify their true costs, as well as weaknesses in the DRG methodology and the DRG rates that were developed.

Based on this study, it appears that hospitals have a greater opportunity to be profitable under Medicare's Prospective Payment System with the following type of DRGs:

— Cardiac catheterizations and percutaneous angioplasties. These procedures are relatively new, and the medicare rates do not reflect the shift to these procedures.
— DRGs that fall into the orthopedic and male reproductive major diagnostic categories.
— Medical cases seem to have a slightly greater profitability than surgical cases.
— Simple, noncomorbid cases. The comorbidities treated in a patient could be quite severe—the extra reimbursement does not adequately cover hospital costs.

Factors which could negatively impact DRGs include:

— Complicated cardiac surgeries.
— Cases assigned to the Major Diagnostic Categories for the Nervous System and Infectious Diseases.
— Complicated/Comorbid DRGs.

To summarize the above, the old truism of "you can't get rich off of sick people" still rings true under DRGs.

CONCLUSION

Hospitals that are under Medicare's Prospective Payment System are probably receiving profitability statements for their DRGs and their physicians. When evaluating physician performance under the Prospective Payment System, financial officers should be sensitive to the discrepancies involved in the DRG rates as well as in the definitions of the DRGs themselves.

For physicians who practice in the potentially "less profitable" specialties, there is valid concern that medicare will not properly recognize the cost of taking care of sick people.

For hospitals considering the implementation of DRG-based payment for PPOs, the potential financial risks (and opportunities) should be known.

Planning and Design Features

CARRIER CONSIDERATIONS FOR PPO PRICING

Brenda P. Roberts, Ed.D.
Executive Director
Cooperative Health Care Plan of New Mexico, Inc.
Albuquerque, NM

☐ A preferred provider product has five major components. They are: a provider network, utilization review system, health benefits package, administration, and marketing. What is typically called a preferred provider organization (PPO) is a legal entity that is developed by the medical community to contract with self-insured employers, insurance companies, third-party administrators, union trusts, and employer coalitions for health care services.

This article discusses the components of preferred provider products and the importance of product definitions and design. Each component can be developed independently and connected through contracting relationships with various types of organizations—or what is called the "loose coupling of components through contractual relationships." Attention is also given to cost control mechanisms and pricing of components.

Understanding what makes up the components of a preferred provider product and elements that affect pricing creates different opportunities for health care providers and purchasers. Providers and vendors can create a cost-effective delivery system for health benefits that maximizes profits. Insurance companies and third-party administrators can effectively maintain or increase market share. Employers as purchasers have an opportunity to tie in with preferred providers who are willing to be price competitive, thereby offering a cost-effective program to their employees.

Some commercial or health insurance carriers have enough market share within a local area or region to develop all components of a preferred provider product. It is common to couple different components together through contracting arrangements with two or more organizations. A contracting arrangement can bring together all the necessary components of a preferred provider product. For example, a PPO typically represents the medical network and utilization components of a preferred provider product, while the insurance carrier provides a health benefits package, administration, and marketing services.

An organization that is developing either some or all components of a preferred provider product should develop a business plan that incorporates clearly defined goals, profit objectives, and health benefit savings levels. The process of developing a business plan begins with first determining what the goal is and how it is related to profits and savings. For an employer, any savings from health benefits contributes directly to bottom line profits. From an insurance standpoint, any cost savings resulting from the claims-paying function contributes to bottom line profits. For a provider, an increase in patient load enhances income and potential efficiencies in business operations.

Creating a preferred provider product for the market is not an easy task. To assure success, a most important ingredient is strong commitment from senior management (including the chief executive officer) to provide the resources necessary in developing the preferred provider product. Resources and commitment are the key to whether the entire product or a component is initiated by an insurance company, a PPO, self-insured employer, employer trust, union trust fund, or business coalition.

PRODUCT DESIGN

Product design takes into consideration both market definitions and product definition. These two factors are interdependent because the product is designed around the needs of purchasers for optimum marketability. The process involves (1) focusing first on the market; (2) determining whether the market is local, regional, or national; (3) identifying the needs of the market; (4) isolating and defining the health services available; and (5) developing product definition around the findings accumulated in steps 1 through 4 of the process.

Each organization's definition and design of the preferred provider product or component will be different because of their unique goals and corporate values. However the basic process for product definition and design is the same. For example, a self-insured employer who is attempting to design a preferred provider product for a 10,000-life group concentrated within a geographic location is quite different from an insurance company that is going to market the product state or nationwide. The goal of the self-insured employer is to minimize health care costs for employees, while the goal of a carrier is to select and underwrite a group whose risk is minimal.

Each component of the product to be developed that will contribute to the goal should then be identified and a plan set out for implementation. Components that need to be defined and identified include insurance risk, management tasks of developing a medical network and its associated costs, elements and cost of a utilization-review process, cost controls with underlying savings assumptions, and marketing strategy with an accompanying budget.

A preferred provider product is only complete when the health services and risk-taking elements are included. Both purchasers and providers have concerns and needs to be met in developing a preferred provider product. Even though the purchaser is the key factor in determining the marketability of the product, the provider remains an essential ingredient by providing cost-effective health services to the marketplace. If the focus is exclusively on providers, the product will be developed isolated from the needs of the marketplace purchasers. Consequently, the viewpoints of both medical profession and risk-taking participants (i.e., insurance company, union trust, and self-insured employer) are addressed for product and market definitions.

For purposes of clarity, definitions of all the components of the preferred provider product will be set out for all participants. Then, different options will be analyzed for using "coupling" arrangements to develop the preferred provider product.

MARKET DEFINITION

The discussion of product design centers on defining a market and a product. In the early stages of the product definition process, it is important to determine to whom the product will be marketed. This is an integral part of designing the benefits package and promoting the preferred provider product. A market analysis enables the product to be built around the needs of clients. The information collected during the analysis makes it easier to identify administrative support needs and to design a program to promote the product. For an insurance company, the market may be employer groups consisting of under 10 lives, 50 to 100, or 500 to over 1,000 lives in larger cases. Marketing and servicing a client with one thousand lives may require representatives going into a company to educate employees. For an insurer that writes under ten life cases, a more appropriate strategy may be to mail information about the preferred provider product directly to the insureds. In either case, there are costs associated with marketing and educating insureds about the program as a prerequisite to enrollment or participation.

For a provider-based organization that plans to market a preferred provider product, the market is most likely the surrounding community. To determine the characteristics of the community, an analysis can be done of the economic environment (e.g., level of unemployment, influence and control of unions, size and financial stability of employers), and the availability of health services within the community and the region. Decisions must, then, be made about whether to market the product to individuals or to groups, through a broker network, or through an insurance company willing to underwrite the health services program of a provider-based organization. Most provider-based organizations find it difficult to provide a total preferred provider product without associating with a trust, insurance company, self-insured employer, or employer coalition because they provide health services and do not typically underwrite the risk. When a PPO develops the health benefits component, the package typically is capitated or an alternate method is pursued, such as creating an insurance company to market the health benefits package.

PRODUCT DEFINITION

Creating a preferred provider product or component begins with a product definition, which can be simple if all that is required is a marketing strategy for health services, but becomes more complex as the product includes additional features such as a provider network and a utilization-review system. Definitions must be set out for each of the preferred provider components. Establishing a basis of understanding is required so that each participant, regardless of level of expertise, has a common reference point.

For the purposes of this article, the following definitions will apply: A preferred provider product includes all elements of the provider network, the health benefits package, a utilization-review program, administrative systems, and marketing strategy. A PPO is an organization that develops a provider network and may or may not provide a full utilization-review menu. The utilization-review process may be a part of the preferred provider organization, or it may be subcontracted through another organization such as a medical foundation or private peer review company. The system for utilization review may contain some or all of the following: preadmission testing, prior authorization of elective surgeries, concurrent review, including setting and tracking length of stay, retrospective review, and data collection and analysis. A benefits package is a range of health care benefits that can be offered to employer groups or individuals and can be underwritten by insurance companies, union trust funds, self-insured employers, third-party administrators, or employer coalitions. Administration systems refers to the provider billing, claims-paying, and data collection capability. Marketing is the promotional program to create public awareness and sell the product as well as the educational program to get insureds to use the preferred providers.

In developing either one or all components of a preferred provider product, a variety of viewpoints are needed to define the product, since it is a complex entity that integrates elements of both the health and insurance businesses. Within an insurance setting, for example, contributions to the product definition will be from contractual, legal, actuarial, underwriting, administration, claims, medical community, and utilization-review personnel. A coordinator is needed to bring together these viewpoints and expertise and incorporate them into the product definition. It is imperative to focus on the expertise and coordinate input from these disciplines in putting together a preferred provider product package. This involves the benefits package, administrative service that supports the standardization and payment of claims, maintenance and recruiting of the provider network, and marketing to the target market.

Consider another example: a hospital-based provider network. Designing a preferred provider product or a component from this perspective should involve each of the following in varying degrees: financial, marketing, legal, billing, surgical, outpatient and inpatient administrative functions, contracted debt collectors, and risk assessment.

There is a need for a team effort from both the health and insurance industries to develop a preferred provider product. Few organizations have the resources or the market share to provide all components. A viable alternative is to dissect the product and form contractual relationships with other entities to create the entire preferred provider product and implement it in the marketplace. For example, once a provider network has contracted with an insurance company, self-insured employer, or business coalition, a subcontracted relationship can be formed with a utilization-review company. These components can be loosely connected through contractual relationships to form a preferred provider product to market in a local area or in a region.

Developing and marketing a preferred provider product should also take into account such additional factors as distinguishing viable rural and urban markets, the competitiveness of the area (e.g., HMO penetration, prepaid/capitation plans), potential volume of patients offered to a provider network, and supply of medical providers.

BENEFITS DESIGN

Two considerations should be emphasized in benefits design: creating incentives or disincentives for the employees to use the program and building the utilization controls to provide cost efficient use of the health system. This section sets out examples of possible additions to a benefits package to encourage an insured to use the preferred provider system.

The discussion also includes approaches to encourage efficient use of the health care system.

Both negative and positive incentives can be used to attract employees to use a preferred provider product. A frequently used positive method is to waive the deductible and reduce the coinsurance provisions or even provide 100 percent coverage. Another tactic is to penalize insureds who do not use the preferred provider system by requiring them to pay a larger portion of the bill (e.g., copayment could be increased to 50 percent).

Benefits design can take a number of directions. In some packages, additional benefits have been added such as well-baby care, pap smears, and physical exams. These are often used as "loss leaders" to get insureds into the system so that they will become familiar with the preferred medical providers and use them subsequently rather than other providers covered by the indemnity option.

Many employers and insurers are restructuring or amending their medical plans. However, changes in benefits design are also being forced by government regulation. An interesting phenomenon that is occurring in the legislative arena is the growing emphasis on employees to control their own health care costs. This legislative trend overlooks the fact that physicians schedule patients for return office visits, admit patients to a hospital, and determine how long a patient should remain within an inpatient setting. In short, the physician is directly responsible for the type of care, length of care, and place in which the patient receives care.

Benefits design should encourage efficient use of the health care system by not rewarding inpatient care when outpatient care may be more appropriate and effective. The insurance industry has often encouraged inpatient care through financial incentives such as full payment for emergency care versus copayment for visits to a physician's office and maintaining the same copayment for a procedure that could be done outpatient rather than inpatient (e.g., dilatation and curettage [D&C], breast biopsy, cataract surgery, renal dialysis, and tubal ligation). As another example, standards have been created to measure the care for alcoholism on an inpatient basis rather than on an outpatient basis. There is a growing body of research that supports the use of outpatient care for alcoholism and suggests a very limited number of days for inpatient care.[1]

Another example of encouraging efficiency through employee incentives is by determining when emergency care treatment is appropriate. Approximately 85 percent of all visits to the emergency room are non-life-threatening. However, it is very risky to eliminate that option, because insureds believe they should have access to medical care when needed. Consequently, building in some financial liability for a visit to the emergency room for a nonemergency condition should provide enough incentive for insureds to consider the matter more carefully. At the same time, the benefits design should provide a negative incentive strong enough to discourage the insured from seeking emergency care unless truly needed.

Risk assumption factors also need to be considered when designing the benefits package. These include medical office service fees for which employees and family members are responsible when using the preferred provider product, savings from coordination of benefits, and preexisting and subrogation investigations. Less traditional features can also be included, such as providing alternatives for home health, hospice, rehabilitation, and wellness care.

COST ISSUES

The focus of the following discussion is on the efficiencies or additional costs associated with administrative functions, cost management activities, and savings issues.

ADMINISTRATIVE FUNCTION

The administrative function of the preferred provider product consists of billing and paying for medical services according to the contractual agreement, and collecting data useful in creating provider and patient profiles for utilization monitoring. The contractual agreement usually requires the provider to bill and be paid directly by the payor of the claim within a stated time period. Interest is paid on accounts not paid within the agreed-upon time period. This arrangement between the provider and the payor typically leaves the patient out of the billing and paying process. This potential efficiency can lead to inefficiency unless the provider agrees to gather adequate information that the payor can use in identifying situations for coordination of benefits, subrogation, and preexisting conditions, and in collecting the data to establish a base for measuring the efficiency of the system. An effective administrative process gathers information on the patient's condition and available insurance coverage through cooperative efforts between the biller and payor. Without adequate planning, a system can be created that is initially more costly rather than more efficient.

PROVIDER NETWORKS

Developing a provider network is a complex undertaking that involves contracting for a wide range of health services that are geographically accessible to a diverse group of insureds.

The medical network is the vehicle by which medical services are marketed on a very selective basis. When an insurance company, employer, or third party administrator contracts with a medical network, the providers' services are linked with a health benefits package and direct-line marketed to a select group of insureds. This is called focus marketing and replaces the marketing of health services through alternative strategies such as billboards or newspaper advertisements. For example, if an insurance carrier has the home addresses of insureds stored and accessible on its computer system, a direct-mail campaign can be designed to furnish information to insureds, thereby serving to "focus in" on the target market.

In marketing a medical network to insureds, it is important both to offer a wide spectrum of medical health services and to ensure their distribution over a broad geographic area. State statutes require that an insurance carrier, an employer, or a trust provide a wide array of health services, including primary care physicians, specialists, hospitals, freestanding laboratories, radiology clinics, allergy clinics, podiatrists, chiropractors, and psychological services. The geographic distribution of providers is important to assure adequate access of the insured to the health care system. Insureds will only elect to use the provider network if they are located within a convenient commuting distance.

CASE MANAGEMENT

Case management is an approach to patient care that includes alternatives to the standard methods of assessing and providing health care. Traditionally, the payor simply received and paid the bill with little understanding or involvement in the health care decision-making process. The utilization-review system of a preferred provider product builds in a means of communication with providers and a method to track appropriate patient care.

As an example of cost-effective case management, discharge planning makes outpatient services available when a patient would otherwise be kept within a hospital setting. In the case of a patient with a cesarian section, who, under normal conditions, would stay within the hospital for four to six days, the patient, the physician, and the discharge planner can agree to another arrangement. The patient can have the option of staying in the hospital for three days, and then being provided with a housekeeper for custodial care for three days thereafter. The cost savings can be substantial, given the difference between the per-diem price of hospital stay (e.g., $900 to $1,100 a day in Los Angeles County) versus the cost of a 24-hour housekeeper (e.g., $70 to $150 a day).

Case management becomes particularly important for a preferred provider product when a health insurance plan lowers the deductibles and/or coinsurance for inpatient care. If the benefits package offered to the insured provides 100 percent hospital benefit, the negotiation of a price with a hospital is imperative. Negotiations can be for a hospital per-diem discount (percent off actual charges) or a diagnostic related grouping (DRG) price. The negotiated price will offset at least a portion of the increased cost of the coinsurance feature that the health benefits package now pays under the provider plan.

Creating a data analysis system to evaluate the hospital and physician by diagnosis and procedure is important in case management because it allows a comparison to other medical service organizations and providers within the area.

COMPARISON OF COST SAVINGS

From a risk-taking position, a cost-savings program should include certain activities such as (1) conducting a review of benefits and their estimated costs, (2) evaluating any "giveaway" benefits against built-in savings features, and (3) establishing measures to evaluate the success of the preferred provider product. A "giveaway" can be construed as an added benefit that is typically not offered in the standard indemnity package or has been offered at another financial level, e.g., raising the inpatient benefit from an 80/20 level to a 90/10 coinsurance with no change in product price. Adding benefits makes it much more difficult to compare the preferred provider package with a standard indemnity product because there is no longer a reference point for comparison.

Using financial incentives in a health benefits package such as waiving deductibles and reducing coinsurance payments to encourage insureds to use preferred providers introduces additional costs. For most preferred provider products, in place of a deductible, the insured is required to pay a service amount per office visit, which typically ranges from $3 to $10. An insured usually does not pay as much with this arrangement as when a deductible has to be met. Secondly, any coinsurance for both the preferred provider and standard indemnity product is only applicable to a certain dollar figure, such as the first $2,500 to $3,000 worth of medical expenses. So, on a standard health benefits package that has an 80/20 coinsurance provision, and a $100 deductible feature with a $3,000 maximum, the total calendar year out-of-pocket cost for an insured would be $700. Under a 90/10 preferred provider plan, that out-of-pocket cost might be reduced to $350. Again, this reduction must be offset by other cost savings features built into the preferred provider product.

To conduct a comparison of a standard health benefits package and a preferred provider product, a number of factors should be included, such as the average number of doctor visits per family per person per year (e.g., 5.0 in 1980; 4.2 in 1981), average number of family members, ratio of females to males per case mix (females have a higher rate of hospitalization and office visits), type and size of group, and level of negotiated fees compared to a standard (the Health Insurance Association of America has a data base for some of this information). After evaluating the potential cost of giveaways and waiving or reducing coinsurance and deductibles, they must be balanced against expected savings by

EXHIBIT 1
Range of Cost-Control Savings

Cost-Control Mechanisms	Savings as a Percent of Paid Claims
Preadmission testing	1–5%
Prior authorization of elective surgery	3–7%
Concurrent review including setting and tracking length of stay	8–15%
Outpatient surgery in lieu of hospitalization	2–7%
Retrospective audit	3–8%
Negotiated fees (physician, ancillary services, hospital)*	5–20%

*In spending a health care dollar, $.20 to $.25 is paid to the physician, $.07 to $.15 is paid to ancillary services, while $.55 to $.70 is paid out for hospital services.

targeting a potential savings goal for each cost-reduction activity. The ranges in Exhibit 1 are based on various data bases. An array of the cost-control programs and range of savings are as shown above.

There is currently insufficient data to substantiate potential savings for specific cost-control programs because the concepts are relatively new. Accumulating baseline data, however, is fundamental to measuring the savings after implementing utilization review and cost-control programs. Few carriers have accumulated such data, although large self-insured employers, business coalitions, and union trusts often have collected the information.

PRICING

The following exhibit (Exhibit 2) outlines an example of a preferred provider product with all components. The hypothetical price ranges that are set out as a percent of premium do not take into consideration dollars spent for development efforts. The underlying assumption is that the entire product is developed and is available for market. The range of pre-

EXHIBIT 2
Price Range of Preferred Provider
Product Components

Component	Price as Percent of Premium
Provider network	2–3%
Utilization-review system	1–1½%
Health benefits package	75–85%
Administrative support	5–7%
Marketing	6–7%
Profit margins	2–8%

mium percentages does not differentiate by employee group sizes (referred to hereinafter as a "case"), which is an important factor in targeting price. For example, very large cases are considered labor intensive and administrative costs are high. Small cases can be handled primarily by clerical and computer support so that administrative costs account for substantially less of the premium dollar. The profit margins on large cases may be only 2 percent of premium, but the premiums are much greater in terms of dollars than a small case. Consequently, adding the percents vertically in Exhibit 2 is not relevant.

The initiating or sponsoring organization must evaluate each component for such factors as case size, type, and level of administrative support; potential amount paid out in claims for health benefits; and targeting savings for cost-control programs. Clearly, profit margins are most dependent on the design of the health benefits package as represented by the high percentage reflected in Exhibit 2. After the relevant factors are evaluated, a pricing strategy can be established.

CONCLUSION

The preferred provider product encourages greater cooperation and understanding between the health and insurance industries. Because of the widespread emphasis on the collection of baseline data for competitive pricing, health care providers are being pressured by both the private and public sector to take a more active role in creating a cost-effective health care system. The health care providers are not only seeing a need to market their services, but are also seeking to take a more active role with insurers in product design and cost-control programs.

Regardless of its sponsor, a preferred provider product is generally made up of the same components. For the product to be successful, it must combine features that represent all interested parties. The risk of providing health benefits and the cost of such programs, must be offset by effective cost-control measures. Sharing responsibility for risk, cost, and medical care by employers, insurers and providers represents the emergence of an alternative health care system acceptable to all.

NOTES

1. *See* Mark Worden, "The Outpatient Alternative," *Alcoholism* July–August 1982, pp. 59–60.

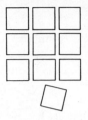

Planning and Design Features

MANAGED HEALTH CARE SYSTEMS AND MEDICAID REFORM

Dennis F. Beatrice

Associate Director
Health Policy Center
Florence Heller Graduate School
Brandeis University
Waltham, MA

Rapid and far-reaching change has become the dominant reality of the health care system in the United States. The system is in a state of flux, marked by challenge and opportunity. The changes that have occurred as a result of these developments go beyond normal adaptation and evolution; they affect the fabric of the health care system as it has existed for 20 years. New forces are at work in a markedly different environment in the health care system:

- The Medicare Hospital Insurance Trust Fund faces depletion by 1989 and the prospect of a $300 billion imbalance by the 1990s.
- Health care costs continue by a wide margin to be the fastest growing component of the Consumer Price Index.
- Medicare has adopted a new prospective payment system, based

on diagnosis-related groups (DRGs), to replace cost reimbursement.

— The increased availability and use of dramatic medical technologies is posing complex ethical, resource allocation, and cost issues to the medical community and payors.

— Care of the publicly financed and uninsured populations has become a major topic of public debate. Financial pressures by payors and providers have made this discussion sharper than at any time since the passage of medicare and medicaid.

— The private sector is becoming increasingly alarmed by rising health care costs and involved in cost-control activities.

— Alternative models of service delivery, such as HMOs and preferred provider organizations (PPOs), are rapidly emerging across the health care system.

— The growth of proprietary hospital, nursing home, and home health providers has been extraordinary. This trend is bringing integration to the health care system, as large firms become providers of many different services.

An additional issue is that states have become principal innovators in health care organization, financing, and delivery. There are two reasons for this development. First, there has been enormous and growing pressure to control medicaid spending. States are finding medicaid programs to be the key items impeding the balancing of their budgets, intensifying pressures for tax increases, and jeopardizing their ability to meet other human service needs. States have tried all manner of initiatives in their medicaid programs to at least slow medicaid budget growth. But these efforts at cost control have not dealt adequately with state budget needs. Medicaid spending is outrunning the capacity of states to continue to fund the program.

A second factor leading to the emergence of states as key decision-makers in health policy is that federal policy has encouraged innovation and flexibility on the part of states. Also, federal policy has sought to devolve authority and decision making to the states. Current federal health care policy is not predicated on national, intervention-oriented solutions. The Omnibus Reconciliation Act of 1981 (OBRA) and The Tax Equity and Financial Responsibility Act of 1972 (TEFRA) show the direction of federal health care policy. That policy is geared toward greater state flexibility and an enlarged state role. Federal funding reductions have also placed states in the difficult position of trying to manage their programs with fewer federal resources while meeting increased needs, growing demand, and increasing costs. The responsibility for medicaid reform has shifted from federal to state officials.

States find themselves increasingly caught between two forces. On the one hand, the desire of the federal government to contain its costs has reduced the flow of funds to the states. This has limited state financial capacity. These changes were designed to limit federal financial exposure while providing the states with the increased flexibility to "do more with less." At the same time, local governments and client advocates are seeking state funds to replace lost federal revenues that had been used to provide local aid and maintain services.

In order to meet their increasing health care responsibilities, states must respond to these conflicting pressures. Creative financing and delivery system solutions will be necessary. Tinkering at the margins of the existing system will not suffice as a response. States must act as prudent and creative purchasers of service rather than passive cashiers if they are to provide adequately for the poor while living within fiscal constraints.

This paper will address eight issues. First, medicaid spending and growth rates are discussed. This spending and growth are putting states in a position where they must control costs. Second, the sources of these medicaid cost pressures are reviewed. Third, the range of potential medicaid cost control options are outlined. Fourth, the development of managed health care in Massachusetts is discussed. Massachusetts is chosen because it was one of the first states to experiment with managed health care, and it has a particularly diverse and active managed health care system in its Medicaid program. Fifth, the models of managed care used in the Massachusetts Medicaid program are described. Sixth, the results of these managed health care initiatives in Massachusetts are outlined. Seventh, the reasons why managed health care constitutes an important state initiative are addressed. Finally, the discussion is broadened, and the development and planning issues that must be addressed in both state managed health care and private sector PPO initiatives are presented.

MAGNITUDE OF MEDICAID SPENDING AND GROWTH RATES

There is a broad and growing awareness that medicaid costs must be controlled and the program restructured if it is to continue to provide quality, accessible service to the eligible population. By 1981, total medicaid expenditures were $30 billion, more than 80 times the expenditures in the first year. By 1992, the medicaid program is expected to grow to approximately $44 billion in federal costs alone, an increase of 132 percent over the 1983 costs of $19 billion.[1] In recent years, state cost-control initiatives have brought national average medicaid cost increases below 10 percent annually. This represents a significant accomplishment and reflects a decrease from the 14 to 17 percent average annual increases experienced in prior years. However, it is not sufficient. State medicaid spending between 1981 and 1983 increased by 22.3 percent while state revenues increased by only 14.2 percent.[2]

Fiscal pressures faced by state medicaid programs and federal policy changes have accelerated the emergence of states as the main laboratories for health care innovation. States are seeking new approaches to cope with the new austerity. They are becoming more creative in their responses, not relying solely on benefit and eligibility cuts. The manner in which states, particularly state medicaid programs, define and implement managed care concepts related to preferred provider arrangements will be an important factor in the growth and shape of these alternative models throughout the health care system.

SOURCES OF MEDICAID COST PRESSURES

A number of factors create medicaid spending pressures in states. These factors make it especially urgent to develop new, more efficient methods of providing care. Some of these factors that fuel cost increases are discussed in the following paragraphs.

STATE AND FEDERAL REVENUE LIMITATIONS

Many states face serious revenue problems, flowing from tax limitation legislation (e.g., Proposition 13 in California and Proposition 2½ in Massachusetts) or high rates of unemployment. Federal revenue for medicaid has also been reduced. The federal budget deficit and federal policy that emphasizes flexibility to states make it unlikely that a major inflow of federal funds into medicaid will be forthcoming. State medicaid programs are so large that it is difficult for a state to meet the inflation increase portion of the budget each year, let alone deal with new needs and emerging costs. This situation becomes even more acute when reduced state and federal revenues are taken into account.

MEDICAL TECHNOLOGY

Funding new medical technology is becoming an issue of increasing concern to policymakers in both the public and private sectors. As new medical procedures move from the realm of the experimental and become routine, the pressure for public and private insurers to pay for these expensive procedures becomes intense. If these new technology procedures are not applied appropriately and efficiently, they will present an insurmountable obstacle to the provision of a broad service package to the medicaid eligible population. Left unchecked, funds will have to be shifted from routine and preventive toward high-intensity services. There will be no other way to meet escalating costs of high technology medicine. All payors must work to see that new technology is appropriately utilized and not excessively duplicated.

CAPITAL CONSTRUCTION

In light of the other upward cost pressures embedded in the health system, capital construction must be controlled. A balance must be struck among several conflicting goals and needs. Facilities must be kept viable and patient access protected, while costs are kept within reasonable limits. If enormous increases in operating costs due to capital construction occur, funds will not be available to maintain present benefits and meet new needs. Moving funds from operating to capital expenses reduces flexibility to adapt to changing circumstances.

HEALTH CARE INFLATION

The inflation rate in the health care industry is the highest of any sector of the economy. Last year, health care costs outran the general inflation rate by almost 300 percent. These cost pressures are felt acutely in medicaid, since they contribute to the medicaid program inflation rate that absorbs funds that might otherwise be available for benefit or eligibility increases.

MEDICARE PROGRAM CHANGES

Changes in the federal medicare program may have a substantial effect on medicaid program costs. For example, if medicare copayments and deductibles are increased, medicaid costs will rise, because medicaid will pay these increased rates for dual entitlees (those with both medicare and medicaid coverage). As the federal government takes steps to avoid crisis in the medicare program, increased cost pressures are likely to fall on state medicaid programs as a result of spill-over effects from medicare changes.

STATUS AS "PAYOR OF LAST RESORT"

Medicaid is required by statute to function as the payor of last resort. Those with no coverage or poor coverage, those who have exhausted other benefits, and those who seek treatments or procedures not reimbursed by other insurers turn to medicaid. As other payors become cost conscious, this pressure on medicaid to step in when others refuse to pay will increase because the status of medicaid as a "welfare" program will leave it as the last hope of those unable to obtain coverage or service through other means.

FEDERAL FUNDING REDUCTIONS IN MEDICAID

Federal matching payments fell three percent in fiscal year 1982, four percent in fiscal year 1983, and are scheduled to be reduced four and one half percent in 1984. There is a perception among state administrators that these reductions will be continued into the future in one guise or another and that Congress has prevented more serious reduction by the Reagan Administration. Eligibility reductions alluded to earlier have fallen disproportionately on women and children in the Aid to Families with Dependent Children (AFDC) program. These federal policies dramatically increase the fiscal pressure on medicaid programs.

GROWING ELDERLY POPULATION

The growth in the elderly population presents the largest likely area of growth in medicaid programs. Medicaid currently provides the only catastrophic insurance coverage for middle-income people who would become impoverished trying to pay nursing home bills without help. It is medicaid, not medicare, that provides full nursing home coverage nationwide. Thirty-seven percent of all medicaid program funds are expended on nursing home services for the elderly, and in many states, this percentage is more than 50 percent.[3] This spending will increase in the face of demographic trends in the elderly population. For example, in Massachusetts, the elderly population and the medicaid resources expended on their behalf are growing rapidly. Between 1970 and 1980, the over-75 population in Massachusetts increased 19 percent and the over-25 population increased 43 percent. The elderly in Massachusetts (12.7 percent of the population), accounted for 35 percent of the state's total health care costs, 60 percent of the medicaid budget, 50 percent of the inpatient hospital spending, and 65 percent of the inpatient hospital days.[4] Demographic and spending trends of this sort are the norm rather than the exception for states.

The inescapable fact is that the highest cost population is also the fastest growing segment of the population. The demographics of the elderly population constitutes a time-bomb for the medicaid program that requires attention in the form of program restructuring and new initiatives. Business as usual is impossible in the face of costs that will be presented by the burgeoning elderly population.

POLITICAL VULNERABILITY AND ACCESSIBILITY

Those who seek to expand program benefits, replace lost federal health care revenue, or maintain current services for an expanding (and aging) population look to medicaid. Medicaid programs are very much subject to lobbying by interest groups. It is easier to identify state decision makers and bring pressure to bear on medicaid programs than it is to pressure private insurers or the federal government. Even individuals bring pressure to bear on medicaid to fund experimental but potentially life-saving techniques that no other insurer will cover. Medicaid programs are thus caught between a desire in the abstract to control costs and pressure to respond to the service needs of particular populations and even individuals.

MEDICAID COST CONTROL OPTIONS

Once the premise is accepted that medicaid costs must be controlled, only a limited number of approaches are available.

First, a strong regulatory approach is possible. Such an approach would mandate government controls on health facilities and service costs. There is and will continue to be an appropriate role for regulation. But regulation alone will not provide an answer. It must be mixed with structural and competitive approaches.

An alternative cost-control mechanism would reduce benefit levels and restrict eligibility. This approach would provide fewer services to fewer people. The difficulty with this method is that it makes recipients the payors in cost-control efforts. Several rounds of federal eligibility policy changes and state administrative actions have already reduced the medicaid caseload. Nationwide, the total number of children and adults enrolled in the AFDC program, and thus eligible for medicaid, dropped about 20 percent from 1976 to 1979.[5] Caseload reductions under the Omnibus Reconciliation Act of 1981 (OBRA) have further reduced these numbers. These caseload reductions suggest that recipients have already borne their share of the cost-control burden.

A third savings strategy would reduce reimbursement to providers. This approach is straightforward. However, it must be very carefully applied to avoid arbitrary impact. In addition, this policy could seriously affect the availability of services to medicaid recipients.

These approaches all have limited utility and do not reform the present fee-for-service system. Fee-for-service reimbursement creates too many perverse incentives to be a long-term solution. Systemic approaches and changes in the way care is organized, financed, and delivered are necessary. Only such broader approaches can deal with cost problems for the long term while maintaining a commitment to high-quality, accessible service for public beneficiaries.

There is a growing recognition that medicaid costs must be controlled. There is also a growing consensus that a central element of this cost-control strategy must be the development of prepaid capitated delivery systems. Other available control options (eligibility or benefit reductions, reimbursement reductions, or tighter regulatory control) are deficient along too many dimensions; system reform is necessary to move from fee-for-service financing toward contracting, bidding, and negotiation strategies. The goals of managed systems are to remove the financial incentive to provide more patient care than is appropriate, to provide necessary care in the most cost-effective and appropriate setting, and to utilize more efficient providers.

Many states have undertaken activity in this area. Arizona, California, Massachusetts, New Jersey, Maryland, New York, and Michigan have active components of their medicaid programs utilizing the principles of capitation, negotiation, bidding, and the construction of "primary care networks," an approach in which physicians are utilized as "gatekeepers" and agents of utilization and cost control.

MANAGED HEALTH CARE IN MASSACHUSETTS

Massachusetts has chosen to seek long-term cost control by constructing primary care networks. This initiative is termed *Managed Health Care*. It seeks:

— To foster competition among providers and plans.
— To incorporate potential provider risk and gain as incentives for efficiency.
— To offer prepaid reimbursement to improve cash flow and increase flexibility.

Managed health provides the opportunity of providing better care at less cost. The coordinated, integrated nature of managed care will improve health outcomes as well as proving to be cost effective.

Managed health draws on six basic conceptual underpinnings:

— Enrollment: To focus care at one site.
— Management: To create a primary care health manager.
— Incentives: To reward appropriate and efficient care.
— Risk: To give the primary care manager a stake in the outcome.
— Capitation: To smooth cash flow and encourage flexibility.
— Competition: To promote high quality, accessible, efficient care.

Under managed health, recipients choose a health care plan (case management site, community health center, health maintenance organization, or health plan administered by an intermediary). Each plan assigns recipients to a primary care case manager. The case manager acts as the "gatekeeper" of the health care system by either providing or authorizing all recipient care.

Massachusetts contracts with health plans to provide needed medical care to enrolled recipients for a target expenditure amount. This target is lower than the current average cost of meeting recipient's medical needs in the fee-for-service system.

The managed health plans have a particular incentive to meet recipient medical needs cost effectively because plans that achieve savings retain these savings as income. Plans that fail to achieve savings are at risk for at least a portion of the overspending. Savings accrue because plans, due to the opportunity to share in the savings, provide care in the most cost-effective settings and reduce unnecessary and duplicative care. This is a significant change from the existing system, under which providers do not benefit from controlling costs and indeed are acting against their own interests to economize, since the less they spend, the less they receive in reimbursement.

MANAGED HEALTH CARE MODELS IN MASSACHUSETTS

A number of program models of managed care are operated in the Massachusetts Medicaid program:

CASE MANAGEMENT SITES

Case management is a model developed for community health centers, hospital outpatient departments, and physicians. This model serves an enrolled population on a fee-for-service basis. The site authorizes all referral services and is at-risk for a percentage of total expenditures for their enrolled population.

Massachusetts is engaged in an ongoing process of contracting with additional sites to provide care in the model of the case management project. The model provides a way to obtain benefits of managed health while using existing organizations. Large-scale expansion would be dramatically slowed if all new enrollment had to be channeled into newly developed managed health organizational settings. Massachusetts currently has 6,000 persons enrolled in case management plans.

MEDICAID ENROLLMENT IN HMOs

Medicaid currently contracts with three HMOs in Massachusetts. They enroll 4,000 medicaid recipients. The state believes it can contract with many of the existing 17 HMOs in Massachusetts, thereby significantly increasing the number of recipients enrolled in managed plans of care. Negotiations with many of these HMOs are underway, and significant expansion is expected. This model provides or arranges for virtually all services for an enrolled population on a full-risk capitation basis at a cost below the regional fee-for-service average.

CONTRACTS WITH INTERMEDIARIES

Massachusetts intends to pursue contracts with intermediaries to provide managed health services. An intermediary arrangement would be based on a health care organization contracting with medicaid to provide health services to a defined medicaid population at a predetermined price. The intermediary organization would then develop and manage the primary care network through which the enrolled recipients would obtain care.

This "broker organization" model will arrange for all services for an enrolled population on a full-risk capitation basis by subcontracting with a series of managed health plans in one area. This will allow recipients to choose among these plans and will allow the coordinating organization to reimburse the subplans for their enrolled populations through a variety of risk-based methods, including fully capitated and voucher plans.

This approach to managed care provides the opportunity for the health care industry to propose and carry out creative options for the organization, financing, and delivery of health care.

AMBULATORY CAPITATION

Ambulatory capitation is a model for use by providers who are able to provide or arrange for all ambulatory services for an enrolled population on a full-risk capitation basis. They will also provide or authorize referral for all inpatient hospital services, on a fee-for-service basis, while accepting risk for a percentage of total inpatient expenditures for their enrollees. This program makes it possible for smaller, ambulatory care-oriented providers to participate in managed health without the need to assume full risk for inpatient hospital services.

MODELS FOR THE ELDERLY AND DISABLED

To meet the health care needs of all medicaid recipients and to realize the fullest savings potential of managed care, programs for the elderly population will also be implemented. These programs are particularly important because older people are more often in need of services, frequently lack primary care providers, are the fastest growing segment of the population, and represent the largest financial investment of the medicaid program. Sixty percent of the medicaid budget is dedicated to serving elderly recipients.

Three programs of managed care are being aimed at the needs of the elderly. The first program concentrates on essentially healthy elderly individuals and links them to a managed care provider in much the same way that current programs integrate younger enrollees. The second program will serve older people who are at risk of going into a nursing home. The program will coordinate health and social services in the community, allowing people to remain at home for as long as possible. Finally, medicaid is expanding managed care for elderly people in nursing homes. In this program, nurse practitioners, under the supervision of physicians, manage the health care of nursing home residents, thus decreasing the incidence of emergency room visits for primary care and the need for inpatient hospital care.

RESULTS OF MANAGED CARE IN MASSACHUSETTS

Medicaid has observed a number of advantages to case-managed care.[6] First, cost and utilization analyses have shown that average health care costs per enrollee per month have been lower at almost every site during case management than before. Expenditures to off-site ambulatory care providers and hospitals were significantly reduced for managed care enrollees. These results suggest that the case management program did alter the utilization patterns of enrollees and reduce costs.

Second, the results showed that individuals could and did change their utilization patterns (even voluntarily) when they became part of a managed health program. Recipient surveys showed that the primary reason for joining a managed health plan was the opportunity to have a personal physician. The cost reduction seemed to result mainly from enrollees changing their care-seeking patterns. However, the disallowance of claims for out-of-plan services may have contributed to the reduction in enrollee's health care costs.

Third, a comparison of the preenrollment period cost and utilization patterns of case-management enrollees to those of a randomly selected control group revealed that program participants differed from the general Aid to Families with Dependent Children (AFDC) population prior to their enrollment in the program. Medicaid recipients who enrolled in case management showed higher health care costs and higher utilization than average recipients. The way in which the demonstration project was marketed seems to be the reason for this difference. Because most marketing took place in the waiting rooms of sites, the program was more likely to attract high utilizers of health care. Enrolling high utilizing families was an advantage, since managed health reached the people whose health care costs most needed to be reduced.

Fourth, patient satisfaction with managed health care has been very high. This has resulted in consistently low rates of voluntary disenrollment. Patient satisfaction surveys indicated that both enrollees and disenrollees were satisfied with the care delivered by program providers.

Fifth, quality of care, as measured by medical record audits, was consistently at least as good as that delivered prior to the program. This standard of no deterioration in quality was a key finding.

Managed health care can be viewed as the best hope to continue to fully and fairly serve medicaid recipients within the cost constraints faced by the states. The development of these models, therefore, should be viewed as the centerpiece of state medicaid reform.

IMPORTANCE OF MANAGED HEALTH CARE

There are a number of reasons why managed care is the innovation chosen by many state medicaid programs. Its effects are positive along a number of dimensions.

COST CONTROL

Systems of managed care can be effective cost-control devices. The health maintenance organization (HMO) experience suggests that HMOs have kept costs from 10 to 40 percent lower than the costs of caring for comparable groups with conventional health insurance.[7] The same principles that guide HMOs are structured into the managed systems of care that are being developed by states; similar results can be obtained through these programs. In Massachusetts, a range of managed health care programs operate. All are geared to reduce spending by at least 10 percent compared to fee-for-service care. Therefore, managed systems of care can play an important role in controlling the growth of spending in state medicaid programs.

MAINTENANCE OF QUALITY

Managed systems of care also provide the opportunity of maintaining high-quality service while controlling costs. The integrated and coordinated nature of care provided under managed health contributes to better health outcomes as well as cost savings. Care received by the medicaid population in the fee-for-service system often results in disjointed service, frequently delivered in hospital emergency rooms, without a clear responsibility for all services located with one provider. This lack of coordination and responsibility mis-serves the medicaid recipient, as it inappropriately utilizes resources.

ALTERNATIVES ARE INADEQUATE

Systemic reform approaches to medicaid cost control are essential. Efforts aimed at marginal changes in the existing financing and delivery system are inadequate, and initiatives that are based on eligibility and service reductions that affect only recipients are unfair. The system reforms represented by managed health care constitute an intelligent approach to the desire to control costs while not resting the burden solely on recipients.

INCENTIVES

A properly structured system of managed care will build the proper incentives into the health care system. The fee-for-service system encourages the provision of high, and perhaps unnecessary, levels of service because only very weak controls exist to monitor and limit reimbursement. Managed care systems reward the delivery of appropriate levels and kinds of service, in the most cost-effective setting. The basic premise underlying managed care systems is that a budget is set in advance for the care of an individual or a population. Profits are made by providing needed care in an efficient manner. This prospective element of reimbursement breaks the link between the provision of more care and the receipt of more reimbursement. This financial incentive is a basic component of managed care and a major rationalization of the system.

COMPETITION

Managed care programs should structure competition among providers of the alternative systems of care. Competition will enhance efficiency, increase the likelihood that savings will accrue to payors, maximize recipient choice, and help maintain quality and patient satisfaction. There is a great deal of discussion about competitive models of health care. It is particularly appropriate that managed health plans be subject to the discipline of the competitive marketplace. The purpose of managed care is to accomplish the objectives that competition is intended to facilitate. Efficiency in resource allocation is the basis on which managed care plans operate, save money for payors, and generate profit. It is wise, therefore, to structure systems of managed care into competitive arrangements that support these efficiencies.

RISK

Provider risk is a key part of managed care. The potential for financial gain if care is managed efficiently is an essential element of an effective system of managed care. Even more importantly, the potential for loss on the part of a provider is crucial. If a provider feels a financial stake in the managed health plan, and if there is financial risk for provider activities, the management of care delivered in the system will be more attentive and stringent. At-risk arrangements are crucial if a state is to realize the maximum savings potential from managed health. Managed care provides the ability to utilize this powerful tool to reform health care and make provider incentives consistent with cost-control goals.

SERVICE INTEGRATION

Managed care provides the motivation and ability on the part of providers to bring together the disparate strands of the health care system. It is increasingly difficult for patients to receive the appropriate mix of services to maintain health and avoid unnecessary and expensive emergency, acute, and long-term care services. This problem is especially severe for elderly patients, whose care needs are often diverse and require the most coordination of diverse services.

Managed care provides the flexibility and incentives to coordinate services and build the most appropriate and cost-effective service package. Since managed health breaks the links to traditional fee-for-service reimbursement, funding sources need not determine the services available and provided. Managed health also provides the incentives—financial risk and potential gain—to encourage providers to undertake the often difficult task of constructing appropriate service packages. These factors make managed care the best way to overcome fragmentation of services.

HEALTH OUTCOMES

A number of elements of managed care work to enhance patient health outcomes. First, the integrated and coordinated nature of services provided in a managed care framework encourage better medical care and improved health status. Second, the likely reduction in unnecessary tests and hospitalization that occurs in managed care systems reduces patient risk. Although the underprovision of service is a danger that must be guarded against in managed care systems, the avoidance of the unnecessary care that is encouraged by the fee-for-service system can substantially improve outcomes. Third, individuals enrolled in managed care systems are more likely to seek needed care, since a primary care manager or gatekeeper is clearly identified to the individual. Increased care-seeking will not necessarily increase costs because the care is provided in a cost-effective setting—the physician's office or health center. The availability of primary care will reduce patient habits of putting off seeking care until expensive acute or emergency episodes are precipitated. Managed care is an important and promising innovation, because it promotes better service and health while containing costs.

MANAGED HEALTH CARE AND PPO DEVELOPMENT DESIGN ISSUES

As a state moves toward providing care to its recipients through managed health systems or as other payors develop PPOs for their employees or beneficiaries, a number of design issues need to be addressed. Initiatives in both the public and private sectors share a set of design issues. How these questions are resolved is critically important to the eventual shape and success of the system.

QUALITY AND ACCESS ASSURANCE MECHANISMS

There is an incentive to underprovide services in managed care or PPO programs. This danger arises because the provider realizes financial benefit if his or her patients do not overutilize. Protocols that assure quality and access are necessary to address this issue. This utilization element of managed health and PPO design should not be ignored. It must be addressed to maintain patient satisfaction and facilitate patient enrollment.

Review procedures can be structured to assure that access and quality are not diminished in a managed health care or PPO system. Simple, usable grievance procedures should be available so that patient difficulties with the system can be easily reported. Appeals mechanisms should be made available to a patient if he or she feels there was an inappropriate denial of care. Patient satisfaction surveys should be conducted to receive input from those in the system. This will serve as an early warning system for problems and provide input on how the managed care or PPO system can be improved and made more attractive to potential enrollees.

Quality and access assurance mechanisms must be built into a managed care or PPO system. Inappropriate underutilization must be controlled, and there should be an avenue for patients to express their dissatisfaction (grievance procedures) and to report on the program in general (patient satisfaction surveys). If these elements are lacking in a system, long-term problems of quality, access, and enrollment are likely to arise.

MANDATORY OR VOLUNTARY ENROLLMENT

An initial decision that managed care or PPO program managers must make is whether to require the enrollment of recipients or beneficiaries or to allow individuals to make a voluntary enrollment decision. A number of differences in program structure and operation will result from this decision. The program will be larger if mandatory enrollment is utilized. Voluntary enrollment will require creative marketing approaches or enhanced benefit packages to entice recipients or beneficiaries to enroll. A mandatory program will require more detailed quality and access assurance mechanisms and grievance procedures because enrollees will be unable to "vote with their feet" and disenroll if they are dissatisfied with the program. Medicaid beneficiaries and employees alike will more strongly resist mandatory enrollment programs. Such programs deny the choice and flexibility allowed by voluntary enrollment.

PROVIDER RISK

Types and amounts of provider risk must be determined. Systems can be structured that range from full provider risk assumption for all services to maintenance of the fee-for-service structure with patient management and limited risk sharing by providers. These issues of risk assumption apply both to PPO and state managed health care development, although a phased-in rather than an immediate use of full provider risk is more likely in state programs. Providers are hesitant to accept full risk for a medicaid population, a population that they believe is more difficult to manage and more in need of service.

CHOICE AMONG PLANS

It must be decided early in the program development process whether recipients or beneficiaries will be guaranteed a choice among PPOs or managed health plans. The availability of choice among plans is important to patient satisfaction, program savings, and quality. It is less desirable to offer only one program to individuals than it is to offer a meaningful choice among competing plans. If mandatory enrollment is utilized, this choice becomes more important. There will be resistance to a proposal that structures only one plan and then requires enrollment into it. The maintenance of choice among plans empowers enrollees. This increases satisfaction and creates an incentive for providers to furnish services appropriately and efficiently. Providers have a powerful incentive to perform if enrollees can exercise the option of leaving an unsatisfactory situation and choosing another plan. The absence of this choice decreases the incentive to operate the plan in a manner that will please enrollees, since they cannot disenroll. This makes program monitoring more difficult for a state or employer, because the program organizer cannot depend on the influence of enrollee response to influence provider behavior.

USE OF COMPETITION

It is not desirable to insert PPO or state managed health activity into the traditional health regulatory environment. The use of competition is an alternative and preferable means of obtaining desired provider response. Competition among plans enhances enrollee choice, serves as a quality control device, encourages provider efficiency, and moves the system away from the regulatory intervention that marks marginal rather than systemic change.

CONSUMER INPUT

Consumer input should be sought in designing managed care and PPO systems. Soliciting consumer response will enhance the ultimate level of acceptance accorded the plan and increase enrollment. In a mandatory enrollment plan, such input is even more essential; if this comment is not sought, there will be greater opposition to the plan. Involving consumers in the planning process will also increase consumer information about the system. This is useful because an important element of a successful PPO or managed health system is changed consumer behavior. If patients know more about the system from their involvement in its design, they will be more educated users of the ultimate program.

CONCLUSION

Managed health and PPO initiatives are the best choices for reforming the current health care delivery system. These arrangements allow significant cost savings while maintaining quality care in an environment of diminishing resources. Cost control and access goals are maintained in managed care systems more effectively than through traditional approaches, such as eligibility, service, or reimbursement reductions, because these marginal adjustments do not alter the underlying structure and incentives of the current system. Proper financial incentives, the appropriate use of competition, and provider risk arrangements can all be utilized in PPO and managed care systems. These elements contribute to making the health care system more efficient. Health outcomes can also be improved through integrated, coordinated service.

These approaches encourage the utilization of the least intensive appropriate care setting and reduce unnecessary care. These are prerequisites to an efficient system of health care that maintains quality and access while controlling costs. State reform efforts in this direction, using primary care networks and other managed health techniques, are essential as states face increased demands for service, higher costs, and reduced federal revenues.

The case for managed care is made eloquently by Robert Blendon and Thomas Moloney of the Robert Wood Johnson Foundation and Commonwealth Fund respectively. In a letter to the editor in the New York Times, Blendon and Moloney note that in the face of pressures to control spending for health programs, public officials are faced with a basic choice of approaches. One approach is administratively simple: reduce the number of poor and near poor who receive medicaid benefits and reduce the comprehensiveness of these benefits. The second approach is to make highly selective program cuts and to change current arrangements for providing health care to the poor. Blendon and Moloney observe:

> Taking the first route may prove extraordinarily expensive over the long haul, in both human and economic terms. Clearly the second option will be selected if the public recognizes the gains achieved by the nation's poor since the inauguration of the medicaid program.[8]

Managed health care and PPO systems facilitate system reform by utilizing incentives. As such, they are superior to reform approaches predicated solely on regulatory change or benefit and eligibility reductions. The problems of the health care system are such that basic change is needed. Managed care makes these changes in a way that is responsible in terms of cost-control, quality, and access goals.

NOTES

1. "Restructuring Medicaid: An Agenda for Change." The National Study Group on State Medicaid Strategies, Executive Summary, The Center for the Study of Social Policy, Washington, D.C., 1984, p. 10.

2. Perspectives, "The State of Medicaid," *Washington Report on Medicine and Health,* March 19, 1984. Washington, D.C.

3. The Commonwealth Fund, "What's Being Done about Medicaid," A Commonwealth Fund Paper, New York, 1982, p. 8.

4. Massachusetts Department of Public Welfare Statistics, Fiscal Year 1983.

5. "What's Being Done about Medicaid," op. cit., p. 6.

6. *Case Management as a Cost-Effective Approach to Improved Health Services Delivery to Medicaid Recipients.* Final Report, Massachusetts Case Management Demonstration Project, November 1982.

7. Harold S. Luft, "How Do HMOs Achieve Their Savings?" *New England Journal of Medicine,* June 15, 1978.

8. "Medicaid Is Vital to the Poor: Cut with Care." *New York Times,* Wednesday, December 22, 1983. Letter, Robert J. Blendon and Thomas J. Moloney.

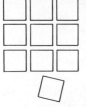 Management Functions

Administrative Requirements for Managing Swing Plan PPOs

Angelo M. Masciantonio

Director of Cost Containment
Advanced Systems Applications, Inc.
Philadelphia, PA

☐ PPOs offer an alternative approach for health benefits payors (insurers, Blue Cross/Blue Shield Plans, TPAs, and corporations) to improve the management of health care costs. Since health benefits costs continue to grow faster than other production costs for U.S. industry, managed health care programs will prosper. This chapter discusses the mechanics of PPOs as a form of managed health care program and outlines several issues worth considering prior to implementing PPO programs.

WHAT IS A PPO?

A PPO is a network of health care providers (hospitals, doctors, or other providers) often associated with a health benefits payor and specifically organized to provide a range of health care services for fees specified in a formal contract and performed according to predetermined protocols or standards.

There are three general distinctions between the various types of PPOs. First, PPOs can be *provider based,* that is, sponsored by a hospital, physician or physician group, or both. Second, PPOs can be *payor based,* that is, sponsored by the payor in association with physician or hospital networks. Finally, PPOs can be sponsored by *independent organizations,* such as consultants, which usually play a role in organizing the PPO and then act as brokers between networks of providers and payors.

SWING AND EXCLUSIVE PPO PLANS

From a benefits design perspective, there are two major types of PPO benefits plans: (1) a "swing" plan in which beneficiaries (or members, subscribers, patients, enrollees, consumers, employees) can, at any time, swing out of the PPO provider network to receive care from a nonparticipating provider and still be eligible for benefits (although usually reduced) under the insurance contract and (2) an "exclusive" provider plan (EPO) where beneficiaries must stay in the network in order to receive benefits. To the general public, an EPO may appear to be the same as an independent practice association model HMO. The rest of the chapter will pertain to swing plan PPOs, since the most difficult implementation problems are associated with the administration of swing-type PPO plans.

COST-CONTAINMENT PROGRAMS TO MANAGE HEALTHCARE DELIVERY

Swing plan PPOs bring traditional indemnity and managed health care programs together under one benefit plan. By incorporating cost-containment strategies used by employers in the last 10 to 15 years, PPOs are a hybrid alternative to HMO and traditional indemnity insurance plans. The following cost-containment activities are typically incorporated in day-to-day PPO operations:

1. Data collection for analysis of benefits utilization and planning.
2. Focused action programs as a part of the benefits structure including:
   a. Preadmission review.
   b. Concurrent review.
   c. Retrospective review.
   d. Mandatory second opinion for select procedures.
   e. Mandatory ambulatory surgery for selected procedures.
3. Selective provider (hospital and physician) contracting to stabilize price.

It is through careful integration of these activities in conjunction with careful benefits plan design that PPOs promise to compete with HMO and traditional indemnity health plan alternatives. (See the Restraining-Driving Forces exhibits following.)

EXHIBIT 1
Healthcare Costs Restraining-Driving Forces:
Traditional Indemnity Plan

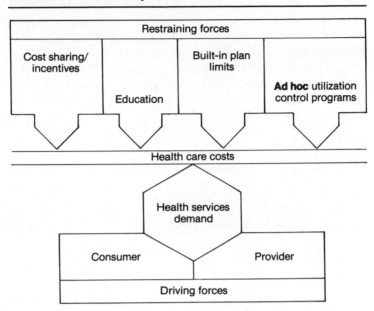

EXHIBIT 2
Healthcare Costs Restraining-Driving Forces: PPO Plan

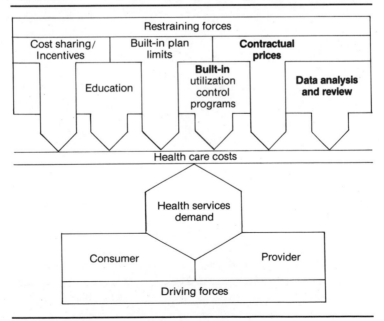

HOW DOES A PPO WORK?

In general, PPOs substantially change the way payors do business with providers of health care services. Like HMOs, PPOs bring price and utilization management to the negotiation table through a formal contracting process between payors and participating providers. This can be accomplished through the principal parties or through a third party. Exhibit 3 illustrates how managed health care programs differ from standard health insurance programs. The key difference is that managed health care programs create formal relationships between all parties in the health care payment and delivery system.

EXHIBIT 3
Traditional versus PPO Program Relationships

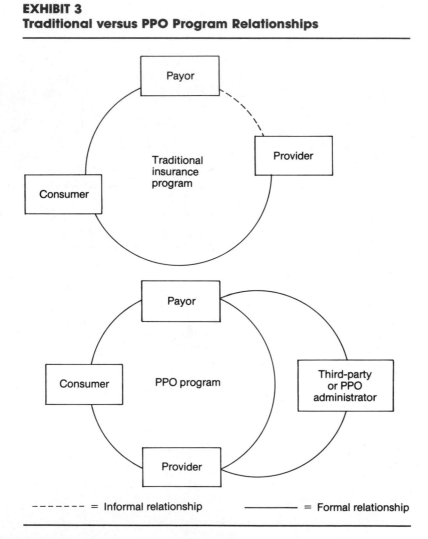

PPOs are an attractive market alternative since they combine several traditional health plan features (freedom to choose providers and flexibility in benefits scope) with the cost-management features of HMOs (predictable costs and utilization-management systems). The formal contracts between payors and participating providers permit this combination, provide the foundation for PPO benefit structures, and hence make PPOs tick.

The notion of a managed health care system implies the ability to control the delivery of health care services. Through the execution of provider contracts, health benefits payors may achieve some control over health care delivery through the performance obligations specified in the contracts. Thus, the formal relationships between the payors and provider offer payors an opportunity to manage health plan utilization and costs, and, to some extent, help control the amount of out-of-pocket costs to beneficiaries. Without this formal relationship, payors must rely solely upon beneficiary and provider behaviors to manage health care delivery.

Formal contracts also create a mechanism for the specification of expectations between providers and payors. Certainly, health cost management requires a change in the expectations of both providers and beneficiaries in order to bring about desired changes in discretionary provider behaviors (situations where providers have several alternatives for treatment or care under circumstances in which these decisions will not endanger the patient). For example, formal contracts can provide a means of defining mutual expectations and establishing guidelines for reasonable charges for medical services as well as for the appropriateness of medical treatment. The importance of provider contracting in managing health care plan costs can be illustrated by examining the cost-containment mechanisms of PPO programs.

COST CONTAINMENT MECHANISMS

PPOs stabilize health expenditures through two primary mechanisms: (1) contractual obligations of providers to accept negotiated fees or rates of reimbursement and meet performance criteria and (2) careful benefit plan design features that provide an array of incentives or disincentives to beneficiaries.

CONTRACTUAL OBLIGATIONS

Participating PPO physicians will agree to accept (or charge) explicit fee schedules or methods of reimbursement. Examples include fixed relative value study (RVS) conversion factors, percent of usual and customary rates (UCR), capitation rate, and Health Insurance Association of America (HIAA) schedule.

Participating hospitals will agree to charge according to a negotiated schedule of rates, including per diem, per admission/discharge, or per DRG (diagnosis related group). Hospitals may also agree to a specified discount from list charges. Finally, participating hospitals may be paid according to a cost-based reimbursement formula using actual costs or reasonable financial requirements based on the PPO's actual utilization of the facility.

The above obligations provide a reimbursement alternative to the traditional "pay as billed" or the "pay what is reasonable and customary" practice of health benefits payors. In economic terms, these obligations stabilize the inflation component in the health care cost equation. A large portion of hospital cost increases in the last 10 years has been attributed to inflation.

PPO contracts between payors and providers can incorporate powerful contractual obligations governing the monitoring and control of the use of health care services. Built-in utilization review (UR) and appropriateness of care protocols often specify that certain procedures and health care settings require review and approval by the payor or by an external peer professional review organization in order to receive full reimbursement.

Depending on the goals of the PPO, these protocols may be designed so that the patient does not perceive a difference in treatment provided under a PPO plan.

The following examples illustrate utilization management protocol or criteria:

— All or selected elective admissions must be preauthorized and/or reviewed prior to admission.
— Lengths of stay on all admissions (by diagnosis, DRG) are established at admission and extensions must be approved.
— Certain procedures require a second opinion.
— Providers contractually agree to direct patients to the appropriate medical setting and facility with the lowest cost in the health service area or in the PPO provider network.
— Providers agree to allow the payors to perform retrospective reviews of provider performance according to negotiated criteria (e.g., appropriateness evaluation protocol) and based on the results of the review, give the payor the right to recover the costs for inappropriate services.

BENEFITS DESIGN

Since PPOs combine the features of traditional health benefits programs with the cost management techniques used by HMOs, they are rightly considered a managed health care system alternative. PPO benefits structures, too, may be designed to reflect a hybrid configuration of indemnity plan/HMO benefits. Like traditional health insurance plans, swing PPO benefits structures allow consumers to receive care at the provider of their choice. Yet, similar to HMO plans, PPOs may provide strong financial incentives or penalties in order to encourage use of PPO providers and compliance with built-in utilization-control programs. This hybrid design of benefits structures in PPO plans is of critical importance.

The nature of the contracts between payors and providers will drive the design of benefits available in PPO plans. For example, a physician-only PPO (where no hospitals are under contract) suggests that benefits be designed to encourage patients to use the "preferred" physicians. Otherwise, the potential cost savings to be gained through negotiated fees and strict utilization-review protocol will not be realized. In such a case, benefits design might incorporate incentives such as higher coinsurance payment, deductible waivers, or waiving the filing of a claim form to encourage beneficiaries to use the participating physicians. Alternatively, disincentives might be built into the benefits design, such as lower coinsurance payment and imposed deductibles for patients who elect to use nonparticipating physicians.

HMOs rely on this incentive/disincentive approach as well. That is, when a patient goes to an HMO physician or facility, benefits are payable, but when a patient seeks care from a non-HMO physician, benefits are not payable except in special circumstances. There can be many variations on this basic approach to benefit payment; however, the type of PPO and PPO contract considerations should dictate how incentive/disincentives are built into PPO benefit structures in order to encourage beneficiaries to use PPO providers and comply with utilization-review program rules. The following samples illustrate how benefit structures were designed to meet the needs of two different PPO models (Benefit Structure: Model I and Benefit Structure: Model II).

Differences Between Model I and Model II

Model I. Model I, aimed at the small employer market, has a simple benefit design that is easy to administer. Since 70 percent of the area physicians were participating in PPO Model I, physician services are paid the same for PPO and non-PPO physicians according to a California Relative Value Study fee schedule. This approach is similar to the old Foundation for Medical Care reimbursement approach developed in the 1970s. With the 70 percent participation, incentives to use PPO physicians in Model I are not necessary, since 7 out of 10 randomly distributed visits to area physicians will result in a visit to a PPO physician.

Model I does contain incentives to use PPO hospitals because it has

EXHIBIT 4
Benefit Structure: Model I

Benefit	PPO Providers	Non-PPO Providers
Hospital (R & B and ancillary services) *Utilization review on all admissions*	80 percent of the negotiated *per diem rate* $200 deductible per year (waived for preauthorization) 3 per family total	80 percent of usual and customary rate $200 deductible per year 3 per family total
Professional services	80 percent of *negotiated fee* (negotiated fee can be based on any schedule, e.g., California Relative Value Study factors)	80 percent of negotiated fee (negotiated fee can be based on any schedule, e.g., California Relative Value Study factors)
Other services	80 percent of usual and customary rates $100 deductible per year 3 per family total	80 percent of usual and customary rates $100 deductible per year 3 per family total
Coinsurance limit (stop loss)	*$10,000 calendar year for all expenses combined*	
Psychiatric	$30,000 lifetime maximum inpatient	
Well-baby	Nursery care for first 5 days of mother's confinement, including physician visits in hospital	
Lifetime maximum	$1,000,000	

agreements with only 10 out of the 30 local hospitals. Also, the hospital contract specifies fixed per-diem rates that are substantially below community average charges. In this example, the benefit structure includes a $200 deductible waiver if a patient uses a participating hospital and the admission is preauthorized by the utilization-review organization.

Model II. PPO Model II has fewer than 10 percent of area physicians under contract. Nonetheless, these physicians have a proven track record in utilization management and have agreed to strict patient management guidelines. Thus, benefits are designed to provide strong incentives to steer patients to participating physicians with 100 percent coinsurance payments, small ($5) copayment on outpatient visits only, and no claim form submission. Hospital services in Model II are capped for each hospital admission under a DRG reimbursement contract. Both Model I and II require utilization review for all inpatient services regardless of provider type. Thus, both benefits plans contain penalties for patients who ignore the utilization-review process. Also, both plans of benefits contain well-baby care benefits in order to compete with comprehensive HMO benefits as well as increase the stop-loss levels in order to keep the incentive/disincentive benefits structure in force.

EXHIBIT 5
Benefit Structure: Model II

Benefit	PPO Providers	Non-PPO Providers
Hospital (R & B, ancillary services)	80 percent of the *DRG schedule*	80 percent of usual and customary rate
Utilization review on all admissions	*70 percent if no utilization review*	*70 percent if no utilization review*
(preadmission review)	$200 deductible per year 3 per family total	$200 deductible per year 3 per family total
Professional services	*100 percent of HIAA fee schedule plus $5 copayment on outpatient visits* *No claim form necessary*	80 percent of HIAA fee schedule Claim form necessary
Other services	80 percent of usual and customary rate $100 deductible per year 3 per family total	80 percent of usual and customary rate $100 deductible per year 3 per family total
Maximum out-of-pocket expenses	*$2,500 per year for all expenses combined*	
Psychiatric	$30,000 lifetime maximum as inpatient 50 percent of first $50 for 50 visits as outpatient	
Well-baby	Nursery care for first 5 days of mother's confinement, including physician visits in hospital	
Lifetime maximum	$1,000,000	

COST SAVINGS

If properly constructed with sound provider/payor contracts and well designed benefit packages, PPOs can achieve significant savings over more traditional plans. The most important factors leading to savings are the current claims experience of the employer group and the extent of historical cost-containment programs within the group's health benefit plan.

For example, a traditional benefits program experiencing 15 to 30 percent inappropriate hospital use, should achieve savings through a PPO program via the following cost savings measures:

1. PPO utilization control programs can lead to a conservative savings of 5 percent of hospital costs.
2. Negotiated fee schedules with physicians often can result in 2 to 3 percent savings in professional services costs.
3. Benefit design features, particularly increased cost-sharing penalties for patients opting to use a nonparticipating provider, can also account for plan savings. These savings will depend upon the size of the penalty (5 percent, 10 percent, etc.) and can often lead to plan savings greater than the savings from built-in utilization review and negotiated fees with PPO providers.

IMPACT ON HEALTHCARE INDUSTRY

PPO plans can represent a radical change in health benefits design, payment, and administration for most health benefits payors, providers, and purchasers. Prior to discussing the specific problems associated with actually implementing these changes, it is helpful to summarize the impact of PPOs on three areas: payor business practices, the provider community where PPOs proliferate, and the consumer faced with yet another alternative health care plan.

PAYORS

Health benefits payors involved in PPO plan administration will be required to modify their business practices considerably, whether the payor is an insurance company, Blue Cross/Blue Shield plan, third-party administrator, or a self-administered corporation.

Payors must become involved in provider contracting. This involvement may range from developing in-house staff to manage and control provider contracting to hiring outside consultants to assume contracting responsibilities. Skills in hospital management and reimbursement, often absent even in large insurance companies, need to be developed if successful contracts are to be negotiated.

This general lack of specialized expertise in payor organizations is probably the most significant technical problem associated with PPO implementation. Health benefits payors require experienced staff to negotiate provider reimbursement agreements, develop effective utilization-control programs, and deal with the challenges brought on by PPO health benefits design, pricing, and payment. Because the technical "know-how" for these activities is still in its infancy, payors may not be fully ready for the changes PPOs will bring in the design and administration of PPO programs.

PPOs also change the way payors design, market, and administer benefits. Incentives, utilization-review conditions, multiple payment schedules, and other variable payment practices need to be integrated into benefits design by knowledgeable staff. Poorly designed, marketed, and administered PPO programs will lead to payor frustration as well as to provider and consumer dissatisfaction.

To support PPOs, benefits contracts, actuarial and underwriting assumptions, marketing, administration, claims systems, and cost-containment activities will have to be modified. Internal planning, coordination, and reporting is critical. Interfaces with providers and with internal or outside organizations that carry out cost-control programs, such as pre-admission review, must be coordinated with benefits payment systems.

Equally important, evaluation methods must be developed to measure the success or failure of PPO programs. Therefore, data to evaluate the PPO program must be captured and reported on a timely basis.

Payors must increase administrative costs in order to implement PPOs. As with providers, payors need to evaluate the likely marketplace scenarios if they decide against PPO participation. Market share and volume analysis are critical to a successful program, and it may prove unprofitable for payors to pursue PPOs in areas where geographic factors, such as isolation, will undermine the success of a PPO venture. In sum, PPO involvement for many payors and providers will mean making a relatively large up-front investment in a volatile and uncertain business environment.

Finally, on the consumer front, payors must face a potential communications problem. Consumers' understanding of the array of built-in incentives and disincentives will determine their utilization of PPO providers. Consequently, payors need to mount an educational campaign and rewrite their benefits literature to better explain the alternatives available under the PPO program.

PROVIDER COMMUNITY

Providers need to adjust to the changing reimbursement methods and utilization monitoring systems in PPO programs. Because PPOs replace "reasonable and customary" or billed charges with fixed reimbursement approaches, adequate pricing of physician and hospital services becomes extremely important in order to maintain financial solvency. Prior to negotiating reimbursement levels for services, providers must understand the value of their services and view their associated costs and charges in the context of a new, competitive environment.

Since PPO programs are aimed at cost containment, some providers will find that reimbursement levels may need to be less than their usual charges in order to offer plan savings. In addition, prospective payment, flat rate, and risk-sharing approaches may be incorporated into provider payment agreements. For example, PPO physicians might be paid according to a flat rate fee schedule that is negotiated only once per year or according to a capitation rate. Similarly, hospitals might be paid according to a DRG, per diem, or prospective payment program.

In addition to negotiated rates, PPO providers will be subject to a variety of utilization-management standards and programs. The ability to comply with special medical management protocol (e.g., admission authorization) will determine each provider's long-range participation in PPOs. Peer review committees will play a major role in how providers manage certain patients. Physicians who do not comply with predetermined medical care guidelines may find that the PPO will no longer request their participation. Practice patterns will be monitored and providers may be held financially accountable.

Contractually, providers may find themselves agreeing to economic as well as medical standards of care. These changes will undoubtedly affect the variability of medical practice. PPO providers will need to balance their malpractice worries with concern (and the potential penalties) associated with excessive use of resources. Thus each medical decision may bear some financial risks under PPO programs. In California, for example, hospitals involved with some PPO contracting programs are subject to retrospective audits where "inappropriate days" can lead to a financial remedy for the payor.

Many providers, too, will be faced with a expertise gap. PPO reimbursement will mean new approaches to pricing, planning, and budgeting. They will have to devise systems that can support the agreements they have made with the various payors. Different billing and payment approaches will mean that providers will need broader expertise in their accounting and billing departments.

Providers will have the additional burden of determining the impact of the PPO on their current and future market share. From the provider perspective, as other external cost-containment strategies place pressure on hospital incomes, monies available for investing in a PPO affiliation may be insufficient, or hospital directors may find the costs prohibitive. The decision to proceed with a PPO should be supported by an analysis of likely scenarios of what might happen if the provider does not proceed.

Depending on the hospital's geographic and competitive environment, some institutions may discover that certain costs associated with PPO participation (such as the cost to perform rigorous utilization review) may need to be incurred regardless of whether or not they enter a PPO agreement, simply because of an increasingly cost conscious marketplace.

CONSUMERS

PPOs offer consumers (corporations and employees) additional choices at benefits plan selection time. Increasingly, multiple choice programs will include PPO options as well as HMO options. If employers move toward fixed contribution levels for employee benefits programs, employees will have greater incentives to select managed health care plans over traditional programs, assuming they are priced below standard industry options. In addition to being price competitive, PPO programs may be broader in scope of benefits than standard plans. PPOs may prove attractive to consumers who are concerned with the rigidity of HMO alternatives but are willing to accept some potential reduction in access in terms of provider selection in exchange for lower out-of-pocket costs.

In addition to being offered greater choice at benefit plan selection time, consumers electing PPO options will have the opportunity to weigh costs versus access when they are seeking care. Choosing participating providers over nonparticipating providers will often mean lower out-of-pocket costs. However, the extent of the change in consumer behavior will depend on a number of important factors, including historical consumer-provider relationships, special medical problems, and PPO benefit plan incentives/disincentives.

POTENTIAL TRANSITION PROBLEMS

Payors and providers must solve several transition problems in order to implement PPO programs effectively. Providers and payors may run into extensive automated system requirements to support PPO provider billing and benefits payment. Potential inadequacies in provider billing systems will center on the capability to support the rates and methods of reimbursement that are negotiated in various provider contracts. If, for example, PPO physicians have agreed to bill fees that are less than their customary charges, their billing systems must be able to identify PPO patients and reduce their billed fees to the proper amount. Otherwise, payors may discover that PPO patients are paying the difference between charges and negotiated fees out of their own pockets, which is an undesirable cost shift.

Tremendous technical and administrative changes must be made to benefits payment systems to support PPO reimbursement. Additional requirements such as identifying eligible PPO claimants, matching them to PPO providers, and then paying according to the proper benefits structure may appear relatively straightforward. However, payors will find that multiple benefits structures, which pay different benefits from plan to plan and vary payment from provider to provider, are cumbersome to administer.

Payors will feel increasing pressure from claims personnel to modify their claims systems with automated techniques to perform the variable deductible and coinsurance calculations and to keep track of multiple accumulations toward new coinsurance rules (stop loss) or other built-in plan maximums. What will be most disappointing to payors will be the realization that there are few "quick and dirty" solutions to these problems that can be employed until automated solutions are developed.

RAISING ADEQUATE RESOURCES AND ANTICIPATING POLITICAL ISSUES

It costs money to attract scarce personnel, address support deficiencies, and intensify training and communications. These costs must be weighed against future opportunities and prospective benefits.

Payors and providers may find that initiating PPO programs has political ramifications. For instance, local providers, who are resistant to change or who are well established in a particular community, may correctly view PPOs as a threat to their market share.

Some physicians clearly view PPOs as a threat while others see them as an opportunity. Public debate around the likely problems associated with PPOs tends to focus upon the impact of PPOs on the quality of care and access to health services. Thus, providers who are leaders in a PPO project should be prepared to address in a public arena how their PPO will not jeopardize access to quality health care. Furthermore, these leaders need to rebuff the consumers' fears of PPOs as a manifestation of discount medicine.

Since PPOs will threaten the marketshare of established managed health care programs and HMOs, serious political jockeying in a target market area can be expected among providers, payors, and employers. Medical practice patterns such as referrals, admitting privileges, and use of outside medical ancillary services may be influenced by PPOs. IPA HMO plans, in particular, may find staff physicians and participating hospitals seeking to associate with one or more PPO programs. Staff model HMOs, which have dominated the managed care market to date, will find certain PPOs offering attractive packages to employees from a marketing perspective (i.e., quality providers, freedom to choose provider, no claim forms, low out-of-pocket costs). It is hard to predict the reaction to this new competition. The important point is to analyze and address possible political ramifications before they develop.

PPOs have been characterized as a "competitive" solution to the national problem of rising health care costs. While PPOs are bound to create a competitive stir in some regions, they will in fact add to some payors' or employers' health cost problems. Incomes reduced through lower volumes or through discounted fees to PPO payors may result in an increase of volume or price to non-PPO payors. This is a form of private sector cost shifting. From a systemwide perspective, the practice of cost shifting will mitigate the likelihood for overall cost containment.

Many health care analysts argue that long range cost management is dependent upon the success of cost-containment programs in "shrinking" a bloated health services sector in some areas of the country. If this is the case, PPOs should be given an opportunity to create competitive pressures to redistribute health care resources in order to shrink or reconfigure a poorly organized, inefficient health care system.

Viewed as an alternative strategy to combat rising health care costs, PPOs can offer flexibility in the face of restrictive private and public financing constraints. But, if PPOs fail to produce cost containment on a systemwide basis or exacerbate systemwide or local cost problems, other strategies such as state or federally mandated prospective regulatory programs and reimbursement controls could prevail.

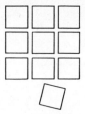

Management Functions

INPATIENT COST CONTROL—THE CRITICAL, UNPROVEN DIMENSION

Frederick S. Fink
Vice President
Booz, Allen and Hamilton
San Francisco, CA

Richard E. Wesslund
Senior Associate
Booz, Allen and Hamilton
San Francisco, CA

☐ One of the most critical and highly touted dimensions of PPOs is an ability to control cost. Objectives of lower health care costs have sparked significant payor interest in the PPO concept. The attractiveness of PPOs is based largely on their ability to retain many of the characteristics of the traditional indemnity/self-insurance payment scheme while controlling its weakest point—cost.

Providers have seized on the PPO concept as an opportunity to improve market share by responding to payors' concerns about cost while maintaining the fee-for-service system. Many providers simply view PPOs as a foray into the wholesale health care business by attempting to market a quantity of services at reduced rates.

EXHIBIT 1
Features of a Successful PPO

Network of low-cost providers
   Stringent utilization-review procedures
   Alternative delivery services as substitutes for inpatient care
   Systems and controls to reduce the cost of hospital products
Comprehensive geographic market coverage
   Strategically placed freestanding local ambulatory care facilities areawide
   Networks with other area providers
Competitively priced services
   Cost-efficient physicians
   Local networks with low-cost primary/secondary care providers
Active marketing to employer groups and insurance companies/TPAs
   Marketing staff
   Marketing research and promotion
Strong management
   Management staff
   Overcome legal barriers in developing physician contracts
   Support systems

EXHIBIT 2
PPO Concept Development Cycle

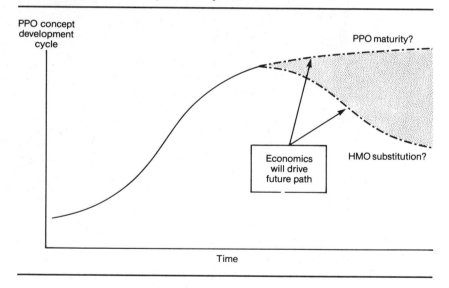

While some short-run shifts in market share may accrue to these wholesale providers as a result of strong marketing efforts, their long-term success or failure will be determined by a broad range of structurally oriented factors, shown in Exhibit 1. A low-cost provider network will be the single most important ingredient just as cost control was the dimension that first stimulated payor interest in PPOs. If providers cannot achieve cost control while maintaining the other favorable characteristics of preferred plan arrangements, the PPO market will dwindle, with payors switching to a system that can demonstrate cost savings. For those PPO subscribers for whom cost is the most critical dimension of their decision, HMOs (or perhaps some other new system) will become most attractive. Thus they will probably substitute an HMO for the PPO, as illustrated in Exhibit 2. Those who find HMOs unpalatable will have no real incentives to continue PPO participation and can be expected to return to traditional insurance payment.

PROVIDER COST CONTROL

At present, however, provider cost control is a critical but unproven dimension of the PPO concept. Properly structured a preferred provider organization has the potential to control cost, but insufficient experience and inadequate data systems prevent most PPO providers and payors from being able to demonstrate actual cost control.

Given this lack of hard data and experience, providers have generally resorted to price discounting schemes. Discounting is essentially a marketing tool used to lure unsophisticated purchasers into the system by superficially reducing their costs. From a provider viewpoint, these discounting approaches offer little tangible results other than instantly reduced per-unit margins for the provider. Providers argue that it brings new patients into their facilities (although few can prove it) and that the increased volume counteracts the reduced margins. This approach simply allows providers to avoid dealing with the real problem, which is costs, not pricing. Price discounting masks the real problem at hand. It can result in a downward spiral in the provider's financial performance as bidding wars emerge among providers, which can potentially drive prices down even below cost.

ACHIEVING COST CONTROL

Achieving cost control requires a focus on hospital and physician inpatient costs, which constitute over 75 percent of total health expenditures, as shown in Exhibit 3. Consequently, these services offer the greatest potential dollar benefit in payor's cost-control efforts.

A number of potential mechanisms are available to control inpatient cost. These mechanisms include both payor and provider approaches and can affect inpatient cost from two directions, shown in Exhibit 4. These mechanisms offer potential for achieving true cost control but they require substantial and sustained investment.

Payor mechanisms, shown in Exhibit 5, include increasing coinsurance, raising deductibles, avoiding expansion of benefits, and offering

EXHIBIT 3
Breakdown of Health Insurance Expenditures

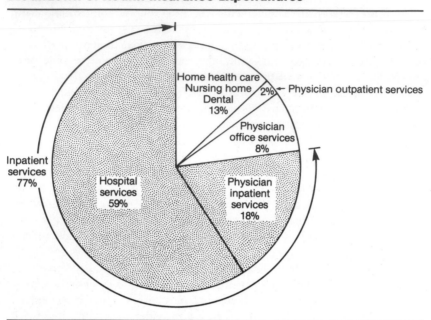

SOURCE: Health Insurance Institute of America, 1981.

incentives to join HMOs and PPOs. These mechanisms are designed to alter consumer/patient incentives regarding choice of provider and level of service use, which affect the payor's costs.

Provider mechanisms, shown in Exhibit 5, focus on inpatient cost and include selective medical staff recruitment, strict utilization review, controlling the cost of hospital products, and integrating alternative delivery systems. These mechanisms focus on changing the cost structure of the provider, the provider incentives, the method of delivery, and policing of the delivery system.

One of the most difficult and complex problems is managing the cost of hospital products. This area offers the most opportunity for improvement but is generally avoided, because so little is understood about it. Just as the information has been lacking in PPOs to indicate market share shifts and demonstrate cost savings, so have the management techniques and information been lacking in hospitals to address inpatient cost problems.

A payor's inpatient costs are driven by price, which is a function of the provider's cost structure and utilization of service. Cost control then must focus both on altering or reducing the cost of providing the services

EXHIBIT 4
Inpatient Cost Control

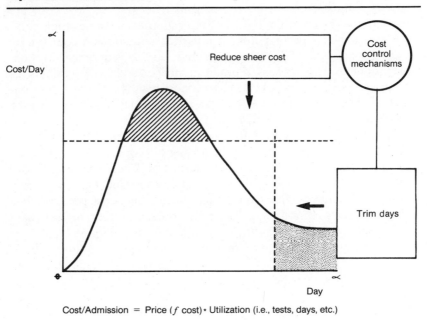

Cost/Admission = Price (f cost) • Utilization (i.e., tests, days, etc.)

EXHIBIT 5
Mechanisms for Long-Term Cost Control

Payor Mechanisms		*Provider Mechanisms*		*Desired Results*

Increase coinsurance
Raise deductibles
Avoid expansion of
  benefits
Offer incentives to join
  PPOs and HMOs
	+	Low-cost providers
		Supportive medical
		  staff—share cost
		  stabilization goals
		Selective staff recruit-
		  ment based on efficient
		  utilization patterns
		Strict utilization review
		Integrated Alternative
		  Delivery Systems (ADS)
			→	Reduce inpatient service
				  costs
				Eliminate unnecessary
				  utilization of hospital
				  services through:
				—A preselected/cost-
				  conscious medical staff
				—Tight utilization-review
				  procedures
				Provide cost-efficient total
				  patient care package sub-
				  stituting lower cost ADS
				  where possible

and on the utilization levels. To truly control cost, both today's cost and the future rate of increase in cost must be addressed. Cost control requires an understanding of the components of cost (i.e., how costs are generated) and an ability to influence utilization and cost generation.

For example, a payor's cost for a particular admission is driven by the number and type of ancillary procedures and days of hospitalization, as well as the provider's cost of producing these services. Essentially, as with any production process, the payor's cost results from both the consumption of services and the cost of the inputs. Practice patterns and the cost structure of delivery often vary markedly between providers, which affords the payor an opportunity to reduce cost through his choice of provider. Hence, by simply channeling patients to the most cost-effective provider, the payor can significantly reduce costs. These cost savings will be sustained because they result from true cost control, not simply purchasing at discounted rates from an inefficient, high-cost provider. If a provider can develop a truly cost-effective operation, then market share can be gained from a PPO without sacrificing profit margins.

Addressing the problem of inpatient costs requires the provider to first understand how costs are incurred on a product-specific basis, and then to develop approaches to reducing these product costs. It is a two-phase process that consists of product costing and profitability analysis (PCP) and product cost management (PCM).

PCPM CONCEPT

Product costing and profitability management (PCPM) is an approach to managing hospital costs that (1) recognizes that hospitals in the 1980s are product-oriented businesses, (2) focuses management attention on the true cost of producing and delivering a product, and (3) provides a framework for strategic management. As such this cost control approach has broad applications in the hospital setting for controlling inpatient costs, which is a necessary element of successful PPOs.

Success as an inpatient care provider in the 1980s will require a better understanding and management of product costs, whether to effectively deliver care in a PPO setting or to manage hospital resources responsibly under Medicare Prospective Pricing. Exhibit 6 illustrates a strategic management framework for providers in the 1980s that internalizes the PCPM concept.

Product costing and profitability (PCP) analysis is the first step in product costing and profitability management. PCP entails product definition, cost allocation, and product cost finding. It represents a necessary data analysis phase that facilitates actual cost management. Once the actual cost and the behavior of cost (i.e., cost generation, cost components, leverage points) are understood, management of cost can begin. PCM then deals with issues of protocols, practices, procedures, product im-

EXHIBIT 6
Strategic Management Framework

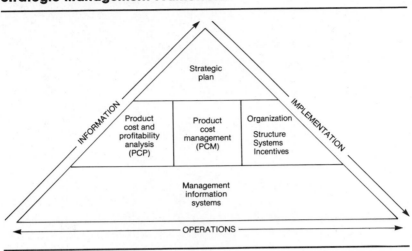

provement, operations improvement, scheduling, and utilization review to affect the product's actual cost.

Two particular points about product costing and profitability management are unique and are critical to success in provider cost control. First, PCPM deals with real economic costs of hospital products rather than costs estimated using medicare cost-to-charge ratio concepts. When cost-to-charge ratios are used to identify product costs, the revenue generated by a patient in each department is multiplied by the ratio of cost-to-charge established by the medicare cost-finding methodology. This is a static process that severely distorts results because (1) revenues are a poor surrogate for actual resource consumption, and (2) the ratios themselves distort true cost because they are a product of the medicare cost-finding process. Consequently, use of medicare cost-to-charge ratios can and often does lead to poor management decisions because cost-to-charge ratios mask the true economics of service delivery in the hospital. An example of the difference between true cost and cost derived through cost-to-charge ratios, is illustrated in Exhibit 7.

Second, PCPM goes beyond the traditional bounds of hospital cost finding. The traditional extent of hospital cost finding is at the intermediate product level (i.e., laboratory test or surgery hours) rather than full end-product costing (e.g., normal delivery). PCPM ties actual costs to end products creating an essential linkage that considers all elements in the delivery of a product or service and involves the key partners in major cost-management programs, as shown in Exhibit 8.

Knowledge of the key components of cost and related leverage points (Exhibit 9) allows managers to understand how costs are incurred and to

EXHIBIT 7
True Economic Cost vs. Cost-to-Charges Results

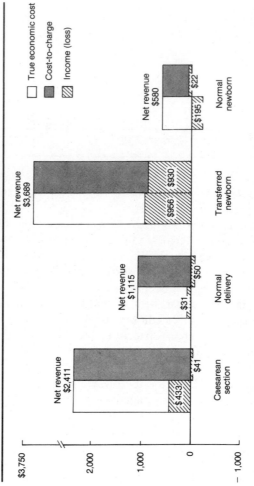

Legend:
- ☐ True economic cost
- ▨ Cost-to-charge
- ▧ Income (loss)

Caesarean section — Net revenue $2,411 — $41, $433

Normal delivery — Net revenue $1,115 — $50, $31

Transferred newborn — Net revenue $3,689 — $930, $956

Normal newborn — Net revenue $580 — $22, $195

EXHIBIT 8

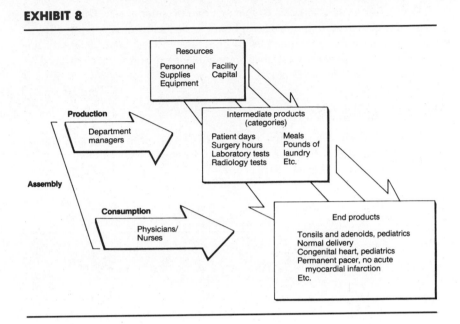

EXHIBIT 9

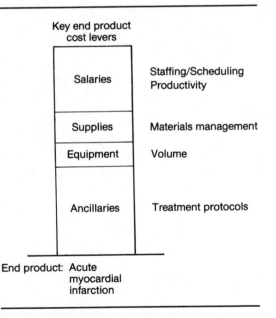

design appropriate strategies to manage end product costs. This information on cost is used in a multidisciplinary group setting, involving clinical and administration professionals to generate cost savings ideas and approaches. Ultimately a total cost-management program for each product is developed and implemented.

PCPM APPROACH

Product Cost and Profitability analysis (PCP) is a relatively straightforward but labor-intensive and time-consuming process. It consists of six steps illustrated in Exhibit 10.

EXHIBIT 10
PCP Approach

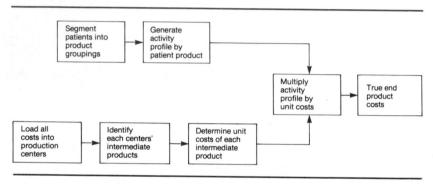

The essential first step of the process is to segment the hospital's patients into product groupings. Most often, a DRG-based approach to product grouping is used because it is consistent with current and future trends in reimbursement and the current development of hospital data systems. These product groupings are called business segments and represent a group of individual end products that can be managed. For example, a business segment might be the routine perinatal program. Within this segment multiple end products exist including normal deliveries, caesarean sections, and nondelivered cases.

Next, an activity profile is generated for each end product. The activity profile is simply a summary listing of intermediate products consumed in producing the end product. In the case of the normal delivery this might include hours in labor and delivery, radiology procedures (e.g., ultrasound), laboratory procedures, and days in the postpartum unit.

Concurrent with business segmentation and generation of activity profiles, a true cost finding for intermediate products is performed. The cost-finding process consists of three steps and deviates significantly, in

EXHIBIT 11
Percent Breakdown of Lab Expenses by Intermediate Product

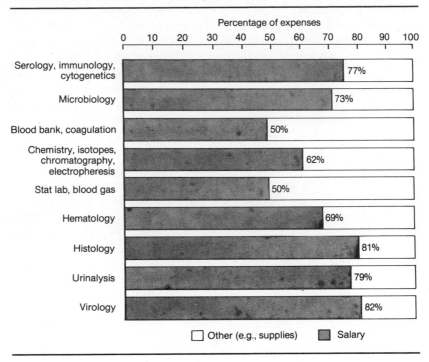

Percentage of expenses

Serology, immunology, cytogenetics	77%	
Microbiology	73%	
Blood bank, coagulation	50%	
Chemistry, isotopes, chromatography, electropheresis	62%	
Stat lab, blood gas	50%	
Hematology	69%	
Histology	81%	
Urinalysis	79%	
Virology	82%	

☐ Other (e.g., supplies)   ■ Salary

method of allocation and level of analysis, from the medicare cost-finding process used in preparing cost reports. As a first step, all direct and indirect costs are loaded into production cost centers. These production cost centers, which actually produce the intermediate products (e.g., tests, meals), are generally subsets of existing hospital departments. This process allows the hospital to break its costs down to the lowest level where meaningful data can be accumulated and where reasonable management action can be taken. For example, calling the entire clinical laboratory a production cost center in most hospitals would diminish the usefulness of the analysis, since the clinical laboratory is actually an aggregation of a number of subdepartments that differ significantly in their operation and cost structure. Hence, more meaningful production centers in the clinical laboratory might be chemistry, microbiology, hematology, virology, etc. An example of how clinical laboratory production cost centers differ in the use of labor, supplies, and other resources is shown in Exhibit 11. These important differences would be overlooked if the analyses stopped at the broad departmental level of the clinical laboratory.

Once costs have been loaded into the production cost center, the appropriate unit of measure for each center's products must be determined. Again it is important to use the most meaningful and practical unit of measure. By breaking the clinical laboratory into subdepartments, the most meaningful unit of measure often becomes what each cost center would call a test. The fact that a test in hematology and a test in chemistry are quite different no longer matters, because the cost to be apportioned to each test has been accumulated at the same subdepartment level.

To complete the intermediate costing process, the production center cost (e.g., hematology) is divided by the number of units or products (e.g., tests) produced in order to compute the unit cost of each intermediate product.

The sixth and final step in the product-costing process is to multiply the activity profile by unit costs. This calculation results in the real economic cost of the hospital's end products. The overall conceptual approach to business segmentation and microcosting analysis is shown in Exhibit 12. In this case the business segment of interest was the routine

EXHIBIT 12
Business Segmentation and Microcosting

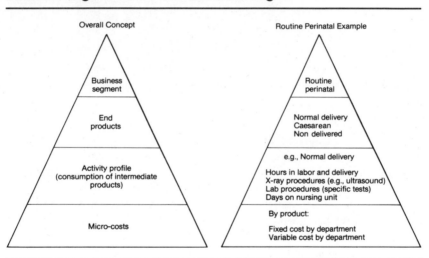

perinatal program that consisted of a number of actual end products including normal deliveries, caesarian sections, and nondelivered cases. Activity profiles were developed for each end product to identify the type and number of intermediate products consumed. Once the intermediate product and usage levels were identified the units consumed were multiplied by the cost of each intermediate product to calculate the cost of the end product, a normal delivery.

While PCP analysis is a worthwhile exercise in and of itself, the real added value comes in the management phase, PCM. Information developed in PCP must be carefully used to facilitate change in the hospital's cost position. Teams of hospital professionals, actively involved in both the production and consumption process, are vital to securing enduring change in the organization.

These PCM teams generally consist of physicians, nurses, and department managers and outside experts in hospital product-cost management under the direction of an experienced project leader. Their common goal is to reduce the cost of service delivery without diminishing the quality of the services delivered. PCM teams can have a major impact on a provider's cost of service as long as they have good information on cost and practice patterns. These teams generally find multiple opportunities to reduce cost and in many cases even improve the quality assurance function. One of the major outcomes of the team's effort is an action-oriented total cost-management program for each product and a revised target cost for the product. Such a cost-management program is illustrated in Exhibit 13.

At the very least the product costing and profitability management approach results in three key outputs for the hospital that are all useful in PPO development efforts: (1) actual costs for hospital products are determined, (2) specific cost-reduction opportunities are identified and action plans developed, and (3) ongoing in-house capabilities and organizational relationships for managing costs are established.

SUPPORT SYSTEMS

Effective PPO management and marketing require up-front investments to first deliver cost control (e.g., PCPM) and then to demonstrate savings to employers.

Support systems are necessary to achieve cost control and facilitate management decision-making in PPO operations. Once the initial two phases of PCPM are complete, systems must be installed to monitor and control cost over time. Specific cost standards for each major product should be developed and performance monitored against these standards. Effective management also requires developing an organization structure and incentive systems consistent with the concept of managing product costs. Further, accomplishing all the elements of a cost-control program requires investments in management information systems to support the cost-finding and cost-management processes.

Pursuit of cost-reduction methodologies and systems requires substantial commitment of managerial and financial resources. A cost-control program of this type enables providers to develop a long-term, sustainable position as a PPO. Implementing PCPM represents only one element of an overall cost-control effort. Utilization-review systems, selective medical staff recruitment, and integration of alternate (non-

EXHIBIT 13
Product Cost Management Program

COST FINDING

EXAMPLE PRODUCT: Cesarean Section

	Direct Expense		Indirect Expense		
	Salary	Non-Salary	ANC/Support*	Overhead	Total
Patient unit	$ 564	16	365	95	$1,038
Labor and delivery	225	62	180	116	583
Anesthesiology	194	30	46	—	270
Laboratory	72	41	22	—	135
Pharmacy	28	53	9	—	90
Central supply	17	55	8	—	80
Other†	—	—	—	55	55
Total	$1,100	257	628	266	$2,251
Percent	48.9%	11.4%	27.9%	11.8%	100%

*Ancillary/support—ancillary and support costs
†Other—miscellaneous costs

ACTION

Reduce average length of stay to 5 days or less (without complications) 6.5 days or less (with complications)
Reduce physician specific variances
Improve scheduling of electives (55% of all)
Do Caesareans in OR suite
Change staff mix: patient unit and labor and delivery
Increase formulary use to 90%
Share nurse anesthetist
Reduce lab test productivity variance

Revised target cost: $1,927 (14.4%)

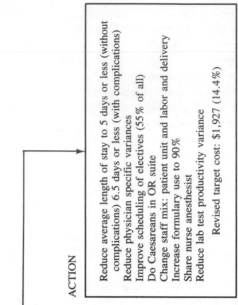

inpatient) delivery settings are other important techniques that also require investment of the hospital's limited resources. Many of these investments are applicable to areas other than PPOs, such as maintaining profitability under medicare prospective pricing.

Once cost control is actually achieved by the hospital the next step is to communicate this success to payors. Payors must be convinced that in fact the PPO can help them control their health care benefits costs. This requires investment in information systems that can track actual cost savings. Over the short term these savings can be computed from a theoretical baseline established by the hospital's past experience or the payor's records. Over a longer time period these savings can be estimated by tracking similar enrollees through different provider systems or can be computed by setting mutually agreed upon goals with payors. For example, target levels of inpatient days/1,000 employees, dollars/employee or total claims paid might be set. Evaluating whether such goals are met requires significant information resources, a large employer base population, and a broad range of services.

Further, payors have additional information needs, including, for example, utilization levels and types of admissions, that are critical to their own planning and control. Providing the payor with desired information is a critical step in strengthening and solidifying the PPO's relationship with its key customers. Investment in these PPO support systems can spell the difference between long-term success or failure as a PPO provider.

Achieving cost control will require two fundamental changes: the nature of both consumer and provider incentives, and the structure of health care delivery with a focus on hospital and physician inpatient costs. To succeed a PPO provider must commit to reducing cost through the use of sophisticated management techniques. One unique approach to reducing inpatient costs is product cost and profitability management (PCPM). This approach is being successfully employed by providers across the country, but PCPM alone is not enough. Effective PPO management and marketing also require up-front investments in PPO support systems. Support systems that facilitate ongoing cost control in operation and management decision-making as well as allow the provider to demonstrate cost savings to payors and meet the payor's critical information needs are fundamental to PPO success.

QUALITY REVIEW AND UTILIZATION MANAGEMENT

Linda L. Kloss
Senior Vice President
InterQual, Inc.
Chicago, IL

☐ The impetus for formation of PPOs grew from increased competition in health care communities among hospitals and among physicians. The PPO offers the marketplace a managed health care alternative. The notion of a managed system, in turn, implies that the quality of the services are maintained at an acceptable level, while the charges for services are controlled. The PPO, similar to prospective payment systems such as medicare's DRG reimbursement, increases the incentives for quality and charge control, incentives that have been lacking under traditional cost plus methods of payment.

As techniques for measuring quality and charge per case have become more sophisticated, data now demonstrates that differences among providers are not all attributable to patient differences. Exhibit 1 illustrates physician-specific differences in charge per case for elective, uncomplicated cholecystectomy patients. The data is case mix adjusted for patient severity of illness. The differences in average charge per case range from a high of $3,899 to a low of $1,794 with a mean of $2,786 for all patients. All cases in this data set were operated on for chronic gallbladder disease, i.e., cholelithiasis and had no comorbidity, hence differences in charge per case are not attributable to patient severity of

EXHIBIT 1
Cholecystectomy Patients: Severity Group 1

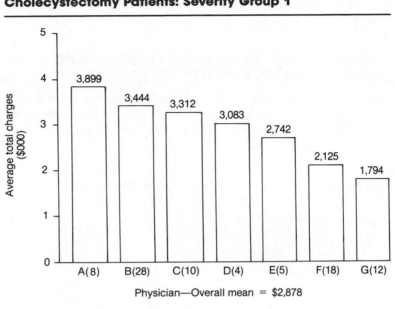

SOURCE: MediQual Systems, Inc., unpublished data from the Medical Illness Severity Grouping System.

illness differences. Further, the data excludes cases with postoperative morbidity or complication, so differences in charge per case cannot be attributed to increased costs of postoperative management. The differences therefore represent differences in physician use of health care resources (ancillary/clinical support service charges and length of stay).

This example encapsulates the quality review and utilization management task of the PPO. To be successful, i.e., maintain its competitive edge, the PPO must be able to demonstrate in the marketplace that it has systems to measure and control:

— Quality or efficacy of services, and
— Efficient use of health care resources.

The essence of the PPO's task is to control the charge per case, in terms of both quality and proper use of resources. Seventy to eighty percent of the charge per case is controlled by the physician's ordering decisions about each patient's care. This chapter describes two organizational models for the PPO quality-review and utilization-management functions: a delegation model, whereby the PPO contracts with the hospital to perform inpatient review, and the external (or nondelegated) review model, whereby the PPO conducts its own review. The advantages and disadvantages of each are presented. Essential quality-review and utilization-management activities under delegated and nondelegated models are also discussed.

EVALUATING EXISTING QUALITY-REVIEW AND UTILIZATION-MANAGEMENT TECHNIQUES

Exhibit 2 summarizes various cost control efforts and illustrates how they fit into the health care expenditure/premium equation. Traditionally, most control mechanisms, both public and private, have focused on the fre-

EXHIBIT 2
Strategies to Control Cost of Health Care Coverage

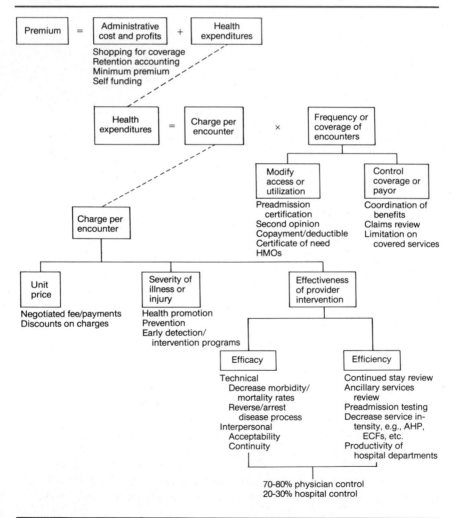

quency, unit cost, or "production" efficiency of the service provided. Examples of review programs to control the frequency of encounters include preadmission authorization or certification and mandatory second opinion programs. Benefits design, including that used in PPOs, also aims at decreasing frequency by changing the patient incentives such as adjusting the copayment, deductible, or range of covered services and by changing the provider incentives by tight claims review, capitation, and rewards for use of outpatient alternatives.

Emphasis on productivity or efficiency of services can be seen in hospital admission and continued stay review programs, preadmission testing, discharge planning, and other programs aimed at evaluating the proper indications for service.

However, review of patterns of iatrogenic illness of both medical and surgical admissions,[1,2] clearly establishes the importance of controlling the quality or efficacy side of the equation as well, both in terms of human and monetary cost. Both studies demonstrate substantial risk to hospitalized patients and suggest the need for improving mechanisms for detecting clinical hazards associated with hospitalization.

Exhibit 3 illustrates clearly the charge per case impact of morbidity

EXHIBIT 3
Average Total Charges by Severity Group for Abdominal Pain Admissions with and without Morbidity
Hospital XYZ
July, 1982—December, 1983

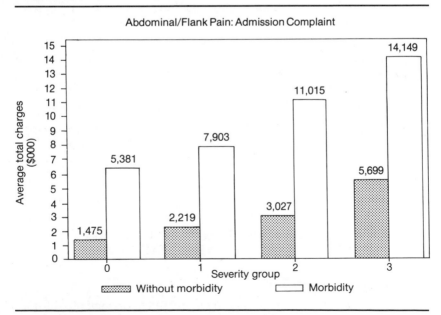

SOURCE: MediQual Systems, Inc., unpublished data from the Medical Illness Severity Grouping System.

or patient complications. Regardless of the severity of illness level on admission (stage 0, 1, 2, or 3), the charge per case doubles or triples as the patient develops new morbidity during hospitalization or fails to improve in an expected timeframe due either to the patient's underlying disease or the quality of provider intervention.

Too often the objective of hospital quality-review and utilization-monitoring activities is to comply with external requirements (JCAH, PSRO), and few hospitals have established a true internal quality/charge control program. The focus is not on charge per case management. Most hospital programs are fragmented, labor intensive, and lacking a clinically relevant database from which to draw conclusions about either patterns of care efficacy or use of resources.

It is important to understand these limitations because in a joint venture PPO between a medical staff group and its associated hospital(s), the PPO may intend to rely on the existing hospital quality review, utilization management, and credentialing mechanisms to act as a control system for inpatient services provided under the PPO. As part of its planning and before delegating these activities to the hospital(s), the PPO must examine the strengths and weaknesses of the hospital(s) existing review programs. Key areas for analysis include:

— Availability of staff support for comprehensive concurrent and retrospective data collection.
— Use of objective screening criteria for quality assessment and resource use monitoring.
— Clinical relevance of the resulting database and availability of pattern and trend data.
— Flexibility of the database to generate PPO patient/provider profiles.
— Evidence that findings are acted upon by the appropriate administrative or medical staff authority.
— Evidence that the Board authority performs the oversight function.

The PPO may elect to contract with the hospital(s) to perform quality review and utilization management for hospitalized PPO patients, or it may set up its own review program apart from the hospitals. This decision should be made after careful evaluation of the hospitals' capability to perform on behalf of the PPO.

DEVELOPING A DELEGATED QUALITY-REVIEW AND UTILIZATION-MANAGEMENT PROGRAM

ADVANTAGES OF DELEGATION

The potential advantages of the joint venture PPO contracting with the hospital(s) for quality-review and utilization-management services include the following:

— Experienced quality review/utilization management (QR/UM) staff and structure is in place.
— A comprehensive database covering all patients is available. A database consisting of only PPO patients may be too limited to enable meaningful pattern or trend data.
— Hospital programs are being tightened to meet the new demands of medicare's prospective payment. These changes are bringing hospital programs closer to the PPOs' management focus.
— Authority, responsibility, and reporting relationships are in place.
— Duplication of effort can be avoided.
— Consistency in review regardless of pay source. Ethical and medicolegal implications require that standards for quality review be uniformly applied to all patients.

DEVELOP A WRITTEN PLAN

Exhibit 4 is a sample quality-review (QR) and utilization-management (UM) plan for use by the PPO that contracts with the hospital(s) to perform or arrange to have performed QR/UM activities on its behalf. The plan itemizes the elements of the QR and UM activities, outlines reporting relationships, and assigns responsibility and authority.

EXHIBIT 4
Sample Quality-Review and Utilization-Management Program Plan

1. PURPOSE

(Name of Hospital) and physicians on its medical staff have established a Preferred Provider Organization (PPO) to negotiate for the hospital(s) and physicians to market a managed health care plan. A critical aspect of the PPO marketing strategy is quality/charge controls to achieve and maintain care effectiveness and efficiency. With respect to inpatient care, the PPO intends to delegate to the hospital to perform, or arrange to have performed, the inpatient Quality-Review and Utilization-Management (QR/UM) activities outlined in this program. With respect to nonhospital physician services, the PPO intends to delegate to the Physicians Association (PA) the responsibility to evaluate data obtained from payors or their third-party administrators on PPO outpatient claims and services relative to the quality and cost of same.

2. QR/UM PROGRAM FUNCTIONS FOR INPATIENTS

The QR/UM program provides for four main functions: data acquisition; data analysis to produce findings; use of findings; and oversight.

Data Acquisition

All QR/UM data acquisition is based on systems endorsed or approved by the appropriate committee of the PPO.

The collection and/or coordination of data acquisition and the related functions of data aggregation, display, reporting, maintenance and storage must be centralized in a hospital Quality Assessment Department or its equivalent.

EXHIBIT 4 *(continued)*

Data Analysis

Data analysis must be performed by a select, knowledgeable, clinical group, and the results of all analysis must be written findings signed by the person or group assigned this responsibility. Findings should underscore areas of hospital practice, professional performance, and patient outcomes and identify

— Differences in patterns among subgroups.
— Range of "acceptable" patterns.
— Those patterns above and below the "acceptable" range.

Such findings are directed to the QR/UM Committee of the hospital medical staff (or its equivalent) that has the responsibility to review data related to medical care given or directed by physicians and other practitioners, and to the PPO.

Use of Findings

The "use" function addresses patterns outside acceptable performance standards and involves action designed to eliminate or reduce the potential impact on quality, utilization, and related charges.

"Use" also requires evidence of follow-up to ensure that the affected practices are brought into conformance with the identified standard of acceptability.

Generally, it is desirable that the clinical department chairman have the primary "use" responsibility, but where local circumstances dictate, this function can be delegated to an individual or committee. Whatever delegation is used, there is regular reporting of data concerning "use" and follow-up to the PPO.

Oversight

Legally, the Hospital Board of Directors or a committee of the Board must perform the oversight function. The function of oversight is to guarantee that

— Information gathering efforts are valid, reliable, and comprehensive.
— Findings are reasonably related to the information gathered.
— Recommended action is taken when indicated.

The Board regularly reports to the PPO concerning its performance of the oversight function.

3. PROGRAM ELEMENTS

Quality Review

The quality review activities must include

— Morbidity Review
— Mortality Review
— Surgical Case Review (including indications for monitoring surgical and invasive procedures) for inpatient and outpatient surgery units
— Antibiotic Use Review
— Medical Record Completeness and Adequacy Review
— Clinical Review of Blood and Blood Product Usage
— Infection Surveillance
— Screening for Unexpected Patient Care Management Events

EXHIBIT 4 *(concluded)*

- — Clinical Support Services Review
- — Emergency Care Review
- — Special Care Unit Review
- — Patient Complaint Review

Utilization Management

The utilization management activities must include control of (append specific procedures)

- — Admissions.
- — Continued stays.
- — Over- and underutilization of patient care resources.

When specifically required by PPO contract and if delegated to the hospital, the program must make provision for:

- — Preadmission authorization.
- — Second opinion for surgery and invasive procedures.
- — Appropriate use of clinical support services, including special care units, emergency room, and other intensive modalities.

Staff support (quality assessment coordinator (QAC) or equivalent) is necessary to assist in the utilization management process including

- — Gathering additional data through timely communication with the patients' attending physician, unit nurses, and other professionals providing care when admission and/or subsequent review criteria are not met.
- — Making early referral for discharge planning.

4. AUTHORITY AND RESPONSIBILITY FOR THE QR/UM PROGRAM

The authority and responsibility for the QR/UM Program must be clearly established in hospital corporate and medical staff bylaws. These documents must establish a QR/UM Committee of the medical staff (or its equivalent) whose charge is to direct the QR/UM Program. From the PPO's perspective, the QR/UM Committee should include physician members representative of the scope and variety of inpatient medical care services provided to PPO patients, and at least one member of the committee should be an active participant in, and acceptable to, the PPO.

5. CONFIDENTIALITY AND REPORTING REQUIREMENTS

The PPO will maintain the confidentiality of all QR/UM Program worksheets, minutes of meetings, findings, and recommendations reported to it. To assist the PPO with this obligation, QR/UM documents provided to the PPO will reference patients by medical record number only and individual practitioners by code number only. The PPO will maintain QR/UM documentation in secured files and will not make them available to any third-party except in aggregate form in accordance with contractual obligations and to the Physician Association for the performance of its delegated quality/cost control obligations. Nothing in this section will prohibit the hospital or PPO from using electronic data processing in its QR/UM procedures, providing that equivalent confidentiality precautions are followed.

EXHIBIT 5
PPO QR/UM Delegation Chart

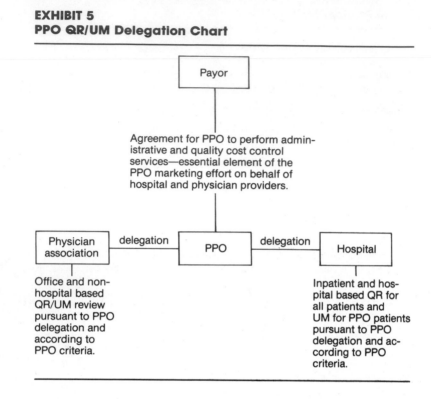

As described in the plan and illustrated in Exhibit 5 a dual delegation relationship exists under this organizational model. Inpatient and hospital-based QR/UM are delegated to the hospital(s). Review of nonhospital ambulatory services and office-based practice is delegated to the Physician Association of the PPO.

With respect to the delegated quality-review activities outlined in Exhibit 4, the PPO requires ongoing evaluation of the effectiveness of patient care. Effectiveness is defined as the achievable outcomes of care. Hence, the hospital must have mechanisms for evaluating:

— Deaths and cases in which the patient develops a complication or fails to improve as expected.
— Clinical indications for surgical intervention, for invasive, expensive, and hazardous diagnostic procedures.
— Clinical indications for drug and other therapeutics, blood transfusions, and use of other expensive, hazardous, ancillary services.
— Incidence of hospital-acquired infections and adherence to care protocols in special care units, including the emergency service.
— Patient complaints.

— Unexpected patient care management events, e.g., unexpected return to surgery, admission following outpatient surgery, adverse reactions to therapy.

Failure to achieve desired outcomes of care has measurable cost consequences, as was shown in Exhibit 3. In addition to the quality and medicolegal consequences, with respect to utilization management, the PPO expects that the hospital will objectively review the following on its behalf:

— Medical necessity for admission as an inpatient.
— Medical necessity for continued stay in the hospital.
— Appropriate use of ancillary resources.

In addition the PPO may contract with the hospital to perform UM activities not ordinarily undertaken by the hospital for its other patients. These include:

— Preadmission authorization for elective admission.
— Mandatory second opinion for surgery or other expensive, hazardous, invasive procedures.
— Screening of admissions to special care units, evaluation of the appropriateness of emergency services, and so on.

EXPLICITLY DEFINE THE
ACCOUNTABILITY RELATIONSHIP

The reporting and accountability relationship should be carefully predetermined. The PPO must receive regular reports of findings and corrective action when supported by findings. Exhibit 6 depicts a sample organizational structure for hospital accountability to the PPO as it relates to the hospital's QR/UM efforts on behalf of the PPO.

It is advisable that the PPO establish a committee for quality review and utilization management. It is this committee that will receive the reports of findings and actions from the hospital and the physicians' association. The PPO QR/UM committee's charge is to monitor the QR/UM Program for the PPO with respect to the PPO patients.

Specifically, the QR/UM Committee is responsible for the following functions:

— Monitoring the concurrent QR/UM Program that includes control of
    Admissions.
    Continued stays.
    Over- and underutilization of patient care resources.
— Monitoring quality-review and utilization-management activities,

EXHIBIT 6
Hospital Organizational Structure—PPO QR/UM Functions

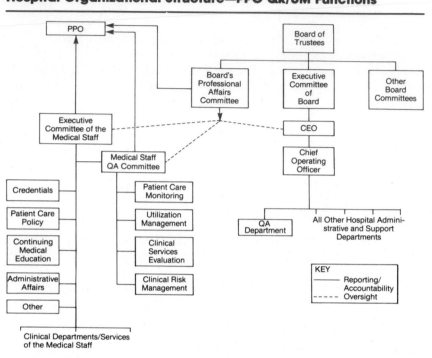

including continuous monitoring and evaluation activities through the QR/UM Program.

— Reviewing and modifying as necessary, screening criteria and the review methodology.

— Monitoring and facilitating the appropriate use of clinical support and ancillary services including special care units, emergency room, and other intensive modalities.

— Analyzing patterns of over- and underutilization.

— Analyzing financial data as it relates to hospital utilization.

— Developing when delegated by the PPO, a methodology for pre-admission authorization.

— Developing when delegated by the PPO, a methodology for second opinion for elective surgery and invasive procedures.

— Recommending changes in hospital policy, procedure, or medical staff practices as indicated by the results of analysis of utilization patterns.

— Establishing and maintaining a mechanism for the review of quality of care issues arising during concurrent review.

— Maintaining complete and accurate minutes of QR/UM activites.

— Reporting all activities to the PPO's governance.

PITFALLS IN THE DELEGATED APPROACH

Despite the advantages of the delegation approach, certain potential pitfalls occur. Most importantly, the hospital's existing review programs may be inadequate. The PPO's objectives may be delayed while the hospital works to strengthten its quality and utilization review programs. Secondly, the PPO that networks with several hospitals will likely find differences among hospitals in the review criteria, procedures and available database. This will compromise the PPO's ability to develop comprehensive, multihospital profiles and do valid interfacility comparisons.

NONDELEGATED QUALITY REVIEW AND UTILIZATION MANAGEMENT PROGRAM

This organizational option can be accomplished in two ways: the PPO can contract with a private review organization, or it can directly hire personnel to perform the requisite quality review and utilization management functions. The nondelegated approach is attractive because it insures that there is PPO-wide standardization of criteria and procedures, and tighter PPO control over the review process.

This approach also has the advantage of overcoming problems in comparability of QR/UM data among hospitals. However it may give rise to a different data problem. New PPOs and those with smaller numbers of enrollees may find that the number of cases in its database is inadequate to detect patterns of differences in effectiveness and efficiency of services. Pattern improvement, not case-by-case questioning, will yield greatest long-term payoffs for the PPO.

The steps in establishing a nondelegated review program are as follows:

DEVELOP AN IMPLEMENTATION PLAN

Through meetings of the PPO's QR/UM committee, review the alternate approaches to staffing and organizational structure approvals.

DRAFT A REVIEW PLAN DOCUMENT AND ESTABLISH ORGANIZATIONAL STRUCTURE

Develop a structure for data flow, including staffing for data collection, data analysis, and accountability for review within the overall PPO organization. Identify review components and methods.

DRAFT AGREEMENT DOCUMENTS FOR SIGNATURE BY PARTICIPATING HOSPITALS

An important component of the agreement is access to PPO patient records and data and the corresponding data confidentiality agreements.

DEVELOP PREADMISSION REVIEW PROGRAM, IF ADOPTED FOR IMPLEMENTATION

Draft criteria and procedures for preadmission review/authorization.

DEVELOP CONCURRENT REVIEW PROCEDURES

Adopt objective criteria for concurrent utilization monitoring and develop protocols for review and referral of questioned cases to the PPO's designated physician advisors.

Incorporate quality review indicators, including surgery indications monitoring and clinical screening for risk management.

IDENTIFY DATA PROCESSING, REPORT GENERATION REQUIREMENTS

DEVELOP METHODS FOR MONITORING OFFICE BASED PRACTICE

Most often this is accomplished by use of a carefully designed claims form incorporating key quality and utilization indicators.

As with review programs, the QR/UM program procedures and methods will evolve with experience. Also, the committee may find that start up can be expedited and trial and error decreased through qualified consultation.

CONCLUSION

To be successful, the PPO's QR/UM program must demonstrate in which areas intensity of service and related cost can be reduced without adverse effect on patient health outcomes. The program must permit control in three critical areas:

— Appropriateness of hospital admission, costly, hazardous procedures, and therapies.
— Effectiveness (quality) of medical care.
— Efficiency of physician use of resources.

To be acceptable the program must be clinically valid and satisfy concerns about the gap between quality and cost evaluation. Tight cost control gives rise to legitimate concern about the impact on quality. Purchasers and providers alike will reject tight cost and utilization controls without corresponding evidence that acceptable quality is being maintained.

NOTES

1. K. Steel, et al., "Iatrogenic Illness on a General Medical Service at a University Hospital," *The New England Journal of Medicine*, 304, no. 11 (March 12, 1981), pp. 638–42.

2. N. P. Couch, et al., "The High Cost of Low-Frequency Events," *The New England Journal of Medicine*, 304, no. 11 (March 12, 1981), pp. 634–37.

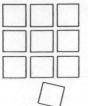

Applying HMO Utilization Control Techniques to PPOs*

Edward M. Bosanac, Ph.D.
President
E. Michael Associates
San Diego, CA

This paper presents a discussion of utilization control and utilization review mechanisms used in HMOs that are applicable in PPOs.

The initial focus of PPOs is often in achieving short-term gains through discounted fee arrangements. While the fees are discounted, the incentive for the provider is to perform additional services to make up for the discounted price. Such a situation eliminates any savings from the discount through increased utilization. Discounted fee-for-service medicine without utilization controls provides no relief from the health care cost problem. To address these issues "full-service" PPOs offering the following types of services to clients are appropriate vehicles to manage indemnity program costs:

— Physician services at an established reimbursement schedule using a discounted usual, customary, and reasonable (UCR) fee sched-

*This work was completed while Dr. Bosanac was the Vice President of Operations for the Greater San Diego Health Plan.

ule or possibly a form of the California Relative Value Study (CRVS). Under the CRVS, each procedure has to be assigned a relative level of difficulty expressed in units. Those unit values multiplied by a dollar conversion factor will yield a reimbursement fee. For example, a limited physician office visit is valued at 5.2 medical units. If the dollar conversion factor was $6.00, the reimbursement for the procedure would be $31.20.

— Hospital services at established rates usually on a per-diem or per-discharge basis for a period of at least one year.

— Claims review of both medical and hospital claims with payment recommendations. The claims review could be total, a sample (10 percent of all cases), or selected procedures (procedures over $500.00).

— Outpatient surgical flat rate fees.

— Utilization-control programs such as prior authorization of services, preadmission certification, concurrent review, and second opinion surgery.

— Retrospective claims audit.

— Extensive retrospective utilization and cost reporting.

UTILIZATION CONTROL MECHANISMS

With the introduction of a PPO, a basic indemnity benefit program continues with the PPO option as an overlay. This new option brings both discounted fees and the utilization-control features to the indemnity program. Many of the utilization control aspects operating in an HMO can be directly applied to the indemnity program through the PPO. This section will concentrate on prospective utilization control functions such as prior authorization of ambulatory services, preadmission certification, concurrent review, and second opinion surgery programs. The following section will detail retrospective utilization review functions that are primarily data driven.

PRIOR AUTHORIZATION PROGRAMS

One of the most effective tools used by HMOs and indemnity dental programs is prior authorization of services. A prior authorization program has multiple effects. The request to authorize various procedures places regulatory checks on the wanton use of service. It also provides the opportunity to direct patients requiring certain procedures to various facilities or types of facilities.

PPOs could authorize certain procedures such as those listed in Exhibit 1 to be done in a physician's office, on a "come and go" basis in a hospital, or in a surgi-center. If these procedures are to be done on an inpatient basis, prior authorization would be required.

EXHIBIT 1
Outpatient Procedures Authorized by HMOs

General Medicine or Surgery:
Breast biopsy
Bronchoscopy
Cervical node biopsy
Colonoscopy
Ganglion excision
Hernia, inguinal child
Hernia, umbilical, child

Lipoma excision
Muscle biopsy
Polypectomy, rectal
Sigmoidoscopy, fiberoptic
Skin lesion excision with primary closure
Upper endoscopy

Gynecology:
Abortion
Abscess drainage
Bartholin marsupialization
Breast biopsy
Cervical conization
Condyloma acuminata, extensive
Culdocentesis or culdoscopy
Dilation and curettage
Hymenectomy

Hysteroscopy
Labia, plastic revision
Laparoscopy
Laser cautery
Ligation, tubal
Vaginal biopsy, cyst or polyp excision
Vulvar biopsy, lesion excision or
  fulguration

Neurosurgery or Orthopedics:
Carpal tunnel release
Fingernail/toenail removal
Fracture, closed reduction
Ganglion excision
Hammertoe repair with both resection
  and tenotomies
Hand, small bones, open reduction

Hand tendon repair
Morton's neuroma excision
Phalangectomy
Plantar wart excision
Tenotomy, hand or foot
Trigger finger, tenovaginotomy

Opthalmology:
Cataract extraction
Ectropion
Entropion
Intraocular lens impact

Iridectomy
Pterygium
Strabismus

Otolaryngology:
Antral puncture
Bronchoscopy without biopsy turbinate
Lacrimal duct probing
Laryngoscopy without biopsy

Myringotomy with or without tubes
Nasal fracture, closed reduction
Navicular bone, excision of

Plastic Surgery:
Blepharoplasty, upper
Closed reduction of nasal fractures
Dermabrasion of skin
Excision of skin tumors, ganglion
Fingernail/toenail removal
Intralesional injections
Mammoplasty

Repair of ectropion, entropion small
  lacerations
Revision of scars
Rhytidectomy
Small skin grafts
Tissue transfer or rearrangement (z-plasty,
  etc.)

Urology:
Circumcision
Cystoscopy, including needle biopsy of
  prostate or retrograde pyelogram
Hydrocele, child

Meatotomy
Urethral dilation
Vasectomy

For example cataract extractions can be contracted for an established fee at a specific eye clinic. Individuals who may need cataract extractions would be directed to that facility even though the physician originally seeing the patient directed them to another physician. Use of the contracted facility could be optional, encouraged through copayment incentives, or required. In such situations, the "sentinel effect" could encourage more conservative use of a service because of the peer-review mechanism.

Other procedures such as hysterectomy, ligation (varicose veins), tonsillectomy and adenoidectomy, or submucous resection (turbinates) would require prior authorization regardless of where performed. The lists can be expanded or contracted to account for local practice patterns or intensity of review desired. Furthermore, the level of documentation required to approve the various procedures can be as brief or extensive as desired. Plastic surgery procedures might require prior authorization with extensive documentation, whereas other procedures such as tonsillectomy or submucous resection (turbinates) might be required to meet only one or two specific criteria in order to be performed on an inpatient basis.

An important aspect of the PPO is the negotiation of flat rates for various surgical procedures. The PPO should be able to offer attractive rates for a number of procedures if done in selected preferred facilities. The prior authorization program directs patients to those facilities.

Prior authorization provides a mechanism to control and direct utilization of selected procedures. While providing additional regulatory burden for the provider, prior authorization programs have been extensively used in HMOs and have direct application and use in a PPO environment.

PREADMISSION CERTIFICATION

Preadmission certification is a form of prior authorization program. It also interjects a regulatory barrier between a physician's decision to admit a patient and the actual admission. While the actual denial of the admission occurs infrequently, there would be an additional sentinel effect that would result in a reduction in admission rates. Furthermore, the redirection of the admission so as to perform the procedure on an outpatient basis could also reduce admission rates and increase savings. With established criteria for specific procedures, a nurse coordinator can easily redirect the admission to be performed on an outpatient basis. The elimination of one- and two-day hospital stays as a result of monitoring such procedures represents significant savings.

Generally, such programs work in conjunction with the physician and do not require direct involvement by the patient. The PPO physician is required to notify the review office approximately one to two weeks in advance of a scheduled admission. When the physician calls the review office, data such as patient ID, hospital, date of procedure, diagnosis, planned surgical procedure (if applicable), and medical indications or risks are collected. These data are compared to specific criteria. An initial length of stay is then assigned and the admission is "precertified." If the appropriateness of the admission is questioned by review personnel (usually a nurse), additional data are collected and the case referred to a physician. Upon review, the requesting physician is notified of the decision. Exhibit 2 illustrates the precertification process by means of a flow chart. Additional responsibility could be placed on patients to notify the PPO of the impending admission since significant savings accrue to the patient by following PPO operating procedures.

In many HMOs, admission on the day of surgery (so called AM admits) is required. The PPO could do likewise. Patients who have anesthesia risks, require in-hospital preoperative procedures, or have medical problems requiring prior hospitalization would be admitted at an earlier time.

The preadmission certification program works hand-in-hand with the prior authorization program to schedule or redirect admissions as outlined by medical criteria.

The effectiveness of the program is also affected by the relationship of the PPO review program and the hospital. Notification of an admission, either emergency or those which were not prior approved, is an important function that the hospital admitting office performs. The contractual relationship between the PPO and the hospital provider should establish penalties for nonnotification. The assessment of financial penalties greatly assists the process.

For an employer operating a PPO or purchasing services from a PPO, an identification card is important. The card contains the appropriate benefit coverage information and notifies the hospital to contact the PPO review program for certification of the admission.

CONCURRENT REVIEW

As part of the overall hospital review program, admission and continuing stay review need to be performed. The concurrent program must be effective because the ability to prevent unnecessary days is of critical importance to the PPO. To be effective, the length of stay criteria must balance frequency of review with length of extensions. A high frequency of review will drive up review costs while long extensions will reduce program effectiveness. Current length of stay books by Professional Activities Survey and other abstracting systems (e.g., Commonwealth Clinical Systems or Hospital Utilization Project) showing distribution of length of stay (LOS) by diagnosis, procedure, or diagnosis related group (DRG) are used to establish and maintain the length of stay criteria. Individual PPO adjustment of the LOS criteria is expected.

The PPO review coordinator does not usually see the patient but rather reviews the chart. Any concern about the continued hospitalization will prompt a call by the review coordinator to the attending physician to

EXHIBIT 2 Hospital Certification Program Flow Chart

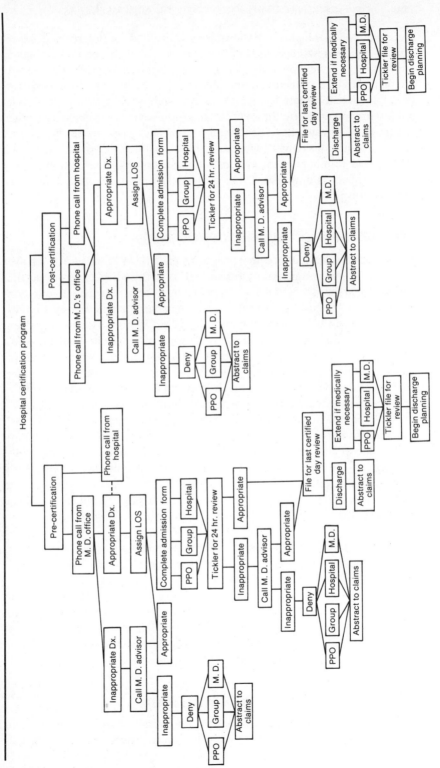

ascertain treatment plans. Extensions are granted as determined necessary by the review coordinator. In cases in which the continued stay is questioned, a review by a physician advisor is carried out, and the results are then provided to the attending physician. Like preadmission certification, concurrent review has long been an established practice and can be readily implemented by the PPO. Concurrent review is especially critical when per-diem rates have been negotiated. The single extra day of stay can wipe out any savings realized in the discounted per-diem rates. In a DRG-based reimbursement system the importance of the continued stay review process is diminished, since the risk for any additional days lies with the hospital.

SECOND OPINION SURGERY PROGRAMS

Second opinion surgical review programs have been in existence for over 10 years. They have generally proven most useful when program participation is mandatory. Voluntary programs have been less effective in containing costs because most health care consumers are unwilling to question a physician via a second opinion program without a sufficient incentive to do so. Studies of second opinion programs have shown the elective surgery was not confirmed in about 20 to 30 percent of all cases reviewed. However, a 5 percent participation rate by consumers in voluntary programs does not make much impact on total health care costs.[1]

The most effective programs financially require consumers to seek a second opinion. For example, if a second opinion is not sought, the elective surgery is not covered. Such a program can ease the potential strain on the doctor-patient relationship by placing the employer or insurance program in the position of requiring the second opinion. Subsequently participation levels are high with corresponding levels of savings. When the provider knows that the decision to perform surgery will be reviewed by a peer, the sentinel effect seems to occur in this review program as well.

Procedures for which some review programs have required a second opinion include hysterectomy, heart surgery, dilation and curettage, laminectomy, tonsillectomy and adenoidectomy, and breast surgery.

The cost benefit of second opinion surgery ranges from a low of $2.50 to $4 per $1 of program cost to as much as $16 per $1 of program cost.[2,3] The elective surgery is not recommended in about 20 percent of the cases studied with the consumer complying with the recommendation to not have the surgery about 75 percent of the time.[4,5]

UTILIZATION REVIEW MECHANISMS

While the utilization control aspects of an overall cost-containment program attempt to regulate use of services on a prospective basis, a balanced program must also retrospectively review those services that have been provided. Retrospective utilization review adds a further dimension to a cost-management program and helps focus the utilization-control components.

There are three major components of utilization review activities: claims review, pricing, and information handling.

CLAIMS REVIEW

The claims payment system used in the administration of any health benefits plan is one of the most important elements of a retrospective utilization review program. Claims payment systems generally contain patient eligibility lists, scope of benefit information, benefit limitations, reimbursement or pricing structure, and provider eligibility lists. These administrative systems maintain tremendous potential for utilization-review activities. With the inclusion of appropriate edits, the system can have an important impact on costs prior to payments being made for those services.

One of the most important features is the ability to detect duplicate claims. Identical services provided by a provider to the same patient on a given date should be denied as duplicates. Billing systems in physicians' offices do not always provide completely accurate claims. Other kinds of problems that require validity checks include the identification of claims in which the procedures are inconsistent with the sex of the patient (obstetric services provided to male patients), procedures that have been performed previously on the same patient (multiple gall bladder removals), and similar types of validity checks.

Eligibility questions deal with who can legitimately receive services under the buyers benefit program. The capture of both employee and dependent information is vital to regulate who receives services under an insurance program. Are family members over age 21 not in school but living at home eligible for coverage under the employee's policy? Can the claims administrator monitor this? Even if the claims administrator for the buyer can and does perform such functions, the PPO could be provided eligibility files by the carrier to facilitate the review process.

CLAIMS PRICING AND AUDITING

Even though it is not a claims administrator, the PPO can perform claim pricing for a buyer. Since the PPO has negotiated rates with a provider network, it would not be unusual for the PPO to price claims. The pricing process could use the California Relative Value Studies (RVS) or Current Procedural Terminology Fourth Revision (CPT4). As part of the RVS ground rules, the established number of units assigned to a particular surgical procedure also includes services provided as follow-up to the original procedure. For example a capsulectomy (wrist) has an RVS unit value of 5.4 surgical units and 60 followup days. Using a surgical conversion factor of $134.00 per unit the procedure would be priced at $723.60. The unit value, however, includes related services provided during a sixty day period subsequent to the original surgery. The review system should be able to identify such services if billed separately and reject payment. Since not all procedures have RVS unit values, the payments have yet to be established. These RNE (relativity not established) and "by-report" procedures generally have their unit values established by the utilization-review committees.

Whether paying claims using billed charges, UCR (usual, customary, and reasonable) or RVS units, the claims review system is a useful component of the overall utilization-review system.

One possible scenario can have the provider submitting claims to an insurer, a third-party administrator (TPA), or to the PPO directly. If submitted to the insurer or the TPA, the claims could be delivered to the PPO for initial screening on a 100 percent basis. After the PPO reviews and enters both hospital and professional claims, a computer tape of all reviewed claims could be provided to the administrator for processing. The PPO is responsible for medical appropriateness, medical necessity, and pricing. The administrator is responsible for final eligibility determination, all benefits administration, and actual payment to the providers. Another option can have the PPO providing review services on a limited basis. Such review includes professional claims over a specific dollar amount, professional claims for selected procedures, and hospital claims. Other claims-related utilization-review activities would be the responsibility of the administrator. A third option would have the claims review performed entirely retrospectively using claims paid tapes from the payors. In most scenarios, however, the PPO is not interested in becoming a claims administrator. The PPO process requires timely and accurate data for buyer reporting and utilization review.

While the auditing of claims (comparing the medical record with the bill) is generally not performed by a PPO, it is a service that can be offered to medical care purchasers. Similar programs are common in both the indemnity and HMO business where they are being performed by an outside firm. Some companies have the employee who received the service review the claim and any savings would be split between the employee and the company.

INFORMATION HANDLING

One of the most important aspects of utilization review is information handling. Buyers have been generally uninformed about the nature of their health care expenditures. Insurers had designed systems to assure accurate turn-around of claims to facilitate the payment process. In most cases, however, patient-specific information and service-specific data were not available for reporting. Information was collected and payments made on a contract basis (employee and dependents) only. Total charges for an entire medical claim were all that was generally available. In recent years as health insurance and claim administration markets became more competitive, insurers have made increased efforts to assist buyers.

Under the current indemnity system, insurers had no incentive to control costs since increased costs represented increased premiums the following year. In contrast, HMOs have had to manage health care delivery costs or face bankruptcy since they did not have access to massive amounts of capital to fund deficits. Since the risk for health care expenditures was directly born by the HMO, strong data systems have been the rule. The need for sophisticated information management techniques has been even more critical for IPA (Independent Practice Association) type HMOs because of their larger numbers of providers and no on-site physician monitoring capability. HMOs have used at least two types of information reporting in operating a review process: trend data and profiles. Trend data provide reference points when interpreting current statistics. A hospitalization rate in isolation is difficult to interpret unless values for prior time periods provide a reference point. Trend data are similarly important for research or statistical analysis. Using trend information on a number of variables permits the application of techniques such as regression analysis or cluster analysis to determine critical variables accounting for cost increases over time. These procedures can also be used to forecast costs or service usage with changes in time, demographic mix, or changes in benefit packages.

The concept of practice profiles has been used in quality assurance for over twenty years. In the hospital area the Commission on Professional and Hospital Activities through its Professional Activities Survey (PAS) has used profile methodology in examining hospital care patterns since its inception. Marketing people have used customer profiles to match against demographic factors to locate potential markets. In the Professional Standards Review Organization program a profile has been defined as "the presentation of aggregated data in formats which display patterns of health care services over a defined period of time."[6]

Profile analysis is a form of retrospective review in which aggregated medical services data are subjected to pattern analysis (e.g., the distribution of a selected diagnosis or the changes in average length of stay at a given hospital compared to community averages over time). The profile generally involves some comparison of patterns of care of a particular physician, hospital, diagnosis, or procedure to some other group of cases. The individual practitioner's use of a procedure could be compared to its use within his or her specialty. Current monthly admission rates could be compared to the admission rate for the same period the previous year.

While most uses of profiling have occurred for inpatient utilization, HMOs have recently done extensive work in ambulatory care profiles.[7,8] Under a PPO arrangement, the data from claims must be available to support extensive profiling for physicians, hospitals, diagnoses, procedures, patients, employer groups, or benefit packages. Without complete and accurate claims data the utilization review process becomes suspect. It requires only one or two instances in which the claims data inaccurately reflect a specific physician's services to place doubt in a reviewer's mind. With any level of doubt, the difficult decision of sanctioning a medical peer is generally not made.

Within the PPO, the profiling methodology should be an integral part of the monitoring process. It is intended to supplement rather than replace the preadmission certification or concurrent review programs. It is used to focus these programs. Similarly, the profiles provide management with summary statistics used to analyze benefit packages, hospital costs, or physician utilization. The profile data is used to establish or modify operating policies or educational programs.

In the development of a preferred provider arrangement the use of trend and profiling techniques can assist in managing the provider network regardless of size. Preadmission certification, concurrent review, or other prior authorization programs maintain their effectiveness regardless of the size of the network.

The utilization review strategy behind trend and profile reporting is to use key variables or indicators such as prescription rate, service rate, or average cost per visit to define aberrant practice patterns. That initial step is then used to scan large numbers of doctors, diagnoses, or patients and subsequently to trigger further analysis about the nature of the problem and possible solution. This permits analysis to focus on a few doctors or diagnoses and to use detail reports to analyze the specific problem (see Exhibit 3).

**EXHIBIT 3
PPO-Focused Review
Strategy**

Utilization review strategy

Scanning reports

Focusing reports

Detail reports

Trend and Profile Review

The physician profile contains both clinical as well as financial data. The clinical data would include rates of referrals, procedure use, prescriptions, and hospitalization. The financial data would include total dollars paid, hospitalization costs, referral costs, average cost per visit, and average cost per service.

The principle behind such a profile methodology is to focus on physicians who exhibit practice patterns that differ from some accepted norm. Historically, review by HMOs and indemnity insurers has been on a claim by claim basis. Such review can be effective but not efficient. A profile and focused utilization-review methodology contains a number of reporting levels.

For physician review, the analytical process begins with aggregation at the specialty level by generating practice norms (specialty averages). While those results are useful for examining costs among the different specialties, they are also used in subsequent steps of the process.

The second type of aggregation would be at the physician-specific level. The merging of physician-specific and specialty-specific data provide the basis for identification of aberrant practice patterns. The PPO can rank physicians on a percentile basis for each item on the profile and provide comparisons to the specialty average (see Exhibit 4). Selection of physicians for more intensive review would be facilitated by a percentile ranking of physicians within their specialty for a number of key indicators such as average visits per patient, average costs per patient or average length of stay for a given diagnosis. Although the percentile ranking is the most lucid measure, other measures such as the standard deviation express a similar concept. The selection of a particular physician for review would involve physicians above the 75th, 80th, or other selected percentile; alternatively, the physician with a number of key variables more than 1 or 1.5 standard deviations above the mean would be targeted for additional review.

A third type of aggregation that is useful is at the patient-specific level. A summarization of all services and charges for each patient seen by each physician provides additional insight into the nature of the aberrant practice pattern identified in the focusing reports. This level of review is only entered if the physician is identified in an earlier level. If the statistics presented in the physician profile were skewed by a single patient, further review might target that patient only. However, if the patient profile shows patterns that would support those found in the physician profile, the final level of review (service specific) is entered.

The examination of bills and services is the final level of analysis under this type of high performance review system. In other review systems this level of reporting represents the entry into the review process. Using the service listing, the actual care provided to each patient is documented (see Exhibit 5). It is at that point that clinical judgment is re-

EXHIBIT 4
Provider Medical Profile of Service Activity

Provider: Doe, Joseph MD [ABC1061]   Specialty: Allergy

For quarter 4 of 1984

	Your Services	Your Percentile in Allergy (AA)	Average for Your Specialty
Number of different patients	100		37
Number of total patient visits	355		151
Number of total services	507		196
Average number services per visit	1.43	79	1.30
Average number services per patient	5.07	46	5.27
Average number visits per patient	3.55	33	4.06
Total: amount paid in services to provider	$4,463.38		
Average cost per visit	$12.57	13	$17.30

	AVG Cost across All Patients				Average Bill Cost			
	Your Services	Your Percentile in AA	Average for Your Specialty	Percent of Bills	Your Services	Your Percentile in AA	Average for Your Specialty	Percent of Bills
All services	$44.63	19	$70.26		$ 8.80	6	$13.33	
Basic care services	31.07	19	43.65	77	7.98	13	10.31	80
Specialty medical service	6.37	46	9.10	7	19.31	38	29.97	6
Surgical services	0.00	49	0.00	0	0.00	49	0.00	
Radiology services	3.83	60	1.60	4	20.20	20	21.95	1
Lab services	3.07	70	1.90	9	6.54	60	6.14	6
Incidental services	0.27	49	13.99	4	1.50	7	39.99	7

EXHIBIT 5 Patient Service Listing for Claims Paid or Denied 84/01/01 through 84/10/01 Doctor Smith (ABC130)

| — Date — | | — RVS — | | | | | | | Ordering | Amount | | | Net |
Service	Register	Code	M1	M2	Bill #	SC	Diag	Diag2	PR#	Billed	Copay	Deduc	Payable
	7114-01	Joan Doe			Eff: 83/11/02			GRP: 30	Age: 17	Sex: F	Prim-Phys: ABC130 William Smith, MD		
84/01/06	84/02/11	00004			10220202	50	574.0	575.1	ABC130	3.00	1.50	0.00	1.50
		Perscription drugs from doctors office											
84/01/06	84/02/11	90050			10220202	50	574.0	575.1	ABC130	24.00	3.00	2.10	18.90
		Limited office visit, established patient											
84/01/06	84/02/11	90730			10220202	50	574.0	575.1	ABC130	10.00	0.00	2.35	7.65
		Therapeutic injection in conjunction with visit											
84/02/01	84/03/11	93000			10220202	50	574.0	575.1	ABC130	30.00	0.00	3.00	27.00
		Electrocardiogram with interpretation and report											
84/02/02	84/07/13	80104			10229203	50	574.0	575.1	ABC130	17.00	0.00	3.50	13.50
		Automated, multichannel tests any three or four tests											
84/02/02	84/07/13	80112			10229203	50	574.0	575.1	ABC130	20.00	3.00	3.50	13.50
•	•	•											
•	•	•											
•	•	•											
84/02/02	84/03/15	90250			10220202	50	574.0	575.1	ABC130	28.00	3.00	5.66	19.34
		Limited hospital visit, established patient											
84/02/06	84/03/15	90260			10220202	50	574.0	575.1	ABC130	35.00	0.00	12.36	19.64
		Intermediate hospital visit, established patient											
		Patient totals:								246.50	17.50	40.00	229.00
	7131-01	Sally Doe			Eff: 83/11/01		GRP 15	Age: 21	Sex: F	Prim-Phys: ABC130	William Smith, MD		
84/9/16	84/9/31	73610			11690651	50			ABC130	40.00	5.00	7.78	27.22
		Diagnostic radiology, ankle, complete											

quired to determine the necessity or appropriateness of a given course of treatment. This level of review is intensive and expensive. It is only done on those few physicians who exceed the established "norm." A data analyst or the computer itself can accomplish all other levels of review. Furthermore, the reviewing physician does not enter the service review level blindly searching for patterns; the process is entered with a "road map" provided by the physician percentile or standard deviation profile. For example, the review physician already knows that the referral rate is excessive or that the use of ancillary services is ten times the specialty average and that this doctor has a higher rate of service per visit than 94 percent of the physician peer group.

After detailed review of the services, the reviewer may find evidence of questionable practices and refer the physician to the PPO utilization-review committee for sanction or expulsion from the PPO. On those services that were not appropriate, the PPO could recommend payment recovery if the physician-PPO contract permits such action. Alternatively, the service review process may find appropriate utilization in all cases. The process is a screening device, and "false positives" are possible. For example, subspecialty internists could appear to be extraordinarily expensive providers when compared to general internists. With this form of review, the intensive analysis is performed on a limited number of cases.

Profiling techniques are similarly possible for hospitals, procedures, diagnoses, or patients. For hospitals, the PPO would usually be dealing with less than 20 or 30 facilities, so the scanning and focusing aspects are not required since examination of this number of hospitals can be accomplished without focusing. For patients or employees, age-sex–specific utilization rates become the key indicators for all services, common procedures, prescriptions, referrals, and surgeries. Comparisons to age-sex–specific groups provide percentile rankings of employees for the key utilization variables (e.g., visits per month, services per visit, services per month, or prescriptions per month) within their age-sex group. An exception report, listing only those patients above the 95th percentile or beyond two standard deviations of the mean for selected items could be reviewed. Those patients' records might be scrutinized because of extraordinary cost or utilization patterns. For procedures and diagnoses, the scanning process is important. The PPO can focus on the 5, 10, or 15 most used or 10, 15, or 20 most expensive procedures or diagnoses and then profile those. This profile would examine the utilization of the selected procedures, by specialty, by doctor, and by time period. In each of these cases the analysis would examine frequency of procedures or repetition of procedures on a patient-specific basis or analyze the use of a particular procedure in concurrence with other procedures. In short, the PPO data should be able to identify the frequency of the procedures, the trend in the use of the procedures, and the appropriate or inappropriate use of the procedures. These summary reports must be keyed to actual claims for detailed medical review. If an unexpected statistic is found in the summary report (e.g., an extraordinary number of Cesarean sections), the actual claims can be recalled for close scrutiny.

In summary, the PPO data system should have a comprehensive trend and profile report capability. The system must support the ability to do exception reporting and enable the analyst to utilize summarized data to key selections of specific claims or services. Ad hoc reporting is important to permit a variety of reports not yet defined.

Health Benefits Management Reporting

From the employers' perspective, the ability to obtain cost information from the carriers on their employees or benefit plans has been wanting. The PPO must have a report series that facilitates the management of health benefits.

A health benefits management system would include reports on service utilization and cost analysis. Reports would generally be for an individual employer group with detailed data on medical, inpatient hospital, and outpatient hospital costs and trends. The medical component should include utilization and trend information for employees and dependents for such items as RVS codes, diagnoses, physician specialties, and hospitals. The difference between billed charges and the PPO pricing should be reported to the buyer as savings from the PPO.

For hospital costs, a PPO-offered health benefits management system should include total charges and actual buyer costs as well as utilization statistics for the group. Comparison of specific employers' costs with averages of other similar or all other groups within the PPO is extremely useful. Items which should be reported include number of admissions, length of stay, total dollar expense, total dollar savings by PPO, average cost per admission, and average cost per day. These reports, while being presented in the aggregate, should also break out similar items for each hospital. Surgical and nonsurgical costs for both employees and dependents provide information useful for benefit design or incentive restructuring. For example, can the employer continue to cover dependents' health costs with a 10 percent copayment? Using rough estimations of savings that might be generated from a second opinion surgery program, how much savings could the employer realize? These are the types of questions such information would tend to generate and assist in answering. Exhibits 6 to 10 show several report examples for hospital length of stay and charges, inpatient hospital utilization, medical claims by type of services, group experience profile, and benefits utilization.

PPO Review Activity Reporting

One final area of reporting that the PPO must support is called activity reports. Activity reports let the employer know what the PPO has done during the month and generally include number of claims reviewed or

EXHIBIT 6 Hospital Length of Stay and Charges Report

Ancillary services are those with a service code ranging from 4040 to 4440. These services include anesthesiology, laboratory, radiology, pharmacy, and various psychiatric, emergency room, and therapy services. The body of this report does not reflect services with deduction codes, i.e., coverage by other carriers. These deduction amounts are given at the bottom of the table.

Group P0201
ABC Manufacturing Company
for November 1984
Total lives: 4,839

Hospital	Total Cost	Admissions	Average Length of Stay	Average Ancillary Cost	Ratio to Community Norm for This Hospital	Average Cost per Admission	Ratio to Community Norm for This Hospital
ABC Hospital	$ 3,304.71	3	2.00	$ 1,733.16	0.61	$ 1,101.57	0.34
Bay Hospital	3,039.75	2	1.50	936.60	0.96	1,519.87	0.85
Childrens Hospital	247.50	1	1.00	—	—	247.50	0.50
Mountain Hospital	23,927.06	15	3.13	925.90	1.36	1,595.14	0.95
Lehr Hospital	30,502.36	21	3.14	1,259.12	1.01	1,452.49	0.63
XYZ Hospital	9,033.62	4	3.25	976.62	1.15	2,258.40	11.22
	•	•					
	•	•					
	•	•					
St. Joseph's Hospital	69,662.20	4	18.75	11,400.72	6.27	17,415.55	5.75
DSP Memorial Hospital	30,410.87	13	3.15	1,128.78	0.93	2,339.30	1.01
Nice View Hospital	7,201.89	1	7.00	6,385.32	3.71	7,201.89	2.54
Mission Hospital	7,205.89	2	4.00	2,570.42	2.44	3,602.94	1.90
St. Louis Hospital	16,329.00	3	7.00	5,443.00	2.02	5,443.00	1.00
Total	$217,371.23	78	4.26	$ 1,888.33	1.406	$ 2,786.81	1.142

EXHIBIT 7
Inpatient Hospital Utilization Summary Report

Group: ABC Manufacturing Company

Reporting period: January–June 1984
Prior period: January–June 1983

	This Period	Prior Period	This Period to Prior Period Ratio	Community This Period	Group to Community Ratio
Admissions per 1,000 in population	11.2	11.3	1.0	8.6	1.3
Age 0–19	8.5	9.3	0.9	4.5	1.9
20–35	6.1	11.2	0.5	13.3	0.5
35–65	19.2	11.9	1.6	7.6	2.5
65+	0.0	0.0	—	0.2	0.0
Average LOS per admission	3.3	3.1	1.1	3.8	0.9
Average cost per admission	$2,003.09	$1,619.48	1.2	$2,309.30	0.9

EXHIBIT 8
Medical Claims and Lag Summary by Type of Service

Medical claims from 3rd quarter 1984
Includes claims on the system and paid as of 10/21/84
Group = P0201

Type of Service	Number of Services	Amount Billed	Percent of Total Billed	Amount Paid	Percent of Total Paid	PPO Savings	Average Days to Pay
Physician office visit	4,315	$139,469.48	29.90	$ 75,198.75	31.36	$ 64,270.73	52.59
Diagnostic lab other	3,089	39,282.03	8.42	18,414.91	7.68	20,867.12	49.22
Allergy testing	669	10,195.25	2.19	7,472.46	3.13	2,722.79	49.19
Other medical	634	17,381.84	3.73	9,004.30	3.76	4,377.54	48.82
Outpatient surgery	608	41,865.05	8.97	19,980.65	8.33	21,884.40	49.97
Diagnostic radiology other	553	33,634.35	7.21	17,469.56	7.29	16,164.79	49.32
Immunization or injection	447	4,571.75	0.98	2,773.10	1.16	1,798.65	53.94
Diagnostic lab inpat hosp	312	1,776.29	0.49	1,178.71	0.49	597.58	31.75
Supplies	256	4,575.75	0.98	3,929.98	1.64	645.77	46.79
Physician hospital visit	243	15,369.00	3.29	7,910.65	3.30	7,458.35	46.00
Outpatient psychiatric	190	16,437.50	3.52	4,901.90	2.04	11,535.60	45.43
Diagnostic radiology inpat hosp	98	3,116.75	0.67	2,106.98	0.88	7,009.77	37.83

Well baby	80	2,912.00	0.62	1,772.58	0.74	1,139.42	57.67
Diagnostic radiology outpat hosp	79	2,921.50	0.63	1,852.89	0.77	1,068.61	47.81
Inpatient surgery	74	55,702.75	11.94	24,459.32	10.20	31,243.43	45.22
Physical therapy	73	1,666.25	0.36	1,172.10	0.49	494.15	32.82
Diagnostic lab outpat hosp	67	461.55	0.10	311.21	0.13	150.34	27.88
Anesthesia inpat hosp	59	22,597.00	4.84	10,494.73	4.38	12,102.27	42.97
Chemotherpay	50	1,040.00	0.22	628.10	0.26	411.90	37.46
Inpatient psychiatric	35	2,730.00	0.59	1,648.38	0.69	1,081.62	72.00
Annual exam	32	2,093.00	0.45	989.50	0.41	1,103.50	53.88
Ambulance transportation	31	968.00	0.21	867.20	0.36	100.80	34.00
Surgical assistant inpat hosp	31	8,560.00	1.83	3,124.75	1.30	5,435.25	42.19
Durable medical equipment	30	812.31	0.17	583.35	0.24	228.96	31.80
Emergency medical treatment	29	1,622.00	0.35	992.20	0.41	629.80	39.48
Maternity care including delivery	27	25,033.60	6.37	15,989.06	6.67	9,044.54	45.15
⋮	⋮	⋮				
Physician home visit	1	40.00	0.01	15.28	0.01	24.72	32.00
Surgical assistant outpat hosp	1	249.00	0.05	95.04	0.04	153.96	39.00
	12,207	$466,506.25		$239,756.24		$226,750.01	

EXHIBIT 9
Group Experience Profile

Group: P125   ABC Manufacturing Company
For November of 1984
Total insured: 236

Inpatient Hospital Care	Group Total	Group/ Community Ratio
Total number admissions	1	
Number admissions per 1,000 insured	4.24	0.64
Total days stay	2	
Number days per 1,000 insured	8.47	0.28
Average length of stay	2.00	0.44
Total expenditures	$1,266.09	
Average cost per admission	$1,266.09	0.51
Average cost per day	$633.04	1.17
Average cost per insured	$5.36	0.33

Outpatient Hospital Care	Group Total	Group/ Community Ratio
Number services	5	
Total expenditure	$120.35	
Average cost per service	$24.07	0.14
Average cost per insured	$0.51	0.11

Drug Services	Group Total	Group/ Community Ratio
Number services	96	
Total expenditures	$778.67	
Average cost per service	$8.11	1.05
Average cost per insured	$3.30	1.49

Medical Services	Group Total	Group/ Community Ratio
Number services	203	
Number office visits per 1,000 insured	322.03	1.36
Total expenditures	$3,698.32	
Average cost per insured	$15.67	1.02
Average visit cost per insured	$8.30	1.69
Average lab cost/insured	$2.58	1.98
Average rad. cost per insured	$1.16	0.96
Total costs	$5,863.43	
Total cost per insured	$24.85	0.65

EXHIBIT 10 Benefits Utilization Report, November 1984

ABC Manufacturing Company
P090

Benefit	Number of Services	Amount Billed	Proposed Amount Paid	PPO Savings	Percent of Total Benefit Costs
Surgery					
Inpatient hospital	81	$ 60,224.75	$ 26,452.57	$ 33,772.18	14.14
Outpatient hospital	16	6,945.00	2,574.54	4,370.45	1.38
Office surgery	591	36,037.05	17,680.70	18,356.35	9.45
Assisted surgery	33	9,327.00	3,420.60	5,907.00	1.83
Anesthesia	61	20,036.00	8,689.39	11,346.61	4.65
Maternity	11	4,374.00	2,580.14	1,793.86	1.38
Hospital visits	157	5,836.50	2,816.97	3,019.53	1.51
Office Visits	4,096	126,787.98	67,260.14	59,527.84	35.96
Psychiatric visits					
Office visits	0	0	0	0	0
Hospital visits	35	2,730.00	1,648.38	1,081.62	0.88
Physical therapy	928	42,388.00	19,015.17	23,372.83	10.17
Laboratory services					
Hospital	314	1,781.39	1,182.73	598.66	0.63
Office	2,036	24,481.20	10,289.86	14,191.34	5.50
Radiology services					
Hospital	98	3,116.75	2,106.98	1,009.77	1.13
Office	444	26,840.45	14,031.22	12,809.23	7.50
Office injections	892	8,642.25	7,299.00	1,343.25	3.90
Office medications	12	47.25	15.80	31.45	0.01
Total	9,805	$379,596.17	$187,064.19	$192,531.98	100.00

*Percents are rounded to two decimal places.

denied, number of admissions certified, and number of concurrent reviews performed. Performance data such as dollars saved and claims lag are also usually included in this report series.

COMMITTEE STRUCTURE AND PROVIDER CONTRACT

The PPO utilization review/quality assurance program incorporates a variety of activities including prior authorization of services, preadmission certification, concurrent review, and reporting. The PPO's management is responsible for tying those pieces together into a consistent program. This is usually done through a committee structure that can vary from a single UR/QA committee reporting to the PPO board of directors to an elaborate committee structure with a host of specialty committees, an overall UR/QA committee, and a judicial committee. The main functions of these committees include recommending selection of providers, development or modification of the medical criteria, review of claims, hearing of appeals, and review of new standards of treatment in the community. These processes establish the boundaries within which the mechanics of the overall review system operate. The UR/QA committee will normally be physician dominated since these issues are primarily medical in nature. However, membership or staff support on the committee is essential from legal, management, and employee benefits experts.

Compliance with PPO rules is governed by the PPO/physician contract. From a utilization review perspective, the contract must explicitly state that the physician will comply with the UR/QA procedures and with the sanction process outlined in the contract. The established rates of reimbursement that will be accepted as payment in full are detailed in the contract. Without such language, the basis for managing the provider network is seriously weakened.

The PPO-hospital agreement must likewise include provisions that establish the terms of compliance with PPO procedures for the hospital. The hospital must notify the PPO of an admission or intent to admit a PPO patient. Authorization for review coordinators to work in the nursing stations and examine patient charts is similarly required as part of the operating procedures.

CONCLUSION

Health maintenance organizations have historically operated a number of programs designed to both control medical utilization through prospective and concurrent methods and to review those same services using claims systems and reporting on a retrospective basis. Some of the differences in medical utilization rates, hospital utilization, and length of stay can be accounted for in the aggressive utilization-control program run by the prepaid plans. The application of those same techniques to the indemnity insurance program is warranted. Contracting with a full-service preferred provider organization to provide that same level of utilization control can effect significant savings to the buyer. When such programs are coupled with favorable contracts for hospital and medical services, the efficiency with which a benefit program operates increases. The result is the provision of more appropriate services at a reduced price.

The utilization control mechanism and utilization review programs are part of PPO management just as they are a fundamental part of the HMO organization. Lack of organizational accountability for costs of services is a major weakness in the current health care system that the HMO has addressed. Although the PPO is not at financial risk for the care provided, the full service PPO accepts "responsibility" to control costs. In order to retain the buyer as a client, the PPO has an incentive to reduce or limit the rate of increase in the cost of health benefit programs. With organized resources, responsibility, and financial incentive the full service PPO shows promise for cost containment. An effective and efficient utilization control and review mechanism is a key to achieving PPO success.

NOTES

1. Eugene G. McCarthy, "Second Opinions in Perspective," *Business and Health* (December 1983), p. 5.

2. Ibid., p. 7.

3. Margaret Sweetland, "CIGNA Reaps Savings with Second Opinions," *Business and Health* (December 1983), pp. 7–8.

4. Ibid., p. 7.

5. Eleanor Tilson, "A Union's Experience with a Second Opinion Plan," *Business and Health* (December 1983), p. 9.

6. Michael J. Goran, "The Evolution of the PSRO Hospital Review System," *Medical Care* (Supplement) 12 (May 1979), pp. 1–47.

7. Edward M. Bosanac, "Utilization Review and Quality Assurance Program Design in IPA HMOs," American Medical Professional Review Association, National Data Assembly, Reno, Nevada. March 1983 (presentation).

8. Gerald Landgraf, "Examples of Goal and Information Based Approaches Using Problem Solving Techniques," American Medical Care and Review Association Data Assembly, February 1984 (presentation).

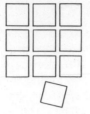

Management Functions

Hospital Quality Control—A Key to Competitive Health Plans[1]

Alan C. Brewster, M.D.
Medical Director
Saint Vincent Hospital, Inc.
Worcester, MA

Robert C. Bradbury, Ph.D.
Director
Master of Health Administration Program
Graduate School of Management
Clark University
Worcester, MA

The basic reason that hospital costs in the United States are out of control is that the predominant incentives to the physician, hospital, and patient reward inefficiency. Physicians and hospitals are paid in ways that reward them for providing more and more costly services. Conversely, reimbursement methods penalize those conservative providers who are judicious in their use of costly resources. Although the trend is toward changing these provider incentives through methods that employ per case payments (e.g., medicare's DRG approach) or all-payor/hospital payment caps (e.g., Massachusetts' Chapter 372), these are regulatory approaches that simply challenge the health care industry to find ways around them. On the consumer side, traditional health insurance plan designs give the patient incentives to use the hospital, even when a substitute setting is equally or more effective, and to demand the most costly services and resources regardless of their cost effectiveness.

Solving the health care cost spiral means reversing these incentives. Health care policy must reward the conservative medical practitioners who hospitalize only when necessary, who do not keep the patient in the hospital any longer than necessary, and whose diagnostic and therapeutic effectiveness is high without overusing expensive ancillary services. There are basically two ways to get the proper incentives in place. The first approach is *price competition,* which involves putting the decision-making burden directly on the patient by requiring significant out-of-pocket payments, usually in the form of deductibles and coinsurance. While this approach may control costs, it is not only operationally difficult given the amount of knowledge patients must acquire in order to be prudent buyers of health services but also politically difficult to sell to employees, and medicare and medicaid recipients.

The second approach is *premium competition,* which puts the decision-making burden on the physician and other health care providers through incentives that reward effectiveness and efficiency. This strategy involves a series of competitive health plans that compete to enroll a large enough share of the market to be financially viable. Each health plan competes in terms of its premium, service package (benefits), service to patients, and effectiveness of care. Once a patient enrolls in a health plan, the plan's providers have financial incentives that promote a conservative medical practice style. What this means is that care is managed so that the patient receives the services that are effective for a given disease or condition and that this care is produced efficiently and is not overutilized. Such case management requires an effective quality control system in order to assure that the health plan remains competitive on both the quality and cost dimensions. Competitive health plans that lack such a system are operating in the dark.

The purpose of this chapter is to demonstrate how hospital quality control can contribute to competitive health plans. To accomplish this, the authors use empirical results from Saint Vincent Hospital, a 578 bed teaching hospital in Worcester, Massachusetts. The development of a sound hospital quality control system requires four key elements:

1. Hospital commitment (Board of Trustees, administration, medical staff).
2. Appropriate database.
3. Corrective action authority.

4. Financial incentives that reward effective and efficient physician behavior.

Each of these is discussed in this chapter, but before doing so, it is important to put this quality control approach into the proper context and define key terms.

As shown in Exhibit 1, hospital systems operate by using a set of resources (inputs) to produce services (processes) that are utilized by a patient population (inputs) for the purpose of improving health status (outputs).

EXHIBIT 1
Basic Components and Linkages of Hospital Systems

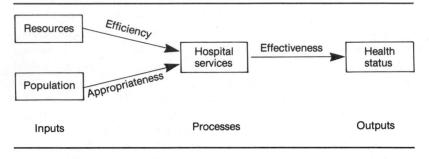

As with any system, tampering with any part of the hospital system can impact the remaining parts. For example, if resource inputs are modified to control costs, this may decrease the effectiveness or may decrease necessary utilization. To avoid unintended results, care must be taken to examine the interactions among the impact on the patient's health (effectiveness), the resources consumed in delivering the service (efficiency), and whether those in need actually receive the service (appropriateness).

When evaluating hospital performance, three interrelated phenomena must be examined:

— Effectiveness: the ability to achieve the desired result, which in the case of hospitals is restoring or maintaining the patient's health status.
— Efficiency: the ability to achieve the desired result at a minimum of cost.
— Appropriateness: the suitability of what is done given the patient's health needs.

It is crucial to recognize that efficiency requires effectiveness. Failure to recognize this relationship has led many physicians and hospital officials to oppose attempts to focus on efficiency or cost-control issues as if they occur in a vacuum. This opposition is expressed in the name of protecting effectiveness or quality. But this debate misses the key point—efficiency demands effectiveness.

Past efforts at hospital utilization review, which is the closest thing in practice to quality control, have consistently made the critical mistake of concentrating on resource use, especially on average length of stay, or charges, or costs, while ignoring effectiveness. But physician efficiency cannot be understood without first determining if the desired results are achieved. This is a crucial issue for efforts like PPOs that select certain physicians to participate while rejecting others.

Going back to this definition of efficiency, several types of efficiency problems should be distinguished. The first is the expenditure of more resources than necessary to deliver the service; e.g., unnecessary days in the hospital or unneeded diagnostic tests. Problems of this type reflect problems of physician behavior and should be addressed as part of quality control. Another issue refers to the classic productivity problem— what is the least expensive way to produce a given test or procedure, for example, a chest x-ray? This problem comes under the control of hospital management not physicians.

Appropriateness relates to whether people who need certain hospital services do in fact receive them, and, conversely, whether persons not in need utilize services. Hospitals can readily address the latter problem if they develop a quality-control system. As far as those in need who are nonusers, this requires an epidemiologic database on the population served by the hospital.

Continuing the definitions, the following are based on Juran's industrial quality-control model.[2] *Quality* is the degree of conformance to a standard. In the case of hospitals, effectiveness, efficiency, and appropriateness standards must be addressed, as discussed above. *Quality control* refers to the process of measuring quality performance, comparing it with standards, and acting on the difference. *Quality assurance* involves providing the evidence to convince all concerned that the quality-control function is being carried out satisfactorily.

INCENTIVES FOR EFFECTIVENESS AND EFFICIENCY

Competitive health plans are organizations that have the responsibility for both insurance and service delivery. They provide a defined list of services for a prepaid premium to those who enroll in the plan. A specified panel of physician, hospital, and other providers deliver these services, and enrollees who use other providers are penalized. Another characteristic is that the providers share in the financial risk of the health plan.

There are a variety of organizational models for competitive health plans including closed panel health maintenance organizations (HMOs) (both staff and group models), open panel HMOs (independent practice associations), and preferred provider organizations (PPOs). While there are many pros and cons relative to each approach, the important issue for this discussion is how the providers are paid. Herein lie the incentives that promote effectiveness and efficiency.

Successful competitive health plans must implement financial incentives that reward conservative medical practice styles. This means abandoning the usual and customary fees approach on the physician side and cost plus methods on the hospital side. There are three basic methods of paying providers: (1) payment according to the volume of services provided or cases treated; (2) payment according to the number of patients for which the physician or hospital is responsible (capitation); and (3) salary. Various combinations of methods are used (e.g., basic physician salaries with productivity incentives). The purpose here is to illustrate how these methods can provide the right incentives, rather than discussing the mechanical details of each method.

If a health plan chooses fee-for-service or fee-per-case reimbursement methods, it is essential that there be a fee schedule that is set in a way that reflects managed care protocols. This means analyzing how conservative practitioners treat each type of patient—the resources used and their costs. As discussed later in this chapter, physician practice patterns may vary greatly. By determining fee schedules based on conservative practice styles, incentives are created that pull other practitioners toward this style or else result in their not participating in the health plan.

Setting fee schedules that will be acceptable to conservative practitioners (and most likely not acceptable to more elaborate style practitioners) is different from discounting. Discounting implies arbitrary, across-the-board reductions in fees or charges, which in turn suggests cost shifting to make up the differences from other payors. This is really a "gas war" phenomenon, which could quickly lead to service or quality sacrifices. Many of the problems with the PPOs developing throughout the country seem to relate to a failure to establish fees based on managed care and instead relying on discounting.

What makes the most sense, in order to provide incentives for effectiveness and efficiency, is to set a fee that covers all costs over a given time period. This is the capitation method of payment, and this will become dominant as premium competition becomes the accepted health policy response to the current pressure for health cost-containment programs. The reason is that capitation provides the most flexibility while providing the right incentives for competitive health plans. Capitating both the hospital and physician is important because systems of conservative providers should be created. While specialists and perhaps tertiary care hospitals in some cases may still require fee schedules, there are a variety of creative ways to modify the capitation payments to the primary care physician or community hospital so that the incentives promote using other levels of care only when cost effective. One way would be a ledger approach, whereby each primary care physician (or community hospital) is debited for each specialist referral (or tertiary hospital referral) and pays a financial penalty to the degree that the referral pattern, with proper severity and case-mix adjustments, exceeds an accepted standard.

Capitation payment does not necessarily mean centralized control by large insurers, whether they are private or government (medicaid and medicare). Actually, this view of capitation means decentralized control, since it refers to hospital-based health plans that receive a capitation payment for both hospital and physician services. Capitation also does not negate fee-for-service payment using fee schedules. Rather, the capitated hospital-based health plan may do well to contract out certain services to less costly providers on a fee-for-service basis. For instance, a large community teaching hospital with such a health plan would have an incentive to relate with one or more small community hospitals in a way that allows referrals of less severely ill patients to the lower cost facility.

Once incentives are in place that reward effectiveness and efficiency, that environment is right for hospital quality-control systems. Unless there is concern about the bottom line, sound control systems will not be developed. Premium competition necessitates such concern.

THE MEDICAL ILLNESS SEVERITY GROUPINGS SYSTEM (MEDISGRPS)

MEDISGRPS uses objective clinical findings to measure severity of illness at hospital admission. These clinical findings are primary data, and thus are of greater validity than such secondary data as diagnosis. It is this primary data on which physicians act. Measuring admission severity provides the basis for evaluating changes in severity that occur during the hospital stay, as well as the resources consumed during the stay. Thus MEDISGRPS has the ability to assess both effectiveness and efficiency, a prerequisite for hospital quality control.

The key clinical findings (KCFs)—laboratory, radiology, pathology, or physical exam findings—on which MEDISGRPS is based indicate the level of illness severity of the patient. Exhibit 2 presents some examples of these KCFs. Each KCF is assigned to one of four severity of illness groups. Patients with multiple findings are assigned to the highest (most severe) group in which the patient has a finding. *Severity Group 0* is for patients that have none of the MEDISGRPS key clinical findings. *Severity Group 1* indicates minimal findings where there is a low potential for organ failure. *Severity Group 2* indicates either acute findings connoting a short time course with an unclear potential for organ failure, or severe findings that involve a high potential for organ failure but when such failure is probably not imminent. *Severity Group 3* indicates both severe

EXHIBIT 2
Examples of Clinical Findings and Their
Assigned Severity Group

Severity Group	Physical Examination	X ray	Laboratory	Pathology
0	Skin tags	Soft tissue swelling	Sedimentation rate (<50)	Endometrial hyperplasia
1	Wheezing	Cardiomegaly	pO_2 (60–70mm/Hg)	Uterine fibroids
2	Ascites	Pneumonia	Albumin (<2.5)	Acute cholecystitis
3	Papilledema	Biliary tract obstruction	Positive blood culture	Ruptured spleen
4	Coma	Intracranial bleeding	ph (<7.1)	—

and acute findings meaning that there is a high potential for organ failure and a short time course is indicated. *Severity Group 4* is for critical findings that indicate the presence of organ failure.

The admission severity grouping is done after the third day in the hospital because it takes that long for the clinical information to get recorded in the medical record. This grouping is repeated on the 10th hospital day to determine whether the desired results (effectiveness) have been achieved. The 10th day was chosen because by this time most patients had improved to the point where they had minimal or no findings.

Morbidity is defined as one or more Severity Group 2, 3, or 4 clinical findings that occur after the third day and before the 10th day. Note that many anatomical findings that are used as KCFs do not disappear over a short time period even if effective treatment is undergone, so the continuance of these KCFs is not counted as morbidity. Rather physiological findings are relied on to indicate continuing morbidity.

EMPIRICAL RESULTS IN A LARGE TEACHING HOSPITAL

All 16,428 admissions to Saint Vincent Hospital between October 1982 and June 1983 were included in the present study.[3] The chief complaint or reason for admission is used as a means of categorizing patients. Although 71 categories are employed, 54.6 percent of all admissions in this study occur in 14 categories (see Exhibit 3). To illustrate the results of this study, this discussion focuses on the four most common medical chief complaints: abdominal/flank pain, shortness of breath, chest pain, and extremity pain. These four complaints represent 27.2 percent of all admissions and 46 percent of all medical service admissions during the study period.

EXHIBIT 3
Most Frequent Chief Complaints or
Reasons for Admission
Saint Vincent Hospital: October 1982 to June 1983

		N	%	Cumulative %
1.	Delivery	1,335	8.1	8.1
2.	Abdominal/flank pain	1,244	7.6	15.7
3.	Shortness of breath	1,170	7.1	22.8
4.	Chest pain	1,058	6.4	29.2
5.	Extremity pain	1,007	6.1	35.3
6.	Changed alertness	628	3.8	39.1
7.	Diffuse weakness	444	2.7	41.8
8.	Fever/chills	372	2.3	44.1
9.	Back pain	358	2.2	46.3
10.	Nausea/vomiting	345	2.1	48.4
11.	Focal defect	334	2.0	50.4
12.	Trauma	283	1.7	52.1
13.	Cough	209	1.3	53.4
14.	Gastrointestinal bleeding	200	1.2	54.6
	All others	7,428	45.4	100.0
	Total	16,428	100.0%	100.0%

ADMISSION SEVERITY AND HEALTH OUTCOMES

The MEDISGRPS approach compares admission severity to subsequent in-hospital mortality and 10th day morbidity (Severity Group 2 or higher on the 10th hospital day) in order to assess effectiveness. Exhibit 4 presents the in-hospital mortality rates for the four most common medical chief complaints. The patient's severity of illness at admission is directly related to the mortality rate, and this relationship is statistically significant (Chi-square: $p < .01$).

EXHIBIT 4
In-Hospital Mortality Rates per 100 Admissions by MEDISGRPS
Severity Groups for Most Frequent Chief Complaints
(Transfers Excluded)

Chief Complaint	# Patients	Admission Severity Group					Total
		0	1	2	3	4	
Abdominal/flank pain	1,244	0.7	1.0	2.9	10.0	33.3	3.0*
Shortness of breath	1,170	0.0	1.0	8.6	11.5	54.2	9.4*
Chest pain	1,057	1.7	0.2	3.9	18.4	69.2	4.8*
Extremity pain	1,007	0.0	0.9	3.0	16.3	50.0	2.4*

*CHI SQUARE: $p < .01$

EXHIBIT 5
10th Day Morbidity Rates per 100 Admissions
by MEDISGRPS Severity (Deaths and Transfers Excluded)

Chief Complaint	# Patients	Admission Severity Group					Total
		0	1	2	3	4	
Abdominal/flank pain	1,196	2.1	10.5	14.3	33.1	62.5	13.5*
Shortness of breath	1,048	0	8.1	19.2	37.5	54.5	22.8*
Chest pain	982	1.8	5.9	14.8	43.0	0	12.8*
Extremity pain	970	1.9	5.6	17.4	40.0	50.0	10.4*

*CHI SQUARE: $p < .01$

This same relationship exists between admission severity and 10th day morbidity rates (Exhibit 5).

ADMISSION SEVERITY AND RESOURCE USE

Admission severity is closely related to resource use, as indicated by total charges, ancillary charges, and length of stay (LOS). Exhibit 6 shows this relationship for the four chief complaints. For all four, the relationship between admission severity and the efficiency indicator is direct and is statistically significant according to the F statistic of the analysis of variance (ANOVA) technique. The experience at Saint Vincent Hospital is that MEDISGRPS creates severity groups that are distinct in terms of average total charges, with the exception of psychiatric admissions. Further refinements of the key clinical findings for mental illnesses are currently underway so that MEDISGRPS can be effectively applied to the psychiatric service.

CLINICAL MANAGEMENT INFORMATION SYSTEM

A sound clinical MIS must provide the basis for assessing performance both in terms of the patient's health outcomes (effectiveness), resource consumption (efficiency), and needs (appropriateness). An important first step is to separate those patients not achieving the desired health status results from those that do. MEDISGRPS accomplishes this by distinguishing the patients who are still acutely or severely ill on the 10th hospital day (patients in Severity Group 2 or higher). To illustrate, Exhibit 7 shows the average total charges for patients with the chief admission complaint of shortness of breath separated into those exhibiting 10th-day morbidity and those who do not.

EXHIBIT 6
Average Total Charges, Ancillary Charges, and Length of Stay by MEDISGRPS Severity Groups for Most Frequent Chief Complaints (Deaths and Transfers Excluded)

Abdominal Pain

Admission Severity Grouping	Patients	Age	Average Total Charges	Average Ancillary Charges	Average LOS
0	144	33.5	$ 1,513	$ 699	4.1
1	501	48.2	2,824	1,302	7.7
2	428	48.3	4,171	2,218	9.6
3	126	57.4	8,460	4,827	16.3
4	8	68.8	29,031	16,876	47.4
Total	1,207	47.9	3,907	2,026	9.1
		$F = 22.6$ $p < .01$	$F = 86.7$ $p < .01$	$F = 90.0$ $p < .01$	$F = 48.3$ $p < .01$

Chest Pain

Admission Severity Grouping	Patients	Age	Average Total Charges	Average Ancillary Charges	Average LOS
0	57	48.6	$ 2,101	$1,070	4.4
1	523	61.9	2,816	1,322	6.4
2	299	61.5	4,873	2,172	11.0
3	124	68.9	6,875	3,349	14.0
4	4	73.5	10,074	5,218	19.0
Total	1,007	61.9	3,918	1,825	8.6
		$F = 19.7$ $p < .01$	$F = 34.0$ $p < .01$	$F = 29.2$ $p < .01$	$F = 28.9$ $p < .01$

Extremity Pain

Admission Severity Grouping	Patients	Age	Average Total Charges	Average Ancillary Charges	Average LOS
0	159	33.8	$ 1,792	$ 997	4.1
1	456	49.6	3,228	1,548	8.6
2	325	62.9	6,555	3,160	17.0
3	41	62.2	10,104	5,458	21.4
4	2	78.0	8,513	4,311	19.0
Total	983	52.1	4,393	2,160	11.2
		$F = 54.2$ $p < .01$	$F = 53.0$ $p < .01$	$F = 49.8$ $p < .01$	$F = 38.7$ $p < .01$

EXHIBIT 6 *(concluded)*

Shortness of Breath

Admission Severity Grouping	Patients	Age	Average Total Charges	Average Ancillary Charges	Average LOS
0	14	29.6	$ 744	$ 296	2.1
1	299	40.7	2,154	930	6.3
2	363	46.6	3,529	1,725	9.3
3	362	69.5	5,374	2,756	12.3
4	22	69.5	9,430	5,100	18.9
		$F = 63.2$ $p < .01$	$F = 30.0$ $p < .01$	$F = 27.6$ $p < .01$	$F = 22.2$ $p < .01$

EXHIBIT 7
Average Total Charges by MEDISGRPS Severity Groups and 10th Day Morbidity Status for Shortness of Breath Chief Complaint (Deaths and Transfers Excluded)
Saint Vincent Hospital: October 1982–June 1983

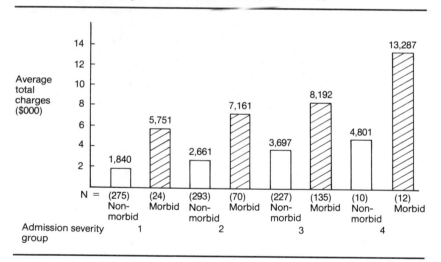

The patients with morbidity have significantly higher average charges, two to three times the average of the nonmorbid patients. Therefore, quality-control efforts should give priority attention to finding out what went wrong with these morbid patients. This is important not only from the perspective of improving their health outcomes but also because of the large cost savings that could be achieved by finding ways of avoiding some of this morbidity.

The ability to separate out those patients with 10th day morbidity is an essential prerequisite for a clinical management information system (MIS). In contrast, discharge diagnosis-based systems neither address the variations in illness severity that often occur among patients with the same diagnosis, nor can they compare a patient's condition at admission to that at discharge.

Using a clinical MIS involves three distinct but related types of studies. First, all 10th day morbidity patients should be systematically reviewed in a manner that searches for effectiveness problems that can be addressed. Second, the relative efficiency of each attending physician in handling the nonmorbid patients should be assessed. Third, the appropriateness of the admission or procedure should be determined.

EFFECTIVENESS STUDIES

One of the most important functions of a clinical MIS is exception reporting, meaning the ability to separate out the group of patients that has the highest proportion of problems. Essentially, the system should determine what to look at, because it is not efficient to review groups of patients in which there are few problems that can be addressed. For example, when patients are in Group 4 (critical findings) there is a high probability of continuing morbidity or even death. Thus the chances are small that reviewing such events will result in improvements. However, we do not expect morbidity or mortality for low severity groups, thus careful and detailed reviews of such events should be conducted when they occur.

In the MEDISGRPS approach, the primary exception reporting involves examining all morbid patients. (Note that similar reviews are done for all in-hospital deaths.) These reviews focus on the key clinical findings that are responsible for the morbidity. The MEDISGRPS software produces patient abstracts that provide this information. The KCFs at both the first review (day 3) and the second review (day 10) are presented, along with the chief admitting complaint, discharge diagnosis, DRG, charges, and other relevant data.

These abstracts enable the quality assessment committee to conduct its reviews without necessitating going back to the medical record. A related advantage is that the name of the attending physician need not be revealed during the discussion of the case, thus adding to the objectivity of the review. The experience at Saint Vincent Hospital is that such reviews are conducted not only with a minimum of wasted time and effort but also with considerable success in identifying and addressing important problems.

In the analysis of all 10th day morbid patients, the focus is on patterns of clinical findings that may indicate medical practice problems. Random events, meaning the occasional occurrence of key clinical findings that are unrelated to the admission complaint, should not be of particular concern. Instead, patterns of findings that could be related to either the admission complaint or the treatment protocol are sought. Postoperative infections or adverse drug reactions are examples of findings to be followed up by physician-specific analysis to see if certain physicians show a pattern of unusual occurrences.

Another approach is to review the 10th day morbidity rates of individual physicians by admission severity group and chief complaint. While this is important, the current database at SVH does not have sufficient numbers of patients to permit meaningful results at this time.

EFFICIENCY STUDIES

Efficiency studies examine variations in medical practice patterns according to such resources use measures as charges or length of hospital stay. To conduct such studies, it is essential to start with a homogeneous group of patients in order to avoid such common critiques as "my patients are sicker" or "I'm treating patients with different medical problems than my colleagues." MEDISGRPS permits the definition of homogeneous groups by classifying patients according to both admission severity and 10th day morbidity. To study efficiency, 10th-day morbid patients are excluded and then comparisons are made of each physician's practice patterns for patients in the same severity group.

The clinical MIS presented in this paper provides the empirical data to describe individual physician practice patterns. This provides the basis for setting efficiency standards by defining the preferred pattern and then comparing each physician to this standard. At Saint Vincent Hospital, a consensus approach to standard setting is employed by the key committees. This approach consists of examining the variations among individual physician's practice patterns; the mean, median, and mode values for all patients; the average for closed panel HMO patients; and the average for non-HMO patients. Standards should be set to reflect judgments about the preferred medical practice patterns rather than simply taking the average of all practitioners. Although oversimplified, the average often reflects a point somewhere between what might be termed good and bad practice patterns, and this is not the standard that should be reflected. Instead, the standard should represent what is acknowledged as good practice patterns.

To illustrate these physician efficiency studies, Exhibit 8 presents each surgeon's average total charges for patients with inguinal hernia repair who were Severity Group 1 on admission.

Patients with complications (morbidity) are excluded in order to focus on efficiency. Patients over 65 years of age are also excluded so that surgeons belonging to a closed panel HMO could be compared to the non-HMO surgeons. These average charges exhibit considerable disparity, ranging from Physician A ($926) to Physician E ($2,045). The over-

EXHIBIT 8
Surgeon Specific Average Total Charges for Patients
Undergoing Inguinal Hernia Repair—Severity Group 1,
Under Age 65 (Excluding 10th Day Morbidity)

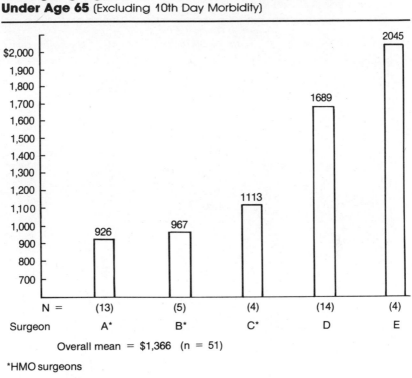

| N = | (13) | (5) | (4) | (14) | (4) |
| Surgeon | A* | B* | C* | D | E |

Overall mean = $1,366 (n = 51)

*HMO surgeons

all mean is $1,366. Note that the three surgeons with the lowest averages are members of a closed panel HMO.

APPROPRIATENESS STUDIES

Appropriateness studies are designed to assure that patients utilizing services have a demonstrated need for them. One approach to determining appropriateness involves patients who are admitted to the hospital but do not exhibit KCFs (Severity Group 0). Physicians are compared in terms of the proportion of their admissions that are classified as Group 0. Exhibit 9 presents the results for patients with chest pain as their chief admission complaint.

The Group 0 proportion ranges from highs of 57.1, 16.7, and 16.7 percent for Physicians A, B, and C to lows of 0 percent for Physicians N, O, P, and Q. Standard setting for this type of study is difficult, since both

EXHIBIT 9
Proportion of Chest Pain Chief Complaint Patients with No
MEDISGRPS Clinical Findings (Severity Group 0) by Physician
(Deaths and Transfers Excluded)

	Number of Group 0 Admissions/ Total Admissions	Percentage
All physicians	58/1,058	5.5
Physician		
A	4/7	57.1
B	8/48	16.7
C	4/24	16.7
D	2/21	9.5
E	3/37	8.1
F	3/38	7.9
G	2/29	6.9
H	3/44	6.8
I	4/60	6.7
J	2/47	4.3
K	1/23	4.3
L	1/25	4.0
M	1/29	3.4
N	0/55	0
O	0/24	0
P	0/24	0
Q	0/22	0

high and low proportions indicate problem situations. Physicians with high proportions may have a tendency to hospitalize some patients that could be treated out of the hospital. On the other hand, physicians with very low proportions could be waiting too long to admit certain patients. From an exception reporting perspective, both high and low physicians should be studied in greater detail.

Two additional types of appropriateness studies can be conducted with the MEDISGRPS clinical MIS. Surgical indications studies determine if there are KCFs that justify particular surgical procedures. Diagnosis validation studies compare the KCFs to the recorded diagnosis.

MEDISGRPS and DRGs

Considerable attention is being given in both the public and private sectors to the use of diagnostic related groups (DRGs) as a means of categorizing patients for reimbursement. Examining physician performance by DRGs is very likely a key activity of many organizations in the process of developing PPOs.

The present study examined MEDISGRPS capability to refine DRGs

EXHIBIT 10
Mean Total Charges by MEDISGRPS Severity
Groups for DRG 140—Angina Pectoris
(Deaths and Transfers Excluded)

Admission Severity Group	N	Mean Total Charges	t-test
0	13	$1,614	
1	211	2,387	$p < .05$
2	40	3,257	$p < .01$
3	27	4,090	$p < .05$
4	0		
Total	291	$2,630	

ANOVA: $F = 19.5$; $p < .01$; $R^2 = 0.17$

by determining if distinct severity groups exist within DRGs. Only 10 medical/surgical DRGs had more than 150 admissions, thus permitting meaningful analysis at this time. In most of these DRGs, at least two statistically significant severity subgroups existed. For example, Exhibit 10 shows the results for DRG 140—angina pectoris.

The direct relationship between admission severity and total charges is statistically significant as indicated by the Analysis of Variance (ANOVA) F statistic ($p < .01$). There is a substantial reduction in variance ($R^2 = 0.17$), and it should be pointed out that this reduction is in addition to that already caused by the DRG method. When both 10th-day morbidity status and admission severity are used to create 10 DRG subgroups, the $R^2 = 0.49$.

These findings indicating that patients within a DRG may differ significantly in their severity of illness have important implications for PPOs. One is that if a PPO uses a DRG scheme for setting hospital prices, it should add a severity-adjustment, or else there will be incentives for hospitals not to take the sicker patients because they will lose money on them. Another problem is that physician cost profiles by DRG are legitimately subject to criticism by those physicians who treat proportionately more of the sicker patients.

ORGANIZATION FOR HOSPITAL QUALITY CONTROL

The preceeding sections addressed both the financial incentives necessary to reward efficient and effective physician behavior and the type of database needed to monitor efficiency and effectiveness. Here, commitment and corrective action authority, the two remaining keys to sound hospital quality control are discussed.

The high level of commitment of Saint Vincent Hospital's Board of Trustees, administration, and medical staff is reflected in the organizational structure of its quality-assurance program (Exhibit 11).

EXHIBIT 11
Saint Vincent Hospital Quality Assurance Organizational Chart

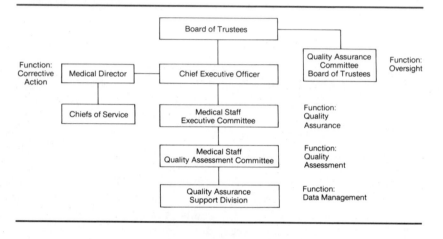

Hospital by-laws place the responsibility for quality assurance oversight with the Board of Trustees and its quality assurance committee. The Board delegates the corrective action authority and responsibility through the chiefs of service to the full-time medical director who must act on the problems identified by the quality control process. The quality assurance support division is responsible for data management, meaning that it must maintain the database necessary to support the clinical management information system. The medical-staff quality-assessment committee used this clinical MIS to set practice standards and identify both effectiveness and efficiency problems by comparing individual physician practice patterns to these standards. The medical staff executive committee has the quality assurance function, which means that it must make sure that quality control is being performed adequately.

Hospitals that seek to develop successful PPOs and other types of competitive health plans must have the capability of managing physicians. This means going far beyond the analysis of data and even the identification of problem areas. It means acting on findings, which is a management function that must be clearly defined. The responsibility and authority for this function should be assigned to an individual, because an individual is more likely to make decisions and carry them out than is a committee. As described above, at Saint Vincent Hospital this management function is assigned to the medical director.

Corrective action in practice at Saint Vincent Hospital concentrates on information feedback to each physician. This feedback focuses on actual practice patterns and comparisons to the adopted standards. This is essentially an educational strategy.

More stringent actions are relied on only if feedback and education fail to provide the necessary change, and this has been rarely necessary. These actions could include denying reappointment to those physicians not meeting the standards or not permitting such physicians to participate in competitive health plans, including developing PPOs and capitation payment plans.

CONCLUSIONS

Health care costs can be controlled without decreasing quality of care when provider and consumer incentives reward the delivery and utilization of services that improve health status without overutilizing expensive resources. Such incentives will become the rule rather than the exception in competitive health plans that develop and grow through keeping their premiums relatively low while providing services in a way that results in a high level of patient satisfaction. To achieve this success, a health plan will have to perform the hospital quality control function effectively.

This chapter has demonstrated how the Medical Illness Severity Grouping System (MEDISGRPS) provides the information necessary for meaningful hospital quality control. MEDISGRPS is an objective method of measuring severity of illness at hospital admission based on key clinical findings. Admission severity is closely related to both health status outcomes (mortality and morbidity) and resource use (charges and length of stay).

MEDISGRPS is used in Saint Vincent Hospital as the basis for a clinical management information system that addresses both effectiveness and efficiency issues. Effectiveness studies focus on those patients not achieving the desired results, defined in this study as having a Severity Group 2 finding on the 10th day and referred to as 10th-day morbidity. All morbid patients are reviewed to determine if there are patterns of findings that indicate medical practice problems. Efficiency studies focus on the nonmorbid patients and demonstrate that physicians may vary greatly in their practice styles. For patients in the same severity group, there are significant differences in average charges among attending physicians. Future research with MEDISGRPS in a variety of hospitals may reveal similar efficiency differences among hospitals. Appropriateness studies examine whether clinical evidence supports physician actions.

Once a PPO or similar type of competitive health plan has the information to describe empirically the differences in physician and hospital practice patterns, it can select those conservative providers that will contribute to the plan's success. The health plan can structure its physician payment practices so that there are incentives for those physicians exhibiting more elaborate practice styles to change their behavior so that it reflects that of the conservative practitioners. The degree to which a PPO can develop such physician profiles should be a good predictor of the plan's success.

NOTES

1. The authors were assisted by Bruce G. Karlin, M.D., Linda A. Hyde, R.R.A., Charles M. Jacobs, J.D., and Young M. Chae, Ph.D.

2. J. M. Juran, "Basic Concepts," in *Quality Control Handbook,* 3d ed. ed. J. M. Juran, F. M. Gryna, and R. S. Bingham (New York: McGraw-Hill, 1974).

3. Alan C. Brewster, B. G. Karlin, L. A. Hyde, C. M. Jacobs, R. C. Bradbury, and Y. M. Chae, "Medical Illness Severity Groupings System (MEDISGRPS): A Clinically-Based Approach to Classifying Hospital Patients at Admission." 1984. (Paper). 24 pp.

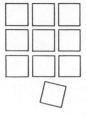

Management Functions

ADMINISTRATIVE INFORMATION SYSTEMS

Robert N. Trombly

President
Mutual Health Services Company
Cleveland, OH

No single aspect of the health care delivery system is less frequently discussed, more poorly understood, more difficult to implement, and more prone to failure than is the administrative information system. Furthermore, it is all but unrecognized that the quality and effectiveness of the information system itself can substantially influence the marketplace acceptance of a PPO product.

In order to have an effective information system, many kinds of data must be recorded, manipulated, combined, analyzed, and reported. If PPOs are to succeed, they must be able to use information to manage the benefit programs that they design and market. This further means that they must employ administrative systems that have a great deal of flexibility, because benefit and plan structures are probably going to be as heterogeneous as the PPOs themselves.

This chapter discusses administrative functions that are common to PPOs and possibly other alternative health delivery models. In order to be as clear as possible, a definition of these functions in a generic sense will be provided. Subsequently, these functions, their importance, the information inputs, and the information outputs from the perspective of the various health administration organizations, such as third-party administrators, health maintenance organizations, insurance companies, and providers of health care, all of whom might become involved with PPO administration, are discussed.

DEFINITIONS OF FUNCTIONS

The major administration information systems are as follows:

1. *Membership administration.* The activity of keeping track of information concerning the identity of covered members. This includes information not only about the employees, contract holders, or subscribers to the health plan but also about their affiliation with an employer or other covered groups and their dependents. The entire process of membership administration includes development, mailing, receipt, control and processing of documents or other media concerning membership, enrollment, and disenrollment.

2. *Billing administration.* The activity involved with charging members, their groups, or other parties the premiums or fees associated with covering members for specific health coverages.

3. *Utilization review.* The activity involved with analyzing and evaluating whether or not health care utilization is consistent with the benefit plan being offered and with good medical practice.

4. *Quality assurance.* The activity of reviewing utilization of health care services in accordance with predetermined norms, criteria, or peer group profiles in order to assure that quality medical care is being delivered (i.e., detecting both over- and underutilization with respect to a diagnosis, age, and sex of the member).

5. *Claims administration.* The activity involved with receipt, control, administration, and adjudication of claims or encounters for health services rendered to members. Claims administration means that *necessary* services provided to *covered* members by *eligible* providers are paid in accordance with *appropriate* fees or rates.

6. *Actuarial administration.* The activity involved with manipulating, grouping, analyzing, and evaluating claims payment or loss experience by type of benefit and by group in order to assure the financial integrity of the benefit program from a premium or cost vantage point.

7. *Financial and accounting.* The activity involved with maintaining the books of the health care administrator with respect to revenues, costs, accounts receivable, accounts payable, taxes, and general ledger functions.

8. *Planning.* The activity involved with manipulating both financial and claims data individually and in the aggregate for purposes of modeling or anticipating the likely impacts of varying deductibles, copays, maximum benefits allowed by member, by contract, and by lifetime fee schedules and premiums impacts on both the administrator and the individual.

9. *Performance monitoring.* The activity involved with maintaining, recording, and reporting on administrative performance factors considered important by the administrator. Some of these factors have to do with claims turnaround (i.e., number of days from receipt to payment) or customer service (number of days to reply to correspondenc), etc.

The above activities represent the major functions conducted by administrators. Each of these functions has a greater or lesser degree of importance according to the organization type. An effective PPO administrative system, however, will contain each of these functions in one form or another. There are additional functions that might also be included in a PPO information system but that are not essential. They will be discussed below.

ADMINISTRATIVE REQUIREMENTS

In this section, administrative considerations and requirements for PPO health care delivery models in a variety of settings are described. Since PPOs are being formed or at least considered by virtually every health care administrative entity—and some who are not yet separate entities—the administrative approaches taken to PPOs will vary widely. Indeed, it is predictable that PPO administrative systems will take on the nature and characteristics of their present organizations, their corporate culture, and administrative orientation and experience.

Adapting current systems and procedures to a new product can be as dangerous as adapting a machine tool designed to produce piston engine parts to one that is expected to produce electric motors. If sufficient information system flexibility is not present, the results can be disastrous. For purposes of illustration, assume that each of the following organizations are considering the formation of a PPO. Further assume that the program will include a defined set of providers who contract with the PPO, an agreement by the providers to render their usual range of services for a discount or a fixed price, some incentive arrangement for accepting patients at a discounted rate, and a penalty for covered members obtaining services outside the network. In addition, assume the need for monitoring the quality of care, reporting savings to the buyer of covered services, and maintaining the financial integrity of the program. Of course, it is necessary to stereotype the administrative capabilities of each organization type.

THIRD-PARTY ADMINISTRATORS

With the exception of a few large national administrators, third-party administrators (TPAs) tend to be small, serving a localized geographic area, and devoted to prompt and accurate payment of claims on behalf of their self-insured clients or on behalf of multiple employer trusts

(METs). Their systems and administrative procedures are typically well adapted to paying claims based on billed charges or some form of usual, customary, and reasonable (UCR) fees. They are generally able to determine a member's eligibility for a given coverage, perform some sort of utilization review and reporting, and account for the financial outlays of the programs. In turn, they are capable of billing clients for the amounts of paid claims and associated administrative fees. They would probably have to modify their administrative systems to accommodate the PPO program as follows:

1. *Membership:* Provide for identification of member and dependents as having PPO coverage; linking PPO members to one or more designated primary care physicians; and maintaining the ability to change primary care physician designation by individual member and/or dependent.

2. *Billing:* Little or no modification should be required to bill groups opting for PPO coverage except: (*a*) a different administrative fee might be charged and (*b*) there would probably be a need to segregate those group members who opted for PPO coverage versus those who did not.

3. *Utilization review:* There would be a general need to strengthen utilization review systems in order to administer the additional limitations and conditions inherent in a PPO arrangement. For example, additional pretreatment, concurrent, and posttreatment utilization-review procedures may need to be added. Examples might be preadmission certification for medical necessity, edits to detect procedures that can be rendered in an ambulatory setting, and comparisons of actual lengths of stay versus predetermined or negotiated norms. Similarly, group-specific reporting is needed to illustrate the effectiveness of the program.

4. *Quality assurance:* Within the PPO setting, there may be a need for administrative procedures that assure that provider incentives are not so attractive as to impair the quality of care. In this regard, there exists the need for evaluating care on a case by case basis vis-à-vis some expected pattern or profile of care. Both underutilization and appropriateness of care must be evaluated on an ongoing basis, with exceptions being referred to professional or peer review committees for further investigation. It is probable that a TPA does not have a module of this type because they have not been required contractually to concern themselves with underutilization.

5. *Claims processing:* Significant modifications are likely to be required in order to comply with the different requirements of a PPO program. For example, it will be necessary to include many, if not all, of the preutilization review edits mentioned above at the front end of the claims systems. The front end implies that segment of the system involved with the first steps in claims entry and adjudication. It will be necessary to verify that the provider rendering service (*a*) belongs to the network (*b*) is the designated provider (if appropriate) or (*c*) for specialty care has been referred by the designated primary care physician and (*d*) has contracted to provide that service. Further, assuming different rates for different providers, the system must maintain and easily refer to each set of negotiated rates by provider. Diagnostic related groupings (DRGs) rates or global fees may also need to be involved. The system also has to be modified in order to pay a percentage of billed charges if the patients exercise their right to use a provider outside the contracted network. Finally, a clear concise explanation of benefits is required to eliminate confusion on the parts of both providers and patients.

6. *Actuarial:* Assuming that third-party administrators handle primarily self-insured PPOs, there will be relatively little modification required to their existing actuarial reporting systems—other than to segregate PPO activity within client accounts.

7. *Financial and accounting:* Again, assuming that similar self-insured accounts will be administered, little modification should be required, except as required to report separately on groups opting for PPO coverage.

8. *Planning:* This activity, from the TPA's perspective, is one offered to clients for the purpose of facilitating their own planning. The planning module should provide for simulation or modeling using both actual data and hypothetical data regarding the account and its experience. It should provide the ability to play "what if" with deductibles, copays, inclusion or exclusion of covered services, changes in preferred rates, and changes in provider mix. It is probably not present in any form within most TPA systems. The embryonic state of PPOs, however, suggests that it is a necessary administrative tool, because benefit structures will be changing and there will be a need to evaluate each contemplated change.

9. *Other considerations:* Provider incentive systems, based on utilization or some other measure of provider performance may be used to distribute "savings" to the providers. These systems can become complicated to administer, depending on their incentive structure and quantity of data needed to distribute the incentive payment. For example, some health care organizations have three different provider incentive "pools" to be distributed using different rules and different stop-loss arrangements for different groups and involving the peer grouping of providers. It is not likely that this kind of administrative module is present within a third-party administrator's system.

HEALTH MAINTENANCE ORGANIZATIONS

The growth of health maintenance organizations has been rapid over the past eighteen months. It is only natural that certain HMOs with existing networks and provider relations are offering or considering the possibility of offering preferred provider networks as an additional product. It is unlikely that staff-model or closed-panel HMOs will offer a preferred provider product since, in a sense, the members of the closed panel are already "preferred." Independent practice associations (IPAs), on the other hand, are increasingly considering subselection of their existing network, designating some providers as "preferred." This would mean that certain providers within an already existing network might be designated as "preferred" in return for negotiated rates or additional incentives. Because they have a network of providers with established relationships already in existence, IPA and group-model HMOs are in position to offer a separate PPO product. They may, nevertheless, have to consider modifications to their systems as follows:

1. *Membership:* Little modification would be needed, since they generally are able to link individual members to primary care or contracted physicians. They would, however, have to modify their systems to identify members and dependents who opt for PPO coverage.

2. *Billing:* Their billing systems will need modification to distinguish groups having PPO rather than standard coverage. They must incorporate the capability of storing multiple premium rates, assuming that PPO rates differ.

3. *Utilization review:* A medium amount of modification will be required, although it is safe to assume that the typical successful IPA already has some of these systems in place. Nevertheless, changes may be required in preutilization edits as well as in group specific reporting.

4. *Quality assurance:* Some level of quality assurance is no doubt already present within the HMO's administrative system. It is also safe to assume that this function will need some strengthening to include additional case evaluation facility and the ability to compare physician practice profiles. Depending on the degree and quality of such administrative procedures already present, changes to these procedures will range from moderate program changes to a complete reimplementation of a new module.

5. *Claims processing:* Claims processing procedures will require significant modification in order to accommodate PPO program provisions as follows. In addition to the more stringent prepayment edits, it will be necessary to identify the provider rendering service as "preferred," link to the appropriate rate table for reimbursement, verify that the service is covered, apply the appropriate adjudication rules, and, if the member exercises freedom of choice, adjudicate the claim altogether differently. DRG, global fees, and other innovative reimbursement schemes may necessitate additional adjustments. Although the modifications here are not as extensive as those for the third-party administrator, this particular function will probably require the greatest number of changes.

6. *Actuarial:* Relatively few changes will need to be made to actuarial systems employed by HMOs except that premiums and losses will have to be segregated for the PPO product line.

7. *Financial accounting:* Successful HMOs already have administrative systems that are capable of keeping track of the financial outcomes of each benefit program. Their systems are also capable of producing cost center and product income and revenue reports. These reports track premium and claims revenue by product. Only minor modifications should be required to break out the PPO product from others.

8. *Planning:* One cannot assume that HMOs have in place a planning procedure or program that allows them to determine the outcome of varying plan design factors, in a PPO or any other program; some do, but most do not. It is, however, a tool that all health care administrators are going to need in the future to be able to adequately predict the impact of changes in benefit structure.

9. *Other considerations:* The nature of an IPA makes it more likely that some sort of "risk pool" accounting or incentive distribution is already present within the administrative structure. Many IPAs currently have risk pool arrangements with their providers. Depending on the flexibility inherent in the calculation of disbursement rules as well as the complexity of the specific rules involved, the existing structure may well be adapted for purposes of administering the PPO. Alternatively, an entirely new module may be needed.

INSURANCE COMPANIES

As insurance companies react to the threat being imposed upon them by PPOs, they are establishing preferred provider networks of their own. Many companies, most notably the Blue Cross and Blue Shield Plans, already have extensive provider networks and existing contracts having many of the attributes inherent in a PPO. Their administrative structures are mature and their systems are fully implemented. Both the administrative structures and the systems tend to be difficult to change, and for this reason, many insurance companies have chosen to purchase or develop stand-alone, mini-computer-based systems designed especially for administration of their PPO products, largely because they perceive that (*a*) the administrative requirements are changing and evolving and (*b*) there is a need to truly differentiate the product in the marketplace. The stand-alone system allows greater ability to change, and fewer resources are required to maintain the system. It also avoids the need for long and costly modification to the "monolithic" computer systems operated by most insurance companies. The ideal functional characteristics of such a stand-alone system are discussed in the next section. If, however, an insurance company plans to administer their PPO product lines using existing procedures and systems, substantial modifications are likely to be required:

1. *Membership:* Members in groups opting for PPO coverage will, of course, have to be distinguished and segregated. The system will need the ability to handle multiple coverages within a group and possibly even within a family. Each member will have to be linked to one or more primary care physicians or specialists.

2. *Billing:* Premiums will need to be maintained at the individual member level, in several tier options (single, family, husband and wife, parent and dependent child), and retroactive changes and adjustments will need to be maintained for accurate billing. PPO members must be billed separately from other group members with appropriate premium detail.

3. *Utilization review:* While most insurance companies talk about utilization review, they actually possess it in varying degrees of sophistication. The requirements set down within a PPO product demand consistency of pretreatment, concurrent, and posttreatment UR procedures. To effectively conduct utilization reviews, insurance companies need automated systems to assist them, and the automation of these procedures requires the ability to easily make changes to edits. The central theme or philosophy of high volume operations within an insurance company is one of standard manual procedures with computerized decision support capabilities. Utilization review systems must accommodate a higher level of edit and review in the PPO product in order to justify and verify the product. It is likely that substantial modifications will be required to the existing UR systems and procedures.

4. *Quality assurance:* Insurance companies conduct varying and sometimes limited levels of quality assurance. Most insurance companies provide for preadmission certification or second surgical opinions, but most do not have procedures and systems in place for determining underutilization, since it is assumed that there is very little underutilization in a fee-for-service system. The pattern of fee-for-service payment has obviated the rationale for monitoring underutilization. In a PPO setting, particularly one that has changed the incentives, there may be a need for the administrator to demonstrate that quality and appropriateness of care are being monitored. Substantial changes in evaluating the quality of care delivered could be required.

5. *Claims processing:* Like third-party administrators, insurance companies have mature, automated systems and procedures in place to pay claims promptly and accurately. Unlike third-party administrators, their systems tend to be large, IBM or other large computers and soft-

ware, and generally are very difficult and expensive to modify. To administer the PPO, additional edits will be needed. There will also be a need for the distinguishing of network versus other providers and accounting for different rates or reimbursement schemes. Other adjudication rules, as covered in other sections, will have to be added. It is further likely that new explanations of benefits and statements of remittance will be required to keep confusion to a minimum. In short, the number of modifications required may be substantial and make the acquisition of a new system or module cost effective.

6. *Actuarial:* The actuarial systems currently in place within insurance companies should be able to handle PPO product analysis with minimum to medium modification requirements. Separate reporting will be required for accurate rate and retention estimating.

7. *Financial and accounting:* Most of these systems are handled separately in large companies and should not be a factor other than to accommodate the bookkeeping and recording of PPO activity.

8. *Planning:* Like all other administrators of health care, insurance companies have not accomplished very much in terms of developing planning and simulation tools to assist benefit design. As also noted above, in a PPO product, this kind of analytical tool is desirable and a new module should be added to the administrative system to provide the necessary decision support.

9. *Other considerations:* Insurance companies have not yet ventured into innovative, incentive payment systems unless they already own HMOs that have incorporated such features. A new module added to the overall administrative system to calculate and distribute incentive payments will probably be required.

PROVIDERS OF HEALTH CARE

Many providers are currently implementing, or at least seriously considering, the formation of PPOs in order to market their services as a body to medium and large employers in their service areas. These include hospitals, clinics, group practices, laboratories, radiology specialists, etc. This activity is known as "backward integration"—from health care delivery to health care financing. In almost every instance, the administrative systems possessed by these organizations are altogether unsuitable to the effective administration of a PPO product because their systems have been geared for administering health care delivery. This will force these organizations to either (*a*) contract with insurance companies, third-party administrators, or other entities for the administration of the service or (*b*) acquire the necessary capability within their own administrative organizations. If a provider-based PPO decides to delegate the administration of its PPO product to an outside party, it should ensure that the features described herein are provided. More than likely, if a group of providers has decided to seriously integrate health care delivery with the financing of health care, it will also wish to be responsible for the "hands on" administration. In that case, a stand-alone administrative system should be acquired.

FUNCTIONAL CHARACTERISTICS OF AN IDEAL PPO ADMINISTRATIVE SYSTEM

OVERVIEW

The system described here represents one of several packaged hardware/ software systems available on the market today that is capable of administering a PPO product. This system design should be of interest to all organizations contemplating the offering of a preferred provider product, including those already having health administration systems in place— albeit systems that were actually designed for other applications.

Ideally, a PPO administrative information system should have the following general characteristics:

— Be cost effective to install and to operate.
— Utilize state-of-the-art hardware and software.
— Allow for a phased-in approach to software implementation.
— Run on hardware that can be expanded as needs increase.
— Accommodate changes and enhancements easily.
— Not require a great deal of technical expertise to operate.

KEY SYSTEM FEATURES

The system should, at minimum, have the following features:

— The system should be menu driven, i.e., each function should be selectable by depressing a single key.
— For ease of use it should have a built in ad hoc report processor. These allow the ability to generate reports as needed without any technical training.
— It should be written in a simple programming language.
— Contain word processing, visi calc, and other generalized software capabilities.
— A fully integrated database that allows access to all files from all system modules.
— System flexibility to allow new or added modules access to any data stored in the database, thereby facilitating a phased-in implementation or future system enhancements. An example of this feature would be a system with one of the new advanced relational database operating systems, such as PICK or UNIX.

— A statistics file containing aggregate data that is updated on line, providing instantaneous access to enrollment, utilization, and financial data.
— Flexible edit specifications and coding criteria as defined by the product and not dictated by systems requirements.
— Communications capability for client access and remote access by providers.
— Hardware expansion capability with no program conversions.
— Security levels that are triggered at both the system level and the menu (applications software) level, thus providing a wide range of capability for controlling access both to data and system functions.

FUNCTIONAL CHARACTERISTICS BY MODULE

Membership. The desired functional characteristics of the membership module are as follows:

— Automatic detection of an attempt to add a duplicate name (subscriber or provider) or number.
— Maintenance of a membership data file of historical eligibility changes.
— Ability to enter and change member/patient and group data in an on-line mode from terminals located at multiple locations.
— Ability to inactivate member/patient or group.
— On-line ability to search and retrieve member records via alphabetic or numeric data.
— Ability to automatically capture and maintain cumulative member months by group and automatically adjust these figures to accurately reflect retroactive additions and terminations of both contracts and members.
— Ability to perform edit checks, with manual override, on the completeness, accuracy, and validity of all enrollment data.
— Ability to suspend transactions failing the edit check and allow for correction and/or re-entry on-line.
— Ability to link primary care physicians (one or more) to a member or dependent.
— Ability to perform edit checks for the completeness, accuracy, and validity of all specified group data.
— Allow for on-line eligibility determination from multiple facilities.
— Ability to transfer members between groups with audit trail.
— Ability to produce over-age dependent reports with choice of age cutoff according to option selected by group; i.e., 19 or 23 and $64\frac{1}{2}$.
— Maintain insurance data for Coordination of Benefits.

— Permit statistical reporting and analysis of enrollment patterns at various hierarchical levels, e.g., group, type of group, benefit coverage.
— Ability to cross reference names, i.e., maintain an audit trail when someone changes their name.
— Ability to code benefit structures, types of coverages, and limitations at the dependent level.

Billing. The desired characteristics of a billing module are as follows:

— Accommodate different tier structures; i.e., two step (single, family), three step (single, double, family), and four step (single, husband/wife, parent/child, family).
— Maintain current and past premium rates in group file to facilitate automatic retroactive billing and adjustments for new and deleted member contracts.
— Provide billing audit trails reflecting additions, terminations, and corrections by group account.
— Ability to suppress full detail on premium bills for specific groups. (Can be used to do summary bills.)
— Permit on-line access to group accounts receivable for the purpose of inquiry and posting cash payments and adjustments.
— Permit posting payments by member for nongroup members.
— Separate maintenance and control of premium amounts, with ability to change.
— Automatic signaling of group anniversaries for reenrollment with member mailing labels upon request.
— Provide regular audit trails supporting all master file changes and transaction processes.
— Maintenance of premium, Accounts Receivable (A/R) payments and aging information by group account—on-line.
— Automatically determine correct premium amount from subscriber contract type, effective date of coverage, and group account information.
— Ability to automatically bill from the first of the month with effective dates other than the first of the month, e.g., a "wash system" where all members enrolling after the 15th of the month would be effective on the enrollment date and billed from the first of the following month.
— Ability to accrue any premium billed in the month as it is earned.

Utilization review. The functional characteristics of a utilization review module are as follows:

— The establishment of a fee schedule that is diagnosis- and procedure-specific (CPT–IV, ICDA–9).
— Automatic linking of inpatient and outpatient data to provide total history capability on individual patients.

— Automatic review of procedures capable of being performed in an ambulatory setting.
— Automatic English translation of diagnosis and service codes for reports and listings.
— Ability to view or print a profile on selected members including ambulatory, inpatient, specialty referral, and emergency treatment. Selection should be on any variable, i.e., age, sex, provider, diagnosis, etc.
— On-line entry and retrieval of all reference files (includes additions, changes, deletions).
— Store utilization data for a period of at least two years on-line for all members.
— Provide audit trails and summarization of all transactions for posting.
— Allow for the retrieval of, or statistical accumulation of, any data element in the utilization/claims file, i.e., fees, procedures, and diagnoses, and accumulate data at different levels, i.e., whole plan, individual facilities, specialty departments, providers, etc.
— Ability to associate utilization data with member data, e.g., to produce utilization reports by group, age, sex, etc. Also to associate the utilization data with various elements in the provider file.
— On-line entry and retrieval of provider, diagnosis, procedure, and fee schedule information.
— Ability to generate diagnosis, provider, and drug-specific profiles.
— Ability to aggregate statistics on the basis of diagnostically related groups, i.e., units of services and costs by diagnosis, age, and sex.

The design of the utilization review and quality assurance module should allow for the following types of reports required for most PPOs:

— Claims by provider and specialty.
— Claims by age and sex.
— Referral reference list.
— Utilization and cost of referral by ordering specialty (detail and/or summary).
— Utilization and cost of referral by referral specialty (detail and/or summary).
— Utilization of referrals by group (detail and/or summary).
— Utilization of referrals by age and sex.
— Provider listings.
— Inpatient admissions by age and sex.
— Claims summary by provider by month.
— Frequency totals by provider and category.
— Members seen by physician more than a specified number of times in a specified time period (criteria set by quality review and utilization review staff).

— Members hospitalized more than a specified number of times in specified time period (criteria set by quality or utilization review staff).

— Members not receiving health services since a specified date.

Quality assurance. The quality assurance module should utilize many of the utilization review module's capabilities and reports, particularly those producing a variety of profiles. In addition, it should possess the following functional characteristics:

— Ability to generate a model treatment pattern by diagnosis and/or "episode of illness."

— Ability to compare all services (medical, hospital, prescription drugs, etc.) by diagnosis.

— Ability to compare all services by members (in a demographic or other selected grouping).

— Ability to compare all services by provider group (specialty, subspecialty).

Claims processing. The functional characteristics of a claims processing module are as follows:

— Uniquely identify each claim.
— Track status of each claim.
— Allow for various claim types.
— Allow for multiservice claims.
— Check for second surgical opinion.
— Check for prior authorization.
— Check for preadmission certification.
— Perform patient eligibility checks.
— Identify potential COB.
— Perform provider eligibility checks.
— Administer provider reimbursement methodology.
— Accommodate multiple pricing schemes, i.e., DRG, global fees, UCR, or fee schedules.
— Apply contract specific pricing considerations.
— Enforce consistent payment policies in accordance with the benefit plan.
— Perform duplicate/conflict benefit determinations and adjudicate claims in accordance with appropriate rules.
— On-line claim correction capability.
— Pend claims for individual consideration, complications, or any other specific reasons, such as flagging claims for suspect provider or suspect member.
— Perform risk contribution and control processing in order to distribute the proceeds of risk pools to participating providers.
— Produce checks on a nonscheduled basis.

— Allow for selection of vouchers to be paid.
— Process adjustments.
— Produce provider claims inventory lists.
— Establish edits for limitations of benefits.
— Ability to provide tape to tape or other magnetic media interaction to expedite claims processing with local hospitals or service bureaus (from their computer to the PPOs).
— Automatically report when predetermined limits of specified services have been reached.
— On-line correction of pending claims data with automatic adjustment of affected statistical information.
— Generate comprehensive explanations of benefits and statements of remittances.

Actuarial. The characteristics of an actuarial module are as follows:

— The ability to review and analyze claims utilization and premium earned by group, member/demographics, type of benefit, and coverage classification.
— The ability to analyze claim development (claims lag report) for determination of incurred but not reported liability.
— The ability to determine additional outstanding liability on all referrals.
— Ability to determine reserve requirements.
— Ability to determine retention (percent of claims payments withheld as reserve for future claims).
— Ability to analyze all data on an ad hoc basis.

Financial and accounting. The functional characteristics of a financial and accounting module are:

— Flexible parameters for defining a chart of accounts and number fields to an unlimited number. At least three hierarchies or levels of reporting should be possible in the chart of accounts. These hierarchies should be capable of being changed by the user at any time.
— Periodic updating of the general ledger files. Updated journals should be provided to ensure timely and accurate postings.
— Complete audit trails, on demand, of each transaction regarding entry origin, account or accounts affected, debit and credit amounts, and date.
— Maintenance controls should protect against hazards such as deleting accounts with dollar balances.
— Journal entries that can be posted automatically and reversed in the subsequent accounting periods.
— The ability to provide all normal standard financial reports automatically. This includes the trial balance, the balance sheet, the

income statement, etc. These are cost center based, and should be capable of being produced routinely or on demand, with extensive cross-sorting options in order to analyze costs and revenues by specific center.

— Provide for automatic storing of data into the current and next accounting period, thus allowing data to be input as prepared.

— Provide for automatic posting of standard fixed journal entries (ones which are the same each month, such as fixed asset depreciation or overhead allocations).

— Complete interface with the budget for comparisons of appropriate reports. A variance analysis of actual performance against the budget should be produced automatically.

— The ability to automatically retain a display of prior year's comparable financial data, once it has been loaded.

— Automatic expense posting of journals to the ledger, allowing flexibility and summarizing expenses for different levels of management.

— Ability to identify beginning balances, monthly activity, and ending balances for each general ledger account.

— The ability to produce responsibility accounting reports. Examples of responsibility accounting would be:

Level 1—consolidated revenue and expense.

Level 2—departmental revenue and expense.

Level 3—revenue and expense by cost center within departments.

— Complete audit control and transaction reporting for both the current monthly and year-to-date periods.

— Reconciliation of any subsidiary ledgers to the general ledger.

— Automatic posting of premium accounts receivable entries to the general ledger.

— Ability to provide a cash requirement report at any point in time. The printed report shows all items on the Accounts Payable file that are due for payment by a specific cycle or period of time.

— Ability to identify all open invoices at any point in time by any vendor.

— Provide for automatic calculation and recording of due dates.

— Maintenance of a comprehensive vendor history for audit trail.

— Flexibility to produce daily, weekly, and monthly audit trails of all transaction activities in order to reconcile various transaction types depending on their frequency.

— Control and edit mechanisms for all invoices, expense distribution, and vendor information.

— Automatic distribution of expenses to the general ledger.

— Allow for the suppressing of payments.

— On-line voucher data entry editing and correction process.

— Controlled issuance of checks with accompanying registers.
— On-line retrieval of vendor file by ID code.
— Inquiry into the accounts payable files to verify the status of particular vendor accounts.
— An ability to post all cash receipts by categories such as employer payment, patient payment, and insurance payment. This includes a process for write-offs, allowances, and/or deductibles.
— Provide for automatic posting of adjustment in group premium billing.
— Ability to handle adjustments to A/R.
— Maintenance of accounts receivable financial history for an adequate period.
— An ability to recover accounts receivable detail for fiscal year-end purposes and also to incorporate revenue received in a new fiscal year with prior year accruals.
— Ability to account for monthly patient refunds.
— Produce a broad range of reports for each billing and monthly processing cycle. These reports should be available by account number, payor, and insurance carrier and should be "aged" to isolate offenders. Considerable flexibility in selecting and sorting account data for production of aging reports.
— Produce daily reports that summarize cash receipts/payments, adjustment transactions, and each input batch.
— Ability to produce separate reports for delinquent and nondelinquent accounts.
— User-initiated general ledger interface. All A/R activity should automatically post to the general ledger.
— Produce daily audit trails.
— Generation of various dunning messages that are user-defined based on prescribed rules established by the users. Include a mechanism to override standard collection messages on an individual basis.
— On-line review of batch payment postings to locate errors if a batch is out of balance.
— Availability of detailed charge and payment information for each accounts receivable transaction to the general ledger.
— Availability of patient collection and contract information for on-line inquiry.
— Similar features available for management of other cash receipts, including those for interest grants, cash loan proceeds, gifts, and other categories.
— On-line account receipt, adjustment, and payment posting.
— On-line inquiry into the A/R financial history.
— Number or name inquiry into an individual guarantor or patient account status.

Planning and budgeting. The characteristics of a planning and budgeting module are as follows:

— Full access to actual system data.
— Facility for input of hypothetical data, such as models.
— Facility for modeling utilization behavior and calculating associated plan liability as a result of different plan structures.
— Capability to reflect the full range of coverage parameters (e.g., deductibles and copays) and service restrictions in a preferred provider context.
— Capability to model "bottom line" impacts of alternative enrollment growth schedules. Also, impacts on financial ratios, such as percent of net income to revenue.
— Capability to model financial impacts of alternative resource allocation (e.g., staffing and facilities) assumptions.
— Integrated ad hoc reporting capability. Reports similar to those mentioned in the utilization review section would be applicable in this module.
— Integrated facility for performing simple statistical analysis (e.g., means, standard deviations, and partial correlations).
— Capability to flexibly generate a data file that can be easily used for more sophisticated statistical analysis (e.g., a data file for input to a statistical software package).
— Facility for time series analysis (i.e., analyzing changes in actual experience over time).
— Capability to simulate future financial experience for at least ten years.

Other considerations. Throughout this chapter, the need has also been highlighted for models that control the distribution of risk pools or otherwise produce a flow of funds to providers of care who are at risk in a PPO. A complete systems administrative package to perform other functions will likely be needed by someone starting a PPO. For example, there could be a need for:

— Capitation fund administration, where a monthly fee is paid to the primary care physician for each insured.
— Referral fund administration, where gross revenues for the referral portion of premiums are matched against discounted fee-for-service payments for referrals and the surplus is distributed to participating physicians or the deficit is assessed to them for future periods.
— Hospitalization fund, where both the hospitalization portion of premium and the outlay for hospital services are compared and the surplus or deficit is distributed or assessed.

In practically every case of a PPO, there will be a need for some type of administrative system which can perform these functions. In every case, the system must be flexible and capable of change.

CONCLUSION

In the general arena of health care administration, the PPO product will impose some serious challenges to existing administrative systems. Unless administrators already possess the most advanced and flexible systems just coming onto the market today, there will be significant costs involved with the proper administration of PPOs. Even the larger insurance companies will seriously consider stand-alone organizations and administrative systems to better serve the PPO product and other alternative delivery models of the future.

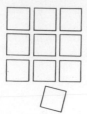

Management Functions

BUSINESS REQUIREMENTS FOR IMPLEMENTING PPOS

Angelo M. Masciantonio
Director of Cost Containment
Advanced System Applications, Inc.
Philadelphia, PA

A PPO can be a transition alternative to managed health benefits programs for payors or purchasers seeking both the cost management features of HMO programs and the flexibility and freedom of choice characteristic of traditional health insurance programs. On the surface, swing PPOs expand on the independent practice association model HMO, adding some level of health benefits for care rendered by nonparticipating providers. But PPOs go beyond most employer cost-containment strategies by using rate or fee negotiation with providers as a counter to the inflationary pressures within the health care industry.

The formal relationships between payors and providers that evolve from PPO development will have a dramatic impact on payor business practices, provider practice patterns, and consumer use patterns, and these changes should not impair the quality or accessibility to needed health care services for PPO members (consumers). The critical problem for administrators, however, is to define the business requirements for implementing a PPO program.

This chapter focuses on the challenges facing benefits payors as they implement swing PPO programs. Special emphasis will be given to the business requirements for manual or computerized systems used to support PPO programs.

SUPPORT SYSTEMS

Once a network of providers (hospitals and physicians) has been established and the benefits payor has designed a plan containing the appropriate incentives, three major systems must be developed in order to implement the PPO program: (1) a PPO benefits payment and administration system, (2) a managed health care program support system, and (3) a data capture and analysis system for performance evaluation and reporting.

BENEFITS PAYMENT AND ADMINISTRATION SYSTEM

The requirements for PPO benefit payment and administration will be driven by the agreements made with providers and the benefits plan structure and design. These agreements plus the benefits programs will determine the reimbursement method, rates or fees, and other special

EXHIBIT 1
Common Options in PPO Creation

Provider agreements

Hospital rates	*Reimbursement rules*
Per diem (multiple)	Periodic interim payment
Per discharge (multiple)	Pay when billed
Per DRG	Prospective payment
Other flat scheduled rates	Retrospective payment
Charges minus discount	Other method
Percent of reasonable financial requirements	

Physician fees or rates	*Managed health care rules*
Conversion factor-relative value study	Outpatient procedures only
HIAA fee schedule	Utilization-review program rules
Percent of UCR	Data submission requirements
Other scheduled rate including DRG	Exclusions
Capitation rate	
Charges minus discount	

Benefits plan structure

Participating provider payment	*Nonparticipating provider payment*
Hospital services	Hospital services
Physician services	Physician services
Other services	Other services
Maximums, limits, exclusions, coinsurance levels	Maximums, exclusions, limits, coinsurance levels
Other rules	Other rules

Other plan features unaffected by provider status

Individual, family, and plan limits
Coinsurance levels

---

conditions for payment. Because flexibility is essential in a rapidly changing business environment, itemizing potential "options" is a first step to defining these requirements. The Common Options in PPO Creation (Exhibit 1) lists the various options available in provider agreements and in the benefits structures that will be used to support PPO programs.

Manual versus Computerized Systems

It would be nearly impossible for a manual system of benefits payment and administration to support any combination of the benefits structure and provider agreement options described in the Common Options in PPO Creation Exhibit. With a manual benefits payment system, PPO options must be made as straightforward and as simple as possible: provider agreements using simple rate schedules; provider bills being the source for negotiated charges for data entry; most, if not all providers, asked to accept the same reimbursement rate and agreeing to the same reimbursement method; anniversary dates for benefits plan renewals timed to coincide with provider negotiations to avoid disruption in benefits processing. Computerized support of PPO programs, on the other hand, permits greater complexity and flexibility of benefits payment and administration and can better handle multiple variable factors.

In either the computerized or manual environment, PPO plan payment and administration represent a radical departure from the traditional approach used for indemnity, fee-for-service health benefits payment. PPO programs require more extensive and accurate records of providers than traditional programs. When bills are submitted, payors need to distinguish participating from nonparticipating providers, the applicable PPO plan, and the appropriate payment for a particular bill as defined by the claimant's benefit plans and claim history. In traditional fee-for-service plan administration, the benefits administrator is concerned with provider eligibility while benefits structures primarily determine payment rules.

Furthermore, benefits structures (and benefits contracts) need to comply with or support provider agreements and interface with one another. For example, the hospital charges negotiated in the provider contract should easily translate into the charges for hospital services under the PPO benefits contract. If a per-diem charge is negotiated, the benefits contract should define whether this rate is a maximum covered charge or a maximum paid amount and define how deductibles, other copayments, and maximums apply. Among the many other questions to be addressed are: When do benefits structures override provider agreements and vice versa? How is COB handled?

These issues must be considered and resolved before the details of the PPO benefits administration and payment system requirements are determined. To provide some direction for these requirements, the following flowchart (Exhibit 2) illustrates the basic functions needed in a system that will support and pay swing PPO plan benefits.

The following flowchart greatly simplifies the potential decisions required of a benfits payor under a swing plan. PPOs add tremendous variation to an already complex benefits payment decision process. Consequently, objectives need to be thought through carefully and automated support is highly desirable.

EXHIBIT 2
PPO Benefits Payment System

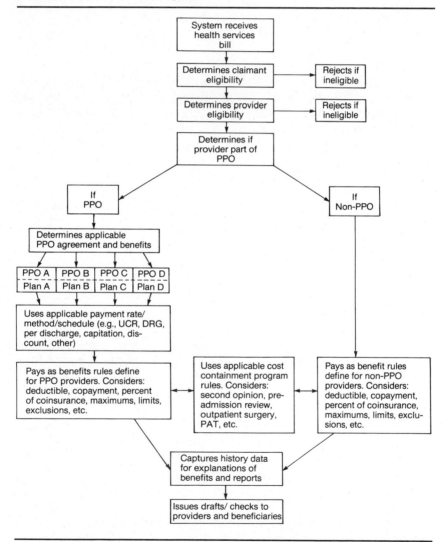

MANAGED HEALTH CARE SYSTEMS

Managed health care systems refer to all business and computerized programs or actions that are specifically aimed at managing or controlling health care utilization and costs. The managed health care systems (e.g., cost-containment programs, provider agreements) required to support a PPO program must be designed so that consumers and providers do not perceive a reduction in quality or access to needed health services. The programs, protocols, and "rules" established to manage health care utilization and costs should not disrupt the benefits administration process. Otherwise, the potential savings will be outweighed by greater claims production costs, consumer dissatisfaction, provider skepticism, and increased risk of bad faith action from beneficiaries or health policy holders.

A PPO's managed care system should also make sense from the standpoint of the overall type and structure of the PPO. For example, a payor-based PPO program that has negotiated reimbursement to hospitals on a per discharge (e.g., DRG) basis should not design a managed health care system that uses a utilization review program focusing on length of stay as its keystone since the length of a patient's hospital stay will not affect the amount of money paid to a hospital under the PPO agreement.

The managed health care systems necessary to support PPO functions can be classified into three general categories:

1. Utilization control systems.
2. Provider contracting.
3. Ongoing provider/payor work programs.

A summary of common activities relating to each category is useful in understanding how PPOs manage health care delivery in order to avoid inappropriate utilization and to stabilize rising costs.

Utilization Controls

It is generally acknowledged that PPO programs that simply offer discounts from normal provider charges risk failure because they do not incorporate precautions against unnecessary utilization of health services. HMOs, in contrast, are known for their success in managing health benefits costs through reducing use of hospital services (as measured by days per 1,000 population, length of stay, admission rates, and tests per admission), rather than through simple discounting. HMOs monitor health care utilization and provide financial incentives to providers. Many PPOs on the other hand will rely solely on utilization controls to manage health care. Therefore, proper design of a PPO's utilization control program is a critical requirement.

In general, utilization controls may be applied on a prospective, concurrent, or retrospective basis. The importance of any of the following programs lies in the creation of ongoing review procedures, which will ensure the success of the PPO in managing utilization of services.

Prospective Review Programs. Prospective review programs attempt to influence health care delivery prior to the actual delivery of services, i.e., preadmission.

1. *Second opinion programs* may be required in the PPO to reduce unnecessary surgery. These programs may be administered by the PPO or by an outside review organization. Active programs require a modification to benefits design in order to provide incentives for consumers to seek a second or third opinion for certain elective procedures, such as knee surgeries, hysterectomies, or hernia repair. Similarly, the benefits payor must have the capability to identify and monitor second opinion claims so that benefits can be paid according to the rules specified in benefits contracts requiring a second opinion. For example, the payment might vary coinsurance, waive or impose deductibles, or vary the stop-loss level.

2. *Preadmission Testing (PAT) protocol* may be a part of preadmission review programs in order to reduce unnecessary prospective hospital days for elective admissions, e.g., admission on Monday for surgery on Wednesday. Modification in benefits payment may be associated with failure or compliance with the rules specified in the PPO benefits contract.

3. *Preadmission authorization* may be required on all elective or nonemergency hospital admissions, including the necessity for the admission, the proposed length of stay, and the proposed setting or facility (e.g., inpatient versus outpatient, Hospital A versus Hospital B). Preadmission review programs may define benefits payment or reimbursement rules according to whether a patient complied or failed to comply with recommended or approved practices.

4. *Mandatory ambulatory (outpatient) surgery* may be required for certain surgical procedures. Exceptions may be approved by a review body (e.g., the PPO or outside review organization). Like mandatory second opinion programs, if a patient fails to comply with the approval rule for exceptions, the benefits paid to the patient or to the provider will be modified accordingly. Thus, benefits payors must have the ability to identify certain procedures and track approvals for benefits calculation and payment.

Concurrent Review. Concurrent review programs aim to monitor and approve utilization of health services during hospitalization or treatment. Concurrent utilization review involves a third-party reviewer who visits the site of treatment to evaluate services, review the necessity of admission (retrospectively), and review or recommend a proposed discharge date and step-down setting.

Increasingly, concurrent programs focus on select medical conditions and attempt to advocate more cost-effective case management approaches or less costly alternative health delivery settings, such as intermediate care facilities. Similarly, focused review programs may try to encourage better case management for more serious and more costly medical problems (e.g., cancer). Like preadmission review, concurrent review requires the capability to track utilization and to vary the way benefits are calculated and paid according to benefits contract rules.

Retrospective Review. Unlike preadmission or concurrent review, retrospective review takes place after treatment and, perhaps, after payment has already been made. Thus, retrospective programs must be tied to educational (e.g., employee and provider awareness of overutilization trends), financial (e.g., providers fined for overcharges), or other sanctions (e.g., period of nonparticipation) in order to change utilization behaviors. These programs typically review the appropriateness of admissions, settings, length of stay, ancillary services, and charges. Meaningful and high-quality data on services provided, length of hospital stay, and other utilization trends and judgment criteria must be available in order to implement a retrospective program.

PPO negotiations provide an opportunity to define the data needed for these reviews, the measurement and the standards to be used in the review, as well as the consequences for inappropriate use or charges in retrospective review. Provider/payor contracts need to specify the approach and sanctions pertaining to retrospective utilization review, since retrospective utilization review can require adjustments to benefits payments and can result in discontinuation of provider participation in the PPO. In many cases, retrospective analyses of claims data may be the first stage in a retrospective utilization-review program. Claims analysis that reveals potentially inappropriate use or charges may be followed by more detailed review of medical records.

Some retrospective review techniques are better than others and each technique should fit into the overall PPO structure. For example, an appropriateness evaluation protocol (AEP) approach is designed to target inappropriate admissions and days of care rather than high charges. Consequently, AEP represents a good retrospective program to monitor hospital contracts that specify per day or per discharge (e.g., DRG) reimbursement methods.

Provider Contracting

Provider contracts formulize utilization management efforts and bring price to the bargaining table.

If the combination of price (unit costs) and utilization (volume) of health care are considered as determinants of the overall costs of health care services, it becomes clear that provider agreements specifying negotiated charges for health services are essential to stabilizing growing health care costs. In addition, these agreements should define the guidelines for medical management of different types of patients seeking care from participating providers.

As indicated earlier, the benefits payment and administration system for PPOs must support a variety of contractual obligations negotiated in provider agreements and thus become a major tool in administering and tracking provider agreements. The benefits payment and administration system must (1) determine the proper hospital, physician, or other negotiated provider rates and method of reimbursement and (2) determine whether providers and patients are adhering to the expressed standards of acceptable medical practice as specified in provider agreements, (e.g., exclusions such as cosmetic surgery considered not billable by participating providers).

Beyond the requirements of benefits payment and administration systems, PPOs must be able to enforce the remedies for inappropriate medical practices described in the provider agreements. For example, PPOs need to define the infractions that will lead to discontinuation of the contract. Second, when financial penalties are involved, PPOs need to develop effective means to recover payments for services later deemed inappropriate. Third, initial or remedial provider education programs need to be established.

An alternative approach to changing provider behavior is through financial incentives for meeting performance standards specified in the contract. Similar to many HMO programs, financial rewards can be constructed to offer providers some share of the profits or savings that result from conforming to the specified managed care standards. For example, physicians paid under a PPO agreement according to a capitation rate will receive a financial reward for successfully reducing costs and utilization beyond predetermined levels.

Joint Provider/Payor Programs

The final requirements for a PPO managed health care system are to define the communication channels and forums of debate for participating providers and payors. One example of an important joint activity is the formation of quality-assurance committees that can monitor both overutilization and underutilization of medical services.

The effectiveness of these quality assurance efforts in PPOs determines the success of the PPO. Indeed, consumers, purchasers, and benefits payors will judge a PPO on ease of access to medical care and quality of care, as well as its price.

Like other businesses, PPO quality assurance programs must address

1. Inputs: provider quality, accessibility of networks, and benefits structure.
2. Process: ongoing review of medical practices, referrals, and payment patterns.
3. Outcomes: review of provider performance, medical experience with focus on readmission rates, and tracer conditions, mortality rates, and consumer satisfaction.

DATA CAPTURE AND ANALYSIS SYSTEM

The third major system to support PPO implementation is a data capture and analysis system. PPO data are essential for selecting providers for PPO participation, measuring benefits utilization and costs, evaluating and monitoring the various managed health care programs, profiling and analyzing provider performance, and providing baseline information for future planning. Again, automated support greatly facilitates data collection, reporting, and analysis given the scope of data required for PPO payment, underwriting, accounting, management reporting, and record-keeping.

In order to avoid duplication of data entry, the PPO benefits payment and administration systems should be the primary facility for capturing critical clinical, demographic, provider, payor, resource utilization, and cost data. Furthermore, data requirements should be designed to accommodate likely technological advances (software, networking, hardware) affecting provider billing and benefits payment and administration systems. For example, electronic data transfer (versus manual data entry) promises to improve the type, scope, and quality of data submitted by health care providers to health benefits payors at a reasonable cost.

Another important consideration in defining data requirements is the types of data the providers are now required to submit to traditional health insurance plans and government programs, particularly Medicare. By using data that providers are readily geared to offer, PPOs will be more likely to receive more accurate data on a timely basis.

Finally, definition of data requirements should occur at the same time as development of software programs for payment or reporting. It makes little sense to define data requirements to support PPO evaluation that differ dramatically from the data required to support payment and reporting. For example, suppose one evaluative study recommended by the PPO sponsor is the comparison of hospital costs of participating and non-participating hospitals for common diagnostic related groups (DRGs). Yet, in analyzing the data from the benefits payment and administration system, the evaluation team discovers that the procedure coding scheme used for payment is inconsistent with the procedure coding scheme used for grouping patients into DRG categories. This type of problem could have been avoided through careful planning.

In response to growing demands from benefits payors for more detailed and uniform data, PPOs should find the data requirements for reporting and analysis satisfied from bills submitted according to standardized hospital abstracts (i.e., UB 82) and outpatient abstracts (i.e., HCFA 1500), as well as from enrollment data required for eligibility determination. Generally, these abstracts will provide more information than will be needed for most PPO reporting requirements but they will provide a wealth of detailed information that can be saved and used, albeit infrequently.

Requirements for Reports and Analysis

If the PPO benefits payment and administration system collects the proper data, PPO reporting and analysis can be broken down into four major reporting categories: provider performance, benefits utilization, charges and costs, and performance. The Reporting Information Chart (Exhibit 3) summarizes these report categories.

EXHIBIT 3
Reporting Information

Report Category	Focus	Example Measurements
1. Provider performance (PPO and non-PPO)	Provider selection	Hospital and physician qualifications record Medical practice patterns Degrees Specialty License, type Association membership Certifications Board standing Malpractice cases Privileges
	Utilization reports	Hospital and physician profiles Hospital use rate (days, admissions) Admitting patterns to hospitals LOS, case mix adjusted DRG profiles Readmission rates Percent short stay elective admissions Outpatient visit rate Ratio inpatient to outpatient procedures Other use measures
	Cost reports	Hospital and physician profiles Charges/admission, charges/day, charges/service Charges/visit Percent distribution of charges by type of service (e.g., medical/surgical, ICU, ancillary) Charges for select procedures or conditions (e.g., DRG)
	Quality assurance reports	Admissions by condition Readmission rates Short stay rates Mortality rate Risky procedure rate

EXHIBIT 3 *(continued)*

Report Category	Focus	Example Measurements
2. Benefits utilization (PPO and non-PPO)	Plan utilization of services	Hospital use report Days, admissions, ALOS Inpatient procedures—outpatient candidates Percent elective admission procedures 2nd opinion surgery candidates Percent greater than or equal to 1 day stays prior to surgery for elective admissions Condition profile including DRGs Outpatient report Visits total and by setting Outpatient ancillary rate
3. Charges and costs associated with benefits utilization (PPO and non-PPO)	Cost reports	Hospital cost report Billed & covered charges/ admission, charges/day, charges/service Paid/admission, paid/day, paid/ service Percent distribution of billed charges covered and paid Number of high cost, serious medical problems Charges/paid per condition, select procedures Outpatient cost reports Charges/paid per visit
	Overall benefits cost profile	Breakdown of charges, covered amount, not covered amounts, COB savings, deductible and other copayment and plan payments, and other payment control savings.
4. Managed health care program performance	Utilization controls evaluation	Second opinion procedure report Number second opinion candidates Number second or third opinions Number confirmations Number subsequent surgeries Costs for second opinion Expected savings for nonconfirmed surgeries, not performed

EXHIBIT 3 *(concluded)*

Report Category	Focus	Example Measurements
		Preadmission and utilization review report
		Certified admissions, LOS, days
		Ratio of inpatient to outpatient procedures
		Number of procedures and days shifted to outpatient setting
		DAYS/1000 population
		ALOS
		Admission rate
		Costs to administer UR
		Ambulatory surgery
		Percent inpatient or outpatient surgeries
		Ratio of inpatient to outpatient procedures for select conditions
		Cost of inpatient versus costs to administer program
	Provider contracting	Normal charges versus negotiated rates
		Days saved via retrospective review
		Number of procedures shifted to outpatient setting

To generate reports with all of the suggested information on a timely basis requires a flexible and user-driven data system: flexible, because it must capture various combinations of the data in different quantities as the user desires, and user driven, because it must be able to produce reports as needed without a long wait between request and receipt.

Descriptive reporting requirements should be designed to identify general trends in PPO utilization and costs. Analytic reporting should provide statistical or professional interpretation of data to troubleshoot problems and identify specific opportunities for improving PPO performance.

The following exhibits describe sample formats for evaluating PPOs.[1] The PPO Physician Report (Exhibit 4) and the PPO Hospital Care Facilities Report (Exhibit 6) are descriptive profiles while Exhibit 5 is an example of an analytic format.

EXHIBIT 4
Claims Administration and Payment Reporting System
Physician's Activity Report for Period 1/1/84 to 12/1/84

(Group 42563 Big Company)
(PPO—Preferred Plan)

(Year-to-Date)

| | | | | | | | Inpatient | | | | | Outpatient | |
PPO	Select Physician	Suf	Policy Number	Employee ID Number	First Name	Rel	Los	Avg Los	Procedure	Hospital Charges	Avg Chrg/ Admission	Visits	Average Charge
Preferred Plan	Dr. Kildare	01	857603	889037423	Jill	sp	3		19120	$3,000			
				204567232	Mary	sp	5	4	19185	6,000	$4,500	20	$28
	Dr. B. Casey	02	333549	990455321	Bill	EE	10		33511	$15,500			
				885543109	Harry	EE	4	7	43844	2,500	$9,000	16	$24
	Dr. Trapper	03	2855543	094833347	Jim	sp	3		42840	$2,000			
				111209453	Jane	ch	2		31090	1,520			
				00098765 3	Elliot	sp	3	2.7	27330	2,500	$2,007	19	$31
All PPO physicians total								3.5		$628,400	$3,100	160	$26
Select Non-PPO physician ID	Dr. Vinnie	00	9000348	184993245	Bob	EE	7		33511	$12,000			
				111209453	Jane	ch	2	4.5	31090	1,520	$6,760	8	$40
All non-PPO physicians total								6.8		$1,634,000	$3,400	28	$36

SOURCE: Advanced System Applications, Inc. Cost Containment Division.

EXHIBIT 5
Appropriateness and Efficiency of Medical Care at PPO Hospitals, 1984

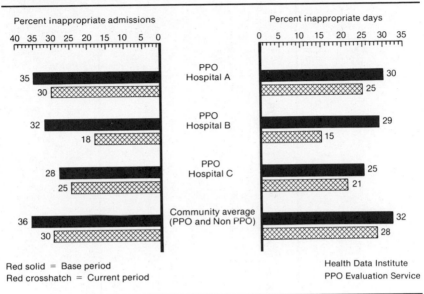

Percent inappropriate admissions

40 35 30 25 20 15 10 5 0

Percent inappropriate days

0 5 10 15 20 25 30 35

PPO
Hospital A — 35 / 30 | 30 / 25

PPO
Hospital B — 32 / 18 | 29 / 15

PPO
Hospital C — 28 / 25 | 25 / 21

Community average
(PPO and Non PPO) — 36 / 30 | 32 / 28

Red solid = Base period
Red crosshatch = Current period

Health Data Institute
PPO Evaluation Service

SOURCE: The Health Data Institute Inc.

EXHIBIT 6
Claims Administration and Payment Reporting System
PPO Hospital Report for Period 1/1/84 to 12/1/84

(PPO—Preferred Plan)

Utilization and Cost Data for Medical/Surgery (Year-to-Date)

PPO	Hospital	Admissions	Days	Avg LOS	Avg Charges	Re-admissions	Total Charges
Preferred Plan	St. Elsewhere	100	600	6.0	$2,000	2	$ 200,000
	General Hospital	220	1,230	5.6	1,500	0	330,000
	Medical Center	70	350	5.0	2,300	0	161,000
	Wayne Memorial	130	500	3.8	1,080	0	140,400
Preferred Plan Total		520	2,680	5.2	$1,600	2	$ 831,400
All PPOs		4,225	25,000	5.0	$2,100	16	$8,872,500
Non-PPO Total		3,000	21,000	7.0	$3,120	63	$9,360,000

SOURCE: Advanced System Applications, Inc. Cost Containment Division.

IMPLEMENTATION GUIDELINE ISSUES FOR MANAGEMENT

BUILD A QUALITY NETWORK

Quality providers plus quality payors will add up to an attractive package for employers and other consumers of PPO services. A critical factor to a PPO's success is the image it projects as a viable and reputable organization in the marketplace. It is important for those organizing the PPO to do their homework and set high standards when contracting with providers. Checking references, seeking medical community leader support, and analyzing available data on medical practice patterns will assist in marketing the PPO and help alleviate the risk of future malpractice exposure.

UNDERSTAND STRENGTHS AND WEAKNESSES OF UTILIZATION MANAGEMENT APPROACHES

A major advantage of programs that use capitation payment as a means to reimburse providers is the direct financial incentive for providers to manage health care utilization. Each medical decision made by a participating doctor under a capitation program bears a potential financial reward or liability. Hence, providers actively reduce the use of medical services under capitation programs. Skeptics of capitated medical programs have raised this important question, "Does capitation result in a reduction of only unneeded or frivolous services or in a reduction of needed services as well?" One balancing factor for capitated providers is the risk of malpractice if needed services are foregone.

On the other hand, most PPOs will rely on utilization controls administered by the PPO or an outside peer review organization to manage utilization. Externally applied utilization controls do not necessarily develop sufficient pressure to achieve changes in participating provider behavior to reduce medical utilization.

In sum, capitation is a powerful weapon against unnecessary health care utilization. Utilization review, although less powerful, poses less of a risk of encouraging underutilization of health services. The important points for PPOs incorporating utilization controls are (1) to assure that medical professionals are involved in the development and implementation of the PPO utilization-review program and (2) to make certain that abusive patterns are investigated quickly and dealt with effectively.

COORDINATE AND PLAN PROGRAM CAREFULLY

Major PPO components such as provider contracts, benefits contracts, data collection, payment, and analyses systems and utilization management programs need to fit together and support each other. This goal can be met by establishing critical project objectives. Below are five sample PPO project objectives:

1. Make sure that the PPO hospital reimbursement methods are consistent with the type of utilization management techniques developed for the PPO. (See the Utilization Review by Reimbursement Method Chart, Exhibit 7.)

EXHIBIT 7
Utilization Review by Reimbursement Method

Reimbursement Method	Hospital Utilization Review Focus
DRG payment	Preadmission review; categorization into DRGs.
Per discharge/admission (all inclusive)	Preadmission review; categorization into service categories if service-specific rates are used.
Per diem	Preadmission review; length of stay review; categorization into service categories if service-specific rates are used.
Charges minus discount	Preadmission review; length of stay review; ancilliary services review; post-hospitalization billing audits.

2. Make certain that medical necessity clauses in PPO benefits policies are similar to the medical necessity conditions negotiated in provider agreements and do not contradict utilization management program protocol. For instance, if PPO benefits policies exclude elective cosmetic surgeries, so should provider agreements and vice versa.

3. Clarification and redesign of coordination of benefits (COB) provisions and payment practices are essential in a PPO environment. Payment rules, in particular, need to be defined. Also, revised rules must be communicated and understood in order to properly pay and underwrite PPO benefits.

4. In order to assure congruency, all hospital benefits outlined in the PPO benefits contracts should be linked to the definition of allowable charges outlined in the PPO provider contracts. For example, typical benefit policy exclusions for private room charges, television sets, and other services not covered by the contract should be excluded from negotiated covered charges as outlined in a DRG or other fixed payment contract.

5. When designing the PPO benefits plan, make certain that family or individual new coinsurance or stop loss levels are set at high enough levels to maintain the incentive/disincentive benefits design for PPO versus non-PPO provider payment. For example, assume that a PPO plan waives all deductibles, pays 100 percent coinsurance for participating physicians' services, but requires a $100 deductible, and pays 80 percent coinsurance for nonparticipating physician services. Individual stop loss should be set at an appropriate level in order to insure that this incentive/disincentive structure remains effective. A level that is too low, (e.g., $2,000) would suggest that only one or two medical episodes (e.g., hospitalization) during a policy year could result in 100 percent payment across the board (and thus, eliminate the effects of the incentive/disincentive feature). As medical costs keep rising, these levels should be adjusted upward.

AVOID OPEN-ENDED PROVIDER ENROLLMENTS

Although attractive from a marketing perspective, including too many providers in the PPO may lead to provider disillusionment with the PPO. As IPAs have discovered, provider behaviors do not change if member patients are too few and too far between.

CONSIDER RESIDUAL EFFECTS OF PPO DEVELOPMENT

Building patient and utilization management systems that result in more efficient use of health care services is an investment that will probably pay off whether or not a PPO is in a payor's or provider's long range plan.

DEFINE PAYMENT RULES FOR REFERRALS OUTSIDE NETWORK

Since PPO providers may direct patients to specialists outside the PPO network, procedures for overriding the disincentives in benefits payment to nonparticipating providers need to be outlined. Approaches include (1) requiring referral approvals from the PPO utilization review organization or the medical practice committee, (2) urging or requiring use of participating specialists and allowing nonparticipating referrals under special conditions (e.g., geographic access or emergency), and (3) offering primary care physicians a capitation payment program wherein they must pay specialists' fees in excess of the normal benefits payment for non-PPO physician services.

PLAN FOR THOROUGH PROVIDER ELIGIBILITY/MAINTENANCE PROCEDURES

It is essential to think through and negotiate the conditions under which a physician can withdraw from the PPO program or under which eligibility can be withdrawn by a payor. Also, the timetable and procedures for renegotiating PPO agreements need to be well planned. Finally, appoint someone full-time to maintain participating provider records.

MAKE AGREEMENTS IN GOOD FAITH

When a payor, provider, or purchaser decides to proceed with and implement a PPO program, the business relationships formed through the PPO with other parties must be made in good faith and with realistic expectations. Payors, providers, or purchasers expecting quick behavior changes from the PPO are bound to be disappointed. Since a PPO is essentially a purchaser-payor-provider partnership in which each partner wins or loses based on the other's performance, there is a tendency to point fingers when problems arise. Thus, as PPO relationships evolve, keep in mind that there is only one way to get along, and that is to get along.

NOTES

1. Reporting formats were developed by Advanced System Applications, Inc. and Health Data Institute.

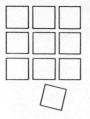
A Business Approach to Contracting with PPOs

Charles H. Harrison
Partner
Arthur Andersen & Co.
Los Angeles, CA

William H. Hranchak
Manager
Arthur Andersen & Co.
Los Angeles, CA

☐ The advent of the PPO, more than any other recent development, is forcing health care providers to view themselves in a traditional business sense. This is because the PPO represents a new, knowledgeable consumer in the marketplace which is contracting for health care services on the basis of price, quantity, and quality. To remain profitable (and possibly to survive) hospitals must now seriously address factors such as product pricing, cost, volume, and other business considerations. If this is not successfully done, and if such arrangements continue to proliferate in the industry, the resulting unmet costs will ultimately cause the hospital's demise because there will be nowhere left to shift these costs. While PPOs have not yet reached this dominant position in the marketplace, the importance of addressing these factors is not lessened.

From the hospital's standpoint, contracts with the PPO would ideally provide increased utilization of low-cost, underutilized services. In fact, the first PPOs were originally formed for this purpose. However, recognizing the existing over capacity at many of the nation's hospitals, health care purchasers have seized upon the PPO concept as a means of "negotiating" with competing hospitals to obtain the broadest health care coverage at the lowest possible cost. Whether the contracting process requires the provider to competitively bid, respond to a quote, or negotiate with purchasers, the provider must understand the effects the contractual provisions will have from a business and financial standpoint. Entering into contracts solely to "meet the competition" may give rise to unintended and potentially disastrous results.

A hospital should enter into a contractual relationship with a PPO on the basis of whether it serves as an appropriate, consistent, and feasible strategy for the achievement of the hospital's mission, objectives, and goals contained in its strategic plan. A strategy is not an end in itself but a means for achieving the specific objectives and goals of an *individual* hospital. What may be an appropriate strategy for one hospital (contracting with a PPO) may not be appropriate for another. Consequently, an evaluation of a strategy must be performed with the hospital's strategic plan in view. This evaluation requires the following tasks to be performed:

- Describe the strategy in sufficient detail to understand the essential components.
- Identify the resources required to implement the strategy.
- Obtain management assumptions on volumes, costs, and revenues.
- Evaluate the strategies against a predetermined set of entity-specific criteria (i.e., need for service, financial viability/consequences, cost effectiveness, medical staff acceptance).

The following discussion is intended to assist in performing this type of evaluation by providing a review of key contractual considerations, their ramifications, and a means of assessing the potential financial viability/consequences of the transaction. These considerations will become more critical as hospitals find themselves dealing with PPOs as the primary purchasers of health care services.

CONTRACTUAL CONSIDERATIONS

SERVICES OFFERED

While PPOs may prefer to contract with hospitals that offer their full line of services to their enrollees, this is usually not desirable to the hospital. Which services are offered and which are not must be based on a hospital's individual assessment of its strengths and weaknesses. This essentially translates to departmental or even subdepartmental profitability and availability.

Particular attention should be given to those high-cost, special services (i.e., open heart surgery, neonatal care) if they will not be separately considered in the rate structure. If fees are negotiated on the basis of an aggregate charge per day and such charge does not adequately anticipate the utilization of such special services, a financial disaster could occur. In such instances, the hospital is essentially serving as an insurance company. Consequently, every effort should be made to either exclude these services or contract at a separate rate to reduce risk.

A hospital would properly want to exclude from the contract those services that are already fully utilized. Including these services under the PPO agreement could result in a revenue loss if a discounted rate structure is adopted, since existing, not new, revenue would be discounted. In addition, if sufficient excess capacity does not exist, this situation may result in turning away existing patients or having to subcontract in order to provide service under the contract.

It should be noted that PPO contracting opportunities may exist for the hospital that wants to become a preferred provider with respect to only specific services that are currently underutilized.

The contract should also address whether "services" include the services of hospital-based physicians. Many PPOs will expect a hospital to develop and present a "medical group." Failure to identify this expectation could result in an understated rate structure. Also, where a hospital has agreed to discount certain services, the hospital-based physicians' contracts should be revised to permit such discounts to be passed through to them.

Since the continued financial cutbacks facing hospitals may prevent them from offering all desired services, a situation might exist where a service desired by the PPO is not currently offered by the hospital. This situation should be specifically allowed for in the contract. Certain PPOs, in a desire to reduce their administrative costs, may require the hospital to directly subcontract for services it does not already provide. If this is the case, the hospital should determine that the subcontracted service can be feasibly obtained in the marketplace. This search for subcontractors may ultimately develop into a *team* or joint venture of subcontractors consisting of several hospitals whereby the PPO contract provides an opportunity for each hospital to more fully utilize its specialized programs.

WHO IS THE PATIENT?

The contract should specifically identify the class of patient who will receive health care services under the PPO agreement. The patient population demographics will determine the unique types of services to be rendered, which in turn will determine the cost to the hospital. The lack of specificity in the contract will create the greatest risk to the hospital where it has entered into an aggregate charge per day arrangement, because case mix changes will be reflected only in costs, not revenues. While many PPOs are publicized as excluding high-risk patients from their plans, this fact should specifically be documented in the contract. Particular concern must be given to the interplay existing when a PPO enrollee is also covered by either medicare or medicaid since different payment procedures may have to be adopted.

PHYSICIANS

Put succinctly, the hospital that is under an aggregate charge per day arrangement must protect itself from physicians who:

— Do not move patients from high-cost units (ICU/CCU) to stepped down units or routine units on a timely basis.
— Over order diagnostic tests and procedures.

While utilization review will protect the PPO from excess days and/ or unnecessary admissions, once the patient is in the hospital, the PPO really has no concern how much is done (as long as the length of stay is reasonable). To protect itself, the hospital needs to utilize some system of medical practice parameters. Such parameters need to be developed (or at least "blessed") by the medical staff who will be working under them. Adherence to such practice parameters should be monitored by a paid medical director who has the trust of the medical staff, as well as an understanding of the economic realities of the PPO agreement.

BASIS FOR RATES

Many PPO agreements will provide for services to be paid on the basis of an aggregate charge per day. Such a rate will typically be lower than the average rate in the community. Consequently, since revenues are fixed, the hospital's ultimate profitabiiity under the agreement will be determined by its costs to provide these services. As previously noted, a case mix shift after the contract is entered into could place the hospital at substantial risk due to the unanticipated costs. The downside exposure from such an occurrence could be limited by providing limits on the volume of certain high-cost services. Another possible solution would involve establishing a separate rate structure to services after a particular volume of services has been rendered, or a contract provision could exist that would allow certain services to be dropped completely, solely at the discretion of the hospital (if it appears that the demographics of the PPO's patients are different than they were represented to be when the contract was negotiated).

Of course, rates do not have to be based on an aggregate charge per day. A fee-for-service arrangement should not be excluded from consideration. While this method is typically coupled with discounting, a hospital should not give a discount on its services until a determination has been made that its fees do not already reflect a discount from the community standard.

As a middle ground between fee-for-service and aggregate charge per day, hospitals might attempt to negotiate fees on the basis of charge per day by type of service, i.e., medical, surgical, obstetrics, pediatrics, surgical ICU, and medical ICU. Such a posture offers a hedge against case mix changes as well as physicians who may not transfer their patients from ICU to medical/surgical as fast as the hospital would desire.

BILLING/PAYMENT TERMS

The agreement should specify a billing schedule between the hospital and the PPO. The hospital should avoid restrictions that would prevent their timely submission of bills. The time period in which payment is to be made by the PPO should also be clearly defined. Where discounts have already been specifically provided, slow payment should not be available to provide another form of discount. In this regard, consideration should be given to reducing or eliminating the otherwise allowed discount if payment is not received within a specified number of days. In addition, the assessment of interest should be applied in the case of late payments. The low margins that can be expected from participation would probably justify inclusion of a termination provision for continued delinquencies.

Another publicized benefit of PPOs is that despite their imposition of discounts for services, the hospital will profit because of increased utilization. That is to say, the lower margins will be offset by volume. Accordingly, if such volume is not generated, the agreement should provide for the imposition of some sort of monetary penalty since the agreed upon rate reflected this expected benefit.

OTHER CONSIDERATIONS

All PPO agreements contemplate some sort of utilization review including prior authorization for inpatient admissions, concurrent review of hospital stays, and retrospective claims reviews. The PPOs typically expect the costs of these administrative procedures to be borne by the hospital. If this is the case, these costs must be considered in determining whether or not the additional volume generated under the PPO agreement will actually increase the hospital's profit.

The utilization review process will also require close coordination with the medical staff in determining how such procedures will be carried out. In certain situations, the PPO will require third parties to perform a review process that was previously performed by staff physicians.

Exclusive agreements with hospital-based and other physicians must be examined to determine whether the PPO arrangement will interfere with their practice patterns by allowing such services to be provided by other physicians.

Medical staff provisions in general must be given consideration since PPO agreement may provide that any participating physician may admit at any participating hospital. Such provisions must be reviewed closely with the medical staff and legal counsel. Regular application requirements should be imposed on these nonstaff participating physicians before granting staff membership and/or any admission privileges.

The financial viability of the PPO should be examined by the contracting hospital to ensure that services rendered will be paid for. The numerous new entries into the PPO arena almost guarantee that some sort of shake-out will occur. Risk from this type of exposure can be minimized by maintaining the timeliness of billings and receivables. In extreme cases, deposits to secure future payments may be advisable. In a similar regard, contractual provisions should address the PPO's liability for payment in the event an enrollee leaves the program while admitted to the hospital; or the case where the PPO terminates the agreement while enrollees are still admitted to the hospital. This and other similar situations must be considered and specifically addressed to insure that the hospital is able to recover fees for the services it renders.

FINANCIAL MODELING

After the various financial factors of the PPO agreement have been established, their overall financial impact to the hospital should be assessed. Financial modeling is a technique by which this can be done. Modeling merely refers to the use of computer programs to assist in the preparation of financial projections thereby simulating or "modeling" actual business activity. This type of analysis provides one method of evaluating the cost or benefit of "meeting the competition" by entering the PPO arrangement.

The first step to utilizing the model would be to develop a set of assumptions involving operations under the agreement. This could include

— Anticipated volume by patient type for all departments with anticipated significant participation from enrollees (i.e., ICU, CCU, open heart surgery, hip surgery).
— Incremental costs of the enrollee patient types considered above as well as the additional direct costs to provide utilization review and other administrative requirements associated with the PPO agreement.
— Revenue by enrollees (by patient type, if applicable).

The model, before considering the PPO agreement, would then be revised to incorporate the above factors to establish the resulting effect on net income.

The impact of potential errors on the assumptions could be evaluated by performing sensitivity analyses. This would involve preparing alternative computations involving variations in the assumptions such as changes in case mix, revisions in cost assumptions, or changes in volume. Such an analysis will highlight the need to contract over short periods of time.

Parameters for purposes of performing the sensitivity analysis aspect of the model should be based in part on an assessment of potential competitors' strengths and weaknesses. This will provide indications of what they can or cannot offer under an agreement with a PPO (i.e., a financially weak hospital with poor occupancy might be more willing to concede discounts to a PPO. This knowledge may encourage a competing hospital to "give up" the contract to the other hospital where it thinks it may further weaken its position). The use of a computer program will greatly facilitate the development and analysis of these types of "what if" scenarios.

In most circumstances, even relatively unsophisticated approaches will provide substantial insight into the potential ramifications of a PPO agreement. However, it must be recognized that such a model, no matter what degree of detail and complexity is incorporated into it, is generally still a guess about the future, and it is essential that hospital management identify key nonfinancial factors.

CONCLUSION

The development of PPOs has forced many hospitals to begin to make financial decisions that they must live with. By using sound business techniques and judgment, hospitals can minimize the inherent risk of such decisions and maximize their profitability.

HOSPITAL CONTRACTING WITH PPOS

Leonard Kalm, M.P.H.
Director of Special Programs
AmeriCare Health Corporation
Sacramento, CA

Paul R. DeMuro, J.D.
Attorney
Carpenter, Higgins & Simonds
Burlingame, CA

☐ This article reviews issues as they relate to hospitals contracting with non-provider-based PPOs. The hospital's unique role in the PPO movement, contracting strategies, and steps to follow in negotiating PPO contracts are discussed.[1]

The development of PPOs has proceeded at a remarkable rate. With purchasers of medical care seeking to curb the rapid escalation of their costs, a myriad of health care coverage options has developed. More noteworthy than the number of participants in these alternative health care delivery systems is the number and wide variety of plans that have been formed. Insurance-based, broker-based, employer-based, and in at least one state, government-based competitive contracting exist, primarily for the purpose of forming preferred networks of cost-effective providers.

The lack of extensive regulation of PPOs and the ease with which they can be established are among the primary reasons why the development of PPOs has proceeded at such a rapid rate. Unlike health mainte-nance organizations (HMOs), no extensive federal and statutory schemes govern the operation of PPOs. HMOs are required, among other things, to offer a minimum benefit structure, maintain certain risk reserves, and apply for new service area designation if they wish to expand. PPOs typi-cally have not been subjected to these kinds of requirements.

Although the future direction of PPOs is uncertain, this new industry exists today as a viable health care alternative for the public. PPOs, if successful, have the ability to reshape business patterns of various seg-ments of the health care community. For this reason alone, hospitals can-not ignore preferred provider organizations.

THE HOSPITAL AND ITS ROLE IN THE PPO MOVEMENT

Hospitals, being the primary source of inpatient care, serve a pivotal role in the development and growth of PPOs. Because of increasing competi-tion among health care facilities, hospital management must consider dual strategies for the future. The first, a defensive posture, must be aimed at preserving existing patient utilization in the hospital. The sec-ond, a more aggressive one, must strive to strengthen or enlarge a hospi-tal's position in the marketplace. PPOs can, in part, assist in employing both these strategies. Specifically, hospitals should be interested in con-tracting with PPOs for the following reasons:

Protection of market share. If a PPO enters into a relationship with a hospital's competitor, a hospital may contract with the PPO to protect its existing market.

Increased volume. Through aggressive marketing or provider exclu-sivity within a region, PPOs offer a hospital an opportunity to serve pa-tients that it might not otherwise serve. This is particularly true in multi-facility, overbedded areas.

More favorable case mix. Most PPOs are primarily interested in en-rolling low medical risk individuals. As a result, a hospital contracting with a PPO may experience a more favorable case mix.

Strengthen hospital-physician relationships. Where physicians es-tablish exclusive relationships with the same PPO as the hospital, new loyalties may be created or existing ones strengthened. Many hospitals have viewed the PPO movement as an opportunity to create joint ventures with their medical staffs in an effort to attract PPOs or to form their own health care plans that can be marketed externally.

Cost containment. As hospitals offer competitive rates to PPOs, they must begin to examine ways to minimize costs. This incentive is desirable in an industry that is being subjected to increasing cost pressures.

HOSPITAL RISKS IN PPO CONTRACTING

In addition to the opportunities that are available for hospitals as they align with PPOs, there is much risk and reason for concern. PPOs exist, in part, to achieve cost savings in the provision of medical care. This can only be accomplished by one or more of the following means: (1) a reduction in the benefit package offered to beneficiaries, (2) a reduction in the consumption of services by beneficiaries, or (3) a reduction in the dollar amount spent for any given unit of service.

PPOs generally achieve a reduction in the benefit package by limiting the scope of services that the plan covers. PPOs can decrease the consumption of services by restricting access, implementing effective utilization review, or encouraging health prevention practices. Finally, PPOs aim to reduce the dollar amount paid for an episode of care by obtaining favorable or discounted rates from providers. In fact, some PPOs address the issue of cost savings by focusing only on this latter strategy. As a result, hospitals must be cautious when approached by PPOs and should consider the following risks prior to any decision to negotiate with a PPO:

Failing PPOs and bad debt. If a PPO's operations are unsuccessful, a hospital may experience bad debts due to services provided for which it will receive no payment. In California, for example, there are cases of bankrupt PPOs that have left both hospitals and physicians without payment for services they have rendered.

Adverse patient mix. As with HMOs, there is always the risk that a PPO may enroll a more acute population than it had originally intended. If a PPO experiences such adverse selection, a hospital could be forced to provide care to a more medically intense population than for which it had negotiated or intended.

PPO credibility and physicians. By contracting with a PPO, a hospital may provide credibility for a particular plan with physicians on its medical staff. If a PPO fails or is mismanaged (e.g., late payment of claims), the hospital may be blamed for leading physicians into a disreputable or poorly managed PPO.

PPO endorsement and the public. The public may view a hospital as an endorser of a particular PPO merely because it has a contract with that plan. This is particularly true when a PPO's marketing strategy targets a limited number of providers from which beneficiaries can receive care. Some plans provide better coverage than others, and a dissatisfied beneficiary, rather than pursuing the insurer, may erroneously look toward the hospital for an explanation.

New industry with many uncertainties. As with any new industry that is evolving there are potential pitfalls that may adversely impact hospitals.

INITIAL CONTACT WITH A PPO

A hospital should view whether to enter into a relationship with a PPO as a business decision. As with other contracting decisions in the hospital environment, it is advisable to develop a consistent strategy. Hospital management would not approve the purchase of an expensive piece of equipment without first determining the need or justification for the item, the reasonableness of its price, and its impact on patient care. Similarly, hospital management must follow a strategy to ensure that any particular PPO contracting decision is an informed and ultimately defensible one.

A necessary component of the hospital's strategy is to obtain as much information as possible about the PPO. Specifically, a hospital should consider the PPO's background and history, financial solvency, overall position in the health care market, and the PPO's plans to enter the hospital's market. As a guide to an initial meeting with a PPO representative, Exhibit 1 lists several questions that can be asked in order to gather such information.

EXHIBIT 1
Questions to Ask When Considering a PPO Arrangement

History and Organization of Plan
1. Who is sponsoring the PPO? Is it insurance-, employer-, union-, provider-, or third-party administrator-based?
2. Is the plan affiliated with any organization? If so, what organization?
3. How long has the plan been in existence?
4. Where is the plan's home office?
5. Where is the plan's nearest office to the hospital?
6. Has the plan sought or obtained any federal and state approvals (e.g., Department of Insurance, Department of Corporations)? If not, does it intend to?

Financial Viability
1. Request the plan's audited financial statements for the past two years. (In cases of newly formed PPOs, request any existing operating statements, and pro formas for the same period.)
2. What is the plan's current premium structure?
3. Is any other entity responsible for the plan's operations in the event that it fails?
4. If the plan is administered by a third party, what organization is responsible for payment and is it financially viable?
5. Does the plan have a reinsurance policy, and if so, at what limits is it operative?

EXHIBIT 1 *(concluded)*

Position in Marketplace
1. In what locations is the plan currently in operation?
2. What is the plan's current enrollment size?
3. Describe the composition of the plan's current enrollment (age, sex, lives per contract, etc.)?

Marketing and Strategic Plan
1. What are the plan's targeted geographic markets?
2. To whom does the plan intend to market its PPO (large employers, small employers, insurance plans, employer trusts, etc.)?
3. What is the plan's projected enrollment size? Do any of these projections represent cross-overs from a previously existing plan in the organization?
4. Who sells the plan (exclusive agents, brokers, inhouse representatives, other)?
5. What is the plan's marketing commitment for the future for the hospital's particular geographic area (both in terms of personnel and dollars)?
6. Are there any marketing brochures or advertising materials that can be reviewed?

Physician Participation
1. Does the plan intend to selectively contract with physicians? If so, in what manner?
2. What role does the plan envision for the hospital in enlisting physicians?
3. How will physicians be reimbursed for their services (fee schedule)?

Utilization Review
1. Does the plan have its own utilization review program? If so, request a copy.
2. Does the plan intend to incorporate the hospital's existing utilization program into that of the PPO?
3. How does the plan intend to integrate physicians into the utilization review system?
4. What is the plan's current experience of hospital days per 1,000 enrollees?

Plan Benefits and Other Considerations
1. Request a copy of the plan's benefit structure.
2. For what services is the plan primarily interested in contracting (inpatient, outpatient, specialty, tertiary)?
3. Describe the incentive subscribers will have to use a PPO provider in lieu of non-PPO providers?
4. If the hospital offers a discounted rate, will this apply only to PPO subscribers, or also to other plans the organization may offer?

In addition to information that can be obtained directly from the PPO, hospital and medical associations, state departments of insurance or corporations, and consumer affairs organizations can sometimes provide information about a particular PPO. Also, when a PPO has been in operation in other areas, a hospital may benefit from the experience of other providers.

THE CONTRACTING PROCESS

A decision to enter into negotiations with a PPO necessitates the formation of a negotiating team. The size and composition of the negotiating team will depend on the complexity of the contract and its importance to the institution. This team, however, will usually include the chief executive officer and chief financial officer, or their representatives, and hospital legal counsel. In addition, the team might also include board members, in cases where the PPO represents a significant portion of the hospital's business or a major departure from one of the hospital's long-term goals, representatives of the medical staff, in cases where there are major physician considerations, or consultants who have experience with PPOs or similar kinds of contracting.

After hospital management or the governing body of the hospital has clearly defined the authority of the negotiating team with respect to contracting, the team should establish its objectives and delineate the role of members. One individual should be designated as the primary contact person, through which all communications with the PPO are channelled. Another member might be responsible for financial considerations, including pricing options, and one individual could compile any additional information requested. The team's legal counsel would be responsible for suggested revisions to the contract.

The hospital's primary contact with a PPO may not be with the plan's administrator. Often, group claims administrators, insurance brokers, marketing representatives, or directors of provider relations act as PPO negotiators. Because of this, knowledge of the negotiator's background, position, and authority is important. In addition, it is helpful to ascertain the PPO negotiator's familiarity with the hospital and its market. The negotiating team may want to educate a less informed PPO negotiator about unique aspects of the hospital and its community.

A PPO negotiator may impose a negotiating schedule on the hospital. The negotiating team should be comfortable with the schedule and should be able to make reasoned decisions within the established time frame. There may be instances in which a PPO has set unreasonably short deadlines for the submission of a bid or proposal. In such a situation the hospital might consider requesting an extension of the time frame or providing some preliminary information that can be supplemented at a later date. Where a PPO has employed as part of its negotiating strategy unreasonable deadlines, such deadlines should not dictate a hospital's actions.

CONTRACT PRICING

The development of a hospital's pricing philosophy is instrumental in submitting PPO bids. Some hospitals will aggressively price their services hoping to achieve increased volumes. Other hospitals will choose not to discount their services understanding that in the future, they may serve fewer patients. A hospital's approach to pricing will depend on the overall contribution margin (revenue less variable costs) it desires to achieve from PPOs and the competitive nature of the hospital's market.

The types of pricing hospitals can propose (or be presented with) range from a simple percentage discount to complex sliding fees based on changes in volume and case mix. The most prevalent methods are per-diem rates (all inclusive and multitiered), per case arrangements, and percentage discounts from charges. In addition to being relatively easy to implement within a hospital's business office, PPOs prefer these methods because they can compare the bids of competing hospitals. Inherent in each of these forms of pricing is a certain degree of risk which a hospital must consider. If a hospital submits a bid on a basis other than full or discounted charges, price must be balanced against additional financial risk.

For example, a hospital that accepts a single per-diem rate of reim-bursement assumes financial risk for any change in usage of ancillary services or any change in case mix. If a patient's daily usage of ancillary services exceeds the level that the hospital had predicted, it could experi-ence a financial loss for each day of such care. Similarly, if patient acuity of the PPO exceeds the level that the hospital had predicted, more inten-sive, and thus, more expensive, daily services may be required that in-crease the hospital's costs.

Exhibit 2 categorizes these and other financial risks.

EXHIBIT 2
Types of Pricing and Hospital Risk

Method of Payment	Change in Admissions	Change in Length of Stay	Change in Usage of Ancillary Services	Change in Case Mix
Full charges	No risk	No risk	No risk	No risk
Single percentage discount from charges	No risk	No risk	No risk	No risk
Multiple percentage discount from charges*	No risk	No risk	No risk	No risk
Single per diem	No risk	No risk	Full risk	Full risk
Multiple per diems†	No risk	No risk	Full risk	Limited risk
Single price per discharge	No risk	Full risk	Full risk	Full risk
Case mix adjusted price per discharge‡	No risk	Full risk	Full risk	Limited or no risk
Capitation	Full risk	Full risk	Full risk	Full risk

*Multiple percentage discount from charges is normally based on either volume (e.g., X percent discount for a certain number of days, Y percent discount for each additional day) or type of service (e.g., X percent discount for general medical-surgical services, Y percent discount for maternity care).

†Multiple per diems can be based on bed classification, type of service provided, or some other meaningful classification.

‡The best example of this payment method is the Medicare Prospective Payment system for hospital inpatient services, based on Diagnosis Related Groups (DRGs).

Eventually, a hospital's bid must take into account the cost of caring for the PPO subscriber. Unfortunately, many hospitals have difficulty competitively pricing their services because they lack the ability to accurately determine their true costs.[2] These facilities must rely on alternative costing methods, including the sampling of patient records and estimated ratios of the cost of services provided to billed charges. It should be noted, however, that such methods are only as accurate as the assumptions upon which they are based. Hospitals will eventually be forced to implement comprehensive cost accounting systems similar to those currently in operation in other industries.

CONTRACT TERMS

In negotiating the terms of a PPO contract, it is important to note that although each contract will exhibit its own unique characteristics, the major elements of most contracts will be similar. The following paragraphs outline some of these provisions:

SERVICES

The contract should clearly define the services that the hospital agrees to provide and the nature and extent of their availability. These services may include all or part of the hospital's available inpatient services, emergency services, or outpatient services. The hospital may also agree to arrange for selected physician services, such as emergency room physician services, radiology, pathology, and anesthesiology.

SUBSCRIBERS

There should be a means to identify subscribers and their eligibility for services under the contract. Subscribers are usually identified by subscriber identification cards or enrollment lists. Eligibility can be determined by contacting the PPO prior to or at the time of admission to verify current status.

UTILIZATION REVIEW

PPOs may incorporate a hospital's existing utilization review procedures, perform these functions on their own, or enlist outside review agencies. The utilization review procedures should be clearly described and, if performed by the PPO or its representative, should not disrupt a hospital's existing utilization-review program. If the PPO's utilization-review procedures involve interaction with a hospital's medical staff, the hospital will want to consult representatives of the medical staff.

COMMITMENT TO MARKETING AND VOLUME

If the PPO is undertaking a commitment to market the plan, the contract should reflect this commitment and the efforts that will be expended to accomplish this. For example, the PPO may be required to expend a certain sum on advertising in a hospital's service area. If the PPO has promised certain volumes of patients, these should be reflected in the contract. This can be achieved by ensuring enrollment size or hospital patient days.

MEDICAL RECORDS AND CONFIDENTIALITY

To ensure that patient records remain confidential in accordance with applicable law, the contract should provide that the records of all subscribers are only accessible by the PPO where the subscriber has consented.

COORDINATION OF BENEFITS

Because a patient may be covered by a plan or insurance in addition to the PPO coverage, the contract should specify mechanisms by which benefits are to be coordinated. The contract should outline which coverages are primary and secondary in nature and who will undertake responsibility for billing other carriers.

INSURANCE; INDEMNITY

The hospital and the PPO should demonstrate that they are sufficiently insured for professional and general liability and liability arising from their duties and obligations under the contract, and those of their employees. In addition, the contract may provide that each party will indemnify the other for liability arising from its wrongful actions.

DISPUTE RESOLUTION

The contract should include a procedure for the resolution of disputes. A separate process for disagreements arising from the utilization-review procedures may be incorporated to preclude lengthy disputes over these issues.

EXCLUSIVITY

If a hospital, in an attempt to increase its volume, is able to obtain a promise from the PPO that it will not contract with another hospital in a particular area, and such a provision would not be in violation of any law, this should be part of the contract.

NONASSIGNMENT

The contract should provide that the PPO cannot assign its rights and obligations to another party without the hospital's permission because the hospital should not unknowingly be subjected to a change in the identity of the patient population or the payor.

TERM OF CONTRACT, RENEGOTIATION

A long contract term can assure a continued relationship with a PPO, thereby reducing uncertainty in long-term planning. A shorter contract term, however, permits a hospital to gain experience with a PPO without the risk of an extended commitment. Long-term contracts may include renegotiation provisions.

TERMINATION

An early termination clause can be incorporated into the contract and can be applicable to either the hospital or PPO or both. Such a clause reduces the risk of a bad bargain for a hospital. It, however, may decrease the value of a more favorable long-term contract where the PPO has a similar clause.

IMPLEMENTATION OF PPO PLAN

A few weeks to several months may elapse from the time a PPO contract is successfully negotiated to when the hospital may provide services to a PPO subscriber. The length of this period is primarily determined by the speed at which a PPO is able to market and sell its plan. In the interim, hospital management has the opportunity to direct its efforts to maximizing its benefits under the contract. An initial step can be the formation of an ad-hoc task force to implement, coordinate, and monitor the operation of the PPO contract. Members of this task force might include a negotiating team member familiar with the PPO and contract, an admitting supervisor, nursing representative, utilization review coordinator, and the business office or claims review manager. Other members could also include the medical records manager, data processing managers, discharge planner, or representatives from the hospital's medical staff.

An effective monitoring system is essential, particularly when a hospital has a contract that provides for risk-based rates. In many instances, hospitals will have existing monitoring systems for other payors under similar arrangements that can be applied to the PPO. In addition, these systems should assist in developing historical data upon which to base pricing or contract changes during renegotiation.

Not only is it necessary to internally monitor the operation of the PPO at the hospital, it is also important to periodically review the PPO's activities. Hospitals should ensure that the PPO markets and operates its plan in the agreed upon manner by requesting quarterly summaries of the PPO's activities. For new PPOs, a hospital may desire interim financial statements to ensure that the PPO continues to be financially viable. Finally, hospital management may periodically review the PPO's enrollment size within the hospital's community. This "external monitoring" may prove useful at the time of renegotiation.

CONCLUSION

Although PPOs afford a hospital many opportunities, risks are inherent in PPO contracting. Therefore, hospitals must be cautious in their approach to this new health care option. Hospital administrators must develop the skills to accurately assess the strengths and weaknesses of PPOs, to offer alternative pricing arrangements, and to negotiate effectively in this competitive environment.

For preferred provider organizations to achieve a dominant position in the marketplace, they will have to establish that they offer a cost-effective solution to the increasing cost of medical care without jeopardizing reasonable access for consumers. The nature of selective contracting and hospital discounting may make this objective increasingly difficult.

NOTES

1. Although this article discusses both financial and legal considerations in PPO contracting, it should not be construed as financial or legal advice. The opinions set forth herein are those of the authors.

2. This is due in part to federal and state regulations providing for payment to hospitals based on a method inconsistent with cost accounting principles.

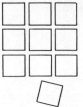

Contracting Requirements

PUBLIC SECTOR CONTRACTING WITH PPOS[1]

Jon B. Christianson, Ph.D.

Associate Professor
Department of Management and Policy
Department of Economics
College of Business and Public Administration
University of Arizona
Tucson, AZ

The current growth in the number of PPOs providing medical care to private sector employees coincides with two important recent developments in indigent medical care programs: a search for new methods of containing cost increases in these programs and a new latitude for program administrators to limit by contract the providers who are allowed to deliver care to indigents. Given these circumstances, it seems inevitable that medicaid administrators will consider selective contracting with PPOs as a means of controlling program costs. Other forms of contracting with fee-for-service providers and with prepaid organizations have already been implemented in several states, most notably California and Arizona.[2] Because of the highly visible, political nature of indigent medical care programs and the legal and procedural constraints that govern such programs, contracting with PPOs raises issues for public sector administrators that differ in nature and importance from those faced by benefit managers in private firms. This chapter identifies these issues and discusses alternative approaches for addressing them.

MOTIVATION FOR PUBLIC SECTOR CONTRACTING WITH PPOs

Between 1972 and 1977 annual Medicaid program costs rose from $6.3 billion to $16.3 billion, while the number of program enrollees increased from 17.6 million to 22.9 million.[3] More important than the level of Medicaid expenditures during this period was their relative growth rate; overall Medicaid costs increased 40 percent faster than total health expenditures during the decade of the 1970s.[4] This trend continued into 1981, when Medicaid outlays increased by 18 percent.[5]

Program administrators initially responded to escalation in program costs by reducing benefits and enforcing stricter eligibility rules. For instance, in the year prior to July, 1982, 23 states adopted proposals to eliminate optional services, limit the duration and scope of services, or restrict eligibility for services.[6] However, while Medicaid rolls in some states did decline modestly in the late 1970s and early 1980s, fiscal year 1983 program expenditures will total approximately $37 billion, of which $19.5 billion are federal funds.[7]

The Reagan Administration has attempted a variety of means to limit federal outlays for Medicaid. Its initial budget recommendations to Congress (1981) included an immediate mandatory ceiling on federal contributions to Medicaid. While this proposal was rejected by Congress, approval was granted for a 3 percent reduction in the federal matching rate for the program. The 1984 budget seeks to continue this reduced rate and proposes additional cost cutting measures including copayments for physician, clinic, and hospital outpatient services ($1 per visit for most program eligibles and $1.50 for the medically needy). It is projected that these changes, if adopted, would reduce federal expenditures by $870 million annually.[8]

The current effort by the federal government to limit its Medicaid program expenditures places a significant burden on state program administrators. To maintain existing levels of benefits and eligibility requirements states would need to increase their own Medicaid expenditures or seek programmatic changes to reduce expenditures for and/or utilization of services by eligibles. Since the pressures to limit budget growth are severe in most states and since Medicaid has been the single largest and fastest growing item in most state budgets in recent years, it seems unlikely that the first alternative would be politically feasible. Until recently, Medicaid statutes that constrained the latitude of state program administrators in dealing with providers made the second approach to cost containment equally unlikely. However, this situation was altered by the Omnibus Budget Reconciliation Act of 1981. While reducing the federal matching rate for Medicaid, this act also provided several avenues by which program administrators could restrict, or otherwise modify, the range of providers available to program eligibles.[9] As a result, a wide range of "experiments" in provider contracting have been instituted in state Medicaid programs. For instance, the California Medi-Cal program negotiates with providers on the basis of price and limits the providers available for Medi-Cal patients. In Arizona, providers engage in competitive bidding for the right to serve indigent patients on a prepaid, capitated basis. In addition, 10 states have established experimental "case management" programs whereby participating primary care physicians serve as entry points into the medical care system for program eligibles. These physicians approve all referrals to specialists and are subject to various degrees of financial risk, depending on the design of the individual programs.[10]

These recent developments in state Medicaid programs increase the likelihood that PPOs could be an important part of future efforts to contain costs. Furthermore, current Medicaid legislation provides administrators with the flexibility to redesign their programs to accommodate contracts with PPOs. Finally, the call for the introduction of copayments for program eligibles could make PPOs easier to implement as program options (as discussed below).

INTRODUCING PPOs INTO INDIGENT MEDICAL CARE PROGRAMS: ONE POSSIBLE SCENARIO

Given the wide variety of possible organizational forms for PPOs,[11] there are likely to be many different means of introducing PPOs into indigent medical care programs. Rather than attempting to enumerate all of these possible alternatives, the rest of this chapter will be based on one possible PPO scenario. This will permit a discussion in greater depth of the issues that are likely to face program administrators who adopt PPOs as options for program beneficiaries.

The scenario adopted assumes that copayments are instituted as cost-containment devices in medicaid programs. Physicians are reimbursed at the previously agreed upon rate—some percentage of usual and customary fees—but are required to collect copayments on a per-service basis, and transfer these monies to program administrators. Alternatively, some mechanism could be established that allowed providers to retain the copayments they collect while accepting per service reimbursements that deduct the copayment amount from the standard fee.

The existence of copayments provides a clear opportunity for the introduction of PPOs into indigent medical care programs. Suppose a PPO offered to provide services to program eligibles at fees that were lower than the standard reimbursement rate minus the designated copayment, while instituting a management information system designed to identify and reduce excessive utilization of services and protect against underservice. An incentive could be provided to program eligibles to choose PPO providers when they need medical care by waiving the copayment requirement if the chosen provider of services were a member of the PPO. The program's total costs could not increase, since PPO providers agree to reduce fees by at least the amount of the copayment; they could decrease if even lower fees are offered by PPO providers and if instances of excessive service utilization could be identified and reduced by the PPO. The ability to reduce excessive service utilization is crucial to the PPO's ability to reduce program costs relative to a system in which indigents can seek care from any provider but are required to copay. In the latter case, the copayment presumably discourages excessive utilization. When the copayment is removed under the PPO option, the PPO's utilization-review system must perform the function of discouraging excessive utilization. If it is ineffective, then total costs under the PPO option could be larger than under a "fee-for-service with copay" system, even if the per-service charges of PPO providers were lower.

Why would this scenario be attractive to providers? That is, why would providers be willing to accept lower fees for Medicaid eligibles, already viewed by many providers as financially unattractive patients, and submit to stringent utilization review to participate in a PPO? The key factor to the attractiveness of PPOs to providers in this case, as in applications to the private sector, is their ability to channel additional patients to participating providers. Lower fees and stringent utilization review may be acceptable to large numbers of providers if they increase provider incomes. However, there clearly is a limit to the amount providers will reduce their fees per unit of service in return for increased patient volume, and the exact nature of the trade off that providers will accept will vary with their own circumstances and the characteristics of the existing indigent medical care program.

PPOs will be most likely to become a viable option in Medicaid programs in communities where the competition for patients is intense because of an excess of hospital beds or a relatively large number of physicians.[12] Hospitals with empty beds are more likely to accept rates approaching the costs of treating additional patients, while physicians are more likely to accept lower fees if they have unoccupied practice time that contributes no revenue toward office overhead costs. Since these conditions will vary on a community by community basis, it seems unlikely that all states or regions within states will have equal success in introducing PPOs as options for indigent medical care.

A second factor in the likelihood that the above scenario will develop relates to the existing characteristics of the indigent medical care program itself. In particular, if reimbursement rates under the existing program are already relatively low compared to fees for private pay patients, PPOs may be unwilling to discount significantly from these rates. Yet unless they offer discounts which are at least equal to the waived copayments, PPOs must rely on their utilization review systems to generate savings for program administrators. While these savings in fact may occur, they are less visible and harder to document than reimbursement-related savings. Thus the PPO option becomes less attractive politically for program administrators.

A third consideration in projecting the likelihood that a favorable PPO scenario will develop is the ability of the program administrator to effectively "market" the option to program eligibles. This requires that information concerning the PPO option be clearly presented and accessible to eligibles. In the private sector, this set of marketing activities is relatively straightforward. Benefit managers have information concerning all employees, there is a regularly scheduled period during which employees have their options explained to them, and employees are relatively easy to contact as a group at the work site. None of these conditions ordinarily pertains in indigent medical care programs. Some groups of program eligibles, such as the medically needy or medically indigent, are not readily identifiable until they actually seek care. They move on and off program rolls depending on changes in their incomes, so it is difficult to accurately identify program eligibles at any point in time. Furthermore, explanation of the PPO option cannot take place during a limited period of time through group presentations; instead it must occur on an individual-by-individual basis when determination of program eligibility occurs. Furthermore, it must continually be reinforced so that program eligibles are kept up to date concerning the participating providers in the PPO. All of these considerations make marketing the PPO a difficult task for program administrators and reduce the likelihood that program eligibles will select PPO providers when care is required. Therefore, the potential for PPOs to generate significant cost savings will depend crucially on the ability of the program administrator to overcome these obstacles and effectively market the PPO option.

ISSUES IN THE DESIGN AND IMPLEMENTATION OF PPO OPTIONS

As the scenario above suggests, a number of thorny design and implementation issues will arise in the development of PPO options for indigent medical care programs. The remainder of this chapter addresses four of these issues: (1) setting the copayment level for non-PPO patients, (2) establishing reimbursement levels for PPO providers, (3) defining the extent of the PPO option, and (4) designing an effective strategy for marketing the PPO to program eligibles.

SETTING THE COPAYMENT LEVEL

Assuming that copayments are introduced for indigent patients as a mechanism for the development of a PPO program option, the level at which copayments are set will be critical to the success of a PPO strategy from the point of view of the program administrator. Exhibit 1 summarizes the trade offs that are inherent in the copayment determination. The level at which copayments are set can affect PPO program participation in a variety of ways (assuming that PPOs are politically attractive only if they offer discounted fees that are lower than state reimbursements to providers net of copayments). A high copayment level is attractive to PPOs, since it increases the likelihood that PPO providers will be successful in securing relatively large numbers of indigent patients. The high copayment level provides a relatively strong incentive for indigent patients to choose PPO providers since the reward for that choice is signifi-

EXHIBIT 1
Considerations for Program Administrators in Setting Copayment Levels

Impacts on Indigent Medical Care Programs	Level of Copayments	
	High	*Low*
Positive	Assuming a PPO option is established, there is a stronger incentive for patients to choose the PPO option, with lower program costs expected.	Easier to get PPOs to participate as less discount in fees is required.
	Utilization of non-PPO providers will be decreased, with lower program costs expected.	Less risk of underutilization of services by non-PPO patients; less political opposition to PPO.
	Easier to get PPO to participate since potential for securing patients is greater.	Mix of PPO and non-PPO providers maintained.
Negative	Risk of underutilization by program participants and a reversal of gains achieved by medicaid in increasing the utilization of health services by indigents; possible political opposition.	Difficulty in getting providers to participate in a PPO since incentive for patients to choose PPO is weak.
	Difficulty in interesting PPOs to participate if large discounts in fees are required to exceed copayment levels.	Assuming a PPO option is established, there is a weaker incentive for patients to choose the PPO option, with little reduction in program costs expected.
	If sufficiently high, copayments could channel large portion of patients to PPO, discourage program participation by non-PPO physicians, and reduce freedom of access of indigents to other providers.	Utilization of non-PPO providers will be relatively unaffected with little reduction in program costs for these patients resulting.

cant. However, a high copayment level is unattractive to the extent that providers must severely discount their fees in return for PPO participation. The key issue is, therefore, the degree to which providers are willing to trade off lower fees for more patients. If program administrators set copayments either "too high" or "too low," they jeopardize PPO participation in their program. (One "solution" to this dilemma is proposed in the following discussion of mechanisms for establishing provider reimbursement levels.)

A second related trade off involves the effect of copayment levels on patient utilization and program costs. High levels for copayments presumably reduce utilization in two ways. First, they channel more patients toward PPO providers (assuming copayments are not so high that PPOs cannot be established) who presumably are subject to more effective utilization review and receive smaller fees for their services. Second, they also can have a relatively large effect on the utilization of patients electing non-PPO providers. The magnitude of this effect will depend on the level at which copayments are set, but it could be substantial. For instance, experiments conducted by the Rand Corporation on a population of predominantly nonindigents suggest that a 25 percent copayment reduces utilization and expenditures by 20 percent, and that utilization falls steadily as cost sharing increases.[13] To the extent that this represents a reduction in previously unnecessary "overutilization" of services, it may be appropriate. However, the Medicaid program was predicated on a belief that the indigent underutilize health services, and one of its significant achievements has been to increase their utilization of services over time.[14] Therefore, the use of relatively high copayments as part of the development of a PPO option could be viewed as a threat to this achievement and generate political opposition from program supporters.

There is obviously no single "correct" copayment level for indigent medical care programs instituting PPO options. The impact of any particular level on a given indigent medical care program will depend on the characteristics of the community in which the program is located as well as the historical development of the program and its present characteristics. Programs in markets where there is substantial competition for patients and where Medicaid reimbursements have been generous may be able to institute large copayments without discouraging PPO participation. Where the opposite conditions occur, large copayments could make PPO participation relatively unattractive for providers and limit the usefulness of PPOs in indigent medical care programs.

DETERMINING REIMBURSEMENT RATES FOR PPO PROVIDERS

In establishing a PPO option, program administrators must develop some mechanism for determining the rate at which PPO providers will be reimbursed for their services. At one extreme, administrators could assume complete responsibility for arbitrarily specifying fees and designing a PPO utilization review system. Individual providers could then be invited to participate in a PPO that would be administered by program officials. This centralized model places the entire burden of PPO design and management on the program administrators but has the advantage of permitting administrators to implement the PPO models that they feel will be the most effective in the context of their own programs. It sacrifices the "better ideas" that might be generated through some process of competition among privately formed PPOs for a contractual relationship with the indigent program but provides, in return, direct control for the program administrator of the structure and operations of the PPO.

At the other extreme, program administrators could invite offers from private PPOs to serve indigents, with reimbursement rates based on these offers. The resulting proposals could be evaluated along such dimensions as fee schedules, provider credentials, service delivery capability, service accessibility, and potential effectiveness of the proposed utilization review system. While this relatively unstructured approach might be successful in encouraging a variety of proposals, the selection of the "best" proposal(s) would be difficult. Some proposals might offer low fees, but have poorly developed utilization review systems and limited service availability. Others might feature elaborate, proven review systems but higher fees. The number of different possible combinations is limitless and the rate at which different features should be "traded off" against each other is not clear. Case studies of the awarding of franchise contracts for cable TV suggest that public officials have great difficulties evaluating these trade offs. Williamson's study (1976) of cable contracting in Oakland, California implies that at least some nonprice features of the PPO should be specified by program administrators in advance to minimize subsequent difficulty in comparing offers.[15]

If this approach is accepted, a middle ground strategy for price determination emerges. Program officials specify in advance such things as the desired capabilities for utilization review systems and geographical areas to be covered by contracts. Then, privately administered PPOs submit offers, or bids, which meet these specifications and include a schedule of prices. While this simplifies the selection problem, there still remains the difficulty of comparing many different price schedules, each consisting of arrays of prices defined over a wide range of services. In the absence of collusion among bidders, these price schedules could exhibit considerable variation, making it difficult for administrators to determine which schedule would ultimately result in the lowest program cost for the state.

There are two relatively straightforward approaches that could be adopted to facilitate price schedule comparisons. The first—an "estimated total cost" approach—would require the state to estimate the number of services of different types that program eligibles will utilize during some specific time period. Each service estimate is then multiplied by the appropriate prices on the submitted price schedules and all of these products are summed to generate an estimated total program cost associated with each submitted schedule. The risk in this procedure is that inaccurate estimates of the numbers of each type of service that will be demanded can lead to the erroneous selection of a price schedule that does not minimize program costs. The potential for this type of error, at least during the initial round of PPO bids, is very real since the utilization review systems that PPOs implement will, if effective, alter historical service delivery patterns.

A second approach requires that program administrators publish a base schedule of prices as part of the request for proposals, request that all bids specify a percentage discount that will be applied "across the board" to this schedule, and require that this discount at a minimum exceed the percentage that the copayments are of the stated prices. For example, PPO-A might propose to deliver services at a 25 percent discount from the published schedule, while PPO-B might offer services at 20 percent off base prices, where copayment requirements are approximately 15 percent of scheduled prices. All else equal, the bid of PPO-A would result in the lowest cost to the state. However, the risk of making an incorrect decision still exists, since PPO-B might contain providers who minimize utilization of some particular high-priced service, or it might be able to operate its utilization review program more effectively than PPO-A. Despite this risk, which seems unavoidable, the base price schedule approach offers a reasonably straightforward mechanism for program administrators to evaluate disparate PPO offers.

Given that appropriate nonprice criteria for evaluating PPOs can be developed and the base price schedule approach is adopted, at what level should the winning PPO be reimbursed? The most obvious answer—at the percentage discount specified by the winning bid—is not necessarily the strategy that will result in the lowest costs to the state. Bidding processes in which winners are reimbursed at the level specified in their sealed bids are labelled "discriminative sealed bid" auctions in the competitive bidding literature. The primary finding of interest concerning these auctions is that bidders have an incentive to "outguess" the bidding process by submitting bids which are lower than the true value they place on the object being auctioned. That is, PPO-A may be willing to accept an indigent contract at 30 percent off the base price schedule but may submit a bid with a 25 percent discount if it believes that its competitors place a lesser value on the contract. The idea that bidders in discriminative auctions have strong incentives to "game" the bidding in this manner was examined in detail by Vickrey and also noted by Friedman in his discussion of treasury bill auctions.[16] Several authors have subsequently provided theoretical and experimental support for gaming behavior in discriminative auctions.[17]

A frequently suggested bidding alternative, which is designed to minimize the prevalence of gaming behavior, requires that the winning bidder be reimbursed at a discounted amount equal to the second best bid. For example, if PPO-A offered a 30 percent discount and PPO-B offered a 25 percent reduction PPO-A would be awarded the contract but would be reimbursed at a 25 percent discount from the base price schedule. This type of auction has been termed a "Vickrey" or "second price" auction. In theory, the dominant strategy for PPOs under this set of reimbursement rules is to offer the maximum discounts from base prices that they would consider in return for the contract. There would be little incentive for PPOs to submit discounts smaller than these amounts: Smaller discounts would not enhance the revenues of providers for the PPO selected as the winning bidder, and they would increase the risk of not winning the contract.

On the surface, it would appear that a Vickrey auction would result in greater total program expenditures than a discriminative auction, but this is not necessarily true. Since there is a stronger incentive in discriminative auctions for less than full value bids to be submitted (that is, for PPOs to specify discounts that are lower than they would actually accept in return for the contract) the discounts submitted in discriminative auctions would likely be less than the discounts submitted in Vickrey auctions. In this situation, the total expenditures by the program under a discriminative auction could exceed expenditures under Vickrey auction rules, depending on the degree to which the two sets of bids differed. A number of researchers have attempted to identify the circumstances under which program administrators might prefer a Vickrey auction to a discriminative auction, and vice versa, with results that depend on a variety of different assumptions.[18] Given this lack of definitive conclusions, many program administrators may find the Vickrey process a relatively unattractive bidding procedure. The reimbursement of the winning PPO at a price schedule that exceeds the schedule offered in its bid gives the *appearance* of wastefulness on the part of program administrators and therefore may be politically unacceptable.

A third alternative—the descending Dutch auction—may prove politically easier to implement than either the discriminative or Vickrey auctions. In this auction, the program administrator announces a discount off the base price schedule (say 40 percent) and then invites any PPO fulfilling all other criteria to accept a contract at this discount. If the initial state-specified discount does not result in a contract, the state reduces the discount until some PPO agrees to the resulting price schedule. The Dutch auction can be characterized as a "game" in which PPO-A needs to take into account information about the probable discounts acceptable to other PPOs, while the discounts offered by others depend in part on expectations about the behavior of PPO-A.[19] The longer the bidder waits in the Dutch auction, the greater the risk of not winning. Without making extreme assumptions about the strategic behavior of the PPOs involved in the process, it is not possible to make definitive statements about how bidders will trade off increased risk against increased profits in making their decisions. However, laboratory experiments suggest that the Dutch auction would elicit even more strategic gaming by bidders, and hence higher program costs, than the sealed bid discriminative auction.[20]

The political attractiveness of the Dutch auction relative to either sealed bid alternative results from the proactive role that the program administrator can play in the bidding process and hence in the determination of the ultimate price schedule. In appearance, the administrator can exert control over the PPO bidders by determining the level of the initial discount announcement and the increments and timing of the subsequent discount decreases. In this sense, the Dutch auction represents a public, formalized negotiation process with potential PPOs.

All these bidding approaches outlined above—discriminative sealed bid, Vickrey, and Dutch—can play a role in addition to establishing reimbursement rates. The bidding organizations could be informed that the winning bidder will not only receive a contract to serve indigents but also that its bid will be used to set copayment levels for visits to non-PPO providers. This gives the bidding organizations greater influence over the number of indigents that will choose the winning bidder, since high PPO discount offers result in high copayments for non-PPO providers and presumably encourage more program participants to seek their care from the winning PPO. One liability to this procedure, from the program administrators' viewpoint, occurs if PPO discount offers prove to be substantial. Then copayment levels may be set so high that appropriate utilization is discouraged for indigents with long established ties to non-PPO providers; political opposition to use of PPOs could increase as a result.

LIMITING THE PPO OPTION

An important issue that program administrators must face in redesigning their programs to accommodate PPOs is the nature of the limits to place on a PPO option. Should a PPO option be available for all services, classifications of indigents, and geographic areas within the program's jurisdiction? Or, at the other extreme, should PPOs be restricted at least initially to a specific service in a limited geographic area for a subgroup of program eligibles? Should multiple PPOs be offered, or should only one PPO option be available to program eligibles?

Limitations on Services

There is nothing in a PPO's design that demands that it offer a full range of services. For instance, physicians could form a PPO to deliver outpatient care only, accepting discounts on fees and a utilization review system for services provided in an outpatient setting. Once patients are admitted to a hospital, they would no longer be affected by the PPO arrangement; they could be admitted to any hospital participating in the program and be subject to the copayments, if any, that were in place. Alternatively, a hospital PPO could be formed to deliver inpatient care only. Patients, in consultation with their physicians, would have the choice of being admitted to a PPO hospital, having their copayments waived, and participating in the PPO's utilization review system or selecting a non-PPO hospital and assuming the responsibility for whatever copayments are required.

In some communities, program administrators may wish to introduce a PPO option by concentrating solely on pharmaceuticals, or on inpatient, outpatient, or laboratory services. There are at least two advantages to this approach. First, it allows the administrator to experiment with the PPO option in a limited way. After experience is gained in designing and implementing a PPO for, say, pharmaceuticals, the administrator can bring this experience to bear on the more complicated problem of introducing a comprehensive PPO for inpatient and outpatient services. Second, a limited service PPO may be feasible in a particular area, where development of a comprehensive PPO would not be possible. For example, consider a community with an excess of hospital beds but a lower than average physician-population ratio. Some hospitals in that community might be willing to form a PPO offering discounted prices, while physicians would be less likely to consider PPO participation as attractive. In this case, requiring a "full service" PPO could inhibit the development of a PPO program option in any form.

Balancing these advantages are the potential complications that could be introduced by limiting the PPO option to specific services. For example, consider further the case where there is a hospital PPO only. Presumably the patient will be influenced to seek hospitals participating in this PPO because copayments are waived for admittance to these hospitals. However, the admitting decision is influenced strongly by the patient's physician. If the physician does not have staff privileges at PPO hospitals or prefers non-PPO hospitals for other reasons, the copayment waiver may be ineffective in influencing patient choice. As a result, the PPO may be relatively unsuccessful in attracting patients. If the PPO covered both inpatient and outpatient services, presumably participating physicians would have access to PPO hospitals and would be required or encouraged by PPO management to use them where medically appropriate.

Limitations on Patient Eligibility

The program administrator may wish to consider limiting the PPO option to a specific subcategory of program eligibles. For instance, a comprehensive PPO could be made available only to individuals qualifying for the program under the medically needy classification (generally a relatively high income group of program eligibles). This restriction could reduce political opposition to the introduction of copayments, since they would be targeted on that category of program eligibles with the greatest ability to pay. If a system of copayments in conjunction with a PPO option were successful with this group, it could be extended to other categories of patients.

One drawback to limiting the PPO option to a subgroup of program eligibles is that it could reduce the likelihood that providers would participate. As stated previously, providers accept discounted fees and stringent utilization review expecting greater patient volume in return. The expected number of patients generated by a subgroup of eligibles might be too small to induce PPO formation and participation. This consideration would be less important if the PPO participating in the public program were simultaneously contracting with other payors. Then the burden of justifying price reductions would not be borne solely by the public program's ability to deliver additional patients.

Limitations on Geographical Area

It may be possible for program administrators to secure the necessary latitude to limit PPO introduction to subregions within the program's overall geographical jurisdiction. This seems appropriate since, although program jurisdictions encompass entire states, medical care market areas typically do not. Conditions may vary among market areas within a state, suggesting that PPOs may be more attractive to providers and easier to implement in some communities than in others. Varying degrees of market competitiveness could also result in different discount arrangements with PPOs in different communities. Program administrators may be able to reduce program costs by exploiting these market differences and establishing separate PPO options on a community by community basis.

The costs of pursuing this policy involve increased administrative complexity. Instead of dealing with one PPO, the public administrator must deal with many, each with different reimbursement schedules, utilization review systems, and participating providers. This results in greater demands on the public administrator with respect to the process of PPO selection, management of reimbursements, evaluation of the effectiveness of utilization review systems, and marketing of options to program enrollees.

Limitations on Number of PPOs

Public managers may wish to accept bids from more than one PPO to provide the same service in a given geographic area. Multiple PPOs would increase the choices available to program enrollees and therefore possibly result in greater numbers of enrollees utilizing PPO providers. Thus, offering program participation to multiple PPOs could reduce program costs, although this may not always occur. Lower total costs may not always result because the degree to which PPO providers are willing to discount prices will depend on their projections of the additional patients that the PPO will generate. Multiple PPO options could reduce the volume of patients expected by any single PPO and therefore reduce the discounts offered by the participating PPOs. The end result, averaged across all participating PPOs, could be higher costs for the program. In addition, it is not clear that multiple PPO options could be marketed effectively to program enrollees or designed in a manner that rewards enrollees for choosing the particular PPO providers who cost the state the least.

MARKETING THE PPO OPTION

Marketing and enrollment problems have long been cited by prepaid plans as obstacles to the introduction of alternative delivery systems into indigent medical care programs, and these obstacles are likely to arise with respect to PPOs as well. Therefore, the development of an effective plan for communicating the PPO option to program eligibles will be a critically important task for program administrators. Fortunately, there is now some relevant experience for program administrators to draw on in developing marketing strategies.

Experiments conducted by the Prepaid Health Research, Evaluation and Demonstration (PHRED) project in assisting California in managing prepaid options for its indigent program have shed some light on potentially effective marketing strategies. The PHRED project was conducted under the assumption that the eligibility determination process is an appropriate vehicle for enrolling program eligibles in alternative plans. It was felt that this approach would yield larger enrollments at a lower per person cost than door-to-door solicitations. Consequently, several marketing techniques were introduced in a select number of welfare offices in California, including

1. A printed brochure with no personal explanation.
2. A film.
3. A personal presentation by a county eligibility worker.
4. A similar presentation by a specifically trained member of the PHRED staff.
5. A personal presentation by an HMO sales representative.[21]

These techniques were supplemented by a mailing of literature to eligibles in the relevant geographic areas.

The initial results of the PHRED project suggest that alternative delivery systems can be marketed effectively in the context of the eligibility determination process. Sufficient enrollments were secured to permit elimination of door-to-door solicitations, but the relative effectiveness of the different strategies seemed to reflect local conditions rather than any inherent superiorities. The welfare office marketing "cost about $9 per person enrolled, where as door-to-door marketing costs between $45 and $50 per person enrolled."[22] Also of importance was the finding that indigents were able to understand the options available to them sufficiently to make a choice; out of 5,913 presentations, only 41 did not result in selection of an option.[23]

The PHRED project findings can be supplemented by less rigorous observations of other demonstrations involving indigent populations. For example, a Massachusett's program used a variety of methods to inform eligibles of their options. Again, it was found that successful marketing strategies needed to be tailored to specific sites. Mailings, public service radio spots, personal presentations by state employees in waiting rooms, and marketing in the welfare office were all utilized in different situations, with direct marketing approaches found to be more effective than mailings.[24]

In summary, the accumulation of evidence from these and other demonstrations suggests that it is possible to conduct PPO marketing efforts for large numbers of program eligibles at a reasonable cost, providing that program administrators are willing to relax "standard operating procedures" to allow variation in the approaches taken across sites and possible incorporation of the marketing process into the eligibility determination process. However, PPOs do present somewhat different marketing problems than do HMO alternatives to which the reported evidence applies. In particular, if actual enrollment in a PPO is not required, then an important issue is the degree to which marketing efforts need to be carried out on a continuous basis to maintain awareness of PPO providers among program eligibles. The necessity to market continuously could add substantially to the cost of implementing a PPO.

CONCLUSIONS

The key assumptions in the scenario described in this chapter were that (1) PPOs would be introduced in programs where copayments for services were also present, (2) program participants would have copayments waived if they chose PPO providers, (3) participants would not be required to "enroll" in a PPO and therefore be "locked in" to PPO providers for a specific time period, and (4) discounts offered by PPO providers would have to meet or exceed, by some criteria, the level of the waived copayments for PPOs to be a politically feasible option for program administrators.

Other scenarios are, of course, possible. However, regardless of how PPOs are actually introduced as options in indigent medical care programs, concerns can be raised with respect to their probable success.

One concern is whether the administrative expertise and enthusiasm is available in public medical care programs to implement PPOs. The introduction of PPOs raises several administrative issues that will be relatively unfamiliar to program managers. It also requires that managers tolerate program diversity and accept new demands on their limited agency resources. Will public managers be capable and willing to make the adjustments necessary to ensure that the PPO alternative is successful? Their review of medicaid experiments with HMOs leads Galblum and Trieger (1982) to caution that, "states may not be willing or able to make changes in their administrative systems that are small in scope but critical to the successful management of organized systems."[25]

A second concern relates to the impact that successful PPO implementation could have on traditional Medicaid program objectives. If PPOs prove to be successful at containing program costs, there will be pressure to encourage as many program participants as possible to utilize only PPO providers. While this is consistent with the desire to contain costs, it conceivably could promote the development of a two-tiered medical care system, with some PPOs serving only medicaid eligibles. This conflicts with one of the initial goals of the Medicaid program: to provide the indigent with access to "mainstream medicine."[26] One means of (at least) delaying the development of a two-tiered system would be to require that PPOs offered to the indigent already be providing a significant amount of care under contracts to private payors.

One final concern relates to the relatively unproven nature of PPO status and performance. Although the number of PPOs nationwide is increasing at a rapid rate, accompanied by the proliferation of a variety of PPO "models," there is as yet little evidence concerning their cost effectiveness and their overall impact that extends beyond the anecdotal. In fact, it is not clear at present which PPO models are legal in different states or which state authorities can exercise licensing and regulatory authority over PPOs. Therefore, it may be appropriate for program administrators to allow evidence to accumulate with respect to PPO performance and legal status—in effect, allow the PPO movement to proceed first among the middle class—before applying the concept to indigent programs. This again suggests that PPOs already contracting with private payors be given preference when program administrators do move to incorporate PPOs into indigent medical care programs.

NOTES

1. The author gratefully acknowledges the financial support of the John A. Hartford Foundation, New York, N.Y., and the Flinn Foundation, Phoenix, Ariz.

2. John K. Iglehart, "Medicaid Turns to Prepaid Managed Care," *New England Journal of Medicine,* 308, no. 16 (April 21, 1983), pp. 976–80; Edward P. Melia, Leonard M. Aucoin, Leonard J. Duhl, and Patsy S. Kurokawa, "Competition in the Health Care Marketplace: A Beginning in California," *New England Journal of Medicine,* 308, no. 13

(March 31, 1983), pp. 788–92; Jon B. Christianson, Diane G. Hillman, and Kenneth R. Smith, "The Arizona Experiment: Competitive Bidding for Indigent Medical Care," *Health Affairs*, 2, no. 3 (Fall 1983), pp. 88–103.

3. L. E. Demkovich, "Government Strives to Change Incentives," *Dupont Context*, 12, 1983, pp. 21–23.

4. D. E. Rogers, R. J. Blendon, and T. W. Moloney, "Who Needs Medicaid?" *New England Journal of Medicine*, 307, 1982, pp. 13–18.

5. John K. Iglehart, "Reagan's Health Policy at Midterm: Fairness Remains Key Issue," *Hospital Progress*, 64, 1983, pp. 32–36.

6. *Recent and Proposed Changes in State Medicaid Programs: A Fifty State Survey*, Intergovernmental Health Policy Project, George Washington University, July, 1982.

7. John K. Iglehart, "Medicaid Turns to Prepaid Managed Care," p. 976.

8. Ibid., p. 976.

9. L. Bartlett, *Medicaid Freedom of Choice: A Review of Waiver Applications Submitted under Section 2175 of the Omnibus Budget Reconciliation Act of 1981*, State Medicaid Information Center, Center for Policy Research, National Governors' Association, Washington, D.C., 1982.

10. John K. Iglehart, "Medicaid Turns to Prepaid Managed Care," p. 978.

11. Joan B. Trauner, *Preferred Provider Organizations: The California Experiment*, Institute for Health Policy Studies, University of California, San Francisco, August 1983.

12. Jon B. Christianson, "The Impact of HMOs: Evidence and Research Issues," *Journal of Health Politics, Policy and Law*, 5, no. 2 (Summer 1980), pp. 354–67.

13. Charles E. Phelps, *Health Care Costs: The Consequences of Increased Cost Sharing*, R-2970-RC, RAND, Santa Monica, California, November 1982, pp. xv–xvi.

14. D. E. Rogers, R. J. Blendon, and T. W. Moloney, "Who Needs Medicaid?"

15. Oliver E. Williamson, "Franchise Bidding for Natural Monopolies—In General and with Respect to CATV," *Bell Journal of Economics*, 7 (Spring 1976), pp. 73–104.

16. William Vickrey, "Counterspeculation, Auctions and Competitive Sealed Tenders," *Journal of Finance*, 16 (March 1961), pp. 8–37; Milton Friedman, "Price Determination in the United States Treasury Bill Market: A Comment," *Review of Economics and Statistics*, 45 (August 1963), pp. 318–20.

17. J. C. Cox, B. Roberson, and V. L. Smith, "Theory and Behavior of Single Object Auctions," and R. Forsythe, and R. M. Issac, "Demand Revealing Mechanisms for Private Goods Auctions," both in *Research in Experimental Economics*, Vol. II, ed. V. L. Smith (Greenwich, Conn.: JAI Press, 1982); J. B. Ramsey, *Bidding and Oil Leases* (Greenwich, Conn.: JAI Press, 1980); V. L. Smith, "Bidding Theory and the Treasury Bill Auction: Does Price Discrimination Increase Bill Prices?" *Review of Economics and Statistics*, 48, 1966, pp. 141–6.

18. J. G. Riley and W. G. Samuelson, "Optimal Auctions," *American Economic Review*, 71, 1981, pp. 381–92; V. L. Smith, "Experimental Studies of Discrimination vs. Competition in Sealed Bid Auction Markets," *Journal of Business*, 40, 1967, pp. 56–82; G. J. Miller, and C. R. Plott, "Revenue Generating Properties of Sealed Bid Auctions: An Experimental Analysis of One-Price and Discriminative Processes," *Research in Experimental Economics*, Vol. III, ed. V. L. Smith (Greenwich, Conn.: JAI Press, 1983).

19. William Vickrey, "Counterspeculation, Auctions, and Competitive Sealed Tenders."

20. J. C. Cox, B. Roberson, and V. L. Smith, "Theory and Behavior of Single Object Auctions."

21. Trudi W. Galblum, and Sidney Trieger, "Demonstrations of Alternative Delivery Systems under Medicare and Medicaid," *Health Care Financing Review,* 3 (March 1982), p. 7.

22. Ibid., p. 7.

23. Ibid., p. 7.

24. Ibid., p. 7.

25. Ibid., p. 5.

26. D. E. Rogers, R. J. Blendon, and T. W. Moloney, "Who Needs Medicaid?"

Legal Issues

LEGAL ISSUES IN CREATING PPOS

Douglas L. Elden, J.D., LL.M.

Richard A. Hinden, J.D.

Both of
Altheimer and Gray
Chicago, IL

The development of alternate delivery and reimbursement mechanisms, particularly those known as *preferred provider organizations* (PPOs), raise a multitude of legal issues. Each PPO will exist in different market conditions and under different state laws. Therefore, while this article seeks to identify and discuss the legal issues, it cannot provide definitive answers. This article can, however, serve as a guideline or checklist for the analysis of a PPO and provide recommendations and alternatives for legal roadblocks that occur in the formation and operation of PPOs. This discussion will be general in nature and cannot be a substitute for specific legal advice regarding particular factual situations encountered in the establishment of a PPO.

ANTITRUST

The emergence of alternative mechanisms such as PPOs represents one innovative response to the competitive and financial pressures currently experienced by the providers of health care. As a result of the new economic pressures and the new approaches designed to counter those pressures, the health care industry has witnessed increased activity in the area of antitrust litigation. These challenges arise due to the formation of cooperative business ventures by existing business enterprises.

Alternative delivery systems, including PPOs, are composed of independent providers who are traditionally competitors or potential competitors. These competitors or potential competitors are now combining in cooperative business ventures. The formation of cooperative business ventures among competitors and potential competitors will result in careful scrutiny by their competitors and federal and state governments who will seek to establish that the combination is an unreasonable restraint of trade in violation of antitrust laws. Antitrust challenges are costly to defend, and the risks of being found in violation of the antitrust laws are heightened, under civil law, by the possibility of treble damages and, under criminal law, by possible fines and imprisonment. It is an area that requires careful analysis by those considering how to establish a PPO.

ANTITRUST STATUTES

The Sherman Antitrust Act[1] provides the principal basis for antitrust scrutiny of PPOs. Section 1 of the Sherman Act prohibits contracts, agreements, combinations, or conspiracies in restraint of trade, which have been held by the courts to include price fixing, group boycotts, tying arrangements, division of markets, and customer allocation. Section 2 of the Sherman Act proscribes monopolization as well as attempts and conspiracies to monopolize. Violation of the Sherman Act is a felony and carries a fine of up to $100,000 or imprisonment for up to three years for an individual, and a fine of up to $1 million for a corporation. Civil remedies under the Act include treble damages to a private claimant, punitive damages, recovery of plaintiff's costs and reasonable attorneys' fees, and injunctive relief.[2]

Section 5 of the Federal Trade Commission Act prohibits unfair methods of competition, which have been held to encompass not only all Sherman Act and Clayton Antitrust Act[3] violations but also any restraint of trade contrary to the policy and spirit of those laws.[4]

The Clayton Act is less likely to pose problems for PPO formation as most of its provisions relate to sales of commodities rather than to the provision of services as generally contemplated by PPOs. Nevertheless, any PPO must be analyzed in light of Section 7 of the Clayton Act,[5] which governs mergers, acquisitions, and joint ventures in restraint of trade.

State antitrust statutes are frequently analogous to federal antitrust laws with respect to the practices they prohibit and the penalties imposed. Some state antitrust statutes, however, provide for different requirements and govern different conduct than do the federal laws. In Texas, for example, an illegal trust is defined as a combination of capital, skill, or acts by two or more persons to "fix, maintain, increase or reduce the. . .cost of insurance."[6] Unless this provision were construed to refer only to the price of insurance premiums, a PPO could be held to violate the terms of this statute. Texas courts have not construed this provision so narrowly, applying the prohibition to any combination that affects insurance costs.[7] The Texas law serves as an example of why creators of PPOs must consult and comply with the antitrust laws of each state in which the PPO or its member organizations do business or, in the case of physicians, each state in which they are licensed to practice medicine.

FEDERAL ANTITRUST JURISDICTION

Prior to the consideration of an antitrust complaint under federal law, a court must determine if a defendant's activity falls within the federal jurisdictional requirements. An antitrust complaint must contain allegations that the plaintiff's business is in, or affects, interstate commerce and that either the defendant's general business activity or the specific challenged activity substantially affects interstate commerce. Traditionally, antitrust defendants, including health care providers or members of the "learned professions," successfully argued that their business or practice was local in character and that any effect on interstate commerce was incidental and remote.[8] Recent U.S. Supreme Court decisions, however, indicate that a defense based upon the absence of an impact on interstate commerce may not suffice to exempt conduct from the federal antitrust statutes. Many such decisions involve health care providers.[9]

METHODS OF CASE ANALYSIS

The U.S. Supreme Court has held that, while most restraints of trade must be analyzed in terms of the nature, purpose, and effect of the restraint, some types of restraints are so inimical to competition and so unjustified that they are conclusively presumed to be illegal. These restraints are called per se violations. They require no inquiry into their effect on competition or their business justification. Per se violations include price fixing, group boycotts, division of markets, and tying arrangements.[10]

In situations where restraints of trade other than per se violations are involved, the legal analysis follows what is called the "rule of reason" approach. The rule of reason approach tests an alleged restraint of trade to determine whether the restraint promotes, suppresses, or destroys competition. The court considers the facts peculiar to the challenged activity, the nature of the restraint and its probable effect on competition, and other relevant information necessary to determine whether the conduct is, in fact, anticompetitive.[11] The courts have not established a special standard for the analysis of the activities of health care providers.

POTENTIAL SUBSTANTIVE ANTITRUST VIOLATIONS

Price Fixing

Inherent in the formation of most PPOs is the creation of contractual arrangements among and between physicians, hospitals, payors, and employers. These agreements raise the concern that they will be viewed under antitrust theory as concerted activity among competing or potentially competing entities that may restrict price, quality, or service in an anticompetitive manner. The antitrust issue most frequently raised when analyzing a PPO is the claim that the participating providers are engaged in illegal price fixing. As noted earlier, price fixing is per se unlawful, and may include agreements to charge uniform prices, set minimum or maximum prices, employ uniform discount or credit policies, or share pricing information.

The Supreme Court, however, in *Broadcast Music, Inc.* v. *Columbia Broadcasting System, Inc.*[12] and other cases, has indicated that the per se rule does not apply to each instance of literal price fixing among competitors. The Court has distinguished between agreements whose predominant purpose is the suppression of price competition and those where the price restraint is incidental to some otherwise valid business purpose. Therefore, the method by which a restraint is characterized is crucial. Those agreements found to be "naked" price fixing arrangements are per se unlawful, whereas agreements where price restraint is "ancillary" to a valid purpose are judged under the rule of reason. An analysis under the rule of reason permits courts to determine whether an arrangement tends to promote competition despite the fact that price restraint may result. The Supreme Court rekindled the possibility that a traditional per se analysis might not be applied to members of the learned professions for what would otherwise be per se unlawful practices of the "learned professions" when, in dicta, it advanced the possibility that the professions may be "treated differently" than other occupations,[13] and that professional services "differ significantly from other business services."[14] Nevertheless, the holdings in these cases indicate that at least price fixing activities by the learned professions would be scrutinized under the per se rule.

The extent of these decisions was subject to debate when the Supreme Court issued its decision in *Arizona* v. *Maricopa County Medical Society.*[15] In *Maricopa* the Court held that agreements among physician members of medical care foundations to accept no more than predetermined maximum prices as full payment for services rendered to policyholders of foundation-approved insurance plans were per se price fixing violations.

In *Maricopa,* organizations composed of and controlled by 70 percent of the physicians in the geographic area canvassed their members to determine what would constitute an acceptable fee schedule. This market dominance, while not relied upon by the Court, is noteworthy. It enabled these competitors "to sell their services to certain customers at fixed prices and arguably to affect the prevailing market price of medical care." The restraint was not "ancillary" to a valid arrangement but rather it "fit squarely in a horizontal price fixing mold."

The Court rejected the defendants' arguments that the public service and professional aspects of health care delivery entitled them to a special exemption from the per se standard. The Court was not persuaded that a different standard should be applied because "cost containment" was an objective of the agreements. It found the fixing of maximum prices to be as objectionable as the fixing of minimum prices: "In this case, the rule is violated by a price restraint that tends to provide the same economic rewards to all practitioners, regardless of their skill, their experience, their training or their willingness to employ innovative and difficult procedures in individual cases."

A careful review of the *Maricopa* decision and its underlying facts, however, suggests that not all agreements that have price fixing components will inevitably be subject to the per se standard. In *Maricopa* the Court could not find a way in which the scheme would enhance competition or foster efficiencies in service. The fee arrangements in *Maricopa* were not ancillary to any other lawful foundation activities. The foundations did not sell insurance or otherwise market health care services, nor were the fee schedules essential to other foundation activities, such as utilization review or claims administration. They merely established a price schedule to be followed by existing insurers in paying providers, with no resultant procompetitive effect. The arrangement in *Maricopa* was not established as a framework to provide for the combination of competing practitioners to permit them to offer a product different from the product which could be offered absent the agreement, nor did it provide for the pooling of capital and sharing of risks by the competitors as in a partnership or joint venture. Instead, the Court found that "the combination has merely permitted [the physicians] to sell their services to certain customers at fixed prices and arguably to affect the prevailing market price of medical care . . . The agreement . . . is [one] among hundreds of competing doctors concerning the price at which each will offer his own services to a substantial number of consumers." [16]

The *Maricopa* decision suggests a spectrum of business organizations. At one end of the spectrum is the professional corporation (i.e., of physicians), at the other end the entity in *Maricopa.* Professional corporations, by statutory definition, pool capital and share risks. The *Maricopa* entity, however, did not pool capital or share the risks of the venture. Their price fixing was a naked restraint, not ancillary to any other lawful activities. Significantly, the Court stated that "each of the foundations is composed of individual practitioners who compete with one another for patients. Their combination. . .does not permit them to sell any different product. The foundations are not analogous to. . .other joint arrangements in which persons who would otherwise be competitors pool their capital and share the risks."

For a cooperative business venture to avoid per se antitrust analysis and fall within the purview of the rule of reason, it must resemble a traditional business entity as much as possible. The cooperative business venture should be established to offer a different, improved product than that offered by the participants individually, and the participants should pool capital and share the risks of the venture.

It is not yet clear what ultimate effect *Maricopa* will have on PPOs and other alternate health care provider arrangements in analyzing antitrust issues generally and traditional per se violations in particular. The Court forcefully rejected arguments that per se treatment was inappropriate because the health care industry is relatively removed from the competitive model, is the object of statutory and voluntary cost containment efforts, is an industry with which the judiciary has had little antitrust experience and that is composed of professions historically immune from such a high degree of antitrust scrutiny. These points suggest an expansive reading of *Maricopa* in assessing its application to the health care industry and to PPOs specifically.

On the other hand, the case was decided by a narrow 4-3 margin, with three vigorous dissents. Most significantly, the factual context of *Maricopa* differs markedly from that of a properly crafted PPO. Using the guidance provided in *Maricopa,* a PPO, if organized as a cooperative business venture between a hospital or hospital group and members of their medical staffs, may minimize antitrust exposure if they then structure the venture substantially as follows:

— The participants pool their capital and share the risk of loss in the venture.
— Each participant has the opportunity to profit from the venture.
— The PPO does not include a high proportion of area physicians.
— The ultimate authority to set the fee schedule is in the hands of the cooperative business venture and not the physicians.
— The cooperative business venture is not subject to unilateral control of the physician competitors.
— The PPO physician fee component of the total discount package is negotiated by the PPO separately with each buyer.

If a PPO is so structured, it appears to avoid the pitfalls of *Maricopa.* Further, if the PPO is a new and perhaps *better* entrant in the health care delivery market and exhibits these characteristics, the price arrangements that accompany the formation and operation of the PPO will probably be viewed as ancillary in nature and subject to examination under the rule of reason.

Group Boycotts; Refusals to Deal

A second potential basis for antitrust liability is the theory of the group boycott or concerted refusal to deal. A refusal to deal arises where an entity is deprived of suppliers, customers, or other essential trade relationships by concerted action among other entities designed to keep the target from competing in the marketplace. Such activity is generally viewed as a per se violation of the antitrust laws.[17] Group boycotts must be distinguished from unilateral refusals to deal. A unilateral refusal to deal is a decision by only one person or entity and has been held to be lawful provided the refusal is not in furtherance of any other anticompetitive purpose. Where the refusal has been supported by legitimate business reasons, it has generally been held to be valid.[18] Nevertheless, even unilateral refusals to deal may be unlawful. In *United States* v. *Parke, Davis & Co.*,[19] Parke, Davis claimed it did no more than maintain resale prices solely through unilateral refusals to deal with noncomplying customers. The Court, however, reviewing a panoply of actions designed to coerce resale price maintenance, concluded that Parke, Davis had embarked on a program to "effect adherence to his resale prices, . . . [forming] a combination [among itself and complying customers] in violation of the Sherman Act."[20]

Many group refusals to deal are upheld upon a finding that the refusal is intended to advance the group's economic interests without being directed at adversely affecting competition. In such cases, where an exclusionary intent is not apparent and the restrictive result is ancillary to the valid business purpose, the courts tend to employ a rule of reason approach. The most likely source of a group boycott claim will emanate from a provider excluded or terminated from membership in the PPO. However, the PPO may exclude or terminate a provider so long as the PPO contracts define objective standards and reasons for termination or nonappointment and the motive for such exclusion is not anticompetitive.[21] The guidelines for such provisions developed in PPO contracts should be based on objective criteria other than economic concerns and should be the least restrictive alternative available to accomplish legitimate objectives. Articulated and consistently applied criteria such as quality of care or the physical limitations of the PPO and its institutional members should survive judicial scrutiny. For example, credentials requirements may be applied in determining provider participation in a PPO if the intent and effect of the requirements are to ensure the efficient rendering of quality patient care and the availability of necessary medical services.[22] Restrictions pertaining to the number of physicians permitted to participate in the PPO may be established if the physical structure of the PPO is self-limiting, or if the hospital(s) involved in the PPO can only service a limited volume of patients.[23]

PPO market share in each health care delivery market will determine whether a refusal to deal is so anticompetitive that it must be analyzed under the per se rule. The greater the PPO's market share, the more sensitive the PPO must be in establishing objective criteria for excluding or terminating physicians. If a PPO possesses a substantial majority of the market (e.g., 60 percent of the patients in the service area are subscribers, or 75 percent of the admitting hospitals are members) and it is clear that there is tangible economic benefit to participation in the PPO, exclusion or termination of providers from the PPO will be scrutinized more closely and the rationale and justification for such actions must be more carefully supported by objective criteria set forth in the PPO contractual arrangement to insure that the overall effect of such provisions are not anticompetitive.

Practical measures that should be considered in avoiding antitrust liability for concerted refusals to deal include (1) objective standards for the appointment of providers to the PPO; (2) comprehensive due process protections for providers challenging exclusions or terminations from the PPO, which should provide for right to notification of a denial, the reasons for denial, the right to a hearing, and a decision on the record of the hearing examiner or committee; and (3) a vote by a nonbiased hearing examiner or, preferably, a vote by a committee composed of individuals other than potential competitors of the provider under scrutiny.[24] Conversely, the criteria should not include, for example, exclusion of entire classes of licensed primary care providers such as osteopaths,[25] nor should it condition PPO membership on membership in a particular professional association.[26] Properly written contracts, procedures, memorandums and communications are essential in establishing the lack of an anticompetitive motive.

Recent cases have indicated that even where competitors of the excluded provider performed the selection of provider members, the rule of reason dictates that no cognizable boycott claim arises merely when competitors are excluded from equal access to a PPO. The Court of Appeals in *Feminists Women's Health Center* v. *Mohammad*[27] acknowledged that standards of ethical and professional responsibility should be governed by the rule of reason absent a showing of a minimal indicia of anticompetitive purpose. Crucial to the defense of the standards would be the genuineness of the justification, the reasonableness of these standards themselves and the manner of their enforcement. The court recognized however that actions of coercion or intimidation that extend beyond the professional standards should not be governed by the rule of reason but rather by the per se rule.

The court also indicated the importance of the relative market share of the entity that excludes the practicing professional. One traditional theory of antitrust law holds that an otherwise defensible activity may be found to be an unlawful concerted refusal to deal where a market is sufficiently small that denial of access to a facility is tantamount to market closure for the applicant. This so-called essential facilities doctrine provides, in essence, that where facilities cannot practically be duplicated by would-be competitors, those in possession must allow the facilities to be shared on fair terms. It is an illegal restraint of trade to foreclose the use of a scarce facility. An essential facility is not necessarily defined as indispensable. It is sufficient if duplication of the facility would be economically infeasible and if the denial of access will inflict a severe handicap on a potential market entrant.[28] However, the doctrine was expressly rejected in *Pontius* v. *Children's Hospital*,[29] involving denial of hospital staff privileges.

Thus, practices that have the effect of excluding providers from PPO participation will not result in group boycott violations where the PPO does not possess excessive market power and the purpose of the rejection of certain providers is not to exclude those providers from essential trade relationships but rather to expand the business opportunities, efficiencies, and professional competencies of the PPO through its member professionals.

Exclusive Dealing

Agreements between providers and PPOs may give rise to an additional antitrust violation commonly referred to as exclusive dealing. Exclusive dealing arrangements ordinarily arise in situations in which a supplier of a product (e.g., the provider or PPO) prohibits a purchaser (e.g., the PPO or payor, respectively) from handling competitive products. Conversely, it may also occur where the purchaser (PPO) prohibits the supplier (provider) from performing services for other purchasers. Generally, exclusive dealing contracts have been viewed by the courts as governed by the rule of reason standard unless the exclusive dealing is in furtherance of some other restraint of trade. Factors such as the length of time of the contract and the extent of the foreclosure of the competitive market have been deemed to be significant in assessing the legality of the arrangement.[30]

In the context of the structure of a PPO, the issue of exclusive dealing arrangements may be initiated where, by contract, a PPO prohibits a provider from contracting with other health care delivery systems such as hospitals, other PPOs, HMOs, and similar entities. These arrangements are generally considered to be without a significant purpose other than the prevention or crippling of competition and, as such, tend to be viewed as per se violations of antitrust law. A more common practice and of more concern is the exclusive contract whereby a PPO or PPO-related organization enters into an agreement with one or a limited number of providers or provider groups to the exclusion of other providers. This situation has been discussed in terms of objective criteria that should be applied to such decisions. However, the factual context also gives rise to questions concerning the possibility that such agreements are exclusive arrangements in violation of Section 1 of the Sherman Act. Numerous courts have found that such exclusive arrangements, at least in the hospital context, are permissible under the rule of reason analysis. The courts have held that the anticompetitive effect of the exclusion of providers who have not contracted with the hospital is outweighed by the efficiencies, availability, responsiveness, and other business-related and quality-of-care-related considerations that may be more effectively addressed through the exclusive arrangement.[31]

Once again, the creators of a PPO must be mindful of the danger underlying such exclusive arrangements. Once the market share foreclosed by the exclusive arrangements reaches a critical level in the view of a court, that court will tend to more closely scrutinize the arrangement for potential anticompetitive effects.[32] By analogy, where an exclusive contract is established by a PPO, by all or a substantial majority of admitting hospitals, and by one group practice of health care providers in a particular specialty, a disenfranchised provider of that health care specialty may be successful in an antitrust lawsuit alleging unlawful exclusive dealing, since the market share circumscribed by the arrangement could be substantial.

Monopolization

Section 2 of the Sherman Act sets forth three separate offenses regarding monopolies: monopolization, attempted monopolization, and conspiracy to monopolize. Unlike Section 1, which requires an agreement between separate entities to establish a violation, Section 2 creates a liability for acts undertaken by one entity alone. Claims against a PPO and its member provider institutions alleging all three Section 2 offenses may be made by physicians and other practitioners who are denied access to hospital facilities by virtue of termination or denial of staff privileges. The excluded practitioner would attempt to show that the PPO and its members have monopolized, attempted to monopolize, or conspired to monopolize the specialty area of that physician or practitioner by refusing to provide access to hospital or PPO member facilities.

Requirements in a PPO agreement preventing providers from joining other PPOs, or requiring a provider to use PPO facilities for medical services that may be performed outside the PPO member institutions, could raise questions of the PPO's monopolization or attempted monopolization of the health care market for those services. The antitrust result in these circumstances would depend upon the PPO's ability to demonstrate that the exclusionary act is justified by some independent procompetitive interest and not the result of monopolization or an attempt to monopolize the market for those services.

The standard test under current law for monopolization is that the entity under scrutiny "(1) possess monopoly power in the relevant market and (2) willfully acquire or maintain that power as distinguished from its growth or development as a consequence of a superior product, business acumen, or historic accident."[33] The current standard for attempts to monopolize requires a "specific intent to monopolize" and the fact that a defendant "has come dangerously near to unlawful monopolization."[34] A substantial amount of one element often substitutes for a lesser quantity of the other element under both monopolization[35] and an attempt to monopolize.[36]

Increasing market share by making participation in an arrangement more attractive than nonparticipation does not imply a specific intent to monopolize. As the court noted in *Hoffman* v. *Doctor Dental Plan of Minnesota, supra,* a PPO's discount rate in its agreements can be a marketing device to increase market share, not a strategy to destroy competitors. Whatever percentage share of the market a PPO gains by such agreements is not in itself sufficient to establish the requisite specific intent for an attempt to monopolize.

POSSIBLE ANTITRUST DEFENSES

Learned Professions Exemption

Participation in a "learned profession" was formerly a ground for antitrust immunity until the U.S. Supreme Court's decisions in *Goldfarb* v. *Virginia State Bar,*[37] and *National Society of Professional Engineers* v. *United States,*[38] which held professionals to the same standards as other commercial entities for antitrust purposes. It is abundantly clear that the health care industry and its various components are no longer immune from antitrust scrutiny. Supreme Court decisions have made it plain that courts are no longer reluctant to intrude into the activities of the learned professions and their associations and organizations.

State Action Exemption

The Supreme Court in *Parker* v. *Brown*[39] held that a state's raisin marketing program that restricted competition was not covered by the antitrust laws. The Court stated that the Sherman Act prohibited acts of individuals, not the acts of the state.[40] After *Parker* v. *Brown,* courts generally applied a blanket antitrust exemption to activities dictated by or closely regulated by the states. Recent decisions, however, have limited the application of *Parker* v. *Brown.* In *Goldfarb* v. *Virginia State Bar,*[41] the Court held that minimum fee schedules of a bar association were illegal, rejecting the state action defense. The Court determined that although the Supreme Court of Virginia regulated the practice of law, it had not acted specifically to fix fees.[42] In *Cantor* v. *Detroit Edison Co.,*[43] the Court held that Detroit Edison illegally had tied sales of electricity and light bulbs.

The Court rejected the argument that since the providing of free light bulbs was approved by the state the practice was thereby exempt as state action. More recently in *Community Communications Co. Inc.* v. *City of Boulder*,[44] the Supreme Court held that the state action doctrine does not extend to municipal subdivisions. In that case the Court stated that the state action doctrine exempts only conduct engaged in as an act of government, or acts undertaken pursuant to state policy where the state policy is *"clearly articulated and affirmatively expressed."*[45]

Despite its limits, the state action exemption to antitrust law has continuing validity especially with regard to the delivery of health care services. Providing, reducing, or expanding health care services is pervasively regulated by state and federal law and agency rule. For example, State Certificate of Need (CON) laws and state acts under the National Health Planning and Resources Development Act of 1974[46] impose state action for the legitimate state interest of providing delivery of necessary health care services. Recent cases have held or suggested that the state action defense may be available in a variety of circumstances. For example, in *Phoenix Baptist Hospital and Medical Center* v. *Samaritan Health Services*,[47] participation by a competitor hospital in Certificate of Need (CON) hearings pursuant to a clearly expressed state policy and an actively supervised regulatory scheme constituted state action rendering its activities immune from antitrust scrutiny. In *Gambrel* v. *Kentucky Board of Dentistry*,[48] the dental association refused to give denture prescriptions and dental laboratory work orders directly to patients where such action was prohibited by state law under a valid exercise of state police power. This conduct was found to be exempt from antitrust scrutiny based on the state action exemption. This line of cases provides support for the proposition that a PPO will be exempt from antitrust review under the state action exemption if the PPO was created pursuant to a clearly articulated state mandate, evidenced by a pervasive regulatory scheme or where the activities of the PPO are regulated pursuant to state law, policy, or rule such as CON regulations.

The health planning laws and regulations, however, do not create a blanket immunity from antitrust laws for the health care planning and CON processes. The Supreme Court in *National Gerimedical Hospital* v. *Blue Cross of Kansas City*[49] reviewed the actions of defendant Blue Cross Association, which refused membership to the complaining hospital because the hospital had not obtained a certificate of need for its construction. The hospital sued, and Blue Cross based its defense on antitrust immunity provided under the health planning laws. The Supreme Court held that the planning act granted no such antitrust immunity and that Blue Cross would have to defend the antitrust charges on the merits. The Court, reiterating its opinion in *Silver* v. *New York Stock Exchange*,[50] stated that where, for example, a state health planning agency has expressly advocated a form of cost-saving cooperation among providers it may be that antitrust immunity is "necessary to make the [National Health Planning Act] work." It restated the congressional intent that state health planning agencies and providers who voluntarily work together to carry out the state's health planning statutory mandate should not be subject to antitrust laws. Congress determined that enforcement of the antitrust laws would prevent the implementation of the Federal health planning law. The Court in *National Gerimedical,* however, determined that such a situation differs substantially from the present one where the conduct at issue was found not to be cooperation among providers, but rather merely an insurer's refusal to deal with a provider that had failed to heed the advice of a state health planning agency.[51]

Relying on *National Gerimedical,* the U.S. Court of Appeals for the Sixth Circuit in *Huron Valley Hospital Inc.* v. *City of Pontiac*[52] upheld the right of plaintiff to proceed with an antitrust lawsuit charging that a competitor hospital had "captured the CON process and caused denial of plaintiff's application for approval of new construction." The plaintiff alleged that the competitor hospital in the community where a CON was sought blocked approval of the CON and manipulated the administrative process to obtain a license for itself to rebuild its existing hospital. The *Huron Valley* Decision reversed a lower court determination that the national health planning laws provided state action immunity from antitrust purview. The Sixth Circuit sought to establish that the mere existence of a CON process does not provide an exemption from the antitrust laws to entities that use or are required to participate in the process. Rather, it is the mandated activities arising out of such regulatory schemes that provide state action immunity from antitrust scrutiny with respect to the practices of those entities that would otherwise be deemed violations of antitrust law.

The case *State of North Carolina* v. *P.I.A. Asheville, Inc.*[53] is instructive in connection with the application of both the state action and implied repeal (see next section) doctrines to health planning laws. At the initial trial stage, a defense based upon the state action doctrine was successful as the court held that a hospital merger is immune from antitrust liability where the state has granted a CON for such merger following due process hearings pursuant to its regulatory powers. A three-judge appellate court panel originally affirmed the lower court decision.

However, after a rehearing before the entire appellate court, the trial court decision was reversed and remanded for a new trial. The court of appeals found that, while the CON requirements constituted a clearly articulated and affirmatively expressed state policy, there was no active state supervision due to an absence of any monitoring of the use of the hospital acquisition after its consummation.

The status of the state action exemption with regard to health care providers remains unclear in the wake of seemingly inapposite lower court decisions in *Samaritan, Gambrel, Huron Valley,* and *P.I.A.*

Asheville. While courts have not entirely repudiated a state action immunity for health care provider activities, those activities must be essentially compelled by a state regulatory or statutory scheme and the intent underlying that scheme. In an effort to resolve this uncertainty, a petition for *certiorari* has been filed with the U.S. Supreme Court in *P.I.A. Asheville.*[54]

The Doctrine of Implied Repeal

Closely related to the state action doctrine is the doctrine of implied repeal. This doctrine provides that where two legislative actions are inconsistent, the subsequent act implicitly repeals the prior act to the extent of the inconsistency.[55] Antitrust immunity may be implied if a subsequent legislative act is deemed to conflict with certain aspects of antitrust law. It is critical to note, however, that "implied antitrust immunity is not favored, and can be justified only by a convincing showing of clear repugnancy between the antitrust laws and a regulatory system."[56] "Only where there is a plain repugnancy between the antitrust and regulatory provisions will repeal be implied. Repeal is to be regarded as implied only if necessary to make the subsequent law work and even then only to the minimum extent necessary."[57] Health care litigants seeking refuge behind this doctrine have met with little success. The Supreme Court recently held in a unanimous decision, discussed in the previous subsection, that the National Health Care Planning and Resources Development Act of 1974 is "not so incompatible with antitrust concerns as to create a 'pervasive' repeal of the antitrust laws as applied to *every action* undertaken in response to the health planning process."[58] Specifically, the court held that defendant Blue Cross' refusal to grant participating status to hospitals that had not obtained approval for construction from the local health planning agency was neither compelled nor approved by any governmental regulatory body, but was rather a spontaneous decision on the part of such hospitals.

This reasoning was followed in *Huron Valley Hospital Inc.* v. *City of Pontiac,*[59] where the court ruled that the authority granted to state planning agencies under the Federal Health Planning Act to review new hospital construction does not include an implied repeal of antitrust law oversight of the hospital marketplace. The court in *Huron Valley,* despite the defense of implied repeal of the antitrust laws for all CON process activities, found that the predatory practices of certain hospitals preventing the issuance to Huron Valley Hospital of a CON were subject to antitrust oversight. Similarly, in *White & White Inc.* v. *American Hospital Supply Corp.,*[60] the court held that a medicare regulation that permits hospitals to engage in the group purchasing of supplies as a form of prudent buying does not conflict with federal antitrust laws and hence held that no repeal would be implied.[61]

The Supreme Court, however, cautioned in *National Gerimedical* that "our holding does not foreclose future claims of antitrust immunity in other factual contexts...where, for example, a [state health planning agency] has expressly advocated a form of cost saving cooperation among providers, it may be that antitrust immunity is necessary to make the [federal health planning statutes] work."[62] Citing *National Gerimedical,* the Fourth Circuit in *Hospital Building Co.* v. *Trustees of Rex Hospital*[63] held that participation by health care providers in local planning activities is immune from antitrust attack if it is done in good faith and aimed at avoiding needless duplication of health care resources. This implied immunity does not require a finding that the health care defendants were required or compelled to engage in the challenged activity, said the court, but only that the health care statute "encouraged" such participation in the planning process.[64] The Fourth Circuit reversed a jury verdict in favor of plaintiff and ordered a new trial on jury instructions concerning implied immunity and Noerr-Pennington immunity (see below). The Supreme Court denied plaintiff's petition for *certiorari* on October 11, 1983.

The appellate court found that both state and federal authorities had advocated health care planning, that federal legislation encouraged cooperation among governmental and private parties in their planning effort and that it would be "potentially impossible to engage in local health care planning" without involving potential competitors in the creation of a rational health planning scheme.[65] The court was able to distinguish *Rex Hospital* from *National Gerimedical.* In *National Gerimedical,* the action by Blue Cross to refuse participating status to hospitals that failed to obtain health planning agency approval for construction had not been implemented into a state plan or mandated by any health planning agency. In *Rex Hospital,* the defendants participated in the local health planning process, as contemplated and encouraged by Congress and state health planning statutes. The defendants participated in the development of a long-range plan for hospital development in the area and opposed plaintiff's application for a CON that conflicted with the plan. Without expanding the holdings of *Silver* and *National Gerimedical* that the health planning statutes do not impose a blanket repeal of antitrust laws, the court in *Rex Hospital* found that health planning statutes and their underlying rationale do repeal antitrust laws to the extent that potential antitrust defendants participate in the health planning process in good faith.

The Fourth Circuit appeared to reinforce its holding in *Rex Hospital* when it handed down its decision in *North Carolina* v. *P.I.A. Asheville Inc.*[66] There the court found that a merger was exempt where a CON authorizing it had been obtained.

However, after a rehearing, the same court reversed the lower court holding and its own affirmance of that holding, finding no implied repeal or state action[67] to immunize the defendant from antitrust liability. The court noted that a change in hospital ownership did not require CON approval under federal health planning laws. The court found, moreover, that no purpose of the federal health planning statute would be furthered by failing to apply antitrust standards to the transaction at issue (a private hospital acquisition) and that the legislative history of that statute shows concern for permitting competition to operate fully. Finally, the court found no clear repugnancy between the health planning and antitrust laws, noting that the standards applicable to the acquisition under both laws could have been satisfied.

To date, health care providers have succeeded in advancing only health planning laws as grounds for the implied immunity of some antitrust statutory regulation. Nevertheless, courts appear willing to permit concerted activities that otherwise would constitute antitrust violations provided those activities are conducted in good faith within the scope of established health planning law and regulations that have the purposes of cost savings, the reduction of duplication, and the rationalization of providing efficient health care services. The increasing efforts by state and federal governments to control the spiraling costs of health care by means of revised reimbursement methods (e.g., the medicare prospective payment system) and stronger state health planning laws (e.g., New York, Wisconsin, and Massachusetts have all recently strengthened their CON statutes) suggest the continued viability of the implied immunity doctrine as espoused in *Rex Hospital*.

The recent advent of PPOs and other alternative delivery systems make their status under state and federal health planning laws somewhat uncertain. However, PPOs in general do not create new entities, add beds, services, or equipment to existing entities or otherwise undertake activities ordinarily within the purview of the health planning regulations. In the event a PPO is required to obtain a CON under a state law and regulations, such CON could, in conjunction with other facts evidencing the anticompetitive nature of the PPO, provide some degree of antitrust comfort to that PPO if the PPO is challenged on the basis of concerted activities among competitors in the PPO's formation or practices. It may even be advisable, particularly in areas where the creation of a PPO involves a large proportion of area providers and may have an adverse impact on those providers not involved in the PPO, for the PPO to seek the imprimatur of the state or local health planning agency before the PPO is constituted. This may be accomplished through the formal CON process or by insertion of the proposed PPO into the state or local health plan. These steps could protect the formation of the PPO from antitrust risk under the *National Gerimedical* and *Rex Hospital* decisions. It is important to note that a petition for *certiorari* has been filed with the U.S. Supreme Court in *P.I.A. Asheville* in an effort to obtain a further dispositive solution to the tension between the health planning and antitrust laws.[68]

Noerr-Pennington Doctrine

This doctrine provides that concerted efforts to persuade either a governmental body or official to take a specific action do not violate the antitrust laws. The doctrine is based on the right of the government to obtain the information it needs to act and on the constitutional right of individuals to petition the government.[69] Actions within the doctrine's scope are protected even if it is based on anticompetitive motives. The doctrine extends to efforts to persuade legislative bodies and courts as well as administrative agencies; however, the doctrine does not protect "sham" efforts to affect governmental policy. Collective efforts to exert undue or improper influence on the decision makers are not protected from antitrust scrutiny, nor are filings of frivolous litigation or commencing administrative proceedings merely to harrass competitors. The Noerr-Pennington doctrine would appear to have limited application in the area of alternate delivery systems such as PPOs. The doctrine was applied in *Rex Hospital* to the defendant hospitals' involvement in the CON process pursuant to state health planning law and regulations. Those concerted activities, arguably violations of antitrust law, were found by the court to be immune from antitrust risk under the Noerr-Pennington doctrine as well as the doctrine of implied immunity, discussed earlier.[70]

The reach of the Noerr-Pennington doctrine should not be overstated however. Advocacy is clearly protected; however, actions designed to achieve those same ends may not be protected. In *Virginia Academy of Clinical Psychologists* v. *Blue Shield,*[71] two insurers were charged with antitrust violations for refusing to pay for services for clinical psychologists unless they were billed through physicians. A state law required direct payment but defendants argued that they were protected under the Noerr-Pennington doctrine because they sought a judicial test of the statute. The Fourth Circuit ruled in favor of plaintiffs stating that "the collaboration in defiance of a statute may have been calculated to provoke a judicial resolution . . . but it amounted to no more than an agreement to persist in economically restricted commercial activity in the face of a state law designed to open up the health care market."[72] Thus, while the defendant's rights to persuade the repeal of the challenged statute may have been protected under Noerr-Pennington, their continued violation of the statute was not protected. Similarly, if an entity seeking to create a PPO requests that a state or local health planning agency include in its health plan the proposed PPO formation, the request should be protected under Noerr-Pennington. The actual PPO formation and activities undertaken by the PPO, however, may not be protected by antitrust law and depends upon the applicability of other antitrust defenses such as implied repeal or state action.

The McCarren-Ferguson Exemption

The McCarren-Ferguson Act[73] exempts the "business of insurance" from antitrust scrutiny to the extent that such business is regulated by state law, provided the challenged acts do not constitute "boycott, coercion, or intimidation."[74] The McCarren-Ferguson Act, however, does not exempt from federal antitrust regulation all activities of insurance companies, as all acts of insurance companies are not considered to be the "business of insurance." The U.S. Supreme Court has held that not all aspects of a third-party provider contract are within the McCarren-Ferguson Act antitrust exemption. In *Group Life and Health Insurance Co.* v. *Royal Drug Co., Inc.*,[75] the Supreme Court in 1979 found that price fixing between Blue Shield and participating pharmacies did not involve an insurance relationship between insurer and insured. In *Royal Drug,* the plaintiffs alleged that the contracts between the Blue Shield plan and individual participating pharmacies were illegal restraints of trade. Blue Shield's prepaid prescription drug policy entitled insureds of Blue Shield to purchase drugs from any pharmacy, and Blue Shield had entered into agreements with pharmacies to provide pharmaceutical products. If the insured purchased pharmaceuticals from a participating pharmacy, the insured paid only $2.00, the policy deductible. If the insured used the nonparticipating pharmacy, however, the insured was required to pay the full price and then was reimbursed to the extent of 75 percent of the price exceeding the $2.00 deductible. Blue Shield argued that the price fixing was directly related to its relationship with the insured because it encouraged cost containment and resulted in reduced premiums. The Court, however, held that the contracts between the Blue Shield plan and the participating pharmacists were not the business of insurance and consequently were not exempt from antitrust scrutiny.[76] The Court in a five to four decision limited the "business of insurance" exemption to insurance contracts between insurers and insureds, risk spreading activities, and practices limited to entities within the insurance industry.[77]

The typical PPO structure is in many ways analogous to the facts in *Royal Drug*. In *Royal Drug,* insureds were given a financial incentive to use "preferred" pharmacists. No such incentive existed for using a nonparticipating pharmacy, although insurance indemnification was nonetheless available for the use of those pharmacies as well. In a PPO model, subscribers are encouraged through economic incentives to use the participating providers. Although PPO subscribers may use other providers, they do not obtain the economic benefits of using the preferred provider.

Having found no McCarren-Ferguson exemption applicable to *Royal Drug,* the Supreme Court remanded the case for trial on the merits. The appellate court affirmed the trial court decision that the prepayment plan constitutes neither horizontal nor vertical price fixing.[78] It found no horizontal combination because the agreements between the group insurer and the participating pharmacies did not run between competitors in either the pharmaceutical or insurance industries. The court did not find vertical price fixing since there was no evidence that Blue Shield had monopoly power or, if it did, that such power had been abused. Absent such evidence, the court held, Blue Shield had the right to bargain for the lowest price for itself and its insureds. The court further found no boycott to exist as each pharmacy had the opportunity to participate in the plan, there was no evidence that Blue Shield conspired with other insurance companies, and Blue Shield did not limit the ability of nonparticipating pharmacies to deal with other insurers or the general public, which purchases a substantial amount of prescription pharmaceuticals.

The McCarren-Ferguson Act exemption appears to be inapplicable to PPOs on two grounds. First, the specific scheme described in *Royal Drug,* which may be analogized to the typical PPO structure, is not the business of insurance under the Court's ruling in that case. Second, even if the Court had determined that the *Royal Drug* scheme was the business of insurance, PPOs should not meet the general criteria for insurance as described hereafter. Nevertheless, the decision on the merits in *Royal Drug* provides significant comfort to PPO organizers.

Antitrust Compliance

The foregoing discussion demonstrates the numerous potential antitrust hazards that may befall an ill-conceived and/or poorly structured PPO. Antitrust lawsuits may be filed by the federal or state governments or by individuals or entities aggrieved by the allegedly unlawful activity. In the few instances where governmental bodies have been asked to review PPO structures for possible antitrust violations, the agencies have found no significant antitrust problems. They have deemed the PPO arrangements presented to them to be generally procompetitive and lacking in those features, discussed above, which could serve as the basis for antitrust litigation.[79] Nevertheless, government agencies may revise their opinions as to the antitrust implications of PPOs as the PPO entities evolve. Agency opinions are merely advisory and should not be viewed as controlling legal precedent. Regardless of favorable opinions by government agencies, private litigants may file lawsuits against PPOs for alleged anticompetitive activities.

Therefore, it is advisable for creators of PPOs to have legal counsel undertake a thorough antitrust audit to illuminate possible antitrust problem areas. Counsel for the PPO should also prepare and assist the PPO in preparing an antitrust compliance manual and implementing an antitrust compliance program. The manual together with an instructive program should highlight areas of antitrust concern and provide the Board and the officers of the PPO with systems for avoiding or reducing antitrust liability.

REGULATORY OVERSIGHT

INSURANCE

Licensure Requirements

A major issue confronting PPO organizers involves the determination of whether the PPO is subject to regulation and licensure as an insurance company under state law. If the PPO is deemed to be an insurance company, the PPO organizers must weigh the cost and expense of compliance with the insurance laws against the expected benefits of the PPO.

The licensing and regulation of insurance companies generally provides for a vigorous regulatory scheme calling for the maintenance of certain levels of financial reserves by the regulated entity, strict regulation of the form and content of health care provider and subscriber agreements, prescribed forms of investments by the regulated entity and other forms of control intended to protect the subscribers, enrollees, or insureds of such an entity.[80] The threshold question for such an analysis is generally whether the proposed PPO would constitute or give rise to a "contract of insurance" under state law. States describe contracts of insurance in different manners. For example, Mississippi defines it as:

> an agreement by which one party for a consideration promises to pay money or its equivalent, or to do some act of value to the assured, upon the destruction, loss, or injury of something in which the assured or other party has an interest, as an indemnity therefor.[81]

Under Georgia law it is defined as:

> a contract which is an integral part of a plan for distributing individual losses whereby one undertakes to indemnify another or to pay a specified amount or benefits upon determinable contingencies.[82]

Although PPOs frequently perform functions traditionally performed by insurance companies, such as claims administration, they generally do not undertake agreements to indemnify patients for health care benefits, or the underwriting or spreading of risks. Still, utilization controls imposed by a PPO, including a possible fee-retention system as a method of spreading risk, should be assessed under relevant state insurance laws to determine whether this constitutes risk spreading for insurance regulatory purposes.

PPOs frequently incorporate billing, claim processing, and other administrative services. A variety of jurisdictions require that insurance claims adjusters and persons performing various other functions relating to the sale, interpretation, and administration of insurance contracts be licensed.[83] At least ten jurisdictions require the registration of third party contract administrators.[84] Therefore, PPO organizers must assess whether their staff requires licensure under these or other statutory or regulatory provisions before doing business in each state.

Freedom of Choice; Antidiscrimination

If the PPO is an insurance company, for state law purposes, the insurance laws and regulations that pose significant problems to PPOs are the "freedom of choice" statutes that prohibit insurers from limiting a beneficiary's selection to only certain providers, and antidiscrimination statutes that prohibit insurers from reimbursing providers at different levels. For example, certain freedom of choice provisions in various states provide that "the policy may not require that the service be rendered by a particular hospital or person." [85] This language is typical of many state statutes including those of Alaska, Arizona, Arkansas, Delaware, Georgia, Hawaii, Idaho, Indiana, Maryland, Oklahoma, Pennsylvania, South Dakota, Texas, Utah, and Wyoming. Connecticut insurance law prohibits interference by any other person with the exercise of free choice in the selection of a physician or optometrist. [86] In Utah, the Insurance Department regulations require that any physician who desires to participate in a PPO health insurance program under the program's terms must be allowed to do so. [87] If a PPO were deemed to fall within the state insurance laws, the freedom of choice provisions would certainly constrain their development. An attractive feature of PPO arrangements is that subscribers retain the freedom to use any provider, although incentives are given for the use of the preferred providers.

Antidiscrimination laws erect a different and potentially more difficult barrier for PPO creation. They provide generally that a payor may not vary the level of reimbursement for a covered expense based on the provider of the service or upon any other discriminatory basis. A number of states have statutes that prohibit insurers from paying different rates to different health care providers, and others prohibit hospitals from charging different rates to different payors unless they can establish that the differences are cost justified. [88] Such statutes necessarily restrict the organization and operation of most PPOs.

However, several states including California, Virginia, Wisconsin, Nebraska, Indiana, Utah, Minnesota, and Florida have adopted statutes or regulations that expressly permit the contractual arrangements contemplated by PPOs to provide discounts only for services of preferred providers participating in the PPO. Soon after Blue Cross and Blue Shield developed and introduced its preferred provider program, Minnesota adopted legislation to permit different benefits for covered services obtained from designated providers avoiding the unlawful discrimination or rebating problems. [89] In Virginia, the law effectively barred development of preferred provider arrangements. When it became clear that Blue Cross and Blue Shield of Virginia was interested in developing such an arrangement and that a possible barrier existed, the Virginia legislature quickly enacted the necessary legislation clarifying the authority of the Virginia Plans and Commercial Insurers to develop and offer such arrangements. [90]

Careful analysis of the insurance laws and regulations of each state are necessary to determine whether these states contain freedom of choice or antidiscrimination provisions. Where such provisions exist, it may be difficult or impossible to establish PPOs along traditional structural formulas. However, recent experience has indicated that those states who wish to encourage the formation of such alternative delivery systems have enacted the laws necessary to permit PPO formation. In fact, on May 9, 1983, Congressman Ron Wyden introduced H.R. 2956 entitled "A Bill to Permit Group Health Care Payors to Provide for Alternative Rates with Providers of Health Care." The bill (which is currently in the Subcommittee on Health and the Environment of the Committee on Energy and Commerce in the House of Representatives) was the subject of hearings in October, 1983. No action on the bill is expected until late in 1984.

The bill provides that group health plan payors, with the agreement of group policyholders and subject to the terms of any applicable collective bargaining agreement, may limit payments under their policies to services secured from health care providers charging alternative rates.[91] Section 2(a)(1) of H.R. 2956 permits group health plan payors to negotiate and contract for alternative rates of payment with, or determine alternative rates of payment for, providers of health care services and in turn offer the benefit of such alternative rates to their beneficiaries selecting such providers. Section 2(b) states that payments with respect to group health plan beneficiaries by the payor of alternative rates under 2(a)(1) and 2(a)(2) shall not constitute a violation of any state law or regulation. This bill therefore supersedes state freedom of choice and antidiscrimination laws and permits such practices in an effort to encourage the formation of PPOs.

HMO Regulations

Creators of PPOs must determine whether the PPO, as contemplated, would be sufficiently similar to a health maintenance organization (HMO) to place it within the class of entities regulated pursuant to state HMO law. The law of one jurisdiction defines a "health care plan" as

> any plan whereby any person undertakes to provide, arrange for, pay for, or reimburse any part of the cost of any health care services, provided, however, a part of such plan consists of arranging for or the provision of health care services as distinguished from indemnification against the cost of such service on a prepaid basis through insurance or otherwise.[92]

The relevant statute then defines a HMO as "any person who arranges for or provides a health care plan to enrollees on a prepaid basis."[93]

Arguably, PPOs "arrange for" the provision of health care services. Nevertheless, PPOs generally do not provide or arrange for the provision of health care services on a prepaid basis to establish the PPO as the indemnitor for the care rendered to beneficiaries. A careful analysis of the state HMO statute is required to avoid inadvertently becoming subject to the HMO statutes for purposes of state regulation.

HEALTH PLANNING LAWS AND REGULATIONS

The application of state health planning laws and regulations to a PPO depends on the statutory definition of "health care provider" in the laws of the particular state. Ordinarily, PPOs constitute a contractual arrangement among separate independent entities that include providers, payors, and subscribers. It is unlikely that the mere contracting process will give rise to a requirement that a CON be obtained for approval of the new entity. However, where additional services are provided or where services, beds, or equipment may be reallocated among or between the various entities of the PPO, state CON law may require that that activity be reported or perhaps even delayed until it is approved by the appropriate agency.

Most state laws currently apply to capital expenditures made by, through, or on behalf of, a hospital, nursing home, or other health care provider. Some states define provider to include free standing, nonacute care facilities such as chemical dependency units and outpatient rehabilitation facilities. Where a PPO maintains any control over a capital expenditure that would ordinarily require the hospital incurring the expense to obtain a CON, the PPO may instead be required to obtain the CON under pertinent state laws. In addition state statutes must be reviewed to insure that a hospital's capital contribution to the PPO in the form of start-up costs or additional payments to the corporation for capital purposes is not a capital expenditure that must be reported to or approved by state health planning agencies.

A proposed PPO may command such substantial market power or have such a significant impact on the health care delivery system in the area in which it is ultimately created that state and local health planning bodies may wish to or may be required by law and regulations to include the proposed PPO in its health plan. (As noted in the state action and implied repeal sections of the antitrust discussion, this may also serve to immunize the PPO from antitrust scrutiny once it is operational.)

STATE PROFESSIONAL LICENSING AGENCIES; STATE DEPARTMENTS OF HEALTH

The majority of states have statutes that prohibit the corporate practice of medicine and proscribe arrangements that constitute fee splitting, illegal discounts, rebates, and referral fees in the provision of health care services. These areas can be avoided provided the contracts executed by the various component members of the PPO do not inadvertently shift their responsibility for providing medical care from the physician and hospital providers to the PPO itself.

PPOs should not be subject to licensure or regulation under the various state departments of health statutory mandates, as a PPO does not directly provide medical services. Operationally, the PPO should seek to insure that other activities overseen by state health departments, such as record keeping and reporting requirements of the providers, remain the province and responsibility of those providers rather than be contractually assigned to the PPO.

ERISA

Employers and unions are key marketing targets for PPO development. Many medical benefit programs operated by unions and employers are those covered by the Employee Retirement Income Security Act of 1974 (ERISA).[94] A PPO entering into an agreement with a benefit plan covered by ERISA risks being deemed, either expressly or impliedly, a fiduciary or administrator of the plan. A plan fiduciary is responsible for managing the assets of the plan in a prudent manner, and the failure to act in accordance with fiduciary standards can result in the breach of fiduciary duties.[95] A PPO found to be a fiduciary will also be liable for the breach of fiduciary responsibility of other fiduciaries named in the plan documents.[96] ERISA, by statute and regulations, includes a comprehensive discussion of transactions prohibited to a fiduciary. Liability for breach of fiduciary duty includes restitution to the plan of any losses resulting from the breach, restoring to the plan any profits of such fiduciary that have been made through use of plan assets by the fiduciary, as well as any other equitable or legal relief available including the removal of the plan fiduciary.[97]

The design of the PPO is not consistent with service as a plan fiduciary and the PPO should seek to avoid being deemed to be serving in that capacity and incurring potential liability as a fiduciary under ERISA. To avoid this potential liability, it is important to understand what functions could cause a court to deem the PPO to be a plan fiduciary. ERISA provides that a person is a fiduciary to the extent that he exercises discretionary authority or control with respect to the management of the plan, exercises any authority or control with respect to the management or disposition of plan assets, renders investment advice for a fee or other compensation, or has discretionary authority or responsibility in administration.[98]

The PPO and the employer or union covered by the ERISA plan should provide in the agreement engaging the PPO (1) that fiduciary status is expressly disclaimed and indicate clearly that it remains the responsibility of the employer or union to expressly name the fiduciary, (2) the name of the actual plan administrator, (3) that the PPO does not have authority or responsibility for the disposition or management of plan assets, (4) an indemnity of the PPO against any liability resulting from claims by plan beneficiaries or others.

Although the PPO may not be a plan fiduciary, it may nevertheless be subject to the bonding requirements contained in 29 U.S.C. §1112 if it handles funds or other property of the plan within the meaning of the regulations pursuant to that section.

MEDICARE

Medicare law, codified at Title XVIII of the Social Security Act of 1965, as amended, does not significantly impact on the operation and organization of a PPO. Medicare imposes Conditions of Participation upon numerous providers, including hospitals and nursing homes, and these providers, if they seek reimbursement under the medicare program, must meet all conditions of participation. Thus far, no conditions of participation have been enacted or proposed to govern PPOs. PPOs must be aware, however, that each provider entity that is a part of the PPO must continue to meet its own conditions of participation under the medicare program. Failure to do so can lead to sanctions that may include decertification as a medicare provider. That action may have a significant impact on the provider's ability to continue to do business, depending on the volume of its medicare patient load, and may be cause to terminate a provider's participation in the PPO.

In many PPO situations, PPO costs and income are allocated to the hospital participants. This should affect the hospital's cost reporting methodology and may change its level of reimbursement. Each hospital must determine which, if any, PPO costs will be allowable under medicare. It is important to note that many of the cost-related questions concerning medicare reimbursement to hospitals affiliated with PPOs will be ameliorated by the implementation now under way of the prospective payment system for medicare reimbursement.

SECURITIES REGULATION

The structure of the PPO and any other affiliated entities, such as physicians' associations, determine whether those entities are subject to securities regulation. The critical factor is whether or not the contribution by the hospital and the physicians to the PPO or to any other corporate entity is considered the sale of a security by the PPO or that other entity. The physicians' association is particularly susceptible to this risk if it sells stock to a significant number of physicians.

The sale of any interest in a PPO or related entity or any contribution made to a PPO or such entity must be reviewed under federal and pertinent state securities law and regulations to determine whether that transaction is in fact a sale of securities. If the transaction is a sale of securities, it gives rise to a panoply of filing, disclosure, and publication requirements under both state and federal securities regulatory schemes unless the transaction falls within an exemption. These provisions must be analyzed prior to the formation of any PPO.

TAX CONSIDERATIONS

Each tax exempt participant in the PPO must determine the effect of the PPO structure on its tax exempt status. While there is no Internal Revenue Service revenue ruling specifically addressing this issue, in analogous fact situations, IRS revenue rulings have generally found the tax-exempt status of hospitals to be undisturbed. To maintain its Internal Revenue Code §501(c)(3) exemption, a hospital must be operated to serve public interests, and no part of its net earnings may inure to the benefit of private individuals. This area has been labeled as the "inurement issue" or the "prohibitions against private benefit and inurement."

The inurement issue frequently arises in situations where a hospital constructs and operates a medical office building. In revenue rulings issued in 1969, the IRS generally held that the operation of a medical office building contributes importantly to a hospital's operation and is therefore substantially related to the performance of hospital tax-exempt functions. More recent private letter rulings continue to reflect this viewpoint, despite the advent of more complex medical office building arrangements.[99] In sustaining the hospitals' tax-exempt status, the IRS generally holds that the arrangement furthers the hospital's tax exempt purposes. An important factor in this analysis is the proximity of the office building to the hospital's emergency room and inpatient beds, which attracts physicians to serve in the emergency room and on the hospital staff, thereby improving the health care delivery system in the community.[100]

Based upon these analogous factural situations, it appears that the tax-exempt status of a hospital would not be necessarily jeopardized because of its membership in a PPO. Both the impetus and effect of hospital membership in a PPO is the enhancement of the provision of cost-conscious medical care to the community without affecting the quality of that care. The hospital that joins a PPO to improve the health care delivery system in the community is a clearly demonstrable justification and any advantages that may accrue to the hospital through the PPO arrangement can be shown to further the hospital's tax-exempt purposes with respect to medical care, rather than constituting merely a private benefit or inurement.

Hospitals considering PPO membership should determine whether any portion of revenue generated from PPO activities will constitute unrelated business income. The critical issue is whether the trade or business, that is, PPO-related business, is substantially related or contributes importantly to the hospital's exempt purposes. As described above, there should be little difficulty in establishing that PPO business is no different than other hospital business and thus revenues derived therefrom are not unrelated business income subject to taxation.

MALPRACTICE LIABILITY CONSIDERATIONS

Liability for medical malpractice arises where a physician, who owes a duty to treat the patient with the requisite standard of care, fails to meet that standard of care and, in so doing, causes physical, mental, or emotional injuries. Historically, malpractice actions brought against hospitals have failed on the basis that physicians, and not hospitals, owed the duty to provide the proper medical care to their patients. During the last several years, however, liability for medical malpractice has been extended to parties other than physicians, including hospitals. This extension of liability has evolved under several theories. First, hospitals have been held responsible for the negligence of their employees, whether they be physicians, nurses, or other health practitioners, under the doctrine of *respondiat superior.* This doctrine provides that an employer is responsible for the acts of its employees. The doctrine of *respondiat superior* should not create problems for PPOs joined with doctors and hospitals in medical malpractice litigation provided that the employer-employee relationship does not exist between the PPO and the affiliated hospitals, physicians' associations, and physicians.

Potentially more troublesome to a PPO is the doctrine of "corporate negligence" which has resulted in liability to hospitals for the medical malpractice of their nonemployed physician staff members. Under the doctrine of corporate negligence, hospitals have been found to owe certain duties to patients, the breach of which constitutes negligence for which plaintiff patients have been permitted recovery in their malpractice litigation against both physicians and hospitals. Courts have determined that a hospital generally owes a duty to its patients to insure the competency of the hospital's medical staff and to periodically evaluate the quality of medical treatment rendered on its premises or through use of its facilities.[101] The courts have determined in many cases that hospitals have the duty to exercise due care in medical staff appointments, reappointments, and termination. In the view of these courts, hospitals have breached their duty by their failure to take reasonable steps to acquire and analyze the information necessary to make informed choices on medical staff appointments. The grant of privileges to a physician on a hospital's medical staff has the effect, according to the courts, of holding that physician out as competent to practice medicine in his field of specialization. The failure of a physician to act in a competent manner gives rise to at least a triable issue of fact with respect to the determination of whether the hospital followed the reasonable and proper procedures necessary to ensure the quality of the medical services rendered by that physician.

The creation of a PPO should not affect the application of these doctrines to the hospital or perhaps to physicians' association entities of the PPO. It is conceivable, however, that these theories of corporate negligence may be applied to the PPO or a physicians' association formed in conjunction with a PPO in the event a lawsuit is brought by a patient against the PPO or the physicians' association alleging medical malpractice of a PPO member hospital or physician. This application of the corporate negligence theory would be more probable if a PPO or the physician association maintains a selection process for determining the acceptance of health care providers as participating providers.

The exposure of a PPO or a physicians' association may be further increased if they administer a quality assurance program. A patient filing a malpractice action against a participating provider might join the PPO and the physicians' association in the lawsuit on the theory that the PPO or physicians' association negligently permitted the allegedly negligent provider to participate in the program. Conversely, if the PPO or physicians' association does not undertake the screening of the credentials or monitor the quality of participating providers, plaintiffs may allege that such screening and monitoring is the duty of the PPO and physicians' association, and that the failure to undertake that duty constitutes negligent conduct. While the latter scenario appears less likely based on current case law, the expansion of the doctrine of corporate negligence could result in the instigation of litigation. Indeed, even the appearance in PPO promotional literature of such terms as "quality care" or "preferred providers" might be found by a court to allow plaintiffs to assume that the PPO guarantees or warrants that it is expressly offering only quality, preferred care. Negligence of a participating provider may then be imputed to the PPO based on the doctrine of corporate negligence or even perhaps on the doctrine of breach of contract where the PPO has failed to live up to its announced standards.

PEER REVIEW

In *Union Labor Life Insurance Co.* v. *Pireno,*[102] the Court held that the use of a peer review committee to determine the reasonableness of chiropractic charges did not constitute the "business of insurance" within the meaning of the McCarren-Ferguson Act. The Court reiterated the three criteria (outlined in *Royal Drug* and discussed above) relevant in determining whether a particular practice is part of the "business of insurance" and found that the peer review procedure met none of the three criteria.

It must be noted, however, the Court in *Pireno* has not indicated its opinion of the legality of the underlying conduct. It merely found that the McCarren-Ferguson Act exemption from antitrust laws was not available to such conduct because the conduct did not constitute the business of insurance.[103] Therefore, while peer review functions of health care entities are not automatically immune from antitrust scrutiny, they nevertheless may be found to be legal under antitrust law. A staff report from the Federal Trade Commission concluded that the potential for abuse in peer review by the professions "seems relatively low." [104] The Supreme Court in *Pireno* remanded the case to the lower court for a full trial on the merits of the underlying claim, i.e., whether the peer review process in question actually violated antitrust laws.

While the final outcome of the legality of peer review arrangements under the antitrust laws must await the decision of the lower court and any appeals therefrom, it would seem that many peer review schemes should be permissible. First, notwithstanding *Pireno,* peer review mandated by federal or state law may well be exempt from antitrust scrutiny under the implied repeal or state action doctrines discussed above. In addition, many peer review plans should be permissible on their merits. In the Federal Trade Commission Advisory Opinion to the Iowa Dental Association, the Commission asserted that voluntary utilization and fee review are permissible under the antitrust laws provided that the power of the physician-controlled organization is limited to making recommendations and that ultimate authority to pay rests elsewhere. The Commission also suggests that a consumer representative be placed on the peer review panel, that the voluntary and advisory nature of the process be stressed, and that no preferred status is conferred upon participants or nonpreferred status conferred upon nonparticipants in the peer review process.

STRUCTURE OF A COOPERATIVE VENTURE PPO

PPOs may be structured according to a variety of organizational models. These include payor-based PPOs (e.g., Aetna Choice, Blue Cross/Blue Shield), PPOs formed by entrepreneurs as brokers between payors and providers, hospital-based PPOs, physician-based PPOs, and cooperative ventures initiated by two or more of the participants described above, most commonly hospitals and physicians. Each of these models has different implications and advantages in terms of its functional characteristics, tax status, ability to earn and disburse a "profit," and potential legal liability (including antitrust and regulatory risks) as well as the financial exposure of the parties and entities involved. This section of the article will describe the legal structure and operation of the cooperative venture PPO organizational model. A discussion of this PPO structure provides the opportunity to address in an operational context a significant number of legal issues described in the preceding sections of this article. The structure and function of the cooperative venture PPO may be used as guidelines for the formation of other PPO models.

The cooperative venture PPO consists of one or more hospitals, one or more physicians' associations (PAs), and a single PPO entity (see Exhibits 1 and 2). The PA and PPO may be for-profit or not-for-profit corporations, however, it may be advisable for these entities to be formed as for-profit organizations. A for-profit structure provides the traditional incentives associated with business ventures and permits the PPO and PA to

EXHIBIT 1

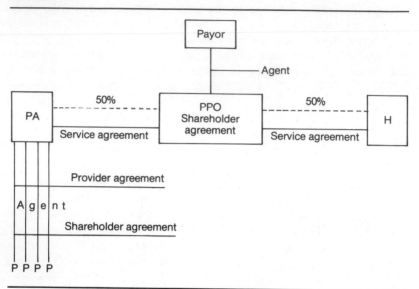

EXHIBIT 2

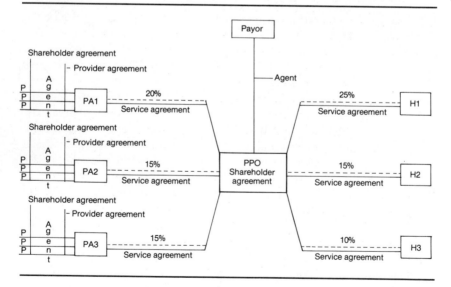

take advantage of opportunities that may exist currently or that may arise in the future to engage in profit-making health care related activities. The PA in particular may be a vehicle for numerous profit-generating singular or cooperative business ventures on behalf of or in conjunction with its members or its affiliated hospital.

Physicians seeking to create the cooperative venture PPO with their hospital will incorporate a PA comprising some or all of the medical staff physicians from that hospital. Ideally, this opportunity will be offered to the entire eligible medical staff to avoid some of the antitrust pitfalls described earlier. Once created, the PA, in conjunction with the PPO, may establish the proper standards of practice to eliminate inefficient and less competent members.

The proponents of the cooperative venture PPO derive their advocacy from the premise that the competitive environment in the health care industry makes it imperative that hospitals and physicians cooperatively participate as business partners, avoiding the traditional animosity between these groups. This PPO structure recognizes the nature and economic independence of these groups and seeks to provide safeguards within the corporate structure to assure, to the extent possible, that neither group is able to dictate the terms of participation in the PPO to the other group. The result of a "takeover" of the PPO by either the hospital or physician, it is theorized, could result in the nonparticipation of the other and thus the destruction of the PPO.

If this premise is accepted, the cooperative venture PPO in the organizational structure should be a corporation created by the cooperative undertaking of physicians' associations and hospitals. The hospital and the PA should each own one half of the stock of the PPO corporation, and each entity should elect one half of the Board of Directors of the PPO. These provisions, and other similar measures described herein, can safeguard the equality of ownership and of voting rights between the PA and hospital and maintain it as a cooperative venture.

The cooperative venture PPO is a restructuring of existing entities. In this PPO, the hospitals and physicians are shareholders in a new corporate structure and are also providers of health care in a system that rearranges functions and incentives to provide cost-efficient, high-quality health care to purchasers. This dual role is best understood by separately describing the PPO corporate structure and the documents that create it, and the PPO operational functions and the agreements that mandate those functions.

CORPORATE STRUCTURE

To structure the cooperative venture PPO, certain provisions should be contained in the Articles of Incorporation and the Bylaws. As noted, the cooperative venture PPO is to be owned and controlled equally by the hospital and PA. Therefore the bylaws should provide for two classes of stock, one ("Class A") owned by the hospital or hospitals involved in the PPO, and one ("Class B") owned by the PAs of those hospitals (see Exhibit 1).

The PPO Board of Directors should consist of an even number of directors, one half elected by the holders of Class A stock, and one half elected by the owners of Class B stock. These proposed PPO bylaws would provide that at shareholder meetings, each class of stock would have one shareholder vote. In this way shareholder decisions reflect the unanimous agreement of both the hospital(s) and the PA(s). Similarly, the vote of 50 percent of the full board of directors plus one director, rather than a simple majority of a quorum, would be required to pass any resolution of the PPO directors. This requirement could prevent the board from taking official action by the vote of all of the directors elected by any one class of stock. For example, if the board of directors consists of 10 directors, 5 of whom are Class A directors and 5 of whom are Class B directors, action should require the approval of 6 directors. At least one director from the "other faction" must join with the other group in order to attain the majority-plus-one vote for board action. Additional protections may be secured by requiring a majority-plus-two or -three vote for board action. In this and other provisions, the flexibility of this corporate structure is such that it may be readily adapted to the PPO as it evolves.

This corporate structure may be used to form a network of hospitals and PAs. The same shareholder and board voting provisions, and the theory that underlies their application to a PPO with only one hospital and PA, applies to a network PPO as well. In a network structure, all the hospitals together own 50 percent of the shares of the PPO, and all the PAs own 50 percent of the PPO stock. The amount of stock in the PPO owned by each hospital and PA is determined by the members of the respective groups by a networking agreement or by the PPO. Regardless of the number of PPO shareholders, all the owners of each class of stock elect one half of the PPO board and have one vote in shareholder matters (see Exhibit 2).

All the hospitals and PAs affiliated with the proposed PPO should execute a PPO shareholder agreement to further secure the equal ownership of each group in the PPO. The shareholder agreement should restrict the transferability of shares of stock in the PPO. The PPO shareholder agreement provides that where the PPO consists of multiple hospitals or PAs (Exhibit 2), the hospital or PA wishing to terminate or being terminated may sell its interest in the PPO only to another member of its PPO shareholder group (i.e., a hospital may sell only to a hospital and a PA only to a PA). It may not sell to a third party, to a member of the other provider group, or to the PPO itself.

There are two basic purposes for these restrictions. First, these restrictions prevent one hospital or PA in the network from transferring its ownership interest in the PPO to a hospital or PA that may be incompatible with the quality, standards, reputation, or ethical requirements of the other shareholder hospitals or PAs in the PPO. Second, if the shareholders could freely transfer their interest, the equal balance maintained between hospitals and PAs in the ownership of the PPO would be destroyed.

Each physician desiring to purchase stock in the PA could execute a PA shareholder agreement. The PA shareholder agreement should restrict the transferability of shares of stock in the PA to prevent a physician from transferring his interest in the PA to a physician who may be unable to meet the standards of the PA or the PPO. The PA shareholder agreement provides that the physician shall cease to be a shareholder of the PA on the occurrence of any of the following: failure to comply with the PPO's quality review and utilization management program (based upon objective standards), desire to transfer ownership of PA shares, loss of medical license, loss of hospital staff membership, or failure to pay dues. In the event of any of the above, the shareholder agreement provides that the PA shall redeem the share of PA stock owned by that physician.

PPO FUNCTIONS

As described above, the legal structure of the PPO is significant in terms of ensuring the continued viability of the cooperative venture in the face of potential conflicts and jealousies among the economically powerful and traditionally independent health care providers that constitute the PPO. Equally important is the proper allocation and performance of the numerous PPO functions among the various PPO entities. Establishing an effective operational framework for the PPO entity is critical to providing cost-efficient, high-quality health care to the consumer (which is the product a PPO has to sell), as well as to reducing or eliminating the PPO's exposure to legal liability. The functions and obligations of the entities comprising the PPO are set forth and described in the provider agreements and service agreements executed by and among those entities. The provider agreements and service agreements are essential to the operation of the PPO. The PPO cannot offer to provide a managed health care plan unless the providers are in place within a structure that operates efficiently.

In general, a PPO is created to provide economic incentives to consumers to utilize the provider members of the PPO. These incentives, usually in the form of reduced deductibles and copayments for patients, reduced costs to payors, and increased efficiencies and claims management for providers, are established by aggressively containing the cost of care provided by the members of the PPO. This is accomplished through intensive and ongoing quality review and utilization management. These controls are implemented by the PPO through the enlistment and retention of cost-conscious health care providers, while avoiding or terminating inefficient providers. One of the central functions of the PPO, therefore, is to implement the quality review and utilization program necessary to the viability of the PPO and to acquire and analyze quality, charge, utilization, and fee data from billing and patient records as part of that program. The PPO then uses the quality, utilization, and cost information to develop and administer the range of services provided by the physician and hospital members of the PPO, referred to as the "PPO managed health care plan."

The cooperative venture PPO provides physicians and hospitals with a powerful structure for negotiating separate agreements with each potential payor. In addition, the cooperative venture PPO provides the flexibility to permit the PPO or its member hospitals and physicians to enter into agreements with payors based upon a set plan separately negotiated with each health care provider or an agreement in which the providers receive customary fees but with utilization controls superimposed upon their services. Regardless of the PPO structure or method of contracting, it is advisable, from both an antitrust and operational standpoint, for the PPO to retain the option of submitting any payor agreement negotiated by the PPO to each hospital and physician in the PPO for their acceptance or rejection. Ultimately, the PPO structure and method of contracting with payors must be determined by the specific organizational dynamics and requirements of the parties forming the PPO.

In the cooperative venture PPO structure, the PPO acts as the agent for the hospitals and physicians (represented in the PPO by the PA) that provide the services comprising the PPO managed health care plan. The PPO negotiates the plan with potential payors (e.g., insurance companies, self-insured employers, union trust funds), seeking the most favorable payment terms for its principals, the PAs and hospitals in the PPO. Only the PPO negotiates the price of the services offered in the plan. Neither the hospitals, the PAs, nor the physicians take part in the price negotiations or fee determinations. In fact, no provider has access to the fee and charge information concerning any other provider used by the PPO to negotiate price with the payor. The PPO would negotiate separately with each payor and would be prepared to negotiate separately the price of each service offered in the plan. These steps are strongly recommended as ways to significantly reduce the PPO's exposure to allegations of antitrust violations based on unlawful price fixing, discussed earlier.

When the negotiations result in a proposed contract, the PPO would submit that contract to the PA(s) and hospital(s). The PAs in turn submit that contract to each physician member. The participants should be more susceptible to allegations of price fixing under antitrust law if individual providers are required to accept whatever arrangement was negotiated by the PPO with the payor. Therefore, each physician and each hospital has the option to accept or reject any or all contracts negotiated by the PPO with any payor. The contracting parties are only the payor and provider; they do not include the PPO or PA. It is contemplated that a contract will not be implemented without some threshold number of provider acceptances. The option retained by each provider to accept or reject a payor contract is critical in the attempt to prevent antitrust liability. It is also critical for the providers themselves to avoid establishing or appearing to establish a set fee for purposes of negotiation with a payor. It is for that reason that it is suggested that the PPO, using fee and pricing information obtained from PPO member and nonmember physicians alike, take such information to the payor to negotiate a reasonable fee for particular medical services. The incorporation of the PPO as a separate entity is all the more important from an antitrust standpoint where the PPO is negotiating fees and charges on behalf of the hospital and physician providers.

Under the operation of the cooperative venture PPO, each patient would be free to obtain services from "nonpreferred" providers who are not members of the PPO, albeit at a higher cost. This prevents further antitrust problems and avoids violation of "freedom of choice" laws that may exist under state insurance codes. The patients' ability to use any provider they wish, coupled with the fact that the providers are paid on the traditional fee-for-service basis rather than through a prepaid mechanism, preclude consideration of the PPO as an HMO for purposes of state HMO statutes. In addition, the PPO should not be subject to state insurance law if it does not indemnify or reimburse any party to the venture or spread the risk of loss over the PPO members. Therefore, payment should be made directly by the payor to the provider based on the provider's claim filed with the payor.

Antitrust problems may also arise if a physician is rejected for or terminated from membership in the PA. It is therefore recommended that the PPO, composed of representatives of all the provider groups as well as nonproviders, have the ultimate decision with regard to the termination or rejection of a provider's application for PPO membership rather than place that decision in the hands of fellow providers. Rejection of one physician by other physicians for PA membership strongly suggests an intent to boycott or monopolize patient care or to refuse to deal with that rejected applicant based upon subjective criteria not reasonably related to the business goals of the PPO venture.

Where a PPO, represented by a panel of objective, disinterested (to the extent possible) decision-makers, applies a set of uniform standards and criteria to any decision involving membership in the PA, that decision will be less vulnerable to antitrust sanction. Certain criteria are relatively free from controversy, such as requiring licensure, staff membership, and other related standards. However, the PPO may also establish criteria related to cost efficiencies, quality of care, the need for certain specialties and not for others, the limitations of the physical facilities of PPO member providers, and other similar requirements. These criteria may survive antitrust scrutiny if they are related to a valid business goal and not established to exclude certain practitioners or groups of practitioners. As the PPO market share increases, the PPO must be especially sensitive to the need for such criteria to be objective, unbiased, and not overtly anticompetitive.

The model PPO's presumed objectivity makes it appropriate for the PPO to administer grievances among the various parties to the PPO venture: patients against providers, providers against payors, providers against patients. The PPO could create an administrative staff with an executive director. The funds for operating the PPO should be derived from the capitalization of the PPO by its hospital and PA shareholders. However, a particularly efficient PPO, that is, one whose members provide cost-effective care, may be able to negotiate with payors for them to provide a portion of the operating expenses of the PPO.

The functions of the member hospitals under the model PPO are set forth in the service agreements between and among the hospitals and the PPO. The hospitals would agree to provide the covered services to eligible persons pursuant to the payor agreements negotiated by the PPOs and accepted by the hospital. The hospitals accept the amount negotiated in the payor agreement as full payment for the services provided to the eligible person. The hospitals agree to treat PPO patients in the same manner as they treat all other patients and to accept or reject PPO patients only on the basis of the same criteria employed for other patients. Significantly, the hospitals would agree to accept and implement the PPO's quality review and utilization management program which is central to insuring the cost effectiveness of the PPO venture. In order for the PPO to negotiate with payors and implement the quality review and utilization management program, the hospital would agree to provide the PPO with all necessary records and information that are in its possession. The hospital's failure to adhere to any provision in its service agreement with the PPO could be grounds for termination of the hospital's membership in the PPO pursuant to the terms of the proposed shareholder agreement.

The functions of the PA are set forth in the service agreement between the PA and the PPO. It is proposed that the PA implement the PPO obligations with respect to monitoring and controlling the provision of office-based physicians' services to the patients covered by the contract between the physician and the payor. The PA would develop and enforce practice-related membership criteria for the PA, but it is recommended that the final decision for a termination from participation of any provider should reside with the PPO. As noted earlier, it is the independence and objectivity of the PPO that enables it to make decisions to terminate PA membership without engendering antitrust liability.

The PA would cooperate in the resolution of grievances filed pursuant to the grievance procedure of the PPO; it is suggested, however, that the PPO render the final decision on any grievance filed by any party. The PA would provide the PPO with a current list of all physician providers and the location where such providers perform services pursuant to payor contracts. Like the PPO member hospitals, the PAs would agree to provide the PPO with all records and information necessary to enable the PPO to negotiate with payors and to perform its administrative obligations. A PA's failure to perform any of these functions could constitute grounds for its termination as a PPO member.

The physician providers execute a provider agreement with their PA. In addition to performing many of the functions that the hospitals must perform, each physician would notify the PA and the PPO of any eligible persons whose behavior jeopardizes the efficient rendering of services by the PPO. Each physician would, within the dictates of good medical practice and in the best interest of his patients, attempt to refer PPO patients to other physician providers who are members. To avoid problems both with antitrust law and with standards governing the ethical practice of medicine, the proposed referral provision would be worded in an advisory rather than mandatory fashion. Each physician member of the PPO would be required to carry insurance at limits set by the PPO. As with hospitals and PAs, any violation of the recommended provider agreement between the physician and the PA or any violation of the physician's obligations under the service agreement between the PA and the PPO should be grounds to terminate the physician's membership in the PA.

In addition to the advantages described above, the foregoing structure and operation of the model cooperative venture PPO may provide other legal benefits. For example, it is proposed that no provider be an employee of the PPO. The stockholder/independent contractor relationship of providers to the PA and PPO, evidenced by the existence of shareholder and service agreements and the absence of employment contracts or any other indicia of employment, would help mitigate against professional negligence liability being imposed upon the PPO for the alleged malpractice of PPO member physicians or hospitals. This does not prevent liability from being imposed on a PPO for the professional negligence of its member providers. Indeed, as discussed above, courts are becoming more sympathetic to claims of "corporate negligence," where an institution fails to properly supervise or negligently grants privileges to a physician who then commits medical malpractice. Nevertheless, the cooperative venture PPO structure provides the PPO with additional insulation against such claims.

As noted earlier, a PPO may take myriad forms. The PPO concept is sufficiently novel that no one particular corporate structure has emerged as clearly superior to any other structure. The PPO organization in this section herein is relatively detailed and contains certain requirements intended to protect the venture from legal liability. However, regardless of what form it takes, a successful PPO must retain the flexibility necessary to respond to the changes that are constantly occurring in the health care industry, and the resulting opportunities for the members of that industry.

NOTES

1. 15 U.S.C. §§1 and 2.

2. 15 U.S.C. §§15, 26.

3. 15 U.S.C. §§12, *et seq.*

4. *See FTC* v. *Brown Shoe Co.*, 384 U.S. 316 (1966).

5. 15 U.S.C. §18.

6. Tex. Bus. & Com. Code Ann. art. 15.02(b)(2) (Vernon 1968).

7. *See Commercial Standard Inc. Co.* v. *Board of Ins.*, 34 S.W.2d 343 (Tex. Civ. App. 1931).

8. *United States* v. *Oregon State Medical Society*, 343 U.S. 326 (1952).

9. *See Hospital Building Co.* v. *Trustees of Rex Hospital*, 425 U.S. 738 (1976); *Goldfarb* v. *Virginia State Bar*, 421 U.S. 773 (1975); *Cardio-Medical Associates, Ltd.* v. *Crozer-Chester Medical Center*, 552 F. Supp. 1170 (E.D. Pa. 1982), *rev'd in part*, 1983-2 Trade Cases ¶65,716 (3d Cir. 1983).

10. *Northern Pacific Railway* v. *United States*, 356 U.S. 1 (1958).

11. *Chicago Board of Trade* v. *United States*, 246 U.S. 231 (1918).

12. 441 U.S. 1 (1979).

13. *Goldfarb* v. *Virginia State Bar*, 421 U.S. 773, 788 n.17 (1975).

14. *Nat'l Soc. of Prof. Engineers* v. *U.S.*, 435 U.S. 679, 696 (1978).

15. 457 U.S. 332 (1982).

16. *Maricopa* at 355–57.

17. *United States* v. *General Motors Corp.*, 384 U.S. 127 (1966).

18. *United States* v. *Colgate & Co.*, 250 U.S. 300 (1919); *Joe E. Seagram & Sons, Inc.* v. *Hawaiian Oke & Liquors, Ltd.*, 416 F.2d 71 (9th Cir.), *cert. denied*, 396 U.S. 1062 (1970).

19. 362 U.S. 29 (1960).

20. *Id.* at 44.

21. *Hoffman* v. *Doctor Dental Plan of Minnesota*, 517 F. Supp. 564 (D. Minn. 1981). *See also Associated Foot Surgeons* v. *National Foot Care Prog., Inc.*, No. 84-271367 CZ, Cir. Ct. Co. of Oakland (MI) (Feb. 1, 1984).

22. *See Robinson* v. *Magovern*, 521 F. Supp. 842 (W.D. Pa. 1981), *aff'd*, 688 F.2d 824 (3d Cir.), *cert. denied*, 103 S.Ct. 302 (1982).

23. *See Deeson* v. *Professional Golfers' Ass'n of America*, 358 F.2d 165 (9th Cir.), *cert. denied*, 388 U.S. 846 (1966).

24. *See Robinson* v. *Magovern, supra; Pontius* v. *Children's Hospital*, 552 F. Supp. 1352 (W.D. Pa. 1982); *Silver* v. *New York Stock Exchange*, 373 U.S. 341 (1963).

25. *See Weiss* v. *York Hospital, Inc.*, 548 F. Supp. 1048 (M.D. Pa. 1982).

26. *See Boddiker* v. *Arizona State Dental Ass'n*, 680 F.2d 66 (9th Cir.), *cert. denied*, 103 S.Ct. 83 (1982).

27. 586 F.2d 530 (5th Cir. 1978).

28. *See Hecht* v. *Pro-Football, Inc.*, 570 F.2d 982 (D.C. Cir. 1977), *cert. denied*, 436 U.S. 956 (1978).

29. 552 F. Supp. 1352 (W.D. Pa. 1982).

30. *Standard Oil Co.* v. *United States*, 337 U.S. 293 (1949); *Tampa Electric Co.* v. *Nashville Coal Co.*, 365 U.S. 320 (1961).

31. *See, e.g.*, *Dos Santos* v. *Columbus-Cuneo-Cabrini Medical Center*, 684 F.2d 1346 (7th Cir. 1982); *Jefferson Parish Hospital District No. 2* v. *Hyde*, 52 U.S.L.W. 4385 (March 27, 1984); *Harron* v. *United Hospital Center Inc.*, 522 F.2d 1133 (4th Cir. 1975), *cert denied*, 424 U.S. 916 (1976).

32. *See Tampa Electric Co.* v. *Nashville Coal Co.*, *supra* (requirements contract for $128 million of coal over 20 years was not unlawful); *Standard Oil Co.* v. *United States*, 337 U.S. 293 (1949) (exclusive arrangement foreclosing 65 percent of market in oil was unlawful).

33. *United States* v. *Grinnell Corp.*, 384 U.S. 563, 570–71 (1966).

34. *Walker Process Equipment Inc.* v. *Food Machinery & Chemical Corp.*, 382 U.S. 172 (1965).

35. *See, e.g.*, *United States* v. *Aluminum Co. of America*, 148 F.2d 416 (2d Cir. 1945) (substantial market power substituted for purposeful conduct).

36. *See, e.g.*, *Lessig* v. *Tidewater Oil Co.*, 327 F.2d 459 (9th Cir.), *cert. denied*, 377 U.S. 993 (1964) (purposeful conduct substituted for market power theories).

37. 421 U.S. 773 (1975).

38. 435 U.S. 679 (1978).

39. 317 U.S. 307 (1943).

40. *Id.* at 351–52.

41. 421 U.S. 773 (1975).

42. *Id.* at 788–89.

43. 428 U.S. 579 (1976).

44. 455 U.S. 40 (1982).

45. *Id.* at 42 (emphasis added). *See also City of LaFayette* v. *Louisiana Power & Light Co.*, 435 U.S. 389, 410–13 (1978).

46. 42 U.S.C. §300(k) *et seq.*

47. 668 F.2d 847 (9th Cir. 1982), *cert. denied*, 103 S.Ct. 3096 (1983).

48. 689 F.2d 612 (6th Cir.), *cert. denied*, 103 S.Ct. 1198 (1982).

49. 442 U.S. 378 (1981).

50. 373 U.S. 341 at 357 (1963).

51. 452 U.S. at 393.

52. 666 F.2d 1029 (6th Cir. 1981).

53. 1982-2 Trade Cases ¶64,764 (W.D.N.C. 1981), *Aff'd* 722 F.2d 59 (4th Cir. 1983), *rev'd and remanded after hearing en banc*, No. 82-1058 (4th Cir., July 16, 1984), *pet. for cert. filed*, No. 84-480, 53 U.S.I..W. 3271 (U.S. Sept. 24, 1984).

54. See note 55.

55. *United States* v. *National Ass'n of Security Dealers*, 422 U.S. 694 (1975); *Gordon* v. *New York Stock Exchange*, 422 U.S. 659 (1975).

56. *United States* v. *National Ass'n of Security Dealers, supra*, 422 U.S. at 719-20.

57. *Silver* v. *New York Stock Exchange*, 373 U.S. 341, 357 (1953).

58. *National Gerimedical & Gerontology Center* v. *Blue Cross of Kansas City*, 452 U.S. 378, 393 (1981) (emphasis added).

59. 666 F.2d 1029 (6th Cir. 1981).

60. 540 F. Supp. 951 (W.D. Mich. 1982).

61. *See also Ballard* v. *Blue Shield of Southern West Virginia*, 529 F. Supp. 71 (S.D. W.Va. 1981) (no implied repeal where complaint alleged a group boycott to refuse health insurance coverage to chiropractic services).

62. 452 U.S. at 393 n. 18.

63. 691 F.2d 678 (4th Cir. 1982), *cert. denied*, 104 S.Ct. 231 (1983), *aff'd on retrial*, No. 4048 (E.D.N.C. 1984).

64. 691 F.2d at 686.

65. 691 F.2d at 685.

66. 722 F.2d 59 (4th Cir. 1983), *rev'd and remanded after hearing en banc*, No. 82-1058 (4th Cir., July 16, 1984), *pet. for cert. filed*, No. 84-480153 U.S.L.W. 3271 (U.S. Sept. 24, 1984).

67. See text at note 55.

68. See note 66.

69. *See Eastern R.R. Presidents Conference* v. *Noerr Motor Freight Inc.*, 365 U.S. 127 (1961); *United Mine Workers* v. *Pennington*, 381 U.S. 657 (1965).

70. 691 F.2d at 688.

71. 624 F.2d 476 (4th Cir.), *cert. denied*, 450 U.S. 916 (1980).

72. 624 F.2d at 482.

73. 15 U.S.C. §§ 1011-1015 (1976).

74. 15 U.S.C. § 1013(b) (1976).

75. 561 F.2d 262 (5th Cir. 1977), *aff'd*, 440 U.S. 205 (1979).

76. 440 U.S. at 214.

77. *Id.* at 211, 215-16, 220-221.

78. *Royal Drug Co.* v. *Group Life & Health Ins. Co.*, 47 Antitrust & Trade Reg. Reptr. 321 (5th Cir., Aug. 6, 1984), *pet. for cert. filed*, No. 84-804, 53 U.S.L.W. 3419 (U.S. Nov. 19, 1984).

79. *See* Federal Trade Commission Advisory Opinion to Health Care Management Associates, 101 F.T.C. 1014 (June 3, 1983); Department of Justice Business Review Letters to Health Care Management Associates and to Hospital Corporation of America (September 21, 1983); Opinion of Ohio Attorney General, 1984-1 CCH Trade Cases ¶65,796 (1983).

80. *See, e.g.*, Florida Insurance Code, Florida Statutes, Chapter 624-632.

81. Mississippi Code, Section 83-5-5 (1972).

82. Georgia Code Annotated, Section 56-102.

83. *See, e.g.,* Florida Statutes, 626; Ga. Code An., Chapter 56–8.

84. Arizona, California, Florida, Indiana, Kansas, Minnesota, Montana, Nevada, Tennessee, and Utah. *See, e.g.,* Arizona Rev. Stat. §20-485 (West 1982–83 Supp.).

85. *See, e.g.,* Kentucky Revised Statutes, Section 304.18-048 (Bobbs-Merrill 1981), Argon Insurance Code Section 743.531 (1979).

86. Connecticut General Statutes Annotated, Section 20-138b (1982).

87. Utah Insurance Department Regulations, Reg. 81-2, §4.

88. *See, e.g.,* Wyoming S.B. 101, Chapter 63, which requires that any hospital discounts, credits, rebates, or other related reductions in price given by a tax-supported state or county hospital or other health care facility must apply uniformly to all persons; *see also* Colorado H.B. 1330 and Iowa H.F. 519, both proposed legislation.

89. *See* Minnesota H.F. 765, *codified at,* Minn. Stat. §72A20(15)(4).

90. S.B. 110, Chapter 464 (1983 Session), *codified at* Va. Code §38.1-347.2 and 38.1-813.4 (1984). *See also* S.B. 28-B (Florida, passed June 24, 1983); 1983 Wisconsin Act 27 (1983–85 Biennial Budget Act, published July 1, 1983), *codified at,* Wis. Stat. §628.36; Indiana Code §27-8-22 (1984); Nebraska L.B.902 (1984). *See also* legislation under consideration in Arizona, Colorado, Kansas, Louisiana, Michigan, Mississippi, Oklahoma, Pennsylvania, South Carolina, Washington and Vermont. *See generally,* State Regulation of Preferred Provider Organizations: A Survey of State Statutes (American Hospital Association, March 1984).

91. H.R. 2956, Section 2(a)(2).

92. Tex. In. Code Ann. art. 20A.02(j) (Vernon 1981).

93. *Id.* art. 20A.02(n).

94. 29 U.S.C. §1001 *et seq.*

95. *See* 29 U.S.C. §§1102–1104.

96. *Id.* §1105.

97. *Id.* §1109.

98. *Id.* §1002(21)(A).

99. *See* LTR 8234029.

100. *See* LTR 8234029 (Private Letter Ruling 1982).

101. *See Darling* v. *Charleston Community Memorial Hospital,* 211 N.E. 2d 253 (Ill. 1965); *Elam* v. *College Park Hospital,* 132 Cal. App. 3d 332, *as modified,* 133 Cal. App. 3d 94(A)(1982).

102. 102 S.Ct. 3002 (1982).

103. *But see Royal Drug Co.* v. *Group Life & Health Ins. Co.,* 47 Antitrust & Trade Reg. Rptr. 321 (5th Cir. Aug. 6, 1984) (underlying conduct did not violate antitrust laws).

104. *Iowa Dental Association,* 3 Trade Reg. Reptr. (CCH) ¶21,918 (April 9, 1982).

PPO PROGRAMS AND THE ANTITRUST LAWS

Arthur N. Lerner, J.D.

Assistant Director for Health Care
Bureau of Competition
Federal Trade Commission
Washington, DC

David M. Narrow,[1] J.D., M.P.H.

Attorney
Bureau of Competition
Federal Trade Commission
Washington, DC

☐ "Preferred provider organization" or PPO programs are the latest form of alternative delivery system to emerge in the health care services and health care financing markets. Like such previous innovations as union welfare plans, prepaid group practices, health maintenance organizations (HMOs), and primary care networks, PPO programs present an alternative to the historically predominant system of solo, fee-for-service medical practice where the patient has had unrestricted freedom to choose among available physicians and hospitals, and third-party payors (both insurers and employers) have been uninvolved in and largely indifferent to that choice in paying for health care services.[2]

PPO programs have significant potential to enhance competition in the markets for both the financing and the provision of health care services. In the financing market, PPO programs offer consumers an additional choice of health care coverages, one that has the attractive features of reducing or eliminating deductibles or copayments when subscribers use the identified "preferred" providers. Unlike HMOs, though, PPO programs still allow the subscriber to use any provider, albeit possibly at the cost of having to pay deductibles or copayments. In addition, by discouraging unnecessary utilization and by obtaining fee discounts from providers, insurers may achieve savings from PPO programs that permit them to set lower policy premiums. This, in turn, creates competitive pressure on other third-party payors' marketing insurance programs to lower prices and to control their programs' health care costs.

Providers of health care services—notably physicians and hospitals—have an economic incentive to participate in PPO programs in order to gain or maintain access to PPO program subscribers as patients.[3] This incentive to participate exists both for providers with current "excess capacity"—empty beds or unfilled appointment slots[4]—and for providers who are concerned about possible future loss of patients to providers participating in PPO programs or other alternative delivery systems.[5]

The market pressure on providers to participate in PPO programs in order to protect their patient supplies may give third-party payors offering PPO programs considerable leverage in setting and enforcing rigorous participation standards for providers. Thus, PPO program sponsors may choose to exclude providers whose charges are judged to be too high or whose patterns of service utilization are considered excessive, inappropriate, or questionable.[6] Likewise, third-party payors offering PPO programs may require adherence by providers to rigorous utilization controls and other cost-containment measures, and in some cases may obtain discounts from the providers' usual fees or charges as a condition of participation. PPO programs therefore can generate market pressure on health care providers to improve their efficiency and lower their prices in order to better compete with other providers in the market for access to PPO program subscribers.

Because of their procompetitive potential, PPO programs have received general endorsement from antitrust law enforcers.[7] In fact, the Federal Trade Commission's antitrust decision in the *American Medical Association*[8] case probably has been an important factor easing PPO programs' way into the marketplace. In that case, the Commission found unlawful, among other things, ethical prohibitions the AMA had imposed on member physicians' participation in arrangements that involve "underbidding by physicians," in plans that preclude the "free choice of physician," and in contracts that pay "inadequate" compensation to physicians because they pay less than the "usual" fees in an area. Since PPO arrangements can involve fee discounts by physicians and competitive bidding, and include incentives discouraging the use of non-PPO physicians, they might well have violated these ethical restrictions and been subject to challenge and condemnation by state or local medical societies. The FTC's order effectively prohibits such anticompetitive restrictive conduct.

Similarly, the antitrust laws would condemn conspiracies or agreements among competing physicians or hospitals to refuse to deal with—or boycott—a PPO program offered by insurers or others.[9] The antitrust laws would also be likely to prohibit concerted efforts by physicians to coerce health care providers to refuse to deal with PPO programs,[10] to deter physicians from joining PPO programs by threatening to obstruct or deny them access to hospital privileges,[11] or to deter participation in PPO programs by conditioning participation in a competitively powerful medically sponsored prepayment program on an agreement to limit or refrain from participation in other prepayment programs, such as competing PPO programs.[12] It is unresolved how the antitrust laws would treat a leading health insurer in a particular market, particularly one controlled by providers, trying to prevent participating providers from granting to competing programs, such as PPOs, discounts from their usual fees.[13]

However, the general support for PPO initiatives and the protections the antitrust laws afford PPO programs from illegal restraints does not mean that there are no potential antitrust concerns that arise from PPO programs. PPO programs can take a variety of forms and incorporate numerous differences in operation. Depending upon their sponsorship, size, structure, and operation, particular PPO programs potentially could raise antitrust questions about horizontal price fixing, vertical price fixing, boycott or concerted refusal to deal,[14] monopolization, territorial allocation of markets, or other types of anticompetitive conduct.

Initially, it may be useful to briefly examine from an antitrust perspective just what a PPO program is and is not. The term "preferred provider organization" has been used to describe a group of providers who together participate in a PPO program, and also to describe the entire program, including the set of contractual relationships it involves. The former usage can be misleading because it suggests that some new, identifiable entity competing in the market is always formed in a PPO program. In reality, however, PPO programs need not involve any new entity. Rather, PPO programs can be offered by third-party payors[15] currently operating in the market. These programs can be implemented by a third-party payor through a series of contractual arrangements[16] involving the third-party payor and subscribers or beneficiaries, on the one hand, and individual participating health care providers who have signed contracts with the third-party payors to provide covered services to subscribers, on the other.[17] Viewed this way, PPO programs are not fundamentally different in structure from Blue Shield plan or some IPA–type HMO[18] programs that have provider participation agreements.[19] The primary differences are that PPO programs generally involve a more limited number of "preferred" health care providers, and unlike HMO programs, PPO subscribers are not restricted to using only the participating providers.[20] In addition, while PPO programs may give providers some positive or negative financial incentives to influence their performance, PPO providers generally do not assume an insurance underwriting risk as HMO providers commonly do when they accept capitation reimbursement, either directly or indirectly through an IPA.

Given the wide variety of structural options available to potential PPO program participants in establishing these programs, the antitrust risks attending many PPO programs actually may be quite small. In many areas of potential antitrust concern PPO programs probably will not raise greater or even different antitrust problems than the operations of any other type of business. Most aspects of PPO programs appropriately will be analyzed under the antitrust "Rule of Reason," which attempts to judge an activity's legality by weighing its procompetitive and anticompetitive effects. Because PPO programs do appear to have significant procompetitive potential and because, as new programs, they are unlikely to have great market power that would enable them to have serious anticompetitive effect (for example, through the maintenance of artificially high fee levels), it is unlikely that aspects of their operation subject to this type of Rule of Reason analysis will be found to violate the antitrust laws. In addition, many of the antitrust questions concerning certain forms of PPO programs will be easily resolved by reference to similar arrangements that have operated in the health care financing and delivery markets. For example, the issue of possible price-fixing by a nonprovider-controlled PPO program that contracts for services with individual health care providers is easily resolved by reference to earlier antitrust cases that unsuccessfully challenged Blue Shield plans' physician participation agreements on that basis.[21]

There is one antitrust issue, however, that is much more troubling and difficult to resolve: Do agreements on prices or price-related terms among health care providers selling their services through PPO programs face significant risk of condemnation under the antitrust laws as horizontal price-fixing similar to that found by the Supreme Court to be per se illegal in *Arizona* v. *Maricopa County Medical Society,* 457 U.S. 332 (1982)?

In *Maricopa,* by a four to three vote, the Supreme Court held that it was per se or automatically unlawful for physician members of a foundation for medical care to agree jointly on the maximum fees to be claimed by them in payment for health services provided to policyholders of insurance plans wishing to be approved or "sponsored" by the foundation. The Court found that the per se rule of automatic illegality applied to the price agreement, and not the Rule of Reason, where legality is determined on a case-by-case basis using a process of balancing competitive effects of the arrangement. The Court based its decision on the fundamental concern of the antitrust laws with price as the "central nervous system" of our economy.[22] This concern is reflected in the courts' long-standing construction of the antitrust laws' ban on unreasonable restraints of trade. "Price-fixing" among competitors is conclusively presumed to be an unreasonable restraint of trade without need for further proof of the participants' market power or intentions,[23] and without regard for the "fairness" or "equitableness" of the prices set.[24]

The precedent set by the Court's decision in the *Maricopa* case is quite clear in its application to some conduct. Nonetheless, the *Maricopa* decision leaves the law somewhat uncertain with regard to some PPO-type systems. This uncertainty arises partly because the decision was not rendered by a majority of the nine justices of the Court. Also, the Court did not seem to articulate a satisfying and self-contained explanation of its reasoning in reaching its conclusion of per se illegality in the face of the possible alternatives.

When does the per se rule of the *Maricopa* case apply? The best start on this question is the language of the Sherman Act. The Act prohibits combinations and conspiracies in restraint of trade.[25] A critical factual element in the *Maricopa* case was the clear existence of a combination or conspiracy among competitors. Absent this element, per se illegality is extremely unlikely in the PPO context. Second, the collective action clearly related to price and fixed a price-related term of contractual dealings affecting the competing participants in the scheme. These two elements established the makings of a per se illegal horizontal price-fixing case. The principal way for a defendant to work its way out of per se illegality in such a case is to show that the agreement among competitors was not a so-called naked restraint of trade, but that it was, in contrast, reasonably related and "ancillary" to a productive joint venture, one offering economic integration or efficiency advantages, whose competitive benefits outweigh the harms from the potential lessening of competition among the participants.[26] The defendants in *Maricopa* did not make that showing.[27]

Where did the defendants in *Maricopa* fall short in showing that their conduct was not a naked restraint of trade? The foundation physicians in *Maricopa* performed peer review and administrative functions. But these did not prevent per se condemnation of their joint agreement relating to pricing, because the price agreement was not necessary for the plans to perform those other functions effectively. Nor did the Court consider the agreement among physicians on the price schedule to be a "natural consequence" of, or "ancillary" to, any efficiency-enhancing productive integration or activity by the member physicians. The health care coverage involved in *Maricopa* was offered and underwritten by independent insurance carriers, not by the physician groups. The physicians were not joint venturers with the insurers and in fact were under no financial risk. It also was clear that the insurers could have offered comparable plans without using fee schedules established or approved by the physician groups. The Supreme Court noted that the insurers themselves, rather than the foundations, could have derived a fee schedule by canvassing individual physicians.[28] Therefore, on the evidence before it, the Court faced a situation in which, without achieving any operational integration or meaningful increase in efficiency *related* to the challenged conduct, most of the physicians practicing in the area had jointly set a maximum fee schedule that had to be adopted by any insurer who wanted their seal of approval. Viewed in this way, it is not surprising that the Court concluded that the conduct was illegal.

The decision makes clear, of course, that different facts could lead to a different result. Under the Court's opinion, competitors who *do* achieve sufficient operational integration by forming some sort of partnership or "joint arrangements in which [they]...pool their capital and share the risk of loss"[29] do not face per se condemnation if they jointly set prices.[30] In that situation, the arrangement would be evaluated under the Rule of Reason, with its procompetitive and anticompetitive effects balanced against each other to determine the arrangement's legality. Most carefully planned PPO programs should pass a Rule of Reason test.

The problem is that the Supreme Court did not provide specific guidance for determining when competitors acting in a joint enterprise have made a *sufficient* integration of their operations, or when joint conduct relating to price is reasonably necessary to significantly enhance the effectiveness of a joint enterprise, so as to receive Rule of Reason treatment rather than swift per se condemnation as price fixing. The Court gave little useful guidance to providers who may be willing to integrate their business operations through a PPO to some limited extent, but who might not wish to form actual partnerships or other joint ownership arrangements or to assume underwriting or insurance risk, as in a group practice or IPA-type HMO. In this situation, can joint rate-setting be permitted, for example, if it is ancillary to an arrangement for the joint marketing of health services by a relatively small proportion of the providers in a local market, who might otherwise face difficulties competing for contracts with group purchasers?[31]

Attorneys providing antitrust counsel can make some predictions on this issue,[32] but doctors, hospitals, and businesses may want a clearer path to legal safety. This can be found by stepping back a little, going back to antitrust basics, and avoiding the structural and operational risks that characterized the conduct of the Maricopa County physicians. Given the uncertainties that the *Maricopa* decision has highlighted, the obvious question is whether potential participants in PPO programs, as a practical matter, can protect themselves against possible antitrust exposure for per se illegal price fixing, and if so, how?

The surest way to eliminate or minimize antitrust risk is to structure the PPO program so that competing providers participating in the program do not agree among themselves on any aspect of the prices they will charge for services or the amounts or levels of payment they will accept from the program.[33] This is perhaps most easily achieved where the PPO program is established and controlled by parties other than competing providers. Thus a PPO program established and run by an insurer, employer, or entrepreneur usually can decide on reimbursement levels to be paid to providers who agree individually to participate in the program without running afoul of *Maricopa* or the antitrust laws generally. Of course, competing providers contracting with such a PPO program still would be subject to antitrust scrutiny, particularly if they agree among themselves on prices or terms of participation in the program and if they collectively negotiated with the PPO program's sponsor or payor concerning these terms.

A second way for a PPO program to avoid the problem of having competing providers agree on prices, and thus avoid the risk of falling under *Maricopa*, is for the participating providers to individually opt in or out of the program or particular group coverages in response to a price term set directly by the payor. In this model, any organization representing the providers would be able to perform certain necessary or desirable joint functions, such as utilization review or claims administration. However, as to price, the provider organization would merely act as a messenger that transmits the payor's offers to its members, but leaves price-setting and negotiation to the payor and the individual provider. The provider organization can provide historical pricing data and offer information and expertise on structuring the program to the insurer or employer so that the PPO program is likely to be acceptable to a sufficient number of providers. The provider organization or payor then can transmit the offer to the members of the provider group, who individually decide whether or not to participate, depending upon whether the terms of the agreement—including the terms of reimbursement—are acceptable to that individual provider. By this approach, the agreement on price by competing providers, which was the crux of the conduct found to be unlawful in *Maricopa*, is eliminated from the PPO program.

Another "safe" course is to build the PPO program around a panel of physicians in a large multispecialty group or clinic who, in antitrust terms, are already a single actor and not competitors. Similarly, a single hospital or a number of hospitals under the same ownership or in different areas so they are not independent competitors of one another can be the core of a PPO program set up to avoid price agreements among competitors.

Finally, there remains the option of establishing a PPO program that does involve agreement on price by competing providers participating in the program. This approach obviously entails risk and guesswork, since it requires the provider participants to predict what types and levels of productive integration, efficiency-enhancing activity, or risk of profit sharing by them, and what arguments for the "reasonable necessity" of joint pricing behavior will be considered legally sufficient to justify excluding that agreement on price from the per se treatment it received in *Maricopa*. If per se condemnation is avoided, the conduct would be upheld as lawful under the antitrust Rule of Reason if its actual or likely anticompetitive effects did not outweigh the procompetitive effects of the whole venture, an analysis that would take into account the purpose of the program, the extent of its market power, and conditions in the local market.

CONCLUSION

The goals of the antitrust laws are practical and purposeful. Congress enacted the antitrust laws, and the courts and antitrust law enforcement agencies seek to apply their strictures to promote competition and thereby serve the public interest. Careful application of the antitrust laws will condemn only that conduct which, in the long run, is truly likely to harm consumers more than it helps them. Consequently, the well-designed and well-run PPO program should be both safe from antitrust condemnation and affirmatively protected by the antitrust laws from anticompetitive conspiratorial interference. Facts and common sense should dictate the course and results of application of the antitrust laws to PPO programs. That is a goal, of course. However, the antitrust laws may appear to many citizens to be a deliberately esoteric, confusing, complex, and highly technical obstacle that can be overcome only by equal parts of luck and recourse to magical incantations of arcane, legalistic mumbo jumbo. This discussion is intended to introduce the antitrust issues relating to PPO programs and to help make the course of their resolution more accessible and comprehensible to interested members of the public.

NOTES

1. The views expressed by the authors are their own and are not necessarily those of the Federal Trade Commission, any individual commissioner, or the Bureau of Competition. The authors wish to acknowledge the valuable contributions to their analysis made by Deputy Director Walter T. Winslow and Assistant to the Deputy Director David A. Giacalone in the Bureau of Competition.

2. Under virtually all states' insurance laws, for example, an insurance company, in effect, must honor the insured's assignment of indemnity health insurance benefits to any licensed physician. State statutes authorizing and regulating Blue Shield plans often require that any licensed physician is eligible to participate, and may prohibit Blue Shield from "interfering" in the doctor-patient relationship. These types of state laws effectively may prevent third-party payors from offering certain forms of PPO programs in many states without legislative changes. Some states, including California, Florida, Indiana, Loui-

siana, Michigan, Minnesota, Nebraska, Virginia, and Wisconsin, have enacted statutes that expressly permit third-party payors to adopt programs with negotiated provider contracts with a limited number of health care providers. For a more detailed survey of state laws affecting PPO programs, see State Legal Initiatives Program, Office of Legal and Regulatory Affairs, American Hospital Association, *Legal Developments Report No. 4, State Regulation of Preferred Provider Organizations: A Survey of State Statutes* (March 1984); T. Brooks, Regulation of PPOs under State Law (unpublished), presented at Conference on Preferred Provider Organizations, The National Health Lawyers Ass'n, Washington, D.C., September 21–22, 1983. Congressman Ron Wyden (D. Or.) also has introduced legislation—H.R. 2956, the "Preferred Provider Health Care Act of 1983"—that would exempt third-party payors of health care benefits from state laws, including insurance regulatory statutes, that would prevent their offering PPO programs.

3. See R. Cassidy, "Will the PPO Movement Freeze You Out?" *Medical World News* (April 18, 1983) pp. 264, 265, 267; D. Lefton, "PPOs: Interest High, Action Low So Far" 26 *American Medical News* 3, no. 33 (July 1 and 8, 1983); M. Waldholz, Discount Medicine" *The Wall Street Journal* (Nov. 22, 1983) pp. 1, 18.

4. *See* R. Cassidy, *supra* note 3 at 267; D. Lefton, *supra* note 3 at 3, 33.

5. *See* D. Lefton, *supra* note 3 at 33, 33–34. Physicians may also find PPO programs' fee-for-service reimbursement and rapid claims payment attractive, although neither of these characteristics is unique to PPO programs. *See* R. Cassidy, *supra* note 3 at 264; J. Bendix, "Employers Prefer Negotiating Fees" 12 *Modern Healthcare* 18, no. 20 (May 1982).

6. *See* R. Cassidy, *supra* note 3 at 270–274.

7. *See, e.g.,* Advisory Opinion Letter from Emily H. Rock, Secretary, Federal Trade Commission to Irwin S. Smith, M.D., President, Health Care Management Associates (June 7, 1983), 101 F.T.C. 1014 (1983), 3 Trade Reg. Rep. (CCH) ¶22,036; Business Review Letter from William F. Baxter, Assistant Attorney General, Antitrust Division, Department of Justice to Dr. Irwin S. Smith, President, Health Care Management Associates (Sept. 21, 1983); Business Review Letter from William F. Baxter, Assistant Attorney General, Antitrust Division, Department of Justice to Donald W. Fish, Esq., Senior Vice President and General Counsel, Hospital Corporation of America (Sept. 21, 1983); Opinion of the Attorney General of Ohio (to Laurel Call) (November 17, 1983), 1984-1 Trade Cas. (CCH) ¶65,796. *See also* Statement of George W. Douglas, Commissioner, on Behalf of the Federal Trade Commission, *Hearings on H.R. 2956: The Preferred Provider Health Care Act of 1983 Before the Subcomm. on Health and the Environment of the House Comm. on Energy and Commerce,* 98th Cong., 1st Sess. (Oct. 24, 1983); Letter from James C. Miller III, Chairman, Federal Trade Commission to Congressman Ron Wyden (July 29, 1983).

8. American Medical Ass'n 94 F.T.C. 701 (1979), *aff'd,* 638 F.2d 443 (2d Cir. 1980), *aff'd mem. by an equally divided Court,* 455 U.S. 676 (1982).

9. *See* Michigan State Medical Soc'y, 101 F.T.C. 191 (1983); Texas Dental Ass'n, 100 F.T.C. 536 (1982) (consent order); Association of Indep. Dentists, 100 F.T.C. 518 (1982) (consent order). *See also United States* v. *North Dakota Hospital Ass'n,* Civ. Action No. 82-131 (D. N. Dak. filed Aug. 25, 1983), Trade Reg. Rep. (CCH) ¶45,083 (Aug. 25, 1983). *But cf. Indiana Fed'n of Dentists* v. *FTC,* 1984-2 Trade Cas. (CCH) ¶66,229 (7th Cir. 1984), *reh'g den.,* No. 83-1700 (7th Cir. Dec. 21, 1984).

10. *See American Medical Ass'n* v. *United States,* 317 U.S. 519 (1943).

11. *Ibid.; United States* v. *Halifax Hospital Medical Center,* 1981-1 Trade Cas. (CCH) ¶64,151 (M.D. Fla. 1981); Forbes Health Sys. Medical Staff, 94. F.T.C. 1042 (1979) (consent order).

12. *See* Medical Serv. Corp. of Spokane County, 88 F.T.C. 906 (1976) (consent order); *Blue Cross of Wash. and Alaska* v. *Kitsap Physicians Serv.,* 1982-1 Trade Cas. (CCH) ¶64,588 (W.D. Wash. 1981). *See also* United States Department of Justice, untitled press release concerning Stanislaus Preferred Provider Organization, Inc. (Oct. 12, 1984), noting that SPPO's board had decided to voluntarily dissolve the physician-controlled PPO upon being informed that the Department of Justice was prepared to file a civil antitrust lawsuit against it. SPPO required its physician members to agree not to contract with any other PPO or health care delivery organization not affiliated with or sponsored by SPPO, and had enrolled 90 percent and 50 percent of the physicians, respectively, in the two Health Facilities Planning Areas in which it operated. The Department of Justice's investigation had led it to conclude that "SPPO's members formed and operated it for the purpose of inhibiting the development of competing PPOs and to suppress price competition and other forms of competition in the delivery of health care services by physicians," *Ibid.* at 2.

13. For example, a leading insurer might adopt so-called "most favored nation" clauses requiring participating providers to charge the leading insurer no more than the lowest fees the providers offer to any other prepayment programs, including a PPO program. Similarly, an insurer might adopt any discounted fee offered by a provider to a PPO program as the "usual" fee for that provider in calculating allowable reimbursement. Resolution of this particular situation might turn on the insurer's (or its controlling providers') intent—whether the policy was adopted to discourage competition from PPO programs or discounting by providers, or, in fact, to obtain the best purchase price in the market for the services of participating providers—or on the effects of the program—for example, whether it represented a use of market power to effectively discourage the development of PPO programs and the offering of discounts by providers in the market, and was not reasonably necessary for effective cost control by the dominant insurer.

14. Private antitrust challenges to PPO programs, brought by excluded providers and raising allegations of boycott or concerted refusal to deal, may be a common concern of many PPO programs. However, absent a showing that such exclusions were motivated by an anticompetitive purpose, rather than for legitimate business reasons, they would not normally be held to violate the antitrust laws, since it is unlikely that excluded providers could show that exclusion by a PPO program without market power would have substantial anticompetitive effects.

15. *E.g.,* insurance companies, Blue plans, employer self-insured health benefits programs, multiemployer trusts, etc.

16. "PPOs are not entities—they are groupings of contractual relationships. Physicians, hospitals, commercial insurance carriers, employers, third-party administrators, or entrepreneurs all can initiate a PPO. As initiators, they act as brokers, obtaining the fundamental agreements between providers—who agree to negotiate rates and/or take cost-containment measures—and employers—who agree to provide a certain volume of patients. Once the agreements are made, any of the parties can administer the PPO." K. Kodner, "PPOs: Should Physicians Do It Themselves?," *The Hospital Medical Staff* 2-3 (July 1983). *See also* K. Kodner, "Competition: Getting a Fix on PPOs," *Hospitals* 59 (Nov. 16, 1982).

17. Provider contracts may be either direct between individual health care providers and the third-party payor or indirect, involving either or both an organization representing providers and an intermediary arranging for provider services on behalf of the payor.

18. Individual practice association–type health maintenance organization.

19. *See* "PPOs Described as 'Same Old Girl in a New Dress,'" 11 *Health Services Information* 7-8 (January 23, 1984); D. Gibbons, "Doctors Hope Cut-Rate 'Preferred

Provider' Organizations Can Fill Empty Waiting Rooms, *Medical World News,* (Feb. 28, 1983) p. 57; "Preferred Providers: Discount Health Care," *Washington Report on Medicine & Health/Perspectives* (July 12, 1982) (unpaginated).

20. In a variation of PPO programs, sometimes called an "exclusive provider organization" or "EPO," subscribers generally are limited to using only participating providers for nonemergency care if they wish the program to pay for the services.

21. *See, e.g., Sausalito Pharmacy, Inc.* v. *Blue Shield of California,* 544 F. Supp. 230 (N.D. Cal. 1981), *aff'd per curiam,* 677 F.2d 47 (9th Cir. 1982), *cert. denied,* 103 S. Ct. 376 (1982); *Medical Arts Pharmacy of Stamford, Inc.* v. *Blue Cross and Blue Shield of Connecticut, Inc.,* 581 F. Supp. 1100 (D. Conn. 1981), *aff'd per curiam,* 657 F.2d 502 (2d Cir. 1982); *Feldman* v. *Health Care Service Corp.,* 562 F. Supp. 941 (N.D. Ill. 1982). *See also Michigan State Podiatry Ass'n* v. *Blue Cross and Blue Shield of Michigan,* 1982-2 Trade Cas. (CCH) ¶64,801 (E.D. Mich. 1982); *Michigan Ass'n of Psychotherapy Clinics* v. *Blue Cross and Blue Shild of Michigan,* 1982-83 Trade Cas. (CCH) ¶65,035 (Mich. Ct. App. 1982). Many of these cases paralleled or relied on analytically similar challenges to automobile insurers' programs of contracting with particular automobile repair shops to provide covered repair services. *See, e.g., Proctor* v. *State Farm Mutual Automobile Insurance Co.,* 1980-81 Trade Cas. (CCH) ¶63,591 (D.D.C. 1980), *aff'd,* 675 F.2d 308 (D.C. Cir. 1982), *cert. denied,* 103 S. Ct. 86 (1982); *Quality Auto Body, Inc.* v. *Allstate Insurance Co.,* 1980-2 Trade Cas. (CCH) ¶63,507 (N.D. Ill. 1980), *aff'd,* 660 F.2d 1195 (7th Cir. 1981), *cert. denied,* 455 U.S. 1020 (1982).

22. *See Maricopa,* 457 U.S. at 351 n.23, *quoting United States* v. *Socony-Vacuum Oil Co.,* 310 U.S. 150, 226 n.59 (1940).

23. *See Maricopa,* 457 U.S. at 342-8; *United States* v. *McKesson & Robbins, Inc.,* 351 U.S. 305, 309-10 (1956); *Socony-Vacuum Oil Co.,* 310 U.S. at 218.

24. *See Maricopa,* 457 U.S. at 350 n.22; *United States* v. *Trenton Potteries Co.,* 273 U.S. 392, 397-8 (1927).

25. 15 U.S.C. §1 (1982).

26. *See, e.g., Broadcast Music, Inc.* v. *Columbia Broadcasting Sys.,* 441 U.S. 1 (1979); *United States* v. *Realty Multi-List, Inc.,* 629 F.2d 1351 (5th Cir. 1980). *See also* Enforcement Policy with Respect to Physician Agreements to Control Medical Prepayment Plans (FTC Sept. 25, 1981), 46 Fed. Reg. 48982 (1981); Harrison, "Price Fixing, The Professions, and Ancillary Restraints: Coping with *Maricopa County,*" 1982 *U. Ill. L. Rev.* 925; Louis, "Restraints Ancillary to Joint Ventures and Licensing Agreements: Do *Sealy* and *Topco* Logically Survive *Sylvania* and *Broadcast Music*?," 66 *Va. L. Rev.* 879 (1980). For example, a merger between two competing firms eliminates the price competition that previously existed between them. The loss of this competition, however, is a necessary consequence of a broader enterprise—the full integration of the two companies—with potential improvements in overall efficiency. The legality of such merger agreements, therefore, depends on a careful assessment of their likely overall effect on competition in the market. No *per se* rule is applied.

27. *See also NCAA* v. *Board of Regents of the Univ. of Okla.,* 104 S. Ct. 2948 (1984), where the Supreme Court condemned the NCAA's policies and practices that limited its members' freedom to individually negotiate and enter into contracts for televising college football games, thereby restricting the output of such televised games. The Court, finding that the imposition by the NCAA of some horizontal restraints on competition by its members was "essential. . .[for] the product [intercollegiate league football]. . .to be available at all," 104 S. Ct. at 2961, did not apply the per se rule to the challenged restrictions. Rather, the NCAA was found liable under the rule of reason because it had failed to meet its "heavy burden" of justifying its horizontal price and output restraints, which are inherently suspect under the antitrust laws. The NCAA did not show either that the restrictions were necessary

to market the college football product at all, that they were necessary to enable the NCAA's individual members to compete in getting their games televised, or that they were so efficiency-enhancing as to increase overall output and promote competition.

28. 457 U.S. at 353-4 n. 28.

29. *Ibid.* at 356.

30. Many IPA-type HMOs are structured so as to meet this standard. *See* Enforcement Policy with Respect to Physician Agreements to Control Medical Prepayment Plans, *supra* note 21.

31. As a general rule, the antitrust risks will be higher whenever so many providers are involved in a venture that its actions might be viewed as reflecting "market power," *i.e.*, dictating, rather than responding to, competitive conditions in the market.

32. Further guidance in framing this type of analysis is contained in the *amicus curiae* brief filed jointly by the Department of Justice and the Federal Trade Commission in *NCAA* v. *Board of Regents of the Univ. of Okla. See* Brief for the United States as *Amicus Curiae* in Support of Affirmance, On Writ of Certiorari to the United States Court of Appeals for the Tenth Circuit, *NCAA* v. *Board of Regents of the Univ. of Okla.*, No. 83-271 (October Term, 1983). In the brief, the Department of Justice and the Federal Trade Commission argue that even where seemingly *per se* illegal horizontal agreements are involved, they should not be condemned outright if there is "a plausible efficiency justification for the practice, *i.e.,*...there [is] reason to believe that the restraint may...have significant efficiency benefits and therefore enhance competition and output." *Ibid.* at 9. For such a restraint to be legal, however, "it is not enough that a restraint accompanies an otherwise legitimate cooperative activity (such as the creation of a new product, or operation of a market exchange). A restraint that appears inherently likely to restrict output or enhance price [such as horizontal price-fixing] can be justified as an efficiency only if it is also 'capable of increasing the effectiveness of that cooperation and no broader than *necessary* for that purpose.' [citation omitted], (emphasis added)." *Ibid.* at 10.

This analysis and the Supreme Court's discussion in the *NCAA* case should help clarify the applicable legal standards. Ultimately, however, the legality of PPO programs involving collective price agreements or negotiations by participating providers will depend on application of those legal standards to varying sets of facts, requiring judgments whether the price agreement was, as a matter of proof, shown to be reasonably necessary for the effective operation of the venture.

33. It should be noted that competitors need not agree on the actual price for their actions to receive *per se* condemnation. For example, in *Catalano, Inc.* v. *Target Sales, Inc.*, 446 U.S. 643 (1980), the Supreme Court held to be *per se* illegal an agreement among competing beer wholesalers to eliminate short-term credit and require retailers to make payment in cash. The beer wholesalers did not integrate any aspect of their operations, and the Court viewed the arrangement as being tantamount to an agreement among competitors to eliminate discounts, which "falls squarely within the traditional *per se* rule against price-fixing." 446 U.S. at 648. In the PPO context, this analysis would probably prevent member providers from agreeing, for example, on a percentage discount from their usual fees that they would offer or accept in treating PPO program patients, unless, of course, the program involved sufficient integration by the providers to distinguish their agreement from the *Maricopa* and *Catalano* situations.

Similarly, providers probably cannot insulate themselves from potential antitrust liability for price fixing by concertedly appointing an agent to set fees or to negotiate on their behalf. Where direct joint fee setting or negotiation is not defensible as being ancillary to productive integration or efficiency-enhancing joint activity, use of such an agent should not change the underlying character of the activity or affect its legality. *See, e.g., Virginia Excelsior Mills, Inc.* v. *FTC*, 256 F.2d 538 (4th Cir. 1958).

Legal Issues

ANTITRUST CONSIDERATIONS RELATING TO PPOS

Richard C. Warmer
Partner
O'Melveny & Myers
Washington, DC

Bertrand M. Cooper
Partner
O'Melveny & Myers
Los Angeles, CA

Christopher W. Savage
Associate
O'Melveny & Myers
Washington, DC

☐ For purposes of this discussion, a PPO will be defined as a contractual arrangement with three basic characteristics: (1) "Preferred" health care providers agree to perform their services for patients referred to those providers by a third-party payor or group of such payors (e.g., insurance companies, unions, self-insured employers). (2) The referring payors agree to provide a financial incentive for their beneficiaries to use the "preferred" providers and may agree to other conditions as well, such as a guarantee of prompt payment.[1] (3) The providers agree to conditions relating to cost containment, typically including utilization review and frequently including discounted fees.[2] A broad range of variations on these basic features is possible, and it appears that each PPO has some distinctive characteristics.

The antitrust laws are designed to prevent private parties from entering into agreements or transactions the purpose or effect of which is to reduce competition in the market for a given product or service. The Department of Justice and the Federal Trade Commission (FTC) share governmental authority in enforcing the antitrust laws. In addition, private parties who claim to have been injured as a result of an alleged violation can sue under the antitrust laws for damages and injunctive relief.[3]

VARIATIONS ON BASIC CONCEPTS

There are basically three types of PPOs: provider-based, payor-based, and third-party based. Each is briefly discussed below.

PROVIDER-BASED PPOs

A provider-based PPO is, in essence, a joint marketing plan in which providers (doctors, hospitals, or both) form an organization through which they offer their services at agreed-upon rates. A provider-based PPO does not involve any new entities not currently present in the health care marketplace (excepting, of course, whatever administrative personnel may be hired), but instead changes the tenor of the relationship among existing marketplace participants. Providers may desire to create a PPO for a number of reasons, including a perceived need to respond to competition from other providers or health maintenance organizations (HMOs), a general desire to increase business, or a commitment to cost containment efforts. To the extent that providers forming a PPO integrate their service offerings and practices (so that they actually share jointly in each other's profits or losses), a provider-based PPO begins to lose its distinction from a traditional group practice that decides to contract directly with third-party payor entities. When the risks and rewards of a provider's practice are not fully shared with other participants in the PPO, substantial antitrust concerns may be raised, as discussed below.

PAYOR-BASED PPOs

A payor-based PPO is formed when a purchaser (or group of purchasers) contracts with providers who are willing to agree to provide more cost-effective care (through discounts, a more efficient style of practice, or utilization review) in return for the payor's agreement to encourage the payor's pool of patients (i.e., insureds, union members, employees) to utilize the participating providers. Unlike the traditional financing system, in which payors passively pay for care, payors in a payor-based PPO take the initiative to select a group of "preferred" providers and normally monitor the efficiency of the providers who are selected. The payor-based PPO thus represents a new role for payors.[4]

THIRD-PARTY PPOs

Finally, a third-party PPO involves a new entity (i.e., neither a provider nor a payor), which acts as a middleman, contracting with providers for reduced rates or an agreement to submit to utilization review and with payors for patients, and then putting the two together for a fee. The providers get more business, the payors get lower costs, and the third party gets revenues for putting the two together.

ANTITRUST ISSUES

Antitrust concerns relevant to PPOs arise primarily under Section 1 of the Sherman Act, which outlaws "[e]very contract, combination...or conspiracy, in restraint of trade."[5] The potentially broad sweep of this language has been narrowed by the courts in several important respects. In particular, most activities to which Section 1 applies are judged under the so-called Rule of Reason, which looks to the purpose and effect of the given restraint in its overall business context.[6] An activity is not illegal under the Rule of Reason unless it has a substantial adverse impact on competition within relevant product and geographic markets.[7]

In contrast, certain activities are judged under a rule of per se illegality. When the activity in question falls within this rule, a court does not inquire into the reasons for the restraint nor the substantiality of its effects on competition. Instead, the restraint is conclusively presumed to be illegal.[8] Activities that are per se illegal include price fixing, division of markets, and group boycotts.

1. *Price-Fixing:* A seller cannot collaborate with its competitors or its suppliers to fix the price of its products or services. Price fixing eliminates customers' ability to shop around for the best price—an essential attribute of competition—so the ban on price fixing is, in general, interpreted broadly by the courts.[9] As discussed below, price fixing concerns potentially affect all PPOs and may affect provider-based PPOs most of all.[10]

2. *Division of Markets:* A seller cannot decide with its competitors which of them gets which customers or territories.[11] The rationale for including division of markets within the per se ban is that, in essence, this practice creates a series of little monopolies, depriving customers within each area of the benefits of competition.

3. *Group Boycott:* Under some circumstances, it is unlawful for sellers to agree among themselves to refuse to deal with another entity or to coerce a third party not to deal with another entity.[12] These sorts of concerns could arise in several contexts relevant to PPOs, although antitrust doctrine relating to group boycotts is somewhat muddled.[13]

The formation and operation of a PPO can potentially raise questions in each of these problem areas.[14] However, the rule of per se illegality should not be applied uncritically to arrangements in this new field, since a PPO will often represent a procompetitive entry into the health care market.[15] As antitrust enforcement officials have noted, "PPOs have the potential to create competition in both the financing and provision of health care by offering price and coverage options that increase the economic incentive to control fee and utilization levels in the health services market."[16]

Another ground for antitrust concern is Section 2 of the Sherman Act, which outlaws monopolization of, or the attempt to monopolize, any market.[17] Section 7 of the Clayton Act may also be relevant.[18] Section 7 prohibits mergers or acquisitions that may tend substantially to lessen competition in a given market. PPO formation itself may be considered to be a "merger" if there is a true pooling of risks among PPO participants to form a new entity. Alternatively, a PPO may be viewed as a joint venture, the formation of which is analyzed under Section 7 standards.[19] The principal test used in analyzing the legality of mergers under Section 7 is the share of the market represented by the merging firms.[20]

SPECIFIC ANTITRUST CONCERNS

This section is organized around the antitrust issues that will confront the three types of PPOs noted above as they undertake several basic activities. These activities are PPO formation, pricing of providers' services, decisions regarding provider or payor membership in the PPO, and marketing the PPO's services. The focus of antitrust concern is slightly different with respect to each type of PPO.

As will be seen, most antitrust issues relating to PPOs are analyzed under the Rule of Reason, based on the detailed facts of a given case. As a rule of thumb, the smaller the percentage of the market held by a PPO—be it the "market" of providers or the "market" of patients—the less the likelihood of an antitrust problem.[21]

PROVIDER-BASED PPOs[22]

Formation

Usually, a provider-based PPO consists of a group of competitors (e.g., doctors or hospitals) acting jointly. Hence, the formation of such a PPO will often raise substantial antitrust issues, and participants should proceed cautiously. The Supreme Court in the *Maricopa* case posed but did not answer the question of how doctors, short of forming a completely integrated group practice, could jointly undertake PPO-related activities in such a way as to permit collaborative action on pricing.[23] Various forms of partial integration by doctors (e.g., risk sharing in the operation of a PPO plan but without merging medical practices) may have the effect of stimulating competition by creating an alternative delivery mechanism to compete with traditional insurance and HMOs.[24] But because *Maricopa* provides no guidance in this area, while at the same time applying conventional per se analysis to strike down the conduct challenged in that case, the decision may have the ironic effect of inhibiting innovative arrangements that have the potential to enhance price competition and efficiency.[25]

Apart from the question of functional integation, antitrust plaintiffs may contend in certain instances that a provider-based PPO has been formed for the purpose of providing a vehicle for actual or tacit collusion among providers.[26] In this respect, two Department of Justice business review letters dealing with proposed PPO plans are instructive.[27] In each case, the Department noted with approval that in connection with its formation the PPO had established procedures to isolate the participating providers from each other with respect to both prices[28] and control of the PPO's operations.[29]

Pricing

After *Maricopa,* a provider-based PPO has several options regarding prices, each with a different level of antitrust risk. Fully integrating the members' practices results in creation of a single entity for antitrust purposes and thereby eliminates the prospect of joint action. The course of action with the next lowest risk is probably a limited agreement among provider-members under which each provider expresses a willingness to negotiate, on an individual basis, some unspecified discount off normal rates.[30] Separate negotiations between the payors and individual providers would appear to solve the problem that was the focus of the Court's attention in *Maricopa,* since this would not involve joint action by competing providers with respect to price.[31]

If the provider-members of a PPO do not want to merge their medical practices but desire nevertheless to make joint decisions regarding the rates they will charge to payors, it is clear that there must be significant sharing in the risk of loss associated with the enterprise. Antitrust officials have observed that a "joint stake in the financial success (or failure) of the PPO venture, if sufficiently substantial, may help remove the arrangement's pricing decisions from *Maricopa's* per se condemnation."[32] But no concrete guidelines have been suggested as to how such a venture should be structured.[33] In general, the goal should be to show that joint pricing is reasonably ancillary to the particular form of operational integration adopted and that overall, the venture will be a procompetitive force in the health care market. The foundations for medical care discussed in *Maricopa* failed this test. The Court found that the doctors had no financial stake in the outcome of the plan and that joint fee-setting by the doctors was not a necessary feature of the arrangement.[34] Until the case law in this area is more fully developed, it is impossible to give any hard and fast rules regarding what forms of partial integration will be sufficient to assure analysis of joint pricing decisions under the Rule of Reason rather than the per se rule. Providers who wish to establish a PPO with a structure that gives provider-members control over prices but does not involve full integration of their practices should consult closely with counsel on alternative approaches that will minimize antitrust risks in light of the particular facts.

Membership

Membership encompasses three kinds of issues for provider-based PPOs. First, the proportion of a given area's providers (or payors) who are members of a given PPO will normally be relevant from an antitrust point of view. Second, if a PPO decides not to allow a given provider or payor to participate, antitrust issues may be raised. Finally, if a PPO seeks to forbid participating providers or payors from participating in other PPOs, this too will raise antitrust issues in most cases.

As to the first of these issues, the larger the proportion of an area's providers who are committed to the PPO, the greater the chance that their association and cooperation will have a negative impact on the competitive process. For example, if two doctors in a large community enter into a joint marketing agreement, this may be procompetitive if it allows those doctors to compete more effectively with a large and established group practice. On the other hand, an agreement among 50 percent of the doctors in an area to market their services jointly may substantially impair the operation of competitive forces.[35]

This issue appears to be of concern to antitrust enforcement authorities.[36] It is not clear just what percentage of providers in an area is enough to raise an antitrust question, but a 20 percent share apparently passes antitrust muster as far as the Department of Justice is concerned, while a 50 percent share does not.[37] The Department's concern over undue market share is probably based on both Section 1 and Section 2 of the Sherman Act. Section 2 will be relevant if the PPO is a vehicle for a dominant group of providers to collaborate and attempt to monopolize the provision of health care services. This may unduly lessen the choices available both to consumers and to group purchasers who are seeking to contract with preferred providers. Section 1 is also relevant here because the Rule of

Reason requires that the challenged practice have a substantial effect on competition,[38] and such an effect becomes more likely as the market share of the PPO increases.

One of the problems in having too great a percentage of area providers connected with a given PPO is. that it may then become difficult to justify excluding particular applicants.[39] A provider-based PPO may be challenged on the ground that by refusing to admit a doctor or hospital to membership the existing members have acted to exclude a competitor from an arrangement of substantial competitive significance.[40] The validity of such a challenge depends on whether PPO membership provides a distinctive competitive advantage that, in the particular community, cannot reasonably be secured in any other way. If that is the case, it may be that the outsider must be allowed in on reasonable terms.[41] It seems unlikely, however, that membership in any one provider-based PPO would have substantial competitive significance unless that PPO was a truly dominant force by virtue of its size or other advantage. Normally, the provider seeking membership could go out and start its own PPO or could join another PPO. At least during this early stage of PPO development, PPOs represent such a small proportion of the overall health care market that the competitive significance of membership in a given PPO would seem to be *de minimis*.

Plaintiffs (e.g., excluded providers) may seek to characterize PPO membership restrictions as a *group boycott* and thus illegal per se. But not all activities that can in some sense be considered a concerted refusal to deal are subject to the per se rule. A conventional illegal boycott involves concerted action to exclude competitors from a trade relationship that they need to compete effectively.[42] Although this type of conduct is subject to per se condemnation, other joint conduct that is plainly exclusionary in nature (e.g., an exclusive dealing contract) and could thus arguably be labelled a boycott is nevertheless judged under the Rule of Reason.[43] If membership in the PPO were required in order for the excluded provider to compete effectively, the classic group boycott situation would be presented.[44] Since this is not likely to be the case, characterizing the typical decision to exclude a provider as a group boycott would be inappropriate.[45]

The final membership issue for a provider-based PPO would arise if a given PPO required its members to agree not to join other PPOs (or HMOs or other alternative health care delivery models).[46] Such an agreement is, in essence, an exclusive dealing contract restricting the access of other PPOs (and their patients) to providers who are thus restrained. The potential plaintiff here would be another PPO that could not recruit a given provider due to the restrictive provision. Exclusive dealing arrangements are judged under the Rule of Reason.[47] The most relevant factor is the degree to which the market has been foreclosed to other entities.[48] This depends upon the proportion of providers in the community who are contractually prevented from joining other PPOs.[49] Under the Rule of Reason, the reasons for which a PPO imposes such a requirement are also relevant. For provider-based PPOs in particular, such a requirement may be reasonable as an ancillary restraint designed to assure maximum effort on behalf of the PPO by its provider-members, analogous to restrictions often imposed by partnerships on partners' outside activities.[50]

Marketing

The marketing focus of a provider-based PPO will be on finding potential users of its members' services, i.e., patients. Such a PPO can reach patients by seeking contracts with employers, unions, and so on, or it may approach a payor such as Blue Cross or a commercial insurance company, seeking to persuade the payor to offer the PPO as an option to the payors' insureds. In either case, the provider-based PPO can be expected to stimulate competition in the health care financing market because, assuming the PPO is a popular option, insurers who do not offer a PPO option will lose business to those who do. (Indeed, to the extent that employees desire a PPO option, even self-insured employers will be under pressure to offer one.) This is, without doubt, procompetitive activity.[51]

Despite this, marketing efforts by independent members of a provider-based PPO must be undertaken with some care. In particular, such provider-members must not agree that Dr. A will try to attract the business of one payor while Dr. B will pursue another payor. Such a marketing plan could be construed as a division of markets among the competing providers, a practice deemed per se illegal.[52] Instead, it would probably be well for a provider-based PPO to market the services of each provider-member to all patient sources. Even this must be done carefully, so that the marketing or negotiation process does not have the effect of allocating the patients from a particular payor to a particular doctor by joint action of the provider-members.

PAYOR-BASED PPOs

Payor-based PPOs face a slightly different set of antitrust concerns. Because payors are purchasers of health care, most (but not all) of these concerns are so-called vertical issues (involving purchaser–seller relationships) rather than horizontal issues (involving purchaser–purchaser and seller–seller relationships).[53]

Formation

Some payors will be large enough to set up their own PPOs. Such a PPO can conduct its activities with no involvement of other purchasers of care. As a result, formation per se of such a PPO would not appear to raise antitrust problems, so long as it does not become a vehicle for collusion among providers, and so long as too high a proportion of a given community's providers are not locked in to such a PPO by exclusive contracts. Smaller payors (e.g., smaller self-insured businesses) may not have a large enough patient base to be in a credible bargaining position with individual providers.[54] To form an effective PPO, several such smaller payors may band together to achieve economies of scale in purchasing. This joint action by buyers of the same products may raise antitrust concerns, since Section 1 of the Sherman Act applies to joint action of competing buyers, as well as sellers.[55]

However, there is considerable latitude under the antitrust laws for buyers to join together to achieve efficiencies in purchasing.[56] If too many payors (i.e., those representing too great a share of the patient pool) join a given PPO, this may present Section 1 or Section 2 problems. The argument would be that these payors have market power, allowing them to force onerous terms on providers and lessen competition among themselves for insureds. As long as the share of the total patient pool represented by the payor-based PPO remains relatively low, however, the arrangement should pass muster under the Rule of Reason.[57] Of course, a multipayor–based PPO (e.g., consisting of a group of self-insured employers) should take care that the practical effect of the operation of the PPO is not to allocate particular providers to particular payors by joint action, thereby lessening the range of options available to interested providers.[58]

Pricing

Payor-based PPOs face fewer antitrust risks with regard to pricing of services than do provider-based PPOs. First, a PPO based on the patient pool of a single payor is free to bargain with providers to reach the best deals possible. Such a PPO will normally be free to set the maximum prices it is willing to pay for given health care services.[59] Although thus setting a fixed price unilaterally will result in less price differentiation among providers, this effect is merely an incident to a legitimate bargaining process. Even a PPO of this type, however, must avoid becoming a vehicle for collusion resulting in standardization of doctor or hospital fees. In this connection, the enforcement authorities seem satisfied with confidentiality plans under which one provider does not know the prices at which other providers have agreed to perform services for PPO beneficiaries.[60]

The antitrust analysis of pricing of services by a PPO composed of several payors is less clear-cut.[61] Such a PPO is, in essence, a joint purchasing arrangement. Although it is clear that the Sherman Act applies to conspiracies among buyers as well as conspiracies among sellers,[62] it has also been held that joint purchasing activity can be procompetitive in the sense of creating efficiencies in the purchasing process. A joint purchasing plan among a group of hospitals has been upheld on this basis.[63] If the buyer group has monopsony power (i.e., if it represents a large proportion of the market), agreement on prices may constitute an antitrust violation, but if the buyer group does not have such power, there should be no antitrust violation, assuming that there are legitimate business reasons for the joint purchasing activity.[64]

Membership

A payor-based PPO comprised of more than one purchaser will face horizontal membership issues, analogous to those faced by provider-based PPOs, concerning the PPO's relationship to the payor marketplace: (1) Can the PPO exclude payors who wish to participate? (2) Can the PPO prevent its payor-members from joining other PPOs? Analysis of these issues is analogous to that discussed above in relation to provider-based PPOs. In general, exclusion of payors should not result in antitrust liability as long as membership in the particular PPO has little or no competitive significance and the excluded payor can join another PPO or form its own;[65] and exclusive dealing arrangements are judged under the Rule of Reason and may thus be justified on the facts of a given case.

Payor-based PPOs (whether comprising one or more payors) also face vertical issues based on the PPO's relationships with the provider marketplace. Here, the issues are: (1) What proportion of providers are under contract to the PPO? (2) What is the antitrust significance of excluding a provider? (3) Can the PPO require that providers under contract not deal with any other PPO?[66] In general, vertical relationships are judged under the Rule of Reason.[67] If a PPO decides not to enter into a contract with a given provider, it is an antitrust problem only if it results in the lessening of competition in a given market. It will be difficult for a provider to show such an effect in most cases. Moreover, as long as there is a clear procompetitive business reason for excluding a provider, such as a reputation for poor quality services or inefficiency, the Rule of Reason should be satisfied. In this regard, the analysis is somewhat analogous to hospital staff privileges cases.[68] In general, a legitimate business reason will suffice to make refusing to deal with a given provider acceptable from an antitrust perspective.[69]

Marketing

As with provider-based PPOs, a payor-based PPO will stimulate competition in the market for health care financing. The focus of marketing for a payor-based PPO will be on potential PPO subscribers, i.e., getting employers to agree to offer the PPO as an option to employees. (From a certain perspective, getting providers to sign up is a "marketing" function as well.) The PPO must of course not collaborate with other payor-based PPOs to set the premiums (or other terms of sale) to employers. Barring such collaboration, as long as the PPO does not encompass too great a share of the payors in a given region, marketing the PPO option should not raise antitrust concerns.

THIRD-PARTY PPOs

Third-party PPOs are new entrants into the health care financing market-place. Consequently, the antitrust concerns they face are somewhat different from those facing provider- or payor-based PPOs. Some issues remain the same, however.

Formation

The entity organizing a third-party–based PPO would not seem to face significant antitrust problems in connection with the formation of the PPO, because by definition this entity is neither a buyer nor a seller of health care. As such, its contracts with buyers (payors) and sellers (providers) are not themselves arrangements among competitors and thus do not raise immediate Section 1 questions. The act of forming such a PPO would raise antitrust issues only if it involved contracts with a substantial percentage of an area's providers. As noted above, the antitrust enforcement authorities seem concerned about this problem.[70]

Pricing

The third-party PPO would naturally want to strike the best deal possible with each provider. From a negotiating perspective, the best way to do this is probably to keep the terms of each individual deal in confidence. This confidential approach is also prudent as a means of alleviating any concerns that the PPO may facilitate collusion among providers. The Department of Justice has commented favorably on such confidentiality arrangements in its business review letters.[71] The only real concern in this area is that the third-party PPO not become a mechanism through which the provider-members learn each others' prices for various items and act to stabilize those prices.

Membership

A third-party PPO faces two main antitrust concerns regarding membership. First, if it contracts with too great a proportion of providers or payors in a given market, it may encounter the antitrust problems discussed previously. Second, if such a PPO restricts the ability of its providers or payors to join other PPOs, it may be challenged as foreclosing too great a share of the market. The resolution of these issues follows now-familiar lines. A third issue that arose in connection with both provider-based and multipayor-based PPOs—the refusal of a PPO to contract with a provider or payor—would not seem to present antitrust concerns for a third-party PPO, as long as the decision not to deal with a given provider or payor is truly unilateral with the PPO. As an independent entity, it is in general free to deal with whomever it chooses.[72]

Marketing

The third-party PPO has to "market" both to providers and payors. The principal antitrust concern here is that the PPO not act in collaboration with other PPOs in its marketing efforts. As long as such collaboration is avoided, however, the antitrust pitfalls in the marketing area for third-party PPOs would appear minimal.

CONCLUSION

As the preceding discussion indicates, antitrust analysis of any given PPO depends heavily on the details of the proposed organizational structure and on the supply of and demand for health care services in the community where the PPO will operate. Difficult questions of judgment may arise, but with careful consideration of these factors it should be possible in most instances to form and operate a viable PPO that can pursue the commercial and medical objectives of its participants without undue antitrust risk.

NOTES

1. Commonly the PPO agrees to pay 100 percent of the providers' fees if "preferred" providers are used, but only a lesser amount (e.g., 80 percent) if the patient chooses a "nonpreferred" provider.

2. For a similar definition, *see Antitrust and Alternative Health Care Systems*, Address by W. T. Winslow, Bureau of Competition, Federal Trade Comm'n, before the Antitrust and Health Care Sections of the Minnesota State Bar Association 19–20 (May 25, 1983) ("Winslow").

3. 15 U.S.C. § 15 (1982).

4. An interesting practical issue here is how the providers are chosen. Fees, style of practice, efficiency, and the quality of care delivered would all appear to be factors relevant to the choice of providers, but reliable information on these factors is often scarce. Insurance company claims records may be one source, and information may be publicly available in some states, especially regarding hospitals.

5. 15 U.S.C. § 1 (1982).

6. *See Arizona* v. *Maricopa County Medical Soc'y,* 457 U.S. 332, 342–43 & n. 13 (1982); *Bd. of Trade of Chicago* v. *United States,* 246 U.S. 231, 238 (1918).

7. *See Gough* v. *Rossmoor Corp.,* 585 F.2d 381, 389 (9th Cir. 1978), *cert. denied,* 440 U.S. 936 (1979). The damage must be to competition itself, not merely to individual competitors. *See Brunswick Corp.* v. *Pueblo Bowl-O-Mat, Inc.,* 429 U.S. 477, 488 (1977); *Blue Cross* v. *Kitsap Physicians Serv.,* 1982-1 Trade Cas. (CCH) ¶64,588 at 73,208 (W.D. Wash. 1982). "Lively legal competition will result in the efficient and shrewd businessman routing the inefficient and imprudent from the field." *Richter Concrete Corp.* v. *Hilltop Concrete Corp.,* 691 F.2d 818, 823 (6th Cir. 1982). This activity is encouraged, not discouraged, by the antitrust laws. *Id.*

8. *See Jefferson Parish Hosp. Dist. No. 2* v. *Hyde,* 104 S. Ct. 1551, 1556 & n. 10 (1984).

9. Not all agreements relating to or affecting price are per se illegal, however. For instance, an agreement among the joint producers of a new product as to the price at which they will sell the product is judged under the Rule of Reason. *See Broadcast Music, Inc.* v. *Columbia Broadcasting Sys.,* 441 U.S. 1 (1979).

10. *See Maricopa, supra* note 6, 457 U.S. at 342–48.

11. *See United States* v. *Topco Assoc., Inc.*, 405 U.S. 596 (1972).

12. *See, e.g., United States* v. *General Motors Corp.*, 384 U.S. 127 (1966); *Klor's, Inc.* v. *Broadway-Hale Stores, Inc.*, 359 U.S. 207 (1959); *Associated Press* v. *United States*, 326 U.S. 1 (1945).

13. *See, e.g., Ron Tonkin Gran Turismo, Inc.* v. *Fiat Distributors, Inc.*, 637 F.2d 1376, 1381–88 (9th Cir.), *cert. denied*, 454 U.S. 831 (1981); *Blue Cross* v. *Kitsap Physicians Serv., supra* note 7, at 73,207; *Pontius* v. *Children's Hospital*, 552 F. Supp. 1352, 1367–71 (W.D.Pa. 1982); *Robinson* v. *Magovern*, 521 F. Supp. 842 (W.D.Pa. 1981), *aff'd mem.*, 688 F.2d 824 (3d Cir.), *cert. denied* 103 S. Ct. 302 (1982); *In re Indiana Fed'n of Dentists*, 101 F.T.C. 57, 167–68 (1983).

14. *See Preferred Provider Organizations and the Antitrust Laws*, Address by A. N. Lerner, Bureau of Competition, Federal Trade Comm'n, before the Washington Health Letters and Business Week Conference on Preferred Provider Organizations 4–5 (Sept. 30, 1983) ("Lerner").

15. "The *per se* rule should not be lightly applied to business relationships with [the] potential for enhancing competition." *Medical Arts Pharmacy* v. *Blue Cross & Blue Shield*, 675 F.2d 502, 505 (2d Cir. 1982). *See In re Michigan State Medical Soc'y*, 101 F.T.C. 191, 289–91 (1983).

16. Winslow, *supra* note 2, at 20. Until the advent of PPOs and similar alternatives to the conventional fee-for-service basis of health care delivery, there was limited potential for genuine economic competition among providers. Under the unique system of third-party payment buyers and sellers have not been price-sensitive, and therefore the industry, particularly the hospital sector, has not responded to normal competitive forces. *See* A. Enthoven, *Health Plan* xvii–xviii (1980); J. Newhouse, *The Economics of Medical Care* 63 (1978).

17. 15 U.S.C. §2 (1982).

18. 15 U.S.C. §18 (1982).

19. *See United States* v. *Penn-Olin Chemical Co.*, 378 U.S. 158 (1964).

20. *See United States* v. *Philadelphia Nat'l Bank*, 374 U.S. 321 (1963); Antitrust Div., Dep't of Justice, Merger Guidelines, 49 Fed. Reg. 26,823 (1984).

21. *See, e.g., Blue Cross* v. *Kitsap Physicians Serv., supra* note 7; *In re Indiana Fed'n of Dentists, supra* note 13, 101 F.T.C. at 173.

22. The FTC's stated enforcement policy regarding "physician agreements to control medical prepayment plans" (e.g., Blue Shield plans) concludes that generally the formation and activities of such plans should be judged under the Rule of Reason. *See* 46 Fed. Reg. 48,982, 48,986 (1981). These plans are somewhat analogous to provider-based PPOs, and FTC officials have indicated that the analysis contained in that statement is applicable to PPOs. *See* Winslow, *supra* note 2, at 27–32.

23. *See Maricopa, supra* note 6, 457 U.S. at 356–57; *Preferred Provider Organizations: How Potential Problems of Horizontal Price Fixing Can Be Avoided or Minimized*, Address by L. B. Costilo, Bureau of Competition, Federal Trade Comm'n, before the American Bar Association Forum Committee on Health Law 11–15 (Feb. 3, 1984) ("Costilo").

24. *See* Advisory Opinion *re* Health Care Management Associates, 101 F.T.C. 1014, 1016 (1983); Winslow, *supra* note 3, at 27–32; Opinion of the Attorney General of Ohio, 1983-2 Trade Cas. (CCH) ¶65,796 (November 17, 1983). *See also* Department of Justice Business Review Letter from W. F. Baxter to D. W. Fish at 3–4 (Sept. 21, 1983) ("HCA Letter"); Department of Justice Business Review Letter from W. F. Baxter to I. S. Smith at 4 (Sept. 21, 1983) ("HCMA Letter").

25. Winslow, *supra* note 2, at 22–23.

26. "Tacit collusion," also referred to as "oligopolistic interdependence" and "conscious parallelism," refers to the behavior of competitors who know that it is to their joint advantage to, say, maintain prices at a high level and therefore do so without any explicit agreement to this effect. Tacit collusion in and of itself is probably not illegal, *see, e.g., Sausalito Pharmacy, Inc.* v. *Blue Shield,* 544 F. Supp. 230, 239–40 (N.D. Cal. 1981), *aff'd per curiam,* 677 F.2d 47 (9th Cir.), *cert. denied,* 103 S. Ct. 376 (1982), but a showing of parallel anticompetitive behavior can provide a basis, in connection with other evidence, for an inference that an actual conspiracy exists. *See id. See also* L. Sullivan, *Handbook of the Law of Antitrust* 315–22 (1977); R. Bork, *The Antitrust Paradox* 101–04 (1978).

27. *See* note 24, *supra.*

28. *See* HCA Letter, *supra* note 24, at 2; HCMA Letter, *supra* note 24, at 2–3.

29. *See* HCMA Letter, *supra* note 24, at 4; HCA Letter, *supra* note 24, at 3.

30. *See* Lerner, *supra* note 14, at 11–13. An agreement among competitors to discount their normal rates by a specified amount or percentage would likely be caught within the ban against price-fixing. *See Catalano, Inc.* v. *Target Sales, Inc.,* 446 U.S. 643 (1980) (agreement among competitors fixing credit terms, but not prices, held illegal per se).

31. 457 U.S. at 351–53. *See* Costilo, *supra* note 23, at 7–9.

32. Lerner, *supra* note 14, at 16.

33. *See* Costilo, *supra* note 23, at 11–15; Lerner and Narrow, *supra* note 30, at 857.

34. *See Maricopa, supra* note 6, 457 U.S. at 340. *See* Winslow, *supra* note 2, at 25–27.

35. The Court in *Maricopa* noted that the medical foundations at issue in that case encompassed 70 percent of the area's doctors. *See Maricopa, supra* note 6, 457 U.S. at 352. The Department of Justice has issued an unfavorable business review letter with respect to a PPO that would have involved 50 percent of the physicians in Modesto, California, and 90 percent of the physicians in neighboring Turlock. Department of Justice, Press Release (Oct. 12, 1984) ("Stanislaus Release").

36. *See* HCA Letter, *supra* note 24, at 4; HCMA Letter, *supra* note 24, at 4–5.

37. *See* HCMA Letter, *supra* note 24, at 4–5; Stanislaus Release, *supra* note 35, at 2.

38. *See Brunswick Corp.* v. *Pueblo Bowl-O-Mat, Inc., supra* note 7, 429 U.S. at 488–89; *Gough* v. *Rossmoor, supra* note 7, 585 F.2d at 389.

39. *See* H. R. Halper & J. Miles, *Antitrust Guide for Health Care Coalitions,* ¶¶3.5, 6.5 (d) (1983) ("Halper & Miles"); Lerner, *supra* note 14, at 15.

40. *See Associated Press* v. *United States, supra* note 12; *United States* v. *St. Louis Terminal R.R. Ass'n,* 224 U.S. 383 (1912); *Hecht* v. *Pro-Football, Inc.,* 570 F.2d 982 (D.C. Cir. 1977), *cert. denied,* 436 U.S. 956 (1978).

41. *See Terminal R.R. Ass'n, supra* note 40, 224 U.S. at 411; *Hecht* v. *Pro-Football, supra* note 40, 570 F.2d at 992–93.

42. *See Langston Corp.* v. *Standard Register Co.,* 553 F. Supp. 632, 638 (N.D.Ga. 1982).

43. *See id.* at 638–39 & n. 13. *See also Handbook of the Law of Antitrust, supra* note 26, at 259.

44. *See, e.g., Klor's Inc., supra* note 12 (conspiracy pursuant to which suppliers would sell to plaintiff only at artificially high prices).

45. Courts will look to the economic substance of the restraint in question to determine if per se treatment is appropriate in a given case. *See Langston Corp.* v. *Standard Register Co., supra* note 42, 553 F. Supp. at 638. *See also Ron Tonkin, supra* note 13, 637 F.2d at 1381–88; American Bar Ass'n, *Antitrust Law Developments (Second)* 40–49 (1984) (*"Antitrust Law Developments"*).

46. A similar issue would arise if a PPO required the payors with whom it dealt not to contract with other PPOs. This issue would be subject to analysis under the principles outlined in this paragraph. It seems unlikely that a PPO would have sufficient leverage to secure such an agreement with a payor having a patient pool large enough to raise a serious antitrust question.

47. *Tampa Elec. Co.* v. *Nashville Coal Co.*, 365 U.S. 320, 333–35 (1961). *See Jefferson Parish, supra* note 8, 104 S. Ct. at 1575 (O'Connor, J., concurring).

48. *Standard Oil Co.* v. *United States*, 337 U.S. 293 (1949). *See Jefferson Parish, supra* note 8, 104 S. Ct. at 1576 (O'Connor, J., concurring).

49. If a given PPO does "control" a large percentage of an area's physicians, a restriction on joining other PPOs may transgress antitrust standards. *See Blue Cross* v. *Kitsap Physicians Serv., supra* note 7. A restriction barring a sole provider hospital in a rural area from serving more than one PPO may fall on the theory that such a hospital is an "essential facility," *see Hecht* v. *Pro-Football, supra* note 40, and even in urban areas some hospitals may as a practical matter be the only source of a given service or specialty.

50. *See Continental T.V., Inc.* v. *GTE Sylvania, Inc.*, 433 U.S. 36 (1977); *United States* v. *Addyston Pipe & Steel Co.*, 85 Fed. 271, 280–81 (6th Cir. 1898), *affirmed in relevant part*, 175 U.S. 211 (1899). In these circumstances, the term of the exclusive contract should not be unduly long. *See Antitrust Law Developments, supra* note 45, at 98.

51. *See* FTC Advisory Opinion, *supra* note 24, 101 F.T.C. at 1016.

52. *See United States* v. *Topco Assoc., Inc., supra* note 11.

53. *See Ron Tonkin, supra* note 13, 637 F.2d at 1383–85 (discussion of significance of vertical/horizontal distinction). *Cf. Medical Arts Pharmacy* v. *Blue Cross & Blue Shield*, 518 F. Supp. 1100, 1106 (D. Conn. 1981), *aff'd per curiam*, 675 F.2d 502 (2d Cir. 1982).

54. Note, however, that such smaller payors may be the most likely customers of provider-based and third-party PPOs.

55. *See Mandeville Island Farms, Inc.* v. *American Crystal Sugar Co.*, 334 U.S. 219 (1948).

56. *See White and White, Inc.* v. *American Hospital Supply Corp.*, 723 F.2d 495, 508 (6th Cir. 1983). *See also Langston Corp.* v. *Standard Register Co., supra* note 42, 553 F. Supp. at 639; *Webster County Memorial Hosp.* v. *United Mine Workers*, 536 F.2d 419, 420 (D.C. Cir. 1976) (*per curiam*); *Antitrust Law Developments, supra* note 45, at 53 & n. 366.

57. *See Medical Arts Pharmacy* v. *Blue Cross & Blue Shield, supra* note 53, 518 F. Supp. at 1108 n. 9 (a "buyer conspiracy" is illegal only if, *inter alia*, the buyers have monopsony power). Professors Areeda and Turner believe that, as long as the total market share of a joint buying plan is relatively low, such a plan should be presumptively legal. V P. Areeda & D. Turner, *Antitrust Law* ¶1104b3 (1980). In a related discussion, they conclude that an aggregation of buyers representing less than 25 percent of a given market would raise no antitrust concerns. *See* IV P. Areeda & D. Turner, *Antitrust Law* ¶¶964b, 965a (1980).

58. *See* Halper & Miles, *supra* note 39, ¶6.4.

59. As long as the market share of the PPO is relatively low and as long as the maximum amount is set unilaterally by the payor rather than collusively by the providers, this practice should be acceptable under antitrust standards. *See* Costilo, *supra* note 23, at 8, *citing Sausalito Pharmacy, Inc.* v. *Blue Shield, supra* note 26; *Medical Arts Pharmacy* v. *Blue Cross & Blue Shield, supra* note 53; and *Feldman* v. *Health Care Service Corp.*, 562 F. Supp. 941 (N.D. Ill. 1982).

60. *See* HCA Letter, *supra* note 24, at 2; HCMA Letter, *supra* note 24, at 2–3.

61. This discussion assumes that the payor-members would operate entirely independently with respect to the determination of premiums and other terms of the benefits they offer.

62. *See Mandeville Island Farms, Inc.* v. *American Crystal Sugar Co.*, *supra* note 55, 334 U.S. at 235–236.

63. *See White and White, Inc.* v. *American Hospital Supply, supra* note 56.

64. *See* notes 56 and 57, *supra*. Moreover, to the extent that a payor-based PPO can properly be characterized as a joint venture among the payor-members, the logic of *Maricopa*, discussed above in connection with pricing by provider-based PPOs, would appear to apply to move purchasing decisions by the payor-based PPO into the realm of the Rule of Reason.

65. *See Blue Cross* v. *Kitsap Physicians Serv.*, *supra* note 7.

66. The analysis of membership issues facing provider-based PPOs is analogous to some degree. *See* discussion at notes 36–50, *supra*, and accompanying text.

67. *See Oreck Corp.* v. *Whirlpool Corp.*, 579 F.2d 126, 131 (2d Cir.) *(en banc)*, *cert. denied*, 439 U.S. 946 (1978).

68. *See* Winslow, *supra* note 2, at 8. *See also Pontius* v. *Children's Hospital, supra* note 13.

69. *See* Lerner, *supra* note 14, at 15–16 ("A non-provider controlled PPO should not face significant antitrust risk from unilateral decisions to exclude particular providers or limit its panel size.") An exception would be if the PPO's decision not to deal with the provider was not based on its own business judgment, but rather on collusive pressure applied by the existing providers under contract. Such conduct is illegal per se. *See United States* v. *General Motors, supra* note 12.

70. *See* HCMA Letter, *supra* note 24, at 4–5; Stanislaus Release, *supra* note 35, at 2.

71. HCMA Letter, *supra* note 24, at 2–3.

72. *See Ron Tonkin, supra* note 13, 637 F.2d at 1387.

Legal Issues

FUNDAMENTALS OF PPO CONTRACTING

Donald A. Jackson

Robert E. Ward

Thomas A. Pedreira
All from
Kimble, MacMichael, Jackson & Upton
Fresno, CA

This article is concerned with legal issues relating to PPO contracts. It will address issues that are fundamental in negotiating a PPO contract and will provide general background information relating to PPO contractual relationships.

OVERVIEW OF CONTRACTUAL RELATIONSHIPS

PPO DEFINED

A PPO may generally be defined for contracting purposes as an entity that contracts with both providers of health care (providers) and payors of health care costs (payors) to establish "preferred rates" of compensation that contracting or "preferred" providers will accept as payment in full for services rendered to patients covered by health benefits of contracting payors. It is also important to define a PPO in terms of the specific PPO contracts that may exist with providers and payors, because these agreements largely establish the legal and functional framework in which a PPO operates.

PPO CONTRACTS

The three principal types of PPO contracts are provider contracts, payor contracts, and provider/payor contracts. However, other PPO contracts for services such as claims administration and utilization review may also be involved in a PPO program. Each of these PPO contracts is briefly summarized below.

Provider Contracts

PPO contracts between providers and a PPO are an important element of a PPO program and are the central focus of this article. A PPO may contract with physician providers, institutional providers (i.e., hospitals), and ancillary providers (i.e., home health care services, ambulance services, laboratory services, physical therapists). The main purpose of provider contracts is to contractually obligate providers on an individual basis to accept preferred rates of compensation for services rendered. Those providers that contract with the PPO will constitute its panel of preferred providers who will accept contracted-for preferred rates of compensation for health services given to patients covered by contracting payors.

Payor Contracts

Fundamental PPO contracts also include the agreements between the PPO and the payors. Contracting payors may include employer groups, insurers, and government entities. The primary purpose of a payor contract is to obligate a contracting payor to make payment to participating providers at preferred rates for services rendered to patients covered by the payor's health benefits.

Provider/Payor Contracts

PPO contracts may be entered into directly between participating providers and participating payors. One reason why these agreements may occur is to allow one contracting party to have direct recourse against the other. In a traditional indemnity situation, this recourse would not be available because there would not be a contract directly between a provider and a payor. The contractual relationships in this latter situation are only those between a provider and a patient or between the patient and the payor. Thus, if a payor failed to compensate a provider for services performed, the provider would need to first seek recourse against the patient for unpaid bills rather than against the responsible payor.

Regulatory considerations may also be involved in determining whether a direct provider/payor contractual relationship should be developed. For example, the California Department of Corporations has taken the position that a PPO may be subject to its regulatory jurisdiction if provider/payor contracts do not exist that supersede any activities of the PPO that may be characterized as "providing or arranging for the provision of health care services." This concern and additional regulatory considerations that may be relevant to PPO contracting are discussed later in this article.

Claims Administration and Utilization-Review Contracts

While the focus of this article is on the three types of PPO contracts discussed above, a PPO may also need to contract with other parties for services that will usually be a part of a PPO program. Such contracts will most often include arrangements to provide claims administration or utilization review services. To illustrate, a PPO may need to contract with a third-party administrator to provide claims processing services for participating payors and providers. Administration of claims will usually be important to a PPO program because prompt payment and administration of claims tend to enhance the successful marketing of a PPO.

Peer review, quality assurance, and utilization review services will also typically be important to a PPO's operations because most PPOs contemplate an effective review of professional services as necessary to promote cost containment objectives inherent in the PPO concept. If a third-party organization is to provide these services, a utilization review contract will be necessary.

PPO SPONSORSHIP

The existence of or need for the contractual relationships described above depends on the sponsorship of the PPO and whether it is established as a separate and distinct legal entity from its sponsoring organization. When a PPO is established as a legal entity separate from that of its sponsoring organization, each of the PPO contracts described above will most likely be necessary. However, as demonstrated in the following paragraphs, there may be some variation required in the operational contracts of a PPO when a sponsoring organization is itself a PPO contracting party.

Third-Party Sponsorship

A PPO may be sponsored by any third party given the proper organizational ability and financial capacity. In this situation, there will be a need for each of the PPO contracts discussed above because the PPO will most likely be a distinct legal entity. A third-party entrepreneur will almost always create a PPO as a separate corporate entity to limit liability exposure.

There does not appear to be much regulatory restriction at the present time in many areas of the country with respect to PPO organizational requirements. Thus, a PPO is in relative terms easier for a third-party entrepreneur to organize than other health care organizations such as HMOs which, unlike PPOs, are clearly regulated. This is especially true when a PPO is structured so that it does not provide or deliver health care services but instead limits its activities to establishing and administering preferred rates of compensation for services that are actually provided or delivered by participating providers (Exhibit 1).

EXHIBIT 1
Third-Party-Sponsored PPO

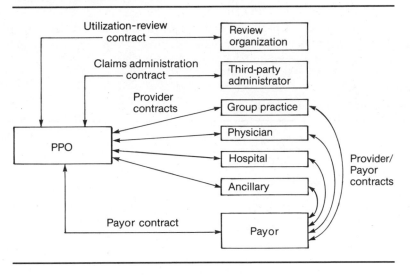

Provider Sponsorship

A provider or provider group organizing a PPO will not generally abrogate the need for provider contracts or the other PPO contracts discussed above. Individual providers will usually continue to independently participate in the PPO, which reasonably dictates that a separate contract should be entered into between each participating provider and the PPO. For example, while a Foundation for Medical Care made up of physician members may sponsor a PPO program by doing business as a PPO, it would probably still require individual physician provider contracts. Participating physician providers would not be rendering professional services on behalf of the PPO through their membership in the Foundation. Their participation should instead involve agreeing as independent contractors to accept payment at preferred rates for services they provide through their own practice to patients covered by a contracting payor's health benefits. For similar reasons, a PPO sponsored by a hospital–

physician joint venture would also require each of the provider joint venturers to contract directly with the PPO.

A situation in which a separate provider contract may not be required would involve a provider who is an employee of an integrated medical group that renders services as a professional corporation. In this case, a physician employment contract may be required, but it should be distinguished from a provider contract that intends an independent contractor relationship. In the event that the medical group was itself acting in the capacity of a PPO, then provider contracts would probably not be required as between the medical group and its employee providers, because the medical group as a single legal entity would be acting in the capacity of both a provider and a PPO. In contrast, the medical group may itself act only as a preferred provider, and in this instance a provider contract would be required between the provider medical group corporation and a PPO operating as a separate legal entity (Exhibit 2).

EXHIBIT 2
Provider-Sponsored PPO

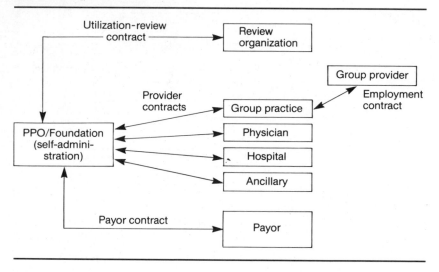

Payor Sponsorship
A PPO may also be sponsored by a payor or by payor groups. In a situation where the sponsoring payor or payor group is, from a legal standpoint, a single integrated entity doing business as a PPO, then there would be no need for a payor contract, because the PPO and the payor or payor group would be characterized as the same entity. For example, an integrated employer group or an insurer operating as a PPO may in either situation be characterized as a single payor entity indistinguishable from

the PPO, and therefore, a PPO payor contract would not be required. (Exhibit 3). However, as long as a participating payor and the PPO are distinct legal entities, an express payor contract should be developed in order to more clearly establish the respective rights and duties of the parties.

EXHIBIT 3
Payor-Sponsored PPO

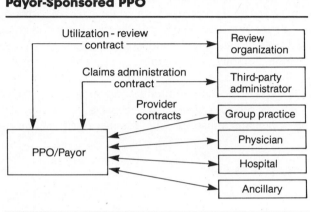

REGULATION OF PPOs

A PPO will contract with providers and payors to establish preferred rates of compensation but generally does not itself directly provide health care services. Therefore, the duties of a PPO should be limited to necessary administrative activity (discussed below) that is involved in coordinating participation by contracting payors and providers. This is a very important consideration in contract drafting, because a PPO may become subject to undesired or unintended regulatory scrutiny by using language in its contracts that implies that it is engaging in regulated activities.

For example, the State of California has adopted legislation regulating any entity that "provides or arranges for the provision of health care services," and this could arguably bring within its scope the activities of certain PPOs. However, it may be persuasively argued that to the extent a PPO limits its activities to those that are administrative in nature and does not impose upon either the professional judgment of the participating providers or upon determinations of contracting payors relating to health benefits coverage, the PPO should not be within the scope of this legislation or similar regulatory provisions. Whether this is the case depends largely on using appropriate language in PPO contracts. To illustrate, a provider contract should probably not refer to "services rendered pursuant to the PPO agreement" but should instead refer to "services rendered for which the provider is compensated pursuant to the PPO agreement."

COMPARISON OF PPOs WITH OTHER HEALTHCARE DELIVERY SYSTEMS

TRADITIONAL INDEMNITY ARRANGEMENTS

The direct contractual relationship between the PPO and a provider generally requires the provider to accept a certain payment for services rendered as payment in full. In contrast, a provider is not limited in a traditional indemnity situation to accepting a payor's rate of compensation as payment in full for services rendered. Thus, a patient may experience substantial and oftentimes unexpected copayments under a standard indemnity situation. Although copayments usually are not completely eliminated in a PPO program, they may be substantially reduced if a participating provider is contractually limited to accepting the preferred rates as payment in full for services given. An exception to this may happen in a coordination of benefits situation, which is discussed later in the article.

PREPAID HEALTH PLANS

Entities such as health care service plans and HMOs generally provide or arrange for the provision of health care services on a capitation or prepaid basis. This places them at financial risk to the extent that they charge only a fixed amount per patient for all services which that patient may require during the premium period. Therefore, in order to control costs, these entities usually contract with providers for a fixed rate of compensation in a manner similar to that used by PPOs. However, a patient's freedom of choice of providers is limited to the extent that payment is often not made for services rendered outside the plan. In contrast, a PPO will generally not limit a patient's freedom of choice but instead contracts for rates of compensation charged by participating providers. This usually allows a patient to limit the copayments for which he or she is responsible by electing to be treated by a participating provider.

PRELIMINARY CONTRACT CONSIDERATIONS

Prior to negotiating a PPO contract, each party to the agreement should consider whether the parties have the capacity to enter into the agreement and be aware of the fact that a PPO contract may not need to be reduced to writing to be legally binding. There are also several economic and administrative considerations to keep in mind prior to entering into an agreement.

CAPACITY OF THE PARTIES

An elementary but nonetheless fundamental issue involved in PPO contracting is whether each contracting party has the legal capacity to enter into a binding agreement. This is especially important in a PPO context from the standpoint that PPO regulatory requirements, if any, are not well delineated at this point in time. Therefore, financial viability and competency of the management staff of a PPO may not be as easily assumed as might be the case with clearly regulated entities such as insurers or institutional providers. Accordingly, prior to negotiating a PPO contract, a contracting party may want to request financial and legal information from the other party sufficient to resolve these concerns and also to have the other party represent in the contract that it has the legal capacity to enter into the agreement.

To illustrate the concerns that may arise, there may be laws in certain states that implicitly prohibit the formation of PPOs. In this regard, the PPO concept of establishing preferred rates of compensation is not a novel concept to the health care field. For example, nonprofit foundations for medical care have for many years been operating as PPOs by establishing preferred rates of compensation that member physicians would accept as payment in full for services rendered to patients covered under health plans administered by the foundations. However, the ability of payors to form their own PPOs and directly enter into contracts with providers for alternative rates of compensation is a relatively new development. It was only recently in California that legislation was enacted that expressly authorized payors to establish preferred provider programs. Prior to this, the development of payor-sponsored PPOs was impeded by limitations on the corporate practice of medicine and statutory provisions requiring complete freedom of choice of providers for patients covered by health benefits of regulated payors.

NEED FOR A WRITTEN AGREEMENT

Another fundamental point to consider prior to negotiating a PPO contract is that such contracts probably do not need to be in writing to be legally binding. An oral PPO contract may be enforceable because provisions relating to the statute of frauds under applicable law generally do not prohibit the enforcement of oral contracts to provide compensation for services delivered. However, it is always advisable to memorialize contractual relationships in writing because it enables more effective interpretation of the agreement between the parties. In the event of a dispute, a written agreement also assists in establishing the duties and obligations of the respective contracting parties, which in many instances will allow for a satisfactory resolution of any disputes that may arise.

ECONOMIC CONSIDERATIONS

In addition to issues relating to compensation that are discussed in the context of specific PPO contracts, an initial determination should be made as to whether a contracting party would be placed at economic risk by participating in the PPO. Unlike an HMO or similar prepaid health care entity, a PPO may not need to place itself or participating providers at economic risk. For instance, if preferred rates are established on a fee-for-service basis, there is generally no need, as is often the case with HMOs, for risk pools or holdbacks in provider compensation.

There may, however, be other considerations that could make some risk sharing desirable. For example, a certain degree of risk sharing is beneficial from an antitrust standpoint. The rationale behind sharing risk to address antitrust concerns relates to the fact that providers who might otherwise be characterized as competitors for price-fixing purposes may not be competitors with each other with respect to PPO participation when there is at least some degree of economic risk sharing.

Another important economic consideration is the extent to which exclusivity is called for in a PPO contract. Generally, a payor participating in or establishing a PPO program will not limit coverage for health benefits so as to provide reimbursement for services given only by participating providers. This type of situation, commonly referred to as an exclusive provider organization, is not discussed in this article other than to note that any PPO contract should be analyzed to determine whether it actually contemplates an exclusive provider arrangement.

A more common issue relating to exclusivity is whether the PPO, for marketing purposes, intends to enhance a provider's competitive position by restricting provider participation in order to increase a provider's relative patient base. From a payor's standpoint, this may also be desirable, because it may encourage participating providers to accept lower reimbursement rates in return for the higher patient volume. At the other extreme, a broad-based provider panel would allow for greater freedom in a patient's choice of providers. This would, however, reduce each provider's relative patient base and may therefore also reduce the incentive of providers to accept lower reimbursement rates.

State legislation may also have an effect in this area. For example, the state of Virginia may prohibit excluding a provider from a PPO under existing law that prohibits the exclusion of a physician from an insurance panel when the physician has agreed to accept the reimbursement schedule offered by the insurer. Legislation has also been introduced in California which, if adopted, would require "every willing provider" be allowed to participate on a PPO panel.

ADMINISTRATIVE CONSIDERATIONS

Providing for the administration of claims will in many instances be a necessary part of a PPO program. The ability of a PPO to contract for the provision of or to provide claims administration itself may be a further incentive for a payor to participate. From the provider's standpoint, the ability of a PPO to assure prompt payment on claims creates an incentive to participate. This would appear to be a necessary element of most PPOs, and all PPO contracts should be reviewed to determine how claims will be administered.

SPECIFIC PROVISIONS OF PPO CONTRACTS

PROVIDER CONTRACTS

This section discusses the specific PPO contracting concerns that should typically be addressed in provider contracts. Specific concerns that may also arise with respect to a particular provider group will be illustrated by way of example. Many of the provider contract issues discussed below will also be relevant to payor and provider/payor contracts and, therefore, should also be considered when reviewing these other agreements. Additional concerns with other PPO contracts that are distinct from provider contracting issues are discussed in following sections.

General Concerns

A provider contract should focus on preferred rates of compensation, and to the extent that it should not intrude upon a provider's professional judgment in rendering health care services, a provider contract may also be a very simple document. However, as provider contracts largely define the legal relationship between contracting parties, these agreements will typically contain a number of other provisions in an attempt to more clearly define and characterize the contractual relationship. The most important of these provisions that may be found in a provider contract are discussed below.

An example of standard provisions not discussed in depth here, but that will be found in most PPO contracts, are those relating to modification, assignment, or delegation of the rights and duties under the contract. Another example would be arbitration provisions that would become important in the event of a dispute. There may also be specific local concerns to consider, such as the provision for annual dues or for certain billing procedures.

Definition of Terms

A provider contract should define those terms of the agreement that carry special significance. For example, the term "payor" should be defined in order to allow the provider to determine which payors of health care costs will be participating in the PPO and to determine whether to elect to participate as to any particular payor. To this end, a provider would probably want a list of the participating payors to be set forth as a part of the agreement.

Another definitive aspect of particular importance in a provider contract is that of the services to which the preferred rates apply. In many instances, and in particular with respect to physician providers, this definition may involve simply those medically necessary services that the provider is licensed to provide and that are covered under applicable benefit agreements. However, this definition may become much more complex with respect to hospital providers that have agreed to accept compensation on a per-diem rate. In order to allow for cost effective provision of services by the hospital and to prevent future disputes, it is critical to establish as clearly as possible those services that are included within the per-diem rate.

Independent Contractor Status

A standard but very important provision in any PPO contract is one establishing that the parties are independent contractors as opposed to employees or agents of each other. This may have a substantial impact from the standpoint of possible liability exposure discussed below with respect to insurance and indemnification.

Third-Party Beneficiary Rights

Another standard but very important provision should be one that establishes that third parties are not intended to be beneficiaries of the PPO contract. This means that the contracting parties to a particular agreement do not intend to bestow upon parties who have not signed the agreement any specific rights, such as the ability to enforce the contract or prevent it from being modified or terminated. An example of what could otherwise happen if this type of provision is not included in a provider contract is that a patient may be able to prevent a provider and the PPO from modifying their agreement to change rates of compensation on the theory that the patient's rights, as a beneficiary to the agreement, would be injured.

Performance

The primary objective of a PPO is to establish preferred rates of compensation and thereby to contain the costs of health care services. With this narrow purpose in mind, PPO provider contracts should not directly impose substantial changes in a provider's normal operating procedures other than those activities related directly to the manner of compensation. While a provider may find it necessary to adopt new procedures in order to be cost effective in providing services at the preferred rates, changes in these procedures should not be mandated by the PPO if this would interfere in any substantial degree with the way a provider exercises professional judgment.

For example, a hospital provider contracting with a PPO to be compensated at a per-diem rate for services may find it necessary to revise the procedures it follows in providing care to patients in order to be more cost effective. However, it should not be the PPO contract that directly mandates a change in these procedures. On the other hand, it would appear to be proper for a provider contract to require changes in a provider's operating procedures that may be characterized as administrative in nature. Thus, a provider may be required to adopt different billing procedures, such as submitting a billing under a certain format not previously required.

Compensation

Rate Structure. Provisions establishing preferred rates of compensation are of critical importance in negotiating provider contracts. From a cost containment standpoint, a PPO's desire may be to establish per diems, diagnostically related group rates (DRGs), or capitation approaches to compensation. As contemplated in government subsidized medical programs, these types of compensation structures place a cap on the cost of health care. This in turn enables payors to more accurately anticipate their health care costs and, therefore, enhances the marketability of the PPO. However, these types of rate structures also put providers at greater economic risk.

Providers tend to favor preservation of a fee-for-service approach for the very reason that it places them at less economic risk. The fact that a PPO may be organized on a fee-for-service basis without placing providers at economic risk would therefore appear to encourage provider participation.

Establishing Rates. Establishing preferred rates of compensation from an antitrust standpoint is a very sensitive issue. It should be stressed that competing providers may not agree upon or otherwise act in concert to negotiate rates. For example, while it would be appropriate for one hospital to negotiate rates with the PPO, it may be inappropriate for two hospitals to jointly negotiate rates. Parallel concerns would be present with respect to competing physicians or competing payors.

The approach utilized to establish rates will vary with the PPO legal structure. To illustrate, a payor that is acting in a PPO capacity would be in the position to establish its own rates. However, a PPO that was physician-sponsored may not be in a position to establish rates for physician compensation, since this activity could constitute price-fixing among the competing physician members. Other alternatives would be to have fees established by an independent fee determination panel or to allow payors to establish their own rate schedules. This latter approach would, however, most likely result in multiple rate schedules that functionally would be very difficult to administer.

Payment of Claims. A PPO may contract to assure prompt payor payment on claims because this would be an incentive for provider participation. Assuming this obligation would emphasize the need for a satisfactory claims administration arrangement. This may require the PPO either to be in the position to effectively administer claims or to contract with a third-party administrator to provide the claims administration called for under each of the PPO's provider and payor contracts.

Billing Format. A sensitive area of the agreement may be the manner in which billings are submitted. The specific problem that would usually arise is whether a provider participating on other than a fee-for-service basis would be required to submit an itemized billing. For instance, it may become an issue whether a hospital on a per-diem rate should have to submit an itemized bill or one that simply sets forth charges at the per-diem rate for each day of stay. This point is subject to negotiation, but it would appear reasonable to require billings with itemized charges in order to allow an accurate determination of whether the preferred per-diem rate is actually containing costs.

Coordination of Benefits. Coordination of benefits (COB) is a very important element of provider contract compensation provisions. The main issue is whether a provider would be entitled to receive compensation beyond that of the preferred rates established under the agreement. In the event preferred rates constitute the base for COB, then the provider would probably be limited to a preferred rate as payment in full. However, providers may negotiate to allow COB up to usual, customary, and reasonable rates (UCR) when there is secondary coverage.

In the situation in which a primary payor is participating in the PPO, this payor should not reasonably be responsible in any situation for payment in excess of the preferred rate. The secondary payor, however, may be responsible for COB payment for remaining amounts up to the provider's UCR. In the event the secondary payor were not participating in the PPO, there would not be a limit as to the payor's COB responsibility. However, if the secondary payor were participating in the PPO, it would appear reasonable to limit COB responsibility to the extent that the PPO would allow COB up to UCR, provided the secondary payor never ended up paying a greater amount than it would be required to pay if it were the primary contracting payor.

It should also be noted that many state laws establish minimum COB requirements. At the present time, most traditional COB statutes do not recognize or take into account PPOs that feature contracted-for reimbursement schedules. The interrelationship in COB between a PPO program with contract benefits based on a negotiated schedule and an indemnity plan with contract benefits based on UCR may have some unintentional or undesirable effects, such as disproportionate cost shifting to the indemnity plan. Likewise, the PPO program may be expected to pay as much or more as a secondary payor than it would as a primary payor utilizing the benefit of its cost-reducing contracts. Accordingly, PPO contracts should focus on COB provisions quite carefully. The cost-saving objectives of the PPO should be preserved to as great an extent as allowed by state law and regulations covering COB.

Insurance and Indemnification

Obtaining adequate insurance to cover potential liability exposure should be an absolute prerequisite to participation in a PPO. This is inherently a required cost of doing business and should be required of each contracting party. It is therefore advisable to expressly set forth in PPO contracts that each party is required to maintain adequate insurance coverage and provide the other party with evidence of the same. This is especially true with respect to PPOs because it is difficult at the present time to quantify the type and extent of liability exposure that may arise from this newly developing alternative to health care delivery. Specifically, a PPO should at least require professional liability coverage as to each provider. Such coverage is currently available to the extent it would cover the liability arising from each provider's errors or omissions.

Another important question with respect to insurance coverage is whether a PPO contract should require each contracting party to indemnify and hold harmless the other party. Typically, an agreement to indemnify and hold harmless another party would involve the indemnified party being held harmless for vicarious or secondary liability imposed for the acts or omissions of the indemnifying party. For example, if it was determined that a contracting provider was an agent or employee of a PPO, as opposed to an independent contractor, the PPO may be exposed to liability for the malpractice of the physician on a vicarious liability theory. Alternatively, a PPO may be held secondarily liable for the malpractice of an independent contractor physician on the basis that the PPO had been negligent in allowing the physician to participate in the PPO in the first instance. In either of these situations, the physician would be ultimately responsible for the liability imposed on the PPO if a physician had agreed to indemnify and hold harmless the PPO.

The major concern with respect to indemnification arises when parties contractually obligate themselves to indemnify and hold harmless each other. In most professional liability policies, this type of liability exposure is generally excluded from coverage. The rationale behind excluding such coverage is that while a policy will cover liability arising out of the insured's negligent acts or omissions, it will not cover that which the insured has intentionally and willfully assumed under contract.

It should clearly be the preference of the contracting parties to have each party expressly agree to indemnify and hold harmless the other with respect to liability imposed on either party arising out of the indemnifying party's own acts or omissions. This makes each party ultimately responsible for the party's own acts and further assures that both parties are independent contractors as opposed to employees or agents of each other. However, to the extent a party is not able to adequately insure against such exposure it is difficult to reasonably require express indemnification as part of the contracting process.

While an express provision to indemnify and hold harmless the other party is desirable, this obligation may in any event be implied by law. To illustrate how this may become an issue if both parties to a provider contract were sued for the malpractice of a provider, the PPO's insurance carrier would undoubtedly sue the provider and the provider's insurance carrier for implied indemnity if there was not an express indemnity provision. Thus, it is unclear why insurance carriers tend to exclude professional liability coverage under express agreements of this nature to indemnify and hold harmless another party. This is an area that will need to be clarified as PPOs continue to develop.

Utilization Review

Utilization review should be an important aspect of every PPO because it is difficult to demonstrate cost containment advantages of preferred rates of compensation if it cannot be shown that providers are effectively delivering services. Provisions requiring participation in any utilization review programs established or adopted by the PPO are, therefore, a central part of any provider contract.

There are at least several utilization review issues related directly to the contracting process that should be kept in mind in negotiating a PPO contract. The first of these is whether the PPO has a review program in place at the time a PPO contract is entered into or whether such a program will be established at a future point in time. If the program is not established and in place at the time of signing a PPO contract, the provider or even a payor may not be in the position to first review the program's specific terms and conditions. In this situation, a contracting party may become obligated to participate in a program that imposes certain restrictions that were not anticipated.

A contracting provider should next determine whether review procedures are well delineated and expressed in clear terms. In particular, a party should be satisfied that there are procedures established for reviewing the appropriateness of services rendered and an adequate appeals process to address any adverse determinations. For example, review procedures should include provisions for concurrent review of services at the time they are performed and preferably should avoid review practices that allow for retroactive denial of payment. A contracting provider should also avoid review procedures that are subject to modification without notice to the provider.

A contracting party should also determine whether utilization review programs will be conducted by the PPO itself or whether these duties will be delegated to a third-party review organization. In the latter instance, a provider may also be placed in a position of being subject to review procedures that are undesirable and unanticipated. For example, a provider may find that the review functions of the delegated program are in the provider's judgment conducted by inappropriate third parties.

Another important concern a contracting provider may have with respect to utilization review is whether the party would be required to participate on any review committees or make determinations as to the appropriateness of particular services rendered. This activity may increase the liability exposure of the particular party. From the provider's standpoint, participation on a review committee may call for undertaking activities that are arguably beyond the scope of standard professional liability coverage. These activities may be characterized as administrative in nature as opposed to professional and, therefore, excluded under a provider's existing professional liability coverage. In this regard, a provider should also determine which party makes the final decision as to payment for a claim. This responsibility should usually rest with the payor.

Term of Agreement

Provisions set forth in a PPO contract relating to the term of the agreement are of substantial importance for several reasons. First, the term of the agreement may have a significant impact on the cost-containment features of the PPO. Second, provisions relating to the term of the agreement in large part determine the alternatives available to a party in the event of a dispute.

The longer the duration of a provider contract, the more potential it may have to contain costs. This would result from the fact that preferred rates are generally established for the term of the agreement which would generally result in cost effectiveness due to the stability of the preferred rates in an inflationary economy. Such stability also allows payors to more accurately assess benefit requirements and, thereby, possibly lower premiums. With this in mind, a PPO will normally attempt to establish a term of the agreement that is as long as possible and further establish that the agreement may not be terminated without cause during this period.

However, every PPO agreement should allow for termination by either party for specified causes such as a major breach of the agreement by the other party. This type of provision in a PPO contract gives each contracting party the ability to protect its position with respect to unforeseen or undesired consequences. In the event there are certain contingencies under which a contracting party would absolutely not want to participate in a PPO, these may be negotiated and specified in a PPO agreement as reasons for termination of the agreement with cause. For example, a provider may want to establish a provision whereby it would be entitled to terminate the agreement immediately or upon providing notice of a certain specified number of days in the event a retroactive denial payment procedure was established as part of the PPO utilization-review program. Another common event that would allow termination for cause would be if payment on a certain number of claims is not made within a specified period by a participating payor.

With respect to this latter point, a PPO contract might also provide that the agreement may be terminated in part regarding certain duties or obligations imposed upon a contracting party. For instance, in order to ensure flexibility in the agreement, it is not unreasonable to allow a provider to partially terminate an agreement by electing not to participate with particular payors for specified reasons.

The substantive importance of adequate provisions regarding the term of a PPO contract becomes apparent when it is realized that negotiated termination provisions may convince an otherwise hesitant party to participate. While a party may have concern with respect to the occurrence of certain undesired consequences, an understanding that the PPO relationship could be terminated upon short notice may tend to lessen such concerns. This point is further emphasized by the fact that most PPO agreements are not on an exclusive basis. Thus, a provider's entire patient base will usually not be lost upon terminating a PPO agreement.

Referral Procedures

Most provider contracts will establish referral procedures whereby a provider giving services to a patient will be required to refer the patient to other participating providers for additional or specialized treatment. This type of provision is probably justified to the extent it requires a provider to refer to other participating providers for cost-containment purposes. However, as discussed previously, the PPO does not provide health care services and, therefore, should not intrude on a provider's professional judgment. Therefore, such clauses should be limited to (or at least interpreted as limited to) requiring referrals to other participating providers only when it is reasonable to do so in the professional judgment of the provider. This is particularly relevant to physician providers. However, it may also be applicable to a hospital provider to the extent that treatment may be necessary at a specialized clinic.

Records

There has been a great deal of recent legislative activity with respect to access to medical records, and a provider contract should be sensitive to these legal developments. For the purposes of flexibility, it is probably not necessary to specifically set forth specific statutory requirements. However, these contracts should at least provide for confidentiality of medical records pursuant to applicable state or federal law.

While similar concerns may exist with respect to financial records to the extent that they contain confidential medical information, there is also an additional concern in this regard as to ownership of these records. In particular, the ownership of financial records in the possession of a PPO or third-party administrator should be delineated. This is important because in the event of a dispute, possession of records and the cost for reproducing them will immediately become an issue. Specifying the ownership of the records avoids such problems at the inception.

Advertising

An important aspect of any PPO is marketing its panel of providers to payors. From this standpoint, it is probably desirable for a provider to be listed as a PPO participant and to have this information made available to patients. Therefore, an express provision should address these issues in a provider contract. The provider should further focus upon the right to prior approval of any advertising or listing of the provider. Another concern would be that the PPO not advertise or list the provider as a PPO participant or solicit a provider to payors prior to the time when the provider actually signs a contract with the PPO.

PAYOR CONTRACTS

General

The specific purpose for a payor contract is to enable contracting payors to take advantage of the preferred rate of compensation that has been established by the PPO. While a payor will be required to make payment at the preferred rates, the payor is already obligated to provide plan benefits to patients. Thus, the incentive for a payor to enter into a PPO contract is to further contain health care costs. PPO participation that reduces a payor's costs in providing plan benefits may ultimately allow the payor to reduce its premiums and enhance the marketability of its health care coverage.

Review of Provider Contracts

A payor contract should also address most of the issues discussed above in the context of provider contracts. In fact, prior to entering into an agreement with a PPO, a payor may further want to review all existing provider contracts. A PPO will usually first contract with providers in order to have an established panel of preferred providers prior to marketing its programs to payors. A payor would want to review existing contracts with the preferred provider panel in order to determine whether these agreements obligated the PPO to impose certain contractual requirements on participating payors. Future disputes are probable if such requirements are not specifically set forth in payor contracts. For example, if a PPO agreed pursuant to a provider contract that payment on all claims would be made within thirty days of billing, this turnaround time is what would be expected of participating payors and should, therefore, be expressly spelled out in payor contracts.

Compensation

The most important issue from a payor's viewpoint in establishing preferred rates of compensation is to determine how the rates of compensation will be set. As to payors contracting on an individual basis with the PPO, these rates would always be subject to negotiation. However, from a marketing standpoint, a PPO may not be willing to accept different rates of compensation from different participating payors. This approach is usually not as desirable as utilizing a single-rate structure, which greatly simplifies the payment and administration of claims process. A single-payment schedule would also provide more consistent statistical data in order to determine whether cost containment objectives are being reached.

Eligibility

Questions of patient eligibility will always arise with respect to payment of claims. A payor contract should specifically address the issue of which party has the final responsibility for establishing eligibility. As this involves professional judgment about a determination of coverage, this obligation may reasonably rest ultimately with the payor. In conjunction with the determination of eligibility, a payor contract should also create a mechanism whereby providers can readily determine the scope of coverage under relevant benefit agreements. This may be easily accomplished by requiring a payor to make available to participating providers copies of all benefit agreements or summaries to these agreements.

Administration of Claims

Claims processing will certainly be an issue addressed in any payor contract because the administration of claims is a necessary aspect of all health care coverage. Thus, payor agreements should clearly spell out the manner in which claims will be administered and which party will provide these services. If licensing of administrators is required under state law, reference should also be made that the administrator should comply with such requirements.

Utilization Review

Another essential aspect of a payor contract in almost every instance will be provisions establishing a utilization-review program. Both contracting parties will most likely choose to leave final decision-making authority with the payor as to whether payment will be made on submitted claims.

Term of Agreement

In addition to the termination provisions discussed above, a provider contract should specifically address the issue of when rates of compensation may be adjusted. As with establishing the rates of compensation, uniformity would likewise be important here. Coordinating modifications or changes to the rate structure between providers and payors would be one of the important administrative functions performed by the PPO once its program is operating.

PROVIDER/PAYOR CONTRACTS

General

This contract establishing a direct relationship between a payor and provider would normally be a very simple agreement. It could incorporate both the provider and payor contracts discussed above by simply referring to these specific agreements and indicating that they would be considered a part of the provider/payor contract.

Third-Party Beneficiary Rights

A principal concern with respect to having a simple provider/payor contract is that it would give one contracting party the right to enforce the terms of the other party's contract with a PPO. For example, incorporating a provider contract into a provider/payor contract may enable the payor to enforce the terms of the agreement between the PPO and the provider. This could result in the payor interceding to prevent the provider and the PPO from modifying the terms of their agreement. Thus, in the situation where a provider and the PPO desire to mutually terminate their agreement, a payor may be able to bring a successful suit to enjoin termination of the agreement if the payor could show it would be injured by this termination.

Administration

The greatest practical problem in establishing provider/payor contracts would be the vast number of agreements that would be required if every provider entered into a direct contract with every payor. This would require an incredible number of agreements and would almost mandate that these agreements be very simple in order to avoid an otherwise impossible administrative burden that would be placed on the PPO. One approach for simplifying this process would be to have each contracting party authorize the PPO as its attorney-in-fact to execute these provider/payor contracts. This may, however, lead to the assertion that the PPO would be acting as a joint marketing agent for competing providers, which could give rise to antitrust problems. It is with these concerns in mind that the benefits obtained through direct provider/payor contracting may be offset by the administrative and liability burdens these agreements may create.

CONCLUSION

PPO contracts play an important role in defining a PPO in addition to establishing the respective rights and duties of the contracting parties. It is therefore necessary to pay close attention to specific provisions in negotiating a PPO contract and to address the major issues discussed above. This will hopefully enable a party to better understand the operations of a PPO and to make an informed decision as to whether or not to enter into a contract to participate in the PPO.

Legal Issues

PURCHASERS' LEGAL CONSIDERATIONS

Charles D. Weller, J.D.
Jones, Day, Reavis & Pogue
Cleveland, OH

☐ This chapter summarizes recent developments and reviews considerations for dealing with PPOs. First, it describes the health care setting from which PPOs have emerged and the PPO concept itself. Second, it discusses some of the principal antitrust questions that have been raised about PPOs from an employer's perspective. Third, it reviews the impact of selected state laws on PPOs. Finally, it suggests general principles for employers to use in dealing with PPOs and discusses selected contractual issues.

HEALTHCARE SETTING

Between 1980 and 1984, national health expenditures grew from $250 billion to $400 billion. In 1984, approximately $160 billion will be spent on hospital care, $80 billion on physician services, and $100 billion on private health insurance.

The present structure of "perverse incentives"[1] facing doctors, hospitals, and patients is generally recognized to be the principal factor contributing to the rapid inflation in health care costs. The efficient use of expensive health care resources is rarely rewarded, and too often the reverse is true. Patients have little incentive to seek out those doctors and hospitals that practice quality care efficiently, as the typical health insurance program does not vary its payments based on the efficiency of the providers. Hospitals are generally paid on the basis of cost and the number of services they provide. Physicians are generally paid on the basis of "usual and customary" fees and the number of services they provide. Thus, the providers of health care services are reimbursed through a system that penalizes efficiency and makes inefficiency profitable. If providers eliminate questionable or unnecessary tests, or days in the hospital, revenues are reduced.

PPOs are but one example of various attempts to change the present structure of perverse incentives. PPOs are also a part of the first major restructuring of the health care industry in 50 years. This age of discontinuity[2] in health care was precipitated by at least eight unprecedented developments:

1. Business efforts to control health care costs have increased exponentially in recent years. The new business focus on reducing health care costs is manifested in many ways, including the formation of more than 100 health care coalitions in the last two years alone, and the evaluation and use of a variety of new cost-containment measures.[3]

2. Antitrust enforcement has come to the health care field. Prior to 1975, the antitrust laws were seldom enforced in the health care industry. Since 1975, more health care antitrust cases have been filed than in the preceding 85-year history of the Sherman Antitrust Act.[4]

3. In 1982, the United States Supreme Court upheld a Federal Trade Commission ruling that the American Medical Association's ethical rules concerning contract practice, "free choice," and advertising illegally restrained trade. Under the AMA rules, it was unethical for a physician to provide medical services under a contract when the compensation was less than "the usual fees paid in the community," when there was "underbidding by physicians in order to secure the contract," or when "free choice of physician" was denied. These rules played an important role in structuring public and private health insurance over the past 50 years.[5]

4. New business entities and actors have entered the health care field, previously dominated by local nonprofit institutions and solo practitioners. These new business entities and actors (including hospitals, health maintenance organizations, emergency centers, and other health care services), organized and operated as for-profit companies on a national or regional basis, have grown rapidly in recent years.

5. Congress recently made the first major changes in medicare and medicaid since these programs were enacted in the mid-1960s. In 1981, states were given freedom for the first time to experiment with alternative methods of financing the medicaid program for the poor. In 1983, medicare began to pay hospitals a flat amount for treatment of a specific diagnosis, through the use of so-called DRGs (diagnosis related groups), in contrast to the cost-based reimbursement of the preceding 17 years.

6. In 1980, a physician surplus began to emerge that is projected to continue throughout the decade of the 1980s. Prior to that time, it was generally thought there was a physician shortage.

7. The absolute level of health care expenditures has reached historic highs. In 1983, national health expenditures approached 11 percent of GNP—double the percentage that they represented in 1960. For employers, health care benefits now average 8 percent of payroll—a 16-fold increase in 20 years.

8. The first systematic thinking about private market reform of the health care industry took place in the 1970s. Competition among doctors and hospitals over efficiency and price was identified as the crucial missing ingredient for private market reform, and several innovative methods for introducing efficiency incentives were developed.

The fundamental restructuring of the health care industry includes major changes in health insurance benefits. Many employers have considered or implemented medical expense accounts, "cafeteria" benefit plans with alternative health insurance plans, benefit design changes requiring such things as second opinions for surgery and precertification for high-cost procedures, and major medical policies with higher deductibles and coinsurance. PPOs are one of the newest ideas for changing health care benefits to create rational economic incentives for doctors, hospitals, and patients.

PPOs DEFINED

A PPO is a group of doctors and hospitals that offers lower cost services under contract to a self-insured employer, an insurance company, or a health and welfare fund. Under the typical PPO plan, employees are given a financial incentive to use these doctors and hospitals (the "preferred providers"), but are not required to use them. In theory, use of the preferred providers will result in lower costs because they will discount their fees or charges, reduce the quantity of services provided, and/or not use high-cost doctors and hospitals.

In concept, PPOs provide employees with a choice between two groups of doctors and hospitals. Employees may use a limited group of providers, the preferred providers, who agree to provide quality health care for a lower cost. Or employees may use any other doctor or hospital, but they have financial incentives to seek out the preferred providers. For example, an employee who uses a preferred doctor may have 100 percent of the bill for covered benefits paid, while only 80 percent of the bill is paid if the employee uses other physicians.

PPOs can be viewed as a combination of two types of health insurance: the "closed panel" health maintenance organization (HMO), and major medical insurance. The employee has financial incentives to use the closed panel of preferred providers but, unlike the situation with a closed panel HMO, does not have to use the closed panel of doctors and other providers. If an employee goes outside the closed panel, coverage in effect switches to a major medical policy with a deductible and co-payment.

PPOs are being developed by insurance companies, hospitals, physicians, and others. Today, preferred providers are paid on a fee-for-service basis and do not bear any insurance risk. The insurance risk is borne either by an insurance company, a self-insured employer, or a health and welfare fund. However, PPOs may evolve into insurance plans, perhaps resembling a closed panel HMO in Minneapolis, where 100 percent of charges are paid when subscribers use the HMO's panel of providers and 80 percent of charges are paid when subscribers use other doctors and hospitals.

In practice, PPOs vary considerably in organization, sponsorship, and performance. As one observer commented, "If you've seen one PPO, you've seen one PPO." In reality, each PPO is a custom arrangement. Two PPOs recently submitted their proposals for review by the Antitrust Division of the Department of Justice. These two plans, one organized by the Hospital Corporation of America (HCA) and the other by Health Care Management Associates (HCMA), are illustrative.

EXAMPLE: HCA PPO

Hospital Corporation of American plans to operate its PPO as a wholly owned subsidiary, which will enter into contracts with physicians and other providers of services (the preferred providers). The PPO will then contract with insurers and self-insured employers. Under the provider contracts, physicians agree to provide services at less than their usual and customary fees, and hospitals give discounts from their standard charges.

As described to the Antitrust Division, the PPO initially will sign contracts with four hospitals owned or managed by HCA in southern Florida. Only physicians with staff privileges at a contracting hospital will be eligible to contract with the PPO. The contracts between the PPO and participating providers will be nonexclusive.

A list of preferred providers will be circulated to all persons enrolled in the PPO. Patients may use any doctor or hospital they choose, including providers not affiliated with the PPO. However, if they wish to be sure that they receive services at the negotiated discount, patients must select a preferred provider and hospital. Patients using other providers may be reimbursed for less than their full cost.

The PPO will negotiate a discount individually with each preferred provider and hospital. As a result, the size of the discount and the resulting price may vary among different providers and hospitals. Participating providers and hospitals will be free to lower their discounted prices at any time, but they will agree not to raise their prices for one year.

HCA's PPO will have a local advisory board of trustees composed of contracting professional providers, representatives of contracting hospitals, and representatives of insurers. The PPO will also have a utilization and peer review committee, which will review medical procedures used in treating patients.

The sponsoring hospital and provider members of the local board and committee will not have access to confidential fee information of their competitors, and neither the local board nor the committee will review the fees or discounts offered by contracting providers or hospitals. The local board and committee will serve only as advisory groups. Final authority for pricing, membership, and other policy decisions will reside with the PPO's Executive Director and board of directors.

EXAMPLE: HCMA PPO

Health Care Management Associates' PPO is called a *broker-type PPO,* in that it is not controlled by or affiliated with purchasers or providers. HCMA's PPO will individually contract with no more than 20 percent of the providers of health care in a local area. "Cooperating providers," as they are called under the plan, will have a choice between two methods of reimbursement determined by the PPO: first, the lesser of the individual provider's charges or a maximum payment schedule developed by the employer or other buyer, and second, the "usual, customary, and reasonable" fee, discounted at least 10 percent. The discount will be negotiated with each provider separately and may vary from purchaser to purchaser. Individual provider fee data will be distributed only to affiliated buyers and otherwise will be kept confidential. The PPO will provide utilization review and quality assurance services through a panel composed of physicians and an HCMA official. The panel will not review fees.

As these examples suggest, PPOs raise a variety of novel antitrust, contractual, and other legal issues. The antitrust questions have generated the most controversy and uncertainty, and are discussed next in some detail.

ANTITRUST CONSIDERATIONS

VIEWS OF THE ENFORCEMENT AGENCIES

The antitrust division of the Department of Justice and the Federal Trade Commission both have recently expressed generally favorable views on PPOs. The Department of Justice, having reviewed the HCMA and HCA programs discussed above, concluded that "as a general matter...the emergence of preferred provider organizations can benefit the public by increasing competition among providers and contributing, to some degree, to a decrease in providers' fees" and that PPOs "may spur greater cost-containment efforts and contribute to lower health care costs." The Ohio Attorney General's Office has taken a similar position.[6]

The fact that the Antitrust Division of the Department of Justice, the Federal Trade Commission, and the Ohio Attorney General are generally receptive to PPOs merely reduces, rather than eliminates, antitrust risk. Those doctors and hospitals who are not included in the group of preferred providers may take a different view. Thus it is prudent for employers to be aware of basic antitrust developments in the health care field that affect PPO contracting and to act accordingly. These developments and suggestions for employers are discussed next.

THE MARICOPA DECISION

In 1982, the U.S. Supreme Court held, in *Arizona* v. *Maricopa County Medical Society,* 457 U.S. 332 (1982), that a maximum fee schedule adopted by physicians controlling an enterprise somewhat similar to provider-controlled PPOs was per se illegal as horizontal price fixing. *Maricopa* involved two nonprofit organizations, called medical care foundations, established by two medical societies. The foundations conducted utilization reviews and developed a maximum schedule of fees to be charged by member physicians under contract with insurers. PPOs also generally provide these two services.

The Supreme Court, in a four-to-three decision, applied standard antitrust principles and held that the foundations' maximum fee agreements were per se illegal. In so ruling, the Court cited several factors. First, the foundations did not in substance provide a new or unique product. Second, there was no evidence that the program could not function if the maximum fee schedules were established in a different way than by horizontal agreement by independent physicians. The maximum fee schedules in question were established by majority vote of the foundation member physicians. Third, the foundations did not constitute a joint venture in which, for example, the participating doctors contributed capital or shared profits and losses. Member doctors had no other financial interest in the operation of the foundations than payment for their services. Fourth, the participating physicians had substantial market power, as they constituted from 30 percent to 80 percent of local physicians.

Maricopa did not involve a PPO, but its reasoning is certainly relevant to an antitrust analysis of PPOs. Fortunately, PPOs can be structured and operated in a variety of ways to eliminate these problems and to avoid antitrust illegality. Some of the relevant factors are: who controls the PPO, providers or nonproviders? If providers control, what percentage of local providers participate? If providers control, do they contribute capital or technology, share business risks of profit or loss, and create a new product? How are provider price levels determined, and by whom? How are preferred providers selected, and by whom? The answers to these questions will vary tremendously, given the great variety of PPO sponsors and structures.

GENERAL PRINCIPLES FOR EMPLOYERS[7]

Antitrust planning and counseling in the health care field is complicated by several factors. The antitrust laws have only recently been applied to this industry, so there are few direct precedents to rely on, and the area is changing rapidly. In addition, doctors and hospitals are often unfamiliar with the antitrust laws, and not infrequently their understanding is at odds with the laws and principles. As a result, there is an increased risk that frivolous antitrust cases will be filed. Finally, the health care industry is fragmented, with health care services provided by many independent firms. As a result, many new arrangements (including PPOs) necessarily involve combinations of independent firms that may be characterized by potential plaintiffs as horizontal "combinations" or "conspiracies."

Significantly, there is a series of court decisions that are instructive on the legal principles that should be used in evaluating PPOs. These cases involve what are called *participating contracts* used by insurance companies and constitute one of the largest group of antitrust cases filed by private parties in the health care field to date.

Under most participating contracts, a doctor or hospital agrees to a set fee or a maximum fee set by an insurance company in return for direct payment from the insurance company. The providers typically charge higher prices than allowed under the insurance company's participating contract. Frequently, the providers allege that the insurer's effort to have them sign a participating contract and therefore lower their prices is a form of price fixing and that the effect of the participating contract, shifting patients to participating providers, is a boycott.

Such allegations reflect a common misunderstanding of private markets and antitrust principles by health care providers. Generally, participating contracts are vertical arrangements between buyers and sellers. They are what the Supreme Court has described as "merely arrangements for the purchase of goods or services." The first court to reach the merits of the price-fixing theory stated: "What plaintiffs describe as price fixing is, in fact, no more than a natural consumer-oriented competitive activity in getting the lowest competitive price." The same court also rejected the boycott claim, observing, "An unlawful boycott will not result from a buyer's refusal to pay a higher price for goods or services where it can buy them at a lower price." In dismissing the case, the court concluded that the plaintiffs were incorrrectly trying to use the antitrust laws to avoid, rather than to promote, competition:[8]

> [P]laintiffs seek to use the antitrust laws as a shield from . . . competition; they seek to avoid "the free play of market forces" . . . to compel the defendants to pay their higher prices. This interpretation of the antitrust laws cannot be enforced.

The participating contract cases support the antitrust legality of selective contracting with doctors and other providers that is an essential element of PPOs. Unfortunately, the cases also reflect the fact that doctors and hospitals frequently misunderstand the antitrust laws; this can lead to the filing of nonmeritorious antitrust actions. Accordingly, employers should carefully consider the extent to which they want to actually participate in the selection of the panel of preferred providers. The risk of suit against an employer can probably be limited by avoiding active involvement in the selection of the panel of preferred providers, but this approach results in less control by the employer over which providers are selected. The proper balance of benefits and risks here must be evaluated in each particular case.

The generally favorable position that the antitrust division of the Department of Justice and the Federal Trade Commission have taken toward PPOs suggests that additional favorable business review letters or advisory opinions could be obtained. Because this can be a lengthy process and because the views of the enforcement agencies are not binding on private parties, the desirability of seeking such a statement should be carefully considered. Obviously, to the extent that additional statements by the agencies reduce uncertainty in the area, they lessen the changes that meritless antitrust cases will be filed.

STATE LAW CONSIDERATIONS

STATE FREE CHOICE LAWS

Numerous states have laws that in some way restrict the development of PPOs. Most of these laws are patterned on the AMA's free choice ethical rules developed many years ago but recently found to be illegal by the FTC. Generally, these laws either prohibit an insurer from influencing or attempting to influence a patient's selection of his or her doctor or hospital or require that patients have free choice of providers. Sometimes the laws apply to all insurers, and other times they apply to Blue Cross or Blue Shield plans but not to commercial health insurers.

To date, these laws do not appear to have raised major barriers to the development of PPOs. The laws, by their terms, may not apply to self-insurers; the statutes may not have anticipated differing financial incentives between preferred and nonpreferred providers; and several states have recently repealed the laws. For example, PPO activity in California was significantly encouraged by a 1982 change in California law that repealed these free choice requirements. It also can be argued that these statutes are preempted by §514 of ERISA.[9] However, since state laws vary significantly on this issue and are subject to change, any employer considering dealing with a PPO should examine each relevant state law and monitor legislative and regulatory developments in those states where it is dealing with a PPO.

INSURANCE LAWS

At the present time, PPOs are not regulated as such by state insurance departments. Most PPOs pay doctors and hospitals on a fee-for-service basis, that is, doctors and hospitals bill separately for each service they provide. Typically, the insurance risk is borne by a self-insurer or an insurance company, not the PPO. Some employers and some PPOs may prefer a capitation basis in order to achieve possibly greater savings. Under a capitation arrangement, a provider is paid a fixed amount per person to provide certain specified benefits. For example, primary care physicians might be paid $15 per month per covered person and agree in return to provide or pay for all primary care services, lab tests, x-rays, and specialist services.

PPOs that use capitation instead of the typical fee-for-service method of payment are a special case and raise different issues under state insurance law. Some state insurance departments take the position that a capitation contract with a physician makes the physician an insurer. In return for a fixed monthly payment, the physician agrees to provide or pay for services in the future if the patient gets sick. As a result, some state insurance departments argue that the physician must be licensed as a health maintenance organization or insurance company. It can be argued—at least in the context of a self-insured employer or a PPO sponsored by a licensed insurer—that no further license is required. The principal argument is that in both instances the patient can be adequately protected by the licensed insurer or self-insurer, and thus the policy concerns of state insurance laws will be met. This issue, however, remains unsettled.

HOSPITAL RATE REGULATION

Several states regulate hospital rates, and some require hospitals to charge all payors the same rates. In those states with this type of hospital rate regulation, PPOs may not be allowed to obtain hospital discounts or may have to justify any discount they grant. Employers seeking discounts from hospitals designated as preferred providers may be informed that hospitals are not permitted by state law to grant discounts. Since state laws vary significantly on this issue and are generally complex, the employer should investigate the applicable state law carefully. It may be possible for the employer to obtain a discount, for example, by demonstrating the cost savings involved or by coming within an exemption under the particular state legislation.

MALPRACTICE AND OTHER SOURCES OF TORT LIABILITY

The operation of PPOs can give rise to a variety of tort actions, and employers could become "deep pocket" targets of this litigation if adequate precautions are not taken.

Hospitals have been held liable for negligently selecting or controlling a physician who later commits malpractice. A similar tort theory could be asserted against an employer who becomes involved in selecting or terminating preferred providers.

"Excluded providers," particularly those who are terminated after being preferred providers, may assert state tort claims, as well as antitrust claims. The tort claims might include, for example, libel, slander, and tortious interference with business relations. The benefits of close involvement with decisions to terminate specific providers who turn out to generate high costs or poor quality care must be weighed against the additional potential liability such involvement may create.

Utilization review can play a critical part in whether or not a PPO actually reduces costs. However, a $500,000 jury verdict was recently rendered against the State of California for the negligent administration of utilization review as part of the state's medicaid program. Thus, again, the benefits of employer involvement in this process must be weighed against potential additional liability.

Claims processing, and the denial of claims in particular, can give rise to a tort "bad faith." The bad faith refusal by an insurance company to pay a valid claim can result in the award of substantial punitive damages. This is a rapidly developing area of law and could possibly be extended to self-insured employers as well. In the PPO context, it is therefore advisable to review carefully the capabilities of the firm doing the claims processing and the firm's procedures for handling claims that are denied.

In general, these matters underscore the care with which employers should approach detailed involvement in the operation of a PPO and in the PPO's actual management of health care costs.

CONFIDENTIALITY OF PATIENT RECORDS

Patient records are subject to varying confidentiality requirements in different states. In addition, special confidentiality requirements almost always apply to patient records that contain information relating to psychiatric illnesses, alcohol abuse, and drug abuse.

Since employers are often interested in obtaining detailed information on a PPO's performance, it is important to determine that the information provided to the employer complies with applicable laws on the confidentiality of patient records.

GENERAL CONSIDERATIONS

State laws vary considerably and need to be considered on a state-by-state basis wherever the PPO operates. State legislative and legal developments also should be monitored for proposals by provider groups, regulatory authorities, and others affecting PPOs and their relationships with employers.

CONTRACTUAL CONSIDERATIONS

GENERAL PRINCIPLES

Obtain Collective-Bargaining Agreement Flexibility

PPOs affect the manner in which health care benefits are provided and will be a mandatory subject of collective bargaining under the National Labor Relations Act. Since each PPO has to be evaluated individually and since new PPOs will become available over time, it is helpful for employers to build flexibility into their collective-bargaining agreements with respect to the manner in which health care benefits are provided. The greatest flexibility would be achieved by including in the collective-bargaining agreement the right of the employer to offer PPOs and to implement other cost-containment measures without negotiation and on a unilateral basis. The next best approach would be to establish in the collective-bargaining agreement a labor–management committee to develop and implement cost-containment measures. One major employer and union, for example, agreed as follows:

> During the course of negotiations, the parties agreed that the unacceptable rate of health care cost escalation is a problem that needs to be addressed. It was also noted that the employee and his family is adversely impacted by rising health care costs.
>
> In recognition of our shared interest in resolving this problem, the Company and the International Union agree to commence discussions on ways to control these rising costs without adversely impacting the employee and his family. Studies have shown that there are a number of ways in which abuses can be eliminated and in which doctors and hospitals can be encouraged to provide quality health care more efficiently and at reasonable rates. Examples of successful programs include requiring second surgical opinions,

greater use of outpatient services, participation in health maintenance organizations and preferred provider organizations and greater emphasis on health education and wellness programs.

Therefore, the parties agree that representatives of the International Union and the Company will meet and will have the authority to develop and implement mutually agreeable changes in the Medical plan which will accomplish our shared objective to contain health care costs.

Preserve Buyer/Seller Relationship

In order to minimize exposure under the antitrust laws and state tort law, including malpractice actions, and in order to best achieve company cost-containment objectives, an employer should maintain an arms-length relationship with the PPO as a purchaser of services and avoid acting as a joint venturer. Responsibility for management of health care services, including control of its costs, should clearly be that of the PPO, not the employer.

Target Adjusted Total Costs per Employee

Health care costs are determined by both the quantity of services provided ("utilization" in health care terminology) and the price. Reduction of health care costs requires close attention not only to the price of services, but to their utilization as well.

Accordingly, employers are best advised to target total costs per employee in measuring PPO performance. Since the PPO may actually see an employer's healthiest group of employees, it is also desirable to adjust the total costs per employee by age, sex, and health status to ensure fair comparisons.

The same symptoms often can be treated in a variety of clinically accepted ways but with considerable variation in the total cost. Obviously the total cost of treating the same patients will be substantially lower if the preferred providers practice conservatively and use fewer hospital days or other expensive services than do other providers.

The opposite is true as well. If the preferred providers utilize more hospital days and other services than do other providers, the total cost of treating patients enrolled in a PPO can be higher. Indeed, a PPO's group of doctors and hospitals conceivably could offer a price discount but practice in such a way as to result in higher total costs for the employer. Even though their prices may be below the community average, they may utilize far more services than the community average. For example, a doctor may agree to charge $900 for a procedure in an area where the average fee is $1,000 but may utilize the procedure three times more frequently than do other doctors. As a result, the total costs generated by the physician will be $2,700 versus $1,000, even though the employer received a 10 percent discount.

For these reasons, an employer's basic criterion should be adjusted total costs per employee, not merely the price of hospital or physician services. This does not mean that discounts should not be sought from PPOs. It does mean, however, that discounts and provider price levels are only a part of the overall issue of whether the PPO will actually reduce total costs.

Periodically Evaluate the PPO's Performance
Given the existing pattern of perverse incentives, doctors and other health care providers have little experience in managing the total costs of health care. Moreover, they have established patterns of clinical practice. If PPOs are to reduce an employer's total health care costs, the doctors and other providers probably will have to make major changes in their established practice patterns. They are not likely to make these difficult changes, no matter how many cost-containment measures the PPO has on paper, without periodic evaluations of their performance by the employer.[10]

Educate the Provider Community
PPOs provide incentives for patients to change doctors and hospitals, from nonpreferred providers to preferred providers, in part on the basis of cost. Although this use of financial incentives is consistent with antitrust principles, it is threatening and considered "anticompetitive" by a significant number of doctors and hospitals. Many doctors, hospitals and other providers are unfamiliar with the antitrust laws and market principles. This misunderstanding can lead to the filing of frivolous antitrust suits that are expensive to defend.

As a result, an employer should take the time to meet with doctors and other providers to educate and open a dialogue with them. In addition to explaining what the company is doing, the company may find it helpful to state its willingness to develop multiple PPOs and to explore other alternative financing arrangements; to describe the company's health care costs and their impact on the company's competitiveness; to compare the fundamental changes in the health care field to the fundamental changes in the company's markets; to explain common interests in preserving a private system of health care and avoiding government regulation; and to discuss antitrust principles and the favorable positions federal enforcement agencies have taken with respect to PPOs. In this way, employers can reduce the chances that frivolous suits will be filed.

SELECTED CONTRACTUAL ISSUES
Provider Selection
To minimize an employer's tort and antitrust exposure, an employer's contract with a PPO should state that the employer is not responsible for, and plays no role in, the selection of physicians, hospitals, or other health

care providers who contract with the PPO. In addition, the contract should state that the arrangement with the employer is an independent contractor relationship. Finally, the employer should act consistently with these representations.

At the same time, the employer is interested in avoiding high-cost providers. If total costs per employee are running unacceptably high, the employer should inform the PPO so that the PPO has an incentive to take corrective action with high-cost providers. This approach has proven effective. The employer should also consistently make clear that the PPO is expected to manage itself; that the employer is not a manager but a purchaser of services; and that it is the PPO's responsibility to determine who will be a participating provider.

Reports

The employer will need regular reports in order to evaluate the PPO's performance. Many employers now obtain detailed reports on their traditional health insurance benefits, and this experience will be helpful in dealing with PPOs. It is easy to be overwhelmed with data that is difficult to analyze and evaluate, and there is often a significant difference between what is promised and what is delivered, given the novelty of the subject and the large number of new vendors. There are no generally accepted standards for evaluating performance in this area. There is also a tendency to obtain partial data, for example, on hospital days per 1,000 employees, rather than data on total costs. Finally, the number of PPO enrollees will usually be relatively small in the beginning, and thus there may not be enough data available to make statistically valid comparisons.

Accordingly, it is advisable for an employer to identify a variety of relatively simple performance measures, so that reports are easily understood and so that normally there will be at least one area in which the PPO can improve its performance. The employer should obtain the adjusted total costs per employee per month, and should specify the timing, content, and cost of the reports in the PPO contract. The option to obtain additional data, at a specific cost, should be included in the PPO contract to allow for an employer's evolving data requirements. The payment of PPO administrative fees should be contingent upon the employer receiving the reports in a timely and adequate manner. Finally, purchasers should be sure that the data received complies with applicable confidentiality requirements.

Incentive Payments

Some PPOs will ask for an incentive payment if they achieve certain cost-containment objectives. Incentive payments are difficult to design, generally are not required, and rarely will be effective. If an incentive payment provision is included, great care must be taken to ensure that no incentive payment is owed by the employer if the PPO does not in fact save money.

For example, a PPO may propose an incentive payment of $100 a day for each day PPO patients spend in the hospital below the company average. That is, if 1,000 company employees enroll in the PPO and use 800 days of hospital care, while the company average is 1,200 days per 1,000 employees, the PPO may ask for an incentive payment of (1,200 days − 800 days) × $100 = $40,000. This type of incentive payment should be avoided, because the PPO patients may be younger and healthier than the company's average employees. In this example, the PPO actually may be increasing rather than decreasing costs, because the efficient delivery of quality care may only require 600 days per 1,000 employees for the type of employees enrolled in the PPO. An employer who agrees to this type of incentive payment would be in the undesirable position of paying higher costs for the employees involved and owing the PPO an incentive payment for its poor performance. Accordingly, it is generally advisable not to include an incentive payment in PPO contracts.

Exclusive Arrangements
Some PPOs will ask to be the employer's exclusive PPO for a period of time. Exclusive arrangements limit an employer's flexibility and deprive the employer of an important means of encouraging a PPO to perform, namely, competition. Competition between two or more PPOs at the same employer has proven to be very productive. Accordingly, exclusive arrangements should be avoided unless the value received is sufficient to outweigh the opportunity for useful competition that nonexclusive arrangements create.

Cancellation Clause
The employer should have the right to cancel the contract in the event that costs per employee turn out to be unacceptably high. Such a provision will encourage the PPO to perform and to provide the employer with the ability to cancel the contract if the PPO's performance proves to be ineffective. At the same time, the PPO ideally should not have the right to cancel the contract for at least one year. The PPO should not need a cancellation clause because it does not bear any risk.

Audit Rights
Many employers are considering or already using a variety of auditing techniques for their existing health care benefit programs. Auditing claims can be an effective cost-containment measure. Accordingly, the PPO contract should ensure that the employer has the right to audit bills from all preferred providers and should describe the procedures to be used. These procedures also must comply with applicable confidentiality laws.

Utilization Review
Preferred providers should agree to be bound by utilization-review determinations, so that neither the employer nor employees may be billed for

hospital or other services found by utilization review to be unnecessary. In addition, the employer should examine the specific standards to be used. These standards, and thus the potential cost savings, can vary considerably. Finally, it is important to consider how the standards will be applied. Since meaningful standards will result in changes in the ways some doctors and hospitals provide care, the standards must be applied in a manner that is acceptable and practical.

Provider Prices

Some PPOs may ask an employer to pay whatever fees the providers individually set (or a discount from those fees). The employer would then have little or no protection from the provider who may charge $5,000 for a service when the community average is $1,000. The contract should make clear that the employer and employees are not bound to pay whatever prices are charged by doctors and other providers.

For example, it may be appropriate to have a clause which provides that, notwithstanding any other provision of the contract, the employer is only obligated to pay reasonable fees and charges for medically necessary services, and that, in the event of a dispute, no collection action may be taken against any employee or retiree.

Benefit Design

The benefit package should be designed to include as many cost-containment features as practical, such as precertification, mandatory second opinions, and outpatient surgery for designated procedures. At a minimum, the PPO benefit package should conform to benefit design changes that the employer has already incorporated in its traditional health insurance benefits. In addition, the employer may want to include other benefit design changes it has identified but not yet implemented in its traditional coverage. Benefit design can significantly influence total health care costs and should be an important part of any PPO contract negotiations.

Malpractice Protection

An employer's potential exposure to malpractice claims against preferred providers was discussed earlier. As a result, the contract with the PPO should specify that each preferred provider will carry an acceptable level of malpractice insurance. The PPO should also agree to hold the employer harmless for any malpractice claims. Finally, the PPO contracts with preferred providers should require the provider to carry the same level of malpractice coverage.

Provider Contracts

A PPO should have contracts with its preferred providers, including doctors and hospitals. The employer should carefully review the provider contracts to assure that the PPO can perform all of its commitments to the employer.

Employee Brochures and Information Materials

The contract should state who has the responsibility to provide specific information and materials for employees. In addition, these materials should be subject to the employer's approval and should be reviewed carefully. It is important that the written materials to employees accurately and clearly describe the benefits. It is also advisable that the materials avoid making representations that the PPO will provide superior quality health care services. Finally, it is important that the materials do not state that the PPO is sponsored by or affiliated with the employer, and it is preferable that the materials affirmatively disclaim any such sponsorship or affiliation.

CONCLUSION

Preferred provider organizations are one of the fastest growing alternatives to traditional health insurance that have emerged recently as part of a fundamental restructuring of the health care industry. PPOs can benefit employers, hospitals, doctors, and patients alike by introducing rational economic incentives that can reduce costs without government intervention. PPOs, however, vary considerably in organization and likely performance. PPOs should be reviewed individually to assure that they will achieve cost-containment objectives and to minimize legal complications.

NOTES

1. This term was apparently first used by Walter McClure. On the general subject, *see, e.g.,* Walter McClure, "The Medical Care System Under National Health Insurance: Four Models," *J. Health Politics, Policy & Law* 1, p. 447 (1978); A. Enthoven, *Health Plan* (1980); and Weller, "Antitrust and Health Care: Provider Controlled Health Plans and the *Maricopa* Decision," *Am. J. Law & Medicine* 8, p. 223 (1983).

2. The last fifty years have been an age of continuity for health care and other sectors of the economy. *See* Weller, "Antitrust, Joint Ventures and the End of the AMA's Contract Practice Ethics: New Ways of Thinking about the Health Care Industry," *N.C. Central L.J.* 14, p. 1401 (1984) and P. Drucker, *The Age of Discontinuity* (1969).

3. *See,* "Business and the Health Marketplace," Fed. American Hospitals *Review* (January/February 1984).

4. *See* Weller, "The Primacy of Standard Antitrust Analysis in Health Care," *Toledo L. Rev.* 14, p. 609 (1983) for a history of government enforcement of the antitrust laws in health care.

5. See generally Weller, "Antitrust, Joint Ventures and the End of the AMA's Contract Practice Ethics."

6. 1984-1 CCH Trade Cases ¶65,796 (1983).

7. General principles for providers are discussed in Weller, "Antitrust Aspects of PPOs" in *Preferred Provider Organizations* ed. D. Cowan, (1984).

8. *Chick's Auto Body* v. *State Farm Mutual Automobile Insurance Co.*, 1979-1 Trade Cases ¶62,642 (N.J. Superior Ct. 1979). Accord *Proctor* v. *State Farm Mutual Automobile Insurance Co.*, 675 F.2d 308 (D.C. Cir. 1982). *See also Feldman* v. *Health Care Service Corp.*, 1982–83 Trade Cases ¶65,042 (N.D. Ill. 1982) (and cases cited therein). But see *Kartell* v. *Blue Shield of Mass.*, 1984-1 Trade Cases ¶65,907 (D. Mass. 1984) (holding a Blue Shield plan's requirement that participating physicians not bill patients for the balance of their fees in excess of Blue Shield payment levels violated Section One of the Sherman Act). This opinion is legally unsound and should be reversed on appeal.

9. One of the factors leading to the enactment of the §514 preemption provision was the existence of similar state laws affecting prepaid legal service plans. Several recent cases have held arguably analogous state laws are preempted by §514.

10. The problems many IPA-HMOs experience in this regard is illustrative. *See, e.g.*, OHMO, *The Physicians Health Plan of Minnesota* & H. Luft, *Health Maintenance Organizations* (1981).

Legal Issues

LIABILITY AND LIMITATION OF RISK

Gerald W. Connor
Wood, Lucksinger & Epstein
Los Angeles, CA

☐ Preferred provider organizations (PPOs) are gaining acceptance as a creative way to provide medical and health care more efficiently and at a lower cost. Frequently the hospitals, skilled nursing facilities, home health agencies, doctors, therapists, and other allied health professionals that make up a PPO system already have been providing care in the community. The PPO is a business entity that establishes a new relationship among these health care institutions and professionals. The PPO markets the combined health care resources of its system to third-party payors such as unions and employee benefit plans.

The PPO may be one of the existing providers that expands the scope of its operations through contract or internal expansion. More commonly the PPO is a new business entity jointly owned by some or all of the providers of the PPO's system. Both situations involve a new potential for liability and the need to consider insurance coverage.

Virtually all existing health and medical providers that join PPOs already have insurance coverage. Can a PPO as a separate business rely upon that insurance? Probably not. Consider the following situation:

A PPO contracts to provide medical care to members of a union. The

PPO then contracts with a physician partnership to provide some of this medical care. An accident occurs while one of the physicians of the partnership is treating a union member. A lawsuit ensues; malpractice and the PPO's negligent selection of its physicians are alleged. The PPO, the medical partnership, and the individual physician are named as defendants.

Existing insurance of the medical partnership will cover, usually, the cost of defending the partnership and its physician and the amount of any liability they may be determined to have, up to specified limits. The PPO in the absence of insurance will have to pay its own attorney and other defense costs, even if the PPO ultimately is found not liable for damages. Of course the PPO may be found liable and may have to pay a judgment.

A PPO's business risks are not limited to malpractice; it faces the same risks other businesses with assets, employees, and an ongoing operation must face. Insurance policies for a health-related business generally are structured along the following lines:

1. Comprehensive general liability.
2. Umbrella general liability.
3. Fire damage to the insured's property.
4. Nonfire damage of the insured's property.
5. Professional liability (malpractice).
6. Business automobile liability.
7. Worker's compensation/employer's liability.
8. Boiler and machinery damage.
9. Directors' and officers' liability.

This chapter will explore the way these types of insurance policies are written and coverage provided.[1]

STRUCTURE OF AN INSURANCE POLICY

There are six principal parts to an insurance policy. They are the following:

1. The declaration page.
2. Definitions.
3. The statement of coverage.
4. The statement of exclusions from coverage.
5. The statement of limits of liability for covered items.
6. The endorsements.

The *declaration page* contains information specific to the insurance policy and the insured. This information includes the name and address of the insured, the insurance broker, the policy number, the policy term, a summary statement of the categories of coverage provided, a summary statement of any limits on liability, the date of signing, and signatures.

The *definitions* section is self-explanatory. Insurance policies use many terms of art. These terms of art include, for example, the "insured," the "named insured," "occurrence," "bodily injury," and "property damage." Because these words are used as terms of art, special care in understanding them is important.

The *statement of coverage* is the section that defines, in broad terms, those liabilities that the policy will cover. The *statement of exclusions from coverage* limits this broad coverage, that is, but for an exclusion, a given liability may be covered under the statement of coverage. It follows, then, that no exclusion is required if there is no coverage in the first instance.

The policy may limit the *amount of liability* against which the insurance company protects when there is coverage. There are two primary types of limitations. The policy may state a specific dollar limitation for each covered occurrence during the policy term. Second, the policy may state an overall dollar limit on liability for all occurrences during a policy term, regardless of the number of occurrences.

Finally, an insurance policy may have endorsements. An *endorsement* is a specific amendment to the insurance policy. It may limit or expand coverage or make any other change in the insurance policy. Endorsements are numbered. Thus one endorsement may modifiy a previously numbered endorsement.

STRUCTURE OF AN INSURANCE PACKAGE

An insurance package, if properly structured, will cover the significant business risks that a PPO faces. Coverage is generally divided among the various types of policies listed above. This chapter will describe each in turn.

COMPREHENSIVE GENERAL LIABILITY INSURANCE
Coverage

This insurance covers bodily injury and property damage. The following statement is a typical scope-of-coverage provision.

> The insurance company will pay on behalf of the insured all sums which the insured shall become legally obligated to pay as damages because of: bodily injury or property damage to which this insurance applies, because of an occurrence which the company shall have the right and duty to defend any suit against the insured seeking damages on account of such bodily injury or property damage, even if any of the allegations in the suit are groundless, false or fraudulent, and the insurance company may make such investigation and settlement of any claim or suit as it deems expedient, but the company shall not be obligated to pay any claim or judgment or to defend any judgment after the applicable limit of the company's liability has been exhausted by payment of judgments or settlements.

Coverage under comprehensive general liability insurance sometimes includes, in addition to bodily injury and property damage liability, personal injury and advertising injury liability, host liquor law liability, and fire legal liability.

Personal injury means injury arising out of a false arrest, detention, malicious prosecution, libel or slander, or an invasion of a right of privacy. Advertising injury covers defamation, violation of a right of privacy, unfair competition, and infringement of copyright where the events giving rise to the alleged liability occur in the course of a named insured's advertising activities.

Host liquor law liability coverage provides protection for the insured for liability arising out of serving alcoholic beverages at functions incidental to the named insured's business. The named insured may not be in the business of manufacturing, distributing, selling, or serving alcoholic beverages.

Finally, fire legal liability coverage provides protection against liability for property damage to structures rented to or leased to the named insured, if the property damage arises out of fire. Damage to the named insured's property ordinarily is excluded from coverage (see exclusions below).

Exclusions from Coverage

Common exclusions from coverage of a comprehensive general liability insurance policy are:

1. Damage to property owned by the insured.
2. Damage to property used by the insured.
3. Damage to property in the care, custody, or control of the insured.
4. Bodily injury or property damage arising out of the discharge, dispersal, release, or escape of various pollutants.
5. Bodily injury to any employee of the insured arising out of and in the course of his/her employment by the insured.

Limits of Liability

Comprehensive general liability insurance policies state dollar limits on the insurance company's liability for each occurrence and in the aggregate for the policy term. Whether there is one occurrence or more than one occurrence can become a significant issue because of the per occurrence limit. For example, if two people talking together and walking side by side slip on a recently washed and still wet floor, is the event a single occurrence?[2]

The term *occurrence* is defined as follows:

> Occurrence means an accident, including continuous or repeated exposure to conditions, which results in bodily injury or property damage neither expected nor intended from the standpoint of the insured.

The significance of there being one occurrence or more than one occurrence is compounded by the selective application of the aggregate limit. The aggregate limit states the maximum liability of the insurance company to the insured during a policy term. The aggregate is applied only to some of the categories of occurrences that are covered by the insurance policy. Also, the aggregate may be applied separately to each of those categories to which it does apply. For many types of occurrence there may be no aggregate. The PPO's protection and the insurance company's liability will be limited only by the number of occurrences times the per occurrence limit.

The categories that are subject to an aggregate may be completed operations hazard, product hazard, liability for independent contractors supervised by the named insured, property damage arising out of premises or operations rated on a remuneration basis, and liability assumed under any incidental contract.

Comprehensive general liability insurance includes the obligation of the insurance company to defend the insured, and to pay for that defense. The insurance company's payment of defense costs supplements any other financial obligations that the company has. The costs of defense are not included within the occurrence and aggregate limits on liability.

UMBRELLA LIABILITY INSURANCE

Coverage

Umbrella liability insurance primarily provides a PPO with protection against liability for bodily injury, property damage, and advertising injury in excess of the limits on liability of specifically identified insurance policies. The most commonly identified underlying policy of insurance is the comprehensive general liability insurance policy. The underlying policies also may include business automobile liability insurance, worker's compensation/employer's liability insurance, boiler and mechanical insurance, and other types.

The insured must keep in effect any specified underlying policies as a condition for coverage. Failure to keep the underlying policies in effect will not terminate the umbrella liability insurance, but it will relieve the insurance company from payments that would not have been required had the underlying policies been kept in effect.

Umbrella liability insurance coverage is not limited to those liabilities covered by the named underlying insurance policies. Where there is no underlying insurance coverage for a particular type of liability, but there is coverage for it under the umbrella liability insurance, the umbrella liability insurance is for amounts in excess of a stated retained limit. The retained limit is stated on the declaration page. The named insured pays the retained limit.

An umbrella liability insurance policy's statement of coverage commonly would read as follows:

> The insurance company will indemnify the insured for all sums that the insured shall become legally obligated to pay as damages and expenses, all as

hereinafter defined as included within the term ultimate net loss, by reason of liability

a.   imposed upon the insured by law,

b.   assumed by the named insured, or by any officer, director, stockholder or employee thereof while acting within the scope of his duties as such, under any contract or agreement other than liability assumed with respect to occurrences taking place prior to the time such contract or agreement became effective because of:

(1)   Personal injury caused by

(2)   Property damage caused by

(3)   Advertising liability arising out of

an occurrence that takes place during the policy period anywhere in the world.

Umbrella liability insurance sometimes will assume the cost of the defense where defense is no longer afforded by a previously exhausted underlying insurance policy.

Exclusions from Coverage

Coverage exclusions commonly extend to the following:

1. Situations that are covered under worker's compensation, unemployment compensation, and disability benefit laws.
2. To any employee of the insured with respect to personal injury to another employee of the insured injured in the course of employment.
3. Certain water craft and aircraft situations.

Limits on Liability

Umbrella liability insurance usually has per occurrence and aggregate limits. These types of limits, as discussed under Comprehensive General Liability Insurance are applicable here.

Umbrella liability insurance is designed primarily to provide coverage in excess of existing underlying policies. Limits on liability include only amounts in excess of the applicable limits of liability of the underlying insurance policies, if applicable. If the amount of insurance available from an underlying policy has been reduced due to prior claims, commonly the umbrella liability insurance will pick up where the reduced coverage leaves off. The modified coverage level of an underlying policy commonly is called "the underlying limit." It is important that an umbrella liability policy not permit a gap to develop between coverage by a partially exhausted underlying policy and the umbrella liability policy.

FIRE DAMAGE TO THE PPO's PROPERTY

Comprehensive general liability insurance covers property damage, but fire damage to the property of the PPO or under the control of the PPO generally is excluded. Some comprehensive general liability insurance policies are written to include fire damage of the PPO's property and of the property under its control (see Coverage in Comprehensive General Liability Insurance).

NONFIRE DAMAGE OF THE PPO's PROPERTY
Coverage
This insurance covers personal and real property of the PPO and property of both types owned by others but under the PPO's control. A personal property coverage statement might read as follows:

> PERSONAL PROPERTY OF THE INSURED: Business personal property owned by the named insured and usual to the occupancy of the named insured, including the named insured's interest in personal property owned by others to the extent of the value of labor, materials and charges furnished, performed or incurred by the named insured; all while in or on the described building(s), or (2) in the open (including within vehicles) on or within 100 feet of the described premises.

The coverage provisions would have a separate but comparable provision for personal property of others under the PPO's custody or control.

The real property coverage provision might read as follows:

> BUILDING(S): Building(s) or structure(s) shall include attached additions and extensions, fixtures, machinery and equipment constituting a permanent part of and pertaining to the service of the building(s), materials and supplies intended for use in construction, alteration or repair of the building(s) or structure(s), yard fixtures, personal property of the named insured used for the maintenance or service of the described building(s), including fire extinguishing apparatus, outdoor furniture, floor coverings and appliances for refrigerating, ventilating, cooking, dishwashing and laundering (but not including other personal property in apartments or rooms furnished by the named insured as landlord), all while at the described premises.

Both types of coverage provisions limit protection to specifically identified locations. This contrasts with comprehensive general liability insurance, which is not location specific. While the limitation as to location is obvious for buildings, it is less so for personal property of the PPO that might be taken away from the premises for any number of appropriate business reasons. Damage to business personal property might not be covered by the nonfire property damage policy, and coverage for liability may be obtained only through a special endorsement or through another policy.

Losses due to business interruption can be covered by special endorsement.

A nonfire property damage policy should have a special provision for newly acquired locations and property. Sometimes the policy requires the insured to notify the insuring company within a specified period of time or coverage lapses.

Property Excluded from Coverage

Common exclusions from nonfire property damage coverage are:

1. Accounts, bills, currency, deeds, evidences of debt, money, and securities;
2. Outdoor signs, whether or not attached to a building or structure.

Furthermore, certain types of property are subject to limitations of coverage. These properties might include steam boilers and related equipment where a burst or rupture originates within the equipment, machines and machinery that rupture or burst because of centrifugal or reciprocating forces, and property undergoing alterations and repair if the loss is directly attributable to the operations or work being performed.

Perils Excluded from Coverage

Nonfire property damage insurance protects a PPO against property damage from all sources unless excluded. These exclusions of peril, that is, the source or origin of the damage, can be significant. In some instances a PPO may need a special endorsement to get adequate protection against a significant, excluded peril.

Excluded perils might include the following:

1. Leakage or overflow from plumbing, heating, air conditioning, or other equipment or appliances.
2. Explosion of steam boilers and related equipment.
3. Rain, snow, or sleet damage to property in the open.
4. Interruption of power or other utility service.
5. Earthquake and earth movement, including earth sinking, rising, or shifting.
6. Flood.

Limits of Liability

A PPO is interested in dollar coverage reasonably related to the value of the property being covered. Any lesser coverage would not give adequate protection. Any greater amount would never be used beyond the value of the property. Property damage insurance typically allocates the amount of coverage to a specific location. If a PPO has more than one location, a schedule will list each location and assign a dollar limit to each location. The dollar amount varies with the value of the particular locations.

PROFESSIONAL LIABILITY (MALPRACTICE) INSURANCE

Coverage

Professional liability insurance covers the PPO for liability when providing medical services. A coverage provision might read as follows:

The company will pay on behalf of the insured all sums which the insured shall become legally obligated to pay as damages because of injury to which this insurance applies caused by a medical incident (1) which occurs during the coverage period and (2) for which the written claim is first presented to the company during the policy period.

A medical incident is defined to include events giving rise to liability which result (1) from furnishing professional health care services or (2) from working as a member of a formal accreditation, standard of review, or similar professional board or committee of the PPO, or as a person charged with executing the directives of such board or committee. This latter includes coverage of liability when the PPO does peer review.

The coverage provision above describes a *claims-made* policy, that is, coverage is limited to events that occur during the policy period and for which a claim is first presented during the policy period. This means that if a claim is made after the policy period but before the statute of limitations runs, the insurance policy will not provide protection from liability.

Claims-made policies give the insured the right to obtain additional reporting periods. This means that claims occurring during the policy period but reported subsequent to it will still be covered if they are made during an additional reporting period. This additional coverage is called a *tail*.

The tail may be purchased in one or more increments. For example, one insurance company allows a tail to be purchased for 1 year, then for a second year, and then for all time.

Formerly, professional liability insurance was obtained on an occurrence basis. As discussed under the Comprehensive General Liability Insurance Section, an event would be covered if it occurred during the policy period, regardless of when the claim was first made against the insured and the insurance company by the injured party. This type of policy is commonly called an *occurrence* policy. Most insurance companies do not write occurrence type policies now for medical liability risks.

Exclusions from Coverage

The following are typcial exclusions from professional liability coverage:

1. Bodily injury of an employee.
2. Obligations which may be covered under workers' compensation, unemployment compensation, or disability benefit laws.

Limits of Liability

Limits of liability are done on the basis of per medical incident and aggregate amount. This is for practical purposes identical to the occurrence/aggregate limits used for comprehensive general liability insurance purposes. The discussion under Limits of Liability in the section on Comprehensive General Liability Insurance is applicable here.

BUSINESS AUTOMOBILE LIABILITY INSURANCE

Coverage

Automobile liability insurance covers the risks that are associated with the operation of an automobile by a business. A coverage provision might read as follows:

> We will pay all of the sums the insured legally must pay as damages because of bodily injury or property damage to which this insurance applies, caused by an accident and resulting from ownership, maintenance or use of a covered auto.

In addition, business automobile insurance policies may cover medical and funeral expenses to or for an insured, uninsured motorist coverage, and specific types of damage to the PPO's own property.

Coverage is individually tailored for a particular business. It reflects the types and numbers of cars and other vehicles that the business may have and the special requirements for automobile insurance coverage of each state where a PPO is located. These requirements can vary significantly.

The policy is limited to specifically identified automobiles. It may also extend under special endorsement to automobiles leased or rented by the PPO in the course of its business.

Exclusions from Coverage

Business automobile liability insurance might exclude the following:

1. Accidents or losses that occur outside the United States of America, its territories or possessions, Puerto Rico, and Canada. Most particularly, Mexico generally is not covered.
2. Liability assumed under any contract or agreement.
3. Bodily injury of the PPO's employees.
4. Any obligation that may be covered by workers' compensation or disability benefit laws.
5. Property damage to property owned or transported by the PPO, or in the PPO's care, custody, or control.

In the nonfire property damage section discussed previously, it was noted that property owned or controlled by the PPO but not at a specifically identified location might not be covered. Business automobile insurance also might not cover this property (see 5. under Exclusions from Coverage above). The PPO might want to cover property under these circumstances by special endorsement.

Limits of Liability

The limits of liability can be stated variously. Most commonly, each of the types of coverage are limited to a stated amount per accident or loss.

The amounts of coverage will vary for the different types of purposes. For example, liability coverage may be a million dollars per accident, while uninsured motorist's coverage may be $60,000 per accident.

WORKERS' COMPENSATION/EMPLOYER'S LIABILITY INSURANCE

Coverage

Workers' compensation laws vary significantly from state to state. A general insurance policy might state the coverage provision in this manner:

> *Workers' Compensation.* To pay promptly when due all compensation and other benefits required of the insured by the Workmen's Compensation Law.

The policy would have appended to it the locations of the PPO's operation, for purposes of identifying the states where it does business. Coverage would be in each of those states.

Commonly, the workers' compensation policy will have special endorsements and restrictions reflecting the particular requirements of each state.

Employer's liability insurance is designed to complement workers' compensation insurance. A coverage provision might read as follows:

> *Employers' Liability.* To pay on behalf of the insured all sums which the insured shall become legally obligated to pay as damages because of bodily injury by accident or disease, including death at any time resulting therefrom,
>
> (*a*) sustained in the United States of America, its territories or possessions, or Canada by any employee of the insured arising out of and in the course of his employment by the insured either in operations in state designated in Item 3 of the declarations or in operations necessary or incidental thereto, or
>
> (*b*) sustained while temporarily outside of the United States, its territories or possessions, or Canada by any employee of the insured who is a citizen or resident of the United States or Canada arising out of and in the course of his employment by the insured in connection with operations in a state designated in Item 3 of the declaration; but this insurance does not apply to any suit brought in or any judgment rendered by any court outside the United States of America, its territories or possessions, or Canada or to an action on such judgment wherever brought.

Exclusions from Coverage

Workers' compensation insurance covers only those items that are required by statute. Employer's liability insurance is not required statutorily and may be subject to a number of exclusions. These exclusions could include:

1. Liability assumed by the insured under any contract or agreement.

2. Punitive or exemplary damages on account of bodily injury or death of any employee employed in violation of law.
3. Any employee employed in violation of the law.
4. Any situation covered by the workers' compensation insurance.

Limits of Liability

Workers' compensation insurance provides only that coverage that is statutorily required. Employer's liability insurance sets a dollar amount of coverage for all losses in connection with a single incident or accident. There may be no aggregate amount.

BOILER AND MACHINERY DAMAGE INSURANCE

Coverage

Nonfire property damage insurance excludes many of the common risks associated with boilers and related equipment. A separate policy ordinarily is obtained for this risk. Coverage would include the loss of the property, plus the cost of temporary repair, and the cost of expediting the repair of damaged property.

As with other property insurance, the policy will identify the specific locations and equipment being insured.

Exclusions from Coverage

The focus of steam boiler insurance is on risks not generally covered by other types of property insurance. Thus, the following are typical exclusions:

1. Loss related to fire.
2. Loss related to a combustion explosion outside the boiler.
3. Loss from interruption of business.
4. Loss from lack of power, light, heat, steam, or refrigeration.
5. Loss from any other indirect result of an accident.

Limits of Liability

The insurance company's limit on its liability may be stated as a dollar amount per accident. The amount of the dollar limit will vary depending upon the extent of the machinery insured.

DIRECTORS' AND OFFICERS' LIABILITY INSURANCE

Coverage

Directors' and officers' liability insurance is designed to protect key members of the PPO from personal liability for operating the PPO. A coverage provision might read as follows:

> The insurer shall pay on behalf of the directors and officers (hereinafter called the insureds) loss arising from any claim or claims made against the

insureds, jointly or severally, during the policy period by reason of any wrongful act (as hereinafter defined) committed, attempted or allegedly attempted or committed by the insureds.

The insurer shall pay on behalf of the company loss arising from any claim or claims made against the insureds, jointly or severally, during the policy period by reason of any wrongful act committed or attempted or allegedly committed or attempted by the insureds, but only when the company is required or permitted to indemnify the directors or officers pursuant to statutory or common law, or pursuant to the charter or bylaws of the company.

Wrongful act might be defined as follows:

Any actual or alleged error, misstatement, misleading statement, act or omission, or neglect or breach of duty by the directors or officers in the discharge of their duties in their capacity as directors or officers of the company, either individually or collectively, or any matter claimed against them by reason of their being directors or officers of the company.

Thus, directors' and officers' insurance recognizes as a normal business risk potential liability of its key persons for operating the business. It insures these key persons directly, or insures the company to the extent it indemnifies these persons, for any liability by reason of directing the company.

Exclusions from Coverage

Directors' and officers' liability insurance does give broad coverage for liabilities arising from directing a PPO. There are some exclusions that are important.

1. Actual or alleged violations of the responsbilities, obligations, or duties imposed upon fidiciaries under the Employee Retirement Income Security Act of 1974 (ERISA).
2. Bodily injury, sickness, or death of any person, or persons, or damage to or any destruction of any tangible property.
3. Pollution or contamination based upon or attributable to violation or alleged violation of any federal, state, municipal or other governmental statute.
4. Claims brought by or on behalf of the Securities and Exchange Commission.
5. Libel and slander.
6. Claims based upon or attributed to the directors and officers gaining in fact any personal profit or advantage to which they were not legally entitled.

Limits of Liability

The insurance company's limit of liability is expressed as a specific dollar amount for each policy period, in excess of a retained amount. The retention may vary depending upon whether the incident giving rise to the claim of coverage concerns a director or officer, or the company.

The amount of the limit of liability will vary with the requirements of the PPO and its perceived risk.

In addition, the insurance company's liability may be limited to a set percent of all amounts owed above the retained limit, subject to the total dollar liability limit of the company.

CONCLUSION

PPOs, like other businesses, face a full range of exposure to liability, including slips and falls, fires, automobile accidents, and workers' compensation situations. As a health-related business, PPOs also face the risk of malpractice liability.

PPOs need to evaluate the risks they face and to consider appropriate insurance to limit their exposure. PPOs should be cautious when thinking of relying on the insurance of their provider members, as those policies might limit coverage and fail to provide real protection. Care is required to be sure that PPOs actually have all the protection their management— and those with whom they deal—believe they need.

NOTES

1. This chapter describes coverage, exclusions from coverage, and limitations on liability provisions that are commonly found in certain types of insurance policies. An individual policy may vary considerably from the typical provisions described here. The reader is cautioned that the terms "typically," "commonly," and "generally" have not been used more only to avoid gross repetition.

2. If each slips independently of the other, generally courts will find two occurrences. If one slips and, while falling, instinctively grabs the other for support, causing the second person to fall, a single occurrence is more likely to be found. This example underscores that coverage and limitations on coverage can depend heavily on the facts.

PART 4

FUTURE TRENDS

Looking Forward: The Future of Preferred Provider Organizations

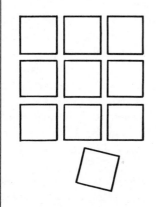

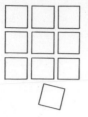

The Future of Preferred Provider Organizations

LOOKING FORWARD: THE FUTURE OF PPOS

Samuel J. Tibbitts

President
Lutheran Hospital Society of Southern California
Los Angeles, CA

Dennis W. Strum, Ph.D.

Vice-President Planning and Development
Lutheran Hospital Society of Southern California
Los Angeles, CA

☐ The PPO is one of the most significant organizational innovations in health care in this decade, but by the year 2000 the PPO may be extinct.

The PPO is a transitional vehicle for a health industry in flux. For hospitals, it provides a bridge to establishing contractual arrangements with consumers and major purchasers. For physicians, the PPO provides a way to stay in solo or small-group office practice and gain the benefits of expanded consumer volume. For insurance carriers, the PPO is the first step toward establishment of their own service delivery network with minimal capital investment. For major purchasers, the PPO provides convenience for employees and the price advantages of large-volume purchasing of health care services.

Whether the PPO survives the "turbulent 1980s" is not in question. The health care industry is in a watershed era of change, and the PPO is one of the key factors in its future.

A FUTURE HISTORY OF
HEALTHCARE REIMBURSEMENT

In the year 2000, historians will look back on the 20th century and see five stages of development in the history of health care reimbursement. (See Exhibit 1.)

EXHIBIT 1
100 Years of Healthcare
Reimbursement

1900
Phase I: Consumer payment out-of-pocket

1935
Phase II: Health insurance

1965
Phase III: Cost-reimbursement

1982
Phase IV: DRGs

1990
Phase V: Capitation

2000

At the beginning of the century, *consumers* paid for health care directly out of their pockets, with the exception of industries such as mining and the railroads, where company hospitals and physicians provided direct care. The needs of the poor were met through private charity. Most hospitals were small, under 25 beds, and physicians practiced solo. The development of Blue Cross during the Great Depression inaugurated a major change in health care reimbursement. Application of the *insurance* principle to health care provided security for millions. Hospitals grew larger and multispecialty groups began to develop in major cities and around teaching hospitals. Religious orders developed the first "hospital chains." Passage of medicare and medicaid in 1966 made government a major force in health care. Hospitals expanded rapidly, acquiring new technology. Physician group practice grew to become common in urban areas. Reimbursed on a *cost basis,* hospital costs rose rapidly. For-profit hospital chains, attracted by lenient government reimbursement policies, began to multiply in the South and West.

Unable to control its health care expenditures, the federal government initiated the fourth era, *DRGs.* Hospitals are now reimbursed on a prospective basis to manage patients on a case by case basis. Physicians are not yet covered by DRG-based payment but may be soon. The government plans to reduce payments over time, by squeezing hospitals into providing lower cost care. Insurers and major employers will begin to "coattail" on the federal government's DRG-based payment system.

During this period the PPO is emerging as a new type of "Alternative Delivery System." Promising to provide services at low-cost prices, the PPOs will flourish, but unable to really control cost, the PPO will eventually wane in popularity. By 1990, many PPOs will have failed or disbanded. The fifth and final phase in the evolution of health care reimbursement may be *capitation*. The health maintenance organization may become the dominant health care provider organization of the future, based on the effectiveness of the capitation payment rather than fee-for-service. To keep health costs down physicians would be allied with the HMOs, sharing financial risk and rewards. Some physicians may be salaried, but most would practice in professional corporations that would contract with the HMOs. Use of inpatient services would be discouraged, and hospital inpatient facilities will shrink. Long-term care, home care, and health promotion services would expand.

Most change is evolutionary—not revolutionary. PPOs are a key step in the evolution of the American health system.

Based on the findings of a new trends report, "Forecast 85," ten driving forces have been identifed that will be powerful factors in tomorrow's health care marketplace.[1] All forces will have a significant impact on the emergence of the PPO as a model for tomorrow's health care organizations. The ten driving forces and their implications for PPOs are:

Aging. Today, one out of nine Americans is over 85, in the year 2030 it will be one of five. Today's elderly are heavy health care users; they are three times as likely to be hospitalized. Tomorrow's elderly will be different. A new generation, the "Young Elders," will be healthier, more fit, better educated, more affluent, and better informed about their health than any generation of our elderly we have ever seen. PPOs that appropriately manage the health needs of the "Young Elders" (50 to 70) can build a solid consumer-base for the future.

Competition. The door to competition in health care has been opened, and there is no closing it. PPOs will compete on price. Major carriers are forming PPOs to compete with their own traditional health plans. By some estimates, 1,000 hospitals will close in this decade due to competitive pressures. PPOs will prosper. The PPOs will have the capacity to be large vendors to major corporations and insurance carriers buying health care in large volumes and at discount prices. Having the needed service capacity, location, and financial strength to compete on a volume/price basis will accelerate the growth of PPOs and leave the freestanding hospital in a precarious position.

Conglomerates. The PPO is a first-stage conglomerate. Today one out of 10 hospitals in the nation is affiliated with a PPO. In five years it will be one of two hospitals. Today's multihospital systems are small; only one owns more than 100 hospitals. By 1990, at least six multihealth corporations will own or manage more than 100 hospitals. Health care expenditures will reach nearly $700 billion by 1990; 20 percent will go to multihealth corporations. The health care industry is about to be totally restructured, and PPOs will be major building blocks of the new very large companies.

Corporate practice. Three forces will combine to fundamentally change medical practice: conglomerates, the information era, and the shifting dollar. One of two physicians practices in a group setting today; in the year 2000 it will be nine out of ten. Physicians will work with hospitals, not for them, through professional medical corporations. Hospitals and physicians will share financial risks and rewards, as reimbursement shifts from fee-for-service to capitation and prospective payment for diagnosis related groups (DRGs). Some PPOs will own or manage medical groups, but most will contract with doctor-owned professional corporations negotiating independently with the PPO. Their case management systems will incorporate the philosophy and style of practice of the PPO. Because it retains fee-for-service payment, the PPO is a bridge to the future of organized medicine. New data systems will fuse case management and cost accounting into powerful corporate management systems for the PPO.

New consumer. Recent opinion polls indicate consumer attitudes are shifting. Consumers have traditionally wanted quality regardless of cost. Today's consumer is more price sensitive. In Houston, there are more urgent care clinics than hospitals. The reason is simple; urgent care prices are only half of the cost for similar care in the hospital emergency room. The Rand study on consumers and health underscores the lesson that consumers are cost conscious.[2] Where deductibles and coinsurance were high, health care utilization was reduced by as much as 50 percent. Employers and insurance carriers are reinstalling front-end deductibles in health plans across the country. This shift in health benefits will have the short-term effect of reducing hospital and physician use. In the long-range, it will drive consumers into PPOs that have few or no coinsurance or deductibles.

Diversification. Most hospitals are still dependent upon inpatient-related revenues (95 to 99 percent of all revenues). The PPO offers hospitals a significant advantage in diversification and new business development. The PPO has the expertise, entrepreneurial experience, and access to major purchasers. Marketing has an expensive learning curve. The

PPO can provide centralized assistance to its hospitals and provider subsidiaries in marketing their services.

Information/telecommunications.   In the new information society, PPOs will be linked on a national and global basis by telecommunications. The American Hospital Supply Corporation is a model of a multinational company that has made extensive use of computer systems and video conferencing to link its worldwide network of facilities and services. Its computer-based links with customers provide a model for the health industry. More fundamentally—health is information. Reconceptualizing the "health" industry as providing information puts a new light on use of cable television, video discs and tapes, and even the telephone as ways of providing information to the consumer. Almost all of these are more cost efficient than the physician-patient encounter. The very large PPO, operating from a regional or national base, will have the capital and expertise to utilize these information technologies to the fullest.

Shifting dollars.   Health care dollars are shifting: from inpatient to outpatient; from fee-for-service to capitation and at-risk contracting; from public to private; and from acute care to long-term care and health promotion. The PPO must establish effective case management systems and have the discipline necessary to use them effectively. The PPOs will have real market advantages with their "preferred" status in being chosen "preferred provider" organizations, having the self-control to be low-cost producers.

Technology.   Technology will continue to be a major driving factor in health care. There is an estimated demand for 34,000 artificial hearts each year. The new alternative organs and joints—hip replacements, knees, livers—will similarly provide new market opportunities for hospitals. On the other hand, as technology becomes less costly and more portable, many procedures will be done out of the hospital using sophisticated new technology such as laser surgery. New "super-drugs" may eliminate procedures such as kidney stones and cardiac bypass surgery. PPOs will take a conservative stance towards high-cost technologies, and embrace lower-cost technological substitutions.

Values.   Today's board rooms are dominated by financial issues. The issues agenda of the first PPOs will be narrow: financial survival. Management values will play a key part in shaping the corporate culture of tomorrow's PPO. The leading companies in tomorrow's health industry will have a distinctive set of values at the core of its management approach. The PPO will have to deal with new bioethical issues raised by technologies such as in utero surgery. Issues of life and death will be highly complex. The PPO may need an in-house ethicist and ethics committee to provide guidance for boards and medical staff. As a very large corporate citizen, the PPO may also need an "issues management" program. Identifying emerging social and environmental issues will be in the best business as well as civic interest of the PPO.

ALTERNATIVE DELIVERY SYSTEMS

One of the most powerful structural factors in tomorrow's health industry is the uniting of financing and service delivery. These new "alternative delivery systems" (ADS) will be the dominant organizational form of the future. The PPO is only one form of ADS and is a transitional vehicle to move the health industry in this direction.

Until now health maintenance organizations, independent practitioner associations, medical foundations, and other forms of "alternative delivery systems" have all been outside the mainstream of modern health care delivery. Today, these alternative delivery systems seem on the threshold of national consumer and employer acceptance. HMO enrollment recently surged past 12 million consumers in the United States, and may rise to 40–50 million in this decade. In the west, where HMOs are best known, they have achieved penetration rates of as high as 25 percent (Los Angeles) and more than 30 percent (San Francisco/Alameda). In the Twin Cities of Minnesota, HMO enrollment has pushed past 25 percent and is still gaining. Estimates of potential HMO and other alternative delivery system penetration are being revised upwards.

In tomorrow's health care system, these ADSs will be the dominant organizational model. Today, the ADSs have 20 percent of the market, and traditional plans 80 percent. That 80-20 ratio may be reversed within 10 years. Traditional indemnity insurance, Blue Cross-type plans, and fee-for-service will see their market shares eroded substantially. By some estimates, the national enrollment in ADSs could reach 50 percent as soon as 1990. The trend is clear. ADS-type systems will not only have joined the mainstream, they will be the new standard against which other health organizations must compete.

STRATEGIC IMPLICATIONS FOR PPOs

Strategically managed organizations anticipate the future and plan for it. For PPOs the future is coming their way. The major driving forces that will most directly affect PPO growth and development are alternative delivery systems, corporate practice, the new consumer, and the shifting dollar.

PPOs and other ADSs are market-driven. The most successful PPOs will be those that can stay "close to the customer." Business will be the major purchaser of PPO services. Major employers are most cost-driven, and have great flexibility in volume purchasing. Union contracts will not be a substantial impediment. Employers will simply shift to lower-cost providers, not down-scale benefits. State government is also a potentially very large buyer of PPO services. In California, the state Medi-Cal program has contracted with a limited number of California hospitals through a process of open competition. The selective contracting program is saving the state of California an estimated $180 million in its first year. Almost certainly, other states will follow California's lead in selective contracting.

The trend toward *corporate practice* will be given impetus by the PPOs, which prefer to contract with physician groups. The professional medical corporation will provide the necessary administrative and data support to the PPO while retaining control for distribution of earnings to its participating physicians.

The *new consumer* is both price- and value-sensitive. As more major employers add coinsurance and deductibles to health plans, there will be a greater incentive for individual consumers to use PPOs where the deductibles or coinsurance provisions are waived.

The *shifting dollar* favors the PPO. As the most flexible organization on the health care scene, the PPO can potentially react more quickly to changes in buying patterns in consumer preferences. As the newest type of health care organization, it will have the least inertia to overcome in responding to market shifts. Entrepreneurs in health care will gravitate towards PPOs.

RECONCEPTUALIZING THE BUSINESS

In the future, the business of the health industry will be *health*. Two powerful trends are converging: capitation will become the dominant form of payment, and alternative delivery systems will be the dominant organizational form.

The business of health care organizations of tomorrow will be the health of their consumers. With a contractual relationship between health plan and consumer, under a pre-set capitation payment, all incentives will operate to keep the consumers healthy and out of the hospital.

These powerful forces from within the industry will align with changing consumer attitudes. The "new consumers" are taking more personal responsibility for their health. Tomorrow's consumers will be better educated, more informed, and better able to make effective use of their health delivery systems. Employers have an economic incentive to keep their work force healthy. Many major corporations are already beginning to provide incentives and support for healthy lifestyles. It is good business.

PATHS TO THE PPO FUTURE

There will be many ways to establish a successful PPO. Here are three scenarios:

1. *The Alliance:* Health care system *alliances* can be easily formed. They require little or no capital investment by the participating organizations. At the heart of the alliance is the promise to provide services on demand, giving priority to the customers of the PPO. Commitment is minimal. This PPO system is loosely linked. For cautious health care organizations and providers, it is a low-risk initiative. In these early days of the PPO concept, there will be many alliances formed, but relatively few will succeed in the marketplace. Potential customers, especially major employers, will regard them with suspicion for their limited track record and lack of cost-management controls. Among providers, the "alliance" will be a popular form, but in the marketplace, it may be a difficult concept to sell.

2. *PPO Association:* Bringing independent practitioners and hospitals into a formal *association* is hardly easy. Joining a PPO association is like joining a club. There are rules by which all must abide for the greater good of all members. Associations need contracts, lawyers, data systems, audits, and controls. Individual practitioners and hospitals are still paid on a fee-for-service basis. Prices are negotiated, usually below market rates. In return, there is additional volume and timely payment. In today's health care marketplace, both are advantageous to any provider. PPO associations must make a critical choice: either they exist for the sake of their members or for long-term organizational survival. PPOs organized only to advance the interests of member practitioners will almost certainly fail when they cannot control expenditures by their members. These PPO associations must make a conscious decision to become permanent organizations with an arms-length relationship with their provider associates.

3. *PPO Organization:* Most difficult to start but most likely to succeed is the PPO *organization.* First and foremost, the PPO is a business. Consumer satisfaction is the "bottom-line" for the PPO organization. Providers will be treated in a fair-handed manner, but the PPO organization is not provider-driven. Many forms of sponsorship can be potentially successful: multi-health corporation, insurer, even government. There are two experiments in California where counties have developed their own PPOs to care for Title 19 Medi-Cal beneficiaries. Existing HMOs can use the PPO organization as a strategy for entering new markets, converting the PPO to a more tightly organized HMO form in the future.

LIFE CYCLE OF THE PPO

All products have life cycles (see Exhibit 2). PPOs are still in the phase of product development and testing. Their growth still lies ahead. The PPO is not a fad, but it will have a limited life cycle. New variations on

EXHIBIT 2
PPO Product Life Cycle

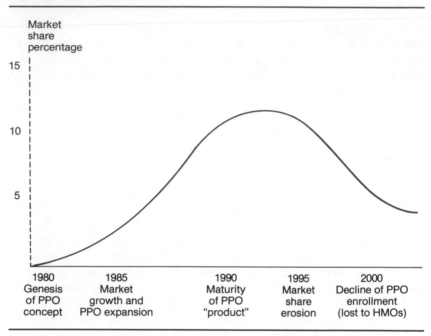

1980	1985	1990	1995	2000
Genesis of PPO concept	Market growth and PPO expansion	Maturity of PPO "product"	Market share erosion	Decline of PPO enrollment (lost to HMOs)

PPO models will continue to come forward. It is not yet clear which form of PPO sponsorship will be most successful.

PPOs are now entering the growth phase. Marketing campaigns are active and beginning to show some success. A number of PPO contracts have been signed in the past year. Conservative estimates for market share potential are between five and ten percent of the health insurance market within five years. The market revenues at stake for PPO developers are very large.

The PPO concept should reach maturity between the years 1990 and 1995 and begin a product decline by the year 2000. As the PPO becomes well-established, PPO price wars are inevitable. As one of the most entrepreneurial types of health care organizations in the industry, the PPO competition could trigger a wave of price competition in the late 1980s and early 1990s. Many PPOs see their primary competitive advantage today in positioning themselves as the lowest cost producer.

As the PPO concept wanes on the product life-cycle curve, new competitors and organizational innovations will overcome it. Cutting through the product life cycle will be the continuing growth of alternative delivery systems (ADS). PPOs will not die, in many cases but convert to more centrally managed structures.

FAD OR MARKET TREND

The PPO concept is new. It is championed by some as the next phase in the evolution of the health care system. Others, especially employers and major purchasers, are more skeptical.

Are PPOs the "hula hoop" of the health care industry of the 1980s? Opinions are divided. The PPO concept is controversial. In some sectors, the response has been enthusiastic; in others, lukewarm or hostile. The following commentary reflects a broad spectrum of opinion on the future of PPOs:

Beware of providers bearing gifts. Willis Goldbeck, Executive Director of the Washington Business Group on Health, reflects the skepticism of some major employers. The business community should be cautious of PPOs.

> Unlike health maintenance organizations which, for better or worse, receive government specified definitions as to structure, obligations and financing, PPOs are the creation of those who buy and sell health and medical care. In simplest terms, the PPO concept is nothing more than a buyer-seller negotiated agreement covering services, conditions of service, and price. The absence of a specific PPO definition should be seen as an advantage. Greater rigidity should be resisted. Regarding discounts, however, as the business community knows, no business offers a discount for any other purpose than to strengthen its economic position. The PPO movement is a healthy development that needs only one guarantee to succeed: information for a truly free market negotiation to exist. Purchasers must insist on, be willing to pay for, and interpret with care, the utilization, quality, cost and price data that will bring them to the table at parity with the sellers. Nothing less than the quality of care for all patients is at stake.

Helping doctors to survive. Martin Dale, a PPO developer based in Los Angeles, links the PPO to the economic survival of medical practice. "As for the doctors, I can't give an example of a PPO they're happy with. They don't like giving up any autonomy. But they do feel the PPO is helping them survive." Contract medicine is not new. Blue Shield first contracted with doctors in 1939, but contracts are changing because of competitive pressures. PPOs are moving to close their panels. Dale reports that the Adolph Coors Company in Colorado recently sent a letter to area doctors inviting them to join the company's health plan. Coors said, "If you sign up you'll continue to see our employees as patients. If you don't, we'll try to direct them away from you." For physicians, the handwriting is on the wall. PPOs do not succeed by discounts alone. They must control their physicians, who will simply bill for more services and procedures without such constraints. Dale tells doctors not to get into PPOs unless they are prepared to dramatically alter the way they practice.

Return of the insurers.   Health insurers have been hardhit by competition from self-insurance and PPOs. PPOs organized by insurers are having more success signing up companies that will offer the PPO to their employees than are PPOs that hospitals have developed. Joan B. Trauner, Ph.D, of the Institute for Health Policy Studies at the University of California, San Francisco, believes that in California, insurers and employers will ultimately have the upper hand in the PPO market. The ability to organize PPOs by providers has outstripped their ability to market them. Employers have been unwilling to gamble that PPOs actually will check rapidly rising health care costs. PPOs do not have enough of a track record yet. Many insurance carriers are unconvinced that hospital-based PPOs have improved cost efficiency enough to warrant shifting the bulk of their subscribers to the preferred providers. Hospitals also are at a disadvantage because they have no way to evaluate a physician's practice outside the hospital. They cannot identify efficient providers before they set up a PPO. Insurer-based PPOs will have the advantage of established claims management systems to weed out high-cost medical practitioners.

Employer-risk equals rewards.   Employers can achieve health care cost savings if they are willing to take a larger role in the direct management of provider relations. Peter D. Fox, Vice President of Lewin and Associates, Inc., Washington, D.C., puts the issue squarely to the employers: "The organization that bears the risk must either manage that risk or continue accepting premium rate increases of the current magnitude or greater. Dealing with Alternative Delivery Systems is a critical element of risk management." Employers must be discriminating in their choice of PPOs. The Denver experience may be instructive. Denver PPO hospitals are among the most expensive in the area. Four of the five highest-cost hospitals are PPO members. There are a number of successful examples where major employers have managed their own health costs. The PPO is one such option.

Corporate PPOs.   One corporation has started its own PPO. In fact, the Cleveland-based Stouffer Corporation has launched four of them. Stouffer's involvement with PPOs began three years ago, with the first PPO contract for dental care. Early results were promising. A second dental PPO was organized. Dental plan 1 has reduced Stouffer's dental cost by 20 percent, and dental plan 2 by 35 percent. The success of those two PPOs encouraged formation of a PPO for medical services. In response to Stouffer's interest, two PPOs were formed: one physician-based, the second hospital-managed. The hospital-based PPO has been particularly successful; its costs are nearly 25 percent below the Cleveland average. The physician-based PPOs' costs are still above the community average. More than 50 percent of Stouffer's local employees have signed with PPOs. The Stouffer Corporation believes PPOs are here to stay. In San Diego, employers took the initiative in forming a new PPO, The Community Care Network. PPOs provide an excellent opportunity to select providers with a desired style of practice and track record of lower costs. Dealing through the PPO gives employers a measure of influence with hospitals and physicians they never had before. In San Diego, employers recognize price is not the only criterion. Hospitals selected must carry their fair share of community care to the poor. The employers hope to use their PPO leverage to ultimately achieve one-price equity across all payors, and end the problem of cost shifting.

Surviving the "Dark Ages." Medieval medicine? By all accounts the draw bridges are closing. But opportunities are rising just as fast. PPOs, IPOs, and other multiple allegiances are being formed. John Pinto, a San Diego health care marketing consultant, calls it the "medievalization of medicine." Physicians as independent tradesmen are forming "guilds" through new physician associations outside the traditional bounds of medical societies to protect their interests. Large physician groups, clinics, and hospitals form a "ruling class," consolidating their power bases by controlling groups of patients and making pacts with neighboring "kingdoms," the employer coalitions and insurance carriers. Small battles for control are breaking out between competing groups; nothing serious yet, but the campaign should intensify as the stakes increase.

LOOKING FORWARD: THE FAR FUTURE OF PPOs

For today, the future of PPOs is bright. It is a fresh and imaginative concept that will invigorate the health care industry. The PPO will be a lively source of competition for established health insurers and organizations.

The PPO movement is part of a larger shift within the health industry towards capitation and ADSs. The PPO is a transitional vehicle. Hospitals and physicians can join PPOs and still maintain much of their independence. The experience of working within the PPO structure will provide a base for the development of more fully developed health care finance and delivery systems.

A closely related development is the growth of large "multihealth corporations." These new health care companies will grow very large, the conglomerates of the future health industry. Some of these new multihealth corporations will own their own PPOs or even take the PPO as their primary organizational form.

In business, as well as athletics, the race goes usually to the swift and the strong. The PPO has demonstrated its ability to develop swiftly. Now the market will test whether the PPO will be strong.

NOTES

1. The Lutheran Hospital Society of Southern California established the first futures research program in the health industry and hired the first corporate futurist. The five-step program for advance planning is called "Foresight." This program has been expanded to serve LHS and the three multihealth corporations that have jointly established the Health Network of America.

2. For additional information on the Rand Study see previous chapter entitled, "Economics of PPO Participation."

PART 5

CURRENT PREFERRED PROVIDER ARRANGEMENTS: CASE STUDIES

1. State Policy
2. Physician Sponsored
3. IPA/HMO Sponsored
4. Hospital Sponsored
5. Health/Hospital Service Plan Sponsored
6. Entrepreneurial/Investor Sponsored
7. Insurance Carrier Sponsored
8. Employer Initiated/Sponsored
9. Labor Organization Initiated/Sponsored

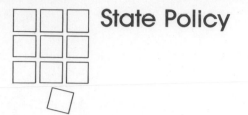 **State Policy**

CASE STUDY: SELECTIVE CONTRACTING IN CALIFORNIA*

Lucy Johns, M.P.H.

*Independent Consultant
Health Care Planning and Policy
San Francisco, CA*

California was the first state to adopt selective contracting by both public and private third-party payors as a preferred policy approach to containment of health care costs. Within only two and a half months in the spring of 1982, selective contracting was conceived, drafted, passed by the legislature, and signed by the governor. Thus was a tactic—the negotiation of a contract between a third-party payor and a provider—raised to the level of state policy. The result of this policy was intended to be the inducement of price competition and the lowering of prices in the health care marketplace. This chapter describes the origin, initial impact, and some important implications of selective contracting as state policy.[1]

Selective contracting means the ability of a third-party payor to contract for delivery of health services to beneficiaries *only* with those pro-

---

*Financed in part by the John A. Hartford Foundation, New York, NY, and sponsored by the National Governors' Association, Washington, DC. All opinions expressed herein are the author's alone. Assistance and support of R. A. Derzon and M. Anderson of Lewin and Associates, Washington, DC, is gratefully acknowledged.

viders agreeing to accept a negotiated price for their services. California third-party payors now permitted to contract selectively include the medicaid program ("Medi-Cal"), Blue Cross, and indemnity carriers (private insurance companies). Although there is wide variation in the potential financial significance of contracting for an individual hospital, revenue from Medi-Cal plus private insurance accounts for about two thirds of the patient revenue of the average hospital.

ORIGIN OF SELECTIVE CONTRACTING

As with many policy changes perceived as abrupt by those affected, selective contracting legislation enacted in California in 1982 permits an unexpectedly sweeping application of a relatively familiar idea.

Selective contracting had appeared in both the public and private sectors during the 1970s. The Medi-Cal program experimented (unsuccessfully) with such contracting with prepaid health plans in the early 1970s, and continued to favor and publicize the concept throughout the decade. In the private sector, selective contracting was viewed by some large employers and business coalitions in southern California as a promising cost-containment option for self-insured firms, and a few such contracts began to appear in the late 1970s.

Widespread use of selective contracting was nevertheless infeasible due to federal and state requirements regarding patients' "freedom of choice." (Selective contracting in practice implies no or diminished reimbursement to a "noncontract" provider. The resulting financial penalty for the patient interferes with freedom of choice.) Federal medicaid regulations prohibited programs designed to limit freedom of choice, except as might be permitted by special waiver, and state law forbade private insurers and Blue Cross[2] from restricting in any manner the "right" of an individual to select a physician or hospital.

By the spring of 1982, however, several political and economic factors combined to override the traditional value placed on freedom of choice. Hospital costs and prices in California were increasing at rates approaching 20 percent per year. Private insurers were losing millions on their health benefits policies. The Reagan administration had made a waiver from medicaid regulations much easier to obtain (Omnibus Budget Reconciliation Act of 1981). Most importantly, the state of California, already reeling from diminution of its taxing powers by Proposition 13 (June, 1978), faced a drastic reduction in its tax revenues due to economic recession. Action to decrease the Medi-Cal budget (more than 15 percent of the state's budget) and to intervene in the inflationary spiral of hospital costs became inescapable.

The result was the 1982 package of bills—AB 799, AB 3480, and SB 2012—enabling selective contracting by the state and by private insurers and Blue Cross. AB 799 established the new position of "special negotiator," appointed by the Governor and empowered to negotiate contracts with hospitals for inpatient care of Medi-Cal beneficiaries as of July 1, 1982.[3] AB 3480 permitted insurers and Blue Cross to negotiate "alternative rates" with both hospitals and physicians as of July 1, 1983 and to ignore, in these cases, the "free choice" provisions otherwise required. SB 2012 was a "cleanup bill" whose major feature was an exemption for the special negotiator from the customary public disclosure required for all state proceedings.

The expectations accompanying the contracting legislation were high. In total, the statutes were intended to introduce "competition" for the first time to a field universally presumed to lack any. Due to the state's surplus of hospital beds and services, it was anticipated that providers, anxious to ensure a steady flow of patients, would engage in price competition to secure contracts. A corollary expectation was that inefficient providers would not survive, thereby ameliorating the state's long-standing problem of excess capacity. It was finally hoped that the insurance industry would utilize AB 3480 to protect itself against the "cost shifting" that would otherwise result from reductions in Medi-Cal reimbursement. In sum, selective contracting was viewed and promulgated as a historic attempt to crack the intractable problem of inflation in the cost of health care.

IMPACT OF SELECTIVE CONTRACTING

The nature of reimbursement to hospitals and physicians is a central organizing principle for the health care system. When the reimbursement mechanism changes significantly, the values, attitudes, behavior, and relationships of health care organizations and professionals can be expected to shift noticeably. With selective contracting elevated to state policy for both public and private payors, the effects on "the system" were immediate, widespread, and diverse.

IMPACT ON STATE GOVERNMENT

The implementation of the Medi-Cal contracting legislation posed an unprecedented challenge to the executive branch in terms of structure, activities, and timetable. A special negotiator, located in the Governor's Office, was to be appointed for a term of only one year, during which the "rates, terms and conditions" of contracts with some 600 hospitals were to be negotiated. The negotiator, quickly dubbed the "Medi-Cal Czar," was accorded "maximum discretion and flexibility" to develop any contracting process deemed expedient. The czar could call on any state department for help, was not subject to review by any state agency, was bound by no accountability procedures, and could function in complete secrecy. The state Department of Health Services (DHS), hitherto the location of all Medi-Cal program administration, had no role in the contracting undertaken by the negotiator, but would be obligated by, and have to monitor the terms of, the contracts. After a year, on July 1, 1983, the negotiator's position would be eliminated, his responsibilities being taken over by a nine-person California Medical Assistance Commission (CMAC). The state's response to this unusual mandate is noteworthy for its speed, simplicity, absence of legal entanglements, and strong sense of priorities.

The major events during the first hectic year of Medi-Cal contracting may be summarized as follows:

1. Appointment of the special negotiator: On July 8, 1982, ten days after the legislation had been signed, Governor Edmund G. Brown, Jr. announced the appointment of William Guy, former President of Blue Cross-Southern California, as the Medi-Cal czar.

2. Establishment of the Governor's Office of Special Health (Care) Negotiations (GOSHN)—Within a few days, Guy recruited two assistants, who in turn recruited a staff of eight over the next two months. This small group of highly committed staff conducted all of GOSHN's activities over the next year.

3. Securing of a federal waiver—Selective contracting by the Medi-Cal program required a waiver from the federal government on a number of issues, including freedom of choice and the typical cost-based, hospital reimbursement methodology. Legally, the negotiator could not proceed without such a waiver. Whereas a waiver request of the significance of California's might ordinarily take at least six months to process, the waiver was granted in September, 1982.

4. Design and disclosure of a negotiating process—By October, 1982, Guy and GOSHN staff had debated and resolved a myriad of complex contracting issues.[4] Most important, it was decided that there would be: face-to-face "negotiations" with every hospital; a "model contract," any proposed changes to which would decrease a hospital's chance of getting one; a preference for an "all-inclusive per diem" form of reimbursement; and protection of beneficiary access by extension of a negotiation invitation to all acute care hospitals in the state.[5] Negotiations would take place in "waves" by hospital planning area, starting with the state's four largest cities. These and numerous other decisions were never put into regulation. They were revealed piecemeal by Guy in a ceaseless round of speeches and interviews.

5. Conduct of negotiations—The first wave of negotiations commenced in October, 1982. By the time Guy departed the special negotiator position on June 30, 1983, 417 hospitals had been involved in the contracting process (72 percent of the total 581), 365 had entered into negotiations, and 245 of these (67 percent) had been awarded contracts.

The outcome of Medi-Cal contract negotiations by month is detailed in Exhibit 1.

6. Appointment of CMAC—One of Gov. Brown's final acts was appointment of the nine CMAC members. Although CMAC had no role to play until July, 1983, it began meeting monthly as of February. It did, however, issue a report to the legislature on Medi-Cal contracting, the only public document produced by GOSHN during its first year.[6]

7. Organization of contract monitoring responsibility—After lengthy consideration of the alternatives, DHS' Medi-Cal activities were not reorganized at all in response to AB 799. The Medi-Cal Operations Division has overall contract monitoring responsibility. Day-to-day contract problems and all utilization review are handled in DHS' 12 field offices scattered around the state. The Division's only new task related to contracting is the management of an "incident reporting" system to track contract implementation problems.

The fiscal impact on the state of the first year of selective contracting is simply stated: an estimated savings on Medi-Cal inpatient expenditures of $165 million in fiscal year 1983-1984,[7] producing a decline of 11.8 percent from comparable inpatient expenditures in the previous year.[8]

EXHIBIT 1
California Hospitals by Final Medi-Cal Contract Status and Contract Effective Date
California, FY 1982–83 (approximate)

Contract Effective Date	Medi-Cal Contract Hospitals	Non-Contract Hospitals	Exempt Hospitals	Other Hospitals*	Total Hospitals
Feb. 1, 1983	43	20†	0	5	68†
March 1, 1983	19	15	2	6	42
April 1, 1983	74	51	1	24	150
May 1, 1983	13	11	0	2	26
June 1, 1983	38	3	0	2	43
July 1, 1983	50‡	23	2	1	82
Aug. 1, 1983	8	2	0	1	11
Total	245	120§	5	47	417§
Open/deferred areas	—	157	—	7	164
State total	245	277	5	54	581

*Nonacute care hospitals (psychiatric, alcoholism, rehabilitation, etc.)

†Includes the five San Francisco hospitals which were noncontract until negotiations were reopened in April.

‡Includes the five San Francisco hospitals awarded contracts in April.

§Nonduplicated count, hence column does not add. Excludes the five San Francisco hospitals originally noncontract in February, 1983, which received contracts effective July 1, 1983.

SOURCE: L. Johns, R. A. Derzon, and M. Anderson, *Selective Contracting for Health Services in California—First Report*, National Governors' Association, 1983, p. 50.

This result was accomplished with minimal disruption of patient flow,[9] a negligible number of documentable "horror stories,"[10] no obvious trend as yet toward "two-tier" care for Medi-Cal patients,[11] only two legal suits, both settled out of court, and no accusations of corruption or shady dealings, even by watchdog agencies inclined to look for same.[12]

The long-term impact on the state can only be surmised. It is unlikely that a nine-member commission will move as forcefully or quickly to pressure hospitals as the Medi-Cal czar did. Further changes in Medi-Cal reimbursement are contemplated but are not certain and would in any case be phased in over several years. There has been some tension over the respective jurisdictions of the CMAC and DHS. Although manageable, it is not likely to disappear. Further inpatient reimbursement savings are anticipated, but of a much lower order than in the first dramatic year.

IMPACT ON THE PRIVATE INSURANCE MARKETPLACE

The impact of AB 3480 on the design and sale of health insurance benefits in California is at once more diffuse and potentially more profound than the impact of AB 799 on state government. A great variety of organizations were affected, including commercial insurers, Blue Cross, Blue Shield, third-party administrators (TPAs), insurance brokers, purchasers of health benefits (employers and union trust funds), already existing "preferred provider organizations" (PPOs), health service providers interested in forming PPOs, and HMOs. The legislation directly enabled action only by insurers and Blue Cross. But in freeing these large entities to engage in selective contracting, it created potential new competition for existing PPOs and HMOs and stimulated purchasers and providers to consider new roles, activities, and structures to effect measurable "cost containment." The result is a pervasive new sensitivity to the price of health care services on the part of both those who buy them and those who furnish them.

At the same time, the number of "players" and problems involved in any concrete response to AB 3480 means that the development of selective contracting approaches and entities by the private sector has been slower than all the talk, press coverage, and seminars would lead one to believe. Interest in contracting is unquestionably high and intentions are vigorous. But real barriers do exist, requiring talent, time, and capital to overcome.

It should be recalled at this point that some contracting between purchasers and individual providers had begun to appear prior to enactment of the legislation. (These activities between private parties required no state permission and they remain unregulated in any way.) Self-insured firms with local market clout and a scattering of TPAs had moved to create a "preferred provider" benefits option, generally encompassing a discount off usual charges, plus a financial incentive for employees to select the "preferred provider" benefit and to use the contract providers when illness occurred. Similarly, a few hospitals were beginning to organize provider networks to make themselves available to TPAs, brokers, and self-insured firms for contract negotiations. The resulting arrangements were very limited in terms of numbers of employees to whom benefits were available, and with the exception of one unsuccessful hospital network in San Francisco, confined to the Los Angeles-San Diego areas. Nevertheless, contracts negotiated independently of AB 3480 are part of the "PPO phenomenon" in California (see Implications, below) and were in fact stimulated by passage of the legislation.

The first insurer to develop and market a preferred provider benefit in direct response to AB 3480 was Blue Cross.[13] Blue Cross mailed a model hospital and a model physician contract to its "first wave" hospitals in March 1983. Uproar ensued. Hospitals were unhappy that the contract looked so much like the Medi-Cal contract, including the undifferentiated per-diem payments. Physicians, encountering their first contract to include negotiated rates and mandatory submission to nondelegated utilization review, were very unhappy. Blue Cross, traditionally closer to hospitals and more vulnerable to informal pressure than the state, met with many hospital groups and county medical societies and did modify the model contracts to some extent. Nevertheless, no hospital could afford to decline Blue Cross' offer, and several, having lost out on Medi-Cal contracts, were desperate. At a jubilant press conference in June 1983 to announce the first contract awards, Blue Cross stated that it had contracted with only 25 percent of the hospitals making offers, and that the contract rates should produce premium savings of 10 to 15 percent. As for physicians, while they did not care for the contract, fear of losing patients to nearby competitors won out in the end. By the end of the year, Blue Cross had contracts with nearly 150 hospitals and over 9,000 physicians statewide and was just beginning to market its "prudent buyer benefit" to its large accounts. The premium for the new policy is comparable to those of Blue Cross's own HMO and to Kaiser (by far the largest HMO in the state) and well below that for traditional fee-for-service policies with comparable benefits.

Contracting activity by other insurers in the state has been more cautious. While Pacific Mutual and Blue Shield were ready to market PPO options in selected areas in early 1984, most insurers were still in developmental stages 20 months after the legislation was passed. The pace of contracting by commercial insurers has thus been relatively slow compared to the expectations and to the very widespread interest reported in the possibility.

Several barriers to rapid implementation of selective contracting by private parties are worth mentioning. From the insurer point of view, a key problem is the selection of providers with whom to contract. The authority to negotiate "alternative rates" puts insurers in the unaccustomed position of having to select a group of providers which can be marketed as a quality source of health care at, nevertheless, lower prices. This role is a major change for insurers, and they generally realize these are not decisions to be made lightly. The typical insurer will be seeking broad geographic coverage, some evidence of commitment to cost containment, and a willingness to submit to (more or less vigorous) utilization review. Whether providers come forth or have to be sought, there is no mechanical technique for testing their suitability or stability as preferred providers. A corollary problem is the creation and analysis of a data base to monitor experience under contracting, in order to identify high-cost problem areas, whether diagnoses, patients, physicians, or hospitals. This is not a simple task, nor is it cheap, and again, it is unfamiliar.

From the provider point of view, contracting presents formidable challenges. The creation of a provider network large enough to appeal to an insurer or a multisite firm requires a substantial effort. Physician staffs and hospitals must work out cooperative arrangements, institutions must seek compatible partners, policies on pricing and utilization review must be developed, and antitrust considerations must be evaluated at every turn. Once a network is in place, care must be exercised in choosing the agents who will carry the news of its existence to employers. Hospitals are not necessarily expert in judging the viability of potential contractors, especially TPAs and multiple-employer trusts (METs). Physicians who look to the California Medical Association (CMA) for assistance are advised to contract with anyone only with extreme caution.[14]

Clearly, risks must be taken and accommodations made on many sides before selective contracting can produce a marketable product, a "PPO." There is a ferment of activity to set up the necessary structures and arrangements. But the real market test of PPOs—their bargaining power vis-à-vis providers, their attractiveness to consumers—was still to come in 1984. The true impact of selective contracting on private expenditures for health care will not be measurable for some time.

IMPACT ON PROVIDERS

Selective contracting as envisioned by the state's political leadership embodies strong incentives for hospitals to adopt more competitive attitudes and more cost-conscious behavior. On a per capita basis, inpatient admissions and patient days have been declining for a decade in California; statewide occupancy of available beds has been under 70 percent for 10 years.[15] Whereas resource inputs to hospital services—staff, physicians, equipment, technology, capital—have been readily available, patients are becoming relatively more scarce.[16] Since a contract has the potential to protect and possibly to enlarge a hospital's patient base, competition for contracts should quickly occur. Further, effective competition means competition on price. This, in turn, implies the need for cost containment. While it cannot be proven that the legislation alone produced them, there is little question that the desired effects are beginning to take place.

Within only a few months after the legislation was passed, competitive assumptions and practices began to color decision making by hospitals in California. Open and direct advertising appeared, and the "marketing" function, previously merely fashionable, became a pivotal management task. Corporate diversification, "product-line management," and financial rewards for efficient departmental management are coming into vogue. CEOs meeting in their regional councils are reluctant now to talk about institutional plans and problems, for concerns about competitive advantage and "antitrust" are rampant. Perhaps most important, there are indications that "cost cutting" has replaced "cost shifting" as the principal strategy for protecting financial viability in the short run. Cost cutting on an unprecedented scale is occurring: hospitals surveyed in a recent study reported budgeted increases of 6.5 to 10 percent,[17] entailing cuts in entire programs and staff decreases of dozens of "full-time equivalent" (FTE) personnel. Statewide data for 1983 show a hospital expense increase of 6.6 percent,[18] compared to 17.8 percent for all of 1981, and 12.8 percent for 1982. Although data showing charges to nongovernmental payors in 1983 and 1984 are not yet available, the combination of medicare per-case reimbursement, Medi-Cal contracts, and the imminence of private payor contracts leaves few patients on whom to shift unreimbursed costs.

The ultimate desired effect, reduction of hospital prices to payors offering contracts, cannot be documented as yet. Medi-Cal contract prices are not public, and private contract prices are not reportable. But there are some indications that price competition was vigorous in the first round of Medi-Cal and Blue Cross negotiations. Over half the hospitals in a recent sample settled for contract prices below their fiscal year 1981–1982 rates, and only two of these hospitals received any notable increase over their previous reimbursement, as shown in Exhibit 2. William Guy has stated that his contract decisions in San Francisco precipitated a frantic revision of "best and final offers" elsewhere in the state.[19] And Blue Cross awarded contracts to a suggestive number of hospitals that had only just failed to win a Medi-Cal contract.[20] Unfortunately, no other payor has issued any official statements on contract prices. The evidence of price competition so far is thus limited and somewhat indirect. But the signs do portend some move in this direction.

The impact of contracting on California physicians has also been dramatic. Although the Medi-Cal program opted not to engage in physician contracting in the first year, private payors began to descend on physicians in droves by mid-1983. Physicians' initial response to contracting evinced "...that complex of emotions—disbelief, fear, anger, resignation—reminiscent of the cycle observed in dying patients."[21] A conviction of helplessness and loss of control in the face of bewildering and hostile

EXHIBIT 2
Medi-Cal Contract Rates (offers)*
as a Percentage of FY 1981–82
Medi-Cal Per Diem Reimbursement †
Sample Hospitals
FY 1982–83

Hospital‡	Rate (offer rejected) as Percent FY 1982 per Diem
Ruby	75
Opal	78
Amber	80
Diamond	(83)
Pearl	92
Garnet	95
Topaz	98
Zircon	(102)
Sapphire	105
Jade	107
Amethyst	108
Emerald	(116)
Coral	(121)
Aquamarine	123
Onyx	(124)
Turquoise	143

*Rate (offer) when HFPA closure was announced. Some rates (offers) were renegotiated before the end of the fiscal year.

†Medi-Cal per diem reimbursement = non-MIA, non–cross-over, actual general acute care reimbursement per day, excluding nursery days, for FY 1981–82, adjusted for 6 percent cap court settlement of July 1982.

‡Since Medi-Cal contracts and prices are not publicly available, the hospitals participating in the NGA study are referred to by code names, and price data are presented only in percentage terms.

SOURCE: L. Johns, R. A. Derzon, M. Anderson, *Selective Contracting for Health Services in California—First Report,* National Governors' Association, 1983, p. 78.

changes was widespread. One early reflection of this distress was an attempt by the CMA to weaken AB 3480 significantly in the spring of 1983. The failure of this bill even to reach the floor of the legislature reflects a noteworthy decline in the political clout of "organized medicine" in the state.

As this realization sank in and the first shock wore off, many physicians have begun to come to grips with contracting and its implications. A "contract evaluation/negotiation service" established by the CMA to advise individual physicians about contracting in general and specific contracts on request has been widely used. Some of the major group practices in the state are organizing a PPO; a number of hospital medical staffs have formed, or soon will, corporate structures to facilitate participation in hospital-sponsored PPOs. One county medical society has mounted an extensive planning and educational effort to help its members understand "the new world."

It remains to be seen, however, how physicians will finally adjust to the challenge of contracting. Their excess number in the state suggests that they will accommodate to selective contracting in some manner. But a successful PPO will require a physician commitment to abide by any utilization-review process established by the PPO. This contractual obligation raises a number of serious issues, the most prominent being malpractice liability and the second-guessing of medical judgment. Who will control the practice of medicine, as fixed price, contractual relationships begin to pervade the field? This question sums up the complex issues of physician responsibility and accountability thrown up by a state policy of selective contracting.

IMPLICATIONS

California's sudden shift away from the traditional reimbursement patterns for health care implies some practical lessons for other states or private parties considering similar approaches.

First, selective contracting will not work unless all (major) payors engage in it. As with any reimbursement change intended to decrease payments, a provider's first response will be to allocate unreimbursed costs to other payors. Only if other payors can and do act to prevent such "cost shift" will the provider be faced squarely with the remaining alternative: to cut costs. While it is true that medicare is not participating in selective contracting, neither is medicare a viable target for cost shifting.

Second, price negotiations in selective contracting will not accomplish cost containment without some form of utilization review. Selective contracting as currently practiced in California does not cap expenditures for payors or revenues for providers. Contract negotiations concentrate on the price to be paid per unit of service (a day, a case, an item like a semiprivate room). Since increased volume can compensate for reduced prices and there is no cap on total reimbursement, utilization must be controlled by utilization review. Such review can be performed by the payor, as with Med-Cal,[22] or it can be contracted to firms specializing in this field.

Third, it must be clear in the legislation that there is no entitlement on the part of providers to receive a contract under any selective contracting process. A provider knowing that some kind of contract is inevitable has less incentive to negotiate seriously. Further, any form of entitlement invites suits and reversals of purchaser decisions by court order. Use of competition for distribution of contracts, on the other hand, offers few grounds for challenge. The terms of a competitive process are simple and straightforward: if the price (and such other conditions as may be specified) is right, a contract will be forthcoming. Failure to win a contract means the price was not right. It does not indicate a violation of "due process" or some other legal right. It can hardly be overstated how serious a reversal this is. Private health insurance evolved under the theory, and medicare and medicaid under a mandate, that universal provider participation was required, necessary, and desirable. With selective contracting, this notion is out the window, with possible serious consequences for some providers.

A corollary is that there must be very strong bipartisan and executive/legislative branch support for contracting. Politicians must understand that no provider can be assured of a contract by virtue of past performance, community role, or political clout. The heat, naturally, will be intense.

Fourth, the medicaid program must have a backup payment system, independent of the contracting process, for medical emergencies. If emergency payments look unfavorable to the provider compared to contracting, an incentive to contract is created. If, on the other hand, providers make unsatisfactory offers, the state negotiator can decline to approve any contracts without totally jeopardizing access to necessary care. If providers decide not to negotiate at all, patients are similarly protected for their most urgent needs.

Fifth, selective contracting and the competition it engenders contain an implicit challenge to any state regulation of health care. "Let the buyer decide" is a persuasive philosophical position in the current climate. Regulation of capital investment via certificate of need (CON) review will be the first regulatory policy to come under scrutiny in a "competitive" environment. Following enactment of the contracting legislation in 1982, California's CON law was virtually gutted in 1983, and the Department of Health Services has made clear its intention to let "market discipline" determine the distribution and ownership of expensive services. Further, the role of areawide planning is not obvious under competitive conditions, and even collection of uniform statistics may be criticized as infringement on "proprietary" information. Thus a policy of selective contracting will raise many questions that policymakers are well advised to consider from the beginning.

Finally, at the same time selective contracting by government can undermine existing regulatory policy, selective contracting by private payors may arouse some demand for new state regulation. This is because reduced prices create an incentive to overtreat and/or not to treat at all (if revenue can be derived from other sources). The California legislation provided for some regulation of that form of PPO in which beneficiaries are "locked in" to certain providers (dubbed "exclusive provider organization," or EPO), i.e., there is no insurance coverage provided for use of noncontract providers. However, since a preferred provider benefit is designed to appeal to consumers used to full freedom of choice, EPOs are not now considered a marketable commodity, none are being developed, and no EPO regulations have been issued. On the other hand, there has been some discussion of the need to regulate nonexclusive PPOs, currently not regulated at all, if only to classify and count them.[23] Physicians in particular have voiced a need to protect both consumers and physicians from unscrupulous PPO developers.[24] Thus far in California, however, "marketplace discipline" remains the preferred regulator. As PPOs take shape and function and real problems materialize, pleas for regulation may take on more substance and find a more sympathetic legislative audience.

A last implication of selective contracting is the potential for conflict with antitrust law. This problem is addressed at length elsewhere in this book.

THE FUTURE

Selective contracting, for all its immediate impact, has the odd property of being widely regarded as an interim measure. Initially, several legislators supported the 1982 bills as a first step toward turning over the administration of the Medi-Cal program to the private insurance industry. There is considerable agreement that selective contracting by Medi-Cal with hospitals for negotiated prices will give way to selective contracting with "capitated health systems" on the basis of prepaid, capitation rates. (Such "systems" could be counties, HMOs, insurance companies, primary care networks, etc.) This reimbursement method would virtually cap state expenditures without having to set utilization standards or provider revenue limits. Capitation is also a way to begin to control physician fees and to align physician and hospital incentives, without direct negotiations with individual physicians. Some private payors likewise see selective contracting on a competitive, fee-for-service basis as a transition to capitation contracts, i.e., HMOs. If hospital use continues to fall, provider interest in HMO contracts may bloom, since such contracts would ensure revenue flow independent of utilization. Thus competitive incentives seem logically to strengthen interest in prepaid health care.

EXHIBIT 3
The Health Insurance Marketplace: Framework for Describing Selective Contracting Activity

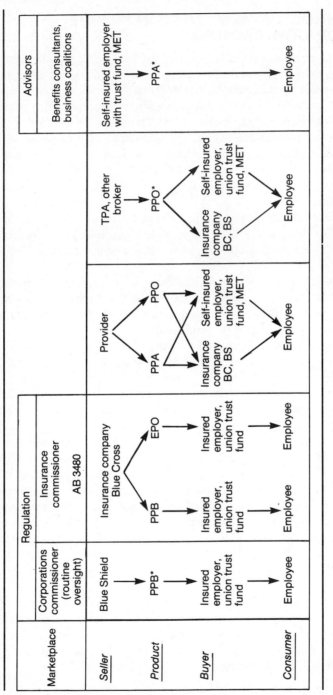

Key: BC = Blue Cross
BS = Blue Shield
TPA = third-party administrator

PPB = preferred provider benefit
PPO = preferred provider organization
EPO = exclusive provider organization

MET = multiple employer trust
PPA = preferred provider arrangement

*Could also offer an EPO.

SOURCE: L. Johns, R. A. Derzon, and M. Anderson, *Selective Contracting for Health Services in California—First Report,* National Governors' Association, 1983, p. 96a.

DEFINITION OF TERMS USED IN PRIVATE SECTOR CONTRACTING[25]

One of the most prominent features of the current California health insurance marketplace is the lack of precise terminology to describe it. The oblique references in AB 3480 to "alternative rates" appeared to authorize selective contracting by insurers with providers and to point to the whole realm of "PPOs." The statute, however, makes no mention of entities other than Blue Cross or commercial insurers that might engage in contracting with providers for "alternative rates," nor does it state precisely how the contracts now permitted differ from contracts already in force between these insurers and providers.

Standard definitions still do not exist. As one commentator noted: "To date, it has been impossible for physicians, lawyers, and health care professionals to agree on a uniform definition of a PPO."[26]

In order to promote understanding of developments in the health insurance marketplace associated with selective contracting and abetted by AB 3480...a simple theoretical framework and a set of working definitions (is proposed).

The framework for ordering the variety of entities and relationships emerging in this corner of the marketplace is shown in Exhibit 3. Using the basic economic concepts of "seller," "product," "buyer," and "consumer," it can be seen that insurers and other "sellers" are now developing "preferred provider products" to sell to employers, union trust funds, and sometimes brokers, TPAs, and other middlemen, all of whom are "buyers," some of whom act as intermediaries for the ultimate "consumer," the employee. It should also be clear that AB 3480 enabled development of only one of several preferred provider products, and that many sellers of these products are currently unregulated in any way. The exhibit further shows that insurers and other purchasers may now have unaccustomed, direct contractual relationships with individual providers. Finally, it is plain that there are two marketing phases involved in selling the new products: the first from seller to buyer, and the second from buyer to consumer.

(It can) be assumed that the essence of a PPO is the existence of a contract between a direct provider of health services (hospital, physician) and a source of payment other than the patient. Beyond this assumption, a variety of incidental characteristics will be ignored to make the following conservative distinctions:

— Preferred provider: "a hospital, physician or other provider that, by virtue of a direct contractual relationship with a

buyer or through a PPO, agrees to accept a fee-for-service price[27] stipulated in the contract, among other provisions";
— Preferred provider organization (PPO): "a legally constituted entity comprised of a hospital or group of hospitals, or a group of physicians, or a group of hospitals and physicians, that offers the providers' services on a contractual basis to a buyer, usually but not necessarily at a fee-for-service price lower than usual charges, among other provisions";
— Preferred provider arrangement (PPA): "a contract between a buyer and a provider, stipulating a fee-for-service price to be paid for services provided, among other provisions";
— Preferred provider benefit (PPB): "a benefit option arranged for and marketed by a commercial insurer, Blue Cross, Blue Shield or third-party administrator, providing access to "preferred providers" who agree to accept a contractual, fee-for-service, "alternative rate" as payment for services rendered, among other provisions; usually includes incentives to purchasers to make it available to employees (e.g., reduced premiums, enriched benefits) and to beneficiaries to choose it (e.g., co-insurance and deductibles reduced or eliminated)";
— Exclusive provider organization (EPO): "a preferred provider *benefit,* as above, but also providing that *no* reimbursement will be paid in the event a beneficiary uses a non-preferred provider";
— Purchaser: "an employer, or union trust fund, that makes PPBs available to employees; an insurer, Blue Cross, or Blue Shield acting to organize a PPB and thus contracting with preferred providers and/or with PPOs."

PPOs and PPAs may stipulate other services: for example, utilization review, reduced turnaround time on claims payment, grievance procedures, etc. The field in California is far too fluid, however, to call such provisions standard, or even common.

The following considerations may be emphasized:

— PPOs, PPAs, PPBs, and EPOs are all loosely referred to as "PPOs";
— Only EPOs are regulated according to provisions of AB 3480;
— There is currently *no* state regulation at all of PPOs or PPAs;
— PPBs arranged by insurers and Blue Cross must be submitted to the Insurance Commissioner for the usual review of proposed insurance benefit packages—AB 3480 added nothing to this longstanding mandate;

— A PPB arranged by Blue Shield must be submitted to the Corporations Commissioner for the usual review of proposed insurance benefit packages—AB 3480 added nothing to this longstanding mandate.

One problem not clarified by these definitions is the type of PPO that prohibits a participating preferred provider from signing up with any other PPO (or PPA or PPB). This form of exclusivity has been dubbed an "exclusive PPO," whereas a PPO having no such requirement is termed a "swing PPO."[28]

NOTES

1. This chapter draws extensively from a detailed report by L. Johns, R. A. Derzon, and M. Anderson, *Selective Contracting for Health Services in California—First Report,* National Governors' Association, Washington, D.C. 1983. (Hereafter, *NGA Report.*)

2. Under a regulatory scheme for third-party payors unique to California, Blue Shield, which is entirely separate from Blue Cross, was never subject to the freedom of choice requirements. It never engaged in selective contracting as a cost-containment measure, however.

3. AB 799 made several other major changes in the Medi-Cal program. *NGA Report,* Appendix A.

4. Ibid, pp. 40–45, for details of alternatives and justifications.

5. Alcoholic, rehabilitation, and psychiatric hospitals were excluded; children's and HMO hospitals are exempt from contracting.

6. Governor's Office of Special Health Care Negotiations, *Report to the Legislature on the Operations of the Office of Special Health Care Negotiations,* Sacramento, May 1983.

7. California Medical Assistance Commission (CMAC). *Report to the Legislature on the Operations of the California Medical Assistance Commission,* Sacramento, May 1984, Figure 1. California's fiscal year is July 1 to June 30.

8. CMAC, personal communication, May 1984.

9. *NGA Report,* pp. 49, 125. The 67 percent of hospitals winning contracts are in areas accounting for 85 percent of historical Medi-Cal expenditures. In the great majority of hospital planning areas, the majority of contract-eligible hospitals have contracts.

10. Ibid., pp. 58, 83–84.

11. Ibid., pp. 143–44.

12. Remarks by William Guy and Hon. Milton Marks, Commission on California State Government Organization and Economy, "Public Hearing on the State's Medi-Cal Hospital Negotiations," Sacramento, January 20, 1983, p. 25.

13. Blue Cross of Southern California and Blue Cross of Northern California merged in 1982.

14. California Medical Association, *Contracting Alert,* 1, no. 1–5, San Francisco, 1983.

15. C. White and L. Morse, *Hospital Fact Book—1983,* California Hospital Association, Sacramento, 1983, pp. 32, 33, 37.

16. Reasons for the decline in hospital use include: growth of HMOs, impact of utilization review, and increased use of hospital substitutes (home care, ambulatory surgery, etc.).

17. *NGA Report,* p. 81.

18. California Health Facility Commission, *Quarterly Financial and Utilization Report, Aggregate Hospital Data, 4th Quarter,* 1983, Sacramento, April 16, 1984, p. 86.

19. *NGA Report,* pp. 124–25.

20. Ibid., pp. 126–27.

21. Ibid., p. 85–86.

22. The Medi-Cal program has long performed utilization review (UR) through the 12 Department of Health Service (DHS) Field Offices. Since UR is a "monitoring" and not a "negotiating" problem, responsibility for UR lies with DHS, not with CMAC.

23. AB 3480 makes no mention of PPOs or EPOs. It merely enables private insurance carriers and Blue Cross to do certain things (*NGA Report,* pp. 28–29). It is not self-evident who can now do what was prohibited before, nor how to recognize what might be a new entity or product, nor how these might relate to or differ from pre-existing entities or products. This accounts for the vast discrepancy in count of PPOs: from "a handful" to "160," (*NGA Report,* p. 95). For one attempt to define and classify current activity in the PPO marketplace, see Definition of Terms Used in Private Sector Contracting at the end of this chapter.

24. *CEO Contracting Bulletin,* Hospital Council of Northern California, No. 19, San Bruno, CA, July 26, 1983, p. 8.

25. Excerpted from *NGA Report,* pp. 95–9.

26. California Medical Association, *Contracting Alert,* 1, no. 2, CMA, San Francisco, May 2, 1983, p. 1.

27. Excludes capitation.

28. Personal communication, R. Stromberg, Esq., Hanson, Bridgett, Marcus, Vlahos and Stromberg. Summer, 1983.

CASE STUDY: CALIFORNIA PREFERRED PROFESSIONALS, FOUNTAIN VALLEY, CA

Edward Zalta, M.D.
Chairman
California Preferred Professionals, Inc.
Fountain Valley, CA

California Preferred Professionals (CaPP CARE) was founded in 1982 by physicians who were aware of the escalation of health care cost and the resultant increasing enrollment in prepaid plans. In an attempt to stem the rate of escalation these physicians, prior to founding CaPP CARE, expended a great deal of time and effort through voluntary approaches such as "economic rounds" in an unsuccessful attempt to modify practice patterns. They had predicted in the late 1970s that the rate of increase of health care costs would soon make indemnity plans unaffordable for the average employer/employee.

There were a multitude of reasons for the spiraling health care costs. An aging population and increased technology were examples of acceptable reasons. There were many unacceptable reasons: first dollar coverage, defensive medicine, absence of competition or positive incentives, and cost shifting. The very nature of the "system" of cost reimbursement for health care had built-in escalation for almost two decades.

Everyone—physicians, hospitals, insurers, employers, unions, and patients—had played a part in the escalation. Physicians, although receiving less than 20 percent of the health care dollar and responsible for most of the remainder, had little knowledge of, or influence over, hospital charges. Yet physicians were being blamed for the hospital cost overruns.

Something had to be done to keep health care affordable. Thus the push by those who pay the health care bill for reform legislation in California and elsewhere.

As physicians, they studied the potential of the new contracting law and arrived at the following conclusions:

1. The increase in the cost of health care was at an unacceptably high rate.

2. Payors were becoming more involved than ever before in health care costs issues. They would enter into contracting if for no other reason than to insulate themselves from the cost shift that was due to escalate with discounting and DRGs.

3. The status quo could not survive. Indemnity programs were fast disappearing. Government intervention and control were inevitable unless a free enterprise response to this new challenge was developed.

4. Competition must be introduced into the health care delivery system.

5. A revolution in health care reimbursement was underway that would benefit patients, payors, and providers if they became informed and could respond intelligently rather than emotionally.

6. If fee-for-service medicine was to survive, a new alternative system of health delivery, which combined the best of both fee-for-service medicine (freedom of choice and accessibility) and prepaid plans (utilization control), had to be developed.

7. A partnership approach involving providers, payors, and patients was needed to cooperatively develop this new system.

8. The dominant health delivery systems of the future would be the prepaid plans at one end of the spectrum and an exclusive provider organization (EPO) at the other with the preferred provider organization as a transitional model. Few if any indemnity plans would remain as an affordable option.

9. A physician-run PPO, working independently but cooperatively with hospitals, insurers, employers, unions, and third-party administrators and their subscribers would be the most effective and acceptable PPO.

CaPP CARE's initial concept was to limit their program to a relatively small geographic area. Discussions with a few industry leaders broadened their perspective. Major employers would bring in the major insurers; major insurers would bring in the smaller insurers and the smaller employers. The only viable alternative to a multitude of differing PPOs with differing programs and requirements would be a statewide physician PPO. CaPP CARE opted to be statewide to serve the needs of major employers, insurers, and third-party administrators.

Physicians reviewed the existing and planned PPOs. Some PPOs merely called themselves one; others relied on "discounts" for cost reduction. CaPP CARE held the belief that a PPO must have an automated quantifiable program of cost reduction, an independent relationship between physicians and hospitals, and a program of utilization control that allowed for objective monitoring and review of physician performance. The objective would be to modify physician practice patterns into more cost-conscious behavior without adversely affecting quality.

CaPP CARE set about developing a quantifiable program of cost containment with the physician as the controlling element. The physician admits, prescribes, discharges, advises—in short, controls—the expenditures for health. CaPP CARE would represent change in a system accustomed to nonconformity to the forces of the marketplace. But in the opinion of the founders, failure to accept the challenge meant that physicians and patients would otherwise become pawns in a contracting war.

CaPP CARE established their goals and objectives as follows:

1. Organizing independent private practitioners into a cohesive, competing, structured entity that would be bound by common cost-efficient practice guidelines. This required development of uniform selection criteria, ongoing educational endeavors, and meaningful disciplinary procedures for noncompliance.

2. Development of a quantifiable program of cost containment.

3. Development of a computerized system of utilization control that would provide tracking of contract compliance by physicians and hospitals, comparison of data for payor reporting as to cost effectiveness, and cybernetic in design to take advantage of the experience of cost-conscious physicians in the development of future standards for length of stay and physician practice patterns.

4. Development of integrated contracts to be used between CaPP CARE and the physician, CaPP CARE and the payor, the payor and the physician, and the payor and the hospital.

5. Development of a marketing program to inform payors of CaPP CARE's administrative capabilities and unique approach to health care cost management through a unique automated utilization review program.

In order to facilitate selection and discipline, CaPP CARE selected a for-profit corporate structure, funded privately by physicians.

Development of uniform criteria for selection of providers was a top priority. They found an absence of reliable data on the cost effectiveness of individual physicians. One of their physician board members involved in data processing had accumulated biographic and disciplinary data on all physicians in California.

Utilizing this data to exclude physicians with known disciplinary problems by governmental agencies, hospitals, or other entities, CaPP CARE selected physicians for participation. The physician application form authorizes release of information concerning professional liability claims. Each applicant was reviewed by a physician review committee before acceptance. The initial rejection rate was approximately 13 percent. Presently, very few applications are arriving from physicians who have past disciplinary problems or significant professional liability claims.

The development of a quantifiable program of cost containment was accomplished by many physicians, representing all specialties, who devoted innumerable hours of their time. These physicians developed a list of over 1,300 surgical procedures which, by agreement, would be performed on an outpatient basis (same day surgery) unless the patient's medical condition required hospital confinement. A list of over 1,700 elective surgical procedures requiring prior authorization was developed by this team. Cosmetic procedures, outmoded or experimental procedures (both nonreimbursable), and those requiring physician assistance at surgery were also identified.

Additionally, the physician committees identified a long list of medical conditions which, in their medical experience, were more appropriately evaluated in an ambulatory setting. Length of stay would be determined by using the age-related guidelines published by the Commission on Physician and Hospital Activity, except where local practice patterns required a modification.

Since effective utilization control is an essential element of any successful PPO, CaPP CARE developed an automated program of utilization review. The interface requires minimal alteration by payors to their existing claims processing software.

Prior authorization is obtained for elective procedures by submission of a written request containing specific indications. Physicians review the request, and if approved, a computer-generated form is returned to the physician indicating the appropriate facility use (inpatient or outpatient) as well as the appropriate length of stay. Computer review of claims data identifies noncompliance.

Using the experience gathered over 17 years and a very large database from a claims administrator, specialty-specific standards for monitoring ambulatory practice patterns of physicians were developed. This allows CaPP CARE to measure a physician's practice patterns against norms by specialty for frequency of visits, injections, radiologic services, use of varied office visit codes to detect upgrading or fragmentation, anesthesia times, nonmedically necessary admissions, length of stay extensions, cost per encounter, and many other things. Exceptions are then selectively reviewed by physicians for contract compliance.

All review of computer-identified exceptions to norms for physician practice patterns, contract noncompliance, and prior authorization requests is performed by physicians in the CaPP CARE automated utilization-review program. The utilization-review program has the capability of indicating changes in the standards used for length of stay and aberrant practice patterns based on the experience of the participating physicians and hospitals.

The utilization programs select out for review both under- and over-utilizers. Underutilization can not only cause a deterioration in quality, but in many instances will be more costly.

Physician monitoring alone was insufficient to measure savings. Payors needed to know why and where savings occurred and how additional savings could be achieved without reduction in quality. CaPP CARE developed management reports for payors, in both detailed and summary format, which identify cost savings in the PPO option as compared to the non-PPO segment.

If cost-efficient quality care is achieved, and to a significant degree, then the PPO will be transitional and lead to a "de facto" EPO through greater differentials in reimbursements or premiums.

Contract development was performed concurrently with the development of the cost-containment and utilization-review programs. To avoid antitrust implications, CaPP CARE separated their contract with physicians from the payor/physician contract that contains a reimbursement schedule. The reimbursement schedule is developed solely by the payor.

Altering physician practice patterns would have the same limited effect on health cost management as in the past unless cost reimbursement for hospital services could be replaced by competition. The cost plus method of reimbursing hospitals, in use for almost two decades, has rewarded the inefficient hospital and penalized the efficient. Thus, in the development of a model hospital contract for use by payors, CaPP CARE recommended hospitals be reimbursed at a per-diem rate by major service and a set fee for outpatient surgeries.

This reimbursement policy brings accountability and introduces positive incentives for economy into the hospital industry. CaPP CARE's independent but cooperative relationship with hospitals affords the payor the opportunity for independent selection, contract negotiation, renegotiation, and performance evaluation. Hospital staff appointment identification is performed by CaPP CARE and supplied to the payor prior to hospital negotiation. See Exhibit 1.

Marketing the concept and eventually the cost-containment and utilization programs was an ongoing activity.

PPOs defied definition, and they were perceived with trepidation by

EXHIBIT 1
Contracting Relationships

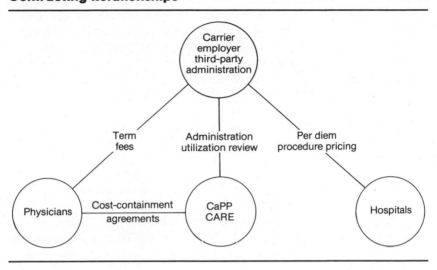

many physicians who opposed change. They were not acceptable to some hospital administrators unless the administrators could somehow control them to maintain or expand market share and avoid competitive pricing of hospital services.

Many cost-conscious and quality-conscious physicians perceived the benefits of being involved with a physician-run PPO. Efficient hospitals realized the potential for increased market share. Employers perceived the benefits to be gained by avoiding a hospital-based PPO ("the fox in the henhouse" to quote one employer). Insurers realized that savings to be derived from a discounted program for physicians or hospitals were illusory.

CaPP CARE developed a complete manual for their physician members and their office staffs explaining the program, the procedures, the limited modification in their present office policies, and the appropriate use of the ICD-9CM, CPT, and CRVS. Through a regular "COMMUNI-QUE" CaPP CARE continually updates their membership on ways to become more efficient, expansion of the physician listing, inauguration of a patient referral service, disciplinary actions for noncompliance, and general information.

Education of the employees who select the PPO option is another ongoing function. Informing employees how to select a primary care physician or specialist, how to enter and use the health delivery system, and tips on wellness programs are all part of the patient education services.

The geographic service area currently served by CaPP CARE includes most of southern California. It is statewide, has been replicated in three other states, and is being reviewed for implementation in six others. CaPP CARE was recently approached by two major national employers interested in providing a national PPO network to their employees.

CaPP CARE became operational in February 1984. They have an administrative and utilization-review agreement with one of the state's largest insurance carriers in the PPO field, Pacific Mutual Life Insurance Company. They have also signed administrative and utilization review agreements with Crown Life Insurance Company, Home Life Insurance Company, Provident Mutual and Union Mutual Life Insurance Company. Their present physician membership (MDs, DOs, and DPMs) exceeds 6,000. The first employer has enrolled approximately 4,000 employees. There are presently over 120,000 eligible employees and dependents in the CaPP CARE program.

CaPP CARE does not contract with hospitals. They advise and provide the model contract. The philosophy is built on the historical relationship between physicians and hospital administrators. Physicians are suspicious of hospital domination and hospitals are suspicious of physician domination. The payor contracts with hospitals in the CaPP CARE program.

Pacific Mutual has negotiated contracts with a large number of hospitals in southern California on behalf of its 1.4 million covered individuals and is expanding to include the entire state by late 1985.

The physician reimbursement formula used by Pacific Mutual and offered to (and accepted individually by almost all) CaPP CARE members was determined solely by Pacific Mutual. It represents a trade-off for physicians—a capped rate representing usual and customary reimbursement for most physicians in exchange for their compliance with CaPP CARE's utilization-control system.

CaPP CARE acts as a "super messenger" by distributing payor contracts to their physician members. Physicians and payors each retain the right to accept or reject on an individual basis.

As in the case of physician and hospital reimbursements, benefits are determined by the payor. Economic incentives for employees are individually tailored to the needs of the employer/payor. Three incentives to encourage employee enrollment are presently being used: differential reimbursement, differential deductibles, and differential premiums.

CaPP CARE physicians are not obligated to any hospital "partner" to retain a patient longer than medically sound judgment dictates. In fact, the contract calls for admission only when medically necessary and for only as long as medically necessary. Their physicians are not "at risk" for delivering care as in a prepaid plan. In the CaPP CARE program, the incentive is to maintain or expand a patient base by delivering quality care at agreed-upon fixed rates for both physicians and hospitals.

EXHIBIT 2
Table of Organization

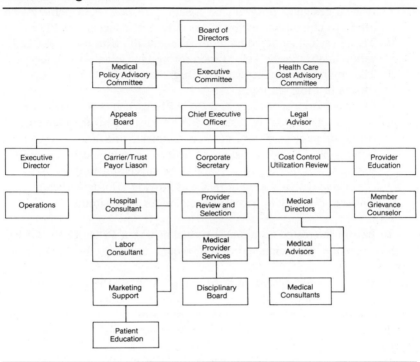

CaPP CARE estimates that its program of health care cost management can save 20 to 40 percent depending on the degree of patient penetration and the sophistication of the claims gathering program used by the payor. These estimated savings are quantified as follows: Same day surgery: 5 to 10 percent; prior authorization: 6 to 10 percent; hospital reimbursement: 5 to 10 percent; utilization control: 5 to 10 percent; stabilization of costs: 1 to 2 percent.

Their low cost for administration and utilization review to achieve this level of savings is dependent on the degree of review desired and the volume of claims to be processed. CaPP CARE is willing to be "at risk" for all of the administrative and utilization-control services.

In developing an alternative delivery system, the principals in CaPP CARE learned the following:

1. An organization cannot be a PPO by just calling itself one.
2. The acceptance by the payors of a hospital-based PPO is limited,

since it does not maximize savings or allow for independent evaluation of physicians and hospitals.

3. A well-designed program of health care cost management and effective utilization review is essential for a successful PPO.
4. The physician is the key to controlling health care costs, and utilization control is the key to monitoring physician performance.
5. The myth that physicians with high fee profiles deliver quality care is just that—a myth.
6. Perhaps most importantly, CaPP CARE learned early that few payors want half a loaf or less. A PPO must have all the elements of administration, selection, cost containment, utilization, computerization, physician and patient education, communication, referral services, and marketing in place to be successful in developing an alternative delivery system that can provide affordable health care without adversely impacting on quality or accessibility.

To payors interested in aiding or establishing a PPO, CaPP CARE recommends the physician-sponsored model utilizing the partnership approach.

To physicians interested in forming a PPO, CaPP CARE recommends that they avoid discussing fees, fund the endeavor themselves, maintain an independent but cooperative relationship with hospitals, employ business expertise, and be prepared to devote considerable time and energy.

To quote one of the physician principals in CaPP CARE, "Here is our opportunity as private practitioners to compete effectively with the prepaid plans and preserve freedom of choice. We may never have another chance."

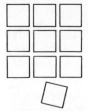

IPA/HMO Sponsored

CASE STUDY: AV-MED, INC., MIAMI, FL

Robert T. Jones

Vice President, Corporate Development
National Medical Management
Miami, FL

☐ AV-MED, Inc. is a medical care management corporation built on the HMO-IPA model that became federally qualified in September, 1977. With over 50,000 members, AV-MED is the largest federally qualified HMO in the southeastern United States. Over 300 employers offer the AV-MED Health Plan option to their employees. AV-MED consists of a network of 1,400 physicians and 40 hospitals operating in seven counties in Florida. Participating nursing homes, home health agencies, dentists, laboratories, and other health service providers complement the physician/hospital network to provide a full range of comprehensive services.

As a result of a special contract awarded by the federal government in 1982, AV-MED also offers a competitive benefit package to medicare beneficiaries that waives the standard medicare deductibles and coinsurance payments. Services ordinarily excluded under the medicare program such as dentistry, eyeglasses, prescription drugs, and hearing aids are also covered.

AV-MED also offers a PPO to major employers and self-insured union trust funds in its service area. The PPO program, unlike the HMO and medicare program, is not a prepaid plan. Under the PPO, employers take advantage of volume purchasing discounts and utilization controls, and AV-MED is paid an administrative or management fee.

The development of the AV-MED PPO was primarily in response to the marketplace. In south Florida, union trust funds as well as business and industry were responding to the alarming increases in health care cost. Major corporations joined to form a business coalition to address the issue. The state legislature authorized indemnity insurance companies and HMOs to develop PPOs. Further, corporations noted that while the HMOs were bringing down health care costs, the vast majority of the savings went to the employees rather than to the employer. PPOs seemed to be a logical alternative.

AV-MED markets its PPO to major employers and union trust funds with a current enrollment of 30,000 members. Marketing to date has been directed towards large, self-insured groups. A major advantage in marketing the PPO is that it affords the employee an opportunity to move

EXHIBIT 1
Health Plan Options Including PPO

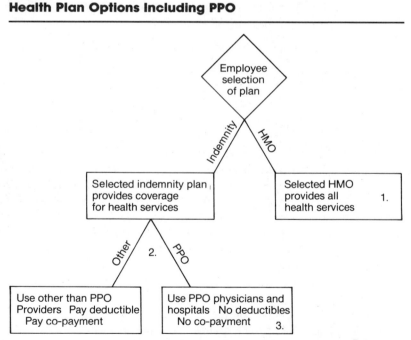

1. Employees selecting HMOs have no incentives to use PPO. Therefore, the PPO option applies only to employees selecting indemnity plan coverage.

2. At each encounter with the health system the employee determines whether or not to use PPO providers.

3. A nominal fee per physician encounter is recommended.

in and out of the system at will. This advantage, however, requires that the employee have indemnity coverage, and efforts are underway to design a wraparound policy that will enable AV-MED to market its program to fully insured medium and small employee groups as well as self-insured larger groups.

While the benefit program of the PPO varies with each employer group, all are designed to influence the employer to encourage utilization of the identified preferred providers. This is usually accomplished by establishing lower deductibles and copayments if the employee selects the identified preferred providers. Exhibit 1 depicts the options available.

AV-MED has also participated in the design and implementation of a PPO for Honeywell Corporation's facility in St. Petersburg. The Honeywell PPO is administered by AV-MED and utilizes all components of its PPO program, including claims processing. Under this program the employee elects the PPO option during the open enrollment period, in a similar manner to selecting between indemnity plans and HMOs.

AV-MED processes all claims for employees selecting the PPO option, including those from providers not participating in the PPO. Exhibit 2 depicts the options under this program.

The AV-MED PPO consists of four basic components: physician services, acute care hospital services, utilization review, and program ad-

EXHIBIT 2
Honeywell PPO Option

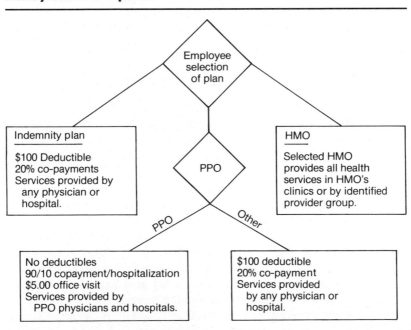

ministration. For the purpose of this case study the focus will be on the Miami-Ft. Lauderdale area PPO. Programs in other areas differ only in the size of the provider network.

PHYSICIAN SERVICES COMPONENT

AV-MED Associates, an association incorporated under the laws of the State of Florida, has agreed to provide comprehensive health care services to members under the medical care programs of AV-MED, Inc. As such, AV-MED Associates has entered into "Physician Agreements" with over 1,000 physicians in the Miami-Ft. Lauderdale area (Dade and Broward Counties).

The agreement between the physician and AV-MED Associates stipulates that the "Physician agrees to use those inpatient, extended care and ancillary service organizations which have agreements with the Association and AV-MED."

The network of physician services offered members provides excellent accessibility for employees and dependents throughout the Dade and Broward County areas. Of the physicians, 260 are primary care physicians in family practice, internal medicine, or pediatrics. The remainder are specialists who provide quality care in their area of expertise. The specialists provide services in all aspects of care normally available to a population group. Chiropractic and podiatric specialties are also offered.

AV-MED, Inc. negotiates with the Association with respect to the appropriate rates for services rendered by the physician members. The current rate of reimbursement approximates 67 percent of the usual and customary charges for the area.

ACUTE CARE HOSPITAL SERVICES COMPONENT

AV-MED, Inc. has entered into contractual agreements with sixteen hospitals in Dade County and ten hospitals in Broward County to provide acute care hospital services to patients affiliated with its programs. These hospitals provide diagnostic and treatment facilities that are geographically accessible to residents of the two counties.

Through its hospital contracts, AV-MED has access to 51 percent of the total acute care hospital beds of the area. The contracts require the hospital to verify the patient's eligibility except in cases of accidental injury or life-threatening acute illness where emergency treatment is rendered. AV-MED in turn assumes responsibility for payment for all services rendered. This payment is based on a negotiated discount from the usual charges for the services. The contract also provides for prompt itemized billing for the services and prompt payment.

The rate of discount with contracting hospitals is negotiated on an annual basis. In carrying out these negotiations, AV-MED is sensitive to the cost of providing a particular service in comparison with similar charges of other area hosptials for the same service. Therefore, AV-MED expects and receives high discounts from those hospitals that traditionally have higher patient costs than other hospitals that provide similar services. The high volume of patients within the system provides the leverage needed to successfully conduct negotiations.

Since the discount is dependent, in part, on patient volume, it is in the interest of AV-MED to concentrate its patient admissions to select hospitals. The Medical Department directs patients to those facilities with lower cost through its interaction with plan physicians during the preadmission certification phase. At the same time it is important to assure patient accessibility and to recognize that all admissions cannot be controlled. Thus AV-MED has contracted with more hospitals than ordinarily needed to provide inpatient care for its members. Discounts average approximately 14 percent of the usual charges of the hospitals.

Discounts, however, are not the *sine qua non* of the PPO. Discounts without proper utilization controls are not discounts. One extra day of hospitalization or one or more additional, unneeded test, wipes out the discount. Utilization remains the key to the control of inflation in health care costs. AV-MED requires contract hospitals to provide access to patient's charts in order to conduct daily monitoring of utilization. This enables concurrent review to be performed in a real time environment and further eliminates unneeded testing and excess hospital days.

UTILIZATION-CONTROL COMPONENT

Over the past six years AV-MED has developed an effective utilization-review program. The patient day per 1,000 rate for HMO enrollees is less than half the community norm. This program focuses on unnecessary utilization, particularly hospital and consultation utilization. Major components of the program are preadmission certification, second surgical opinion, concurrent review, and retrospective review.

At the time preadmission clearance is requested, the medical department considers and discusses with the physician the diagnosis, the proposed admitting hospital, and the length of stay. If approved, an authorization number is given and immediately put into the computer. The hospital can then rapidly verify patient eligibility and approval for admittance by use of the authorization number. The number is also used later by the hospital on the claim form.

Should questions arise concerning the appropriateness of hospitalization, AV-MED's medical director discusses the proposed admission with the patient's physician. Physicians are encouraged to utilize outpatient surgery, home health care, or other less costly treatment resources where medically indicated.

When hospitalization is the only appropriate response, the medical department assures that necessary tests are performed prior to admission whenever possible. Physicians are not authorized to admit patients on Saturdays for operations on Monday.

Once the patient is admitted, the utilization manager has responsibility for monitoring inpatient care. These individuals visit the hospitals and monitor the patient's charts to assure that the care being given and the tests being ordered are appropriate for the patient's diagnosis and signs and symptoms.

The concurrent review process allows the medical director to closely monitor the progress of each patient. The medical director frequently contacts the patient's physician to discuss the patient's progress. Every effort is made to assist the physician in scheduling ancillary patient services as the discharge planning phase is entered. Through this supportive process, the patient receives the appropriate treatment in the most appropriate and least expensive setting.

Second surgical opinion and retrospective review programs are other important components of the utilization control program. AV-MED's quality assurance program is an integral part of the activities. The program is built on the database of an in-house IBM 38 computer with software programs designed to capture significant data.

The plan's focus is on identifying physicians whose practice patterns are markedly variant from the norm. The number of physician visits per patient is captured as well as the percent of visits referred to specialized medical consultants. Norms are established, and follow-up through office record review is accomplished when significant variances are identified.

Hospital utilization data by diagnosis, length of stay, and total charges are also captured. The norm for the diagnostic protocol for the appropriate specialty is established, and again, there is follow-up for those providers who markedly differ from the norm. Hospital utilization data is also captured on normal or ceasarean section deliveries and providers markedly at variance from the norm are identified.

The information system for utilization review has the capability of compiling utilization review data by employer group, hospital, age, sex, diagnosis, length of stay, charges, and other components that might be useful to a particular employer. The PPO is designed to be flexible in order to meet employer's needs, and occasional specific program requests can be accommodated. Further, historical record of all claims of a particular member can be captured at any time.

AV-MED's utilization system is an integral part of the management information system. Patient eligibility and provider payments are linked to the preadmission certification requirements. Data notes relating to various providers are linked to member and provider services. Aberrant utilization patterns are flagged by the computer when claims entered demonstrate such patterns.

PROGRAM ADMINISTRATION COMPONENT

Management of the provider network is a continuing responsibility. Recruitment and retention of physicians requires constant attention. Similarly, hospital rate negotiations must be carried out routinely. AV-MED's experience and financial database, which provides the necessary information to identify differences in costs and charges of various facilities, contribute to successful negotiations. The program's high membership provides significant leverage and enables negotiation from a position of strength.

Consumer relations is the key to a successful PPO program and an important administrative task. The plan's computer program lists all providers participating in the network and identifies pertinent facts about each. The computer program also incorporates a geographic scan to refer to providers located near their home or place of employment.

Another program administrative component, member/provider services, assists marketing in enrollment processing, distribution of member I.D. cards and materials, and provides eligibility verification of members to providers. This section also responds to requests for physician selection assistance, benefit inquiries, membership verification, authorization to treat, information on hospital benefits, and member complaints.

Participating employers are provided detailed information regarding claims processed and paid in addition to information regarding individuals and their claims. Employers are also provided with a detailed listing of all hospital disbursements for their employees. The printout identifies the hospital, the member, claim number, received date, admission date, check number, total charges, noneligible charges, C.O.B., copayment, discount, and net fee paid. Similarly, another printout identifies claims and payments to physicians.

AV-MED's management fee is paid in a variety of ways, individually negotiated with the different corporations. Fees can be based on a per member per month rate, percentage of claims, or percentage of discounts. Fees take into account whether AV-MED provides all claims processing services.

POTENTIAL PROBLEMS

The development of a PPO is a natural extension of the IPA model HMO, as all necessary components are in place. Problems do exist.

First, there is likely to be confusion in the minds of the employer and members as to the difference between the two programs. While the concept of the PPO is very simple, it is difficult for those who are used to dealing with indemnity plans to immediately grasp. Understanding "risk" is the key.

Further, unless a total packet can be developed that includes wraparound indemnity type coverage, marketing is limited to major self-insured groups. The volume of health care cost to an employer has to be high for the PPO to be effective and to offset the cost of loss of employer payments of part or all copayments and deductibles.

Finally, PPO plans must be tailored to meet the needs of major employers, and this presents numerous administrative problems, particularly in claims processing. The benefit package for employers selecting the PPO is usually identical to that of coworkers selecting indemnity coverage with the exception of lower copayments and deductibles. Inasmuch as benefit packages vary by corporation, PPO benefits must also vary. This means numerous edit checks and other accommodations must be made in order to appropriately administer the program.

FUTURE

During 1984 AV-MED, Inc. was acquired by National Medical Enterprises, Inc. (NME). A new division of NME, National Medical Management was established and serves as the holding company directing the expansion of alternative delivery systems program to other states. The PPO program is currently being marketed as Preferred Medical Systems in California, Florida, Louisiana, and Massachusetts. Under development is expansion to New York, Chicago, St. Louis, Dallas, and a number of other sites.

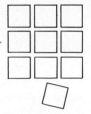

IPA/HMO Sponsored

CASE STUDY: HEALTH PLAN OF AMERICA, EMERYVILLE, CA

Sandra W. Smith, MBA

President and Chief Executive Officer
Health Plan of America
Emeryville, CA

☐ The Health Plan of America (HPA) was developed to provide Catholic hospitals and their medical staffs with a mechanism that would allow them to maintain their patient base in an increasingly competitive health care marketplace, while retaining their high quality of care standards and community service values. In 1978 the California Association of Catholic Hospitals, an organization representing 46 Catholic hospitals throughout the state, began exploring the development of a prepaid health plan that would provide services through a network of Catholic hospitals. The Health Plan of America (HPA) is the result.

HPA is a statewide alternative health care delivery system that provides medical and hospital services to contracted subscribers through the HPA participating hospitals and physicians. It began operating in November 1980 at a pilot site and, as of early 1984, its network consisted of 23 hospitals, nearly 3,000 physicians, and multiple institutions that provide ancillary services (e.g., laboratories, outpatient x-ray facilities, home health agencies) in four major metropolitan areas of the state: greater San

Francisco Bay area, greater Los Angeles area, Sacramento, and Fresno. Both Catholic and selected non-Catholic institutions are included in the network. HPA projects expansion of its provider capability by 50 percent during 1984.

HPA is licensed as a nonprofit corporation by the California Department of Insurance and is federally qualified as an IPA model HMO. HPA's primary line of business is the marketing of its HMO product to employers and unions on a statewide, regional, and local basis within the service areas of its contracted hospitals. Employers responding favorably to the HPA system cite the statewide network, the quality of participating hospitals and physicians, and the financial protections afforded by statutory reserve requirements.

In 1982 the California legislature passed enabling legislation for PPO activity. This was occasioned by health care costs that were among the highest in the country and the resulting concern of employers and insurance companies as to the impact on corporate bottom lines. The legislation generated a flurry of activity in the state as insurers, existing delivery systems, hospitals, physicians, and entrepreneurs investigated and initiated PPO activity. HPA conducted an analysis of the PPO environment, developed a business plan, and ascertained that the corporation was in a good position to develop a PPO product as a separate line of business that utilized its existing network of hospitals and physicians.

As a delivery system, HPA is unique in terms of both its licensure and its relationship with providers. HPA's licensure permits it to operate on a statewide basis and gives it specific authority to negotiate payment rates with hospitals and physicians. This authority is important to HPA in its PPO activities, as it provides certain protections against antitrust concerns. The HPA delivery system consists of contracted hospitals and IPA corporations (for-profit professional corporations of physicians) whose members are selected from the medical staff of the contracting hospital. The system has been formulated to promote a working partnership between the hospital, physicians, and HPA in order to achieve common goals of high quality, cost-effective care. Through the application of financial incentives and utilization monitoring, HPA has established a system whereby physicians in the hospital-based IPA work cooperatively with hospital personnel to prevent overutilization of expensive levels of care and ancillary services. This cooperative relationship, which promotes the most efficient use of required services, places HPA in a competitive position in selling both its HMO and its PPO products to cost conscious third-party payors.

KEY ISSUE

The legislation passed at both state and national levels within the past two years has significantly altered the mechanisms that govern how and how much hospitals and physicians are paid. Both Medi-Cal and medicare have established formulas that limit the dollars they will pay for treatment rendered an individual, regardless of the actual cost of the treatment. Private insurers and Blue Cross, in an effort to control the "cost shift," are negotiating for reduced rates of payment with hospitals and doctors. All indications are that the payment squeeze will intensify within the next two years as government payors move toward capitation and private industry directs patients to health care providers that offer quality service at lower cost.

In this environment, hospital and physician survival and/or success may be dependent on two things:

1. *The ability to control cost* through predictable cost levels, operational efficiency within the hospital, and most important, through a working partnership with the medical staff physicians who determine the nature, volume, and cost of services provided to patients.
2. *The ability to preserve market share,* as increased volume will be necessary to offset losses from decreased admissions and length of stay.

In addition, both public and private payors are beginning to contract with networks or systems of providers that are able to provide services to employees or recipients over a large geographic area. The PPO networks that are being established either by insurers or by providers themselves have appeal to the extent that services are available in most areas where constituents reside or work.

HPA is positioned to act as a principal mechanism for participating hospitals and physicians to control costs and preserve market share in this new marketplace. Its utilization-control programs, which include the physician in a significant role, will enable the hospital to be paid at an appropriate level for services delivered and thereby keep its price increases moderate. With price-competitive hospitals, HPA expects to attract private sector payors who want quality service, but who want that quality at lower cost.

HPA also offers to the health benefits payor fiscal stability and a track record of quality care. It has been in operation since 1980, is federally qualified, and meets the fiscal requirements of the California Department of Insurance. The fact that HPA is a financially stable organization is attractive to both private and public payors who are concerned about the fiscal viability and quality of their providers.

ORGANIZATIONAL STRUCTURE

HPA contracts with a sister corporation, HPA Management Systems, Inc., for all administrative and marketing services. All staff functions, marketing and finance activities, and claims and member administration are handled by the management company. HPA holds all contracts with purchasers and providers and oversees the utilization control and quality assurance activities. See organizational and contractual exhibits (Exhibits 1 and 2).

EXHIBIT 1
Organization Chart

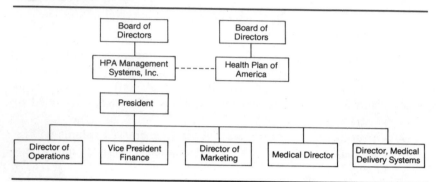

EXHIBIT 2
Contractual Chart

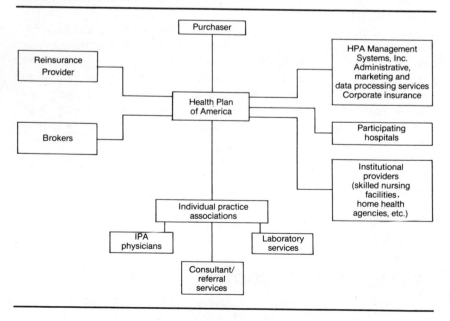

MARKETING

Because of its licensure and its internal claims administration, HPA is able to design its PPO program to meet the particular needs of the purchaser. Thus, marketing is targeted both toward purchasers (insurance companies, self-insured employers, unions) who wish to hold contracts directly with hospitals and physicians and simply to use the PPO organization as an intermediary and toward those that wish to hold a master contract with the PPO organization and to delegate to the PPO all pricing and contractual functions. Marketing is handled by internal staff, and prospects are approached both on a direct basis and through brokers.

PAYMENT MECHANISMS

All-inclusive per-diem rates have been negotiated by HPA with hospitals on a service category basis (e.g., medical-surgical, ICU, CCU). Fee maximums by procedure code have been negotiated with physicians. In addition, HPA maintains discounted rates with outside laboratories, x-ray facilities, and some health services.

UTILIZATION MANAGEMENT AND QUALITY ASSURANCE

The heart of the HPA system is strong utilization control, which has been centrally developed and receives central oversight, but is locally administered at each hospital site by the physician corporation (IPA). While HPA will modify its basic utilization-control system if necessary to meet an individual purchaser's needs, the preferred system to ensure control of medical costs is as follows:

- Each eligible PPO individual must access the system through a *primary care physician* (or PCP) who will see the patient for all routine medical care. Normally, that physician's specialty will be either Family Practice, Internal Medicine, Pediatrics, or Obstetrics-Gynecology.
- *Referrals* to any other physician (another primary care doctor or a specialist) must come from the PCP.
- *Prior authorization* from the IPA is required to refer to non-IPA physicians or to refer for other specific services that the IPA wants to monitor. Each IPA determines for which specific services it will require prior authorization. The utilization control chairman or his/her designee usually gives the authorization.
- *Preadmission certification* from the IPA is required for all elective hospital admissions. The utilization control chairman, through the hospital utilization review nurse, usually gives the certification to

hospitalize. If the admitting physician is other than the PCP, the PCP must give a referral to the other physician. Emergency admissions are certified as soon after admission as possible.

— *Utilization monotoring* is a joint responsibility of the IPA and the Health Plan. HPA provides both routine and "special order" monthly computer recaps of utilization activity, as well as guidance in resolving local utilization issues. However, each local IPA is responsible for establishing effective local utilization-control policies and then implementing those policies.

— *The health plan utilization-control nurse coordinator and the medical director* work closely with each IPA to implement an effective utilization-control program.

The same basic structure is used for quality assurance activities. Both the IPA and HPA medical director review records for appropriateness of service provided. HPA also maintains a customer grievance mechanism to handle any complaints from patients.

LESSONS LEARNED

The process of developing a PPO is lengthy, even when the basic provider system is in place. Issues related to payment, antitrust and other legal issues, the product to be delivered, contractual relationships, and the prospective marketplace all are complex, time consuming, and expensive. In addition, the old marketing adage to "find out what the customers want and give it to them" doesn't work here, because the concept of a PPO is new to purchasers who often do not know what they want. HPA's experience has been that each prospective customer must work through numerous conceptual and political issues before it is possible for them to decide upon a PPO structure and product that will meet their requirements.

Recommendations for those beginning a PPO endeavor would be to develop an excellent market feasibility study and a business plan that identifies income needs and expense projections. Adequate capitalization is extremely important, as the PPO will expend significant dollars upfront and may not generate revenue for one to two years after its formation. In spite of a great deal of press recently about the PPO movement, we have found that many insurers and employers are taking a "wait and see" attitude and are proceeding very cautiously in investigating PPO relationships.

An additional recommendation is that organizations that are considering a PPO should design it to be flexible in order to meet a myriad of purchasers' needs. A PPO that can operate in only one way may be compared to an insurance company with only one benefit package; it will eliminate itself from a large portion of the potential market.

Finally, the prospective PPO must confront the issue of *effective* utilization control head-on. A system that either explicitly or implicitly assumes that, except for modest discounts from usual and customery payment levels, the PPO will operate in a business as usual manner simply will not survive. Purchasers will look critically at the record of PPO organizations in terms of the PPO's ability to control health care cost inflation, and those that are the most successful will be those who receive the contracts.

Hospital Sponsored

CASE STUDY: FAMILY HEALTH PLAN, INC., MINNEAPOLIS, MN

Stephen A. Gregg

President
Family Health Plan, Inc.
Edina, MN

☐ After several months of discussions in 1981, seven Twin City hospitals initiated the development of an organizational design for the purposes of directly marketing their institutional services to various buyers of health care services. The term "PPO" was relatively unknown at the time; however, alternative delivery systems in the form of health maintenance organizations were well established in the Twin Cities.

The initial study was completed in early 1982 and was quickly rejected by powerful elements of the medical community because it lacked traditional physician control of design and operation. In the ensuing months, several other "PPO" initiatives were introduced and quickly conceived in the renewed race to the marketplace. This response over a period of several months legitimized the initial study and what today is Family Health Plan, Inc. (FHP).

Family Health Plan is an independent, for-profit corporation representing client relationships with eight hospitals and 630 physicians located in the seven county Minneapolis-St. Paul area. The plan accepted its first enrollment in January 1984 and has approximately 8,000 plan members. Family Health Plan has received all of its developmental funding from the participating hospitals and physicians. Providers were strategically selected to accomplish objectives associated with geographic distribution, cost effectiveness, and identity.

This chapter highlights important considerations of design and organizational commitments of Family Health Plan, Inc. (see Exhibit 1).

EXHIBIT 1
Family Health Plan Organizational Model

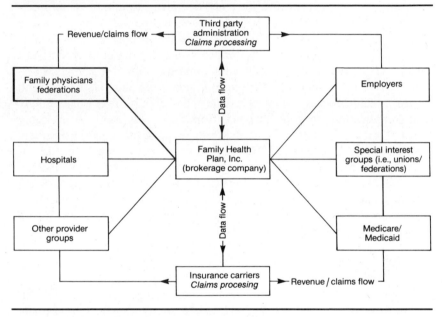

PLAN DESIGN

If the PPO concept is to be successful, it must be more than a marketing device for a collection of aggressive providers. Enlightened providers initiating a PPO should design a plan that serves the differing vested interests of consumers, payors, and providers—probably in that order. Simply stated, the consumer appears to be interested in a product that offers quality (as they perceive it), convenience, affordable out-of-pocket expenses, and a product that is better than the alternatives. The payor (employer) is interested in a product that offers employee satisfaction, *assurance* of cost effectiveness, and in some cases, a reconciliation of the value delivered for the dollars expended. The provider wants to protect or increase existing patient volume and obviously wants to receive "fair" payment for services rendered. Some provider-initiated PPOs do not appear to attend adequately to the interests of consumer and payor.

The following is intended to inventory the major design elements of Family Health Plan that are critical to long-term effectiveness.

ENROLLMENT

Almost all PPO designs introduced so far provide the "dual option" approach and as such do not require a separate enrollment process as is the case with the health maintenance organization. The "option" provides the user with the ability to elect the preferred provider, or not, on each occasion of service. Typically, the employee elects to join the employer's indemnity plan (if there is an option), and each time the employee uses a "preferred provider," he or she receives an incremental benefit such as reduced copay requirement. This appears to offer the employer a very quick and easy method of introducing some possible cost savings; however, since there is no consumer commitment to the plan, as there is with an enrollment process, the PPO has no membership. This presents several complications to a health plan effort that holds itself out as being able to "manage" health care behavior and expenditures more effectively than traditional health care delivery systems, because there is no denominator for measurable performance standards, i.e., patient days, average length of stay for PPO member versus the other plan. In addition, PPO management cannot contact a membership routinely to assess satisfaction or introduce them to better behavioral patterns. FHP is a distinct health plan requiring separate enrollment.

GOVERNANCE

Provider-initiated plans must be careful in their eagerness to assure control that the governance structure achieves a configuration of appropriate expertise, value systems, and authority to act decisively to assure plan performance. Governance structures that are provider-controlled would seem to have particular difficulty with the implications of dealing firmly with the "problem provider," negotiating favorable fee structures with their own changes in the delivery system that reduces their cash flow. Realistically, these are all necessary functions of a properly designed PPO. Family Health Plan is sponsored totally by provider financing but independently owned by 12 to 15 people representing different backgrounds and fields of expertise (e.g., physicians, legal, business, labor, insurance, and employed staff).

Another important aspect of governance is the question of organizing as a for-profit, or not-for-profit operation. Typically, the nonprofit route achieves greater acceptance from providers and is easier to introduce politically; however, Family Health Plan elected the for-profit approach to improve the prospects of organizational decisiveness and business motivation.

COMPREHENSIVE PROVIDER PARTICIPATION

This principle of design suggests a plan with geographic distribution of service points, a full spectrum of specialization, and the inclusion of both physicians and hospitals in the plan design. Selection of these providers from the available population was a critical step to the formation of Family Health Plan. Approximately 20 percent of the available physicians and hospital beds in the community are involved in the plan. This has enabled a geographic distribution of providers and employer and employee recognition of the capacities of the plan. More provider involvement has been discouraged, as it could reduce the atmosphere of competitive advantage, result in an unmanageable number of provider participants, and even introduce antitrust problems.

The involvement of hospitals in the provider configuration is believed by some to be unnecessary or even undesirable. It is often stated that almost all of the health care economy is controlled and directed by the physician; however, it is important to recognize that hospital costs comprise 50 to 60 percent of the premium dollar. With known variations in productivity, contractual allowances, costs of teaching programs, and costs of capital, Family Health Plan concluded that there is substantial variation in the costs and charges of hospitals beyond factors of patient mix or physician utilization patterns. Family Health Plan has accomplished considerable effect on premium costs through its hospital selection.

The "gatekeeper" concept is another optional design feature affecting the provider organization. In varying ways, this places greater control of the patient in the hands of a primary care practitioner on the theory that the practitioner will know how to use health care resources more effectively than the user. The actual outcome of this approach understandably is difficult to measure and involves considerable debate between primary practitioners and specialist.

BENEFIT DESIGN

This is important for two reasons. First, it has obvious influence on whether the buyer decides to select the preferred provider plan from a list of competitive alternatives. Second, benefit configuration has much to do with how the consumer elects to use health care resources and, therefore, the resulting costs to the employer. Unfortunately, some PPO benefit designs, in effect, reintroduce first-dollar coverage by saying to the consumer, use PPO providers and receive 100 percent coverage; use someone else and be subject to an 80 percent/20 percent copay arrangement. Placing some financial responsibility on the user of services is an important retardant to overutilization. PPOs should maintain this incentive; selecting other methods, if necessary, to create encouragement for the employee to elect the PPO option. If the plan is structured to provide for separate enrollment, it is conceivable that a "savings" could be retrospectively determined and, in part, passed on to the employee. Particular possibilities may exist in returning savings to an employee's medical expense account or a 401K program, which are both relatively new benefit innovations.

Family Health Plan offers three optional approaches to benefit design: (1) adjust the employer's existing indemnity plan, reducing benefits and introducing the PPO under the prior more favorable benefit configuration, (2) add incremental benefits to the PPO plan that are over and above the existing indemnity plan, and (3) disregard the existing plan and offer a very lean package that returns much of the savings to the participating employee. The preferred method varies greatly depending on the circumstances of each employer.

COMMITMENT TO PERFORMANCE

There are four ways Family Health Plan seeks to contain costs: (1) careful selection and elimination, if necessary, of certain providers, (2) negotiation of favorable rates, (3) application of strict utilization controls, and, (4) long-term alteration of provider and consumer behavior not viewed as adverse to qualitative outcome. It is a pure management task to design systems, policies, and cultures supporting each of these areas. The traditional fee-for-service system has always lived with the handicap of not being able to organize itself to accomplish these management tasks.

When providers were solicited to join Family Health Plan, the obligation to performance and required systems were clearly communicated. Current levels of competition in many communities will lead providers to join efforts that have any prospect of influencing the disposition of patients. While this level of uneasiness has made it generally easier to solicit provider participation, it is not necessarily a commitment to cooperation to the specific policies and procedural restrictions of the plan. In the ideal circumstances, the participating providers should recognize that they are electing to sponsor and encourage changing individual provider behavior. The more understanding achieved at the front end in this regard, the better.

There are, obviously, many aspects of favorable performance; but today's business climate stresses cost, and this must be in the forefront of a PPO's consideration. Family Health Plan has a goal of maintaining at least a 15 percent favorable differential between its costs and those of the relevant competing indemnity plan. Its efforts will not be considered complete until it achieves that level of performance. Goals such as these need to be firmly expressed and serve as a focal point for effort.

BEHAVIORAL OBJECTIVES

By now most providers are somewhat familiar with the three components of utilization review: preadmission certification, concurrent review (length of stay review), and retrospective review (appropriateness review). These are necessary elements of a PPO and represent the beginnings of behavioral modification. In addition, Family Health Plan will focus on certain targeted goals that the insurance underwriters indicate account for significant premium costs and yet are discretionary patterns of behavior. As an example, in Minneapolis-St. Paul a patient undergoing a normal uncomplicated delivery will stay in the hospital on the average slightly over three days. In Oregon, that same patient would be expected to stay one day less on the average. Since obstetrics accounts for a significant percentage of premium dollars, some special focus on this issue would be appropriate. Other opportunities exist with outpatient surgery, second surgical opinions, chemical dependency, mental health, and other diagnostic-specific procedures. The inadequacy of traditional utilization review is that it is simply a process that yields indefinite and variable outcomes.

PROVIDER INCENTIVES

One of the common issues that surfaces very quickly in PPO design is the matter of incentives. Will providers change their ways without direct economic incentives? Why should they participate if they do not have the opportunity for gain as well as loss? Unless the provider is at risk, can the employer possibly believe that the preferred providers will in fact perform as indicated? These are all legitimate issues that frame a basic attraction to including some incentive plan in the design of the PPO.

There are two risks to designing incentives into the PPO at the outset. The first is that direct economic incentives never seem to work like they should in retrospect. A PPO that depends on that methodology to produce the results promised may be in for a surprise. Second, the mere process of developing and implementing an incentive program can be protracted and raise unnecessary anxieties among physicians that one would like to avoid in the early days of a PPO.

Incentives policies have been deferred for future consideration by Family Health Plan after the organization has matured to some degree.

CAPITALIZATION

Family Health Plan's operating expenses are approximately $400,000 per year with an estimated three-year time-frame before achieving operational breakeven from its routine fee structure. As with any new enterprise, adequate working capital for development is an essential consideration. These requirements can be easily underestimated, and this can be deadly to a well-conceived design.

MARKETING

The marketing plan has been a very important consideration, and the following lessons have been learned so far:

1. Employers are not as ready to buy as providers have calculated them to be.
2. Meaningful feasibility studies are difficult to do since employer attitudes seem highly dependent on whose opinion is assessed within the company, the current financial condition of the company, its most recent experience in health care cost increases, its experiences with other alternative delivery systems, its current management-union relationships, the distribution of its work force, and current intentions relative to health benefit reform within the company.
3. It usually takes about 15 to 20 meetings with the typical large employer to arrive at an employer commitment.
4. The sales force may have problems understanding the conceptual aspects of the plan and its differences from the competition.
5. Plan sponsors need to be able to prospectively identify how a 15 to 20 percent savings can be achieved.
6. A number of employers still want to see providers at risk.
7. The plan must have geographic distribution of recognizable providers (helps considerably if the benefit manager's physician is in the network).
8. High-quality brochures and support material appear to be important.
9. A thorough understanding of the competition is essential.

SUMMARY

Organizational concept, philosophy, and policy are as essential to Family Health Plan's future success as they are to any other business. These value systems will also distinguish it from other PPO efforts. It is very important that PPO initiatives allocate significant thought to these principles, even at the expense of more elaborate feasibility studies and market plans.

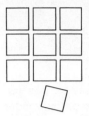

Hospital Sponsored

CASE STUDY: PRIMED NASHVILLE, TN

Terry Warren
Director of Marketing
PriMed
Nashville, TN

☐ PriMed is Hospital Corporation of America's (HCA) response to the HMO, PPO, and IPA movements. The factors that distinguish it from a PPO are discussed later in this case study. PriMed is a health care cost-management system developed to achieve these goals:

— To develop a competitively priced alternative health care delivery system package to market directly to other businesses and employers.
— To develop a vehicle for reducing the annual rate of health care cost increases for industry.
— To reduce the annual rate of increase in health care cost of HCA employees.
— To encourage HCA employees, by the use of incentives, to use HCA facilities and physicians instead of non-HCA facilities and physicians.
— To develop opportunities to enhance the patient care practices of physicians utilizing HCA facilities.
— To explore the utilization of more cost-effective health care alternatives such as home care and outpatient treatment.

BACKGROUND

In 1983, this country was expected to spend about $360 billion on health care, which was more than was spent on national defense.

Since the majority of people who use health care services are covered under some kind of employer-provided insurance plan, it is little wonder that corporate America, including HCA, is paying record amounts for health care. HCA's own health care expense for its employees approached $100 million in 1983.

Business and governement alike have, in the last year, frequently asked HCA what efforts it has made to help get control of health care costs. HCA made a decision to commit the necessary time and resources to study and react to the problem. Over the past year, HCA carefully reviewed how health care costs are affecting business and government and what actions are being taken. As a means of getting at the problem, for itself and for other employers, HCA has developed a program to show that it is possible for employees to get top-quality health care delivered in a cost-efficient way.

PriMed is an innovative alternative to traditional insurance coverage programs. While health care coverage is still the primary focus, PriMed goes beyond traditional insurance by encouraging employees to be wise consumers of health care services, to take care of themselves, and to use HCA hospitals and physicians when it is necessary to seek health care.

DESCRIPTION

Essentially, PriMed is built around two facts: (1) the greatest savings can be achieved in the long run through changing the way people utilize and physicians provide health care and (2) that HCA can do the best job of controlling costs in the facilities over which it has control (namely, HCA owned or managed hospitals).

PriMed attempts to control health care costs by encouraging more efficient utilization of the health care system and by changing utilization.

It is a total approach to controlling health care costs while delivering quality health care. The PriMed concept (see Exhibit 1) includes these elements:

— Benefit design.
— Benefit administration.
— Utilization control.
— Claims administration and control.
— A management information system.
— An employee assistance program.
— A wellness program.
— A total communication plan.

EXHIBIT 1
Basic Design of PriMed

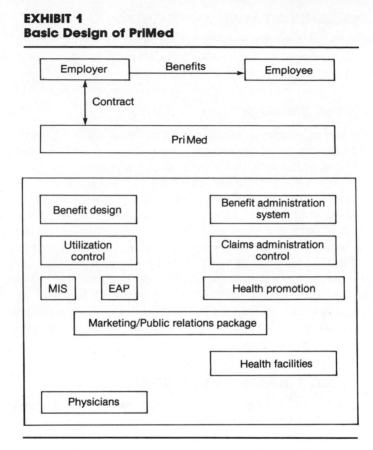

— Hospitals.
— Physicians.

Each of these elements are described briefly as follows:

BENEFIT DESIGN

PriMed staff work with employers to design a benefit plan that meets the employer's and employee's needs but provides appropriate incentives for wise use of health care.

BENEFIT ADMINISTRATION

Policies, procedures, forms, etc. necessary to support the efficient implementation and operation of the Plan are all part of benefit administration.

CLAIMS ADMINISTRATION AND CONTROL

Through its third-party administrator, PriMed can provide claims processing for an employer. Data from claims is stored as a portion of a total database. Tight controls are established to assure appropriate payments.

UTILIZATION CONTROL

This consists of a series of medical reviews consisting of a preadmission certification, concurrent review, retrospective review, and selected mandatory second opinions and outpatient surgery programs. Admission certification assures the necessity of inpatient admission and encourages outpatient care as appropriate. Concurrent review involves frequent case review during confinement. It seeks to minimize lengths of stay and identify candidates for more cost-effective alternative settings for care such as home care. Retrospective review utilizes historical data to identify problems.

The key to the utilization control is the oversight by the medical coordinator. The medical coordinator can authorize payment for cost-effective treatment that may not be specifically covered in the plan design. The medical coordinator communicates outpatient programs to physicians.

MANAGEMENT INFORMATION SYSTEM

This system provides information with which management can make decisions about health care cost management. Specific summary and detail reports are generated from the database. The database is broad-scoped and includes data from claims, utilization control, enrollment, the medical coordinator, and other appropriate sources. PriMed staff assist the employer in report analysis and action planning.

EMPLOYEE ASSISTANCE PROGRAM

This provides a comprehensive confidential counseling and referral service for employees. Counseling is available on virtually any problem related to performance (e.g., stress management, marital difficulties, alcohol and drug abuse, financial problems, etc.).

WELLNESS PROGRAM

Programs and materials are available to encourage prevention of illness. Programs are available in stress management, smoking cessation, nutrition, weight control, etc. While large short-term results are not expected, significant long-term results can be achieved.

COMMUNICATIONS PACKAGE

Videotapes, audio/slide programs, brochures, and other communication tools are available to assist in communicating the problem and solution to employees and providers. Most of the communication tools have been generically designed and can be personalized to the individual company identity.

HOSPITALS

In locations where HCA has sufficient concentration and appropriate geographic dispersion, HCA hospitals are considered the participating providers. It may be both appropriate and necessary in some locations for PriMed to serve as a broker in organizing participating providers.

PHYSICIANS

In locations where HCA is concentrated, medical staff who practice at HCA hospitals are considered participating providers. In other locations it may be necessary to structure agreements with other physicians.

DISTINGUISHING FEATURES

PriMed is a unique approach in that it places greatest emphasis on achieving savings through changing utilization patterns of employees. Effective cost savings measures can be employed while preserving the fee-for-service concept.

OPERATIONAL STATUS

The PriMed program was implemented on October 1, 1983 for HCA corporate and hospital employees in Nashville, Tennessee and on March 1, 1984 for HCA employees in Richmond, Virginia. PriMed will be implemented throughout the remaining HCA-owned hospitals over the next year.

Highlights of the benefit design implemented in Nashville appear in Exhibit 2.

MARKETING

One of the original goals of PriMed was to develop a cost-management product that could be marketed directly to business. To this end HCA has developed a marketing orientation to the organization of PriMed.

PriMed is a for-profit subsidiary of HCA. Marketing and operational staff are located in various cities across the country. These people have

EXHIBIT 2

	Participating Provider	Nonparticipating Provider
Service	(HCA affiliated hospitals and medical staffs)	(Non-HCA affiliated hospitals and medical staffs)
Deductibles	$200 per person per policy year $400 per family per year	$400 per person per policy year
Copayment hospital outpatient, and inpatient services	90 percent (covered hospital outpatient and inpatient services at semi-private rates)	70 percent (covered hospital outpatient and inpatient services at semi-private rates)
Physicians' fees	80 percent (reasonable and customary charges)	70 percent (reasonable and customary charges)
Out-of-pocket limits	$1,000 per year per individual $2,000 per year per family	$3,000 per year per individual $5,000 per year per family
Lifetime maximum benefit	$500,000	$250,000

responsibility for local sales and service. Staff at the corporate office are responsible for national accounts marketing, product management, information system design and development, finance, and administration.

LESSONS LEARNED

Critical to the success of any cost management system are a utilization-control program and a complete management information system. To be successful, the utilization-control program should include all the elements of preadmission certification, concurrent review, and retrospective review. Additionally, these programs must be directly linked to the amount of benefit paid.

The management information system is essential to monitoring the effectiveness of changes over time. Good data is critical to future discussions about changes that may need to be made.

Another valuable lesson learned is the importance of good employee communications. Employees should first be made aware of the health care cost problem. Next, they need to clearly understand how their health care program will change. Finally, it is important to help them become smarter shoppers for health care.

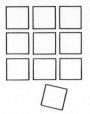
Case Study: California Health Network, San Francisco, CA

Philip M. Levine

Contract Manager
Saint Francis Memorial Hospital
San Francisco, CA

The California Health Network (CHN), based in San Francisco, was one of the first provider-based preferred provider organizations in the United States. This case study will present a brief summary of the development, operation, and ultimate closing of the network. In the short span of three years, CHN witnessed dramatic changes in its own structure and purpose as the health care environment in California underwent similar changes. The events described in this case study are illustrative of how rapidly converging influences affected and helped determine the course of CHN's existence. Although many of the factors that relate to the CHN story and the lessons learned from the experience are unique to it, some can be generalized and thus be useful to those just entering this new realm in other settings.

BACKGROUND

The concept of a network of hospitals and physicians arose out of the concerns of a group of Bay Area hospital administrators who foresaw the need to respond to competitive pressures in their communities and to do something to position themselves to be more competitive as health care providers.

Some of the specific reasons for their decision to form an alternative delivery system included the growth of HMO activity, particularly the Kaiser Plan; impending cutbacks in medicare payments to hospitals; the continuing problem of the existence of too many hospital beds and physicians relative to the general population in the community; and an increasing demand for health care cost containment from payors in the private sector. For example, the local professional standards review organizations had begun contracting with private payors to provide preadmission authorization and concurrent hospital utilization review services for any of their beneficiaries entering hospitals.

ORGANIZATION

The predecessor to CHN was an alliance of four Bay Area hospitals and physicians on their medical staffs that was formed in 1980. The purpose of this venture was to contract with third-party payors in order to establish preferred provider relationships, although the term PPO was not applied at the time since it had not come into popular use yet. The concept underlying this arrangement was to be able to provide a competitive alternative to the HMO or IPA system by creating a network of quality, private, nonprofit hospitals in different Bay Area locations (geographically distant enough from each other to be noncompetitive) and using the services of physicians in private practice who were on the medical staffs of those hospitals.

In this arrangement, the hospitals were contributing the funds necessary to make the plan operational, including providing staff time and office space available for administrative functions. They were in agreement that each would agree to set rates and participate in cost-control activities such as concurrent review and preadmission authorization for elective admissions. They expected to eventually be able to see a positive impact on patient volume at their facilities.

CONTRACT WITH FAR WEST ADMINISTRATORS

In order to put this concept into action and to see if it would be a viable means to accomplish the goal of being competitive, the alliance contracted with a third-party administrator called Far West Administrators, which conducted its business on behalf of an uninsured multiple employer trust (MET). Far West was responsible for administering the benefit plan, marketing it to employers, and paying claims for medical and hospital services.

Through aggressive marketing, Far West was able to sell its dual option benefit plan to many small employers throughout the Bay Area. The hospitals and physicians in the alliance did begin to see new patients in exchange for their acceptance of reduced fees and the other conditions of the contracts. The development of a PPO was underway. As time passed, however, problems with claims payment arose, and soon it became apparent to the alliance that Far West was not satisfactorily performing its contractual obligations. The contract was terminated with the anticipation that all the current outstanding claims would be paid. A short time later Far West went out of business, and since there was no insurance backing the plan, outstanding claims were never paid.

BIRTH OF CHN

This put the organizers of the alliance in a very difficult position. The bankruptcy of Far West did more than leave unpaid claims; it raised the fundamental concern of some participants of the advisability of participating in such a contractual arrangement. By this time, in early 1981, the term PPO was entering more common usage in the literature and was beginning to gain the interest of payors and providers alike as a way to preserve the fee-for-service system while still addressing cost containment. There was a strong enough interest on the part of the hospitals in the alliance to reorganize and formalize their network. Thus, the California Cooperative Health Network was incorporated in June, 1981. Doing business as the California Health Network, the new organization was structured as a nonprofit, shared services organization with the four hospitals as founding members of the cooperative corporation (see Exhibit 1). A Board of Directors was created, composed of the administrator from each member hospital and, later, a physician from each medical staff. The underlying assumption for having a Board composed of both physicians and hospital administrators was that it was necessary to have input and support from both to determine the course of operation for the network. As health care providers, both groups had certain common interests, such as containing costs, preserving quality, and assuring accessibility for patients. Likewise, the interests of the physicians on the panel needed representation in policy decisions.

A network administrative office was established separately from any of the hospitals, and an executive director was hired to manage the day-to-day activities. Initially, these activities concentrated on establishing procedures for recruiting new physicians, bringing new hospitals into the network, marketing the CHN concept to payors, developing a utilization-review plan, and creating data monitoring systems. CHN spent many months exploring possible payor partners and discussing its concepts and capabilities with experts in the insurance and benefits consulting fields. One very important consideration for contracting with a new payor was to make certain that the payor was financially sound. This was an obvi-

EXHIBIT 1
California Health Network
Organization Chart-Relationships of Participants

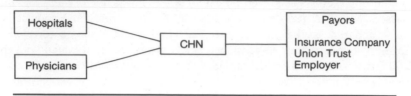

ous outgrowth of the earlier experience with Far West Administrators.

Meanwhile, efforts were also directed at increasing the membership of CHN by bringing more hospitals and physicians into the network. Hospitals were considered on the basis of their general reputation, service capability (such as having ambulatory surgery), commitment to cost containment (having active utilization review committees and quality assurance programs), and location. This last aspect was important because the network planned to have a hospital and physicians available in every part of the greater Bay Area and yet still make sure that the hospitals were not competing with others in the network. It was felt that this would make it far more likely that common interests would not be in conflict with pressures of competition with each other.

Physician recruitment was based on having the panel composed of a range of primary and specialty care physicians geographically situated in order to provide access and convenience to patients. Each physician needed to be on the medical staff of a member hospital. These requirements were felt to be necessary to assure that the physician had the qualifications and credentials to be considered a good candidate. Each was required to sign a participation agreement containing provisions that the physician abide by utilization review and other cost-control measures.

Plans called for the creation of a physician advisory committee that would oversee and monitor the CHN utilization-review plan. This committee was to be made up of two CHN physicians from each hospital in the network.

AMERICAN BENEFITS ADMINISTRATORS

By early 1982, work on the development of internal structures and procedures was progressing at the same time as CHN was discussing potential contracts with a number of payors. The one that appeared most ready to do business with CHN was a third-party administrator from southern California, American Benefits Administrators (ABA). CHN was careful to explore the underwriting status of ABA and made sure that there was insurance for the benefit plans being administered and marketed through ABA. Information was provided that showed that ABA was acting as an agent for Associated International Insurance Company, a company licensed by the California Department of Insurance to operate in the state. A contract was signed between CHN and ABA in May 1982.

The basic agreement was to have CHN negotiate terms of agreements for fees and cost-control mechanisms on behalf of its member hospitals and its physician panel. Furthermore, CHN would provide administrative services to its providers to coordinate and facilitate billing and referrals and would oversee utilization review. ABA, on the other hand, would market benefit plans to employers, pay claims, and thus provide prospective patients for CHN. They opened an office in the Bay Area so that communication was improved for CHN, and payments could be processed more quickly for providers.

AB 3480 AND MARICOPA

It is important to describe the impact of the passage of AB 3480 and the Maricopa decision on CHN, since both occurred during the summer of 1982. At this time, Medi-Cal selective contracting was introduced as a cost-containment effort by the state of California. The legislation, AB 799, was quickly passed and signed by the governor. It meant that a special Medi-Cal "czar" would contract with selected California hospitals for the right to continue to be paid for services provided to Medi-Cal beneficiaries.

The insurance and employer groups in the state reacted by backing the passage of AB 3480, which granted the same powers to private payors of health care benefits such as insurance carriers, self-insured employers, Blue Cross, and union trust funds. Their mutual concern was that Medi-Cal payment decreases would lead to greater cost shifting onto the private payor sector.

A great deal of concern had been expressed by organized hospital and medical groups who had fought unsuccessfully against AB 3480. Issues of access and quality of care were two that did not sway the final outcome. Nevertheless, many questions continued to be raised about the bill, because it apparently gave private payors the authorization to selectively contract with health care providers to establish exclusive arrangements; there was no wording in the bill pertaining directly to preferred provider arrangements. Through the efforts of the California Medical Association, additional legislation, SB 2012, was enacted as an attempt to clarify AB 3480. The question of PPO regulation was still open, and it represented a "gray" area in the minds of many people, especially physicians.

At the same time, the U.S. Supreme Court handed down a decision in *Arizona* v. *Maricopa County Medical Society* in which the court declared that price agreements among nonintegrated groups of physicians constituted a per se violation of federal antitrust laws. Moreover, the court determined that horizontal price-fixing could be avoided by having the payor offer individual agreements to competing providers. Thus, the original concept of CHN of negotiating fees and rates was struck down. The existing contracts between CHN and each of its hospitals and physicians were altered so as to avoid antitrust implications. CHN then accepted the role of coordinating and facilitating the fee agreement negotiations between payor and provider. This particular change in CHN's function would not have been that major had it not been for the events that occurred in late September 1982.

THE ABA COLLAPSE

During the summer of 1982, CHN had grown to five hospitals and about 75 physicians. By this time, ABA had stepped up its marketing efforts, and there were an estimated 6,000 to 7,000 beneficiaries in the Bay Area. Some physicians on the CHN panel had begun to see many new patients, and the hospitals were also benefiting from their CHN relationship.

The CHN option was an attractive one for small employers because the employees using it paid only a small service charge at the time they saw a CHN physician, and they did not have to pay any deductible or copayment. Employers were able to pay lower monthly premiums partly due to the reduced (about 15 percent to 20 percent lower) fees paid to physicians and hospitals and partly due to the anticipated savings from the utilization-review program that would control unnecessary admissions and lengths of stay in the hospitals.

Overall, the operation of the CHN was proceeding well, and other payors continued to express a lot of interest in the concept. CHN stepped up its plans to conduct educational seminars for ABA brokers and agents so that they could be more knowledgeable about CHN and thus be more effective in their marketing. Then, on September 27, 1982, CHN learned that the California Department of Insurance had placed a temporary restraining order against ABA requiring it to suspend its operations until a hearing could be held to hear their explanation of several allegations brought against them by the state of California. There were questions about the relationship of ABA to their underwriter and their ability to guarantee payment of outstanding claims. There was some question as to whether or not ABA still had a contract with Associated International, or if it had signed one with another carrier. One week later, at the hearing, ABA filed for bankruptcy, and a trustee was named to be responsible for the long-term conduct of its business.

The CHN hospitals and physicians were shocked by this news. All of the patients covered through ABA using CHN providers as preferred providers were now suddenly left without any coverage. The employers quickly signed up with other traditional insurance plans, but CHN was not available as a preferred provider network for any of them.

These developments led to quick action by the CHN board. The CHN executive director resigned, and an immediate legal inquiry into the situation was initiated. A decision was also made to allow a minimum of three months for CHN to attempt to recover from this setback and to try to resume normal operation. While the ABA situation was being monitored by CHN's legal counsel, discussions that had previously begun with Fireman's Fund American Life Insurance Company (FFAL) were intensified in order to finalize negotiations. This effort was successful, and a contract was signed in early November 1982.

ATTEMPTS AT RECOVERY

Fireman's Fund had been developing a dual option benefit package called "Health Plus." They intended to market it as a PPO option to their existing and potential group health insurance customers in the Bay Area (and other parts of California). The contract specified that FFAL would use CHN as its source of hospitals and physicians in its own contract offerings to providers. Consequently, CHN now had a linkage with a large, well-established insurance company. The major task of CHN was to coordinate the contracting between FFAL and the existing CHN hospitals and physicians. It was also important to enlarge the physician panel by adding physicians in geographic areas where they were needed on the CHN panel and to include specialists. CHN relied on a "gatekeeper" approach to case management, wherein primary care physicians were at the point of access to medical care for beneficiaries and controlled referrals to specialists. It was still necessary to have specialists of all types on the panel in each hospital service area so that referrals could be made to specialists on the panel.

This task turned out to be more difficult and time-consuming than at first anticipated. The questions raised by individual physicians and organized medical groups created the need for a well-planned and deliberate process for bringing new physicians onto the CHN panel. One basic issue that seemed to be of concern to almost every physician had to do with the wording in AB 3480 concerning the dates when contracting could begin. The legislation stipulated that contracting for the type of arrangements described in the bill could not begin with physicians until July 1, 1983. CHN had been advised by its legal counsel that AB 3480 did not affect PPO contracting and that it should be permissible for physicians to sign CHN and FFAL contracts.

Also, CHN itself was being questioned about its past relationships with Far West Administrators and American Benefits Administrators. There was a concern about the credibility of the organization that had to be addressed. This was done in combination with explanations about

CHN's role and purpose, the utilization review plan, and CHN contracts during meetings with individual physicians, medical society leaders, and medical staff leaders. CHN staff worked hard to contact and inform physicians about itself and the opportunities that existed through the FFAL contract. A new staff person was hired to assist in this effort so that personal visits could be made to physicians offices. This staff member was a nurse with an MBA who had previous experience working in a physician's office and who had assisted in utilization review work with a peer review organization.

A special consultant was retained to assist in contracting efforts in one hospital service area where the medical staff had turned over all of the CHN material to the local medical society for further study.

Even though these activities took months to unfold, progress was being made, and CHN was preparing to add more of the needed physicians to its panel. By this time, in early 1983, CHN had five hospitals (one previous hospital had dropped out of the network in November 1982 because of lack of physician support, and another hospital had joined in January 1983). Physician membership on the panel had grown to 130, although the geographic distribution was uneven among the hospital service areas.

FINAL DAYS

Several important issues internal to CHN remained to be resolved. One of these involved the designation of a permanent executive director. This was in progress while the Board underwent changes in representatives due to changes in administration at several of the member hospitals. Soon after the Board had elected new officers, CHN was presented with a proposal to merge with a newly developing provider-sponsored network also based in San Francisco. The proposal suggested that a larger, stronger provider-based PPO would more likely succeed in competition with prepaid systems, which also had wide geographic accessibility. Furthermore, it was reasoned that a new network identity would resolve the problem of CHN's negative image. Lastly, it was argued, a major reorganization of corporate structure would be required to respond more effectively to the ramifications of the Maricopa decision.

After several months of discussion, the CHN members voted to reject the proposal, because one of the key issues in the merger could not be agreed upon. This issue was the suggestion that all of the CHN hospitals except one would be included in the new organization to be created by the merger. The hospital to be excluded had been an original founding member of the network and had contributed a great deal to CHN over the years. The other CHN members voted in favor of a merger that included this hospital, but this was rejected by the other group. The discussions that had taken place because of the merger proposal had created differences of opinion about the best direction for the future of CHN. Once the merger failed, two of the CHN hospitals elected to terminate their CHN membership. The first decided to join the new group with whom the merger had been proposed. The second hospital had only been in the network a few months and felt its interests would be better served by working with several IPAs to which many of its physicians belonged and to join with them in joint efforts involving health plans in their local area.

Compounding these organizational problems, FFAL was planning to market "Health Plus" in the service area of the first of the hospitals to drop out of CHN. Their own research had indicated that they could be most successful in their marketing efforts by starting in this locale and then spreading into the rest of the CHN regions.

Several months prior to this, CHN had attempted to attract the interest of Blue Cross to be a network for their new Prudent Buyer Plan. It had eventually been learned that Blue Cross did not intend to go through a network such as CHN to offer contracts to Bay Area hospitals but was instead directing their negotiations directly at individual hospitals.

These events led the remaining three CHN hospitals to the conclusion that their continued investment of time and money necessary to maintain network operations was not going to benefit their institutions any further. The public image of CHN was viewed as a disadvantage at this point. Each hospital still faced competitive pressures, and each needed a means to address those pressures. The first step towards this was to close down the CHN office. This was done on June 30, 1983. At the same time, the hospitals decided to wait before dissolving the corporation in order to see if it might be worth maintaining the network legal structure in order to resume operations at some time in the future. The consensus was that if marketplace forces, such as the interest of insurance companies to contract with a provider-based network, determined that there was still sufficient need to resurrect the network, it could be done without starting from the beginning again.

Eight months later, it became evident that each of the hospitals had embarked on similar but different efforts to work more closely with their own physicians to consider the issues of contracting and preferred provider arrangements. In fact, it did not appear at all advantageous to attempt to network with each other at this time (and certainly not using the CHN identity), so dissolution proceedings began.

An example of the way in which the market had evolved is the emergence of a new PPO from Transamerica-Occidental Life Insurance Company called "Transamericare." This company sought contracts either with individual hospitals or with hospitals based on their membership in a provider-based PPO. In this case, there was no competitive advantage for the former CHN hospitals to be in a network; they could negotitate contracts directly with Transamerica-Occidental.

CONCLUSIONS

There were many important lessons learned from the CHN experience. Each participant, whether it was the hospital, the physician, the insurance company, or the broker, came away from it with an appreciation for the complexity of PPO organization and functioning.

The major lesson for hospitals and physicians was the realization of the importance of working together as equal participants in developing contractual relationships. Key issues such as who was going to control utilization review and how new physicians were to be selected for the panel were of great concern and caused a great deal of debate.

Another lesson was that developing a network of hospitals can be a time-consuming and costly proposition if the hospitals are financing the venture themselves. The CHN hospitals contributed an initial membership fee when they formed the network, and each subsequent member paid the same initial fee. Monthly dues were divided among the member hospitals according to a formula that spread some of the expenses evenly to each hospital and some of the expense according to a computation based on the operating revenue at each hospital. This was designed to make the individual hospital contribution equitable. Naturally, each planned to derive added revenue from membership, and this would offset the monthly dues expense.

A third major lesson has to do with utilization review. There is a strong case to be made for local control of this vital component of the PPO. Local physicians are more sensitive to their communities and their peers. They have more insight into particular problems. Conversely, some payors regard this approach as being like the proverbial "fox guarding the chicken coop." In any case, this is an area so important to the success of the PPO that it is mandatory that arrangements be developed that accommodate all participants without sacrificing the intent of the process.

Taking a retrospective view of CHN, it is possible to identify several things that could have been done to make the outcome of the network a different one. It is important to keep in mind the unique set of circumstances in which CHN was developed, especially the environmental factors that have been identified in this case study. It is clear that PPOs offer an opportunity for health care professionals and insurance and employer representatives to discuss common concerns in an attempt to construct a meaningful plan to meet their own needs and those of the others. This dialogue needs to be encouraged. CHN was one early attempt to do this; it will certainly not be the last.

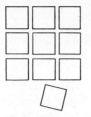

CASE STUDY: THE CARECARD EXPERIENCE

Gary D. Aden, J.D.

Senior Vice President
Pennsylvania Hospital
Philadelphia, PA

In the summer of 1982, Pennsylvania Hospital in Philadelphia undertook an environmental scan to provide direction for the hospital's next five years. It soon became clear that there were new developments afoot which would have a dramatic impact on the health care field. There was an obvious change underway in the public's perception of health providers, particularly hospitals.

The environmental assessment highlighted two key changes: (1) market pressure coming from a variety of payors and (2) pressure for organizational change. Among the strategies determined to be appropriate to address these factors was one that would place the hospital in a broader role than that of a traditional deliverer of health services. It appeared that a preferred provider organization might make sense.

The hospital asked the president of the Hospital Association of Pennsylvania (HAP) to spearhead an effort to bring the hospital and others like it together in creating a PPO. Although secure in his position, he agreed to join the effort. His rationale was that he had been directed by the HAP membership to develop a competitive health care model in

Pennsylvania and he could not do it as an association executive representing many different types of hospitals. By creating a PPO, he could help bring about meaningful change on the health care scene.

Tentatively committed, he and representatives from Pennsylvania Hospital visited the Forbes Health System in Pittsburgh and Harrisburg Hospital in Harrisburg, Pennsylvania. Both joined the effort immediately. York Hospital in York, Pennsylvania, joined later. The hospitals formed a corporation named Health Alternatives Development to develop the PPO.

This combination of hospitals allowed the endeavor to capitalize on some important common characteristics. The hospitals provided geographical coverage across the commonwealth of Pennsylvania. Each hospital had high-quality professional staff. All were moderate-cost hospitals. All were service oriented. These strong characteristics were essential to market any successful PPO.

The keystone of the program, however, was to be the close involvement of hospitals and physicians in the financing as well as delivery of health care. If these elements could all be brought together successfully, the PPO would have hospitals with similar characteristics working with their medical staffs to bring new patients into the system.

DEVELOPMENT OF CARECARD

The endeavor was formally underway in March 1983. Health Alternatives Development quickly developed as its objective the provision of affordable health care coverage. Incentives for doctors and hospitals to provide quality care in an efficient manner were to be key to the success of the endeavor.

Various models were examined to see which might best achieve the objective. The elements of a PPO which the new company examined were as follows:

— Provider network.
— Negotiated fee schedule.
— Utilization/claims review.
— Rapid claims turnaround.
— Consumer choice somewhat restricted.
— No risk.

To Health Alternatives Development, a sound program mandated that providers bear risk. It did not seem possible to the founders that any program could be operated well and deliver care efficiently if there were no risk for the providers. Therefore, the other PPO elements were combined with risk to set the stage for the development of a preferred provider insurance company.

The model evolved as follows. An insurance company was to be established in Harrisburg (in central Pennsylvania) to provide marketing, support services and insurance functions to health care delivery organizations under a contractual agreement. The delivery organizations, called "local provider organizations," were to be spread across the state in various population centers. These elements would come together to form a company called Carecard.

EXHIBIT 1

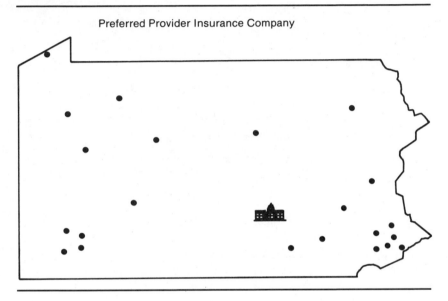

Preferred Provider Insurance Company

The mechanism for Carecard's operation took shape as illustrated on page 1016.

The key to successful operation was the local provider organizations (LPOs). LPOs were to provide physicians with a strong voice in the operation of Carecard. Each LPO was comprised of primary physicians, specialists, and their hospital. Marketing to employers would be handled by Carecard. The employee who chose the Carecard option would then select a primary care physician. The primary care physician selection would lock the patient into a given hospital. The primary care physician would be the gatekeeper responsible for controlling the use of specialists, hospital utilization (in conjunction with the specialists), and other resources such as rehabilitation services, home care, and pharmacy.

The risk account shown in the illustration symbolizes the mechanism for implementing the provider incentives. A determination was to be made for each local provider organization projecting the cost of resources needed to provide care for the individuals selecting the LPO. If funds remained in the account at the end of the fiscal year, they would be divided up in the form of

EXHIBIT 2

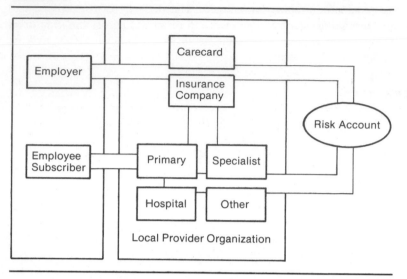

bonuses to the primary physicians, the specialists, and the hospital. If the account was overspent before the end of the fiscal year, all providers would be paid 50 percent of their usual payments.

The result of the efforts of Health Alternatives Development was to be quality care at a better price. The future looked bright.

PERFECT SOLUTIONS

Carecard never achieved its future. It was an excellent idea brought forth by intelligent, aggressive people, but it still did not succeed. One of the most important reasons why it did not succeed was that Health Alternatives Development set out to do far more than was necessary to penetrate the market.

Part of the reason for this "search for perfection" may have been the hospital association experience that was pervasive among the Carecard founders. On the positive side, the *association factor* did provide much needed contacts. Carecard's president had been heavily involved with business and industry through the Governor's Task Force on Health Care Cost Containment. This provided an entree to the market. His contacts with the hospitals were just as important since Carecard was to focus on them to attract the quality providers needed for its success.

Carecard's president was not the only one with association experience. Out of the 12 board members, one was a past chairman of the American Hospital Association, he and two others had served as past chairmen of the Hospital Association of Pennsylvania, and three others were heavily involved in committee work for the hospital association. All knew each other and all worked well together. Their association experience was part of the glue that held them together.

However, there was a negative side to the association factor. Associations strive to satisfy all members and treat them fairly. Associations also prepare idealistic solutions for important issues, which then are the starting point in negotiating a resolution.

At Carecard, there was a tendency to think in terms of societal solutions rather than business objectives. For example, the strategy developed to achieve overall objectives was:

> To generate mutual commitments by hospitals and participating doctors to the common goal of growth and progress by using a health care financing mechanism that (1) improves patient mix, (2) discourages regulatory expansion, (3) produces stable healthcare financing, and (4) supports the delivery of quality health care.

Carecard worked hard to develop perfect solutions. There were perfect benefits, perfect payment mechanisms, and perfect incentives, which all took extensive time to develop and implement. In the end, there was such a wealth of good ideas that Carecard may have choked on them.

ELEMENTS OF CARECARD

Several substantial concepts were built into the Carecard plan. These were:

— Hospital network.
— Physician/hospital partnership.
— Statewide market.
— Insurance.
— Incentives/risk.
— Provider ownership.
— Prompt payment.
— Strong utilization control.
— Data feedback.
— Multiple products.

The first concept was *networking* with hospitals. This was important because of the hospital's role as the focus for provider involvement with Carecard. Hospitals of high caliber were expected to be associated with doctors of equal quality. These quality providers were essential for the Carecard marketing strategy.

The second good idea was the *hospital/physician partnership*. Hospitals had long struggled to bring the physicians closer to institutional goals and objectives. If physicians could be joined in a business enterprise with hospitals, substantial progress could be made. The local provider organization envisioned a major role for physicians in the management of its affairs and was the mechanism designed to accomplish this task.

The third item of great interest was a *statewide* market. There was a window open for gaining substantial market share and the company wanted to take advantage of it before it closed. The frenzy of activity from HMOs that has since surfaced was not even rumored at that time. The Blue Cross plans were doing little in alternative delivery programs. In addition, there are five Blue Cross plans in the commonwealth, and they seldom worked in concert. Carecard felt that if it could move into the market before other plans developed, there was a chance to break into the business without serious competition. By being able to serve employers with multiple locations, the company could attract many of the larger employers and build its market share.

The next good idea was the *insurance* company. The PPO concept avoided risk. Carecard embraced provider risk and felt it important to have an insurance function under Carecard's control if the company was going to deal ably with the risks and incentives in the program. The expertise needed to establish the insurance function was available in-house. Carecard's president had the experience of establishing a hospital-sponsored malpractice insurance company in 1975, and it had since grown to a multimillion dollar company serving 14 states.

The fifth element involved the *incentives*. It was determined that there would be incentives for providers and subscribers. The final product probably had more opportunities for risk than a roulette wheel. For openers, the hospitals and the physicians were required to make a cash commitment. Hospitals would commit $200 per bed to participate. Physicians were to commit $1,000 apiece. This formula produced a 50/50 split of capitalization between doctors and hospitals. Secondly, the payment mechanism contained risk. Gatekeepers were to be paid on a capitation basis. Specialists were to receive 80 percent of usual and customary charges with a cap at approximately the 95th percentile. Twenty percent of their fees would be held back in a risk pool for later payment. Hospitals were to be paid an amount that would provide a slight operating margin, the extent of the margin to be based on how competitive their prices were with other Carecard hospitals. The higher-cost hospitals would receive a margin in the range of 6 percent. The lower-cost hospitals would receive approximately 10 percent. The result would be hospital payments at 84–88 percent of charges. Finally, the funds remaining in the local risk account at the end of the year would be distributed to the providers.

Subscribers also had incentives. Among other benefit packages, there was a basic benefit plan that incorporated deductibles to encourage the subscriber to utilize fewer services. Included were a $250 deductible for hospitalization, a $7.50 deductible for physician visits, and no outpatient psychiatric care. The difference in premiums between the basic and expanded benefit plans was about 15 percent. There were also the usual incentives of any PPO to encourage subscribers to stay within the Carecard system. Subscribers would pay 50 percent of charges out-of-pocket if they went to a provider outside of the system.

Provider ownership was another important concept. Doctors and hospitals were to have a stake in the company to establish commitment. In addition, provider ownership directed the distribution of profits. At this time, new issues of health stocks were being issued at very attractive price to earnings (P/E) ratios. If there was to be a potential stock bonanza, it was fair that those who made the enterprise successful should receive some benefit related to their stock ownership. Thus a stock option was discussed for those providers who were more efficient in using resources in the delivery of patient care.

The next two concepts, *prompt payment* and strong *utilization control,* are cornerstones of any PPO. Prompt payment was an incentive to the physicians and the hospitals to join the system. Utilization control was an incentive to the purchasers to buy into the system.

There was also to be a management *information* system developed to assist the local provider organizations in monitoring utilization. The management information system would also allow the company to supply data to the employers to enable them to take an active role in controlling their costs.

The final concept among the good ideas was *multiple products.* Carecard was preparing to offer the insurance line including basic and expanded options (the preferred products). Second, there was an administrative services only (ASO) option for those employers who were self-insured and not yet sure of Carecard. An ASO arrangement would build the employer's confidence in Carecard and give the Carecard staff the opportunity to identify and demonstrate the savings potential associated with its preferred products. Third, the Carecard staff was eager to develop an HMO option because they sensed that a strong market existed. Finally, as Carecard was about to be implemented, it again became evident that there were companies more interested in a basic PPO involving no risk. The staff was directed to develop one. There was a product for everyone.

PROBLEM 1: COMPLEXITY

Those ideas were good then and still are. Despite that, the promise of Carecard did not materialize. The strength of the concept was overwhelmed by four factors: complexity, time, risk, and capital.

First of all, Carecard became much too complex. This relates to the drive for perfect solutions. Carecard probably became somewhat intimidating because of its many elements. Of the 10 good ideas, there were some straightforward elements. *Prompt payment, utilization control,* and *information management* were all easily understandable. So too was the *insurance* mechanism.

The next group of good ideas, however, had elements with differing levels of appeal to different groups. The *hospital network* did not appeal across the board. In addition, hospital/physician *partnerships* were a new concept in Pennsylvania. Thirdly, the *incentives* were so numerous that they became confusing. Finally, *provider ownership* was not as attractive as expected. Some physicians objected to putting any money into the program. Others objected because they were not given the opportunity to put in more. Provider ownership would have been more appealing if it had been offered on a voluntary basis.

There were a few elements that turned out to be of little value. *Multiple products* seemed to make sense but complicated the development phase. The *statewide market* became a problem because the company could not deliver.

Providers who looked at Carecard primarily as a means of attracting new patients found it very acceptable. Those who analyzed its every element were put off by its apparent complexity. Employers eagerly awaited a product that never reached the market.

PROBLEM 2: TIME

Trying to develop and implement a complex program is difficult. It became impossible in this case because of the time constraints the company placed upon itself. Not only was Carecard striving to take advantage of the window of opportunity that existed, but business and industry representatives on the Governor's Task Force on Health Care Cost Containment were creating tremendous pressure for the speedy development of a competitive system in Pennsylvania. The company was incorporated in February of 1983. The target date to be operational was September 1983.

The concept of the hospital network illustrates the difficulties encountered. To incorporate the desired hospitals into a PPO, there was to be a selection process. Carecard's desire for fairness required that an elaborate set of criteria be developed as the basis to bring those hospitals in. Developing the criteria absorbed a tremendous amount of consulting time, staff time, and money. The staff probably knew within four or five hospitals those that were acceptable. To develop a list of criteria that could withstand public scrutiny was overkill. Most PPOs target the desired hospitals and ask them to sign a contract. Carecard spent a lot of time developing quantitative criteria.

In addition, any time one talks about a hospital network and selected providers, it becomes imperative to obtain an antitrust opinion. The company expended precious funds and several weeks obtaining the opinion. Once produced, it indicated that the direction the company was taking in selective contracting was permissible. This level of comfort was achieved at the expense of time and money for other developmental activities. The ubiquitous fear of antitrust dictated that course.

Time also affected the creation of the physician/hospital partnerships. The local provider organization was new, and a structure had to be developed for it. To formalize that structure, contracts were needed between the LPO and Carecard, the LPO and the hospital, and the LPO and the physicians. There were also model contracts developed for other LPO relationships. The company concentrated on time-consuming legal work rather than on the actual development of the LPOs. Consequently, none were developed.

The development of multiple products also consumed time. The achievements here were monumental, however. The company was set to receive its certificate from the state insurance commissioner once it was determined what the book of business would be. This was a substantial accomplishment. Most new companies, however, utilize existing insurance companies to provide underwriting services, claims management, and data processing services. The time and effort saved is substantial.

As for incentives, a substantial amount of time was spent on developing the payment systems. Primary care physicians could receive three different levels of capitation depending on the type of service they provided in their offices; i.e., whether they offered basic office services, performed basic tests, or handled more sophisticated tests. The hospital payment mechanism also required a substantial effort to produce.

There was also the issue of the distribution of surpluses. It was resolved that LPOs would have to handle this on an individual basis. Working out the proper percentage of stock ownership, value of stock, and voting rights also took time that encroached on implementation of the Carecard product.

Utilization controls had to be developed. The basic matter of selecting computer hardware and software took considerable time, especially because it was done in-house.

Statewide marketing also consumed time. In order to be in a position to provide the products statewide, the enterprise needed a geographical spread of hospitals across the commonwealth. In late August, the Carecard staff visited 12 cities in Pennsylvania and made presentations to hospitals who wanted to hear about Carecard. That process consumed the period through the end of September, not only to make presentations but also to obtain feedback from the hospitals and to answer a variety of questions from hospital management, board, and medical staff. Over 200 meetings were held during this period.

Forty-three hospitals signed up to reserve the opportunity to participate. To do that, $2.4 million was collected and placed in escrow. Unfortunately, when it came time to infuse more capital into the enterprise, these monies could not be used. They were to remain in escrow until the hospital was actually selected as a participant. That could not be done until the company was operational. Carecard had money in the bank, hospitals ready to participate, and nowhere to go.

The next time-consuming exercise involved the Physician Advisory Committee. This issue arose in a most unusual manner. One of the founding hospitals had a more volatile relationship with its physicians than the other three. (As an aside, even cozy relationships start to be battered a bit when something new like Carecard is brought on line.)

At the beginning of 1983, the founders had been cautious about publicly announcing Health Alternatives Development. They wanted to be sure that it was going to go forward before the news broke. In addition, they did not want to expose the president's plans prematurely. The date set to make the announcement was January 27, 1983.

The administrator of the hospital in question had a longstanding commitment to go to Jamaica for two weeks on January 28. The announcement was made on the 27th. On the morning of the 28th, he boarded a plane to Jamaica. No one could reach him. Some of the hospital's medical staff decided that the administrator had orchestrated events so that the announcement would be made one day and he would leave the country the next. For the sake of a vacation, Carecard never really recovered. This issue became a bone of contention between the management of that hospital and its medical staff. In the final analysis, Carecard would have fared better with only three hospital founders. The management input from the fourth was solid, but it was negated by the impact of the medical staff squabble. This issue festered and never went away.

The issue was important, however, in another way. It reinforced the idea that physicians must be involved in the design of the delivery system. To provide physician input, four physicians were selected to serve on the board—one from each founding hospital.

In addition to board input, the Physician Advisory Committee was created. It was comprised of three physicians from each hospital resulting in a committee of 12 physicians who were to advise the Carecard staff on issues relating to medical affairs.

To understand how this effort failed, one must appreciate how difficult it is to bring any 12 physicians together at any one given time. Add to that the problem of bringing three from Philadelphia and three from Pittsburgh—each halfway across the commonwealth—into Harrisburg for half-day meetings, and it becomes clear that all were never present or were somewhat unhappy when present.

At the meetings, their reaction to the material presented by the Carecard staff was either that: (1) the material was set up by the staff to co-op the physicians and allow Carecard to proceed to do what it wanted regardless of their input, or (2) the material was so elementary that the physician's time was wasted. The result was that the Physician Advisory Committee, even though staffed by a physician, the Carecard medical director, never worked. That does not mean that physician input is unimportant, only that obtaining it on a group basis is difficult. This exercise consumed valuable time and netted the enterprise little.

The last problem relating to time also relates to capital. When Carecard realized that it needed to raise capital, time had become critical. Unfortunately, a filing with the Pennsylvania Securities Commission was required because other investors were being sought. Legal counsel was able to turn the filing around in just four weeks. However, the four weeks were devastating for a company on the brink of a cash shortage. The potential investors had given a day of their time to hear about Carecard. They were unimpressed with a company which then took four weeks to return to them with a prospectus.

The problems with time were clearly crucial for Carecard. Why was such a short time frame set? The founders did not want to be in development too long. They wanted to take advantage of the window of opportunity, which was a constant reminder of the need to move fast. However, because the time frame was unrealistic, $1.2 million was expended and nothing was achieved. And, in retrospect, the window stayed open much longer than projected.

PROBLEM 3: RISK

The third element that came into play in Carecard's demise involved risk. The founders were totally committed to risk as an important element in Carecard. It was needed to produce an effective program. All of the people involved in the inception of Carecard considered themselves risk takers; they clearly were not afraid to be at the cutting edge of health care management.

Others a little more distant from the enterprise were not necessarily as comfortable with this risky undertaking, and this turned out to be critical. If the founders had been entrepreneurs working out of a garage, the enterprise would have fared better. As it was, the founders each had their own organizational relationships to satisfy. This placed the Carecard president in the position not only of dealing with his board members but of handling issues raised by four hospital medical staffs and four boards. It created a nearly impossible situation.

First, as the amount of money invested rose, the risk adverseness of some of the founding hospitals' boards came to the fore. Secondly, the situation with the physician unrest did not do anything to add to the comfort level of those boards. Finally, there was a great deal of concern about starting an insurance company. Carecard was cast as ill equipped to handle the risk that the insurance mechanism entailed. Concern was also expressed that the well-established insurance companies had not tried to take advantage themselves of this window of opportunity. (In retrospect, all of the major insurance companies were working quietly on an alternative delivery system strategy.) The support that founders had received from their boards began to wane as these three elements grew in importance. The result was that the hospital boards told the founders to put a limit on the capital investment. The lid was shut at $281,000 apiece.

PROBLEM 4: CAPITAL

The last problem in the development of Carecard was capital. In the fall of 1983, Carecard was close to becoming operational. In fact, with the money in hand, it appeared that Carecard had sufficient funds to commence operations. The problem came when just completed cash flow projections showed a $1.3 million deficit before it would turn positive.

The founding hospitals' boards had already capped their investment. The $2.4 million in escrow was included in these financial projections. No cash was available from these sources to save the company. Another vehicle designed to generate cash flow was Carecard's management of the founding hospital's health care benefits on an administrative services only basis. Because of the company's tenuous financial position, only one of the founders was willing to take this risk. Carecard decided quickly that it had to raise additional cash. This began in the second week in October.

Hospitals were the first investor groups approached. Carecard had identified six hospitals who were very strong supporters of the concept and had indicated some desire to invest. A meeting was convened on October 9. In early November, when the lawyers had completed their four-week effort to prepare the prospectus, the results were that one hospital did not respond, one could not make up its mind, three said no, and one could not write the check fast enough. That was clearly insufficient.

Doctors were not approached because it did not appear that there was enough time to deal with hundreds of investors. Furthermore, because the hospitals had not yet been selected, it was unclear which doctors the company could approach. Therefore, Carecard approached venture capitalists. Again, the problem with venture capitalists was time. In addition, while the Carecard staff had a missionary zeal about Carecard, they were all on salary. None of their compensation was based on the success of the company. Stock provisions had been discussed but had not been implemented. The venture capitalists walked away. They were only interested in enterprises with hungry management.

The last resort was the insurance companies. It was now the period between Thanksgiving and New Year's. The Carecard staff was told that insurance companies never make a decision in a month. And even if they could find one that could make a decision within a month, nobody in the insurance business makes decisions between Thanksgiving and Christmas. One company was willing to put up $250,000, but Carecard ended up far short of raising the funds to continue.

The problem with the hospital investors was not as clearcut as it was with the venture capitalists and the insurance companies. It would appear that the hospitals could not deal with the idea of writing out a check for $281,000. It is important to note that the four founders had phased their investment in over a period of months and were committed from the first day. Carecard was now asking hospitals to put $281,000 into a company that was on the ropes. The risk adverseness of hospital boards in this regard was understandable.

CONCLUSION

On December 18, 1983, the Carecard board decided that it could not run the risk of a bankruptcy and the resulting embarrassment to their hospitals. The board voted to close down the operation, pay off the debts, and put the company up for sale. That was the end for Carecard.

Almost all those who were involved in Carecard remain strongly committed to the idea of alternative delivery systems. Four of the key executives are working in positions with HMOs or insurance companies developing alternative delivery systems. Three of the hospitals are involved in new activities to develop alternatives to traditional health care delivery. Time is proving the founders of Carecard right in terms of the changes they forecasted even if it was not so kind to Carecard.

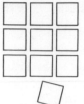

Health/Hospital Service Plan Sponsored

CASE STUDY: BLUE SHIELD PREFERRED PLAN—BLUE SHIELD OF CALIFORNIA

Charles L. Parcell

Senior Vice President
Marketing Group
Blue Shield of California
San Francisco, CA

☐ When California preferred provider legislation was passed in 1982, Blue Shield of California was in the unique position of already having preferred provider relationships. Blue Shield's contracts with California physicians—by which they accept Blue Shield's payment determinations as payment-in-full—were the forerunner and prototype of the contracts authorized by the new legislation (AB 3480 and AB 799). In a sense, Blue Shield has already been a preferred provider organization for almost 45 years. The preferred provider conception was not revolutionary and has even been called "the reinvention of Blue Shield."

Despite an inherent head start, however, Blue Shield was determined not to rush into the marketplace with a hastily assembled PPO package. There were too many concerns about cost-controlled medicine in general, and PPOs in particular, to be solved before introducing the Blue Shield Preferred Plan. In California, concerns and doubts centered on four issues:

1. Quality of Care—How could employers or indeed anyone considering a PPO be certain that for the reduced fee they were not purchasing inferior services? Would the discount, in the final analysis, turn out to be an illusion?

2. Inconvenience—Could a way be devised to avoid the limitations so often associated with HMOs and other forms of cost-controlled medicine, i.e., the limited (or no) choice of physicians, the one or two (often inaccessible) hospitals, the long hours in the waiting room?

3. Utilization Controls—Without utilization controls, a PPO would amount to nothing more than a fancy marketing scheme; a PPO without these controls could not favorably impact on a group's basic experience. But what are the most effective utilization controls? What is the most effective way to administer them?

4. Equity and Cost Shifting—On whose behalf would the PPO contracts be made? There was concern that PPOs, while slowing down the spiraling increase of employer health costs, would do nothing for individuals and families. In the same vein, would preferred providers raise their rates and fees for other Blue Shield patients to compensate for the lower rates to PPO plan members? This kind of cost shifting had been common earlier under Medicare and Medi-Cal.

Blue Shield has designed a plan, creating the contracts and the benefits, to meet these specific concerns. The Blue Shield Preferred Plan attempts to ensure the quality of service by setting explicit criteria its providers must meet. It avoids inconveniences and limitations by giving subscribers a choice of over 40 percent of the hospital beds and over 85 percent of the physicians in California. These figures represent the widest choice provided by any PPO in the state. Blue Shield supervises the effectiveness of its utilization controls and reviews. Rather than contracting them out to a third party, the hospital administers them under Blue Shield Supervision, or Blue Shield itself administers them through its own medical staff. The Preferred Plan attempts to avoid the perils of cost shifting, first by ensuring that the contracted fee amounts from physician members applies to every Blue Shield subscriber and, secondly, by passing on the savings from using preferred hospitals to its standard business. Finally, Blue Shield fulfills its obligation to all its members by making a PPO plan available to individuals as well as groups. These points are discussed in more detail below.

DISTINGUISHING FEATURES

The Blue Shield Preferred Plan has several features that distinguish it from other PPOs in California. For example, the Preferred Plan:

1. *Combines a 15 to 20 percent rate reduction with wide choice of physicians.* All Blue Shield Physician Members are automatically preferred physicians, which gives Preferred Plan subscribers a choice among 37,000 physicians in California. In most cases, subscribers will simply continue using their present physician.

2. *Markets to individuals and families as well as groups.* PPO-type arrangements are available to individual customers who can receive the same benefits as other Blue Shield plans but at 15 percent savings.

3. *Passes savings on to standard business.* The rate advantage Blue Shield negotiated with its preferred hospitals applies to all Blue Shield group subscribers, not just Blue Shield Preferred Plan groups. That means that every group with Blue Shield coverage—even those organizations that self-insure and have Blue Shield administer their plan—will receive credit for the lower cost of care when their employers use preferred hospitals. This savings will be reflected in lower care charges to the group, which in turn will affect renewal rates. By the end of the first year, four major groups covering nearly 150,000 people were offering cash incentives ranging from $100 to $250 for either using Blue Shield Preferred Hospitals or for joining the Blue Shield Preferred Plan.

One year of development effort was spent researching the different geographic markets in California, making cost-effective contractual arrangements and creating a competitive benefit package. Blue Shield considered it unadvisable to try blanketing the whole state with a single plan all at once. The agenda for introducing the Plan brought it to Sacramento in March, San Diego in April, Los Angeles in May, San Francisco and the Bay Area in late summer, and by the year's end, most of the remaining state would be covered.

COST-SAVING FEATURES

Any serious attempt at cost control depends on utilization review to insure that medically unnecessary treatment is not provided. Most PPOs take a wholesale approach to utilization review, contracting most or all of it out to a third-party administrator. Blue Shield's medical staff however performs the preadmission review, and the hospital itself under Blue Shield supervision performs the necessary concurrent review during and after admission. The purpose of this approach is to maintain a higher degree of sensitivity to individual physician judgments and to exceptional cases than would be possible under a utilization management approach that followed strictly set guidelines.

Renewal rates for Preferred Plan groups are expected to become more competitive as group experience becomes better. This expectation is based on the Plan's utilization controls curtailing medically unnecessary services and costly but inappropriate techniques. Blue Shield's utilization controls include:

1. *Required ambulatory surgery* for over 45 procedures that may be performed just as safely on an outpatient basis. This list of procedures was researched and developed by the Blue Shield Medical Policy Committee and is already widely known within the trade.

2. *Required second opinions* before certain types of elective surgery are performed. To increase cost effectiveness, Blue Shield selected only those procedures for which there is a very high degree of elective determination by the patient and for which there are often less expensive alternative treatments. Requiring a second opinion for every elected surgical procedure is *not* cost effective. The cost of the second and possibly third opinions must be added to the cost of the ultimate medical and surgical treatment for the patient's condition.

3. *Preservice and preadmission review* to determine if the admission or if the surgery (for example cosmetic surgery), is medically necessary and thus covered under the plan.

4. *Concurrent review,* which determines first, if admission was appropriate and after admission, whether the hospital services being provided are medically necessary and are performed at the most economical level consistent with accepted standards of medical practice.

MEMBERSHIP AND SELECTION

Most preferred hospitals follow a policy of opening their facilities to any of the 37,000 Blue Shield Preferred Plan physicians in their area who qualify for staff privilege. Other providers such as dentists and x-ray specialists also participate in the Plan. Together they make the Blue Shield Preferred Plan the least restrictive PPO in California.

In different market areas, almost every hospital submitted a bid to be a Preferred Plan Hospital. The selection process for preferred hospitals was based on criteria for (1) quality of service, (2) accessibility, (3) management, (4) reputation, and (5) price. In these categories, Blue Shield investigated over 500 items of data from each hospital. The following discussion of this selection process is based on a summary of the methodology for evaluating each criteria.

Quality of service. Blue Shield examined each hospital's range of service, its physical plant, its medical staff, its capacity for utilization review, as well as its average length of stay. For range of service Blue Shield used data gathered by the California Health Facilities Commission, to determine the exact services the hospital did provide and weighted them in a total evaluation of the scope of service. The Commission also categorized hospitals for Blue Shield on a sliding scale ranging from a rural hospital to a university teaching hospital.

The physical plant evaluation was done through on-site inspections. Factors such as the date of the buildings, last renovations, and proposed building schedules were taken into consideration. Medical staff evaluations took into consideration the number and kinds of specialists and their board certification.

For utilization review Blue Shield received from each hospital a formal protocol describing its approach to utilization reviews. These protocols were evaluated by Blue Shield's medical staff using information gathered by the regional PSRO. Determining whether the hospital was under medicare's Waiver of Liability also provided a means of indicating if the hospital had an acceptable percentage of disputed denial days (less than 2.5 percent).

Accessibility. The objective was to ensure that the hospitals chosen provided geographic coverage convenient to all area residents. Proximity is a relative matter and is defined differently for a rural area than for an urban area. Blue Shield's maximum driving time and mileage to a preferred hospital thus varied from county to county. One standard guideline is provided by the Health Facilities Planning Areas (HFPAs) into which the federal government has divided each state to promote cost-effective travel time and equal access to medical services. The placement of Blue Shield preferred hospitals is considerably denser than one facility per each HFPA. For example, there are four HFPAs in San Diego County as opposed to the seventeen Blue Shield preferred hospitals there. Blue Shield also made certain that specialized services, such as open-heart surgery, were provided in at least one of the selected hospitals in each area.

Management. Under scrutiny in this category were the hospital's ownership, its history, whether it was for-profit or nonprofit, and whether it belonged to a chain and how old the chain was. These factors taken together gave an indication of the hospital's stabililty. Also the cooperative attitude of the hospital management was important. Were they enthusiastic, for example, or did they object to some Blue Shield's provisions for cost control and quality-of-care control?

Reputation. Feedback was solicited from a wide variety of relevant sources throughout each community: hospital councils, the medical society, health services agencies, PSROs, business coalitions, and even from Blue Shield's own marketing and professional relations staff who lived in the area. Hospitals excluded because of a pervasive negative reputation were generally found to be deficient in other areas as well, such as their scope of service or their physical plant.

Price. Each hospital submitted to Blue Shield a flat rate per patient per day. These "flat rates" were scrutinized to make sure the same components were in each case being included, such as the participation of hospital-based physicians (i.e, radiologists, pathologists). Blue Shield employed specialized outside consultants to evaluate the hospital's cost sheets, its costs and revenues, and to assess whether the proposed flat rate was viable, competitive, and justified. An additional guide to the hospital's cost effectiveness was based on Blue Shield's payments for existing hospital claims, which provided a cost comparison of hospitals by procedure.

CLAIMS PROCESSING SYSTEM

It was not necessary for Blue Shield to develop a claims processing system specifically for the Preferred Plan. The Preferred Plan is backed by all statewide Blue Shield support systems, including those for claims processing.

Preferred Plan claims are processed at a centralized automated processing center, designed and operated by Electronic Data Systems in conjunction with Blue Shield.

One major indication of a claims system's effectiveness is the savings effected on coordination of benefits (COB). On standard business in 1983, Blue Shield reported a COB savings of 7.65 to 15.0 percent. Other categories of savings that Blue Shield claims processing systems passed on to its clients in 1983 are shown in Exhibit 1.

Preferred Plan claims are subject to the same Blue Shield processing systems, and similar savings are projected under the Plan.

EXHIBIT 1

Category	Percentage Saved (of total claims submitted)
Usual, customary, and reasonable requirement with physician members	11.31
Unnecessary services	1.03
Ineligibility	4.85
Noncontract service	3.95
Prevention of duplicate claims	5.64

BENEFIT PACKAGE

The basic benefit package includes the following features:

Lifetime maximum. The subscriber and each covered dependent have a lifetime maximum benefit of $2,000,000.

Deductibles. For illnesses, there is a $250 calendar year deductible, with a maximum of $500 per family, regardless of the number of dependents. For injuries, the deductible is $50 per person (family maximum of $150 per calendar year). The combined maximum deductible for illness and injury shall not be greater than $250 for individuals each calendar year and $500 for entire families covered under the program each calendar year. The deductible does not apply to charges for second opinions prior to surgery for specified procedures. Other variations on the deductible and nonpreferred doctor payment are available based on the size of the group.

Physician services.   When services are provided by a preferred physician, the plan pays 80 percent of the usual fee not to exceed the customary or reasonable fee. The subscriber is responsible for the remaining 20 percent of the fee. When, however, the subscriber uses a nonpreferred physician in a nonemergency situation, the plan pays only 60 percent of the usual, customary, or reasonable fee. The subscriber is responsible for the remaining 40 percent and for any balance billing from the nonpreferred doctor who does not accept Blue Shield's allowed amount. Here again options are available depending on group size.

Hospital services.   The plan pays for services provided by a preferred hospital at the negotiated amount established by the preferred hospital and Blue Shield, less 20 percent of billed charges for all covered services. Subscribers are responsible for this 20 percent of billed charges. When services are provided by a nonpreferred hospital in a nonemergency situation, the plan pays 50 percent of billed charges, and subscribers are responsible for the remaining 50 percent of billed charges.

If services are not available in a preferred hospital (verified by preadmission review), the plan pays 80 percent of billed charges. The subscriber is responsible for the remaining 20 percent.

Emergency admission.   When services incident to an emergency admission are provided by a nonpreferred hospital, the plan pays 80 percent of billed charges. Subscribers are responsible for the remaining 20 percent of billed charges.

Copayment.   After a subscriber has made copayments of $2,500 ($5,000 per family) in a calendar year for covered services, Blue Shield pays 100 percent of the usual, customary, or reasonable charges for all further covered services. Preferred physicians and preferred hospitals accept this payment determination as payment-in-full so that subscribers have no further liability when they use preferred providers.

Nonpreferred physicians and hospitals may not accept Blue Shield's payment limitations, so subscribers are responsible for any difference between what Blue Shield allows and the actual charge.

Larger groups may negotiate specific options, such as the deductible and copayment to nonpreferred providers.

EXHIBIT 2
Blue Shield of California Preferred Plan Organizational Chart (Physicians, Subscribers, Brokers, Agents, Hospitals)

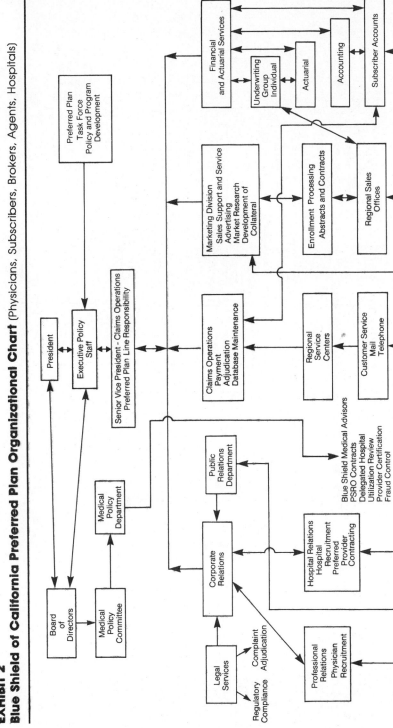

EXHIBIT 3   Blue Shield of California Preferred Member Contracting

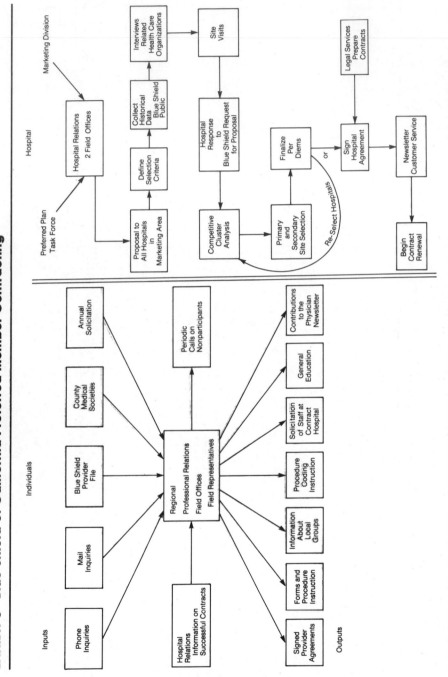

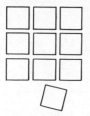

CASE STUDY: BENEFIT PANEL SERVICES, LOS ANGELES, CA

W. Mark Jasper, M.P.H.

President
Benefit Panel Services
Los Angeles, CA

A number of market conditions had fully ripened in 1982 to make way for a cost-effective health care product that could benefit carriers, employers, employees, and providers. In Southern California, HMOs had been in existence for 10 years and had captured 20 percent of the market. As in many places around the country, employers were faced with a dilemma: rising health care costs and an inability to meet budgets without passing these costs on to employees and risking employee alienation. Southern California had an oversupply of both doctors and hospitals.

Benefit Panel Services' (BPS) founders were aware of all these trends and reached five conclusions about the new marketplace that was emerging in the state:

— Contract medicine was the wave of the future.
— Medical groups were the best-positioned to take advantage of new market conditions, in part because of experienced lay management.
— A "team" approach of strong medical leadership and strong administrative leadership was essential to any new health care venture.

— Ambulatory care would gradually supplant a great deal of institutional care.

— Purchasers of health care services were quite naive and uncertain about how to improve their "purchasing" of health care services.

When landmark legislation was passed in California in August 1982 allowing carriers to selectively contract with providers, they moved quickly to organize the company. When it incorporated in November 1982, the task of BPS was to develop a structure and strategy that would make the PPO concept actually work.

The first task was a definition of a PPO product. Definition of types of PPOs still remains the most problematic issue for purchasers of health care services because the structural characteristics as well as the experience, and the expertise of the principals are the major determinants of success. It was on this premise that the BPS business plan was first created.

The business plan was based on the obvious fact that physicians control health care and, thus, health care expenditures. Potentially, all concerned parties could work together for mutual advantage, i.e., the win/win scenerio. Insurance carriers with billions of dollars of premium at stake could ideally get doctors to change their practice styles so their costs would go down and their loss of clients to HMOs would be reduced. Employers could either directly or indirectly contract to achieve lower rates. Employees could be given an additional benefit with no additional cost by going to the preferred provider with less-out-of-pocket and no claims form a la the HMO. (The PPO is an "HMO without walls.") Physicians could attract more patients simply by keeping those patients out of the hospital. (Physicians do not normally benefit economically from hospital admissions; the hospitals benefit.)

DEVELOPMENT STAGES

BUSINESS PLAN—IMAGE AND ROLE FOR COMPANY

The missing ingredient in order to obtain the win/win scenerio was the management skill and expertise to identify the initial insurance companies, employers, physicians and others who could be organized to achieve the ideal of cost containment in a fee-for-service setting. This is the fundamental test for a PPO. Can fee-for-service medicine, which is preferred by the majority of the population with its inherent freedom of choice, also yield cost reductions without placing physicians financially at risk? BPS answered that question affirmatively but conditionally. The conditions were correct leadership, correct organizational structure, and correct strategy in areas of provider contracting, marketing, and pricing.

The central issue with image was "credibility" based on proven experience of cost control and *based* on ownership and control. In southern California, independently contracted medical groups had proven (with HMOs) their ability to reduce costs despite the fact that they were mainstream, reputable fee-for-service physicians. Selective contracting for health care, on the other hand, lacked credibility between providers and purchasers and had been attacked by medical associations and provider organizations. The most effective approach for overcoming the skepticism of purchasers and the adversarial position of providers was to develop a credible image. Image became not just a marketing concept but an operational one as well.

BPS founders and owners initially felt that they could deal most effectively as an independent, closely held corporation in order to establish a nonadversarial role with payors and providers.

The model of the "interface" management company was established as BPS' image that would have the greatest potential for credibility. (See Exhibit 1.) The medical group model of provider contracting and utilization control via the "gatekeeper" concept was established as the basis for credibility from a product point of view. Statistics could be used to dem-

EXHIBIT 1
Benefit Panel Services'
Organizational "Interfaces"

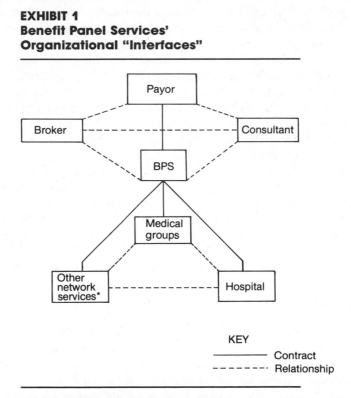

KEY

——————— Contract
- - - - - - - Relationship

*Home health, referral laboratory, other
© Copyright 1984, Benefit Panel Services, Inc.

onstrate that the providers who subsequently contracted to BPS actually had achieved meaningful reduction inpatient days-per-thousand from an average 700 in fee-for-service to 300 in contract to HMOs (400,000 enrollees distributed among 23 medical groups).

BPS' goal was to become a public company that would attract investor capital once it demonstrated the cost savings that would be achieved through a well-managed alternative delivery system.

By 1982, there had been some preliminary PPO-type organizations, but they were largely "mail order" operations made up of physicians agreeing to discounted fees in return for being placed on a list marketed by a third-party administrator. The major flaw in this arrangement was the lack of selectivity of the so-called preferred providers. There were no utilization controls and no protection for the patients or purchasers.

There were also some fledgling hospital-based PPOs that offered discounts as marketing tools to compensate for declining admission rates. The major drawbacks of these initial PPOs were lack of credibility and an inability to exert meaningful controls over physicians who actually generate admissions and cost patterns.

These failures created skepticism and fear of PPOs from the provider sector. Some hospitals lost hundreds of thousands of dollars from contracting with uninsured plans. The skepticism was overcome the following year by increasing competition in the marketplace, which led numerous hospitals to form some sort of PPO or PPO alliance for self-preservation.

It was evident by early 1983 that, despite the unregulated PPO environment, provider-based PPOs could potentially result in legal entanglements. It is particularly the fear of legal entanglements that inhibits insurance carriers and employers from exercising their new freedom to contract for services. The role of BPS was to become an independent vehicle to bring the parties together for common gain.

Since BPS was independent, it did not have to preserve or protect physician or hospital interests. Its pricing strategy was based on reimbursing primary care providers who were accountable for managing all of each patient's medical care under the PPO option. BPS could also establish a range of data analysis capabilties, which insurance companies did not have.

Carriers in southern California were reeling from the demands of many employers, who had received excessive premium increases, to negotiate price discounts with providers. Carriers did not have the contracting expertise in-house nor did they have computer systems flexible enough to compare provider profiles with enough detail to assess utilization behavior. The PPO benefit option requires software changes not easily or quickly made by carriers. They did have a large patient base, however, which became the initial marketing thrust of BPS.

The "image" and strategy were to be independent and nonadversarial and to use truly "preferred" providers—medical groups with HMO experience. BPS would charge the payor for the cost-savings results of the contracting, utilization review, claims review, and other functions provided by BPS to the payors.

Like all PPOs, BPS became a marketing tool, but for payors rather than providers. BPS could only be successful as a for-profit company (in terms of return on private investment) by actually achieving documented cost savings. The marketing strategy of BPS to carriers was designed to meet their needs for PPO contracting in terms of:

— Business risk taken by nonproviders.
— Independent utilization monitoring.
— Full service including claims audit.
— Flexible computer system.
— Nonadversarial approach to provider contracting.

The first carrier contract was signed in June 1983 with Firemen's Fund. This established sufficient credibility to obtain additional carrier contracts which, in turn, established an economic base sufficient to attract quality hospitals. Initially, these hospitals were not approached because they played a minor role in generating health care costs compared with physicians. Although most health insurance expense occurs in hospitals, it is largely based on doctor-initiated orders. It became clear, however, that the inclusion of quality hospitals was a significant factor to employer acceptance of the PPO.

FINANCING, STAFFING AND CONTRACTING

After marketing criteria were set, operational standards were established. Provider networking, staffing and financing steps were planned. The provider contracting strategy was to sign up many HMO medical groups that had low rates of hospitalization. Also, their lay managers understood business aspects of contractual medicine and competition, which facilitated the contracting process. Ambulatory care procedures are essential for meaningful utilization control and were already well-established in targeted group practices. Where these groups were unavailable, other provider contracting criteria were applied such as ownership and control by primary care physicians rather than by other high cost/high-tech specialists with adverse incentives.

Another major criteria was to not over contract any given area. This would enable participating providers to gain financially by cost-effective case management practices so that they would want to remain contract providers. This is based on the marketplace model that purchaser "demand" (claims dollars) must be channeled to providers of good quality who are cost effective. This adds the additional factor of peer pressure, which can only be found in medical groups and not in solo practice physicians.

Once the network of providers was in place, target carriers were approached indirectly through health care consultants to the insurance industry. Two carriers were identified who had developed progressive cost-containment programs, had begun preliminary planning for PPO development as an alternative delivery system, and were planning to offer a dual choice benefit option on a fully insured basis. They were also relatively noncompetitive due to differences in case sizes and product lines. A third carrier was targeted based on its competitive position to Blue Cross (which has its own captive payor-based PPO) and because of its large market share among carriers based in southern California. A cost-

EXHIBIT 2
Financial Model (Sample Cost Containment Analysis)

Savings from utilization management and reduced fee schedules compared to cost of providing incentives to use the system.

	Description	Usual Cost	Increased Cost	Savings
(1)	Monthly total cost (experience) for comparison; amount does not include commissions or administrative charges	$100.00		
(2)	Charge for use of the system ($2.25 member)		$2.25	
(3)	Use of nonpanel services; with a well-designed plan approximately 50 percent of membership will continue to use nonpanel physicians and hospitals	$50.00		
(4)	Use of panel physicians for primary care services (25 percent of panel services)	$12.50		
	10 percent savings from average negotiated fixed rates			$1.25
(5)	Use of panel specialists and ancillary services for referred care (25 percent of panel services)	$12.50		
	Savings from utilization reduction (10 percent)			$1.25
	Savings from 15 percent fee reduction			$1.88
(6)	Use of panel hospitals (50 percent of panel services)	$25.00		
	Savings from 25 percent utilization reduction			$6.25
	Savings from average 17 percent negotiated fixed rates			$4.25
(7)	Cost to health plan for providing incentives to use panel. Eliminate $100 deductible$^{(100/12 \times .5)}$ (net panel physician cost)		$4.16	
	Increased primary care physician use, 10 percent		$1.25	
	Savings from copayment revenue, $5.00 payment/visit, 50 percent panel, 5 visits/year			$2.00
	Sub-totals		$7.66	$16.88
	Net savings as a percent of plan experience	9.22%		

containment model, which quantified benefit plan design changes, administrative fees, and projected bottom-line savings, was developed by BPS and presented to targeted carriers. (See Exhibit 2.)

BPS pricing was based on the philosophy of selling cost-containment services to payors. Pricing was based on the capitation method for several reasons. It was an established method used by carriers for commission purposes in prepaid plans and was easy to administer. The level of capitation had to be below the rate for third-party administrators whose services were quite different (such as the adjudication and payment of claims) and yet sufficient to meet the operating requirements of BPS and achieve a break-even below 10,000 lives (two-year forecast). The pricing strategy established wholesale capitation rates for BPS services to carriers or payors with sizable enrollment and a higher retail level for solo employers.

The marketing philosophy was intended to be nonadversarial with the established brokerage and consulting community and to allow targeted carriers their normal marketing channels to "distribute BPS." One partially self-funded employer was targeted to test whether the preferred provider benefit was sufficient to cause an employer to change carriers and prompt employees to leave the HMO for the PPO. This was accomplished and a higher proportion of employees consequently selected the indemnity plan PPO option than had enrolled in the HMO option the year before.

Financing came entirely from the founding individuals with an initial capital commitment of about a million dollars.

PITFALLS AND EXPERIENCES

The first pitfall was distribution of stock and whether providers, employees, outside investors, or others should become owners. The Board of Directors decided that control and ownership should be limited until such time as an initial public offering was anticipated. Thereafter, a controlling interest was to be retained by the founders to ensure that its long-term goals were achieved.

The next pitfall was in marketing strategy. The approach to insurance carriers proved to be incredibly time-consuming (nine to 18 months), expensive, and slow to come to fruition (between the period of initial endorsement and actual implementation). This process resulted in reducing a complex set of interactions, decisions, and planning strategies that needed to be addressed into a simple checklist format that could be applied with any third-party payor. The checklist format condenses the period from endorsement to implementation to about three months.

The next pitfall was power struggles between members of the initial staff who had personal goals and agendas that were not in keeping with the organizational goals and objectives of the founding members. This resulted in some staff turnover, which ultimately demonstrated that BPS had the ability to manage change without jeopardizing service to carriers or to their client insureds. Management stability was greatly enhanced during this shakedown period of nearly a year.

The next challenge was competition from hospitals that were beginning to obtain contracts with carriers and employers simply because their rates were discounted and because the purchasers were somewhat naive about the importance of price reductions. Provider charges can be reduced at the same time that intensity of services can be increased by both physicians and hospitals so that the total dollar outlay (the medical revenue) is the same or greater. Utilization is a much more significant cost factor than charges. Once BPS became visible in the community, there was a split among local hospitals and physicians. Some of the medical community were willing to work with BPS because of its reputable client base and others were not because it was competitive with their own preferred provider arrangements.

To summarize BPS' pitfalls and experiences, the most important management lessons are that:

— Marketing strategy is crucial.
— Equity issues must be settled as early as possible.
— Power struggles are inevitable.
— Allegiances and alliances must be established with providers based on personal and professional reputation and affiliations.
— More capital will almost certainly be needed than initially forecast.
— Selection of the CEO and Medical Director are the most important PPO formative decisions.
— Substantial flexiblity is required in establishing the provider contracting criteria and operational staffing needs (e.g., specific qualifications, numbers, and sequencing).
— Computer software is one of the most important tangible assets to develop since it will be the PPO's principal investment in research and development.

Forming marketing plans and successful operating procedures requires a long-term philosophy. The most practical advice for starting a PPO is to select the right medical leadership and the right management leadership with direct experience and knowledge of the service area. Recognize that a significant investment of time, money, and energy will be necessary. The decision-making process for a health care purchaser is quite complicated and all elements of the health insurance industry must be thoroughly evaluated and analyzed from every perspective (including political) before attempting a PPO initiative in a particular service area.

STRATEGIC ADJUSTMENTS

BPS decided to restrict its initial operations to southern California through 1984 and then establish itself in northern California during 1985. Future operations are intended to be based upon a "guaranteed" revenue stream from established carrier clients. BPS expects to attract business from competing preferred provider arrangements because it has greater "buying power" due to *multiple* payor clients. Other PPOs will not be as competitive because they:

— Cannot generate offsetting cost savings greater than the cost of increased employee benefits.
— Are not structured appropriately.
— Do not have the right incentives.
— Have too many "preferred providers" to actually establish utilization control.

FUTURE

It will be years before most corporate benefits managers or insurance carriers are sophisticated enough to make knowledgeable decisions about preferred provider arrangements. PPOs will continue to proliferate for some time before the inevitable shakeout occurs. PPOs unable to build an effective management reporting system and a database for medical accountablity will fail.

Eventually, PPOs will most likely become EPOs in the future. However, PPOs will not be able to make this transition without a sufficient data system to allocate provider revenues based on quality measures and resource allocation methods.

At present, employers should be aware that most PPOs are marketing shells without sufficient operational substance. Employers should be cautious, while benefits consultants, brokers, and insurance carriers should be even more cautious to protect their own credibility and business base when choosing a PPO. It will take at least two years to document empirical results, and many employers will likely get burned during this period.

The PPO option will probably parallel the HMO experience and take at least ten years to take hold and even then will be available only in urban areas that have an oversupply of physicians and hospitals.

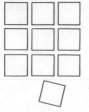

Insurance Carrier Sponsored

CASE STUDY: MASSACHUSETTS MUTUAL LIFE INSURANCE COMPANY

Janett C. Greenberg

Vice President
Group Life and Health Cost-Containment
Massachusetts Mutual Life Insurance Co.
Springfield, MA

☐ The decision to offer a PPO alternative to Massachusetts Mutual's policy and self-funded contract holders was driven by three environmental factors: (1) the state of the medical care system, (2) internal corporate direction, and (3) the business needs of Mass Mutual and its insured/self-funded policy and contractholders.

The state of the medical care system set the stage for PPO consideration. Mass Mutual recognized that the health care system's growth and subsequent financing crisis had to be resolved and that if the private sector did not respond to this problem more aggressively, the public sector would. The nature of the public sector response could jeopardize the future role of the insurance industry in the health care system. In 1983, the public sector did respond by restructuring medicare benefits and the program's payment structure. These actions created the spectre of increased cost shifting to the private sector and provided further reason for Mass Mutual to more aggressively seek alternative solutions to the problem of providing quality care cost effectively.

Internal corporate changes facilitated the decision. In 1981 Mass Mutual's Group Division was reorganized. Executive management of the Group Life and Health Division, as part of its corporate strategy, decided to make significant investments in the cost-containment area and created a separate Cost Containment Department. This department was to develop and implement a broad spectrum of cost-containment programs: indepth claims experience analysis and consulting services; employee benefit communications programs; private review programs, health promotion, and educational services; catastrophic claims management services; and alternative reimbursement programs. The decision to become involved with PPOs was a natural extension of the 1981 strategy.

Both Mass Mutual and its policyholders had significant business needs that PPO involvement could address. Clients needed a method to control the cost of their health insurance plan and mitigate the increasingly negative impact of this employee benefits line item on their corporate budget. Mass Mutual wanted to provide its policyholders with a solution that would have this effect and, at the same time, avoid cost shifting to the insured, protect freedom of provider choice, and assure high quality care.

PPOs were important to Mass Mutual for three other business reasons. First, a carrier's ability to retain and expand market share would be tied to its ability to offer an effective PPO option. Second, PPOs would be a competitive alternative to HMOs since the insured could receive services from a preferred provider with minimal out-of-pocket expense (similar to an HMO), yet not be locked into receiving services from a specific group of providers. Furthermore, a well-designed PPO option could improve the indemnity plan's risk pool by attracting employees from the HMO back into the indemnity plan. It would do so by providing insureds with coverage for services normally available only through an HMO when a preferred provider was used, e.g., well-baby care, Pap smears. Third, PPOs have potential for demonstrating the value of commercial insurers and securing their place and role in the future health delivery system.

The catalytic event that led to the design and development of Mass Mutual's PPO option, PREFERRED PLUS, was the elimination of the legal barrier that had heretofore prevented commercial carriers from entering into contractual arrangements with medical care providers. That legislation, A.B. 3480, was introduced and passed in California in 1982. A bevy of similar bills were introduced subsequent to A.B. 3480 in other states, as well as in the U.S. Senate.

In the fall of 1983 an aggressive effort began within Mass Mutual to design and develop a PPO option for policyholders and self-funded contractholders. The design and developmental issues are the focus of this chapter.

GENERAL CRITERIA

Before tackling the PPO developmental and design issues, the Group Life and Health Division decided what criteria the Mass Mutual PPO option would have to meet. Seven were set forth. The PPO option would have to: (1) save dollars, (2) control inappropriate utilization, (3) render high quality care, (4) have "staying power," (5) lend itself to reasonable prediction of savings over time, (6) operate at minimum unit costs, and (7) be standardized and duplicatable.

The first and second criteria, saving dollars and controlling inappropriate utilization are intimately related. Dollar savings could not be realized in the absence of *strong* utilization controls. Since dollars expended on health services are equal to the price per unit of service multiplied by the number of units rendered or consumed (utilization), it was essential that the PPO institute and properly administer programs and procedures targeted to control both the price per service and the number and types of services rendered to maximize dollar savings.

Third, ensuring that high-quality care is rendered by PPO providers was an important criteria since it directly reflects the quality of the insurance product. Equally important, when insureds know that high-quality care is available through the PPO their use of preferred providers will increase. Increased PPO provider utilization will maximize the potential of the PPO to negotiate better financial arrangements and influence provider behavior and compliance with utilization-control programs.

"Staying power," the fourth criteria, refers to a PPO's ability to survive the PPO "shakeout," which Mass Mutual believes will occur in the 18 to 24 month period following enabling legislation. For example, following the passage of A.B. 3480 in California there was a flood of PPO development. As of March, 1983, the California Department of Corporations had received over 150 applications for PPO licensing. Of those, 38 were designated operational, 21 developmental, and the remainder were not classified. While the bulk of PPO activity is provider-based, significant entrepreneurial, and some carrier-based activity, has and is currently taking place. Not all will survive. Many PPOs will fail because they will not save dollars, and in some cases, will cost the insurer or self-funded employer more. They will fail because they lack either effective utilization controls, or the patient volume required to control price and utilization. This requirement to survive is essential to assuring continuity of care. It is both unjust and detrimental to the continuity of care concept to provide incentives for individuals to switch medical providers, and, subsequently find that the providers are no longer preferred when the PPO fails. Moreover, when this happens the PPO concept will lose credibility with insureds, participation levels will decrease, and the PPO's potential cost savings impact will be diminished. For these reasons it was essential that PREFERRED PLUS be designed to survive and grow in effectiveness over time.

The fifth requirement, that the PPO must lend itself to reasonable prediction of savings over time was necessary to project claims and rate plans with a PPO option.

The last two criteria, that the PPO operate at minimum unit cost and be standardized and duplicatable, are interrelated. National carriers and multi-location employers who wish to eventually extend the PPO option to all geographic areas cannot operate at minimum unit cost if each location-specific PPO does not administer similar control programs, collect and report similar information, and have similar administrative interfaces.

DESIGN ISSUES

The seven general criteria defined what the PPO option was to do. The design and developmental issues defined how the PPO option was to do it. The major design issues Mass Mutual addressed, and their resolutions are summarized below. The developmental issues are reviewed in the next section.

The first design problem was to define the operational factors that would maximize effective PPO functioning and decide which programs, procedures, and policies needed to be in place. The following operational factors were defined: (1) discounts; (2) utilization controls; (3) data systems to support controls; (4) administrative interfaces with claim paypoints, operations, and management; (5) panel selection criteria; (6) provider contract provisions; and (7) strong PPO management. An expanded discussion of these is in order.

Discounts are a factor in effective PPO functioning, but they have been oversold as *the* principal underpinning of PPO cost savings. Private sector patients are already paying more than their share of the bill, so a discount is still not an equitable or acceptable solution. The discounted rate may not offset the differential that already exists. More important, when discounts are used as the principal means for saving dollars, there are clear incentives for providers to increase the number or intensity of services rendered to offset or exceed income lost through discounts. This is not to say that discounts are not an important operational factor. They are an integral part of the PPO concept.

Discounts can be viewed in two ways: by level and type. The *level* of discount refers to the percent discounted, as well as what the discount base is. For example, one could negotiate a discount off charges or off a percentile of prevailing fees. There are different *types* of discounts as well—a percentage discount is one of them. Examples of other discounts include flat per diems, per diems tied to bed type, and diagnosis related groups (DRGs).

Mass Mutual decided to pursue a fee schedule based upon a discounted conversion factor for professional medical services. As part of the company's philosophy to encourage "gatekeeping" responsibility among primary care physicians the conversion factor for their payment was slightly higher. With respect to hospital charges the goal was to reimburse based on DRGs, and begin with a combination of negotiated per diems and flat discounts off of regular charges, whichever was less.

Strong and *effectively administered utilization-control programs* were considered to be the single most important operational factor. Accordingly, it was decided that network physicians would be contractually bound to use preadmission testing, second surgical consultations for elective surgery, and outpatient testing and surgery, as well as preadmission certification and concurrent review. As a matter of policy it was decided that responsibility or the latter two programs could not be delegated back to the providers of care. Further, to insure that these programs were adhered to, a system had to be in place to regularly profile the utilization behavior of network providers. The profiling system was to review provider quality, referral patterns, and ambulatory ordering patterns, as well as compliance with control programs.

An information system to support the administration and management of these control programs was identified as a critical operating requirement. In addition to standard utilization reporting, the system was to regularly report selected information to support early identification of aberrant providers and provide backup data for problem discussion with those providers.

As a carrier Mass Mutual was extremely concerned about the administrative interfaces among the PPO network, claim paypoints, home office administrative operations, and home office management. Parties not directly involved in daily plan maintenance have a tendency to overlook this aspect of PPO operation. For example, the manner and speed in which employee eligibility information reaches providers in the PPO network is important. If termination information is delayed in getting to the providers and they render services based upon presentation of a PPO ID card, the carrier or self-funded employer could be liable to pay for services at 100 percent as well as for services (e.g. well baby care, Pap smears) covered only under the PPO option. If such delays occur regularly, and particularly if there are large numbers of insureds involved, unnecessary costs to the plan could be high.

It was essential to Mass Mutual that the procedures for linking with PPOs be uniform among the different PPO networks in various geographic areas. This requirement had to be met to minimize unit cost and maximize quality. The system's enhancement costs alone, not to mention the management and actuarial problems that come with different interfaces (e.g., interpretation and comparison of different utilization and management reports), made this a straightforward policy decision.

To support utilization control and administrative interfaces between the network and payor a comprehensive medical information system that provided administrative, financial, and medical-management capabilities was needed to maximize effective PPO operations. An automated system had to exist that could profile provider behavior and track and report cost savings attributable to specific utilization-control programs, as well as support claims handling, eligibility, fee billing/collections, and provider contract negotiations.

Early in the design phase it was determined that panel selection criteria would play an important role in the ongoing success of the PPO option. Review of the criteria used by most developmental and operational PPOs in California was disappointing. Some were "mail order" (i.e., providers were solicited to participate by virtue of a mailing list); some had restrictions on the number of providers in the panel and accepted them on a first come-first serve basis; and some required a membership fee and fee payment was the criteria for panel participation. Others were marriages of convenience, such as groups of affiliated hospitals and their medical staffs or all members of a Foundation for Medical Care.

Since PPOs by design should only include a segment of the provider community, Mass Mutual decided that its panel would be limited in size in accordance with a standard physician to insured population ratio. This was based on the premise that providers would not be concerned about their standing in the panel (i.e. whether their contracts would continue), and consequently their utilization behavior, unless the PPO patients represent a significant portion of their income, i.e., 10 percent to 20 percent. If the network has too many providers the number of patients per provider becomes too small and consequently diminishes the PPO's impact on the provider's revenue and influence over their behavior. It was decided that the only time the provider to patient ratio criteria could be violated would be if there was inadequate PPO provider representation in a given geographic area. Patients would have to have access to a PPO doctor within five miles or fifteen minutes driving time, and access to hospitals and referral services within seven miles or thirty minutes driving time.

In addition to panel size and accessibility criteria, Mass Mutual decided that its providers would be selected on quality criteria other than state licensing. Members would be selected based upon their utilization track record, reputation among peers in the community, malpractice history, and attitude towards utilization-control programs.

Finally, it was decided that provider contracting would be designed to implement the "gatekeeper" concept wherein the primary care physician would control and manage utilization of expensive diagnostic and specialty services. This would be accomplished by contracting mostly with primary care physicians. While a full range of contracted specialists would be on the panel, insureds would be directed to the primary care panel providers vis-à-vis the PPO directory, which would list only primary care provider groups. This approach would place another external control on excessive or unnecessary use of costly specialty services.

While the importance of carefully selecting the initial PPO panel in a given geographic area was understood, it was recognized that some mistakes in panel selection would be made in the process, particularly in geographic areas where data on providers was inadequate. Mass Mutual anticipated that agreements would have to be terminated with providers who did not deliver high quality care or who did not comply with utilization-control programs. The only way to accomplish this was through the provider contract—another key operational factor in maximizing the effectiveness of the PPO. The contract must contain clear and comprehensive utilization review and termination provisions that specify the control programs the provider agrees to comply with, as well as conditions and time frame for termination based on noncompliance.

The last major operational factor was the nature and strength of the PPO's management. The presence of strong, highly specialized administrative management was a prerequisite to effective panel selection, utilization-control monitoring, provider relations, claims handling, and financial management. Experienced provider relations staff would be required to select the panel, train and communicate with their administrative staffs, discuss utilization problems, and maintain positive relations. Specialized staff who can profile and monitor provider practice patterns and identify and evaluate providers who are not complying with control programs would be required to assure maximum panel, and consequently, program effectiveness. Typically, this would require the skills of a R.N. Review Coordinator and a physician review committee. Strong financial managers would be needed to assure the ongoing operating efficiency of the PPO and maximize its growth potential. Finally, highly competent administrative managers would be required to assure efficient daily execution of eligibility, claims handling, and external employer/employee relations functions.

The second major design issue that needed to be resolved was what the PPO insurance option should include to maximize insureds' use of panel providers. Mass Mutual recognized that the degree of insureds' participation in the PPO would directly affect its success as a cost-containment alternative. The greater the number of insureds who use the network, the greater the PPO impact on the providers and costs of the plan.

Mass Mutual sought maximum participation by structuring its option to attract employees already in HMOs back into the indemnity plan and, at the same time, provide clear financial incentives for indemnity plan members to use the PPO network. To provide financial incentives for insureds to use the PPO, all deductible and coinsurance liabilities were waived. In their place a $5 per visit copayment for physician services was required. This latter provision is similar to the copayment normally required by HMOs. To both attract employees back from the HMO and provide further incentives to insureds to use the PPO, Mass Mutual added coverage for the first two years of routine well-baby care, including immunizations and Pap smears.

The third design issue the company addressed was education. Employers, providers, and the public must all be educated about PPOs and how they work. Mass Mutual, however, was most concerned with educating the employee and their dependents, since it was these individuals who ultimately would make the decision as to where to seek care.

To accomplish this, materials to support an employee awareness campaign would have to be prepared. Brochures that explained the PPO benefit option, how the PPO program works, and directories of preferred providers would have to be available. In addition, arrangements for information hotlines within a company (to the benefits department) and to the PPO organization would have to be in place.

The fourth design issue was to determine whether both comprehensive and base plus plan types could realize maximum PPO savings and decide which benefit plans could carry the PPO option. There are basically two types of health insurance benefit plans: (1) those that provide first dollar coverage (base plans), and (2) those that provide dollar coverage following deductible and some level of coinsurance (major medical plans). It is most common for employers to have comprehensive major medical plans (all medical services covered subject to deductible and coinsurance), or have base plus major medical plans (some services, such as hospital and surgical, covered at first dollar and the remaining services covered subject to deductible and coinsurance). The richer benefit provided by the base plus plan insulates the insured from costs and, therefore, produces different utilization and consumption behavior than would be generated by an insured under a comprehensive major medical plan.

Since it had been decided that Mass Mutual's PPO benefit would waive the insured's deductible and coinsurance liability, in order for the employer with a comprehensive major medical plan to benefit from the PPO, savings would have to exceed what the insured would have paid in a non-PPO environment. Base plus plans would experience dollar savings immediately, but their first dollar coverage would neutralize any financial benefit to the insured for use of the PPO. Consequently, participation levels would be low, and the probabilities of dollar savings slim.

Using both internal and external utilization data, negotiated rates, and a range of participation assumptions, Mass Mutual's actuaries determined which comprehensive major medical plans would financially benefit by having the PPO option available. Based on their study the PPO would be highly recommended to employers with certain types of comprehensive major medical plans. It was also decided that the PPO option would be available to employers with base plus plans, if this was insisted upon. The comparative experience of these two groups will be evaluated over time.

Maximum PPO savings that could be expected and the anticipated time frame required to reach that savings level were also addressed at this point. Many PPOs market themselves by claiming the ability to save 15 percent to 20 percent in overall plan costs. While Mass Mutual concluded that such savings are achievable, it also concluded that they would not be realized immediately. Savings in the 15 percent to 20 percent range are achievable with high PPO participation (minimum 50 percent) for at least a twelve-month period. On day one of PPO operation very few insureds will use preferred providers. It will take time for plan members to change physicians, and consequently, it will take time for utilization-control programs to have a measurable cost impact. In addition PPO programs will be subject to a learning curve, and so their effectiveness and ability to achieve cost savings will grow with their maturation.

DEVELOPMENTAL ISSUES

Two major developmental issues were dealt with in the formative stages of PREFERRED PLUS. The first was whether Mass Mutual would create its own PPO or link up with one or more existing PPOs. The second was the nature of the changes that would have to be made to the claims processing, management reporting, and administrative systems to support the PPO. Systems issues could not be defined until the first issue was resolved.

Mass Mutual believed that the PPO concept would spread to most states and become an integral part of the health delivery system. The company had three basic needs that drove its decision to either create its own PPO or link up with one or more existing PPOs: (1) to minimize unit cost; (2) to create a basis for a national PPO network to service the company's national distribution of policyholders and self-funded contract-holders; and (3) to standardize the PPO between geographic areas for policyholders whose employees were geographically dispersed and promote consistency in program quality. With this as background, the following discussion on the appeal of the carrier-based, provider-based, or entrepreneurial model to Mass Mutual and the subsequent decision on how to proceed will be more meaningful.

A PPO can be organized by carriers, providers, or entrepreneurs. Each model has distinct characteristics, advantages, and disadvantages.

In the carrier-based model the insurance company performs all PPO development and administrative functions. The carrier selects the providers, negotiates and executes contracts, processes PPO claims, monitors individual provider behavior, maintains professional relations with providers, runs utilization-control programs, and maintains and periodically updates preferred provider directories.

The appeal of this model to carriers will vary according to the carrier's characteristics—whether they are regional or national; number of in-house specialists available to manage the program, conduct utilization review, select and negotiate with providers; and resources available to enhance in-house computer systems to accommodate PPO fee schedules and claims processing and market share in any given geographic area.

The perceived advantages of this model were: (1) it provided carriers with complete control of the PPO program; (2) it facilitated development and fine-tuning of the PPO insurance product option; (3) the carrier controlled selection of providers it wanted to participate in the program; (4) the carrier could direct the growth of its PPO product by channeling internal resources to develop PPOs in other geographic areas consistent with its marketing strategies; and (5) if the carrier had a large client base in a given geographic area its potential for negotiating larger discounts on its own behalf would be improved.

The disadvantages of this model were significant. It depends on the carrier's market share to finance the PPOs development and maintain its operation. Since the fixed costs are considerable, the unit cost of a carrier-based PPO would be prohibitive unless the carrier had considerable market share over which the fixed costs could be spread.

The issue of market share is important since market share provides the leverage needed to negotiate favorably with providers. Providers expect an increase in patients in return for their PPO participation. A carrier whose client base does not represent a significant portion of the geographic market would be unable to negotiate arrangements that provide for maximum discount and tight utilization control.

In the provider-based model the physicians and/or hospitals perform all PPO development and administrative functions. The providers form a corporation that ministers the affairs of the participating providers. Participating providers are contractually tied to the corporation (PPO network) through membership agreements. Insurers, self-insured employers, third-party administrators, and self-insured trusts contract with the PPO corporation and gain access to all of its participating members.

The provider owned and operated PPO corporation usually handles payment between payor and providers and is responsible for monitoring individual provider utilization behavior and operating utilization-control programs.

From a carrier's standpoint linkage with a provider-based PPO has a few advantages. First, insurers would not have to incur the costs associated with selecting and contracting with individual providers. They could develop a PPO option in a given geographic area quickly by contracting with a provider-based PPO.

Second, since a PPO corporation is responsible for conducting utilization-review programs and monitoring provider performance, the insurer's cost of offering a PPO product would be reduced.

While the model offers advantages, it also has a number of disadvantages from the carrier's perspective. First, the panel of physicians or hospitals available through the provider-based PPO corporation may not have been carefully selected based upon their performance records. For example, in some provider-based models, participating providers pay annual or one-time membership fees on a first come-first serve basis. Some do not limit the number of participating providers. Some consist of all specialists. Chances of maximizing cost control are jeopardized if the panel is not carefully selected and if it is too large.

Second, with regard to utilization-control programs, the provider-based model could be in conflict with the interests of its members. This raises the risk of the carrier linking into a program that may demonstrate less effectiveness in saving money through utilization controls.

Third, because provider-based models are typically local, carriers who want to offer a PPO product in more than one geographic area will have to contract with more than one PPO network. This will mean greater internal administrative expense to coordinate with multiple PPOs, since each network has its own unique administrative, data collection, claims handling, utilization control, and management reporting systems.

In the entrepreneurial model a business entity forms a PPO corporation that selects and contracts with a network of providers and acts as an "agent" for these providers by marketing their services to payors. The corporation may provide panel members with administrative services such as claims handling and financial reporting for a fee.

The payor contracts directly with the providers through the corporation, which acts as a facilitator for developing fee schedules, negotiations, and contract execution. The payor also contracts (for a fee) with the corporation to provide utilization control and provider monitoring services, provider relations, cost-effectiveness reporting, claims handling, and employer/employee education regarding panel use.

The entrepreneurial model has a significant number of advantages. First, it is not controlled by providers who tend to act in their own self-interest. This maximizes the potential for effective utilization-control programs.

Second, it is not controlled by payors who also act in their own self-interest. This is an important feature because providers are wary of getting "trapped" and controlled by payors. High quality providers will be more willing to join the panel if it is being run and they are being monitored by an independent third party.

Third, the entrepreneurial model is more likely to be transportable. While both provider-based and entrepreneurial model PPOs may be developed for a specific geographic area, entrepreneurial ventures are characteristically less tied to a particular geographic area's provider community. Transportability provides a distinct financial advantage to carriers who want to introduce their PPO product in multiple locations, since administrative interfaces with the PPO remain consistent in each location.

Fourth, it is able to attract more experienced executives due to financial incentives such as ownership or profit sharing.

Fifth, the entrepreneurial model is driven by the profit motive. Since its profit will be made through administrative fees charged for each employee covered by the PPO product, its objective is to incresse the number of employees who have access to the panel. Such growth can only occur if costs are controlled and dollars saved. Therefore, it is in the entrepreneurial model's interest to select a panel of providers with a history of efficient practice patterns, conduct effective utilization-control programs, carefully monitor provider practice patterns, and terminate agreements with providers who do not control costs.

While the model has many advantages, it also has weaknesses that could result in PPO failure. First, the PPO corporation could collapse if the partners or management team lack financial skills, experience in claims handling and utilization review, or knowledge of health insurance benefits. This is also true for the provider-based PPO corporation.

Second, the entrepreneurial model must have a method of becoming knowledgeable about local practice patterns in each area where it selects and organizes a panel. If its staff is unable to identify who the best providers are in a community, it will not be able to organize the best panel; consequently, it will handicap program effectiveness.

Third, in order for an entrepreneurial model to succeed, it must have employee (patient) volume. In order to gain volume it will have to market and enlist multiple carrier participation. The disadvantage here is that the individual carrier loses its competitive edge since it does not have a PPO that is unique to the market.

Mass Mutual had three options for developing a PPO: (1) create its own (carrier-based); (2) contract with many PPOs (provider or entrepreneurial); and (3) contract with one entrepreneurial organization.

Given the advantages and disadvantages previously discussed, Mass Mutual decided to contract with an entrepreneurial organization because of its significant cost and administrative advantages. An entrepreneurial model would provide cost control, program effectiveness, and consistency for policyholders with employees in multiple geographic locations.

Beginning in January 1983, the Cost Containment Department carefully monitored PPO activity and evaluated a number of PPO organizations. The organizations were assessed on the basis of organizational structure and ownership, provider influence on activities, experience and quality of management staff, utilization-control programs and procedures, range of administrative services provided, number and types of providers under contract, criteria applied in selecting panel members, and data systems/management report capabilities.

Once the decision had been made to link up with an entrepreneurial PPO organization and once that organization had been chosen (Benefit

Panel Services), Mass Mutual needed to determine what changes would be required to its claims processing, management reporting, and administrative systems.

The claims system needed to be able to identify groups or subgroups of PPO eligible insureds, process preferred payment amounts, and collect cost savings information. Coordination of benefits adjudication procedures and payment calculation methods needed to be modified.

The management reporting system had to be enhanced to generate cost-savings reports for use by administrative managers, policy and contractholders, actuaries, and underwriters.

Administrative systems and procedures that support policy issue services and contracts needed to be changed to facilitate the update of contracts and certificate booklets, as well as the issue of PPO ID cards and employee educational material.

FUTURE

After operating in southern California for a six-month period Mass Mutual plans to expand and offer the PREFERRED PLUS option to policyholders in northern California and other geographic areas.

Home office staff will carefully evaluate the accuracy and workability of the initial design and developmental decisions. The PREFERRED PLUS option will be fine-tuned to reflect changes dictated by the outcomes of such study. Major questions remain. The company is anxious, for example, to determine how transportable PPOs are. Mass Mutual expects that it will take two to four years to reach a final conclusion about the PPO's ability to control costs and render high-quality care. At that time Mass Mutual, its policy and contractholders, and the nation will have sufficient experience with PPOs to determine whether they will have a permanent role in the American health care system as an effective alternative form of medical care delivery.

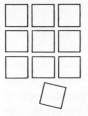
CASE STUDY: FLORIDA HEALTH NETWORK, JACKSONVILLE, FL

Patricia R. Sher, M.P.A.

Vice President
Cost Containment
Gulf Group Services Corporation
Jacksonville, FL

Frank J. Greaney, M.P.A.

Vice President
Cost Containment
American General Group Insurance Company
Dallas, TX

☐ The Florida Health Network (FHN) is the tradename for the preferred provider operations within Gulf Group Services Corporation, which performs the group insurance functions for Gulf Life Companies in Jacksonville, Florida. These companies were acquired by the American General Corporation in January of 1984.

FHN was conceived and initiated in 1983 in response to the growing dissatisfaction among group clients with the escalation in health care costs. Important preferred provider concepts that these employers found attractive were the freedom of choice among providers for employees, fee-for-service for physicians, and utilization review of health care resources.

The employer "market" appeared to need very little convincing that an alternative approach to health care delivery was well advised. A significant portion of the group business handled by Gulf Group Services is self-funded with administrative services contracts. Since these employers were bearing the risk of health care costs, they were most interested in controlling expenditures. The provider community, however, was ill-prepared and only peripherally familiar with PPO formulations. Duval County's experience with an HMO in the mid-1970s had been negative from all perspectives. This perception suffused all proposed alternative systems with hostility. The initial overtures to the hospital community were met with "polite disinterest." With one notable exception, final contractual agreement was achieved only through aggressive pursuit with repeated phone calls, letters, and visits. Geographic location of the hospitals was of primary concern. Since the employees were located throughout Duval County, a hospital was required in at least three accessible sites. In most traffic situations, employees should not have to drive longer than 20 minutes to reach a PPO hospital.

Scope of hospital services was another key consideration. To enhance acceptability among clients and to achieve maximum cost savings FHN assumed that every necessary service had to be available in at least one participating hospital. These objectives were thwarted to a degree, however, when it was found that only one hospital in the city had full pediatric services. The fact that this hospital was not a candidate for the panel was a complication. It was determined that FHN's inability to supply certain services should not penalize the employee/patient. When necessary care was not available within the PPO, favorable benefits would still apply for that employee.

Measures of cost effectiveness such as length of stay and cost per admission and per day were examined using FHN's claims data system. There were clearly some hospitals with higher than area average charges.

Assessment of the needs of the employee market was an important planning concern. Historical data regarding the number and types of admissions for the population of employees and dependents to specific hospitals was extracted from the claims systems. FHN's negotiating stance would be enhanced with knowledge regarding how many of which employer group clients used which hospitals. Utilization experience by zip code was similarly accessed.

Employee communications were deemed critical. In addition to the obvious need to educate potential enrollees regarding this new concept, the manner in which it was to be presented would be important. If employers and/or their unions viewed the benefit differentials as punitive or discriminatory, there would be marketing problems.

The first FHN PPO became operational in Jacksonville on October 1,

1983. It was piloted with the employees of the City of Jacksonville and their dependents totaling approximately 20,000 lives. FHN staff included a General Manager, Director of Professional Relations, Utilization Review Registered Nurse, key Claims, Phone Unit and Systems personnel from Gulf Group Services, and Marketing support (see Exhibit 1). The General

EXHIBIT 1

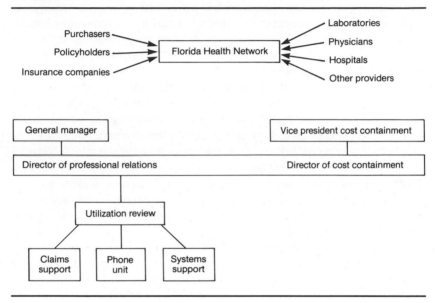

Manager's responsibilities include hospital contract negotiations, policy and procedure development and approval, systems oversight, and planning. The Director of Professional Relations contacts the active staff of each of the participating hospitals, individually negotiates physician contracts, educates office staff, and maintains communications with hospital administration, physicians, and their staffs, employers, and employees.

Utilization-review (UR) nurses conduct preadmission review, concurrent hospital review, and retrospective analysis of claims and bills.

As the pilot program demonstrated its acceptability and administrative problems were corrected, expansion to other markets became desirable and feasible. Marketing Regional Managers throughout the Southeast and particularly in Florida began calling on employer groups as well as third-party administrators in their areas to inform them regarding the PPO concepts and their potential for restraining the rate of cost increases. As of spring of 1984, hospital negotiations were underway for the establishment of FHN PPOs in five Florida cities as well as in Mississippi. Plans for the next year include sites in Texas, California, and Georgia.

There are currently four acute care general hospitals actively participating in Jacksonville. The commitment to the provision of volume to these institutions precludes the admission of other hospitals. These hospitals must have JCAH accreditation and demonstrated cost effectiveness for FHN insureds, where FHN has accumulated a historical database. Their administrations agreed contractually to discounts from charges for Gulf Group Services clients as well as firm cooperation with utilization-review procedures established by FHN utilization-review nurses in consultation with many sources throughout the nation. Contractual termination without cause, by either party, with 90 days written notice was a protective mechanism incorporated in lieu of disciplinary procedures.

Physicians were contacted after the hospitals signed participation contracts. All active staff physicians of participating hospitals were invited to become FHN members. This facilitated the credentialing process, as well as the institution of necessary procedures and practices for cost-effective health care. It clearly required the cooperation of both the hospital and the physician, for example, to successfully implement same-day surgery for selected procedures. Interested physicians were encouraged to call for information or a visit from Professional Relations staff. Because preferred provider concepts were essentially unknown in this area, substantial effort was devoted to educating, and in some instances, reassuring the medical community.

Contracts were signed individually with physicians, again with the 90-day termination clause incorporated. Disciplinary procedures were deemed unnecessary with this mechanism in place. Although rarely encountered, noncooperative physicians are merely notified that their contracts will be terminated in 90 days. Examples of problems include repeated failure to notify FHN prior to an elective admission, failure to communicate with UR staff, or admission to a nonparticipating hospital. Physicians agree to discounted fee-for-service with their current fee schedules fixed and incorporated into the contract for one year. Each physician receives a list of procedures to be performed on an outpatient basis as well as a list of those to be admitted on the day of surgery. It is made eminently clear that mitigating or complicating factors preventing adherence to these policies need only be documented to the UR staff.

Payment to hospitals and physicians is guaranteed within five days from receipt of bill. Bills are submitted on the provider's usual form in the usual amount. There is no additional paperwork. Special envelopes identified for priority handling are supplied each participant for mailing of FHN claims. The fully adjudicated computerized claims system is programmed with each provider's discount, and bills are paid accordingly.

There are currently 150 participating physicians or about 15 percent of the area medical community. As long as there are fewer than 20 percent of the total physician population, FHN expects that sufficient patient volume can be delivered to the providers, given representive specialty and subspecialty participation.

The client population currently encompasses approximately 25,000 employees and their dependents in the Jacksonville area. Gradual addition of other large employer clients is planned over the next year.

FHN recommends financial consumer incentives to the maximum level acceptable to the State Insurance Commissioner. There is currently a $100 difference in deductibles to the employee who utilizes FHN hospitals and physicians, as well as a 20 percent versus 25 percent coinsurance level. Although several employer groups are interested in increasing these incentives to much higher levels, they have yet to be approved by the Insurance Commissioner.

Group clients of GGS receive a "FOCUS" report that details utilization and cost data for a given "prior" and "current" period. Based on the accompanying analysis, specific cost-containment strategies and recommendations are advanced for each group's particular needs or desires. Second opinion surgery programs, outpatient testing or surgery benefits, and health education programs may be recommended. Consultation may be provided for the institution of many cost-containment programs. Many of these techniques are also incorporated into the preadmission review component of the utilization-review program such as mandatory second opinion at the discretion of the health care professional performing preadmission review.

Registered nurses with hospital utilization-review expertise comprise the UR staff of FHN. All elective admissions must be reported prior to admission, at which time a length of stay is assigned. A list of 110 procedures are designated for outpatient performance, as well as 40 surgery on day of admission (SODOA) procedures. FHN has found that in most cases physicians are eager to cooperate in efficient and less costly health care delivery practices.

Concurrent review, which tracks the progress of hospitalized patients, is conducted in cooperation with the hospital UR staff. FHN nurses contact the hospital's UR nurses when notification of pending admission is received. Discharge planning is then initiated. If for example, the patient is expected to be discharged to a nursing home, those arrangements are initiated at this time. The day prior to expected discharge, communication between the hospital and FHN nurses establishes that there have been no complications to jeopardize discharge. If it is necessary, the physician's office is contacted to reassign the length of continued stay. Retrospectively, FHN UR staff visits the hospital to examine the patients medical record, assuring that hospital review was communicated accurately by phone. Any misinformation or misunderstandings are rectified at this point.

FHN has made a corporate commitment to automated systems that expedite claims processing and provide data on costs and utilization to client groups.

Claims are paid within three to five days after submission. The PPO is recognized as an enhancement to group health insurance services. Claims forwarded in the specially designated envelopes are handled in a priority manner. Claims examiners refer questions regarding PPO claims directly to FHN utilization review or professional relations staff for expedient resolution.

The GGS Fully Automated Claims Tracking System captures 3,300 bytes of information, enabling FHN to capture, analyze, and display client experience in conventional group health insurance use within and outside the framework of the PPO.

The FOCUS reports are generated for PPO health care encounters and are compared with non-PPO encounters. Utilization and cost data can then be compared and savings in both days of hospitalization and financial data can be assessed. A cumulative record of days saved is maintained on a personal computer by the utilization review professionals. Hospitals and physicians are also profiled regarding cost effectiveness for FHN internal use. This information is potentially useful during provider enrollment and at contract evaluation time.

Quality assurance is accomplished through the provider selection process, the contracting process, and through the ongoing care review process.

In selection, FHN recognizes the steps taken by hospitals to achieve quality assurance, such as JCAH accreditation and medical school affiliation. Participation is offered only to physicians on the staff of PPO-participating hospitals. The PPO is selective in designating hospitals. In turn, these hospitals are selective about granting and continuing medical staff privileges. In effect, this credentialing process serves to secure physicians for the PPO panel. Prudence would dictate in any case that the PPO purchase malpractice insurance for this risk.

Physician contracts include representations by the physicians that they are appropriately licensed by the State and qualified to admit to a participating PPO hospital. Participating physicians also agree to notify the PPO of any disciplinary proceeding initiated against them by any government agency, medical staff, medical society, or hospital. The privacy and exclusivity of the physician-patient relationship is also affirmed in the participation contract.

Practitioners' and hospitals' respective responsibility for quality assurance is emphasized in the contract, as is PPO access to records to review all care.

Group decision-makers are sometimes concerned about quality in PPOs. They fear contingent malpractice liability for this new intervention in the delivery of care. Some employers also fear that the PPO will contract only with marginal hospitals and physicians. Their anxieties are relieved as the PPO contracts with prestigious and effective hospitals and as its list of prominent physicians grows.

A PPO is discriminatory by nature because it seeks to promote the use of a small number of cost-effective providers. Caution is needed at all steps of PPO development to ensure the operator and the purchaser that such discrimination is based upon sound factual data and promotes cost-effective care within the confines of the law.

FHN assumes responsibility for the total administration of the PPO. Employers who sign contracts with FHN are provided with communication materials for employees, consultation for implementation of employee orientation, a hot-line for employee questions, and a list of participating providers that is updated regularly. All provider negotiations and contracts and communications are part of the administrative agreement. Claims processing and adjudication are handled within three to five days, and the day to day management of isolated problems or questions are coordinated by FHN staff.

A fixed fee for implementation and administration of the PPO is charged. Fees usually equal about 1 percent of the group's previous year's claims experience. It is expected that the group's first-year savings will exceed the first-year fee.

LESSONS LEARNED

During early stages of negotiations with unions and employers, union leaders must be solidly convinced of the benefits of participation and in agreement about the necessity for benefit incentives. Enforcing benefit differentials can be politically difficult, and unions must be fully cognizant of the ramifications.

FHN recommends that PPO benefits be applied only to health care provided by a PPO physician, *in* a PPO hospital, if admission is required. It is tempting for an employer to focus on the cost savings achieved by the discount, and to allow PPO benefits for either participating hospitals *or* participating physicians. This approach abdicates the control over utilization that is achieved *only* when both the hospital and the physician are participants. Examples of this would be the following:

— A participating physician wants to comply with same-day surgery policies, but a nonparticipating hospital has no incentive to administratively facilitate an early morning admission for the procedure.
— A nonparticipating physician may admit a patient for several days to a participating hospital for a procedure that should be conducted in the outpatient setting.

Physicians frequently have little familiarity with the financial conduct of their office. Frequently, the concept of deductibles and coinsurance are unknown to them.

Experience is still the best instructor. Lessons learned in the first round of provider selection and contracting rapidly expedite subsequent PPO implementations.

Benefits must be designed to handsomely reward conservative behavior by physicians, patients, and hospitals.

Establishment of the first PPO in an area is most difficult, and can trigger some unusual competitive reactions, such as hospital "sales" featuring waiver of copayments and deductibles even within the PPO panel.

Legal counsel experienced in PPO implementation is essential during the development of the PPO. The ongoing consultative role of the law firm should also be emphasized.

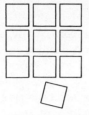

CASE STUDY: PACIFIC MUTUAL LIFE INSURANCE COMPANY, NEWPORT, CA

Robert L. Broaddus, FLMI

President
California Preferred Professionals, Inc.
Fountain Valley, CA

Walter Wieners

Account Representative
Health Systems International
New Haven, CT

☐ The uncontrollable rising costs of medical care have been a particularly perplexing problem to companies in the group health insurance market. On one hand, health costs produce a continuing need for indemnity coverage, but on the other, profit margins were so thin many insurers contemplated withdrawal from the health market.

This marginal profit situation was aggravated by many large corporate clients deciding to assume risk for numerous reasons, including retaining investment income on reserves, eliminating premium tax, and reducing insurance company expenses. This trend affected the insurers as administrative expenses were distributed over a decreasing book of business.

Pacific Mutual, after a difficult year with group health insurance losses in 1980, reevaluated these problems to assess on what basis, if any, the company should continue in the health market. The firm decided to recommit to group health but only in a new role that could exert more control over medical expenditures.

Corporate commitment to health cost control is important because the financial resources necessary to develop specialized health cost control programs are substantial. Resources were expended to recruit health care finance specialists, upgrade the claims payments system, and conduct significant health expenditure analysis. This internal activity enabled the firm to greatly improve capability in the health field and prepare senior corporate management to embrace provider contracting.

LEGISLATIVE IMPACT

Coincident to Pacific Mutual's business decisions, the California legislature, reacting to budgetary deficit problems, enabled insurers to prospectively contract with medical providers. Hospitals were allowed to contract effective January 1, 1983, and physicians to join preferred provider organizations (PPO) beginning July 1, 1983.

Since Pacific Mutual had already developed significant cost-containment programs, the company began examining the most advisable means of contracting with providers to further control health expenditures.

PREFERRED PROVIDER ORGANIZATIONS

While examining the varied forms PPOs were taking, Pacific Mutual concluded that most of these start up organizations had significant shortcomings. Hospital-based PPOs appeared to be formed primarily as a means of protecting market share and involved no meaningful utilization review or aberrant physician practice pattern controls. Clinic or university medical center based PPOs typically were limited in area of coverage and would be difficult to network on a statewide basis. Entrepreneurial based PPOs did not appear to offer thoroughly documented retrospective utilization review or hospital preadmission certification programs. Physician groups involved in an existing prepaid plan or panel were attractive because of their successful HMO track record. Viewing the physician as the key element in cost-effective medicine, Pacific Mutual's attention focused on the type of organization thought to be most successful over the long run in providing quality and cost-effective care.

Pacific Mutual selected CaPP CARE as the principal PPO to develop a network for reasons that are instructive to health care practitioners. First, the basic approach of using independent physicians offered a broad base of geographical coverage acceptable to benefit managers and employees.

Second, CaPP CARE's automated utilization review system, mandatory hospital precertification, and strong physician agreement enforcing cost-effective treatment patterns, provided what the firm believed to be an excellent opportunity to control costs. Third, the flexibility of adding to the geographic network outside California by licensing the data system and administrative operations provided the insurer a uniform product to offer large clients and simplified the task of comparing and analyzing physician performance. Provider arrangements are described in Exhibit 1.

EXHIBIT 1
Pacific Mutual/CaPP CARE

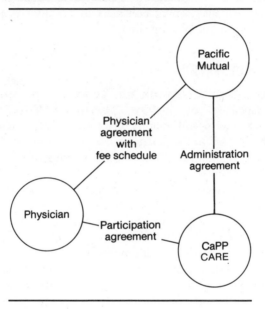

Three written agreements were developed: the administrative relationship between Pacific Mutual and CaPP CARE; the Pacific Mutual's Physician Agreement with Fee Schedule; and, the Participation Agreement between CaPP CARE and the physician. Pacific Mutual elected to establish fees keyed to the California Relative Value Scale (CRVS) and to make additional fee adjustments by region to account for variation in the cost of medical practice. Fee discounts are not requested of physicians because Pacific Mutual believes the utilization controls are the key to reducing expenditures. The agreement between the carrier and CaPP CARE addresses compensation for administrative expenses, obligations of parties for data security and confidentiality, and other standard legal business concerns.

The participation agreement between the PPO and the physician is of critical importance because the contract obligates the physician to comply with preadmission certification, concurrent review, peer review, and guidelines for agreement determination for inefficient practices are clearly delineated.

The PPO, as a new cost-control product, is a start towards developing a health care delivery capability that may evolve to exclusive provider arrangements as benefit manager and employee acceptance increase. PPOs bring to insurers cost controls previously only available through health maintenance organizations. The PPOs hospital preadmission certifications, concurrent review, and retrospective data analysis can be combined with independent hospital contracts to provide an alternative delivery system for indemnity programs.

HOSPITAL NETWORK

Pacific Mutual's hospital network was planned to be broad-based and subject to competitive cost analysis. The firm preferred developing a partnership relationship with quality institutions rather than an adversarial relationship based on the absolute lowest per-diem rate available. In the long run the company will increase the volume of business provided to these selected hospitals and reduce expenditures.

Pacific Mutual is assisting selected hospitals to become competitive with analysis of utilization patterns and hospital length of stay characteristics. Contracts require the hospital to participate in Appropriateness Evaluation Protocol (AEP) conducted by nurse analysts and a supporting data analysis firm. Pacific Mutual's intention, after the first year's contracting, is for hospitals to be completely at risk for unnecessary patient days; however, this concept was not instituted in the first contract year. Pacific Mutual felt hospital administrators must understand that a renewable contract with the firm would be based on genuine reductions in expenditures per patient. Some hospitals welcomed the use of these analytical data tools and purchased AEP analysis, which enabled administrators to identify problem areas in advance.

Once an effective contract and retrospective review policy was developed, Pacific Mutual began developing a capability to precertify inpatient admissions for all insured employees not participating in an HMO or PPO and expanded geographic coverage of contracted hospitals.

The hospital contracts were individually negotiated by Pacific Mutual with the individual hospitals (see Exhibit 2). Preadmission certification and concurrent review are provided by an independent utilization-control organization under direct contract with Pacific Mutual. For any employer who has purchased the utilization-control service, employees and their physicians are required to acquire preadmission authorization. The combination of inpatient controls and per-diem rates are being used to contain institutional expenditures.

EXHIBIT 2
Hospital Network

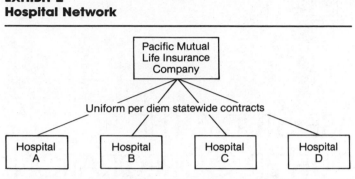

COST-CONTAINMENT OUTLOOK

Pacific Mutual views the preferred provider organization as one integral product within a total cost-containment program and the one element that fundamentally alters medical practice. Pacific Mutual believes the PPOs preadmission certification, concurrent review, and utilization controls, can only be monitored and operated effectively when supported with up-graded and modified claims processing and data reporting systems. The PPO and hospital contracts must be supported with automated means of early catastrophic case identification, analysis of second surgical opinion costs and benefits, and the balance of the health program features.

Pacific Mutual believes the actual performance of the PPO must be clearly demonstrated. The benefits of the total cost-containment program will support achieving a genuine reduction in health costs for the large corporation and smaller group client. Pacific Mutual knows short-term success in cost control has been realized and believes continued progress is essential to remain in the group health market.

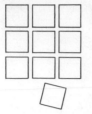
CASE STUDY: THE STOUFFER CORPORATION, SOLON, OH

Donald C. Flagg

Vice President, Human Resources
Corporate Relations
The Stouffer Corporation
Solon, OH

Nearly three years ago, the Cleveland-based Stouffer Corporation launched a campaign to slow the advance in health care costs through use of a newly emerging phenomenon, PPOs.

At the time, aggressive medicine and its allies—ignorance, apathy, and deference—posed a formidable threat to Stouffer's financial health. Worse yet, the quality of health care employees received was steadily deteriorating. Health care providers, constituting one of the nation's largest industries, were enjoying a captive market in which they created both supply and demand and determined market prices. Providers also enjoyed immunity from traditional marketplace constraints brought on by competition and the need to be cost-effective.

Stouffer responded by playing a major role in the development of four PPOs offered to its employees. The company's experience with its two dental and two medical PPO options, detailed following, exemplify why it feels this health care delivery approach, through a reliance on utilization review and provider incentives, will make it victorious in combating rising costs.

DENTAL PPOs—A START

Stouffer's involvement with PPOs began three years ago, when a 10-member dental group in Cleveland proposed that the company designate it as a panel of preferred dental care providers. In return, Stouffer employees would obtain dental care at discounted prices. As its dental costs were zooming beyond control at the time, the company listened.

Stouffer supplied the dental group with benefit plan and claims experience data, from which it eventually formulated a prepaid capitated plan providing broader coverage than Stouffer's traditional plan. Stouffer's claims went from $15.78 per beneficiary per month under its standard plan to a monthly per-capita rate of $13.06 under the dental PPO. In addition, about 240 employees, scattered throughout the Cleveland area, signed up with the PPO, despite its single location (see Exhibit 1).

Peer review was performed on a spot-check basis by an independent local dentist who did not detect any problems with quality of care.

Stouffer's positive experience with one preferred dental provider panel led to selection of another multisite dental group that offered even broader benefits, such as fewer copayments and deductibles, for a greater number of basic and specialized dental services.

At the end of one year, Stouffer had negotiated a 5 percent increase with the first dental PPO and added the second panel. A comparison of dental care rates per employee per month showed its traditional plan paid $14.84; dental group I, $13.74; and dental group II, $9.64.

Today approximately 24 percent of Stouffer's Cleveland work force voluntarily has enrolled with the two dental PPOs. While the overall dollar savings are not huge, they are significant.

EXHIBIT 1
Comparison of Stouffer Corporation Dental Plan and Preferred Provider Dental Plan

Traditional Dental Plan	*PPO Dental Plan*
1. Single deductible of $25	All preventive and diagnostic dentistry done without a deductible
Family deductible of $25 per person	Then a $25 per person deductible with a family maximum of $100
2. Yearly maximum of $1,000	Yearly maximum of $1,250
3. Plan pays:	
80 percent on routine dentistry	Supplemental fee schedule given to
50 percent on prosthetics	employees and guaranteed for one year
4. Requires completion of claim forms	No claim forms needed

Dental plan II has reduced Stouffer's dental costs by as much as 35 percent, and Dental plan I by more than 20 percent—with no employee relations problems. The success of these two PPOs has prompted competing dental groups to approach Stouffer with PPO proposals.

MEDICAL PPOs—TWO APPROACHES

Not long after Stouffer's started its dental PPO plans, and at a time when it was trying to organize a coalition to undertake utilization review of health care delivery in the private sector, the company was approached by a few physicians interested in starting a PPO.

The company was concerned that the PPO should not just offer discounted medical care, but that it be used to reward physicians who practiced "conservative medicine," that is, not overusing medical services, facilities, and drugs. Stouffer, at the time, favored a physician-based PPO over a hospital-based model, which it saw as merely a device for hospitals to capture market share. It felt a PPO made up of doctors not obligated to specific hospitals would be preferable.

A draft plan to include a small pilot group of about 20 physicians was scrapped as impractical, however, because of objections from competing physicians. Membership in the PPO had to be offered to all physicians on the staff of the hospital where a key organizer of the PPO did most of his work. The hospital, itself, did not contract to become a provider under the PPO at this time.

The task of organizing the PPO also seemed monumental. The lead physician had little time to spend on the project, but provided secretarial service and seed funds of about $5,000 to cover start-up costs. Meetings were difficult to arrange and rushed.

As this physician-based PPO was developing, another company approached Stouffer suggesting that a few companies get together and ask an area hospital to form a PPO. Stouffer was lukewarm toward the concept but felt it might be good to compare a hospital-based PPO with its physician-based model.

The companies, AmeriTrust and Mannesmann Demag, along with Stouffer, approached a nearby suburban hospital. The facility had been operating at 100 percent capacity for years and was a leader in the area for home nursing care, hospice, and preadmission testing, a sign that it was conscientious about use of outpatient services and reducing hospital lengths of stay. The hospital also had a reputation for delivering quality care and its average cost-per-case was in the low to mid range of Cleveland hospitals.

Representatives of the three companies met with the hospital's administrators, and it was decided to pursue the PPO concept. Unlike the physician-based PPO, start up of the hospital-based plan went much more smoothly because the hospital devoted full administrative resources to the project, did a thorough job of educating its physicians, and established the necessary computer support. The hospital's outstanding coordination demonstrated the importance of having and using the proper resources.

For its PPO medical director, the hospital selected a highly respected obstetrician-gynecologist who was phasing out his practice and who became an integral part of the organization.

Stouffer eventually signed identical contracts with both the physicians' and hospital's PPOs that took effect April 1, 1983. In its initial contracts, there was a complex formula that gave the providers an incentive to keep down costs. If company health care costs are reduced by the PPOs, Stouffer paid the PPOs 40 percent of the difference between the average cost per person under the PPOs and the average cost per person under its traditional health plan. This incentive did not appear in subsequent contracts by mutual agreement.

Carefully avoiding a hard sell, Stouffer then launched a comprehensive employee communication program through slide presentations, bulletin boards, and meetings to introduce the new PPOs and emphasize the benefits of having a family doctor, such as continuity of care and improved preventive medicine. Employees electing the PPO option for a minimum of one year were told they could choose or change doctors within the PPO. Under the plan, Stouffer pays 80 percent of the cost of office visits to physicians, unlike Stouffer's traditional plan, which required a $100 deductible. The company subsequently found that the 80 percent-20 percent coverage ratio was unpopular with doctors because it was inconvenient to make change and is switching to a flat fee of $5 per office visit.

Despite the newness of the PPO concept and the fact that both Stouffer plans offered only limited geographic coverage, approximately 10 percent of eligible employees enrolled in the PPOs. This 10 percent represented over 50 percent of the employees living in the geographic area served by the plans. More employees have joined as Stouffer expanded the PPOs to cover hotel employees.

Generally speaking, employees have accepted the PPO concept and understand it. There have been no complaints about being locked into a PPO. Employees whose regular doctors were participating PPO providers were among the first to join.

RESULTS

The following statistics relate our PPO experience to date (see Exhibit 2). These figures cannot be accepted without question because there are simply too few people involved over too short a time to provide clear-cut answers to the many questions that arise. Regardless of an inability at present to statistically validate the results, Stouffer's is thrilled with what is taking place.

EXHIBIT 2
Cost Comparisons
PPOs versus non-PPO Employees
Costs per Benefited Person

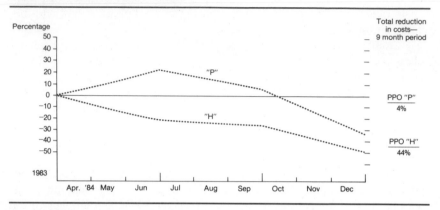

NOTE: These figures are not statistically valid but represent data compiled to date.

Specifically, the one hospital-based PPO has produced a reduction in costs exceeding 40 percent. Two other companies dealing with this PPO reported cost reductions surpassing our findings. The second physician-only PPO that later converted to a hospital-based PPO showed a reduction of 4 percent. This PPO is now at a 40 percent rate of reduction but because of its early problems showed a total reduction of 4 percent at the end of the period. The wide difference in results between PPOs reflects the effectiveness of the PPOs' medical director in firmly monitoring utilization. Initially the physician's PPO had no medical director and only installed one after interim results showed excessive utilization and costs. Immediately following his appointment, inappropriate utilization—and costs—began to plummet.

Stouffer's experience with this PPO illustrates the necessity to examine each PPO and its method of operation before inputing effectiveness. Inasmuch as this PPO was one of the first of this type to operate in the county, the initial difficulties can be attributed to a normal learning curve. As experience was gained and trends developed, this group's response in making the necessary changes was excellent. Stouffer's confidently expects that this and other PPOs will reach and maintain a level of costs of at least 35 percent below the costs of non-PPO participants. Such a reduction will allow Stouffer's to increase our incentives to employees to join a PPO, thus "rewarding" PPO physicians with additional patients. Currently an employee who selects a PPO is locked into the PPO for a year and must obtain medical treatment from the PPO (or their referrals) to have insurance coverage.

LESSONS LEARNED

Stouffer experiences to date indicate the following basic premises: (1) If hospital-based, the hospital selected should be in the lower 50 percent range of hospital costs. In most cases this obviates a discount. (2) Effectiveness of a PPO is related to the degree of trust and mutual respect that is enjoyed by the hospital administrators and its medical staff. (3) Whether hospital- or physician-based, a medical director who has knowledge, courage, and sufficient peer respect to enforce conservative utilization is the key to successful operation—from both cost and quality viewpoints.

At this point in time, Stouffer's believe that PPOs offer an excellent long-range means of providing quality health care at an affordable price. From a *quality* viewpoint the careful selection of a PPO plus the monitoring of a good medical director provide quality standards that are simply not available to our non-PPO employees today. From a *utilization* viewpoint the PPOs have already demonstrated that significant reductions are possible.

The reduction of inappropriate and unnecessary care also enhances quality. While *price* is not addressed directly in nondiscount PPOs, it enters into the equation through a good medical director's monitoring of heavy utilizers and high-cost physicians and through the competitiveness of PPOs with each other. Reduction of utilization and PPO price competitiveness should force hospitals to reduce excessive *capacity* over the long haul. To effectively bring about these results it is felt that PPOs should be relatively small (not city-wide or statewide) and numerous in order to provide the competition between PPOs that is necessary to achieve maximum results.

To Stouffer's, the long-range relationship that will develop between the company (the buyer) and the medical profession (the vendor) through the PPO offers advantages heretofore unattainable. For the first time, a vehicle has been provided where the buyer and vendor of health care can communicate and gain understanding of each other's problems. For the first time, vendors of health care can be held accountable for the quality and cost of their services. For the first time, the company has the ability to reward conservative practitioners by increasing their business.

There are many possibilities yet to be explored in PPO relationships that can benefit both parties. Home nursing, drug formularies, employee education in the use of the health care system, wellness techniques, management of individual long-term acute care situations, and consultation in the layout of plants and equipment are but a few of the many different ways in which a close relationship between medical professionals and industry people can work to aid the consumer in obtaining quality health care at an affordable cost. After a few years of collecting data, it is conceivable that some PPOs would see a greater financial future for themselves by becoming prepaid or capitated programs. However, one of the current advantages of a PPO over an HMO or capitated plan is that it is easily overlaid on current benefit plans and can be implemented quickly.

While there will be evolution in the details of PPOs (or whatever they may be called in the future) there is no doubt that the concept of a direct buyer-vendor relationship in health care is here to stay—a relationship that can be positive in every sense of the term. A relationship where the provider of services can deal directly with the buyer of services in a joint, mutually beneficial association to provide quality, affordable health care to employees and their families without the intercession of governmental bodies. Truly a worthy goal!

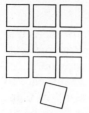

Employer Initiated/Sponsored

CASE STUDY: SECURITY PACIFIC CORPORATION, LOS ANGELES, CA

Esther Wu, MSPH

Senior Employee Benefits Representative
McDonnell Douglas Corporation
Long Beach, CA

Alan Jeffery, BA

Vice President, Manager
Employee Benefits
Security Pacific Bank
Los Angeles, CA

Security Pacific Corporation is a diversified financial institution that owns California's second largest bank. The Security Pacific Health Care Plan (SPHCP) is a self-insured and self-administered indemnity plan offered to employees of SPC. Security Pacific also offers the option of 13 health maintenance organizations, nine of which are in California.

Security Pacific Health Care Plan, which serves approximately 18,500 employees, retirees, and their families, provided over $24.2 million in benefits in 1983, a 50 percent increase over 1981. Approximately 30 percent of these corporate health care expenditures were paid by staff members, the remaining amount was contributed by SPC.

The most viable means of reducing the rate of increase of health care costs to the corporation was determined to be the reduction of the actual patient charges for this care. This was considered a more attractive cost-management option for the staff member than a reduction in benefits. A reduction in benefits would only shift more of the cost of health care to the employee; it would not affect the factors that cause health care increases. A change of this nature affects the employer in the form of reduced costs of providing health benefits, and affects employees in terms of reduced out-of-pocket expenses. To accomplish this type of change requires the involvement of both physicians and hospitals. This is because consumer demand for expensive health services is largely dependent on hospital and physician decisions.

PREFERRED PROVIDER PLANS

The PPO was the system that best fit the criteria of reducing patient charges for health care. Employees were expected to use the PPOs, since they would receive services at more attractive rates than the normal fee-for-service office visit. One of the major employee complaints in dealing with health maintenance organizations, freedom of choice when selecting a provider, was eliminated. With the PPO the selection of a provider was more at the discretion of the participating staff member. Also, at each incidence of illness or disability, the participating employees were free to choose the PPO or the indemnity plan.

Three types of PPOs were identified by Security Pacific:

— Provider-based PPOs are initiated by hospitals and/or groups of physicians. The advantage is that providers generally have more direct incentive to make the PPO a success. The disadvantages are that utilization review is generally done internally, and there may be prior allegiances to providers that may preclude selection of the most cost efficient.

— Purchaser-based PPOs are generally initiated by insurance companies. The advantage is that they normally have a larger client base with which to negotiate service agreements with providers.

— Entrepreneurial-based PPOs are initiated by independent third-party administrators of health care. The advantage is that they have no allegiance to any provider and their incentive is to contract with the most cost-efficient physicians and hospitals. However, the lack of a close working relationship with the providers may discourage some physicians and hospitals from participating in such an endeavor.

SELECTION CRITERIA

Because Security Pacific is self-insured and self-administered, the criteria for selecting a PPO was unencumbered by any previous provider relationships. The following selection criteria were used.

First, the ability to serve a geographically dispersed population was of major concern. With over 650 banking offices spread throughout the state and an additional 1,200 subsidiary employees in California, it was important that Security Pacific require California-wide coverage as a minimum criterion. It was also important that there be sufficient number of medical offices and capacity to care for staff members and their families. Although initial utilization during the introduction of the PPO was expected to be low, it was assumed that utilization of medical services would increase as word spread about the convenience and low cost of the PPO. Therefore, the capacity to meet the needs of an expanding enrollee population would become of paramount importance.

Second, the selection of a third-party administrator to manage the PPO would protect Security Pacific Corporation from alienating physicians and hospitals that had a pre-existing financial relationship with SPC.

Third, an acceptable track record with a history of experience in health care cost containment was sought. The fact that the organization sponsoring the preferred provider organization had previously been active in the health care field would greatly aid in the contracting process with cost-conscious providers and give them more confidence in dealing with the organization.

Fourth, previous experience in the operation of a PPO was desired because the corporation wished to have at least preliminary data from the organization upon which to evaluate the effectiveness of different PPOs. Companies that were already utilizing the PPOs under considertion were contacted and asked about their experience. Utilization and cost data were requested to be used in projecting anticipated cost savings for Security Pacific.

The fifth criterion was the assurance of fiscal viability of the project. Since the association to be developed was expected to be a long-term relationship, Security Pacific Corporation had to be reasonably certain that the organization sponsoring the PPO had a proven track record in the market to ensure that no one participant group (i.e., the physicians, hospitals, Security Pacific Corporation, or the sponsoring organization) would assume the total risk for the venture. If the venture exposed one interest group to more risk than the others, this would decrease the willingness of quality providers and purchasers to participate. Research on the financial solvency of the sponsoring organization included verification of such information as a reasonable breakeven point for the sponsoring organization of the PPO, a reasonable administrative cost to Security Pacific Corporation, and adequate financial agreements with the participating providers.

Sixth, the most important criterion was the additional cost-containment procedures used by the PPO such as utilization review, precertification for elective hospitalization, concurrent review of hospital stays, and second opinion surgery programs. These procedures had to be already in place at the time Security Pacific reviewed the different PPOs in order to determine the adequacy of the cost-containment procedures. As PPOs grow in popularity, the fee schedule (the initial selling point of PPOs) will become the adjusted amount charged by physicians in a highly competitive provider market, and the cost-saving factor will be the behavior modification of providers. The utilization-review procedures will also aid in ensuring that doctors do not increase the number of procedures to make up for the reduced fee schedule.

The PPO option was designed to operate on a dual system or "swing" plan, which means that if participants did not choose to utilize the PPO, they were covered under the standard indemnity plan as before (see Exhibit 1). A dual system or swing plan provides some of the cost savings of a health maintenance organization and the convenience of the standard indemnity plan.

Since the PPO was available only to those staff members enrolled in

EXHIBIT 1
Comparison of Benefits

	PPO	SPHCP Standard Indemnity Plan*
Claim forms required	No	Yes
Deductible required	No	Yes
Doctor charges for illness or accident		
Home,† office,† and hospital calls	100%	80%
Surgery, including assistant surgeon	100%	80%
Maternity	100%	80%
Outpatient facilities for surgery	100%	80%
Radiotherapy, X-ray, and lab	100%	80%
Prescription drugs	100%‡	80%
Well care benefits for		
Annual gynecological exam†	100%	None
Well-baby care to age 1†	100%	None
Childhood immunizations to age 2†	100%	None
Other Medical Charges		
Deductible required	Yes	Yes
Hospital charges		
Room and board	80%	80%
Intensive care	80%	80%
Services and supplies, anesthetist	80%	80%
Emergency room	80%	80%
Accident expense	100%	First $300 of covered charges are payable at 100%

*After deductible.

†There is a $10 fee per encounter with a MedNetwork doctor.

‡There is a $5 per prescription filling fee at a MedNetwork Pharmacy. This benefit is for prescriptions issued by a MedNetwork doctor only.

Security Pacific Health Care Plan, the result was a 3 percent shift during the health care open enrollment period for 1984. This was a sharp contrast to 1983 when approximately 3 percent shifted to health maintenance organizations.

The PPO ultimately chosen had previous experience in operating PPOs for other companies and as a result of this experience, had developed relationships with over 40 California hospitals that were willing to provide discounts for inpatient services. The patient's point of contact with the provider was not a high-priced specialist, but by design, the primary care physician. If a specialist were required, a referral form would be completed by the primary physician justifying the referral. The referral forms would ensure prompt reimbursement because the medical justification for the use of the specialist had already been established. Security Pacific's contract with the PPO chosen was a nonexclusive one, allowing for contracting with other preferred provider groups if it was favorable for the corporation to do so. This flexibility ensured that Security Pacific was not locked into a PPO that might not be as efficient as others in the market as time went on.

Seventy percent of Security Pacific Corporation's staff members are female. Therefore, the preferred provider organization benefit package was designed to be more attractive to women than the standard indemnity plan by offering annual gynecological examinations. The expectation was that if the staff member switched to a PPO physician for that examination, the employee might stay with the PPO physician for more expensive, long-term health problems and thus generate savings for the corporation further down the road. The additional dollars necessary to fund this added benefit were comparatively small, since this and similar procedures were frequently paid for under the SPHCP, disguised as medical problems. This reasoning also justified the well-baby and immunization coverage for infants. If the baby's initial entry into health care was through the PPO system, it was more likely that the baby would remain in that system and receive more efficient health care services. Another incentive to participate in the preferred provider option was the use of a generic prescription drug plan that cost employees only $5.00 per prescription.

For hospital utilization-review and precertification programs, the PPO worked with one of its own corporate subsidiaries that had been doing utilization review for insurance companies. This subsidiary was part of the same corporation as the PPO, but there were separate management teams, and Security Pacific felt that the advantage of immediate enforcement of utilization-review procedures outweighed the question of conflict of interest. The major tool used by the utilization-review organization was the prior authorization forms that the participating providers submitted for review of elective hospital admissions, hospital stay extensions, and emergency hospitalizations within 48 hours of admission.

IMPLEMENTATION

The initial publicity campaign began six weeks before the actual introduction of the PPO. Teaser ads were placed strategically in the corporate newspaper. Front page articles appeared for a two-week period and were followed by a question and answer article the next week. The next step was the introduction of the PPO benefit package to Security Pacific staff members. This was done in the form of an orientation packet that presented the preferred provider option as an added benefit under the Security Pacific Health Care Plan. This approach was intended to stimulate interest in the product as a new, broader, more comprehensive health plan. The orientation materials included the PPO identification cards and a booklet with the addresses of participating physicians, maps denoting the location of the primary care physicians (see Exhibit 2), and examples of how much could be saved by using the PPO. Embossed plastic identification cards that resemble credit cards were chosen to replace the computer-generated paper cards used previously. The impression that Security Pacific wished to foster was that this was a new payment mechanism. The cards were bright red to attract attention. This color was used repeatedly in the articles and teaser ads announcing the PPO in the weekly corporate newspaper.

CLAIMS PROCESSING

Eligibility is verified at the time of each office visit. Participating physicians are instructed to call the Security Pacific Health Programs office by utilizing the telephone number on the back of the identification card. All PPO health plan claims are initially sent by providers to the PPO offices where they are reviewed for completeness of billing and verification that the physician or hospital actually is a participating provider. The approved charges are then entered, and the claim is sent to the SPHCP for processing on the online computer system used for claims adjudication.

LESSONS LEARNED

In the enthusiastic response to the introduction of the PPO, some situations occurred that had not been anticipated. They included the following:

— The identification cards had been stamped with the original effective date of eligibility for the indemnity plan, not the effective date of the PPO. These identification cards were used for both the PPO and the standard indemnity plan and were sent a week early so the staff member would be able to take advantage of the PPO as soon as it was available. However, when the staff members received the identification cards and introductory booklets, some were overly enthusiastic and went to a PPO provider prior to Security Pacific's participation date.

— The comparison between the standard indemnity plan and the PPO stated that claim forms were no longer necessary. While this was true, the processing of the PPO bills did necessitate an employee statement, which employees did not file, and thus caused delays in payment to some providers.

EXHIBIT 2

LOS ANGELES COUNTY

DOCTORS

Arcadia
Arcadia Medical Clinic (#107)
1108 S. Baldwin Ave.
(213) 446-8831

Bell
Bell Medical Clinic (#68)
3649 E. Florence Ave.
(213) 583-6333

Bellflower
Bellflower Medical Group (#42)
17027 S. Clark Ave.
(213) 920-9641

Beverly Hills
Dr. Daniel V. Ehrensaft (#78)
300 S. Beverly, #407
(213) 277-6222

Dr. Michael W. Rubottom (#97)
8920 Wilshire, #545
(213) 652-0656

Burbank
Burbank Medical Clinic (#43)
2301 W. Magnolia Blvd.
(213) 842-4863

Canoga Park
West Hills Medical Group (#149)
7230 Medical Center Dr.
(213) 347-7800

Canyon Country
L.R. Leiter, MD (#120)
18915 Soledad
(805) 251-7000

Henry Mayo Newhall
Family Medical Center (#152)
27141 Hidaway Ave.
(805) 251-7800

Cerritos
Cerritos Plaza
Medical Group (#108)
18327 Grindley Rd.
(714) 521-1980
(213) 860-5180

Compton
West Alondra
Medical Group (#77)
1410 W. Alondra Blvd.
(213) 537-5605

Downey
Noble Medical Group (#61)
11015 Downey Ave.
(213) 773-5263

Glendale
Donald D. Doty, MD (#146)
1560 E. Chevy Chase,
(213) 241-2121

Glendale Family
Medicine Center (#156)
801 S. Chevy Chase
(213) 247-5733

Douglas Olson, MD (#147)
601 S. Glendale Ave.
(213) 241-1196

Glendora
Glendora Primary Care (#88)
150 E. Meda Ave.,
(213) 335-4079

Granada Hills
Granada Hills Associated
Physicians Medical Group (#47)
10339 Balboa Blvd., #200
(213) 368-6621

Granada Hills Medical Group (#125)
10660 White Oak Ave.
(213) 368-5851

Hacienda Heights
Med Site Medical Group (#132)
15906 Haliburton Rd.
(213) 330-0683

Hawthorne
Health Care Center (#116)
13252 S. Hawthorne Blvd.
#101-102
(213) 675-7175

Huntington Park
Southeast Medical Center (#56)
2675 E. Slauson Ave.
(213) 589-6681

Inglewood
Century Medical Group (#70)
11311 Inglewood Ave.
(213) 673-2222
      678-5068

Lancaster
Lancaster Medical Clinic (#82)
44469 N. 10th Street, West
(805) 942-1421

La Puente
La Puente Valley
Medical Group (#58)
18335 E. Valley Blvd.
(213) 964-2308

Long Beach
Seaview Medical Group (#50)
900 Pine Ave.
(213) 432-4461

Los Angeles
Axminster Medical Group (#93)
4314 W. Slauson Ave.
(213) 293-7171

California Primary
Physicians Group (#94)
929 S. Georgia
(213) 623-3065

Century City
Ambulatory Care Center (#117)
2070 Century Park East
(213) 203-0320

Highland Park Family
Medical Group (#100)
5823 York Blvd.
(213) 255-1575

Moore-White Medical Group (#71)
266 S. Harvard
(213) 386-8440

Olympic-Western
Medical Group (#74)
3323 W. Olympic Blvd.
(213) 733-0121

Perez Medical Group (#67)
3521 Whittier Blvd.
(213) 263-9541

Pico Medical Clinic (#110)
8615 W. Pico Blvd.
(213) 652-8010

Herman Ricketts, MD
A.H. Kahn, MD & Associates (#154)
1700 Brooklyn Ave.
(213) 269-7537
Pediatrics only:
414 N. Boyle Ave.
(213) 263-9866

Whittier Garfield
Medical Clinic (#69)
6425 E. Whittier Blvd.
(213) 728-0101

North Hollywood
Laurel Canyon Urgency Room
and Medical Group (#148)
8020 Laurel Canyon Blvd.
(213) 767-9623

Norwalk
Rosecrans Medical Group (#65)
11832 E. Rosecrans
(213) 868-0481

Panorama City
Van Nuys Medical Group (#51)
9628 Van Nuys Blvd.
(213) 893-7961

Pasadena
Roy Jackson, MD (#127)
185 S. Euclid Ave., #11
(213) 792-4147

Pasadena Family
Medical Group (#96)
931 North Lake Ave.
(213) 791-2410

Washington Professional
Medical Group (#151)
2595 E. Washington Blvd.
(213) 798-7338

Pico Rivera
Ritchard Fishman, MD (#136)
9505 E. Telegraph Rd.
(213) 949-6565

EXHIBIT 2 *(concluded)*

LOS ANGELES COUNTY

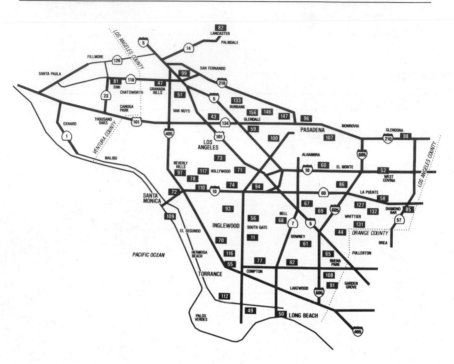

San Fernando
Case Medical Group (#99)
321 N. Maclay St.
(213) 361-7325

San Gabriel
Noble Medical Group (#60)
1323 S. San Gabriel Blvd.
Suite B
(213) 280-5343

Simi Valley
Simi Doctors Medical Clinic (#81)
1854 Cochran St.
(805) 526-8360

South El Monte
Dalton Medical Group (#86)
10414 Vacco St.
(213) 443-3163

Sunland
F. Morada, MD (#133)
8424 Foothill Blvd.
(213) 352-3146

Torrance
Centro Medico (#112)
3655 Lomita Blvd., #309
(213) 378-4294

Emergency Medical Group
of Torrance (#137)
19000 Hawthorne, #100
(213) 542-6982

North Torrance
Medical Group (#55)
16636 S. Crenshaw
(213) 324-4975

Venice
Rose Medical Group (#109)
604 Rose Ave.
(213) 396-5974

West Covina
West Covina
Medical Group (#52)
741 S. Orange Ave.
(213) 960-5311
          337-1241

West Hollywood
Citizens Medical Group (#73)
1300 N. La Brea
(213) 464-1336

West Los Angeles
Shelley Medical Group (#72)
11545 W. Olympic Blvd.
(213) 477-8285

Whittier
Colima Internal
Medical Group (#44)
10155 Colima Rd.
(213) 945-3671

Family Practice Associates (#131)
16315 Whittier Blvd., #105
(213) 697-6793

Wilmington
Seaview Medical Group (#49)
1127 N. Avalon Blvd.
(213) 830-3130

CONCLUSION

The preliminary reports investigating the effectiveness of the PPO instituted at Security Pacific Corporation are currently being evaluated. Early
results appear to indicate some cost savings for the Corporation.

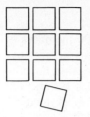

Labor Organization Initiated/Sponsored

CASE STUDY: TEAMSTERS CENTRAL STATES HEALTH AND WELFARE FUND,[1] HOUSTON, TX

Judith D. Bentkover, Ph.D.
Research Fellow in Health Policy
Center for Health Policy and Management
Harvard University

Ann Venable, M.A.
Senior Health Care Staff
Arthur D. Little, Inc.
Cambridge, MA

☐ The Central States, Southeast, and Southwest Areas Health and Welfare Fund, which provides health benefits to members of Teamsters local unions, began an experimental preferred provider arrangement with a dental clinic in Miami in 1978 and has since made similar arrangements with dental groups in Minneapolis and St. Louis. In 1980, it established two programs in Houston: another dental contract and the Fund's first preferred provider contract for medical services. This case study focuses on the medical contract, which is with the Kelsey-Seybold Clinic, P.A., a multispecialty physician's group. The preferred provider arrangement with Kelsey-Seybold is available to the approximately 3,600 members of Teamsters Local 988 in the Houston area and their families who are covered by the C5 Benefit Plan. This is the most comprehensive benefits plan offered by the Fund; its health care component provides 100 percent coverage of "reasonable and customary" charges for most medical services.

PROGRAM PARTICIPANTS

THE HEALTH AND WELFARE FUND

The Central States, Southeast, and Southwest Areas Health and Welfare Fund, established under the provisions of the Taft-Hartley Act, provides health and other benefits to about 140,000 Teamsters local union members and their families in the Midwest, Southwest, and Southeast. The Fund is headquartered in Chicago. Amalgamated Insurance Agency Services, Inc. processes claims for the Fund. Other trust funds handle benefits for the Northeast and the West Coast. The benefits provided cover life insurance, disability, accident and health, dental, and vision.

The Health and Welfare Fund is a trust fund, legally and financially separate from the Union. It has a Board of Trustees with equal representation from local unions and employers. Benefits are paid out of a fund made up of employer contributions, with each employer contributing an amount negotiated with the Union. For Teamsters employed in long-haul trucking, contribution rates are negotiated nationally between the Union and the three large associations of motor carriers and are embodied in the Teamster Master Freight Contract. Contribution rates for other Team-

EXHIBIT 1
C5 Benefit Plan

Basic benefits:

Loss of time	$125 per week up to 26 weeks
Hospitalization	100 percent of covered charges
Surgery/obstetrics	100 percent of reasonable and customary charges (R&C)
Outpatient diagnostic x-ray and lab	100 percent of R&C (including the related doctor's visit)
Outpatient accidental bodily injury	100 percent of covered charges (first day of treatment only)
Psychiatry	
Inpatient	If nonhospital: 100 percent up to $10,000 or 90 days per person per year
Outpatient	50 percent up to $1,000 per person per year
Prescription drugs	80 percent of covered charges

Major medical (includes nondiagnostic-related physicians' fees and a variety of other charges)

Deductible	$100 per person; $200 per family
Maximum	80 percent up to $250,000 per person per year

sters are negotiated either with associations or, at the local level, with individual employers. This bargaining process determines which benefit package the employees will receive; individual employees do not have any choice of benefits.

The Central States Fund offers five benefit packages with different levels of benefits. The most comprehensive, Plan C5, covers all Teamsters covered by the Master Freight Contract and is the plan of interest to this case study. Plan C5 includes the medical benefits listed in Exhibit 1.

The other plans—C4, A, B, and L, in descending order—offer reduced benefits. The Fund also has a plan called R4 for retired employees between ages 57 and 65.

KELSEY-SEYBOLD CLINIC, P.A.

The Kelsey-Seybold Clinic was founded in 1949 and now has more than 120 physicians, representing most medical and surgical specialties and subspecialties. It has a wide array of medical equipment and its own laboratory and pharmacies. Since 1963, it has occupied its present main facility in the Texas Medical Center. It also has a satellite office with 17 physicians and seven other satellites with six to eight physicians each. There are plans to open two similar satellites soon.

The clinic is physician-owned and operated, with 62 of its physicians participating as shareholders. Physicians are paid salaries based on their specialties, and stockholders in addition receive incentive payments reflecting their contribution to total revenues.

The clinic has several contracts with area employers to perform physical exams for executives and provide limited follow-up services. However, the arrangement with the Health and Welfare Fund is its only contract for comprehensive health care services.

TEAMSTERS LOCAL 988

Teamsters Local 988 is one of six Teamsters locals in the Houston area. About 3,600, or 80 percent of its members, are covered by Benefit Plan C5 (the rest are in C4) and are therefore eligible to participate in the preferred provider program.

PROGRAM PURPOSE AND INCENTIVES FOR UNION AND CLINIC PARTICIPATION

From the viewpoint of Central States, the purpose of the preferred provider dental and medical experiments is cost containment. In the past, the only approach used for cost containment has been HMOs, and in some locations these have incurred higher costs than the indemnity plans. In one location, the Fund is experimenting with a risk-sharing arrangement with an HMO, whereby the Fund pays an amount based on its own forecast of utilization, which is lower than the amount based on the HMO's forecast: if costs exceed the payment, the Fund pays half the difference. However, an additional problem with HMOs has been complaints about HMO practices such as triage and the use of nurse practitioners from union members who formerly had their own family physicians. The Fund hopes that contracts negotiated with the provider groups of its own choosing can avoid these problems. Eventually, it might try converting some of these into capitation contracts.

The Health and Welfare Fund is also interested in promoting competitive incentives other than the equal contribution/multiple choice model being discussed as a possible basis for federal legislation. The benefit packages administered by Central States are established through the collective bargaining process that determined the amount of the employer contribution. Arrangements with providers offer an alternative approach to containing costs.

For the clinic, the Central States' contract helps to keep patient volume high. There are high fixed costs for clinic operations, and rapid population turnover in the area requires the clinic to market its services constantly in order to attract patients. A second incentive for the clinic is the potential for simplified billing and expedited payment under the program. Finally, the clinic hopes that program data will demonstrate reduced hospitalization costs through use of its services. Such data would be very valuable in the competition with HMOs.

PROGRAM DESCRIPTION

Under this program, the Kelsey-Seybold Clinic agrees to accept a discounted fee schedule as full payment for covered services to Local 988 members with Plan C5 coverage and their families, and the Fund agrees to pay this amount. The clinic bills the Fund directly rather than via the patient.

Eligible union members are now free to use the clinic physicians for any service and can alternate between clinic and outside physicians as they wish. The advantages to them of using the clinic are: (1) no out-of-pocket cost for covered benefits and (2) no insurance forms to be filled out and submitted by the patient for covered benefits. When members use other physicians, or when they use Kelsey-Seybold physicians for services that are not included in the program (see below), the regular provisions of Plan C5 apply. Hospital charges are not affected by the program, and again the C5 provisions apply.

COVERED SERVICES

The agreement with Kelsey-Seybold includes most of the physician services covered by Plan C5 and listed above; exceptions are listed later.

As indicated earlier, the arrangement does not affect hospital charges. It also does not affect the following physician services covered under C5:

— Psychiatric services.
— Drug and alcohol abuse services.
— Prescription drugs.
— Dental services (the focus of another preferred provider program in which Local 988 is participating).
— Vision services.
— Referral to specialists not on the staff of Kelsey-Seybold.

Patients using these services obtain the normal Plan C5 benefits and follow the C5 claims procedures, whether or not the services are obtained through Kelsey-Seybold.

PRICING AND DIRECT BILLING

Kelsey-Seybold physicians charge for their services on the basis of a fee schedule. For this contract the Fund compares the Kelsey-Seybold fees for covered services with the "reasonable and customary rates" that it normally uses for reimbursement, and wherever the Kelsey-Seybold fees are higher (in practice, this is true of only a few procedures), resolves the difference by negotiation with the clinic. The agreed-upon fees are then discounted by 8 percent for covered services to eligible Teamster families; i.e., the Fund pays 92 percent of the scheduled fee and the clinic accepts this amount as full payment for services. The patient, who under normal reimbursement practices has to pay the deductible and coinsurance required under Plan C5 Major Medical as well as any difference between "reasonable and customary" and actual charges, pays nothing.

Normally, a Teamsters member or dependent who obtains health services is charged for the services. The member must then complete a claim form and turn it in to the local union headquarters to be forwarded to the Fund for processing and payment. Often the member must pay the charge out-of-pocket and then collect from the Fund. Under the Kelsey-Seybold Central States contract, the clinic bills the Fund directly, without the patient and local union as intermediaries. This benefits the patient, who is relieved of both the paperwork and the initial cash outlay, and it benefits the clinic by speeding up payment. It also saves some of the time spent by the Local in reviewing and forwarding claims.

It should be noted that Kelsey-Seybold is not at risk for hospitalization. The incentives for the clinic to reduce hospitalization rates for Teamsters are (1) to retain the arrangement with the Health and Welfare Fund and (2) to demonstrate the potential for cost savings by fee-for-service organizations.

ADMINISTRATION

Eligibility

All members of Local 988 in Plan C5 and their covered dependents are eligible for the program. Eligibility information is provided on the Local 988 Insurance Identification Card and on a plastic card available from the Health and Welfare Fund; both cards were in use prior to the program, and both are used by the clinic as identification of Teamster membership. The clinic must call the Fund on special toll-free lines to verify eligibility. The clinic is responsible for asking about dependent status (for example, child over 19 who is a full-time student) and determining whether other insurance policies exist.

Program Information for Members

Union members are informed about the program in a letter sent annually by Local 988, accompanied by a clinic brochure. The program is also described at company and general membership meetings, and notices are put on bulletin boards. Shop stewards are supplied with copies of the information letter.

Claims Processing and Payment

For services provided under the program, the Kelsey-Seybold Clinic sends a monthly itemized bill to the Fund on computer tape. For each Teamster family, the bill indicates the date of each visit during the month, whether the visit was by the member or by a dependent, nature of the visit by ICDA code, and charge. Fund personnel make a copy of the tape for their own computer and print out a hard copy for billing. The information is edited post-processing to verify the person's eligibility for coverage and to make sure that Social Security number, ICDA code, and other required information are all present. The bills are then forwarded to Amalgamated Insurance Agency Services, Inc., which reviews them to make sure the services are covered, denies ineligible claims, and processes the claim. At present, a separate check is sent for services during the month for each Teamster member or dependent; the Fund hopes eventually to streamline this so that a single check covering all approved claims will be paid each month.

Administrative Costs

Administrative costs consist mainly of staff time and travel expenses. In the current year, staff time is estimated at one full-time person plus smaller contributions of time by four others, for a total cost of $21,795. Travel is estimated at $2,000. The total of $23,795 comes to $6.50 per eligible Teamster member. Program staff feel that most of the cost is incurred in resolving reporting and computer problems between the Fund and the clinic. Next year they hope to cut the cost in half and eventually it should be still lower.

PROGRAM HISTORY

ORIGIN AND STARTUP

The program grew out of previous activities of both the Fund and Local 988. At the Fund, growing interest in cost containment had led to establishment of preferred-provider dental programs and an interest in a similar arrangement for medical services. At the local union, the President was interested in innovations that might improve health care services to union members. Around 1971, he and representatives of the other local unions began to plan a jointly operated clinic, but there was not enough support from local leadership to pursue this. He also had a high regard for the Kelsey-Seybold Clinic and was interested in the possibility of some kind of service arrangement with this group that would permit an increase in health benefits.

When the Health and Welfare Fund began planning the medical program, it asked the American Group Practice Association to recommend appropriate physician groups, and Kelsey-Seybold was among the recommendations. The presence of Kelsey-Seybold and the interest of the local union President were the reasons for the Fund's choice of Houston as a site for the program. At the request of the Fund, the Union also explored other candidate physician groups in the area, but it preferred Kelsey-Seybold. The clinic agreed to participate mainly because of the volume incentive, though initially it had concerns about being unaccustomed to a blue-collar and largely black population.

One drawback to the Kelsey-Seybold arrangement is that the clinic does not have its own hospital, and the arrangement therefore does not extend to hospital charges. The Fund approached area hospitals about a potential contract but was not successful. The hospitals approached are tertiary care hospitals with an international reputation, and they indicated that they did not need service contracts as a source of patients.

The agreement with Kelsey-Seybold was worked out and the initial contract signed August 1, 1980. The program went into effect September 1.

Fund personnel estimate the startup costs of the program at about $4,500. This reflects time contributed by four professional staff, some clerical time, and about $1,200 in travel costs.

EXPERIENCE TO DATE

Program Acceptance

According to the President of the Local, this program has been very well received by the membership. At the beginning, some members were apprehensive about dealing with the "high-class doctors" at the clinic, reciprocating the concern of clinic physicians about the union clientele. Also, some of those who first went to the clinic thought that the medical history taking and annual physicals were probably a waste of money.

Then some serious illnesses were detected early, and attitudes changed. There have been no recent complaints.

The President of the Local thinks that the incentive that is most important in getting members to use the program is "elimination of the cash-flow barriers"; i.e., the fact that members do not have to pay for care and then collect from the Fund. He thinks that the reasons for non-use of the clinic are, in order of importance, lack of proximity to a clinic site, an established relationship with another physician, and a long-ingrained habit of seeking care in a hospital emergency room.

Word-of-mouth, he reports, is the best advertising for the program. There is an adage, "Telephone, telegraph, tell-a-truck-driver," and the program response is an example.

Clinic representatives are generally pleased with the program. There were a few problems initially with no-shows for appointments, or program eligibles who forgot to identify themselves as such, but these have diminished. Physicians report a high level of medical care need among the user population; this is consistent with the experience of the dental programs whose utilization in the first year is typically very heavy as people with little or no history of dental care get "caught up."

Utilization and Impact

Analysis of data tapes from the program will provide an accurate picture of the extent to which members use the Kelsey-Seybold and the impact to date on hospitalization rates and program costs. The President of Local 988 believes that about one third of the families who live within reasonable geographic access of the Kelsey-Seybold Clinic or a satellite make at least some use of the program. He estimates that between 50 percent and 75 percent of the C5 families in the area are appropriately located. The clinic is heavily used for child care, with many families apparently taking their children to Kelsey-Seybold without using it for their own care.

Although about half the members of Local 988 are black or Hispanic, the clinic estimates that 75 percent of program users are white. Clinic representatives think the main reason is geographic; Houston is a fairly segregated city, and the main clinic facility is in a white area.

The President of Local 988, the Fund, and the clinic all believe that the program will reduce hospitalization, mainly because the clinic is equipped to provide many specialized diagnostic services on an outpatient basis that are often available only in the hospital. Preliminary figures from the Fund show lower hospitalization rates among Kelsey-Seybold users than among nonusers. If this proves to be the case and is not explained by differences in patient characteristics, hospitalization costs to the Fund should be reduced.

Administration

Both for the Fund and for the clinic, the billing and payment arrangement has necessitated a learning process. Clinic staff need to learn to handle

Teamsters' bills differently and Fund staff need to learn to handle Kelsey-Seybold differently. Fund staff audit the clinic annually in order to resolve small differences between clinic and Fund claims records, primarily consisting of claims recorded by the clinic as outstanding and by the Fund as paid or denied. Most of these appeared to result from errors in certifying eligibility—mainly relating to dual coverage, stepchild coverage, and the status of children over 19. In addition, there are incompatabilities between the computer systems of the Fund and the clinic. Problems of these kinds still make the billing and payment process slower than desired. Fund staff were still investing considerable time in administrative "de-bugging."

FUTURE PLANS

A second medical group arrangement is planned in Oklahoma City, where there is another clinic recommended by the American Group Practice Association. This clinic is affiliated with a hospital, which will provide a discount under the program. Additional activities that the Fund contemplates down the road include:

— Possibly converting some of the medical or dental contracts to closed panel—i.e., patient enrolls and then uses this facility for all services—and possibly also capitation contracts.
— Exploring potential hospital contracts with hospital management companies.
— Establishment of a similar program for Plan C4, with some co-payment by the patients.
— Further streamlining of the billing and payment process in order to achieve a single itemized bill, paid with a single check.

The clinic is considering doing a study of where nonusers of the program live, as a possible guide to location of a new satellite office. Another change contemplated is adding Family Practice to the clinic's list of specialities.

NOTE

1. Much of this work was undertaken pursuant to DHHS contract HHS-100-81-0067, Evaluation of the Impact of Competitive Incentives on Employees' Choice of Health Care Coverage. However, the views expressed above are those of the authors.

INDEX